Guide to the U.S. Supreme Court

Guide to the U.S. Supreme Court

THIRD EDITION • VOLUME I

JOAN BISKUPIC AND ELDER WITT

 CONGRESSIONAL QUARTERLY INC.
WASHINGTON, D.C.

Joan Biskupic is Supreme Court reporter for the *Washington Post* and previously served as legal affairs reporter for the *Congressional Quarterly Weekly Report.* She is the author of three editions of CQ's annual *Supreme Court Yearbook.* She won the 1991 Everett McKinley Dirksen Award for Distinguished Reporting of Congress. She holds a law degree from Georgetown University Law Center.

Elder Witt is an award-winning writer and deputy publisher on the staff of CQ's *Governing* magazine. She spent eighteen years as Supreme Court reporter for the *Congressional Quarterly Weekly Report* and was the primary writer and editor of the two previous editions of CQ's *Guide to the U.S. Supreme Court.* She is also the author of *A Different Justice: Reagan and the Supreme Court.*

Copyright © 1997 Congressional Quarterly Inc.
1414 22nd Street, N.W., Washington, D.C. 20037

Book design and production by Kachergis Book Design, Pittsboro, North Carolina

Printed and bound in the United States of America

The paper used in this publication meets the minimum requirements of the American National Standard for Information Science—Permanence of Paper for Printed Library Materials, ANSI Z 39.48-1984.

Acknowledgments: HoweData Supreme Court Reports provided the text of the five Supreme Court decisions appearing in Appendix A. Lee Epstein and Thomas G. Walker contributed their research on natural courts, which is part of Appendix B. This research was published previously in their book *Constitutional Law for a Changing America: Institutional Powers and Constraints,* 2d ed. (Washington, D.C.: CQ Press, 1995), 617. Lee Epstein, Jeffrey A. Segal, Harold J. Spaeth, and Thomas G. Walker provided the map of the federal court system, which is part of Appendix B. The map was published previously in their book *The Supreme Court Compendium: Data, Decisions, and Developments,* 2d ed. (Washington, D.C.: Congressional Quarterly, 1996), 651.

Illustration credits and acknowledgments begin on page 1161, Volume II, which is to be considered an extension of the copyright page.

LIBRARY OF CONGRESS CATALOGING-IN-PUBLICATION DATA
Biskupic, Joan.
    Congressional Quarterly's guide to the U.S. Supreme Court /
Joan Biskupic and Elder Witt — 3rd ed.
       p. cm.
    Rev. ed. of: Congressional Quarterly's guide to the U.S. Supreme Court /
Elder Witt. 2nd ed. 1990.
    Includes bibliographical references and index.
    ISBN 1-56802-130-5 (set). — ISBN 1-56802-236-0 (v. 1).
— ISBN 1-56802-237-9 (v. 2)
    1. United States.   Supreme Court.   I. Witt, Elder.   II. Title.
KF8742.W567   1996
347.73'26—dc20   96-8222
[347.30735]

Summary Table of Contents

Table of Contents

VOLUME II

Preface to the Third Edition

THE VAST POWER of the modern Supreme Court could hardly have been imagined when the first six justices convened for the first time on February 1, 1790. Only three of the justices were in New York to attend the opening day, and the term lasted just nine days. No cases were argued or decided. When the national government moved to Washington in 1801, the Court was such an insignificant body that those who planned the new capital city forgot to provide a place for it to meet.

But just two years later, in 1803, the Court staked out its power to shape the course of American government. Asserting its role as a check on the exercise of legislative authority in *Marbury v. Madison,* the Court became a defining force in the new democracy and arbiter of the balance of powers. With each decade and each major decision, the Court's influence on America grew. In the early years of its second century, the Supreme Court exercised its authority to guarantee the individual rights promised in the Constitution. Into the fabric of American life the Court wove the right to liberty and property, free speech, free press, and the freedom to worship and assemble. Often at odds with public opinion and the interests of the powerful, the Supreme Court decision by decision enhanced each individual American's dignity and worth.

This book tells the story of how the Court grew from modest beginnings to a singularly powerful court of justice. And even today, in the first years of its third century, the Court continues to alter significantly the balances of power. After six decades of expanding national authority at the expense of the states, the Court has begun to trim congressional power and to give states more sway. Breathing new life into state sovereignty, the Court is redefining the boundaries of power and, consequently, what protections individuals may expect from their governments. At the same time, the Court remains engaged in today's most difficult social dilemmas, a powerful force in the debate over equal protection for gays and lesbians, the right of seriously ill patients to choose to die, and freedom of speech in the computer age.

When the first edition of Congressional Quarterly's *Guide to the U.S. Supreme Court* appeared in 1979, the Court was in a period of quiet stability. Eight of the nine justices had served together for eight years. Warren E. Burger was in his tenth year as chief justice. The 1970s had seen a slowing of the Court's liberal momentum but no real change in direction.

Seventeen years later, William H. Rehnquist is in his tenth year as chief justice, having succeeded Burger in 1986 and overseen a sharp conservative shift in direction. Only three of today's justices have served together for more than ten years. Since 1986, six new justices have taken their seats.

The nation has also seen two fractious confirmation fights over high court nominations: Robert H. Bork, who was defeated in 1987, and Clarence Thomas, who narrowly won Senate approval in 1991. The change in personnel, the political spotlight of confirmation hearings, the calendar of continuing social dilemmas such as abortion, and the bitter divisions among the justices themselves have intensified public attention to the Court.

In 1996, Rehnquist, appointed by Richard Nixon and elevated to chief justice by Ronald Reagan, shared the bench with fellow Republican appointees John Paul Stevens, Sandra Day O'Connor, Antonin Scalia, Anthony M. Kennedy, David H. Souter, and Clarence Thomas. Only two justices, Ruth Bader Ginsburg and Stephen G. Breyer, were placed on today's Court by a Democratic president. But this is no lopsided Court. On some of the most controversial cases of the day, the Court divides 5–4, reflecting the close balance that could be shifted by the next presidential election.

The Court's development, its people and their decisions, are covered in this completely updated and redesigned third edition of Congressional Quarterly's award-winning *Guide to the U.S. Supreme Court.* The work is now in two volumes, reflecting additional substantive explanations of the Court's work, more than 150 new cases, and the additional biographies of all the new justices. The main sections of the book have been converted into numbered chapters for quick and easy reference. New illustrations have been added as well. The third edition contains more than 270 photos, editorial cartoons, drawings, and maps that personalize and explain the Court's history.

What has not changed is our commitment to providing the reader with accurate, thoughtful, highly readable information and analysis of all aspects of the Court and its work. For those who wish to pursue their own research on a particular decision or legal issue, extensive notes are included as well as a selected bibliography listing scholarly and general sources of additional information. Both volumes contain detailed case and subject indexes. The case index includes every decision mentioned in the book, along with a complete legal citation for each case.

In Volume I, Part I (chapters 1–3) introduces the reader to the Court's origins and development, tracing the growth of the

Court from an idea into a powerful institution. Part II (chapters 4–7) in this volume examines the Court's influence on the American system of government, the rulings affecting the powers of Congress, the president, the lower federal courts, and the states. Part III (chapters 8–12) explains the impact of the Court's rulings on the rights and freedoms of the individual—the freedom to hold and express ideas and beliefs, the rights of political participation and voting, the due process guarantee, and the promise of equal protection.

In Volume II, Part IV (chapters 13–15) examines the influence of public opinion and the press on the Court. Part V (chapters 16–18) reviews the history of the Court's operations and functions. Part VI (chapters 19–20) contains biographical sketches of each of the individual justices. The reference materials section contains documents and texts that trace the Court's history as well as the full text of five landmark rulings and summaries of more than four hundred major decisions. Also included are a table of natural courts, a nominations chart, a glossary, and a complete list of the acts of Congress the Court has found unconstitutional.

We are most thankful for the assistance of Supreme Court public information officer Toni House and her associates at the Court. They provided accurate, timely information on the past workings and modern operation of the Court.

We are also grateful to our editors at Congressional Quarterly, especially Chris Karlsten, who professionally and cheerfully coordinated our work as well as the efforts of the several editors handling these volumes. Other Congressional Quarterly staffers made valuable contributions to the project, including Megan Campion, Ann Davies, Carolyn Goldinger, Talia Greenberg, Kerry Kern, Gwenda Larsen, Jon Preimesberger, Sabrina Salcito, and Kathleen Walton. Freelance editor Barbara de Boinville copyedited most of the book, and freelance photo researcher Jamie Holland selected the illustrations. The indexes were prepared by freelancer Jan Danis.

They, as well as we, have been guided by a respect for this venerable institution and a belief in the value of public understanding of the Court's traditions, its calling, and its place in American life.

Joan Biskupic and Elder Witt

Origins and Development of the Court

CHAPTER 1

The First Century: Origins of Power

W E MUST NEVER FORGET that it is a constitution we are expounding," Chief Justice John Marshall admonished his fellow justices in 1819.[1] To modern ears, Marshall's words may seem at first a truism, yet through them rings with clarity the mission that gives the Supreme Court such a significant role in American life and government. The Court's unique role in the United States is a direct outgrowth of the new meaning the word *constitution* assumed in the American experiment.

In 1789 every government had a constitution. The word simply referred to whatever principles and assumptions underlay the existing system. But in the new nation called the United States the word was invested with added significance.

"A Constitution, in the American sense of the word," Justice Samuel Miller would write a century later, "is a written instrument by which the fundamental powers of the government are established, limited, and defined, and by which these powers are distributed among several departments, for their more safe and useful exercise for the benefit of the body politic."

In the U.S. Constitution, Miller continued, "the people themselves have undertaken to frame an organic law governing the relations of the whole people, as well as of the individual states, to the federal government, and to prescribe in many cases the limits and rules of private and personal rights. It is the fundamental law pursuant to which the government is permanently organized and conducted."[2]

In the United States, then, the Constitution is far more than a description of the existing system. It is an active instrument, the charter of the national system, the source of power and of the limits of power.

But the Constitution of the United States is hardly self-enforcing. Chief Justice Marshall described it as a document whose "great outlines should be marked, its important objects designated, and the minor ingredients which compose those objects be deduced from the nature of the objects themselves."[3]

The next question was obvious. Who would undertake these all-important deductions? Who would implement the limits the Constitution set? Who would fill in the broad outlines of the powers it granted? The answer was not long in doubt. The Supreme Court would serve this function, it declared in *Marbury v. Madison*. The "weakest branch" of the new system would assume this critical responsibility; the Court would be "the particular guardian of the terms of the written constitution."[4]

In the ensuing two centuries, the Supreme Court—by virtue of its exercise of this responsibility—has become the most pow-

erful court the world has ever known. It can override the will of the majority expressed in an act of Congress. It can remind a president that in the United States all persons are subject to the rule of law. It can require the redistribution of political power in every state. And it can persuade the nation's citizens that the fabric of their society must be rewoven into new patterns.

There have been mistakes and contradictions along the way. Constitutional development in the United States follows no tidy pattern. The Court does not initiate cases or solicit issues; it must take them as they come. When it decides cases, it often seems tentative and hesitant, zigging and zagging from case to case within a particular issue. The pattern is quintessentially human. For all its remoteness, the Court is the most human of government institutions. It is nine individuals, men and women whose names and faces and histories are publicly known. Issues come to the Court when individuals disagree. Black and white, merchant and consumer, prisoner and warden, president and pauper—they come before the Court to seek resolution of their disputes.

The justices who decide these cases are neither monks nor oracles. They respond to the same concerns and influences as their fellow citizens. They hear the arguments; then they meet, talk, and vote. The Court has decided. The justices write, comment, edit. The opinions are signed. The decision is announced. The dispute is resolved—and the role of the Court in the continuing development of the American system is once again affirmed.

The Court is the nation's balance wheel. Justice Robert H. Jackson explained:

In a society in which rapid changes tend to upset all equilibrium, the Court, without exceeding its own limited powers, must strive to maintain the great system of balances upon which our free government is based. Whether these balances and checks are essential to liberty elsewhere in the world is beside the point; they are indispensable to the society we know. Chief of these balances are: first, between the Executive and Congress; second, between the central government and the States; third, between state and state; fourth, between authority, be it state or national, and the liberty of the citizen, or between the rule of the majority and the rights of the individual.[5]

This is the story of that Court and those balances.

The Foundations

The contrast in the amount of detail is striking. Articles I and II of the Constitution set out in considerable length the powers

3

and prerogatives of Congress and the executive branch. Article III simply sketches the outline of a federal judiciary.

One scholar, Julius Goebel Jr., suggests that at least for some delegates to the Constitutional Convention, "provision for a national judiciary was a matter of theoretical compulsion rather than of practical necessity . . . more in deference to the maxim of separation [of powers] than in response to clearly formulated ideas about the role of a national judicial system and its indispensability."[6]

At any rate, with little discussion and less debate, the convention approved language that declared:

The judicial Power of the United States, shall be vested in one supreme Court, and in such inferior Courts as the Congress may from time to time ordain and establish.

Section 1 provides that federal judges will hold their posts during good behavior and that their salaries may not be diminished during their terms in office.

Article II already provided that the members of the Supreme Court would be appointed by the president by and with the advice and consent of the Senate—and that judges, along with all other civil officers of the new national government, "shall be removed from office on Impeachment for, and Conviction of, Treason, Bribery, or other high Crimes and Misdemeanors."

Section 2 of Article III describes the reach of federal judicial power. Some cases were included because of their subject—"all Cases, in Law and Equity, arising under this Constitution, the Laws of the United States, and Treaties made, or which shall be made, under their Authority . . . all Cases of admiralty and maritime Jurisdiction." Other cases were included because of the parties involved—"all Cases affecting Ambassadors, other public Ministers and Consuls; . . . Controversies to which the United States shall be a Party; . . . Controversies between two or more States."

The Supreme Court would have original jurisdiction—the power to hear the initial arguments—in cases involving foreign dignitaries and those involving states. In all other cases, the Court's jurisdiction was appellate—it would hear appeals from rulings of lower courts.

There ended the Constitution's description of the nation's judicial branch. The remaining sections of Article III dealt with jury trials, the place of trials, and the crime of treason.

The brevity of the constitutional description left to Congress and the Court itself the task of filling in much of the substance and all of the details of the new judicial system. One early observer commented, "The convention has only crayoned in the outlines. It is left to Congress to fill up and colour the canvas."[7]

AN INDEPENDENT BRANCH

Although the Articles of Confederation had not provided for a system of national courts, the concept of a separate and relatively independent judiciary was generally accepted by the delegates to the Constitutional Convention. At the time of the adoption of Article III, six of the original thirteen states had such judicial branches.[8]

There was some debate over the need for any inferior federal courts. Some delegates argued that state courts were adequate to handle all judicial business other than that which the Supreme Court would consider. That debate was resolved by leaving the final decision to Congress.

Delegates also disagreed over whether Congress or the president should appoint the members of the Supreme Court—and whether the Court should try impeachments. A compromise resulted in giving the president the power to name the Court's members with the advice and consent of the Senate, the same body given the power to try impeachments.

To safeguard judicial independence, the "good behavior" and salary provisions were added. Alexander Hamilton wrote in *The Federalist Papers:*

The standard of good behavior for the continuance in office of the judicial magistracy is certainly one of the most valuable of the modern improvements in the practice of government. In a monarchy it is an excellent barrier to the despotism of the prince; in a republic it is a no less excellent barrier to the encroachments and oppressions of the representative body. And it is the best expedient which can be devised in any government to secure a steady, upright, and impartial administration of the laws.[9]

By providing for impeachment of judges, Hamilton wrote, the Constitution ensured their responsible conduct.[10]

FEDERAL SUPREMACY

Neither the separateness nor the independence of the Supreme Court is truly unique. The most notable and peculiar of its characteristics is its power of judicial review, the power to review and nullify state and federal laws that collide with the Constitution.

The need for judicial review grew out of the convention's adoption, in Article VI, of the declaration that

This Constitution, and the Laws of the United States which shall be made in Pursuance thereof; and all Treaties made, or which shall be made, under the Authority of the United States, shall be the supreme Law of the Land; and the Judges in every State shall be bound thereby, any Thing in the Constitution or Laws of any State to the Contrary notwithstanding.

Article VI also states that all officials of the national and state governments were to take an oath to support the Constitution. Left unsaid—again—was who would enforce the provisions and prescriptions of the Constitution if some officials chose to ignore that oath.

Insofar as state actions were concerned, Congress remedied that omission in the Judiciary Act of 1789. This act gave the Supreme Court the power to review rulings of state courts rejecting claims that state laws or actions conflict with the U.S. Constitution, federal laws, or treaties. It also specified that the Supreme Court would consist of a chief justice and five associate justices, meeting twice each year, in February and in August.

This provision for judicial review of state rulings was contained in the famous Section 25 of the Judiciary Act, the subject of much criticism and many repeal efforts over the next three decades.

JUDICIAL REVIEW

Congress did not grant the Supreme Court the power of judicial review over acts of Congress, the power to measure challenged federal laws against constitutional standards. Nor does the Constitution address this aspect of the Court's power.

In 1803 the Court simply claimed this role. In *Marbury v. Madison* the Court struck down a portion of the same Judiciary Act that granted it the power to review state court rulings. The offending section, wrote Chief Justice Marshall, purported to enlarge the original jurisdiction of the Court—something Congress had no power to do.

Marbury v. Madison sparked a long scholarly debate over whether the Court was undertaking a role the Framers intended it to fill or was usurping power it was never intended to possess. Despite its sporadic intensity, the debate is irrelevant. The Court's power to review acts of Congress is firmly established and has never been seriously challenged.

Most scholars think that the members of the Constitutional Convention intended the Court to exert this power. They point to various remarks during the convention debates—and during the ratification conventions in the states—as indicating that many members of the convention simply assumed that the Supreme Court would have this power.

Most enduring of the arguments of this early period are those set out by Alexander Hamilton in *The Federalist Papers*. Hamilton reasoned that this function of the Court was essential to the existence of a limited constitutional government. The federal courts, he said, would serve as "bulwarks of a limited Constitution."[11]

After his often-quoted description of the judicial branch as "incontestably . . . beyond comparison the weakest of the three departments of power," Hamilton continued:

The complete independence of the courts of justice is peculiarly essential in a limited Constitution. By a limited Constitution, I understand one which contains certain specified exceptions to the legislative authority; such, for instance, as that it shall pass no bills of attainder, no ex post facto laws, and the like. Limitations of this kind can be preserved in practice no other way than through the medium of courts of justice, whose duty it must be to declare all acts contrary to the manifest tenor of the Constitution void. Without this, all the reservations of particular rights or privileges would amount to nothing.[12]

Hamilton rejected the argument that to allow the Court to declare acts of Congress invalid would elevate the "weakest branch" to a position superior to that of Congress:

. . . every act of a delegated authority, contrary to the tenor of the commission under which it is exercised, is void. No legislative act, therefore, contrary to the Constitution, can be valid. To deny this would be to affirm . . . that the representatives of the people are superior to the people themselves; that men acting by virtue of powers may do not only what their powers do not authorize, but what they forbid. . . .

. . . the courts were designed to be an intermediate body between the people and the legislature in order, among other things, to keep the latter within the limits assigned to their authority. The interpretation of the laws is the proper and peculiar province of the courts. A constitution is, in fact, and must be regarded by the judges as, a fundamental

"Where the will of the legislature . . . stands in opposition to that of the people, declared in the Constitution, the judges ought to be governed by the latter."

Alexander Hamilton, *The Federalist Papers*

law. It therefore belongs to them to ascertain its meaning as well as the meaning of any particular act proceeding from the legislative body. If there should happen to be an irreconcilable variance between the two, that which has the superior obligation and validity ought, of course, to be preferred; or, in other words, the Constitution ought to be preferred to the statute, the intention of the people to the intention of their agents.

Nor does this conclusion by any means suppose a superiority of the judicial to the legislative power. It only supposes that the power of the people is superior to both, and that where the will of the legislature, declared in its statutes, stands in opposition to that of the people, declared in the Constitution, the judges ought to be governed by the latter.[13]

A Slow Start: 1790–1800

On September 24, 1789, President George Washington signed the Judiciary Act into law and sent the Senate his nominations of six men to serve as the first members of the Supreme Court. One of the men so honored declined to accept a state post; another accepted but never attended a formal session; and John Jay, the first chief justice, spent much of his tenure abroad, engaged in diplomatic duties; he resigned after six years to become governor of New York.

Washington's original selections—all active participants in the founding of the new government—were:

• Chief Justice John Jay, age forty-four, of New York, coauthor with Hamilton and James Madison of *The Federalist Papers*.

• John Rutledge of South Carolina, fifty, a member of the Constitutional Convention.

• Robert Hanson Harrison of Maryland, forty-four, who declined the post to become chancellor of Maryland.

• John Blair of Virginia, fifty-seven, a member of the Constitutional Convention and a leader in the effort to obtain Virginia's ratification of the new national charter.

• James Wilson of Pennsylvania, forty-seven, signer of the Declaration of Independence, member of the Constitutional Convention, and a leader in obtaining ratification of the new charter by his state.

• William Cushing of Massachusetts, fifty-seven, a state judge and leader of the state ratification effort.

After Harrison's refusal, Washington selected James Iredell of North Carolina, thirty-eight, for the fifth associate justice's seat. Iredell had led the initially unsuccessful effort to win North Carolina's vote in favor of the new Constitution.

Confirmation of these first nominees came within two days, on September 26. Iredell was nominated early the next year, February 9, 1790, and confirmed the next day.

The tenure of five of these original members was brief. Jay resigned in 1795. Two other men followed him as chief justice within the Court's first decade. Rutledge resigned in 1791. He had never attended a formal session of the full Court. Blair, after several years of irregular attendance, resigned because of poor health in 1796. Wilson died in 1798. Iredell, the only member of the first Court to move his family to the new nation's capital, New York, resigned in 1799.[14] Cushing alone served into the nineteenth century, remaining on the Court for twenty-one years until his death in 1810.

FIRST TERMS

"The status of the federal judiciary in the 1790s," wrote political scientist Robert G. McCloskey, "was ambiguous and . . . comparatively minor. . . . The paramount governmental tasks were legislative and executive."[15]

The record of the Supreme Court's first decade bears out that statement. Only three of the six justices were present for the Court's opening session February 1, 1790. Jay, Wilson, and Cushing, wearing robes and, at least in Cushing's case, a wig, met briefly in the Royal Exchange Building in New York.

By February 2 Blair had arrived, making the quorum needed for transaction of business. But there was no business, aside from organizational matters, chief among which was the appointment of a clerk. After several days of admitting attorneys to practice before it, the Court adjourned its first term on February 10, 1790.

The second term lasted two days—August 2–3, 1790. Iredell, confirmed in February, was present.

In 1791 the capital and the Court moved to Philadelphia where the Court shared, with the mayor's court, a room in the new City Hall. No cases were decided by the Court in 1791 or 1792. The Court met in Philadelphia until 1800. Three times—in

1793, 1794, and 1797—it was forced by epidemics of yellow fever to cancel its August term.[16]

In 1791 Justice Rutledge resigned to take a state judgeship. Two of the men offered his seat declined, preferring to retain their seats in state legislatures.[17]

President Washington then selected Thomas Johnson of Maryland, at fifty-nine, one of the Court's oldest members. Johnson would hold the seat only fourteen months.

In 1792 Chief Justice Jay campaigned unsuccessfully from the bench for the post of governor of New York. He described his Court post as "intolerable."[18]

On February 18, 1793, the Court announced its decision in *Chisholm v. Georgia*, its first major case. Within five years, the country overturned that decision.

Reading Article III literally in *Chisholm*, the Court upheld the right of citizens of one state, South Carolina, to bring original suits in the Supreme Court against another state, Georgia. The vote of the Court was 5–1. Iredell dissented. Each justice announced his opinion orally.

The states were shocked, seeing in this decision the potential for their economic ruin. Early in 1798 the Eleventh Amendment was ratified. This amendment declared that states could not be sued, without their consent, in federal Courts by citizens of another state.

Despite the lack of many notable decisions during these first years, the justices found themselves quite busy—and rather unhappy—with the demands of their duty as circuit judges. For a full century, the justices worked to convince Congress to abolish this role, which fell to the justices because the Judiciary Act of 1789 provided no separate set of judges for the federal circuit courts. The act instead provided that Supreme Court justices would travel to hold circuit court where and when necessary.

This aspect of judicial duty, although onerous, served an important function in the new nation. Historian Charles Warren notes that "it was . . . almost entirely through their contact with the judges sitting in the circuit courts that the people of the country became acquainted with this new institution, the federal judiciary."[19]

But the distances the justices were required to travel were long, conditions were difficult, and questions were raised about the propriety of the justices participating in cases at the circuit level that were then reviewed by the Supreme Court. As early as 1790 Chief Justice Jay asked Congress to remove this burden. Congress responded with minor changes in 1793; the Judiciary Act of 1801 (which was quickly repealed) abolished the duty temporarily; but until late in the nineteenth century the requirement that justices fill this function remained on the statute books.[20]

COURT, CONGRESS, AND PRESIDENT

During its first decade, the Court made clear its character as a purely judicial branch, declining to perform nonjudicial functions assigned by Congress or to issue advisory opinions in re-

John Jay

Oliver Ellsworth

sponse to executive queries. "In other words," wrote Goebel in summarizing the Court's first years, "it left the formulation of policy to the branches of government where it conceived such belonged."[21]

In 1792 Congress gave circuit courts the duty of ruling upon claims of invalid pensioners. Justices Iredell, Blair, and Wilson, sitting as circuit judges, refused to carry out that duty, declaring that Congress had overstepped itself by requiring them to undertake such nonjudicial responsibilities. As a result of their protest, Congress amended the pension law.[22]

In 1793 President Washington asked the Court for advice on certain questions of foreign policy, neutrality, and treaty law. The justices politely declined, citing "the lines of separation, drawn by the Constitution between the three departments of the government" and "our being Judges of a Court in the last resort." Thereby, the Court established its policy of issuing no advisory opinions.[23]

Earlier that year Johnson had resigned. He was replaced by William Paterson of New Jersey, age forty-four, one of the two senators who had been primarily responsible for drafting and enacting the Judiciary Act of 1789. Paterson would serve until 1806.

During the February 1794 term the Court heard *Georgia v. Brailsford,* one of a handful of cases tried before it by a jury.[24] And in the last major case in which John Jay participated, the Court rejected the assertion that a foreign country had the right—independent of any treaty or other legal guarantee—to set up a prize court in the United States to decide the disposition of captured vessels.[25]

In April 1794 Jay accepted an appointment as special ambassador to England; he never returned to his seat on the Court. After concluding a treaty of "amity, commerce, and navigation" (the Jay treaty) with Britain, he resigned in June 1795 to become governor of New York.

John Rutledge of South Carolina, the absentee justice of the Court's first terms, was nominated by Washington—at Rutledge's own suggestion—to succeed Jay. Appointed while the Senate was in recess in 1795, Rutledge presided over the Court's August 1795 term but was refused confirmation by the Senate in December. The Senate acted upon reports of Rutledge's criticism of the Jay treaty and on rumors of his mental instability, rumors to which Rutledge gave new credibility by attempting suicide after his rejection by the Senate.

Washington, early in 1796, named Cushing, the senior justice, to lead the Court. Although he was confirmed, Cushing declined the post on the basis that at sixty-four he was too old. He would serve for fourteen more years.

President Washington next offered the post of chief justice to Sen. Oliver Ellsworth of Connecticut, who, with Paterson, had drafted the Judiciary Act. Ellsworth, fifty-one, was nominated March 3, 1796, confirmed the following day, and took his seat March 8.

TREATIES AND TAXES

Without Ellsworth, who was sworn in too late to take part in the decisions, the Court during the February 1796 term decided the two most significant cases of the decade—the treaty case of *Ware v. Hylton* and the tax case of *Hylton v. United States.* John

Marshall argued *Ware v. Hylton,* apparently his only appearance as an advocate before the tribunal he would lead for more than three decades. He lost the case.

In *Ware v. Hylton* the Court established the supremacy of federal treaty provisions over conflicting state laws. A Virginia law that allowed the confiscation, or payment in depreciated currency, of debts owed by Virginians to British subjects was invalid, held the justices, because it conflicted with provisions of the peace treaty with Britain, which ensured the collection of such debts.

Hylton v. United States brought to the Court the first clear challenge to an act of Congress as unconstitutional. There was no debate over the Court's power to rule on that point. Each of the sitting justices—while on circuit duty—had indicated his belief that federal courts were empowered to resolve such challenges.[26]

Congress had imposed a tax on carriages. The tax was challenged as a direct tax, which the Constitution required be apportioned among the states by population. The definition of "direct tax" was unclear, but the Court declared that the carriage tax was not a direct tax and thus was not subject to the apportionment requirement. The Court said that direct taxes were only those on land and on individuals, a definition that would stand for a century, until its repudiation by the Court in 1895.

A new member of the Court took part in these two decisions—Samuel Chase of Maryland. Chase, a political maverick, would be the only justice in history to be impeached and tried by the Senate. Chase was Washington's surprise choice to fill the seat left vacant by the resignation, in mid-1795, of Justice Blair. A signer of the Declaration of Independence, Chase had opposed ratification of the Constitution, arguing that it was an undemocratic document.

Nominated and confirmed in January 1796, he took his seat as the February 1796 term began—and voted with the majority in both the tax and the treaty cases. Chase and Ellsworth were the last of Washington's appointments to the Court. With Cushing and Paterson, Chase would serve well into the next century.

THE ADAMS YEARS

During the administration of John Adams, the Court issued one major decision, declaring in *Calder v. Bull* that the constitutional ban on ex post facto laws applied only to criminal, not civil, laws. Few other decisions of lasting significance were announced during the 1797–1801 terms.

With the deaths of Justices Wilson and Iredell, Adams had the opportunity to fill two seats on the Court. To succeed Wilson, Adams named Bushrod Washington of Virginia, thirty-five, President Washington's nephew. To succeed Iredell, he chose Alfred Moore, forty-four, of North Carolina. Washington would serve for more than three decades; Moore resigned in 1804 after barely five years on the bench.

The 1799 and 1800 terms of the Court were uneventful. The August 1800 term was the last to be held in Philadelphia. Only three justices attended—Paterson, Moore, and Washington.

Ellsworth, named ambassador to France in February 1799, was abroad—as he would be for the remainder of his time as chief justice. Cushing was ill. Chase was campaigning, unsuccessfully, for Adams's reelection.

In the election of 1800 the staunch nationalist position of the Court became a campaign issue, coupled with complaints about the ambassadorial service of Chief Justices Jay and Ellsworth, acting as agents of the Federalist administrations.

The Court's first decade was a cautious time. As Goebel concludes:

Its posture toward acts of Congress, except for a few instances of individual critique, was one of respect. There were, indeed, occasions . . . that invited inquiry into the constitutional basis for congressional action where less deference would have been appropriate. These opportunities were not seized, nor was there succumbing to the temptation to a loose construction of statutory language sometimes advanced by counsel in argument.

When the Court was constrained to explore the intendment of statutory language, it did so as a court of law in terms familiar to the profession and not by flights of fancy about the "spirit" of the Constitution.[27]

Establishment of Power: 1801–1835

With the year 1801 the new nation began a new century with a new president, Thomas Jefferson, and a new chief justice, John Marshall. Although Jefferson and Marshall shared a home state, they were life-long antagonists, and that personal tension further heightened the natural strains between the young nation's executive and judicial branches.

That same year the government moved to a permanent home, Washington, D.C. The Capitol was under construction as the home of Congress, a residence was planned for the president, but no one thought to provide a place for the Supreme Court to meet. At the last minute, it was allotted a small room in the unfinished Capitol. There it convened for its February 1801 term, the first of Marshall's thirty-four-year tenure.

Oliver Ellsworth, still in France on diplomatic assignment, resigned as chief justice in 1800. President Adams first named former chief justice Jay to the seat. Confirmation was immediate; so was Jay's letter declining the honor. Jay noted his failing health and the continuing responsibilities of the justices for holding circuit court. He wrote:

. . . the efforts repeatedly made to place the Judicial Department on a proper footing have proved fruitless. I left the bench perfectly convinced that under a system so defective, it would not obtain the energy, weight and dignity which are essential to its affording due support to the National Government, nor acquire the public confidence and respect which, as the last resort of the justice of the nation, it should possess.[28]

Adams was a lame duck, defeated for reelection in 1800, but he was not about to relinquish this opportunity. On January 20, 1801, he named John Marshall chief justice. Marshall was then secretary of state, after having served for a time on diplomatic assignment and in the House of Representatives.

Thomas Jefferson

After a brief delay by Federalist advocates of Justice Paterson's elevation to the chief justiceship, the Senate confirmed Marshall January 27.

MARSHALL AND *MARBURY*

Chief Justice Marshall was sworn in February 4, 1801, the second day of the Court's first term in Washington. He was forty-five years old. He would serve thirty-four years, until his death in 1835.

On the day set for the opening of the term, February 2, only Justice Cushing was present. By February 4 four members were present—Cushing, Chase, Washington, and Marshall. No cases were reported as decided during the term.

But events outside the Court's makeshift chamber were moving quickly with broad implications for the Court and its new chief justice. In February the House broke the electoral deadlock between Aaron Burr and Jefferson, choosing Jefferson as the new president. He took office March 4, 1801.

Only a few days before Jefferson's selection, Congress enacted the Circuit Court Act of 1801. The act eliminated circuit duty for the justices, providing for a separate staff of circuit judges. It shifted the Court's schedule, providing for June and December terms, instead of February and August; and it reduced to five the number of seats on the Court.

The law was widely viewed as a Federalist plan to allow Adams to name a last group of Federalist judges and to protect the Supreme Court from any immediate change through Jefferson's appointments. Adams filled the new judgeships with Federalist loyalists, confirming Jefferson's view that the federal judiciary would indeed remain a "strong fortress in the possession of the enemy."[29]

Another late-session law produced the situation that brought the case of *Marbury v. Madison* to the Court. This law created a number of justice-of-the-peace positions for the District of Columbia. On March 2 outgoing president Adams appointed men to fill those posts; they were confirmed the following day. Their commissions were made out and signed. But still-acting secretary of state John Marshall (also by now the sitting chief justice) failed to deliver all the commissions to all the nominees before the end of the Adams administration at midnight March 3.

President Jefferson appointed a number of these people to their sought-after posts, but not William Marbury, who came to the Supreme Court late in 1801, asking the justices to order Secretary of State James Madison to deliver him his commission. Marbury filed an original suit with the Court, asking that the justices use the authority granted them by the Judiciary Act of 1789 and issue a writ of mandamus to Madison.

The Court was already pursuing a path quite independent of the Jefferson administration. In August the justices demurred when Jefferson offered to give them his views on how to apply a law at issue in a pending case. The president's position, the Court indicated, was not relevant. Then, in December, the Court agreed to hear Marbury's case, setting arguments for the June 1802 term.

Jefferson was convinced that the Court would use *Marbury* as a vehicle for interfering in executive branch business. That view—and the Jeffersonians' distaste for the 1801 Circuit Court Act—sparked the law's repeal early in 1802. Circuit court duty was reinstated for the justices, and a single annual term was set for the Court, beginning each year in February.

Because the change in schedule was enacted after February 1802, this last provision delayed for fourteen months the term at which *Marbury v. Madison* would be argued. The Court did not meet from December 1801 until February 1803.

Two major decisions were announced in the 1803 term. In both their coupling and their resolution the skilled leadership of John Marshall was evident. Marshall's legal training was meager; he had little experience in the practice of law and none as a judge. Before his appointment as chief justice, he had been a politician and a diplomat. The skills gained from those posts characterized his tenure on the Court. For three decades his personality dominated the Court and the men who served with him.

More than at any other time in the Court's history, the personal characteristics of the chief justice were of considerably more importance than his legal talents. The Court operated as a family firm, not a federal institution. The justices, most of whom came to Washington for only a few months each year, leaving their wives and families at home, lived together in a boardinghouse. After their dinners together, they often, over wine, discussed and resolved the cases brought before them.[30]

These men, under the leadership of John Marshall, shaped

the Court and the federal judiciary, act by act and decision by decision. As Alexander M. Bickel described it:

Congress was created very nearly full blown by the Constitution itself. The vast possibilities of the presidency were relatively easy to perceive and soon, inevitably, materialized. But the institution of the judiciary needed to be summoned up out of the constitutional vapors, shaped and maintained; and the Great Chief Justice, John Marshall—not singlehanded, but first and foremost—was there to do it and did.[31]

The most famous example of Marshall's effect on the shaping of the court's role came just two years after he became chief justice. *Marbury v. Madison* was decided February 24, 1803. With that ruling, the Court at once claimed, exercised, and justified its power to review and nullify acts of Congress it found in conflict with the Constitution. And in so doing it neatly avoided an expected collision with Jefferson, although it did rebuke him for not delivering Marbury's commission.

Marbury was due his commission, the Court held: it should be delivered to him. But the Court also held that it was powerless to order the delivery, that the section of the Judiciary Act authorizing it to issue such orders was unconstitutional and void, an impermissible expansion of its original jurisdiction.

This decision "became authority . . . for the proposition—which had already been adopted in a majority of the states and which was destined to form a distinct feature of the whole political system of the United States—that a constitution is a fundamental law, that legislative and executive powers are limited by the terms of this fundamental law, and that the courts as interpreters of the law are expected to preserve and defend constitutions as inviolable acts, to be changed only by the people through the amending process."[32]

During congressional debate over repeal of the 1801 Circuit Court Act, the possibility was raised that the Court might declare the repeal unconstitutional, an improper effort by Congress to encroach on the independence of the Court. One week after *Marbury,* the Court made clear that it would exercise its newly affirmed power with care. The Court upheld the Repeal Act of 1802.[33]

It would be more than fifty years before the Court again declared void an act of Congress.

THE CHASE IMPEACHMENT

The business before the Court steadily increased during the first decade of the nineteenth century, but few of its decisions were of as much significance as some of the extrajudicial matters affecting the Court. Most notable of these was the impeachment, trial, and acquittal of Justice Samuel Chase.

Chase, a maverick at the time of his selection, continued to make enemies. He actively campaigned for President Adams in 1800. He strongly supported the hated Sedition Act of 1798—and presided as the judge in the trials of a number of persons charged with violating it.

After a particularly partisan speech to a grand jury in Baltimore in May 1803, Chase became the object of an impeachment drive. The charges against him involved both his conduct during the Sedition Act trials and this particular charge to the Baltimore grand jury. On March 12, 1804, the House impeached Justice Chase by a vote of 73–32.

His trial in the Senate began early in 1805. Chase, who continued to participate in the Court's functions, appeared in the Senate with his attorneys. Presentation of the evidence and arguments consumed a month. On March 1, 1805, he was acquitted. More than a majority of the senators voted to find him guilty on three of the charges against him, but the vote fell short of the two-thirds required for conviction.

Chase's acquittal ended any rumored Republican plans to impeach all four remaining Federalist justices—Marshall, Cushing, Paterson, and Washington. Furthermore, wrote Charles Warren, the acquittal represented a rejection of the Republican argument that impeachment could be used as "a means of keeping the courts in reasonable harmony with the will of the nation, as expressed through Congress and the executive, and that a judicial decision declaring an Act of Congress unconstitutional would support an impeachment and the removal of a judge."[34]

REPORTING THE DECISIONS

At the end of the 1804 term, William Cranch, then chief justice of the circuit court in the District of Columbia, began publication of Cranch's *Reports* of the decisions of the Supreme Court.

Alexander J. Dallas, a noted attorney in Pennsylvania, had reported some of the Court's decisions during its terms in Philadelphia, along with those of other courts in the state. But after the Court moved to Washington, Dallas discontinued this service.

Cranch, who would perform this public service for a dozen years, first published a volume including the decisions from 1801 through 1804. Until that time, the Court's opinions were little known by the bar and less by the general public. The exception was *Marbury,* which had been widely reported and discussed in the newspapers.

In his preface to the first volume, Cranch expressed the hope that publication of the Court's decisions would eliminate "much of that uncertainty of the law, which is so frequently, and perhaps so justly, the subject of complaint in this country."

Furthermore, he wrote, making public a permanent record of the Court's decisions might also limit judicial discretion:

Every case decided is a check upon the judge. He cannot decide a similar case differently, without strong reasons, which, for his own justification, he will wish to make public. The avenues to corruption are thus obstructed, and the sources of litigation closed.[35]

Early in Marshall's tenure—undoubtedly with the encouragement of Cranch—the Court began to write down its decisions and opinions. In addition, Chief Justice Marshall exerted all his considerable personal influence to convince his fellow justices to speak with one voice in these decisions. He persuaded them to drop the practice of *seriatim* opinions, under which each justice wrote and read his own views, and to adopt the

William Johnson

"opinion of the Court" approach, usually allowing him to write that opinion.

Appropriately enough, however, William Johnson, the first Republican justice, who served for most of Marshall's tenure, provided a counterbalance to the chief justice's push for judicial unanimity. Johnson, known as the "father of dissent," was only thirty-two at the time of his appointment to the Supreme Court, but he nevertheless did not hesitate to voice his disagreement with the chief justice and the Court.

Jefferson filled two other seats on the Court during his two terms in office. In 1806 Justice Paterson died, and Jefferson named John Jay's brother-in-law, Brockholst Livingston of New York, forty-nine, as Paterson's successor. Livingston served on the Court for sixteen years.

In 1807 increases in territorial and judicial business spurred Congress to create a new circuit that took in Kentucky, Tennessee, and Ohio, thus raising to seven the number of seats on the Supreme Court. Jefferson, after polling the members of Congress from those three states, named Thomas Todd, Kentucky's chief justice, to the new seat. Todd, forty-one, was nominated and confirmed in 1807, seated at the 1808 term, missed the 1809 term, and issued his first opinion—a dissent—in 1810. He served until 1826 but, like Livingston, his judicial career was notable mainly for his steady support of Chief Justice Marshall.

THE BURR TRIAL

In 1807 the Jefferson administration charged former vice president Aaron Burr with treason. The charge was related to Burr's alleged efforts to encourage an uprising in and a movement for the independence of the western states from the United States. The actions of the Supreme Court and its chief justice in this affair further heightened the animosity felt by the president for the Court.

Early in 1807 the Supreme Court, affirming its power to issue a writ of habeas corpus to challenge the detention of an individual by federal officials, held that there was insufficient evidence for the government to prosecute two of Burr's accomplices for treason.[36]

Jefferson, wrote Charles Warren, regarded this ruling as "another deliberate attack by the Court upon his executive authority" while the Federalists viewed it as "a noble example of the judicial safeguards to individual liberty."[37]

After the Supreme Court's term ended, Chief Justice Marshall traveled to Richmond to preside personally as circuit judge over the trial of Burr. His rulings that the government's evidence was insufficient to support a charge of treason were seen as directly contributing to Burr's acquittal later in the year. Jefferson, irate at the rulings and the outcome, suggested that the Constitution be amended to provide other means than impeachment for removing justices from the bench. The amendment was not approved.

Jefferson's feelings toward the Court were exacerbated during the national resistance to his administration's Embargo Act imposed during the conflict with Britain. Justice Johnson—one of Jefferson's appointees to the Court—declared illegal and void the president's effort to instruct customs officials to detain all vessels thought to be intending to evade the embargo.[38]

CONTRACTS AND CONFLICTS

In 1810 the Supreme Court for the first time exercised its power to strike down a state law as unconstitutional.

In *Fletcher v. Peck* the Court invalidated a law passed by Georgia's legislature in 1796 to repeal a 1795 land grant law obtained through bribery of the members of the 1795 legislature. The repeal was challenged by the innocent third parties who had acquired land under the 1795 grant and who now found their titles null and void. They argued that the legislative nullification was unconstitutional, a clear violation of the Constitution's language, which forbids states to impair the obligation of contracts.

The case was argued twice, in 1809 and 1810. One of the attorneys for the property owners bringing the challenge was thirty-two-year-old Joseph Story of Massachusetts.

On April 16, 1810, the Court—for whom Chief Justice Marshall spoke—held unconstitutional the legislative repeal of the land grant law and the nullification of the titles granted under it.

Story won his case, and the following year he was appointed to the Supreme Court.

In September 1810 Justice Cushing died—the last of the original six justices named to the Court in 1790; he had outlived all his original colleagues by a decade or more.

The interest that attended the search for Cushing's successor on the bench provided some indication of the status the Court had attained in its first decades. The Court was then evenly divided between Federalists (Marshall, Washington, Chase) and Republicans (Johnson, Todd, and Livingston).

President Madison received much advice on the selection of a nominee, including some from his predecessor, Thomas Jefferson. Despite all the advice—or perhaps because of it—Madison required four tries to fill Cushing's seat.

His first selection was Levi Lincoln, who had served as attorney general to Jefferson. Lincoln declined, but Madison nominated him anyway. The Senate confirmed the nomination, and Lincoln again declined, early in 1811.

In February Madison named Alexander Wolcott, a Republican leader in Connecticut, to the seat. Criticized as unqualified, Wolcott was rejected by the Senate: only nine votes were cast in favor of his confirmation. Madison subsequently nominated John Quincy Adams, then ambassador to Russia; Adams was confirmed but declined the appointment.

Madison then waited for most of 1811 before making another choice. The 1811 term—for which there was neither a quorum of justices present nor any business—passed virtually unnoticed.

At midyear Justice Chase died, creating a second vacancy. In November Madison nominated Gabriel Duvall of Maryland, comptroller of the treasury for almost a decade, to fill the Chase seat; he named Story to the Cushing seat. Both were confirmed and would serve long terms—Duvall, twenty-three years and Story, thirty-four.

For the next several years, the conflict with England—the War of 1812—was a dominant factor in the work of the Court. After the Capitol was burned by the British in August 1814, the Court met in temporary quarters for the next four terms, even holding some sessions in a tavern.

The cases before the Court largely involved wartime issues—neutral rights, ship seizures, and foreign affairs. The Court made clear in these rulings that violations of neutral rights were to be resolved diplomatically, not judicially. And it affirmed broad power for the federal government over the person and property of enemies during wartime.

One result of *Fletcher v. Peck* was considerable state resistance to the Court's exercise of its power to invalidate state actions. States began to question whether in fact Congress could authorize the Court to curtail state power in such a final manner. In 1816 the Court itself considered that question. The case presenting it was *Martin v. Hunter's Lessee*, a long-running dispute over the ownership of a large parcel of land in Virginia. Chief Justice Marshall did not participate in the Court's consideration of the case because of his own ties to the matter.

In 1813 the Court had ruled on the substance of the case, deciding in favor of the British claim to the land, rejecting the Virginian's claim. But the Virginia courts refused to obey the decision, ruling that the Supreme Court could not constitutionally tell a state court what to do.

This direct challenge to its authority returned to the Court in 1816. On March 20, 1816, it was firmly rebuffed. Justice Story wrote the Court's opinion, upholding the power of Congress to grant the Supreme Court appellate jurisdiction over all matters involving federal laws, treaties, and the U.S. Constitution—regardless of the court in which such cases had first been heard. This opinion, declared Charles Warren, "has ever since been the keystone of the whole arch of federal judicial power."[39]

In another 1816 ruling, however, the Court left the large and controversial area of criminal law almost entirely to state courts. In *United States v. Hudson and Goodwin* the justices declared that federal courts had no jurisdiction over criminal activity—except for matters that Congress had specifically declared to be federal crimes.

Warren described the end of the 1816 term as the end of an era. With the end of the War of 1812, he wrote, the attention of the people turned toward industrial and manufacturing endeavors, transportation, communication, and economic change. Questions of war, prize vessels, and embargo acts—which had taken so much of the Court's attention during the first years of the century—faded from the docket, replaced by questions of contract obligations, commerce regulation, and state powers.

Also at the end of this term, Cranch ended his work as unofficial reporter of the Court's work, and an official reporter, Henry Wheaton, was appointed. Congress authorized him a salary of $1,000 a year. He would hold that post for eleven years.

In their history of the Court, George L. Haskins and Herbert A. Johnson characterized the period 1801–1815 as one in which the Court, both in its dealings with the executive and Congress and in its internal development, established the foundations of the judicial power it would exercise with increasing visibility in the remaining decades of the Marshall era. With *Martin v. Hunter's Lessee*, Haskins and Johnson explained, the Court reinforced its power and the supremacy of the still-new federal government, and it did so even though the only Federalist still on the Court—Chief Justice Marshall—took no part in the ruling. That decision, they concluded, was "a victory for his [Marshall's] efforts to extricate the Court from partisan politics, and to establish a rule of law in the United States. The foundations of judicial power had been fixed firmly in place."[40]

1819: A REMARKABLE TERM

Three major constitutional decisions were announced by the Court in the term that convened February 2, 1819. This term, which brought the Court's rulings in *Dartmouth College v. Woodward, Sturges v. Crowninshield,* and *McCulloch v. Maryland,* was one of the most notable in history. With those decisions, the Court dramatically illustrated its view that the Constitution imposed far more stringent limitations on state actions than on the actions of Congress.

The Court was back in its permanent quarters in the rebuilt courtroom under the Senate chamber. Here the Court would meet until the Civil War.

The *Dartmouth College* decision was announced on the opening day of the term. Argued for three days in the preceding term, the case had drawn little attention in the nation's press. The dispute between a small college in New Hampshire and that state's legislature hardly seemed notable. But the issue was of major significance for the nation's economic development: Did the Constitution's contract clause protect private corporate charters—as well as public grants—against impairment by the state? "Yes, indeed!" responded the Court with only Justice Duvall dissenting. Not only did the decision protect Dartmouth College from a legislature that wished to reshape its structure and purpose; it also promised embryonic American corporations that they were secure against such tampering with charters.

Two weeks later the states received another blow. On February 17 the Court held invalid New York's insolvency law—enacted to ease the difficulties of debtors in default. The Court held that it violated the ban on state action impairing the obligation of contracts because it allowed the discharge of debts contracted before its passage.

The day before, the *National Intelligencer* of Washington, D.C., became the first newspaper in the country to begin printing daily announcements of the actions of the Supreme Court. Even so, the insolvency decision, *Sturges v. Crowninshield,* was misreported and misunderstood. Until a second ruling in 1827, it was generally thought that the states lacked any power to afford debtors this sort of relief.[41]

After these two rulings, the Court heard arguments—for nine days in late February and early March 1819—in *McCulloch v. Maryland.* Daniel Webster, a young member of Congress from Massachusetts who had argued successfully for Dartmouth College, argued for the Bank of the United States in this case. Again, he won.

McCulloch v. Maryland posed two questions: Could Congress charter a national bank? Could states tax its operations? The Court announced its decision on Saturday, March 6. Congress won and the states lost. The Court, with Chief Justice Marshall as its spokesman, was unanimous. Congress, Marshall declared, has broad power under the "necessary and proper" clause to decide the means by which it implements its powers. "Let the end be legitimate, let it be within the scope of the Constitution," he wrote, "and all means which are appropriate . . . which are not prohibited . . . are constitutional."[42] The bank was a useful fiscal instrument for national economic stability, so Congress might properly decide to incorporate it.

Furthermore, states could not hamper the exercise of this power. They could not tax the bank, for by taxing it, they could destroy it and frustrate the congressional purpose in chartering it. This decision aroused intense opposition, especially in the South and the West where the bank was particularly hated.

McCulloch v. Maryland, wrote Robert McCloskey, "is by almost any reckoning the greatest decision John Marshall ever handed down." In upholding the constitutionality of the bank's incorporation, Marshall "set down the classic statement of the doctrine of national authority. The argument he advanced was not new; its main outlines had been endlessly debated since the first Congress. . . . But Marshall deserves the credit for stamping

"Let the end be legitimate, let it be within the scope of the Constitution, and all means which are appropriate . . . which are not prohibited . . . are constitutional."

Chief Justice John Marshall, *McCulloch v. Maryland,* 1819

it with the die of his memorable rhetoric and converting it from a political theory into the master doctrine of American constitutional law."[43]

REVIEW AND REACTION

With its 1821 decision in *Cohens v. Virginia,* the Court for the second time reaffirmed its power to review state court decisions. *Cohens,* like *Martin v. Hunter's Lessee,* presented the Court with a basic challenge to its power under Section 25 of the Judiciary Act.

With great firmness, Chief Justice Marshall reiterated the points Justice Story had made in the 1816 ruling. When a state court held that state action did not conflict with the U.S. Constitution, federal law, or U.S. treaties, it was the constitutional obligation of the U.S. Supreme Court to review that decision.

Those who approved the decision considered it "one of the chief bulwarks of American unity." Critics—still led by former president Jefferson—saw it as one more blow to state sovereignty. Jefferson complained that the Court was "working like gravity . . . to press us at last into one consolidated mass."[44]

By 1825 the Court had nullified as unconstitutional at least one law from each of ten states. These rulings set off an effort to remove or at least restrict this power. Advocates of such a restriction considered repealing Section 25, amending the Constitution to have the Senate, not the Court, review all cases involving a state, and passing a law to require that five—or all seven—justices concur in holding a state law invalid.

Jefferson proposed that each justice be required to issue a separate opinion—as in the pre-Marshall days. He suggested that Congress then denounce the views of those with whom it disagreed—and impeach the justices who did not change their views. None of these proposals was approved by both chambers of Congress.

The years from 1811 until 1823 were remarkably stable at the Court. There was no change in the Court's membership. Then in March 1823 Justice Livingston died. President James Monroe chose Secretary of War Smith Thompson, also of New York and related by marriage to the Livingston clan, to fill the seat. Confirmed late in the year, Thompson took his seat in the February 1824 term. The most important case of his twenty-year-tenure would be the commerce power case of *Gibbons v. Ogden,* decided in his first term. But because of Thompson's close relationship to the Livingston family—to whom the contested steamboat monopoly involved in the case had been granted—Thompson would not participate in that landmark ruling.

CONGRESS AND COMMERCE

From the first day of its existence, Congress had—by constitutional grant—the power to regulate interstate and foreign commerce, but it scarcely exercised this power until well into the nineteenth century.

In contrast, the states had passed a variety of laws regulating commerce and transportation within their borders. In 1824, with its decision in *Gibbons v. Ogden,* the Court began the long process of defining the reach of federal commerce power and the limits it imposed on state power.

Gibbons v. Ogden was a challenge to New York's grant of a steamboat monopoly giving the Fulton-Livingston partnership exclusive rights to run steamships on New York waterways. The monopoly provoked considerable interstate animosity threatening to destroy both the national peace and any sort of incipient national commercial network.

The monopoly, challengers argued, interfered with federal power to regulate interstate commerce because it excluded from New York waterways vessels licensed under the federal coasting law, the most notable early law passed by Congress to implement its commerce power.

The case divided Republican against Federalist. It was argued for five days in February 1824. Daniel Webster represented the challengers. On March 3, 1824, Chief Justice Marshall announced the Court's opinion. Commerce, he explained, was not merely buying and selling of goods; it embraced "intercourse" of all sorts, including navigation. Congress had licensed vessels in the coasting trade. The state monopoly conflicted with the free operation of those federally licensed vessels and so must be held invalid.

Gibbons v. Ogden ranks with *McCulloch v. Maryland* as one of the two major rulings of the Marshall era establishing national power and national supremacy. Furthermore, *Gibbons v. Ogden* served as the "emancipation proclamation of American commerce,"[45] giving impetus to the development of the port of New York, the railroads, and a national system of commerce.

A few weeks after *Gibbons,* the Court approved further extension of federal authority at the expense of state prerogatives—holding in *Osborn v. Bank of the United States* that the bank could sue state officials in federal court even if the state did not consent. The Court declared that a state official who acted in reliance upon an unconstitutional state law—or exceeded his proper authority—was not immune from being sued in federal court for his actions. The justices thus began to narrow the effect of the Eleventh Amendment.

In response to the Court's steadily increasing workload, Congress lengthened the Court's term. Beginning in 1827, the Court convened its term a month earlier, on the second Monday in January.

When the 1827 term began, the Court had a new member. Justice Todd had died in 1826, and President John Quincy Adams named federal judge Robert Trimble of Kentucky as his successor. Trimble would serve only two terms before his death in 1828.

The 1827 term was a busy one. The Court resolved 77 cases during the two-month session, leaving 109 for resolution in the next term.[46]

With the January 1828 term a new reporter, Richard Peters Jr., took over publishing the Court's opinions. He would fill that post for fifteen years.

STATE POWERS

With federal supremacy firmly established by *Marbury, McCulloch,* and *Gibbons,* the Court in 1827 recognized that in some areas states could act concurrently with the federal government.

In *Ogden v. Saunders* the Court clarified the power of states to enact laws to help debtors. By an unusually close 4–3 vote, the justices upheld New York's revised insolvency law, which—as amended after the 1819 ruling in *Sturges v. Crowninshield*—applied only to debts contracted after its passage. For the first and only time in his career, Chief Justice Marshall was on the losing side in a constitutional case. Emphasizing the deference the Court owed to the decision of state legislators, Justice Washington wrote the majority opinion. Justices Duvall and Story joined Marshall in dissent.

Later in the term, the Court upheld a state's power to abolish the penalty of imprisonment for debtors. This change did not impair the obligation of a contracted debt, held the Court in *Mason v. Haile;* it simply modified the remedy for defaulting on that obligation.

Advocates of state powers did lose a major case. *Brown v. Maryland* posed the question of state power to tax imported goods. The state's advocate was Roger B. Taney, who would follow Marshall as Chief Justice. As Marshall had lost *Ware v. Hylton,* so Taney came out on the losing end of *Brown.*

States, the Court held in *Brown,* could not tax persons who sold imported goods; that tax interfered with the federal regulation of imports. So long as imported goods remained in their original package, held the Court, they could not be taxed by the state.

In 1828 Justice Trimble, the Court's junior member, died. Defeated for reelection, President Adams nonetheless named John J. Crittenden of Kentucky to fill the Trimble seat. The Senate refused to consider the nomination.

A week after his inauguration, President Andrew Jackson named John McLean of Ohio, Adams's postmaster general, to the empty seat. McLean, who would be a perennial presidential candidate during his thirty-one years as a justice, had already served in the House, run unsuccessfully for the Senate, and expanded the Post Office into the largest department in the executive branch. One of the most political of all the justices, McLean never hesitated to use his judicial opinions for political ends.

There was at least one other unsettling member of the Court during this period, wrote G. Edward White in *The Marshall Court and Cultural Change.* "If McLean's political concerns sometimes made him a distracted presence on the Court, Henry Baldwin's presence was surely a distracting one."[47]

Baldwin was President Jackson's choice to fill the seat left vacant in 1829 when Justice Washington died after thirty-two years on the Court. A Pennsylvanian, Baldwin was one of the most eccentric men ever to serve on the Court. His fourteen years as a justice were characterized by bouts of mental illness, vociferous quarrels with his colleagues, and bizarre constitutional writings.

Four times in the 1829 term, the Court spoke to questions of state power. The effect of three of the rulings was to restrict state authority. In *Providence Bank v. Billings* the Court held that a state that intended to grant a corporation a tax exemption must expressly include that privilege in the corporation's charter. In *Weston v. City of Charleston* the Court held that cities and states could not tax U.S. stock, finding such a tax an impermissible interference with the federal borrowing power. And in *Craig v. Missouri* the Court held that the constitutional ban on state bills of credit prohibited states from issuing loan certificates.

States, however, did win a ruling in *Willson v. Blackbird Creek Marsh Co.,* in which the Court upheld state power to regulate waterways and navigation thereupon, as long as Congress had not done so.

A slavery case was considered in the 1829 term. In *Boyce v. Anderson* the justices held that a slave who drowned in a steamboat accident was a passenger, not freight. Slave owners were disappointed; their recovery would have been greater had the slave been considered freight.

THE CHEROKEE CRISIS

Georgia and the Supreme Court collided in the waning years of the Marshall era over the state's effort to exert its authority over the Cherokee Indians by enacting stringent laws affecting the Indians and their land. The Cherokees asked the Supreme Court to order Georgia to stop enforcing these laws. While their request was pending before the Court late in 1830, Georgia ig-

nored a Court-ordered stay of execution for a Cherokee convicted of murder under the challenged laws and executed the man.

In 1831 the U.S. House of Representatives refused again to repeal the statute authorizing the Supreme Court to review state court rulings. In March the Court held that the Cherokees' case, brought as an original suit, could not proceed in that fashion because the tribe was not a separate nation in the eyes of federal law.

A second case arose quickly. Georgia had charged and convicted two missionaries, Samuel Worcester and Elizur Butler, for violating the state law that forbade white persons to live in Indian territory without a state license. Worcester and Butler took their case to the Supreme Court, arguing that the state lacked the power to impose or enforce such a requirement.

On March 3, 1832, Chief Justice Marshall announced that the Court found the state law unconstitutional, a usurpation of exclusive federal jurisdiction over Indian matters. The missionaries' conviction was reversed, and they should be released, the Court declared.

Georgia refused to comply. President Jackson openly sympathized with the state, allegedly remarking, "Well, John Marshall has made his decision, now let him enforce it."

For eight months the confrontation persisted. Worcester and Butler remained in jail. Jackson was reelected. Chief Justice Marshall was most depressed, writing to Justice Story that he doubted the Union would survive in the face of such rebellion by state authority.

But late in 1832 South Carolina's legislature, unhappy with a protectionist federal tariff, adopted a declaration "nullifying" the new tariff with which it had refused to comply. This placed Jackson in a highly contradictory position. He was supporting Georgia's resistance to the Supreme Court's decision while labeling South Carolina's resistance to the tariff as treason. Jackson made his choice and asked Congress to increase the power of federal courts to enforce federal laws in the face of such nullification.

It was clear to Georgia that its resistance to the Supreme Court's order would no longer have presidential support. The governor pardoned the missionaries, and the case ended. In 1833 Congress approved Jackson's request for expanded federal judicial power.

END OF AN ERA

Marshall's last major constitutional opinion was the 1833 ruling in *Barron v. Baltimore* that the Bill of Rights limited only federal, not state, action. "It is a striking fact," wrote Charles Warren, "that this last of Marshall's opinions on this branch of law should have been delivered in limitation of the operations of the Constitution whose undue extension he had been so long charged with seeking."[48]

As a result of *Barron v. Baltimore,* it was a full century before the Court addressed itself at length to questions of the rights of individuals rather than of institutions. And this decision made

Andrew Jackson

Roger B. Taney

In January 1835 the aged Duvall resigned. Jackson named Roger B. Taney, former attorney general and Treasury secretary, to succeed him. Taney had played a major role in Jackson's war on the Bank of the United States, implementing the president's order to remove U.S. funds from the bank. In that post he had made many enemies. Whig opposition to the nomination convinced the Senate, on the last day of its 1835 session, to postpone consideration of the Taney nomination. The vote was 24–21. The Duvall seat remained empty.

Then, on July 6, 1835, Chief Justice John Marshall died. The Court's great center chair was vacant.

Eulogies were numerous and elaborate. But perhaps the most objective assessment of his accomplishment as chief justice came from abroad. After traveling through the United States in the last years of the Marshall era, Alexis de Tocqueville wrote of the Supreme Court:

The peace, the prosperity, and the very existence of the Union are vested in the hands of the seven Federal judges. Without them the Constitution would be a dead letter: the executive appeals to them for assistance against the encroachments of the legislative power; the legislature demands their protection against the assaults of the executive; they defend the Union from the disobedience of the states, the states from the exaggerated claims of the Union, the public interest against private interests, and the conservative spirit of stability against the fickleness of the democracy. Their power is enormous, but it is the power of public opinion.[49]

No one had done more than John Marshall to establish that enormous power or to win the essential public respect for the still-young Supreme Court of the United States.

States' Rights: 1836–1860

Perhaps it indicates how infrequently presidential nominees to the Supreme Court adhere to the views of their patron, but the Court has rarely been known by the name of a president, even if he named all or most of its members. Washington select-

necessary the enactment of the Fourteenth Amendment, which would eventually, in the twentieth century, extend the guarantees of the Bill of Rights against state action and thus serve as the basis for an expansion of federal judicial power comparable to that of the Marshall era.

Three major cases were argued in the early 1830s but carried over to later terms because the Court was unable to resolve the questions they posed. They were *Charles River Bridge v. Warren Bridge, Briscoe v. Bank of the Commonwealth of Kentucky,* and *New York v. Miln.*

The Court's pace had slowed: Marshall was nearing eighty, and Johnson and Duvall were ill and absent much of the time.

An era was ending. In August 1834 Justice Johnson, the independent soul who fathered the Court's tradition of dissent, died. To succeed him, Jackson named James M. Wayne of Georgia. Wayne would serve for thirty-three years, until 1867.

Daniel Webster

Joseph Story

ed the entire original Court; it was never referred to as the "Washington Court."

The next president to name more than half the tribunal's members was Andrew Jackson. Of the six he named in eight years, four served for more than a quarter of a century, well into the Civil War years. McLean, Baldwin, and Wayne were Jackson's first three nominees. The fourth was Taney.

After consideration of Taney's nomination as an associate justice was postponed by the Senate early in 1835, Chief Justice Marshall's death created another vacancy on the Court. When Congress returned to town late in 1835, Jackson sent it a second Taney nomination. This time he named Taney chief justice.

To fill the other vacant seat Jackson chose Philip P. Barbour of Virginia, who had argued the state's case in *Cohens v. Virginia* (1821), in which the Court reaffirmed its power to review state court rulings denying federal claims. Barbour had served several terms in the House, during which he had advocated requiring five of seven justices to concur in holding a statute unconstitutional. He also had served as a state and a federal judge. Barbour would have the briefest tenure of all the Jackson appointees. He died in 1841 after five years on the Court.

The same political opposition that delayed action on Taney's first nomination to the Court delayed confirmation of him as chief justice until March 15, 1836. Leading the opposition were two of the foremost Supreme Court advocates of the era, Daniel Webster and Henry Clay. Nevertheless, the Senate confirmed Taney's nomination by a 29–15 vote.

While the Senate considered the nomination, the Court met without a chief justice for its 1836 term. Story, the senior sitting justice, presided.

CONTRACTS, CREDIT, AND COMMERCE

During Taney's first term, the 1837 term, the Court decided three major constitutional cases that had been pending throughout the last years of the Marshall era—*Charles River Bridge v. Warren Bridge*, *New York v. Miln*, and *Briscoe v. Bank of the Commonwealth of Kentucky*. All three went in favor of the states, and many saw the cases as evidence that the Taney Court would favor the rights of the states, which had been consistently curtailed by the Court under Chief Justice Marshall.

A more balanced assessment is provided by Carl B. Swisher, who wrote:

The work of the 1837 term . . . marked the beginning of a new order. The transition was not a sharp one, and those who saw it as such were mistaken. In spite of the radical doctrines sponsored by some Jacksonians of the time, the Court was careful to adhere to traditional patterns. . . . The change was limited . . . and yet it was there. There was a greater tendency to look to items of local welfare and to emphasize the rights of the states, a greater concern with living democracy in a rapidly changing society.[50]

First and most famous of these decisions is the case of Boston's Charles River Bridge, first argued before the Court in 1831. At issue was the constitutional ban on state action impairing the obligation of contracts. The Charles River Bridge Company, chartered by Massachusetts to build a bridge for pedestrian traffic across the Charles River, challenged a subsequent state decision allowing a second bridge. Daniel Webster argued for the original company that implicit in its charter was the exclusive privilege to carry such traffic. After five days of argument in January 1837, the Court announced its opinion in February. Chief Justice Taney wrote the Court's decision.

The Court did not undercut its earlier rulings protecting contracts, but it ruled against the Charles River Bridge Company. A charter, Taney explained, would not be construed to be more favorable to its corporate recipient, at public expense, than it explicitly required. In the absence of an explicit grant of monopoly privilege, the state had not infringed the first charter by granting a second to another company.

A few days later, the Court held that a state could require shipowners to report all passengers on ships arriving in its ports. This reporting requirement had been challenged in *New York v. Miln* as an infringement of the federal power to regulate foreign commerce. But the Court held the requirement a legitimate exercise of the state police power.

The term's third major ruling came in *Briscoe v. Bank of the Commonwealth of Kentucky,* which, like *Miln,* was first argued in the 1834 term. In it the Court upheld a state law that authorized a state-chartered bank to issue bank notes. Henry Clay had argued for the victorious bank.

This law, like that struck down seven years earlier in *Craig v. Missouri,* had been challenged as infringing the constitutional ban on state bills of credit. But where the Marshall Court had struck down the law in *Craig,* the Taney Court upheld that in *Briscoe.* Justice Story dissented, as he had in *Miln* and *Charles River Bridge,* saying that Chief Justice Marshall would have disagreed too.

On the last day of President Jackson's term, Congress expanded the Court to nine seats. Jackson immediately nominated John Catron of Tennessee and William Smith of Alabama to fill the two new seats.

Catron, the Tennessee campaign manager for the newly elected president, Martin Van Buren, was confirmed and served until 1865. Smith declined the second seat. Van Buren then named Alabama senator-elect John McKinley to the seat. He was confirmed and served fifteen years, although illness curtailed his participation for half that period.

During Taney's tenure, the Court continued to assert its own power and that of lower federal courts to resolve the increasingly frequent questions of the allocation of governmental authority. The decision reached in *Dred Scott v. Sandford* (1857) provides a dramatic example of the extreme to which this point could be carried. But unlike that ruling, most of the Court's pronouncements in this area simply consolidated and reinforced the position the Court already had assumed in earlier years.

In 1838 Rhode Island asked the justices to resolve a boundary dispute with Massachusetts, the first such case to come to the Court. Massachusetts moved to dismiss the case, arguing that the Court lacked the power to hear it. Over the dissent of the chief justice, the Court rejected the motion and proceeded with the case, which finally was resolved in favor of Massachusetts in 1846.

Also in the 1838 term the Court decided the case of *Kendall v. United States,* upholding the power of a federal court to issue an order directing an executive branch official to perform certain "ministerial" duties—even if the court order directly conflicted with presidential instructions. Such orders, held the Court, did not breach the separation of powers.

The increase in the number of corporations in the United States brought questions of corporate rights to the Court, and in 1839 the Court held that states could forbid out-of-state companies to do business within their borders. But in the same case the Court effectively moderated that holding; it declared that without clear evidence that a state intended to exercise this power, it would be assumed to consent to the operations of such "foreign" corporations.[51]

Five years later, the Court opened the doors of the federal courts to corporate litigation by modifying the strict view of a corporation's "residence" adopted early in the Marshall era. The new rule allowed more cases involving corporations to be heard in federal courts, rather than state courts, on the basis that the corporation and the opposing party were residents of different states.[52]

SLAVERY AND THE STATES

The early victories of the Taney era for advocates of state sovereignty were followed by a number of defeats in the 1840s. In *Holmes v. Jennison,* in 1840, the Court held that states had no power to engage in foreign affairs.

Two years later it held that federal courts were not bound by state judges' interpretations of state laws. In another case the Court held that states could not tax the income of federal officials.[53]

By this time virtually all questions of states' rights were linked to the increasingly sensitive issue of slavery. The Court had carefully avoided addressing this issue in any but peripheral ways, but in 1841, Swisher wrote, "the Court found itself in the thick of the slavery discussion, from which it did not actually escape until the close of the Civil War period, even though there were intervening years in which no such cases were actually decided."[54]

Thus, even when the issue was commerce in general, with no evident tie to slavery, the Court's opinions were closely perused and construed for their effect on state power to deal with slavery.

The double-edged nature of the issue—and all judicial efforts to deal with it—was evident in the 1841 and 1842 rulings of the Court and their public reception.

In 1841 the Court decided *Groves v. Slaughter* on a point other than the slavery questions presented. But Justice McLean's opinion, declaring the right of a state to exclude slavery, was interpreted by some southerners as upholding the right of a state to exclude free blacks as well.

The following year the Court decided *Prigg v. Pennsylvania,* striking down a Pennsylvania law setting up procedures for determining whether a black person was a sought-after fugitive before he or she was taken out of the state. Federal power over fugitive slaves was exclusive, leaving states no opportunity to pass such laws, held the Court. But, wrote Swisher, while upholding the power of the federal government to provide for the return of fugitive slaves, it nullified the obligations and seemed to nullify the power of the states to aid in the process, [and] it at once gave incentive to abolitionist activities and led the South to demand enactment of a Fugitive Slave Act which could be effectively administered without the aid of the states. Thereby it added to the furor of sectional conflict and the hysteria of competing parties.[55]

The Court's efforts to deal with increasingly difficult issues were hampered by the illness and disability of some of its members and then by long-vacant seats, the product of political turmoil outside the courtroom.

One of these vacancies was the longest in Supreme Court history. After the death of the eccentric Justice Baldwin, his seat remained empty for more than two years. This situation resulted from the political disaffection that marred the relationship between President John C. Tyler and Congress. Tyler had more nominations to the Court rejected than any other president. Of his six nominations, only one was confirmed.

Before Tyler took office, another new justice filled a seat. Justice Barbour died during the 1841 term. The lame-duck president, Van Buren, nominated—and the Senate confirmed—Peter V. Daniel of Virginia, a federal judge, to Barbour's seat. Daniel served until 1860.

Tyler had his first chance to name a justice when Justice Smith Thompson died in 1843. He chose Secretary of the Treasury John Spencer, who was rejected by the Senate in January 1844. Tyler next nominated Reuben Walworth of New York, state chancellor. Before its midyear adjournment, the Senate tabled that nomination.

In April, Justice Baldwin died. Tyler nominated Philadelphia lawyer James Edward King for that seat. The King nomination was also tabled by the Senate. Both nominations finally were withdrawn.

Early in 1845, Tyler, now a lame duck in addition to his other political disabilities, sent two more names to the Senate. To fill the Thompson seat he chose Samuel Nelson, a New York judge. Nelson, a well-respected figure, was quickly confirmed; he would serve on the Court for twenty-seven years, until 1872. But Tyler's selection of John M. Read as Baldwin's successor was ignored by the Senate. That seat remained empty for another full year.

Early in James Polk's administration, Justice Story died. He had served thirty-four years—longer than any other justice up to that time. Late in 1845 Polk nominated George W. Woodward of Pennsylvania to fill the Baldwin seat—and Sen. Levi Woodbury of New Hampshire to fill Story's chair. Woodbury—Taney's successor as secretary of the Treasury—was confirmed early in 1846; he would serve only six years before his death in 1851. Woodward, his nomination opposed by one of his state's senators, was rejected.

Finally, in August, Polk named Pennsylvania judge Robert C. Grier to the Baldwin seat. Grier's confirmation ended the twenty-eight-month vacancy on the Court. He served for twenty-four years, until his resignation in 1870.

For the next five years, the Court's membership was complete and stable.

CONFUSION AND CHANGE

Despite stability of membership, the Court's performance on the interlocking issues of commerce and slavery was confusing, to say the least. In the December 1846 term, the Court upheld the federal fugitive slave law.[56]

But in the same term, it backed state power to regulate commerce in intoxicating liquor. The diversity of reasoning among the justices in these latter cases—known as the *License Cases*—from Massachusetts, Rhode Island, and New Hampshire reflected the Court's increasing division over the proper allocation of state and federal power over commerce. Six justices wrote nine opinions.

In 1849 this uncertainty flowered into complete confusion with the Court's ruling in the so-called *Passenger Cases*. These two cases, from New York and Boston, involved challenges to state laws that required masters of vessels to post bonds and to pay a tax for each immigrant landed in the state. The laws were challenged as infringing upon federal power to regulate foreign commerce. They were defended as a proper exercise of the state's police power to protect its public health and welfare.

After hearing each case argued three times, the Court found these laws unconstitutional as in conflict with federal power over foreign commerce. But beyond that point the Court splintered, with eight justices writing separate opinions that took seven hours to read from the bench. The justices could not agree on whether the federal power over foreign commerce was exclusive, leaving no room for state regulation, or whether there might be such room if Congress had not exercised its power in a particular area.

There was no opinion of the Court in these cases, and Reporter Benjamin C. Howard, exercising considerable wisdom, declined to summarize the ruling beyond the fact that it struck down the challenged laws. For details and reasoning, he simply referred the reader to the "opinions of the judges."

In the 1829 case of *Foster v. Neilson*, the Court had refused to resolve an international boundary dispute because it said such a disagreement presented a "political question" that should be resolved by the more political branches of the government. Twenty years later the Court applied this doctrine in *Luther v. Borden* and refused to decide which of two competing factions was the legitimate government of Rhode Island. This too was a political question, held the Court, suitable for resolution by Congress, not the Court.

In 1844 Congress responded to the Court's increasing workload by once again lengthening its term. Opening day was moved back from January to the first Monday in December.

Other procedural changes during this time reflected the end of the days when the Court considered only a few cases and did so at a leisurely pace that allowed time for lengthy arguments and required less record keeping. In 1839 the Court required that all motions to it be filed in writing with the clerk. In 1849 the

Court limited the time for arguments, giving counsel for each side two hours to present his case, but no more, without special leave.

In 1843 Richard Peters, for fifteen years the Court's reporter, was fired by four of the justices acting in the absence of the chief justice and their other colleagues. Peters had fallen out of favor with several of the justices as a result of differences over the inclusion of their opinions in the reports. Peters was replaced by Benjamin Howard of Maryland, a former member of Congress and a college friend of Justice Wayne. Howard would serve until 1861.

CONFIDENCE AND CLARITY

Despite the personnel changes and philosophical difficulties endured by the Court during the 1840s, public confidence in it continued to grow. Charles Warren noted that public esteem for the Supreme Court was at a peak in the last years of that decade: "While there were extremists and radicals in both parties who inveighed against it and its decisions, yet the general mass of the public and the Bar had faith in its impartiality and its ability."[57]

The first decisions of the next decade appeared to bear out this confidence. The Court exercised restraint in dealing with the slavery issue—and appeared to be clarifying its position on commerce matters.

In the December 1850 term the Court heard arguments in *Strader v. Graham.* The basic question would arise again in *Scott v. Sandford* a few years later: Were slaves still slaves after they had worked for a time in a free state but then returned to a slave state?

The Court held that this matter should be resolved by the laws of the state in which the slaves were residing. This was not a matter for federal courts to resolve, held the justices.

In 1851 Justice Woodbury died. As his successor, President Millard Fillmore chose Benjamin R. Curtis, forty-one, a noted Boston attorney. Confirmed in December 1851, Curtis would serve only six terms, but in that brief tenure he would leave his mark on history.

During his first term, the Court decided *Cooley v. Board of Wardens of the Port of Philadelphia,* a commerce clause challenge to a Philadelphia ordinance regulating the use of pilots in its harbor. The Court upheld the ordinance, with Curtis as its spokesman. There are two categories of interstate and foreign commerce, he explained. One was essentially local and could be regulated locally, at least so long as it was not regulated by Congress; the other was essentially national and needed a uniform rule if it was to be regulated at all. This category could never be regulated by the states.

In one sense, Curtis' opinion was no more than "an eloquent statement of indefiniteness," wrote Swisher a century later, but "with the statement the indefiniteness came to seem in some way manageable, by contrast with the confusion of multiple opinions in the *License Cases* and the *Passenger Cases.* The opinion promised to give a more pragmatic, less conceptual and cat-

John A. Campbell

egorical direction to the Court's thinking concerning state regulation of commerce."[58]

This term brought two other commerce and navigation decisions of importance. In *Pennsylvania v. Wheeling & Belmont Bridge Co.,* the Court held that a bridge built by the state of Virginia across the Ohio River was too low and thus obstructed interstate commerce. The Court ordered the bridge torn down. But Congress in 1852 passed a law that declared the bridge did not obstruct interstate commerce, allowing the bridge to stand. This was the first example of Congress overturning a Court decision by legislation.

Also that term, the Court responded to the growing network of national commerce and transportation, substantially enlarging the federal government's admiralty jurisdiction to include all the nation's navigable waterways, not just those subject to the ebb and flow of tides.[59]

In July 1852 Justice McKinley died. To fill his place, President Fillmore chose Edward Bradford of Louisiana, who failed to win Senate confirmation. Fillmore next named Sen. George E. Badger of North Carolina, whose nomination was effectively killed when the Senate, in an unusual breach of tradition, postponed consideration of it, by a one-vote margin, early in 1853. In the last week of his term, Fillmore sent still a third name to the Senate, that of Louisianan William C. Micou—but the Senate refused to confirm him.

The new president, Franklin Pierce, chose John A. Campbell of Alabama, forty-one, well known both for his scholarship and for his advocacy before the Supreme Court. Campbell was confirmed and served until the outbreak of the Civil War.

Benjamin R. Curtis

In 1856 the Court began the long process of defining due process. In *Murray's Lessee v. Hoboken Land & Improvement Co.,* the Court held that the Fifth Amendment guarantee of due process applied to the actions of Congress, as well as to those of the executive and judicial branches.

And Justice Curtis, writing for the Court, defined due process as procedures that did not conflict with specific written provisions of the Constitution or with the established practice in England at the time of the settlement of the New World.

SCOTT V. SANDFORD

In 1856 the Court heard arguments in the case involving Dred Scott, a Missouri slave who claimed that he was free as a result of a sojourn in Illinois and other territories that were "free states" under the Missouri Compromise of 1820. Scott's case was first argued February 11. In May the Court ordered the case argued again. Reargument took place early in the December 1856 term. Justice Curtis's brother was one of the attorneys appearing in the case.

Chief Justice Taney was aging. This factor, along with health and family problems of other members of the Court, slowed its operations. Not until February 1857—a year after the first arguments—was *Scott v. Sandford* discussed at conference.

The Court agreed the decision would follow that in *Strader v. Graham* a few years earlier—holding that Scott's status should be resolved under state law. The majority agreed not to consider the larger issue—whether Congress had the power to exclude slavery from some territories, as it had done in the now-repealed Missouri Compromise. Justice Nelson was assigned to write the majority opinion.

But Justices McLean and Curtis, both adamant abolitionists, dissented and announced their intention to declare that the Missouri Compromise was proper, that Congress indeed had the power to ban slavery from the territories. The majority was compelled to revise its plan. Nelson's assignment was withdrawn, and Chief Justice Taney assumed the task of writing the majority's opinion.

Taney's illness delayed its announcement until March 6, 1857, just after President James Buchanan was inaugurated. Each justice wrote a separate opinion in this case; the reading of the opinions in Court took two days. The majority declared black people forever disabled from attaining citizenship, the Missouri Compromise unconstitutional, and Congress powerless to halt the spread of slavery.

The Court had overreached its power in setting such limits to the hopes of blacks and the powers of Congress. It forced the issue of slavery out of the courtroom and the legislative chambers and onto the battlefield. This was also the first of the "self-inflicted wounds" of the Court. One scholar summarized its impact:

During neither the Civil War nor the period of Reconstruction did the Supreme Court play anything like its role of supervision, with the result that during the one period the military powers of the President underwent undue expansion, and during the other, the legislative powers of Congress. The Court itself was conscious of its weakness. . . . [A]t no time since Jefferson's first administration has its independence been in greater jeopardy than between 1860 and 1870.[60]

The *Scott* decision was endorsed by southern Democrats and denounced by northern Democrats, dividing the party and enabling the Republican Party to win the White House in 1860. Of this development, Charles Warren wrote, "It may fairly be said that Chief Justice Taney elected Abraham Lincoln to the presidency."[61]

Another result of that decision was Justice Curtis's decision to resign after only six years on the Court. His philosophical disagreement with his colleagues and his general lack of confidence in the Court, compounded by an acrimonious exchange with Chief Justice Taney over access to the *Scott* opinions, spurred him to leave the bench and return to his more lucrative practice of law. He resigned in September 1857. He would argue more than fifty cases before the Court in subsequent years, including the first of the *Legal Tender Cases,* which he lost.

To replace Curtis in the "New England" seat President Buchanan nominated former attorney general Nathan Clifford. Clifford, considered a party hack by some in the Senate, was confirmed early in 1858 by a three-vote margin. He served until his death in 1881.

Although Chief Justice Taney's name became almost synonymous with his opinion in *Scott v. Sandford*—and the damage it did to the nation and the Court—his last major prewar opinion was both far more eloquent and more enduring in its impact.

Two years after the Scott ruling, the Court decided *Ableman v. Booth.* In speaking for the Court, Chief Justice Taney delivered a ringing reaffirmation of federal judicial power.

Ableman v. Booth involved an abolitionist in Wisconsin who was tried and convicted of violating the federal Fugitive Slave Act. Both before his trial and after his conviction, state judges ordered federal officials to release him, using the writ of habeas corpus and declaring his detention improper.

The case came before the Supreme Court in January 1859. The state did not send anyone to argue its side. On March 7, 1859, the unanimous Supreme Court declared that state judges lacked the power to interfere in such a manner in federal judicial proceedings. To allow such interference, wrote Taney, "would subvert the very foundations of this Government." As long as the Constitution endured, he continued, "this tribunal must exist with it, deciding in the peaceful forms of judicial proceedings the angry and irritating controversies between sovereignties, which in other countries have been determined by the arbitrament of force."[62]

The *Scott* case and the conflict that followed so colored historians' view of the Taney Court that only after a century had passed was an objective assessment of its accomplishments attempted.

In the concluding chapter of his history of the Taney era, Swisher described the Court's decisions and operations during this period:

By contrast with the work of the same tribunal in various other periods, the essence of its contribution was seldom focused in eloquent philosophical statement from the bench. The Taney Court was peculiarly unphilosophical. . . . [I]t tended to be assumed that the federal constitutional system was now generally understood so that the earlier forms of judicial explanation were unnecessary. The government was no longer experimental but was a going concern. . . .

The Taney Court fell upon evil times not because of Jacksonianism or even because of lack of ability on the part of its members, but because it was caught in the grinding pressures of sectional conflict. A Court committed to the application of the law was bound to crash into difficulties when the nation itself divided over whether there was indeed a surviving body of constitutional law binding on all the states and all the people.[63]

War and Recovery: 1861–1872

The Civil War decade brought the Supreme Court to a new low in public esteem. It was, Swisher explained,

not merely because it had handed down the *Scott* decision but because the rule of law as interpreted by the judiciary had given way to a rage for unrestricted exercise of power—which seemed to flare with even greater violence once the battlefields were stilled. There could be a restoration of the prestige of the judiciary only with restoration of respect for the rule of law.[64]

During the last years of Chief Justice Taney and the tenure of his successor, Chief Justice Salmon P. Chase, the Court underwent considerable change.

It moved into a new courtroom, grew to ten members and then shrank to eight, gained five new members—including the new chief justice—and found itself facing extremely sensitive questions of executive power.

In mid-1860 Justice Daniel died. His seat remained empty for almost two years. Late in his term, President Buchanan named his former attorney general and secretary of state, Jeremiah S. Black, to fill Daniel's seat. But in February 1861 political opposition within both parties brought the rejection of Black's nomination by a vote of 25–26.

The Civil War broke out in April. That month Justice McLean died, and Justice Campbell resigned when his home state, Alabama, seceded. The Court's other southern members, Wayne and Catron, continued to hold their seats through the war.

President Abraham Lincoln thus had three seats to fill as soon as he arrived at the White House. In January 1862 he selected Noah H. Swayne, an Ohio attorney, fifty-seven, to fill the McLean seat. Swayne would serve nineteen years. In July 1862 Lincoln filled the empty Daniel seat by naming Samuel Freeman Miller of Iowa, forty-six, the only justice trained in medicine as well as law. Miller would serve for twenty-eight years, until 1890, writing 616 opinions.[65]

To the third seat Lincoln named his close friend and political adviser David Davis of Illinois, forty-seven. Davis would serve fourteen years, until he resigned to take a Senate seat.

In March 1863 Congress added a tenth seat to the Court, giving Lincoln a fourth appointment. To that new seat he named Stephen J. Field, chief justice of the California Supreme Court, who would serve almost thirty-five years and be the only justice ever the target of an assassination attempt as a result of his rulings. When Field was appointed he had to travel to Washington by steamship and railroad across Panama—the transcontinental railroad was not completed until 1869.

When the Court met for its December 1860 term, it met in a new courtroom. After four decades in the basement room under the Senate chamber, the Court moved upstairs. The new wings of the Capitol housing the Senate and House had been completed; the old Senate chamber had been refurbished for the Court at a cost of $25,000. The Court would meet in this room for the next seventy-five years, until it moved into its own building.

The Court had a new reporter in 1861. Benjamin Howard resigned to run a losing race for governor of Maryland. He was followed by Jeremiah Black, Buchanan's unsuccessful nominee for the Daniel seat. Black served for only two years, resigning in 1863 to resume his private law practice. He was succeeded in 1864 by John William Wallace of Pennsylvania, who held the post until 1875.

PRESIDENTIAL WAR POWERS

The Civil War began in April 1861. Congress was not in session and did not meet until midsummer. In the interim President Lincoln called for troops, imposed a blockade on southern ports, and in some circumstances authorized military commanders to suspend the writ of habeas corpus. These actions were the most dramatic expansion of executive power in the nation's history to that point and, not surprisingly, they were challenged as exceeding the president's constitutional authority.

Chief Justice Taney was among the first to declare Lincoln's actions unconstitutional. In May, the month after war had bro-

THE COURT IN 1865
From left: Court Clerk Daniel W. Middleton, Justices David Davis, Noah H. Swayne, Robert C. Grier, James M. Wayne, Chief Justice Salmon P. Chase, Justices Samuel Nelson, Nathan Clifford, Samuel F. Miller, Stephen J. Field

ken out, a military commander in Baltimore refused to comply with Taney's order—issued as a circuit judge, not a Supreme Court justice—to produce in court one John Merryman, a civilian imprisoned by the Union army for his anti-Union activities.

The commander cited, as grounds for his refusal, Lincoln's instructions allowing him to suspend the privilege of the writ of habeas corpus, the instrument used to inquire into the reasons justifying an individual's detention by government authority. Taney responded with an opinion, which he sent to Lincoln himself, declaring that only Congress could suspend this privilege and that Lincoln's actions were unconstitutional. If such authority can be "usurped by the military power . . . the people of the United States are no longer living under a government of laws, but every citizen holds his life, liberty, and property at the will and pleasure of the army officer in whose military district he may happen to be found."[66]

Lincoln, undeterred, continued to insist that emergency conditions required the exercise of extraordinary power. Five years later, after both Taney and Lincoln were dead, the Supreme Court in *Ex parte Milligan* confirmed Taney's position.

The legality of Lincoln's blockade of southern ports was the major war issue resolved by the Court during the war years. These *Prize Cases* were decided in favor of presidential power, although only by a vote of 5–4.

Had the vote tipped the other way, all of Lincoln's wartime actions would have been called into question, seriously undermining his ability to lead the nation in the conflict. The majori-

ty upheld the president's power to institute the blockade even before Congress officially had authorized such an action. The vote made clear the importance of Lincoln's appointments to the Court. The majority consisted of his first three nominees—Swayne, Miller, and Davis—and Wayne and Grier, who wrote the majority opinion. Dissenting were Taney, Nelson, Catron, and Clifford.

Having resolved that critical question, the Court retreated to a position of restraint in dealing with issues of war. In the December 1863 term, Taney's last, the Court held that it lacked jurisdiction to hear a challenge to the use of paper money as legal tender (necessary to finance the war),[67] or over a petition of habeas corpus ordering military officials to justify their detention of a civilian.[68] Within six years, the Court would reverse both holdings.

In October 1864, as the war neared its end, Chief Justice Taney died. He was eighty-seven years old and had served the nation as its chief justice for twenty-eight years.

President Lincoln wished to name a man who would back the administration on the critical issues of emancipation—another exercise of extraordinary presidential powers that lacked any clear base in the Constitution—and legal tender. Congress had passed laws making paper money legal tender in place of gold to enable the Union to finance its war effort.

Lincoln chose Salmon P. Chase, a potential political rival who had, nevertheless, served until mid-1864 as secretary of the Treasury. After his reelection in 1864, Lincoln nominated Chase as chief justice. He was confirmed and seated as the Court began its December 1864 term. Chase was fifty-six, three years younger than Taney when he had assumed the post, yet he would serve only nine years before his death in 1873.

"Never again would there be a term wherein so few questions of importance were answered as in that of 1864–65," wrote historian Charles Fairman.[69]

But the following term brought another facet of the *Merryman* issue that had confronted Chief Justice Taney five years earlier: Can a president in wartime replace the nation's civilian courts with courts-martial, to which civilians as well as military personnel are subject?

In April 1866 the Supreme Court answered this question with an emphatic no—just as Taney had. The justices were unanimous in holding that Lincoln had acted illegally when he instituted trial by military commission for civilians in nonwar areas where the civil courts continued to function.

The Court divided 5–4 on whether Congress and the president acting together could replace civilian justice with courts-martial in such areas.

The Court's full opinions in *Ex parte Milligan* were not released until December 1866—eight months later. The majority opinion was written by Lincoln's personal friend, Justice Davis, who warned as Taney had that suspension of constitutional guarantees during wartime would lead to despotism.

These opinions and this ruling provoked violent criticism in Congress, where they were viewed as evidence that the Court would—at its first opportunity—hold unconstitutional the military regimes imposed by Congress upon the defeated South as its Reconstruction program.

Congressional criticism took a variety of forms—proposals for impeachment of the justices in the majority, "reorganization" of the Court through the addition of new seats, curtailment of the Court's appellate jurisdiction, and the requirement that the Court be unanimous on constitutional rulings.

In fact, the Court did undergo some reorganization at this point, due, however, more to the unpopularity of President Andrew Johnson than to the Court's own rulings. In May 1865 Justice Catron died after twenty-eight years on the Court, the last of which he had spent in virtual exile from his southern home. Johnson's April 1866 nomination of his close friend, Attorney General Henry Stanbery, died after the Senate abolished the vacant seat and reduced the size of the Court to eight by providing that both Catron's seat and the next one becoming vacant not be filled.

In mid-1867 Justice Wayne, the Court's other southern member, died after thirty-two years on the bench. He was the last of the Jackson justices; his service had spanned the Taney era. His seat was not filled; the Court was now eight members.

RECONSTRUCTION AND REVIEW

The apprehensiveness of Reconstruction architects about the Court was heightened early in 1867. The Court struck down an act of Congress requiring persons wishing to practice law before the federal courts to take a "test oath" affirming their loyalty, past and present, to the Union.

Augustus H. Garland, a noted Supreme Court advocate who had served in the Confederate government, challenged this requirement. A similar state law also was challenged.

In *Ex parte Garland* and *Cummings v. Missouri,* the Court in 1867 held both state and federal oaths unconstitutional, in violation of the bans on ex post facto laws and bills of attainder. The only Lincoln justice voting with the majority against the oaths was Field, who apparently was persuaded by the arguments of his brother, David Dudley Field, who had argued one of the cases before the Court.

After *Milligan* and the *Test Oath Cases,* however, the Supreme Court showed no stomach for battle with Congress on the overall issue of Reconstruction.

In the 1867 term—only months after the *Garland* case—the Court unanimously refused Mississippi's request that it order President Johnson to stop enforcing the Reconstruction Acts. Such an order, the Court held in *Mississippi v. Johnson,* was outside its power and its jurisdiction.

In 1868, however, a southern editor named McCardle asked the Court to order his release through a writ of habeas corpus to military authorities in Mississippi. This case brought to a peak the concern of Reconstruction advocates in Congress.

McCardle was being held for trial by a military commission on charges that his anti-Reconstruction articles were impeding the process of "reconstructing" the South. The Court heard arguments the first week of March 1868, just as the Senate opened its impeachment trial of President Johnson. Three days after the Court had taken *McCardle* under advisement, Congress revoked its jurisdiction over such cases. Johnson vetoed the bill. It was immediately repassed over his veto.

The Court then considered a new issue, the impact of the repeal of its jurisdiction on the pending case. In May the Senate acquitted President Johnson. In April 1869 the Court dismissed the *McCardle* case, finding unanimously that once Congress revoked its jurisdiction over a category of cases, all it could do was dismiss all pending cases of that type.

The same day, in *Texas v. White,* the Court majority endorsed the view that as a matter of law the seceding states never had left the Union—that states had no power to secede—a moot point in 1869. Justices Swayne, Grier, and Miller objected that the majority was endorsing a legal fiction and ignoring political reality.

GOLD OR GREENBACKS

To finance the war, Congress had passed the Legal Tender Acts, allowing the use of paper money to pay debts. These laws, which resulted in drastic change in the nation's economic system, repeatedly were challenged in federal courts.

In the December 1867 term, the Supreme Court heard a challenge in the case of *Hepburn v. Griswold.* A second round of arguments took place in December 1868; one of the attorneys arguing for the acts was former justice Benjamin R. Curtis. The Court was expected to uphold the acts. After all, Chief Justice

Chase had been Treasury secretary when they were approved. But no decision was announced during the December 1868 term.

The justices apparently did not reach a decision until November 1869—and then their efforts were hampered by the vacillations of the aged justice Grier, who voted in conference first to uphold the acts, then to strike them down.[70] The final vote was 5–3 against the Legal Tender Acts. The majority was Chase, Nelson, Clifford, Field, and Grier.

Congress in 1869 provided that a justice might retire and continue to receive half his salary. In December—before the Court announced its decision in *Hepburn v. Griswold*—Justice Grier, seventy-six, was persuaded to retire, effective February 1, 1870. Six days after his resignation, on February 7, 1870, the Court announced that by a 4–3 vote it found the statutes unconstitutional. They were inappropriate means for the exercise of the war powers, held the majority, and, as applied to debts contracted before the passage of the laws, they were a clear impairment of contract obligations. The dissenters were Justices Miller, Swayne, and Davis.

Even as Chase was reading the opinion, the most effective Court packing in the nation's history was under way—or at least the best-timed appointments.

After Ulysses S. Grant's election as president in 1868, Congress increased the size of the Court to nine, giving Grant a new seat to fill. Grier's decision to retire opened a second vacancy. Grant first chose Attorney General Ebenezer Hoar of Massachusetts for the new seat, but personal and political opposition developed to block his nomination in the Senate. To smooth the way for Hoar's confirmation, Grant nominated former secretary of war Edwin M. Stanton—the choice of most members of Congress—for the Grier seat. Stanton was confirmed immediately, but died four days later. Hoar's nomination was rejected in February 1870; the vote was 24–33.

And so on February 7, 1870, Grant sent two more nominations to the Senate—Joseph P. Bradley of New Jersey, fifty-seven, a railroad attorney, and Grier's personal choice; and William Strong of Pennsylvania, a state judge. Bradley and Strong were confirmed and seated in March 1870.

Within weeks of their seating the Court announced it would rehear the constitutional challenge to the Legal Tender Acts. The second of these cases, *Knox v. Lee,* was argued in the December 1870 term.

On May 1, 1871, fifteen months after *Hepburn v. Griswold,* the Court overruled itself. By a 5–4 vote, the Court reversed the 4–3 vote in the earlier case. The majority upheld the Legal Tender Acts as a proper exercise of the power of Congress. Justice Strong, who with Bradley converted the dissenters in *Hepburn* into the majority in *Knox,* wrote the opinion. The full opinions were not released until January of the following year.

This abrupt about-face—so clearly the result of a change in the Court's membership—damaged the public confidence the Court had been slowly regaining after the *Scott* ruling and the war decade. It was, in the words of Charles Evans Hughes, the second of the Court's self-inflicted wounds. Hughes declared that "there was no ground for attacking the honesty of the judges or for the suggestion that President Grant had attempted to pack the court." But he added, "Stability in judicial opinions is of no little importance in maintaining respect for the court's work."[71]

The Balance of Power: 1873–1888

The Union had been preserved. Indeed, in *Texas v. White* a majority of the Supreme Court endorsed the legal fiction that it never had been disrupted. Now as the war issues faded from its docket, the Court set about restoring the state-federal balance of power.

Concern for the states as effective functioning units of the federal system was paramount in the minds of the justices. And so, to enhance state power, the Court curtailed federal authority.

The Court's power of judicial review of acts of Congress was wielded with new vigor. Between *Marbury* in 1803 and the *Slaughterhouse Cases* in 1873, the Court held unconstitutional ten acts of Congress. Six of the ten were struck down between 1870 and 1873.

Another sign of the Court's sensitivity to the claims of states was its decision in 1871 that, even as the salaries of federal officials were not subject to state taxes, so state officials' salaries were immune from federal taxes.[72]

THE FOURTEENTH AMENDMENT

No better example of the Court's view of the proper balance between state and federal power can be found than its rulings interpreting the Civil War Amendments, in particular the Fourteenth Amendment.

In 1865 the Thirteenth Amendment formally abolished slavery. In 1868 the Fourteenth Amendment gave added protection to the rights and liberties of persons threatened by state action. And in 1870 the Fifteenth Amendment guaranteed blacks the right to vote.

Intended as instruments of radical change in the nation's social fabric, these amendments were so narrowly construed by the Court in the decades immediately after their adoption that they lay virtually useless for most of the ensuing century.

The effect of these rulings was to preserve state power over the rights of individuals by denying any expansion of federal authority in that area.

The Court's first ruling on the scope of the Fourteenth Amendment came in the 1873 *Slaughterhouse Cases.* It was indicative of the direction in which Fourteenth Amendment protections would first be extended that these cases were brought by butchers seeking to protect their businesses rather than by blacks seeking to assert their newly granted civil rights.

Louisiana had granted one company a monopoly on the slaughtering business in New Orleans. That grant was challenged by other butchers as denying them the right to practice their trade. They argued that this right was protected by the Fourteenth Amendment's guarantee of the privileges and im-

THE COURT IN 1876

From left: Justices Joseph P. Bradley, Stephen J. Field, Samuel F. Miller, Nathan Clifford, Chief Justice Morrison R. Waite, Justices Noah H. Swayne, David Davis, William Strong, Ward Hunt

munities of U.S. citizenship, of equal protection of the laws, and of due process.

The *Slaughterhouse Cases* were first argued in January 1872, just before the Court's opinions in the second *Legal Tender Case* were read. But those arguments were before an eight-man Court. Justice Nelson, now eighty, was absent. The Court apparently was evenly divided and ordered the cases reargued in the following term.

Before the December 1872 term began, Nelson resigned after twenty-seven years of service. President Grant named Ward Hunt, a New York judge—as Nelson had been—to the seat. Hunt was seated in December 1872.

The *Slaughterhouse Cases* were reargued over a three-day period in February 1873. Attorney for the butchers was former justice John Campbell. The Court announced its decision April 14, 1873. By 5–4, the Court held that Louisiana had not violated the Fourteenth Amendment by its grant of a slaughtering monopoly.

Writing for the Court, Justice Samuel Miller stated that the amendment did not increase the number of rights an individual possessed, but only extended new protection to those few rights, privileges, and immunities that had their source in one's federal, rather than state, citizenship. The right to do business did not derive from one's U.S. citizenship, held the majority.

Any other decision, wrote Miller, would convert the Court into "a perpetual censor upon all legislation of the States on the civil rights of their own citizens."[73]

Chief Justice Chase dissented, as did Justices Swayne, Field, and Bradley. The next day, over Chase's lone dissent, the Court held that a state did not deny a woman the privileges or immunities of U.S. citizenship when it refused, because of her sex, to license her to practice law in its courts.[74]

Within the month, Chief Justice Chase was dead of a sudden stroke. His seat remained vacant for most of the following year.

President Grant tried unsuccessfully to place two of his personal friends in the seat, naming first George Williams, attorney general of Oregon, and then Caleb Cushing, a former attorney general of Massachusetts. Finally, he chose a little-known Ohio attorney, Morrison R. Waite, fifty-eight. Waite, who never had argued a case before the Supreme Court and who had no judicial experience, was confirmed. He was seated in March 1874.

The term in which Waite began his fourteen years as chief justice was the first to begin in October. Early in 1873 Congress had provided that the Court's term would begin the second Monday in October rather than in December as it had since 1844.

Unlike Chief Justice Chase, Waite agreed fully with the Court's narrow view of the privileges and immunities of federal citizenship. In 1875 he wrote the Court's opinion reinforcing its decision in the *Slaughterhouse Cases,* holding that the right to vote was not a privilege of U.S. citizenship.[75]

The Court remained reluctant to acknowledge either that the Civil War Amendments had expanded federal power to enforce individual rights or that the amendments had expanded the list of federally protected rights.

Illustrating that view, the Court in 1876 voided portions of laws Congress intended to ensure the Fifteenth Amendment's guarantee of the right to vote and the Thirteenth Amendment's abolition of slavery. Again, Waite spoke for the Court to declare that Congress had overreached itself in enacting a broad statute penalizing persons who used violence to deny blacks the right to vote. That right, the Court reiterated, came from the states; only the right to be free of racial discrimination in voting came from the U.S. Constitution. These rulings left Congress powerless to protect the newly enfranchised black Americans.[76]

The disputed presidential election of 1876 drew the Court directly into political controversy when five of its members—Bradley, Miller, Strong, Field, and Clifford—served on the commission that resolved the dispute over electoral votes and paved the way for the election of Republican Rutherford B. Hayes. Hayes subsequently placed Stanley Matthews—the man who had helped negotiate the compromise that elected him—on the Supreme Court.

STATE POWER

Not surprisingly, the Court of the 1870s, which refused to acknowledge a broadening federal power to enforce the rights of individuals, was quite hospitable to state claims of a far-reaching police power operative in ever-widening fields.

As large manufacturing and transportation companies grew rapidly after the Civil War, their customers organized to use state regulation to curtail the power of those businesses over individual consumers. Among the most successful were farm groups, including the Grange, which in some states obtained the passage of "Granger laws" limiting how much railroads and grain elevator companies could charge for hauling or storing farm products.

Despite the failure of the butchers to win Fourteenth Amendment protection of their right to do business in the *Slaughterhouse Cases,* the railroad and grain storage operators mounted a similar challenge to these Granger laws. They argued that the state, in passing these laws, deprived them of their liberty and property without due process of law.

In a group of cases known as the *Granger Cases,* and by the title of one of them, *Munn v. Illinois,* the Court in 1877 rejected this challenge to state regulatory laws. Upholding the laws, Chief Justice Waite explained that some private property, by virtue of its use, was so invested with a public interest that states could properly exercise their police power to regulate it. Justices Field and Strong dissented.

The majority also rejected the idea that federal courts should review such laws to determine if they were reasonable. Waite acknowledged that the state might abuse this power, but found that insufficient argument "against its existence. For protection against abuses by Legislatures the people must resort to the polls," he concluded, "not to the courts."[77]

Three years later, the Court found in the state police power a substantial qualification of the Constitution's ban on state impairment of contract obligations. In *Stone v. Mississippi* the Court held that a legislature could never by contract place a subject outside the reach of this power. It upheld a decision of the Mississippi legislature to ban lotteries, even though this de-

THE COURT IN 1882
Seated from left: Justices Joseph P. Bradley, Samuel F. Miller, Chief Justice Morrison R. Waite, Justices Stephen J. Field, Stanley Matthews. *Standing from left:* Justices William B. Woods, Horace Gray, John Marshall Harlan, Samuel Blatchford

cision nullified the charter of a lottery corporation granted by a previous legislature.

A week after *Munn v. Illinois*, Justice Davis resigned to take a Senate seat. As his replacement President Hayes chose John Marshall Harlan, a forty-four-year-old lawyer and a namesake of the fourth chief justice. Harlan's own namesake also would sit on the Court. Harlan would serve well into the twentieth century, his thirty-four-year tenure characterized by a long line of opinions dissenting from the Court's narrow view of the Fourteenth Amendment.

At the turn of the decade, the Court's personnel underwent further change. By 1881 only three of the justices who participated in the 1873 *Slaughterhouse* decision remained on the bench: Miller from the majority and Field and Bradley from the dissent.

By 1880 the Court was operating with three members who were no longer able to fill their proper roles. Swayne, now seventy-five, had been in failing mental health for three years.[78] Hunt suffered a stroke in 1879 and never returned to the bench. Clifford had been disabled for some time but refused to resign until a Democratic president could choose his successor.

But the first departure from the Court of the 1880s was none of these but Justice Strong, who, although in his seventies, still was at the peak of his abilities. President Hayes chose William B. Woods of Georgia as Strong's successor. Woods, a federal circuit judge, was the first southerner named to the Court since Justice Campbell was selected in 1853. Although just fifty-six at the time of his appointment, he served only six years before his death.

In January 1881, shortly after Woods was confirmed, Swayne resigned. To succeed him, Hayes selected Sen. Stanley Matthews, fifty-six, also of Ohio. Matthews had been instrumental in the compromise that placed Hayes in the White House in 1877. Nominated first by Hayes and then by incoming President James J. Garfield, Matthews was confirmed by the narrow margin of one vote, 24–23. He served on the Court for seven years, until his death in 1889.

Later in 1881 Justice Clifford died. To replace him President Chester A. Arthur selected Horace Gray, chief justice of the Massachusetts Supreme Court. Gray, fifty-three at the time, served for twenty years.

Finally in 1882, after three years of absence from the bench, Justice Hunt resigned. After Arthur's first choice, Roscoe Conkling, declined, Arthur chose federal judge Samuel Blatchford of New York to fill the seat. He served for eleven years.

PERSONAL RIGHTS

The Fourteenth Amendment, ratified in 1868, eventually became a mother lode of litigation. In the fifteen years between the *Slaughterhouse Cases*, the Court's first Fourteenth Amendment decision, and the end of Chief Justice Waite's term in 1888, the Court decided some 70 cases on the basis of that amendment. In the ensuing thirty years there would be ten times as many—some 725 Fourteenth Amendment cases.[79]

In general, individuals who sought to invoke the protection of the Fourteenth Amendment had little success. The Court was generally unresponsive to "social" legislation or to claims of individual rights. In 1878, for example, the Court struck down a state law that required equal access for black and white passengers to railroads operating in the state. The law was impermissible state interference with interstate commerce, held the Court in *Hall v. De Cuir*.

In 1880 the Court used the Fourteenth Amendment to deny states the freedom to restrict jury service to white persons. But three years later, in the *Civil Rights Cases,* the Court made clear that it would condone use of the amendment only to reach clearly discriminatory state action.

In the *Civil Rights Cases* the Court declared Congress powerless to reach acts of private discrimination against black persons. With Justice Bradley writing the majority opinion, the Court struck down the far-reaching Civil Rights Act of 1875, enacted to implement the guarantees of the Civil War Amendments.

The Fourteenth Amendment, the Court declared, did not give Congress the power to regulate matters that traditionally had been left to state control. Congress could act only to correct—not to prevent—discrimination by the state.

In 1884, however, the Court upheld the power of Congress to provide for the punishment of persons who beat up a black man to keep him from voting in a federal election.[80]

But the same day, the Court reaffirmed the view, first set out by Chief Justice John Marshall in *Barron v. Baltimore*, that the Bill of Rights did not apply against state action, even though there was clear evidence that the authors of the Fourteenth Amendment intended it to change the *Barron* view. Joseph Hurtado was convicted of murder under California law, which did not provide for a grand jury indictment in serious crimes. Citing the Fifth Amendment guarantee of charge by indictment for serious federal crimes, Hurtado challenged his conviction as a violation of the Fourteenth Amendment's due process guarantee. That guarantee, he argued, applied the indictment provision to the states.

The Court rejected Hurtado's argument. The Fifth Amendment, it reiterated, applies only against federal, not state, action. The Fourteenth Amendment, held the Court, did not extend the right to an indictment to persons charged with state crimes. Justice Harlan dissented from this ruling in *Hurtado v. California*.

In its first major ruling interpreting the guarantees of the Fourth and Fifth Amendments against *federal* authority, however, the Court just two years later read those provisions to give broad protection to the individual.

The Court's decision in *Boyd v. United States*, decided in 1886, was a ringing defense of individual privacy against the threat of governmental invasion. Justice Bradley, for the Court, declared that "constitutional provisions for the security of person and property should be liberally construed. A close and literal construction deprives them of half their efficacy and leads to gradual depreciation of the right."[81]

And later that year, in one of the first successful equal protec-

THE COURT IN 1888
Seated from left: Justices Joseph P. Bradley, Samuel F. Miller, Chief Justice Melville W. Fuller, Justices Stephen J. Field, Lucius Q. C. Lamar. *Standing from left:* Justices Stanley Matthews, Horace Gray, John Marshall Harlan, Samuel Blatchford

tion cases brought by an individual, the Court held that the equal protection guarantee extended to all persons, not just citizens, and meant that city officials could not deny Chinese applicants the right to operate laundries.[82]

PROPERTY RIGHTS

In the 1870s—most notably in the *Slaughterhouse* and *Grange* cases—the Court steadfastly had rejected the efforts of businessmen to use the Fourteenth Amendment as a shield against government regulation. But in the 1880s that stance began to weaken.

In 1869 the Court had held that corporations were not *citizens* and so could not invoke the Amendment's privileges and immunities clause.[83] Seventeen years later, in 1886, Chief Justice Waite simply announced—before the Court heard arguments in *Santa Clara County v. Southern Pacific Railway*—that there was no need for the arguing attorneys to discuss whether corporations were *persons* under the protection of the Amendment's equal protection clause: the Court had decided they were.

That same year the Court limited state power over railroad rates. In *Wabash, St. Louis and Pacific Railway Co. v. Illinois,* the Court held that states could not set rates for railroads that were part of an interstate network without infringing federal power over interstate commerce. This ruling cut back sharply the power the Court had granted the states just nine years earlier in *Munn v. Illinois.*

Yet in other areas the Court continued to support the exercise of state police power. It upheld state laws regulating intoxicating liquors and colored oleomargarine, refusing to find them in violation of due process or the commerce clause.[84]

In 1887 Justice Woods died. President Grover Cleveland filled this "southern seat" with Lucius Quintus Cincinnatus Lamar of Mississippi. Lamar, sixty-two, had served both in the House and the Senate and was secretary of interior at the time of his selection to the Court. He was the first Democrat placed on the Court in twenty-five years. Although the Republican-dominated Senate Judiciary Committee opposed him, he was confirmed, 32–28. He served only five years, until his death in 1893.

In March 1888 Chief Justice Waite, seventy-two, died of pneumonia.

President Cleveland selected Melville W. Fuller to be the new chief justice. Fuller was a successful Chicago attorney whose clients included several major railroads. He had argued a number of cases before the Court and was fifty-five years old at the time of his selection. Nominated in May 1888, he was confirmed in July by a vote of 41–20. He would lead the Court for twenty-two years, until his death in 1910.

By the end of its first century, the Court had become more institutional and less personal in its operations. No longer did the justices live, as well as work, together. That practice had ended soon after the Civil War. And after Reporter Wallace left that post in 1875, the volumes of the Court's decisions were no longer cited by the name of the reporter but by the impersonal "U.S." designation.

NOTES

1. *McCulloch v. Maryland,* 4 Wheat. 316 at 407 (1819).

2. Samuel F. Miller, *Lectures on the Constitution of the United States* (New York and Albany: Banks & Brothers, 1891), 71, 73–74.

3. *McCulloch v. Maryland,* 4 Wheat. 316 at 407 (1819).

4. Charles Grove Haines, *The American Doctrine of Judicial Supremacy* (Berkeley: University of California Press, 1932; reprint ed., New York: Da Capo Press, 1973), 23.

5. Robert H. Jackson, *The Supreme Court in the American System of Government* (Cambridge: Harvard University Press, 1955), 61.

6. Julius Goebel Jr., *History of the Supreme Court of the United States,* Vol. 1, *Antecedents and Beginnings to 1801* (New York: Macmillan, 1971), 206.

7. Quoted in ibid., 280.

8. Charles Warren, *Congress, the Constitution and the Supreme Court* (Boston: Little, Brown, 1925), 23.

9. James Madison, Alexander Hamilton, and John Jay, *The Federalist Papers.* Introduction by Clinton Rossiter (New York: New American Library, Mentor Books, 1961), No. 78, 465.

10. Ibid., No. 79, 474.

11. Ibid., No. 78, 469.

12. Ibid., 466.

13. Ibid., 467–468.

14. Goebel, *Antecedents and Beginnings,* 554.

15. Robert G. McCloskey, "James Wilson" in *The Justices of the United States Supreme Court, 1789–1969: Their Lives and Major Opinions,* 4 vols., ed. Leon Friedman and Fred L. Israel (New York: Chelsea House Publishers in association with R. R. Bowker, 1969), I: 93.

16. Charles Warren, *The Supreme Court in United States History,* rev. ed., 2 vols. (Boston: Little, Brown, 1922, 1926), I: 102.

17. Ibid., 57.

18. Ibid., 89.

19. Ibid., 58.

20. Goebel, *Antecedents and Beginnings,* 556–559, 566–569.

21. Ibid., 792.

22. Ibid., 560–565; Warren, *Supreme Court in U.S. History,* I: 70–82.

23. Warren, *Supreme Court in U.S. History,* I: 108–111.

24. Ibid., 104, note 2.

25. *Glass v. The Sloop Betsey,* 3 Dall. 6 (1794).

26. Goebel, *Antecedents and Beginnings,* 589–592.

27. Ibid., 792.

28. Warren, *Supreme Court in U.S. History,* I: 173.

29. Ibid., 194.

30. Ibid., 791–792.

31. Alexander M. Bickel, *The Least Dangerous Branch* (Indianapolis: Bobbs-Merrill, 1962), 1.

32. Haines, *Judicial Supremacy,* 202–203.

33. *Stuart v. Laird,* 1 Cr. 299 (1803).

34. Warren, *Supreme Court in U.S. History,* I: 293.

35. William Cranch, Preface to Vol. 1 of *Reports of Cases Argued and Adjudged in the Supreme Court of the United States in August and December Terms, 1801, and February Term, 1803.*

36. *Ex parte Bollman,* 4 Cr. 75 (1807).

37. Warren, *Supreme Court in U.S. History,* I: 307.

38. Ibid., 326.

39. Ibid., 339.

40. George L. Haskins and Herbert A. Johnson, *History of the Supreme Court of the United States,* Vol. 2, *Foundations of Power: John Marshall, 1801–1815* (New York: Macmillan, 1981), 365.

41. Ibid., 494.

42. *McCulloch v. Maryland,* 4 Wheat. 316 at 421 (1819).

43. Robert G. McCloskey and Sanford Levinson, *The Modern Supreme Court,* 2d ed. (Chicago: University of Chicago Press, 1994), 43.

44. Warren, *Supreme Court in U.S. History,* I: 550.

45. Ibid., 616.

46. Ibid., 699.

47. G. Edward White, *History of the Supreme Court of the United States,* Vols. 3–4, *The Marshall Court and Cultural Change, 1815–1835* (New York: Macmillan, 1988), 298.

48. Warren, *Supreme Court in U.S. History,* I: 780–781.

49. Alexis de Tocqueville, *Democracy in America* (New York: Alfred A. Knopf and Random House, Vintage Books, 1945), 156–157.

50. Carl B. Swisher, *History of the Supreme Court of the United States,* Vol. 5, *The Taney Period, 1836–1864* (New York: Macmillan, 1974), 97.

51. *Bank of Augusta v. Earle,* 13 Pet. 519 (1839).

52. *Louisville Railroad v. Letson,* 2 How. 497 (1844).

53. *Swift v. Tyson,* 16 Pet. 1 (1842); *Dobbins v. Erie County,* 16 Pet. 435 (1842).

54. Swisher, *The Taney Period,* 535.

55. Ibid., 546.

56. *Jones v. Van Zandt,* 5 How. 215 (1847).

57. Warren, *Supreme Court in U.S. History,* II: 207.

58. Swisher, *The Taney Period,* 407.

59. *Propeller Genesee Chief v. Fitzhugh,* 12 How. 443 (1851).

60. Edward S. Corwin, "The *Dred Scott* Decision in the Light of Contemporary Legal Doctrine," *American Historical Review* 17 (1911), quoted in Warren, *Supreme Court in U.S. History,* II: 316–317.

61. Warren, *Supreme Court in U.S. History,* II: 356.

62. *Ableman v. Booth,* 21 How. 506 at 525, 521 (1859).

63. Swisher, *The Taney Period,* 973–974.

64. Ibid., 974–975.

65. William Gillette, "Samuel Miller" in Friedman and Israel, *Justices of the Supreme Court,* II: 1023.

66. *Ex parte Merryman,* Federal Cases 9487, 152.

67. *Roosevelt v. Meyer,* 1 Wall. 512 (1863).

68. *Ex parte Vallandigham,* 1 Wall. 243 (1864).

69. Charles Fairman, *History of the Supreme Court of the United States,* Vol. 4, *Reconstruction and Reunion, 1864–1888* (New York: Macmillan, 1971), 32.

70. Frank Otto Gatell, "Robert C. Grier" in Friedman and Israel, *Justices of the Supreme Court,* II: 883.

71. Charles Evans Hughes, *The Supreme Court of the United States* (New York: Columbia University Press, 1928), 53.

72. *Collector v. Day,* 11 Wall. 113 (1871).

73. *The Slaughterhouse Cases,* 16 Wall. 36 at 78 (1873).

74. *Bradwell v. Illinois,* 16 Wall. 130 (1873).

75. *Minor v. Happersett,* 21 Wall. 162 (1875).

76. *United States v. Reese, United States v. Cruikshank,* 92 U.S. 214, 542 (1876).

77. *Munn v. Illinois,* 94 U.S. 113 at 134 (1877).

78. William Gillette, "Noah H. Swayne" in Friedman and Israel, *Justices of the Supreme Court,* II: 998.

79. Warren, *Supreme Court in U.S. History,* II: 599.

80. *Ex parte Yarbrough,* 110 U.S. 651 (1884).

81. *Boyd v. United States,* 116 U.S. 616 at 635 (1886).

82. *Yick Wo v. Hopkins,* 118 U.S. 356 (1886).

83. *Paul v. Virginia,* 8 Wall. 168 (1869).

84. *Mugler v. Kansas,* 123 U.S. 623 (1887); *Powell v. Pennsylvania,* 127 U.S. 678 (1888).

CHAPTER 2

The Second Century: Court and Controversy

MELVILLE W. FULLER became chief justice as the Court's first century ended. His tenure spanned the chronological, political, and social transition to the world of the twentieth century. Vast changes occurred during this period, changes that brought new challenges to the Supreme Court. William Swindler explained:

The passing of the frontier, the rise of an interstate industrialism, the shift from a rural to an urban distribution of population, the breakdown of nineteenth-century capitalism and the efforts to construct in its stead a twentieth-century capitalism, the breakthrough in science and technology, the change in the society of nations brought about by global wars and the militant dialectic of totalitarianism—the constitutional posture of the American people had to be readjusted in response to each of these.

Fuller's court stood upon the watershed, with a powerful pull of ideological gravity toward the past. At least three of his colleagues when he came onto the bench dated from the constitutional golden age: Justices Bradley, Field and Miller all had begun their careers under men who in turn had known John Marshall and Joseph Story. From these venerated predecessors, who interpreted the Constitution with reference to a pioneer economy and an ante-bellum concept of the Federal function, Fuller and his intimate associates undertook to derive a jurisprudence to apply to issues never imagined by the early Federalist jurists.[1]

Four other new justices joined the Court within Fuller's first five years there. All were chosen by President Benjamin Harrison; all were men of conservative bent.

The first of Harrison's selections was the most notable. Justice Matthews died in March 1889. As his successor, Harrison chose federal circuit judge David J. Brewer of Kansas, Justice Field's nephew. Brewer, fifty-two, was confirmed late in the year. During his twenty years on the Court he would be one of its most articulate members.

On March 3, 1890, Justice Brewer delivered his first major opinion for the Court. In *Louisville, New Orleans and Texas Railway Co. v. Mississippi*, the majority upheld a state law requiring railroads to provide separate accommodations for black and white passengers on trips within the state. Justices Harlan and Bradley dissented.

Accepting the state court's view that the state law applied only to intrastate trips, the Supreme Court majority held that it did not burden interstate commerce. This ruling distinctly foreshadowed the Court's acceptance, six years later in *Plessy v. Ferguson*, of the "separate but equal" doctrine, an action that established the racial segregation of U.S. society well past the midpoint of the next century.

Three weeks after the *Mississippi* ruling, on March 24, 1890, the era of "substantive due process" began. For the first time the Court endorsed the belief that the due process clause of the Fifth and the Fourteenth Amendments gives federal courts the power to review the *substance* of legislation, not just the *procedures* it sets up. At issue in the case of *Chicago, Milwaukee & St. Paul Railway Co. v. Minnesota* was a Minnesota law that prescribed the rates that the railroad could charge—and did not provide for judicial review of the reasonableness of these rates. The Court held that this law denied the businessmen their right to due process, declaring by its action that it would no longer defer to legislative judgment in rate setting, as it had in *Munn v. Illinois*. Now it assumed for itself and other courts the power to review the wisdom of these economic decisions.

This ruling extended the protection of the Fourteenth Amendment to business, adopting a view the Court had rejected in the *Slaughterhouse Cases*. Six months later, Justice Miller, author of the *Slaughterhouse* opinion, died after twenty-eight years on the bench. Harrison chose federal judge Henry B. Brown, a Yale classmate of Brewer's, to succeed Miller. Brown, from Michigan, would serve for fifteen years.

For the nation's first century, the Supreme Court was essentially the only federal court of appeals, the only court that heard appeals from the decisions of other federal courts. As a result of increasing litigation, its workload mushroomed. From the end of the Civil War until 1891 it was not at all uncommon for a case to wait two or three years after being docketed before it was argued before the Court.

The Court made various changes in its operations to promote more expeditious handling of cases, but all its efforts were of little avail to deal with the increasing volume of business.

Finally, in 1891, Congress eliminated the justices' obligation to ride circuit. It set up a system of federal appeals courts between the old district and circuit courts, on the one hand, and the Supreme Court on the other. The decisions of these new circuit courts of appeals were final in many cases. When a decision was appealed from one of these new courts, the Supreme Court had complete discretion in deciding whether to review it. The result, at least for a time, was a reduction in the press of business at the Court.

Early in 1892 the Supreme Court decided *Counselman v. Hitchcock*, one of its rare nineteenth-century rulings interpreting the Bill of Rights. And, as in *Boyd v. United States* six years earlier, the Court gave individuals broad protection against federal authority. The immunity provisions of the Interstate Commerce Act were constitutionally insufficient, the Court held. The Fifth Amendment, said the unanimous Court, required that a witness could be compelled to testify and give evidence against himself only if the government promised not to use that evidence in any way against him.

Within days of *Counselman,* Justice Bradley died. As his successor, President Harrison chose George Shiras Jr., a Pennsylvania lawyer whose clients included the great iron and steel companies of Pittsburgh and the Baltimore & Ohio Railroad. Despite opposition from his home state senators, Shiras was unanimously confirmed. He served for a decade.

In January of the following year, 1893, Justice Lamar died. To succeed him, Harrison chose a friend from his Senate days, Howell Jackson of Tennessee, a federal circuit judge. Jackson, however, became ill within a year of his appointment and died a year later.

In mid-1893 Justice Blatchford, the author of *Counselman,* died. The seat he had filled had been held by a New Yorker since 1806. With his death this tradition ended. President Cleveland tried twice, without success, to place another New York attorney in the seat, but the opposition of the senators from New York blocked the nominations of both William Hornblower and Wheeler Peckham.

Finally, in February 1894, Cleveland nominated Sen. Edward D. White of Louisiana, forty-eight, to the seat. He was confirmed the same day. White would serve on the Court twenty-seven years. After seventeen years as an associate justice, he would become the first sitting justice promoted to chief justice, a post in which he would serve for a decade more.

Business at the Court: 1889–1919

The conservative character of the Court of the 1890s was demonstrated with stunning force in the October 1894 term, one of the most notable single terms in Court history. With three landmark decisions, the Court placed itself firmly on the side of business, defending the interest of property against federal power and organized labor.

On January 21, 1895, the Court, 8–1, held that the Sherman Antitrust Act did not outlaw manufacturing monopolies. The Court reasoned that manufacturing was not commerce and so was not reachable under the federal commerce power, upon which the Sherman Act was based.

Chief Justice Fuller wrote the majority opinion in *United States v. E. C. Knight & Co.,* agreeing with the argument of the "sugar trust"—the sugar refining monopoly—that the United States could not challenge its concentrated power. The monopoly remained intact, and the antitrust law lay virtually useless.

On May 20, 1895, the Court struck down the act of Congress imposing the nation's first general peacetime tax on personal income. The decision came in the twice-argued case of *Pollock v. Farmers' Loan and Trust Co.* By a 5–4 vote, the Court overturned a century-old precedent and declared the income tax a direct tax, subject to—and, in this case, in conflict with—the constitu-

tional requirement that direct taxes be apportioned among the states according to population. Again Chief Justice Fuller wrote the majority opinion. Dissenting were Justices Harlan, Brown, Jackson, and White.

The ruling, which Justice Brown described as "nothing less than a surrender of the taxing power to the moneyed class,"[2] resulted in the Sixteenth Amendment, added to the Constitution in 1913, which lifted the apportionment requirement for income taxes.

It had fended off assaults upon property from trustbusters and the tax laws, but the Court was not yet finished. A week after *Pollock,* the Court gave federal judges the power to stop strikes.

In *In re Debs* the Court unanimously upheld the contempt conviction of labor leader Eugene V. Debs for disobeying a court order to call off a Pullman strike that halted rail traffic. Justice Brewer wrote the Court's opinion. As a result of this ruling, such court orders were frequently used by employers against labor unions. In the thirty-seven years between *Debs* and passage of a law forbidding judges to use injunctions in this way, they were sought in more than 120 major labor cases.[3]

In August 1895 Justice Jackson died. President Cleveland in December chose Rufus W. Peckham of New York—brother of his earlier unsuccessful nominee—for the seat. Peckham, fifty-seven, and a state judge, was quickly confirmed. During his thirteen years on the Court, he would serve as its spokesman in some of its most notable rulings defending property rights.

SEPARATE AND EQUAL

The social views of the Court of the 1890s were no more liberal than its economic beliefs. *Plessy v. Ferguson,* decided May 18, 1896, made that point clear: The Court, 8–1, upheld a Louisiana law requiring railroads operating in the state to provide separate cars for white and black passengers. This law was not in violation of the Fourteenth Amendment's equal protection clause, declared Justice Brown for the majority. It was a reasonable exercise of the state police power to preserve the public peace and public order.

Reflecting the view that laws are inadequate social instruments, Brown wrote that social equality of the races could not be accomplished by laws that conflicted with general community sentiment. The government can secure its citizens equal legal rights and equal opportunities, but it can and should go no further. "Legislation is powerless to eradicate racial instincts or to abolish distinctions based upon physical differences, and the attempt to do so can only result in accentuating the difficulties of the present situation. If the civil and political rights of both races be equal one cannot be inferior to the other civilly or politically. If one race be inferior to the other socially, the Constitution of the United States cannot put them upon the same plane."[4]

In lonely if prophetic dissent, Justice Harlan warned that this decision would "in time, prove to be quite as pernicious as the decision made by this tribunal in the *Dred Scott* case."[5] He continued:

THE COURT IN 1897
From left: Justices Edward D. White, Henry B. Brown, Horace Gray, Stephen J. Field, Chief Justice Melville W. Fuller, Justices John Marshall Harlan, David J. Brewer, George Shiras Jr., Rufus W. Peckham

If evils will result from the commingling of the two races upon public highways . . . they will be infinitely less than those that will surely come from state legislation regulating the enjoyment of civil rights upon the basis of race.[6]

This law, Harlan concluded, "is inconsistent with the personal liberty of citizens, white and black . . . and hostile to both the spirit and letter of the Constitution."[7]

Abraham Lincoln had nominated Justice Stephen Field of California to the Court in 1863 to hold the new "western" seat. In 1897 Field was eighty-one years old, his health was failing, and his irritability growing. Justice Harlan was selected by his colleagues to suggest that Field consider retirement. His reminder that Field had made such a suggestion to Justice Grier twenty-five years earlier was met with an angry rejoinder. But after thirty-four years and nine months—the longest service of any man in the Court's history, and a record unsurpassed for another seventy-five years—Field resigned in October 1897.

To succeed him President William McKinley named Attorney General Joseph McKenna of California, fifty-five, a political protégé of railroad magnate Leland Stanford, then a U.S. senator. McKenna, a former member of Congress, was confirmed, was seated early in 1898, and served on the Court well into the next century.

After McKenna filled Field's seat, there was no change in the Court's membership for the next four years.

FREEDOM OF CONTRACT

With its last decisions of the nineteenth century, the Court discovered a new aspect of the liberty protected by the Constitution, a freedom of contract that provided additional doctrinal foundation for rulings protecting property rights, rather than individual rights, against governmental power.

On March 1, 1897, the Court in *Allgeyer v. Louisiana* declared that the liberty protected by the Fourteenth Amendment included "the right of the citizen . . . to earn his livelihood by any lawful calling; to pursue any livelihood or avocation, and for that purpose to enter into all contracts which may be proper, necessary and essential" to those ends.[8]

This doctrine provided the Court, for forty years, with one of its most potent weapons against state laws intended to protect individual workers by setting the maximum hours they might work and the minimum wage they should be paid.

In a second ruling announced that day, *Chicago, Burlington & Quincy Railway Co. v. Chicago,* the Court in a business context acknowledged that some of the guarantees of the Bill of Rights might be of such a nature as to be included in the Fourteenth Amendment's guarantee of due process.

With Justice Harlan writing for the Court, the justices upheld state police power to require railroads to maintain certain safety measures. In so doing, it stated that due process required the government to compensate the owner of private property for property "taken" for use in the public interest.

Despite its new freedom-of-contract doctrine, the Court in 1898 upheld the first state maximum-hour law challenged as violating that freedom. In *Holden v. Hardy* the justices found that a law limiting the hours persons could spend working in underground mines was a proper exercise of the state's power to protect the health of its citizens.

The following week, however, the Court in *Smyth v. Ames* reaffirmed the judicial role in reviewing such state laws. When states set the rates that railroads could charge, wrote Justice Harlan, those rates must be set high enough to ensure the railways a fair return on their investment. And the courts will decide what return is fair.

In 1898 the Court also demonstrated its continuing willingness to leave to the states regulation of the suffrage, even if the states effectively denied blacks that right. In *Williams v. Mississippi* the Court found no constitutional flaw in a law that required voters to pass a literacy test before being allowed to cast their ballot. Justice McKenna wrote the Court's opinion, one of his first.

THE TURN OF THE CENTURY

What were the privileges and immunities of U.S. citizenship protected against state action by the Fourteenth Amendment? In 1873 the Court had held that the right to do business was not one of these. In later rulings it held that the right to vote was not such a privilege either.

But what about the guarantees of the Bill of Rights that protected U.S. citizens against federal action? In one of its first rulings of the twentieth century, the Court answered that these were not privileges or immunities of federal citizenship either. That ruling came in *Maxwell v. Dow,* decided in 1900. Justice Peckham, for the Court, rejected the argument that the Fourteenth Amendment required states to provide twelve-person juries to try persons accused of crimes. Justice Harlan dissented.

In 1901 the Court showed similar reluctance to extend constitutional protections to any new groups of persons. In the *Insular Cases* the Court held that it was up to Congress to decide whether the Constitution and its guarantees applied to persons residing in territory newly acquired by the United States.

Late in 1902 Justice Gray resigned. As his successor President Theodore Roosevelt chose Oliver Wendell Holmes Jr., sixty-one, chief justice of the Massachusetts Supreme Judicial Court. Holmes served on the Court for more than twenty-nine years, through the terms of three chief justices and into a fourth. He was, by all measures, one of the nation's greatest justices. Like Harlan, he was often in dissent from the rulings of the conservative Court; also like Harlan, many of his dissents later became the prevailing view of the modern Court.

The following year Justice Shiras resigned. Roosevelt chose Judge William R. Day, of the federal circuit court of appeals, as Shiras's successor. Day, fifty-three, a successful railroad lawyer and McKinley's secretary of state before moving to the bench, would serve for nineteen years.

The first few years of Holmes's service saw the Court give a broader reading to the federal commerce power than it had been willing to give earlier. In 1903 the Court recognized the existence of a federal police power, upholding in *Champion v. Ames* an act of Congress forbidding the use of the mails for transmitting lottery tickets. But the vote was close—5–4. Justice Harlan wrote the majority opinion; the dissenters were Chief Justice Fuller and Justices Brewer, Peckham, and Shiras.

The following year the Court enlarged on that ruling as it upheld a "police" use of the federal tax power to discourage the marketing of colored oleomargarine, holding that it would not inquire into the purposes of such a tax.[9]

In 1904 the Court began to revive the usefulness of the Sherman Antitrust Act, ruling for the government in *Northern Securities Co. v. United States.* Four of the justices, for whom Justice Harlan again spoke, read the Sherman Antitrust Act literally—forbidding all restraints of trade. The four dissenting justices—White, Holmes, Peckham, and Chief Justice Fuller—argued that the law forbade only unreasonable restraints of trade. The Harlan group became the majority through the concurrence of Justice Brewer and ruled in this case that the securities company was so powerful that it imposed an unreasonable restraint on trade.

In a separate dissenting opinion, Justice Holmes set out one of his most often-quoted epigrams:

Great cases, like hard cases, make bad law. . . . For great cases are called great, not by reason of their real importance in shaping the law of the future, but because of some accident of immediate overwhelming interest which appeals to the feelings and distorts the judgment.[10]

Holmes's comment appeared to be aimed directly at the man who had placed him on the bench—Theodore Roosevelt—whose intense interest in the success of the government's trust-busting effort, and this case, was well known. Roosevelt disregarded his appointee's comment and hailed the decision as a reversal of the 1895 holding in the sugar trust case.

In 1905 the Court unanimously backed the government's prosecution of the beef trust. Justice Holmes wrote the opinion in *Swift & Co. v. United States,* basing the ruling on a broad concept of commerce as a "current" among the states, a "stream" of which meatpacking was a part—and so was within the reach of the antitrust laws.

Although the Court was still willing to support the exercise of the state police power over a subject such as the public health, in 1905 its decision in *Lochner v. New York* signaled its distaste for state efforts to interfere with wage and hour bargaining between employer and employee.

In February 1905 the Court upheld state power to compel its citizens to be vaccinated against smallpox. This requirement, wrote Harlan, was a proper use of the police power.[11] Six weeks later, the Court—over the dissent of Harlan, Holmes, Day, and White—ruled in *Lochner* that New York's law setting an eight-hour maximum work day for bakery employees interfered with the freedom of contract.

Justice Peckham wrote the majority opinion declaring "that there is a limit to the valid exercise of the police power by the state." This law overstepped that limit: "Clean and wholesome bread does not depend upon whether the baker works but ten hours per day or only sixty hours a week."[12]

In 1906 Justice Brown resigned. President Roosevelt named his attorney general and close friend, William Moody, fifty-two, as Brown's successor. Only four years later, Moody would retire, disabled by acute rheumatism. Congress passed a bill allowing him to retire with special benefits.

LABOR AND THE COURT

With its unsympathetic ruling in the 1895 case of Eugene Debs and the Pullman strike, the Supreme Court expressed a profound distaste for the arguments and the tactics of the workers' labor movement. In 1908, it reaffirmed that view.

On January 6, 1908, the Court struck down an act of Congress enlarging the liability of railroads for injuries to their employees. By 5–4 the Court held that the law was invalid because it applied to intrastate aspects of interstate commerce.[13]

Three weeks later, the Court invalidated another law that outlawed "yellow-dog" contracts, which railroads used to make their employees promise, as a condition of keeping their jobs, not to join labor unions. Justice Harlan wrote the opinion of the Court in *Adair v. United States,* finding this federal law an undue restriction on freedom of contract. Holmes and McKenna dissented.

On February 3, 1908, the Court unanimously agreed that the Sherman Antitrust Act forbade secondary boycotts by labor unions; Chief Justice Fuller wrote the Court's opinion in *Loewe v. Lawlor,* known as the *Danbury Hatters* case.

This term did bring workers one major victory, a victory in which a Boston lawyer named Louis D. Brandeis played a significant role. Oregon law set the maximum hours that women should work in laundries. The law was challenged, on the basis of *Lochner,* as a violation of the liberty of contract. The state engaged Brandeis as its counsel. He submitted a brief full of factual data supporting the argument that long hours of hard labor had a harmful effect upon women, and thus, through mothers, upon their children.

Brandeis won a unanimous decision in favor of Oregon's law, modifying *Lochner* by finding some state interference with freedom of contract justified to protect the public health. Justice Brewer wrote the opinion in *Muller v. Oregon.* And the term "Brandeis brief" came to be used to refer to briefs filled with factual, as well as legal, arguments.

Throughout the early years of the new century, the Court continued to hold a narrow view of the Constitution's protection for individual rights. In May 1908—over the dissent of Justices Day and Harlan—the majority upheld a state law that required Kentucky's Berea College to separate black and white students in classes.[14]

And in November 1908 the Court reaffirmed its point made in *Maxwell v. Dow,* that the Fourteenth Amendment did not automatically extend the guarantees of the Bill of Rights to state defendants. In *Twining v. New Jersey* the Court refused to hold that a defendant was denied his constitutional rights when the judge in his case commented on his failure to testify in his own defense. The Fifth Amendment guarantee against self-incrimination, the Court held, did not apply in state trials. Justice Moody wrote the opinion; Justice Harlan dissented alone.

THE TAFT JUSTICES

William Howard Taft always wanted to be chief justice. But on March 4, 1909, he was sworn in as president instead. During his term he appointed six members of the Court, the greatest number named by a single president since George Washington. A dozen years later, he finally did become chief justice.

In 1909 Justice Peckham died. To succeed him Taft chose Horace H. Lurton, sixty-five, with whom he had served on the Court of Appeals for the Sixth Circuit. Lurton served only four years before his death in 1914.

In 1910 Taft placed three more new members on the Court and elevated Justice White to the seat of chief justice. Justice Brewer died in March after twenty years of service. Taft chose Charles Evans Hughes, forty-eight, governor of New York, as his successor. Hughes would serve six years before resigning to run unsuccessfully for president in 1916. He would return to the Court in 1930, Taft's successor as chief justice.

In July 1910 Chief Justice Fuller died after twenty-two years in his post. Taft broke precedent and named Justice White as the Court's new chief. White was immediately confirmed and served for more than ten years in his new seat.

To replace White, Taft chose Joseph R. Lamar, fifty-three, a Georgia attorney, whom he had met playing golf in Augusta. Lamar died after only five years on the Court.

In November 1910 Justice Moody resigned. Taft named to the seat Willis Van Devanter of Wyoming, fifty-one, a member of the Court of Appeals for the Eighth Circuit. Van Devanter would serve for twenty-six years, Taft's longest serving appointee.

In October 1911 Justice Harlan died after a long and distinguished, if often lonely, career on the Court. As his successor, Taft chose Mahlon Pitney of New Jersey, fifty-four, a member of that state's supreme court. Pitney served until 1922. With Harlan's death, only two members remained from the Court of the 1890s—White and McKenna.

TRUSTS AND TAXES

For a few years after White had replaced Fuller as chief justice, the Court relaxed its conservative stance.

In Harlan's last term the Court adopted the "rule of reason" for applying the Sherman Antitrust Act against restraints of trade, the rule that Harlan had so vigorously rejected in the *Northern Securities* case seven years earlier. By an 8–1 vote in mid-May 1911 the Court declared that the antitrust act outlawed only unreasonable restraints of trade, not all restraints of trade. The majority ordered the breakup of the Standard Oil trust, which they found to be an unreasonable restraint. Chief Justice White wrote the majority opinion, declaring reasonableness the standard, which the courts would apply. Justice Harlan dissented.[15]

Two weeks later the Court ordered the dissolution of the tobacco trust. Again Harlan dissented, arguing that the Court was acting as a legislature, rewriting the law by adding the rule of reason.[16]

Nevertheless, the rule of reason would stand through most of the twentieth century as the standard by which the federal antitrust laws would be applied against combinations charged with restraint of trade.

THE COURT IN 1914

Seated from left: Justices William R. Day, Joseph McKenna, Chief Justice Edward D. White, Justices Oliver Wendell Holmes Jr., Charles Evans Hughes.
Standing from left: Justices Mahlon Pitney, Willis Van Devanter, Joseph R. Lamar, James C. McReynolds

The federal police power continued to win backing at the Court, which upheld the Pure Food and Drug Act in 1911, a revised employers' liability act in 1912, and the White Slave Act in 1913.[17]

Other aspects of the federal commerce power were broadly construed as well. In the *Shreveport Rate Case* of 1914, the Court held that in some situations Congress, through the Interstate Commerce Commission, could set rates for railroads operating entirely within a state.

With the antitrust rulings culminating in the oil and tobacco trust decisions, the Court had resuscitated the Sherman Antitrust Act, which its sugar trust ruling of 1895 had seemed to leave useless.

Congress and the states overrode the second of those landmark 1895 rulings—the income tax decision. In 1913 Congress and the states added to the Constitution the Sixteenth Amendment, which declared that a federal income tax was not subject to the Constitution's apportionment requirement. Congress enacted a statute taxing incomes of more than $3,000 and $4,000 for single and married persons, respectively.

In the 1916 case of *Brushaber v. Union Pacific Railroad Co.,* the Court upheld the act as constitutional. Chief Justice White wrote the opinion for the Court, acknowledging that the clear intent of the new amendment was to overturn the Court's reasoning in the 1895 *Pollock* case.

RIGHTS AND REMEDIES

In 1914 the Court adopted the "exclusionary rule" to enforce the Fourth Amendment promise of personal security against unreasonable searches and seizures by federal agents. In *Weeks v. United States* the unanimous Court held that persons whose rights were violated by such searches could demand that any evidence so obtained against them be excluded from use in federal courts. Half a century later, when the Court applied this rule against state action as well, it would become one of the most controversial of the Court's rulings.

In 1915 the Court applied the Fifteenth Amendment to strike down Oklahoma's grandfather clause, which made it difficult for blacks to register to vote in the state. This decision in *Guinn v. United States,* however, did not settle the matter. Twenty-four years later, in *Lane v. Wilson,* the Court struck down a similarly discriminatory law Oklahoma adopted in place of the grandfather clause.

President Woodrow Wilson named three men to the Court, one of whom refused to speak to the other two for most of their tenure.

In 1914 Justice Lurton died. To succeed him, Wilson nominated his attorney general, James C. McReynolds, fifty-two, of Tennessee. McReynolds, one of the most conservative men to serve on the Court in the twentieth century, also was one of the most difficult. He went out of his way to avoid dealing with Justices Louis Brandeis and Benjamin Cardozo—both Jewish—and he refused to speak to Justice John H. Clarke, whom he considered unintelligent.[18]

Brandeis was Wilson's second nominee to the Court, chosen to fill the seat left vacant by Justice Lamar's death in 1916. The nomination of Brandeis, fifty-nine, was opposed by a number of leaders of the American bar, including former president Taft, who considered him a dangerous radical. After lengthy and contentious hearings, he was confirmed in June 1916 by a vote of 49–22. He served on the Court for twenty-three years.

As soon as Brandeis was confirmed, Justice Hughes resigned to run unsuccessfully against Wilson for the White House. Federal judge John Clarke of Ohio, fifty-eight, was Wilson's choice to fill this seat. Clarke resigned after six years on the bench to work for U.S. entrance into the League of Nations. He lived for thirty-three more years, dying in 1945. After Clarke joined the Court, there were no other changes in its membership until 1921.

By 1917 the Court appeared to have silently overruled *Lochner v. New York*. In two decisions early in the year, the Court upheld maximum-hour statutes. In *Wilson v. New* it approved a federal law setting an eight-hour work day on interstate railroads, and in *Bunting v. Oregon*, a state law setting maximum hours for all industrial workers. The law upheld in *Bunting* also set minimum wages for women and child workers; by implication the Court sustained those provisions as well.

But the votes were close. Day, Pitney, Van Devanter, and McReynolds dissented from *Wilson. Bunting*, decided by only eight justices, found White, Van Devanter, and McReynolds in disagreement with the majority.

CONSERVATISM CONFIRMED

The years in which the nation fought World War I ended the Court's liberal interlude.

In 1918 the Court abruptly halted the steady expansion of federal police power striking down, 5–4, a 1916 act of Congress intended to outlaw child labor by barring from interstate commerce goods produced by child workers.

Justice Day wrote the Court's opinion in *Hammer v. Dagenhart*, returning to the distinction between manufacturing and commerce set out in 1895. This child labor law attempted to regulate manufacturing and so overreached the commerce power. Child labor was a subject left to state regulation, Day proclaimed. The Court's most senior members, McKenna and Holmes, and its most junior ones, Brandeis and Clarke, dissented.

World War I also brought the Selective Service Act and the military draft. In June 1917, 9.5 million men were registered for military service.[19] The law was immediately challenged, and in January 1918, it was unanimously upheld by the Court in its decisions in the *Selective Draft Law Cases*.

Wartime also brought enactment of an espionage act and a sedition act, the most repressive legislation since the Alien and Sedition Acts of 1798. But unlike their predecessors—which were not challenged before the Court—the World War I legislation was contested as violating the freedom of speech protected by the First Amendment.

In 1919 the Court unanimously sustained the espionage act in *Schenck v. United States*. Justice Holmes wrote the Court's opinion, setting out the famous—if little-used—"clear and present danger" test for determining when government might permissibly curtail an individual's freedom of speech.

The First Amendment, Holmes wrote, would "not protect a man . . . [who] falsely shout[ed] fire in a theater and caus[ed] a panic." The question to be asked, he continued, "is whether the words are used in such circumstances and are of such a nature as to create a clear and present danger that they will bring about the substantive evils that Congress has a right to prevent. It is a question of proximity and degree."[20]

Schenck was quickly followed by decisions upholding convictions under these challenged wartime statutes. The Court soon divided over the use of the clear and present danger test—but *Schenck* remains notable for its declaration that the First Amendment does not provide an absolute protection for free speech and as the first step in the Court's effort to find and define the standards for deciding when government may permissibly curtail free speech.

New Times, Old Court: 1920–1937

In May 1921 Chief Justice White died suddenly. Former president William Howard Taft, who had made no secret of his long-held ambition to be chief justice, was chosen by President Warren G. Harding as the tenth man to hold that post. Taft was confirmed in June 1921. He would serve for nine years, during which he would play a pivotal role in winning passage of the Judiciary Act of 1925, giving the Court more control over its workload, and in initiating work on the Court's own building.

Under Taft the Court's conservatism intensified even further. It revived the *Lochner* doctrine of freedom of contract and used it vigorously to restrain state efforts to regulate economic matters. And it curtailed federal authority, persisting in the view that Congress could not regulate matters such as agricultural production and manufacturing, and converting the seldom-invoked Tenth Amendment into a potent instrument for protecting state sovereignty and business matters from federal power.

During the Taft era the Court accelerated its use of its power of judicial review. While the Court had struck down only two acts of Congress in the years between the nation's founding and the Civil War, it struck down twenty-two federal laws in the period between 1920 and 1932.[21]

Despite such clearly conservative views, it was this same Court that set the nation on its course toward the "due process revolution" of the 1960s.

RESTRAINT OF REGULATION

Three acts of Congress struck down by the Taft Court in its first years exemplify the Court's tendency to put certain subjects outside the reach of federal power.

In 1921 the Court, in *Newberry v. United States,* held that Congress could not regulate spending in primary elections. Federal regulatory power reached only to general election campaigns for federal office; all other aspects of the electoral process were left to the states. One effect of this decision, which invalidated part of the 1911 Federal Corrupt Practices Act, was to leave the way open for states to exclude black voters from the electoral process, by hindering or blocking their participation in the primary elections. The successful attorney in this case was former justice Charles Evans Hughes.

In 1904 the Court, in *McCray v. United States,* declared that so long as a subject taxed by Congress was properly within federal power, the justices would not look behind the tax to ascertain its purpose. With this assurance, Congress responded to the Court's 1918 ruling striking down its commerce-based effort to outlaw child labor by using its tax power to achieve that same end. The result: the Child Labor Tax Act—placing a high tax on products made by industries that employed children. The Court in 1919 had upheld a similar tax measure intended to outlaw narcotics.[22]

But the Taft Court found a new tool to wield against federal regulation: the Tenth Amendment. Part of the original Bill of Rights added to the Constitution in 1791, the amendment states that "the powers not delegated to the United States by the Constitution, nor prohibited by it to the States, are reserved to the States respectively, or to the people."

In May 1922 the Court invoked this amendment to strike down the 1918 child labor tax law. Chief Justice Taft wrote the majority opinion in *Bailey v. Drexel Furniture Co.* By using the tax power to ban child labor, Congress was infringing upon the reserved rights of the states to regulate such topics, held the Court. Justice Clarke was the only dissenter.

The same day, with the same Tenth Amendment argument, the Court invalidated a 1921 law in which Congress had used its tax power to regulate the commodities futures trade. This too was a matter reserved to state control, wrote Chief Justice Taft.

If this sort of law were upheld, Taft wrote,

all that Congress would need to do hereafter, in seeking to take over to its control any one of the great number of subjects of public interest, jurisdiction of which the states have never parted with and which are reserved to them by the Tenth Amendment, would be to enact a detailed measure of complete regulation of the subject and enforce it by a so-called tax. . . . To give such magic to the word "tax" would be to break down all constitutional limitation of the powers of Congress and completely wipe out the sovereignty of the states.

THE COURT IN 1925
Seated from left: Justices James C. McReynolds, Oliver Wendell Holmes Jr., Chief Justice William Howard Taft, Justices Willis Van Devanter, Louis D. Brandeis. *Standing from left:* Justices Edward T. Sanford, George Sutherland, Pierce Butler, Harlan Fiske Stone

(Congress then passed a new grain futures regulatory law based on the commerce power; the Court upheld it in 1923.)[23]

Continuing to evidence an antilabor bias, the Court during these years made it even easier for management to use the antitrust laws against labor union efforts to organize and improve the conditions of workers.

Responding to earlier Court decisions, Congress in 1914 had included in the Clayton Act specific language exempting labor unions from the reach of the antitrust laws. But in the 1921 decisions—*Duplex Printing Press v. Deering* and *American Steel Foundries v. Trades Council*—the Court interpreted this exemption into uselessness. It was ten more years before Congress finally and effectively forbade the use of federal injunctions in labor disputes.

After the close of Taft's first term, three justices resigned: first Clarke in September 1922, followed by Day and Pitney, who had suffered a stroke several months earlier. To fill the empty seats President Harding chose former Utah senator George Sutherland, sixty; Minnesota corporate attorney Pierce Butler, fifty-six; and federal judge Edward T. Sanford of Tennessee, fifty-seven. Sutherland would serve for sixteen years, Butler, seventeen, and Sanford, seven.

Early in 1925 Justice McKenna—the last of the nineteenth-century justices—resigned after twenty-six years on the Court; he was eighty-two years old.

President Calvin Coolidge named Attorney General Harlan Fiske Stone to that seat. Stone, fifty-three at the time of his appointment, had been a law professor at Columbia Law School for fifteen years before entering government. He would serve for sixteen years as an associate justice before becoming chief justice in 1941, a post he held until his death five years later. After Stone's confirmation, there were no further changes in the Court's membership until Taft's death in 1930.

Taft's second term brought a surprise to those who assumed that the Court's rulings upholding state maximum-hour laws reflected the Court's abandonment of the *Lochner* principle that a state violated the Fourteenth Amendment guarantee of due process when it interfered with this "freedom of contract." In April 1923 *Lochner* was revived. In *Adkins v. Children's Hospital* the Court, 5–3, struck down as invalid a minimum-wage law for women workers in the District of Columbia.

With Justice Sutherland writing one of his first and most important opinions, the Court held that such a law unconstitutionally infringed on the freedom of contract of employer and employee. Chief Justice Taft and Justices Sanford and Holmes dissented; Brandeis did not participate in the case.

The same year brought two other notable decisions. In *Frothingham v. Mellon* the Court found that a federal taxpayer lacked sufficient personal interest in the use of tax moneys to justify a federal suit challenging the way Congress raised and spent money. For forty-five years this decision protected federal spending from taxpayer challenges.

Foreshadowing the role that federal courts would assume later in the century—of insisting that state procedures adhered to fundamental standards of fairness—the Court in *Moore v. Dempsey* approved the intervention of a federal judge to vindicate the rights of persons convicted in state courts dominated by a mob. In that situation, wrote Justice Holmes, where "the whole proceeding is a mask—that counsel, judge and jury were swept to the fatal end by an irresistible wave of public passion, and . . . the state courts failed to correct the wrong," the federal courts must act.[24]

DUE PROCESS AND FREE SPEECH

The Court's role as balance wheel can give its work a paradoxical character. So it was in 1925 when the conservative Court ignited the spark that eventually would flare into the "due process revolution" of the 1960s.

Benjamin Gitlow, a socialist, did not convince the Court to overturn his conviction for violating New York's criminal anarchy law by distributing a pamphlet calling for the overthrow of the government. Gitlow had challenged his conviction as violating the First Amendment, which, he contended, the Fourteenth Amendment extended to protect individual rights against state, as well as federal, action.

But although the Court in *Gitlow v. New York* upheld Gitlow's conviction, it accepted this argument. Almost in passing, Justice Sanford stated that the Court now assumed "that freedom of speech and of the press . . . are among the fundamental personal rights and 'liberties' protected by the due process clause of the Fourteenth Amendment from impairment by the states."[25]

During the 1930s this declaration would form the foundation for the Court's first decisions striking down state laws as encroaching upon First Amendment freedoms.

Federal law enforcement practices, however, survived constitutional challenge in two significant cases during the 1920s. The Court upheld routine searches, without search warrants, of cars that agents suspected were used in violating a law; and it upheld federal use of wiretaps, again without warrants, to obtain evidence. Neither practice, held the Court in *Carroll v. United States* and *Olmstead v. United States*, violated the individual's right to be secure from unreasonable search and seizure. *Carroll* remains in effect; *Olmstead* protected electronic surveillance from constitutional challenge until it was overturned in 1967.

The Court's first decision overturning a state conviction because it was obtained in violation of the Fourteenth Amendment's due process guarantee came in 1927. In *Tumey v. Ohio* the Court held that due process meant that a person charged with a violation of the law be tried before an impartial judge. It overturned the conviction of a person tried before a city court, where the judge was the mayor and the fines collected went into the city treasury.

The Court's definition of the liberty protected by the Fourteenth Amendment was slowly beginning to expand in the area of personal rights, even as it had expanded earlier in the area of property rights.

In 1923 the Court had struck down a state law forbidding a

teacher to use any language other than English.[26] The Fourteenth Amendment protected the right of teachers to teach a foreign language—and of parents to engage teachers to teach their children another language, held the Court.

In 1925 the Court in *Pierce v. Society of Sisters* invalidated a state law that required all children to attend public schools. Again, the Court found that parental freedom to choose private schools was within the protected area of personal liberty.

Black citizens, however, continued to meet with little success in asserting their rights under this amendment. In 1926 the Court in *Corrigan v. Buckley* clung to its nineteenth-century view that the Fourteenth Amendment did not reach private discrimination and so left unaffected the use of restrictive covenants limiting the sale of real estate to blacks.

When state action was involved, however, the Court was willing to exercise the power of the Civil War Amendments. In 1927 the Court in *Nixon v. Herndon,* the first in a long line of "white primary" cases, struck down Texas's efforts to exclude blacks from participating in the all-important Democratic primary elections.

THE ALLOCATION OF POWER

Local government won strong affirmation from the Court in 1926 of its power to control the use of its land through zoning. In *Euclid v. Ambler Realty Co.* the Court upheld such regulation as a legitimate use of the police power. The following year, in *Buck v. Bell,* the Court went even further, approving the use of the state's police power to sterilize some mentally defective state residents.

But when a state asserted its power over economic transactions, it again collided with the Court's insistence upon the freedom of contract. *Adkins* (1923) was followed by *Burns Baking Co. v. Bryan* (1924), which struck down a state law regulating the weight of loaves of bread sold to the public. In 1927 the Court held that states could not regulate the resale of theater tickets, and the following year it placed employment agency practices beyond state reach as well.[27]

The power of the chief executive was twice challenged and twice upheld. Confirming a virtually unlimited power of the president to remove appointees from office, the Court in the 1926 case of *Myers v. United States* held that Congress could not deny the president the power to remove postmasters without its consent. The power to remove was a necessary corollary of the power to appoint, held Taft in the majority opinion. Congress could not require a president to retain subordinates whom he wished to remove.

Two years later, in *Hampton v. United States,* the Court upheld Congress's delegation of power to the president to adjust tariff rates in response to the competitive conditions.

In February 1930 Chief Justice Taft resigned, a dying man. President Hoover selected Charles Evans Hughes, sixty-one, to return to the Court as chief justice. Hughes would serve through the turbulent decade of the New Deal, resigning in 1941.

Taft died March 8, 1930. So did Justice Sanford. To replace Sanford Hoover chose federal judge John J. Parker of North Carolina. But opposition to the nomination from labor and black groups resulted in Senate rejection of Parker's nomination in May. The vote was 39–41. It was the first time in the twentieth century that the Senate had refused to confirm a presidential nominee to the Court and the first such occurrence since Cleveland's New York nominees were blocked in 1894 by Senator Hill.

Hoover then chose Owen J. Roberts of Pennsylvania to fill the Sanford seat. Roberts, fifty-five, was a Philadelphia lawyer who had served as one of the two government prosecutors in the Teapot Dome scandal. He would serve on the Court for fifteen years.

In 1931 Justice Holmes was ninety, the oldest man to serve on the Court in its history. Hughes was the fourth chief justice with whom Holmes had served in his twenty-eight years on the Court. Age had slowed Holmes, and Chief Justice Hughes gently suggested to him that the time for retirement had come. On January 12, 1932, Holmes resigned. He died, at ninety-three, in 1935, leaving his estate to the nation; it eventually would be used to fund a history of the Court.

To replace Justice Holmes, Hoover selected New York judge Benjamin Cardozo, sixty-two, who had been almost unanimously proposed as Holmes's successor by leaders all over the nation. Cardozo's selection clearly represented the victory of merit over more mundane geographic or ethnic criteria. At the time there were two New Yorkers already on the Court—Hughes and Stone—and there was already a Jewish justice. Cardozo served only six years before his death in 1938.

After Cardozo took his seat on the Court in early 1932, there were no further changes in the Court personnel for more than five years.

FREEDOM, FAIRNESS, AND THE STATES

The first years of the 1930s were quiet at the Supreme Court. A nation devastated by the economic crash of 1929 and the resulting depression was preoccupied with survival and had little time for litigation.

In 1931 the Court for the first time struck down a state law because it infringed upon the freedoms protected by the First Amendment. In *Stromberg v. California* the Court divided 7–2 to strike down California's law forbidding citizens to display a red flag as a symbol of opposition to organized government. Chief Justice Hughes wrote the opinion, declaring that the opportunity for free political discussion was a fundamental principle of the U.S. constitutional system, both in itself and as a means of achieving lawful change and responsive government. Justices Butler and McReynolds dissented.

Two weeks after *Stromberg,* the Court struck down a second state law on similar grounds. In *Near v. Minnesota* the Court, 5–4, found that a state law penalizing newspapers for criticizing public officials violated the guarantee of a free press. Joining Butler and McReynolds in dissent were Sutherland and Van Devanter. Hughes again wrote the majority opinion.

Twice in the first half of the 1930s the Court considered constitutional questions arising from the case of the "Scottsboro boys," several young black men arrested in Alabama, away from their homes, and charged with raping two white women.

In 1932 *Powell v. Alabama* came to the Court. At issue was the right of these defendants, who were tried in state court, to have the effective aid of a lawyer in preparing a defense. This right is guaranteed defendants in federal trials by the Sixth Amendment, but the Court had not yet read the Fourteenth Amendment guarantee of due process as extending this right to state defendants.

In November 1932 the Court, 7–2, held that these black men, represented only at the last minute by a local lawyer, had been denied their constitutional right to due process. In these particular circumstances, wrote Justice Sutherland for the Court, the Constitution guaranteed these defendants the effective aid of an attorney. Justices Butler and McReynolds dissented.

Three years later—in the busy term of 1935—the second Scottsboro case came to the Court. In *Norris v. Alabama* the issue was not the right to counsel but the right to trial by a fairly chosen jury.

On April 1, 1935, a unanimous Court held that the Scottsboro defendants were denied their Fourteenth Amendment rights when they were indicted and tried by all-white juries, the result of the state's consistent practice of excluding blacks from jury duty. Chief Justice Hughes wrote the Court's opinion.

On the same day as *Norris v. Alabama*, the Court decided *Grovey v. Townsend*, the third of its rulings concerning Texas's persistent effort to keep blacks from voting in primary elections, the only significant elections in the Democratic-dominated South.

After the Court in *Nixon v. Herndon* (1927) struck down a state law barring blacks from voting in primary elections, the state handed over to state political parties the task of determining who could vote in its primary. In *Nixon v. Condon* (1932) the Supreme Court held that this delegation denied black voters equal protection. The state took no further action, but the Texas Democratic party barred all blacks from membership. In *Grovey v. Townsend* the Court held that the party's exclusion of blacks was beyond the reach of the Fourteenth Amendment. The party's action, it reasoned, was not state action. The Court was unanimous; Justice Roberts wrote the opinion.

In 1934 the Court lifted one long-standing restriction on state power to regulate business—and loosened another. The Court abandoned the view, first set out in *Munn v. Illinois* fifty-seven years earlier, that the only businesses states could regulate

THE COURT IN 1932
Seated from left: Justices Louis D. Brandeis, Willis Van Devanter, Chief Justice Charles Evans Hughes, Justices James C. McReynolds, George Sutherland.
Standing from left: Justices Owen J. Roberts, Pierce Butler, Harlan Fiske Stone, Benjamin N. Cardozo

were those "affected with a public interest." In its new case of *Nebbia v. New York* the Court, 5–4, upheld a New York law setting milk prices and declared that any business was subject to reasonable regulation. Roberts wrote the Court's opinion; McReynolds, Butler, Sutherland, and Van Devanter dissented. This decision was followed by rulings overturning the Taft Court's decisions nullifying state regulation of bread weights, ticket sales, and employment agencies.[28]

The Court also upheld a state mortgage moratorium law against a challenge that it violated the Constitution's contract clause. Again the vote was 5–4; the dissenters were the same as in *Nebbia*. Chief Justice Hughes wrote the opinion, finding the law a reasonable means of responding to the economic emergency of the Great Depression.[29]

THE COURT AND THE NEW DEAL

"The Court is almost never a really contemporary institution. The operation of life tenure in the judicial department, as against elections at short intervals of the Congress, usually keeps the average viewpoint of the two institutions a generation apart. The judiciary is thus the check of a preceding generation on the present one; a check of conservative legal philosophy upon a dynamic people, and nearly always the check of a rejected regime on the one in being." The man who wrote those words in 1941 was Attorney General Robert H. Jackson, an active participant in the New Deal battles between the Court and the president, and later a member of the Court.[30]

Never was Jackson's point more dramatically made than by the events of 1935, 1936, and 1937. A Court made up of men born in the mid-nineteenth century, and appointed to their seats by Presidents Wilson, Harding, Coolidge, and Hoover, looked with distaste upon radical legislative measures espoused by President Franklin D. Roosevelt and the Congress elected in the midst of national economic depression.

The Old Court

The Court of 1935 was five septuagenarians and four men only a few years their junior. Roberts, sixty, was the Court's youngest member. President Roosevelt was only fifty-three.

The Court's first decision on a New Deal measure came the first week of January 1935. Part of the National Industrial Recovery Act (NIRA) was invalidated, because in it Congress delegated power to the executive without setting specific standards for its use. The vote in *Panama Refining Co. v. Ryan* was 8–1. Chief Justice Hughes wrote the opinion; only Cardozo dissented.

Six weeks later, in mid-February 1935, the Court in the three *Gold Clause Cases* upheld the power of Congress to shift the nation away from the use of gold as its standard currency. The vote was 5–4: Hughes wrote the opinion; Sutherland, McReynolds, Butler, and Van Devanter dissented. McReynolds, distressed by the rulings, added to his dissenting opinion the extemporaneous lament: "As for the Constitution, it does not seem too much to say that it is gone. Shame and humiliation are upon us now!"[31]

But the *Gold Clause Cases* would be the administration's solitary victory before the Court in this October 1934 term. On May 6, 1935, the dissenters in the gold cases were joined by Justice Roberts to strike down the comprehensive retirement system Congress had set up for railroad employees. In *Railroad Retirement Board v. Alton Railway Co.,* the Court held that the commerce power did not provide a sufficient basis for such a system.

This decision was a harbinger of "Black Monday," three weeks later. On May 27 a unanimous Court handed Roosevelt three major defeats. In *Schechter Poultry Corp. v. United States,* the Court held invalid other major provisions of the NIRA, finding them an unconstitutional delegation of power from Congress to the president.

The Court also held the Federal Farm Bankruptcy Act in violation of the due process guarantee, and in a third decision the justices sharply limited the president's removal power, which it had envisioned as virtually unlimited only nine years earlier when it decided the *Myers* case.[32]

The 1936 Term

When the Court began its next term, in early October 1935, it met for the first time in its own building. Chief Justice Taft had persuaded Congress to approve the idea in 1929; the cornerstone had been laid by Chief Justice Hughes in October 1932; and the Court moved into the handsome marble building across from the Capitol for its 1936 term.

It was clear this would be a crucial term. Several cases testing the validity of New Deal legislation were pending; and the justices—even before they addressed these cases—were clearly divided. As historian Arthur M. Schlesinger Jr. described it:

They were already forming into distinct personal as well as constitutional blocs. The four conservatives used to ride to and from the Court together every day of argument and conference. To offset these riding caucuses, Stone and Cardozo began to go to Brandeis' apartment in the late afternoon on Fridays before conferences. Each group went over cases together and tried to agree on their positions.[33]

Hughes and Roberts were the two "swing men" between these two blocs. On January 6, 1936, they joined Sutherland, Van Devanter, Butler, and McReynolds to strike down the Agricultural Adjustment Act, which adopted crop controls and price subsidies as measures to stabilize the agricultural produce market. By 6–3 the Court held that Congress in this legislation intruded upon areas reserved by the Tenth Amendment for state regulation. Justice Roberts wrote the opinion in *United States v. Butler.*

On May 18 the Court by the same division struck down the Bituminous Coal Conservation Act. In *Carter v. Carter Coal Co.* the Court nullified a law designed to control working conditions of coal miners and to fix prices for the sale of coal. Coal mining was not commerce and so was outside the reach of federal authority, held the Court. The same day, the Court, 5–4, struck down the Municipal Bankruptcy Act.[34]

The administration claimed just one victory in the spring of

1936: the Court upheld—as a proper exercise of the commerce power—the creation of the Tennessee Valley Authority.[35]

As the term ended, Justice Stone commented:

I suppose no intelligent person likes very well the way the New Deal does things, but that ought not to make us forget that ours is a nation which should have the powers ordinarily possessed by governments, and that the framers of the Constitution intended that it should have. . . . We finished the term of Court yesterday, I think in many ways one of the most disastrous in its history.[36]

In this same term, so devastating in its impact on the effort of federal authority to deal with the nation's economic difficulties, the Court once again wielded the due process guarantee to strike down a state minimum-wage law. In *Morehead v. New York ex rel. Tipaldo* the same conservative majority that struck down the bankruptcy act struck down New York's law setting the minimum wage to be paid women workers. Such a law, wrote Butler for the Court, impaired the liberty of contract. Dissenting were Hughes, Stone, Brandeis, and Cardozo.

Almost overlooked amid the New Deal controversy, the Court in February 1936 took one more step toward imposing constitutional requirements on state criminal procedures. In *Brown v. Mississippi* the unanimous Court held that the Fourteenth Amendment guarantee of due process denied states the power to use as evidence against individuals any confession wrung from them by torture.

In December 1936 the Court, which held such a dim view of the president's efforts to deal with domestic crises, endorsed virtually unlimited power for the president in foreign affairs. In *United States v. Curtiss-Wright Export Corp.* the justices declared the president to be the sole negotiator of U.S. foreign policy. Justice Sutherland, author also of the opinions curtailing the removal power and striking down the coal act, described this aspect of presidential power as "plenary and exclusive."

PACKING THE COURT

Frustrated by the Court's adamant opposition to his efforts to lead the nation toward economic recovery, President Roosevelt began to look for a way to change the Court's views. His entire first term had passed without a vacancy there, despite the age and length of service of many of the justices. In part this state of affairs may have been due to the fierce opposition of the conservative justices to Roosevelt's New Deal, but it also was due to much more practical considerations.

In 1936 there was no "retirement" system for justices; they could withdraw from full-time active service only by resigning. Upon resignation the largest pension a justice could draw was $10,000. Chief Justice Hughes later would say that he felt that both Van Devanter and Sutherland would have retired earlier had the provisions for retirement income been more generous.[37]

Roosevelt decided to create vacancies by convincing Congress that the Court's functioning was hampered by the advanced age of its members. Early in February, just after his second inauguration, Roosevelt sent Congress a "judicial reform" proposal, quickly labeled his "Court packing" plan. He asked Congress to

authorize him to appoint an additional member of the Supreme Court for each justice over age seventy who did not resign. This plan would have enabled Roosevelt immediately to appoint six new justices (Butler had turned seventy in 1936), and in all likelihood, assured him a majority in favor of the New Deal.

The reaction to the proposal was adverse on all sides, yet Congress began formal consideration of it. In a move that would prove crucial, Congress immediately separated out and passed a new Supreme Court Retirement Act on March 1. It provided that Supreme Court justices could retire and continue to receive their salary, just as other federal judges already were able to do.

The Senate Judiciary Committee then turned to consideration of the proposal's more controversial items.

THE TURNABOUT

Unknown to any but the justices themselves, however, the Court already had begun to abandon its conservative effort to protect business from state and federal regulation. Signaling this change was its decision, reached before the Court-packing proposal was made known, to abandon the *Lochner-Adkins* line of reasoning and uphold state minimum-wage laws.

Implicit in this reversal was the willingness of a majority of the Court to accept government authority to act to protect the general welfare of society—and to withdraw the Court from any role as the censor of economic legislation.

On March 29, 1937, while the Senate committee was still considering the Roosevelt plan, the Court announced its decision in *West Coast Hotel Co. v. Parrish*. By 5–4, the Court upheld Washington State's minimum-wage law, overruling *Adkins* and effectively reversing the previous year's ruling in *Morehead v. New York*. Justice Roberts, who had voted to strike down the New York law, now voted to uphold the Washington law. His changed position was popularly described at the time as "the switch in time that saved the Nine." Chief Justice Hughes wrote the majority opinion; Sutherland, Butler, McReynolds, and Van Devanter dissented.

In his opinion, Chief Justice Hughes interred the doctrine of freedom of contract. No such freedom was mentioned in the Constitution, he pointed out. The "liberty" protected by the due process clauses of the Fifth and Fourteenth Amendments, he continued, was not liberty of contract, but instead "liberty in a social organization which requires the protection of the law against the evils which menace the health, safety, morals and welfare of the people."[38] That liberty was protected by the minimum-wage law, which thus was fully constitutional.

The same day the Court unanimously upheld two New Deal statutes—a second Federal Farm Bankruptcy Act, virtually identical to the one struck down on Black Monday, and a provision of the Railway Labor Act encouraging collective bargaining.[39]

Two weeks later, on April 12, the Court—by the same 5–4 vote as in *Parrish*—upheld the National Labor Relations Act. Writing the majority opinion in *National Labor Relations Board v. Jones & Laughlin Steel Corp.*, Chief Justice Hughes declared that the right to organize for collective bargaining was a fundamental right well within the scope of Congress's power over commerce.

On May 18 the Senate Judiciary Committee reported Roosevelt's legislation adversely, recommending against its enactment.

Almost simultaneously, Justice Van Devanter, age seventy-eight, informed President Roosevelt that he intended to retire at the end of the current term.

Less than a week later, on May 24, the Court confirmed the completeness of its turnabout. In *Steward Machine Co. v. Davis* and *Helvering v. Davis,* the Court by votes of 5–4 and 7–2 upheld the unemployment compensation and old-age benefits programs set up by the Social Security Act. The Court upheld the first as a proper use of the taxing power and the second as an appropriate means of acting to protect the general welfare. Justice Cardozo wrote the majority opinions in both cases.

To replace Van Devanter, Roosevelt chose Alabama senator Hugo L. Black as his first nominee to the Court. Black, fifty-one, was confirmed in August 1937. He would serve on the Court until a week before his death in 1971.

In December 1937, soon after Black took his seat, the Court announced its decision in *Palko v. Connecticut.* With Cardozo writing for the majority, the Court firmly declined to rule that the due process clause of the Fourteenth Amendment automatically extended all the guarantees of the Bill of Rights against state, as well as federal action.

Only those rights essential to a scheme of ordered liberty were binding upon the states through the due process guarantee, stated Cardozo. In Black's thirty-four years on the Court, the justices would, one by one, place almost all of the guarantees of the Bill of Rights in this "essential" category.

The Court, Civil Rights, and Society: 1938–1968

On October 4, 1937, Justice Hugo Black took his seat as the Supreme Court's most junior justice, ushering in a new era. President Roosevelt's Court-packing bill had been deflated into a judicial procedure bill, signed into law in August 1937. Van Devanter, one of the conservative quartet of justices so staunchly opposed to the New Deal approach, had left the bench; the others would follow shortly. The Court had resigned as arbiter of the wisdom of economic legislation; it would now turn its attention to questions of individual rights and liberties.

Over the next six years Roosevelt would name eight justices and elevate a ninth to chief justice. The men he would place on the Court were young enough to be the sons of the men they succeeded, and the views of the Court would change accordingly.

A few months after Black was seated, Justice Sutherland, seventy-five, retired. To succeed him, Roosevelt named Solicitor General Stanley F. Reed, fifty-four. Reed served nineteen years until he retired in 1957.

In mid-1938 Justice Cardozo died. In his place Roosevelt chose his close friend and adviser, Felix Frankfurter, fifty-six, a Harvard law professor. Seated early in 1939, Frankfurter served for twenty-three years on the Court.

Soon after Frankfurter took his seat, Justice Brandeis resigned. He was eighty-two years old and had served on the Court twenty-three years. He was succeeded by a man literally half his age; William O. Douglas, the forty-year-old chairman of the Securities and Exchange Commission, would serve for thirty-six and one-half years—longer than any man in the Court's history.

Late in 1939 Justice Butler died at seventy-three. He was replaced by Attorney General Frank Murphy, fifty, who served until his death in 1949. With Murphy's arrival in January 1940, Roosevelt nominees became a majority of the Court. Of the four staunch conservatives who had blocked Roosevelt's New Deal plans, only McReynolds remained.

FROM COMMERCE TO CIVIL RIGHTS

The philosophical shift evident in the decisions of 1937 was reinforced by the rulings of the succeeding terms. Not only did the Court redirect its efforts away from matters of property rights and toward issues of personal rights, but also it began to evolve different standards for the two types of cases.

The change was illustrated in *United States v. Carolene Products Co.,* decided April 25, 1938. Over McReynolds's lone dissent, the Court upheld a federal law barring the interstate transportation of certain milk products.

In the majority opinion, Justice Stone tentatively set out a double standard for constitutional cases. When a law was challenged as impinging upon economic rights, he said, the Court would presume the law to be valid, unless the challenger could prove otherwise. But if a law was challenged as impinging upon personal liberties protected by the Bill of Rights, the Court might be less inclined to assume the law's validity. As Stone worded it, "there may be narrower scope for operation of the presumption of constitutionality when legislation appears on its face to be within a specific prohibition of the Constitution, such as those of the first ten amendments."[40]

The reasoning behind such a double standard, Stone explained, was based upon the relationship of economic rights and personal rights to the political processes. Laws infringing upon the individual rights guaranteed by the Bill of Rights restricted the operation of the very processes that could be expected to produce the repeal of repressive legislation. Laws operating to curtail economic freedom, on the other hand, did not hinder the political processes that therefore could be used to repeal or modify the offending laws.

This new set of standards—plus the extension of the guarantees of the Bill of Rights to the states, begun with *Gitlow*—provided the doctrinal underpinnings for the civil rights revolution to come. One observer calls the *Carolene Products* standard, set out in a footnote, "the manifesto in a footnote."[41]

In a steady line of decisions beginning with those announced on March 29, 1937, the Court upheld revised versions of virtually all the major New Deal legislation it had struck down in 1935 and 1936.[42]

Abandoning its restrictive view of the relationship between states' rights and federal power, the Court overturned its earlier decisions granting the incomes of federal officials immunity from state taxes and granting those of state officials similar immunity from federal taxation.[43]

This line of rulings—in which the Court also renounced many of the doctrines it had invoked to curtail state and federal power over economic matters—culminated on February 3, 1941. By a unanimous vote the Court upheld the Fair Labor Standards Act of 1938, which prohibited child labor and set a maximum forty-hour workweek and a minimum wage of forty cents an hour for workers in interstate commerce.

This decision, in *United States v. Darby Lumber Co.,* specifically overruled *Hammer v. Dagenhart,* the 1918 ruling placing child labor beyond the reach of the federal commerce power. The Court implicitly reaffirmed Hughes's earlier statement discarding the "freedom of contract" doctrine and declared the Tenth Amendment of no relevance to questions of federal power. Writing for the Court, Justice Stone explained that the justices viewed that amendment as "but a truism [stating] that all is retained which has not been surrendered."[44]

With this decision, legal scholar William F. Swindler wrote, the Court returned to Marshall's view of the broad commerce power:

[A]fter half a century of backing and filling, the Court had come unequivocally to acknowledge that a plenary power over interstate commerce was vested in Congress, and that Congress was the sole judge of the appropriate use of this power. The new constitutionalism, in this, was returning to the concept enunciated by John Marshall a century before, that the commerce power "is complete in itself, may be exercised to its utmost extent, and acknowledges no limitations other than are prescribed in the Constitution."[45]

Later this term, in May, the Court reversed another precedent and extended federal power in another direction. In *United States v. Classic* the Court acknowledged that Congress could regulate primary elections when they were an integral part of the process of selecting members of Congress. This decision overturned the Court's holding to the contrary in *Newberry v. United States,* decided twenty years earlier. Chief Justice Hughes, the attorney who had won the *Newberry* ruling, did not participate in the *Classic* decision.

Already in Black's first term questions of civil rights and individual freedom were beginning to occupy more of the Court's attention.

In March 1938 the Court unanimously held in *Lovell v. Griffin* that the First Amendment guarantee of freedom of religion was abridged when a city required Jehovah's Witnesses to be licensed before they could distribute religious literature to city residents.

THE COURT IN 1940

Seated from left: Justices Owen J. Roberts, James C. McReynolds, Chief Justice Charles Evans Hughes, Justices Harlan Fiske Stone, Hugo L. Black.
Standing from left: Justices William O. Douglas, Stanley F. Reed, Felix Frankfurter, Frank Murphy

In May the Court confirmed the broad scope of the Sixth Amendment right to counsel for federal defendants. The justices in *Johnson v. Zerbst* held that federal courts were constitutionally bound to provide defendants with legal counsel unless they waived that right.

And in December the Court began seriously to test the constitutional validity of the "separate but equal" doctrine, which had made possible the pervasive racial segregation of American life.

In *Missouri ex rel. Gaines v. Canada* the Court held that the Constitution required a state providing white residents the opportunity for higher education to offer it to blacks as well. This promise of equal protection, wrote Chief Justice Hughes, was not fulfilled by a state's offering to pay the tuition for a black student to attend law school in another state.

The following term the Court decided *Hague v. CIO*, striking down a city ordinance used to prevent union organizers from meeting and discussing labor union membership and related subjects. The First Amendment guarantee of free speech and assembly forbids such official restrictions, held the Court. And in 1940 the Court in *Thornhill v. Alabama* extended this rationale to strike down a state law forbidding labor picketing.[46]

Also in 1940 the Court in *Cantwell v. Connecticut* held that a state could not, without offending the First Amendment guarantees, convict persons for breach of the peace simply as a result of their making provocative statements about religion.

WAR AND PATRIOTISM

The war in Europe encouraged a resurgence of patriotic display in the United States. In 1940 the Court's emerging views on state power and religious freedom were tested by *Minersville School District v. Gobitis*. State efforts to inculcate patriotism prevailed, at least temporarily, over religious freedom. By 8–1 the Court upheld a state's right to require public school students to recite daily the national Pledge of Allegiance to the flag, even if the recitation conflicted with their religious beliefs. Justice Frankfurter wrote the majority opinion; only Justice Stone dissented.

Early in 1941 Justice McReynolds resigned after twenty-six years on the Court. He was seventy-eight years old, the last of the conservative foursome of the New Deal to leave the bench. At the end of the 1941 term, Chief Justice Hughes retired.

Roosevelt chose Justice Harlan Fiske Stone, a Republican who had sat on the Court as an associate justice for sixteen years, to move to the center chair. Stone, then sixty-nine, served in that post until his death in 1946.

To fill McReynolds's seat, Roosevelt chose Sen. James F. Byrnes of South Carolina, sixty-two. Byrnes did not find the post a satisfying one and resigned after one term, in October 1942, to take a more active role in the Roosevelt administration's war effort.

As Byrnes's successor Roosevelt chose federal judge Wiley B. Rutledge, forty-eight. Rutledge took his seat in February 1943 and served until his death six years later.

To fill the seat Stone left vacant upon becoming chief justice, Roosevelt in 1941 chose Attorney General Robert H. Jackson, forty-nine, who served for thirteen years.

The United States was forcibly brought into World War II early in Stone's first term as chief justice. War issues of personal liberty and governmental power dominated the Court's work during his tenure in that post.

After his first term, a special session was called in July 1942 so that the Court might consider the constitutional challenge brought by Nazi saboteurs, arrested in the United States, to Roosevelt's decision to have them tried by a military commission, not civilian courts. In *Ex parte Quirin* the Court upheld the president's actions as within the scope of the authority delegated to him by Congress.

In three later decisions in 1943 and 1944, the Court also upheld against constitutional challenge the actions of the president and Congress restricting the liberty of persons of Japanese descent living on the West Coast through a program of curfews and removal from the coast to inland camps. The Court conceded the odious nature of ethnic distinctions, but found them justified in this particular wartime situation.[47]

In one of these cases, however, *Korematsu v. United States,* the Court for the first time declared that "all legal restrictions which curtail the civil rights of a single racial group are immediately suspect . . . the Courts must subject them to the most rigid scrutiny."[48] Thus, even in condoning severe infringements of personal liberty and individual rights in the war years, the Court laid the foundation for later decisions expanding those rights.

A primary characteristic of the Court in the early 1940s, unlike its immediate predecessor, was its experimental approach to constitutional law, its "readiness to change new landmarks as well as old" ones.[49]

This readiness was amply demonstrated in the term that began in October 1942. In that term the Court reversed two of its own recent rulings concerning the First Amendment rights of Jehovah's Witnesses, a sect whose particular beliefs and evangelistic fervor brought its members into frequent collision with state and local authority.

In the 1940 *Gobitis* case the Court had upheld Pennsylvania's rule that schoolchildren participate in the Pledge of Allegiance to the U.S. flag each day.

In 1942 the Court had upheld, in *Jones v. Opelika,* a city ordinance requiring street vendors—including Jehovah's Witnesses passing out religious material—to obtain city licenses for their activity.[50] The vote was 5–4. Justice Reed wrote the majority opinion.

But three of the dissenters in *Opelika*—members of the majority in *Gobitis*—announced that they were ready to reverse the flag salute case. This unusual public confession of error came from Justices Black, Murphy, and Douglas.

Eleven months later, on May 3, 1943, the Court reversed *Jones v. Opelika,* returning to the view set out initially in *Lovell v. Griffin* that licenses could not be required of religious pamphleteers.

THE COURT IN 1943
Seated from left: Justices Stanley Reed, Owen R. Roberts, Chief Justice Harlan Fiske Stone, Justices Hugo L. Black, Felix Frankfurter.
Standing from left: Justices Robert H. Jackson, William O. Douglas, Frank Murphy, Wiley Blount Rutledge

By 5–4 the Court in *Murdock v. Pennsylvania* struck down licensing requirements similar to those upheld in *Opelika,* finding that they burdened the free exercise of religion when they were applied to the Jehovah's Witnesses. Justices Frankfurter, Reed, Roberts, and Jackson dissented.

Six weeks after *Murdock* the Court reversed *Gobitis.* The vote in *West Virginia Board of Education v. Barnette* was 6–3. The majority was composed of Stone, the lone dissenter in *Gobitis,* now joined by Black, Douglas, and Murphy, and two new justices—Jackson and Rutledge. Dissenting were Frankfurter, Reed, and Roberts.

The new majority's view was eloquently stated by Jackson:

If there is any fixed star in our constitutional constellation, it is that no official, high or petty, can prescribe what shall be orthodox in politics, nationalism, religion, or other matters of opinion or force citizens to confess by word or act their faith therein.[51]

In 1941 the Court refused to hold that the Fourteenth Amendment required states to provide all criminal defendants the aid of an attorney. Justices Black, Douglas, and Murphy dissented from the ruling in *Betts v. Brady;* twenty-two years later, Black would write the opinion overruling it.

In 1944 the Court in *Smith v. Allwright* expanded its definition of state action to strike down, once again, Texas's effort to maintain its "white primary." Relying on *United States v. Classic,* the Court effectively nullified *Grovey v. Townsend* (1935) by holding that when a primary election is an integral part of the electoral process, exclusion of black voters by a political party is state action within the reach of the Fourteenth Amendment.

THE POSTWAR COURT

In mid-1945 Justice Roberts resigned. President Harry S. Truman selected a friend, Republican senator Harold Burton of Ohio, fifty-seven, to fill the seat. Burton, the first Republican justice named by a Democratic president, served on the Court for thirteen years.

Despite the addition of Justice Burton, the Court operated for its October 1945 term with only eight members present. Justice Robert Jackson was absent for the term, acting as prosecutor at the Nuremberg trials of German war criminals.

On April 22, 1946, the Court, over dissenting votes by Stone, Reed, and Frankfurter, overruled several earlier decisions to permit conscientious objectors to become naturalized citizens, even if they were unwilling to bear arms in the defense of their adopted country. As Stone spoke from the bench to register his dissent in *Girouard v. United States,* his voice faltered. He had to be helped from the bench. He died that evening.

"The bench Stone headed was the most frequently divided, the most openly quarrelsome in history," wrote an observer.[52] That point was quickly borne out by events following his death. A long-distance feud erupted between Jackson, still absent in Europe, and Justice Black, now the Court's senior member. Many assumed that Truman would elevate Jackson to the post of chief justice; rumors flew that two other justices had said they would resign if he were appointed.

Hoping to smooth over these differences, Truman chose Secretary of the Treasury Fred M. Vinson to head the Court. Vinson, fifty-six, served for seven years, until his death in 1953.

After Stone's death, the Court—now with only seven participating members—announced its decision to strike down state laws requiring separate seating for black and white passengers on interstate buses. In *Morgan v. Virginia* the Court held such a rule a burden on interstate commerce. Seating rules for interstate vehicles was a matter for uniform national regulation, said the Court. This decision effectively reversed *Louisville, New Orleans and Texas Railway Co. v. Mississippi,* the Court's 1890 ruling upholding such requirements.

Also late in the October 1945 term, the Court by 4–3 in *Colegrove v. Green* declined to enter the "political thicket" of electoral malapportionment.

Questions of individual freedom came before the Court in increasing numbers during the postwar years. In its first rulings on the application of the First Amendment's establishment clause to state action, the Court in 1947 began a long effort to determine when and in what manner a state may provide aid to parochial schools or students at such schools without infringing on the amendment's guarantee.

In 1947 the Court reaffirmed its view that the due process clause of the Fourteenth Amendment did not require states to abide by all the provisions of the Bill of Rights. In that same term, however, the Court simply assumed that the Eighth Amendment ban on cruel and unusual punishment applied to state action.[53]

In 1949 the Court in *Wolf v. Colorado* declared that the states, like the federal government, were bound by the Fourth Amendment guarantee of security against unreasonable searches and seizures. But the Court rendered this declaration of little practical effect by refusing to require state judges to exclude evidence obtained in violation of the guarantee.

In 1948 the Court had effectively curtailed the use of restrictive covenants to perpetuate housing segregation. In *Shelley v. Kraemer* the Court held that although the Fourteenth Amendment did not reach the covenant itself, an agreement between private individuals, it did reach—and forbid—state court action enforcing those agreements.

In mid-1949 Justice Murphy died. President Truman selected Attorney General Tom C. Clark to fill the seat. Clark, forty-nine, served on the Court for eighteen years. Almost as soon as Clark was confirmed, Justice Rutledge died. Truman named Sherman Minton, fifty-nine, a colleague from his days as a senator, to that seat. Minton, who had become a federal judge, served on the Court for seven years.

SUBVERSION, SEGREGATION, AND STEEL SEIZURE

Cold war issues and the emerging civil rights movement dominated the work of the Supreme Court during most of the 1950s. Intense national concern over the threat of world communism produced a variety of laws and programs intended to prevent domestic subversion. Many of these antisubversive efforts were challenged as infringing on freedoms of belief and expression protected by the First Amendment.

In May 1950 the Court ruled on the first of these challenges. In *American Communications Association v. Douds* the Court upheld the Taft-Hartley Act's requirement that all labor union officers swear they were not members of the Communist Party. Chief Justice Vinson explained that Congress, under its commerce power, had the authority to impose such a requirement to avoid politically based strikes impeding the flow of interstate commerce. Justice Black in dissent argued that the commerce clause did not restrict "the right to think."

The following year the Court in *Dennis v. United States* upheld the Smith Act, which made it unlawful to advocate or teach the violent overthrow of government in the United States or to belong to an organization dedicated to the accomplishment of these ends. The Court upheld the convictions of eleven leaders of the U.S. Communist Party under the act. Chief Justice Vinson wrote the opinion; Justices Black and Douglas dissented.

During this term the Supreme Court also upheld the power of the attorney general to prepare a list of organizations considered subversive—and backed state power to require public employees to take an oath denying membership in the Communist Party.[54]

In a special term called in the summer of 1953, the Court considered a stay of execution granted by Justice Douglas for Julius and Ethel Rosenberg, convicted under the Espionage Act of 1917 of passing atomic secrets to the Soviet Union. The Court—over the dissents of Black and Douglas—lifted the stay, allowing the Rosenbergs to be executed.[55] Douglas's action in granting the stay sparked the first of several unsuccessful impeachment attempts against him.

By 1950 President Truman had named four justices, including the chief justice. Thus, when he found himself before the Court in May 1952, defending his decision to seize the nation's major steel companies to avoid a strike and disruption of steel production during the Korean conflict, he might have expected a favorable decision.

Instead, on June 2, 1952, the Court rebuked Truman, ruling that he had acted illegally and without constitutional authority. The vote was 6–3. In an opinion by Justice Black, the majority upheld a lower court's order blocking the seizure. Justices Burton and Clark voted against Truman; Chief Justice Vinson and Justice Minton voted for him.

The decision in *Youngstown Sheet & Tube Co. v. Sawyer* marked one of the rare instances where the Supreme Court flatly told the president he had overreached the limits of his constitutional power. And it was a mark of the Court's power that President Truman, fuming, complied.

In June 1951 the Court announced two unanimous decisions that called further into question the continuing validity of the "separate but equal" doctrine it had espoused in *Plessy v. Ferguson,* fifty-five years earlier.

In *Sweatt v. Painter* the Court ordered the University of Texas law school to admit a black student. The Court found the educational opportunity provided by a newly created "black" law school in the state in no way equal to that at the university law

THE COURT IN 1950
Seated from left: Justices Felix Frankfurter, Hugo L. Black, Chief Justice Frederick M. Vinson, Justices Stanley F. Reed, William O. Douglas.
Standing from left: Justices Tom C. Clark, Robert H. Jackson, Harold H. Burton, Sherman Minton

school. Therefore, the state did not fulfill the promise of equal protection under the Fourteenth Amendment by providing a separate black law school, held the Court in an opinion written by Chief Justice Vinson. In *McLaurin v. Oklahoma State Regents* the Court rebuffed the effort of the University of Oklahoma, forced by court order to accept a black student, to segregate that student in all phases of campus life.

A year and a half later, in December 1952, the Court heard arguments in a group of five cases challenging the segregation of public elementary and secondary schools. The cases are known by the title of one—*Brown v. Board of Education of Topeka*. In June 1953 the Court ordered reargument in the October 1953 term. Before the reargument took place, however, the Court had a new chief justice.

CHIEF JUSTICE WARREN

Chief Justice Vinson's last years were difficult ones. In addition to sensitive questions of antisubversive legislation, the face-off with Truman over the steel seizure and the tense special session considering the Rosenberg case confirmed Holmes's description of the Court as the quiet center of national storms.

In September 1953, less than three months after the Rosenberg decision, Vinson died. President Dwight D. Eisenhower then had the task of selecting a new chief justice within his first year of taking office. He looked to California, and chose that state's governor, Earl Warren.

Dwight D. Eisenhower

Earl Warren

Warren, a Republican, had run unsuccessfully for vice president on Thomas Dewey's ticket in 1948. As governor during World War II he had supported the relocation of residents of Japanese ancestry. He had just announced that he would not run for a fourth gubernatorial term when Vinson died. Explaining his choice, President Eisenhower said that he had selected Warren, then sixty-two, for his "integrity, honesty, middle-of-the-road philosophy."[56]

Warren received a recess appointment and began serving as the October 1953 term opened. He was confirmed in March 1954. He served for sixteen years, retiring in June 1969.

Brown v. Board of Education

When the *Brown* cases were reargued in December 1953, Warren presided over the Court. When they were decided on May 17, 1954, Warren spoke for the Court. In his brief opinion, the unanimous Supreme Court reversed *Plessy v. Ferguson,* decided fifty-eight years earlier when Earl Warren was five years old.

Concluding this, his first major opinion, Warren said:

We conclude that in the field of public education the doctrine of "separate but equal" has no place. Separate educational facilities are inherently unequal.[57]

Richard Kluger, twenty years later, assessed the impact of *Brown* this way:

Having proclaimed the equality of all men in the preamble to the Declaration of Independence, the nation's founders had then elected, out of deference to the slave-holding South, to omit that definition of equalitarian democracy from the Constitution. It took a terrible civil war to correct that omission. But the Civil War amendments were soon drained of their original intention to lift the black man to meaningful membership in American society. The Court itself would do much to assist in that process, and *Plessy* was its most brutal blow. Congress passed no civil rights laws after the Court-eviscerated one of 1875, and those that remained on the books were largely ignored by the states and unenforced by federal administration. . . .

It was into this moral void that the Supreme Court under Earl Warren now stepped. Its opinion in Brown v. Board of Education, for all its economy, represented nothing short of a reconsecration of American ideals.[58]

In April 1955 rearguments were held on the question of implementing the *Brown* decision. In May 1955 *Brown II* set out the standard—the states should proceed to end segregation in public schools with "all deliberate speed." Again the Court was unanimous; again Warren was its spokesman.

Although the Court had carefully limited its opinion to the subject of schools, "it became almost immediately clear that *Brown* had in effect wiped out all forms of state-sanctioned segregation."[59]

The impact of *Brown* was so fundamental—and public reaction to it so broad and deep—that it tends to dominate all descriptions of the Court's work during the 1950s. Yet with the exception of its 1958 ruling in *Cooper v. Aaron*, rebuking Gov. Orval Faubus of Arkansas for his resistance to desegregation, the Court did not hand down another major civil rights decision until the 1960s.

In case after case challenging various forms of segregation, the Court did not hear arguments but simply told lower courts to reconsider them in light of *Brown*. Resistance to these rulings was fierce, and was soon felt in Congress. The period from 1954 to 1960, writes William Swindler, was one of "tension between the high tribunal and Congress unparalleled even by the early years of the 1930s."[60] But now the roles were reversed: the Court was the vanguard of change—and Congress the bulwark of reaction.

The tension between Congress and the Court created by the school desegregation decisions was further heightened by subsequent decisions invalidating federal and state antisubversive programs and imposing new due process requirements upon police practices.

In 1956 the Court struck down a state sedition law, holding in *Pennsylvania v. Nelson* that Congress in passing the Smith Act had preempted state power to punish efforts to overthrow the federal government. The same term, the Court in *Slochower v. Board of Education* held that a state could not automatically dismiss employees simply because they invoked their Fifth Amendment right to remain silent when questioned by congressional committees.

And in the same term the Court applied the equal protection guarantee to require that a state provide an indigent defendant

THE COURT IN 1954

Seated from left: Justices Felix Frankfurter, Hugo L. Black, Chief Justice Earl Warren, Justices Stanley F. Reed, William O. Douglas.
Standing from left: Justices Tom C. Clark, Robert H. Jackson, Harold H. Burton, Sherman Minton

with a free transcript of his trial so that he might appeal his conviction. In *Griffin v. Illinois,* as in *Slochower,* Burton, Minton, Reed, and John Marshall Harlan, the newest justice, dissented.

The Eisenhower Justices

Just as the October 1954 term opened, Justice Jackson died. As his second nominee to the Court, President Eisenhower chose John Marshall Harlan, grandson and namesake of the famous dissenting justice whose career spanned the turn of the century. Harlan, a distinguished New York attorney, was fifty-five when he was appointed to the Supreme Court. He was confirmed in March 1955 and served for sixteen years.

Two years later, in October 1956, Justice Minton retired. As his successor, Eisenhower named William Joseph Brennan Jr., fifty, a judge on the New Jersey Supreme Court. Brennan was the first member of the Court born in the twentieth century. He would become a key strategist of Warren Court liberalism and serve thirty-four years before stepping down in 1990.

Early in 1957 Justice Reed retired after almost two decades on the bench. Eisenhower nominated federal judge Charles Whittaker, fifty-six, of Kansas. Whittaker would serve only five years before resigning in 1962.

In October 1958 Justice Burton retired, giving Eisenhower his fifth and last vacancy to fill. Eisenhower chose Potter Stewart of Ohio, a forty-three-year-old federal judge. Seated in the fall of 1958 as a recess appointment (as were Harlan and Brennan), Stewart was confirmed in May 1959. He served until 1981.

CASES AND CONTROVERSY

Criticism already aroused by *Brown* and some of the Court's other decisions during Warren's early years intensified in reaction to several lines of decisions in the late 1950s.

In 1951 the Court in *Dennis v. United States* had upheld the Smith Act, under which the leaders of the U.S. Communist Party were prosecuted for advocating the violent overthrow of the federal government. On June 17, 1957, the Court in *Yates v. United States* set such a strict standard for convictions under the Smith Act that it made successful prosecutions under the law almost impossible. Justice Harlan wrote the Court's opinion, making clear that only advocacy of subversive *activity* could be penalized without infringing on the First Amendment. The same day the Court in *Watkins v. United States* reversed the contempt citation of a witness who had refused to answer questions from the House Un-American Activities Committee about the Communist Party membership of other persons.

These opinions and two others announced that day led conservative critics to label June 17, 1957, "Red Monday"—as May 27, 1935, had been "Black Monday" and March 29, 1937, "White Monday" for supporters of the New Deal.[61]

Public and political criticism of the Court was intense. Legislation was proposed to reverse or circumvent the June 17 decisions and to withdraw the Court's jurisdiction over all matters of loyalty and subversion. Southerners critical of *Brown* joined others unhappy over the antisubversive rulings to raise congressional hostility toward the Court to a point unprecedented in the twentieth century.[62]

A week after Red Monday the Court in *Mallory v. United States* overturned a young man's conviction for rape because he had been interrogated too long without being informed of his rights and held too long between arrest and arraignment. The Court was unanimous in this ruling; the criticism was almost as unified.

The same day the Court in *Roth v. United States* made clear that obscene material did not have First Amendment protection, embarking on the long and difficult process of describing what is and what is not obscene.

In a special session in July 1957, the Court cleared the way for Japanese courts to try an American soldier for killing a Japanese woman on an Army rifle range, another ruling that won the Court few friends.[63]

In 1958 the Court began to give full constitutional recognition to the freedom of association—striking down Alabama's efforts to force the National Association for the Advancement of Colored People (NAACP) to disclose its membership lists.[64]

A second special session was called late in the summer of 1958 to consider the Little Rock, Arkansas, desegregation case. The Court in *Cooper v. Aaron* unanimously rejected city officials' request for delay in implementing the desegregation plan for the city's schools.

THE REAPPORTIONMENT REVOLUTION

In *Brown v. Board of Education* the Supreme Court set off a long overdue revolution in civil rights. But after *Brown* the Court played only a secondary role in the accelerating civil rights movement, leaving Congress to implement, at last, the guarantees of the Civil War Amendments through effective legislation. The Court's role was crucial but secondary. When civil rights legislation was challenged, as it had been during Reconstruction, the Court upheld it as constitutional.

But in the area of voting rights, the Court—unexpectedly—took the lead. In 1946 the Court had rebuffed a constitutional challenge to maldistribution of voters among electoral districts, declaring such a matter a political question beyond its purview.

In 1962 the Court abandoned that cautious stance and held that constitutional challenges to such malapportionment of political power were indeed questions the Courts might decide. This ruling was foreshadowed in the 1960 decision in *Gomillion v. Lightfoot,* in which the Court unanimously agreed that a state, in gerrymandering a district to exclude all blacks, had clearly violated the Fifteenth Amendment. Because such state action violated a specific constitutional guarantee, held the Court, it was properly a matter for federal judicial consideration.

It was from that ruling only a short step to *Baker v. Carr,* announced March 26, 1962. Tennessee's failure to redistrict for most of the twentieth century had produced electoral districts for the state legislature of grossly unequal population. This maldistribution of electoral power was challenged as violating the Fourteenth Amendment guarantee of equal protection. Abandoning the "political thicket" view of *Colegrove v. Green,* the majority held that this was clearly a constitutional case within the jurisdiction of the federal courts.

Later in 1962 Justices Whittaker and Frankfurter retired. President John F. Kennedy named Deputy Attorney General Byron R. White, forty-four, and Secretary of Labor Arthur Goldberg, fifty-four, to fill the empty seats. White took his seat in April 1962; Goldberg was seated at the beginning of the October 1962 term. Although Goldberg would serve only three years, White remained on the bench for more than three decades.

In March 1963 the Court set out the standard for constitutionally valid reapportionment plans. In *Gray v. Sanders* Justice Douglas wrote for the Court that the promise of political equality, contained in the nation's most basic documents, meant "one person, one vote." A year later, in February 1964, the Court applied that rule to congressional redistricting in *Wesberry v. Sanders.* Four months later in the June 1964 ruling in *Reynolds v. Sims,* the justices held that the same standard applied to the electoral districts for the members of both houses of the states' legislatures.

The result of these rulings, which Warren considered the most important of his tenure, was the redistribution of political power in Congress and every state legislature. In 1969 the Court in *Kirkpatrick v. Preisler* reaffirmed its commitment to this standard, requiring congressional districts within a state to be mathematically equal in population.

THE DUE PROCESS REVOLUTION

Involving itself in still another area traditionally left to state control, the Court in the 1960s accelerated the step-by-step application of due process requirements to state law enforcement and criminal procedures. By 1969 the Court had required states to abide by virtually every major provision of the Bill of Rights.

The first major ruling in this "due process revolution" came on June 19, 1961. By a 5–4 vote the Court held in *Mapp v. Ohio* that evidence obtained in violation of the Fourth Amendment guarantee of security against unreasonable search and seizure must be excluded from use in state, as well as federal, courts. Justice Clark wrote the opinion; Justices Stewart, Harlan, Frankfurter, and Whittaker dissented.

A year later the Court for the first time applied the Eighth Amendment ban on cruel and unusual punishment to strike down a state law. In *Robinson v. California* the Court held that a state could not make narcotics addiction a crime.

In 1963 the Court declared in *Gideon v. Wainwright* that states must provide legal assistance for all defendants charged with serious crimes. If defendants are unable to pay for an attorney, the state must provide one for them, wrote Justice Black for the unanimous Court, overruling the Court's 1941 refusal, in *Betts v. Brady,* to extend this right to state defendants.

On June 15, 1964, the same day it decided *Reynolds v. Sims*, the Court held that states must observe the Fifth Amendment privilege against compelled self-incrimination. The vote in *Malloy v. Hogan* was 5–4; Brennan wrote the opinion; Harlan, Clark, Stewart, and White dissented.

A week later, by the same vote, the Court held, in *Escobedo v. Illinois*, that suspects have a right to legal assistance as soon as they are the focus of a police investigation.

In April 1965 the Supreme Court overruled *Twining v. New Jersey* (1908) and held that state judges and prosecutors may not comment adversely upon the failure of defendants to testify in their own defense. Such comment infringes upon the Fifth Amendment right to remain silent, declared the Court in *Griffin v. California.*

The most controversial single Warren Court criminal law ruling came the following term, on June 13, 1966. In *Miranda v. Arizona* the Court held 5–4 that police may not interrogate suspects in custody unless they have informed them of their right to remain silent, of the fact that their words may be used against them, and of their right to have the aid of a lawyer. If suspects wish to remain silent or to contact an attorney, interrogation must cease until they wish to speak or until their attorney is present. Statements obtained in violation of this rule may not be used in court. Chief Justice Warren wrote the majority opinion; dissenting were Harlan, Clark, Stewart, and White.

The next term, as criticism of the Court mounted in Congress and in statehouses across the nation, the Court extended to state defendants the right to a speedy trial, enlarged the due process guarantees for juvenile defendants, and brought wiretapping and electronic surveillance under the strictures of the Fourth Amendment warrant requirement.[65]

This step-by-step process of applying the Bill of Rights against state, as well as federal, action was completed with the 1968 ruling in *Duncan v. Louisiana* and the 1969 ruling in *Benton v. Maryland*. In *Duncan* the Court announced that it was extending the right to a jury trial to state defendants. On Warren's last day as chief justice, the Court announced *Benton*, extending the guarantee against double jeopardy to states.

CIVIL RIGHTS, PERSONAL LIBERTY

Questions of freedom of belief and association, arising from the antisubversive measures of the 1950s, were still before the Court during the 1960s. Generally, the Court scrutinized these restrictive measures closely, and often it found some constitutional flaw.

In 1961 the Court upheld the constitutionality of the Subversive Activities Control Act of 1950, under which the Communist Party was required to register with the Justice Department. But this ruling in *Communist Party v. Subversive Activities Control Board (SACB)* came by a 5–4 vote. Four years later a unanimous Court held in *Albertson v. SACB* that individuals could not be compelled to register under the law without violating the Fifth Amendment protection against self-incrimination.

In 1966 the Court closely circumscribed the use of state loyalty oaths, and in 1967 it struck down the portion of the Subversive Activities Control Act that made it a criminal offense for a member of a "subversive" group to hold a job in the defense industry.[66]

In 1964 Congress at last reasserted its long-dormant power to implement the promises of the Civil War Amendments through legislation. Passage of the comprehensive 1964 Civil Rights Act was followed in 1965 by the Voting Rights Act and in 1968 by the Fair Housing Act. The modern Supreme Court, unlike the Court of the 1870s and 1880s, reinforced congressional action, finding these revolutionary statutes clearly constitutional.

In late 1964 the Court upheld the contested public accommodations provisions of the 1964 act in *Heart of Atlanta Motel v. United States*. Justice Clark wrote the opinion for a unanimous Court.

In 1966 the Court rebuffed a broad challenge to the Voting Rights Act of 1965 as violating states' rights. In *South Carolina v. Katzenbach* the Court, with only Justice Black dissenting in part, upheld the sweeping statute as within the power of Congress to enforce the Fifteenth Amendment guarantee against racial discrimination in voting. And even as Congress was debating the modern Fair Housing Act, the Court in *Jones v. Mayer* reinterpreted the Civil Rights Act of 1866 to prohibit racial discrimination in the sale of real estate.

Throughout the 1960s the Court exercised a supervisory role over the desegregation efforts of school systems across the country. In its first major school ruling since 1954, the Court in the 1964 case of *Griffin v. County School Board of Prince Edward County* said that a state could not avoid the obligation of desegregating its public schools by closing them down.

Four years later, in *Green v. County School Board of New Kent County*, the Court declared that "freedom of choice" desegregation plans were acceptable only when they were effective in desegregating a school system. The Court made clear that, in its view, there had been entirely too much deliberation and not enough speed in the nation's effort to implement *Brown*.

The Court during this decade also substantially expanded constitutional protection for the exercise of personal rights to choose a course of individual action.

In 1965 the Court in *Griswold v. Connecticut* struck down as unconstitutional a state law that forbade all use of contraceptives, even by married couples. The justices could not agree on the exact constitutional basis for this ruling, but they did agree there were some areas so private that the Constitution protected them from state interference. Two years later the Court, using similar reasoning in *Loving v. Virginia*, held it unconstitutional for a state to forbid a person of one race to marry a member of another race.

The criticism the Warren Court engendered by its rulings on security programs, segregation, and criminal procedures reached a new crescendo after the Court's "school prayer" decisions. On the basis of the First Amendment's ban on state action "establishing" religion, the Court in 1962 held that a state may not prescribe a prayer or other religious statement for use in public schools. This ruling in *Engel v. Vitale* was followed in 1963 by a second ruling denying a state power to require Bible reading as a daily religious exercise in public schools.[67]

The Supreme Court also expanded the meaning of other First Amendment provisions. In the landmark libel case of *New York Times v. Sullivan,* decided in March 1964, the Court enlarged the protection the First Amendment provided the press by stating that public officials and public figures could recover damages for libelous statements made by the news media only if they could prove the statements were published with "actual malice."

And early in 1969 the Court held that the First Amendment's protection for symbolic speech guaranteed students the right to engage in peaceful nondisruptive protest of the war in Vietnam, through the wearing of black armbands to school.[68]

Also during the 1960s, in decisions that drew far less public attention, the Court made it easier for state prisoners, federal taxpayers, and persons threatened by state action to come into federal court for assistance.

On March 18, 1963, the same day it announced its decisions in *Gray v. Sanders* and *Gideon v. Wainwright,* the Court in *Fay v. Noia* relaxed the requirements placed upon state prisoners who wished to challenge their detention in federal courts. Two years later, in *Dombrowski v. Pfister,* the Court indicated that federal judges should not hesitate to intervene and halt ongoing state proceedings under a law challenged as violating the First Amendment.

And in 1968 the Court in *Flast v. Cohen* substantially modified its 1923 bar against federal taxpayer suits challenging the use of tax moneys.

Impatient to place a man of his own choosing on the Supreme Court, President Lyndon B. Johnson in 1965 persuaded Justice Goldberg to leave the Court for the post of ambassador to the United Nations. In the empty seat Johnson placed Washington attorney Abe Fortas, his close friend and adviser and the successful advocate in *Gideon v. Wainwright.* Fortas, fifty-five, was seated just before the October 1965 term began.

Two years later, when his son, Ramsey Clark, became attorney general, Justice Tom Clark retired. To fill Clark's seat, Johnson nominated the nation's first black justice, Thurgood Marshall, who had argued the *Brown* cases for the NAACP Legal Defense Fund. Marshall, fifty-nine, began his service just before the opening of the October 1967 term. He would serve on the high Court for twenty-four years.

At the end of that term, in 1968, Chief Justice Warren informed President Johnson that he intended to retire as soon as a successor to him was confirmed. Johnson promptly nominated Justice Fortas chief justice.

Johnson was a lame duck; he had announced in March 1968 that he would not run for reelection. The Republicans had hopes of winning the White House and wished to have their candidate, Richard Nixon, select the new chief justice. These hopes were given added significance by the fact that the Court itself was a major campaign issue. Nixon criticized the Court for "coddling criminals" and promised to appoint justices who would turn a more receptive ear to the arguments of the police and prosecutors.

Charges of cronyism—related to Fortas's continued unofficial role as adviser to Johnson—and conflict of interest further compounded the difficulties of his nomination as chief justice. After a filibuster stymied the nomination in October 1968, Johnson withdrew it at Fortas's request. Simultaneously, Johnson withdrew his nomination of federal judge Homer Thornberry of Texas to succeed Fortas as associate justice.

The following May, Fortas resigned his seat under threat of impeachment, the result of a magazine article charging him with unethical behavior. Fortas asserted his innocence in his letter of resignation and said he left the Court to avoid placing it under unnecessary stress.

The Court in Transition: 1969–1989

On June 23, 1969, Chief Justice Warren retired. He left behind a Court and a country dramatically changed since 1953, changed in significant part by the decisions of the Supreme Court during his sixteen years there. Many of those decisions were still hotly controversial, as was the strain of judicial activism which they had encouraged in lower federal courts across the country. Under Warren's leadership, the Court had exerted a strong liberalizing force on American life. Its rulings had initiated and accelerated the civil rights movement, ignited a reapportionment revolution, reformed police procedures, and curtailed state powers over controversial matters such as birth control and school prayer.

For twenty years after Warren's retirement, two presidents, Richard Nixon and Ronald Reagan, worked hard to undo his legacy, to return the Court—and the country—to a more conservative stance. Their appointments and their arguments moved the Court into an extended period of transition as it completed its second century.

CHIEF JUSTICE BURGER

Warren's successor, Warren Earl Burger of Minnesota, the nation's fifteenth chief justice, was sworn in June 23, 1969. President Nixon had chosen Burger, he said, to reverse the "liberal activism" of the Warren era. As an appeals judge, Burger had earned a reputation as a "strict constructionist" of the Constitution and federal laws. He usually sided with the state in criminal law cases and had publicly criticized the Warren Court for rulings showing leniency toward defendants. But Burger was more moderate on civil rights issues. Sixty-one at the time of his nomination, he was easily confirmed by the Senate.

Fortas's seat would remain vacant for a full year, however, as Nixon's effort to appoint a successor ran into unexpected difficulties. Three months after Fortas resigned, Nixon nominated a conservative South Carolinian, appeals court judge Clement F. Haynsworth Jr. In November a liberal backlash to the Fortas affair generated charges of conflict of interest against Haynsworth and denied him confirmation by a vote of 45–55. It was the first time since 1930 that a presidential nominee to the Court had been rejected.

Early in 1970 Nixon named G. Harrold Carswell of Florida, another appeals court judge, to the empty seat. Carswell, whose qualifications were mediocre at best, was rejected, 45–51, in April 1970. His nomination had drawn opposition from a wide variety of groups because of his views on racial issues and his undistinguished career.

Soon after the Carswell defeat, Nixon selected Harry A. Blackmun, an appeals court judge from Minnesota and a longtime friend of Chief Justice Burger, as his third choice for the seat. Blackmun, sixty-one, was confirmed unanimously, and he joined the Court in June 1970. He would serve as a justice for twenty-four years.

CONSERVATIVE CHOICES

President Nixon had promised to appoint justices who would give the Court a more conservative character. During his first term he named four justices, and some of the Court's rulings in the 1970s did lessen the impact of some of the landmarks of the Warren era. But none of those landmarks was overturned—and the Burger Court established a few more important rulings of its own on the liberal landscape.

The October 1970 term was an eventful one. In *Swann v. Charlotte-Mecklenburg County Board of Education* the Court made clear that it had no intention of retreating from its *Brown* ruling that racial segregation of public schools was unconstitutional. With Burger writing the opinion, it unanimously upheld the use of controversial methods such as busing, racial balance ratios, and gerrymandered school districts to remedy school segregation.

During this term the Court for the first time held invalid a state law discriminating against women and ushered in a line of decisions that would bring increasing pressure on laws that treated the sexes differently. The Court also declared alienage, like race, to be a suspect classification or category when used by lawmakers. It said statutes relating to alienage deserve the highest judicial scrutiny.[69]

In *Harris v. New York* the justices allowed limited in-court use of statements obtained from suspects who were not given their *Miranda* warnings. And in a set of cases known as *Younger v. Harris* the Court curtailed the power of federal judges to halt enforcement of state laws challenged as infringing the First Amendment.

The most dramatic ruling of the term came June 30, 1971. The Court resoundingly rejected the Nixon administration's effort to halt publication of newspaper articles based upon the classified "Pentagon Papers."[70]

Just two weeks before the opening of the October 1971 term, Justices Black and Harlan, in failing health, resigned. Black, eighty-five, had served thirty-four years; Harlan, seventy-two, had served almost seventeen.

Nixon chose Lewis F. Powell Jr., a former president of the American Bar Association and a successful Virginia attorney, to

fill Black's seat, and William H. Rehnquist of Arizona, an assistant attorney general, to fill Harlan's. Powell, sixty-four, and Rehnquist, forty-seven, were confirmed in December 1971. Not since Warren Harding had one president in his first term placed four men on the Court.

Although these justices were picked by President Nixon for their conservative views, the Court's decisions continued to move in the liberal direction set by the Warren Court. In 1972—the first term in which all four Nixon nominees participated, the Court struck down all existing death penalty laws, expanded the right to counsel, and refused to allow the administration to use electronic surveillance without a warrant, even in cases involving the nation's security.[71]

The most controversial decision of the decade came early the following year. President Nixon opposed abortion rights. Yet in January 1973, in the same week as his second inaugural, the Supreme Court, 7–2, legalized abortion. Justice Blackmun wrote the Court's opinion. Only Justices Rehnquist and White dissented from the Court's ruling in the case of *Roe v. Wade*.

Also in that term, the Court rejected a constitutional challenge to the property-tax system for financing public schools, told nonsouthern schools they too must desegregate, formulated a new definition of obscenity, and held that state legislative districts need not always meet the standard of strict equality applied to congressional districts.[72]

The last and most stunning decision of the Court during the Nixon administration was a peculiarly personal blow for President Nixon. The Watergate scandal had set off full-scale investigations on Capitol Hill, as well as by a special prosecutor. In the course of his investigation, the special prosecutor subpoenaed the president for certain taped recordings of White House conversations that could be used as evidence in the trial of former White House aides charged with obstruction of justice.

Nixon refused to comply, asserting executive privilege—the president's privilege to refuse with impunity to obey such an order when that refusal was necessary to protect the confidentiality of conversations with his aides. In June 1974 the case came to the Supreme Court. *United States v. Nixon* was argued in a special late-term session in July. On July 24 the Court, 8–0, ruled that Nixon must comply with the subpoena and turn over the tapes. Rehnquist did not participate; the opinion was delivered by Chief Justice Burger.

With this ruling the Court reasserted the power first claimed for it by Chief Justice John Marshall: to say what the law is. In doing so, the Court flatly denied the president of the United States the right to operate outside the law.

Nixon said he would comply. Because of the contents of those tapes, he resigned the presidency, two weeks later, after the House Judiciary Committee had approved articles of impeachment against him.

DISABILITY, DEATH, AND DISCRIMINATION

In 1973 Justice William O. Douglas surpassed Justice Stephen Field's record to become the country's longest-serving justice.

Two years later he was disabled by a stroke and retired from the bench in November 1975. He had served on the Court thirty-six and one-half years since his appointment by President Roosevelt in 1939. He was seventy-seven years old.

To succeed him, President Gerald R. Ford—who as House minority leader had once led an effort to impeach Douglas—selected John Paul Stevens, fifty-five, a federal appeals court judge from Chicago. Stevens was sworn in December 19, 1975.

Stevens's first term was a busy one. In January 1976 the Court held invalid several major portions of the 1974 Federal Election Campaign Act Amendments intended to regulate campaign spending. In *Buckley v. Valeo* the Court invalidated spending limits, ruling that limits diminished political expression in violation of the First Amendment.

Also in 1976 the Court appeared ready to roll back the clock on the division of authority between the federal government and the states. For the first time in almost forty years, it used the Tenth Amendment to limit the power of Congress over interstate commerce. In *National League of Cities v. Usery* the Court, 5–4, nullified the 1974 act of Congress that required states and cities to pay their employees in line with federal minimum wage and overtime laws. Such matters, wrote Justice Rehnquist, are for state, not federal authority, to resolve.

Ten days later the Court cleared the way for executions of convicted murderers to resume in the United States after a four-year hiatus, as it upheld certain carefully drafted death penalty laws enacted by states in the wake of its 1972 ruling striking down all capital punishment statutes. But the Court also declared that states could not make death the mandatory penalty for first-degree murder. On this point the Court again divided 5–4.[73]

The justices also made it more difficult for state prisoners to challenge their convictions in federal court. The Court ruled that if their challenge was based on the argument that illegally obtained evidence was used to convict, it could succeed only if the state had failed to give them an opportunity to make that claim earlier.[74]

The most publicized decisions of the late 1970s involved "reverse discrimination"—claims by white men that they were denied fair treatment as a result of the efforts of schools and employers to implement affirmative action programs to remedy past discrimination against women, blacks, and other minority group members.

The Court was as divided as the country on that issue. In 1978 the Court in *University of California Regents v. Bakke* held, on the one hand, 5–4, that racial "quotas" were invalid—but, on the other, also 5–4, that moderate affirmative action policies were permissible. A majority refused to hold all consideration of race unconstitutional in school admissions decisions. Justice Powell—who would more and more often in succeeding years be the pivotal vote on close cases—was the swing vote on this issue.

The following year the Court in *United Steelworkers v. Weber* held, 5–2, that private corporations were free to adopt voluntary affirmative action programs to eliminate clear racial imbalances in certain job areas. In 1980, in *Fullilove v. Klutznick,* the Court

THE COURT IN 1979
Seated from left: Justices Byron R. White, William J. Brennan Jr., Chief Justice Warren E. Burger, Justices Potter Stewart, Thurgood Marshall.
Standing from left: Justices William H. Rehnquist, Harry A. Blackmun, Lewis F. Powell Jr., John Paul Stevens

upheld, 6–3, congressional power to set aside a certain percentage of federal funds under the 1977 Public Works Employment Act for contracts with minority-owned businesses.

CAMPAIGN FOR CHANGE

In 1981 Ronald Reagan became president, convinced that he had a mandate from the American people to change the way government related to the governed. The Supreme Court was a major focus of his campaign for change throughout his eight years in the White House.

Reagan disagreed with the substance of many of the modern Court's liberal decisions—and with the judicial activism that informed them. He believed that federal judges were intruding into controversial matters that, in a democracy, should be left to elected officials. The phrase *judicial restraint* was his administration's shorthand for the belief that courts should leave most major controversies to legislatures and elected officials to resolve.

Reagan used his appointments and his administration's power of argument to move the court in this direction.

The Reagan Appointments

President Jimmy Carter, Reagan's predecessor, had the unhappy distinction of being the only full-term president to enter and leave the White House without having the chance to name a member of the Supreme Court. There was no change in the Court from December 1975, when Justice Stevens took Justice Douglas's seat, until June 1981.

At that point, just five months into the Reagan presidency,

Sandra Day O'Connor

Ronald Reagan

Justice Potter Stewart announced that he was retiring, after twenty-three years on the Court. Three weeks later, President Reagan made history by announcing that he would send to the Senate the name of a woman—Sandra Day O'Connor, fifty-one, an appeals court judge from Arizona—as Stewart's successor.

O'Connor, who had served in all three branches of Arizona government before her nomination, was easily confirmed, 99–0, in September. She was sworn in September 25, 1981, the 102d justice and the first woman member of the nation's highest court. She soon proved to be a reliable conservative vote and an articulate conservative voice on many issues before the Court.

Several years passed before another vacancy occurred. By 1984 the Court was one of the oldest in history: the average age of the justices was seventy; O'Connor was the only justice under sixty.

In March 1986 Justice Brennan turned eighty; he had served on the Court thirty years. As the liberal spokesman in a time of conservative resurgence, his continued presence on the Court was a focus of considerable speculation. But a happy second marriage after the death of his first wife and his continuing energy and enthusiasm for his job made his departure from the Court an unlikely prospect, heartening to liberals and discouraging to conservatives.

In June 1986 Chief Justice Burger, about to celebrate his seventy-ninth birthday, announced that he would retire. Three days after Burger's announcement, Reagan named Justice Rehnquist, then sixty-one, as Burger's successor. He selected Antonin

William H. Rehnquist

Scalia, fifty, a member of the U.S. Court of Appeals for the District of Columbia Circuit, to take Rehnquist's seat.

Rehnquist's confirmation came with more difficulty than the White House had anticipated. Liberal criticism focused less on his opinions as a justice and more on allegations of discriminatory conduct years before he had come to the bench. Civil rights groups mounted an all-out fight to deny him confirmation. But he was confirmed September 17, 65–33. Scalia was confirmed the same day, 98–0.

The Court that presided over the October 1986 term was unique. The nine justices who sat together from late September of 1986 until July of 1987 did so for only those nine months. As the term ended, Justice Powell, seventy-nine, announced that he was retiring from the Court.

Public attention focused on the selection of Powell's successor with an intensity unlike that accorded the earlier three Reagan appointments, primarily because of Powell's pivotal position on several important issues. A reserved, courtly, and inherently conservative man, Powell had nonetheless cast several critical votes against school prayer, for freedom of choice in abortion, and for permitting the continued use of affirmative action. The person who took his seat would inherit the opportunity to swing the Court's position on those and other issues that divided the sitting justices.

President Reagan first nominated Robert H. Bork, sixty, a colleague of Scalia's on the Court of Appeals for the District of Columbia Circuit. Bork was well known for the strength of his intellect and his conservative views—and for the role he had

played in 1974 as solicitor general, when it fell to him to fire Special Prosecutor Archibald Cox during the Watergate tapes controversy. Bork's nomination was highly controversial, and in October 1987 the Senate denied him confirmation, 42–58.

Reagan moved quickly, announcing he would name another member of that same appeals bench, Douglas H. Ginsburg, forty-one, to the empty seat. His proposed nomination was short-lived; within two weeks, before it was officially sent to Capitol Hill, the nomination was withdrawn in the wake of Ginsburg's admission that he had used marijuana during his years as a student and professor at Harvard Law School.

Four days later, on November 11, Reagan named Anthony M. Kennedy of California, as his nominee to fill Powell's seat. Kennedy, fifty-one, was a member of the U.S. Court of Appeals for the Ninth Circuit. Kennedy's nomination created no controversy and he was confirmed by the Senate February 3, 1988, by a vote of 97 to 0.

The Reagan Arguments

Through his solicitors general, President Reagan for eight years argued his policy views consistently to the Court—on abortion, civil rights, and church and state. He was not successful in convincing the Court to change its mind on these issues during his time in the White House.

Twice the administration suggested to the justices that it was time to overturn *Roe v. Wade,* the landmark ruling legalizing abortion—and leave that decision to the states instead. Twice, in 1983 and in 1986, the Court rejected that suggestion and reaffirmed *Roe v. Wade.* But the margin was narrowing. In 1973 seven justices formed the majority in *Roe v. Wade,* with White and Rehnquist dissenting. Ten years later, the Court's 1983 ruling in a case from Akron, Ohio, came by a 6–3 vote as Justice O'Connor joined the dissenters with an opinion strongly critical of the logic of the *Roe* ruling.[75] When the Court revisited the issue in 1986, the margin had shrunk to one vote—that of Justice Powell. The reaffirmation of *Roe* came that year, 5–4; Powell then retired.[76]

The administration met with some limited success in its battle against affirmative action. In Reagan's first term, the Court held that affirmative action should not apply to override the traditional rule for layoffs—last hired, first fired.[77] But the administration's effort to stretch that ruling into a broad ban on affirmative action crumbled in 1986 and 1987, when the Court ruled decisively in four separate cases that, carefully applied, affirmative action was an appropriate and constitutional remedy for documented discrimination.[78]

The Court initially seemed receptive to Reagan's arguments urging it to relax its view that the First Amendment required strict separation of church and state. In 1984 the Court, 5–4, upheld a city's decision to include in its holiday display a nativity scene. The majority, in the words of Chief Justice Burger, declared that the Constitution "affirmatively mandates accommodation, not merely tolerance, of all religions, and forbids hostility toward any."[79]

Encouraged, the administration backed Alabama's bid in the next term for approval of its "moment of silence" law, permitting teachers to set aside a period in each public school classroom each day for quiet meditative activity.[80] But the theory of accommodation did not stretch that far and the Court, 6–3, held Alabama's law unconstitutional. A few weeks later, the Court told Grand Rapids, Michigan, and New York City that they too were in violation of the First Amendment for supplying remedial and enrichment services to disadvantaged children who attended parochial schools.[81]

SEPARATION OF POWERS

The doctrine of separated powers is implicit in the federal government set up by the Constitution. It allocates powers among the judicial, legislative, and executive branches so that they act as a check upon each other. As the federal government adapted to the increasingly complex demands of modern life, it experimented with new devices for governing—the legislative veto, a new budget-deficit-reduction mechanism, and the independent prosecutor. In the 1980s each was challenged before the Supreme Court as violating the separation of powers. Two fell to that challenge; one survived.

For half a century, Congress had found it useful to include in various laws—more than two hundred by 1983—a legislative veto provision requiring or permitting certain administrative actions implementing the law to return to Congress for approval before taking effect. The executive branch had long criticized this device as encroaching on its functions, and in 1983 the Court agreed. Not since the New Deal collisions had Congress felt so keenly the power of the Court to curtail its actions. The Court's ruling in *Immigration and Naturalization Service v. Chadha* invalidated parts of more federal laws than the Court had struck down up to that time in its entire history.[82]

Three years later the executive branch won another separation of powers victory, when the Court held unconstitutional a new mechanism that Congress had devised for forcing the president to reduce the ever-growing budget deficit. In *Bowsher v. Synar* the Court held that the comptroller general, head of the General Accounting Office, which the Court said was an arm of Congress, could not be given authority to dictate budget cuts to the president.

But Congress won the last big separation of powers argument with the Reagan administration when the Court, in 1988, upheld as appropriate the law that gave a special three-judge court the authority to appoint an independent counsel, a special prosecutor outside the Justice Department, to investigate alleged wrongdoing by high government officials. Written by Chief Justice Rehnquist, the Court's 7–1 opinion in *Morrison v. Olson* was decisive in upholding the power of Congress to grant this authority to the special court. The ruling had particular sting for President Reagan, for it left standing the convictions of two of his close former White House aides, both obtained by independent counsel.

REVERSALS AND EXCEPTIONS

In 1985 the Court reversed its 1976 ruling in *National League of Cities v. Usery*, which had revived the Tenth Amendment as a means for keeping certain state prerogatives from the reach of federal power. States, delighted with its promise, had tried repeatedly to convince the Court to apply the principle in other areas, without success. Its demise was anticipated. Justice Blackmun, who had voted with the five-man majority in *Usery*, changed his mind to cast the critical fifth vote to reverse it nine years later. The Tenth Amendment sank back into constitutional oblivion.[83] Three years later states suffered another blow, in *South Carolina v. Baker*, when the Court abandoned a position taken almost a century earlier in the *Pollock* ruling of 1895 and declared that nothing in the Constitution forbade Congress to tax the interest earned on municipal bonds.

For the first time, the Court in 1984 approved a clear exception to the exclusionary rule forbidding the use of illegally obtained evidence in court and a narrow but definite exception to the *Miranda* rule that suspects must first be warned of their rights before being questioned by police.[84]

In *Davis v. Bandemer* (1986), a decision akin to *Baker v. Carr*, decided twenty-four years earlier, the Court opened the doors of federal courthouses to constitutional challenges to political gerrymandering.

Also in 1986 the Court ruled 7–2 that prosecutors may not use peremptory challenges to exclude African Americans from serving on juries. The justices said in *Batson v. Kentucky* that rejecting someone on the basis of race violated the guarantee of equal protection of the laws.

Finally, in one of the most difficult cases of the term, the Court, 5–4, said that the Constitution's guarantees of personal liberty and privacy do not protect private consensual homosexual conduct between adults. Written by Justice White, *Bowers v. Hardwick* upheld Georgia's law against sodomy. Justice Powell, who was in the majority, would later state publicly that he regretted his vote. It would be nearly a decade before the Court decided another case involving gay rights.

A CONSERVATIVE CONCLUSION

For eight years President Ronald Reagan worked to bring about a change of direction in the Supreme Court. Despite four appointments and innumerable arguments, that change did not take place until he left the White House.

The October 1987 term, the last full term of the Court during Reagan's presidency, was a holding action. For more than half of it, the Court operated with only eight members. Reagan's last nominee, Justice Kennedy, did not join the Court until February 1988.

But the October 1988 term brought Reagan's campaign for change closer to fruition. Kennedy proved a powerful conservative force, allied with Scalia, O'Connor, White, and Rehnquist, who showed an increasing mastery of the power of the chief. By the end of the term, even the most cautious observers were call-

THE COURT IN 1989
Seated from left: Justices Thurgood Marshall, William J. Brennan Jr., Chief Justice William H. Rehnquist, Justices Byron R. White, Harry A. Blackmun.
Standing from left: Justices Antonin Scalia, John Paul Stevens, Sandra Day O'Connor, Anthony Kennedy

ing it a watershed in the Court's history. "Rarely has a single Supreme Court term had such an unsettling effect on the political landscape," declared the *New York Times*.[85]

The first signal of the Court's conservative shift came in January 1989, when the justices struck down a Richmond, Virginia, minority set-aside plan. The city's plan required that 30 percent of city funds granted for construction projects go to firms with black owners. The Court, 6–3, said that the set-aside, challenged by a white contractor, was too rigid and that the city had not sufficiently justified it with specific findings of past discrimination.[86]

The Court moved away from its usual emphasis on concern for the victims of discrimination. It returned to a more neutral stance, balancing the needs of employer and worker, minority and majority.[87]

On questions of criminal law, the Court took a tough stand, refusing to find it unconstitutional for a state to execute criminals who were juveniles at the time of their crime—or to execute a mentally retarded criminal.[88] In addition, two federal drug testing programs won the Court's approval, despite its acknowledgment that obligatory urine tests for drug use fell within the meaning of the constitutional promise of security against unreasonable searches. In these cases—the testing of railroad workers after accidents and the mandatory testing of customs officials involved in drug interdiction—the public interest out-

weighed the private right, the Court held. Justice Kennedy wrote both opinions.[89]

The single notable liberal ruling of the October 1988 term was a highly controversial one. In line with its precedents from the Vietnam era, the Court held in the case of *Texas v. Johnson* that Texas could not punish an individual who burned an American flag in protest. The Court said that the law violated the First Amendment's protection for freedom of expression. Not only did this ruling align the Court in unusual ways—Justice Kennedy joined the Court's liberal members in the majority and Stevens found himself in dissent with Rehnquist, White, and O'Connor—but it also set off calls for a constitutional amendment to reverse the ruling.[90]

In the most closely watched case of the term, the Court gave states power to regulate abortions more thoroughly than the states had for sixteen years. Although it did not reverse *Roe v. Wade* outright—the Court's willingness to uphold a ban on abortions in publicly funded hospitals and tests for fetal viability was widely viewed at the time as a step toward repudiation of *Roe*.

The vote in *Webster v. Reproductive Health Services* was 5–4. Chief Justice Rehnquist wrote the opinion without mentioning the right of privacy, which he previously had stated he had never located in the Constitution. Joining him in the majority were White, his fellow dissenter from *Roe*, Scalia, Kennedy, and

O'Connor. In bitter dissent were Brennan, Marshall, Stevens, and Blackmun, the author of *Roe*.[91]

As the Court's second century ended, it appeared likely that the most controversial decision of its latter decades—*Roe v. Wade*—would soon be reversed and discarded as precedent. The Court's rulings upholding increased state regulation of abortions, narrowing the reach of federal antidiscrimination laws, and strengthening the prosecutor's hand in criminal cases all indicated a clear conservative trend.

But the sweep of history now stretching back two hundred years bore testimony to the difficulty of predicting the Court's future path: Was the conservative coalescence of 1988–1989 merely a temporary deviation from the more liberal path of the second half of the Court's second century? Or was it evidence of a strong new force that would control the first years of the Court's third century?

NOTES

1. William F. Swindler, *Court and Constitution in the 20th Century: The Old Legality, 1889–1932* (Indianapolis: Bobbs-Merrill, 1969), 1–2.

2. *Pollock v. Farmers' Loan and Trust Co.*, 158 U.S. 601 at 695 (1895).

3. Swindler, *Court and Constitution: 1889–1932*, 60.

4. *Plessy v. Ferguson*, 163 U.S. 537 at 551–552 (1896).

5. Id. at 559.

6. Id. at 562.

7. Id. at 563.

8. *Allgeyer v. Louisiana*, 165 U.S. 578 at 589 (1897).

9. *McCray v. United States*, 195 U.S. 27 (1904).

10. *Northern Securities Co. v. United States*, 193 U.S. 197 at 400 (1904).

11. *Jacobson v. Massachusetts*, 197 U.S. 11 (1905).

12. *Lochner v. New York*, 198 U.S. 45 at 57 (1905).

13. *First Employers Liability Case*, 207 U.S. 463 (1908).

14. *Berea College v. Kentucky*, 211 U.S. 45 (1908).

15. *Standard Oil Co. v. United States*, 221 U.S. 1 (1911).

16. *United States v. American Tobacco Co.*, 221 U.S. 106 (1911).

17. *Hipolite Egg Co. v. United States*, 220 U.S. 45 (1911); *Second Employers Liability Case*, 223 U.S. 1 (1912); *Hoke v. United States*, 227 U.S. 308 (1913).

18. David Burner, "James C. McReynolds" in *The Justices of the United States Supreme Court, 1789–1969: Their Lives and Major Opinions*, ed. Leon Friedman and Fred L. Israel (New York: Chelsea House Publishers in association with R. R. Bowker, 1969), III: 2023.

19. Swindler, *Court and Constitution, 1889–1932*, 197.

20. *Schenck v. United States*, 249 U.S. 47 at 52 (1919).

21. Arthur M. Schlesinger Jr., *The Politics of Upheaval* (Cambridge, Mass.: Houghton Mifflin, 1960), 455.

22. *United States v. Doremus*, 249 U.S. 86 (1919).

23. *Hill v. Wallace*, 259 U.S. 44 at 67–68 (1922); *Chicago Board of Trade v. Olsen*, 262 U.S. 1 (1923).

24. *Moore v. Dempsey*, 261 U.S. 86 at 91 (1923).

25. *Gitlow v. New York*, 268 U.S. 652 at 666 (1925).

26. *Meyer v. Nebraska*, 262 U.S. 390 (1923).

27. *Burns Baking Co. v. Bryan*, 264 U.S. 504 (1924); *Tyson & Bro. v. Banton*, 273 U.S. 418 (1927); *Ribnik v. McBride*, 277 U.S. 350 (1928).

28. *Petersen Baking Co. v. Burns*, 290 U.S. 570 (1934); *Olsen v. Nebraska*, 313 U.S. 236 (1941).

29. *Home Building & Loan Association v. Blaisdell*, 290 U.S. 398 (1934).

30. Robert H. Jackson, *The Struggle for Judicial Supremacy* (New York: Knopf, 1941), 315.

31. Quoted in William F. Swindler, *Court and Constitution in the 20th Century: The New Legality, 1932–1968* (Indianapolis: Bobbs-Merrill, 1970), 37.

32. *Louisville Joint Stock Land Bank v. Radford*, 295 U.S. 555 (1935); *Humphrey's Executor v. United States*, 295 U.S. 602 (1935).

33. Schlesinger, *Politics of Upheaval*, 468.

34. *Ashton v. Cameron County District Court*, 298 U.S. 513 (1936).

35. *Ashwander v. TVA*, 297 U.S. 288 (1936).

36. Quoted in Schlesinger, *Politics of Upheaval*, 483.

37. Swindler, *Court and Constitution: 1932–1968*, 5.

38. *West Coast Hotel Co. v. Parrish*, 300 U.S. 379 at 391 (1937).

39. *Wright v. Vinton Branch*, 300 U.S. 440 (1937); *Virginia Railway Co. v. System Federation*, 300 U.S. 515 (1937).

40. *United States v. Carolene Products Co.*, 304 U.S. 144 at 152 (1938).

41. Leo Pfeffer, *This Honorable Court: A History of the United States Supreme Court* (Boston: Beacon Press, 1965), 342.

42. *NLRB v. Jones & Laughlin Steel Corp.*, 301 U.S. 1 (1937); *Steward Machine Co. v. Davis*, 301 U.S. 548 (1937); *Helvering v. Davis*, 301 U.S. 619 (1937); *Alabama Power Co. v. Ickes*, 302 U.S. 464 (1938); *United States v. Bekins*, 304 U.S. 27 (1938); *Mulford v. Smith*, 307 U.S. 38 (1939); *United States v. Rock Royal Cooperative*, 307 U.S. 533 (1939); *Chicot County Drainage District v. Baxter State Bank*, 308 U.S. 371 (1940); *Sunshine Coal Co. v. Adkins*, 310 U.S. 381 (1940).

43. *Helvering v. Gerhardt*, 304 U.S. 405 (1938); *Graves v. New York ex rel. O'Keefe*, 306 U.S. 466 (1939).

44. *United States v. Darby Lumber Co.*, 312 U.S. 100 (1941) at 124.

45. Swindler, *Court and Constitution: 1932–1968*, 104.

46. *Thornhill v. Alabama*, 310 U.S. 88 (1940).

47. *Hirabayashi v. United States*, 320 U.S. 81 (1943); *Korematsu v. United States*, 323 U.S. 214 (1944); *Ex parte Endo*, 323 U.S. 283 (1944).

48. *Korematsu v. United States*, 323 U.S. 214 at 216 (1944).

49. Swindler, *Court and Constitution: 1932–1968*, 139.

50. *Jones v. Opelika*, 316 U.S. 584 (1942).

51. *West Virginia Board of Education v. Barnette*, 319 U.S. 624 at 642 (1943).

52. Alpheus T. Mason, *The Supreme Court from Taft to Warren* (Baton Rouge: Louisiana State University, 1958), 154.

53. *Louisiana ex rel. Francis v. Resweber*, 329 U.S. 459 (1947).

54. *Joint Anti-Fascist Refugee Committee v. McGrath*, 341 U.S. 123 (1951); *Garner v. Board of Public Works*, 341 U.S. 716 (1951).

55. *Rosenberg v. United States*, 346 U.S. 273 (1953).

56. Anthony Lewis, "Earl Warren" in Friedman and Israel, *Justices of the Supreme Court*, IV: 2728.

57. *Brown v. Board of Education*, 347 U.S. 483 at 495 (1954); see also Richard Kluger, *Simple Justice* (New York: Knopf, 1976), 707.

58. Kluger, *Simple Justice*, 709–710.

59. Ibid., 750.

60. Swindler, *Court and Constitution: 1932–1968*, 235.

61. Ibid., 243.

62. Ibid., 246.

63. *Wilson v. Girard*, 354 U.S. 524 (1957).

64. *NAACP v. Alabama ex rel. Patterson*, 357 U.S. 449 (1958).

65. *Klopfer v. North Carolina*, 386 U.S. 213 (1967); *In re Gault*, 387 U.S. 1 (1967); *Katz v. United States*, 389 U.S. 347 (1967).

66. *Elfbrandt v. Russell*, 384 U.S. 11 (1966); *United States v. Robel*, 389 U.S. 258 (1967).

67. *Abington School District v. Schempp*, 374 U.S. 203 (1963).

68. *Tinker v. Des Moines Independent Community School District*, 393 U.S. 503 (1969).

69. *Reed v. Reed*, 404 U.S. 71 (1971); *Graham v. Richardson*, 403 U.S. 365 (1971).

70. *New York Times Co. v. United States, United States v. The Washington Post*, 403 U.S. 713 (1971).

71. *Furman v. Georgia*, 408 U.S. 238 (1972); *Argersinger v. Hamlin*, 407 U.S. 25 (1972); *United States v. U.S. District Court, Eastern Michigan*, 407 U.S. 297 (1972).

72. *San Antonio Independent School District v. Rodriguez*, 411 U.S. 1

(1973); *Keyes v. Denver School District No. 1*, 413 U.S. 921 (1973); *Miller v. California*, 413 U.S. 15 (1973); *Mahan v. Howell*, 410 U.S. 315 (1973).

73. *Gregg v. Georgia, Proffitt v. Florida, Jurek v. Texas*, 428 U.S. 153, 242, 262 (1976); *Woodson v. North Carolina, Roberts v. Louisiana*, 428 U.S. 280, 325 (1976).

74. *Stone v. Powell, Wolff v. Rice*, 428 U.S. 465 (1976).

75. *City of Akron v. Akron Center for Reproductive Health Inc.*, 462 U.S. 416 (1983).

76. *Thornburgh v. American College of Obstetricians and Gynecologists*, 476 U.S. 747 (1986).

77. *Firefighters Local #1784 v. Stotts*, 467 U.S. 561 (1984); see also *Wygant v. Jackson Board of Education*, 476 U.S. 267 (1986).

78. *Local #28 of the Sheet Metal Workers' International v. Equal Employment Opportunity Commission*, 478 U.S. 421 (1986); *Local #93, International Association of Firefighters v. City of Cleveland and Cleveland Vanguards*, 478 U.S. 501 (1986); *United States v. Paradise*, 480 U.S. 149 (1987); *Johnson v. Transportation Agency of Santa Clara County*, 480 U.S. 616 (1987).

79. *Lynch v. Donnelly*, 465 U.S. 668 (1984).

80. *Wallace v. Jaffree*, 472 U.S. 38 (1985).

81. *Aguilar v. Felton*, 473 U.S. 402 (1985); *Grand Rapids School District v. Ball*, 473 U.S. 373 (1985).

82. *Immigration and Naturalization Service v. Chadha*, 462 U.S. 919 (1983); see in particular Justice White's dissenting opinion for list of affected laws.

83. *Garcia v. San Antonio Metropolitan Transit Authority*, 469 U.S. 528 (1985).

84. *United States v. Leon*, 468 U.S. 897 (1984); *New York v. Quarles*, 467 U.S. 649 (1984); *Nix v. Williams*, 467 U.S. 431 (1984).

85. Linda Greenhouse, "The Year the Court Turned to the Right," *New York Times*, July 7, 1989, A1.

86. *City of Richmond v. J. A. Croson Co.*, 488 U.S. 469 (1989).

87. *Wards Cove Packing Co. v. Atonio*, 490 U.S. 642 (1989).

88. *Stanford v. Kentucky*, 492 U.S. 361 (1989); *Penry v. Lynaugh*, 492 U.S. 302 (1989).

89. *Skinner v. Railway Labor Executives' Association*, 489 U.S. 602 (1989); *National Treasury Employees Union v. Von Raab*, 489 U.S. 656 (1989).

90. *Texas v. Johnson*, 491 U.S. 397 (1989).

91. *Webster v. Reproductive Health Services*, 492 U.S. 490 (1989). *Allegheny County v. American Civil Liberties Union, Greater Pittsburgh Chapter*, 492 U.S. 573 (1989).

CHAPTER 3

The Third Century: New Challenges

THE SUPREME COURT began its third century speaking in a decidedly conservative voice. Two decades of pressure from three Republican presidents and an increasingly conservative Congress at last had their impact. Led by Chief Justice Rehnquist, the Court adopted a narrow view both of affirmative action and other remedies for race discrimination and, in many cases, of federal governmental power itself.

But during these same years, the Court affirmed *Roe v. Wade,* which had made abortion legal nationwide, endorsed earlier rulings against sex discrimination, and sanctioned equal rights for lesbians and gay men. These rulings drew considerable public notice, both because of their substance and their divergence from the contemporary Court's overall conservative direction.

Within the first five years of the Court's third century, its four senior members—including the three most liberal justices—retired. William J. Brennan Jr., Thurgood Marshall, and Byron R. White, the lone conservative of this group, had served since the days of Chief Justice Earl Warren. The fourth retiree and third liberal, Harry A. Blackmun, was the author of *Roe v. Wade.* Once the voices and votes of Brennan, Marshall, and Blackmun were no longer part of the Court's discussions, the conservative justices took control.

Brennan left the Court in 1990 and Marshall in 1991. One of Marshall's final dissents proclaimed a mournful epitaph for the liberal precedents he saw discarded: "Power, not reason, is the new currency of this Court's decisionmaking."[1] Brennan and Marshall were succeeded by David H. Souter and Clarence Thomas, conservative jurists selected by President George Bush from the federal appellate bench.

White and Blackmun retired in 1993 and 1994, respectively. As their successors, President Bill Clinton named Ruth Bader Ginsburg and Stephen G. Breyer, federal appeals court judges

THE COURT IN 1995
Seated from left: Justices Antonin Scalia, John Paul Stevens, Chief Justice William H. Rehnquist, Justices Sandra Day O'Connor, Anthony Kennedy.
Standing from left: Justices Ruth Bader Ginsburg, David H. Souter, Clarence Thomas, Stephen G. Breyer

with reputations for pragmatic moderation. They were expected to strengthen the Court's middle and reverse the conservative trend.

But on the most fractious issues, that did not happen.

Ginsburg and Breyer tended to be more centrist than liberal, and their choice of the court's middle ground coincided with moves by Justices Sandra Day O'Connor and Anthony M. Kennedy away from the center to a more conservative posture. The result was a Court characterized by a new fervor to check government's race-conscious decision making, to curb the reach of the federal government, and to shore up state sovereignty.

After decades of approving the uninterrupted expansion of the power of Congress to regulate interstate commerce, the Court in 1995 held that Congress had exceeded its commerce power when lawmakers banned the possession of guns near local schools.

The following term, in 1996, the Court significantly reduced the authority of Congress to subject states to lawsuits for failure to enforce federal rights. Both cases were decided by a majority led by Rehnquist, and made up of the three Reagan appointees (O'Connor, Kennedy, Antonin Scalia) and Bush-appointee Thomas.

Rehnquist had argued for the curtailment of federal power from the time he joined the Court a quarter-century earlier, but his views had been no more than dissenting opinions for most of that time. The passing of the liberal era finally gave him a majority as the Court returned to fundamental questions of the balance of power between the central government and the states.

But if the liberal stalwarts were no longer on the bench, the difficult social problems of prior decades remained central to the docket. The issue of school desegregation, which Marshall had argued as a young civil rights advocate and Brennan had helped decide a quarter-century earlier, was back before the Court in 1995. School prayer, first decided soon after White arrived on the Court in 1962, was the topic of one of the major cases of his last term in 1992.[2] These three justices, joined by Blackmun, also had voted together in the first affirmative action case in 1978, to permit consideration of race as a positive factor in school admissions. With all four gone by 1995, one of the major decisions that year set in place a far stricter standard for affirmative action in federal contracting.

Review of voting rights issues, begun in the 1960s, continued to be a staple of court business through the 1990s. But there was a modern-day twist. Instead of scrutinizing poll taxes and other government practices that had disadvantaged racial minorities, the Court heard challenges by white voters to electoral districts drawn to include a majority of racial minorities and boost their chances of electing one of their own. Over a series of cases from 1993 to 1996, the justices struck down several such districts. Justice O'Connor, who became the voice of the Court in this area, said, "Racial gerrymandering, even for remedial purposes, may balkanize us into competing racial factions; it threatens to carry us further from the goal of a political system in which race no longer matters—a goal that the Fourteenth and Fifteenth Amendments embody, and to which the Nation continues to aspire."[3]

The Contemporary Court: 1989–1996

The first term of the Court's new century, which began in October 1989, provided evidence of the growing conservatism and deep divisions within the Court. In two separate cases, the Court allowed states to require that parents be notified when a teenaged daughter seeks an abortion. Illustrative of their wrenching disunity on the questions of personal privacy, the justices issued nine separate opinions in the two cases.[4]

The Court also confronted the issue of withdrawing artificial life support from a comatose patient. Although the justices ruled against withdrawal from a patient who had not made it clear earlier that she would have chosen to end her life under such circumstances, the Court for the first time said that the Constitution protects an individual's right to make such a decision.[5]

In one notable, if short-lived, victory for liberals, the Court, 5–4, upheld preferential treatment of minorities seeking federal broadcast licenses. The Court said "benign race-conscious measures" are constitutional if they further important government objectives. The ruling in *Metro Broadcasting v. Federal Communications Commission* marked the first time the Court had upheld an affirmative action program that was not devised to relieve the effects of past discrimination.

THE LAST LIBERALS

This affirmative action decision turned out to be the last hurrah for Brennan, a champion for individual rights and liberties who had tried—and succeeded to a remarkable extent—to keep alive the activism of the Warren era. Brennan retired July 20, 1990, after suffering a minor stroke. His departure gave President Bush the opportunity to appoint his first justice. Bush chose David H. Souter, a dry-witted, twelve-year-veteran of New Hampshire state courts. Souter, a newly appointed judge on the U.S. Court of Appeals for the First Circuit, was fifty-one when he took his seat in October 1990.

During his first term, Souter helped carry out Bush's law-and-order agenda. With his vote, a five-justice majority reversed precedent to hold that a coerced confession used at trial does not automatically taint a verdict. The Court also ruled that a death row prisoner has only one chance to challenge the constitutionality of his state conviction and sentence in federal court, absent extraordinary circumstances. And it allowed evidence of a victim's character and the effect of a crime on her family to be used against a defendant at sentencing.[6]

Souter also voted with the majority to uphold administration regulations barring abortion counseling in publicly funded clinics. In a separate decision involving reproductive rights, the

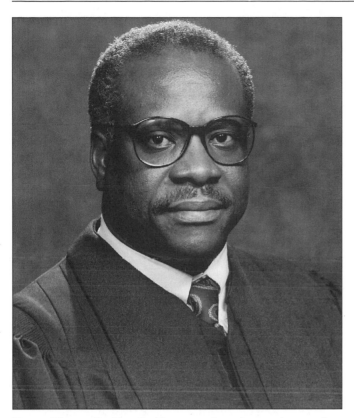

Clarence Thomas, President Bush's 1991 appointee, became the second African-American justice in Court history.

For his first Supreme Court nomination, President Clinton selected Ruth Bader Ginsburg. She became the Court's second woman justice.

Court ruled unanimously that companies—in this case, a battery manufacturer—may not exclude women from jobs that might harm a developing fetus.[7]

At the end of the term, Justice Marshall, whose six-decade legal career had shaped the country's civil rights laws, retired. As Marshall's successor, Bush chose Clarence Thomas, forty-three, the second black man named to the Court. Opposition to his conservative views and highly public (but unproven) charges by a former employee that he had sexually harassed her made Thomas's confirmation the closest of the twentieth century. The Senate approved his appointment by a four-vote margin, 52–48.

The October 1991 term saw O'Connor, Kennedy, and Souter emerge as the Court's center, exerting a steadying influence born out of concern for the Court's institutional stability. Their effectiveness was most notable in the abortion case that was the single most visible decision of the term. In an unusual joint opinion they emphasized the importance of precedent and the need to preserve the integrity of the Court. In *Planned Parenthood of Southeastern Pennsylvania v. Casey*, the Court essentially affirmed the central ruling of *Roe v. Wade*, which established a constitutional right to end a pregnancy.

In the opinion, O'Connor, Kennedy, and Souter said *Roe* could not be discarded without serious social repercussions, because for nearly twenty years people had lived with the idea that abortion is available if contraception fails. But the Court made it somewhat easier for states to impose restrictions on the exer-

cise of this right as long as the regulation did not put an "undue burden" on a woman seeking an abortion.

The following term was a conservative reprise. On its final day, the Court signaled an end to its traditionally broad interpretation of the Voting Rights Act, allowing white voters to bring constitutional challenges to congressional districts that appeared to have been drawn solely on racial lines. "We believe that reapportionment is one area in which appearances do matter," said Justice O'Connor in *Shaw v. Reno*. "A reapportionment plan that includes in one district individuals . . . who may have little in common with one another but the color of their skin bears an uncomfortable resemblance to political apartheid."[8]

White retired in the summer of 1993, concluding a thirty-one-year career on the bench. As his first nominee, President Clinton chose the Court's second female justice, Ruth Ginsburg, age sixty, a federal appeals judge in Washington. The first successful Democratic nominee since Lyndon Johnson named Marshall in 1967, Ginsburg was easily confirmed by the Senate.

In her first term, Ginsburg, a legal strategist in the women's rights movement of the 1960s and 1970s, joined the majority to prohibit lawyers from using their peremptory challenges to exclude people from a jury pool based on sex and stereotypes of how men and women decide cases.[9] The Court also upheld the use of "buffer zones" around abortion clinics to protect them from antiabortion demonstrations. Chief Justice Rehnquist, a consistent opponent of abortion rights, wrote the opinion in

Madsen v. Women's Health Center. He stressed that judges have the authority to protect public safety and order with narrowly tailored injunctions.

At the end of the 1993–1994 term, Justice Blackmun retired at the age of eighty-six. Blackmun's evolution as a justice reflected the changes that had taken place in the Court during his twenty-four-year tenure. When he took his seat in 1970, an appointee of President Richard Nixon, Blackmun was an addition to the Court's conservative bloc. By the time he retired in 1994, he was its liberal pole. Blackmun was succeeded by President Clinton's second appointee, Stephen Breyer, fifty-seven, a judge on the U.S. Court of Appeals for the First Circuit in Boston. He was easily confirmed.

CONSERVATIVE CONSOLIDATION

For most of its existence, the Court has been slow to change. Rarely has a new majority emerged dramatically in a single term. But the October 1994 term, Breyer's first, was such a term. With Blackmun's departure, a bold conservative majority took control. Its members were Rehnquist, the Nixon appointee who had been elevated to chief justice in 1986 by Reagan; O'Connor, Kennedy, and Scalia, also Reagan appointees; and Thomas, named by Bush.

Voting together, they set a strict new legal standard for affirmative action programs and set in motion a new round of challenges to "majority minority" congressional districts. In both rulings, they criticized government decisions made on the basis of race. "Government may treat people differently because of their race only for the most compelling reasons," Justice O'Connor wrote for the majority in *Adarand Constructors Inc. v. Peña.* She said the Constitution's guarantee of equal protection of the laws protects "persons, not groups." "It follows from that principle that all governmental action based on race . . . should be subjected to detailed judicial inquiry to ensure that the personal right to equal protection of the laws has not been infringed." [10]

Similar reasoning was adopted when the Court struck down a black-majority voting district in Georgia. [11] The justices said that courts should apply "strict scrutiny" to the constitutionality of redistricting maps when the race of voters was the predominant factor in deciding how to draw the boundaries. The decision threw into doubt numerous voting districts that had produced a doubling of African American and Hispanic representation in Congress since the 1990 redistricting.

Taken with its school desegregation decision restricting the ability of a federal judge to order remedies to integrate a school district, the Court seemed to say that the time had come for the nation to stop seeking remedies for its history of segregation and put race aside. [12]

A similar retrenchment on a different front came in the Court's opinion striking down a federal ban on guns near schools. For the first time since the New Deal, the Court set a limit on Congress's power to regulate interstate commerce. Emphasizing the Framers' belief in limited congressional powers,

Chief Justice Rehnquist wrote that upholding the gun ban "would convert congressional authority under the commerce clause to a general police power of the sort retained by the states." [13]

The only notable victory for the more liberal justices, Souter, Ginsburg, Breyer, and John Paul Stevens, was the Court's rejection of state-imposed term limits for members of Congress. Joined by Kennedy in the majority, those justices declared that the only qualifications for persons seeking to be U.S. senators and members of the U.S. House of Representatives are those explicitly set out in the Constitution, relating to age, residency, and citizenship. [14]

Throughout the first years of its new century, the Court continued to wrestle with the issues of religious freedom and of separation of church and state. [15] By the end of the watershed 1994–1995 term, there was a new attitude of tolerance for government involvement with religion and a new ability for church groups to express their messages in the public arena. [16]

The 1995–1996 term echoed the Court's earlier actions invalidating minority voting districts and hemming in federal power. The Court struck down three more majority black and one majority Hispanic voting districts, emphasizing that voters are "more than mere racial statistics." [17]

The justices also restricted congressional authority to allow individuals to sue states to enforce federal rights. The Court struck down as a violation of the Eleventh Amendment the Indian Gaming Regulatory Act, which allowed tribes to sue states that had not negotiated in good faith toward a gaming contract. [18] The voting rights and Indian gambling cases were decided by the same five-justice majority: Rehnquist, Scalia, O'Connor, Kennedy, and Thomas. Dissenting were Stevens, Souter, Ginsburg, and Breyer.

In the blockbuster ruling of the term, the Court nullified an amendment to the Colorado constitution that barred localities from protecting homosexuals from discrimination. The justices said the amendment violated the federal Constitution's guarantee of equal protection. [19]

Justices O'Connor and Kennedy made the difference in the outcome. Their votes and Kennedy's opinion for the majority, asserting that "a state cannot so deem a class of persons a stranger to its laws," reflected their belief that government should not single out minorities, whether for preferential treatment as in the situation of federal contracting preferences, or for disfavored treatment as occurred in Colorado.

And so the Court began its third century—still nine controversial, independent individuals, working to maintain the great balances of order and freedom, still the balance wheel of the national system.

NOTES

1. *Payne v. Tennessee,* 501 U.S. 808 (1991).
2. *Lee v. Weisman,* 505 U.S. 577 (1992).

3. *Shaw v. Reno,* 509 U.S. 630 (1993).

4. *Hodgson v. Minnesota,* 497 U.S. 417 (1990), *Ohio v. Akron Center for Reproductive Health,* 497 U.S. 502 (1990).

5. *Cruzan v. Director, Missouri Department of Health,* 497 U.S. 261 (1990).

6. *Arizona v. Fulminante,* 499 U.S. 279 (1991); *McCleskey v. Zant,* 499 U.S. 467 (1991); *Payne v. Tennessee,* 501 U.S. 808 (1991).

7. *Rust v. Sullivan,* 500 U.S. 173 (1991); *International Union, United Automobile, Aerospace & Agricultural Implement Workers of America, UAW v. Johnson Controls,* 499 U.S. 187 (1991).

8. *Shaw v. Reno,* 509 U.S. 630 (1993).

9. *J. E. B. v. Alabama ex rel. T. B.,* 114 S. Ct. 1419 (1994).

10. *Adarand Constructors Inc. v. Peña,* 115 S. Ct. 2097 (1995).

11. *Miller v. Johnson,* 115 S. Ct. 2475 (1995).

12. *Missouri v. Jenkins,* 115 S. Ct. 2038 (1995).

13. *United States v. Lopez,* ____ U.S. ____ (1995).

14. *U.S. Term Limits v. Thornton,* 115 S. Ct. 1842 (1995).

15. *Lee v. Weisman,* 505 U.S. 577 (1992); *Board of Education of Kiryas Joel Village School District v. Grumet,* 512 U.S. ____ (1994).

16. *Board of Education of the Westside Community Schools (Dist. 66) v. Mergens,* 496 U.S. 226 (1990); *Lamb's Chapel v. Center Moriches Union Free School District,* 508 U.S. 384 (1993); *Zobrest v. Catalina Foothills School District,* 509 U.S. 1 (1993); *Rosenberger v. Rector and Visitors of University of Virginia,* 115 S. Ct. 2510 (1995); *Capitol Square Review and Advisory Board v. Pinette,* 115 S. Ct. 2440 (1995).

17. *Bush v. Vera,* ____ U.S. ____ (1996).

18. *Seminole Tribe of Florida v. Florida,* ____ U.S. ____ (1996).

19. *Romer v. Evans,* ____ U.S. ____ (1996).

The Court and the Federal System

CHAPTER 4

The Court and the Powers of Congress: Article I

THE NEW GOVERNMENT created by the Constitution included an executive to carry out the laws and a judiciary to resolve conflicts, but it was the legislature—Congress—that was the heart of the new democracy. The House of Representatives was the only part of the federal government originally elected by the people. Not unexpectedly then, it was to Congress that the people looked for a direct response to their needs and concerns.

And so it was that the Framers entrusted to the legislature the lion's share of the power necessary to govern. The Constitution granted Congress the power to tax, to control commerce, to declare war, to approve treaties, and to raise and maintain armies.

Congress also was granted some authority over its coequal branches. Congress had the power to set up whatever federal courts, other than the Supreme Court, became necessary. And it was empowered to impeach, convict, and remove from office the president, Supreme Court justices, and other federal officers for treason, bribery, or other high crimes and misdemeanors.

Specific constitutional limitations were placed on Congress's exercise of power.

Congress was forbidden to single out individuals for punishment through the passage of ex post facto laws or bills of attainder. It was denied the power to impose a direct tax that is unapportioned or an indirect tax that is not uniform. Perhaps the most significant limits were added by the First Amendment, prohibiting Congress from interfering with the free exercise of speech, the press, assembly, or religion, and the Fifth Amendment, prohibiting the taking of life, liberty, or property without due process of law. In addition, the Tenth Amendment reserved to the states and the people all powers not granted to Congress.

Nothing was said in the Constitution about who would enforce these limitations on Congress. Was Congress to police itself, or would the judiciary—most particularly, the Supreme Court—have this role?

Indeed, said Alexander Hamilton, writing as Publius in *The Federalist Papers,* this role belonged to the courts. "[T]he courts," Hamilton wrote, "were designed to be an intermediate body between the people and the legislature in order, among other things, to keep the latter within the limits assigned to their authority."[1]

Most constitutional scholars agree that a majority of the Framers expected the Supreme Court to assume this role, but the question of whether the Court could actually nullify an act of Congress as unconstitutional remained unanswered until 1803 and the Court's decision in *Marbury v. Madison.* Then, as he ruled that Congress had impermissibly enlarged the Court's original jurisdiction, Chief Justice John Marshall declared that "a law repugnant to the Constitution is void."

In so doing, he firmly asserted the power of the Supreme Court to make such determinations: "It is, emphatically, the province and duty of the judicial department, to say what the law is."[2]

While scholars have questioned the legal reasoning in *Marbury,* its significance has never been challenged. The nation might have survived if the Court had not claimed this power to review and declare invalid acts of Congress, but without the power of judicial review, a clear check on the exercise of legislative power, wrote historian Charles Warren,

the Nation could never have remained a Federal Republic. Its government would have become a consolidated and centralized autocracy. Congress would have attained supreme, final and unlimited power over the Executive and the Judiciary branches and the States and the individual citizens could have possessed only such powers and rights as Congress chose to leave or grant to them. The hard-fought-for Bill of Rights and the reserved powers of the States guaranteed by the Constitution would have been subject to the unlimited control of the prejudice, whim or passion of the majority as represented in Congress at any given moment. Though such a government might possibly have operated in this country, it would not have been the form of government which the framers of the Constitution intended, but a government with unlimited powers over the States.[3]

Having claimed this power, the Marshall Court never again exercised it to nullify an act of Congress. Rather than confine the exercise of legislative powers, the Marshall Court consistently defined the power of Congress in broad terms. Perhaps most important of these decisions was the Court's declaration that the clause giving Congress the power to make all laws "necessary and proper" to the exercise of its specific powers gave the legislature the authority to enact any measure that was an appropriate means to a constitutional end.

Two decades after *Marbury,* the Court further broadened the scope of congressional power when it acknowledged the authority of Congress to delegate some legislative responsibility to other branches. In 1828 the Court acknowledged that Congress had, in addition to its enumerated powers, powers that were inherent in the fact of national sovereignty.

THE COMMERCE POWER

Even as the Marshall Court established the supremacy of the Constitution over acts of Congress, it was careful to protect congressional power from encroachment by the states. This point was made forcefully by the famous steamship monopoly decision, *Gibbons v. Ogden* (1824). The Court ruled that a federal permit overrode a state-granted monopoly. Navigation between two states was interstate commerce, Marshall wrote, and state action would not be permitted to limit Congress's power to regulate interstate commerce.

The congressional power over commerce, the Court emphasized in *Gibbons,* was not limited to transportation but extended to all commercial intercourse affecting two or more states. The only commerce Congress could not reach, Marshall said, was that wholly within one state not affecting any other state.

The importance of this broad definition was not fully apparent until the late nineteenth century when Congress exercised this power to regulate not only the railroads, but also the huge trusts that monopolized many of the nation's major industries. Although some of the railroads and many of the trusts operated within single states, Marshall's definition left room for Congress to regulate them, because they affected more than one state. The Court, sympathetic to business interests, temporarily narrowed Marshall's definition to hold that Congress could only regulate those intrastate matters that directly affected interstate commerce. Intrastate matters affecting interstate commerce indirectly were for the states to regulate. And it was the Court that determined which effects were direct and which indirect.

From these two versions of Marshall's view, the Court developed two lines of precedent that it applied in unpredictable and conflicting fashion. Using the narrow view in 1895, for example, the Court held that a trust processing 98 percent of all refined sugar did not violate the antitrust law. Sugar refining was manufacturing, the Court held, and manufacture was not commerce and did not affect commerce directly. Ten years later the Court, taking the broad view, ruled that an intrastate stockyard operation did violate the antitrust act. Even though it was an intrastate processing operation, the Court said the stockyard was an integral part of a stream of interstate commerce.

During this same period, Congress began to use its commerce and tax powers for social as well as economic purposes, developing a federal "police" power used to protect public health and morals. In 1903 the Supreme Court sustained a congressional prohibition on the interstate sale and shipment of lottery tickets. In 1904 it upheld a tax placed on colored oleo to remove this competition to butter from the market. In subsequent terms, the Court sanctioned other uses of this new federal power. Encouraged, Congress exercised this power to bar from interstate commerce goods made by child labor.

In 1918, however, the Court returned to the narrow view of the commerce power and struck down the child labor law. Congress, the Court ruled, had attempted to regulate manufacture, not commerce. True, but the child labor law was quite similar to the ban on lottery tickets. The Court distinguished the two cases by saying that lottery tickets were harmful in themselves while goods made by children were not.

Congress responded by imposing a heavy tax on the profits of any company that employed children. The Court in 1922 struck down the tax as a penalty, not a revenue-raising device. The Court distinguished the child labor tax from the oleo tax by refusing to acknowledge that the oleo tax had any other purpose than to raise revenue. For the next few years, the two child labor cases stood as anomalies, while the Court upheld other uses of the federal police power, including some wider federal regulation of intrastate matters.

Only against labor unions did the Court maintain a consistently conservative stance, ruling repeatedly that many strikes and boycotts were illegal restraints of trade under the antitrust law and diluting the force of new laws designed to protect the rights of organized workers. By 1930, however, the Court was rethinking its position on labor. It upheld a federal law guaranteeing collective bargaining rights to railway workers.

With the advent of the Great Depression, the president proposed and Congress enacted recovery laws regulating business to an unprecedented degree. When these laws were challenged as unconstitutional, in almost every instance the Supreme Court struck them down, ruling that Congress did not have the broad power necessary to cope with the national crisis.

The Court struck down a law encouraging wage and hour standards for coal miners on the grounds that mining was an intrastate operation with no direct effect on interstate commerce. It struck down fair competition codes because they affected some industries that did not directly affect interstate commerce. The Court invalidated a plan to tax food processors and use the revenue to pay benefits to farmers who curtailed production of certain crops as an unconstitutional scheme to regulate agricultural production, which was not, it held, in interstate commerce. It declared that a federal pension plan for retired railroad workers was outside the reach of the interstate commerce power. In other words, a majority of the Court in the New Deal period refused to acknowledge that local economic conditions had any direct bearing on the health of the national economy or that Congress had the authority, through its commerce and tax powers, to try to ameliorate local conditions.

Apparently responding to the president's "Court-packing" threat, the Court in 1937 reassessed the scope of the commerce power and returned to Marshall's broad view. In quick succession, the Court upheld acts of Congress banning unfair labor practices and regulating wages and hours and agricultural production. It approved federal laws establishing the Social Security pension system and the federal/state unemployment compensation system. It even upheld application of agricultural marketing regulations to a farmer who produced wheat not for sale either intrastate or interstate but for his own consumption.

In the words of Justice Benjamin N. Cardozo, the Court finally "confronted . . . the indisputable truth that there were ills to be corrected, and ills that had a direct relation to the maintenance of commerce among the states without friction or diversion."[4] And Congress, using its commerce power, could reach those problems.

At this point, the Court gave up its effort to judge whether Congress had acted *wisely* in exercising its commerce power. It returned to simply deciding whether Congress had acted *constitutionally.*

Unless its choice is clearly arbitrary, the Court said, Congress has the power to determine whether an intrastate matter affects interstate commerce to a sufficient degree to require federal regulation.

For well over half a century after 1937, that deferential view of the commerce power governed. Only twice did the Court declare an act of Congress an unconstitutional exercise of the commerce power. During the same period, it sustained the commerce power as a tool to reach and prohibit racial discrimination in public places and to guarantee the right to travel within the United States.

It seemed that Congress had virtually unlimited discretion to regulate commercial intercourse. Writing in 1963, constitutional scholars Alan F. Westin and C. Herman Pritchett articulated the prevailing view: "[I]f we moved into an era of novel economic measures or major nationalization programs, the Court might reassert its authority, but the decades since 1937 have been years of consolidation rather than innovation in economic regulation, and the Court's withdrawal from constitutional intervention is therefore not likely to change in the immediate future."[5]

Three decades later, as the century came to an end, the period of deference appeared to be ending. In 1995 the Court struck down a 1990 act of Congress banning guns near schools, declaring that this law was impermissible and unjustified intervention in local affairs (*U.S. v. Lopez*). The peculiarities of this particular law, the 1990 Gun-Free School Zones Act, made it vulnerable, and left uncertain the reach of the Court on commerce clause questions. Congress had made no explicit findings of a connection between interstate commerce and the dangers of guns on school grounds, nor had it distinguished the law from state gun-control statutes applicable to school grounds. To uphold this law in the face of those facts, wrote Chief Justice William H. Rehnquist for the Court, would convert Congress's commerce power to a general police power.

Some scholars said they thought the Court was not truly retreating from an approach that had ushered in the modern national economy.

Others hailed this ruling as the beginning of a new era in commerce clause interpretation. Among them, Douglas W. Kmiec, a law professor at the University of Notre Dame, declared: "*Lopez* is the first step in nearly 60 years toward the restoration of a constitutional order premised upon a national government of enumerated and, therefore, limited powers.

"The legal riddle of what precisely falls within the national commerce power has not been solved," he acknowledged, but "*Lopez* supplies some useful clues."[6]

FISCAL AND MONETARY POWERS

The Court has sustained most congressional decisions concerning taxes, spending, and currency. In three instances, the Court declared such laws unconstitutional only to have the declarations overturned.

Those three decisions occurred between 1870 and 1936, the same period in which the Court was delivering its often contradictory opinions on the commerce and federal police powers. All three favored business interests and states' rights at the expense of congressional authority.

In the 1870 *Legal Tender* case, the Court, 4–3, declared that Congress had unconstitutionally exercised its war powers during the Civil War to substitute paper money for gold and silver as legal tender for the payment of debts. Even as the decision was being announced, President Ulysses S. Grant named two new justices. Within fifteen months, the Court, 5–4, overturned its 1870 decision. That quick reversal pleased debtors, the government, and many businesses, but there was considerable public criticism of its speed, the narrow margin of the vote, and the role of the two new justices.

In 1895 the Court declared the first general peacetime income tax unconstitutional. A tax on income from real estate was a direct tax, it held. Because the Constitution required that direct taxes be apportioned among the states on the basis of population, and this tax was not, it was unconstitutional. This flaw, the Court then held, invalidated the entire tax statute. To reach this conclusion, the Court overlooked both its earlier declaration that the only direct taxes were head and property taxes and its earlier decision sustaining a wartime income tax. The Sixteenth Amendment overturned the decision in 1913, exempting income taxes from the apportionment requirement.

In 1936 the Court ruled for the first time on the scope of Congress's power to spend for the general welfare. It struck down a New Deal effort to raise farm prices by taxing food processing companies and using the revenue to pay benefits to farmers who reduced their production of certain crops. The Court held that the tax-benefit scheme was unconstitutional because it was intended to regulate production, which was beyond the scope of congressional power. This decision was one of many during the New Deal that precipitated the "Court-packing" threat; although the decision was never specifically overruled, its value as a precedent largely vanished when the Court in 1937 approved similar tax-benefit plans contained in the federal Social Security Act.

There has been no subsequent move by the Court to limit Congress's fiscal and monetary powers.

KEEPING THE POWERS SEPARATE

In the last decades of the twentieth century, the Supreme Court was unusually busy reviewing acts of Congress that were challenged as infringing on the separation of powers among the three branches of the federal government. More often than not, the Court agreed with the challenge and struck down the law as infringing too far on the sphere of the executive or the courts.

The Court's decisions in these cases included:
- *Buckley v. Valeo* (424 U.S. 1, 1976) - The 1974 Federal Election Campaign Act Amendments infringed executive power by giving Congress the power to appoint four of the five members of the Federal Election Commission that would enforce the law.
- *Nixon v. General Services Administration* (433 U.S. 425, 1977) - The Presidential Recordings and Materials Preservation Act of 1974, placing the tapes and papers of the Nixon administration in federal custody, did not violate the separation of powers.
- *Northern Pipeline Construction Co. v. Marathon Pipe Line Co., United States v. Marathon Pipe Line Co.* (458 U.S. 50, 1982) - The 1978 Bankruptcy Reform Act infringed on the independence of the federal courts by creating a corps of bankruptcy judges who had the authority, but not the independence (life tenure and fixed compensation), of federal judges.
- *Immigration and Naturalization Service v. Chadha, United States House of Representatives v. Chadha, United States Senate v. Chadha*

(462 U.S. 919, 1983) - The one-house legislative veto, under which Congress claimed the power to review and veto executive branch decisions implementing the laws, violated the separation of powers between the executive and legislative branches.
- *Bowsher v. Synar, United States Senate v. Synar, O'Neill v. Synar* (478 U.S. 714, 1986) - Congress impinged on the prerogatives of the president when it included in the 1985 Balanced Budget and Emergency Deficit Control Act a provision giving the comptroller general, an officer removable from office only at the initiative of Congress, the power to tell the president where to cut federal spending.
- *Morrison v. Olson* (487 U.S. 654, 1988) - The 1978 Ethics in Government Act did not usurp executive power when it authorized a panel of judges to appoint independent prosecutors to investigate charges of misconduct by high government officials.
- *Mistretta v. United States, United States v. Mistretta* (488 U.S. 361, 1989) - The Sentencing Reform Act of 1984, which created an independent commission in the judicial branch with power to set forth binding guidelines for sentencing, did not violate the separation of powers by delegating too much legislative power to judges.
- *Metropolitan Washington Airports Authority v. Citizens for the Abatement of Aircraft Noise* (501 U.S. 252, 1991) - Congress violated the separation of powers by giving a congressional review board the power to veto the directors of an interstate airport authority, created in the 1986 Metropolitan Airports Act as an independent entity.

FOREIGN AFFAIRS

Though it played an active role in shaping the commerce and federal police powers, the Supreme Court has taken little part in defining congressional powers in the field of foreign affairs.

Responsibility for exercising these powers, including the war powers, is shared by the executive and the legislature. The president as commander in chief conducts war, but Congress declares war and raises and maintains the army. The president negotiates treaties; the Senate must ratify them. While the president has great discretion to deal with foreign nations on a wide range of issues, many presidential actions ultimately must be approved by Congress through appropriation of funds.

In many instances, the Supreme Court has refused even to review a foreign affairs or war powers issue, describing it as a political question solvable only by the political branches of government. The Court first adopted this stance in *Foster v. Neilson* (1829), which involved an international dispute over title to part of the Louisiana Territory.

In cases the Court has agreed to hear, it generally has upheld exercise of the power in question. This has been particularly true of the war powers, where the Court has sustained establishment of the draft and large delegations of discretionary power to the executive branch to conduct war. In the rare instances in which the Court has felt compelled to declare a wartime statute unconstitutional, it has done so usually on a ground other than the war power and after combat has ceased.

In short, the Court for the most part has refused to limit congressional flexibility to exercise its powers over foreign affairs. It undoubtedly realizes that a decision contrary to the will of the political branches and the people might go unobeyed. "[F]or better or for worse," observed political scientist Robert G. McCloskey, "the fact remains that [the powers over foreign affairs] are now subject to constitutional limits only . . . by legislative and executive self-restraint and by the force of public opinion."[7]

STATES AND CITIZENS

Congress is authorized by the Constitution to admit new states to the union, to govern territories, and to make rules for the naturalization of aliens. The Supreme Court has been steadfast in its insistence that new states be admitted on an equal political footing with those already in the Union, a precept now clearly established. But questions of citizenship in the United States and territories have posed continuing problems.

In its most infamous opinion, the Dred Scott decision, the Court declared that blacks were not and could not become citizens. The Civil War overturned that decision, and ratification of the Fourteenth Amendment made citizens of all persons born in the United States and subject to its jurisdiction.

Residents of the territories of the continental United States generally enjoyed the guarantees and protections of the Constitution as those areas were prepared for statehood. But in the

1890s and 1900s the nation acquired several new territories in the Caribbean and the Pacific, and a debate ensued as to whether the Constitution automatically followed the flag there.

In a series of decisions known as the *Insular Cases,* the Court adopted a rule still in use in 1996. If Congress formally incorporated the territory into the United States, the rights, responsibilities, and protections of the Constitution would devolve on the inhabitants of the territory. If Congress did not incorporate the territory, its residents were not guaranteed those protections.

Congressional control over citizenship is extensive. In addition to setting conditions for naturalization, Congress, with the Court's approval, has prohibited several categories of people from entering the country or applying for citizenship. It was Congress that wrote the Fourteenth Amendment, the first definition of citizenship to appear in the Constitution.

Following that language, the Court has sustained the citizenship of any person born in the United States, even if the child's parents were not and could not become citizens. Not fully resolved by the Court, however, is the question of whether Congress may revoke the citizenship of a native-born or naturalized citizen against his or her will. The ruling case holds that Congress may not revoke citizenship.

AMENDING POWER

As with foreign policy, the Court views the adoption of constitutional amendments as political decisions in which it is reluctant to interfere. Most of its decisions in this area concern procedural questions of ratification, although it has ruled that liquor was proper subject matter for a constitutional amendment and that the amendment extending suffrage to women did not destroy the political autonomy of those few states that refused to ratify it.

Several of the twenty-seven amendments to the Constitution confer political rights and give Congress specific power to enforce them. The most significant of these are the Civil War Amendments (Thirteen, Fourteenth, and Fifteenth), which extended citizenship and political rights to blacks. To enforce these newly won rights and freedoms, the Reconstruction Congress quickly enacted several civil rights statutes, but the Supreme Court, construing the enforcement power narrowly, struck down almost all of them.

In general, the Court held that Congress could act only to correct, not prevent, discriminatory action. It had no power, the Court said, to reach discriminatory actions by private individuals.

These restrictive rulings, coupled with a waning public concern, meant that blacks remained victims of political and social discrimination in many states of the Union for almost a century, until an activist Court began to reassess national authority to enforce the rights guaranteed by the three amendments. In the 1950s and 1960s, the Court sustained congressional power to prevent state discrimination before it occurred and to reach certain private discrimination, particularly in public places and housing.

INVESTIGATIONS AND INTERNAL AFFAIRS

The Court has never questioned the right of Congress to investigate its own members for possible misconduct, nor has it denied the use of such power to examine issues so that Congress might legislate more effectively. In aid of both kinds of investigations, the Court has sustained the right of Congress to compel witnesses to testify and to punish those who refuse.

The Court has even been reluctant to curb the exercise of the investigatory power in order to protect constitutionally guaranteed individual rights. To protect witness rights, the Court requires that the investigations serve a valid legislative purpose and that the questions asked of witnesses be pertinent to the investigation. At the same time, the Court, in the interests of national security, has upheld investigations that were clearly designed only to focus publicity upon witnesses holding unpopular political beliefs.

The Constitution gives Congress powers over its own internal affairs. By no means insignificant, these powers include judging the qualifications of members, punishing members it finds guilty of misconduct, regulating federal elections, and establishing rules of procedure.

Congress has taken few of its internal problems to the Court. In only one major case has the Court clearly limited Congress's power over its own affairs. In 1969 it held that Congress did not have the authority to add to the Constitution's list of qualifications for membership in the House and Senate. The Court in 1995 cited those specific criteria, relating to age, citizenship, and residency, when it ruled that neither Congress nor the states could impose term limits on members of Congress.

The Court has guarded zealously the institutional integrity of Congress. Nowhere has this been more apparent than in its interpretation of the "speech or debate" clause. The Court has extended this constitutional grant of immunity for actions taken during the course of legislating to cover criminal acts and certain actions of employees.

Judicial Review and Legislative Power

The Constitution does not expressly grant the Supreme Court the power of judicial review—the right to measure acts of Congress against constitutional standards and to nullify those that do not fit. The implicit justification for this judicial role lies in the supremacy clause (Article VI, Section 2), which states:

This Constitution, and the Laws of the United States which shall be made in Pursuance thereof; and all Treaties made, or which shall be made, under the Authority of the United States, shall be the supreme Law of the Land; and the Judges in every State shall be bound thereby, any Thing in the Constitution or Laws of any State to the Contrary notwithstanding.

Few constitutional scholars believe that the omission of an express grant of power of judicial review from the Constitution meant that the Framers intended to deny this power to the Court. The concept of judicial review was relatively well established in the colonies. The Privy Council in London had reviewed the acts of the colonies for compliance with English law prior to the Revolution. Several state courts had struck down state laws they had found inconsistent with their state constitutions.

The Constitutional Convention considered and rejected the proposal that the Supreme Court share the veto power over acts of Congress with the president. The major reason this idea was voted down seems to have been the feeling that the Court should not be involved in enacting a law it might later be required to enforce, rather than any strong opposition to the concept of judicial review.

According to the records of the Constitutional Convention compiled by Max Farrand, only two Framers of the Constitution expressed reservations about judicial review, although other scholars feel that the number of opponents was larger.[1] During the ratification period, both James Madison (who would later qualify his endorsement) and Alexander Hamilton supported the concept in *The Federalist Papers.* Future Supreme Court chief justices Oliver Ellsworth and John Marshall endorsed the principle at their state ratification conventions. *(See box, The Proper and Peculiar Province, p. 77.)*

The First Congress, in Section 25 of the Judiciary Act of 1789, specifically granted the Supreme Court the right of judicial review over state court decisions

where is drawn in question the validity of a treaty or statute of, or an authority exercised under, the United States and the decision is against their validity; or where is drawn in question the validity of a statute of, or an authority exercised under any State, on the ground of their being repugnant to the constitution, treaties, or laws of the United States, and the decision is in favor of their validity, or where is drawn in question the construction of any clause of the constitution, or of a treaty, or statute of, or commission held under the United States, and the decision is against the title, right, privilege, or exemption, specially set up or claimed by either party, under such clause of the said constitution, treaty, statute or commission.

Most of the early Supreme Court justices seemed to believe that they enjoyed a similar power of judicial review over federal statutes. Several of the justices, sitting as circuit court judges, refused to administer a 1792 federal pension law, arguing that the administrative duties it required of them were not judicial and so were in conflict with the constitutional separation of powers.[2]

Sitting as the Supreme Court in 1796, the justices assumed that they had this power of judicial review when they held valid a federal tax on carriages.[3] The ruling, since it upheld the law rather than nullified it, occasioned little comment. A few days later, the Court for the first time invalidated a state law because it conflicted with a federal treaty.[4]

By the time John Marshall was appointed chief justice in 1801, the Court already had exercised the power of judicial review although it had not tested the extent of that power by declaring an act of Congress unconstitutional. When it did find the opportunity, the occasion arose as much from the politics of the day as from a clear-cut reading of the law.

Marbury v. Madison

The aftermath of the bitter presidential election of 1800 brought forth the Court's decision in *Marbury v. Madison,* which many believe is the single most important ruling in the Court's history. In 1800 Republican Thomas Jefferson defeated incumbent Federalist John Adams for the presidency. Unwilling to relinquish the power they had held since the founding of the Union, the Federalists sought to entrench themselves in the only branch of government still open to them—the judiciary. One of Adams's first acts in the interim between his electoral defeat and his departure from office was to appoint Secretary of State John Marshall, a committed Federalist, as chief justice.

Congress speedily confirmed Marshall, who continued to serve as secretary of state until Adams left office on March 4, 1801. Congress, at Adams's behest, also approved legislation creating sixteen new circuit court judgeships, authorizing Adams to appoint as many justices of the peace for the newly created District of Columbia as he deemed necessary, and reducing the number of Supreme Court justices from six to five at the next vacancy. The last was intended to deprive Jefferson of a quick appointment to the bench.

Adams named and Congress confirmed the sixteen new circuit court judges and forty-two justices of the peace. On March 3, Adams's last night in office, he signed the commissions for the new justices of the peace and had them taken to Marshall, who was to attach the Great Seal of the United States and have the commissions delivered to the appointees. Marshall affixed the seal but somehow failed to see that all the commissions were actually delivered.

"THE PROPER AND PECULIAR PROVINCE"

Writing in No. 78 of *The Federalist Papers*, Alexander Hamilton made a strong case for the principle of judicial review in the new government. Reminding his readers that the Constitution limited legislative authority, Hamilton wrote:

Limitations . . . can be preserved in no other way than through the medium of courts of justice, whose duty it must be to declare all acts contrary to the manifest tenor of the Constitution void. Without this, all the reservations of particular rights or privileges would amount to nothing. . . .

. . . There is no position which depends on clearer principles than that every act of a delegated authority, contrary to the tenor of the commission under which it is exercised, is void. No legislative act, therefore, contrary to the Constitution, can be valid. To deny this would be to affirm that the deputy is greater than his principal; that the servant is above his master; that the representatives of the people are superior to the people themselves; that men acting by virtue of powers may do not only what their powers do not authorize, but what they forbid.

If it be said that the legislative body are themselves the constitutional judges of their own powers and that the construction they put upon them is conclusive upon the other departments it may be answered that this cannot be the natural presumption where it is not to be collected from any particu-

lar provisions in the Constitution. It is not otherwise to be supposed that the Constitution could intend to enable the representatives of the people to substitute their will to that of their constituents. It is far more rational to suppose that the courts were designed to be an intermediate body between the people and the legislature in order, among other things, to keep the latter within the limits assigned to their authority. The interpretation of the laws is the proper and peculiar province of the courts. A constitution is, in fact, and must be regarded by the judges as, a fundamental law. It therefore belongs to them to ascertain its meaning as well as the meaning of any particular act proceeding from the legislative body. If there should happen to be an irreconcilable variance between the two, that which has the superior obligation and validity ought, of course, to be preferred; or, in other words, the Constitution ought to be preferred to the statute, the intention of the people to the intention of their agents.

Nor does this conclusion by any means suppose a superiority of the judicial to the legislative power. It only supposes that the power of the people is superior to both, and that where the will of the legislature, declared in its statutes, stands in opposition to that of the people, declared in the Constitution, the judges ought to be governed by the latter rather than the former.

SOURCE: *The Federalist Papers*, with an Introduction by Clinton Rossiter (New York: Mentor, 1961), 466–468.

William Marbury, an aide to the secretary of the navy, was one of the appointees who did not receive his commission. With three other men in the same position, he asked Jefferson's secretary of state, James Madison, to give him the commission.

When Madison, at Jefferson's direction, refused, Marbury asked the Supreme Court to issue a writ of mandamus ordering Madison to give the four men their commissions. In December 1801 Chief Justice Marshall asked Madison to show cause at the

next session of the Court why he should not comply with the order.

The Republicans were already talking of repealing the 1801 act creating the new circuit court judgeships, and in March 1802 Congress did so. To forestall a challenge to the repeal as invalid, Congress also delayed the next term of the Supreme Court for almost a year—until February 1803.

Exacerbating the antagonism between the two political par-

President John Adams signing judicial commissions, the so-called midnight appointments, on his last night in office. Several appointees, including William Marbury, did not receive their commissions. The Jefferson administration's refusal to deliver them led to the famous case of *Marbury v. Madison* (1803) in which the Supreme Court clearly asserted its power of judicial review.

ties was considerable personal animosity between Chief Justice Marshall and President Jefferson. Marshall did not relish the thought that Jefferson would best him in this contest. Under modern standards, Marshall, whose oversight had led to Marbury's suit in the first place, probably would have had to disqualify himself. And there also would be some suggestion that the case was moot by the time the Court heard it argued. But neither factor deterred Marshall from taking it up.

His insistence created an apparent dilemma. If the Court ordered delivery of the commission, Madison might refuse to obey the order, and the Court had no means to enforce compliance. It seemed likely that Madison would refuse; the government did not even argue its viewpoint before the Court. And if the Court did not issue the writ, it would be surrendering to Jefferson's point of view. Either way, the Court would be conceding its lack of power.

Marshall resolved his problem with a remarkable decision that has been called a "masterwork of indirection, a brilliant example of Marshall's capacity to sidestep danger while seeming to court it, to advance in one direction while his opponents are looking in another."[5]

Ignoring the question of jurisdiction, Marshall ruled that once the president had signed the commissions and the secretary of state had recorded them, the appointments were complete. He also ruled that a writ of mandamus was the proper tool to use to require the secretary of state to deliver the commissions.[6]

Having thus rebuked Jefferson, Marshall turned to the question of whether the Supreme Court had the authority to issue the writ—and concluded it did not. Congress, Marshall said, had added unconstitutionally to the Court's original jurisdiction when, under the Judiciary Act of 1789, it authorized the Court to issue such writs to officers of the federal government.

To justify striking down a section of a federal statute, Marshall drew heavily on Hamilton's reasoning in No. 78 of *The Federalist Papers*. The chief justice wrote:

The powers of the legislature are defined and limited; and that those limits may not be mistaken or forgotten, the constitution is written. To what purpose are powers limited, and to what purpose is that limitation committed to writing, if these limits may, at any time, be passed by those intended to be restrained? The distinction between a government with limited and unlimited powers is abolished, if those limits do not confine the persons on whom they are imposed, and if acts prohibited and acts allowed, are of equal obligation. It is a proposition too plain to be contested, that the constitution controls any legislative act repugnant to it.[7]

Having established the Constitution's supremacy over legislative enactments, Marshall turned to the question of whether the judiciary had the authority to determine when acts of Congress conflicted with the Constitution:

It is, emphatically, the province and duty of the judicial department to say what the law is. Those who apply the rule to particular cases, must of necessity expound and interpret that rule. If two laws conflict with each other, the courts must decide on the operations of each. So, if a law be in opposition to the constitution; if both the law and the consti-

tution apply to a particular case, so that the court must either decide that case, conformable to the law, disregarding the constitution; or conformable to the constitution, disregarding the law; the court must determine which of these conflicting rules governs the case: this is of the very essence of judicial duty. If then the courts are to regard the constitution, and the constitution is superior to any ordinary act of the legislature, the constitution, and not such ordinary act, must govern the case to which they both apply. . . .

. . . The judicial power of the United States is extended to all cases arising under the constitution. Could it be the intention of those who gave this power, to say, that in using it, the constitution should not be looked into? That a case arising under the constitution should be decided, without examining the instrument under which it arises? This is too extravagant to be maintained.[8]

While refusing the power to issue writs of mandamus in such cases, Marshall claimed for the Court the far more significant power of judicial review.

Marshall's claim of authority was not generally viewed by his contemporaries with the same importance that future scholars would confer. In fact, Jefferson, who believed that the legislature was the only branch capable of determining the validity of its actions, apparently did not find Marshall's claim of power particularly significant. According to historian Charles Warren, "Jefferson's antagonism to Marshall and the Court at that time was due more to his resentment at the alleged invasion of his Executive prerogative than to any so-called 'judicial usurpation' of the field of Congressional authority."[9]

Moreover, Marshall himself may have been willing to sacrifice the Court's role as the final authority on the constitutional validity of federal statutes in the face of a later political threat from the Republicans. Attempting to remove Federalist judges from office, the Republican Congress impeached and tried Justice Samuel Chase in 1805. Chase escaped conviction by the Senate, but not before Marshall, plainly concerned about the security of his own position, wrote in a letter to Chase:

I think the modern doctrine of impeachment should yield to an appellate jurisdiction in the legislature. A reversal of those legal opinions deemed unsound by the legislature would certainly better comport with the mildness of our character than [would] removal of the Judge who has rendered them unknowing of his fault.[10]

THE POWER EXERCISED

The Court's next two major rulings striking down acts of Congress both had decidedly negative effects on the Court itself. The ill-conceived decision in the 1857 *Scott v. Sandford* case (Dred Scott) invalidating the already repealed Missouri Compromise of 1820 was followed in 1870 by the Court's holding in *Hepburn v. Griswold* that Congress could not make paper money legal tender for the payment of certain debts. Listed as two of three "self-inflicted wounds" by Charles Evans Hughes (the third was the 1895 invalidation of the federal income tax), the two opinions severely strained public confidence in the Court. Both were subsequently reversed—the Dred Scott case by the Fourteenth Amendment and the *Legal Tender* case by the Court itself. *(See "Dred Scott's Case," p. 145; "First Legal Tender Decision," pp. 129–131.)*

More than half a century elapsed between *Marbury* and the Dred Scott decision. During that time, the Court reviewed and upheld several federal statutes. Each time, it reinforced the power it had claimed in *Marbury*. And each time that the government appeared in Court to argue for the federal statute, it again conceded the Court's right of review.

As Congress began to exercise its powers more fully in the late nineteenth century, the number of federal laws the Court found unconstitutional increased. In several instances—such as the *Legal Tender* cases and the *Income Tax* case—judicial opinion ran directly contrary to popular opinion and stirred bitter public animosity against the Court. Yet the Court's authority to review these statutes was never directly assaulted. As two constitutional historians observed:

It is interesting to note that at no time in our history has the power of judicial review been seriously endangered. Despite attacks on the Court's decisions, on its personnel, and even on the procedures by which review is exercised, no major political party has ever urged the complete abolition of the power of review itself. The resounding defeat in Congress of the so-called "Court Packing Plan," suggested by President Franklin D. Roosevelt at the height of his popularity, indicates that popular dissatisfaction with the use of the power of judicial review does not necessarily imply a feeling that the Court should be dominated by the political branches of the government.[11]

RULES OF RESTRAINT

The Supreme Court has forestalled successful challenge to its power of judicial review by its own recognition of the need for restraint in its exercise. *(See "Judicial Restraint," pp. 35–44, in Chapter 6.)*

The Court has developed several rules to guide its deliberations.

The Court will not hear a case unless it involves a real controversy between real adversaries. The Court generally refuses to take "friendly" or collusive suits, although, as with most of these rules of restraint, the rule is often honored in the breach. Major exceptions to this rule were the 1895 *Income Tax* cases, in which a stockholder in a bank sought to prevent the bank from paying the income tax. It was clear that neither party wanted to pay the tax and that both wanted to test the constitutionality of the tax law. *(See "The Income Tax Cases," pp. 118–121.)*

The Court will not pass on the constitutionality of a federal statute if it can decide the issue without doing so. A major exception to this rule was the Dred Scott case, in which the Court invalidated the already repealed Missouri Compromise in order to make a pronouncement on slavery in the territories when it might have decided the case on much narrower grounds. *(See "Dred Scott's Case," p. 145.)*

If there are two reasonable interpretations of a statute, one upholding it and one striking it down, the Court will favor the one upholding it. By corollary, if the constitutionality of a statute must be considered, the Court will make every effort to find it valid. A major exception to these two rules was John Marshall's opinion in *Marbury v. Madison*. In this first case asserting the judiciary's right to strike down acts of Congress, Marshall held that in authorizing the Court to issue writs of mandamus to federal officials, Congress had added impermissibly to the Court's original jurisdiction. Most scholars agree that Marshall could have found the statute valid by viewing the power to issue this order to federal officials as incidental to the Court's original jurisdiction.

If a statute is valid on its face, the Court will not look beyond it to examine Congress's motives for enacting it. Two exceptions to this rule are the opinions striking down congressional attempts to eliminate child labor. In *Hammer v. Dagenhart* (1918) the Court said Congress did not design the Child Labor Act of 1916 as a regulation of interstate commerce but to discourage the use of child labor, an impermissible objective. A subsequent attempt to tax goods manufactured by children was struck down in *Bailey v. Drexel Furniture Co.* (1922) on identical reasoning: the tax was not intended to raise revenue, the Court said, but to penalize employers of children.

If the rest of a statute can stand on its own when part of it has been invalidated, the Court will strike down only the unconstitutional portion. Major exceptions to this rule of separability were the *Income Tax* cases and *Carter v. Carter Coal Co.* (1936), the case invalidating New Deal legislation regulating coal production. In both cases the Court found one section of the law invalid, and then, without further examination, used that infirmity to strike down the rest of the statute. *(See box, Severability: Divided It Stands, p. 123; "The Income Tax Cases," pp. 118–121; "Coal Codes," pp. 107–109.)*

The Court will not review cases that present so-called political questions—those that involve matters regarded as within the discretion of the political branches of government. Intervention by the Courts in such questions has been considered a violation of the principle of separation of powers. A major exception to this rule was the Court's decision in *Baker v. Carr* (1962), in which it held that federal courts could review state apportionment plans for violations of federally guaranteed rights. Until that landmark decision, the federal courts had consistently refused to review challenges to both federal and state apportionment. *(See "Baker v. Carr," pp. 520–522, in Chapter 10.)*

The primary significance of these rules of judicial restraint, wrote constitutional scholar Robert K. Carr,

probably lies in the conscious strategic use which the Court has made of them. They are often available as props to strengthen the particular decision which the Court has chosen to render and have frequently had no small value in enabling the Court to support the view that judicial review is subject to many limitations which have been self-imposed by the justices.[12]

Exceptions to the rules are probably inevitable. Carr continues:

For the most part these rules are of such a character that they cannot always be followed in an absolutely consistent manner. At the same time they have been followed so often that it would be misleading to suggest that they have had no significance at all.[13]

Implied Powers

The first seventeen clauses of Article I, Section 8, of the Constitution specifically enumerate the powers granted to Congress, but the eighteenth clause is a general grant to Congress of the power "To make all laws which shall be necessary and proper for carrying into Execution the Foregoing Powers, and all other Powers vested by this Constitution in the Government of the United States, or in any Department or Officer thereof."

Does this "elastic" clause restrict or expand the enumerated powers of Congress? That was a major question before the Court early in its history.

Thomas Jefferson and Alexander Hamilton in 1791 argued opposing viewpoints on this question after Congress passed legislation establishing the first national bank. Before deciding whether to sign the bill, President George Washington solicited opinions on its constitutionality and then placed them before Hamilton, chief advocate of the bank, for rebuttal.

Jefferson viewed the legislation as invalid; the Constitution did not specifically give Congress the power to incorporate a bank. He said that the phrase "necessary and proper" meant Congress could only enact those laws that were *indispensable* to carrying out one of the other enumerated powers.

Hamilton, on the other side, contended that Congress had two sorts of implied powers—those derived from the fact of the national government's sovereignty, such as its autonomous control over territories, and those derived from the necessary and proper clause. The criterion for determining if an act of Congress is constitutional, Hamilton said,

is the end, to which the measure relates as a mean. If the end be clearly comprehended within any of the specified powers, and if the measure have an obvious relation to that end and is not forbidden by any particular provision of the Constitution, it may safely be deemed to come within the compass of the national authority.[14]

The Marshall Court early on indicated that it would adopt Hamilton's broader view. In 1805 the Court upheld a federal statute that gave payment priority to the United States in cases of bankruptcies. It "would produce endless difficulties if the opinion should be maintained that no law was authorized which was not indispensably necessary to give effect to a specified power," Marshall said. "Congress must possess the choice of means and must be empowered to use any means which are in fact conducive to the exercise of a power granted by the Constitution."[15]

"NOT A SPLENDID BAUBLE"

Marshall's view on this point would not be fully developed until 1819, when it emerged in the case of *McCulloch v. Maryland* with the unanimous support of the Court.

McCulloch v. Maryland involved the second national bank.[16] Chartered in 1816, the bank was extremely unpopular, particularly in the eastern and southern states, many of which tried to keep it from opening branches at all or, failing that, tried to tax branches out of existence. The latter strategy was chosen by Maryland, which imposed a hefty tax on the notes issued by the bank's Baltimore branch. James McCulloch, a bank cashier, refused to pay the tax. McCulloch claimed the state tax was an unconstitutional infringement on the federally chartered bank, while Maryland contended that Congress had exceeded its pow-

Despite the Supreme Court's decision in *McCulloch v. Maryland* (1819) the Bank of the United States remained under criticism. This cartoon depicts President Andrew Jackson attacking the bank with his veto stick. Vice President Martin Van Buren, center, helps kill the monster, whose heads represent Nicholas Biddle, bank president, and directors of the state banks.

ers when it chartered the bank. The state also claimed that in any event it had the power to tax the bank within its borders.

For the Court, Marshall first upheld the power of Congress to incorporate the bank. He noted that the national government is "one of enumerated powers," but asserted that "though limited in its powers [it] is supreme within its sphere of action."[17]

The Constitution said nothing about the power to establish a bank and create corporations, Marshall acknowledged. But, he wrote,

there is no phrase in the instrument which, like the articles of confederation, excludes incidental or implied powers; and which requires that everything granted shall be expressly and minutely described. Even the 10th amendment, which was framed for the purpose of quieting the excessive jealousies which had been excited, omits the word "expressly," and declares only that the powers "not delegated to the United States, nor prohibited to the states, are reserved to the states or to the people"; thus leaving the question, whether the particular power which may become the subject of contest has been delegated to the one government, or prohibited to the other, to depend on a fair construction of the whole instrument.[18]

Although the Constitution did not specifically authorize Congress to incorporate banks, Marshall said, it did grant it "great powers"—to tax, to regulate commerce, to declare war, and to support and maintain armies and navies. Therefore, he said,

it may with great reason be contended, that a government, entrusted with such ample powers, on the due execution of which the happiness and prosperity of the nation so vitally depends, must also be entrusted with ample means for their execution.[19]

Incorporation, Marshall said, was one of these means. "It is never the end for which other powers are exercised, but a means by which other objects are accomplished," he said.[20]

Marshall then turned to the meaning of the word "necessary" as it is used in the Constitution. The attorneys for Maryland had used Jefferson's argument that the word limited Congress to those means indispensable for implementing a delegated power. "Is it true that this is the sense in which the word 'necessary' is always used?" asked Marshall. He continued:

Does it always import an absolute physical necessity, so strong that one thing to which another may be termed necessary, cannot exist without the other? We think it does not. . . . To employ the means necessary to an end, is generally understood as employing any means calculated to produce the end, and not as being confined to those single means, without which the end would be entirely unattainable. . . .

. . . It must have been the intention of those who gave these powers, to insure, so far as human prudence could insure, their beneficial execution. This could not be done by confiding the choice of means to such narrow limits as not to leave it in the power of Congress to adopt any which might be appropriate, and which were conducive to the end. This provision is made in a constitution intended to endure for ages to come, and, consequently, to be adapted to the various crises of human affairs. . . . To have declared that the best means shall not be used, but those alone without which the power given would be nugatory, would have been to deprive the legislature of the capacity to avail itself of experience, to exercise its reason, and to accommodate its legislation to circumstances.[21]

The central government had already relied on the concept of implied powers in exercising its delegated powers, Marshall pointed out. The Constitution specifically empowers Congress to punish only a few federal crimes such as counterfeiting currency and crimes committed on the high seas, Marshall said. Yet, he added, no one has questioned the power of Congress to provide punishment for violations of other laws it passes. The Constitution, while it gives Congress authority to establish post roads and post offices, does not specify that the government has the authority to carry the mail, Marshall noted; yet the government assumed that authority.

In conclusion, Marshall wrote:

The result of the most careful and attentive consideration bestowed upon this clause is, that if it does not enlarge, it cannot be construed to restrain the powers of Congress, or to impair the right of the legislature to exercise its best judgment in the selection of measures to carry into execution the constitutional powers of the government. If no other motive for its insertion can be suggested, a sufficient one is found in the desire to remove all doubts respecting the right to legislate on that vast mass of incidental powers which must be involved in the constitution, if that instrument be not a splendid bauble.

We admit, as all must admit, that the powers of the government are limited, and that its limits are not to be transcended. But we think the sound construction of the constitution must allow to the national legislature that discretion, with respect to the means by which the powers it confers are to be carried into execution, which will enable that body to perform the high duties assigned to it, in the manner most beneficial to the people. Let the end be legitimate, let it be within the scope of the constitution, and all means which are appropriate, which are plainly adapted to that end, which are not prohibited, but consist with the letter and spirit of the constitution, are constitutional.[22]

In the remainder of the opinion Marshall developed the now-famous doctrine that because "the power to tax involves the power to destroy," the state tax on the federal bank threatened the supremacy of the federal government. "[T]here is a plain repugnance, in conferring on one government a power to control the constitutional measures of another, which other, with respect to those very measures, is declared to be supreme," Marshall wrote.[23] *(See "A Limited Power," p. 344, in Chapter 7.)*

In the eyes of constitutional scholar Robert G. McCloskey, *McCulloch v. Maryland* was "by almost any reckoning the greatest decision John Marshall ever handed down—the one most important to the future of America, most influential in the court's own doctrinal history, and most revealing of Marshall's unique talent for stately argument."[24]

McCulloch forcefully upheld the supremacy of federal law over conflicting state law, reaffirmed the Supreme Court's judicial review powers, and espoused a broad construction of the necessary and proper clause in particular and congressional power in general that has been in use ever since. Hardly a bill passed by Congress does not rely to some extent on the necessary and proper clause for its validity. It has been especially significant to congressional control over fiscal affairs and to the establishment of the vast network of regulatory agencies. As Marshall pointed out, it is the basis of the federal power to punish violations of the law. It is also the foundation for the doctrine of eminent domain.

All these powers have in one way or another touched the life of every citizen of the United States. Marshall's contribution was summarized by R. Kent Newmyer:

As in *Marbury v. Madison,* the genius of the *McCulloch* opinion lay not in its originality but in its timing, practicability, clarity and eloquence. Original it was not. . . . Marshall did not create these nationalist principles. What he did do was seize them at the moment when they were most relevant to American needs and congenial to the American mind, and (aided by the rhetoric of Alexander Hamilton) he translated them gracefully and logically into the law of the Constitution. Basing his interpretation of the law on the needs and spirit of the age, Marshall gave it permanence. Hamilton himself was unable to do as much.[25]

INHERENT POWERS

In addition to its implied powers, the Court has acknowledged that Congress has certain inherent powers derived from the fact of the nation's sovereignty. In his *Commentaries on the Constitution of the United States,* Justice Joseph Story defined this authority as that which results "from the whole mass of the powers of the National Government, and from the nature of political society, [rather] than a consequence or incident of the powers specially enumerated."[26]

Chief Justice John Marshall relied on these inherent powers in 1828 to declare that the absolute authority conferred on the central government to make war and treaties gave it the power to acquire territory by either war or treaty.[27]

The principle of inherent power has also been used to justify federal authority to acquire territory by discovery, to exclude and deport aliens, and to legislate for Indian tribes.[28]

Inherent power has generally been invoked only to rationalize an exercise of power over external affairs. As Justice George Sutherland wrote in 1936:

[S]ince the states severally never possessed international powers, such powers could not have been carved from the mass of state powers but obviously were transmitted to the United States from some other source. . . . The powers to declare and wage war, to conclude peace, to make treaties, to maintain diplomatic relations with other sovereignties, if they had never been mentioned in the Constitution would have vested in the federal government as necessary concomitants of nationality.[29]

Delegation of Power

The Latin phrase *delegata potestas non potest delegari* summarizes an old legal doctrine—"a power once delegated cannot be redelegated." Some have used this doctrine to contend that because Congress's powers have been delegated to it by the Constitution, it cannot in turn delegate them to any other body. Practically speaking, however, Congress does delegate its power and has done so almost from the beginning of its history.

While it occasionally pays lip service to the doctrine, the Supreme Court acknowledges that it has little meaning for Congress. "Delegation by Congress has long been recognized as nec-

essary in order that the exertion of legislative power does not become a futility," the Court has said.[30]

FILLING IN THE DETAILS

There are two types of legislative delegation. In the first, Congress sets an objective and authorizes an administrator to promulgate rules and regulations that will achieve the objective. The administrator may have only the broadest standards to guide the regulation making, or the administrator may be required to incorporate a host of congressionally approved details in regulations.

This type of delegation was first upheld in 1825. Congress had granted authority to the federal courts to set rules of practice so long as they did not conflict with the laws of the United States. The Court approved this delegation:

The difference between the departments undoubtedly is, that the legislature makes, the executive executes, and the judiciary construes the law; but the maker of the law may commit something to the discretion of the other departments, and the precise boundary of this power is a subject of delicate and difficult inquiry, into which a court will not enter unnecessarily.[31]

Nonetheless, Chief Justice John Marshall felt capable of distinguishing between "those important subjects, which must be entirely regulated by the legislature itself, from those of less interest, in which a general provision may be made, and power given to those who are to act under such general provisions to fill up the details."[32] Congress and the Court have found few subjects to require "entire regulation" by Congress, viewing most as amenable to delegation.

Congress enacted and the Court in 1904 sustained a law that gave the secretary of the Treasury authority to appoint a board of tea inspectors to set standards for grading tea. The statute also barred the import of any tea that did not meet the inspection standards. The act was challenged as an unconstitutional delegation of a policy-making function, that is, the establishment of the standards. But the Court said no, that Congress had set a "primary standard" that was sufficient.[33]

Justice Edward D. White explained:

Congress legislated on the subject as far as was reasonably practicable, and from the necessities of the case was compelled to leave to executive officials the duty of bringing about the result pointed out by the statute. To deny the power of Congress to delegate such a duty would, in effect, amount but to declaring that the plenary power vested in Congress to regulate foreign commerce could not be efficaciously exerted.[34]

In another case, the Court upheld congressionally mandated penalties for violations of administrative regulations, while making clear in a subsequent case that the administrative agency could not impose additional punishments.[35]

One major use by Congress of the delegation power has been the creation of agencies to regulate the nation's transportation and communications systems, trade practices, securities, and interstate power distribution and sales. The authority of Congress to make this delegation of power was first upheld in 1894, soon after the creation of the Interstate Commerce Commission.[36]

AUTHORIZING ACTION

A second type of legislative delegation authorizes an administrator to take a certain course of action if and when he or she determines that certain conditions exist. This contingency delegation was first upheld by the Supreme Court in 1813 when it sustained the right of Congress to authorize the president to reinstate the Non-Intercourse Act of 1809 under certain conditions. "[W]e can see no sufficient reason, why the legislature should not exercise its discretion in reviving the act . . . either expressly or conditionally, as their judgment should direct," the Court declared.[37]

Expansion of this contingency delegation came in 1892 when the Court upheld congressional delegation of authority to the president to prohibit free entry of certain items when he determined that foreign governments were imposing unreasonable duties on U.S. imports. The Court held that the president was not making law but finding fact. The president, the Court said, was a "mere agent of the lawmaking department to ascertain and declare the event upon which its expressed will was to take effect."[38]

In 1928 the Court sustained a delegation of tariff authority to the president. Upholding the Fordney-McComber Act, which authorized the president to raise or lower tariffs by as much as 50 percent to equalize production costs between the United States and competing countries, Chief Justice William Howard Taft offered an oft-quoted "common sense and inherent necessities" doctrine to govern the delegation of powers:

The well-known maxim (Delegata potestas non potest delegari), applicable to the law of agency in the general and common law, is well understood and has had wider application in the construction of our Federal and State Constitutions than it has in private law. The Federal Constitution and the State Constitutions of this country divide the governmental power into three branches. . . . [I]n carrying out that constitutional division . . . it is a breach of the national fundamental law if Congress gives up its legislative power and transfers it to the President, or to the Judicial branch, or if by law it attempts to invest itself or its members with either executive power or judicial power. This is not to say that the three branches are not co-ordinate parts of one government and that each in the field of its duties may not invoke the action of the other two in so far as the action invoked shall not be an assumption of the constitutional field of action of another branch. In determining what it may do in seeking assistance from another branch, the extent and character of that assistance must be fixed according to common sense and the inherent necessities of the governmental coordination.[39]

CONGRESSIONAL STANDARDS

When the Court has examined a challenge to a particular legislative delegation, it has usually considered the guidelines and standards Congress set out for the delegated agency to follow. Most of the time, it has found them sufficient. Occasionally, it has upheld a delegation when the law provided no standards at all.[40]

But the Court whose conservatism clashed with the New Deal philosophy of President Franklin D. Roosevelt found inadequate congressional standards ample reason to negate two major elements of the New Deal program.

"Hot" Oil

The first of these was a provision of the National Industrial Recovery Act (NIRA) that authorized the president to ban "hot oil" from interstate commerce. The term described oil produced in violation of state limits on production.[41]

In the 1935 case of *Panama Refining Co. v. Ryan,* this delegation of power was challenged from several angles, including the argument that this delegation to the president was too broad. But the Court had never held an act of Congress invalid as too broad a delegation of power, and so the government gave only 13 pages of its 427-page brief to refuting that charge.[42]

To the government's surprise, the Court struck down the provision on the ground that it transferred too much legislative power to the president. The Court said:

Among the numerous and diverse objectives broadly stated [in the act], the President was not required to choose. The President was not required to ascertain and proclaim the conditions prevailing in the industry which made the prohibition necessary. The Congress left the matter to the President without standard or rule, to be dealt with as he pleased. The effort by ingenious and diligent construction to supply a criterion still permits such a breadth of authorized action as essential to commit to the President the functions of a Legislature rather than those of an executive or administrative officer executing a declared legislative policy.[43]

The only dissenting justice, Benjamin N. Cardozo, found enough "definition of a standard" in the statute's declaration of intent to justify the delegation. "Discretion is not unconfined and vagrant," Cardozo wrote. "It is canalized within banks that keep it from overflowing."[44]

Sick Chickens

But the next time the Court struck down a law on the delegation issue, Cardozo agreed that Congress had left the president "virtually unfettered" in his exercise of the delegated power.[45] The case of *Schechter Poultry Corp. v. United States,* popularly known as the "Sick Chicken" case, involved a challenge to the fair competition codes set for various industries under the NIRA. The statute authorized the president to approve an industry code if he had been asked to do so by at least one association representing the industry. The Schechters had been charged with violating the poultry code; they responded by challenging this delegation of power. *(See "Black Monday," pp. 106–107.)*

Cardozo conceded that the "banks" set up by the NIRA were not high enough, that discretion was "unconfined and vagrant," and that, in short, it was a case of "delegation running riot."[46]

Congress quickly caught on to this test. When it passed the Fair Labor Standards Act in 1938, it added what two commentators referred to as "a rather detailed, though uninstructive, list of factors to guide the administrator's judgment,"[47] and the Court upheld this delegation.[48]

SPECIFIC CONSTITUTIONAL LIMITS ON CONGRESSIONAL POWERS

Article I, Section 9, of the Constitution contains specific prohibitions on congressional action with regard to taxes, the writ of habeas corpus, bills of attainder, ex post facto laws, export duties, and several matters which, over time, have become less and less important.

TAXES

One prohibition of prime importance in the nation's first century forbids Congress to levy a direct tax unless it is apportioned among the several states on the basis of population.

Until 1895 the Supreme Court defined only capitation taxes and taxes on land as direct taxes. In that year, however, the Court struck down a general income tax, holding that a tax based on the income from land was a direct tax and that this one was invalid because it had not been apportioned.[1]

This decision was overturned by adoption of the Sixteenth Amendment, which specifically exempted income taxes from the apportionment requirement. *(See box, The "Income Tax" Amendment, p. 120.)*

The second tax requirement stipulated that all indirect taxes be uniform throughout the United States. The requirement has presented little difficulty since the Court in the early twentieth century defined it to mean only that indirect taxes must be applied uniformly to the group being taxed.[2] *(See "Uniformity," p. 121.)*

HABEAS CORPUS

Section 9 also forbids Congress to suspend the privilege of the writ of habeas corpus "unless when in Cases of Rebellion or Invasion the public Safety may require it." Intended to protect citizens against illegal imprisonment, a writ of habeas corpus commands whoever is holding a prisoner to bring him before the court to justify his continued detention.

The clause does not state who has the authority to suspend the writ in emergencies. In the early Civil War years, President Lincoln suspended the privilege. That action was challenged by Chief Justice Roger B. Taney in the case of *Ex parte Merryman.*[3] Despite Taney's ruling, Lincoln continued to assert this power until March 1863 when Congress specifically authorized him to do so.

In three instances, Congress has asserted its power to suspend the writ—in nine South Carolina counties during a conflict with the Ku Klux Klan in 1871, in the Philippines in 1905, and in Hawaii during World War II.

The full Supreme Court has not ruled on this aspect of presidential power. Clinton Rossiter, noted scholar of the American presidency, has written that the lesson of Lincoln's assertion is that "in a condition of martial necessity," the president has this power. "The most a court or judge can do is read the President a lecture," he wrote.[4] *(See "Merryman and Milligan," pp. 198–199, in Chapter 5.)*

BILLS OF ATTAINDER

The Constitution's third clause of prohibition forbids enactment of bills of attainder and ex post facto laws. The Court has defined a bill of attainder as "a legislative act which inflicts punishment without a judicial trial."[5]

In 1867 the Court struck down, as a bill of attainder, an 1865 law that barred attorneys from practicing before federal courts unless they had sworn an oath that they had remained loyal to the Union throughout the Civil War. Persons taking the oath falsely could be charged with and convicted of perjury.

A. H. Garland of Arkansas had been admitted to practice law before the federal courts during the 1860 Supreme Court term. When Arkansas subsequently seceded, Garland went with his state, becoming first a representative and then a senator in the Confederate Congress.

In 1865 Garland received a full pardon from the president for his service to the Confederacy, and his case, *Ex parte Garland,* came to the Court two years later when he sought to practice in federal courts without taking the required loyalty oath.[6] *(See "The Effect of a Pardon," pp. 232–234, in Chapter 5.)*

Justice Stephen J. Field explained the Court's position: lawyers like Garland who had served with the confederacy could not take the oath without perjuring themselves, he said. Therefore,

the act, as against them, operates as a legislative decree of perpetual exclusion. And exclusion from any of the professions or any of the ordinary avocations of life for past conduct can be regarded in no other light than as punishment for such conduct.[7]

Eighty years later, in 1946, the Court nullified as a bill of attainder an act of Congress barring appropriations to pay the salaries of three government employees, who had been declared by Rep. Martin Dies, D-Texas (1931–1945, 1953–1959), chairman of the House Committee on Un-American Activities, to be affiliated with communist front organizations.[8]

The Supreme Court struck down this law, declaring that "Legislative acts, no matter what their form, that apply either to named individuals or to easily ascertainable members of a group in such a way as to inflict punishment on them without a judicial trial are bills of attainder."[9]

Twenty years later, in *United States v. Brown* (1965), the Court again found that Congress had enacted a bill of attainder when it approved a provision of the Labor Management and Reporting Act of 1959, which declared it a crime for a present or former member of the Communist Party to serve as an officer or employee of a labor union.[10] Designed to prevent politically motivated strikes, this provision replaced a section of the 1947 Taft-Hartley Act that had required labor unions to swear that none of their officers was affiliated with the Communist Party. That requirement had been upheld.[11]

The Supreme Court, however, found the successor provision unconstitutional. Chief Justice Earl Warren explained that the former provision was permissible and the latter not, because one could be escaped simply by resigning from the Communist Party, while the offending act applied to persons who had been members of the party for the last five years.

EX POST FACTO LAWS

An ex post facto law makes illegal an act that has already taken place, or it makes the punishment greater than it was at the time of the act. In *Calder v. Bull* (1798), the earliest Supreme Court discussion of ex post facto laws, the Court held that the constitutional prohibition did not apply to civil statutes but only to criminal laws.[12]

In *Ex parte Garland* the Court also found the loyalty oath requirement an ex post facto law because to prohibit an attorney from practicing before federal courts without taking the oath was to punish him for past acts not defined as illegal at the time they were committed.

In other instances, however, the Court has upheld, against charges they were ex post facto laws, statutes that denied to polygamists the right to vote in a territorial election, that deported aliens for criminal acts committed prior to the deportation law's enactment, and that revoked naturalization papers obtained fraudulently before passage of the law.[13]

EXPORT DUTIES AND OTHER LIMITS

The Constitution also prohibits Congress from imposing duties on items exported from any state. Using this prohibition, the Court has declared invalid a stamp tax on foreign bills of lading and a tax on charter parties that operated from ports in the United States to foreign ports.[14]

The Court, however, has said that the prohibition does not extend to a general property tax that affects goods intended for export so long as the tax is not levied only on goods for export and so long as the goods are not taxed in the course of exportation.[15]

The Court has also held that a tax on corporate income, including income from exportation, was not forbidden by the constitutional limitation.[16]

The remaining restrictions on congressional authority have required little interpretation. The first barred Congress from banning the importation of slaves for the first twenty years after the Constitution was ratified. Others stipulate that Congress shall give no preference to the ports of one state over those of another, that it should not grant titles of nobility, and that Congress must appropriate all money before it can be drawn from the Treasury.

1. *Pollock v. Farmers' Loan & Trust Co.*, 157 U.S. 429 (1895), 158 U.S. 601 (1895).

2. *Knowlton v. Moore*, 178 U.S. 41 (1900).

3. 17 Fed. Cases 9487 (1861).

4. Clinton Rossiter, *The Supreme Court and the Commander-in-Chief* (Ithaca, N.Y.: Cornell University Press, 1951), 25.

5. *Cummings v. Missouri*, 4 Wall. 277 (1867).

6. *Ex parte Garland*, 4 Wall. 333 (1867).

7. Id. at 377.

8. *United States v. Lovett*, 328 U.S. 303 (1946).

9. Id. at 315.

10. *United States v. Brown*, 381 U.S. 437 (1965).

11. *American Communications Association v. Douds*, 339 U.S. 382 (1950).

12. *Calder v. Bull*, 3 Dall. 386 (1798).

13. *Murphy v. Ramsey*, 114 U.S. 15 (1885); *Rahler v. Eby*, 264 U.S. 32 (1924); *Johannessen v. United States*, 225 U.S. 227 (1912).

14. *Fairbank v. United States*, 181 U.S. 283 (1901); *United States v. Hvoslef*, 237 U.S. 1 (1915).

15. *Cornell v. Coyne*, 192 U.S. 418 (1904); *Turpin v. Burgess*, 117 U.S. 504 (1886).

16. *Peck & Co. v. Lowe*, 247 U.S. 165 (1918); *National Paper Co. v. Bowers*, 266 U.S. 373 (1924).

DELEGATIONS TO PRIVATE PARTIES

In the "Sick Chicken" case, the Court also struck down the provisions of the NIRA that authorized trade associations to recommend fair competition codes to the president for approval.

Writing for the Court, Chief Justice Charles Evans Hughes asked whether Congress had this power. "The answer is obvious," he wrote. "Such a delegation of legislative power is unknown to our law, and is utterly inconsistent with the constitutional duties and prerogatives of Congress."[49]

Similar concern about delegating legislative power to private parties moved the Court to strike down the Guffey Coal Act of 1935, which authorized the coal industry to establish mandatory wage and hour regulations for the industry.

In *Carter v. Carter Coal Co.* (1936), the Court explained its decision:

The power conferred upon the majority [of the coal industry] is, in effect the power to regulate the affairs of an unwilling minority. This is legislative delegation in its most obnoxious form; for it is not even delegation to an official or an official body . . . but to private persons whose interests may be and often are adverse to the interests of others in the same business.[50]

The Court, however, later upheld a federal law that required two-thirds of tobacco growers to approve the markets to which the growers could sell in interstate commerce. The justices said this was not an attempt to delegate power, but simply a condition of the federal regulation.[51]

Prior to *Schechter* and *Carter*, the Court had sustained federal statutes giving the force of law to local customs regarding miners' claims on public lands and to the determination by the American Railway Association of the standard height of freight car draw bars.[52] The Court has not reconciled these seemingly conflicting rulings.

WARTIME DELEGATIONS

Since 1827, when it first upheld an act of Congress delegating to the president the power to decide when to call out the militia, the Supreme Court has steadily affirmed all wartime delegations of legislative power.[53] This is particularly striking since the discretion given by Congress to the president during times of war has far exceeded any peacetime delegation.

The reason that wartime legislative delegations are viewed differently was explained in *United States v. Curtiss-Wright Corp.* (1936). The Court upheld a grant of authority to the president allowing him to bar the sale of arms to warring countries in South America if he thought the ban might help restore peace.[54] Justice George Sutherland wrote:

It is important to bear in mind that we are here not dealing alone with an authority vested in the President by an exertion of legislative power, but with such an authority plus the very delicate, plenary and exclusive power of the President as the sole organ of the federal government in the field of international relations—a power which does not require as a basis for its exercise an act of Congress. . . . It is quite apparent that if, in the maintenance of our international relations, embarrassment . . . is

COURTS AND BASE CLOSING DECISIONS

Once Congress delegates to the president power to decide to close certain military bases, courts have no authority to review those decisions, held the Supreme Court in 1994. If Congress does not explicitly provide for judicial review of those decisions, that power cannot be assumed by the courts.

Under the Defense Base Closure and Realignment Act of 1990, a special commission developed a list of unneeded military and naval facilities and submitted its recommendations for those bases to be closed to the president. The president could accept or reject the package as a whole. If the president accepted the commission's decision, Congress similarly could disapprove the package only as a whole.

The law was designed to reduce political maneuvering over the issue. Yet, several members of Congress from Pennsylvania brought a lawsuit seeking to prevent the recommended closure of the Philadelphia Naval Shipyard. They alleged that the base-closing commission and military personnel who had recommended various installations be closed had violated several substantive and administrative requirements of the 1990 act. Republican senator Arlen Specter personally argued the case before the Court.

The justices ruled unanimously that courts had no power to review decisions under the base-closing law. Chief Justice William H. Rehnquist wrote for the Court, "Where a statute . . . commits decisionmaking to the discretion of the President judicial review of the President's decision is not available." (*Dalton v. Specter,* 114 S. Ct. 1719, 1994)

to be avoided and success for our aims achieved, congressional legislation which is to be made effective through negotiation and inquiry within the international field must often accord to the President a degree of distinction and freedom from statutory restriction which would not be admissible were domestic affairs alone involved.[55]

(For details on specific cases involving wartime delegations, see "Wartime Legislation," pp. 137–139; "President Wilson and World War," pp. 199–200; and "President Roosevelt and Total War," pp. 200–203, in Chapter 5.)

DELEGATIONS TO STATES

Sometimes Congress delegates power to the states, a delegation that the Court has also upheld while generally refusing to call it a delegation. One leading case involved the Federal Assimilative Crimes Act of 1948, which made any crime committed on a federal enclave and not punishable under federal law punishable under state law.

The Court reasoned that because Congress had the power to assimilate state laws on a daily or annual basis, it also had the power to do it on a permanent basis. "Rather than being a delegation by Congress of its legislative authority to the States, it is a deliberate continuing adoption by Congress for federal enclaves of such unpreempted offenses and punishments as shall have been already put in effect by the respective States for their own government," the Court held.[56]

Earlier the Court had upheld a 1913 law that prohibited the shipment of liquor in interstate commerce into any state that was dry. Because the same law allowed states to ban liquor, the federal statute was challenged as an unconstitutional delegation of power. The Court disagreed, declaring it was not a delegation because the act established the precise conditions under which it would take effect.[57] *(See "Public Health and Morals," pp. 338–340, in Chapter 7.)*

Power and Process

Article I spells out the lawmaking process in clear and certain terms: for a measure to become law it must be approved by both the House and the Senate and then be presented to the president for signature. Almost two hundred years of constitutional history had passed before the Court struck down an act of Congress because it deviated too far from that process. That occasion came in 1983, and the subject was the legislative veto.

RETAINING POWER

The legislative veto, which enabled Congress to retain a measure of control over the implementation or execution of a law, originated during the Hoover administration. The first legislative veto was part of the fiscal 1933 legislative appropriations bill; it provided that either house of Congress could veto President Hoover's executive branch reorganization proposal by a vote of disapproval. This device, controversial from the start, was used the very next year to disapprove a reorganization plan.

Over the next fifty years, legislative veto provisions were included, in one guise or another, in more than two hundred laws. Some permitted a veto by a single chamber or even a committee; others required action by both chambers. All legislative vetoes, however, were alike in that they permitted Congress to block executive action—with or without the president's approval.

Presidents from Hoover on protested the veto as an encroachment on their power, but it was not until the early 1980s, during President Reagan's first term, that a challenge to this device reached the Court. The case of *Immigration and Naturalization Service v. Chadha* began in 1974 when Jagdish Rai Chadha, a Kenyan East Indian who had overstayed his student visa, persuaded the Immigration and Naturalization Service (INS) to suspend his deportation.

But Congress had amended the Immigration and Nationality Act of 1952 to give either of its chambers the power to veto an INS decision to suspend an individual's deportation. In December 1975 the House exercised its power to veto Chadha's stay of deportation. Chadha contested the House veto, arguing that it was unconstitutional for the House to overrule the INS in this way. In 1980 the U.S. Court of Appeals for the Ninth Circuit agreed, holding the one-house veto unconstitutional.

The Supreme Court heard arguments appealing that ruling in February 1982. On the last day of that term, the Court ordered a second round of arguments, which were held on the opening day of the October 1982 term. (Chadha, in the meantime, had married an American, fathered a child, and settled down in the United States.)

SEPARATING POWERS

It took the Court all term to reach a decision. On June 23, 1983, it held the legislative veto unconstitutional by a 7–2 vote. The majority found the device an impermissible abrogation of "the Framers' decision that the legislative power of the Federal Government be exercised in accord with a single, finely wrought and exhaustively considered, procedure." That procedure required that bills be passed by both houses and presented to the president for signature.[58]

Chief Justice Warren E. Burger wrote for the majority that in only four specific situations had the Framers authorized one chamber to act alone with the force of law, not subject to a presidential veto: in initiating an impeachment, in trying a person impeached, in approving presidential appointments, and in approving treaties.

Legislative vetoes might indeed be useful and convenient, Burger acknowledged, but "convenience and efficiency are not the primary objectives—or the hallmarks—of democratic government and our inquiry is sharpened rather than blunted by the fact that congressional veto provisions are appearing with increasing frequency in statutes which delegate authority to executive and independent agencies."[59]

Burger concluded:

The choices . . . made in the Constitutional Convention impose burdens on governmental processes that often seem clumsy, inefficient, even unworkable, but those hard choices were consciously made by men who had lived under a form of government that permitted arbitrary governmental acts to go unchecked. There is no support in the Constitution or decisions of this Court for the proposition that the cumbersomeness and delays often encountered in complying with explicit Constitutional standards may be avoided, either by the Congress or by the President. With all the obvious flaws of delay, untidiness, and potential for abuse, we have not yet found a better way to preserve freedom than by making the exercise of power subject to the carefully crafted restraints spelled out in the Constitution.[60]

In dissent, Justice Byron R. White wrote one of the longest dissenting opinions of his career, equaling the majority's in length. The legislative veto, he said, was "an important if not indispensable political invention that allows the president and Congress to resolve major constitutional and policy differences,

assures the accountability of independent regulatory agencies and preserves Congress' control over lawmaking."[61]

To deny Congress the use of this device, he continued, the Court required Congress "either to refrain from delegating the necessary authority, leaving itself with a hopeless task of writing laws with the requisite specificity to cover endless special circumstances across the entire political landscape, or in the alternative, to abdicate its lawmaking function to the executive branch and independent agencies."[62]

Describing the decision as destructive, he pointed out that "in one fell swoop," the Court had struck down provisions in more acts of Congress—about 200—than it had invalidated in its entire history to that point. As of the end of the 1988–1989 term, the Court had invalidated all or part of 124 federal laws.[63]

Among the laws containing legislative vetoes were the War Powers Resolution of 1973, the Congressional Budget and Impoundment Control Act of 1974, the Nuclear Non-Proliferation Act of 1978, the Airline Deregulation Act of 1978, and the Federal Election Campaign Act Amendments of 1979. In 1987, in a case concerning the legislative veto in the Airline Deregulation Act, the Court held unanimously that in most of these laws, only the legislative veto provision itself was nullified by its ruling.

The remainder of the law could stand, unless the inclusion of the veto was critical to the decision of Congress to pass the law in the first place. "The unconstitutional provision must be severed unless the statute created in its absence is legislation that Congress would not have enacted," said the Court in *Alaska Airlines v. Brock*.[64]

But the limits of the Supreme Court's power to change the way Congress and the president relate to each other soon became apparent. Legislative veto provisions continued to appear in acts of Congress, and, five years after *Chadha,* scholar Louis Fisher of the Congressional Research Service wrote that "the practical effect was not nearly as sweeping as the Court's decision."

Indeed, in his book *Constitutional Dialogues*, Fisher said:

The Court's decision simply drove underground a set of legislative and committee vetoes that used to operate in plain sight. No one should be misled if the number of legislative vetoes placed in statutes gradually declines over the years. Fading from view will not mean disappearance. In one form or another, legislative vetoes will remain an important method for reconciling legislative and executive interests.[65]

The Commerce Power

The Constitution grants Congress the power to regulate interstate commerce, that is, all commercial intercourse that is not wholly within one state, wrote Chief Justice John Marshall in *Gibbons v. Ogden* (1824). This grant of power "is complete in itself, may be exercised to its utmost extent, and acknowledges no limitations other than those prescribed by the Constitution."[1]

With that declaration, Marshall laid the basis for the Supreme Court's subsequent interpretations of the commerce clause. This broad view gives Congress virtually unfettered authority to regulate all interstate matters and any intrastate matter—production, business practices, labor relations—that in any way affects interstate commerce.

But more than a century passed until the Court gave full approval to Marshall's expansive interpretation. That did not happen until its insistence on a narrower interpretation, more protective of states' rights and business interests, prompted President Franklin D. Roosevelt's Court-packing plan that threatened the independent existence of the Court itself. From the late nineteenth century until well into the twentieth, the Court rulings described manufacture and labor relations as intrastate matters outside the reach of Congress.

For several decades after *Gibbons v. Ogden,* Congress found little need to regulate commerce. Most cases before the Supreme Court involved the question of state power to regulate commerce in the absence of federal controls. In 1851 the Court adopted the *Cooley* doctrine under which the federal government would regulate those matters of commerce that required a uniform national approach such as immigration. Matters in interstate commerce but of primarily local concern, such as insurance, would be reserved for state regulation. It was up to the Court to determine which matters were national and which local in scope.

Regulation and Concentration

Only in the last decades of the nineteenth century did Congress begin actively to regulate interstate commerce. With the Interstate Commerce Act of 1887 and the Sherman Antitrust Act of 1890, Congress responded to a changing economic scene in which post–Civil War industrial growth produced interstate railroads and large national corporations and trusts. Concentration meant less competition and higher prices. The laissez-faire doctrine of little or no government regulation of business became less acceptable to farmers, laborers, consumers, and owners of small businesses. With states foreclosed by the Constitution from regulating businesses that spread over more than one state, the farmers and laborers sought relief from Congress.

Many of this era's Supreme Court justices were disinclined to favor government regulation of business. Some had been corporation and railroad company lawyers before their appointment.

Several were part of the majority that construed the Fourteenth Amendment to protect business from state regulation.

But the conservative Court did not view all federal regulation as inherently bad. In order to uphold regulation it approved while striking down that which it disapproved, the Court developed two lines of contradictory precedent.

In 1895, the year that it declared a federal income tax unconstitutional and sanctioned the use of federal troops to quell the Pullman strike, the Supreme Court held that a sugar trust, which processed 98 percent of all refined sugar in the country, did not violate the antitrust law because processing was not a part of, and did not directly affect, interstate commerce. In other words, the federal commerce power did not reach intrastate manufacture unless that manufacture directly affected interstate commerce.

With this ruling the Court took a narrow view of Marshall's 1824 statement that Congress could regulate intrastate matters that "extended to or affected" other states. For the 1895 Court to allow regulation, that effect must be direct.

The Court, in claiming for itself the power to determine direct effect, seemed to some to usurp the power to legislate. Such judicial legislation was sharply criticized by Justice Oliver Wendell Holmes Jr., an economic conservative and an advocate of judicial restraint. "It must be remembered," Holmes told his colleagues in 1904, "that legislators are the ultimate guardians of the liberties and welfare of the people in quite as great a degree as the courts."[2]

THE LABOR EXCEPTION

Labor law was the one area in which the Court consistently refused to heed Holmes's admonition. In 1908 the Court converted the antitrust law into an antiunion weapon, ruling that a union-organized secondary boycott was an illegal restraint of interstate trade. Congress subsequently exempted unions from the reach of antitrust law, but the Court in 1921 narrowed that exemption to normal union activities. Secondary boycotts still were a restraint of trade in violation of the antitrust act, the Court said.

In a second 1908 case the Court ruled that Congress exceeded the scope of the commerce power when it outlawed "yellow dog" contracts that required employees to abstain from union membership. Union membership had no direct effect on interstate commerce, the majority declared.

While it sustained federal worker safety laws and even upheld an emergency and temporary minimum wage for railway workers to avert a nationwide strike in 1917, the Court generally viewed unions and labor relations as intrastate matters that could not be regulated by Congress. At the height of its pre–New Deal efforts to protect business from government-imposed labor regulations, the Court in 1918 struck down the act of

Congress that prohibited the transportation in interstate commerce of any goods made by child laborers. Congress was not regulating transportation, the Court said in *Hammer v. Dagenhart,* but manufacture, which its power did not reach.

INNOVATION

These restrictions on the exercise of the commerce power, however, were in large part exceptions to the Court's fundamentally broad view of that power. For during this same period, the Court endorsed innovative uses of the commerce power. Beginning with a 1903 decision upholding a federal ban on interstate sale of lottery tickets, the Court, with the notable exception of the child labor case, sanctioned the use of the commerce power as a federal police power to protect the public health and morals. Among the police power statutes sustained were those prohibiting transportation across state lines of impure food and drugs, women for immoral purposes, and stolen cars.

In 1905 the Court modified its sugar trust decision to hold unanimously that the federal antitrust act did reach a combine of stockyard operators even though the individual stockyards were wholly intrastate. Because the yards received shipments of cattle from out of state for slaughter and sale in other states, the Court found that they were part of a stream of interstate commerce subject to federal regulation. Although the Court still further modified its antitrust position in 1911, ruling that the antitrust act applied only to unreasonable combinations and restraints of trade, the "stream-of-commerce" doctrine was subsequently applied to other intrastate businesses that were part of a larger interstate enterprise and so held subject to federal regulation. *(See box, The Court, Congress, and Commerce: A Chronology, p. 102.)*

Extending federal power over intrastate commerce in another direction, the Court in 1914 held that the Interstate Commerce Commission could regulate intrastate rail rates when necessary to achieve effective interstate regulation. To do otherwise, the Court said, would make the federal power to regulate subordinate to the state's power to regulate.

THE NEW DEAL

By 1930 the Court had begun to retreat from its reluctance to protect organized labor, sustaining that year a law providing for collective bargaining in the railway industry.

But the Court had not specifically overturned any of its restrictive rulings on the federal commerce power and so it had both sets of precedents to draw on when it came to review New Deal legislation that called for unprecedented federal regulation of the economy. That regulation proved too pervasive for a majority of the Court, which struck down as unconstitutional eight of the first ten statutes enacted to reinvigorate the economy. Among these were three acts based on the commerce clause—a railway workers pension plan, the National Industrial Recovery Act, and the Bituminous Coal Conservation Act of 1935. In all three instances, the Court held that Congress had unconstitutionally intruded into intrastate matters.

Irate that the Court had blocked most of his economic recovery programs, President Roosevelt offered his famous Court-packing plan, and the initial likelihood of support by Congress apparently had an impact on the Court.

By a 5–4 vote, the Court in 1937 abandoned its distinction between direct and indirect effects on interstate commerce. In upholding federal regulation of labor-management relations, the Court sustained the federal power to regulate intrastate matters, even if their effect on interstate commerce was only indirect. Four years later the Court upheld a federal minimum wage law, acceding to the congressional opinion that substandard labor conditions unconstitutionally burdened interstate commerce.

These two decisions were capped in 1942 by the Court's ruling that even a farmer's production of goods for his own consumption—in this case, wheat—directly affected the demand for those goods in interstate commerce and was thus subject to federal regulation.

One commentator summarized this series of decisions:

The Commerce Clause was now recognized as a grant of authority permitting Congress to allow interstate commerce to take place on whatever terms it may consider in the interest of the national well-being, subject only to other constitutional limitations, such as the Due Process Clause. The constitutional grant of power over commerce was now interpreted as enabling Congress to enact all appropriate laws for the protection and advancement of commerce among the states, whatever measures Congress might reasonably think adopted to that end, without regard for whether particular acts regulated in themselves were interstate or intrastate. No mechanical formula any longer excluded matters which might be called "local" from the application of these principles.[2]

At least until the mid-1990s, this summary continued to be an accurate description of the Court's view of the commerce power. Only twice between 1937 and 1996 did a majority find unconstitutional a congressional exercise of the commerce power. In 1976 the Court struck down, 5–4, federal wage and hour standards for state employees. But nine years later that decision was reversed. By a 5–4 vote in 1985, the Court reaffirmed Congress's domination over commerce.

More significant as an indication that the contemporary Court may be inclined to restrict federal authority in the years to come is the 1995 ruling in *United States v. Lopez.* Striking down a law that prohibited people from carrying guns near local schools, the Court—again with a one-vote majority—declined to defer as much to Congress as it had in the past, saying that federal lawmakers had overstepped their authority to intervene in local affairs.

While the 1976 ruling limited federal power relative to the states, invoking the Tenth Amendment, the *Lopez* case posed a greater threat to congressional authority by narrowing the definition of what activity constituted commerce.

FEDERAL CONTROL

The necessity for federal control over interstate and foreign commerce was one of the primary reasons for the Constitutional Convention in 1787. "Most of our political evils may be traced

The lawsuit of one-time business partners Aaron Ogden *(left)* and Thomas Gibbons *(right)* led to a landmark Commerce Clause decision in 1824. John Marshall's opinion for the Court defined commerce and stated that Congress has the power to regulate interstate commerce.

to our commercial ones," James Madison had written to Thomas Jefferson the previous year.[4] Under the Articles of Confederation, adopted in 1781 during the Revolutionary War, Congress had power to regulate trade only with the Indians. Control of interstate and foreign commerce was left to the individual states, and each state attempted to build its own prosperity at the expense of its neighbors. State legislatures imposed tariffs upon goods coming in from other states as well as from foreign countries. New York levied duties on firewood from Connecticut and cabbages from New Jersey.

Different currencies in each of the thirteen states likewise hampered commercial intercourse. And if a merchant were able to carry on interstate business despite tariff and currency difficulties, he often had trouble collecting his bills. Local courts and juries were less zealous in protecting the rights of distant creditors than those of their neighbors and friends.

This condition was universally recognized as unacceptable. Even those like Samuel Adams and Patrick Henry, who feared that a federal executive would repeat the tyranny of the English monarch, favored regulation of commerce by Congress. As a result, the inclusion of the congressional power "to regulate Commerce with foreign Nations, and among the several States, and with the Indian Tribes" as Clause 3 of Article I, Section 8, occasioned comparatively little discussion at the Philadelphia convention.

It is ironic, therefore, that the commerce clause should have generated more cases, if not more controversy, than any other power the Framers granted to Congress.

Gibbons v. Ogden

Not until 1824 did the Supreme Court rule on the scope of the commerce power. And it was precisely the sort of commer-

cial warfare at issue in *Gibbons v. Ogden* that had prompted the drafting of the Constitution in the first place.[5]

New York in 1798 granted Robert R. Livingston, chancellor of the state, a monopoly over all steamboat operations in New York waters. Taking on the inventor Robert Fulton as a partner, Livingston turned the steamship monopoly into a viable transportation system. So successful were they that in 1811, the pair was granted similar exclusive rights to operate in the waters of the territory of New Orleans. The monopoly, therefore, controlled transportation on two of the nation's largest waterways and ports.

Attempts to break the monopoly were frequent but unsuccessful. Connecticut, New Jersey, and Ohio enacted retaliatory measures closing their waters to ships licensed by the New York monopoly, while five other states granted steamship monopolies of their own. The ensuing navigational chaos brought the states to what one attorney would describe as "almost . . . the eve of war."[6]

Aaron Ogden, a former New Jersey governor (1812–1813), ran a steam-driven ferry between Elizabethtown, New Jersey, and New York City in uneasy partnership with Thomas Gibbons. In 1815 Ogden had acquired a license from the Livingston-Fulton monopoly, and Gibbons held a permit under the federal Coastal Licensing Act of 1793 for his two boats. Despite the partnership, Gibbons ran his boats to New York in defiance of the monopoly rights that Ogden held. In 1819 Ogden sued for an injunction to stop Gibbons's infringement of his rights to monopoly. New York courts sided with Ogden, ordering Gibbons to halt his ferry service. Gibbons appealed to the Supreme Court, arguing that his federal license took precedence over the state-granted monopoly license and that he should be allowed to continue his ferrying in New York water.

Public interest in the case ran high during the four years between the time the Court said it would take the case and the time it heard arguments. The steamboat monopolies were unpopular with many who were eager for the Court to prohibit them. In addition, the case fueled the public debate between the nationalist beliefs of the Federalists and the states' rights beliefs of the Republicans. As historian Charles Warren wrote, the New York monopoly "had been created by Republican legislators, owned by Republican statesmen and defended largely by Republican lawyers."[7] Those lawyers, some of the ablest in the land, argued their case before Chief Justice John Marshall, a leading exponent of a strong centralized government. It was widely assumed that Marshall would side with Gibbons, but whether the remainder of the Court would follow Marshall was uncertain.

ARGUMENT AND DECISION

The case presented several questions. Did Congress have power under the commerce clause to regulate navigation and, if so, was that power exclusive? Could federal regulation of commerce leave room for the states to act and still be supreme?

In Gibbons's behalf, Daniel Webster argued "that the power of Congress to regulate commerce was complete and entire, and, to a certain extent, necessarily exclusive."[8] Navigation was one of the areas where federal power precluded all state action, Webster claimed.

But the attorneys for Ogden construed the commerce power narrowly, contending that it applied only to "transportation and sale of commodities," not to navigation, a matter left to the states to regulate.[9]

Delivering the Court's opinion on March 2, 1824, Chief Justice Marshall refused to construe the federal commerce power narrowly or to omit navigation from its scope:

The subject to be regulated is commerce; and . . . to ascertain the extent of the power, it becomes necessary to settle the meaning of the word. . . . Commerce undoubtedly is traffic, but it is something more; it is intercourse. It describes the commercial intercourse between nations, and parts of nations, in all its branches, and is regulated by prescribing rules for carrying on that intercourse. The mind can scarcely conceive a system for regulating commerce between nations, which shall exclude all laws concerning navigation. . . . All America understands, and has uniformly understood, the word "commerce" to comprehend navigation. . . . The power over commerce, including navigation, was one of the primary objects for which the people . . . adopted their government, and must have been contemplated in forming it.[10]

To what commerce does the power apply? asked Marshall. The first type was commerce with foreign nations. The second, he said:

is to commerce "among the several states." The word "among" means intermingled with. A thing which is among others, is intermingled with them. Commerce among the states cannot stop at the external boundary line of each state, but may be introduced into the interior.[11]

But Marshall did not find that the commerce power foreclosed all state regulation:

It is not intended to say that these words comprehend that commerce which is completely internal, which is carried on between man and man in a state, or between different parts of the same state, and which does not extend to or affect other states. Such a power would be inconvenient or unnecessary.

Comprehensive as the word "among" is, it may very properly be restricted to that commerce which concerns more states than one. . . . The completely internal commerce of a state, then, may be considered as reserved for the state itself.[12]

With regard to the supremacy of the federal power, Marshall said:

This power, like all others vested in congress, is complete in itself, may be exercised to its utmost extent, and acknowledges no limitations, other than are prescribed in the constitution. . . . If, as has always been understood, the sovereignty of congress, though limited to specified objects, is plenary as to those objects, the power over commerce with foreign nations, and among the several states, is vested in congress as absolutely as it would be in a single government, having in its constitution the same restrictions on the exercise of the power as are found in the constitution of the United States.[13]

Marshall did not address whether states could regulate areas Congress has not regulated. Here, he said, Congress had acted when it passed the Coastal Licensing Act. Nor did he answer the question of whether states could regulate commerce simultaneously with Congress. Marshall did say that in exercising its police powers a state might take actions similar to those Congress adopted in the exercise of its commerce power. But if the state law impeded or conflicted with the federal law, the federal law would take precedence. The chief justice then enumerated the ways in which the New York law interfered with the federal act and declared the state law invalid.

Justice William Johnson's concurring opinion argued that the commerce power "must be exclusive . . . leaving nothing for the states to act upon."[14]

REACTION

The decision in *Gibbons v. Ogden* was politically popular. But staunch Republicans, including Thomas Jefferson, were appalled. In 1825 Jefferson wrote a friend that he viewed "with the deepest affliction, the rapid strides with which the federal branch of our government is advancing towards the usurpation of all the rights reserved to the states."[15] Also disturbed were slave owners who feared that Congress might exercise the commerce power to wrest control over slavery from the states and then abolish it.

Marshall's opinion settled only one point: where state exercise of its power conflicts with federal exercise of the commerce power, the state must give way. But in reaching that pronouncement, Marshall laid the groundwork for extending the commerce power to forms of transportation and communications not yet contemplated. By leaving the power to regulate wholly internal commerce to the states only so long as that commerce did not "extend to or affect" other states, he planted the seeds that would eventually allow Congress to regulate manufacture of goods and matters that themselves were not in commerce but were deemed to affect interstate commerce.

Scholars have wondered why Marshall, having gone so far,

did not go on to claim exclusivity for the federal commerce power. To do so would have avoided many of the inconsistencies, confusions, and contortions that found their way into constitutional law as the Court sought to determine what was in or affected interstate commerce and how far Congress could reach to regulate that commerce. And why did the Marshall Court not adopt, as a later Court would, Daniel Webster's argument that congressional power over some areas of commerce was exclusive? Professor Felix Frankfurter provided perhaps the best answer when he noted the double-edged potential of Webster's argument: Marshall may have "ignored Webster's formula not because it would have failed to serve in his hands as an instrument for restricting state authority, but because its very flexibility was equally adaptable in hands bent on securing state immunity." Frankfurter also postulated that Marshall did not endorse Webster's theory because it would then be apparent what "large powers of discretion . . . judges must exercise" in determining over which subjects Congress had exclusive control.[16]

COMMERCE AND THE STATES

Congress did not use the power claimed for it by Marshall until later in the century. Between 1824, when *Gibbons v. Ogden* was decided, and the 1880s, when need for federal regulation of the interstate railroads and interstate corporations became apparent, the Court's rulings on the commerce power focused primarily on determining when state actions impinged unconstitutionally on the federal commerce power.

Before Marshall's death in 1835, the Court handed down two more major decisions defining the range of state power to affect commerce. In *Brown v. Maryland* (1827), it forbade states to tax imports as long as they remained unopened in their original packages.[17] In *Willson v. Blackbird Creek Marsh Co.* (1829), it held that a state could exercise its police power over matters affecting interstate commerce in the absence of conflicting federal legislation.[18]

The commerce power rulings by Marshall's successor—Roger B. Taney—reflected the Court's uncertainty as to the proper line between state regulation and federal power. At various times, different judges put forth various doctrines as a standard for determining that line. Taney, for instance, maintained that Congress and the states held the commerce power concurrently; Justice John McLean held it exclusive to Congress. Rarely did any one doctrine win a majority. If it did, the majority dissolved when the next case was heard.[19]

The conflict was temporarily resolved in *Cooley v. Port Wardens of Philadelphia* (1852), when the Court upheld state regulation of city harbor pilots and adopted the so-called selective exclusiveness doctrine first enunciated by Webster in 1824.[20]

In his majority opinion, Justice Benjamin R. Curtis shifted the focus of judicial scrutiny from the power itself to the nature of the subject to be regulated. Some fields of commerce were of necessity national in nature and demanded a uniform regulation provided by Congress, he said. Others demanded local regulation to accommodate local circumstances and needs. This doctrine left it up to the Court to determine on a case-by-case basis what matters were reserved to Congress and which were local in nature. *(See "The Control of Commerce," pp. 328–336, in Chapter 7.)*

Commerce and Navigation

The opinion in the steamboat monopoly case also settled a second issue: navigation was commerce. Then, the question became one of state power: Was the federal power over navigation exclusive, or were there some situations in which states could regulate traffic on the waterways?

Five years after *Gibbons v. Ogden* the Marshall Court sustained Delaware's right to build a dam across a small but navigable tidal creek as an exercise of its police power in the absence of conflicting federal legislation.[21]

The chief justice conveniently ignored the fact that the owner of the ship protesting the dam as an obstruction to interstate commerce was licensed under the same federal coastal licensing act that figured so prominently in Marshall's reasoning in the monopoly case. *(See "Gibbons v. Ogden," pp. 90–92; box, The Coastal Licensing Act, p. 93.)*

But in the next major navigation case, the Court held that Congress could use its commerce power to override both state law and an earlier Court decision. In 1852 the Court ruled that a bridge on the Ohio River must either be raised so that ships could pass under it or be taken down altogether. The Court held that the bridge not only obstructed interstate commerce but also violated a congressionally sanctioned compact between Virginia and Kentucky agreeing to keep the river free of such obstructions.[22]

However, Congress immediately overruled the Court by declaring that the bridge was not an obstruction and requiring instead that ships be refitted so they could pass under the bridge. In 1856 the Court upheld this act of Congress:

So far . . . as this bridge created an obstruction to the free navigation of the river, in view of the previous acts of Congress, they are regarded as modified by this subsequent legislation; and although it still may be an obstruction in fact, [the bridge] is not so in the contemplation of law. . . . [Congress] having in the exercise of this power, regulated the navigation consistent with its preservation and continuation, the authority to maintain it would seem to be complete.[23]

In the same period, the Court held that navigation on a river wholly in one state and involving commerce that was not connected to interstate or foreign commerce could not be regulated by Congress.[24]

In 1866 the Court reaffirmed Congress's complete control over navigable waters "which are accessible from a State other than those in which they lie."[25] In 1871 congressional authority over navigation was further extended to permit federal regulation of a boat that transported goods in interstate commerce even though the boat operated solely on waters entirely within one state. The Court issued an opinion that was clearly a forerunner of the "stream of commerce" doctrine. *(See "The 'Stream of Commerce,'" p. 100).* It stated:

THE COASTAL LICENSING ACT

In one of the earliest exercises of its commerce power, the First Congress in 1789 enacted a statute "for enrolling or licensing ships or vessels to be employed in the coasting trade and fisheries, and for regulating the same." Partly because the major commercial transportation system in the country for the next fifty years was water-based and partly because Congress seldom exercised its commerce power until late in the nineteenth century, this federal coastal licensing act played a major role in several important Supreme Court cases interpreting the commerce power. Among them were:

• *Gibbons v. Ogden* (1824) in which the Court ruled that Congress's power to regulate navigation between two states preempted the state's power to regulate that subject. *(See "Gibbons v. Ogden," pp. 90–92.)*

• *Willson v. Blackbird Creek Marsh Co.* (1829) in which the Court held that the states could regulate interstate commerce in the absence of conflicting federal legislation. *(See "An Exclusive Power?" p. 330, in Chapter 7.)*

• *Pennsylvania v. Wheeling and Belmont Bridge Co.* (1852) in which

the Court held that a bridge too low to allow ships to pass interfered with Congress's power to regulate commerce through the coastal licensing act. Congress overturned this decision by declaring that the bridge was not an obstruction. *(See "Commerce and Navigation," pp. 92–94.)*

• *Veazie v. Moor* (1852) in which the Court held that the federal act did not automatically entitle licensed vessels to operate on waters that are wholly intrastate.

The 1789 licensing act has been renewed repeatedly but is substantially unchanged in modern times and is still the subject of Supreme Court cases. In *Douglas v. Seacoast Products Inc.* (431 U.S. 265, 1977), for example, the Court ruled that a Virginia law denying certain fishing rights to federally licensed noncitizens was invalid because it conflicted with the act. In *Ray v. Atlantic Richfield Co.* (435 U.S. 151, 1978), the Court struck down a Washington state law requiring state-licensed pilots on tankers entering and leaving Puget Sound. The Court said the law was in conflict with federal power to regulate pilots on tankers licensed under the coastal act.

So far as [the ship] was employed in transporting goods destined for other States, or goods brought from without the limits of Michigan and destined to places within that State, she was engaged in commerce between the States, and however limited that commerce may have been, she was, so far as it went, subject to the legislation of Congress. She was employed as an instrument of that commerce; for whenever a commodity has begun to move as an article of trade from one State to another, commerce in that commodity between the States has commenced.[26]

Control over the nation's waterways eventually led to disputes over who controlled the power generated by those waterways. In 1913 the Court sustained an act of Congress allowing the federal government to sell excess electricity generated as a result of a plan to improve the navigability of a stream. "If the

primary purpose [of the legislation] is legitimate," the Court wrote, "we can see no sound objection to leasing any excess of power."[27]

The Court in 1931 ruled in *Arizona v. California* that it would not inquire into the motives behind congressional waterways projects—in this case the Boulder Canyon Project Act—so long as the waterway concerned was navigable and the project not unrelated to the control of navigation.

Whether the particular structures proposed are reasonably necessary is not for this Court to determine. . . . And the fact that purposes other than navigation will also be served could not invalidate the exercise of the authority conferred even if those other purposes would not alone have justified an exercise of congressional power.[28]

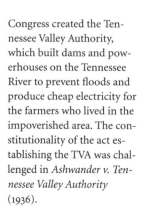

Congress created the Tennessee Valley Authority, which built dams and powerhouses on the Tennessee River to prevent floods and produce cheap electricity for the farmers who lived in the impoverished area. The constitutionality of the act establishing the TVA was challenged in *Ashwander v. Tennessee Valley Authority* (1936).

The Constitution gives Congress no express authority over admiralty and maritime matters. The only mention of the subject is in Article III, Section 2, which states that the "judicial power shall extend . . . to all Cases of admiralty and maritime jurisdiction. . . ." This phrase implies that a body of admiralty and maritime law existed; the question was whether Congress had any power to modify this law.

In the case of *The Lottawanna* (1875), the Court sought to answer the question. The Framers of the Constitution could not have meant to leave changes in this law to the states, Justice Joseph P. Bradley said:

One thing . . . is unquestionable; the Constitution must have referred to a system of law coextensive with, and operating uniformly in, the whole country. It certainly could not have been the intention to place the rules and limits of maritime law under the disposal and regulation of the several states, as that would have defeated the uniformity and consistency at which the Constitution aimed on all subjects of a commercial character affecting the intercourse of the States with each other or with foreign states.[1]

Nor, wrote Bradley, can it be "supposed that the framers . . . contemplate that the law should forever remain unalterable. Congress undoubtedly has authority under the commercial power, if no other, to introduce such changes as are likely to be needed."[2]

But in two cases denying states authority in this field, Bradley declared for the Court that Congress's power over maritime law was based not on the commerce clause but on Article III, Section 2, supplemented by the necessary and proper clause. "As the Constitution extends the judicial power of the United States to 'all cases of admiralty and maritime jurisdiction,' and as this jurisdiction is held to be exclusive, the power of legislation on the same subject must necessarily be in the national legislature and not in the state legislatures," Bradley wrote in 1889.[3] Two years later, he wrote:

It is unnecessary to invoke the power given to Congress to regulate commerce in order to find authority to pass the law in question. The act [being challenged in the case] was passed in amendment of the maritime law of the country, and the power to make such amendments is coextensive with that law. It is not confined to the boundaries or class of subjects which limit and characterize the power to regulate commerce; but, in maritime matters, it extends to all matters and places to which the maritime law extends.[4]

1. *The Lottawanna*, 21 Wall. 558 at 574–575 (1875).
2. Id. at 577; see, for example, *Providence and New York Steamship Co. v. Hill Manufacturing Co.*, 109 U.S. 578 (1883); *The Robert W. Parsons*, 191 U.S. 17 (1903).
3. *Butler v. Boston & S. Steamship Co.*, 130 U.S. 527 at 557 (1889).
4. *In re Garnett*, 141 U.S. 1 at 12 (1891).

In 1933 Congress created the Tennessee Valley Authority (TVA), a three-member board authorized to set up a comprehensive development program for the Tennessee Valley that included flood control, power generation, and agricultural and industrial development. Although its establishment involved no extension of federal authority over navigation, the TVA represented a major source of government-sponsored competition for the private power companies in the area, and its constitutionality was immediately challenged.

In *Ashwander v. Tennessee Valley Authority* (1936), the stockholders of a power company challenged the validity of a contract between the company and the TVA for the sale of the excess energy generated by a TVA-operated dam.[29] The stockholders hoped the Court would declare the act authorizing the TVA unconstitutional, but the Court restricted itself to the narrower issue before it, upholding the TVA's authority to make the contract.

Direct challenges to the constitutionality of the TVA by the power companies failed in 1939 when the Court ruled that the companies did not have a right to be free from competition and therefore had no standing to bring the challenge.[30]

Congressional power over the nation's waterways was made virtually complete in 1940 when the Court held that federal authority even extended to some waters that were not at the time navigable. In *United States v. Appalachian Electric Power Co.*, the Court said the Federal Power Commission had the authority to regulate dam construction on a portion of Virginia's New River that might be made navigable by the dam. "A waterway, otherwise suitable for navigation, is not barred from that classification merely because artificial aids must make the highway suitable for use before commercial navigation may be undertaken," wrote the Court.[31]

Congress, Commerce, and the Railroads

While the extension of Congress's commerce power over the nation's railroads came less directly than over navigation, ultimately it was just as complete.

Like ships, railroads were clearly carriers in interstate commerce. Although privately owned, the rails were public in nature, a fact recognized by the Supreme Court. As it observed in 1897 that interstate railroads were public corporations organized for public reasons and supported by public grants and the use of public lands, the Court clearly viewed the railroads as owing "duties to the public of a higher nature even than that of earning large dividends for their shareholders. The business which the railroads do is of public nature, closely affecting almost all classes in the community."[32]

The first railway lines were strictly local ones, and most early regulation came from the states. As late as 1877, the Court upheld the authority of the states to set rates for hauling freight and passengers within their boundaries.[33] *(See "Railroad Rates," pp. 331–333, in Chapter 7.)*

The business panics of the 1870s and 1880s and the nation's westward expansion led to consolidation of railroads into vast interstate networks. As a result, state regulation became less effective even as the public was demanding tougher rules to prohibit rebate and price-fixing practices that resulted in high costs for shippers and passengers and favored certain companies and regions over others.

Two events shifted the responsibility of regulating the railroads from the states to the federal government. In 1886 the Court essentially ended state authority over interstate railroads by holding that the states could not set even intrastate freight rates for goods traveling interstate. Basing its decision in part on the selective exclusiveness doctrine accepted in the 1851 *Cooley* decision, the Court found that "this species of regulation is one which must be, if established at all, of a general and national character, and cannot be safely and wisely remitted to local rules and local regulations."[34]

CREATION OF THE ICC

That decision in *Wabash, St. Louis & Pacific Ry. Co. v. Illinois* made it necessary for Congress to regulate interstate railroads. The Interstate Commerce Act of 1887 did just that, stipulating that all rates should be reasonable and just, and prohibiting rebate and price-fixing practices. To enforce the law, Congress set up the Interstate Commerce Commission (ICC), which could issue cease-and-desist orders to halt any railroad violating the act's provisions. The ICC was not given specific power to set rates or adjust those it found to be unreasonable, and it was unclear whether Congress intended the commission to have these powers.

At the time the ICC was created and for several years thereafter, a majority of the members of the Supreme Court endorsed the principles of economic laissez-faire, opposing regulation that impinged on the free development of business and industry. Moreover, many of the justices came to the bench from careers in corporate law; three—Chief Justice Melville W. Fuller and Justices Henry B. Brown and George Shiras Jr.—numbered major interstate railroads among their clients. Therefore, it was not surprising that the Court viewed the ICC with little pleasure.

Nonetheless, in 1894 the Court upheld the ICC as an appropriate delegation of congressional power.[35] But three years later, the Court stripped the fledgling commission of its essential regulatory authority, holding that it had no rate-fixing powers. "There is nothing in the act fixing rates," said the Court, and so "no just rule of construction would tolerate a grant of such power by mere implication."[36] The Court majority also thought that the power to establish rates was a legislative function that could not constitutionally be delegated to an executive agency without violating the separation of powers. "The power given [by Congress to the ICC] is partly judicial, partly executive and administrative, but not legislative," the majority wrote.[37] In another 1897 decision, the Court rendered the commission's findings of fact subject to judicial review and reinterpretation.[38]

These cases left the ICC toothless, and the practices that it was created to control resumed with full force. Renewed demands from the public as well as some of the rail companies encouraged Congress to attempt to revive the ICC as an enforcement mechanism. In 1906 it passed the Hepburn Act, which among other things specifically authorized the commission to adjust rates it judged to be unreasonable and unfair.

The following year, the Court signaled that these new powers would pass constitutional muster when it curtailed the extent of review authority it claimed, saying that it would accept the commission's findings of fact as true, confining its review of the commission's decisions to constitutional questions.[39]

In 1910 the Court upheld the commission's authority to adjust interstate railroad rates. The case arose after the ICC substituted a lower rate schedule for that set by several western lines. The Court said that the "commission is the tribunal intrusted with the execution of the interstate commerce laws, and has been given very comprehensive powers in the investigation and determination of the proportion which the rates charged shall bear to the service rendered."[40]

With the agency's rate-adjusting power established, Congress then gave the ICC authority to set original rates. The railroads challenged the act as an unconstitutional delegation of legislative authority, but the Court in 1914 found the contention "without merit." How could it be, the Court asked, that the authority to set rates "was validly delegated so long as it was lodged in the carriers but ceased to be susceptible of delegation the instant it was taken from the carriers for the purpose of being lodged in a public administrative body?"[41]

The Court had now sanctioned what it had forbidden less than twenty years earlier. As one commentator noted, "The Court, which had long accepted the principle of rate regulation by the states, could find no constitutional reason to refuse to accept the same power when exercised unambiguously by the national government."[42]

With federal control established over interstate rail rates, the next question was when and whether the federal government could regulate intrastate rates. The Court addressed this question in the 1913 *Minnesota Rate Cases.* Justice Charles Evans Hughes wrote:

[T]he full control by Congress of the subjects committed to its regulation is not to be denied or thwarted by the commingling of interstate and intrastate operations. This is not to say that the nation may deal with the internal concerns of the State, as such, but that the execution by Congress of its constitutional power to regulate interstate commerce is not limited by the fact that intrastate transactions may have become so interwoven therewith that the effective government of the former incidentally controls the latter.[43]

This statement was extraneous to the case at hand and did not have the full force of law. But it was a harbinger of the Court's ruling the following year in the *Shreveport Rate Cases,* which concerned a railroad based in Shreveport, Louisiana, that carried freight and passengers into East Texas in competition with two Texas-based railroads. The rail rates set by Texas officials for the state lines were substantially lower than those set by the ICC for the interstate Shreveport line, giving the Texas railroads a decisive competitive edge. To equalize the competition, the ICC required the intrastate lines to charge the same rates as the interstate rail company. They protested, but the Court upheld the ICC order:

Wherever the interstate and intrastate transactions of carriers are so related that the government of the one involves the control of the other, it is Congress, and not the State, that is entitled to prescribe the final and dominant rule, for otherwise Congress would be denied the exercise of its constitutional authority and the States, and not the Nation, would be supreme in the national field.[44]

In time, the Court expanded the so-called Shreveport doctrine beyond transportation to justify congressional intervention in other intrastate matters, such as manufacture, that touched on interstate commerce.

The Court endorsed an even greater expansion of federal control over intrastate rail rates in 1922 when it upheld the section of the 1920 Transportation Act that authorized the ICC to set intrastate rates high enough to guarantee the railroads a fair income based on the value of their railway property. The 1920 law had been passed to return the railroads to private control; they had been run by the government during World War I. The Court held that a state burdened interstate commerce by lowering its intrastate rates to undercut interstate rates. Lower intrastate rates meant proportionately less income from intrastate companies, which in turn could force interstate rates higher in order to guarantee the congressionally mandated rate of return. Noting that intrastate systems used the same tracks and equipment as the interstate systems, Chief Justice William Howard Taft wrote: "Congress as the dominant controller of interstate commerce may, therefore, restrain undue limitation of the earning power of the interstate commerce system in doing state work."[45]

On the other hand, the Court in 1924 also upheld the profits recapture clause of the 1920 Transportation Act. This provision authorized the federal government to recover half of all railroad profits above 6 percent. The excess profits were put into a fund to compensate those rail lines earning less than a 4½ percent profit. Stressing the public nature of railroads, a unanimous Court declared that a railroad "was not entitled, as a constitutional right, to more than a fair operating income upon the value of its properties."[46] The recapture provisions proved ineffective, however, and were repealed in 1933.

RAILWAY LABOR

The Court's initial antipathy to organized labor was particularly evident in railway union cases. In 1895 the Court upheld contempt citations against Eugene V. Debs and other leaders of the Pullman strike and sanctioned the use of federal troops to control strike-related violence.

In 1908 the Court handed down two major decisions adverse to labor and its unions. In *Loewe v. Lawlor* it held that certain labor practices, such as organized boycotts, were illegal restraints of trade under the Sherman Antitrust Act of 1890. In *Adair v. United States* it struck down a federal law aimed at strengthening the organized railway labor movement. *(See details of In re Debs, pp. 227–228, in Chapter 5; details of Loewe v. Lawlor, p. 101.)*

"Yellow-Dog Contracts"

To ensure collective bargaining rights for railway employees, an 1898 railway labor law contained a provision prohibiting employers from making contracts that required an employee to promise not to join a union as a condition of employment. These so-called yellow-dog contracts had been effective in management's fight against the railway brotherhoods, and the statute barring them was challenged as exceeding congressional power over interstate commerce and violating the Fifth Amendment "freedom of contract."

In *Adair* the Supreme Court sustained the challenge, striking down that portion of the law. "In our opinion," said Justice John Marshall Harlan, "the prohibition is an invasion of the personal liberty, as well as of the right of property, guaranteed by that [Fifth] Amendment." As to the commerce clause, Harlan said that there was not a sufficient "connection between interstate commerce and membership in a labor organization" to justify outlawing the yellow-dog contracts.[47]

Justice Oliver Wendell Holmes Jr. disagreed, saying that "it hardly would be denied" that labor relations in the railroad industry were closely enough related to commerce to rationalize federal regulation. He also chastised the majority for interfering with congressional policy: "Where there is, or generally is believed to be, an important ground of public policy for restraint [of the freedom of contract], the Constitution does not forbid it, whether this Court agrees or disagrees with the policy pursued."[48]

The same year, the Court, 5–4, declared unconstitutional a second effort to regulate labor-management relations in the rail industry.[49] The 1906 Employers' Liability Act made every common carrier liable for the on-the-job deaths of employees. This act modified two common law practices that held the employer not liable if the employee died through negligence on his own part or on the part of fellow workers.

Finding the law invalid, the Court said the statute infringed states' rights because it covered railway employees not directly involved in interstate commerce as well as those who were. Congress shortly thereafter enacted a second liability act that covered only railway workers in interstate commerce. The Court upheld the modified law in 1912.[50]

As part of the Transportation Act of 1920, Congress created the Railway Labor Board to review and decide railway labor disputes. But in two subsequent cases, the Court held that the board had no power to enforce its decisions.[51]

Congress then enacted the Railway Labor Act setting up new procedures for settling railway labor disputes. Among the provisions of the act was a prohibition against employer interference with the right of employees to select their bargaining representatives.

In 1930 the Court upheld an injunction against railway employers who had violated this ban by interfering with the representative selection process. In so doing, it upheld the constitutionality of the Railway Labor Act as a valid means for Congress to avoid interruptions of interstate commerce by resolving disputes before they resulted in strikes. The Court also distinguished the case from the 1908 *Adair* ruling, rejecting the railroad company's claim that the statute infringed on the employers' Fifth Amendment freedom of contract.

The Railway Labor Act of 1926 does not interfere with the normal exercise of the right of the carrier to select its own employees or to discharge them. The statute is not aimed at this right of the employers but at the interference with the right of employees to have representatives of their own choosing. As the carriers subject to the act have no constitutional right to interfere with the freedom of the employees in making their selections, they cannot complain of the statute on constitutional grounds.[52]

Railway Safety

In 1911 the Court, which already had approved the use of both the federal tax and commerce powers as police tools to regulate such matters as the color of oleo and the interstate shipment of lottery tickets, upheld the application of this same police power to encourage railway safety, even if that meant federal regulation of intrastate equipment and employees. In *Southern Railway Co. v. United States* the Court upheld the federal Safety Appliance Act, which required safety couplers on railroad cars used in interstate commerce. In an opinion that foreshadowed its reasoning in the Minnesota and Shreveport rate cases, the Court ruled that this law also applied to intrastate cars because the cars used in interstate and intrastate traffic were so intermingled that to regulate one necessitated regulation of the other.[53] *(See Minnesota and Shreveport cases, p. 95.)*

In the same year the Court upheld as an appropriate use of the federal police power a federal safety measure setting maximum hours that interstate railway employees could work.

In its power suitably to provide for the safety of employees and travelers, Congress was not limited to the enactment of laws relating to mechanical appliances, but it was also competent to consider, and to endeavor to reduce, the dangers incident to the strain of excessive hours of duty on the part of engineers, conductors, train dispatchers, telegraphers, and other persons embraced within the class defined by the act.[54]

Minimum Wage

In 1917—just a year before the Court would hold that Congress did not have the power to set minimum wages and maximum hours for child laborers—the justices upheld congressional authority to set temporary wage and permanent hour standards for interstate railway employees.[55]

The case of *Wilson v. New* arose after unionized rail workers asked that they be permitted to work eight, not ten, hours, for the same wages they made for the longer day. When their employers refused, the unions threatened a nationwide strike. To avoid such an economic calamity, President Wilson urged Congress to establish an eight-hour workday for railway employees with no reduction in wages pending a six-to-nine-month commission study.

With U.S. entry into World War I imminent, the Court, 5–4, ruled the emergency legislation constitutional. Congress's power to set an eight-hour workday was "not disputable," the Court said, although the question of wages was not so clear-cut. Acknowledging that wage agreements were "primarily private," but emphasizing the public nature of the railways and the failure of the unions and management to settle the dispute, the Court concluded that Congress had the authority

to exert the legislative will for the purpose of settling the dispute, and bind both parties to the duty of acceptance and compliance, to the end that no individual dispute or difference might bring ruin to the vast interests concerned in the movement of interstate commerce.[56]

The four dissenters said the act went beyond the power granted by the commerce clause and furthermore was a violation of due process guaranteed by the Fifth Amendment because it took property (wages) from one party (employers) and gave it to another (employees) by legislative proclamation.

Pensions

The Railroad Retirement Pension Act, which set up a comprehensive pension system for railroad workers, was one of the major pieces of legislation struck down by the Court during its anti–New Deal period of the mid-1930s. A majority of the Court in 1935 found that several parts of the pension plan violated the guarantee of due process. It also held that the pension plan was unrelated to interstate commerce. Speaking for the Court, Justice Owen J. Roberts wrote:

The theory [behind the legislation] is that one who has an assurance against future dependency will do his work more cheerfully, and therefore more efficiently. The question at once presents itself whether the fostering of a contented mind on the part of any employee by legislation of this type, is in any just sense a regulation of interstate commerce. If that question be answered in the affirmative, obviously there is no limit to the field of so-called regulation.[57]

For the minority, Chief Justice Charles Evans Hughes agreed that parts of the plan were unconstitutional. But he refused to hold that the plan itself was altogether outside the scope of congressional commerce powers. "The fundamental consideration which supports this type of legislation is that industry should take care of its human wastage, whether that is due to accident or age," said Hughes, adding that the "expression of that conviction in law is regulation."[58]

Because railroads are interstate carriers and their employees are engaged in interstate commerce, said Hughes, regulation of pension benefits falls under the interstate commerce power.

Federal legislation passed in 1935, 1937, and 1938 set up a railroad employees' pension fund financed by a tax on both employers and employees. The constitutionality of the pension plan was not challenged in the ensuing forty years.

OTHER COMMON CARRIERS

Once it established that Congress has broad authority to regulate the railroads, the Court did not hesitate to permit Congress to regulate other common carriers. The *Pipe Line Cases* (1914) upheld its inclusion of oil pipelines under the coverage of the Interstate Commerce Act. The Standard Oil Company, either through complete or almost complete stock ownership of several pipeline companies, had made itself, in the words of Justice Oliver Wendell Holmes Jr., "master of the only practicable oil transportation between the oil fields east of California and the Atlantic Ocean."

Standard Oil required that any oil transported through the pipelines it owned be sold to it. The Court, speaking through Holmes, rejected the oil company's contention that it was simply transporting its own oil from the well to the refinery.

Holmes said that the "lines we are considering are common carriers now in everything but form" and that Congress has the power under the commerce clause to "require those who are common carriers in substance to become so in form."[59]

The Court subsequently held that the transmission of electric power from one state to another was interstate commerce and that rate regulation of that power by the original state was an interference with and a burden on interstate commerce. The Court also upheld the right of the Federal Power Commission to set the price for natural gas found in one state and sold wholesale to a distributor in another state.[60]

The Court furthermore ruled that forms of communication crossing state borders, though intangible, were nonetheless interstate commerce. In 1878 the Court held that Florida's attempt to exclude out-of-state telegraph companies by granting a monopoly to a Florida company was a burden on interstate commerce.[61] In 1933 the Court upheld federal regulation of radio transmissions. "No state lines divide the radio waves, and national regulation is not only appropriate but essential to the efficient use of radio facilities," the Court said.[62]

Congress and the Trusts

The development of the nation's railroads into interstate networks paralleled and facilitated the growth of "combinations" or "trusts" in many areas of business and industry. Designed to forestall the vicious competition that so often resulted in bankruptcy, the trusts frequently eliminated all competition of any significance and drove the smaller entrepreneur out of the market. By 1901 trusts dominated the steel, oil, sugar, meat packing, leather, electrical goods, and tobacco industries.

The clear threat this development posed to the traditional concept of the free enterprise system and the unsavory methods frequently used by trusts to gain control and enlarge their hold on the industry involved generated considerable public outcry. Congress responded in 1890 by passing the Sherman Antitrust Act, which made illegal "[e]very contract, combination in the form of trust or otherwise, or conspiracy, in restraint of trade or commerce among the several states, or with foreign nations."

COMMERCE AND MANUFACTURE

Like the Interstate Commerce Act, the Sherman Antitrust Act represented a major assumption of power by Congress. Not only the trusts but also economic conservatives in general warned of the day when laissez-faire principles would fall to congressional attempts to control all phases of commercial enterprise, including manufacture and production.

The Court had already spoken to this issue. In *Veazie v. Moor* (1852) it had asserted that the federal power over commerce did not reach manufacturing or production, even of products to be sold in interstate or foreign commerce:

A pretension as far reaching as this, would extend to contracts between citizen and citizens of the same state, would control the pursuits of the planter, the grazier, the manufacturer, the mechanic, the immense operations of the collieries and mines and furnaces of the country; for there is not one of these avocations, the results of which may not become the subject of foreign [or interstate] commerce, and be borne either by turnpikes, canals or railroads, from point to point within the several States, towards an ultimate destination.[63]

This viewpoint became law with the 1888 decision in *Kidd v. Pearson* upholding a state prohibition on producing liquor for interstate shipment. In that case, the Court said:

No distinction is more popular to the common mind, or more clearly expressed in economic and political literature, than that between manufactures and commerce. Manufacture is transformation—the fashioning of raw materials into a change of form for use. The functions of commerce are different. The buying and selling and the transportation incident thereto constitute commerce.[64]

The full significance of *Kidd* became apparent seven years later in 1895 when the Court delivered its first antitrust ruling in *United States v. E. C. Knight Co.*[65]

Defendants in the suit were the American Sugar Refining Company and four smaller Philadelphia processors. Through stockholders' agreements, the larger company had purchased stock in the smaller ones, and the resulting trust controlled more than 90 percent of all the sugar processed in the United States. The federal government's case, prosecuted less than vigorously by Attorney General Richard Olney, who had opposed passage of the Sherman Act and later worked for its repeal, challenged the sugar combination as an illegal restraint of trade in interstate commerce designed to raise sugar prices.

Relying on the narrow interpretation of commerce expounded in *Veazie v. Moor* and *Kidd v. Pearson*, Chief Justice Melville W. Fuller declared again that manufacture was not part of interstate commerce:

Doubtless, the power to control the manufacture of a given thing involves in a certain sense the control of its disposition, but this is a secondary and not the primary sense; and although the exercise of that power may result in bringing the operation of commerce into play, it does not control it, and affects it only incidentally and indirectly.[66]

The fact that the sugar was manufactured for eventual sale, possibly in another state, also had only an indirect effect on interstate commerce, Fuller said:

The fact that an article is manufactured for export to another state does not of itself make it an article of interstate commerce, and the intent of the manufacture does not determine the time when the article or product passes from the control of the state and belongs to commerce.[67]

This view basically limited the definition of interstate commerce to transportation. "Slight reflection will show," said Fuller, that if the federal antitrust law covers all manufacturing combinations "whose ultimate result may effect external commerce, comparatively little of business operations and affairs would be left for state control."[68]

The majority claimed that the combination in question related solely to the acquisition of refineries in Pennsylvania and to sugar processing in that state and was therefore not in interstate commerce and not touchable by the Sherman Act. The state had authority under its police power to relieve the situation if the monopoly burdened intrastate commerce, the Court said.

Fuller's insistence that the states were the proper instruments to deal with manufacturing monopolies ignored the reality that

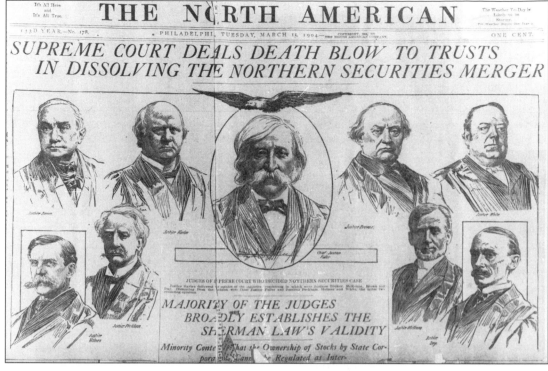

Melville W. Fuller presided over the Supreme Court when it decided a series of cases determining the strength of the Sherman Antitrust Act, which Congress had passed to break up monopolies. When President Theodore Roosevelt dissolved the Northern Securities Company, which held the stock of three major railroads and enjoyed a monopoly over transportation in the Northwest, the Court upheld his action. It ruled that stock transactions were within the realm of interstate commerce, which the federal government may regulate.

states were incapable of regulating the gigantic trusts, which meant there was no effective mechanism for regulation at either the state or national level. As Justice John Marshall Harlan wrote in his vigorous dissent, the public was left "entirely at the mercy" of the trusts.[69]

Fuller's rather artificial distinction between the direct and indirect effects of manufacture on interstate commerce significantly qualified Marshall's opinion that sanctioned congressional regulation of intrastate matters that "affect" other states. It would provide a handy tool for future Courts that wished to thwart congressional regulation of intrastate matters. As Justice Wiley B. Rutledge wrote in 1948: "The *Knight* decision made the [antitrust] statute a dead letter for more than a decade and, had its full force remained unmodified, the Act today would be a weak instrument, as would also the power of Congress to reach evils in all the vast operations of our gigantic national industrial system antecedent to interstate sale and transportation of manufactured products."[70]

While the *Knight* ruling seriously limited the scope of the Sherman Act, it did not declare it unconstitutional, and the Court in 1897 readily applied the law to strike down a combination of railway companies joined together to set freight rates that all the companies would charge.[71]

In 1899 the Court sustained for the first time the use of the Sherman Antitrust Act against an industrial combine. It held that a regional marketing agreement drawn up by six corporations that made and sold iron pipe interstate was an illegal restraint of trade in violation of the act. Justice Rufus W. Peckham said the situation in this case was unlike that in the sugar trust case because the pipe combine "was clearly involved in selling as well as manufacturing."[72]

The Holding Company Case

In 1904 the Court moved further away from the narrow view set out in the sugar ruling. A result of President Theodore Roosevelt's trustbusting campaign, the case of *Northern Securities Co. v. United States* involved the government's challenge to a holding company set up by the major stockholders of two competing railroads to buy the controlling interest of the roads.

By a 5–4 vote, the Court ruled that the holding company was clearly intended to eliminate competition between the two rail lines. "This combination is, within the meaning of the act, a 'trust'; but if not, it is a combination in restraint of interstate and international commerce and that is enough to bring it under the condemnation of the act," wrote Justice Harlan for the majority.[73]

In an important modification of its decision in the sugar trust case, Harlan declared that the holding company, unlike the sugar company, was really in commerce.

The antitrust act, he maintained, applied to "every combination or conspiracy which would extinguish competition between otherwise competing railroads engaged in interstate trade or commerce, and which would in that way restrain such trade or commerce."[74]

Harlan was unimpressed with the defendants' contention that, because the holding company was incorporated by a state, the attempt to enforce the antitrust act was an undue interference with the internal commerce of the state:

An act of Congress constitutionally passed under its power to regulate commerce among the States . . . is binding upon all. . . . Not even a State, still less one of its artificial creatures, can stand in the way of its enforcement. If it were otherwise, the Government and its laws might be prostrated at the feet of local authority.[75]

The four dissenters adhered to the reasoning in the *Knight* case, contending that commerce did not extend to stock transactions or corporations even if they were indirectly involved with matters in interstate commerce.

The "Stream of Commerce"

The following year, with its adoption of the "stream of commerce" doctrine, the Court did away almost entirely with the distinction it had drawn between direct and indirect effects on commerce. *Swift & Co. v. United States* (1905) concerned the "beef trust"—meat packing houses that had made extensive agreements among themselves to control livestock and meat prices in many of the nation's stockyards and slaughtering houses.[76] Swift claimed that its livestock was bought and sold locally and was therefore not in interstate commerce. Justice Oliver Wendell Holmes Jr. wrote the unanimous opinion rejecting that claim: "Although the combination alleged embraces restraint and monopoly of trade within a single State, its effect upon commerce among the States is not accidental, secondary, remote or merely probable," Holmes wrote. He then enunciated what became known as the "stream of commerce" doctrine:

When cattle are sent for sale from a place in one state, with the expectation that they will end their transit, after purchase, in another, and when in effect they do so, with only the interruption necessary to find a purchaser at the stock yards, and when this is a typical constantly recurring course, the current thus existing is a current of commerce among the states, and the purchase of the cattle is a part and incident of such commerce.[77]

This stream of commerce doctrine eventually would be used to rationalize federal regulation of actual production. But long before that, the significance of the *Swift* case had been acknowledged. Chief Justice William Howard Taft wrote in 1923:

[The Swift] case was a milestone in the interpretation of the commerce clause of the Constitution. It recognized the great changes and development in the business of this vast country and drew again the dividing line between interstate and intrastate commerce where the Constitution intended it to be. It refused to permit local incidents of great interstate movement, which, taken alone, were intrastate, to characterize the movement as such. The Swift case merely fitted the commerce clause to the real and practical essence of modern business growth.[78]

The stream of commerce doctrine was reinforced and applied to questions outside the realm of antitrust in 1922 when the Supreme Court upheld federal regulation of business practices that might contribute to an illegal interference with interstate commerce. *Stafford v. Wallace* (1922) concerned the validity of the Packers and Stockyards Act of 1921, which prohibited certain unfair and discriminatory practices believed to lead to restraint of trade.

The Court backed federal regulation, ruling that packers and stockyards were part of the stream of interstate commerce. As Chief Justice Taft put it, the stockyards were "a throat through which the current flows, and the transactions which occur therein are only incidents to this current."[79]

The Court also used the stream of commerce doctrine to uphold the Grain Futures Act of 1922. The shipment of grain to market, its temporary storage, sale, and reshipment in large part to other states were all parts of the flow of interstate commerce, Taft wrote in *Board of Trade of Chicago v. Olsen* (1923). This opinion was somewhat ironic since it effectively overturned an earlier decision, also written by Taft, that held unconstitutional a congressional attempt to regulate boards of trade dealing in commodities futures.[80] *(See details of Board of Trade of Chicago v. Olsen, p. 124.)*

The Court's adoption of this doctrine restricted state power to regulate commerce. This restriction was illustrated in *Lemke v. Farmers Grain Co.* (1922), in which the Court held that wheat delivered and sold by farmers to North Dakota grain elevators and then resold mostly to buyers in Minnesota was in a stream of interstate commerce. Therefore, the Court said, a state statute regulating the price and profit of wheat sales interfered with the free flow of interstate commerce.[81]

THE "RULE OF REASON"

In 1911 the Court abandoned the literal interpretation of the language of the Sherman Antitrust Act set out by Justice Harlan in the *Northern Securities* case. A slim majority of the Court in *Standard Oil Co. v. United States* adopted the controversial "rule of reason," under which only unreasonable combinations and undue restraints of trade are considered illegal.

The Court first discussed the rule in *United States v. Trans-Missouri Freight Association* (1897). There the majority held that a combination of railroads that set freight rates was illegal even though the rates were reasonable. The majority flatly rejected the argument that the Sherman Antitrust Act applied only to unreasonable combinations. Justice Peckham wrote for the Court:

When, therefore, the body of an act pronounces as illegal every contract or combination in restraint of trade or commerce among the several States . . . the plain and ordinary meaning of such language is not limited to that kind of contract alone which is unreasonable restraint of trade, but all contracts are included in such language.[82]

Disagreeing with this interpretation, Justice Edward D. White wrote a dissenting opinion:

The theory upon which the contract is held to be illegal is that even though it be reasonable, and hence valid under the general principles of law, it is yet void, because it conflicts with the act of Congress already referred to. Now, at the outset, it is necessary to understand the full import of this conclusion. As it is conceded that the contract does not unreasonably restrain trade, and that if it does not so unreasonably restrain, it is valid under the general law, the decision, substantially, is that the act of Congress is a departure from the general principles of law, and by its terms destroys the right of individuals or corporations to enter into very many reasonable contracts. But this proposition, I submit, is tantamount to an assertion that the act of Congress is itself unreasonable.[83]

Over the next few years, the majority continued to apply the antitrust act to all combinations, not only those considered unreasonable. But in 1911, in the case that broke up the Standard

Oil complex, the advocates of the rule of reason became the majority.

In an elaborate and lengthy opinion, White, now chief justice, traced the development of the rule of reason in English common law and its use in the United States at the time the antitrust act was enacted. He then declared that because the act did not enumerate the kinds of contracts and combines it embraced, the act "necessarily called for the exercise of judgment which required that some standard should be resorted to" for determining whether the act had been violated.[84] Clearly, he said, Congress meant that standard to be the rule of reason.

Although he concurred with the majority's conclusion that the Standard Oil combination violated the antitrust act, Justice Harlan criticized the majority for "usurpation . . . of the functions" of Congress. By endorsing the rule of reason, Harlan said,

the Court has now read into the act of Congress words which are not to be found there, and has thereby done that which it adjudged . . . could not be done without violating the Constitution, namely, by interpretation of a statute, changed a public policy declared by the legislative department.[85]

Two weeks later the Court again endorsed the rule of reason when it decided that the tobacco trust must be dissolved. White wrote that the rule "was in accord with all the previous decisions of this Court, despite the fact that the contrary view was sometimes erroneously attributed to some of the expressions" in prior decisions.[86]

Harlan's fear, expressed in his *Standard Oil* dissent, that unreasonableness would prove a difficult standard to apply, was not unwarranted. In 1913 the Court found reasonable a combination of manufacturers of shoemaking equipment that controlled between 70 and 80 percent of the market. Because the three manufacturers involved individually controlled about the same percentage of the market before they joined forces, the Court found that their combination sought only greater efficiency.[87]

Under this rule, the Court held in 1920 that the U.S. Steel Corp. was not in violation of the antitrust act, despite the fact that the corporation had attempted to create a monopoly and failed. "It is against monopoly that the statute is directed, not against an expectation of it," the Court wrote.[88]

Declaring in 1918 that "[e]very agreement concerning trade, every regulation of trade, restrains," the Court enunciated the procedure it still uses to determine whether a combination or trust is reasonable. Justice Louis D. Brandeis, for the Court in *Chicago Board of Trade v. United States,* wrote:

The true test of legality is whether the restraint imposed is such as merely regulates and perhaps thereby promotes competition or whether it is such as may suppress or even destroy competition. To determine that question the court must ordinarily consider the facts peculiar to the business to which the restraint is applied; its condition before and after the restraint was imposed; the nature of the restraint and its effect, actual or probable. The history of the restraint, the evil believed to exist, the reasons for adopting the particular remedy, the purpose or end sought to be attained, are all relevant facts.[89]

ANTITRUST AND LABOR

Efforts to include a specific exemption for labor unions in the 1890 Sherman Act were unsuccessful, and, as a result, the act was used almost from its passage against labor, justifying the issuance of orders halting strikes by labor unions. In 1894 a federal circuit court relied partially on the Sherman Act to uphold an injunction against Eugene V. Debs and other leaders of the Pullman strike on the grounds that the railroad workers had conspired to restrain trade. *(See details of In re Debs, pp. 227–228, in Chapter 5.)*

The Supreme Court upheld the injunction against the strike and the resulting convictions for contempt of the order, resting its opinion on the broad grounds that the federal government's responsibility for interstate commerce and the mails gave it the authority to interfere with the strike to prevent obstruction of those functions. Of its failure to look to the antitrust act for authority to issue the injunction, the Court said: "It must not be understood from this that we dissent from the conclusion of that [circuit] court in reference to the scope of the act."[90]

That the Court agreed in the application of the antitrust act against labor unions was made abundantly clear in its 1908 decision in the Danbury Hatters' case *(Loewe v. Lawlor).* A union attempting to organize workers at a hat factory in Danbury, Connecticut, was supported by the American Federation of Labor, which set up boycotts of stores selling the hats in several states.

Speaking for the Court, Chief Justice Melville W. Fuller asserted that because the antitrust act covered "any combination whatever" in restraint of trade, it extended to labor unions whose activities—as in this case—were "aimed at compelling third parties and strangers involuntarily not to engage in the course of trade except on conditions that the combination imposes."[91]

Fuller also employed the stream of commerce doctrine to show that the boycotts, although intrastate, had a direct effect on interstate commerce. "If the purposes of the combinations were, as alleged, to prevent any interstate transportation [of the hats] at all, the fact that the means operated at one end before the physical transportation commenced and at the other end after the physical transportation ended was immaterial," Fuller wrote.[92]

As a result of that decision Congress inserted provisions in the Clayton Antitrust Act of 1914 exempting labor unions from antitrust actions. Section 6 of the act stipulated that labor was "not a commodity or article of commerce." Section 20 provided that "no restraining order or injunction shall be granted by any court of the United States . . . in any case between an employer and employees . . . unless necessary to prevent irreparable injury to property, or to a property right."

The Court did not consider the validity of these sections until 1921 when it narrowed the Clayton Act labor exemption in *Duplex Printing Press Co. v. Deering.* An interstate union wanted to organize workers at a press manufacturer in Michigan. It struck the Michigan plant and also set up a secondary boycott of

The following lists in chronological order major Supreme Court decisions on the power of Congress to tax and regulate commerce.

1824—*Gibbons v. Ogden*—Definition of commerce power: Congress may regulate all commerce affecting more than one state.

1851—*Cooley v. Port Warden of Philadelphia*—"Cooley doctrine" gives Congress authority to regulate areas of commerce national in scope while allowing state to regulate areas local in nature.

1871—*The Daniel Ball*—Forerunner of the "stream of commerce" doctrine: Congress may regulate boat operating solely intrastate but transporting goods in interstate commerce.

1888—*Kidd v. Pearson*—Manufacture is not commerce.

1895—*United States v. E. C. Knight Co.*—Processing is manufacture, not commerce, and does not affect commerce directly; therefore, a sugar processing trust is not a restraint of trade under federal antitrust law.

1903—*Champion v. Ames*—Congress may use commerce power as police power to outlaw interstate sale and shipment of lottery tickets.

1904—*McCray v. United States*—Congress may use tax power as police power to impede sale of yellow oleo.

1905—*Swift & Co. v. United States*—"Stream of commerce" doctrine: Congress may regulate intrastate commerce that is a part of a stream of interstate commerce.

1908—*Adair v. United States*—Labor relations do not directly affect interstate commerce; therefore, Congress may not use its commerce power to prohibit "yellow dog" contracts.

—*Loewe v. Lawlor*—Union boycott is restraint of trade and interstate commerce in violation of antitrust act.

1909—*First Employers' Liability Case*—Congress lacks power to make employers liable for on-job death of railway employees not involved with interstate commerce.

1911—*Standard Oil of New Jersey v. United States*—Adoption of "rule of reason": only unreasonable trusts are violations of antitrust act.

1914—*Shreveport Rate Cases*—Congress may regulate intrastate rail rates when such regulation is necessary to ensure effective regulation of interstate rates.

1917—*Wilson v. New*—Congress may set emergency wage and hour standards for railway workers.

1918—*Hammer v. Dagenhart*—Congress may not use commerce power as police power to set hour standards for child laborers; such use is unconstitutional attempt to regulate manufacturing, which is not commerce.

1921—*Duplex Printing Co. v. Deering*—Clayton Act does not exempt unions involved in boycotts from prosecution under antitrust act.

1922—*Stafford v. Wallace*—"Stream of commerce" doctrine expanded: Congress may regulate unfair business practices in intrastate industries that are part of flow of interstate commerce.

—*Bailey v. Drexel Furniture Co.*—Congress may not use tax power as police power to place high tax on profits of companies employing child laborers; such a use of the tax power is unconstitutional imposition of a penalty, not an effort to raise revenue.

1935—*Schechter Poultry Corp. v. United States*—"Stream of commerce" doctrine does not allow Congress to regulate company receiving goods from out of state but selling them locally.

—*Railroad Retirement Board v. Alton Railroad Co.*—Law establishing pension system for railroad workers exceeds commerce power.

1936—*Carter v. Carter Coal Co.*—Mining is not commerce and does not affect it directly; therefore, Congress may not regulate labor relations in coal mining industry. Tax on coal, refundable if producer complies with regulations, is an unconstitutional penalty.

—*United States v. Butler*—Congress may not regulate agricultural production by taxing food processors in order to pay benefits to farmers who reduce production of certain crops.

1937—*National Labor Relations Board v. Jones & Laughlin Steel Corp.*—Congress may regulate labor relations in manufacturing to prevent possible interference with interstate commerce; *Carter, Schechter* rulings overturned.

—*Helvering v. Davis, Steward Machine Co. v. Davis*—Congress has authority to use tax and spending powers to enact benefit plans as part of Social Security and unemployment compensation statutes; *Butler, Alton* rulings overturned.

1939—*Mulford v. Smith*—Congress may set marketing quotas for agricultural production, regulating commerce at beginning of stream.

1941—*United States v. Darby Lumber Co.*—Congress may use commerce power to prohibit from interstate commerce goods made under substandard labor conditions; *Dagenhart* overturned.

1942—*Wickard v. Filburn*—Congress may regulate agricultural production affecting interstate commerce even if produce is not meant for sale.

1964—*Heart of Atlanta Motel v. United States*—Congress may use commerce power to bar private individuals operating public accommodations that cater to interstate clientele or use goods made in interstate commerce from discriminating on basis of race.

1976—*National League of Cities v. Usery*—Congress exceeds commerce power when it establishes wage and hour standards for state employees; such standards are unconstitutional infringement on state sovereignty.

1985—*Garcia v. San Antonio Metropolitan Transit Authority*—Congress may apply federal minimum wage and hour standards for state employees; the Constitution does not limit this exercise of the commerce power to curtail the power of states; *Usery* overturned.

1995—*United States v. Lopez*—Congress overstepped its authority to regulate interstate commerce when it passed a law banning guns within one thousand feet of a public school; statute had "nothing to do with commerce or any sort of economic enterprise"; Court refers to previous commerce clause rulings: "some of our prior cases have taken long steps down that road, giving great deference to congressional action. The broad language in these opinions has suggested the possibility of additional expansion, but we decline here to proceed any further."

the press markets, primarily in the New York City area. The question was whether the Clayton Act prohibited the issuance of an injunction against those persons engaged in the secondary boycott. With three dissenting votes, the Court ruled that it did not, holding that the Clayton Act exemptions pertained only to legal and normal operations of labor unions. There was nothing in the act, the Court said, "to exempt such an organization or its members from accountability where it or they depart from its normal and legitimate objects and engage in an actual combination or conspiracy in restraint of trade."[93] The secondary boycott was such a restraint, the justices held.

The *Duplex Printing Press* decision was only the first in a series of cases in the 1920s in which the Court continued to use the antitrust laws against labor unions. In 1925 the Court held that an intrastate strike against a coal company directly affected commerce and violated the antitrust laws. In 1927 the Court overruled two lower federal courts to grant an injunction against a stonecutters union that had instituted a secondary boycott of stone cut by nonunion workers.[94]

To force the Court to expand its interpretation of the labor exemption in the Clayton Act, Congress in 1932 passed the Norris-LaGuardia Act, which prohibited the issuance of injunctions by federal courts in labor disputes except where unlawful acts were threatened or committed.

The Court in *Lauf v. E. G. Shinner & Co.* (1938) upheld the act on the grounds that it was within congressional power to determine the jurisdiction of the federal courts.[95] The Court has maintained that ruling in the face of several subsequent challenges to the law.[96]

In 1941 the Court gave additional vigor to the Clayton Act when it sustained a provision of Section 20 that stated that certain acts such as strikes and secondary boycotts would not be considered violations of any federal law.[97]

In 1945 the Court ruled that a union that conspired with manufacturers to boycott a nonunion competitor was violating the Sherman Act.[98] But a union's refusal to work for a trucking firm or to take as members any of the persons who worked for the firm did not violate the antitrust law but was a proper exercise of union rights under the Clayton and Norris-LaGuardia Acts.[99]

The Federal Police Power

The Constitution does not authorize Congress to protect the health, welfare, or morals of the public. Those responsibilities are traditionally left to the states acting through the police power. Nonetheless, Congress in the late 1800s began to develop a federal police power to deal with a growing list of social and economic problems that were national in scope.

The national legislature used its constitutional grant of authority over interstate commerce to justify much of this regulation, claiming power to regulate any matter that at any point was a part of interstate commerce. As scholar Robert K. Carr described it:

Where the commerce power had previously been used primarily to regulate, foster or promote commerce for its own sake, . . . it now seemed that Congress might seek to regulate social and economic practices within the states, provided only that at some point they involved a crossing of state lines.[100]

Congress's initial attempts to exercise a police power were largely unsuccessful; the Court ruled that such regulations could apply only in areas of the United States outside of state boundaries, such as the District of Columbia. In 1870, for example, the Court vitiated most of a federal statute barring the sale of certain illuminating oils "except so far as the [prohibition] operates within the United States, but without the limits of any State."[101]

The Court explained:

[The] grant of power to regulate commerce among the States has always been understood as limited by its terms; and as a virtual denial of any power to interfere with the internal trade and business of the separate states; except, indeed, as a necessary and proper means for carrying into execution some other power expressly granted or vested.[102]

The first sign of change in the Court's view on this matter came in 1902, when it upheld a federal statute prohibiting the transportation of diseased cattle in interstate commerce.[103] But it was a controversial 1903 case that was of greater significance. The Court heard arguments three times in *Champion v. Ames (The Lottery Case)*, a challenge to Congress's 1895 act making it illegal to transport lottery tickets from a state or foreign country into another state.[104] The statute had been challenged on the grounds that lottery tickets were not commerce, that it was up to the states to regulate them, and that Congress could not prohibit commerce, in any case.

The five-man majority, speaking through Justice John Marshall Harlan, declared that lottery tickets were commerce subject to regulation by Congress. Federal regulation, Harlan said, did not interfere with intrastate commerce in lottery tickets and so did not infringe on states' right to regulate that traffic. In effect, he said, federal regulation supplemented state regulation:

As a State may, for the purpose of guarding the morals of its own people, forbid all sales of lottery tickets within its limits, so Congress, for the purpose of guarding the people of the United States against the "wide-spread pestilence of lotteries" and to protect the commerce which concerns all the States, may prohibit the carrying of lottery tickets from one State to another.[105]

Recalling John Marshall's declaration that the commerce power is plenary and complete, Harlan said that the power to regulate included the power to prohibit.

If Congress finds a subject of interstate commerce noxious, "can it be possible that it must tolerate the traffic, and simply regulate the manner in which it may be carried on?" Harlan asked.[106] On the contrary, he said, "we know of no authority in the Courts to hold that the means thus devised [prohibition of shipment] are not appropriate and necessary to protect the country . . . against a species of interstate commerce which . . . has become offensive to the entire people of the nation."[107] Harlan also noted that the Court had sustained the Sherman Antitrust Act, which prohibited contracts that restrained interstate commerce. *(See "Congress and the Trusts," pp. 98–103.)*

COMMERCE AND PROSTITUTION

Congressional efforts to curb prostitution were thwarted at first by the Supreme Court. In 1907 Congress made it illegal for anyone to harbor an alien woman for purposes of prostitution within three years after her arrival in the country. But two years later the Court held, 6–3, that regulating houses of prostitution was an internal state affair beyond the reach of Congress.[1]

Continuing concern over reports of women held as virtual slaves and forced to engage in prostitution led to adoption in 1910 of the Mann Act, which punished any person found guilty of transporting women for immoral purposes in interstate or foreign commerce. The Court in *Hoke v. United States* (1913) unanimously upheld the act, without referring to its decision in the earlier prostitution case. "Of course, it will be said that women are not articles of merchandise but this does not affect the analogy of the cases," wrote Justice Joseph McKenna. He added:

[I]f the facility of interstate transportation can be taken away from the demoralization of lotteries, the debasement of obscene literature, the contagion of diseased cattle or persons, the impurity of food and drugs, the like facility can be taken away from the systematic enticement to and the enslavement in prostitution and debauchery of women, and, more insistently, of girls.[2]

In subsequent cases, the Court backed enforcement of the Mann Act against persons transporting women across state lines for immoral purposes, although there was no commercial gain involved, and against Mormons who transported their plural wives across state lines.[3]

1. *Keller v. United States,* 213 U.S. 138 (1909).
2. *Hoke v. United States,* 227 U.S. 308 at 322 (1913).
3. *Caminetti v. United States,* 242 U.S. 470 (1917); *Cleveland v. United States,* 329 U.S. 14 (1946).

Justice Harlan anticipated the dissenters' predictions that the use of the commerce power as a police tool would "defeat the operation" of the Tenth Amendment, which reserved to the states powers not granted to the federal government. While plenary and complete, the power of Congress over interstate commerce is not arbitrary, Harlan said, and may not infringe rights protected by the Constitution.

This decision, as historian Charles Warren wrote, "disclosed the existence of a hitherto unsuspected field of national power." Warren continued:

The practical result of the case was the creation of a federal police power—the right to regulate the manner of production, manufacture, sale and transportation of articles and the transportation of persons, through the medium of legislation professing to regulate commerce between the states. Congress took very swift advantage of the new field thus opened to it.[108]

The Court sustained many of the statutes Warren referred to, including the Pure Food and Drug Act of 1906, the Mann Act, which penalized persons convicted of transporting women across state lines for immoral purposes, and two statutes regulating safety for railway workers.[109] (*See box, Commerce and Prostitution, this page.*)

For a dozen years the federal police power appeared well entrenched. But in 1918 the Court rendered a decision that left further expansion of that power in doubt. The federal police power collided with states' rights and came out the loser.

CHILD LABOR

In *Hammer v. Dagenhart* the Court struck down a 1916 act of Congress that sought to discourage employment of children by prohibiting the shipment in interstate commerce of any products made in factories or mines that employed children under age fourteen or allowed children aged fourteen to sixteen to work more than a limited number of hours per week.[110] The statute was contested by Roland Dagenhart, whose two teenage sons worked in a North Carolina cotton mill. Dagenhart sought an injunction against U.S. District Attorney W. C. Hammer to prevent him from enforcing the act and costing his sons their jobs. (*See box, Doubtful Victory, p. 105.*)

By a 5–4 vote the Court declared the 1916 law unconstitutional. Congress, Justice William R. Day said, had exceeded its authority when it prohibited goods made by children from interstate commerce. The power to regulate commerce is the authority "to control the means by which commerce is carried on," and not the "right to forbid commerce from moving," Day said.[111]

This statement required Day to distinguish his holding in the child labor act from the cases in which the Court had sanctioned a congressional prohibition against the movement of items such as lottery tickets and adulterated food in interstate commerce. Day did so by declaring these latter articles harmful in themselves and asserting that their regulation "could only be accomplished by prohibiting the use of the facilities of interstate commerce to effect the evil intended." That "element is wanting in the present case," he said; the goods manufactured by children "are of themselves harmless."[112]

Day did not stop at this point but went on to examine the reasons Congress enacted the law. "The act in its effect does not regulate transportation among the states," Day said, "but aims to standardize the ages at which children may be employed in mining and manufacturing within the states."[113]

Retreating to the earlier distinction between commerce and manufacture, Day said mining and manufacture were subject only to state regulation. The fact that goods "were intended for interstate commerce transportation does not make their production subject to federal control under the commerce power," he maintained.[114]

In conclusion, the justice stated that the act "not only transcends the authority delegated to Congress over commerce but also exerts a power as to a purely local matter to which the federal authority does not extend."[115]

Justice Oliver Wendell Holmes's dissenting opinion left little doubt that the minority believed the majority's ruling had been motivated by the five justices' personal opposition to the law. On its face, Holmes said, the act was indisputably within the federal commerce power. That being the case, he said, "it seems to me that it is not made any less constitutional because of the indirect effects that it may have (that is, the discouragement of child labor), however obvious it may be that it will have those effects."[116]

In support of this proposition, Holmes cited a number of cases in which the Court had upheld a regulatory measure without considering the probable effect of the measure.

Nor was it important that the evil was not itself in interstate transportation. "It does not matter whether the supposed evil precedes or follows the transportation," Holmes declared. "It is enough that in the opinion of Congress that transportation encourages the evil."[117]

Holmes also maintained that Congress and not the Court should determine when prohibition was necessary to effective regulation, adding that "if there is any matter upon which civilized countries have agreed . . . it is the evil of premature and excessive child labor."[118]

DOUBTFUL VICTORY

Five years after the Supreme Court's decision in *Hammer v. Dagenhart* striking down the child labor law, a journalist interviewed Reuben Dagenhart, whose father had sued to prevent Congress from interfering with his sons' jobs in a North Carolina cotton mill. Reuben was twenty when he was interviewed. Excerpts follow:

"What benefit . . . did you get out of the suit which you won in the United States Supreme Court?"

"I don't see that I got any benefit. I guess I'd have been a lot better off if they hadn't won it.

"Look at me! A hundred and five pounds, a grown man and no education. I may be mistaken, but I think the years I've put in the cotton mills have stunted my growth. They kept me from getting any schooling. I had to stop school after the third grade and now I need the education I didn't get."

"Just what did you and John get out of that suit, then?" he was asked.

"Why, we got some automobile rides when them big lawyers from the North was down here. Oh yes, and they bought both of us a Coca-Cola! That's all we got out of it."

"What did you tell the judge when you were in court?"

"Oh, John and me never was in court. Just Paw was there. John and me was just little kids in short pants. I guess we wouldn't have looked like much in court. . . . We were working in the mill while the case was going on."

Reuben hasn't been to school in years, but his mind has not been idle.

"It would have been a good thing for all the kids in this state if that law they passed had been kept. Of course, they do better now than they used to. You don't see so many babies working in the factories, but you see a lot of them that ought to be going to school."

SOURCE: *Labor*, November 17, 1923, 3, quoted in Leonard F. James, *The Supreme Court in American Life*, 2d ed. (Glenview, Ill.: Scott, Foresman, 1971), 74.

The federal law did not interfere with the state police power, asserted Holmes, and in any event the Court had made clear that the exercise of the federal commerce power could not be limited by its potential for interfering with intrastate regulation of commerce. States, he said,

may regulate their internal affairs and their domestic commerce as they like. But when they seek to send their products across the State line they are no longer within their rights. . . . Under the Constitution such commerce belongs not to the States but to Congress to regulate. It may carry out its views of public policy whatever indirect effect they may have upon the activities of the state.[119]

Congressional efforts to circumvent the *Hammer v. Dagenhart* ruling proved unsuccessful. Congress in 1919 sought to use its tax power to discourage the use of child labor by placing a high tax on goods that had been manufactured in factories employing youngsters, but the Court declared the tax unconstitutional.[120] Congress then passed a constitutional amendment forbidding the employment of children, but the states had not ratified it by the time the Court itself in *United States v. Darby Lumber Co.* (1941) overturned its own ruling.[121] (*See* "Child Labor," pp. 104–105; "Wages and Hours," pp. 110–111.)

EFFECT OF *DAGENHART*

The Court did not rely on the *Dagenhart* ruling much as a precedent, the major exception being the invalidation of the child labor tax law. The justices continued to sanction use of the commerce power as a police tool when it was applied to universally recognized social evils. A few weeks after the child labor case decision, the Court unanimously upheld the constitutionality of the 1906 Meat Inspection Act, which called for local inspection of meat products and banned those rejected or not inspected from interstate commerce.[122] Subsequent decisions approved federal statutes prohibiting the interstate transportation of stolen cars, making transportation of kidnapped persons in interstate commerce a federal crime, and preventing the interstate shipment of convict-made goods to those states that prohibited them.[123] Like child labor, the goods involved in these three cases—cars, kidnapped persons, and horse collars—were not in and of themselves harmful. Yet the Court upheld the federal regulation in all three cases. As it explained in the stolen cars case:

Congress can certainly regulate interstate commerce to the extent of forbidding and punishing the use of such commerce as an agency to promote immorality, dishonesty or the spread of any evil or harm to the people of other states from the state of origin. In doing this, it is merely exercising the police power, for the benefit of the public, within the field of interstate commerce.[124]

More recently, the Court sanctioned use of the police power in 1971 when it sustained provisions of the 1968 Consumer Credit Protection Act that prohibited loan-sharking. Although individual loan-sharking activities might be wholly intrastate, the Court said that it was in a "class of activity" that affected interstate commerce and thus could be regulated under the commerce power.[125]

New Deal and Old Power

In the decades between the *Dagenhart* ruling and the Great Depression, Congress made little use of the commerce power to regulate business. When, under President Franklin D. Roosevelt's guidance, Congress attempted to use federal regulation to stimulate economic recovery, the Supreme Court, still dominated by a small majority strongly disposed toward protection of private property rights—and states' rights—again resisted. The resulting collision—and the threat by President Roosevelt to increase the size of the Court to ensure approval of his New Deal legislation—marked the birth of the modern commerce power. In 1937 the Court accepted Justice Benjamin N. Cardozo's view that the power was equal to the nation's problems. In subsequent years, the Court has upheld the use of the commerce power to deal with problems ranging from civil rights violations to environmental pollution.

BLACK MONDAY

The centerpiece of Roosevelt's recovery program was the National Industrial Recovery Act (NIRA) of 1933. It declared a "national emergency productive of widespread unemployment and disorganization of industry, which burdens interstate and foreign commerce, affects the public welfare and undermines the standards of living of the American people." To speed industrial recovery, the NIRA authorized the president to approve codes of fair competition. Each of these codes, among other conditions, had to contain hour and wage standards for workers in the particular industry.

The first inkling of how the Supreme Court would treat the NIRA came in January 1935 when it declared the "hot oil" section of the law an unconstitutional delegation of legislative authority. The provisions permitted the president to prohibit the interstate transportation of oil produced in excess of amounts allowed by the states. The Hot Oil case did not deal, however, with the codes of fair competition which the NIRA authorized.[126] *(See "'Hot' Oil," p. 83.)*

Five months later, on what came to be known as "black Monday," the Court declared the entire NIRA invalid. *Schechter Poultry Corp. v. United States* was a test case brought by the government in hope that a favorable response from the Court would encourage industry compliance, which had been flagging.[127] The circumstances involved, however, made it less than an ideal test.

The Schechter brothers bought live poultry shipped into New York City largely from points outside of the state, slaughtered it, then sold it locally. They were accused of violating several provisions of the New York City live poultry industry code, including the wage and hour standards and the prohibition against "straight killing" or allowing a customer to select individual poultry for slaughter. They were also charged with selling an "unfit chicken" to a local butcher. As a result, the suit was quickly dubbed the "Sick Chicken" case.

The Supreme Court unanimously held that the Schechters' operation was a local concern that did not directly affect interstate commerce. Federal regulation through the fair competition codes was, therefore, an unconstitutional abridgment of states' rights.

The Court noted that the provisions of the code the Schechters were charged with violating applied to the slaughtering operation and subsequent sale in local markets, activities that the Court said were not in interstate commerce. The Court also denied that these activities were part of the stream of commerce. Chief Justice Charles Evans Hughes wrote:

The Court in *Schechter Poultry Corp. v. United States* (1935) declared unconstitutional the National Industrial Recovery Act, a major piece of New Deal legislation. In this photograph, A. L. A. Schechter *(center)* of Schechter Poultry Corporation confers with his attorneys Joseph Heller *(left)* and Frederick Wood, May 2, 1935.

The mere fact that there may be a constant flow of commodities into a state does not mean that the flow continues after the property has arrived and has become commingled with the mass of property within the state and is there held solely for local disposition and use.[128]

The Court acknowledged that Congress had power not only to regulate interstate commerce but also to protect interstate commerce from burden or injury imposed by those engaged in intrastate activities. The effect of the burden must be direct, however, said the Court, recalling the Court's distinction between direct and indirect effects first discussed in the 1895 sugar trust case. Said Hughes:

In determining how far the federal government may go in controlling intrastate transactions upon the ground that they "affect" interstate commerce, there is a necessary and well-established distinction between direct and indirect effects. The precise line can be drawn only as individual cases arise, but the distinction is clear in principle.[129]

That distinction, the Court said, was essential to maintenance of the federal system. Without it the federal government would have complete power over domestic affairs of the states and there would be a centralized government. "It is not the province of the Court," Hughes wrote, "to consider the economic advantages or disadvantages of such a centralized system. It is sufficient to say that the Federal Constitution does not provide for it."[130]

The Court found no way that the alleged violations by the Schechters directly affected interstate commerce. It also held that the delegation to the president by Congress of the authority to establish the codes of competition was excessive and therefore unconstitutional. On both these grounds, it declared the NIRA invalid. *(See "Delegations to Private Parties," "Wartime Delegations," and "Delegations to States," pp. 85–86.)*

Some scholars have argued that the Court could have upheld the NIRA so far as it was based on the federal power over interstate commerce. Robert Carr, for instance, has suggested that the justices could have extended the stream of commerce doctrine to cover the Schechters' business even though it was at the end of the stream.[131]

It should not be overlooked, however, that the Court was unanimous and that the justices considered more likely to approve the New Deal legislation found the NIRA, as presented in the sick chicken case, unconstitutional. Justice Benjamin N. Cardozo, in a concurring opinion for himself and Justice Harlan Fiske Stone, claimed that the distinction between direct and indirect effects on commerce was a matter of degree. But, he added, "[t]o find immediacy or directness [in this case] is to find it almost everywhere."[132]

COAL CODES

No such unanimity marked the next New Deal decision. In *Carter v. Carter Coal Co.* (1936) the Court struck down the 1935 Bituminous Coal Conservation Act, which declared that the production and distribution of coal so closely affected interstate commerce that federal regulation was necessary to stabilize the industry.[133] Passed despite the adverse ruling in *Schechter*, the act authorized fixed prices for coal, provided for collective bargaining rights for coal miners, allowed a two-thirds majority of the industry to establish wage and hour standards for the entire industry, and established a tax scheme to ensure compliance with the regulations.

Divided 6–3, the Court in May 1936 declared the act unconstitutional. Justice George Sutherland, speaking for the majority, focused first on the labor relations provisions. He declared that mining was production, not commerce, and that the relation between a mine operator and mine workers was purely local in character.

Since mining itself was not in interstate commerce, Sutherland continued, it became necessary to determine if its effect on that commerce was direct. Here, Sutherland set forth a definition of a direct effect that turned not on the degree to which a thing affected interstate commerce but on the manner in which the effect occurred. Sutherland wrote:

The word "direct" implies that the activity or condition invoked or blamed shall operate proximately—not mediately, remotely, or collaterally—to produce the effect. . . . And the extent of the effect bears no logical relation to its character. The distinction between a direct and an indirect effect turns, not upon the magnitude of either the cause or the effect, but entirely upon the manner in which the effect has been brought about.[134]

It made no difference, said Sutherland, whether one man mined coal for sale in interstate commerce or several men mined it. Labor problems were local controversies affecting local production. "Such effect as they have upon commerce, however extensive it may be, is secondary and indirect," Sutherland proclaimed.[135]

Nor was mining a part of the stream of commerce. Looking to *Schechter*, Sutherland said:

The only perceptible difference between that case and this is that in the Schechter case, the federal power was asserted with respect to commodities which had come to rest after their interstate transportation; while here, the case deals with commodities at rest before interstate commerce has begun. That difference is without significance.[136]

Having declared the labor provisions an invalid exercise of federal power under the commerce clause, Sutherland proceeded to hold the price-fixing provisions invalid on the grounds that they were so dependent on the labor provisions, they could not stand on their own. This he determined despite a severability clause in the legislation that said the price-fixing provisions could stand if other provisions were found unconstitutional. *(See box, Severability: Divided It Stands, p. 123.)*

The majority also held the statute an unconstitutional delegation of legislative powers to the executive branch and to the coal industry. It further invalidated the taxes on the basis that the tax provisions were not for the purpose of raising revenue but to coerce compliance with the regulations. Because the commerce power had been exercised unconstitutionally, the tax provisions were also invalid, the majority said.

In a concurring opinion, Chief Justice Hughes disagreed with the majority ruling that the price-fixing provisions were

REGULATION OF FOREIGN COMMERCE

From the beginning, the federal power to regulate foreign commerce has been complete.

The constitutional grant "comprehend[s] every species of commercial intercourse between the United States and foreign nations. No sort of trade can be carried on between this country and any other, to which this power does not extend," wrote Chief Justice John Marshall in *Gibbons v. Ogden* (1824), the classic interpretation of the commerce clause.[1]

Congress may set tariffs, regulate international shipping, aviation, and communications, and establish embargoes against unfriendly countries. In conjunction with its powers to coin money, regulate its value, and borrow it, Congress may authorize U.S. participation in international financing, banking, and monetary affairs.

Exercise of the power has seldom been challenged in the courts; it was not until 1928 that protective tariffs, long a matter of controversy, came before the Supreme Court and then as a test of the taxing power.[2]

Congressional grants of authority to the president to adjust tariff schedules at his discretion have been upheld against challenges that they were improper delegations of power.[3] *(See "Delegation of Power," pp. 226–227, in Chapter 5.)*

Federal power over foreign commerce includes the power to prohibit that commerce. "The Congress may determine what articles may be imported into this country and the terms upon which importation is permitted. No one can be said to have a vested right to carry on foreign commerce with the United States," wrote the Court in 1933.[4]

Under this principle, the Court upheld federal statutes prohibiting the importation of inferior and impure tea, prize fight films, and natural sponges from the Gulf of Mexico and the Straits of Florida.[5]

The federal authority over foreign commerce is exclusive. The Constitution expressly forbade the states to enter into treaties with foreign nations or to lay imposts and duties on foreign imports and exports.

The "original package" doctrine first put forward by Chief Justice Marshall in 1827 undergirds the prohibition against state duties on imports, although that doctrine has been diluted in recent years and some state taxing of imported goods permitted.[6] *(See "Taxing Imports," pp. 344–346, in Chapter 7.)*

However, in the absence of federal regulation, the Supreme Court has allowed state inspection and quarantine laws to stand, even though they might affect foreign commerce.[7]

1. *Gibbons v. Ogden,* 9 Wheat. 1 at 193–194 (1824).
2. *J. W. Hampton Jr. & Co. v. United States,* 276 U.S. 394 (1928).
3. *Field v. Clark,* 143 U.S. 649 (1892); *Buttfield v. Stranahan,* 192 U.S. 470 (1904); *J. W. Hampton Jr. & Co. v. United States,* 276 U.S. 394 (1928).
4. *Board of Trustees v. United States,* 289 U.S. 48 at 57 (1933).
5. *Buttfield v. Stranahan,* 192 U.S. 470 (1904); *Weber v. Freed,* 239 U.S. 325 (1915); *The Abby Dodge,* 223 U.S. 166 (1912).
6. *Brown v. Maryland,* 12 Wheat. 419 (1827); *Michelin Tire Corp. v. Wages,* 423 U.S. 276 (1976); *R. J. Reynolds Tobacco Co. v. Durham County, N.C.,* 479 U.S. 130 (1986).
7. *Gibbons v. Ogden,* 9 Wheat. 1 (1824); *Compagnie Francaise de Navigation a Vapeur v. Louisiana State Board of Health,* 186 U.S. 380 at 385 (1902).

inseparable from the labor provisions. But he agreed that the distinction between direct and indirect effects on interstate commerce was a matter of kind and not degree.

"The power to regulate interstate commerce embraces the power to protect that commerce from injury," Hughes said, then added:

But Congress may not use this protective authority as a pretext . . . to regulate activities and relations within the states which affect interstate commerce only indirectly. . . . If the people desire to give Congress the power to regulate industries within the State, and the relations of employers and employees in those industries, they are at liberty to declare their will in the appropriate manner, but it is not for the Court to amend the Constitution by judicial decision.[137]

As historians Alfred H. Kelly and Winfred A. Harbison noted:

The most extraordinary thing about Sutherland's opinion was the absurdity of his contention that while the labor provisions of the act were only indirectly related to interstate commerce, they were nonetheless so intimately related to those portions of the law dealing with interstate commerce as to be inseparable from them.[138]

In fact, Sutherland never discussed whether the price-fixing provisions were in interstate commerce or directly affected it. If he had, he would have had to reconcile his opinion with the *Shreveport Rate Cases* precedent permitting federal regulation of intrastate matters that are inextricably mingled with interstate commerce. *(See "Creation of the ICC," pp. 95–96.)*

Cardozo in dissent used this precedent to prove the validity of the price-fixing provisions. The provisions, he wrote, were valid as they applied to transactions in interstate commerce and to transactions in intrastate commerce if such local transactions "directly or intimately affected" interstate commerce.

Joined by Justices Stone and Louis D. Brandeis, Cardozo then reiterated his *Schechter* opinion that the distinction between direct and indirect effects was one of degree, not kind. "At all events," wrote Cardozo, "'direct' and 'indirect' . . . must not be read too narrowly. The power is as broad as the need that evokes it."[139]

In this instance, Cardozo said, that need was great:

Congress was not condemned to inaction in the face of price wars and wage wars. . . . Commerce had been choked and burdened; its normal flow had been diverted from one state to another; there had been bankruptcy and waste and ruin alike for capital and for labor. . . . After making every allowance for difference of opinion as to the most efficient cure, the student of the subject is confronted with the indisputable truth that there were ills to be corrected, and ills that had a direct relation to the maintenance of commerce among the states without friction or diversion. An evil existing, and also the power to correct it, the lawmakers were at liberty to use their own discretion in the selection of the means.[140]

Cardozo's opinion recognized what the majority failed to acknowledge—that the local but widespread economic problems of the depression were national in scope. In protecting state sovereignty and private property rights, the majority almost totally rejected the concept of national supremacy.

It did reject the theory that Congress might act to protect

what it perceived to be the general welfare. It was this attitude that led to Roosevelt's attempt to moderate the conservative voice of the Court through his Court-packing plan. *(See "The Court and the Roosevelt Revolution," pp. 248–252, in Chapter 5.)*

Roosevelt, to use an apt cliché, lost the battle but won the war.

Congress rejected his Court-packing scheme, but not before one of the justices who generally voted with the conservative majority, Owen J. Roberts, did an about-face to convert the more liberal minority into a majority. In April 1937, Cardozo's reasoning in the *Carter* dissent became the majority opinion in a case upholding the 1935 National Labor Relations Act (NLRA).[141]

A NATIONAL LABOR LAW

Passed in 1935, the NLRA declared that denying the rights of workers to organize and bargain collectively caused strikes and other labor problems that directly burdened and obstructed interstate commerce. To eliminate the obstruction and guarantee workers' rights, Congress prohibited both employees and employers from engaging in specified unfair labor practices. The act also established the National Labor Relations Board (NLRB) to administer the law and hear charges of violations.

In view of the precedents established in the *Schechter* and *Carter* cases, it seemed likely that the Supreme Court would also invalidate the NLRA's application to employers and employees engaged in manufacturing and production. The question was put to the Court in 1937 in the midst of public and congressional debate over Roosevelt's Court-packing plan.

The case of *NLRB v. Jones & Laughlin Steel Corp.* arose after the steel company fired ten union employees from one of its Pennsylvania factories. The employees claimed they had been let go solely because they were union members. The NLRB agreed and ordered the steel company to stop discriminating against its union workers. When the company failed to comply, the NLRB asked a court of appeals to enforce its order.

Relying on the *Carter* decision, the court refused the petition, saying Congress did not have the power to regulate local labor relations.

Arguing the case before the Supreme Court, attorneys for the NLRB contended that the Pennsylvania factory was in a stream of commerce, receiving raw materials from and transporting its products to other states through interstate commerce. The corporation argued that the NLRA was regulating labor relations, a local concern not subject to federal regulation.

The Supreme Court, 5–4, reversed the lower court, sustaining the National Labor Relations Act. Joining Justices Cardozo, Brandeis, and Stone to make a majority were Chief Justice Hughes and Justice Roberts. Hughes wrote the majority opinion, relying to a great extent on the reasoning of Cardozo's dissent in the *Carter Coal* case.

Reiterating that Congress has the authority to regulate intrastate matters that directly burdened or obstructed interstate commerce, Hughes said the fact that the employees were en-

gaged in the local activity of manufacturing was not "determinative."

The question was what effect a strike of the factory would have on interstate commerce. Chief Justice Hughes continued:

In view of respondent's far-flung activities, it is idle to say that the effect would be indirect or remote. It is obvious that it would be immediate and might be catastrophic. We are asked to shut our eyes to the plainest facts of our national life and to deal with the question of direct and indirect effects in an intellectual vacuum. . . . When industries organize themselves on a national scale, making their relation to interstate commerce the dominant factor in their activities, how can it be maintained that their industrial labor relations constitute a forbidden field into which Congress may not enter when it is necessary to protect interstate commerce from the paralyzing consequences of industrial war? We have often said that interstate commerce itself is a practical conception. It is equally true that interferences with that commerce must be appraised by a judgment that does not ignore actual experience.[142]

Hughes's majority opinion did not specifically overturn the Court's holdings in *Schechter* and *Carter Coal*. But it did do away with Justice Sutherland's artificial and unrealistic definition of what intrastate matters directly affected interstate commerce.

Once again the Supreme Court held that the distinction was a matter of degree to be determined on a case-by-case basis, and not a matter of kind, which did not take into account the realities of the economic system and the nation's needs.

For the four dissenters, Justice James C. McReynolds said he found no material difference between the *Jones & Laughlin* case and those of *Schechter* and *Carter Coal*. "Every consideration brought forward to uphold the Act before us was applicable to support the Acts held unconstitutional in causes decided within two years," he wrote.[143]

The steel company was not in the middle of the stream of commerce but at the end of one stream when it received the raw materials and at the beginning of a second when it shipped its finished product, the minority justices wrote. As a result, the company was not in interstate commerce, and its labor relations were not regulable by the federal government but by the states, McReynolds said. To uphold the NLRA was to give its board "power of control over purely local industry beyond anything heretofore deemed permissible."[144]

Other Labor Cases

The same day as *Jones & Laughlin,* the Supreme Court upheld the NLRB in four other cases. One case involved a large trailer manufacturing company, and another a men's clothing manufacturer, both of which sold a large portion of their products interstate.[145] Nevertheless, a labor strike in either of these businesses would not have the catastrophic effect on the national economy of a steel strike, and so the effect of these decisions was to broaden the Court's holding in the steel case.

The third case involved the Associated Press (AP).[146] Holding that interstate communication of any sort was interstate commerce, the Court rejected the AP's argument that the labor law violated the news association's First Amendment right to freedom of press. The NLRA, the Court said, has "no relation whatever to the impartial distribution of news." In the fourth case, the Court held that a small company running buses between Virginia and the District of Columbia was an instrumentality of interstate commerce subject to the labor relations act.[147]

Three later NLRB cases also are noteworthy. In *Santa Cruz Fruit Packing Co. v. National Labor Relations Board* (1938), the Court upheld enforcement of the NLRA against a California fruit and vegetable packing company that sold less than 50 percent of its goods in interstate and foreign commerce. A company lockout of union employees resulted in a strike and refusal by warehouse workers, truckers, and stevedores to handle the packed food.

"It would be difficult to find a case in which unfair labor practices had a more direct effect upon interstate . . . commerce," the Court wrote.[148] The *Santa Cruz* case is significant because the labor problem stopped the goods at the beginning of the stream of interstate commerce—unlike *Jones & Laughlin* where a strike would have stopped the goods in midstream.

In the second case, *Consolidated Edison v. National Labor Relations Board* (1938), a utility that was not in interstate commerce was nevertheless subject to the NLRA because of "the dependence of interstate and foreign commerce upon the continuity of the service."[149] The utility provided electricity, gas, and steam to three railroads, the Port of New York, several steamship piers, two telegraph companies, and a telephone company.

In the third case, *National Labor Relations Board v. Fainblatt* (1939), the Court ruled that the NLRA covered unfair labor practices by a clothing manufacturer that resulted in a strike that reduced significantly the amount of goods normally available for shipment in interstate commerce. The manufacturer's contention that he only indirectly affected interstate commerce because only a small portion of his product was shipped interstate was to no avail. The Court said:

The power of Congress to regulate interstate commerce is plenary and extends to all such commerce be it great or small. . . . The amount of the commerce regulated is of special significance only to the extent that Congress may be taken to have excluded commerce of small volume from the operation of its regulatory measure by express provision or fair implication.[150]

With these decisions, the Court drew the powers of the NLRB so broadly that few cases have since challenged its authority. Its declaration that labor problems in any industry at all dependent on interstate commerce could burden interstate commerce effectively demanded their regulation under the NLRA.

Wages and Hours

Given the newfound willingness of the Supreme Court—evidenced by the NLRB rulings—to construe the commerce power broadly, Congress decided to try again to set federal minimum wage and maximum hours standards. Since the Court in 1918 had held hours limitations for child workers an unwarranted

federal intrusion into intrastate matters, wage and hour reform attempts had been restricted to the individual states. For almost two decades, the Court had approved state maximum hour statutes, but not until 1937 did it abandon its opposition to state minimum wage laws with a decision upholding Washington State's minimum wage law.[151] *(See details of West Coast Hotel Co. v. Parrish, pp. 342–343, in Chapter 7.)*

The next year Congress passed the Fair Labor Standards Act of 1938, which set a forty-hour work week and an eventual minimum wage of forty cents an hour with time and a half for overtime. The act covered most workers "engaged in commerce or in the production of goods for commerce." It barred production of goods by workers paid less or working more than the standards prescribed, and, in a provision almost identical to that struck down by the Court in the child labor case, *Hammer v. Dagenhart,* it barred the shipment in interstate commerce of any products made in violation of the standards.

A test of this statute came to the Court in 1941 after the government charged Fred W. Darby with violating it.[152] Darby ran a lumber company in Georgia, converting raw wood into finished lumber and selling a large part of it in other states. The Court unanimously upheld the federal minimum wage statute. Justice Harlan Fiske Stone, writing the opinion in *United States v. Darby Lumber Co.,* first considered the power of Congress to prohibit shipment of goods manufactured in violation of the standards:

While manufacture is not of itself interstate commerce, the shipment of manufactured goods interstate is such commerce and the prohibition of such shipment by Congress is indubitably a regulation of the commerce. . . .

The motive and purpose of the present regulation is plainly to make effective the Congressional conception of public policy that interstate commerce should not be made the instrument of competition in the distribution of goods produced under substandard labor conditions, which competition is injurious to the commerce and to the states from and to which the commerce flows. The motive and purpose of a regulation of interstate commerce are matters for the legislative judgment upon the exercise of which the Constitution places no restriction and over which the courts are given no control.[153]

Although based on different precedents, Stone realized that this conclusion was directly contrary to the finding in *Hammer v. Dagenhart.* Of that case, Stone wrote:

The distinction on which the decision was rested that Congressional power to prohibit interstate commerce is limited to articles which in themselves have some harmful or deleterious property—a distinction which was novel when made and unsupported by any provision of the Constitution—has long since been abandoned. . . . The thesis of the opinion that the motive of the prohibition or its effect to control in some measure the use or production within the states of the article thus excluded from commerce can operate to deprive the regulation of its constitutional authority has long since ceased to have force. . . .

The conclusion is inescapable that *Hammer v. Dagenhart* was a departure from the principles which have prevailed in the interpretation of the commerce clause both before and since the decision and that such vitality, as a precedent, as it then had has long since been exhausted. It should be and now is overruled.[154]

The Court also held that the prohibition of the actual production of goods in violation of the standards was a proper means of protecting interstate commerce. This conclusion, said Stone, did not violate the Tenth Amendment reserving to the states those powers not delegated to the federal government. He added:

There is nothing in the history of its [the amendment's] adoption to suggest that it was more than declaratory of the relationship between the national and state governments as it had been established by the Constitution before the amendment, or that its purpose was other than to allay fears that the new national government might seek to exercise powers not granted, and that the states might not be able to exercise fully their reserved powers. . . .

From the beginning and for many years the amendment has been construed as not depriving the national government of authority to resort to all means for the exercise of a granted power which are appropriate and plainly adapted to the permitted end.[155]

With this decision the Court reestablished a strong federal police power and further extended federal opportunities for regulation of production. The idea that the Tenth Amendment restricted the full exercise of federal power was dead. As several scholars have noted, Stone's opinion brought back to prominence the nationalistic interpretation of the commerce clause first outlined by John Marshall, and the Court has not swerved significantly from it since.

A year later, the Court went beyond *Darby* to uphold wage and hour standards applied to employees who maintained a building in which tenants produced goods for sale in interstate commerce.[156] In subsequent cases, the Court held that the standards applied to operators of oil well drilling rigs, night watchmen, and elevator operators.[157] A few employees were not covered, however. In 1943 the Court said the minimum wage did not apply to workers for a wholesaler who brought goods outside the state but sold them locally.[158] Nor did the standards apply to maintenance workers in an office building in which some tenants were executives and sales personnel for manufacturing goods sold in interstate commerce but where no actual manufacturing occurred.[159]

Writing in 1942 Robert Carr said that after the *Darby* decision, "about the only further step the Court might take in its general reasoning concerning the commerce power would be to cease denying that manufacture is not of itself commerce and conclude that where goods are produced for, or affect, interstate trade, the act of production is a phase of the total process of commerce."[160]

The Court took that step the same year.

AGRICULTURE AND COMMERCE

To replace the Agricultural Adjustment Act, which the Court had declared an unconstitutional infringement on state power in 1936, Congress passed a similar law in 1938. Rather than paying farmers to produce less of certain commodities as the first act had, the second act established marketing quotas for the various commodities and penalized producers who exceeded them. *(See details of United States v. Butler, p. 127.)*

The following year the Court upheld the 1938 act against the challenge that it too infringed on the reserved powers of the states by attempting to regulate production. Ironically, the opinion was written by Justice Owen J. Roberts, who had written the Court's opinion in the 1936 case. The Court found that the 1938 act did not regulate production, but marketing, which was at the "throat" of interstate commerce.[161]

The same broad interpretation was given to the 1937 Agricultural Marketing Act, which established milk marketing agreements to control milk prices. The Court upheld the act twice in 1939 and again in 1942, rejecting in all three cases the argument that Congress lacked authority to regulate milk produced and sold within a single state.[162] In the 1942 case, *United States v. Wrightwood Dairy Co.,* Chief Justice Harlan Fiske Stone wrote for the Court:

Congress plainly has power to regulate the price of milk distributed through the medium of interstate commerce . . . and it possesses every power needed to make that regulation effective. The commerce power is not confined in its exercise to the regulation of commerce among the States. It extends to those activities intrastate which so affect interstate commerce, or the exertion of the power of Congress over it, as to make regulation of them appropriate means to the attainment of a legitimate end, the effective execution of the granted power to regulate interstate commerce. The power of Congress over interstate commerce is plenary and complete in itself, may be exercised to its utmost extent, and acknowledges no limitations other than are prescribed in the Constitution. . . . It follows that no form of State activity can constitutionally thwart the regulatory power granted by the commerce clause to Congress. Hence the reach of that power extends to those intrastate activities which in a substantial way interfere with or obstruct the exercise of the granted power.[163]

Just how "substantial" that intrastate activity had to be was tested later in the year in *Wickard v. Filburn.*[164] Under the 1938 agricultural adjustment act, Wickard had been allotted eleven acres of wheat. He planted twenty-three acres and harvested 269 bushels more than his quota permitted. He intended to sell what he was allowed, and use the excess for feed and for seed for future crops. Although he did not sell the excess in either intrastate or interstate commerce, he still was penalized for raising more than his quota. Wickard challenged the penalty.

The Court's opinion was written by Justice Robert H. Jackson who, after the case was first argued, professed bewilderment as to how Congress could regulate "activities that are neither interstate nor commerce."[165]

Reargument apparently erased his doubts. Upholding Congress's authority to regulate Wickard's production, Jackson wrote:

Whether the subject of the regulation in question was "production," "consumption," or "marketing" is . . . not material for purposes of deciding the question of federal power before us. . . . But even if appellee's activity be local and though it may not be regarded as commerce, it may still, whatever its nature, be reached by Congress if it exerts a substantial economic effect on interstate commerce, and this ir-

THE RIGHT TO TRAVEL: FIRMLY ESTABLISHED ON SHIFTING BASE

The right of a citizen to travel freely in the United States has been acknowledged by the Supreme Court for almost a century and a half. As early as 1849, Chief Justice Roger B. Taney wrote in the *Passenger Cases*:

For all great purposes for which the Federal government was formed we are one people, with one common country. We are all citizens of the United States; and, as members of the same community, must have the right to pass and repass through every part of it without interruption, as freely as in our own States.[1]

But the Court has not been consistent in locating the source of this right. The Court has struck down some restrictions on an individual's right to travel as impermissible burdens on interstate commerce and others as a violation of the Fourteenth Amendment's "privileges and immunities" clause.

Both arguments were offered in the 1941 case of *Edwards v. California,* which involved the state's "anti-Okie" law penalizing people who brought indigents into the state. Edwards was charged with bringing his penniless brother-in-law into California from Texas. The Court was unanimous in its decision that the California law must fall, but divided in its reasoning. A majority of five claimed that the state statute was a burden on interstate commerce. The purpose and effect of the law, the majority wrote,

is to prohibit the transportation of indigent persons across the California border. The burden upon interstate commerce is intended and immediate; it is the plain and sole function of the statute. Moreover, the indigent nonresidents who are the real victims of the statute are deprived of the opportunity to exert political pressure upon the California legislature in order to

obtain a change in policy. . . . We think this statute must fall under any known test of the validity of State interference with interstate commerce.[2]

But the other four justices believed the state law invalid because it conflicted with the clause of the Fourteenth Amendment that states: "No State shall make or enforce any law which shall abridge the privileges or immunities of citizens of the United States. . . ." "This Court," wrote Justice Robert H. Jackson, "should . . . hold squarely that it is a privilege of citizenship of the United States, protected from state abridgement, to enter any state of the Union, either for temporary sojourn or for the establishment of permanent residence therein and for gaining resultant citizenship thereof. If national citizenship means less than this, it means nothing."[3]

The Court has never made a choice between these two lines of reasoning. In cases upholding the Civil Rights Act of 1964 it said that refusal of public accommodations to blacks traveling interstate was an unconstitutional burden on interstate commerce.[4] *(See "Civil Rights and Commerce," p. 65.)*

In another case, the Court struck down state laws requiring persons to live in a state for a certain period before becoming eligible for welfare payments. Such laws violated the right to travel, the majority said, adding that it felt no need to "ascribe the source of this right . . . to a particular constitutional provision."[5]

1. *The Passenger Cases,* 7 How. 283 at 492 (1849).
2. *Edwards v. California,* 314 U.S. 160 at 174 (1941).
3. Id. at 183.
4. *Heart of Atlanta Motel v. United States,* 379 U.S. 241 (1964); *Katzenbach v. McClung,* 379 U.S. 294 (1964).
5. *Shapiro v. Thompson,* 394 U.S. 618 at 630 (1969).

---

respective of whether such effect is what might at some earlier time have been defined as "direct" or "indirect."[166]

Jackson then pointed out that by growing his own wheat, Wickard would not buy wheat and thus would reduce the market demand:

That appellee's own contribution to the demand for wheat may be trivial by itself is not enough to remove him from the scope of federal regulation where, as here, his contribution, taken together with that of many others similarly situated, is far from trivial. . . . Home-grown wheat in this sense competes with wheat in commerce. The stimulation of commerce is a use of the regulatory function quite as definitely as prohibitions or restrictions thereon. This record leaves us in no doubt that Congress may properly have considered that wheat consumed on the farm where grown, if wholly outside the scheme of regulation, would have a substantial effect in defeating and obstructing its purpose to stimulate trade therein at increased prices.[167]

The Court had found a rationale to uphold regulation by Congress of production that was not in commerce. Constitutional historian C. Herman Pritchett has called this case the "high-water mark of commerce clause expansionism."[168]

THE MODERN COMMERCE POWER

Once reaffirmed by the Supreme Court in 1937, Marshall's original broad view of the commerce power has shaped the life

of the nation in the twentieth century. Not only is it the foundation for ever more detailed supervision of the commercial life of the nation by Congress and executive agencies; it also has been used to prohibit racial discrimination in public accommodations, remove restrictions on interstate travel, and justify federal regulation of environmental pollutants. In one instance, the Court used the commerce clause to give Congress control of a field of commerce it did not want and quickly returned to the states. Only twice in sixty years did the Court find that Congress had overreached this power, and one of those decisions was reversed by the Court itself.

Racial Discrimination

Early in the nation's history slaveholders realized that Congress might use its power over interstate commerce to prohibit slavery, but it was never wielded for that purpose. After the Civil War, however, Congress attacked racial discrimination in public accommodations through several different means, all with little success. An 1875 statute, based on the Fourteenth Amendment's guarantees of due process and equal protection of the laws, barred segregation in public accommodations. The Supreme Court in the 1883 *Civil Rights Cases* struck down that law, holding that the Fourteenth Amendment applied only to discriminatory actions by states, not by individuals.[169] Therefore, the amendment could not be used to reach discriminatory action on railroads and other privately owned public carriers and accommodations.

Opponents of segregation also tried to use the commerce power to reach discriminatory practices. The Interstate Commerce Commission (ICC), however, dismissed a challenge to segregated railroad facilities based on a section of the Interstate Commerce Act that prohibited "undue or unreasonable prejudice or disadvantage" in such facilities. "The disposition of a delicate and important question of this character, weighted with embarrassments arising from antecedent legal and social conditions, should aim at a result most likely to conduce to peace and order," said the commission, in effect ruling that it would not enforce the prohibition.[170]

An attempt to reach racial segregation on public carriers was successful in *Hall v. DeCuir* (1878) but produced the opposite result—the Louisiana law that was voided would have prohibited segregation.[171] Using the *Cooley* rule, the Court said prohibition of segregation was a matter on which there should be national uniformity and thus only Congress could act. Congress acted in passing the Civil Rights Act of 1875, but as already noted, the Court struck it down.

A state statute that required segregation on public carriers was challenged with the hope that the Court would apply the reasoning of *Hall v. DeCuir,* but instead the Court in 1890 ruled that the law affected only intrastate traffic and imposed no burden on interstate commerce.[172] This case was cited in *Plessy v. Ferguson* (1896) as precedent for denying the claim that separate but equal facilities for blacks and whites in railway cars unduly burdened interstate commerce.[173] (*See box, The Court and the Issue of Slavery: A Question of Legality, Not Morality, p. 396.*)

Although there were subsequent sporadic attempts at ending segregation through the commerce clause, congressional and public interest in resolving the problem waned in the first decades of the twentieth century.

Civil Rights and Commerce

Then in 1946 the Supreme Court ruled that segregation on a public carrier burdened interstate commerce. The case of *Morgan v. Virginia* involved a black woman traveling on a bus from Virginia to Maryland.[174] She refused to move to the back of the bus to make her seat available to a white. The Court upheld her refusal.

In 1950 the Court ruled that separate dining facilities on interstate trains were a violation of the long-unenforced provision of the Interstate Commerce Act.[175] In 1955 the ICC announced that it was prohibiting racial discrimination in all trains and buses that crossed state lines.

But it was not until the 1964 Civil Rights Act that Congress attempted again to prohibit racial discrimination in all public accommodations. Title II of the 1964 act barred discrimination on grounds of race, color, religion, or national origin in public accommodations if the discrimination was supported by state law or official action, if lodgings were provided to transient guests or if interstate travelers were served, or if a substantial portion of the goods sold or entertainment provided moved in interstate commerce.

This portion of the act was immediately challenged as unconstitutional. Six months after the statute was enacted, the Supreme Court upheld Title II. *Heart of Atlanta Motel v. United States* (1964) involved a motel in downtown Atlanta that served out-of-state travelers.[176] The motel challenged the validity of the act on the grounds that Congress had exceeded its power to regulate interstate commerce and had violated Fifth Amendment guarantees by depriving businesses of the right to choose their own customers.

Despite the motel's contention that its business was purely local in character, the Court upheld the application to it of Title II. Justice Tom C. Clark explained that Congress's power to regulate interstate commerce gave it the authority to regulate local enterprise that "might have a substantial and harmful effect" on that commerce.[177]

The fact that Congress intended to correct what it considered a moral and social evil in no way undercut the law's constitutionality, Clark continued. The moral implications of the discrimination did "not detract from the overwhelming evidence of the disruptive effect" that discrimination had on interstate commerce, he said.[178]

In a companion case, *Katzenbach v. McClung,* decided the same day, the Court upheld Title II as applied to a restaurant in Birmingham, Alabama.[179] Ollie's Barbeque did not cater to an interstate clientele but 46 percent of the food it served was meat supplied through interstate commerce.

Five years later, the Court in *Daniel v. Paul* (1969) upheld the application of Title II to a small rural recreation area that attracted few interstate travelers and that offered few food products sold in interstate commerce.[180] Justice Hugo L. Black dissented, saying he would have supported the majority if it had used the Fourteenth Amendment to reach the discriminatory practices at the recreational facility but that he objected to the lengths to which the majority went to find a nexus between that discrimination and interstate commerce.

Insurance

Once the Court used the commerce clause to give Congress control of a field of trade it did not want and quickly gave away. Since its 1869 decision in *Paul v. Virginia,* the Supreme Court had held consistently that purely financial or contractual transactions such as insurance were not in commerce, even if the transactions involved parties in different states.[181] This left the state full authority to regulate the insurance business.

In 1944 the Justice Department sought to use the Sherman Antitrust Act to break up a conspiracy of insurance companies that sought to monopolize fire insurance sales in six southern states. Using the precedent established by *Paul v. Virginia,* the companies, all members of the South-Eastern Underwriters Association, defended themselves with the argument that they

BANKRUPTCY LAWS

The Constitution authorizes Congress to make "uniform Laws on the subject of Bankruptcies." Federal laws were enacted in 1800, 1841, and 1867 to meet specific economic crises, but each survived public criticism and political pressure only a few years before being repealed. In the intervals between passage of federal laws, state bankruptcy laws were controlling.

When Congress chose to act in the field, however, it interpreted its powers broadly, and this interpretation was usually sanctioned by the Supreme Court.

Rather than restrict the coverage of bankruptcy laws to tradesmen as was the English practice, Congress in its first bankruptcy law extended coverage to bankers, brokers, commodities agents, and insurance underwriters.

The belief that the grant of power was broad enough to cover such categories of bankrupts was sanctioned by the Court in 1902, and the Court has since given its implicit approval to laws extending bankruptcy coverage to almost every class of person and corporation.[1] The Court also has approved federal laws to rehabilitate the debtor as well as to provide appropriate relief to creditors.[2]

Despite its liberal interpretation of this clause, the Supreme Court in the 1930s recognized some limitations on the power. Congress must be mindful of a creditor's due process rights guaranteed by the Fifth Amendment. Because the states have incorporation power, a corporation dissolved by a state court decree may not file a petition for reorganization under the federal bankruptcy laws. Nor may Congress place the fiscal affairs of a city, county, or other state political unit under the control of a federal bankruptcy court.[3]

In 1982 the Court for the first time struck down a federal bankruptcy law because it violated the constitutional standard of uniformity. A 1980 law passed to protect the employees of the Rock Island Railroad was held invalid by a unanimous Court because it gave the employees protection not available to people who worked for other bankrupt railroads.[4] The same year the Court sent Congress back to the drawing board in its effort to reform the nation's bankruptcy laws. The Court held that a comprehensive reform law passed in 1978 violated Article III—which provides that federal judicial power be exercised only by federal judges whose independence is assured—by creating a new corps of bankruptcy judges with broad powers but without the guarantees of life tenure and fixed compensation.[5]

1. *Hanover National Bank v. Moyses*, 186 U.S. 181 (1902); *Continental Bank v. Chicago, Rock Island & Pacific Railway Co.*, 294 U.S. 648 (1935); *United States v. Bekins*, 304 U.S. 27 (1938).

2. *Continental Bank v. Chicago, Rock Island & Pacific Railway Co.*, 294 U.S. 648 (1935); *Wright v. Vinton Branch*, 300 U.S. 440 (1937); *Adair v. Bank of America Association*, 303 U.S. 350 (1938).

3. *Louisville Bank v. Radford*, 295 U.S. 555 (1935); *Chicago Title & Trust Co. v. Wilcox Building Corp.*, 302 U.S. 120 (1937); *Ashton v. Cameron County District*, 298 U.S. 513 (1936).

4. *Railway Labor Executives' Association v. Gibbons*, 455 U.S. 457 (1982).

5. *Northern Pipeline Construction Co. v. Marathon Pipe Line Co., United States v. Marathon Pipe Line Co.*, 458 U.S. 50 (1982).

were not reachable in this way because they were not engaged in commerce.

Overturning *Paul*, the Court, 4–3, rejected that argument. "No commercial enterprise of any kind which conducts its activities across state lines has been held to be wholly beyond the regulatory power of Congress under the Commerce Clause," wrote Justice Hugo L. Black. "We cannot make an exception for the business of insurance."[182] Congress, not the Court, must make the exceptions to the antitrust act, Black concluded.

This ruling called into question the validity of all state insurance regulations. In response, Congress in 1945 passed the McCarran Act which stated that "no Act of Congress shall be construed to invalidate, impair or supersede" a state law regulating or taxing insurance unless the federal act specifically related to insurance. In 1946 the Court upheld the McCarran Act.[183]

Environmental Law

Congress's police power, derived mainly from the commerce power, has become the constitutional basis for federal legislation regulating air and water pollution.

The Water Quality Improvement Act of 1970, the primary vehicle for water pollution prevention and control, states in its declaration of policy that it is enacted in "connection with the exercise of jurisdiction over the waterways of the Nation and in consequence of the benefits resulting to the public health and welfare by the prevention and control of water pollution." Likewise, the primary purpose given for passage of the Air Quality Act of 1967 is "to promote health and welfare and the productive capacity of [the nation's] population."

While various regulations promulgated under these statutes have been challenged in the courts, the Supreme Court has not sustained any direct challenge to the authority of Congress to exercise its commerce power in these areas.

State Sovereignty

In 1976 the Court for the first time in forty years struck down an act of Congress based on the commerce power, a law that required state and local governments to pay their employees the minimum wage and overtime pay as well.[184] Congress, a five-man majority said, interfered too far into the essential business of state and local government by imposing these requirements. The Court overruled *Maryland v. Wirtz* (1968), which upheld the minimum wage requirement for employees of state schools and hospitals.[185]

Writing for the majority in this case, *National League of Cities v. Usery*, Justice William H. Rehnquist explained:

We have repeatedly recognized that there are attributes of sovereignty attaching to every state government which may not be impaired by Congress not because Congress may lack an affirmative grant of legislative authority to reach the matter, but because the Constitution prohibits it from exercising the authority in that manner. . . .

One undoubted attribute of state sovereignty is the state's power to determine the wages which shall be paid to those whom they employ in order to carry out their governmental functions, what hours those

---

PATENTS AND COPYRIGHTS

Congressional authority over patents and copyrights comes from Article I, Section 8, Clause 8, which empowers Congress "To promote the Progress of Science and useful Arts, by securing for limited Times to Authors and Inventors the exclusive Right to their respective Writings and Discoveries."

In fashioning copyright and patent laws, Congress must balance two interests.

As described by the Library of Congress, these are "the interest of the public in being protected against monopolies and in having ready access and use of new items versus the interest of the country, as a whole, in encouraging invention by rewarding creative persons for their innovations."[1]

There have been no serious challenges to the right of Congress to set standards and conditions for the granting of patents and copyrights within the constitutional limits. But numerous Court cases have turned on the question of whether a particular invention meets the standards.[2]

These decisions made the Court and not Congress in large measure the final judge of what those standards are.

In one case the Court established three tests an item must pass to be patentable: "Innovation, advancement and things which add to the sum of useful knowledge are inherent requisites in a patent system which by constitutional command must 'promote the Progress of . . . useful Arts.' This is the standard expressed in the Constitution and it may not be ignored."[3]

In the famous *Trademark Cases* of 1879, the Court held that trademarks could not be defined either as writing or discoveries and thus were not capable of being copyrighted or patented.[4] Congress could only regulate trademarks through the exercise of its power over interstate commerce.

But in exercising that power, Congress has considerable latitude. The Court in 1987 held that the decision of Congress to give the U.S. Olympic Committee the power to deny other groups the right to use the word *Olympic* for commercial or promotional purposes was within the traditional scope of its power to make trademark law.[5]

1. U.S. Congress, Library of Congress, Congressional Research Service, *The Constitution of the United States: Analysis and Interpretation* (Washington, D.C.: U.S. Government Printing Office, 1973), 316.

2. *Funk Bros. Seed Co. v. Kalo Co.*, 333 U.S. 127 (1948); *Sinclair & Co. v. Interchemical Corp.*, 325 U.S. 327 (1945); *Marconi Wireless Co. v. United States*, 320 U.S. 1 (1943); *Keystone Manufacturing Co. v. Adams*, 151 U.S. 139 (1894); *Diamond Rubber Co. v. Consolidated Tire Co.*, 220 U.S. 428 (1911); *A&P Tea Co. v. Supermarket Equipment Corp.*, 340 U.S. 147 (1950).

3. *Graham v. John Deere Co.*, 383 U.S. 1 (1966).

4. *Trademark Cases (United States v. Steffens)*, 100 U.S. 82 (1879).

5. *San Francisco Arts & Athletics Inc. v. United States Olympic Committee*, 483 U.S. 522 (1987).

---

persons will work, and what compensation will be provided where these employees may be called upon to work overtime.[186]

"Congress," Rehnquist concluded, "may not exercise that [commerce] power so as to force directly upon the states its choices as to how essential decisions regarding the conduct of integral governmental functions are to be made."[187]

In dissent, Justice William J. Brennan Jr. described the ruling as a "catastrophic judicial body blow at Congress' power under the Commerce Clause."[188]

Also in dissent, Justice John Paul Stevens wrote that it was difficult to perceive the principle on which the Court based a ruling that "the Federal Government may not interfere with a sovereign state's inherent right to pay a substandard wage to the janitor at the state capitol," since the federal government already regulated so many other aspects of the janitor's job, from the withholding of taxes from his paycheck to the environmental regulations he must observe in maintaining the capitol's furnace.[189]

"*National League of Cities v. Usery* may portend a modest resurrection of judicial limitation upon congressional exercise of the commerce power," wrote the authors of the Library of Congress's annotated Constitution. "But, despite the broad phrasing of the opinion, . . . [its] potential . . . may be quite restrained."[190]

The Garcia Ruling

Events proved that statement prophetic. Nine years after the *Usery* ruling, the Court, 5–4, reversed itself. Justice Harry A. Blackmun's was the swing vote, moving from concurrence supporting *Usery* to opposition. He wrote the Court's opinion in the 1985 case of *Garcia v. San Antonio Metropolitan Transit Authority*. The issue was virtually the same as in *Usery*: this time the Court upheld the power of Congress to require that a city pay federal minimum wage and overtime pay to the employees of its transit system.

"We continue to recognize that the States occupy a special and specific position in our constitutional system and that the scope of Congress' authority under the Commerce Clause must reflect that position," wrote Blackmun. "But the principal and basic limit on the federal commerce power is that inherent in all congressional action—the built-in restraints that our system provides through state participation in federal governmental action. The political process ensures that laws that unduly burden the States will not be promulgated."

In *Usery*, Blackmun explained, "the Court . . . attempted to articulate affirmative limits on the Commerce Clause power in terms of core governmental functions and fundamental attributes of state sovereignty. . . . Attempts by other courts since then to draw guidance from this model have proved it both impracticable and doctrinally barren. In sum, in *National League of Cities v. Usery*, the Court tried to repair what did not need repair."

"We do not lightly overrule recent precedent," Blackmun added. "We have not hesitated, however, when it has become apparent that a prior decision has departed from a proper under-

POSTAL POWERS

Clause 7 of Article I, Section 8, gives Congress the power "To establish Post Offices and post Roads." Whether this phrase meant that Congress had the power actually to construct post offices and post roads or simply to designate those that would be used as postal facilities was settled in 1876 when the Supreme Court upheld federal appropriation of land on which to build a post office.[1] The postal power has been interpreted to include the authority to ensure the speedy delivery and protection of the mail.[2] This principle was the basis for the federal government's winning an injunction against leaders of the 1894 Pullman strike, which had halted mail delivery along with the trains.

At the same time, federal troops were sent to Illinois to quell the violence that had erupted. Eugene V. Debs and other labor leaders were convicted of contempt for violating the injunction. The Supreme Court upheld the convictions and the use of federal troops in 1895, declaring that "[t]he strong arm of the national Government may be put forth to brush away all obstructions to the freedom of interstate commerce or the transportation of the mails."[3]

The postal power also has been interpreted to allow Congress to bar items from the mails that it believes might defraud the public or injure its morals. The first such case was *Ex parte Jackson* (1878), in which the Supreme Court sustained congressional action barring from the mails certain circulars relating to lotteries.[4]

In more recent cases, the Court has said that the federal power to exclude matter from the mails is limited by other constitutional guarantees. In 1965, for example, the Court struck down a federal law authorizing the post office not to forward mail it regarded as communist propaganda unless the addressee specifically said he wanted to receive it.[5]

Declaring the statute a violation of the First Amendment, the Court said the law impinged on the right of a person to receive whatever information he or she wanted to receive. The Congressional Research Service of the Library of Congress notes that this case was the first in which the Court had invalidated a federal statute because it conflicted with the First Amendment.[6] *(See box, Freedom to Circulate, p. 457, in Chapter 9.)*

Congress frequently has invoked its postal power to aid it in the exercise of other express powers. In 1910 the Court held that correspondence schools were in interstate commerce and therefore susceptible to federal regulation because of their reliance on the mails.[7] In 1938 the Court upheld provisions of the Public Utility Holding Company Act requiring gas and electric utilities to register with the Securities and Exchange Commission partially on the grounds that such holding companies conducted a large and continuous portion of their business through the mails.[8]

1. *Kohl v. United States,* 91 U.S. 367 (1876).
2. *Ex parte Jackson,* 96 U.S. 727 (1878).
3. *In re Debs,* 158 U.S. 564 at 582 (1895).
4. *Ex parte Jackson,* 96 U.S. 727 (1878).
5. *Lamont v. Postmaster General,* 381 U.S. 301 (1965).
6. U.S. Congress, Library of Congress, Congressional Research Service, *The Constitution of the United States: Analysis and Interpretation* (Washington, D.C.: U.S. Government Printing Office, 1973), 310, n. 10.
7. *International Textbook Co. v. Pigg,* 217 U.S. 91 (1910).
8. *Electric Bond & Share Co. v. Securities and Exchange Commission,* 303 U.S. 419 (1938).

standing of congressional power under the Commerce Clause. Due respect for the reach of congressional power within the federal system mandates that we do so now."[191]

Blackmun was joined in the majority by Brennan, Stevens, Byron R. White, and Thurgood Marshall. Dissenting were Rehnquist, Lewis F. Powell Jr., Warren E. Burger—all members of the *Usery* majority—and the newest member of the Court, Sandra Day O'Connor.

The Lopez Case

The Court's next major ruling on the commerce clause—a surprising rejection of congressional authority in 1995—arose from a case involving a twelfth-grade student in San Antonio, Texas, who sneaked a gun into school.

Alfonso Lopez Jr. was caught with a .38 caliber handgun and five bullets. He was arrested and charged under the Gun-Free School Zones Act of 1990. That law, passed in the wake of several highly publicized schoolyard incidents, made it illegal for anyone to possess a firearm within one thousand feet of a school.

Lopez's lawyer sought to have the indictment dismissed, arguing that Congress was unconstitutionally trying to control activities in local schools. A trial judge nonetheless found Lopez guilty and sentenced him to six months in prison. The U.S. Court of Appeals for the Fifth Circuit reversed. And on April 26, 1995, the Supreme Court agreed, 5–4, that Congress had overreached the commerce clause. In the majority were Rehnquist, now chief justice, and O'Connor, two dissenters from *Garcia*, and three new members of the court—Justices Antonin Scalia, Anthony M. Kennedy, and Clarence Thomas. Dissenting were Justice Stevens and three other justices who had joined the Court since the *Garcia* ruling, David H. Souter, Ruth Bader Ginsburg, and Stephen G. Breyer.

Rehnquist wrote for the majority in *United States v. Lopez*: "We start with first principles. The Constitution creates a Federal Government of enumerated powers. . . . As James Madison wrote, '[t]he powers delegated by the proposed Constitution to the federal government are few and defined. Those which are to remain in the State governments are numerous and indefinite.'"[192]

The chief justice noted that modern precedents had broadly expanded congressional power under the commerce clause to regulate, for example, loan-sharking, hotels, and the production of home-grown wheat. But, said Rehnquist, as far reaching as those examples might be, they involved economic activity in a way that possession of a gun in a school zone did not. The Gun-

Free School Zones law "is a criminal statute that by its terms has nothing to do with 'commerce' or any sort of economic enterprise, however broadly one might define those terms."[193]

In concluding that the activities of Lopez, "a local student at a local school,"[194] had no substantial impact on interstate commerce, the Court said:

To uphold the Government's contentions here, we would have to pile inference upon inference in a manner that would bid fair to convert congressional authority under the Commerce Clause to a general police power of the sort retained by the States. Admittedly, some of our prior cases have taken long steps down that road, giving great deference to congressional action. . . . The broad language in these opinions has suggested the possibility of additional expansion, but we decline here to proceed any further. To do so would require us to conclude that the Constitution's enumeration of powers does not presuppose something not enumerated . . . and that there will never be a distinction between what is truly national and what is truly local. This we are unwilling to do.[195]

Justice Kennedy, joined by Justice O'Connor, wrote separately to stress the limits of the *Lopez* decision and that the Court was not discarding precedent. Rather, said Kennedy, this unusual type of federal legislation requires the Court's unusual rejection of congressional action:

While it is doubtful that any State, or indeed any reasonable person, would argue that it is wise policy to allow students to carry guns on school premises, considerable disagreement exists about how best to accomplish that goal. In this circumstance, the theory and utility of our federalism are revealed, for the States may perform their role as laboratories for experimentation to devise various solutions where the best solution is far from clear.[196]

Kennedy noted that more than forty states already had statutes outlawing the possession of firearms on or near school grounds.

Breyer wrote for the four dissenting justices that the gun control statute fell within the scope of the commerce power as it has been understood for the last half-century. He said courts should give Congress more leeway in this area because the Constitution delegates commerce power directly to federal lawmakers, and they are in a better position than judges to assess social needs in this area. Breyer said the legal test should be not whether the regulated activity sufficiently affects interstate commerce, but rather whether Congress could have had a rational basis concluding that it did so.

From 1976 to 1995, the Court had issued three important commerce clause rulings, all decided by 5–4 votes, all with conflicting messages. *Usery* temporarily raised the hopes of states that the Court would indeed limit federal power to intervene in state affairs, but it was *Lopez* that promised greater restriction on federal power with its narrowed definition of what constituted commerce subject to federal regulation. Whether the post–New Deal era of nearly limitless federal involvement at the local level would be coming to an end as the twentieth century closed was not clear. Only future lawmaking and court cases would determine how much power Congress might lose and states gain at the hands of the Rehnquist Court.

Recognizing that an effective national government must have unquestioned power to raise and spend money, the Framers gave Congress clear authority to lay and collect taxes, pay the national debt, and spend for the common defense and general welfare. That power is the first enumerated in Article I, Section 8. To make congressional control over fiscal and monetary matters complete, the Framers then gave Congress the power to coin money and regulate its value.

The Constitution places one prohibition and three limitations on the federal tax power. The prohibition: Congress may not tax exports. Of the three explicit limits, only two have had any lasting significance.

The first limiting clause requires that all duties, imposts, and excises be levied uniformly throughout the country. The second requires that all direct taxes be apportioned among the states on the basis of their relative populations. The third limited a federal tax on the importation of slaves to $10 per person. One major implied limitation has restricted federal power to tax state government.

Both Congress and the Supreme Court have interpreted the taxing and spending power liberally. C. Herman Pritchett noted in *The American Constitution* that because adequate revenue and broad power to spend it were absolutely necessary to the conduct of an effective central government, "the first rule for judicial review of tax statutes is that the heavy burden of proof lies on anyone who would challenge any congressional exercise of fiscal power. In almost every decision touching the constitutionality of federal taxation, the Supreme Court has stressed the breadth of congressional power and the limits of its own reviewing powers."[1]

Three times in its history the Court has disapproved a major act of Congress involving the fiscal and monetary powers. Each one of those rulings has had negligible effect on the power of Congress, and each has caused the Court considerable embarrassment. In each case, the Court's decision was eventually negated.

The Court ruled in 1870 that paper money could not be substituted for gold as legal tender; fifteen months later it reversed that decision. The Court's 1895 decision barring a federal income tax was nullified by adoption of the Sixteenth Amendment in 1913. Forty years later the Court attempted to limit the power of Congress to spend for the general welfare, striking down the Agricultural Adjustment Act of 1933. But that decision too was soon disavowed by a Court faced with President Franklin D. Roosevelt's Court-packing plan.

Direct Taxes

The Court wrestled for a century with the definition of direct taxes. The Constitution is of little assistance, referring only to "capitation, or other direct taxes." Nor is the history of the Constitutional Convention helpful. The apportionment limitation was inserted at the urging of southern states to prevent heavy taxation of their lands and slaves, but the convention did not discuss what sorts of levies were direct.

As early as 1796 the government asked the Court to define this phrase in a test case concerning a federal tax on carriages.[2] The government's intense interest in having an answer was evident in the fact that the government paid the attorneys on both sides of the case.[3]

Only head taxes and taxes on land were direct taxes required to be apportioned by population, the Court held, finding the carriage tax an indirect use tax. This definition remained in place until the Court in 1895 struck down an income tax as unconstitutional on the grounds that it was a direct tax not levied proportionately among the states.[4]

THE *INCOME TAX CASES*

In the first half of the nineteenth century the federal government's revenue needs were modest, easily met by excise taxes and duties on imports. A federal tax on personal income was first imposed during the Civil War to meet the need for additional revenue. The statute, enacted in 1862, levied a tax on individual incomes in excess of $600; the exemption rose to $2,000 in 1870. The law expired in 1872.

That tax, as applied to attorneys' income, was upheld unanimously by the Court in 1881 as an indirect tax. The justices once more agreed: the only direct taxes were head taxes and taxes on land.[5]

During the 1870s and 1880s there was little interest in a second income tax law. But as the nation's economic base shifted from wealth based on land to wealth based on earnings, the 1890s saw increasing pressure for an income tax. After the depression of 1893 reduced federal revenues, Congress yielded and in 1894 levied a tax of 2 percent on personal incomes in excess of $4,000. Only about 2 percent of the population earned more than this amount.[6] The tax was immediately challenged.

The First Case

Charles Pollock, a stockholder in the Farmers' Loan and Trust Company, sought to enjoin that New York bank from paying the new tax. He claimed the tax was direct and therefore invalid because it was not apportioned on the basis of state populations. It was clear that both Pollock and the bank wanted the law struck down, and that the case had been deliberately arranged to evade the federal ban on suits seeking to stop the collection of taxes.

Although it generally refuses to hear cases in which the opposing parties have agreed to bring the suit, the Court set aside its rule in this instance. Because so much was at stake, Pollock

This 1895 editorial cartoon, published after the Supreme Court's decision in *Pollock v Farmers' Loan and Trust,* illustrates the Court's invalidation of the federal income tax law. In 1913, however, the situation was reversed when the states ratified the Sixteenth Amendment, which gave the federal government the power to tax incomes regardless of source.

and the bank hired the best available attorneys, and the Court allowed the U.S. attorney general to appear in behalf of the law even though the government was not a party to the suit.

Attorneys for Pollock argued two basic points. First, they said that a tax on the income from land was indistinguishable from a tax on the land itself, and therefore was an unconstitutional direct tax since it had not been apportioned. Second, they claimed that even if the tax was indirect it was still unconstitutional because as a tax applied only to incomes over a certain amount it did not meet the uniformity test.

Most historians agree that these arguments were weak at best. But the plaintiff's attorneys also portrayed the income tax as a weapon that could be used by a populist government to destroy private property rights, a political argument calculated to appeal to the more economically conservative justices on the bench. "I believe there are private rights of property here to be protected," the prominent attorney Joseph H. Choate declaimed. The income tax law "is communistic in its purposes and tendencies, and is defended here upon principles as communistic, socialist—what should I call them—populistic as ever have been addressed to any political assembly in the world."[7]

Only eight justices heard the arguments. Justice Howell E.

Jackson was absent, ill with tuberculosis, which would prove fatal. The Court handed down its decision April 8, 1895. Six of the eight agreed with Choate that the tax on the income from land was identical to a tax on the land and was thus unconstitutional. But the eight divided evenly on the issue of whether a tax on income from personal property was also a direct tax and whether the law failed to meet the uniformity test.[8]

The Second Case

Pollock's attorneys asked for reargument so that the Court might settle these crucial points. The Court agreed; the arguments were heard, and a full Court rendered its second decision only six weeks after the first on May 20, 1895. By a 5–4 vote, the Court struck down the entire income tax law as unconstitutional.[9] (Justice Jackson voted with the minority, which meant that one justice who voted to uphold the law in the first case reversed his opinion in the second. Because there was no opinion written and no breakdown given in the earlier 4–4 decision, just who the justice was has been the subject of great speculation.)

Chief Justice Melville W. Fuller, speaking for the majority, reaffirmed the point settled in the first case: "Taxes on real estate being indisputable direct taxes, taxes on the rents or income of real estate are equally direct taxes."[10]

Fuller next declared that the majority was "of the opinion that taxes on personal property, or on the income from personal property, are likewise direct taxes."[11] Fuller finally held that the remainder of the law was invalid on the principle that the parts of the legislation were so inseparable that if any of them were voided, all of them must fall. Since "it is obvious that by far the largest part of the anticipated revenue" was to come from the tax on income from real estate and personal property, Fuller said, it was equally obvious that the Court's decision to strike down those taxes "would leave the burden of the tax to be borne by professions, trades, employments, or vocations; and in that way what was intended as a tax on capital would remain in substance a tax on occupations and labor."[12]

The majority still avoided the question of what constituted uniformity for indirect taxes.

To reach its conclusions the Court found it necessary to gloss over the precedents. Fuller said that the Court's statement in the carriage tax case—that the only direct taxes were head taxes and those on land itself—was only a comment that did not have the force of law. The decision upholding the Civil War income tax involved a tax on earned income, Fuller rationalized, not on income from land. In the second opinion, Fuller did not even mention the earlier *Income Tax* case.

The extralegal argument in defense of private property rights had its intended effect: Justice Stephen J. Field's concurring opinion in the first *Pollock* case warned: "The present assault upon capital is but the beginning . . . the stepping stone to others . . . till our political contests will become a war of the poor against the rich."[13]

The four dissenters submitted separate opinions, sharply reproving the majority for disregarding a century of precedent

THE "INCOME TAX" AMENDMENT

Despite the Supreme Court's 1895 holding that a tax on personal income was unconstitutional, agitation for an income tax continued. Laborers and farmers overburdened by regressive federal taxes, such as tariffs, and incensed at the accumulation of greater and greater wealth by fewer and fewer people, kept the issue alive, electing to Congress a steadily increasing number of Democrats and progressive Republicans who favored an income tax.

Proposals for an income tax followed one of three strategies. One was that Congress simply reenact an income tax statute and hope that the Supreme Court—with several new justices since 1895—would overturn its 1895 decision. The second called for adoption of a constitutional amendment to eliminate the requirement that direct taxes be apportioned among the states. The third alternative was to fashion an income tax as an indirect excise tax and in that way avoid the apportionment problem.

Little action was taken on any of these proposals until 1909, the first year of William Howard Taft's presidency. When he took office, a two-year-long depression had depleted government revenues. At the same time, the Republicans had promised during the 1908 campaign to do something about the high tariffs. When the tariff bill was introduced in the Senate, the Democrats offered an income tax rider almost identical to the law declared unconstitutional. "Instead of trying to conform the amendment to the decision of the Court, the amendment distinctly challenges that decision. I do not believe that that opinion is a correct interpretation of the Constitution and I feel confident that an overwhelming majority of the best legal minds in the Republic believe it was erroneous," said Joseph W. Bailey, D-Texas (House, 1891–1901; Senate, 1901–1913), its chief sponsor.[1]

Fearful that the Democrats and insurgent Republicans had enough strength to pass the Bailey proposal, the conservative Senate Republican leadership countered with a proposed constitutional amendment that would permit an income tax without apportionment. Even if the amendment were approved by Congress, the conservatives did not believe enough state legislatures could be persuaded to ratify it.

Taft supported the constitutional amendment because he be-

lieved that passage of a simple income tax statute would injure the Supreme Court by forcing it to choose between loss of prestige (if it overturned its earlier decision) or loss of popularity (if it found a new income tax law unconstitutional).

Despite their fears that the conservative Republicans were correct and that the states would not ratify an income tax amendment, the Democrats and progressive Republicans nonetheless favored the amendment in principle and felt bound to vote for it. It passed the Senate, 77–0, in July 1909. The House approved it, 318–14, a week later.

Contrary to expectation, state legislatures did approve the amendment; it became the Sixteenth Amendment to the Constitution on February 23, 1913.

In November 1912 the Democrats won majorities in both houses of Congress. They quickly passed a law reducing tariffs on a number of imports and made up the consequent deficit in revenue by enacting an income tax law. The statute levied a 1 percent tax on all net income above $3,000 for individuals and above $4,000 for married couples living together. An additional graduated tax was levied on incomes above $20,000. According to the Internal Revenue Service, 437,036 income tax returns were filed for 1916, the first tax year.[2] The Court upheld the income tax law in 1916.

The Sixteenth Amendment was the third constitutional amendment ratified especially to overturn a decision of the Supreme Court. The Eleventh Amendment was passed to nullify the decision in *Chisholm v. Georgia* (1793) that allowed a citizen of another state or a foreign citizen to sue a state in federal court. The Fourteenth Amendment was passed in part to overturn the decision in *Scott v. Sandford* (1857), which held that blacks could not be citizens of the United States. *(See details of Chisholm v. Georgia, pp. 316–317, in Chapter 7; details of Scott v. Sandford, pp. 145–147.)*

1. Alpheus T. Mason and William M. Beaney, *The Supreme Court in a Free Society* (Englewood Cliffs, N.J.: Prentice-Hall, 1959), 133. Other sources include Alfred H. Kelly and Winfred A. Harbison, *The American Constitution: Its Origins and Development*, 5th ed. (New York: Norton, 1976); Sidney Ratner, *American Taxation: Its History as a Social Force in Democracy* (New York: Norton, 1942).

2. Interview with the Statistics of Income Branch, Statistics Division, Internal Revenue Service, September 19, 1978.

and even more sharply criticizing it for the political implications of its ruling. Justice John Marshall Harlan was most forceful:

The practical effect of the decision today is to give certain kinds of property a position of favoritism and advantage inconsistent with the fundamental principles of our social organization, and to invest them with power and influence that may be perilous to that portion of the American people upon whom rests the larger part of the burden of the government, and who ought not to be subjected to the dominion of aggregated wealth any more than the property of the country should be at the mercy of the lawless.[14]

Criticism of the Court's decision was widespread and blunt. The editor of the generally conservative *American Law Review* wrote:

[I]t appears, at least from one of the opinions which was rendered, that the Justice [Field] who rendered it proceeded with an imagination inflamed by the socialistic tendencies of the law, as involving an attack upon private property; a consideration which lay totally outside the scope of his office as a judge interpreting the Constitution. It is speaking truthfully, and therefore not disrespectfully, to say that some of the judges of the Court seem to have no adequate idea of the dividing line between judicial and legislative power, and seem to be incapable of restraining themselves to the mere office of judge.[15]

Dissatisfaction with the decision resulted eighteen years later in enactment of the Sixteenth Amendment. It also cost the Court prestige. Along with its refusal to apply the Sherman Antitrust Act to sugar manufacturers and its affirmance of Eugene V. Debs's conviction for his involvement in the Pullman strike, the decision, Pritchett wrote, "earned the Court a popular reputation as a tool of special privilege which was not dispelled for forty years."[16]

Retreat

Not deaf to the outcry, the Fuller Court did not apply the *Pollock* precedent to succeeding tax cases. Instead the Court found the taxes on certain kinds of incomes "incidents of ownership" and thus excise or indirect taxes rather than direct taxes. This reasoning was applied to uphold taxes on commodity exchange sales, inheritances, tobacco, and stock sales.[17] The Fuller Court also considered indirect a tax on the business of refining sugar based on gross receipts from the sale of refined sugar.[18] These modifications allowed the Court in 1911 to call a tax on corporate income an excise tax "measured by income" on the privilege of doing business.[19]

Ratification of the Sixteenth Amendment in 1913 gave Congress power to impose taxes on income "from whatever source derived, without apportionment among the several States, and without regard to any census or enumerations." *(See box, The "Income Tax" Amendment, p. 120.)*

Congress later that year enacted an income tax law that was upheld by the Court in 1916.[20] Implicitly criticizing its 1895 position, the Court said that the Sixteenth Amendment gave Congress no new powers of taxation but simply guaranteed that the income tax would never again be "taken out of the category of direct taxation to which it inherently" belongs.[21]

After 1916 the Court's concern shifted from whether a tax was direct or indirect to a determination of what was properly considered income.

A major case on this point was *Eisner v. Macomber* (1920) in which the Court invalidated part of the income tax law providing that "a stock dividend shall be considered income, to the amount of its cash value." The Court held that stock dividends (as opposed to cash dividends) could not be treated as income. Instead they were capital, and taxes on them were direct and had to be apportioned. Only when the dividends were converted or sold did they become taxable as income. This holding has been modified, but its basic premise is still operative.[22]

UNIFORMITY

In 1884 the Court held that a tax met the Constitution's requirement of uniformity if it operated in the same way on all subjects being taxed. A tax, the Court held in the *Head Money Cases*, was not non-uniform simply because the subject being taxed was not distributed uniformly throughout the United States.[23]

The question whether the tax rate had to be uniform—left unanswered in the *Income Tax Cases*—was finally settled in 1900.

Congress had imposed an inheritance tax during the Spanish-American War on legacies of more than $10,000; the tax rate varied with the amount of the bequest and the relationship of the heir to the deceased. The law was challenged on grounds that if it was a direct tax, it was not apportioned, and that if it was an indirect tax, it was not uniform.

The Court ruled that the tax was not direct, but was uniform so long as it applied in the same manner to the class throughout the United States.[24]

In 1927 the Court held that geographic uniformity was not violated by the fact that Florida residents were not able to take advantage of a federal tax deduction for state inheritance taxes because that state did not impose such a tax.

Fifty-six years later, the Court upheld a windfall profits tax on domestic oil production against a challenge that it violated this requirement by exempting new oil produced on Alaska's North Slope. Such a geographic exemption did not violate the uniformity requirement, the Court held, 9–0.[25]

Taxing as Police Power

Since the inception of the nation, Congress has used the taxing power as a regulatory tool as well as a revenue source. The protective tariff was an early example of a regulatory tax.

The second statute passed by the First Congress provided that "it is necessary for the support of government, for the discharge of the debts of the United States and the encouragement and protection of manufacturers, that duties be laid on goods, wares and merchandise imported."

The validity of such tariffs was much debated and not conclusively settled until 1928. Writing for the Court then, Chief Justice William Howard Taft said:

Whatever we may think of the wisdom of a protection policy, we cannot hold it unconstitutional. So long as the motive of Congress and the effect of its legislative action are to secure revenue for the benefit of the general government, the existence of other motives in the selection of the subject of taxes cannot invalidate Congressional action.[26]

FRUIT OR VEGETABLE?

The Supreme Court has declared that the tomato is a vegetable, not a fruit. The question arose in a nineteenth-century tariff case because fruits could be imported duty free under an 1883 tariff act, but vegetables were required to pay a duty equal to 10 percent of their value.

Maintaining that tomatoes were fruits, an importer sued the New York port collector to recover back duties. But in 1893 the Court, in *Nix v. Hedden* (149 U.S. 305), held that tomatoes were vegetables. Delivering the opinion of the Court, Justice Horace Gray wrote:

Botanically speaking, tomatoes are the fruit of a vine, just as are cucumbers, squashes, beans and peas. But in the common language of the people, whether sellers or consumers of provisions, all these are vegetables, which are grown in kitchen gardens, and which, whether eaten cooked or raw, are, like potatoes, carrots, parsnips, turnips, beets, cauliflower, cabbage, celery and lettuce, usually served at dinner in, with, or after the soup, fish or meats which constitute the principal part of the repast, and not, like fruits generally, as dessert.

When the tax power has been used as a regulatory tool to support or enforce another constitutional power, the Court has generally sustained it, even if the tax was designed to eliminate the matter taxed. A landmark decision illustrating this view is *Veazie Bank v. Fenno,* decided in 1869.[27]

Congress had placed a 10 percent tax on the circulation of state bank notes in order to give the untaxed national bank notes the competitive edge and drive the state notes out of the market. The Court upheld the statute on the ground that it was a legitimate means through which Congress could exercise its constitutional authority to regulate the currency.

The taxing power has also been upheld as an auxiliary to the commerce power. In 1884 the Court held that a 50-cent tax on each immigrant levied on shipowners and used to support indigent immigrants was not a use of the tax power as such but rather the exercise of the foreign commerce power.[28] *(See box, Regulation of Foreign Commerce, p. 108.)*

In 1940 the Court upheld the Bituminous Coal Act of 1937, which imposed a stiff tax on sales of coal in interstate commerce but exempted those producers who agreed to abide by industry price and competition regulations. The Court acknowledged that the exemption was intended to force compliance with the code, but said that Congress "may impose penalties in aid of the exercise of any of its enumerated powers," in this case, the commerce clause.[29]

The 1940 ruling effectively overturned the Court's decision in *Carter v. Carter Coal Co.* (1936), which held a similar tax in the 1935 Bituminous Coal Conservation Act to be an unconstitutional penalty for noncompliance with the industry regulations rather than a tax designed to raise revenues.[30] *(See "Coal Codes," pp. 107–109.)*

COLORED OLEO

Where Congress used the taxing power on its own to achieve a desired social or economic goal, the Court developed two distinct lines of precedents, just as it had in its early review of the use of commerce power as a policing mechanism.

The first line essentially held that so long as the tax produced some revenue, the Court would not examine the motives behind its imposition. One year after the Court sustained use of the commerce power as a police tool in the *Lottery Case,* it upheld use of the taxing power to attain similar objectives. *McCray v. United States* (1904) involved a federal statute that placed a tax of 10 cents per pound on oleo colored yellow to resemble butter, but taxed uncolored oleo only a one-fourth of a cent per pound. The tax was clearly intended to remove the competition to butter by making it too expensive to manufacture colored oleo. It was challenged as an invasion of state police powers and as a violation of due process.[31]

But the Court disagreed, holding that the tax was an excise tax and therefore was permissible. "The decisions of this Court," wrote Chief Justice Edward D. White, "lend no support whatever to the assumption that the judiciary may restrain the exercise

of a lawful power on the assumption that a wrongful purpose or motive has caused the power to be exerted."[32]

Similar reasoning was used by the Court to uphold the Harrison Anti-Narcotics Act of 1914. This statute required people dealing in narcotics to pay a small annual registration fee and to keep certain records. It also made manufacture, sale, and shipment of narcotics illegal.

A five-man majority in *United States v. Doremus* upheld the narcotics registration tax in 1919. "The Act may not be declared unconstitutional because its effect may be to accomplish another purpose as well as the raising of revenue," wrote Justice William R. Day.[33] The four dissenters contended that the tax was an exercise of the police power that they believed was reserved to the states.

CHILD LABOR

Three years later, that dissenting view in *Doremus* became the majority position, beginning the second line of precedents. In the next major tax regulation case, the Court decided that a tax was unconstitutional if its primary purpose was the punishment of a certain action, not the raising of revenue.

Bailey v. Drexel Furniture Co. (1922) focused on Congress's second attempt to end child labor.[34] After the Court ruled in 1918 that the commerce power could not be used to reach what many considered a despicable practice, Congress turned to the taxing power, imposing a 10 percent tax on the net profits of any company that employed children under a certain age. Although similar to statutory tax schemes the Court had approved before, the Court nevertheless declared the tax unconstitutional. *(See "The Commerce Power, Child Labor," p. 104.)*

Chief Justice William Howard Taft, for the eight-justice majority, said the child labor tax was a penalty intended to coerce employers to end their use of child labor.

Taxes are occasionally imposed . . . on proper subjects with the primary motive of obtaining revenue from them and with the incidental motive of discouraging them by making their continuation onerous. They do not lose their character as taxes because of the incidental motive. But there comes a time in the extension of the penalizing features of the so-called tax when it loses its character as such and becomes a mere penalty with the characteristics of regulation and punishment. Such is the case in the law before us.[35]

Linking that ruling with its holding in the 1918 case, *Hammer v. Dagenhart,* Taft said that just as use of the commerce power to regulate wholly internal matters of the state was invalid, so was use of the taxing power to achieve the same purpose. The consequences of validating such a law were grave, Taft continued. "To give such magic to the word 'tax,'" he said, "would be to break down all constitutional limitation of the powers of Congress and completely wipe out the sovereignty of the States."[36]

Taft distinguished the ruling in the child labor tax case from the holdings in *McCray* and *Doremus* by asserting that the primary purpose of the taxes in the later case was to raise revenue. He further distinguished the *Doremus* case by claiming that the regulations outlined in the narcotics control statute were neces-

Severability refers to the ability of part of a law to survive even after another part of the same statute has been held invalid. Without this capability, an entire statute would become void because of a single flawed provision. As one authority wrote:

Whether or not the judicial determination of partial validity will so disembowel the legislation that it must fall as a whole, or whether the valid portion will be enforced separately is a question of importance second only to the initial determination of validity. That parts of a statute may be enforced separately provided certain conditions are met has become a fundamental legal concept.[1]

Severability, or separability as it is also called, grows out of the concept that the judiciary should uphold the constitutionality of legislative acts where possible. For a court to find a statute separable, that finding must coincide with legislative intent and the design of the law. To determine intent, the court may examine the act's history, its object, context, title, and preamble. Legislative intent was one of the reasons the Court gave for striking down the general income tax in 1895. Having declared that the tax on income from property was unconstitutional, the Court said that would leave only taxes on occupations and labor, adding: "We cannot believe that such was the intention of Congress."[2] *(See "The Income Tax Cases," pp. 118–121.)*

Despite a severability clause in the Bituminous Coal Conservation Act of 1935, the Supreme Court in 1936 ruled that the price-fixing provisions of the act were inseparable from the labor regulations provisions it had declared unconstitutional. "The statutory mandate for a [coal industry] code upheld by two legs at once suggests the improbability that Congress would have assented to a code supported by only one," wrote the Court.[3] *(See "Coal Codes," pp. 107–109.)*

To be severed, the valid portion of the law must be independent and complete in itself. If eliminating part of the law would defeat or change its purpose, the entire act should be declared void. The Court applied this principle in 1935 when it declared the Railroad Retirement Pension Act of 1934 unconstitutional. Finding certain portions of the act invalid, the Court said that those portions "so affect the dominant aim of the whole statute as to carry it down with them."[4] *(See "Pensions," p. 97.)*

Congress commonly includes a severability or saving clause in legislation, declaring that if one part of the statute is found unconstitutional, the rest of the act may stand. The clause is of relatively modern usage and is not critical to a court determination as to separability. Justice Louis D. Brandeis wrote that the saving clause was sometimes an aid in determining legislative intent, "but it is an aid merely, not an inexorable command."[5]

The general rule followed by the Court on separability clauses was enunciated in 1929. When a separability clause is included, wrote Justice George Sutherland, the Court begins with the presumption that the legislature intended the act to be divisible; and this presumption must be overcome by considerations which make evident the inseparability of its provisions or the clear probability that the invalid part being eliminated the legislature would not have been satisfied with what remains.[6]

Riders to appropriations or revenue bills are the most typical examples of severability. For instance, the sections of the 1919 Revenue Act imposing a tax on articles made by child labor were ruled unconstitutional in 1922, but the rest of the statute was unaffected.[7] Robert E. Cushman observes that the Court has never invalidated an appropriations or revenue bill just because one rider was found invalid.[8]

The Court reiterated its severability doctrine in 1992 when it reviewed an innovative federal law making states responsible for the disposal of low-level radioactive waste generated within their borders and severed a provision that violated the Tenth Amendment guarantee of state sovereignty.[9] The section deemed unconstitutional said states that failed to provide for disposal of low-level radioactive waste became the legal owners of the waste and assumed liability for any injuries caused by it.

The Court went on to uphold the Low-Level Radioactive Waste Policy Amendments Act of 1985, saying that severance of the unconstitutional clause would not prevent enforcement of the rest of the act or defeat its purpose of encouraging the states to be responsible for the disposal of radioactive waste.

Justice Sandra Day O'Connor wrote for the Court, citing precedent: "The standard for determining the severability of an unconstitutional provision is well established: Unless it is evident that the Legislature would not have enacted those provisions which are within its power, independently of that which is not, the invalid part may be dropped if what is left is fully operative as a law."

Although the act contained no severability clause, she continued, "Common sense suggests that where Congress has enacted a statutory scheme for an obvious purpose, and where Congress has included a series of provisions operating as incentives to achieve that purpose, the invalidation of one of the incentives should not ordinarily cause Congress' overall intent to be frustrated."[10]

1. C. Dallas Sands, *Statutes and Statutory Construction*, 4th ed. (Chicago: Callaghan, 1973), II: 335.
2. *Pollock v. Farmers' Loan and Trust Co.*, 158 U.S. 601 at 637 (1895).
3. *Carter v. Carter Coal Co.*, 298 U.S. 238 at 314 (1936).
4. *Railroad Retirement Board v. Alton Railway Co.*, 295 U.S. 330 at 362 (1935).
5. *Dorchy v. Kansas*, 264 U.S. 286 at 290 (1924).
6. *Williams v. Standard Oil Co. of Louisiana*, 278 U.S. 235 at 242 (1929).
7. *Bailey v. Drexel Furniture Co.*, 259 U.S. 20 (1922).
8. Robert E. Cushman and Robert F. Cushman, *Cases in Constitutional Law*, 3d ed. (New York: Appleton-Century-Crofts, 1968), 70.
9. *New York v. United States*, 112 S. Ct. 2408 (1992).
10. Id.

CRIME PAYS . . . TAXES

The Internal Revenue Service just does not believe the old saying that "crime doesn't pay," and the Supreme Court has consistently held that income from illegal activities is taxable.

"We see no reason . . . why the fact that a business is unlawful should exempt it from paying the taxes that if lawful it would have to pay," wrote Justice Oliver Wendell Holmes Jr. in 1927.[1] The Court has held taxable the income from illegal sales of liquor, extortion, and embezzlement.[2]

If taxes are due on illegal incomes, are illegal expenses, such as bribery, deductible? "This by no means follows," said Holmes, "but it will be time enough to consider the question when a taxpayer has the temerity to raise it."[3]

A taxpayer finally did. In 1958 the Court was asked to determine if a bookmaking operation could deduct as ordinary and necessary business expenses the salaries of its bookies and the rent it paid. Both paying employees and renting space to conduct illegal activities were against the law in Illinois where the case arose.

Writing for the Court, Justice William O. Douglas held that the expenses fit the meaning of the Treasury regulations regarding taxable income and were therefore deductible.[4]

1. *United States v. Sullivan*, 274 U.S. 259 (1927).
2. Ibid.; *Rutkin v. United States*, 343 U.S. 130 (1952); *James v. United States*, 366 U.S. 213 (1961).
3. *United States v. Sullivan*, 274 U.S. 259 at 264 (1927).
4. *Commissioner of Internal Revenue v. Sullivan*, 356 U.S. 27 (1958).

sary to the collection of the tax "and not solely to achievement of some other purpose plainly within state power."[37]

Commentators have questioned the logic of Taft's reasoning. If it was clear that Congress wanted to stop child labor, it was just as clear that Congress intended to terminate the colored oleo industry and closely regulate the manufacture and sale of narcotics. But the significant factor was Taft's implicit claim that the Court would determine when a tax became a penalty; the Court would be the final authority in determining the primary motive of Congress in imposing a tax.

Taft reinforced the reasoning laid out in the child labor decision by applying it to a second case decided the same day. In an attempt to stop some unethical practices by some commodity exchanges, the Futures Trading Act of 1921 imposed a tax of 20 cents per bushel on all contracts for sales of grain for future delivery, but exempted those sales arranged through boards of trade that met certain requirements set out in the act.

The Court struck down the statute. When the stated purpose of the statute is to regulate the boards of trade, wrote Taft, and when the purpose "is so clear from the effect of the provisions of the bill itself, it leaves no ground upon which the provisions . . . can be sustained as a valid exercise of the taxing power."[38] The Court in 1923 approved a second attempt to regulate commodity exchanges when it upheld the Grain Futures Act of 1922 as a

valid exercise of the commerce power.[39] *(See details of Board of Trade of Chicago v. Olsen, p. 100.)*

The *Bailey* precedent was applied again in 1935 to invalidate a provision of the 1926 Revenue Act that imposed a $1,000 excise tax on liquor dealers doing business in violation of state or local prohibition laws. The Court held that the tax was actually a penalty and was valid only so long as Congress had the authority under the Eighteenth Amendment to enforce nationwide prohibition. When the amendment was repealed (by adoption of the Twenty-first Amendment in 1933), the $1,000 penalty also fell.[40]

This line of precedent culminated in two 1936 New Deal cases involving the taxing power. In *Carter v. Carter Coal Co.* the Court struck down the Bituminous Coal Conservation Act of 1935 partly because of its provision reducing a coal tax for coal producers who complied with labor regulations set out in the statute. The Court found this provision a penalty on producers who refused to comply.[41] In *United States v. Butler* the Court invalidated a tax on certain food processors, the revenue from which was used to pay farmers to cut their production of certain foods. The Court said the tax was part of an unconstitutional regulatory scheme.[42] *(See "Coal Codes," pp. 107–109; details of United States v. Butler, p. 127.)*

REGULATORY TAX UPHELD

A few months later, following Roosevelt's "Court-packing" plan, the Court abandoned this line of precedent and retreated to the reasoning in the oleo case. It upheld the National Firearms Act of 1934, which imposed an annual license tax on manufacturers of and dealers in certain classes of firearms, such as sawed-off shotguns and machine guns, likely to be used by criminals. The act, which also required identification of purchasers, clearly was intended to discourage sales of such weapons.

Upholding the validity of the tax, the Court directly criticized Taft's opinion in the *Bailey* child labor tax case. Noting that the license tax produced some revenue, the Court added:

Every tax is in some measure regulatory. . . . But a tax is not any the less a tax because it has a regulatory effect, . . . and it has long been established that an Act of Congress which on its face purports to be an exercise of the taxing power is not any the less so because the tax is burdensome or tends to restrict or suppress the thing taxed.

Inquiry into the hidden motive which may move Congress to exercise a power constitutionally conferred upon it is beyond the competency of the courts. . . . They will not undertake . . . to ascribe to Congress an attempt, under the guise of taxation, to exercise another power denied by the Federal Constitution.[43]

Taxes on marijuana and on gamblers were subsequently upheld with similar reasoning.[44] However, the statute authorizing a tax on persons in the business of accepting wagers also required them to register with the Internal Revenue Service. The Court refused to find the registration requirement a violation of the Fifth Amendment's self-incrimination clause, even where the gambler was doing business in a state that prohibited gambling.

In 1968 and 1969 the Court reversed this part of the decision, holding that registration requirements of regulatory tax laws did in fact compel self-incrimination where the activity taxed was unlawful. These decisions in no way diminished the ability of Congress to use the tax power as a regulatory or penalty mechanism, however.[45] *(See "Self-Incrimination," pp. 589–598, in Chapter 11.)*

JUDGES AND TAXES

Would the salaries of federal judges—including Supreme Court justices—be immune from the federal income tax? That question was offered by Justice Howell E. Jackson in 1895 during the Court's consideration of the 1890 income tax law.

In a letter to Chief Justice Melville W. Fuller, Jackson asked if the income tax conflicted with the constitutional prohibition against reducing a judge's salary during his term of office. "Does that [1890] Act include our salary as members of the Supreme Court?" Jackson queried. "It seems to me that it cannot. That Congress cannot do indirectly what it is prohibited from doing directly."[1]

The question was put aside after the Court declared the income tax unconstitutional, but it came up again shortly after the federal income tax law implementing the Sixteenth Amendment was enacted. In 1920 the Court agreed with Jackson's assessment and ruled that the salaries of sitting federal judges were immune from the federal income tax.[2] *(See "Direct Taxes," pp. 118–121.)*

Joined by Justice Louis D. Brandeis, Justice Oliver Wendell Holmes Jr. dissented: "[T]he exemption of salaries from diminution is intended to secure the independence of judges on the ground, as it was put by Hamilton in the *Federalist* (No. 79), that 'a power over a man's subsistence amounts to a power over his will. . . .' That . . . seems to me no reason for exonerating [a judge] from the ordinary duties of a citizen, which he shares with all others."[3]

In 1925 the Court expanded this immunity to include judges who were appointed after the income tax law was enacted.[4] Congress subsequently passed a law providing that salaries of judges appointed after its passage would be subject to the income tax. The Court upheld this statute in 1939, specifically overruling the earlier cases.[5]

To impose a nondiscriminatory income tax on judges' salaries "is merely to recognize that judges are also citizens, and that their particular function in government does not generate an immunity from sharing with their fellow citizens the material burden of the government whose Constitution and laws they are charged with administering," the Court wrote.[6]

Holmes until his retirement in 1932 and Brandeis until his retirement in 1939 voluntarily paid federal income tax.

1. Quoted by Leo Pfeffer in *This Honorable Court* (Boston: Beacon Press, 1965), 223; see also Carl Swisher, *American Constitutional Development*, 2d ed. (Cambridge, Mass.: Houghton Mifflin, 1954), 437.
2. *Evans v. Gore*, 253 U.S. 245 (1920).
3. Id. at 265.
4. *Miles v. Graham*, 268 U.S. 501 (1925).
5. *O'Malley v. Woodrough*, 307 U.S. 277 (1939).
6. Id. at 282.

FEDERAL-STATE TAX IMMUNITIES

"The power to tax involves the power to destroy," declared Chief Justice John Marshall in 1819, setting out the basis for the major implied limitation on the federal government's taxing power.[46] Marshall announced this maxim as the Court ruled that a state could not tax the national bank, intending by this holding to prevent the states from taxing the new and still fragile central government out of existence. In 1842 federal immunity from state taxation was expanded further when the Court ruled that states could not tax the incomes of federal officers.[47]

But the immunity conferred by these holdings cut two ways. In 1871 the Court held that the federal government could not tax the income of state officials. If the states could not threaten the sovereignty of the federal government by taxing its officers, instrumentalities, and property, then neither could the national government use the taxing power to threaten the sovereignty of the states, the Court declared.[48]

For a century the Court applied this doctrine extensively. In 1829 it held that a state could not tax federally owned real estate.[49] In 1895 the Court ruled, as part of the *Income Tax Cases*, that the national government could not impose a tax on state or municipal bonds.[50] At various times the most tangential of relationships with one or the other level of government conferred immunity upon the taxpayer. For example, in 1931 a federal tax on the sales of motorcycles to a city police department was held invalid.[51]

But gradually, the Court began to limit immunities granted to both the federal and state governments. State immunity from federal taxation was restricted to activities of a "strictly governmental nature." States generally were no longer immune from federal taxes on activities that, if performed by a private corporation, would be taxable. Federal contractors were much less often granted immunity from state taxation, and income tax immunity for state and federal officials was overturned in 1938 and 1939.[52]

As the doctrine of immunity stood in the late 1970s, the federal government was prohibited from taxing state government property and instrumentalities. The most significant of the prohibitions continued to bar federal taxation of state and municipal bonds, but this limit was nullified in 1988 with the Supreme Court's decision in *South Carolina v. Baker*. Effectively burying the doctrine of intergovernmental tax immunity, the Supreme Court declared that nothing in the Constitution restrained Congress from taxing the interest paid on state and municipal bonds. States and cities wishing to preserve that immunity must do so by working through the political process to convince their representatives in Congress to refrain from taxing the funds, the Court held.[53]

Federally owned property remains generally immune from state taxation.[54] States may not tax congressionally chartered fiscal institutions without the consent of Congress, although they may assess property taxes on other federally chartered corporations.[55] Income from federal securities and tax-exempt bonds may not be taxed by the states, although the Court has ruled that a state may tax the interest accrued on government bonds and estates that included U.S. bonds.[56]

Government contractors are generally subject to state taxes, even if the taxes increase the cost of the contract to the federal government. States generally, however, cannot levy a property tax on government property used by a private person in the fulfillment of a government contract, although a privilege tax measured by the value of the government property held is permissible.[57] (See "Intergovernmental Immunity," p. 372, in Chapter 7.)

The Power to Spend

The authority of Congress to appropriate and spend money under the necessary and proper clause to carry out any of its enumerated powers has been broadly interpreted by the Court. From the early days of the Union, the power to spend money for internal improvements has been justified by the authority given Congress over war, interstate commerce, territories, and the mails.

Use of the spending power rarely has been challenged, partly because the Court, by finding that neither a taxpayer nor a state has standing to sue, has made it extremely difficult to bring a challenge. In a pair of cases considered together in 1923, a taxpayer, Frothingham, and a state, Massachusetts, questioned the validity of a federal grant-in-aid program, a mechanism whereby the federal government gives a certain amount of money, generally for a certain purpose and usually with the requirement that the states meet certain conditions, such as matching the grant. Such programs were just coming into use and were considered by many an infringement of states' rights.

Because Frothingham's "interest in the moneys of the Treasury . . . is comparatively minute and indeterminate" and because "the effect upon future taxation, of any payment out of the funds . . . [is] remote, fluctuating and uncertain," the Court held that the taxpayer did not have sufficient injury to sue.[58] This holding was modified subsequently to permit some taxpayers' challenges. (See "'Standing to Sue,'" pp. 300–302, in Chapter 6.)

The Court also ruled that the state, which had sought to sue in behalf of its citizens, had no standing. "It cannot be conceded that a state . . . may institute judicial proceedings to protect citizens of the United States from the operation of the statutes thereof," the Court said.[59]

Challenges to spending for internal improvements or public works projects also were rebuffed by the Court. In 1938 the Court upheld federal loans to municipalities for power projects, ruling that the state-chartered power companies that had questioned the loans had no right to be free from competition and had not suffered sufficient damages to have standing to bring the case as federal taxpayers.[60]

The Court also has refused to limit congressional use of grants-in-aid programs. The first challenge came in the two 1923 cases and concerned the Sheppard-Towner Act, which subsidized state maternity and infant welfare programs. The plaintiffs claimed that the grant-in-aid was a subtle form of federal invasion of state sovereignty and that if a state refused the grant, it was a burden on the state's citizens, whose federal taxes supported the grants in participating states.

Neither the taxpayer nor the state had standing to challenge the statute in the eyes of the Court, but, in his majority opinion, Justice George Sutherland implied the Court would uphold grants-in-aid as constitutional. "Probably," Sutherland said, "it would be sufficient to point out that the powers of the state are not invaded, since the statute imposes no obligation, but simply extends an option which the state is free to accept or reject."[61]

With the passage of time, Sutherland's dicta gained the force of law. In 1947 Oklahoma challenged a provision of the Hatch Act under which its federal highway funds would be reduced if it did not remove a state highway commission officer who had actively participated in partisan politics in violation of the act. The state challenged this requirement as improper federal control over its internal political matters. The Court rejected the claim:

While the United States is not concerned with, and has no power to regulate local political activities as such of State officials, it does have power to fix the terms upon which its money allotments to States shall be disbursed.[62]

This point was reaffirmed in the case of *South Dakota v. Dole* (1987). The Court held that Congress may condition a state's receipt of the full allocation of federal highway funds upon the state's decision to raise the drinking age to twenty-one. South Dakota had challenged this condition as barred by the Twenty-first Amendment's grant to states of the authority to control the sale and consumption of liquor within their boundaries.[63]

Spending for the General Welfare

Article I, Section 8, Clause 1, also gives Congress the power "to provide for the common defense and general welfare." From the beginning there were differences over what that clause meant. One view limited it to spending for purposes connected with the powers specifically enumerated in the Constitution. This was the strict interpretation associated with James Madison. "Nothing is more natural nor common," Madison wrote in No. 41 of *The Federalist Papers*, "than first to use a general phrase, and then to explain and qualify it by recital of particulars."[64]

The other view, associated with Alexander Hamilton, was that the general welfare clause conferred upon the government a power independent from those enumerated. This broad construction eventually came to be the accepted view, but not for quite a while—it was almost 150 years before the Court found it necessary to interpret the clause at all.

The first time the Court addressed the interpretation of the general welfare clause, it gave lip service to Hamilton's stance, but then limited the interpretation by claiming that the power to spend had been combined in this instance with the power to tax to regulate a matter outside the scope of the federal government's powers—agricultural production. In other words, the

In *United States v. Butler* (1936) the Court invalidated one of the pillars of the New Deal, the Agricultural Adjustment Act. Pictured is William M. Butler, whose refusal to comply with the act's provisions gave rise to the case.

Court said Congress had combined the two powers in an improper exercise of the federal police power.

The question before the Court was the constitutionality of the Agricultural Adjustment Act of 1933 (AAA), the New Deal measure passed during the first hundred days of Roosevelt's presidency to boost farm prices and farmers' purchasing power. The statute provided that an excise tax would be levied on the processors of seven food commodities and the proceeds of the tax would be used to pay benefits to farmers who reduced their production of those commodities. The case of *United States v. Butler* arose when William M. Butler, a receiver for a bankrupt cotton mill company, refused to pay the processing tax.[65]

In addition to determining whether the benefit payment scheme was a valid exercise of the power to spend for the general welfare, the Court also was required to choose between two lines of precedent to determine the validity of the tax portion of the statute. Under one set of cases, the Court could find the tax valid; under the other, it could declare it invalid because in reality it was a penalty designed to regulate a wholly intrastate matter.

As in earlier New Deal cases, the Court chose the more restrictive interpretation. Writing for the six-man majority, Justice Owen J. Roberts said the tax was not a tax in the normal sense of the word, but "an expropriation of money from one group for the benefit of another" as part of a regulatory device.[66]

The tax was unconstitutional under the taxing power, although, Roberts said, it might be valid if it were enacted as "an expedient regulation" of another enumerated power.[67] This was not the case here either, Roberts continued. Clearly, the enumerated power could not be the power over interstate commerce since agricultural production was an intrastate matter, he said, noting that the government had not argued the validity of the act on the basis of the commerce power.

Roberts then turned to the benefit payments and the general welfare clause. Reviewing the interpretations placed on the clause by Madison and Hamilton, Roberts concluded that Hamilton's was correct. "[T]he power of Congress to authorize is not limited by the first grants of legislative power found in the Constitution," Roberts declared.[68]

Notwithstanding this point, Roberts next declared the crop benefit payments an unconstitutional invasion of the rights reserved to the states. The AAA, he said,

is a statutory plan to regulate and control agricultural production, a matter beyond the powers delegated to the federal government. The tax, the appropriation of funds raised, and the direction of their disbursement, are but parts of the plan. They are but means to an unconstitutional end.[69]

In contrast to Justice Sutherland's dicta in the 1923 grant-in-aid cases, Roberts rejected the argument that compliance with the federal statute was voluntary. "The power to confer or withhold unlimited benefits is the power to coerce or destroy," Roberts said.[70]

He also rejected the contention that the national economic emergency empowered Congress to regulate agricultural production.

It does not help to declare that local conditions throughout the nation have created a situation of national concern; for this is but to say that whenever there is a widespread similarity of local conditions, Congress may ignore constitutional limitations upon its own powers and usurp those reserved to the states. . . . If the act before us is a proper exercise of the federal taxing power, evidently the regulation of all industry throughout the United States may be accomplished by similar exercises of the same power.[71]

For the minority, Justice Harlan Fiske Stone argued that regulation contemplated under the AAA was not accomplished by the tax, but by the way the proceeds were used. The same regulation could be achieved by spending any Treasury funds, no matter what their source, he said, adding that the processing tax simply defrayed the public expense of the benefit payments.

Stone also castigated the majority's weakening of the spending power and invalidation of the benefit payments. "It is a contradiction in terms to say that there is a power to spend for the national welfare, while rejecting any power to impose conditions reasonably adopted to the attainment of the end which alone would justify the expenditure," he said.[72]

Stone's dissent presaged the stand the Court, chastened by President Roosevelt's Court-packing plan, would take a year and

THE BORROWING POWER

The federal government's power to borrow money is not only expressly conferred in the Constitution, but, scholars have noted, it is one of the very few federal powers "entirely unencumbered by restrictions—with the result that Congress may borrow from any lenders, for any purposes, in any amounts, or on any terms, and with or without provision for the repayment of loans, with or without interest."[1]

The power to borrow is so broad that it has been rarely challenged. The Supreme Court cases dealing with this power have produced decisions that give the widest possible latitude to the government in exercising it. For example, the Court has struck down state taxes on federal bonds and securities because such taxes would impair the central government's ability to borrow money.[2] (See "The Taxing Power," pp. 371–372, in Chapter 7.)

The only restriction the Court has placed on the power to borrow came in one of the 1935 Gold Clause Cases, which held that Congress may not change the terms of a loan.[3] (See "The Currency Powers," pp. 128–133.)

1. Frederick A. Ogg and P. Orman Ray, Introduction to American Government (New York: Appleton-Century-Crofts, 1951), 527.
2. Weston v. City Council of Charleston, 2 Pet. 449 (1829).
3. Perry v. United States, 294 U.S. 330 (1935).

a half later. In 1937 the Court upheld in two separate cases portions of the 1935 Social Security Act. Although the Court did not formally overturn its decision in Butler, it effectively left it a dead letter.

The first case, Steward Machine Co. v. Davis (1937), was a test of the unemployment compensation provisions of a statute that taxed employers; employers could earn a tax credit if they contributed to a federally approved state unemployment compensation insurance system.[73] The law was challenged on the grounds that the tax was not intended to raise revenue but to regulate employment, which was an internal matter for the states, and that the states had been coerced into yielding a portion of their sovereignty to the federal government.

The challenges were rejected, 5–4. Justice Roberts, who had written the opinion in Butler, now joined the majority in minimizing its impact.

Justice Benjamin N. Cardozo for the majority first explained its view that Congress had the power to tax employment. "Employment is a business relation ... without which business could seldom be carried on effectively," he said, adding that the power to tax business extended to the power to tax any of its parts.[74]

The Court found the statute no invasion of states' rights or sovereignty but rather an example of cooperation between the national government and the state to overcome the common evil of unemployment. The statute represented a national means to solve what had become a national problem insoluble by the states acting independently of each other. "It is too late

today for the argument to be heard with tolerance that in a crisis so extreme the use of the moneys of the nation to relieve the unemployed and their dependents is a use for any purpose narrower than the promotion of the general welfare," Cardozo wrote.[75]

The justice acknowledged that the tax credit granted on the basis of fulfillment of certain conditions was "in some measure a temptation. But to hold that motive or temptation is equivalent to coercion is to plunge the law into endless difficulties." In any event, Cardozo added, the point of coercion had not been reached in the case at hand.[76] Nor were the conditions themselves coercive, he continued. The states were given a wide range of choice in enacting laws to fulfill the requirements, and they could withdraw at any time from the state-federal cooperative arrangement.

Cardozo distinguished the unemployment compensation case from Butler on two other points. First, unlike the agricultural production case, the proceeds from the employment tax were not earmarked for a specific group of people, but instead went into the general revenues of the country. Second, the states specifically had to approve the tax credit by passing a law allowing it, unlike the AAA, which attempted to regulate without permission from the states.

In the second case, Helvering v. Davis, decided the same day by a 7–2 vote, the Court upheld the constitutionality of federal old age benefits.[77] In this opinion, Cardozo acknowledged that in spending for the general welfare, a

line must still be drawn between one welfare and another, between particular and general. Where this shall be placed cannot be known through a formula in advance of the event. There is a middle ground ... in which discretion is at large. The discretion, however, is not confided to the courts. The discretion belongs to Congress, unless the choice is clearly wrong, a display of arbitrary power, not an exercise of judgment.[78]

Cardozo then showed that Congress had not been arbitrary in this case but that the statute was warranted by a need to solve a national problem that the states could not cure individually. Nor could the states oppose what Congress determined to be the national welfare, Cardozo said. "[T]he concept of welfare or the opposite is shaped by Congress, not the states. So [long as] the concept be not arbitrary, the locality must yield."[79]

The Currency Powers

The power "[to] coin Money, regulate the Value thereof, and of foreign Coin, and fix the Standard of Weights and Measures" has been construed, with one brief but significant exception, to give Congress complete control over the nation's currency.

As the Court upheld creation of the national bank, established largely to give some stability to the various state and foreign currencies in use during the Union's early history, John Marshall gave his classic definition of the necessary and proper clause.[80] (See "Implied Powers," pp. 80–82.)

A national currency did not exist until the Civil War when

Congress authorized the printing of paper money or "greenbacks" and made them legal tender for the payment of debts. In 1869 the Court upheld a federal tax that was intended to drive state bank notes out of circulation and leave a single uniform national currency.[81] (See details of Veazie Bank v. Fenno, p. 122.)

Also in 1869 the Court ruled that greenbacks could not be substituted as payment in cases where the contract specifically stipulated payment in gold, which was then the preferred medium of exchange.[82] Left unanswered was whether a creditor could refuse payment in greenbacks if the contract did not specify gold.

This question was raised as early as 1863 in *Roosevelt v. Meyer*, but the Court refused to take the case, claiming it did not have jurisdiction.[83] Constitutional scholar Robert G. McCloskey, in his book *The American Supreme Court*, found this claim contrived. "We must assume," McCloskey wrote, "either that the judges were unfamiliar with the law that furnishes their very basis for being, or that they deliberately chose a Pickwickian interpretation in order to avoid deciding, in wartime, a question so central to the conduct of war."[84] The government had issued the paper money to finance its war debts, including the salaries of its fighting men. It could not have afforded to pay them in gold.

FIRST LEGAL TENDER DECISION

But when the war ended, the Court no longer avoided deciding the issue, at least so far as it pertained to contracts entered into prior to 1862, when the paper currency was first issued. The case of *Hepburn v. Griswold* came to the Court in 1865.[85] It was argued in 1867 and reargued in 1868. In the words of historian Charles Warren:

The probable action of the Court had been the subject of long and excited debate in the community. On the one side, were the National and the State banks, the mortgagees and creditors who demanded payment in gold; lined up with these interests were those men who, on principle, denied the right of the Federal Government to make paper currency legal tender, and opposed legalized cheating through the enforced payment of debts in depreciated currency. On the other side, were the railroads, the municipal corporations, the mortgagors of land and other debtors who now sought to pay, with a depreciated legal tender currency, debts contracted on a gold basis before the war; and with these interests, there were associated all those men who felt strongly that the Government ought not to be deprived of a power which they considered so necessary to its existence in time of war.[86]

The Court was not ready to deliver its opinion until February 7, 1870. At the time the Court had only seven justices because Congress in 1866 had reduced its size to deprive President Andrew Johnson of an appointment. When Ulysses S. Grant succeeded to the presidency, Congress returned the number of justices to nine, but then refused to confirm Grant's first nominee, Attorney General Ebenezer R. Hoar. And a week before the Court announced its *Hepburn* decision, Justice Robert C. Grier retired. Therefore, it was by a 4–3 split that the Court invalidated the law. It was the third major act of Congress the Court had found unconstitutional. (See box, *Significant Acts of Congress Struck Down as Unconstitutional, pp. 130–131.*)

Rejecting the government's claim that the legal tender laws were a valid means of exercising the war power, the Court ruled against the constitutionality of using paper money to pay debts contracted prior to 1862. The opinion was delivered by Chief Justice Salmon P. Chase, who, ironically, as President Lincoln's secretary of the Treasury, had advocated enactment of the legal tender statutes. Lincoln in fact had nominated Chase to the Court because, he said, "we wish for a Chief Justice who will sustain what has been done in regard to emancipation and the legal tenders."[87]

For the Court, Chase acknowledged that Congress in the exercise of its express powers had the unrestricted right to choose "among means appropriate, plainly adapted, really calculated."[88] But, he said, it was up to the Court, not Congress, to decide whether the means chosen was appropriate.

Chase denied that the express power to issue currency implied a power to make that currency legal tender in the payment of debts. Furthermore, Chase said, whatever benefit might come from allowing paper money to be used as legal tender was "far more than outweighed by the losses of property, the derangement of business, the fluctuations of currency and values, and the increase of prices to the people and the government and the long train of evils which flow from the use of irredeemable paper money."[89]

Given that, Chase continued, "[W]e are unable to persuade ourselves that an expedient of this sort is an appropriate and plainly adapted means for the execution of the power to declare and carry on war."[90] Chase concluded that the statutes were not an appropriate use of Congress's implied powers under the necessary and proper clause.

Chase then noted that the statute could be viewed as impairing the obligations of contracts. He acknowledged that Congress under its express power to establish national bankruptcy laws incidentally had the right to impair contract obligations. But, Chase said, "we cannot doubt that a law not made in pursuance of an express power, which necessarily and in its direct operation impairs the obligation of contracts, is inconsistent with the spirit of the Constitution."[91] The legal tender acts were also a similar spiritual violation of the Fifth Amendment's prohibition against taking private property for public use without due process of law, Chase added.

While the decision applied only to contracts made before the paper currency was issued, Chase's reasoning brought into serious question the validity of using paper money to pay debts incurred after 1862. The consequences, if this were found to be true, were grave. The Court itself in the very near future would describe them:

It is also clear that if we hold the acts invalid as applicable to debts incurred . . . which have taken place since their enactment, our decision must cause, throughout the country, great business derangement, widespread distress, and the rankest injustice. The debts which have been contracted since . . . 1862 . . . constitute, doubtless, by far the greatest portion of the existing indebtedness of the country. . . . Men have bought and sold, borrowed and lent, and assumed every variety

SIGNIFICANT ACTS OF CONGRESS STRUCK DOWN AS UNCONSTITUTIONAL

From its first declaration that an act of Congress was unconstitutional in *Marbury v. Madison* (1803), the Supreme Court has found 135 particular federal laws to be in violation of the Constitution. (This number does not take into account the hundreds of laws containing legislative veto provisions that were indirectly held unconstitutional when the Court invalidated that device in 1983.)

Only a handful of the laws struck down have been of major significance for the Court and the country. Following is a brief explanation of those statutes and the Court's decisions. *(See "Acts of Congress Held Unconstitutional," p. 1102, in Reference Materials.)*

MISSOURI COMPROMISE

In *Scott v. Sandford* (1857) the Supreme Court declared unconstitutional the recently repealed Missouri Compromise of 1820, which prohibited slavery in the Louisiana territories lying north of 36° 30'. Chief Justice Roger B. Taney wrote that slaves were property and that Congress had no authority to regulate local property rights. Taney also held that even free blacks were not and could not become citizens of the United States.

The opinion seriously damaged the Court's prestige, and, rather than settling the slavery question, the decision probably hastened the onset of the Civil War. The Dred Scott decision was undone by the Thirteenth Amendment, ratified in 1865, prohibiting slavery, and by the Fourteenth Amendment, ratified in 1868, making citizens of all persons born in the United States.

TEST OATH LAW

The Court in 1867 declared invalid an 1865 act that required attorneys, as a condition for practicing in federal courts, to swear that they had never engaged in or supported the southern rebellion against the Union. In *Ex parte Garland* the Court said that the statute was an unconstitutional bill of attainder because it punished persons by prohibiting them from practicing their professions. The Court also held the statute to be an ex post facto law because it was enacted after the commission of the offense.

The Court's opinion in this case and other cases coming from the states indicated that it would not review other federal Reconstruction legislation favorably. To avoid this possibility, Congress removed from the Court's jurisdiction cases arising under certain of those laws; it is the only time in the Court's history that Congress specified a group of laws the Court could not review.

LEGAL TENDER ACTS

The Legal Tender Acts, passed in 1862 and 1863, made paper money a substitute for gold as legal tender in the payment of public and private debts. In the case (*Hepburn v. Griswold*, 1870), the Supreme Court ruled that Congress had exceeded its authority by making paper money legal tender for the payment of debts incurred before passage of the laws. The outcry from debtors and the potential economic repercussions from this decision were so great that within fifteen months the Court—with two new members—reconsidered and overturned its earlier decision, thus establishing paper money as a legal currency (*Knox v. Lee*, 1871).

CIVIL RIGHTS ACT OF 1875

One of several federal statutes enacted in the first decade after the Civil War to end discrimination against blacks, the Civil Rights Act of 1875 barred discrimination in privately owned public accommodations such as hotels, theaters, and railway cars. The Court held that neither the Thirteenth nor the Fourteenth Amendment gave Congress the power to act to bar private discrimination of this type. The decision was one in a series that vitiated Congress's power to enforce effectively the guarantees given to blacks by the two amendments. It would be almost a century before Congress and the Court effectively overturned this series of rulings.

FEDERAL INCOME TAX

The Court in 1895 struck down the first general peacetime income tax enacted by Congress (*Pollock v. Farmers' Loan and Trust Co.*). The Court held that the section of the statute taxing income from real estate was a direct tax and violated the Constitution's requirement that direct taxes be apportioned among the states. This defect, the Court held, was inseparable from the rest of the tax provisions and as a result they all fell. The ruling was overturned in 1913 with the ratification of the Sixteenth Amendment specifically exempting income taxes from an apportionment requirement.

---

of obligations contemplating that payment might be made with such notes. . . . If now . . . it be established that these debts and obligations can be discharged only by gold coin; . . . the government has become an instrument of the grossest injustice; all debtors are loaded with an obligation it was never contemplated they should assume; a large percentage is added to every debt, and such must become the demand for gold to satisfy contracts, that ruinous sacrifices, general distress and bankruptcy may be expected.[92]

The narrow margin of the vote, and public perception of such horrors as the Court eventually described, intensified criticism of the Court, which was still suffering the loss of prestige resulting from its ill-fated decision in the Dred Scott case thirteen years earlier. *(See box, Dred Scott Reversed: The Fourteenth Amendment, p. 149.)*

Even as Chase was delivering the Court's opinion striking down the Legal Tender Act, President Grant sent to the Senate for confirmation the names of his nominees to fill the Court's two vacancies. They were William Strong and Joseph P. Bradley.

In light of subsequent events President Grant was charged with "packing" the Court with these appointments.

"YELLOW-DOG" CONTRACTS

Exhibiting its early antipathy to organized labor, the Court in 1908 declared unconstitutional a section of the 1898 Erdman Act making it unlawful for any railway employer to require as a condition of employment that his employees not join a labor union (*Adair v. United States*). The act was an infringement on property rights guaranteed by the Fifth Amendment, the Court said. Congress exceeded its authority under the commerce clause, the Court added, because labor relations were not in interstate commerce and did not directly affect it. It was not until 1930 that the Court sanctioned a federal law guaranteeing railway employees collective bargaining rights and not until 1937 that the Court acknowledged that labor relations affected interstate commerce.

CHILD LABOR LAWS

The Court in 1918 struck down a 1916 law that sought to end child labor by prohibiting the shipment in interstate commerce of any goods made by children under a certain age who had worked more than a specified number of hours (*Hammer v. Dagenhart*). The majority said that Congress was not regulating commerce but manufacture, an authority it did not possess.

Congress then passed a second statute placing a heavy tax on any goods made by children. The Court struck down this statute, too, declaring that the tax was not intended to raise revenue but to penalize employers of children (*Bailey v. Drexel Furniture Co.*, 1922). *Hammer v. Dagenhart* was reversed in 1941 when the Court upheld a federal minimum wage and maximum hour law that applied to children and adults (*United States v. Darby*).

AGRICULTURAL ADJUSTMENT ACT OF 1933

Designed to restore farm prices and farmers' purchasing power, the Agricultural Adjustment Act levied an excise tax on seven basic food commodities and used the revenue to pay benefits to farmers who reduced their production of the commodities. Striking down the act in 1936, the majority held that Congress had no constitutional authority to regulate agricultural production. The following year, after President Roosevelt's Court-packing threat, the majority approved similar tax benefit schemes when it upheld federal Social Security and unemployment compensation legislation (*Helvering v. Davis, Steward Machine Co. v. Davis*, 1937). In 1938 Congress passed a second agricultural adjustment act, which substituted marketing quotas for the processing tax and production quotas of the first act. This second act was upheld in *Mulford v. Smith* (1939).

NATIONAL INDUSTRIAL RECOVERY ACT OF 1933

The centerpiece of President Roosevelt's economic recovery program, the National Industrial Recovery Act (NIRA) authorized the president to approve industrywide fair competition codes containing wage and hour regulations. In the Hot Oil case (*Panama Refining Co. v. Ryan*, 1935), the Court struck down as an unconstitutional delegation of legislative power a section that authorized the president to prohibit from interstate commerce so-called "hot" oil produced in violation of state regulations controlling production. The Court held that Congress had not drawn specific enough standards to guide the president in exercising his discretionary authority.

Panama was followed quickly by the "Sick Chicken" case (*Schechter Poultry Corp. v. United States*, 1935) in which a unanimous Court struck down the entire NIRA, both because it gave the president too much discretion in establishing and approving the fair competition codes and because it exceeded congressional power by applying to intrastate as well as interstate commerce.

COAL CONSERVATION ACT OF 1935

Passed despite the adverse ruling in *Schechter*, the 1935 coal act authorized fixed prices for coal, provided collective bargaining rights for miners, allowed two-thirds of the industry to establish mandatory wage and hour regulations for the whole industry, and set up a tax system to ensure compliance. Divided 6–3, the Court in *Carter v. Carter Coal Co.* declared the act an invalid delegation of powers to private industry and an unconstitutional extension of the interstate commerce power. While not directly overruled, this case and the ruling in *Schechter* were effectively nullified in *National Labor Relations Board v. Jones & Laughlin Co.* (1937) when the Court accepted congressional assertion of its power to regulate intrastate production.

SECOND LEGAL TENDER DECISION

Strong was confirmed February 18; Bradley, March 21. On April 1, 1870, the Court announced that it would hear two more pending legal tender cases (*Knox v. Lee, Parker v. Davis*), and in so doing, would review its decision in the *Hepburn* case.[93] And on May 1, 1871, by another slim majority, 5–4, the Court overruled *Hepburn*. That decision enjoyed the shortest life—fifteen months—of any major decision of the Court in the nineteenth century.

Strong wrote the Court's opinion in the *Second Legal Tender Cases*, rebutting point by point the arguments Chief Justice Chase had made in the first decision. With regard to the weakest point of Chase's opinion, his claim that it was the Court's duty to determine if Congress had used an appropriate means to implement an express power, Strong responded:

Is it our province to decide that the means selected were beyond the constitutional power of Congress, because we may think other means to the same ends would have been more appropriate and equally efficient? . . . The degree of the necessity for any congressional enactment, or the relative degree of its appropriateness, . . . is for consideration in Congress, not here.[94]

President Ulysses S. Grant was accused of packing the Court when his first two appointees, William Strong and Joseph Bradley, voted to overturn the ruling in the first Legal Tender case.

No matter where one stood on the merits of the legal tender issue, the Court's quick reversal was almost universally deplored. A later chief justice, Charles Evans Hughes, was to call the reversal one of the Court's "self-inflicted wounds," and a serious mistake with respect to its effect on public opinion.[95] That effect was summarized in the well-respected *Nation*:

The present action of the Court is to be deplored, first, because this sudden reversal of a former judgment which had been maturely considered after full argument, will weaken popular respect for all decisions of the Court including this one; second, because the value of a judgment does not depend on the number of Judges who concur in it—Judges being weighed, not counted, and because of the rehearing of a cause, in consequence of the number of Judges having been increased, is peculiarly, and for obvious reasons, objectionable, where the number is dependent on the will of the very body whose acts the Court has to review, and which in this very case it is reviewing; and third, because the Judges who have been added to the Bench since the former decision are men who were at the Bar when that decision was rendered, and were interested professionally and personally in having a different decision. We do not mean to insinuate that this has affected their judgment, but we do say that it is not enough for a Judge to be pure; he must be likewise above suspicion; that is, he must not only be honest, but must give no man any reason for thinking him otherwise than honest.[96]

The decision in the *Second Legal Tender Case* was reaffirmed in 1884 when the Court upheld the use of legal tender notes in peacetime.[97] The Court in 1872 also reaffirmed its 1869 decision that creditors holding contracts specifically calling for payment in gold did not have to accept paper money in repayment.[98] As a consequence, more and more creditors insisted on gold clauses and they were eventually contained in almost every private and public bond.

GOLD CLAUSE CASES

In 1933, to counter gold hoarding and exporting and speculation in foreign exchange, Congress required all holders to surrender their gold and gold certificates to the Treasury in return for an equivalent amount of paper currency. In an effort to raise prices, Congress next devalued the dollar by lowering its gold content.

With a third law, Congress then nullified all gold clauses in contracts. The clauses could not be enforced since gold was no longer in circulation, and the statute also prevented creditors from enforcing collection in enough of the devalued currency to make up the value of the gold stipulated in the contract.

The nullification statute was challenged on several grounds —taking private property without compensation, violating the Fifth Amendment's due process clause, and invading the powers of the states. But in a series of four cases, the Court handed Congress and the president one of their few victories of the early New Deal period.

A FISCAL MISSTEP . . .

Although the Court has found that Congress can do almost no wrong in regulating fiscal matters, at least once in the nation's history it decided that Congress chose the wrong way to go about trying to reduce the national deficit.

In 1985 Congress passed the Balanced Budget and Deficit Reduction Act, which gave considerable power to the comptroller general, the head of the General Accounting Office. Among the duties the law gave the comptroller general was the power to tell the president how much spending must be reduced in various areas in order to meet the deficit reduction targets for the year. The president was obliged to follow the comptroller's suggestions.

This arrangement was quickly challenged by members of Congress who had opposed the act, and in only six months the Court had ruled that this portion of the Deficit Reduction Act, commonly referred to as Gramm-Rudman-Hollings for its three Senate sponsors, was an unconstitutional violation of the separation of powers (*Bowsher v. Synar*, 478 U.S. 714, 1986).

Congress had foreseen this possibility and had already written into the law a "fallback" process to replace the one found unconstitutional. The Court "severed" the unconstitutional provisions and left the remaining structure of the Gramm-Rudman-Hollings mechanism intact.

In the first two cases, the Court upheld the power of Congress to regulate the value of currency. Chief Justice Charles Evans Hughes, who wrote the 5–4 majority opinions in all four cases, said:

We are not concerned with consequences, in the sense that consequences, however serious, may excuse an invasion of constitutional right. We are concerned with the constitutional power of the Congress over the monetary system of the country and its attempted frustration. Exercising that power, the Congress has undertaken to establish a uniform currency, and parity between kinds of currency, and to make that currency, dollar for dollar, legal tender for the payment of debts. In the light of abundant experience, the Congress was entitled to choose such a uniform monetary system, and to reject a dual system, with respect to all obligations within the range of the exercise of its constitutional authority. The contention that these gold clauses are valid contracts and cannot be struck down proceeds upon the assumption that private parties, and States and municipalities, may make and enforce contracts which may limit that authority. Dismissing that tenable assumption, the facts must be faced. We think that it is clearly shown that these clauses interfere with the exertion of the power granted to the Congress and certainly it is not established that the Congress arbitrarily or capriciously decided that such interferences existed.[99]

In the third case, the plaintiff sought to recover the difference between the gold content of $10,000 in gold certificates and the gold content of the currency he had been issued in replacement for the certificates. Chief Justice Hughes explained that the certificates were a form of currency, rather than a receipt for gold, the implication being that Congress could replace the certificates with another form of currency. But the Court held that the plaintiff had not sustained sufficient damage to sue in the Court of Claims where the case had originated, and thus avoided deciding whether the gold certificates were actually contracts with the federal government, and whether their required surrender was a violation of due process.[100]

In the last case, the holder of a government bond sued for the difference between its gold value and the amount he had received for it in devalued dollars.

In this instance, the Court ruled against the government, declaring that although Congress had the right to abrogate the gold clauses in private contracts, it had no power to do so with regard to contracts to which the government itself was a party. Wrote Hughes:

By virtue of the power to borrow money "on the credit of the United States," the Congress is authorized to pledge that credit as an assurance of payment as stipulated,—as the highest assurance the Government can give, its plighted faith. To say that the Congress may withdraw or ignore that pledge, is to assume that the Constitution contemplates a vain promise, a pledge having no other sanction than the pleasure and convenience of the pledgor. This Court has given no sanction to such a conception of the obligations of our Government.[101]

Hughes, however, softened the blow to the government by holding that the plaintiff, as in the previous case, had not sustained sufficient damages to be entitled to standing in the Court of Claims.

Speaking for the four dissenters in all four cases, Justice James C. McReynolds wrote what has been called "one of the bitterest minority opinions ever recorded."[102] "Just men regard repudiation and spoliation of citizens by their sovereign with abhorrence; but we are asked to affirm that the Constitution has granted power to accomplish both," McReynolds lamented.[103]

The Power over Foreign Affairs

To the Framers of the Constitution foreign policy was the making of treaties and the waging of war. Wary of entrusting all authority for the conduct of foreign relations to the president, they divided these responsibilities. Congress would declare war, and the president would conduct war with armies raised and maintained by Congress. The president would negotiate treaties; Congress would approve treaties.

But congressional influence over foreign policy has ranged far beyond these shared and somewhat limited powers. Congress's power to regulate foreign commerce and its other express powers have played a role, in conjunction with the necessary and proper clause, in shaping numerous facets of the nation's foreign policy. Despite the widely recognized prerogatives of the president in foreign relations, Congress has significant power to undergird or undercut presidential foreign policy decisions.

The Supreme Court's part in this area has been minor. Challenges to the foreign policy decisions of Congress and the president come to the Court infrequently, and the Court rarely has found fault with the actions Congress has taken in the exercise of its foreign affairs powers.

The War Power

The Constitution divides responsibility for waging war between the president and Congress. The president is commander in chief of the army and navy when they are called into actual service, while Congress is expressly granted power to declare war, raise and support armies, provide and maintain a navy, and make rules and regulations to govern the armed forces. Congress also may organize, arm, and discipline the state militias, but the states have express authority to train them. *(See "The Commander in Chief," pp. 194–208, in Chapter 5.)*

The war powers of the federal government have never been seriously questioned, although their source has been disputed. Chief Justice John Marshall implied in *McCulloch v. Maryland* (1819) that the power to declare war carried with it the power to conduct war.[1] Others have contended, as did Justice George Sutherland in *United States v. Curtiss-Wright Corp.* (1936), that the power to wage war is inherent in the fact of the nation's sovereignty and is not dependent on the enumerated powers of the Constitution.[2] Still others, among them Alexander Hamilton, contended that the power to wage war comes from the enumerated powers amplified by the necessary and proper clause.[3]

Whatever the source of the power, the Supreme Court has been extremely reluctant to place any limits on it as exercised by either Congress or the president. Rarely has it heard cases challenging the exercise of the war power during an ongoing war. By the time it ruled, there was usually little chance that an adverse decision could impede the war effort. The Court has sanctioned substantial congressional delegation of power to the executive—

a wartime delegation of power has never been held unconstitutional—and has supported large-scale intrusions into state sovereignty and the rights of private citizens and corporations. In those cases where it has declared a statute drawn in wartime unconstitutional, it has almost always done so on the grounds that the law abused some other power besides the war power. *(See "Wartime Legislation," pp. 137–139.)*

"In short," constitutional scholar Robert E. Cushman wrote, "what is necessary to win the war Congress may do, and the Supreme Court has shown no inclination to hold void new and drastic war measures."[4]

But at least some of the justices have acknowledged the dangers inherent in such an unchecked power. "No one will question that this power is the most dangerous one to free government in the whole catalogue of powers," wrote Justice Robert H. Jackson in 1948. "It usually is invoked in haste and excitement when calm legislative consideration of the constitutional limitation is difficult. It is executed in a time of patriotic fervor that makes moderation unpopular. And, worst of all, it is interpreted by the Judges under the influence of the same passions and pressures."[5]

DECLARATION OF WAR

While the president as commander in chief has the primary responsibility to conduct war, Congress has the express power to declare it. However, it has formally done so in only five of the nation's conflicts: the War of 1812, the Mexican War, the Spanish-American War, World War I, and World War II. No formal declaration was made in the Naval War with France (1798–1800), the First Barbary War (1801–1805), the Second Barbary War (1815), the Civil War, the various Mexican-American clashes of 1914–1917, the Korean War, or the Vietnam War.

In January 1991 Congress authorized the use of force against Iraq, which had invaded Kuwait. The authorization allowed the president to use U.S. military personnel to enforce an ultimatum against Iraq set by the United Nations. While far more limited than earlier declarations of war, the congressional resolution marked the first time since World War II that lawmakers had confronted the issue of sending large numbers of American forces into combat. Passage of the resolution put the political and constitutional weight of the legislative branch behind President Bush as he prepared the nation for a battle. (The administration's most immediate concern—and the public's—was the threat to oil supplies in the Mideast and to stable oil prices.) The fighting lasted six weeks and the allies swept to triumph.

From time to time the absence of a formal declaration of war has been challenged before the Supreme Court. In 1800 the Court held that Congress need not declare full-scale war but could provide for a limited conflict. "Congress is empowered to declare a general war, or Congress may wage a limited war; limited in place, in objects and in time," wrote Justice Samuel Chase in reference to the Naval War with France.[6]

With Congress in recess when the Civil War broke out, President Abraham Lincoln declared a blockade of Confederate ports in April 1861. In May 1861 he issued a proclamation increasing the size of the army and the navy and calling for eighty thousand volunteers. He also ordered nineteen new vessels for the navy and requested $2 million from the Treasury to cover military requisitions.

In July 1861 Congress passed a measure acknowledging that a state of war existed and authorizing the closing of southern ports. On August 6, 1861, Congress adopted a resolution providing that "All the acts, proclamations, and orders of the President respecting the Army and Navy . . . and calling out or relating to the militias or volunteers . . . are hereby approved and in all respects made valid . . . as if they had been issued and done under the previous express authority and direction of the Congress of the United States."

The Supreme Court upheld this retroactive ratification in a group of rulings known as the *Prize Cases* (1863).[7] The cases were brought by owners of vessels that attempted to run the blockade of the southern ports before Congress acted to ratify the blockade but had been seized and condemned as "prizes." The owners sued for redress on the ground that no war had been declared between the North and the South.

Observing that "civil war is never solemnly declared," the Court said that while a president does not initiate war, he is "bound to accept the challenge without waiting for any special legislative authority."[8] Justice Robert C. Grier for the 5–4 majority continued:

If it were necessary to the technical existence of a war, that it should have a legislative sanction, we will find it in almost every Act passed at the extraordinary session of the Legislature of 1861, which was wholly employed in enacting laws to enable the Government to prosecute the war with vigor and efficiency. . . . Without admitting that such [a ratification] Act was necessary under the circumstances, it is plain that if the President had in any manner assumed powers which it was necessary should have the authority or sanction of Congress, . . . this ratification has operated to perfectly cure the defect.[9]

Although none of them involved declarations of war, the Court has ruled in several cases that subsequent ratification of an executive action or appropriation of money to carry out that action is equivalent to a prior authorization of that action.[10] One of these cases involved a challenge to the president's authority to create war agencies under the First War Powers Act of 1941. The Court in 1947 said that "the appropriation by Congress of funds for the use of such agencies stands as confirmation and ratification of the action of the Chief Executive."[11]

MODERN UNDECLARED WARS

During debate on the controversial Vietnam War of the 1960s and 1970s, it was contended that declarations of war were outmoded, given the existence of modern nuclear weapons and the need to commit troops overseas in emergencies on a limited war basis. Testifying before the Senate Foreign Relations Committee in 1971, Professor Alpheus T. Mason of Princeton University commented:

The Framers, with deliberate care, made war-making a joint enterprise. Congress is authorized to "declare war"; the President is designated "commander in chief." Technology has expanded the President's role and correspondingly curtailed the power of Congress. Unchanged are the joint responsibilities of the President and Congress. The fact that a congressional declaration of war is no longer practical does not deprive Congress of constitutionally imposed authority in war-making. On the contrary, it is under obligation to readjust its power position.[12]

The Supreme Court, however, refused to inject itself in the argument over whether the war in Vietnam should have been formally declared. Lower federal courts in several instances ruled that challenges to the war as undeclared by Congress raised political questions not resolvable in the courts. The Supreme Court refused all appeals that it review the lower court rulings.[13] (*See box, Court, Congress, and Cambodia, p. 136.*)

The Court, however, was not unanimous in its denials. In *Mora v. McNamara* (1967), brought by three enlisted men seeking to stop their transfer to Vietnam, Justices Potter Stewart and William O. Douglas dissented from the Court's refusal to hear the case. Whether a president can commit troops to combat in an undeclared war and whether Congress had in effect declared war by appropriating funds, Stewart wrote, were

large and deeply troubling questions. Whether the Court would ultimately reach them depends, of course, upon the resolution of serious preliminary issues of justiciability. We cannot make these problems go away simply by refusing to hear the cases.[14]

Douglas quoted from the majority opinion in another "political question" case, *Nixon v. Herndon* (1927):

"The objection that the subject matter of the suit is political is little more than a play upon words. Of course the petition concerns political action but it alleges and seeks to recover for private damage. That private damage may be caused by such political action and may be recovered for in a suit at law hardly has been doubted for over two hundred years . . . and has been recognized by this Court."[15]

The Constitution makes no provision for terminating a state of war. While the Supreme Court has indicated there must be some sort of formal termination, it has left the appropriate means to the two political branches. In 1948 the Court wrote:

"The state of war" may be terminated by treaty or legislation or Presidential proclamation. Whatever the mode, its termination is a political act. . . . Whether and when it would be open to this Court to find that a war though merely formally kept alive had in fact ended, is a question too fraught with gravity even to be adequately formulated when not compelled.[16]

RAISING ARMIES, ADMINISTERING JUSTICE

Although the federal government conscripted men into the army during the Civil War, its authority to raise armies through a compulsory draft was not tested in the federal courts until after Congress adopted the Selective Service Act of 1917. The law

COURT, CONGRESS, AND CAMBODIA

The Supreme Court's reluctance to become involved in disagreements between the president and Congress over war powers issues was clearly demonstrated in a series of events in 1973.

Rep. Elizabeth Holtzman, D-N.Y., and several Air Force officers challenged as unconstitutional the continued bombing of Cambodia after the United States had signed cease-fire agreements in Vietnam. Later that year, Congress cut off funds as of August 15 for further bombing operations.

Late in July, federal district judge Orrin G. Judd, ruling in the Holtzman suit, issued a permanent injunction halting all military operations in Cambodia after July 27. Judd stated that he found no congressional authority to fight in Cambodia.[1]

He rejected the government's argument that congressional acceptance of the August 15 bombing cutoff amounted to legislative approval of Cambodian military activities until then.

"It cannot be the rule," Judd said, "that the President needs a vote of only one-third plus one of either House in order to conduct a war, but this would be the consequence of holding that Congress must override a Presidential veto in order to terminate hostilities which it has not authorized."[2]

On July 27, the effective date of Judd's order, the Court of Appeals for the Second Circuit, at the request of the government, delayed the injunction and agreed to hear the government's appeal. Holtzman appealed this delaying order to Supreme Court justice Thurgood Marshall. Marshall refused to reinstate the injunction.

Acknowledging that he might well find continued combat in Cambodia unconstitutional, Marshall said he could not make such a momentous decision alone:

It must be recognized that we are writing on an almost entirely clean slate in this area. The stark fact is that although there have been numerous lower court decisions concerning the legality of the war in Southeast Asia, this Court has never considered the problem, and it cannot be doubted that the issues posed are immensely important and complex.

Lurking in this suit are questions of standing, judicial competence, and substantive constitutional law which go to the roots of the division of power in a constitutional democracy. These are the sort of issues which should not be decided precipitously or without the benefit of proper consultation.[3]

Holtzman then appealed to Justice William O. Douglas who was at his home in Goose Prairie, Washington. Her attorney flew to Seattle, drove five hours toward Goose Prairie, and walked the last mile through the woods to deliver the appeal to Douglas's cabin. Douglas August 4 reinstated the bombing halt.

The government immediately asked Chief Justice Warren E. Burger to call the full Court into session to reverse Douglas's order. Under the Court's rules, this request went to Marshall, who reversed Douglas's action on August 4. That same day, the Court of Appeals for the Second Circuit reversed the district court's original ruling halting military operations in Cambodia. The Supreme Court August 9 refused to review that decision.

Although all bombing of Cambodia ceased as of August 15, the congressionally mandated cutoff date, it is interesting to note that the Department of Defense did not comply with Douglas's reinstatement of the injunction halting the bombing even for the few hours it was in effect.

1. *Holtzman v. Schlesinger,* 361 F. Supp. 553 (1973).
2. Id. at 565.
3. *Holtzman v. Schlesinger,* 414 U.S. 1304 at 1313–1314 (1973).

---

was challenged on several grounds, including the charge that it violated the Thirteenth Amendment's prohibition against involuntary servitude.

In 1918 the Supreme Court unanimously upheld the law in a series of cases known collectively as the *Selective Service Draft Law Cases.* The authority to institute the compulsory draft, said Chief Justice Edward D. White, was derived from the express war powers and the necessary and proper clause, strengthened by historical practice. It also derived from the nature of a "just government" whose "duty to the citizen includes the reciprocal obligation of the citizen to render military service in case of need and the right to compel it."[17]

Conscription was not involuntary servitude, said White, reaffirming a 1916 decision in which the Court held that the Thirteenth Amendment was intended to cover the kinds of compulsory labor similar to slavery and not those "duties which individuals owe to the States, such as service in the army, militia, on the jury, etc. . . ."[18]

The Court has never ruled on whether a "peacetime" draft is constitutional. Lower federal courts, however, have upheld the draft in the absence of declared war.[19]

The draft continues to be a fertile source of legal questions, however. In 1981 the Court upheld the power of Congress—without violating the Constitution—to exclude women from the military draft. In *Rostker v. Goldberg* the Court held, 6–3, that because women were barred by law and policy from combat, they were not "similarly situated" with men for the purposes of draft registration. Three years later the Court held that Congress did not violate the ban on bills of attainder when it denied federal student aid to male college students who had failed to register for the military draft.[20] *(See box, Specific Constitutional Limits on Congressional Powers, pp. 84–85.)*

In the exercise of its power to govern and regulate the armed services, Congress has established a military justice system complete with its own laws, courts, and appeals.

The Supreme Court has held that it has no jurisdiction to review courts-martial through writs of certiorari but may do so through writs of habeas corpus.[21] Traditionally, the Court has only reviewed those cases challenging the jurisdiction of military courts over the person tried and the crimes committed.

The Fifth Amendment guarantee of indictment by a grand jury in any capital case specifically exempts cases involving "land or naval forces, or . . . the Militia, when in actual service in time of War or public danger." The Court also has indicated that such cases might be exempted from the Sixth Amendment guarantee of trial by jury.[22] This exemption has left in question whether someone serving in the military is entitled to a civilian trial for a capital offense when he or she is not in actual service and it is not wartime. In deciding this question the Court generally has restricted the instances in which courts-martial are appropriate.

In 1955, for example, the Court ruled that once discharged, a soldier may not be court-martialed for an offense committed when he was in the service.[23]

In 1969 a serviceman challenged the jurisdiction of a court-martial to try him for a nonmilitary offense (attempted rape) committed off post while he was on leave. In *O'Callahan v. Parker* the Court said that courts-martial could try only service-connected crimes.

The justices did not explain what they meant by service-connected crimes, but in holding that the serviceman had been improperly court-martialed, the majority pointed out that his offense was committed during peacetime in a territory held by the United States, that it did not relate to his military duties and that the victim was not engaged in any military duties, that the crime was traditionally cognizable by civilian courts, which were available to try the offense, and that the commission of the crime did not directly flout military authority or violate military property.[24]

In 1971 another serviceman was court-martialed for the rape and kidnapping on a military post of two women; one woman worked on the base, and the other was visiting her serviceman brother. Although several of the conditions present in *O'Callahan* were present in this case, the Court held that a crime by a serviceman on a military post violating the security of persons on the post was service-connected and that he could be court-martialed.[25]

That narrowing of rights became of increased importance for the military after the Court in 1987 overturned *O'Callahan v. Parker* and ruled that courts-martial had jurisdiction to try any member of the armed forces for any crime. Jurisdiction depended not upon the "service-connected" nature of the crime but upon the status of the defendant as a member of the armed forces.[26]

While the Uniform Code of Military Justice provides many due process rights to military personnel comparable to those enjoyed under the Constitution by civilians, the Court in 1976 held that persons undergoing summary courts-martial did not have a constitutional right to legal counsel.[27]

The Court in 1994 rejected a constitutional challenge to the method of appointing military judges. By a unanimous vote, it refused to require that officers be given a separate presidential appointment before serving as military judges or that military judges have fixed terms of office. The decision in *Weiss v. United States* upheld procedures by which any commissioned military officer who was also a lawyer could be appointed a judge by the judge advocate general of his or her branch of service.[28]

Wartime Legislation

During wartime Congress often adopts legislation placing extraordinary controls and regulations on all phases of the economy, including matters over which the federal government has doubtful authority in peacetime. Relatively few of these statutes have been challenged before the Supreme Court; almost always the Court has upheld the extraordinary exercise of power.

An 1862 greenback. No national currency existed until the Civil War, when Congress authorized the printing of paper money, called "greenbacks," and made it legal tender for the payment of debts. In 1870, in the first of the *Legal Tender Cases,* the Court ruled against the constitutionality of using paper money to pay debts contracted before passage of the greenback legislation in 1862. Amid great political controversy, the Court reversed itself on the issue just fifteen months later.

CIVIL WAR

Desperately in need of money to pay the armed forces and to finance the war effort, Congress in 1862 and 1863 passed laws making Treasury notes legal tender, meaning that creditors had to accept paper money, rather than gold or silver, in the payment of debts. Challenged in Court, the statutes were defended by the government as necessary and proper means of exercising the federal powers over war, commerce, and the borrowing of money.

Five years after the war had ended, the Supreme Court in 1870 disagreed. It struck down the Legal Tender Acts claiming that they carried "the doctrine of implied powers very far beyond any extent hitherto given to it."[29] Little more than a year later, the Court reversed itself and upheld the Legal Tender Acts. That the acts were appropriate to an exercise of the war powers, that they achieved the desired effect was "not to be doubted," the Court said in 1871. "[W]hen a statute has proved effective in the execution of powers confessedly existing, it is not too much to say that it must have some appropriateness to the execution of those powers," the majority wrote.[30] *(See details of Legal Tender Cases, pp. 129–132.)*

WORLD WAR I

War measures enacted during World War I authorized the federal government to force compliance with war contracts, to operate factories producing war goods, and to regulate the foreign language press. In conjunction with other express powers, the federal government also ran the nation's railroads, censored mail, and controlled radio and cable communication.

Among the more important war measures—and the one that most significantly impinged on traditional state authorities—was the Lever Act of 1917, which authorized the federal government to regulate all phases of food and fuel production, including importation, manufacturing, and distribution.

In 1921 the Court held unconstitutional a section of the Lever Act that provided penalties for anyone who sold necessary food items at an unreasonable price. The section was so vague as to violate the accused's right to due process under the Fifth Amendment and the right to be informed of the nature and cause of the accusation guaranteed by the Sixth Amendment, the Court said, adding that "the mere existence of a state of war could not suspend or change the operation upon the power of Congress of the guarantees and limitations" of the two amendments.[31] *(See details of the Lever Act, p. 200.)*

The decision was of relatively little significance to the war effort since it came three years after the war had ended and involved language that would have been easily correctable by Congress. In a 1924 case involving a price-fixing provision of the Lever Act, the Court, by deciding the case on other grounds, carefully avoided discussing the constitutional issue of whether the government could set coal prices that resulted in uncompensated losses to the sellers. As one commentator wrote, "it is to be noted that the Court avoided an adverse action on the war

measure, in a decision handed down more than five years after the cessation of hostilities."[32]

In a third World War I case the Court firmly upheld the federal takeover of the railroads against a challenge that it violated states' rights. The specific challenge was to the authority of the Interstate Commerce Commission to set intrastate rail rates. In *Northern Pacific Railway Co. v. North Dakota ex rel Langer* (1919), the Court wrote that if a conflict occurs in a sphere that both the federal government and the states have authority to regulate, federal power is paramount.[33]

WORLD WAR II

Mobilization of private industry and delegation of authority to the president to conduct the war were even more extensive during World War II than they had been in World War I. Among the more important measures passed by Congress were the Selective Service Act of 1940; the Lend-Lease Act of 1941, which allowed the president to ship supplies to U.S. allies; the First War Powers Act of 1941, which gave the president power to reorganize executive and independent agencies when necessary for more effective prosecution of the war; the Second War Powers Act of 1942, which gave the president authority to requisition plants and to control overseas communications, alien property, and defense contracts; the Emergency Price Control Act of 1942, which established the Office of Price Administration (OPA) to control the prices of rent and commodities; the War Labor Disputes Act of 1943, which authorized seizure of plants threatened by strike or other labor dispute; and the Renegotiation Act, which gave the executive branch authority to require compulsory renegotiation to recapture excessive profits made on war contracts.

During the war itself, the Supreme Court agreed to hear only one major case involving these enormous grants of power. *Yakus v. United States* (1944) challenged the Emergency Price Control Act as an unconstitutional delegation of legislative power to the executive branch.[34] But the Court upheld Congress's power to delegate to the OPA the authority to set maximum prices and to decide when they should be imposed. The Constitution, the Court said,

does not require that Congress find for itself every fact upon which it desires to base legislative action or that it make for itself detailed determinations which it has declared to be prerequisite to the application of the legislative policy to particular facts and circumstances impossible for Congress itself properly to investigate. The essentials of the legislative function are the determination of the legislative policy and its formulation and promulgation as a defined and binding rule of conduct—here the rule, with penal sanctions, that prices shall not be greater than those fixed by maximum price regulations which conform to standards and will tend to further the policy which Congress has established. These essentials are preserved when Congress has specified the basic conditions of fact upon whose existence or occurrence, ascertained from relevant data by a designated administrative agency, it directs that its statutory command shall be effective.[35]

Only if there were an absence of standards for judging whether the OPA administrator had obeyed the will of Congress in administering the law would this price-fixing statute be unconstitutional, the Court said. In this case, the Court continued, the standards, "with the aid of the 'statement of the considerations' required to be made by the Administrator, are sufficiently definite . . . to enable Congress, the courts and the public to ascertain whether the Administrator . . . has conformed to those standards."[36]

As in World War I, the Court avoided answering the question of whether Congress had the authority under its war powers to empower the executive branch to fix prices. But in the postwar case of *Lichter v. United States* (1948), the Court gave some indication of how extensive it believed congressional powers during wartime to be:

Congress, in time of war, unquestionably has the fundamental power . . . to conscript men and to requisition the properties necessary and proper to enable it to raise and support its Armies. Congress furthermore has a primary obligation to bring about whatever production of war equipment and supplies shall be necessary to win a war.[37]

In *Lichter* the Court upheld the Renegotiation Act, which authorized the executive branch to recover excessive profits from war industries, against a challenge of unconstitutional delegation of powers. "A constitutional power implies a power of delegation of authority under it sufficient to effect its purposes," the majority wrote. In no less sweeping terms, the majority continued:

This power is especially significant in connection with constitutional war powers under which the exercise of broad discretion as to methods to be employed may be essential to an effective use of its war powers by Congress. The degree to which Congress must specify its policies and standards in order that the administrative authority granted may not be an unconstitutional delegation of its own legislative power is not capable of precise definition. In peace or in war it is essential that the Constitution be scrupulously obeyed, and particularly that the respective branches of the Government keep within the powers assigned to each by the Constitution. On the other hand, it is of the highest importance that the fundamental purposes of the Constitution be kept in mind and given effect in order that, through the Constitution, the people of the United States may in time of war as in peace bring to the support of those purposes the full force of their united action. In time of crisis nothing could be more tragic and less expressive of the intent of the people than so to construe their Constitution that by its own terms it would substantially hinder rather than help them in defending their national safety.[38]

Postwar Legislation

In the wake of the Civil War, the Supreme Court stated that "the [war] power is not limited to victories in the field. . . . It carries with it inherently the power to guard against the immediate renewal of the conflict and to remedy the evils which have arisen from its use and progress."[39] This reasoning has allowed the Court to sanction enforcement of measures based on the war powers long after the actual hostilities have ended.

For example, the Court in 1921 upheld a federal statute continuing rent control in the District of Columbia first imposed during World War I when a housing shortage occurred in the

nation's capital.[40] The Court said the statute's extension was made necessary by the continuing housing shortage resulting from the war emergency. However, in 1924 the Court denied another extension of the rent control law.[41] "A law depending upon the existence of an emergency or other certain state of facts to uphold it may cease to operate if the emergency eases or the facts change even though valid when passed," the Court said.[42] In this case, the facts had changed—the government was hiring fewer people and there was more new housing available in the District. If an increased cost of living was all that remained from the war, the Court said, that was no justification for a continuation of the rent control measure.

The Court has also sanctioned a measure based on the war powers but not enacted until after the hostilities had ended. Ten days after the World War I armistice was signed, Congress passed a law prohibiting the production, sale, and transportation of liquor for the duration of the war emergency. Finding that it was within congressional power to require prohibition in order to conserve manpower and increase efficiency during the demobilization period, the Court upheld the law in 1919 and 1920.[43]

A similar issue was addressed in the 1948 case of *Woods v. Miller Co.* questioning the validity of a 1947 statute continuing the rent control program established under the Emergency Price Control Act.[44] The Court upheld the statute on the basis of the World War I precedents. But Justice William O. Douglas, writing for the majority, added a note of caution:

We recognize the force of the argument that the effects of war under modern conditions may be felt in the economy for years and years, and that if the war power can be used in days of peace to treat all the wounds which war inflicts on our society, it may not only swallow up all other powers of Congress but largely obliterate the Ninth and Tenth Amendments [reserving rights and powers to the people of the states] as well.[45]

In a separate concurring opinion, Justice Robert H. Jackson also voiced his misgivings: "I cannot accept the argument that war powers last as long as the effects and consequences of war for if so they are permanent—as permanent as the war debts."[46]

Treaty Powers

The 1787 Constitutional Convention considered giving the Senate sole authority to make treaties with foreign countries. Ultimately, that power was shared with the president, who had the "Power, by and with the Advice and Consent of the Senate, to make Treaties." How equal a partner this phrasing made the Senate in the actual negotiation of treaties was debated for several decades.

Some senators advocated that the Senate actually direct treaty making by proposing negotiations. Such initiative, they said, was the right and duty of the Senate under the Constitution, and showed the United States was united in its demands.

This debate was laid to rest in 1936 when the Supreme Court declared: "The President alone negotiates. Into the field of negotiation the Senate cannot intrude, and Congress itself is pow-erless to invade it."[47] *(See "The 'Sole Negotiator,'" p. 211, in Chapter 5.)*

But if the president has the primary treaty powers, Congress plays a crucial role through Senate ratification, congressional implementation, and repeal.

APPROVAL

Although the Constitution is silent on the subject, the Senate since 1795 has claimed the right to amend and modify treaties once they have been submitted for approval. Twice this power has been reviewed and sanctioned by the Supreme Court. Speaking in 1869, the Court said:

In this country, a treaty is something more than a contract, for the Federal Constitution declares it to be the law of the land. If so, before it can become a law, the Senate, in whom rests the authority to ratify it, must agree to it. But the Senate are [sic] not required to adopt or reject as a whole, but may modify or amend it.[48]

In 1901 the Court reiterated that the Senate might make approval conditional upon adoption of amendments to the treaty.[49]

CONGRESSIONAL IMPLEMENTATION

Some treaties are self-executing and when ratified become the law of the land equivalent to legislative acts. Others once ratified still require Congress to pass enabling legislation to carry out the terms and conditions of the treaty.

Chief Justice John Marshall in 1829 described the kinds of treaties needing additional implementation as those where "the terms of the stipulation import a contract—when either of the parties engages to perform a particular act—the treaty addresses itself to the political . . . department; and the legislature must execute the contract, before it can become a rule for the Court."[50]

If the treaty deals with a subject outside the coverage of its enumerated powers, Congress may use its authority under the necessary and proper clause to justify enactment of implementing legislation. It is under this authority that Congress, for example, has conferred judicial power upon American consuls abroad to be exercised over American citizens and has provided for foreign extradition of fugitives from justice. Without a treaty on these subjects, Congress would have no power to act.

An extreme example of the use of the necessary and proper clause in conjunction with treaty making came in *Missouri v. Holland* (1920).[51] Congress wished to protect certain migratory birds from hunters. When lower federal courts ruled an act of Congress to this effect unconstitutional as an invasion of state sovereignty, the federal government negotiated a treaty with Canada for the protection of the birds. The Senate ratified it, and Congress again passed legislation barring hunting of the birds and providing other protections. Because this legislation was to implement the treaty, the Supreme Court upheld it:

We do not mean to imply that there are no qualifications to the treaty-making power; but they must be ascertained in a different way. It is obvious that there may be matters of the sharpest exigency for the national well-being that an act of Congress could not deal with but that a treaty followed by such an act could, and it is not lightly to be assumed, that in matters requiring national action, "a power which must belong to and somewhere reside in every civilized government" is not to be found.[52]

Several commentators have noted that this opinion "is one of the most far-reaching assertions of national power in our constitutional history."[53] Historians Alfred Kelly and Winfred Harbison found the implications of the case "astounding." They wrote: "If a treaty could accomplish anything of a national character so long as its subject matter were plausibly related to the general welfare, what limits were there to federal authority, if exercised in pursuance of the treaty-making power?"[54]

REPEAL

The Court has ruled that a treaty may supersede a prior act of Congress and that an act of Congress may in effect repeal prior treaties or parts of them.[55] In the *Head Money Cases* (1884) the Court wrote that there was nothing in a treaty that made it

. . . irrepealable or unchangeable. The Constitution gives it no superiority over an act of Congress in this respect, which may be repealed or modified by an act of Congress of a later date. Nor is there anything in its essential character, or in the branches of the government by which the treaty is made, which gives it this superior sanctity. . . . In short, we are of opinion that, so far as a treaty made by the United States with any foreign nation can become the subject of judicial cognizance in the courts of this country, it is subject to such acts as Congress may pass for its enforcement, modification or repeal.[56]

General Powers

In addition to its war and treaty powers, Congress, as Louis Henkin points out, has general powers that

enable it to reach virtually where it will in foreign as in domestic affairs, subject only to constitutional prohibitions protecting human rights. The power to tax (Article I, Section 8, Clause 1) has long been a power to regulate through taxation. . . . Major programs depend wholly on the "spending power" . . . —to "provide for the common Defence and general Welfare of the United States"—and it has been used in our day for billions of dollars in foreign aid.

Other, specialized powers also have their international uses: Congress has authorized a network of international agreements under its postal power (Article I, Section 8, Clause 7), and there are international elements in the regulation of patents and copyrights. The express power to govern territory (Article IV, Section 3) may imply authority to acquire territory, and Congress determines whether territory acquired shall be incorporated into the United States. Congress can exercise "exclusive legislation" in the nation's capital, its diplomatic headquarters (Article I, Section 8, Clause 17). The power to acquire and dispose of property has supported lend-lease and other arms programs and sales or gifts of nuclear reactors or fissionable materials. . . . By implication in the Constitution's grant of maritime jurisdiction to the federal judiciary (Article III, Section 2), Congress can legislate maritime law.[57]

(See box, Maritime Law: A Matter of Commerce? p. 94.)

In addition, the fact that the appointment of ambassadors, public ministers, and other diplomatic officers requires the advice and consent of the Senate gives that body a degree of control over foreign relations. The power to appropriate funds for defense, war, and the general execution of foreign policy rests solely with Congress.

In those cases where it has reviewed these powers the Supreme Court has supported their exercise; for instance, regulation of foreign imports through tariffs was upheld in 1928.[58] As early as 1828 the Court endorsed the power to acquire territory through conquest or treaty, and in 1883 it supported the power to acquire territory through discovery.[59] In a series of cases in the early 1900s, the Court left it up to Congress to determine whether to incorporate a territory into the United States.[60] The power of Congress to dispose of federal property was deemed absolute in 1840.[61] (See "Taxing as Police Power," pp. 121–126; "The Insular Cases," pp. 148–150; box, Power over Federal Property, p. 150.)

The Court has never invalidated a spending program or appropriation passed for the common defense.

The Power to Admit States, Govern Territories, and Grant Citizenship

The Constitution gives Congress the authority to admit new states, govern territories, and establish uniform rules for naturalization of foreign-born persons as citizens.

These three seemingly straightforward grants of power have raised some of the most difficult questions the Court has ever been asked to answer. One of these questions was whether Congress had the power to prohibit slavery in the territories. A second was whether the residents of territories automatically enjoyed the rights and privileges guaranteed by the Constitution. A third was who qualified for citizenship in the United States. And a fourth, still not finally resolved, is whether Congress may revoke someone's citizenship against his or her will.

New States

Article IV, Section 3, of the Constitution gives Congress the power to admit new states to the Union so long as it does not form a new state by dividing an existing state or by joining parts or all of two or more states without their consent.

Five states were formed from land that was originally part of the first thirteen states. In the first four cases—Vermont, Maine, Kentucky, and Tennessee—the ceding states agreed to the division. The fifth state, West Virginia, was formed when the western counties of Virginia that wanted to remain in the Union split away from the rest of the state, which had joined the Confederacy. A special legislature composed of people from the western counties was convened to give its approval to the split, but Virginia did not formally agree until after the Civil War ended. Texas was an independent nation before its admission to the Union in 1845, and California was carved from a region ceded by Mexico in 1848. The remaining thirty states were all territories before being granted statehood.[1]

When it adopted the Northwest Ordinance of 1787 providing for the eventual transition of the Northwest Territory into states, the Confederation Congress stipulated that these new states would enter the Union on equal footing in all respects with the original states. The Constitutional Convention formally rejected insertion of a similar phrase into Article IV, Section 3, but the "equal footing" principle, at least as it concerns political standing and sovereignty, has nevertheless remained a valid guide for Congress and the courts.

In *Pollard v. Hagan* (1845) the Court declared that the "right of . . . every . . . new state to exercise all the powers of government, which belong to and may be exercised by the original states of the Union, must be admitted, and remain unquestioned."[2] "Equality of constitutional right and power is the condition of all the States of the Union, old and new," the Court declared again in 1883.[3]

Relying on the equal footing doctrine, Oklahoma challenged

a provision in the congressional resolution granting it statehood. The provision required that the state's capital remain at Guthrie for at least seven years. The state legislature moved it to Oklahoma City after only four years. In *Coyle v. Smith* (1911) the Court held that Congress could not place in statehood resolutions restrictions on matters wholly under the state's control. Writing for the Court, Justice Horace H. Lurton said:

The power is to admit "new States into this Union." "This Union" was and is a union of States, equal in power, dignity and authority, each competent to exert that residuum of sovereignty not delegated to the United States by the Constitution itself. To maintain otherwise would be to say that the Union, through the power of Congress to admit new States, might come to be a union of States unequal in power, as including States whose powers were restricted only by the Constitution, with others whose powers had been further restricted by an act of Congress accepted as a condition of admission.[4]

In most instances, the equal footing theory has worked to give new states constitutional rights and powers they did not possess as territories.

But in one instance, it required a new state to give up some of its sovereignty. In 1947 the Court held that the ocean bed beneath the three-mile coastal limit along the Atlantic Ocean did not belong to the original states, but to the federal government, so states subsequently admitted to the Union did not own the ocean soil along their coasts either. *(See box, The Tidelands Oil Controversy, p. 143.)*

In 1950 Texas challenged that decision on the grounds that as an independent nation before its admission to the Union it had owned its coastal strip. The Court acknowledged Texas's original sovereignty but ruled that entry into the Union "entailed a relinquishment of some of her sovereignty," including the coastal strip, in order that the new state be on an equal footing.[5]

Justice William O. Douglas for the Court explained:

The "equal footing" clause [in the statehood resolution] prevents extension of the sovereignty of a State into a domain of political and sovereign power of the United States from which the other States have been excluded, just as it prevents a contraction of sovereignty . . . which would produce inequality among the states.[6]

The doctrine has been held inapplicable to nonpolitical conditions imposed prior to admission. Before it became a state, Minnesota had agreed not to tax certain lands held by the federal government at the time of Minnesota's admission. Afterwards, some of these lands were granted to a railroad that Minnesota sought to tax. The Court sustained the tax restriction agreement, saying it was unaffected by the equal footing doctrine. "[A] mere agreement in reference to property involves no question of equality of status, but only of the power of a state to deal with the nation . . . in reference to such property," the Court ruled in 1900.[7]

THE TIDELANDS OIL CONTROVERSY

When oil was discovered off the coasts of California, Texas, and Louisiana, the question of who owned the submerged land just off the coastal states developed into a raging controversy. Presuming that it owned the land, California leased drilling rights to oil companies as early as 1921. The federal government, however, also claimed ownership of the land and in 1945 brought an original suit against California in the Supreme Court asking the Court to prevent the state from further exploiting the oil.

The suit was decided by the Supreme Court in 1947. California argued that the thirteen original coastal states held title to the three-mile strip of sea adjacent to their shores and because California entered the Union on an equal footing with the original states, it too held title to the three-mile belt.[1] The federal government contended that it had the right to control the offshore lands because of its responsibility to protect and defend the nation. Moreover, in its exercise of its foreign relations, the federal government asserted it had a right to make whatever agreements were necessary concerning the offshore lands without interference by commitments made by the states.

The Supreme Court found in favor of the federal government. Writing for the majority, Justice Hugo L. Black denied that the thirteen original states had title to the three-mile ocean zone. On the contrary, he said,

the idea of a definite three-mile belt in which an adjacent nation can, if it chooses, exercise broad, if not complete dominion, has apparently at last been generally accepted throughout the world. . . . That the political agencies of this nation both claim and exercise broad dominion and control over our three-mile marginal belt is now a settled fact. . . . And this assertion of national dominion over the three-mile belt is binding upon this Court.[2]

Even without this acquisition by assertion, Black said, the federal government would control the offshore lands as "a function of national external sovereignty."

The three-mile rule is but a recognition of the necessity that a government next to the sea must be able to protect itself from dangers incident to its location. It must have powers of dominion and regulation in the interest of its revenues, its health, and the security of its people from wars waged on or too near its coasts. And insofar as the nation asserts its rights under international law, whatever of value may be discovered in the seas next to its shores and within its protective belt, will most naturally be appropriated for its use.[3]

The Court in 1950 applied its ruling in the California case to assert federal control over Louisiana's coastal lands.[4] In another 1950 case the Court denied Texas's claim that because it was an independent and sovereign nation prior to its admission as a state, it had in fact owned the three-mile strip along its shores.[5] The Court acknowledged that this was so, but said that when Texas came into the Union it did so on an equal footing with the other states and thus relinquished its claim to the coastal lands.

These controversial rulings became a campaign issue in the 1952 presidential contest, with the Republicans promising to turn over the three-mile zone to the states if elected.

In 1953 the Republican-controlled Congress passed the Submerged Lands Act ceding to the states the mineral rights to lands lying offshore between the low tide mark and the states' historic boundaries, which stretched to between three and ten and one-half miles from the shore. Congress's authority to overturn the effect of the Supreme Court's 1947 ruling and relinquish the lands was upheld in 1954.[6]

1. *United States v. California*, 332 U.S. 19 (1947).
2. Id. at 33–34.
3. Id. at 35.
4. *United States v. Louisiana*, 339 U.S. 699 (1950).
5. *United States v. Texas*, 339 U.S. 707 (1950).
6. *Alabama v. Texas*, 347 U.S. 272 (1954); see also *United States v. Louisiana*, 363 U.S. 1 (1960).

The Power to Govern the Territories

There is no express constitutional authority for the federal government to acquire territory. It is implied in some enumerated powers and inherent in the nation's sovereignty.

"The Constitution confers absolutely upon the government of the Union, the powers of making war and of making treaties; consequently, that government possesses the power of acquiring territory, either by conquest or treaty," declared Chief Justice John Marshall in a frequently cited 1828 case.[8] The Court also has held that the nation has an inherent power to acquire territory by discovery.[9]

The only specific constitutional grant of power over territories conferred on Congress is contained in Article IV, Section 3, Clause 2. It authorized the federal legislature "to dispose of and make all needful Rules and Regulations respecting the Territory or other Property belonging to the United States." With one important exception, the Court has consistently interpreted this power broadly and upheld its exercise. Congress, the Court said in 1880, "has full and complete legislative authority over the people of the Territories and all the departments of the territorial governments. It may do for the Territories what the people, under the Constitution of the United States, may do for the States."[10] In 1899 the Court again ruled that Congress had the same full legislative powers over activities within the territories as state legislatures had in the states.[11] The Court also has approved Congress's delegation of its legislative powers over local territorial affairs to a territorial legislature elected by citizens.[12]

SLAVERY IN THE TERRITORIES

The one exception to congressional control was the Court's 1857 ruling that Congress did not have the authority to prohibit slavery in the territories.[13] The decision in *Scott v. Sandford*, which also denied blacks citizenship in the United States, was possibly the Court's greatest strategic error. Instead of resolving the conflict that had divided the nation for decades, as many of

"An overseer doing his duty. Sketched from life near Fredericsburg," 1798, by Benjamin Latrobe. The Court ruled in 1857 that Congress did not have the authority to prohibit slavery in the territories. The decision in *Scott v. Sandford* has been seen over history as a great Court error, reflecting political rather than judicial motivations.

the justices participating in the decision apparently had hoped, the ruling contributed to further division of North and South. Three years after the decision the country plunged into civil war.

The Dred Scott decision was equally damaging to the Court itself—a "gross abuse of trust," as one eminent historian would describe it[14]—for, rightly or wrongly, much of the public believed that the decision had been motivated by narrow political concerns and that the Court had not acted with the judicious dispassion the public expected of the men who were the final interpreters of the nation's laws.

Background

Slavery in the territories did not become an issue until 1819. With support from both northern and southern delegates, the Confederation Congress prohibited slavery in the Northwest Territory when it passed the Northwest Ordinance in 1787.[15]

But when the Missouri Territory applied for statehood in 1819, slavery in the territories became a serious political and constitutional question. At the time there were eleven free states and eleven slave states. Northerners in the House of Representatives pushed through an amendment to the statehood resolution that would have prohibited slavery in the new state even though many Missourians were slaveholders. Dominated by southerners, the Senate objected to the amendment, claiming that Congress had no constitutional right to impose such a condition on a new state. Ironically, few southerners questioned Congress's right to prohibit slavery in the territories.

The stalemate between the two chambers was not resolved until Maine applied for statehood the following year. The Missouri Compromise of 1820 provided for the entry of Maine as a free state and Missouri as a slave state, which maintained the numerical balance. The compromise also prohibited slavery in

the remainder of the Louisiana Purchase area that lay north of 36° 30' north latitude, a line that was an extension of Missouri's southern boundary.

A second compromise became necessary when Missouri's constitution was presented to Congress for approval later in 1820. A section of the document barred the entry of free blacks into the new state. Representatives from several northern states that had given free blacks rights of citizenship objected to the provision, claiming it violated the comity clause (Article IV, Section 2, Clause 1) of the Constitution, which gave citizens of one state "all Privileges and Immunities of Citizens in the several States." Southerners, on the other hand, contended that free blacks did not have the same rights as whites—they could not vote in federal elections, for example—and therefore were not citizens under the Constitution.

The Constitution did not define either federal or state citizenship, nor did it clearly stipulate whether those persons defined as citizens by one state retained that status when they moved to another state. In the immediate controversy, Congress reached a compromise that essentially barred Missouri from passing any law that would ban the entry of citizens of another state. Although the two Missouri compromises relieved sectional tensions at the time, they did not answer the greater questions of whether Congress actually had the authority to prohibit slavery in the territories and whether blacks, free or slave, were citizens with all the rights and privileges guaranteed by the Constitution.

With the formal acquisition of Texas in 1846 and the prospect of obtaining more land from Mexico, extension of slavery into the territories again became an issue. The extension of slavery was in reality a thin shield for the real issue of whether slavery could continue to exist at all.

Once again, northern representatives proposed to bar slavery in the newly acquired territories. They contended that Congress, under the "rules and regulation" clause of Article IV and under the treaty and war powers, had the power to prohibit slavery in the territories. They also noted that Congress had exercised this authority throughout its existence.

Southern opponents argued that slaves were property and that all the sovereign states owned the territories in common. The federal government, they continued, had no right to act against the interest of the sovereign states by barring their property in slaves from any of the territories. A corollary argument was that abolition of slavery was a violation of the Fifth Amendment's due process clause because it took property without just compensation.

The controversy over the western lands was settled in 1850 when Congress produced a three-part compromise. California would enter the Union as a free state. Enforcement of the controversial Fugitive Slave Act would be turned over to the federal government. And the citizens of the newly organized Utah and New Mexico territories would determine whether they would allow slavery at the time those territories became states.

Dred Scott's Case

It was at the beginning of this crisis in 1846 that the slave Dred Scott sought his freedom in the courts.

Scott was owned originally by a family named Blow who in 1833 sold him to an army surgeon, Dr. John Emerson of St. Louis. In 1834 Emerson was transferred to Rock Island, Illinois, and later to Fort Snelling in the Wisconsin Territory, returning to St. Louis near the end of 1838. Scott accompanied Emerson throughout this period.

Some time later Emerson died, leaving Scott to his widow, who in the mid-1840s moved to New York, depositing Scott into the care of his original owners, the Blows. Opposed to the extension of slavery into the western territories, Henry Blow lent financial support to Scott to test in court whether his residence on free soil in Illinois and the Wisconsin Territory made him a free man. A lower state court found in favor of Scott, but in 1852 the Missouri Supreme Court reversed the decision, holding that under Missouri law, Scott remained a slave.

Strader v. Graham: Precedent

The Missouri Supreme Court may have relied on an 1851 decision of the U.S. Supreme Court that dealt with the precise question whether a slave's sojourn in free territory made him a free man if he returned to a slave state.[16] That case was brought by a man named Graham of Kentucky who owned three slaves. These three were traveling minstrels whom Graham had taken into Ohio to perform. In 1841 the slaves escaped by boat across the Ohio River to Cincinnati, and Graham sued Strader, the boat's captain. Strader argued that he had done no wrong because the minstrels were free by virtue of their earlier travels.

The Court unanimously dismissed the case for lack of jurisdiction. Wrote Chief Justice Roger B. Taney for the Court:

Every state has an undoubted right to determine the status, or domestic or social condition, of the persons domiciled within its territory. . . . There is nothing in the Constitution of the United States that can control the law of Kentucky upon this subject. And the condition of the negroes, therefore, as to freedom or slavery, after their return depended altogether upon the laws of the State, and could not be influenced by the laws of Ohio. It was exclusively in the power of Kentucky to determine for itself whether their employment in another state should or should not make them free on their return. The Court of Appeals have determined, that by the laws of the state they continued to be slaves. And this judgment upon this point is . . . conclusive upon this court, and we have no jurisdiction over it.[17]

1820 Compromise Repealed

In 1854 the issue of the extension of slavery into the territories flared up once more. Sen. Stephen A. Douglas (D 1847–1853, PSD 1853–1861) of Illinois and his supporters wanted to organize the area known as Nebraska into a territory and encourage its settlement to improve the feasibility of building a railroad from Illinois to the Pacific Coast.

Under the Missouri Compromise, Congress had barred the introduction of slavery into the Nebraska area. But to secure southern support in Congress for his project, Douglas wrote a bill that repealed the 1820 compromise on slavery and substituted for it popular or squatters' sovereignty, which allowed newly organized territories to decide for themselves whether they would allow slavery.

Antislavery members of Congress were outraged by the proposal, but, with strong pressure from the executive branch, the bill was passed. It led to growing extremism on both sides and to a civil war in Kansas in 1856 between the proslavery government at Shawnee, which was regarded by the federal government as legitimate, and the antislavery government at Topeka.

A Matter for the Court

During these years more and more people began to look to the Supreme Court for a solution to the slavery question. Historian Carl B. Swisher wrote of the period that while there was skepticism about entrusting a final decision to the courts,

the belief was growing [that] there might be some point in turning to the judiciary in the hope that it could resolve a conflict which Congress was unable to settle. Many Southerners hoped and expected that the judiciary would decide their way and perhaps give a security which politics could not provide. Many Northerners hoped the courts could in some way find a pattern of rightness not too different from the pattern of their own beliefs.[18]

A court settlement of the issue was clearly what those around Dred Scott were seeking. In 1854 Mrs. Emerson arranged for the sale of Scott to her brother, John F. A. Sanford (misspelled in the court records as Sandford), and Scott's attorney brought suit for his freedom in the federal circuit court for Missouri. Suits may be brought in federal court by a citizen of one state against a citizen of another, so Scott's first task was to show that he was a citizen of Missouri. The circuit court held that Scott, as a black slave, was not a citizen of Missouri and therefore did not have the right to bring suit in federal court. Scott appealed to the Supreme Court.

Faced with a civil war in Kansas over the precise issue of slavery in the territories, a Congress increasingly less able to find a political solution, and mounting demands for some final judicial solution, the Court agreed to hear the case. The Court first heard arguments in February 1856. But because the justices disagreed on a number of the issues presented and because they feared their disagreement would be used for political ends in the upcoming presidential campaign, adding to the controversy rather than quieting it, the Court decided to have the case reargued later in the year.

Although the circumstances of the two cases were not identical, most historians agree that the Court could have dismissed Dred Scott's suit on the same reasoning that it employed in *Strader v. Graham,* that is, that it was up to Missouri to determine whether Scott was slave or free and the Court had no authority to interfere with that decision.

After the case was reargued, seven of the nine justices were prepared to restrict themselves to this narrow judgment, and Justice Samuel Nelson was assigned to write the opinion. But the two dissenters—John McLean, a Republican from Ohio, and Benjamin R. Curtis, a Whig from Massachusetts—announced that their dissents would cover all the issues: whether Dred Scott was a citizen, whether his stay on free soil made him a free man, and whether Congress had the authority to prohibit slavery in the territories.

Unwilling to let the dissents go unanswered, each of the seven majority justices decided to write an opinion answering those issues he thought to be in question. Several were anxious to address the territorial question, partly out of personal belief, partly because they thought a decision might help resolve the dilemma, and partly because they thought the public expected the Court to address the issue. Several northern papers already had chided the Court for an opinion the papers assumed would favor the South. This assumption was not unreasonable in those days of intense regional feeling because five of the nine justices were from the South.

Newly elected President James Buchanan also put some pressure on the Court to decide the territorial slavery issue. In letters to Justices John Catron and Robert C. Grier, Buchanan urged the Court to take up this issue so that at his inauguration he might say, as he finally did, that the issue was "a judicial question, which legitimately belongs to the Supreme Court . . . before whom it is now pending and will, it is understood, be speedily and finally settled. To their decision, in common with all good citizens, I shall cheerfully submit, whatever that may be." [19]

Taney's Opinion

The Court announced its decision March 6, 1857, two days after Buchanan's inauguration. By a 7–2 vote, the Court ruled against Scott. Of the seven opinions written by members of the majority, Chief Justice Taney's is considered to present the formal view of the Court.

Taney first dealt with the issue of whether Dred Scott, or any slave or descendant of slaves, could be a citizen under the Constitution. It was Taney's opinion that:

they are not, and that they are not included, and were not intended to be included, under the word "citizens" in the Constitution, and can, therefore, claim none of the rights and privileges which that instrument provides for and secures to citizens of the United States. [20]

Taney drew this conclusion from an examination of historical practices and the intent of the Framers of the Constitution. Slaves, he said,

had for more than a century before [the Constitution was ratified] been regarded as being of an inferior order, and altogether unfit to associate with the white race, either in social or political relations; and so far inferior, that they had no rights which the white man was bound to respect; and that the negro might justly and lawfully be reduced to slavery for his benefit. . . . This opinion was at that time fixed and universal in the civilized portion of the white race. [21]

Even the words "all men are created equal" in the Declaration of Independence did not encompass the black race. The authors of that declaration, Taney said,

perfectly understood the meaning of the language they used, and how it would be understood by others; and they knew that it would not in any part of the civilized world, be supposed to embrace the negro race, which, by common consent, had been excluded from civilized Governments and the family of nations, and doomed to slavery. [22]

Taney also touched on the question of whether a person declared a citizen by one state was automatically a citizen of the United States, concluding that this was not so since the Constitution gave the federal government exclusive control over naturalization.

With regard to whether other states were bound to recognize as citizens those granted citizenship by a single state, Taney said:

Each state may still confer [citizenship rights] upon an alien, or anyone it thinks proper. . . ; yet he would not be a citizen in the sense in which the word is used in the Constitution . . . nor entitled to sue as such in one of its courts, nor to the privileges and immunities of a citizen in the other States. [23]

Taney also used an examination of pre–Revolutionary War laws in the states to show that slaves, far from being citizens, were actually considered property:

The unhappy black race were separated from the whites by indelible marks, and laws long before established, and were never thought of or spoken of except as property, and when the claims of the owner or the profit of the trader was supposed to need protection. [24]

That slaves were considered property was reflected in the only two provisions of the Constitution that specifically mentioned them, he continued. These provisions, Taney said, "treat them as property, and makes it the duty of the government to protect it; no other power, in relation to this race, is to be found in the Constitution." [25]

Taney might have ended the matter right there, declaring that because Scott was not a citizen under the meaning of the Constitution, he could not bring suit in federal court. But the chief justice felt it necessary to discuss whether Scott's residence in the Wisconsin Territory made him a free man. In this way he was able to reach the question of whether Congress had the constitutional authority to bar slavery in the states.

Taney first declared that Congress did not have that power under Article IV, Section 2, of the Constitution. This language, he said, allowed Congress to make rules and regulations only for the territories held at the time the Constitution was ratified. "It applied only to the property which the States held in common at that time and has no reference whatever to any territory or other property which the new sovereignty might afterwards itself acquire."[26]

Taney acknowledged that the federal government had the power to acquire new territory for preparation for statehood, and that Congress could in its discretion determine the form of government the territory would have. But Congress must exercise that power over territories within the confines prescribed by the Constitution. Congress, Taney said,

has no power of any kind beyond [the Constitution]; and it cannot, when it enters a territory of the United States, put off its character, and assume discretionary or despotic powers which the Constitution has denied to it. It cannot create for itself a new character separated from the citizens of the United States, and the duties it owes them under the provisions of the Constitution.[27]

Among those duties was the obligation to protect property, Taney said. Noting that the Fifth Amendment provided that no persons should be deprived of life, liberty, or property without due process of law, Taney concluded that

an Act of Congress, which deprives a citizen . . . of his liberty or property, merely because he came himself or brought his property into a particular Territory of the United States, and who had committed no offense against the laws, could hardly be dignified with the name of due process of law.[28]

Therefore, Taney said, the portion of the Missouri Compromise that prohibited slavery in the northern portion of the Louisiana Purchase was void and Dred Scott had not been freed by his residence there.

Nor was Scott free because of his residence in Illinois. Using the reasoning in *Strader v. Graham*, Taney said that because

Scott was a slave when taken into the State of Illinois by his owner, and was there held as such, and brought back in that character, his status, as free or slave depended on the laws of Missouri, and not of Illinois.[29]

Justices Grier and James M. Wayne for the most part concurred with Taney's opinion. Justice Nelson submitted the original opinion he had written for the Court, dismissing the case on the basis of the ruling in *Strader v. Graham*. Justices Peter V. Daniel, John A. Campbell, and Catron, using different reasoning, all agreed that Congress had no authority to prohibit slavery in the territories. The dissenters, McLean and Curtis, also filed lengthy opinions, setting out their opposition to the majority.

But it was Taney's opinion that, in historian Bruce Catton's words, "reverberated across the land like a thunderclap."[30] Northern papers were quick to criticize the decision and the Court. For example, the Washington correspondent for the *New*

York Tribune wrote March 7, 1857: "If the action of the Court in this case has been atrocious, the manner of it has been no better. The Court has rushed into politics, voluntarily and without other purpose than to subserve the cause of slavery."[31]

Northern abolitionists particularly scored Taney's statement that blacks were so inferior to whites "that they had no rights which the white man was bound to respect." Taney had said this, but in the context that this was the general belief at the time the Constitution was written and with the caveat that the accuracy or inaccuracy of the belief was not a question before the Court.

As Taney's biographer, Carl B. Swisher has noted, the "phrase was torn from its context by critics of the decision and published as a statement by Taney that the Negro had no rights which the white man was bound to respect. The error found its way into the history of the period, was repeated in the classrooms of the country and persists to the present day."[32]

Legal scholars and constitutional historians generally agree that Taney's opinion was questionable in several respects. He made no mention of the fact that Congress had been prohibiting slavery in territories for seventy years or of the fact that Missouri courts had accorded citizenship rights to several blacks considered citizens by other states.

By the modern canons of judicial restraint, Taney erred grievously. He decided on the constitutionality of a federal law when it was not strictly necessary to do so. His opinion applied the law more broadly than was required by the facts of the case. And the Court could have observed the rule that no matter how grave the constitutional questions, the Court will try to put a construction on a federal law that will make it valid. *(See "Judicial Restraint," pp. 297–306, in Chapter 6.)*

It also seems apparent that the justices allowed their own political persuasions to influence their decisions. Constitutional historian Edward S. Corwin wrote: "When . . . the student finds six judges arriving at precisely the same result by three distinct processes of reasoning, he is naturally disposed to surmise that the result may possibly have induced the processes rather than that the processes compelled the result."[33]

What was the significance of the Dred Scott decision? Rather than dampening the controversy over slavery, the ruling fueled it, perhaps hastening the onset of civil war. The finding that blacks, both slave and free, were not and could not be citizens under the Constitution led to the adoption of the Fourteenth Amendment, which itself would play a very complicated role in the development of constitutional law. *(See box, Dred Scott Reversed: The Fourteenth Amendment, p. 149.)*

But perhaps its greatest impact was on the Court itself. A contemporary editorial in the *North American Review* of October 1857 stated:

The country will feel the consequences of the decision more deeply and more permanently in the loss of confidence in the sound judicial integrity and strictly legal character of their tribunals, than in anything beside; and this, perhaps, may well be accounted the greatest political calamity which this country, under our forms of government, could sustain.[34]

THE INSULAR CASES

Because the territory acquired in the early decades of the nation's history was intended for eventual statehood, questions of imperialism and colonization over foreign peoples did not arise. But with the acquisition of Hawaii, Puerto Rico, Guam, and the Philippines in 1898, the likelihood of statehood was not assumed, and the ensuing debate over American imperialism raised a difficult question.

Did the constitutional rights and guarantees afforded residents of the United States extend to residents of these new territories? In other words, did the Constitution follow the flag? The Court discussed the issue in the *Insular Cases* in the early 1900s before reaching a final conclusion.

No Foreign Country

In the first case, the collector for New York's port continued to collect duties on sugar imported from Puerto Rico after it was annexed, as if it were still a foreign nation. Contending that the island was no longer a foreign country, the sugar owners sued for return of the paid duties.

The Court by a 5–4 vote held in *DeLima v. Bidwell* (1901) that Puerto Rico had ceased to be a foreign country so far as the tariff laws were concerned and that the duties had been illegally collected.[35] The controlling precedent, wrote Justice Henry B. Brown, was the decision in *Cross v. Harrison* (1853) in which the Court recognized that California had lost its status as a foreign country as soon as ratification of the annexation treaty was officially announced in the new territory.[36] While that opinion did not directly involve the issue at hand in *DeLima*, Brown said, "it is impossible to escape the logical inference from that case that goods carried from San Francisco to New York after the ratification of the treaty would not be considered as imported from a foreign country."[37]

Not the United States

But if Puerto Rico was not a foreign country so far as tariffs were concerned, neither was it part of the United States, said a majority of the Court in a second case decided the same day. *Downes v. Bidwell* (1901) upheld a provision of the Foraker Act of 1900 that established special import duties for Puerto Rican goods.[38] The New York port collector imposed the duty on a shipment of oranges, and the owners sued, citing the constitutional stricture that all duties must be uniform throughout the United States.

With another 5–4 division, the Court ruled against the orange owners. However, the majority could not agree on its reasons. In the official opinion of the Court, Justice Brown held that the Constitution applied only to the states and that it was up to Congress to decide if it wished to extend it to the territories. In passing the Foraker Act, Congress had clearly stated its decision not to extend the Constitution to Puerto Rico, Brown said. Thus the duties were not required to be uniform and were therefore legal.

In a concurring opinion, Justice Edward D. White, joined by Justices George Shiras Jr. and Joseph McKenna, put forth for the first time the theory that the Constitution fully applied only to residents in territories that had been formally "incorporated" into the United States either through ratified treaty or an act of Congress.

In his opinion White envisioned a series of awful consequences that could ensue if the Constitution was automatically extended to acquired territory. He imagined discovery of an unknown island "peopled with an uncivilized race," yet desirable for commercial and strategic purposes. Automatic application of the Constitution could "inflict grave detriment on the United States . . . from . . . the immediate bestowal of citizenship on those absolutely unfit to receive it," White wrote.[39]

He also imagined a war in which the United States would occupy enemy territory. "Would not the war . . . be fraught with danger if the effect of occupation was to necessarily incorporate an alien and hostile people into the United States?" he asked.[40] Once a treaty containing incorporation provisions is ratified by Congress, the full range of constitutional rights would be effective in the territory, White said. But, he added,

where a treaty contains no conditions for incorporation, and, above all, where it . . . expressly provides to the contrary, incorporation does not arise until in the wisdom of Congress it is deemed that the acquired territory has reached that state where it is proper that it should enter into and form a part of the American family.[41]

Dissenting, Justice John Marshall Harlan argued that the Constitution must follow the flag:

In my opinion, Congress has no existence and can exercise no authority outside of the Constitution. Still less is it true that Congress can deal with new territories just as other nations have done or may do with their new territories. This nation is under the control of a written constitution, the supreme law of the land and the only source of the powers which our Government, or any branch or officer of it, may exert at any time or at any place. . . . The idea that this country may acquire territories anywhere upon the earth, by conquest or treaty, and hold them as mere colonies or provinces—the people inhabiting them to enjoy only such rights as Congress chooses to accord to them—is wholly inconsistent with the spirit and genius as well as the words of the Constitution.[42]

Two years later, White again offered his incorporation theory in a concurring opinion. A Hawaiian named Mankichi had been convicted of manslaughter by a nonunanimous jury during the period after the annexation of Hawaii in 1898 but before its incorporation into the United States in 1900. The annexation act had specified that Hawaiian laws not contrary to the Constitution would apply until such time as the islands were incorporated. Conviction by less than a unanimous jury, legal under Hawaiian law, was challenged as a violation of the Fifth and Sixth Amendments of the Constitution.

The majority opinion, written by Brown, contended that although the annexation act said so, Congress had not really intended to provide the guarantees of the Fifth and Sixth Amendments to Hawaiians. To do so would have required the release of

DRED SCOTT REVERSED: THE FOURTEENTH AMENDMENT

It took a constitutional amendment to overturn the 1857 Supreme Court ruling in *Scott v. Sandford*, known as the Dred Scott case, that blacks were not and could not be citizens under the Constitution.

Congress in early 1865 passed the Thirteenth Amendment abolishing slavery. It was ratified toward the end of the year, but hopes that its adoption would encourage the southern states to protect the civil rights of their former black slaves went unrealized. In fact the southern states passed so-called black codes, which contained harsh vagrancy laws and sterner criminal penalties for blacks than for whites and set up racially segregated schools and other public facilities.

Fearing that these actions indicated the southern states were unchastened by the war and that the Thirteenth Amendment would prove a hollow promise, Republicans, both radical and moderate, began to push for stronger guarantees of black rights. To secure political dominance in the South, the radical Republicans also wanted to ensure that blacks had the right to vote and to keep former prominent Confederates out of state and federal office.

To these ends, the Republican-controlled Congress passed the Freedmen's Bureau Act and the Civil Rights Act of 1866. Both sought to protect basic rights, and the latter attempted to void by legislation the Supreme Court's denial of citizenship to blacks. But the Civil Rights Act was passed over President Andrew Johnson's veto, and its constitutionality was doubtful. So Republicans looked to enactment of a constitutional amendment. In April of 1866 the Joint Committee on Reconstruction reported the Fourteenth Amendment. With few changes, the five-part amendment was submitted to the states for ratification in June 1866.

The third and fourth sections of the amendment were of only temporary significance. They prohibited anyone from holding state or federal office (unless authorized by Congress) who had participated in rebellion after taking an oath to support the U.S. Constitution, and denied the responsibility of federal or state governments for debts incurred in aid of rebellion.

The second section of the amendment in effect eliminated the clause of Article I, Section 2, of the Constitution, which directed that only three-fifths of the slave population of a state be counted in apportioning the House of Representatives. This section also provided that if any state abridged the right of its citizens to vote for federal or state officers, the number of its representatives in the House would be reduced in proportion to the numbers denied the vote. In addition to ensuring blacks the right to vote, this language was intended to dilute the strength of the southern states and Democrats in Congress. But it did not specifically give blacks the right to vote because moderate Republicans feared that such an outright grant might jeopardize ratification of the amendment in those northern states that still restricted black voting rights. As a result, the southern states ignored this section of the amendment, and its inadequacy led quickly to adoption of the Fifteenth Amendment in 1870. *(See details of Fifteenth Amendment, p. 505, in Chapter 10.)*

The first section of the Fourteenth Amendment directly overruled the Dred Scott decision. It declared that all persons born or naturalized in the United States and subject to its jurisdiction are citizens of the United States and the state in which they live. It also prohibited the states from making any law that abridged the privileges and immunities of citizens of the United States, deprived any person of life, liberty, or property without due process of law, or denied anyone equal protection of the laws.

In addition to protecting the civil rights of blacks, the original sponsor of this section, Rep. John A. Bingham (R-Ohio, 1855–1863, 1865–1873), intended it to override the 1833 Supreme Court ruling in *Barron v. Baltimore,* which held that the first eight amendments of the Bill of Rights protected individual rights only from infringement by the federal government, not by state governments. Bingham intended that the Fourteenth Amendment also would protect these rights from infringement by the states. But the final wording of the section was a prohibition on the states and not a positive grant to Congress to protect civil rights against state encroachment, and the Court initially limited Congress's authority to enforce these protections against state infringement. Not until 1925, in *Gitlow v. New York,* would the Court begin to apply the Fourteenth Amendment to secure the guarantees of the Bill of Rights against state action. *(See "Rights and the States," pp. 410–411, in Chapter 9.)*

The Court was to frustrate the authors of the Fourteenth Amendment even further by applying the rights guarantees intended for persons to businesses instead. This interpretation of the Fourteenth Amendment's due process clause was not abandoned until the New Deal era. *(See introduction to Chapter 12, Equal Rights and Personal Liberties, pp. 621–624.)*

After World War II the Supreme Court ruled that the equal protection clause prohibited racial segregation in the schools; and almost one hundred years after its ratification, the Court upheld federal civil rights legislation based in part on the Fourteenth Amendment. *(See "Racial Equality," pp. 625–668, in Chapter 12.)*

---

everyone convicted of crimes by nonunanimous juries after the annexation. "Surely such a result could not have been within the contemplation of Congress," Brown said.[43]

White agreed with Brown's result but reasoned that since the islands were not incorporated at the time of Mankichi's trial, the guarantees of the Fifth and Sixth Amendments did not extend to him.

For the four dissenters, Chief Justice Melville W. Fuller wrote: "The language [of the annexation act] is plain and unambiguous and to resort to construction or interpretation is absolutely uncalled for. To tamper with words is to eliminate them."[44]

Incorporation Theory Prevails

A few months later, a majority of the Court subscribed for the first time to White's incorporation doctrine. *Dorr v. United*

POWER OVER FEDERAL PROPERTY

In addition to granting Congress power over territories, Article IV, Section 3, Clause 2, also gives Congress the power "to dispose of and make all needful Rules and Regulations respecting . . . other Property belonging to the United States."

The power to dispose of public property is considered absolute by the Supreme Court. In an 1840 case the Court denied a contention that Congress could only sell federal land and not lease it. "The disposal must be left to the discretion of Congress," the Court asserted.[1]

The authority over disposal of federal property was expanded in 1913 when the Court held that the federal government could sell or lease any excess hydroelectric power it might generate in the process of improving the navigability of a stream.[2] And in 1936 the Court held that because the construction of a federal dam created the energy from which electric power could be generated, the government had the authority to generate and sell the power.[3]

Congressional authority to make rules and regulations for federally owned property is also absolute and may be delegated to the executive branch.[4] States may not tax federal lands within their boundaries nor may they take actions that would interfere with the federal power to regulate federal lands.[5]

In the late 1970s, sixty members of the House of Representatives attempted to use this grant of power as a base from which to carve out for themselves a role in the ratification of the treaty ceding the Panama Canal and the Canal Zone to Panama. They argued that because the land in question was owned by the United States, the consent of the House, as well as the Senate, was required for its disposal. Their efforts proved futile. The Court of Appeals for the District of Columbia ruled that the Senate's constitutional power to ratify treaties included the power to dispose of U.S. property.[6]

1. *United States v. Gratiot*, 14 Pet. 526 at 538 (1840).
2. *United States v. Chandler-Dunbar Water Co.*, 229 U.S. 53 (1913).
3. *Ashwander v. Tennessee Valley Authority*, 297 U.S. 288 (1936).
4. See, for example, *United States v. Fitzgerald*, 15 Pet. 407 at 421 (1841); *Sioux Tribe v. United States*, 316 U.S. 317 (1942).
5. *Van Brocklin v. Tennessee*, 117 U.S. 151 (1886); *Gibson v. Chouteau*, 13 Wall. 92 (1872); *Irvine v. Marshall*, 20 How. 558 (1858); *Emblem v. Lincoln Land Co.*, 184 U.S. 660 (1902).
6. *Edwards v. Carter*, 436 U.S. 907 (cert. denied, 1978).

States (1904) involved circumstances similar to the Mankichi case. The question was whether a criminal trial in the Philippines, held without indictment and heard by a jury of fewer than twelve persons, was a violation of the defendant's rights under the Constitution.

It was not, held the Court. Justice William R. Day's majority opinion offered a succinct statement approving the incorporation doctrine:

That the United States may have territory, which is not incorporated into the United States as a body politic, we think was recognized by the framers of the Constitution in enacting the Article [Article IV] already considered, giving power over the territories, and is sanctioned by the

opinions of the Justices concurring in the judgment in *Downes v. Bidwell*. . . .

Until Congress shall see fit to incorporate territory ceded by treaty in the United States, we regard it as settled by that decision that the territory is to be governed under the power existing in Congress to make laws for such territories and subject to such constitutional restrictions upon the powers of the body as are applicable to the situation.[45]

The incorporation doctrine was reinforced when the Court in 1905 voided trial by six-person juries in Alaska on the grounds that Alaska had been largely incorporated into the United States.[46] In 1911, eight justices—Harlan continued to dissent—agreed that since Congress had not incorporated the Philippines, criminal trials did not require twelve-member juries.[47] The incorporation theory remained into the 1970s the rule for determining when constitutional rights and guarantees are extended to territorial residents.

Citizenship and Naturalization

"Citizenship," declared Chief Justice Earl Warren, "*is* man's basic right for it is nothing less than the right to have rights. Remove this priceless possession and there remains a stateless person, disgraced and degraded in the eyes of his countrymen."[48]

Although it refers to "citizens" in several instances, nowhere does the main body of the Constitution define who is a citizen and how one acquires citizenship. The prevailing assumption was that a citizen was a person who was born in the country and who remained under its jurisdiction and protection. This definition, followed in England and known as *jus soli,* was in contrast to the common practice of *jus sanguines* in the rest of Europe, where citizenship was determined by parental nationality.

In its 1857 Dred Scott decision, the Supreme Court adopted an extremely narrow definition of citizenship that stood for less than a dozen years. Not only did the Court exclude blacks, even native-born free blacks, from citizenship, but also it held that national citizenship was dependent on and resulted from state citizenship. Chief Justice Roger B. Taney wrote:

[E]very person, and every class and description of persons who were at the time of the adoption of the Constitution recognized as citizens in the several States, became also citizens of this new political body; but none other; it was formed by them, and for them and their posterity but for no one else.[49]

This ruling led ultimately to the Fourteenth Amendment, ratified in 1868 at the conclusion of the Civil War. Its first sentence stated: "All persons born or naturalized in the United States and subject to the jurisdiction thereof, are citizens of the United States and of the State wherein they reside." *(See details of Dred Scott case, pp. 145–147; box, Dred Scott Reversed: The Fourteenth Amendment, p. 149.)*

Designed primarily to confer citizenship on blacks, the Fourteenth Amendment made the concept of *jus soli* the law of the land. This concept was confirmed and further defined in the case of *United States v. Wong Kim Ark* (1898) in which the Supreme Court declared that—under the Fourteenth Amendment—children born in the United States to resident alien par-

"The right of eminent domain, that is, the right to take private property for public uses, appertains to every independent government," said the Supreme Court in 1879. "It requires no constitutional recognition; it is an attribute of sovereignty."[1] Evidence that the Framers of the Constitution believed the federal government to possess this power is found in the clauses of the Fifth Amendment that prohibit the taking of private property without due process of law and payment of just compensation.

An attempt to extend these Fifth Amendment guarantees to the taking of private land by the states failed when the Supreme Court in 1833 held that the first eight amendments to the Constitution protected rights only against infringement by the federal government and not by state governments.[2]

The Fourteenth Amendment, ratified in 1868, prohibited the states from depriving a person of property without due process of the law, but made no mention of just compensation. At first the Court interpreted this omission to mean that the states did not have to make compensation.[3] But in 1897 the Court reversed itself, holding that a state had not provided due process of law if it had not made just compensation: "The mere form of the proceeding instituted against the owner . . . cannot convert the process used into due process of law, if the necessary result be to deprive him of his property without compensation."[4]

PUBLIC USE

By virtue of their authority to review eminent domain cases, the courts are the final arbiters of what uses of private land may be considered public. The Supreme Court traditionally has given great weight to the federal legislature's designation of what constitutes a public use, even suggesting in 1946 that the Court might not have the authority to review a congressional determination of public use. "We think that it is the function of Congress to decide what type of taking is for a public use and that the agency authorized to do the taking may do so to the full extent of its statutory authority," the Court observed.[5]

Public uses include lands used for public buildings, highways, and parks and for preserving sites of historical interest, such as battlefields. In 1954 the Court upheld the right of Congress to use its power of eminent domain to facilitate slum clearance, urban renewal, and the construction of public housing, even though only a small portion of the public would be eligible to live in the housing.[6]

In addition to exercising the eminent domain power itself, Congress may delegate it "to private corporations to be exercised by them in the execution of works in which the public is interested," such as railroad and utility companies.[7]

JUST COMPENSATION

The general standard set by the Court for determining whether the compensation paid is adequate is the amount a willing buyer would pay to a willing seller in the open market.[8]

That amount may be adjusted to account for various contingencies. For instance, the compensation may be reduced if the owner receives a benefit from the taking of the property greater than the benefit to the public at large.[9]

In those instances in which the government has infringed on a person's property without actually taking it—for example, where noise from a nearby airport makes land unfit for the uses its owners intended—the Court has established another general rule: "Property is taken in the constitutional sense when inroads are made upon an owner's use of it to an extent that, as between private parties, a servitude [subjecting the property owned by one person to the use of another] has been acquired either by agreement or in the course of time."[10]

In some instances, the Court has held that federal or state regulations prohibiting the use of property for certain purposes in order to protect the public welfare are exercises of the police power and not the taking of property under the eminent domain power, which would require compensation. In 1962 the Court wrote:

A prohibition simply upon the use of property for purposes that are declared, by valid legislation, to be injurious to the health, morals or safety of the community, cannot, in any just sense, be deemed a taking or appropriation of property for the public benefit. Such legislation does not disturb the owner in the control or use of his property for lawful purposes, nor restrict his right to dispose of it, but is only a declaration by the State that its use by one, for certain forbidden purposes, is prejudicial to the public interests.[11]

In times of war or emergency, the Court has held that government actions destroying property or preventing its use for the purposes intended did not constitute a taking entitling the owners to compensation.[12]

In the latter years of the twentieth century, the Court increased the level of scrutiny it applies to cases based on this requirement of just compensation. It rejected a state plan that made a landowner's building permit contingent upon his allowing the public access across his private beachfront property.[13] Unless that permit requirement substantially advanced a legitimate state interest, the state must pay just compensation for the easement, said the Court. Several years later, the Court held that municipal governments must show a connection and a rough proportionality between conditions imposed on landowners with development permits and the claimed public harm from the development.[14]

1. *Brown Co. v. Patterson*, 98 U.S. 403 at 405 (1879).

2. *Barron v. Baltimore*, 7 Pet. 243 (1833).

3. *Davidson v. City of New Orleans*, 96 U.S. 97 (1878).

4. *Chicago, Burlington & Quincy Railroad Co. v. City of Chicago*, 166 U.S. 226 at 236–237 (1897).

5. *U.S. ex rel. Tennessee Valley Authority v. Welch*, 327 U.S. 546 at 551–552 (1946).

6. *Berman v. Parker*, 348 U.S. 26 (1954).

7. *Boom Co. v. Patterson*, 98 U.S. 403 at 405 (1879); see also *Noble v. Oklahoma City*, 297 U.S. 481 (1936); *Luxton v. North River Bridge Co.*, 153 U.S. 525 (1894).

8. *United States v. Miller*, 317 U.S. 369 at 374 (1943); *United States ex rel. Tennessee Valley Authority v. Powelson*, 319 U.S. 266 at 275 (1943).

9. *Bauman v. Ross*, 167 U.S. 648 (1897).

10. *United States v. Dickinson*, 331 U.S. 745 at 748 (1947).

11. *Goldblatt v. Town of Hempstead*, 369 U.S. 590 at 593 (1962).

12. *United States v. Caltex*, 344 U.S. 149 (1952); *United States v. Central Eureka Mining Co.*, 357 U.S. 155 (1958); *National Board of YMCA v. United States*, 395 U.S. 85 (1969).

13. *Nollan v. California Coastal Commission*, 483 U.S. 825 (1987).

14. *Dolan v. City of Tigard*, 114 S. Ct. 2481 (1994).

ents were citizens even if their parents were barred from becoming citizens. The Court wrote:

The Fourteenth Amendment affirms the ancient and fundamental rule of citizenship by birth within the territory, in the allegiance and under the protection of the country, including all children here born of resident aliens, with the exceptions or qualifications . . . of children of foreign sovereigns or their ministers, or born on public ships, or of enemies within and during hostile occupation of part of our territory, and with the single additional exception of children of members of the Indian tribes owing direct allegiance to their several tribes.[50]

This last exception was eliminated in 1925 when Congress granted citizenship to Indians living in tribes.

NATURALIZATION

Wong Kim Ark's parents could not become citizens because Congress, under its power "to establish a uniform rule of naturalization," in 1882 specifically prohibited citizenship by naturalization to Chinese. The Court has allowed Congress to establish whatever conditions it deems necessary for citizenship through naturalization. "Naturalization is a privilege, to be given, qualified or withheld as Congress may determine and which the alien may claim as of right only upon compliance with the terms which Congress imposes," the Court said in 1931. In this case, the Court was upholding denial of naturalization to a pacifist who wanted to qualify his oath of allegiance by refusing to support war unless he believed it morally justified.[51]

The Court has held that Congress may exclude an entire class or race of people from eligibility for citizenship and may expel aliens from the country. Upholding a statute expelling Chinese laborers from the country if they did not obtain a required residence certificate within a specified time the Court wrote:

The right of a nation to expel or deport foreigners, who have not been naturalized or taken any steps toward becoming citizens . . . is as absolute and unqualified as the right to prohibit and prevent their entrance into the country. . . .

. . . The power to exclude or expel aliens, being a power affecting international relations, is vested in the political departments of the government, and it is to be regulated by treaty or by act of Congress, and to be executed by the executive authority according to the regulations so established.[52]

Exclusions

After ratification of the Fourteenth Amendment, Congress enacted laws limiting naturalized citizenship to whites and to blacks of African descent. Citizenship was extended to the residents of some, but not all, of the U.S. territories. The residents of Hawaii became citizens in 1900, those of Puerto Rico in 1917, and those of the Virgin Islands in 1927. But the residents of the Philippines were denied citizenship throughout the period the United States held the islands as a trust territory. Other Asians did not fare any better in winning citizenship through naturalization; the final barriers were not removed until passage of the 1952 Immigration and Nationality Act, which barred the use of race as a reason for denying citizenship.

Other conditions set by Congress have excluded from natu-

ralization anarchists, members of the Communist Party, and others who advocate the violent overthrow of the government. To qualify for naturalization, an alien must have been a resident of the country for five years and be of good moral character. The latter phrase has been interpreted to exclude drunks, adulterers, polygamists, gamblers, convicted felons, and homosexuals. The Court has generally sustained these exclusions.[53]

One exclusion the Court disapproved was for conscientious objectors who refused to swear an oath of allegiance requiring them to bear arms. Initially, the Court agreed that this exclusion was valid. In one extreme case, the Court denied citizenship to a fifty-year-old female pacifist, who would not have been required to bear arms in any event.[54] This ruling and two others like it were specifically overturned in the 1946 case of *Girouard v. United States.*

Girouard was a Seventh-day Adventist who refused to swear he would bear arms but said he would serve in a noncombatant position. In a ruling based entirely on its interpretation of the law, not the Constitution, the majority said it could not believe that Congress meant to deny citizenship in a country traditionally protective of religious freedom to those who objected to war on religious grounds.[55]

Four years later, the Court ruled that citizenship could be granted to a pacifist who refused to serve in the army even as a noncombatant.[56] In 1952 Congress formally took notice of the 1946 and 1950 rulings by allowing naturalization of conscientious objectors so long as they agreed to perform approved alternative service.

Denaturalization

As early as 1824 the Supreme Court, speaking through Chief Justice John Marshall, declared there was no difference between a naturalized citizen and one who was native born. A naturalized citizen, wrote Marshall,

becomes a member of the society, possessing all rights of the native citizens, and standing, in the view of the constitution, on the footing of a native. The constitution does not authorize Congress to enlarge or abridge those rights. The simple power of the national Legislature is to prescribe a uniform rule of naturalization, and the exercise of its power exhausts it, so far as respects the individual.[57]

Aside from not being qualified to run for the presidency, naturalized citizens enjoy the same rights, privileges, and responsibilities as do native-born citizens. The exception is that naturalized citizens may be denaturalized.

Fraud. The Court has repeatedly held that a naturalized citizen may lose his or her citizenship if it was obtained fraudulently. "An alien has no moral or constitutional rights to retain the privileges of citizenship" won through fraud, the Court said in 1912.[58] The Court also has ruled that the lapse of time between naturalization and the time when the fraud is discovered is of no significance. In one case, the Court sustained deprivation of naturalization for a man who claimed to be in real estate when in fact he was a bootlegger. The fact that more than twenty-five years had lapsed between his naturalization and discovery of his fraud made no difference, although the Court subsequently barred his deportation.[59]

Bad Faith. Naturalization also may be lost if it was obtained in bad faith. In *Luria v. United States* the Court upheld denaturalization of a man who apparently never intended to become a permanent resident of the United States at the time he was naturalized. The decision upheld an act of Congress that made residence in a foreign country within five years of naturalization prima facie evidence of bad faith.[60]

In 1943, however, the Court established a rule that a naturalized citizen could not be denaturalized unless the government could demonstrate by "clear, unequivocal and convincing" evidence that the citizenship had been fraudulently obtained. In *Schneiderman v. United States* the government sought Schneiderman's denaturalization on the grounds that he had been a member of a Communist organization five years prior to and at the time of his naturalization in 1927. The Court acknowledged the existence of a statute that foreclosed naturalization to those who advocated the violent overthrow of the government but said that the government had not proved sufficiently whether the organizations Schneiderman belonged to advocated such violence in a manner that was a clear and present public danger or merely in a doctrinal manner that put forward overthrow of the government simply for consideration and discussion.[61]

It was not until 1946 that the Court assented to the denaturalization of a person under the *Schneiderman* rule. Finding clear evidence that Paul Knauer, a naturalized citizen, was a Nazi before, at the time of, and after his naturalization, the Court said that "when an alien takes the oath with reservation or does not in good faith forswear loyalty and allegiance to the old country, the decree of naturalization is obtained by deceit."[62]

In a dissenting opinion that was eventually to gain support of a slim majority of the Court, Justice Wiley B. Rutledge, joined by Justice Frank Murphy, said he did not believe a naturalized citizen could be stripped of his citizenship in such a case. "My concern is not for Paul Knauer," Rutledge said. "But if one man's citizenship can thus be taken away, so can that of any other. . . . [A]ny process which takes away their [naturalized] citizenship for causes or by procedures not applicable to native born citizens places them in a separate and an inferior class."[63] Rutledge said he did not believe such a difference was contemplated by the Framers when they gave Congress the power to establish uniform naturalization rules.

Eighteen years later Rutledge's dissent became the majority position in the 1964 case of *Schneider v. Rusk.*[64] The case tested the validity of a provision of the 1952 immigration law that revoked the citizenship of any naturalized citizen who subsequently resided in his or her native land for three continuous years.

Born in Germany, Mrs. Schneider came to the United States as a child and acquired derivative citizenship when her parents were naturalized. As an adult she returned to Germany, married a German national, and visited the United States only twice in eight years. Her case came to the Court after she was denied a U.S. passport on the grounds that she had lived in Germany for three continuous years. By a 5–3 vote the Court struck down the 1952 provision allowing revocation of Mrs. Schneider's citizenship. Echoing Rutledge and Murphy, and John Marshall before them, Justice William O. Douglas said: "We start from the premise that the rights of citizenship of the native born and of the naturalized person are of the same dignity and are coextensive."[65]

The 1952 provision, Douglas continued, "proceeds on the impermissible assumption that the naturalized citizens as a class are less reliable and bear less allegiance to this country than do the native born. This is an assumption that is impossible for us to make. . . . The discrimination aimed at naturalized citizens drastically limits their rights to live and work abroad in a way that other citizens may."[66]

EXPATRIATION

The *Knauer* and *Schneider* decisions set out the arguments in a continuing debate over whether Congress has the power to revoke the citizenship of any citizen, whether naturalized or native born.

That citizens may voluntarily expatriate themselves has never been questioned. The Court also has held that Congress may stipulate certain acts, the voluntary performance of which would be the equivalent of voluntary expatriation. In 1915 the Court upheld a provision of the Citizenship Act of 1907 by which any female citizen who married an alien surrendered her citizenship in the United States.[67] That provision was repealed in 1922, but in 1950 the Court ruled that a woman who had voluntarily sworn allegiance to Italy in order to marry an Italian citizen had, in essence, forsworn her allegiance to the United States and effectively renounced her citizenship in the United States.[68]

The Immigration and Nationality Act of 1952 contained a long list of circumstances under which a citizen would lose his or her citizenship. These included voting in a foreign election, being convicted for desertion during time of war and being discharged from the armed services, and leaving or remaining outside the country to avoid military service. The question was whether the performance of any of these actions amounted to voluntary renunciation of citizenship. If it did not, then their validity turned on whether Congress had the power to revoke citizenship.

Foreign Elections

In the first case to deal fully with this question—*Perez v. Brownell*—a divided Court in 1958 upheld the provision revoking citizenship of a person who voted in a foreign election.[69] The majority held that Congress could revoke citizenship as a necessary and proper means of exercising its other powers. In this case the Court viewed this provision as enacted pursuant to Congress's implied power over foreign affairs. Justice Felix Frankfurter said the Court could not deny Congress the authority to regulate conduct of Americans—such as voting in foreign

THE CONSTITUTION ON CITIZENSHIP

The Constitution contains few specific references to citizens and citizenship. The body of the Constitution states only that the president, senators, and representatives must be citizens, that citizens of each state shall enjoy the privileges and immunities of all other states, and that citizens may bring certain suits in federal court. The latter was modified by the Eleventh Amendment.

Not until ratification of the Fourteenth Amendment in 1868 was language added to the Constitution defining eligibility for citizenship. The Constitution does not even specifically restrict the right to vote to citizens, but citizens are the only people whose right to vote is constitutionally protected.

Following are the passages in the Constitution that refer to citizens:

Article I, Section 2. No Person shall be a Representative who shall not have . . . been seven Years a Citizen of the United States. . . .

Article I, Section 3. No Person shall be a Senator who shall not have . . . been nine Years a Citizen of the United States. . . .

Article II, Section 1. No Person except a natural born Citizen, or a Citizen of the United States, at the time of the Adoption of this Constitution, shall be eligible to the Office of President. . . .

Article III, Section 2. The judicial Power shall extend to all Cases . . . between a State and Citizen of another State;*—between Citizens of different States;—between Citizens of the same State claiming Lands under Grants of different States, and between a State, or the Citizens thereof, and foreign States, Citizens or Subjects.*

Article IV, Section 2. The Citizens of each State shall be entitled to all Privileges and Immunities of Citizens in the several States.

Amendment XI. The Judicial power of the United States shall not be construed to extend to any suit in law or equity, commenced or prosecuted against one of the United States by Citizens of another State, or by Citizens or Subjects of any Foreign State.

Amendment XIV, Section 2. All persons born or naturalized in the United States and subject to the jurisdiction thereof, are citizens of the United States and of the State wherein they reside. No State shall make or enforce any law which shall abridge the privileges and immunities of citizens of the United States. . . .

Amendment XIV, Section 2. Representatives shall be apportioned among the several States according to their respective numbers, counting the whole number of persons in each State, excluding Indians not taxed. But when the right to vote at any election for the choice of electors for President and Vice President of the United States, Representatives in Congress, the Executive and Judicial officers of a State, or the members of the Legislature thereof, is denied to any of the male inhabitants of such State, being twenty-one years of age, and citizens of the United States, or in any way abridged, except for participation in rebellion, or other crime, the basis of representation therein shall be reduced in the proportion which the number of such male citizens shall bear to the whole number of male citizens twenty-one years of age in such State. . . .

Amendment XV, Section 1. The right of citizens of the United States to vote shall not be denied or abridged by the United States or by any State on account of race, color, or previous condition of servitude.

Amendment XIX. The right of citizens of the United States to vote shall not be denied or abridged by the United States or by any State on account of sex.

Amendment XXIV, Section 1. The right of citizens of the United States to vote in any primary or other election for President or Vice President, for electors for President or Vice President, or for Senators or Representative in Congress, shall not be denied or abridged by the United States or any State by reason of failure to pay any poll tax or other tax.

Amendment XXVI, Section 1. The right of citizens of the United States, who are eighteen years of age or older, to vote shall not be denied or abridged by the United States or by any State on account of age.

* These phrases were modified by the Eleventh Amendment.

elections—that might prove embarrassing or even jeopardize the conduct of foreign relations.

Frankfurter also rejected the argument that the Fourteenth Amendment denied Congress the power to revoke citizenship. "[T]here is nothing in the terms, the context, the history or the manifest purpose of the Fourteenth Amendment to warrant drawing from it a restriction upon the power otherwise possessed by Congress to withdraw citizenship."[70]

Chief Justice Earl Warren dissented:

The Government is without the power to take citizenship away from a native-born or lawfully naturalized American. The Fourteenth Amendment recognizes that this priceless right is immune from the exercise of governmental powers. If the Government determines that certain conduct by United States citizens should be prohibited because of anticipated injurious consequences to the conduct of foreign affairs or to some other legitimate governmental interest, it may within the limits

of the Constitution proscribe such activity and assess appropriate punishment. But every exercise of governmental power must find its source in the Constitution. The power to denationalize is not within the letter or the spirit of the powers with which our Government was endowed. The citizen may elect to renounce his citizenship, and under some circumstances he may be found to have abandoned his status by voluntarily performing acts that compromise his undivided allegiance to his country. The mere act of voting in a foreign election, however, without regard to the circumstances attending the participation, is not sufficient to show a voluntary abandonment of citizenship. The record in this case does not disclose any of the circumstances under which this petitioner voted. We know only the bare fact that he cast a ballot. The basic right of American citizenship has been too dearly won to be so lightly lost.[71]

Desertion

The same day it handed down its decision in *Perez*, the Court invalidated the provision of the immigration law that revoked citizenship for persons convicted for desertion and discharged from the armed services. In *Trop v. Dulles* five justices agreed that the provision was unconstitutional, but only four agreed on one line of reasoning. For them, Warren again said he did not believe Congress had the power to revoke citizenship. Moreover, he said, revocation of citizenship in this instance was a violation of the Eighth Amendment's proscription against cruel and unusual punishment. This punishment was more cruel than torture, Warren said, for it was "the total destruction of the individual's status in organized society."[72]

Justice William J. Brennan Jr. agreed with the outcome but not with Warren's reasoning. He admitted that his support of the majority in the *Perez* case was paradoxical judged against his position in the present case. But, he said, revocation of citizenship for voting in a foreign election was within the authority of Congress under its powers to regulate foreign affairs. In the *Trop* case, revocation for desertion went beyond any legitimate means of regulation in exercise of the power to raise and maintain armies, he said.

The four dissenters maintained the position they had espoused in the majority opinion in *Perez.*

Draft Evasion

Five years later in *Kennedy v. Mendoza-Martinez* (1963), the Court struck down the provisions of the immigration act that revoked the citizenship of anyone who left or remained outside the country to evade military service.

The sections were invalid, the Court said, "because in them Congress has plainly employed the sanction of deprivation of nationality as a punishment . . . without affording the procedural safeguards guaranteed by the Fifth and Sixth Amendments."[73] Deciding the case on these grounds made it unnecessary for the Court to choose between the powers of Congress and the rights of citizenship.

Foreign Elections Again

In 1967 the Court, again divided 5–4, made the choice between Congress's powers and the right to citizenship, declaring the government powerless to revoke citizenship.

The case of *Afroyim v. Rusk* turned on the same issue involved in the *Perez* case.[74] Polish-born Beys Afroyim was a naturalized U.S. citizen who in 1951 voluntarily voted in an Israeli election. He was denied renewal of his passport for that reason.

Urging the Court to review its decisions in the *Perez* case, Afroyim maintained that he could lose his U.S. citizenship only through voluntary renunciation. Following the *Perez* precedent, the lower courts ruled that Congress through its implied power over foreign affairs could revoke the citizenship of Americans voting in foreign elections.

Overturning *Perez,* the majority rejected the idea

that, aside from the Fourteenth Amendment, Congress has any general power, express or implied, to take away an American citizen's citizenship without his assent. . . . In our country the people are sovereign and the government cannot sever its relationship to the people by taking away their citizenship.[75]

Nor could Congress find power to revoke citizenship in the citizenship clause of the Fourteenth Amendment. That clause, the majority said,

provides its own constitutional rule in language calculated completely to control the status of citizenship: "All persons born or naturalized in the United States . . . are citizens of the United States. . . ." There is no indication in these words of a fleeting citizenship, good at the moment it is acquired but subject to destruction by the government at any time.[76]

In a footnote the majority made an exception for those who obtained their naturalization through fraud.

CONTROL OF ALIENS

The congressional power over aliens is absolute and derives from the fact of the nation's sovereignty. This power was recognized by the Supreme Court in 1889 as it upheld an act of Congress barring entry of Chinese aliens into the country:

That the government of the United States, through the action of the legislative department, can exclude aliens from its territory is a proposition which we do not think open to controversy. Jurisdiction over its own territory to that extent is an incident of every independent nation. It is a part of its independence. If it could not exclude aliens, it would be to that extent subject to the control of another power. . . . The United States, in their relation to foreign countries and their subjects or citizens, are one nation, invested with powers which belong to independent nations, the exercise of which can be invoked for the maintenance of its absolute independence and security throughout its entire territory.[1]

Under this authority, Congress has barred entry to convicts, prostitutes, epileptics, anarchists, and professional beggars. It has excluded people because of their race and established national origin quotas.

The authority also empowers Congress to regulate to a large extent the conduct of aliens in the country and to provide that aliens convicted of certain crimes be deported.

The Supreme Court has held that aliens involved in deportation proceedings are entitled to certain constitutional rights, including protections against self-incrimination, unreasonable searches and seizures, cruel and unusual punishment, ex post facto laws and bills of attainder, and the rights to bail and procedural due process.[2]

Nevertheless, the Court did uphold a provision of the Internal Security Act of 1950 that authorized the attorney general to jail without bail aliens who were members of the Communist Party pending a decision on whether they would be deported.[3]

1. *Chae Chan Ping v. United States (Chinese Exclusion Case),* 130 U.S. 581 at 603–604 (1889). See also *Fong Yue Ting v. United States,* 149 U.S. 698 (1893); *Lem Moon Sing v. United States,* 158 U.S. 538 (1895); *Harisiades v. Shaughnessy,* 342 U.S. 580 (1952); *Shaughnessy v. United States ex rel Mezei,* 345 U.S. 206 (1953).
2. *Kimm v. Rosenberg,* 363 U.S. 405 (1960); *Abel v. United States,* 362 U.S. 217 (1960); *Marcello v. Bonds,* 349 U.S. 302 (1955); *Carlson v. Landon,* 342 U.S. 524 (1952); *Wong Yang Sung v. McGrath,* 339 U.S. 33 (1950).
3. *Carlson v. Landon,* 342 U.S. 524 (1952).

The four dissenters held to the reasoning of the majority in the *Perez* case. "The Citizenship Clause . . . neither denies nor provides to Congress any power of expatriation," wrote Justice John Marshall Harlan. He continued:

Once obtained, citizenship is of course protected from arbitrary withdrawal by the constraints placed around the Congress' powers by the Constitution; it is not proper to create from the Citizenship Clause an additional, and entirely unwarranted, restriction upon legislative authority. The construction now placed on the Citizenship Clause rests, in the last analysis, simply on the Court's *ipse dixit*, evincing little more, it is quite apparent, than the present majority's own distaste for the expatriation power.[77]

Nonresidence

Decided by such a narrow vote, the *Afroyim* decision was not considered a definitive answer to the question of congressional power to expatriate citizens. And while it did not overturn the *Afroyim* decision, the case of *Rogers v. Bellei*, decided in 1971, clouded the issue even further.[78]

Bellei was born overseas in 1939 of one American parent and one alien parent. The 1953 immigration law stated that a person of such parentage would be considered a citizen of the United States so long as he or she lived in the United States for five continuous years between the ages of fourteen and twenty-eight. Bellei only visited the United States briefly on five occasions. Because he did not meet the residence requirement, his citizenship was revoked. He challenged the requirement, but by a 5–4 vote the Court upheld the provision.

Writing for the majority, Justice Harry A. Blackmun maintained that Bellei did not qualify for U.S. citizenship under the Fourteenth Amendment. Bellei "was not born in the United States. And he has not been subject to the jurisdiction of the United States," said Blackmun. "All this being so, it seems indisputable that the first sentence of the Fourteenth Amendment has no application to plaintiff Bellei. He simply is not a Fourteenth-Amendment-first-sentence citizen."[79]

The decision in *Afroyim*, Blackmun continued, was based on the fact that Afroyim was a citizen by virtue of the Fourteenth Amendment. But Bellei was a citizen by an act of Congress, and if Congress may impose conditions that such a person must meet before he can become a citizen, Blackmun said, the majority could see no constitutional reason why it could not impose conditions that must be met after he became a citizen. Blackmun wrote:

Our National Legislature indulged the foreign-born child with presumptive citizenship subject to subsequent satisfaction of the reasonable residence requirement, rather than to deny him citizenship outright, as concededly it had the power to do, and relegate the child, if he desired American citizenship, to the more arduous requirements of the usual naturalization process. The plaintiff here would force the Congress to choose between unconditional conferment of United States

DISTRICT OF COLUMBIA

The power "to exercise exclusive Legislation in all Cases whatsoever, over . . . the Seat of Government of the United States" has been interpreted to mean that Congress may make the laws and appoint the administrators of the District of Columbia or delegate the lawmaking powers to a locally elected government. The local government was partially elected from 1802, when the District was established, until 1874, when Congress, in the wake of financial scandals involving city officials, substituted a presidentially appointed commission to administer it under laws passed by Congress. In 1967 this form of government was changed to a presidentially appointed mayor and city council. In 1973 Congress once again turned over administration of the capital city to a locally elected government, although it retained a tight rein on the city's financial affairs and its judicial system and may enact laws for the District at any time. The reality of that power came home to residents of the District in 1995, when Congress responded to the District's precarious financial state by appointing a financial control board with broad powers to oversee the actions of the city's political leaders.

Residents of the District, although citizens of the United States entitled to all constitutional guarantees, were unable to vote for president until the Twenty-third Amendment was ratified in 1961.

Congress in 1970 authorized the District to elect one nonvoting delegate to the House of Representatives. Because the District is not a state, a constitutional amendment is considered necessary to give it a voting member in the House and representation in the Senate. Congress approved such an amendment late in 1978 and sent it to the states for ratification. But the proposed amendment expired in 1985 after only sixteen states had approved it.

The Supreme Court has had almost no occasion to review the federal administration of the District of Columbia.

citizenship at birth and deferment of citizenship until a condition precedent is fulfilled. We are not convinced that the Constitution requires so rigid a choice.[80]

The minority held that the *Afroyim* decision controlled this case and that Congress could not revoke Bellei's citizenship. In an unusually bitter dissent, Justice Hugo L. Black wrote:

Congress could not, until today, consistent with the Fourteenth Amendment enact a law stripping an American of his citizenship which he has never voluntarily renounced or given up. Now the Court, by a vote of five to four through a simple change in its composition, overturns the decision. . . . This precious Fourteenth Amendment American citizenship should not be blown around by every passing political wind that changes the composition of this Court. I dissent.[81]

Congress repealed the residence requirement in 1978.

The Power to Amend the Constitution

Only a few times in the nation's history has the Supreme Court been asked to resolve questions concerning the power of Congress to propose amendments to the Constitution. More of the Court's rulings in this area have focused on the power of Congress to enforce the guarantees of new amendments.

Several of the twenty-seven amendments to the Constitution, primarily those conferring a political right, such as voting, empower Congress to enforce them through legislation. The three Civil War amendments, giving citizenship and political rights to blacks, were the first to include such enforcement provisions.

But the Court of the 1870s and 1880s severely weakened Congress's power to execute these guarantees, ruling that Congress could regulate state discrimination only after it had occurred and could not reach private discrimination at all. It was almost one hundred years before the Court, playing a leading part in the civil rights revolution of the 1950s and 1960s, reversed this posture, sustaining a broad enforcement role for Congress.

The Amending Power

Article V of the Constitution states: "The Congress, whenever two thirds of both Houses shall deem it necessary, shall propose Amendments to this Constitution, or, on the Application of the Legislatures of two thirds of the several States, shall call a Convention for proposing Amendments, which, in either Case, shall be valid to all Intents and Purposes, as Part of this Constitution, when ratified by the Legislatures of three fourths of the several States, or by Conventions in three fourths thereof, as the one or the other Mode of Ratification may be proposed by the Congress. . . ."

By mid-1996 more than 11,000 proposed amendments to the Constitution had been introduced in Congress. Most of them were duplicate proposals; some were introduced repeatedly in successive Congresses. Only thirty-three of these amendments have been submitted to the states for ratification: twenty-seven have been ratified, four are still pending, and two were not ratified within the period Congress set for their approval.[1]

The four pending amendments include one, relating to apportionment of the House, that was originally introduced in 1789 by James Madison along with the ten that became the Bill of Rights. The two amendments that were not ratified and died were the Equal Rights Amendment and a proposal to give the District of Columbia voting representation in Congress.

There has not yet been a constitutional convention called to propose an amendment. All of the thirty-three amendments submitted so far were approved by a two-thirds vote of Congress.

However, as of mid-1996, thirty-two states had petitioned Congress for an amendment requiring that the federal budget be balanced, and nineteen had petitioned for an amendment outlawing abortion. Earlier, in the years immediately following the Supreme Court's ruling in *Reynolds v. Sims* (1964), thirty-three states—one short of the necessary two-thirds required to call a convention—had petitioned Congress for an amendment allowing one chamber of a state legislature to be apportioned on the basis of geographic or political subdivisions, rather than strictly by population. *(See "Abortion," pp. 691–693, in Chapter 12; "'One Person, One Vote,'" p. 522, in Chapter 10.)*

Viewing constitutional amendments as political decisions, the Supreme Court has been reluctant to interfere in the process. Nonetheless, the Court has heard several cases challenging the constitutionality of ratified amendments and has handed down a number of decisions relating to amendment procedures.

CONSTITUTIONAL CHALLENGES

The first challenge to a constitutional amendment came in 1798, after ratification of the Eleventh Amendment, which prohibited the citizens of one state from suing another state in federal court without the latter state's consent. The question was: What effect did ratification of the amendment have on such suits pending at the time of ratification? To apply the amendment to pending suits, said petitioners, would give it the unconstitutional character of an ex post facto law.

In *Hollingsworth v. Virginia* the Court ruled that once the amendment took effect upon ratification, the Court had no jurisdiction to hear any case of the type described by the amendment—including pending ones. Therefore, the Court dismissed the case.[2]

The constitutional amendment prohibiting the manufacture, sale, and transportation of alcoholic beverages enjoyed only a brief life but engendered more Supreme Court cases testing its validity than any other amendment. Most of these cases involved challenges to the way the Eighteenth Amendment was ratified, but in one case the Court was asked to decide whether liquor was a proper subject for a constitutional amendment. The Court in 1920 ruled it was.[3]

The Nineteenth Amendment, granting the vote to women, was challenged on the grounds that it made such a large addition to the electorate of the few states that had refused to ratify it that it undercut their political autonomy. The Supreme Court held that the Nineteenth Amendment affected the electorate no more than the Fifteenth Amendment, which forbade voting discrimination on the basis of race, color, or previous condition of servitude.[4] The Court observed at the time that the latter amendment had been considered valid and enforced by the judiciary for a half-century.

EXTENSION AND RESCISSION

Once Congress has set a time period for ratification of a proposed constitutional amendment, may it extend that deadline? Opponents of the Equal Rights Amendment (ERA) posed that question in their challenge to a thirty-nine-month extension of the amendment's ratification deadline, approved by Congress in October 1978.

The proposed amendment, which would give men and women equal rights under the law, originally provided seven years for ratification; that time period was set to expire March 22, 1979. The 1978 extension moved the deadline to June 29, 1982. At the time Congress passed the extension thirty-five states had ratified the amendment. Three more states were needed to ratify the ERA for it to become the Twenty-seventh Amendment.

Debate on the extension centered on its constitutionality. The question had not at that time been considered by the Supreme Court. However, in *Dillon v. Gloss* (1921), the Court ruled that Congress has the authority to fix a reasonable time period in which the states must ratify a proposed constitutional amendment.[1] And in *Coleman v. Miller* (1939), the Court held that the question of what constituted a reasonable time period was a nonjusticiable political matter for Congress to determine.[2]

A corollary question concerning the ERA ratification was whether states that had ratified the amendment could subsequently rescind the ratification. As of July 1979, four states—Idaho, Nebraska, South Dakota, and Tennessee—had done just that. In *Coleman,* the Court had written that such a question "should be regarded as a political question pertaining to the political departments, with the ultimate authority in the Congress in the exercise of its control over the promulgation of the adoption of the amendment."[3]

In 1981 a federal judge in Idaho ruled that Congress had exceeded its power in extending the ERA ratification deadline. He also ruled that states could rescind their approval of the amendment if they acted during the ratification period. Early in 1982 the Supreme Court agreed to hear an appeal from those rulings, but, after the ratification period expired on June 30, it dismissed the case as moot, leaving the questions still unresolved.

1. *Dillon v. Gloss,* 256 U.S. 368 (1921).
2. *Coleman v. Miller,* 307 U.S. 433 (1939).
3. Id. at 450.

FEDERAL RATIFICATION PROCEDURES

The president is not required to sign and cannot block a congressional resolution proposing a constitutional amendment to the states. "The negative of the President applies only to the ordinary cases of legislation: He has nothing to do with the proposition, or adoption of amendments to the Constitution," wrote Justice Samuel Chase in 1798.[5]

The Court also has ruled that the two-thirds requirement for adoption of a proposed constitutional amendment applies to two-thirds of those members present and voting and not to two-thirds of the entire membership.[6]

Whether a constitutional amendment has to be ratified within a certain time period is unclear. Congress first added a time limit in 1917 when it required that the prohibition amendment be ratified within seven years of its submission to the states. That requirement was contested in *Dillon v. Gloss* (1921).[7]

The Court rejected the challenge, saying that "the fair inference or implication from Article V is that the ratification must be within some reasonable time after the proposal," and that Congress's power to set a time limit was "an incident of its power to designate the mode of ratification."[8]

Not until 1939 did the Court hear a case asking what consti-

IT'S NEVER TOO LATE: THE RATIFICATION OF THE 27TH AMENDMENT

The Twenty-seventh Amendment was ratified on May 7, 1992, 203 years after it was first proposed, taking the modern Congress and many constitutional experts by surprise. The Madison Amendment, named after its original proponent, prohibits midterm pay raises for members of Congress.

The new constitutional provision states: "No law varying the compensation for the services of the Senators and Representatives shall take effect, until an election of Representatives shall have intervened."

This is the language that James Madison wrote in 1789, when this measure was first sent to the states as part of a package of twelve proposed amendments. Ten of them became the Bill of Rights, but the pay raise amendment was ratified by only six states between 1789 and 1792. It languished until 1873 when Ohio affirmed it. (The other amendment in the original package, relating to apportionment of the House, has never been ratified.)

The Madison Amendment was revived in the late 1970s, and thirty-three states approved it between 1978 and 1992, as a steady pace of congressional pay raises drew increasing public criticism. The final drive for ratification began in August 1991 when thirty-five members of the House of Representatives introduced a resolution calling on state legislatures to reexamine the amendment. The state of Michigan pushed it over the required three-quarters threshold May 7, 1992. The Twenty-seventh Amendment was officially certified by the U.S. archivist on May 18, printed in the *Federal Register* on May 19, and at that time effectively became part of the Constitution.

Most modern amendments proposed are sent to the states with a deadline for ratification. But the Madison amendment and the eleven others sent to the states in 1789 had no deadline. So contemporary supporters of the amendment argued that the extensive gaps between state ratifications did not invalidate the proposal.

The Supreme Court has ruled that it is up to Congress to determine whether the time span between introduction and ratification of a particular amendment is too long. In the 1939 case of *Coleman v. Miller,* the Court concluded that questions of timeliness were political in nature, not within the jurisdiction of the courts.

tuted a reasonable time period for ratification. Such a determination, the Court said in *Coleman v. Miller,* was a political question for Congress, not the Court, to decide.[9]

Moreover, four justices in a concurring opinion called into question the Court's finding in *Dillon v. Gloss* that ratification should occur within a reasonable time. Since Congress has exclusive power over the amending process, they wrote, it "cannot be bound by and is under no duty to accept the pronouncements upon that exclusive power by this Court. . . . Therefore any judicial expression . . . is a mere admonition to the Congress in the nature of an advisory opinion, given wholly without constitutional authority."[10]

Although six amendments have been added to the Constitution since this 1939 decision, the Court has not, as of mid-1996, heard any more cases concerning Article V. The timeliness of the proposed Equal Rights Amendment became a public issue but never was resolved by the high court.

STATE RATIFICATION PROCEDURES

The Court has repeatedly held that ratification of constitutional amendments by a state must be accomplished either through the state legislature or by a state convention and that Congress has the sole authority to determine which method will be used for each amendment submitted to the states.[11] In 1920 the Court ruled that a provision of the Ohio constitution requiring a popular referendum to approve its legislature's ratification of the Eighteenth Amendment was in violation of the federal Constitution.[12] In a second case, the Court held that state-required procedures that barred two state legislatures from ratifying the Nineteenth Amendment were in conflict with the federal Constitution.[13] In both cases the Court held that "the function of a state legislature in ratifying a proposed Amendment to the Federal Constitution, like the function of Congress in proposing the Amendment, is a federal function, derived from the Federal Constitution; and it transcends any limitations sought to be imposed by the people of a state."[14]

The Court has indicated that whether a state may rescind its ratification of a constitutional amendment is a political question for Congress. Tennessee challenged the women's suffrage amendment on the grounds that it was counted as ratifying the Nineteenth Amendment despite the fact that its legislature had subsequently rescinded the ratification. Basing its decision on narrow procedural grounds, the Court in 1922 held that official notice of the ratification to the secretary of state was conclusive upon him, and that his certification of ratification was binding on the courts.[15] Similarly, in *Coleman v. Miller* (1939), when asked whether a state legislature that had first rejected an amendment could reverse itself and ratify it, the Court said this was a question only Congress could answer.[16] *(See box, Extension and Rescission, p. 158.)*

The answers Congress has given to such questions have not been consistent. At the direction of Congress, the secretary of state counted the ratifications of the Fourteenth Amendment by Ohio, New Jersey, and Oregon despite votes by the three state legislatures to withdraw the ratification. But the secretary of state apparently accepted North Dakota's rescission of its ratification of the Twenty-fifth Amendment.[17]

Enforcement Power

Seven constitutional amendments contain language conferring on Congress the power to enforce them by "appropriate legislation." These amendments are the three Civil War amendments (the Thirteenth, Fourteenth, and Fifteenth); the Nineteenth, giving women the vote; the Twenty-third, permitting residents of the District of Columbia to vote for president; the Twenty-fourth, abolishing the poll tax in federal elections; and the Twenty-sixth, setting the minimum voting age at eighteen years. The Eighteenth Amendment, prohibiting the sale of liquor, divided enforcement power between Congress and the states. It was repealed fourteen years after its ratification, partly because enforcement proved so ineffective.

The Civil War amendments have required the most significant exercise of the enforcement power. The Thirteenth Amendment, ratified in 1865, abolished slavery. The Fourteenth Amendment, ratified in 1868, made blacks citizens and prohibited states from denying citizens due process and equal protection of the laws. The Fifteenth Amendment, ratified in 1870, prohibited federal and state governments from denying the right to vote to citizens on the basis of race, color, or previous condition of servitude. By 1875 Congress had passed seven statutes to implement and enforce these three amendments.

But in its first considerations of the enforcement power the Supreme Court ruled that Congress had exceeded its authority when it passed many of these statutes. The Court narrowed the congressional enforcement power in two ways: Congress could carry out the guarantees of these amendments only against official state acts of discrimination, not against the discriminatory actions of private persons; furthermore, the enforcement power was corrective, to be exercised only after the discriminatory state action occurred.

THE *CIVIL RIGHTS CASES*

Striking down the Civil Rights Act of 1875, which sought to prohibit discrimination against blacks in public accommodations, the Court in 1883 wrote that the power to enforce the due process and equal protection guarantees of the Fourteenth Amendment

does not invest Congress with power to legislate upon subjects which are within the domain of State legislation; but to provide modes of relief against State legislation, or State action, of the kind referred to. It does not authorize Congress to create a code of municipal law for the regulation of private rights; but to provide modes of redress against the operation of State laws and the action of State officers, executive or judicial, when these are subversive of the fundamental rights specified in the amendment.[18]

In the same case, the Court also curbed congressional power to enforce the Thirteenth Amendment's abolition of slavery. The Court acknowledged that Congress had the authority "to

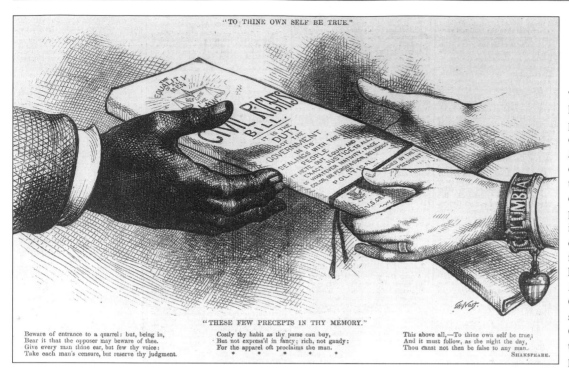

"TO THINE OWN SELF BE TRUE."

"THESE FEW PRECEPTS IN THY MEMORY."

Beware of entrance to a quarrel: but, being in,
Bear it that the opposer may beware of thee.
Give every man thine ear, but few thy voice:
Take each man's censure, but reserve thy judgment.

Costly thy habit as thy purse can buy,
But not express'd in fancy; rich, not gaudy:
For the apparel oft proclaims the man.
*   *   *   *   *

This above all,—To thine own self be true;
And it must follow, as the night the day,
Thou canst not then be false to any man.
SHAKSPEARE.

This engraving depicts Columbia (the United States) passing the Civil Rights Act of 1875 to the hands of black Americans. The act protected blacks from discrimination by state and city governments and prohibited private businesses, such as inns and theaters, from denying blacks access. In five companion cases, collectively known as the *Civil Rights Cases* (1883), the Court struck down provisions of the act, ruling that Congress had no authority to protect blacks against private discrimination.

pass all laws necessary and proper for abolishing all badges and incidents of slavery in the United States." Such laws could guarantee blacks "fundamental rights which are the essence of civil freedom, namely the same right to make and enforce contracts, to sue parties, give evidence and to inherit, purchase, lease, sell and convey property, as is enjoyed by white citizens."[19] But having said this, the Court then held that these fundamental rights did not extend to the right of access to public accommodations. "It would be running the slavery argument into the ground to make it apply to every act of discrimination which a person may see fit to make," the Court wrote.[20]

VOTING RIGHTS

The Court generally recognized that Congress had an inherent power to protect a person's right to vote in federal elections. And once it was established that a person had the right to vote in state elections, the Court generally upheld Congress's power under the Fifteenth Amendment to enforce that right.

In other rulings, however, the Court eased the way for the states to continue to discriminate against blacks. In *United States v. Reese* (1876), the Court ruled that the Fifteenth Amendment did not confer the right to vote on anyone but simply prohibited racial discrimination in voting.[21] As a result, southern states wrote statutes that prevented blacks from voting even though on their face the laws were not discriminatory. Such statutes required voters to pass literacy tests or pay poll taxes. Occasionally, a state or locality would gerrymander voting districts to dilute the strength of the black vote. Some of the more obviously discriminatory of these state statutes were declared unconstitutional only to be replaced by other forms of discrimination. *(See "The Right to Vote," pp. 505–518, in Chapter 10.)*

As a result of this body of rulings, Congress was limited to

enforcing the Civil War amendments against state infringements through remedial legislation alone. One common form of such corrective legislation was to authorize persons denied their rights in state courts to bring their cases into federal court. Another method was to provide federal civil and criminal penalties for state officials who deprived persons of their rights. *(See box, The Right to Remove Cases from State into Federal Court, pp. 268–269, in Chapter 6.)*

MODERN ENFORCEMENT

This situation prevailed until the civil rights movement of the 1950s and 1960s prompted passage of new legislation to enforce the guarantees of the Civil War amendments. In reviewing this legislation, the Supreme Court interpreted the amendments' enforcement clauses expansively, sanctioning congressional authority to prohibit state action before it occurred and, in certain cases, prohibiting racial discrimination by private individuals.

Voting Rights

Two of the cases concerned the constitutionality of the Voting Rights Act of 1965. This statute abolished literacy tests for five years (the abolition was later made permanent) and required certain states and local political units to clear any changes in their election laws with the Justice Department before they took effect. Areas covered by key remedial provisions of the law—primarily in southern states—were those that had invoked literacy tests or other practices that excluded black voters and where a substantial percentage of the voting-age population was not registered to vote. The bill also authorized sending federal examiners into particular areas to supervise voter registration.

In *South Carolina v. Katzenbach* (1966) the Court upheld the law as a proper exercise of Congress's enforcement powers granted by the Fifteenth Amendment. South Carolina challenged the act as infringing on powers traditionally reserved to the states.

"As against the reserved powers of the States, Congress may use any rational means to effectuate the constitutional prohibition of racial discrimination in voting," the Court wrote. While the means used by Congress were "inventive," the Court found them appropriate to prohibit voting discrimination.[22]

The second case challenged a provision of the Voting Rights Act that prevented states from excluding persons who had completed a certain number of years in an accredited foreign language school even if they could not speak or write English. The question arose over a New York requirement that voters be able to speak and write English—a law that disenfranchised most of the state's large Puerto Rican population.

The Court upheld the federal provision as a proper means of enforcing both the equal protection clause of the Fourteenth Amendment and the guarantee of the Fifteenth Amendment.

In both instances, the Court said, the question was not whether the Court agreed with the provision barring such literacy requirements but whether "we perceive a basis upon which Congress might predicate a judgment that the application of New York's English literacy requirement . . . constituted an invidious discrimination in violation of the Equal Protection Clause."[23] That the requirement violated the equal protection clause was plain, the Court said. "Any contrary conclusion would require us to be blind to the realities familiar to the legislators."[24]

In several important cases in the 1990s, the Court assessed the constitutionality not of the Voting Rights Act itself but of the way in which states and the federal government invoked it to increase the political participation of racial minorities.

Private Discrimination

The Court in 1968 broadened its interpretation of the enforcement power conferred by the Thirteenth Amendment. The case of *Jones v. Alfred H. Mayer Co.* concerned an 1866 civil rights law enacted to ensure blacks the same right as whites to make and enforce contracts, sue, inherit, and buy, lease, sell, and occupy real estate. Persons who denied others these rights on the grounds of race or previous condition of servitude were guilty of a misdemeanor. The question was whether this law was violated by the refusal of a private individual to sell a house to a black. Although the Court had never directly ruled on that issue, it had been assumed that the Thirteenth Amendment, like the Fourteenth and Fifteenth, reached only discrimination by state officials.

The Court by a 7–2 vote ruled that the statute did apply to private acts of discrimination. When Congress first enacted the statute granting blacks the right to buy and sell property, "it plainly meant to secure that right against interference from any source whatever, whether governmental or private," the majority wrote.[25]

The issue then was whether the 1866 statute was a proper exercise of the Thirteenth Amendment's enforcement power. The Court held that it was:

Surely, Congress has the power under the Thirteenth Amendment rationally to determine what are the badges and the incidents of slavery, and the authority to translate that determination into effective legislation. Nor can we say that the determination Congress has made is an irrational one.[26]

The Court extended the effect of this enforcement power when it held in 1971 that a section of the 1866 act prohibited private individuals, such as members of the Ku Klux Klan, from conspiring to prevent blacks from exercising their constitutional rights such as freedom of speech and assembly.[27] In a 1976 decision the Court held that racially segregated private schools that refused to admit black students solely on account of their race violated the provision of the 1866 statute, which gave blacks "the same right . . . to make and enforce contracts . . . as is enjoyed by white citizens."[28]

STATE SOVEREIGNTY

Furthermore, in 1976 the Court held that the enforcement power granted by the Fourteenth Amendment acts as a limit on the protection that the Eleventh Amendment provides to the states from undue federal interference in their affairs. By shielding states from federal suits brought by citizens without their consent, that amendment serves as a guarantee of state sovereignty. *(See "Liability to Lawsuits," pp. 367–369, in Chapter 7.)*

In *Fitzpatrick v. Bitzer* the Court held that under the enforcement power of the Fourteenth Amendment, Congress acted properly when it amended the 1964 Civil Rights Act to authorize federal judges to hear civil rights complaints brought by citizens against a state—and, upon a finding of discrimination, to order the state to make retroactive payments of benefits to the victims of discrimination.

The affected state—Connecticut—challenged the power of Congress to authorize such federal court orders, arguing that the Eleventh Amendment protected it from such federal interference in the spending of state funds. The Court rejected the state's argument, declaring:

[W]e think that the Eleventh Amendment, and the principles of state sovereignty which it embodies . . . are necessarily limited by the enforcement provisions . . . of the Fourteenth Amendment. . . . We think that Congress may, in determining what is "appropriate legislation" for the purpose of enforcing the provisions of the Fourteenth Amendment, provide for private suits against States or state officials which are constitutionally impermissible in other contexts.[29]

The Power to Investigate

It is perhaps indicative of the history of congressional investigations that the development of this particular power of Congress began with a disaster.

In 1791 some fifteen hundred soldiers commanded by Maj. Gen. Arthur St. Clair were on a road- and fort-building expedition in the Northwest Territory when they were attacked by Indians. Some six hundred men were killed, and another three hundred were wounded.

The following year, the House of Representatives decided that, rather than ask the president to investigate this tragedy, it would establish its own special committee to inquire into the circumstances surrounding it.

The special committee subpoenaed the War Department's papers concerning the expedition and witnesses, including St. Clair, Secretary of War Henry Knox, and Secretary of the Treasury Alexander Hamilton. The committee's report absolved St. Clair. Blame for the episode was placed on the War Department, particularly the quartermaster and supply contractors, who were accused of mismanagement, neglect, and delay in supplying necessary equipment, clothing, and munitions to the troops. The House took no action on the report, and the Federalists prevented its publication because of its reflections on Knox and Hamilton. So began congressional exercise of the right to investigate, one of Congress's most controversial powers.[1]

The power to investigate is an implied power based on the constitutional assignment in Article I, Section 1, of "all legislative powers herein granted." The authority for legislative bodies to conduct inquiries was established as early as the sixteenth century by the British House of Commons. The Commons first used this power in determining its membership. It then made increasing use of investigations to assist it in performing law-making functions and in overseeing officials responsible for executing the laws and spending funds made available by Parliament.

Investigating committees of the House of Commons had authority to summon witnesses and examine documents, and the Commons could support its committees by punishing uncooperative witnesses for contempt. American colonial legislatures, the Continental Congress, and state legislatures relied on these parliamentary precedents in carrying out their own investigations. The power to investigate, to compel the attendance of witnesses, and to demand the production of documents was regarded by most members of the early Congresses as an intrinsic part of the power to legislate.

Writing as a graduate student in 1884, Woodrow Wilson asserted that "the informing function of Congress should be preferred even to its legislative function."[2] Serving as the eyes and ears of the two chambers of Congress, investigations have gathered information on the need for legislation, tested the effectiveness of already-enacted legislation, inquired into the qualifications and performance of members and executive branch officials, and laid the groundwork for impeachment proceedings.

The practices of some investigatory committees, however—particularly those looking into what were termed un-American activities—have been challenged in the courts. While generally giving Congress wide latitude in the exercise of its investigatory power, the Supreme Court has drawn some limits, primarily to protect the rights of witnesses and to maintain the separation of the legislative and judicial powers.

The investigating power and its limits were described in 1957 by Chief Justice Earl Warren:

> The power of Congress to conduct investigations is inherent in the legislative process. That power is broad. It encompasses inquiries concerning the administration of existing laws as well as proposed or possibly needed statutes. It includes surveys of defects in our social, economic or political system for the purpose of enabling the Congress to remedy them. It comprehends probes into departments of the Federal Government to expose corruption, inefficiency or waste. But broad as is this power of inquiry, it is not unlimited. There is no general authority to expose the private affairs of individuals without justification in terms of the functions of Congress. . . . Nor is the Congress a law enforcement or trial agency. These are functions of the executive and judicial departments of government. No inquiry is an end in itself; it must be related to and in furtherance of a legitimate task of the Congress.[3]

The Contempt Power

Like the investigative power it reinforces, the congressional power to punish for contempt has its source in parliamentary precedents dating from Elizabethan times. No express power to punish for contempt of Congress, except in the case of a member, was granted Congress in the Constitution. But Congress assumed that it had inherent power to jail nonmembers for contempt without a court order because such power was necessary to enforce its investigatory powers and to protect the integrity of its proceedings.

The House issued its first contempt citation in 1795 against two men who had tried to bribe several members of Congress to support a grant of land to them. It was not until 1821, however, that the Supreme Court was asked whether Congress has the power to punish nonmembers for actions it considers contempt. In *Anderson v. Dunn* the Court upheld the constitutionality of the summary use of the contempt power of Congress. A denial of power to punish for contempt, the Court said, "leads to the total annihilation of the power of the House of Representatives to guard itself from contempts, and leaves it exposed to every indignity and interruption that rudeness, caprice, or even conspiracy, may meditate against it."[4]

The Court limited the contempt power, however, "to the least power adequate to the end proposed," and said that imprisonment for contempt of Congress could not extend beyond the adjournment of Congress.[5]

Considering imprisonment only to the end of a legislative session inadequate, Congress in 1857 passed a law, still in effect in amended form, making it a criminal offense to refuse information demanded by either chamber of Congress. (*See box, Contempt of Congress, this page.*)

Even after passage of the 1857 law, Congress preferred to remain the agent of punishment for persons in contempt, reasoning that a few days of confinement might induce a witness to cooperate, while turning him over to a court might put him out of the reach of the investigating committee. However, as the press of legislative business mounted and as court review of summary congressional punishment grew more frequent, Congress increasingly relied on criminal prosecution for contempt under the 1857 statute. The last time either house of Congress itself punished someone for contempt was in 1932. Since then, all contempt citations have been prosecuted under the criminal statute.[6]

The Supreme Court first asserted the right of federal courts to review congressional contempt citations in *Kilbourn v. Thompson* (1881).[7] The case originated with the refusal of a witness, Hallet Kilbourn, to produce papers demanded by a House committee investigating the failure of the banking firm of Jay Cooke. The House ordered Kilbourn jailed for contempt. Released on a writ of habeas corpus, Kilbourn sued the Speaker, members of the investigating committee, and the sergeant-at-arms, John Thompson, for false arrest. In defense they contended that congressional exercise of the contempt power must be presumed legitimate and that the courts had no authority to review the exercise.

Sustaining Kilbourn's claim, the Court held that the chambers of Congress do not have a general power to punish for contempt:

If they are proceeding in a matter beyond their legitimate cognizance, we are of the opinion that this can be shown, and we cannot give our assent to the principle that, by the mere act of asserting a person to be guilty of contempt, they thereby establish their right to fine and imprison him, beyond the power of any court or any other tribunal whatever to inquire into the grounds on which the order was made.[8]

In 1897 the Court upheld the validity of the 1857 statute making contempt of Congress a criminal offense. The act was challenged as an illegal delegation of power from Congress to the courts. The Court wrote:

We grant the Congress could not divest itself, or either of its Houses, of the essential and inherent power to punish for contempt, in cases to which the power of either House properly extended; but because Congress, by the Act of 1857, sought to aid each of the Houses in the discharge of its constitutional functions, it does not follow that any delegation of the power in each to punish for contempt was involved.[9]

The Court reiterated this position in 1935 when it ruled that the 1857 statute did not replace but supplemented Congress's authority to bring its own contempt citations. The case concerned a witness who had destroyed papers after a congressional investigating committee had issued a subpoena for them.[10]

The Court in 1917 held that Congress may not use its con-

CONTEMPT OF CONGRESS

Congress in 1857 enacted a statute that allowed it to turn over congressional contempt cases to the federal courts for indictment and trial.

Under this statute, as it has been amended and interpreted, the courts are obligated to provide the defendant all the protections guaranteed defendants in other criminal actions.

The language of the statute, now known as Section 192, says:

Every person who having been summoned as a witness by the authority of either House of Congress to give testimony or to produce papers upon any matter under inquiry before either House, or any joint committee established by a joint or concurrent resolution of the two Houses of Congress, or any committee of either House of Congress, willfully makes default, or who having appeared, refuses to answer any question pertinent to the question under inquiry, shall be deemed guilty of a misdemeanor, punishable by a fine of not more than $1,000 nor less than $100 and imprisonment in a common jail for not less than one month nor more than twelve months. (2 United States Code, Section 192).

tempt power as punishment for punishment's sake. *Marshall v. Gordon* arose out of a New York State grand jury investigation and indictment of a member of the House for violations of the Sherman Act.[11]

Upon his indictment, the member asked a House Judiciary subcommittee to investigate Marshall, the district attorney responsible for the member's prosecution. The subcommittee went to New York to make inquiries, whereupon Marshall wrote a letter accusing the subcommittee of interfering with the grand jury proceedings. In the letter, which was made public, Marshall used highly abusive language, and the House cited him for contempt.

Ruling that the contempt power could be used only where there was actual interference with or resistance to the legislative process, the Court wrote:

[W]e think from the very nature of that power it is clear that it does not embrace punishment for contempt as punishment, since it rests only upon the right of self-preservation, that is, the right to prevent acts which in and of themselves inherently obstruct or prevent the discharge of legislative duty or the refusal to do that which there is an inherent legislative power to compel in order that legislative functions may be performed.[12]

Judicial Review

With its assertion in *Kilbourn* of authority to review the validity of congressional contempt citations, the Court also assumed the power to review the legitimacy of congressional investigations. The Court held that the House could not punish Kilbourn for contempt because the investigation in which Kilbourn was required as a witness was beyond the authority of the House to conduct.

The House investigation of a bankruptcy case that was still pending in the courts was a judicial exercise that infringed on

Scandals plagued the Harding administration, including the revelation that Attorney General Harry M. Daugherty *(above)* had failed to prosecute those implicated in the Teapot Dome oil lease fraud. The congressional committee charged with the investigation subpoenaed Daugherty's brother, Mally. He refused to appear, and challenged the Senate's power to compel him to testify. The Court in *McGrain v. Daugherty* (1927) broadly interpreted Congress's power to secure needed information by compelling private citizens to testify, even without an explicitly stated legislative purpose.

the separation of powers, said the Court in *Kilbourn*. Not only could Congress not validly legislate in this area, but in its resolution establishing the investigating committee Congress had shown no interest in developing legislation as a result of the investigation.

The Court said that it was sure

no person can be punished for contumacy as a witness before either House, unless his testimony is required in a matter into which the House has jurisdiction to inquire, and we feel equally sure that neither of these bodies possess the general power of making inquiry into the private affairs of the citizen.[13]

Having asserted the right to review congressional inquiries, the Court then ruled that congressional power to investigate had at least three limits. Investigations had to be confined to subject areas over which Congress had jurisdiction, their purpose had to be enactment of legislation, and they could not merely inquire into the private affairs of citizens.

In the next Supreme Court test of the investigation power, the Court relaxed two of the limits it had established in *Kilbourn*. *In re Chapman* (1897) involved New York stockbroker Elverton R. Chapman, convicted of contempt after he refused to answer an investigating committee's questions about senators' trading in sugar stocks during action on a sugar tariff measure.[14]

The Court held that in this instance the Senate had a legitimate interest in knowing whether any of its members had been involved in sugar speculations. As a result it could compel testimony from Chapman on matters he considered private:

The [committee's] questions were not intrusions into the affairs of the citizen; they did not seek to ascertain any facts as to the conduct, methods, extent or details of the business of the firm in question, but only whether that firm, confessedly engaged in buying and selling stocks, and the particular stock named, was employed by any Senator or buy or sell for him any of that stock, whose market price might be affected by the Senate's action.[15]

Because the investigation was legitimate, the Court said that "it was certainly not necessary that the resolution should declare in advance what the Senate meditated doing when the investigation was concluded."[16] With this decision the Court removed its requirement that Congress must state the legislative purposes of its investigative committees, and it narrowed the category of situations in which witnesses might refuse to answer questions put to them by such committees.

In 1927 the Court issued a landmark decision, *McGrain v. Daugherty,* in which it affirmed the *Chapman* decision and firmly established the power of Congress to conduct legislative and oversight investigations.[17] The case arose during a Senate investigation of Harry M. Daugherty's activities as attorney general under President Warren G. Harding from 1921 to 1924, and particularly his failure to prosecute the primary instigators of the Teapot Dome oil lease scandal. The Senate subpoenaed the former attorney general's brother, Mally S. Daugherty, but he refused to appear. The Senate then had its sergeant-at-arms, John McGrain, take Daugherty into custody, but Daugherty won release on a writ of habeas corpus and challenged the Senate's power to compel him to testify.

Upholding the Senate inquiry, the Court ruled that the Senate and the House had the power to compel private persons to appear before investigating committees and answer pertinent questions in aid of the legislative function. The "power of inquiry—with process to enforce it—is an essential and appropriate auxiliary to the legislative function," the Court said.[18] It continued:

A legislative body cannot legislate wisely or effectively in the absence of information respecting the conditions which the legislation is intended to affect or change, and where the legislative body does not itself possess the requisite information . . . recourse must be had to others who possess it. Experience has taught that mere requests for such information are often unavailing, and also that information which is volunteered is not always accurate or complete, or some means of compulsion are essential to obtain what is needed.[19]

The Court denied Daugherty's contention that the inquiry was actually a trial of his actions, holding instead that it was an inquiry into the "administration of the Department of Justice—whether its functions were being properly discharged or were being neglected and misdirected," an area in which Congress was competent to legislate. "The only legitimate object the Senate could have in ordering the investigation was to aid it in legislating," the Court concluded, "and we think the subject-matter was such that this was the real object. An express avowal of the object would have been better; but . . . was not indispensable."[20]

Witness Rights

At the same time it gave Congress a broad field in which to conduct investigations, the Court limited the investigatory power by reaffirming that witnesses in such investigations did have rights. Neither the House nor the Senate has authority to compel disclosures about private affairs, said the Court in *Daugherty*. "[A] witness rightfully may refuse to answer where the bounds of inquiry are exceeded or the questions are not pertinent to the matter under scrutiny."[21]

PERTINENCY

In the next case involving a congressional investigation, the Court confirmed both the broad power and the witness rights set out in *Daugherty*. It upheld a Senate inquiry even though the matter under investigation was also pending in the courts.

Sinclair v. United States (1929) also grew out of the Teapot Dome scandal. Observing that Congress had authority over the naval petroleum reserves, the Court said it was legitimate for the Senate to conduct an inquiry into whether legislation to recover the leased oil lands was necessary or desirable, despite the fact that a suit for recovery of the lands had already begun. While Congress may not compel testimony to aid the prosecution of court suits, the Court said, its authority "to require pertinent disclosures in aid of its own constitutional power is not abridged because the information sought to be elicited may also be of use in such suits."[22]

The Court also used the *Sinclair* case to spell out further what the rights of witnesses appearing before investigating committees were. It reaffirmed the right of a witness to refuse to testify where the question was not pertinent to the matter at hand. If a witness who refused to answer a question was brought to trial under the 1857 contempt statute, the Court said, it was "incumbent upon the United States to plead and show that the question pertained to some matter under investigation."[23] Finally, the Court ruled that the pertinency of an inquiry is a question for determination by the courts as a matter of law.

But, the Court added, a witness who refused to answer questions could be punished for contempt, as in this case, if he were mistaken as to the law on which he based his refusal. It was no defense that the witness acted in good faith on the advice of counsel, the Court held.

PERTINENCY VERSUS BALANCE

The post–World War II quest to uncover subversion in the United States produced a new style of congressional investigation and a host of lawsuits challenging it. Ostensibly seeking to discover the extent of communist infiltration into the government, the labor movement, and various other areas of American life, these investigations were used primarily to expose publicly persons suspected of belonging to or being affiliated with the Communist Party.

This purpose was openly acknowledged by Rep. Martin Dies Jr., D-Texas (1931–1945, 1953–1959), chairman of the House Special Committee to Investigate Un-American Activities: "I am not in a position to say whether we can legislate effectively in reference to this matter, but I do know that exposure in a democracy of subversive activities is the most effective weapon that we have in our possession."[24]

As Chief Justice Earl Warren put it in 1957:

This new phase of investigative inquiry involved a broad-scale intrusion into the lives and affairs of private citizens. It brought before the courts novel questions of the appropriate limits of congressional inquiry. . . . In the more recent cases, the emphasis shifted to problems of accommodating the interest of the Government with the rights and privileges of individuals.[25]

The first case the Supreme Court heard in the postwar era that tested the right of a congressional committee to investigate against the right of a witness did not involve a member of the Communist Party; rather, it involved a publisher of politically conservative books. Edward A. Rumely refused to tell the House Select Committee on Lobbying Activities the names of individuals making bulk purchases of the books he published, which were distributed by the Committee for Constitutional Government, an archconservative organization. Rumely was convicted of contempt of Congress, but a court of appeals reversed the conviction. The Supreme Court upheld the appeals court ruling in *United States v. Rumely* (1953).[26]

A majority of the Court avoided the constitutional issue of whether the committee's questions violated Rumely's First Amendment rights by narrowly construing the authority granted by the resolution establishing the committee. The majority held that the mandate to investigate "lobbying activities" was limited to "representations made directly to the Congress, its members or its committees," and excluded attempts to influence Congress directly through public disseminations of literature.[27] Therefore, its interrogation of Rumely had been outside the committee's power. To interpret the resolution to cover indirect lobbying "raises doubts of constitutionality in view of the prohibition of the First Amendment," wrote Justice Felix Frankfurter for the majority.[28] It was this same narrow interpretation of the meaning of lobbying activities that allowed the Court in 1954 to uphold the federal lobby registration act. (*See "Lobby Regulation," pp. 181–182.*)

Justices William O. Douglas and Hugo L. Black did not shy away from the First Amendment issues of the case. Claiming that the authorizing resolution in fact did intend the investigating committee to look into indirect lobbying activities, Douglas and Black said the demand for Rumely's book distribution list was a violation of the First Amendment guarantees of free speech and press. "If the present inquiry was sanctioned, the press would be subjected to harassment that in practical effect might be as serious as censorship," wrote Douglas.[29]

WATKINS V. UNITED STATES

The most severe limitations placed by the Supreme Court on the power of congressional investigating committees to inquire into the affairs of private citizens came in the 1957 decision in *Watkins v. United States.*[30]

Watkins was a regional officer of the Farm Equipment Workers Union. Appearing before the House Un-American Activities Committee in 1954, Watkins answered fully the questions pertaining to his association with the Communist Party. He also answered questions about individuals he knew to be present members of the party.

But Watkins refused to answer questions about people who, to the best of his knowledge, had disassociated themselves from the party. "I do not believe that such questions are relevant to the work of this committee nor do I believe that this committee has the right to undertake the public exposure of persons because of their past activities. I may be wrong and the committee may have this power, but until and unless a court of law so holds and directs me to answer, I most firmly refuse to discuss the political activities of my past associates," Watkins said.[31] Convicted of contempt of Congress under the amended 1857 statute, Watkins appealed.

Speaking for the majority, Chief Justice Warren held Watkins not guilty of contempt of Congress. The situation, Warren said, demanded that the Court balance the congressional need for particular information with the individual's interest in privacy. The critical element in this courtly juggling act, he said, "Is the existence of, and the weight to be ascribed to, the interest of the Congress in demanding disclosures from an unwilling witness."[32]

The majority, Warren said, had "no doubt that there is no congressional power to expose for the sake of exposure."[33] The only legitimate interest Congress could have in an investigation such as Watkins was subjected to was the furtherance of a legislative purpose. And that required that the instructions authorizing the investigation fully spell out the investigating committee's purpose and jurisdiction.

Claiming that it "would be difficult to imagine a less explicit authorizing resolution" than the one establishing the Un-American Activities Committee, Warren said that such an "excessively broad" authorizing resolution

places the courts in an untenable position if they are to strike a balance between the public need for a particular interrogation and the right of citizens to carry on their affairs free from unnecessary governmental interference. It is impossible in such a situation to ascertain whether any legislative purpose justified the disclosures sought and, if so, the importance of that information to the Congress in furtherance of its legislative function. The reason no court can make this critical judgment is that the House of Representatives itself has never made it.[34]

The majority also reaffirmed the holding in *Sinclair* that the questions asked must be pertinent to the matter under inquiry. A witness deciding whether to answer a question, Warren wrote, "is entitled to have knowledge of the subject to which the interrogation is deemed pertinent."[35] Such subject matter was not revealed by the authorizing resolution or by the resolution establishing the subcommittee. Although the matter under inquiry was communist infiltration of labor unions, that was not apparent to a majority of the Court, and, if it was not apparent after trial and appeal, he said, it was doubtful the subject matter was apparent at the time of the interrogation.

Warren then stated a rule for ascertaining pertinency of questions in the matter under inquiry:

Unless the subject matter has been made to appear with indisputable clarity, it is the duty of the investigative body, upon objection of the witness on grounds of pertinency, to state for the record the subject under inquiry at that time and the manner in which the propounded questions are pertinent thereto. To be meaningful, the explanation must describe what the topic under inquiry is and connective reasoning whereby the precise questions relate to it.[36]

As the committee had not made its topic clear, Warren said, Watkins could not be held in contempt.

Once again the Court had said that the congressional power to investigate was broad but not unlimited. One of the limits was that the investigation had to serve a legislative purpose; its purpose could not be solely to expose publicly people who held unpopular political beliefs or associations. The legislative purpose had to be spelled out in sufficient detail that a witness might know what the purpose was, and the investigating body was required to explain to the witness, if he asked, the relevance of its questions to that purpose.

Most of these limitations already had been set out in previous decisions. The importance of the *Watkins* case was that the Court reaffirmed these individual rights in an era fraught with fear that the exercise of those rights could doom the existence of the nation itself.

BARENBLATT V. UNITED STATES

The Court cited this need for self-preservation two years later when it retreated somewhat from its defense of the rights of witnesses. By a 5–4 vote, the Court ruled that First Amendment rights may be limited where the public interest outweighs the private interest.[37]

Justices John Marshall Harlan and Felix Frankfurter deserted the majority in the *Watkins* case to join the only dissenter in that case, Justice Tom C. Clark. The other two justices making up the majority in *Barenblatt v. United States* (1959) were Charles E. Whittaker, who did not participate in *Watkins,* and Potter Stewart, who had replaced Harold H. Burton on the Court. Burton had not participated in *Watkins.*

Barenblatt refused to answer questions put by a House Un-American Activities subcommittee that was investigating communist infiltration into higher education. Barenblatt's challenge to his subsequent contempt conviction rested largely on the *Watkins* precedent. He claimed that the committee's authorizing resolution was too vague to determine whether the particular inquiry aimed at him was directed toward a legitimate legislative purpose. He also claimed that he was not adequately apprised of the relevance of the questions asked to the subject matter of the inquiry and that the questions he refused to answer were an encroachment on his First Amendment rights.

Upholding Barenblatt's contempt conviction, the majority denied all three claims. First, Harlan wrote, Watkins's conviction had been reversed only because he had not been informed fully of the pertinency to the subject under investigation of the questions he was asked. The vagueness of the mandate establishing the committee was only one facet the Court examined in its search for the subject matter of the investigation and was not determinative.

In the case at hand, the majority did not agree with Barenblatt's contention that the vagueness of the mandate deprived the subcommittee of its authority to compel his testimony:

Granting the vagueness of the committee's charter, we may not read it in isolation from its long history in the House of Representatives. Just as legislation is often given meaning by the gloss of legislative reporters, administrative interpretations, and long usage, so the proper meaning of an authorization to a congressional committee is not to be derived alone from its abstract terms unrelated to the definite content furnished them by the course of congressional actions.[38]

As to the pertinence of the questions asked to the subject of the investigation, the Court said the record showed that Barenblatt was well aware of their relevance. Thus, Harlan continued, the only constitutional issue at stake was "whether the Subcommittee's inquiry into petitioner's past or present membership in the Communist Party transgressed the provisions of the First Amendment, which of course reach and limit congressional investigations."[39]

As the Court recognized in *Watkins,* an answer to that question, Harlan said, "involves a balancing by the courts of the competing private and public interests at stake in the particular circumstances shown."[40]

The Supreme Court upheld the conviction of Lloyd Barenblatt *(left)* for contempt of Congress. Barenblatt had refused to testify about his beliefs and his membership in a university club. Shown at a rally November 5, 1959, with Willard Uphaus, another defendant, Barenblatt thanked the ACLU and other organizations that helped him fight his case.

On the public side, Harlan observed that Congress had the power to legislate in the field of communist activity in the United States:

In the last analysis, this power rests on the right of self-preservation. . . . To suggest that because the Communist Party may also sponsor peaceable political reforms the constitutional issues before us should now be judged as if that Party were just an ordinary political party from the standpoint of national security is to ask this Court to blind itself to policy since the close of World War II.[41]

In other words, Barenblatt's right to conduct theoretical classroom discussions on the nature of communism did not outweigh the committee's right to investigate those who might have advocated the overthrow of the government. "We conclude," Harlan said, "that the balance between the individual and the governmental interests here at stake must be struck in favor of the latter, and that therefore the provisions of the First Amendment have not been offended."[42]

Justice Black, speaking for himself, Chief Justice Warren, and Justice Douglas, charged that the majority had rewritten the First Amendment to read:

"Congress shall pass no law abridging freedom of speech, press, assembly and petition, unless Congress and the Supreme Court reach the joint conclusion that on balance the interests of the Government in stifling these freedoms is greater than the interest of the people in having them exercised."[43]

The majority's balancing test, Black continued,

leaves out the real interest in Barenblatt's silence, the interest of the people in being able to join organizations, advocate causes, and make political "mistakes" without later being subject to governmental penalties for having dared to think for themselves. . . . It is these interests of society, rather than Barenblatt's own right to silence, which I think the Court should put on the balance against the demands of the Government.[44]

In a separate dissent, Justice William J. Brennan Jr. said that no purpose for the investigation of Barenblatt is revealed by the record except exposure purely for the sake of exposure. This is not a purpose to which Barenblatt's rights under the First Amendment can validly be subordinated. An investigation in which the process of law-making and law-evaluating are submerged entirely in exposure of individual behavior—in adjudication, of a sort, through the exposure process—is outside the constitutional pale of congressional inquiry.[45]

SUCCEEDING CASES

In subsequent cases, the Court has continued to employ this balancing approach with mixed results, coming down some times for the witness and other times for Congress.

In *Wilkinson v. United States* and *Braden v. United States,* decided the same day in 1961, the Court again found national interests to outweigh individual rights. These cases involved two men who had followed an Un-American Activities subcommittee to Atlanta where the panel conducted an inquiry into the extent of communist propaganda in the South.[46] Both men actively and publicly protested the subcommittee proceedings and were subsequently subpoenaed to appear before it. Wilkinson and Braden refused to answer questions about their Communist Party affiliations and consequently were convicted of contempt. The two men complained that the subcommittee had intended to harass them rather than to elicit any information pertinent to its investigation. The Court upheld their convictions, saying the investigation was properly authorized and that the questions were pertinent to the subject matter on which legislation could be based.

Four months later, the balance tipped the other way. In *Deutsch v. United States* (1961), the Court overturned the contempt conviction of a man who, like Watkins, refused to answer questions on the possible un-American activities of some of his acquaintances.[47] The Court held that the government had not proved the pertinency of these questions to the inquiry at hand. Not only must the witness be aware of the relevance of the question at the time he refuses to answer, but also the relevance must be proved at the contempt trial, the majority said.

In 1962 the Court reversed another contempt conviction, because the indictment for contempt failed to state the subject under investigation at the time of the interrogation. To omit this statement from the indictment violated the Fifth Amendment guarantee of due process and the Sixth Amendment right to be informed of the cause and nature of the accusation, the Court said in *Russell v. United States.*[48]

In 1963 the Court overturned a contempt conviction on the grounds that the committee involved had violated its own rules when it refused a witness's request for a closed hearing.[49]

In 1966 a unanimous Court held that a person could not be convicted of contempt in a criminal proceeding if the investigation at which he refused to answer questions was not authorized by the full committee, as required by its own rules, and if the full committee had not made a "lawful delegation" to the subcommittee authorizing the inquiry. Justice Abe Fortas wrote that the "jurisdiction of the courts cannot be invoked to impose criminal sanctions in aid of a roving commission."[50]

Of this series of reversals, constitutional scholar C. Herman Pritchett has written:

These reversals were accomplished for the most part without challenging the scope of investigatory power or querying the motives of the investigators. They were achieved primarily by strict judicial enforcement of the rules on pertinency, authorization, and procedure, plus strict observance of the constitutional standards governing criminal prosecutions.[51]

The Fifth Amendment

Some witnesses in the early cold war years invoked the Fifth Amendment guarantee against self-incrimination when they refused to answer investigating committee questions. This portion of the Fifth Amendment states that no person "shall be compelled in any criminal case to be a witness against himself." The Court previously had interpreted this guarantee to mean that a person could not be required to divulge information that might make him liable to a criminal proceeding. *(See "Self-Incrimination," pp. 589–598, in Chapter 11.)*

The Supreme Court did not consider any contempt of Congress cases against witnesses who invoked the self-incrimination clause until 1955. Prior to that it had handed down two important rulings dealing with grand jury investigations. In the first case, *Blau v. United States* (1950), the Court acknowledged that admission of communist activity might be incriminating.[52]

In the second case, *Rogers v. United States* (1951), the Court ruled that a witness could not invoke the Fifth Amendment privilege after already having answered questions about materially incriminating facts. That case arose after Jane Rogers told a grand jury that she had been treasurer of the Communist Party in Denver. After making this admission she sought to end her testimony and refused to give the name of the person to whom she had turned over the party's books. A divided Supreme Court ruled that she had waived the right to silence by her initial testimony and that the further questions she had refused to answer did not involve a "reasonable danger of further incrimination."[53]

The validity of the Fifth Amendment as a defense against a contempt of Congress citation was considered by the Court in two cases decided the same day in 1955. The circumstances in *Quinn v. United States* and *Emspak v. United States* were similar. Both men had refused to answer certain questions from congressional committees pertaining to their affiliation with the Communist Party. Quinn did not expressly invoke the self-incrimination clause, and Emspak's primary defense was that the questions infringed on his First Amendment rights. The Court held that the intent of each man to plead the Fifth Amendment was clear.

There is not a "ritualistic formula" involved in invoking the protection, Chief Justice Warren said in Quinn's case. "If an ob-

THE COMPLICATIONS OF CONGRESSIONAL IMMUNITY

Congress has rarely exercised its power to grant immunity from prosecution to obtain testimony from individuals who would otherwise claim their Fifth Amendment right to remain silent. And the complications that arose from the grant of immunity to former White House aide Oliver L. North in the sensational Iran-contra affair demonstrated how congressional immunity can cripple subsequent prosecutions.

During the 1973 Senate hearings on the Watergate scandal, more than two dozen witnesses were granted immunity. Special Prosecutor Archibald Cox had tried in vain to derail those grants, but in the end they did not impede his prosecutions. Most of the major figures pleaded guilty or were convicted in criminal trials.

Not so after the 1987 Iran-contra hearings.

The Iran-contra operation was a complex triangular affair in 1985 and 1986 involving the sale of weapons by the United States to Iran, in part to obtain the release of U.S. hostages. Some of the profits from that arms sale were then diverted and used, in contravention of a clear congressional ban, to aid the contra rebels in Nicaragua. This elaborate scheme was secretly orchestrated by the Reagan White House. North, a former Marine officer and National Security Council aide, helped mastermind the operation and therefore became a central focus of the joint House-Senate congressional hearings. He and some twenty other witnesses received grants of immunity to testify at the hearings. Committee members insisted at the time that the witnesses would not necessarily escape prosecution.

The 1970 law governing such grants of immunity forbids the use of any compelled testimony against an immunized witness. But a witness can be prosecuted for crimes mentioned in his testimony if the evidence used to prosecute him was developed independently of his congressional testimony. This type of "use" immunity was challenged and upheld in the 1972 Supreme Court case of *Kastigar v.* *United States.*[1] The Court said the government must show in any subsequent prosecution that it obtained its evidence from sources independent of testimony given under grant of immunity.

The criminal probe of the Iran-contra affair was led by Special Independent Counsel Lawrence E. Walsh. In May 1989, through Walsh's investigation and prosecution, North was convicted of three felony counts: altering and destroying National Security Council documents, aiding and abetting the obstruction of a November 1986 congressional inquiry into the Iran-contra affair, and illegally accepting a home security system as a gift.

On appeal, a three-judge panel of the U.S. Court of Appeals for the District of Columbia Circuit set aside the convictions, largely because the court found trial witnesses had been tainted by their exposure to the immunized congressional testimony.[2] "A central problem in this case is that many grand jury and trial witnesses were thoroughly soaked in North's immunized testimony, but no effort was made to determine what effect, if any, this extensive exposure had on their testimony," the appeals panel said.[3]

The appeals court said the trial judge should not have focused on what Walsh and other prosecutors might have learned from North's congressional testimony, but on what all witnesses might have picked up from the televised hearings or how their memories might have been refreshed by hearing North. The full appeals court rejected Walsh's petition to rehear the case as did the Supreme Court.[4] Former national security adviser John M. Poindexter, who was found guilty of lying to Congress about the Iran-contra affair, also won a reversal of his conviction based on similar grounds.

1. *Kastigar v. United States,* 406 U.S. 441 (1972).
2. *United States v. North,* 910 F. 2d 843 (1990).
3. Id. at 863.
4. *United States v. North,* 920 F. 2d 940 (1990), *United States v. North,* 500 U.S. 941 (1991)

---

jection to a question is made in any language that a committee may reasonably be expected to understand as an attempt to invoke the privilege, it must be respected," he added.[54]

In the *Emspak* case, Warren said:

[I]f it is true in these times a stigma may somehow result from a witness' reliance on the Self-Incrimination Clause, a committee should be all the more ready to recognize a veiled claim of the privilege. Otherwise, the great right which the Clause was intended to secure might be effectively frustrated by private pressures.[55]

To counter the frequent use of the Fifth Amendment by witnesses before congressional committees, Congress in 1954 amended an immunity statute that had been on the books since 1857. The Immunity Act of 1954 permitted either chamber of Congress by majority vote, or a congressional committee by a two-thirds vote, to grant immunity to witnesses in national security investigations, provided an order was first obtained from a U.S. district court judge and also provided the attorney general was notified in advance and given an opportunity to offer ob-

jections. The bill also permitted the U.S. district courts to grant immunity to witnesses before the court or grand juries. Witnesses thus immunized were faced with the choice of testifying or going to jail. The Fifth Amendment claim could not be raised.

The Supreme Court upheld the immunity act in *Ullmann v. United States* (1956). Affirming the conviction of William L. Ullmann, who had refused to testify before a grand jury despite a grant of immunity, the Court held that the Fifth Amendment self-incrimination clause protected witnesses only against testimony that might lead to conviction on criminal charges. This possibility was ruled out by the grant of immunity. "Once the reason for the privilege ceases, the privilege ceases," Justice Felix Frankfurter wrote for the majority.[56]

Observing that there was no indication that this immunity would protect a person forced to admit he was a communist from the loss of his job or other consequences, Justice Douglas entered a sharp dissent for himself and Justice Black. "My view

POWER OF SUBPOENA

The Supreme Court has never questioned the power of the House and Senate and their authorized committees to issue subpoenas to ensure the attendance of witnesses or the production of papers and other documents for examination at congressional investigations.

"Issuance of subpoenas . . . has long been held to be a legitimate use by Congress of its power to investigate," the Court wrote in *McGrain v. Daugherty* (1927). "Experience has taught that mere requests for . . . information often are unavailing."[1]

In 1975 use of the congressional subpoena power was challenged on First Amendment grounds. The 1975 case arose when the Senate Judiciary Subcommittee on Internal Security issued a subpoena for the bank records of the United States Servicemen's Fund (USSF), a group that protested American involvement in the Vietnam War.[2] The records included lists of contributors to the organization. The USSF claimed the subpoena was intended to impede the exercise of First Amendment rights because contributors, fearing that their association with the organization might be made public, would withdraw their support.

The Supreme Court rejected the claim, holding that on its face the subpoena was issued to further a legitimate legislative inquiry. Because members of Congress are constitutionally protected from being questioned for legislative actions, the Court said it could not inquire into the motivations for issuing the subpoena. Concurring, Justices Thurgood Marshall, William J. Brennan Jr., and Potter Stewart said they did not read the majority opinion to mean "that the constitutionality of a congressional subpoena is always shielded from more searching judicial inquiry."[3]

1. *McGrain v. Daugherty,* 273 U.S. 135 at 175 (1927).
2. *Eastland v. United States Servicemen's Fund,* 421 U.S. 491 (1975).
3. Id. at 515.

is that the framers put it beyond the power of Congress to compel anyone to confess his crimes," Douglas wrote.[57]

Investigating Elections

Congress has investigative powers inherent in the constitutional right of each chamber to judge the elections, returns, and qualifications of its members. That point was settled in two cases involving the 1926 senatorial election in Pennsylvania in which Republican William S. Vare was declared the winner over Democrat William B. Wilson.

The first case, *Reed v. County Commissioners of Delaware County, Pa.* (1928), arose when the Senate established an investigating committee to look into reports of corruption in the election. Chairman James A. Reed, D-Mo., and his committee filed suit to compel local officials to produce the ballot boxes for inspection. Their right to do so was challenged. The Court upheld the right of each chamber "to secure information upon which to decide concerning elections," but held that the committee did not have the right to subpoena the ballot boxes because the resolution establishing the committee did not contain the proper authorization.[58]

The second case, *Barry v. United States ex rel. Cunningham* (1929), arose because Thomas W. Cunningham refused to answer certain questions concerning Vare's campaign contributions. The Senate ordered Cunningham taken into custody. He petitioned for a writ of habeas corpus, charging that the Senate had exceeded its power when it arrested him. The Court, writing through Justice George Sutherland, disagreed:

Exercise of power [to judge elections, returns and qualifications] necessarily involves the ascertainment of facts, the attendance of witnesses, the examination of such witnesses, with the power to compel them to answer pertinent questions, to determine the facts and apply the appropriate rules of law, and, finally, to render a judgment which is beyond the authority of any other tribunal to review.[59]

The Power over Internal Affairs

The first seven sections of Article I of the Constitution set out the duties of the House and the Senate and the powers each chamber has over its internal affairs. Among these are the authority of each house to judge the qualifications and elections of its members, to punish its members, to set the time, place, and manner of holding congressional elections, to establish its own rules for conducting official business, and to impeach, try, and convict or acquit federal civilian and judicial officers. Observing the doctrine of separation of powers, the Supreme Court has found little necessity to intervene in these internal prerogatives of Congress.

Congress and the Court also have recognized a power that is not expressly mentioned in the Constitution—the power of self-preservation. This authority is implicit in the clause that grants senators and representatives immunity from being questioned by the executive or judicial branch for any legislative action. The necessity for Congress to be protected from intimidation and harassment by the other branches has led the Court to give a broad interpretation to Article 1, Section 6, known as the speech or debate clause, to the extent that immunity has been granted to members of Congress charged with criminal activity.

CONGRESS AND OFFICIAL CONDUCT

In addition to its authority over the conduct of its members, Congress has also been the primary branch responsible for overseeing the conduct in office of executive branch employees below the presidential appointment level.

In 1882 the Court upheld a law that forbade officers and government employees to give or receive any money, property, or "other thing of value for political purposes." That law, the Court held in an opinion by Chief Justice Morrison R. Waite, was clearly an appropriate exercise of the legislative power "to promote efficiency and integrity in the discharge of official duties, and to maintain proper discipline in the public service."[1]

Similar provisions appeared in the Civil Service Act in 1883, the Hatch Act of 1939, and its later amendments and revisions. The Court consistently has upheld the power of Congress to regulate such conduct, including severe restrictions on the political activities of civil servants.[2] (See box, Politics and Public Employees, p. 549, in Chapter 10.)

In 1995, however, the Court ruled that Congress had gone too far in passing the Ethics Reform Act of 1989. That law, the Court held, had breached the First Amendment rights of executive branch employees by barring them from earning money for speeches or articles written on their own time and completely unrelated to their official positions.[3]

1. *Ex parte Curtiss*, 106 U.S. 371 at 373 (1882).
2. *United Public Workers v. Mitchell*, 330 U.S. 75 (1947).
3. *United States v. National Treasury Employees Union*, 115 S. Ct. 1003 (1995).

The power of self-protection also has been used as the authority for enacting laws regulating campaign financing and requiring lobby registration. The Court sustained both laws against challenges that they conflicted with First Amendment rights. The Court, however, has held that some specific campaign financing regulations impermissibly conflicted with First Amendment guarantees. Moreover, it has insisted that the lobby registration law be applied only to certain narrow categories of lobbyists and lobbying activity.

Qualifications

Clause 1 of Article 1, Section 5, of the Constitution states in part: "Each House shall be the judge of the . . . qualifications of its own members." The Constitution also requires that members meet certain age, citizenship, and residency requirements. *(See box, Constitutional Qualifications for Membership in Congress, p. 172.)*

Whether Congress, or either house of Congress, had power to add qualifications for membership beyond those listed by the Constitution, or power to overlook the absence of one of the constitutional requirements, were questions answered sometimes in the affirmative and sometimes in the negative. Until the Supreme Court's negative answer in the 1969 case concerning Rep. Adam Clayton Powell Jr. (D-N.Y., 1945–1967, 1969–1971), Congress acted from time to time as if it were entitled to add qualifications as well as to wink at failure to fulfill a constitutional requirement.

Alexander Hamilton initiated discussion of the question in No. 60 of *The Federalist Papers*. "The qualifications of the persons who may . . . be chosen are defined and fixed in the Constitution, and are unalterable by the legislature," Hamilton wrote.[1] However, later authorities contended that the Constitutional Convention intended to empower Congress to add to the listed qualifications.

Of the three senators-elect the Senate has excluded, only one was refused his seat because he did not meet a qualification added by the Senate—loyalty to the Union during the Civil War. (Loyalty was later made a constitutional requirement by the Fourteenth Amendment.) The other two failed to meet the citizenship requirement. Of the ten excluded representatives-elect, four were excluded for disloyalty during the Civil War. One was excluded because he did not live in the district he represented. Another House member-elect was excluded because he was a polygamist, a second was excluded for malfeasance, a third for misconduct, and two more for seditious activities.

EXCLUSION

In 1967 the House voted to exclude Representative Powell. The exclusion ended one of the stormiest episodes in congres-

Rep. Adam Clayton Powell Jr. gives an impromptu news conference January 9, 1967. That year the House of Representatives voted to exclude him from its chambers, even though he had been duly elected to office. In *Powell v. McCormack* (1969) the Court held that because Powell met the constitutional standards for membership, the House could not refuse to seat him.

sional history and precipitated a Supreme Court ruling that Congress could not add to the constitutional qualifications for membership in Congress.

Pastor of the Abyssinian Baptist Church in Harlem, one of the largest congregations in the country, Powell, a New York Democrat, was elected to the Seventy-ninth Congress in 1944. Powell was reelected regularly, served as chairman of the House Committee on Education and Labor from 1961 to 1967, and was considered by many observers to be the most powerful black legislator in the United States.

Powell's downfall was brought about in part by his flamboyant personality and his apparent disregard for the law. In 1958 he was indicted for income tax evasion, but the case was dismissed when the jury was unable to reach a verdict. In 1960 he was convicted of libel. Powell eventually paid the libel judgment, but not before he had been held in contempt of court four times and had been found guilty of fraudulently transferring property to avoid paying.

But Powell's real troubles began when some of his questionable congressional activities came to light. In the 1950s and early 1960s Powell enjoyed several costly pleasure trips at government expense. He was criticized for taking a female staff member on many trips to Bimini Island in the Bahamas. He paid his wife out of government funds almost $21,000 a year as a clerk while

she lived in Puerto Rico. Additionally, in the late 1960s Powell indulged in long absences from Congress. These apparent misuses of public funds and continuing legal problems in New York created a great furor among the public and members of the House, who felt he was discrediting the institution.

Reelected in 1966, Powell arrived in Washington only to have the House Democratic Caucus strip him of his committee chairmanship. The following day, January 10, 1967, the House voted to deny Powell his seat pending an investigation. The investigating committee recommended that Powell be censured for his misconduct and fined to offset the public funds he had misspent. But the full House rejected these recommendations, voting 307–116 on March 1, 1967, to exclude Powell from Congress.

Powell ran successfully in the special election to fill his vacancy but did not try to claim his seat. He ran again in 1968, was elected, and was seated in Congress, subject to loss of seniority and a $25,000 fine.

Meanwhile Powell and several of his constituents had challenged his 1967 exclusion in the courts. Powell sought a declaratory judgment that his exclusion was unconstitutional, a permanent order forbidding House Speaker John W. McCormack, D-Mass. (1928–1971), to refuse to administer the oath of office to Powell, the House clerk to refuse to perform duties due a representative, the House sergeant-at-arms to refuse to pay Powell his salary, and the House doorkeeper to threaten not to admit him to the House chamber.

There were two main issues involved in this suit. Could the House add to the Constitution's qualifications for membership? Could the courts properly examine the actions of the House in such cases, order the House not to add to those qualifications, and enforce the order?

CONSTITUTIONAL QUALIFICATIONS FOR MEMBERSHIP IN CONGRESS

• A senator must be at least thirty years old and have been a citizen of the United States not less than nine years (Article I, Section 3, Clause 3).

• A representative must be at least twenty-five years old and have been a citizen not less than seven years (Article I, Section 2, Clause 2).

• Every member of Congress must be, when elected, an inhabitant of the state that he is to represent (Article I, Section 2, Clause 2, and Section 3, Clause 3).

• No one may be a member of Congress who holds any other "Office under the United States" (Article I, Section 6, Clause 2).

• No person may be a senator or a representative who, having previously taken an oath as a member of Congress to support the Constitution, has engaged in rebellion against the United States or given aid or comfort to its enemies, unless Congress has removed such disability by a two-thirds vote of both houses (Fourteenth Amendment, Section 3).

The federal District Court for the District of Columbia dismissed the suit because it said it did not have jurisdiction over the subject matter. The Court of Appeals for the District of Columbia Circuit affirmed in February 1969 the action of the lower court in dismissing the suit. The court of appeals held that the lower court did have jurisdiction over the subject matter but that the case involved a political question, which, if decided, would constitute a violation of the separation of powers and produce an embarrassing confrontation between Congress and the courts. Judge Warren E. Burger wrote the court of appeals decision.

The Supreme Court, however, did consider the case, handing down its ruling in *Powell v. McCormack* in June 1969.[2] The vote was 7–1. For the Court, Chief Justice Earl Warren stated that the House had improperly excluded Powell. The case was not moot, Warren said, because of Powell's claim for back salary. Nor did the speech or debate clause protect all those named by Powell in his suit from judicial review of their actions pertaining to his exclusion. Warren dismissed the action against McCormack and the other members involved, but allowed Powell to maintain his suit against the House employees.

Warren then dismissed the argument that this was a political question the Court should not decide. Determination of Powell's right to his seat in the Ninetieth Congress, the Court held, required only interpretation of the Constitution, the traditional function of the Court.

Turning to that interpretation, Warren said: "Our examination of the relevant historical matters leads us to the conclusion that . . . the Constitution leaves the House without authority to exclude any person, duly elected by his constituents, who meets all the requirements for membership expressly prescribed in the Constitution."[3] Because Powell met these requirements, he could not be excluded.

The Court did not deny the unquestionable interest of Congress in maintaining its own integrity. In most cases, however, the Court felt that that interest could be properly safeguarded by use of each chamber's power to punish or expel its members.

The Supreme Court sent the case back to the court of appeals with instructions to enter a declaratory judgment stating that the House action was unconstitutional and to conduct further proceedings on the unresolved issues of seniority, back pay, and the $25,000 fine.

Justice Potter Stewart dissented, holding that the end of the Ninetieth Congress and the seating of Powell in the Ninety-first Congress rendered the case moot.

TERM LIMITS

Twenty-six years later, in 1995, the Court relied on its ruling in *Powell v. McCormack* to strike down a state law limiting the number of terms members of Congress could serve. By a 5–4 vote in *U.S. Term Limits v. Thornton*, the Court said the three qualifications set out in the Constitution, relating to age, citizenship, and residency, are exclusive.[4] If individual states were allowed to adopt term limits, the Court said that it would lead to a patchwork of state tenure qualifications, undermining the uniformity and national character of the Congress.

Although term limits had been debated since the nation's founding, the Arkansas law at issue in this case was the first of its kind to come before the high Court. Anti-incumbency fever swept the country in the 1990s, and at the time of the ruling twenty-three states had approved limits on the tenure of their members of Congress. The Arkansas rule, adopted as an amendment to the state constitution in 1992, prohibited candidates from serving more than three terms in the House of Representatives and two terms in the Senate.

To permit such state limits would effect a fundamental change in the Constitution, Justice John Paul Stevens wrote for the Court. "Any such change must come not by legislation adopted either by Congress or by any individual state, but rather . . . through amendment procedures."[5]

Chief Justice William H. Rehnquist and Justices Antonin Scalia, Sandra Day O'Connor, and Clarence Thomas dissented. Writing for them, Thomas said it was "ironic" that the majority referred to the right of the people to choose who governs as the majority was voiding a "provision that won nearly 60 percent of the votes cast in a direct election and that carried every congressional district in the state."[6]

Power to Punish Members

Article I, Section 5, Clause 2, of the Constitution empowers each chamber of Congress to "punish its Members for disorderly Behavior, and with the Concurrence of two thirds, expel a Member."

Expulsion has been a power little exercised by Congress. Fifteen senators have been expelled, one in 1797 for engaging in a conspiracy against a foreign country and fourteen during the Civil War for supporting a rebellion. In the House only four members have been expelled, three of them in 1861 for Civil War activities and one in 1980 for corruption.

As of 1996, the Senate had used the milder punishment of censure to discipline nine of its members; the House has censured twenty-two of its members. From time to time, each chamber has employed other less severe forms of discipline to punish various kinds of misconduct.[7]

The Supreme Court has not been called upon to mediate directly in any of these punishment cases. It is likely the Court would consider such a case a nonjusticiable political question. The Court has indicated that it considers the power to expel a broad one. "The right to expel extends to all cases where the offense is such as in the judgment of the Senate is inconsistent with the trust and duty of a member."[8]

In a 1906 case touching on expulsion, the Court upheld a law providing that a member of Congress found guilty of accepting payment for services rendered in connection with a government proceeding "shall . . . be rendered forever thereafter incapable of holding any office . . . under the government of the United States." Convicted under that statute, Sen. Joseph R. Burton, R-

Kan. (1901–1906), challenged the act's constitutionality on the grounds that it deprived the Senate of its right to decide on expulsion of its members. The Court disagreed, writing that the "final judgment of conviction did not operate *ipso facto,* to vacate the seat of the convicted Senator nor compel the Senate to expel him or to regard him as expelled by force alone of the judgment."[9]

Although neither the House nor the Senate has ever found it necessary, the Supreme Court in 1881 indicated that both chambers of Congress had the power to imprison members for misconduct. In *Kilbourn v. Thompson* the Court said:

[T]he Constitution expressly empowers each House to punish its own members for disorderly behavior. We see no reason to doubt that this punishment may in a proper case be imprisonment, and that it may be for refusal to obey some rule on that subject made by the House for the preservation of order.

So, also, the penalty which each House is authorized to inflict in order to compel the attendance of absent members may be imprisonment, and this may be for a violation of some order or standing rule on the subject.[10]

Another court test of the congressional power to punish members came in 1969. Two years earlier, the House of Representatives had refused to seat Adam Clayton Powell, a member of Congress since 1944, because he allegedly misspent government funds and committed other misdeeds. In *Powell v. McCormack* (1969) the Court held that Congress could not exclude a member-elect for any reason other than failure to meet one of the constitutionally specified requirements for membership in Congress.[11] Powell met the requirements of age, residence, and citizenship. In essence, the Court said the House could not punish Powell for his indiscretions until after it had seated him. *(See details of Powell v. McCormack, pp. 171–173.)*

Congressional Immunity

The concept of legislators' having some immunity from legal actions was well established in England and in the colonies by the time it was made part of the American Constitution. Article I, Section 6, provides that "Senators and Representatives shall . . . in all Cases, except Treason, Felony and Breach of the Peace, be privileged from Arrest during their Attendance at the Session of their respective Houses, and in going to and returning from the same; and for any Speech or Debate in either House, they shall not be questioned in any other Place."

The privilege from arrest clause has become practically obsolete, as various court decisions have narrowed its protection. As presently interpreted, the clause applies only to arrests in civil suits, such as nonpayment of debts or breach of contract. Even this protection is of little significance because most states do not arrest people in such actions. Civil arrests were more common at the time the Constitution was written.

The Supreme Court has declared that the privilege from arrest clause does not apply to service of process—the delivery of writs or summons—in either civil or criminal cases.[12] Nor does

it apply to arrest in criminal cases. In 1908 the Court interpreted the phrase "treason, felony or breach of the peace" to exclude all criminal offenses from the privilege's coverage.[13]

SPEECH OR DEBATE CLAUSE

Adopted by the Constitutional Convention without discussion or opposition, the speech or debate clause was intended to protect the independence and integrity of Congress and reinforce the separation of powers by preventing the executive and judicial branches from looking into congressional activities for evidence of criminality. Repeatedly, the Supreme Court has stated that the "immunities of the Speech or debate Clause were not written into the Constitution simply for the personal or private benefit of Members of Congress, but to protect the integrity of the legislative process by insuring the independence of individual legislators."[14]

To ensure that integrity, the Court has seen fit to apply the clause to a broader range of legislative activities than just speech and debate and even to protect legislative aides in certain instances. But the Court has not construed the clause so broadly as to grant complete immunity from all prosecution or to preclude all judicial review of the activities of individual legislation.

More than Speech

In its first interpretation of the speech or debate clause in *Kilbourn v. Thompson* (1881), the Supreme Court refused "to limit it to words spoken in debate."[15]

The case involved a contempt of Congress citation against Hallet Kilbourn, manager of a District of Columbia real estate pool, for refusing to answer questions before a House committee investigating the bankrupt Jay Cooke and Company and its interest in the real estate pool. The House ordered Kilbourn jailed for contempt. He sued the Speaker of the House, members of the investigating committee, and Sergeant at Arms John G. Thompson for false arrest. The Supreme Court sustained Kilbourn's claim of false arrest on the grounds that the investigation was not a legitimate one. *(See details of Kilbourn v. Thompson, pp. 163–164.)*

The Court concluded, however, that the Speaker and the members of the investigating committee could not be prosecuted for the false arrest because the report recommending contempt and the vote to direct Kilbourn's arrest were covered by the speech or debate clause. The Court wrote:

The reason of the rule is as forcible in its application to written reports presented in that body [the House] by its committees, to resolutions offered which, though in writing, must be reproduced in speech, and to the act of voting, whether it is done vocally or by passing between the tellers. In short, to things generally done in a session of the House by one of its members in relation to the business before it.[16]

Extension to Aides

In its *Kilbourn* decision the Court did not extend the protection of the speech or debate clause to the sergeant at arms, who, as a result, was liable to prosecution for false arrest. A similar holding was made in 1967 in the case of *Dombrowski v. East-land.*[17] Petitioners charged that Sen. James O. Eastland, D-Miss. (1941, 1943–1979), chairman of the Judiciary Committee's Internal Security Subcommittee, and the subcommittee counsel conspired with Louisiana officials to seize the property and records of the petitioners in violation of the Fourth Amendment.

The Court, in a per curiam decision, held that Eastland was not liable to prosecution but that the subcommittee counsel was. Noting that the record contained no evidence of Eastland's involvement in any activity that he might be liable for, the Court said that "legislators engaged in the sphere of legislative activity . . . should be protected not only from the consequences of litigation's results but also from the burden of defending themselves."[18]

As to the subcommittee counsel, the Court said there was enough dispute over the facts involved in his alleged collaboration with the state officials to warrant prosecution. The speech and debate clause, though applicable to congressional employees, was not absolute, the Court said.

In 1972 the Court elaborated on this opinion. *Gravel v. United States* involved Sen. Mike Gravel, D-Alaska (1969–1981), and his actions in releasing portions of the then-classified *Pentagon Papers* history of U.S. involvement in the Vietnam War.[19]

During the controversy over publication of the *Pentagon Papers* in 1971 by several newspapers, Gravel on June 29, 1971, convened a special meeting of the Public Works Subcommittee on Public Buildings, of which he was chairman. With the press and public in attendance, Gravel read classified documents from the *Pentagon Papers* into the subcommittee record. Subsequently, the senator arranged for the verbatim publication of the subcommittee record by Beacon Press.

In August 1971 a federal grand jury in Boston, investigating release of the *Pentagon Papers,* ordered Gravel aide Leonard S. Rodberg to appear before it. Rodberg had been hired the night Gravel called the session of his subcommittee to read excerpts from the secret documents. He subsequently helped Gravel edit and make arrangements for publication of the papers. Rodberg moved to quash the subpoena on the grounds that he was protected from questioning by the speech or debate clause.

In a 5–4 decision on June 29, 1972, the Supreme Court held that the constitutional immunity of members of Congress from grand jury questioning extended to their aides if the conduct in question would be a protected legislative act if performed by the member. "The day-to-day work of such aides is so critical to the Member's performance that they must be treated as [the member's] alter ego," wrote Justice Byron R. White for the majority.[20]

However, the majority agreed that this protection did not extend to arrangements that were made for the publication of the subcommittee report or to information about the source of the classified documents. Gravel, as well as Rodberg, could be required to testify to the grand jury about these nonlegislative matters, the majority said:

While the Speech or Debate Clause recognizes speech, voting and other legislative acts as exempt from liability that might attach, it does not

"TO SUPPORT THE RIGHT OF THE PEOPLE"

The basic interpretation of the speech or debate clause comes not from the Supreme Court of the United States but from the Supreme Court of Massachusetts, which included an immunity clause in its 1780 constitution. Charged with slander during a private conversation on the floor, three members of the state's lower chamber invoked the immunity clause. Speaking to the plea, Chief Justice Parsons of Massachusetts wrote in 1808:

These privileges [of immunity] are thus secured, not with the intention of protecting the members against prosecutions for their own benefit, but to support the right of the People, by enabling their representatives to execute the functions of their office without fear of prosecutions, civil or criminal. I therefore think that the article ought not to be construed strictly, but liberally, that the full design of it may be answered. I will not confine it to delivering an opinion, but will extend it to the giving of a vote, to the making of a written report, and to every other act resulting from the nature and the execution of the office. And I would define the article as securing to every member exemption from prosecution for everything said or done by him as a representative, in the exercise of the functions of that office, without inquiring whether the exercise was regular, according to the rules of the House, or irregular and against those rules. I do not confine the member to his place in the House; and I am satisfied that there are cases in which he is entitled to this privilege when not within the walls of the Representatives' Chamber. (*Coffin v. Coffin,* 4 Mass. 1, at 27, 1808)

privilege either senator or aide to violate an otherwise valid criminal law in preparing for or implementing legislative acts.[21]

Justice Potter Stewart dissented from the ruling because it held that a member of Congress could be forced to tell a grand jury about the sources of information used to prepare for legislative activity. Justices William O. Douglas, William J. Brennan Jr., and Thurgood Marshall argued in dissent that the constitutional immunity protected Gravel, Rodberg, and the Beacon Press even from questions concerning the publication of the papers read into the subcommittee record.

IMMUNITY VERSUS INDIVIDUAL RIGHTS

The speech or debate clause would appear to protect legislators and their aides from prosecution even in cases where their legislative activities have infringed on the constitutional rights of private individuals.

A major case, *Tenney v. Brandhove* (1951), involved the California state legislature, but the Court's ruling seems applicable to Congress.[22] In this case Brandhove sued members of a legislative committee investigating un-American activities. Brandhove said their questioning of him was not for a legislative purpose but to harass and intimidate him and to prohibit him from exercising his right of free speech.

The Court dismissed Brandhove's suit. "The claim of an unworthy purpose does not destroy the privilege" of congressional immunity, wrote Justice Felix Frankfurter. He continued:

Legislators are immune from deterrents to the uninhibited discharge of their legislative duty, not for their private indulgence but for the public good. One must not expect uncommon courage even in legislators. In times of political passion, dishonest and vindictive motives are readily attributed to legislative conduct and as readily believed. Courts are not the place for such controversies. Self-discipline and the voters must be the ultimate reliance for discouraging or correcting such abuses. The Courts should not go beyond the narrow confines of determining that the committee's inquiry may fairly be deemed within its province.[23]

Justice Douglas dissented: "It is one thing to give great leeway to the legislative right of speech, debate, and investigation. But when a committee perverts its power, brings down on an individual the whole weight of government for an illegal or corrupt purpose, the reason for the immunity ends."[24]

In *Doe v. McMillan* (1973) the Court held that members of Congress and their employees—chiefly John McMillan, D-S.C. (1939–1973), chairman of the House District of Columbia Committee, the committee's members, and employees—were immune from charges that they violated the privacy rights of certain children by naming them as disciplinary and absentee problems in a committee report on the District of Columbia school system. Wrote Justice White:

The business of Congress is to legislate; Congressmen and aides are absolutely immune when they are legislating. But when they act outside the "sphere of legitimate legislative activity" . . . they enjoy no special immunity from local laws protecting the good name or the reputation of the ordinary citizen.[25]

Because the committee members and employees had included the names of the children in a report that was a legitimate legislative activity, they were immune from prosecution. But the Court held that this immunity might not extend to the public printer and the superintendent of documents, also named in the suit. This protection did not cover persons, the Court said, "who publish and distribute otherwise actionable materials beyond the reasonable requirements of the legislative function."[26] It was left to the trial court to determine if these defendants had gone beyond those requirements.

In 1975 the Court held that a valid subpoena from a congressional committee fell within the protected sphere of legislative activity even if it was claimed that the subpoena was intended to impede the exercise of First Amendment rights.[27] The case involved Sen. James O. Eastland, D-Miss. (1941, 1943–1978), the Judiciary Subcommittee on Internal Security, and the subcommittee counsel. Eastland, chairman of the subcommittee, had issued a subpoena for the bank records of the United States Servicemen's Fund (USSF) as part of the subcommittee's inquiry into the enforcement of the Internal Security Act of 1950. The USSF set up coffeehouses and aided underground military base newspapers, both vehicles for protest against American involvement in Indochina. The courts could not investigate the propriety of the inquiry into the fund's activities beyond determining that such an inquiry was within the jurisdiction of the subcommittee, said the Court. If that is determined, "the speech or debate clause is an absolute bar to interference," the Court concluded.[28]

In dissent, Justice Douglas claimed that "no official . . . may invoke immunity for his actions for which wrongdoers normally suffer."[29]

In *Hutchinson v. Proxmire* (1979) the Court held that the speech or debate clause did not immunize a member of Congress from libel suits for allegedly defamatory statements he made about a person in press releases and newsletters, even though the statements had originally been made on the Senate floor. "Valuable and desirable as it may be" to inform the public of a member's activities, the Court said, transmittal of such information in press releases "is not part of the legislative function or the deliberations that make up the legislative process."[30]

CRIMINAL PROSECUTIONS

The Supreme Court in 1966 held, 7–0, that in prosecuting a former member of Congress the executive branch could not inquire into the member's motive for making a speech on the floor, even though the speech was allegedly made for a bribe and was part of an unlawful conspiracy.

United States v. Johnson arose out of the conviction of Rep. Thomas F. Johnson, D-Md. (1959–1963), in June 1963 by a federal jury in Baltimore.[31] The government charged that Johnson, Rep. Frank W. Boykin, D-Ala. (1935–1963), and two officers of a Maryland savings and loan company then under indictment entered into a conspiracy in which Johnson and Boykin would approach the Justice Department to urge a "review" of the indictment and Johnson would make a speech on the floor of the House defending savings and loan institutions in general. Johnson made the speech in June 1960, and it was reprinted by the indicted company and distributed to the public. Johnson and Boykin allegedly received money in the form of "campaign contributions." Johnson's share was put at more than $20,000.

The four men were convicted on seven counts of violating the federal conflict of interest law and one count of conspiring to defraud the United States (President Lyndon B. Johnson, on December 17, 1965, granted Boykin a full pardon).

The Court of Appeals for the Fourth Circuit in September 1964 set aside Johnson's conspiracy conviction and ordered a retrial on the other counts.

The Supreme Court essentially affirmed the court of appeals ruling. The opinion was written by Justice John Marshall Harlan who said that the precedents did not deal

with a criminal prosecution based upon an allegation that a member of Congress abused his position by conspiring to give a particular speech in return for remuneration from private interests. However reprehensible such conduct may be, we believe the Speech or Debate Clause extends at least so far as to prevent it from being made the basis of a criminal charge against a member of Congress of conspiring to defraud the United States by impeding the due discharge of government functions. The essence of such a charge in this context is that the Congressman's conduct was improperly motivated, and . . . that is precisely what the Speech or Debate Clause generally forecloses from executive and judicial inquiry.[32]

Emphasizing the narrowness of its holding, the Court said the decision did not address whether congressional immunity would extend to a prosecution based on a specifically drawn statute passed by Congress to regulate the conduct of its own members. Nor did it speak to a prosecution for a general criminal statute that did not rely for its proof on the member's motivation for performing his legislative activities. The Court said it would allow a new trial of Johnson on the conspiracy charge only if the executive branch could purge all parts of its prosecution offensive to the speech or debate clause. The government chose to drop the conspiracy charge. (On a retrial of the seven conflict-of-interest charges, Johnson was convicted a second time and sentenced to six months in prison.)

Brewster Case

The question of whether the government could—without violating congressional immunity under the speech or debate clause—successfully prosecute a member of Congress for taking a bribe in return for casting a vote came before the Court in 1972.

Former senator Daniel B. Brewster, D-Md. (1963–1969), was indicted in 1969 on charges of accepting $24,000 in bribes between 1966 and 1968 from the mail order firm of Spiegel Incorporated. During that time, Brewster was a member of the Senate Post Office and Civil Service Committee, which was considering proposed changes in postal rates. The indictment alleged that the bribes influenced Brewster's legislative action on these proposals.

In November 1970 a federal district judge in the District of Columbia dismissed the charges against Brewster, stating that the speech or debate clause shielded him from prosecution for bribery related to the performance of legislative acts. The Justice Department immediately asked the Supreme Court to review this decision.

By a 6–3 vote the Court reversed the lower court ruling and held that Brewster could indeed be prosecuted on the bribery charge. Observing that a broad interpretation of the speech or debate clause would immunize almost all legislators' activities, Chief Justice Warren E. Burger stated:

In its narrowest scope, the Clause is a very large, albeit essential, grant of privilege. It has enabled reckless men to slander and even destroy others with impunity, but that was the conscious choice of the framers. . . . [B]ut the shield does not extend beyond what is necessary to preserve the integrity of the legislative process.[33]

The Court has never interpreted the clause "as protecting all conduct *relating* to the legislative process," said Burger. "In every case thus far before this Court, the Speech or Debate Clause has been limited to an act which was clearly part of the legislative process—the due functioning of the process."[34]

Turning specifically to the *Brewster* case, Burger separated the act of taking a bribe from the act of casting a ballot:

The illegal conduct is taking or agreeing to take money for a promise to act in a certain way. There is no need for the government to show that [Brewster] fulfilled the alleged illegal bargain; acceptance of the bribe is the violation of the statute, not performance of the illegal promise.

The Court in *United States v. Brewster* (1972) upheld the bribery conviction of former senator Daniel B. Brewster, D-Md. (1963–1969). The Court held that the speech or debate clause did not shield Brewster from prosecution for bribery related to the performance of legislative acts.

Taking a bribe is, obviously, no part of the legislative process or function; it is not a legislative act.[35]

By this construction, the Court found that, unlike the *Johnson* case, it would not be necessary for the government in prosecuting Brewster to inquire into the legislative acts or their motivations in order to provide a violation of the bribery statute.

In dissent, Justice Brennan said the majority had taken an artificial view of the charges. The indictment, Brennan said, was not for receipt of money, but for receipt of money in exchange for a promise to vote a certain way. To prove this crime, he continued, the government would have to inquire into Brewster's motives, and this it was prevented from doing by the immunity clause.

The three dissenters also said that Congress, not the courts, was the proper forum for disciplining the misconduct of its members. "The speech or debate clause does not immunize corrupt congressmen," wrote Justice Byron R. White. "It reserves the power to discipline [them] in the houses of Congress."[36]

Brewster stood trial and was convicted, but the conviction was reversed. Before a second trial could begin, Brewster pleaded no contest to a felony charge of accepting an illegal gratuity while he was a senator.

Dowdy Case

Little more than a year later, the Court in 1973 refused to review an appellate court ruling that had reversed the conviction of Rep. John Dowdy, D-Texas (1952–1973), on five of eight conspiracy, bribery, and perjury charges. The Fourth Circuit Court of Appeals held that the evidence used in Dowdy's trial directly related to the legislative process. The evidence "was an examination of defendant's actions as a Congressman, who was chairman of a subcommittee investigating a complaint, in gathering information in preparation for a possible subcommittee investigatory hearing," the appeals court said.[37]

Although the alleged criminal act—bribery—was the same in the *Dowdy, Johnson,* and *Brewster* cases, the major difference was the source of the evidence. In Brewster's case the Court found sufficient evidence available outside of Brewster's legislative activities to let the case go forward. In the *Dowdy* and *Johnson* cases, so much of the evidence was based on their legislative activities that introduction of that evidence violated their immunity and was therefore unconstitutional.

Elections Regulation

The Constitution gives the states the authority to set the time, place, and manner of holding elections for Congress with the proviso that "Congress may at any time by law make or alter such Regulations, except as to the Places of chusing Senators" (Article I, Section 4, Clause 1).

The first law that Congress passed regulating the time, place, or manner of a federal election was an 1842 act requiring that representatives be elected by districts. Congress's first comprehensive regulation of elections was the Enforcement Act of 1870, adopted to enforce the right of blacks to vote granted under the Fifteenth Amendment. Together with two 1871 statutes, the Enforcement Act made it a federal offense to register falsely, bribe voters, interfere with election officials, and make false counts of ballots cast. Any election officer who failed to perform a duty required of him in a federal election under either federal or state law was also guilty of a federal offense.

In 1880 the act was challenged as an unconstitutional infringement on the states' right to conduct elections. The suit also questioned whether Congress had the authority to punish state election officers for violations of state election law affecting federal elections.

In *Ex parte Siebold* the Court upheld the Enforcement Act:

There is no declaration [in Article I, Section 4] that the regulations shall be made wholly by the State legislature or wholly by Congress. If Congress does not interfere, of course they may be made wholly by the State, but if it chooses to interfere, there is nothing in the words to prevent its doing so, either wholly or partially. On the contrary, their necessary implication is that it may do either. It may either make the regulations, or it may alter them. If it only alters, leaving . . . the general organization of the polls to the State, there results a necessary cooperation of the two governments in regulating the subject. But no repugnance in the system of regulations can arise thence; for the power of Congress over the subject is paramount. It may be exercised as and when Congress sees fit to exercise it. When exercised, the action of Congress, so far as it extends and conflicts with the regulations of the State, necessarily supersedes them.[38]

It stood to reason that if Congress could regulate elections, it had the power to enforce its regulations, the Court continued. State election personnel officiating at a federal election have a responsibility to the federal government as well as to the state, and the fact that an official is a state official does not shield him from federal punishment for failure to perform his duty to the United States.

To the argument that Congress cannot punish violations of state election law pertaining to federal elections, the Court said: "The State laws which Congress sees no occasion to alter, but which it allows to stand, are in effect adopted by Congress. It simply demands their fulfillment."[39]

In subsequent cases, the Court has upheld Congress's authority under Article I, Section 4, to protect against personal violence and intimidation at the polls, and against failure to count all the votes cast.[40]

PRIMARY ELECTIONS

Although the Court had ruled that congressional authority to regulate the time, manner, and place of holding elections was paramount to state authority, in 1921 it ruled that party primaries were not elections, and that Congress consequently had no right to regulate them. *Newberry v. United States* arose when Truman H. Newberry, R-Mich. (1919–1922), was convicted for having spent more money than he was allowed under the 1911 campaign expenditure law in his primary race against Henry Ford for the 1918 Republican Senate nomination in Michigan.

Newberry's case was argued before the Supreme Court. However, on the constitutional question of whether Congress had the power to regulate primaries the Court divided, 4–4. Justice Joseph McKenna, who voted to reverse the conviction, was unsure how ratifications of the Seventeenth Amendment in 1913 affected Congress's power to act under the 1911 statute.

The four justices who claimed that Congress did not have authority to regulate primaries wrote that the word election "now has the same general significance as it did when the Constitution came into existence—final choice of an officer by duly qualified electors."[41] Primaries, the four continued, "are in no sense elections for an office but merely methods by which party adherents agree upon candidates whom they intend to offer and support for ultimate choice by all qualified electors."[42] The manner in which candidates are nominated for federal office "does not directly affect the manner of holding the election," they concluded.[43]

This politically naive view of the role of the primary was assailed by Justice Mahlon Pitney, who observed that the primary had no reason to exist except as preparation for an election. Congressional authority to regulate the manner of holding an election "can mean nothing less," Pitney said, than the ability to regulate "the entire mode of procedure—the essence, not merely the form of conducting the elections."[44]

SERVICE IN CONGRESS

Twenty-seven of the 108 Supreme Court justices served in the Senate, the House, or both before being seated on the Court.

Only one, David Davis, left the Court to serve in Congress. In 1877 the Illinois legislature elected Davis to the U.S. Senate; Davis had served on the Court since 1862. Davis was in the Senate for only one term, serving as president pro tempore from 1881 to 1883, when he retired.

A list of individuals who served both in Congress and on the Supreme Court follows:

Justice	Congressional Service	Court Service
SENATE		
William Paterson	1789–November 13, 1790	1793–1806
Oliver Ellsworth	1789–March 8, 1796	1796–1799
Levi Woodbury	1825–1831; 1841–1845	1845–1851
David Davis	1877–1883	1862–1877
Salmon P. Chase*	1849–1855; March 4–6, 1861	1874–1873
Stanley Matthews	March 21, 1877–1879	1881–1889
Howell E. Jackson	1881–April 4, 1886	1894–1895
Edward D. White*	1891–March 12, 1894	1894–1921
Hugo L. Black	1927–August 19, 1937	1937–1971
Harold H. Burton	1941–September 30, 1945	1945–1958
Sherman Minton	1935–1941	1949–1956
HOUSE		
John Marshall*	1799–June 7, 1800	1801–1835
Joseph Story	May 23, 1808–1809	1811–1845
Gabriel Duvall	November 11, 1794–March 28, 1796	1812–1835
John McLean	1813–1816	1829–1861
Henry Baldwin	1817–May 8, 1822	1830–1844
James M. Wayne	1829–January 13, 1835	1835–1867
Philip B. Barbour	September 19, 1814–1825	1836–1841
Nathan Clifford	1839–1843	1858–1881
William Strong	1847–1851	1870–1880
Joseph McKenna	1885–1892	1898–1925
William H. Moody	November 5, 1895–May 1, 1902	1906–1910
Mahlon Pitney	1895–January 10, 1899	1912–1922
Fred M. Vinson*	January 12, 1924–1929; 1931–May 12, 1938	1946–1953
BOTH CHAMBERS		
John McKinley	S: November 27, 1826–1831; March 4–April 22, 1837 H: 1833–1835	1837–1852
Lucius Q. C. Lamar	H: 1857–1860; 1873–1877 S: 1877–March 6, 1885	1888–1893
George Sutherland	H: 1901–1903 S: 1905–1917	1922–1938
James F. Byrnes	H: 1911–1925 S: 1931–July 8, 1941	1941–1942

*Denotes a chief justice.

Pitney's dissent became the majority position twenty years later when the Court, in the 1941 case of *United States v. Classic,* reversed its *Newberry* decision. The 1941 case involved a government prosecution, under the 1870 Enforcement Act, of Louisiana election commissioners for altering and falsely counting votes in a primary election. For the most part, winning the Democratic nomination to Congress in Louisiana was tantamount to winning the general election.[45]

Writing for the 5–3 majority, Justice Harlan Fiske Stone stated: "[W]e think that the authority of Congress, given by [Article I, Section 4], includes the authority to regulate primary elections when as in this case, they are a step in the exercise by the people of their choice of representatives in Congress."[46]

The three dissenting justices based their disagreement not on the grounds that Congress did not have the authority to regulate primary elections, but on the grounds that the statute making alteration and miscounting of ballots criminal offenses was not specific enough to encompass primaries.

CAMPAIGN FINANCING

Sensitive to charges that corporations exerted undue influence on Congress through unrestrained spending on favored candidates, Congress in 1907 passed the first law regulating campaign financing. The Tillman Act prohibited corporations and national banks from making any money contributions to any candidate for federal office. A 1910 law required every political committee seeking to influence the election of House members in two or more states to file contribution and spending reports with the clerk of the House. A 1911 law provided similar regulation for Senate races.

In 1925 Congress passed the Federal Corrupt Practices Act setting limits on the amounts candidates for the Senate and House could spend in general elections. Primary elections were omitted because of the Court's ruling in the *Newberry* case. The 1925 act also required political committees seeking to influence the election of presidential electors in two or more states to file contribution and spending reports that would be available to the public.

This last provision was challenged in *Burroughs and Cannon v. United States* (1934) as an infringement on the right of the states to appoint their presidential electors in the manner they deemed appropriate (Article II, Section 1, Clause 2).[47] In upholding the federal disclosure provisions as they pertained to presidential electors, the Supreme Court implicitly sanctioned federal regulation of campaign financing in congressional elections.

The provisions, observed Justice George Sutherland for the majority, applied to committees operating in two or more states. Such committees, "if not beyond the power of the state to deal with at all, are beyond its power to deal with adequately."

Turning to the authority of Congress to supply adequate regulation, Sutherland said that the importance of the election of the president and the vital character of its relationship to and effect upon the welfare and safety of the whole people cannot be too strongly stated. To say that Congress is without the power to pass appropriate legislation to safeguard such an election from the improper use of money to influence the result is to deny to the nation in a vital particular the power of self-protection.[48]

First Amendment Conflict

But congressional authority to regulate campaign spending is not unchecked. In the 1976 decision in *Buckley v. Valeo* the Court held that certain provisions of a 1974 campaign financing law violated First Amendment rights.[49]

Among the plaintiffs challenging the 1974 statute were Sen. James L. Buckley, C/R-N.Y. (1971–1977), former senator Eugene J. McCarthy, D-Minn. (1959–1971), the New York Civil Liberties Union, and *Human Events,* a conservative publication. The plaintiffs did not question Congress's power to regulate campaign financing but claimed that the law's new limits on campaign contributions and expenditures curbed the freedom of contributors and candidates to express themselves in the political marketplace.

The Supreme Court handed down its ruling January 30, 1976, in an unsigned 137-page opinion. In five separate, signed opinions, several justices concurred with and dissented from separate issues in the case.

In its decision, the Court upheld provisions that:

• Set limits on how much individuals and political committees may contribute to candidates.

• Provided for the public financing of presidential primary and general election campaigns.

• Required the disclosure of campaign contributions of more than $100 and campaign expenditures of more than $10.

But the Court overturned other features of the law, ruling that the campaign spending limits were unconstitutional violations of the First Amendment guarantee of free expression. For presidential candidates who accepted federal matching funds, however, the ceiling on expenditures remained intact.

"A restriction on the amount of money a person or group can spend on political communication during a campaign necessarily reduces the quantity of expression," the Court stated, "by restricting the number of issues discussed, the depth of their exploration and the size of the audience reached. This is because virtually every means of communicating ideas in today's mass society requires the expenditure of money."[50] Only Justice White dissented on this point; he would have upheld the limitations.

Although the Court acknowledged that both contribution limits and spending limits had First Amendment implications, it distinguished between the two by saying that the act's "expenditure ceilings impose significantly more severe restrictions on protected freedom of political expression and association than do its limitations on financial contributions."[51] The $1,000 ceiling on the amount an individual could spend on behalf of a candidate was a clear violation of the First Amendment, the opinion said.

Sen. James L. Buckley, C/R-N.Y. (1971–1977), was among the plaintiffs challenging a 1974 campaign financing law in *Buckley v. Valeo* (1976). The Court ruled that key provisions of the law violated First Amendment rights.

While the . . . ceiling thus fails to serve any substantial government interest in stemming the reality or appearance of corruption in the electoral process, it heavily burdens core First Amendment expression. . . . Advocacy of the election or defeat of candidates for federal office is no less entitled to protection under the First Amendment than the discussion of political policy generally or advocacy of the passage or defeat of legislation.[52]

The Court struck down the limits on how much of their own money candidates could spend on their campaigns. "The candidate, no less than any other person, has a First Amendment right to engage in the discussion of public issues and vigorously and tirelessly to advocate his own election and the election of other candidates," the opinion said.[53]

White dissented on expenditure limits. Rejecting the argument that money is speech, he wrote that there are "many expensive campaign activities that are not themselves communicative or remotely related to speech."[54]

Justice Thurgood Marshall rejected the Court's reasoning in striking down the limit on how much candidates may spend on their own campaigns. "It would appear to follow," he said, "that the candidate with a substantial personal fortune at his disposal is off to a significant 'head start.'"[55]

Separation of Powers

The Court in *Buckley v. Valeo* also held unanimously that the Federal Election Commission, the agency established to oversee and enforce the campaign financing laws, was unconstitutional. The Court said the method of appointment of commissioners violated the Constitution's separation-of-powers and appointments clauses because some members were named by congressional officials but exercised executive powers.

According to the decision, the commission may exercise only those powers Congress is allowed to delegate to congressional committees—investigating and information gathering. Only if the commission's members were appointed by the president, as required under the Constitution's appointments clause, could the commission carry out the administrative and enforcement responsibilities the law originally gave it, the Court ruled.

The justices stayed their ruling for thirty days to give the House and Senate time to "reconstitute the commission by law or adopt other valid enforcement mechanisms."[56] As events developed, Congress took more than three months to act and instead of merely reconstituting the commission it passed a considerably expanded campaign financing law.

Election Returns

Because the Constitution makes each house the judge of the election returns of its members, disputed elections have been considered political questions that the Court will not review. Only once has the Court felt obliged to answer whether a state law interfered with this congressional right.

Roudebush v. Hartke (1972) arose when Rep. Richard L. Roudebush, R-Ind. (1961–1972), lost the 1970 Senate election to incumbent senator Vance Hartke, D-Ind. (1959–1977), by a slim margin.[57] Roudebush asked for a recount by the state, and Hartke challenged it on the grounds that the state's recount procedure would interfere with the Senate's right to judge the disputed election returns.

Denying Hartke's challenge, the Court said that the state "recount does not prevent the Senate from independently evaluating the election any more than the initial count does. The Senate is free to accept or reject the apparent winner in either count, and, if it chooses, to conduct its own recount."[58]

Hartke was seated by the Senate pending the outcome of the recount, which did not change the election results. In an earlier case, however, the Senate refused to seat the apparent victor of a disputed election until the investigation into alleged misdoings in his campaign were completed. *Barry v. United States ex rel. Cunningham* involved the contested 1926 election of William S. Vare of Pennsylvania to the Senate. One of the issues involved was whether the Senate's refusal to seat Vare pending the outcome of the investigation deprived Pennsylvania of its equal representation. The Court concluded it did not:

The equal representation is found in Article V, which authorizes and regulates amendments to the Constitution, "provided, . . . that no state, without its consent, shall be deprived of its equal suffrage in the Senate." This constitutes a limitation upon the power of amendment and has nothing to do with a situation such as the one here presented. The temporary deprivation of equal representation which results from the

refusal of the Senate to seat a member pending inquiry as to his election or qualifications is the necessary consequence of the exercise of a constitutional power, and no more deprives the state of its "equal suffrage" in the constitutional sense than would a vote of the Senate vacating the seat of a sitting member or a vote of expulsion.[59]

Lobby Regulation

The right to lobby Congress—to assert rights, or to win a special privilege or financial benefit for the group applying the pressure, or to achieve an ideological goal—is guaranteed by the First Amendment to the Constitution. It provides that "Congress shall make no law . . . abridging the freedom of speech or of the press; or the right of the people peaceably to assemble and to petition the Government for redress of grievances."

Pressure groups, whether operating through general campaigns designed to sway public opinion or through direct contact with members of Congress, help to inform both Congress and the public about public issues and make known to Congress the practical aspects of proposed legislation—whom it would help or hurt, who is for or against it. Against these benefits, there

The right to lobby Congress is guaranteed by the Constitution. Lobbyists line up to get into a Senate Banking Committee meeting in August 1991.

are serious liabilities. The most serious is that in pursuing their own objectives, the pressure groups may lead Congress into decisions that benefit the groups but that do not necessarily serve other parts of the public. Occasionally, lobbyists resort to bribery or other unethical tactics in their efforts to influence legislation.

To guard against such lobbying methods, the House in 1876 passed a resolution requiring lobbyists to register with the clerk of the House. Congress subsequently passed a handful of specialized measures regulating certain kinds of lobbying activities, but it was not until 1946 that it enacted a general lobbying regulation law.

Because of the difficulty of imposing meaningful regulation on lobbying without infringing on the constitutional rights of free speech, press, assembly, and petition, the 1946 act did not actually regulate. Instead it simply required any person who was hired by someone else for the principal purpose of lobbying Congress to register with the secretary of the Senate and the clerk of the House and to file certain quarterly financial reports so that the lobbyist's activities would be known to Congress and the public. Organizations that solicited or received money for the principal purpose of lobbying Congress did not necessarily have to register, but they did have to file quarterly spending reports with the clerk detailing how much they spent to influence legislation.

The National Association of Manufacturers (NAM) brought a test suit in 1948 challenging the validity of the 1946 law. A federal court in the District of Columbia in 1952 held the act unconstitutional because its provisions were "too indefinite and vague to constitute an ascertainable standard of guilt."[60] Late in the same year, the Supreme Court reversed the lower court on a technicality, leaving the 1946 law in full force but open to future challenge.[61]

The challenge came in *United States v. Harriss,* actually begun at the same time the NAM case was being pursued.[62] In June 1948 the federal government obtained indictments against several individuals and an organization for alleged violations of the registration and reporting sections of the 1946 lobbying law.

It was charged that, without registering or reporting, New York cotton broker Robert M. Harriss had made payments to Ralph W. Moore, a Washington commodity trader and secretary of the National Farm Committee, for the purpose of pressuring Congress on legislation, and that Moore had made similar payments to James E. McDonald, the agriculture commissioner of Texas, and Tom Linder, the agriculture commissioner of Georgia. A lower court in 1953 held the lobbying law unconstitutional on grounds that it was too vague and indefinite to meet the requirements of due process, and that the registration and reporting requirements violated the rights of free speech, free press, assembly, and petition.

In June 1954 the Supreme Court, by a 5–3 vote, reversed the lower court and upheld the constitutionality of the 1946 statute. To do so, it had to interpret the act very narrowly. The statute, the majority said, applied only to lobbyists or organizations who solicited, collected, or received contributions in order to conduct their lobbying, and then only to those lobbyists and organizations whose main purpose was to influence legislation.

Furthermore, the Court interpreted the act "to refer only to 'lobbying in its commonly accepted sense'—to direct communications with members of Congress on pending or proposed federal legislation."[63]

This limited interpretation omitted from coverage several categories of lobbying organizations, including those that spent money from their own funds to conduct lobbying activities rather than collecting funds specifically for the purpose of lobbying, those who could claim that their primary purpose was something other than attempting to influence legislation, and those whose lobbying activities were confined to influencing the public on legislation or issues—so-called grassroots lobbying.

But it was only under this limited construction that a majority of the Court would find the act constitutional. Sympathetic to the congressional dilemma, the majority observed that Congress was not trying to prohibit lobbying activities but merely wanted to find out

> who is being hired, who is putting up the money and how much. It acted in the same spirit and for a similar purpose in passing the Federal Corrupt Practices Act—to maintain the integrity of a basic governmental process. . . . Under these circumstances, we believe that Congress, at least within the bounds of the Act as we have construed it, is not constitutionally forbidden to require the disclosure of lobbying activities. To do so would be to deny Congress in large measure the power of self-protection.[64]

In dissent, Justices Douglas, Hugo L. Black, and Robert H. Jackson complained that to uphold the lobbying act, the Court had in essence rewritten it. The dissenters also contended that the majority's construction made the statute no less vague than it had been:

> The language of the Act is so broad that one who writes a letter or makes a speech or publishes an article or distributes literature or does many of the other things with which appellees are charged has no fair notice when he is close to the prohibited line. No construction we give it today will make clear retroactively the vague standards that confronted appellees when they did the acts now charged against them as criminal.[65]

Rules

The power of the House and Senate each to make its own rules for the conduct of its business was described by Justice David J. Brewer in 1892:

> The Constitution empowers each house to determine its rules of proceedings. It may not by its rules ignore constitutional restraints or violate fundamental rights, and there should be a reasonable relation between the mode or method of proceeding established by the rule and the result which is sought to be attained. But within these limitations all matters of method are open to the determination of the house, and it is no impeachment of the rule to say that some other way would be better, more accurate or even more just. It is no objection to the validity of the rule that a different one has been prescribed and in force for a length of time. The power to make rules is not one which once exer-

cised is exhausted. It is a continuous power, always subject to be exercised by the house, and within the limitations suggested, absolute and beyond the challenge of any other body or tribunal.[66]

Twice the Court has ruled that where a rule of the House or Senate conflicts with the rights of a private person, the rule must give way. In *United States v. Smith* (1932) the Court held that the Senate rules on confirming nominees to executive agencies could not be construed to allow the Senate to reconsider its confirmation of a person already sworn into the office.[67] The Court was careful to say that the question before it was how the rule should be interpreted and not its constitutionality.

In the second case, *Christoffel v. United States* (1949), a divided Court overturned the perjury conviction of a witness who claimed before a House committee he was not affiliated with the Communist Party.[68] The majority held that although there was a quorum of the committee present at the time the hearing began, there was no proof that the quorum still existed at the time the alleged perjury occurred. Therefore, it was not proved that the committee was a "competent tribunal" before which an erroneous statement would amount to perjury.

The four dissenters contended that, once established, a quorum was presumed to continue until a point of no quorum was raised.

Article I, Section 5, of the Constitution states that a majority of each house constitutes a quorum to do business.

In *United States v. Ballin* (1892) the Court held that in disputes over whether a majority was present, the *Congressional Record*, the official journal of the proceedings in each chamber, would be the unchallengeable proof of how many members were present.[69] This ruling upheld the most controversial of a new set of rules and procedures adopted by the House in 1890—the counting of present but nonvoting members to make a quorum.

In a second case decided in 1892, the Court upheld a federal statute that had been authenticated by both houses and signed into law by the president despite a showing in the *Congressional Record* that the enacted statute omitted a section that had been passed by both chambers.[70]

In the 1927 case of *McGrain v. Daugherty* the Court sustained the Senate's claim that it was a continuing body that did not need to reauthorize its committees with each new Congress. It may be true that the House must dissolve because its members "are all elected for the period of a single Congress," the Court said, "but it cannot well be the same with the Senate, which is a continuing body whose members are elected for a term of six years and so divided into classes that the seats of one-third only become vacant at the end of each Congress, two-thirds always continuing into the next Congress."[71]

The Court declared in 1993 that a Senate rule permitting evidence in impeachment proceedings to be heard by a fact-finding committee instead of the full Senate cannot be challenged in federal court.[72] The unanimous decision upheld a procedural shortcut that the Senate had used in the recent instances in which the impeachment process had been invoked to remove

three federal judges from office. The Constitution is clear: the "Senate shall have the sole Power to try all Impeachments."

Emphasizing the Senate's "sole power" to try impeachments, Chief Justice William H. Rehnquist said that this issue was beyond the reach of the Court: "The common sense meaning of the word 'sole' is that the Senate alone shall have authority to determine whether an individual should be acquitted or convicted." Rehnquist added that there was no evidence that the Framers thought the courts should play a role in the impeachment process. The decision upheld the 1989 removal of Walter L. Nixon, formerly the chief judge in Mississippi, who was impeached and convicted following a criminal conviction for perjury. The same procedure had been used in removing Judge Harry T. Claiborne of Nevada in 1986 and Judge Alcee Hastings of Florida in 1989.

NOTES

INTRODUCTION (PP. 71–75)

1. *The Federalist Papers*, with an Introduction by Clinton Rossiter (New York: Mentor, 1961), 467.

2. *Marbury v. Madison*, 1 Cr. 137 at 177 (1803).

3. Charles Warren, *The Supreme Court in United States History*, rev. ed., 2 vols. (Boston: Little, Brown, 1922, 1926), 1:16–17.

4. *Carter v. Carter Coal Co.*, 298 U.S. 238 at 332 (1936).

5. C. Herman Pritchett and Alan F. Westin, *The Third Branch of Government: Eight Cases in Constitutional Politics* (New York: Harcourt, Brace and World, 1963), 3.

6. Douglas W. Kmiec, "Supreme Court Restores the Constitutional Structure," *Chicago Tribune*, May 2, 1995.

7. Robert G. McCloskey, *The Modern Supreme Court*, ed. Sanford Levinson, 2d ed. (Chicago: University of Chicago Press, 1994), 127.

JUDICIAL REVIEW AND LEGISLATIVE POWER (PP. 76–87)

1. Max Farrand, *The Records of the Federal Convention of 1787*, rev. ed. (New Haven: Yale University Press, 1937), vol. 1, quoted in Library of Congress, Congressional Reference Service, *The Constitution of the United States of America: Analysis and Interpretation*, S. Doc. 92-82, 92d Cong., 2d sess. (Washington, D.C.: U.S. Government Printing Office, 1973), 670 n. 5. For summary of discussions on the topic, see Raoul Berger, *Congress v. The Supreme Court* (Cambridge: Harvard University Press, 1969), 37–143.

2. *Hayburn's Case*, 2 Dall. 409 (1792).

3. *Hylton v. United States*, 3 Dall. 171 (1796).

4. *Ware v. Hylton*, 3 Dall. 199 (1796).

5. Robert G. McCloskey, *The Modern Supreme Court*, ed. Sanford Levinson, 2d ed. (Chicago: University of Chicago Press, 1994), 25.

6. *Marbury v. Madison*, 1 Cr. 137 (1803).

7. Id. at 176–177.

8. Id. at 177–179.

9. Charles Warren, *The Supreme Court in United States History*, rev. ed., 2 vols. (Boston: Little, Brown, 1926), I: 232.

10. Albert J. Beveridge, *Life of Marshall*, 4 vols. (Boston: Houghton Mifflin, 1916–1919), III: 177, quoted by Robert H. Jackson in *The Struggle for Judicial Supremacy* (New York: Random House, Vintage Books, 1941), 28.

11. Robert E. Cushman and Robert F. Cushman, *Cases in Constitutional Law*, 3d ed. (New York: Appleton-Century-Crofts, 1968), 23.

12. Robert K. Carr, *The Supreme Court and Judicial Review* (New York: Farrar and Rinehart, 1942), 20.

13. Ibid.

14. Alfred H. Kelly and Winfred A. Harbison, *The American Constitution: Its Origins and Development,* 5th ed. (New York: Norton, 1976), 169.

15. *United States v. Fisher,* 2 Cr. 358 at 396 (1805).

16. *McCulloch v. Maryland,* 4 Wheat. 316 (1819).

17. Id. at 405.

18. Id. at 406.

19. Id. at 408.

20. Id. at 411.

21. Id. at 413–415.

22. Id. at 421.

23. Id. at 431.

24. McCloskey, *Modern Supreme Court,* 43.

25. R. Kent Newmyer, *The Supreme Court under Marshall and Taney* (New York: Crowell, 168), 45–46.

26. Joseph Story, *Commentaries on the Constitution of the United States* (Boston: Hilliard, Gray, 1833; reprint ed., 3 vols. New York: Da Capo Press, 1970), III: 124, Section 1251.

27. *American Insurance Company v. Canter,* 1 Pet. 511 (1828).

28. *United States v. Jones,* 109 U.S. 513 (1883); *Fong Yue Ting v. United States,* 149 U.S. 698 (1893); *United States v. Kamaga,* 118 U.S. 375 (1886).

29. *United States v. Curtiss-Wright Corp.,* 299 U.S. 304 at 316, 318, passim (1936).

30. *Sunshine Anthracite Coal Co. v. Adkins,* 310 U.S. 381 at 398 (1940); see also *Mistretta v. United States,* 109 S. Ct. 647 (1989).

31. *Wayman v. Southard,* 10 Wheat. 1 at 43 (1825).

32. Ibid.

33. *Buttfield v. Stranahan,* 192 U.S. 470 at 496 (1904).

34. Ibid.

35. *United States v. Grimaud,* 220 U.S. 506 (1911); *L. P. Steuart & Bro. v. Bowles,* 322 U.S. 398 (1944).

36. *Interstate Commerce Commission v. Brimson,* 154 U.S. 447 (1894).

37. *The Brig Aurora v. United States,* 7 Cr. 382 (1813).

38. *Field v. Clark,* 143 U.S. 649 (1892).

39. *J. W. Hampton Jr. & Co. v. United States,* 276 U.S. 394 at 405–406 (1928).

40. See, for example, *Fahey v. Mallonee,* 332 U.S. 245 (1947); *Arizona v. California,* 373 U.S. 546 at 583 (1963).

41. *Panama Refining Co. v. Ryan,* 293 U.S. 388 (1935).

42. C. Herman Pritchett, *The American Constitution* (New York: McGraw-Hill, 1959), 176.

43. *Panama Refining Co. v. Ryan,* 293 U.S. 388 at 418 (1935).

44. Id. at 440.

45. *Schechter Poultry Corp. v. United States,* 295 U.S. 495 at 542 (1935).

46. Id. at 551, 533, passim.

47. Alpheus T. Mason and William M. Beaney, *The Supreme Court in a Free Society* (Englewood Cliffs, N.J.: Prentice-Hall, 1969), 33.

48. *Opp Cotton Mills v. Administrator of Wage and Hours Division,* 312 U.S. 126 (1941).

49. *Schechter Poultry Corp. v. United States,* 295 U.S. 495 at 537 (1935).

50. *Carter v. Carter Coal Co.,* 298 U.S. 238 at 311 (1936).

51. *Currin v. Wallace,* 306 U.S. 1 (1939).

52. *Jackson v. Roby,* 109 U.S. 440 (1883); *Erhardt v. Boaro,* 113 U.S. 527 (1885); *Butte City Water Co. v. Baker,* 196 U.S. 119 (1905); *St. Louis, Iron Mountain & Southern Railway Co. v. Taylor,* 210 U.S. 281 (1908).

53. *Martin v. Mott,* 12 Wheat. 19 (1827).

54. *United States v. Curtiss-Wright Corp.,* 299 U.S. 304 (1936).

55. Id. at 319–320.

56. *United States v. Sharpnack,* 355 U.S. 286 at 294 (1958).

57. *Clark Distilling Co. v. Western Maryland Railway Co.,* 242 U.S. 311 (1917).

58. *Immigration and Naturalization Service v. Chadha,* 462 U.S. 919 at 951, 952 (1983).

59. Id. at 944.

60. Id. at 959.

61. Id. at 972.

62. Id. at 968.

63. Id. at 1002.

64. *Alaska Airlines v. Brock,* 480 U.S. 678 at 685 (1987).

65. Louis Fisher, *Constitutional Dialogues* (Princeton, N.J.: Princeton University Press, 1988), 224–229.

THE COMMERCE POWER (PP. 88–117)

1. *Gibbons v. Ogden,* 9 Wheat. 1 at 196 (1824).

2. *Missouri, Kansas & Texas Railway Co. of Texas v. May,* 194 U.S. 267 at 270 (1904).

3. Robert L. Stern, "The Commerce Clause and the National Economy," *Harvard Law Review* LIX (May, July 1946): 946.

4. Charles Warren, *The Making of the Constitution* (Boston: Little, Brown, 1928), 16.

5. *Gibbons v. Ogden,* 9 Wheat. 1 (1824).

6. Id. at 184.

7. Charles Warren, *The Supreme Court in United States History,* rev. ed., 2 vols. (Boston: Little, Brown, 1926), I: 597.

8. *Gibbons v. Ogden,* 9 Wheat. 1 at 9 (1824).

9. Id. at 76.

10. Id. at 189–190.

11. Id. at 194.

12. Id. at 194–195.

13. Id. at 196–197.

14. Id. at 227.

15. Warren, *Supreme Court in History,* I: 620–621.

16. Felix Frankfurter, *The Commerce Clause under Marshall, Taney and Waite* (Chapel Hill: University of North Carolina Press, 1937), 25.

17. *Brown v. Maryland,* 12 Wheat. 419 (1827).

18. *Willson v. Blackbird Creek Marsh Co.,* 2 Pet. 245 (1829).

19. See, for example, *New York v. Miln,* 11 Pet. 102 (1837); *The License Cases,* 5 How. 504 (1847); *The Passenger Cases,* 7 How. 283 (1849).

20. *Cooley v. Port Wardens of Philadelphia,* 12 How. 299 (1852).

21. *Willson v. Blackbird Creek Marsh Co.,* 2 Pet. 245 (1829).

22. *Pennsylvania v. Wheeling and Belmont Bridge Co.,* 13 How. 518 (1852).

23. *Pennsylvania v. Wheeling and Belmont Bridge Co.,* 18 How. 421 (1856).

24. *Veazie v. Moor,* 14 How. 568 (1852).

25. *Gilman v. City of Philadelphia,* 3 Wall. 713 (1866).

26. *The Daniel Ball,* 10 Wall. 557 at 565 (1871).

27. *United States v. Chandler-Dunbar Water Co.,* 229 U.S. 53 at 73 (1913).

28. *Arizona v. California,* 283 U.S. 423 at 455–456 (1931).

29. *Ashwander v. Tennessee Valley Authority,* 297 U.S. 288 (1936).

30. *Tennessee Electric Power Co. v. Tennessee Valley Authority,* 306 U.S. 118 (1939).

31. *United States v. Appalachian Electric Power Co.,* 311 U.S. 377 at 407 (1940).

32. *United States v. Trans-Missouri Freight Assn.,* 166 U.S. 290 (1897).

33. *Munn v. Illinois,* 94 U.S. 113 (1877).

34. *Wabash, St. Louis & Pacific Railway Co. v. Illinois,* 118 U.S. 557 at 577 (1886).

35. *Interstate Commerce Commission v. Brimson,* 154 U.S. 447 (1894).

36. *Interstate Commerce Commission v. Cincinnati, New Orleans & Texas Pacific Railway Co.,* 167 U.S. 479 at 494–495, passim (1897).

37. Id. at 501.

38. *Interstate Commerce Commission v. Alabama-Midland Railway Co.,* 168 U.S. 144 (1897).

39. *Illinois Central Railroad Co. v. Interstate Commerce Commission,* 206 U.S. 41 (1907).

40. *Interstate Commerce Commission v. Chicago, Rock Island and Pacific Railway Co.,* 218 U.S. 88 at 108 (1910).

41. *United States v. Atchison, Topeka and Santa Fe Railroad Co.,* 234 U.S. 476 at 486 (1914).

42. Loren P. Beth, *The Development of the American Constitution, 1877–1917* (New York: Harper & Row, Harper Torchbooks, 1971), 151.

43. *Minnesota Rate Cases,* 230 U.S. 252 at 399 (1913).

44. *Shreveport Rate Cases*, 234 U.S. 342 at 351–352 (1914).

45. *Railroad Commissioner of Wisconsin v. Chicago, Burlington & Quincy Railroad Co.*, 257 U.S. 563 at 589–590 (1922).

46. *Dayton-Goose Creek Railway Co. v. United States*, 263 U.S. 456 (1924).

47. *Adair v. United States*, 208 U.S. 161 at 172, 179, passim (1908).

48. Id. at 191.

49. *First Employers' Liability Cases*, 207 U.S. 463 (1908).

50. *Second Employers' Liability Cases*, 223 U.S. 1 (1912).

51. *Pennsylvania Railroad Company v. U.S. Railroad Labor Board*, 261 U.S. 72 (1923); *Pennsylvania Railroad System and Allied Lines Federation No. 90 v. Pennsylvania Railroad Company*, 267 U.S. 203 (1925).

52. *Texas & New Orleans Railroad Co. v. Brotherhood of Railway & Steamship Clerks*, 281 U.S. 548 at 571 (1930).

53. *Southern Railway Co. v. United States*, 222 U.S. 20 (1911).

54. *Baltimore & Ohio Railroad Co. v. Interstate Commerce Commission*, 221 U.S. 612 at 619 (1911).

55. *Wilson v. New*, 243 U.S. 332 (1917).

56. Id. at 350.

57. *Railroad Retirement Board v. Alton Railroad Co.*, 295 U.S. 330 at 368 (1935).

58. Id. at 384.

59. *Pipe Line Cases*, 234 U.S. 548 at 559, 561, passim (1914).

60. *Public Utilities Commission of Rhode Island v. Attleboro Steam & Electric Co.*, 273 U.S. 83 (1927); *Federal Power Commission v. Natural Gas Pipeline Co.*, 315 U.S. 575 (1942).

61. *Pensacola Telegraph Co. v. Western Union Telegraph Co.*, 96 U.S. 1 (1878).

62. *Federal Radio Commission v. Nelson Bros.*, 289 U.S. 266 at 279 (1933).

63. *Veazie v. Moor*, 14 How. 568 at 574 (1852).

64. *Kidd v. Pearson*, 128 U.S. 1 at 20 (1888).

65. *United States v. E. C. Knight Co.*, 156 U.S. 1 (1895).

66. Id. at 12.

67. Id. at 13.

68. Id. at 16.

69. Id. at 43.

70. *Mandeville Island Farms v. American Crystal Sugar Co.*, 334 U.S. 219 at 230 (1948).

71. *United States v. Trans-Missouri Freight Assn.*, 166 U.S. 290 (1897); *United States v. Joint Traffic Assn.*, 171 U.S. 506 (1898).

72. *Addystone Pipe & Steel Co. v. United States*, 175 U.S. 211 at 241 (1899).

73. *Northern Securities Company v. United States*, 193 U.S. 197 at 327 (1904).

74. Id. at 331.

75. Id. at 333.

76. *Swift & Co. v. United States*, 196 U.S. 375 (1905).

77. Id. at 396–399, passim.

78. *Board of Trade of Chicago v. Olsen*, 262 U.S. 1 at 35 (1923).

79. *Stafford v. Wallace*, 258 U.S. 495 at 518 (1922).

80. *Board of Trade of Chicago v. Olsen*, 262 U.S. 1 (1923), overturning *Hill v. Wallace*, 259 U.S. 44 (1922).

81. *Lemke v. Farmers Grain Co.*, 258 U.S. 50 (1922); see also *Eureka Pipeline Co. v. Hallanan*, 257 U.S. 265 (1921); *United Fuel Gas Co. v. Hallanan*, 257 U.S. 277 (1921); *Western Union Telegraph Co. v. Foster*, 247 U.S. 105 (1918).

82. *United States v. Trans-Missouri Freight Assn.*, 166 U.S. 290 at 328 (1897).

83. Id. at 344.

84. *Standard Oil Co. v. United States*, 221 U.S. 1 at 60 (1911).

85. Id. at 103, 104–105, passim.

86. *United States v. American Tobacco Co.*, 221 U.S. 106 at 179 (1911).

87. *United States v. Winslow*, 227 U.S. 202 (1913).

88. *United States v. United States Steel Corp.*, 251 U.S. 417 (1920).

89. *Chicago Board of Trade v. United States*, 246 U.S. 231 at 238 (1918).

90. *In re Debs*, 158 U.S. 564 at 600 (1895).

91. *Loewe v. Lawlor*, 208 U.S. 274 at 293–294 (1908).

92. Id. at 301.

93. *Duplex Printing Press Co. v. Deering*, 254 U.S. 443 at 469 (1921).

94. *Coronado Coal Co. v. United Mine Workers*, 268 U.S. 295 (1925); *Bedford Cut Stone Co. v. Journeymen Stone Cutters' Assn.*, 274 U.S. 37 (1927).

95. *Lauf v. E. G. Shinner & Co.*, 303 U.S. 315 (1938).

96. *New Negro Alliance v. Sanitary Grocery Co.*, 303 U.S. 552 (1938); *Brotherhood of Railroad Trainmen v. Chicago River and Indiana Railroad Co.*, 353 U.S. 30 (1957); *Boys Market v. Retail Clerks Union*, 398 U.S. 235 (1970).

97. *United States v. Hutcheson*, 312 U.S. 219 (1941).

98. *Allen Bradley Co. v. Local Union No. 3*, 325 U.S. 797 (1945).

99. *Hunt v. Crumboch*, 325 U.S. 821 (1945).

100. Robert K. Carr, *The Supreme Court and Judicial Review* (New York: Farrar and Rinehart, 1942), 108.

101. *United States v. DeWitt*, 9 Wall. 41 at 45 (1870).

102. Id. at 44.

103. *Reid v. Colorado*, 187 U.S. 137 (1902).

104. *Champion v. Ames*, 188 U.S. 321 (1903).

105. Id. at 357.

106. Id. at 355.

107. Id. at 358.

108. Warren, *Supreme Court in History*, II: 735–736.

109. *Hipolite Egg Co. v. United States*, 220 U.S. 45 (1911); *Hoke v. United States*, 227 U.S. 308 (1913); *Southern Railway Co. v. United States*, 222 U.S. 20 (1911); *Baltimore & Ohio Railroad Co. v. Interstate Commerce Commission*, 221 U.S. 612 (1911).

110. *Hammer v. Dagenhart*, 247 U.S. 251 (1918).

111. Id. at 268–269.

112. Id. at 271.

113. Id. at 271–272.

114. Id. at 272.

115. Id. at 276.

116. Id. at 277.

117. Id. at 279–280.

118. Id. at 280.

119. Id. at 281.

120. *Bailey v. Drexel Furniture Co.*, 259 U.S. 20 (1922).

121. *United States v. Darby Lumber Co.*, 312 U.S. 100 (1941).

122. *Pittsburgh Melting Co. v. Totten*, 248 U.S. 1 (1918).

123. *Brooks v. United States*, 267 U.S. 432 (1925); *Gooch v. United States*, 297 U.S. 124 (1936); *Kentucky Whip & Collar Co. v. Illinois Central Railroad Co.*, 299 U.S. 334 (1937).

124. *Brooks v. United States*, 267 U.S. 432 at 436–437 (1925).

125. *Perez v. United States*, 401 U.S. 146 (1971).

126. *Panama Refining Co. v. Ryan*, 293 U.S. 388 (1935).

127. *Schechter Poultry Corp. v. United States*, 295 U.S. 495 (1935).

128. Id. at 543.

129. Id. at 546.

130. Id. at 549.

131. Carr, *Supreme Court and Judicial Review*, 118–122.

132. *Schechter Poultry Corp. v. United States*, 295 U.S. 495 at 554 (1935).

133. *Carter v. Carter Coal Co.*, 298 U.S. 238 (1936).

134. Id. at 307–308.

135. Id. at 309.

136. Ibid.

137. Id. at 317–318.

138. Alfred H. Kelly and Winfred A. Harbison, *The American Constitution: Its Origins and Development*, 5th ed. (New York: Norton, 1976), 707.

139. *Carter v. Carter Coal Co.*, 298 U.S. 238 at 328 (1936).

140. Id. at 331–332.

141. *National Labor Relations Board v. Jones & Laughlin Steel Corp.*, 301 U.S. 1 (1937).

142. Id. at 41–42.

143. Id. at 77.

144. Id. at 78.

145. *National Labor Relations Board v. Fruehauf Trailer Co.*, 301 U.S. 49 (1937); *National Labor Relations Board v. Friedman-Harry Marks Clothing Co.*, 301 U.S. 58 (1937).

146. *Associated Press v. National Labor Relations Board*, 301 U.S. 103 (1937).

147. *Washington, Virginia & Maryland Coach Co. v. National Labor Relations Board*, 301 U.S. 142 (1937).

148. *Santa Cruz Fruit Packing Co. v. National Labor Relations Board*, 303 U.S. 453 at 469 (1938).

149. *Consolidated Edison v. National Labor Relations Board*, 305 U.S. 197 at 220 (1938).

150. *National Labor Relations Board v. Fainblatt*, 306 U.S. 601 at 606 (1939).

151. *West Coast Hotel v. Parrish*, 300 U.S. 379 (1937); *Morehead v. New York ex rel. Tipaldo*, 298 U.S. 587 (1936); *Adkins v. Children's Hospital*, 261 U.S. 525 (1923); *Bunting v. Oregon*, 243 U.S. 426 (1917).

152. *United States v. Darby Lumber Co.*, 312 U.S. 100 (1941).

153. Id. at 113, 115, passim.

154. Id. at 116–117.

155. Id. at 124.

156. *A. B. Kirschbaum v. Walling*, 316 U.S. 517 (1942).

157. *Warren-Bradshaw Co. v. Hall*, 317 U.S. 88 (1942); *Walton v. Southern Package Corporation*, 320 U.S. 540 (1944); *Borden v. Borella*, 325 U.S. 679 (1945).

158. *Walling v. Jacksonville Paper Co.*, 317 U.S. 564 (1943).

159. *10 East 40th St. Bldg. v. Callus*, 325 U.S. 578 (1945).

160. Carr, *Supreme Court and Judicial Review*, 135.

161. *Mulford v. Smith*, 307 U.S. 38 at 47 (1939).

162. *United States v. Rock Royal Cooperative*, 307 U.S. 533 (1939); *H. P. Hood & Sons v. United States*, 307 U.S. 588 (1939); *United States v. Wrightwood Dairy Co.*, 315 U.S. 110 (1942).

163. *United States v. Wrightwood Dairy Co.*, 315 U.S. 110 at 118–119 (1942).

164. *Wickard v. Filburn*, 317 U.S. 111 (1942).

165. Quoted in Alpheus T. Mason and William M. Beaney, *The Supreme Court in a Free Society* (Englewood Cliffs, N.J.: Prentice-Hall, 1959), 98.

166. *Wickard v. Filburn*, 317 U.S. 111 at 124–125 (1942).

167. Id. at 128–129.

168. C. Herman Pritchett, *The American Constitution*, 3d ed. (New York: McGraw-Hill, 1977), 198.

169. *Civil Rights Cases*, 109 U.S. 3 (1883).

170. Quoted in C. Herman Pritchett, *The American Constitution*, 1st ed. (New York: McGraw-Hill, 1959), 604.

171. *Hall v. DeCuir*, 95 U.S. 485 (1878).

172. *Louisville, New Orleans & Texas Railway Co. v. Mississippi*, 133 U.S. 587 (1890).

173. *Plessy v. Ferguson*, 163 U.S. 537 (1896).

174. *Morgan v. Virginia*, 328 U.S. 373 (1946).

175. *Henderson v. United States*, 339 U.S. 816 (1950).

176. *Heart of Atlanta Motel v. United States*, 379 U.S. 241 (1964).

177. Id. at 258.

178. Id. at 257.

179. *Katzenbach v. McClung*, 379 U.S. 294 (1964).

180. *Daniel v. Paul*, 395 U.S. 298 (1969).

181. *Paul v. Virginia*, 8 Wall. 168 (1869).

182. *United States v. South-Eastern Underwriters Association*, 322 U.S. 533 at 553 (1944).

183. *Prudential Insurance Co. v. Benjamin*, 328 U.S. 408 (1946).

184. *National League of Cities v. Usery*, 426 U.S. 833 (1976).

185. *Maryland v. Wirtz*, 392 U.S. 183 (1968).

186. *National League of Cities v. Usery*, 426 U.S. 833 at 845 (1976).

187. Id. at 855.

188. Id. at 880.

189. Id. at 880.

190 U.S. Congress, Library of Congress, Congressional Research Service, *The Constitution of the United States: Analysis and Interpretation*, 1976 supplement (Washington, D.C.: U.S. Government Printing Office, 1977), S.10.

191. *Garcia v. San Antonio Metropolitan Transit Authority*, 469 U.S. 528 at 556–557 (1985).

192. *United States v. Lopez*, 115 S. Ct. 1624 (1995).

193. Ibid.

194. Ibid.

195. Ibid.

196. Ibid.

FISCAL AND MONETARY POWERS (PP. 118–133)

1. C. Herman Pritchett, *The American Constitution*, 3d ed. (New York: McGraw-Hill, 1977), 167.

2. *Hylton v. United States*, 3 Dall. 171 (1796).

3. Alpheus T. Mason and William M. Beaney, *The Supreme Court in a Free Society* (Englewood Cliffs, N.J.: Prentice-Hall, 1959), 129.

4. See, for example, *Veazie Bank v. Fenno*, 8 Wall. 533 (1869); *Schley v. Rew*, 23 Wall. 331 (1875).

5. *Springer v. United States*, 102 U.S. 586 (1881).

6. Carl B. Swisher, *American Constitutional Development*, 2d ed. (Cambridge, Mass.: Riverside Press, 1954), 448.

7. Quoted by Mason and Beaney in *Supreme Court in a Free Society*, 131.

8. *Pollock v. Farmers' Loan and Trust Co.*, 157 U.S. 429 (1895).

9. *Pollock v. Farmers' Loan and Trust Co.*, 158 U.S. 601 (1895).

10. Id. at 637.

11. Ibid.

12. Ibid.

13. *Pollock v. Farmers' Loan and Trust Co.*, 157 U.S. 429 at 607 (1895).

14. *Pollock v. Farmers' Loan and Trust Co.*, 158 U.S. 601 at 685 (1895).

15. Editor's Notes, *American Law Review*, May–June 1895, 472; cited by Leo Pfeffer in *This Honorable Court, A History of the United States Supreme Court* (Boston: Beacon Press, 1965), 222.

16. Pritchett, *American Constitution*, 169.

17. *Nicol v. Ames*, 173 U.S. 509 (1899); *Knowlton v. Moore*, 178 U.S. 41 (1900); *Patton v. Brady*, 184 U.S. 608 (1902); *Thomas v. United States*, 192 U.S. 363 (1904).

18. *Spreckles Sugar Refining Co. v. McClain*, 192 U.S. 397 (1904).

19. *Flint v. Stone Tracy Co.*, 220 U.S. 107 (1911).

20. *Brushaber v. Union Pacific Railroad Co.*, 240 U.S. 1 (1916); *Stanton v. Baltic Mining Co.*, 240 U.S. 103 (1916); *Tyee Realty Co. v. Anderson*, 240 U.S. 115 (1916).

21. *Stanton v. Baltic Mining Co.*, 240 U.S. 103 at 112 (1916).

22. *Eisner v. Macomber*, 252 U.S. 189 (1920).

23. *Head Money Cases*, 112 U.S. 580 (1884).

24. *Knowlton v. Moore*, 178 U.S. 41 (1900).

25. *Florida v. Mellon*, 273 U.S. 12 (1927); *United States v. Ptasynski*, 462 U.S. 74 (1983).

26. *J. W. Hampton Jr. & Co. v. United States*, 276 U.S. 394 at 412 (1928).

27. *Veazie Bank v. Fenno*, 8 Wall. 533 (1869).

28. *Head Money Cases*, 112 U.S. 580 (1884).

29. *Sunshine Anthracite Coal Co. v. Adkins*, 310 U.S. 381 at 393 (1940).

30. *Carter v. Carter Coal Co.*, 298 U.S. 238 (1936).

31. *McCray v. United States*, 195 U.S. 27 (1904).

32. Id. at 56.

33. *United States v. Doremus*, 249 U.S. 86 at 94 (1919).

34. *Bailey v. Drexel Furniture Co.*, 259 U.S. 20 (1922).

35. Id. at 38.

36. Ibid.

37. Id. at 43.

38. *Hill v. Wallace*, 259 U.S. 44 at 66–67 (1922).

39. *Board of Trade of Chicago v. Olsen*, 262 U.S. 1 (1923).

40. *United States v. Constantine*, 296 U.S. 287 (1935).

41. *Carter v. Carter Coal Co.*, 298 U.S. 238 (1936).

42. *United States v. Butler*, 297 U.S. 1 (1936).

43. *Sonzinsky v. United States*, 300 U.S. 506 at 513–514 (1937).

44. *United States v. Sanchez*, 340 U.S. 42 (1950); *United States v. Kahriger*, 345 U.S. 22 (1953).

45. *Marchetti v. United States*, 390 U.S. 39 (1968); *Grosso v. United States*, 390 U.S. 62 (1968); *Haynes v. United States*, 390 U.S. 85 (1968); *Leary v. United States*, 395 U.S. 6 (1969).

46. *McCulloch v. Maryland*, 4 Wheat. 316 at 431 (1819).

47. *Dobbins v. Erie County*, 16 Pet. 435 (1842).

48. *Collector v. Day*, 11 Wall. 113 (1871).

49. *Weston v. City Council of Charleston*, 2 Pet. 449 (1829); *Van Brocklin v. Tennessee*, 117 U.S. 151 (1886).

50. *Pollock v. Farmers' Loan & Trust Co.*, 157 U.S. 429 (1895).

51. *Indian Motorcycle Co. v. United States*, 283 U.S. 570 (1931).

52. *South Carolina v. United States*, 199 U.S. 437 (1905); *Helvering v. Gerhardt*, 304 U.S. 405 (1938); *Graves v. New York ex rel. O'Keefe*, 306 U.S. 466 (1939).

53. *South Carolina v. Baker*, 485 U.S. 505 (1988).

54. *Clallam County v. United States*, 263 U.S. 341 (1923).

55. *Maricopa County v. Valley Bank*, 318 U.S. 357 (1943); *Pittman v. Home Owners' Corporation*, 308 U.S. 21 (1939); *McCulloch v. Maryland*, 4 Wheat. 316 (1819); *Thomson v. Union Pacific Railroad Co.*, 9 Wall. 579 (1870); *Union Pacific Railroad Co. v. Peniston*, 18 Wall. 5 (1873).

56. *Northwestern Mutual Life Insurance Co. v. Wisconsin*, 275 U.S. 136 (1927); *Miller v. Milwaukee*, 272 U.S. 173 (1927); *Hibernia Savings Society v. San Francisco*, 200 U.S. 310 (1906); *Plummer v. Coler*, 178 U.S. 115 (1900); *Blodgett v. Silberman*, 277 U.S. 1 (1928); *Rockford Life Insurance Co. v. Illinois Department of Revenue*, 482 U.S. 182 (1987).

57. *Alabama v. King and Boozer*, 314 U.S. 1 (1941); *James v. Dravo Contracting Co.*, 302 U.S. 134 (1937); *United States v. Allegheny County*, 322 U.S. 174 (1944); *United States and Borg-Warner Corp. v. City of Detroit*, 355 U.S. 466 (1958); *United States v. Township of Muskegan*, 355 U.S. 484 (1958); *United States v. New Mexico*, 455 U.S. 720 (1982).

58. *Frothingham v. Mellon, Massachusetts v. Mellon*, 262 U.S. 447 (1923) at 487.

59. Id. at 485–486.

60. *Alabama Power Co. v. Ickes*, 302 U.S. 464 (1938); *Tennessee Electric Power Co. v. Tennessee Valley Authority*, 306 U.S. 118 (1939).

61. *Frothingham v. Mellon, Massachusetts v. Mellon*, 262 U.S. 447 (1923).

62. *Oklahoma v. Civil Service Commission*, 330 U.S. 127 at 143 (1947).

63. *South Dakota v. Dole*, 483 U.S. 203 (1987).

64. *The Federalist Papers*, with an Introduction by Clinton Rossiter (New York: Mentor, 1961), No. 41, 263.

65. *United States v. Butler*, 297 U.S. 1 (1936).

66. Id. at 61.

67. Ibid.

68. Id. at 66.

69. Id. at 68.

70. Id. at 71.

71. Id. at 74–75.

72. Id. at 85.

73. *Steward Machine Co. v. Davis*, 301 U.S. 548 (1937).

74. Id. at 581.

75. Id. at 586–587.

76. Id. at 589–590.

77. *Helvering v. Davis*, 301 U.S. 619 (1937).

78. Id. at 640.

79. Id. at 645.

80. *McCulloch v. Maryland*, 4 Wheat. 316 (1819).

81. *Veazie Bank v. Fenno*, 8 Wall. 533 (1869).

82. *Bronson v. Rodes*, 7 Wall. 229 (1869).

83. *Roosevelt v. Meyer*, 1 Wall. 512 (1863).

84. Robert G. McCloskey, *The Modern Supreme Court*, ed. Sanford Levinson, 2d ed. (Chicago: University of Chicago Press, 1994), 75.

85. *Hepburn v. Griswold*, 8 Wall. 603 (1870).

86. Charles Warren, *The Supreme Court in United States History*, rev. ed., 2 vols. (Boston: Little, Brown, 1926), II: 499.

87. Ibid., 401.

88. *Hepburn v. Griswold*, 8 Wall. 603 at 622 (1870).

89. Id. at 621.

90. Id.

91. Id. at 623.

92. *Knox v. Lee, Parker v. Davis*, 12 Wall. 457 at 529–530 (1871).

93. *Knox v. Lee, Parker v. Davis*, 12 Wall. 457 (1871).

94. Id. at 542.

95. Charles Evans Hughes, *The Supreme Court of the United States* (New York: Columbia University Press, 1928), 52–53.

96. *Nation*, April 27, 1871, quoted by Warren, in *The Supreme Court in U.S. History*, II: 525–526.

97. *Julliard v. Greenman*, 110 U.S. 421 (1884).

98. *Trebilcock v. Wilson*, 12 Wall. 687 (1872).

99. *Norman v. Baltimore & Ohio Railroad Co., United States v. Bankers Trust Co.* (*The Gold Clause Cases*), 294 U.S. 240 at 316 (1935).

100. *Nortz v. United States* (*The Gold Clause Cases*), 294 U.S. 317 (1935).

101. *Perry v. United States* (*The Gold Clause Cases*), 294 U.S. 330 at 351 (1935).

102. Alfred H. Kelly and Winfred A. Harbison, *The American Constitution: Its Origins and Development*, 7th ed. (New York: Norton, 1991), 696.

103. *The Gold Clause Cases*, 294 U.S. 240 at 362 (1935).

THE POWER OVER FOREIGN AFFAIRS
(PP. 134–141)

1. *McCulloch v. Maryland*, 4 Wheat. 316 (1819).

2. *United States v. Curtiss-Wright Export Corp.*, 299 U.S. 304 (1936).

3. *The Federalist Papers*, with an Introduction by Clinton Rossiter (New York: Mentor, 1961), No. 23, 152.

4. Robert E. Cushman, *Leading Constitutional Decisions*, 12th ed. (New York: Appleton-Century-Crofts, 1963), 373.

5. *Woods v. Miller Co.*, 333 U.S. 138 at 147 (1948).

6. *Bas v. Tingy*, 4 Dall. 37 at 43 (1800).

7. *Prize Cases*, 2 Black 635 (1863).

8. Id. at 666.

9. Id. at 670–671.

10. See, for example, *Wilson v. Shaw*, 204 U.S. 24 (1907); *Brooks v. Dewar*, 313 U.S. 354 (1941); *Isbrandtsen-Moller Co. v. United States*, 300 U.S. 139 (1937).

11. *Fleming v. Mohawk Wrecking Co.*, 331 U.S. 111 at 116 (1947).

12. Senate Foreign Relations Committee, *Hearings on War Power Legislation*, 91st Cong., 1st sess., 1971 (Washington, D.C.: U.S. Government Printing Office, 1972), 254.

13. See, for example, *Luftig v. McNamara*, 373 F. 2d 664 (D.C. Cir.), cert. denied, 387 U.S. 945 (1967); *Mora v. McNamara*, 387 F. 2d 862 (D.C. Cir.), cert. denied, 389 U.S. 934 (1967).

14. *Mora v. McNamara*, 389 U.S. 934 at 935 (1967).

15. Id. at 939, quoting from *Nixon v. Herndon*, 273 U.S. 536 at 540 (1927).

16. *Ludecke v. Watkins*, 335 U.S. 160 at 168–169 (1948).

17. *Selective Service Draft Law Cases*, 245 U.S. 366 at 378 (1918).

18. *Butler v. Perry*, 240 U.S. 328 at 333 (1916).

19. See, for example, *Hart v. United States*, 382 F. 2d 1020 (C.A. 3, 1967), cert. denied, 391 U.S. 956 (1968), 391 U.S. 936 (1968).

20. *Rostker v. Goldberg*, 453 U.S. 57 (1981).

21. *Ex parte Vallandigham*, 1 Wall. 243 (1864); *Ex parte Milligan*, 4 Wall. 2 (1866); *Ex parte Yerger*, 8 Wall. 85 (1869); *Ex parte Reed*, 100 U.S. 13 (1879).

22. *Ex parte Milligan*, 4 Wall. 2 (1866); *Ex parte Quirin*, 317 U.S. 1 (1942).

23. *United States ex rel Toth v. Quarles*, 350 U.S. 11 (1955).

24. *O'Callahan v. Parker*, 395 U.S. 258 (1969).

25. *Relford v. Commandant*, 401 U.S. 355 (1971).

26. *Solorio v. United States*, 483 U.S. 435 (1987).

27. *Middendorf v. Henry*, 425 U.S. 25 (1976).

28. *Weiss v. United States*, 114 S. Ct. 752 (1994).

29. *Hepburn v. Griswold*, 8 Wall. 603 at 617 (1870).

30. *Knox v. Lee, Parker v. Davis*, 12 Wall. 457 at 543 (1871).

31. *United States v. L. Cohen Grocery Co.*, 255 U.S. 81 at 88 (1921).

32. *Matthew Addy Co. v. United States*, 264 U.S. 239 (1924); Carl B. Swisher, *American Constitutional Development*, 2d ed. (Cambridge, Mass.: Houghton Mifflin, Riverside Press, 1954), 638, n. 51.

33. *Northern Pacific Railway Co. v. North Dakota ex rel Langer*, 250 U.S. 135 (1919).

34. *Yakus v. United States*, 321 U.S. 414 (1944).

35. Id. at 424.

36. Id. at 426.

37. *Lichter v. United States*, 334 U.S. 742 at 765–766 (1948).

38. Id. at 778–780.

39. *Stewart v. Kahn*, 11 Wall. 493 at 507 (1871).

40. *Block v. Hirsh*, 256 U.S. 135 (1921).

41. *Chastleton Corp. v. Sinclair*, 264 U.S. 543 (1924).

42. Id. at 547–548.

43. *Hamilton v. Kentucky Distilleries and Warehouse Co.*, 251 U.S. 146 (1919); *Ruppert v. Caffey*, 251 U.S. 264 (1920).

44. *Woods v. Miller Co.*, 333 U.S. 138 (1948).

45. Id. at 143–144.

46. Id. at 147.

47. *United States v. Curtiss-Wright Export Corp.*, 299 U.S. 304 at 319 (1936).

48. *Haver v. Yaker*, 9 Wall. 32 at 35 (1869).

49. *Fourteen Diamond Rings v. United States*, 183 U.S. 176 (1901); as to House efforts to assert some role in treaty ratification, note *Edwards v. Carter*, 1978, decided by the U.S. Court of Appeals for the District of Columbia.

50. *Foster v. Neilson*, 2 Pet. 253 at 314 (1829).

51. *Missouri v. Holland*, 252 U.S. 416 (1920).

52. Id. at 433.

53. Henry Steele Commager, *Documents of American History*, 9th ed., 2 vols. (Englewood Cliffs, N.J.: Prentice-Hall, 1973), II: 163.

54. Alfred H. Kelly and Winfred A. Harbison, *The American Constitution; Its Origins and Development*, 7th ed. (New York: Norton, 1991), 644.

55. *The Cherokee Tobacco*, 11 Wall. 616 (1871); *Foster v. Neilson*, 2 Pet. 253 (1829).

56. *Head Money Cases*, 112 U.S. 580 at 599 (1884).

57. Louis Henkin, *Foreign Affairs and the Constitution* (New York: Norton, Norton Library, 1975), 76–77.

58. *J. W. Hampton Jr. & Co. v. United States*, 276 U.S. 394 (1928).

59. *American Insurance Co. v. Canter*, 1 Pet. 511 (1828); *United States v. Jones*, 109 U.S. 513 (1883).

60. *Downes v. Bidwell*, 182 U.S. 244 (1901); *Darr v. United States*, 195 U.S. 138 (1904).

61. *United States v. Gratiot*, 14 Pet. 526 (1840).

THE POWER TO ADMIT STATES, GOVERN TERRITORIES, AND GRANT CITIZENSHIP (PP. 142–156)

1. C. Herman Pritchett, *The American Constitution*, 3d ed. (New York: McGraw-Hill, 1977), 55.

2. *Pollard v. Hagan*, 3 How. 212 at 224 (1845).

3. *Escanaba Co. v. Chicago*, 107 U.S. 678 at 689 (1883).

4. *Coyle v. Smith*, 221 U.S. 559 at 567 (1911).

5. *United States v. Texas*, 339 U.S. 707 at 718 (1950).

6. Id., at 719–720.

7. *Stearns v. Minnesota*, 179 U.S. 223 at 245 (1900).

8. *American Insurance Co. v. Canter*, 1 Pet. 511 at 542 (1828).

9. *United States v. Jones*, 109 U.S. 513 (1883).

10. *First National Bank v. Yankton County*, 101 U.S. 129 at 133 (1880).

11. *Simms v. Simms*, 175 U.S. 162 (1899).

12. *Binns v. United States*, 194 U.S. 486 (1904).

13. *Scott v. Sandford*, 19 How. 393 (1857).

14. Edward S. Corwin, *The Doctrine of Judicial Review, Its Legal and Historical Basis and Other Essays* (Princeton, N.J.: Princeton University Press, 1914; reprint ed., Gloucester, Mass.: Peter Smith, 1963), 157.

15. General sources for historical background of the Dred Scott case include Alfred H. Kelly and Winfred A. Harbison, *The American Constitution: Its Origins and Development*, 7th ed. (New York: Norton, 1991), 234–256, 333–367; Carl B. Swisher, *History of the Supreme Court of the United States*: vol. 5, *The Taney Period, 1836–64* (New York: Macmillan, 1974), 528–652; Bruce Catton, "The Dred Scott Case," in *Quarrels That Have Shaped the Constitution*, ed. John A. Garraty and Don Fehrenbacher, rev. ed. (New York: Harper and Row, 1987), 87.

16. *Strader v. Graham*, 10 How. 82 (1851).

17. Id. at 93.

18. Carl B. Swisher, *American Constitutional Development*, 2d ed. (Cambridge: Houghton Mifflin, Riverside Press, 1954), 588–589.

19. James D. Richardson, ed., *A Compilation of the Messages and Papers of the Presidents* (New York: Bureau of National Literature, 1927), vol. 7, 2962.

20. *Scott v. Sandford*, 19 How. 393 at 404 (1857).

21. Id. at 407.

22. Id. at 410.

23. Id. at 405.

24. Id. at 410.

25. Id. at 425.

26. Id. at 436.

27. Id. at 449.

28. Id. at 450.

29. Id. at 452.

30. Catton, "Dred Scott," 85.

31. Quoted by Charles Warren in *The Supreme Court in United States History*, rev. ed., 2 vols. (Boston: Little, Brown, 1922, 1926), II: 304.

32. Swisher, *American Constitutional Development*, 248.

33. Corwin, *Doctrine of Judicial Review*, 156.

34. Quoted by Warren in *Supreme Court in History*, II: 316.

35. *DeLima v. Bidwell*, 182 U.S. 1 (1901).

36. *Cross v. Harrison*, 16 How. 164 (1853).

37. *DeLima v. Bidwell*, 182 U.S. 1 at 187 (1901).

38. *Downes v. Bidwell*, 182 U.S. 244 (1901).

39. Id. at 306.

40. Id. at 307–308.

41. Id. at 339.

42. Id. at 380.

43. *Hawaii v. Mankichi*, 190 U.S. 197 at 216 (1903).

44. Id. at 223.

45. *Dorr v. United States*, 195 U.S. 138 at 143 (1904).

46. *Rasmussen v. United States*, 197 U.S. 516 (1905).

47. *Dowdell v. United States*, 221 U.S. 325 (1911).

48. *Perez v. Brownell*, 356 U.S. 44 at 64–65 (1958), Chief Justice Earl Warren dissenting.

49. *Scott v. Sandford*, 19 How. 393 at 406 (1857).

50. *United States v. Wong Kim Ark*, 169 U.S. 649 at 693 (1898); see also *Perkins v. Elg*, 307 U.S. 325 (1939).

51. *United States v. Macintosh*, 283 U.S. 605 at 615 (1931).

52. *Fong Yue Ting v. United States*, 149 U.S. 698 at 707, 713, passim (1893).

53. *Galvan v. Press*, 347 U.S. 522 (1954); *Berenyi v. District Director*, 385 U.S. 630 (1967), Communist Party membership; *Boutilier v. Immigration and Naturalization Service*, 387 U.S. 118 (1967), homosexuals.

54. *United States v. Schwimmer*, 279 U.S. 644 (1929).

55. *Girouard v. United States*, 328 U.S. 61 (1946), overturning *United States v. Schwimmer*, 279 U.S. 644 (1929); *United States v. Macintosh*, 283 U.S. 605 (1931); and *United States v. Bland*, 283 U.S. 636 (1931).

56. *Cohnstaedt v. Immigration and Naturalization Service*, 339 U.S. 901 (1950).

57. *Osborn v. Bank of United States*, 9 Wheat. 737 at 827 (1824).

58. *Johannessen v. United States,* 225 U.S. 227 at 241 (1912).

59. *Costello v. United States,* 365 U.S. 265 (1961).

60. *Luria v. United States,* 231 U.S. 9 (1913).

61. *Schneiderman v. United States,* 320 U.S. 118 (1943).

62. *Knauer v. United States,* 328 U.S. 654 (1946).

63. Id. at 675–677.

64. *Schneider v. Rusk,* 377 U.S. 163 (1964).

65. Id. at 165.

66. Id. at 168–169.

67. *MacKenzie v. Hare,* 239 U.S. 299 (1915).

68. *Savorgnan v. United States,* 338 U.S. 491 (1950).

69. *Perez v. Brownell,* 356 U.S. 44 (1958).

70. Id. at 58, note.

71. Id. at 77–78.

72. *Trop v. Dulles,* 356 U.S. 86 at 101 (1958).

73. *Kennedy v. Mendoza-Martinez,* 372 U.S. 144 at 165–166 (1963).

74. *Afroyim v. Rusk,* 387 U.S. 253 (1967).

75. Id. at 257.

76. Id. at 262.

77. Id. at 292–293.

78. *Rogers v. Bellei,* 401 U.S. 815 (1971).

79. Id. at 827.

80. Id. at 835.

81. Id. at 836–837.

THE POWER TO AMEND THE CONSTITUTION
(PP. 157–161)

1. Interview with David Huckabee of the Congressional Research Service, June 1996.

2. *Hollingsworth v. Virginia,* 3 Dall. 378 (1798).

3. *National Prohibition Cases,* 253 U.S. 350 (1920).

4. *Leser v. Garnett,* 258 U.S. 130 (1922).

5. *Hollingsworth v. Virginia,* 3 Dall. 378 at 381, note (1798).

6. *National Prohibition Cases,* 253 U.S. 350 (1920).

7. *Dillon v. Gloss,* 256 U.S. 368 (1921).

8. Id. at 375, 376.

9. *Coleman v. Miller,* 307 U.S. 433 (1939).

10. Id. at 459.

11. *United States v. Sprague,* 282 U.S. 716 (1931).

12. *Hawke v. Smith,* 253 U.S. 221 (1920).

13. *Leser v. Garnett,* 258 U.S. 130 (1922).

14. Id. at 137; see also *Hawke v. Smith,* 253 U.S. 221 at 230 (1920).

15. *Leser v. Garnett,* 258 U.S. 130 (1922).

16. *Coleman v. Miller,* 307 U.S. 433 at 450 (1939).

17. Robert E. Cushman and Robert F. Cushman, *Cases in Constitutional Law* (New York: Appleton-Century-Crofts, 1968), 8.

18. *Civil Rights Cases,* 109 U.S. 3 at 11 (1883).

19. Id. at 22.

20. Id. at 24.

21. *United States v. Reese,* 92 U.S. 214 (1876).

22. *South Carolina v. Katzenbach,* 383 U.S. 301 at 324 (1966).

23. *Katzenbach v. Morgan,* 384 U.S. 641 at 656 (1966).

24. Id. at 653.

25. *Jones v. Alfred H. Mayer Co.,* 392 U.S. 409 at 424 (1968).

26. Id. at 653.

27. *Griffin v. Breckenridge,* 403 U.S. 88 (1971).

28. *Runyon v. McCrary,* 427 U.S. 160 (1976).

29. *Fitzpatrick v. Bitzer,* 427 U.S. 445 at 456 (1976).

THE POWER TO INVESTIGATE (PP. 162–170)

1. For general information on St. Clair inquiry, see Marshall E. Dimock, *Congressional Investigating Committees* (Baltimore: Johns Hopkins University Press, 1929; reprint ed., New York: AMS Press Inc., 1971), 87–89; Congressional Quarterly, *Guide to Congress,* 4th ed. (Washington, D.C.: Congressional Quarterly, 1991), 234 .

2. Woodrow Wilson, *Congressional Government* (Cleveland: World Publishing, Meridian Books, 1965), 198.

3. *Watkins v. United States,* 354 U.S. 178 at 187 (1957).

4. *Anderson v. Dunn,* 6 Wheat. 204 at 228 (1821).

5. Id. at 231.

6. Interviews with the offices of the parliamentarians of the Senate and the House, September 18, 19, 1978.

7. *Kilbourn v. Thompson,* 103 U.S. 168 (1881).

8. Id. at 197.

9. *In re Chapman,* 166 U.S. 661 at 671–672 (1897).

10. *Jurney v. MacCracken,* 294 U.S. 125 (1935).

11. *Marshall v. Gordon,* 243 U.S. 521 (1917).

12. Id. at 542.

13. *Kilbourn v. Thompson,* 103 U.S. 168 at 190 (1881).

14. *In re Chapman,* 166 U.S. 661 (1897).

15. Id. at 669.

16. Id. at 670.

17. *McGrain v. Daugherty,* 273 U.S. 135 (1927).

18. Id. at 174.

19. Id. at 175.

20. Id. at 177–178.

21. Id. at 176.

22. *Sinclair v. United States,* 279 U.S. 263 at 295 (1929).

23. Id. at 296–297.

24. Quoted by August Raymond Ogden in *The Dies Committee* (Washington, D.C.: Catholic University Press, 1945), 44.

25. *Watkins v. United States,* 354 U.S. 178 at 195 (1957).

26. *United States v. Rumely,* 345 U.S. 41 (1953).

27. Id. at 47.

28. Id. at 46.

29. Id. at 57.

30. *Watkins v. United States,* 354 U.S. 178 (1957).

31. Quoted by Robert E. Cushman and Robert F. Cushman in *Cases in Constitutional Law,* 3d ed. (New York: Appleton-Century-Crofts, 1968), 112.

32. *Watkins v. United States,* 354 U.S. 178 at 198 (1957).

33. Id. at 200.

34. Id. at 205–206.

35. Id. at 208–209.

36. Id. at 214–215.

37. *Barenblatt v. United States,* 360 U.S. 109 (1959).

38. Id. at 117.

39. Id. at 126.

40. Ibid.

41. Id. at 127–129.

42. Id. at 134.

43. Id. at 143.

44. Id. at 144.

45. Id. at 166.

46. *Wilkinson v. United States,* 365 U.S. 399 (1961); *Braden v. United States,* 365 U.S. 431 (1961).

47. *Deutsch v. United States,* 367 U.S. 456 (1961).

48. *Russell v. United States,* 369 U.S. 749 (1962).

49. *Yellin v. United States,* 374 U.S. 109 (1963).

50. *Gojack v. United States,* 384 U.S. 702 at 715 (1966).

51. C. Herman Pritchett, *The American Constitution,* 3d ed. (New York: McGraw-Hill, 1977), 161.

52. *Blau v. United States,* 340 U.S. 159 (1950).

53. *Rogers v. United States,* 340 U.S. 367 at 374 (1951).

54. *Quinn v. United States,* 349 U.S. 155 at 162–163 (1955).

55. *Emspak v. United States,* 349 U.S. 190 at 195 (1955).

56. *Ullmann v. United States,* 350 U.S. 422 at 439 (1956).

57. Id. at 445.

58. *Reed v. County Commissioners of Delaware County, Pa.*, 277 U.S. 376 at 380 (1928).

59. *Barry v. United States ex rel. Cunningham*, 279 U.S. 597 at 613 (1929).

THE POWER OVER INTERNAL AFFAIRS

(PP. 171–183)

1. *The Federalist Papers*, with an Introduction by Clinton Rossiter (New York: Mentor Books, 1961), 371.

2. *Powell v. McCormack*, 395 U.S. 486 (1969).

3. Id. at 522.

4. *U.S. Term Limits Inc. v. Thornton*, 115 S. Ct. 1842 (1995).

5. Ibid.

6. Ibid.

7. *Congress A to Z: A Ready Reference Encyclopedia*, 2d ed. (Washington, D.C.: Congressional Quarterly, 1993), 464–465.

8. *In re Chapman*, 166 U.S. 661 at 669–670 (1897).

9. *Burman v. United States*, 202 U.S. 344 at 369 (1906).

10. *Kilbourn v. Thompson*, 103 U.S. 168 (1881).

11. *Powell v. McCormack*, 395 U.S. 486 (1969).

12. *Long v. Ansell*, 293 U.S. 76 (1934); *United States v. Cooper*, 4 Dall. 341 (C.C. Pa. 1800).

13. *Williamson v. United States*, 207 U.S. 425 (1908).

14. *United States v. Brewster*, 408 U.S. 501 at 507 (1972).

15. *Kilbourn v. Thompson*, 103 U.S. 168 at 204 (1881).

16. Ibid.

17. *Dombrowski v. Eastland*, 387 U.S. 82 (1967).

18. Id. at 85; also see *Powell v. McCormack*, 395 U.S. 486 at 505 (1969).

19. *Gravel v. United States*, 408 U.S. 606 (1972).

20. Id. at 616–617.

21. Id. at 626.

22. *Tenney v. Brandhove*, 341 U.S. 367 (1951).

23. Id. at 377.

24. Id. at 383.

25. *Doe v. McMillan*, 412 U.S. 306 at 324 (1973).

26. Id. at 315–316.

27. *Eastland v. United States Servicemen's Fund*, 421 U.S. 491 (1975).

28. Id. at 503.

29. Id. at 518.

30. *Hutchinson v. Proxmire*, 443 U.S. 111 (1979).

31. *United States v. Johnson*, 383 U.S. 169 (1966).

32. Id. at 180.

33. *United States v. Brewster*, 408 U.S. 501 at 516–517 (1972); see also *United States v. Helstoski* (1979).

34. Id. at 515–516.

35. Id. at 526.

36. Id. at 563.

37. *United States v. Dowdy*, 479 F. 2d 213 at 224 (1973); cert. denied, 414 U.S. 823 (1973).

38. *Ex parte Siebold*, 100 U.S. 371 at 383–384 (1880).

39. Id. at 388–389.

40. *Ex parte Yarbrough*, 110 U.S. 651 (1884); *United States v. Mosely*, 238 U.S. 383 (1915).

41. *Newberry v. United States*, 256 U.S. 232 at 250 (1921).

42. Ibid.

43. Id. at 257.

44. Id. at 280.

45. See Louisiana House election results, 1920–1942, in *Guide to U.S. Elections*, 3d ed. (Washington, D.C.: Congressional Quarterly, 1994), 1140–1195.

46. *United States v. Classic*, 313 U.S. 299 at 317 (1941).

47. *Burroughs and Cannon v. United States*, 290 U.S. 534 (1934).

48. Id. at 544–545.

49. *Buckley v. Valeo*, 42 U.S. 1 (1976).

50. Id. at 19.

51. Id. at 23.

52. Id. at 47–48.

53. Id. at 52; see also *Federal Election Commission v. National Conservative Political Action Committee*, 470 U.S. 480 (1985); *Federal Election Commission v. Massachusetts Citizens for Life*, 479 U.S. 238 (1986); *Austin v. Michigan State Chamber of Commerce*, 494 U.S. 652 (1990); and *Colorado Republican Federal Campaign Committee v. Federal Election Committee*, ____ U.S. ____ (1996).

54. Id. at 263.

55. Id. at 288.

56. Id. at 143.

57. *Roudebush v. Hartke*, 405 U.S. 15 (1972).

58. Id. at 25–26.

59. *Barry v. United States ex rel. Cunningham*, 279 U.S. 597 at 615–616 (1929).

60. *National Association of Manufacturers v. McGrath*, 103 F. Supp. 510 (D.C. 1952).

61. *McGrath v. National Association of Manufacturers*, 344 U.S. 804 (1952).

62. *United States v. Harriss*, 347 U.S. 612 (1954).

63. Id. at 620.

64. Id. at 625.

65. Id. at 632–633.

66. *United States v. Ballin*, 144 U.S. 1 (1892).

67. *United States v. Smith*, 286 U.S. 6 (1932).

68. *Christoffel v. United States*, 338 U.S. 84 (1949).

69. *United States v. Ballin*, 144 U.S. 1 (1892).

70. *Field v. Clark*, 143 U.S. 649 (1892).

71. *McGrain v. Daugherty*, 273 U.S. 135 at 181 (1927)

72. *Nixon v. United States*, 113 S. Ct. 732 (1993)

CHAPTER 5

The Court and the Powers of the President: Article II

PRESIDENTIAL POWER developed virtually unchecked by the Supreme Court from the nation's founding until the New Deal.

The gradual alteration in the balance of federalism—the shifting of power from the states to federal jurisdiction—broadened the scope and the range of executive authority. Thirty years of continuous crisis, from the New Deal to the cold war, further accelerated the expansion of presidential power.

The Constitution, Justice Robert H. Jackson once reminded the Court, was an eighteenth-century sketch for a government—not a finished blueprint.[1] The growth of executive authority could not have been foreseen in 1787, and the accrual of presidential power became far more than the original sum of the executive roles set out by the Constitution.

The twentieth century has seen a few major Court rulings curbing presidential power. Most dramatic of these were the short-lived series of anti–New Deal rulings, the 1952 *Steel Seizure* decision, and the 1974 Watergate tapes decision that resulted in President Richard Nixon's early departure from the White House.[2]

Such cases—and such decisions—have been infrequent in the nation's history.

GENERAL RESPONSIBILITIES

Two factors contribute to the infrequency of Supreme Court rulings on the authority of the chief executive. The constitutional language describing the powers of the president is phrased in very general terms of roles and responsibilities: the president is vested with the executive power, is commander in chief, and is directed to take care that the laws are faithfully executed. The language provides an uncertain basis for constitutional challenges to presidential action.

Concurring in the Court's action in the *Steel Seizure* case, Justice Jackson commented on the imprecision of the language employed in the debate over the scope of the president's powers:

Loose and irresponsible use of adjectives colors all non-legal and much legal discussion of presidential powers. "Inherent" powers, "plenary" powers, "war" powers and "emergency" powers are used, often interchangeably and without fixed or ascertainable meanings.

The vagueness and generality of the clauses that set forth presidential powers afford a plausible basis for pressures within and without the administration for presidential action beyond that supported by those whose responsibility it is to defend his actions in court. The claim of inherent and unrestricted presidential powers has long been a persuasive dialectical weapon in political controversy.[3]

A SPECIAL POSITION

The aura that surrounds the office of the president and its occupant insulates it somewhat from court challenges. George Reedy, a former aide to President Lyndon B. Johnson, noted the monarchic dimension of the modern presidency. Reedy observed that "the life of the White House is the life of a court," and the people who make up the court "serve the material needs and the desires of a single man."[4]

Political scientist Louis Koenig remarked in this respect that even if the president "lags in donning monarchic trappings, others will put them on him. . . ."[5]

The advantages the presidency therefore possesses over other branches of government in capturing the public eye and political support, Justice Jackson has pointed out, make the task of curbing presidential power even more difficult:

Executive power has the advantage of concentration in a single head in whose choice the whole Nation has a part, making him the focus of public hopes and expectations. . . . No other personality in public life can begin to compete with him in access to the public mind through modern methods of communications. By his prestige as head of state and his influence upon public opinion he exerts a leverage upon those who are supposed to check and balance his power which often cancels their effectiveness.[6]

In light of these characteristics, the Court has been cautious in locking constitutional horns with the chief executive on matters that juxtaposed its authority and prestige against the president's will.

Divergent Views of Power

Even presidents have held strikingly divergent views on the limits of presidential power. William Howard Taft viewed executive power as limited to the specific powers granted in the Constitution:

The true view of executive functions . . . is, as I conceive it, that the President can exercise no power which cannot be fairly and reasonably traced to some specific grant of power or justly implied and included within such grant as proper and necessary.[7]

Taft's constitutional view of executive authority prevailed throughout much of the nineteenth century.

Theodore Roosevelt viewed the presidential office differently. His "stewardship" theory of presidential leadership envisioned an active president acting responsibly on behalf of the public welfare.

Roosevelt believed

every executive officer . . . was a steward of the people. . . . My belief
was that it was not only his right but his duty to do anything that the
needs of the nation demanded unless such action was forbidden by the
Constitution or by the laws. . . . In other words, I acted for the public
welfare . . . whenever and in whatever manner was necessary, unless
prevented by direct constitutional or legislative provision.[8]

The broadest assertion of executive authority, however, was
Franklin D. Roosevelt's—based on the concept of executive prerogative described by the seventeenth-century English political
philosopher John Locke as "power to act according to discretion
for the public good, without the prescription of the law, and
sometimes even against it."[9]

Acting on this prerogative theory Roosevelt took steps to
cope with the Great Depression and world war, arguing that, as
the Court itself finally noted, extraordinary times demanded extraordinary measures. The prerogative concept of presidential
power carried over into the cold war, but the Court slowed its
development when it rejected Harry S. Truman's claim of the
authority to seize and operate the nation's steel mills.

The Shield of Joint Action

It is always possible in confrontations with the Court that the
president will ignore or defy it. Both Andrew Jackson and Abraham Lincoln, for example, did so. But early in the nation's history, presidents realized that they held the strongest possible position against judicial challenge when they acted in conjunction
with Congress. Joint action by the two political branches of government has consistently provided a high degree of insulation
from Court challenge.

Again Justice Jackson wrote:

Presidential powers are not fixed but fluctuate, depending upon their
disjunction or conjunction with those of Congress. . . .

When the President acts pursuant to an express or implied authorization of Congress, his authority is at its maximum, for it includes all
that he possesses in his own right plus all that Congress can delegate.
In these circumstances, and in these only, may he be said . . . to person-
ify the federal sovereignty. If his act is held unconstitutional under
these circumstances, it usually means that the Federal Government as
an undivided whole lacks power.[10]

When presidents act without the backing of Congress, supported only by their claim of inherent power, they run the high
risk of rejection by the Court.

The Foreign Role

In foreign and military matters, the Court has upheld the
presidential exercise of sweeping power. In the midst of its rulings denying the president authority to cope with the economic
crisis at home, the Court, in 1936, upheld the president's inherent and virtually unlimited authority to conduct the nation's
foreign affairs.[11]

Justice George Sutherland's opinion in this case claimed that
the foreign affairs powers emanated from sources different from
other presidential powers. This reasoning provided the basis for
Sutherland's view that the president could act entirely alone in
foreign relations matters. Though Sutherland's historical analysis has been criticized, the Court has not modified the broad
grant of executive power sanctioned by this ruling.

Domestic Power and Privilege

The Court, on the other hand, has denied the president such
broad inherent power in domestic affairs. When President Truman seized the steel mills during the Korean War to prevent interruption of steel production and supplies, the Court rejected
the president's claim of the power to take such action, in part
because Congress had, some years earlier, decided not to grant
the president the power he sought to exercise here.

The Court's ruling denying President Nixon an absolute executive privilege to withhold White House tapes sought for use
as evidence in a trial specifically recognized the need for a limited privilege to protect documents and information related to
foreign affairs. This decision, it is worth noting, came at a time
when Congress—far from supporting the president's claim—
was considering articles of impeachment against Nixon.

Presidents and Justices

As Nixon learned, presidents can never be certain the individuals they appoint to the Court will support their views when
the Court is faced with a challenge to the exercise of presidential
power. Thomas Jefferson made several appointments to the
bench whom he hoped would counteract Chief Justice John
Marshall's control over the Court's decisions. But Jefferson's
effort to reduce Marshall's effectiveness with the Court's personnel failed.

President Lincoln appointed Salmon P. Chase to the bench to
deflect his presidential ambitions and to harness his legal talents
for the administration. Chase, who had advocated passage of
the Legal Tender Acts as Treasury secretary, later opposed the
Lincoln administration in the first *Legal Tender* case, holding
those acts unconstitutional.

Two of the four Truman appointments to the bench, Justices
Tom C. Clark and Sherman Minton, appointed in October 1949,
were close friends of the president. In the *Steel Seizure* decision,
Clark joined with the majority, which included two other Truman appointees, and Minton dissented.

President Nixon appointed Warren E. Burger chief justice
because—apart from his judicial qualifications—Burger had
been outspoken in his criticism of the Warren Court's rulings
limiting prosecutors' efforts to convict criminals. Ironically,
Burger wrote the Court opinion that forced Nixon to resign or
face impeachment and trial.

"Although history teaches that Presidents are sometimes surprised by the Supreme Court, the surprise is almost always of
their own making," wrote Harvard law professor Laurence Tribe
in *God Save This Honorable Court*. Examining what he calls "the
myth of the surprised president," Tribe contends that "for the
most part, and especially in areas of particular and known concern to a President, Justices have been loyal to the ideals and
perspectives of the men who have nominated them."[12]

Some presidents have ensured such loyalty by maintaining close ties with sitting justices. President James Buchanan sought and obtained information from fellow Pennsylvanian Robert C. Grier about how the Court would vote on the pending decision in the Dred Scott case. Theodore Roosevelt continued his friendship with Justice William H. Moody after he appointed him to the bench in 1906.

Perhaps the most famous friendship between a president and a justice was that of Franklin Roosevelt and Felix Frankfurter. Friends since undergraduate days at Harvard, Roosevelt and Frankfurter maintained a lively correspondence throughout most of their respective careers. After Roosevelt appointed Frankfurter to the Supreme Court in 1939, the two men communicated freely, offering advice and criticism on politics and legal matters. Their correspondence ranged over every conceivable subject from Washington society gossip to matters of administration patronage and political strategy.

President Lyndon Johnson appointed his longtime adviser Abe Fortas to the Supreme Court. The congressional investigation of Johnson's nomination of Fortas for the post of chief justice revealed that Johnson and Fortas also had continued an active political association after Fortas had been appointed to the bench. Concern over this relationship compounded by political concerns eventually forced Johnson to withdraw the nomination.

The interplay between law and politics—between the Court and the president—reaches back to the Court's beginnings. It shows no signs of halting.

The Court is never unaware of the political consequences of the decisions it makes or chooses not to make with regard to the powers of the chief executive, the individual who, more than any other single person, represents the nation and its government at home and abroad.

This has always been the case; it is just an enhanced sensitivity of the Court's character which Charles Warren described more than sixty years ago:

The Court is not an organism dissociated from the conditions and history of the times in which it exists. It does not formulate and deliver its opinions in a legal vacuum. Its Judges are not abstracted and impersonal oracles, but are men whose views are . . . affected by inheritance, education and environment and by the impact of history past and present.[13]

The Commander in Chief

The president is the commander of the nation's military forces. The Constitution vests the executive with the role and title of "Commander in Chief of the Army and Navy of the United States, and of the Militia of the several States, when called into the actual service of the United States."

"These cryptic words have given rise to some of the most persistent controversies in our constitutional history," wrote Justice Robert H. Jackson more than 150 years after the Framers placed those phrases into the Constitution. Jackson, speaking from his experience as attorney general under President Franklin D. Roosevelt as well as Supreme Court justice, continued by saying, "Just what authority goes with the name has plagued Presidential advisors who . . . cannot say where it begins or ends."[1]

One of the first to note the potentially vast scope of this executive role was Alexander Hamilton. Although he wrote initially that it "would amount to nothing more than the supreme command and direction of the military and naval forces, as first general and admiral of the Confederacy,"[2] he soon amended his statement to acknowledge that "the direction of war most peculiarly demands those qualities which distinguish the exercise of power by a single hand."[3]

The men who wrote the Constitution divided the war power between the executive and the legislative departments of government. They gave Congress the power to declare war and the president the power to conduct it. Mistrust of executive power vested in a single individual led to the creation of a unique divided institutional structure for making war.[4] *(See "The War Power," pp. 134–137, in Chapter 4.)* Subsequent experience, however, has led to the blurring of the lines between the constitutionally distinct functions, a blurring that has effectively insulated most exercises of the war power from judicial review.

Between 1789 and 1861 presidents regarded their role as commander in chief as purely military in nature.[5] Faced with a civil war, however, President Abraham Lincoln began to expand the presidential war power beyond the original concept. He found constitutional justification for the exercise of broad discretionary powers by fusing the powers of the commander in chief with the executive's general constitutional responsibility to take care that the laws are faithfully executed.[6] The national emergency of secession and war, Lincoln said, required the swift and firm exercise of extraordinary powers by the chief executive.[7]

In two world wars in the twentieth century, Presidents Woodrow Wilson and Franklin Roosevelt took a similar view of presidential war powers as they further expanded the sphere of those powers in wartime. Faced with war emergencies, Wilson and Roosevelt controlled the economy, fixed prices, set priority production targets, ran the transportation system, the mines, and industrial plants, detained individuals and groups on the basis of their ethnic origin—many of whom were American citizens not guilty of any crime—and threatened to ignore certain laws that did not comply with their objectives.[8]

Moreover, this assertion of broad emergency power blurred the constitutional distinction between Congress's authority to declare war and the president's power to direct it. Congress delegated power and provided funds; the president directed policy. Fiscal and legislative support for the president was regarded as congressional sanction of the president's decisions. In this way, the two political branches fused their war-making powers, and the Court declined to challenge policies adopted and supported by them.[9]

Political scientist Glendon Schubert described the trend:

One very interesting aspect which emerged from the World War II cases . . . was the consistency with which the courts came to conceptualize the fusion or merging of the power of the political branches of the national government so that either the President or the Congress might individually or cojointly exercise any power attributable to the United States as a sovereign state at war. Under this theory, agreement between the President and Congress places any action in time of war beyond the pale of judicial review.[10]

Although the exercise of the war power in such a manner insulated the president's acts from judicial scrutiny, it has not prevented the Supreme Court from denying the president the right to use those war powers in time of peace. In the 1952 *Steel Seizure* case the Court rejected President Truman's claim of authority to seize the nation's steel mills during the Korean War. The Court ruled that without congressional authorization the president lacked the power to seize the mills.

All in all, the Court has looked at only a small portion of presidential actions taken under the war powers clause. As Clinton Rossiter observed, the Court has examined only "a tiny fraction of [the president's] significant deeds and decisions as commander in chief, for most of these were by nature challengeable in no court but that of impeachment."[11]

And, after two centuries, that judicial reluctance to review war powers, asserted Louis Fisher in 1995, "created a climate in which Presidents have regularly breached constitutional principles and democratic values."[12] He observed that federal judges in the last quarter of the twentieth century readily sidestepped lawsuits brought by members of Congress challenging presidential war powers.

As a consequence, wrote Fisher:

So great is the magnitude of executive power that President Bush invaded Panama in 1989 without any involvement by Congress, and he threatened to take military action against Iraq in 1991 solely on the basis of resolutions adopted by the UN Security Council. Only at the eleventh hour did he obtain authority from Congress. . . .

The best that can be argued in support of presidential war power after World War II is that the language of the Constitution, the intent of the framers, and the republican values operating at the time are no longer relevant, having been superseded by twentieth-century conditions and pressures.[13]

UNDECLARED WARS

The Constitution provides Congress with power to declare war, but only five of the eleven major conflicts fought by the United States abroad have been formally declared wars.

The others were undeclared engagements commenced under presidential claims of authority as commander in chief, custodian of executive power, and, after World War II, under Article XLIII of the United Nations Charter. The effect of these undeclared wars was to dim further the Constitution's separation of congressional and presidential war powers. The modern distinction might be: the president directs the war, Congress funds it.

Congress acted in response to the president's acts or recommendations to declare the War of 1812, the Mexican War (1846–1848), the Spanish-American War (1898), and the two world wars (1917–1918, 1941–1945).

Presidents engaged in hostilities without prior congressional sanction in an undeclared war with France (1798–1800), two Barbary wars (1801–1805, 1815), Mexican-American border clashes (1914–1917), the Korean War (1950–1953), and the Vietnam War (1964–1973). Two conflicts—the War of 1812 and the Spanish-American War—were clearly products of congressional policy.[1]

According to the State Department, there have been more than 125 instances since 1789 when a president has authorized the use of armed forces abroad without congressional assent.[2] Among the most recent examples are President Ronald Reagan's use of force against Libya, Grenada, and Nicaragua.

In 1991 President George Bush obtained last-minute authority from Congress to use military force against Iraq, which had invaded Kuwait. The congressional vote over whether to approve U.S. military force in the Persian Gulf was taken in an atmosphere of almost mournful solemnity and marked the first time since World War II that Congress had publicly debated sending large numbers of U.S. forces into combat.

1. Louis Koenig, *The Chief Executive*, 5th ed. (San Diego: Harcourt Brace Jovanovich, 1986), 207.
2. U.S. Dept. of State, Research Project 806A (August 1967), "Armed Actions Taken by the United States Without a Declaration of War, 1798–1967."

Early in its history the Supreme Court was careful to distinguish between the power of Congress to declare war and the power of the president to conduct it.[14] In 1795 Congress granted part of its declaratory power to the president when it authorized him to call out the militia of any state to quell resistance to the law. The Court sanctioned the president's exercise of discretion to determine when an emergency existed and then to order out the state militia to meet the exigency.[15]

During the War of 1812, several New England states challenged that statute, claiming that neither Congress nor the president had the authority to determine when the state militia should be called out. The New Englanders opposed the war and had refused to place their state troops under federal control.

In *Martin v. Mott*, decided in 1827, the Court upheld the delegation of that authority as a limited power, "confined to cases of actual invasion, or of imminent danger of invasion."[16] Justice Joseph Story, who wrote the Court's opinions, stated:

[A]uthority to decide whether the exigency has arisen, belongs exclusively to the President, and . . . his decision is conclusive upon all other persons. We think that this construction necessarily results from the nature of the power itself, and from the manifest object contemplated by the act of Congress. . . .

Whenever a statute gives a discretionary power to any person, to be exercised by him, upon his own opinion of certain facts, it is a sound rule of construction that the statute constitutes him the sole and exclusive judge of the existence of those facts.[17]

While conceding that the president possessed a limited discretionary power to declare that a crisis existed, the Court, nevertheless, continued to regard the president's war power as primarily military in nature. As late as 1850 Chief Justice Roger B. Taney observed that under the war power clauses the president's

duty and his power are purely military. As Commander in Chief, he is authorized to direct the movements of the naval and military forces placed by law at his command, and to employ them in the manner he may deem most effectual to harass and conquer and subdue the enemy. He may invade the hostile country, and subject it to the sovereignty and authority of the United States. But his conquests do not enlarge the boundaries of this Union, nor extend the operation of our institutions and laws beyond the limits before assigned them by legislative power.[18]

The Supreme Court has never opposed the president's deployment of forces abroad as commander in chief. During the nineteenth century presidents assigned naval squadrons to cruise in the Mediterranean (1815), in the Pacific (1821), in the Caribbean (1822), in the South Atlantic (1826), in the waters of the Far East (1835), and along the African coast (1842). These deployments showed the flag, encouraged trade, and protected shipping. However, no American bases were established on foreign soil as a result of these actions.[19]

During the nineteenth century, presidents controlled policy in time of war; in peacetime presidents generally deferred to Congress. Between 1836 and 1898, with the exception of the wartime administrations of James K. Polk, Abraham Lincoln, and Grover Cleveland, Congress provided the initiative in foreign policy. When the chief executive in peacetime advocated expansionist policies that threatened war—for example, Franklin Pierce in Cuba, Secretary of State William H. Seward in Alaska, and Ulysses S. Grant in Santo Domingo—Congress blocked such projects.[20]

Polk's Mexican policy forced a declaration of war with that country in 1846. The president directed General Zachary Taylor to occupy disputed territory claimed by Mexico. As a result of an alleged provocation by Mexican troops, Polk asked Congress to declare war.[21] Congressional opposition led a young Whig member of Congress named Abraham Lincoln to introduce resolutions demanding to know the exact spot where the armed forces clashed. The House censured the president for a war "unnecessarily and unconstitutionally begun," but Congress funded the war anyway.[22]

President William McKinley's decision to send the battleship

Maine into Havana's harbor led to war with Spain over Cuban independence in 1898. Congress passed a joint resolution authorizing the use of armed force to obtain Cuba's separation from Spain, then followed with a declaration of war when Spain recalled its ambassador and refused to leave Cuba.[23]

But McKinley made the decision to insist on Spain's surrender of the Philippines without congressional consultation. Later he deployed more than one hundred thousand troops to put down the insurrection, led by Emilio Aguinaldo, as part of the movement for Philippine independence. This deployment led to charges in Congress of unilateral war making by the president.[24]

McKinley also sent several thousand U.S. troops to join an international brigade that rescued Americans trapped in Peking by a Chinese nationalist uprising. Democrats criticized this action, but Congress was out of session and calls for a special session in an election year were to no avail.[25]

President Theodore Roosevelt engineered the revolution in Panama against Columbia to make the "dirt fly" on construction of the Panama Canal. But Roosevelt's less-than-subtle sanction of the Panamanian revolution in November 1903 raised few objections from Congress or the public.[26]

Early in the twentieth century, the Supreme Court considered and resolved questions of citizenship and constitutional rights for the inhabitants of newly acquired noncontiguous U.S. territories. The Court, however, never challenged the president's prerogative to conduct war or acquire the territories. *(See "The Insular Cases," pp. 148–150, in Chapter 4.)*

Most of the instances of presidential use of troops without congressional authorization between 1815 and 1912 involved small contingents of forces for limited purposes that had strong public support.

President Lincoln and the Civil War

The first major Supreme Court pronouncement on the war powers of the president came as a result of the broad exercise of those powers by President Abraham Lincoln during the Civil War.

From the outbreak of hostilities at Fort Sumter on April 12, 1861, until Congress convened in special session July 4, President Lincoln prepared the nation for war without authority from Congress. He acted under his power as commander in chief and his presidential oath to maintain the Constitution and preserve the Union.

On his own authority Lincoln declared the existence of a rebellion, called out the state militia to suppress it, and proclaimed a blockade of southern ports—the legal equivalent to a declaration of war. In May he called for forty regiments of U.S. volunteers to serve for three years. He ordered increases made in the size of the army and navy, paid out two million dollars from the federal treasury without specific authorization, and indebted the government about a quarter of a billion dollars in pledged credit. Lincoln also ordered suspension of habeas corpus in certain parts of the United States. He directed military

commanders to arrest persons engaged in or likely to engage in "treasonable practices."[27]

When Congress convened, Lincoln's July 4, 1861, message to the special session explained the measures taken and recommended steps for the exercise of additional power. Bolstered by a corroborative opinion from Attorney General Edward Bates, Lincoln informed Congress that public necessity and the preservation of the Union required swift and bold action, "whether strictly legal or not." The president said he felt certain Congress would "readily ratify" his actions. He noted that public safety required the "qualified suspension of the privilege of the writ [of habeas corpus] which was authorized to be made."[28]

During the special session Congress intermittently debated a joint resolution that sanctioned Lincoln's acts. Nagging doubts about the legality of habeas corpus suspension and the port blockades prevented a vote on the approbatory resolution. But a rider attached to a pay bill for army privates, rushed through Congress at the close of the session, gave approval to the president's acts pertaining to the militia, the army, the navy, and the volunteers, stating that they were "in all respects legalized and made valid, to the same intent and with the same effect as if they had been issued and done under the previous express authority and direction of Congress."[29]

Congress made no challenge to Lincoln's management of the war until the December 1861 session. The Joint Committee on the Conduct of the War, established at first to investigate the Union disaster at the first battle of Bull Run, soon expanded the scope of its investigations. Headed by Radical Republican senator Benjamin F. Wade of Ohio, the committee tried unsuccessfully to wrest control of war policy from the president.[30]

THE *PRIZE CASES*

When it faced the questions raised by Lincoln's assumption of broad wartime powers, the Supreme Court was sharply divided.

But by a 5–4 vote in 1863, the Court in the *Prize Cases* upheld the president's exercise of the war power to impose the blockade on southern ports.[31] The cases arose as a challenge to Lincoln's unilateral proclamation of a blockade of the ports, a proclamation made in April 1861 and not in any way ratified by Congress until July.

Several neutral vessels were captured and brought to Union ports as prizes early in the blockade. They had been captured as they tried to pass the blockade. Under international law, ships could legally be taken as prizes only when a conflict had been recognized as a war between two belligerent powers.

Lincoln had consistently refused to recognize the Confederate government as a sovereign—and belligerent—power. He insisted that the conflict was an insurrection, not a war. This view effectively denied the South sovereign status or the possibility of recognition by neutral governments. If the Court adopted Lincoln's view that the South was not a belligerent, it would have to rule that under international law the blockade was illegal and the vessels improperly seized.

President Abraham Lincoln on the battlefield of Antietam in October 1862. Lincoln's assumption during the Civil War of broad wartime powers was challenged in three important Supreme Court cases.

The Opinion

The cases were argued for twelve days in February 1863. Two weeks later, the Court announced its decision in favor of Lincoln's position, upholding his power to impose the blockade.

Lincoln's three appointees to the Court—Justices Noah H. Swayne, Samuel F. Miller, and David Davis—joined with Robert C. Grier and James M. Wayne to form the majority. Grier wrote the opinion, which accepted both the president's definition of the conflict and his power to impose the blockade. The majority acknowledged that Congress has the power to declare war, but ruled that the president had to meet the challenge in the emergency until Congress could act:

By the Constitution, Congress alone has the power to declare a national or foreign war. It cannot declare war against a State or any number of States, by virtue of any clause in the Constitution. The Constitution confers on the President the whole executive power. He is bound to take care that the laws be faithfully executed. He is Commander-in-Chief of the Army and Navy of the United States, and of the militia of the several States when called into the actual service of the United States. He has no power to initiate or declare a war either against a foreign nation or a domestic State. But by the Acts of Congress of Feb. 28th, 1795 . . . and 3rd of March, 1807 . . . he is authorized to call out the militia and use the military and naval forces of the United States in case of invasion by foreign nations, and to suppress insurrection against the government of a State or of the United States.

If a war be made by invasion of a foreign nation, the President is not only authorized but bound to resist force, by force. He does not initiate the war, but is bound to accept the challenge without waiting for any special legislative authority. And whether the hostile party be a foreign invader, or States organized in rebellion, it is none the less a war, although the declaration of it be "unilateral." . . .

This greatest of civil wars was not gradually developed by popular commotion, tumultuous assemblies, or local unorganized insurrections. However long may have been its previous conception, it nevertheless sprung forth suddenly from the parent brain, a Minerva in the full panoply of war. The President was bound to meet it in the shape it presented itself, without waiting for Congress to baptize it with a name; and no name given to it by him or them could change the fact.

It is not the less a civil war, with belligerent parties in hostile array, because it may be called an "insurrection" by one side, and the insurgents be considered as rebels or traitors. It is not necessary that the independence of the revolted province or State be acknowledged in order to constitute it a party belligerent in a war according to the law of nations. Foreign nations acknowledge it as war by a declaration of neutrality. The condition of neutrality cannot exist unless there be two belligerent parties.[32]

The Dissent

Chief Justice Roger B. Taney and Justices Samuel Nelson, John Catron, and Nathan Clifford found Grier's analysis inadequate. The dissenters argued that the war power belonged to Congress and that the blockade was illegal from the time of Lincoln's April proclamation until Congress approved it in July. As to the matter of whether a war existed, Nelson wrote:

[B]efore this insurrection against the established government can be dealt with on the footing of a civil war, within the meaning of the law of nations and the Constitution of the United States, and which will draw after it belligerent rights, it must be recognized or declared by the war making power of the government. No power short of this can change the legal status of the government or the relations of its citizens from that of peace to a state of war, or bring into existence all those duties and obligations of neutral third parties growing out of a state of war. The war power of the government must be exercised before this changed condition . . . can be admitted. . . .

. . . [W]e find there that to constitute a civil war in the sense in which we are speaking, before it can exist, in contemplation of law, it must be recognized or declared by the sovereign power of the State, and which sovereign power by our Constitution is lodged in the Congress of the United States—civil war, therefore, under our system of government, can exist only by an Act of Congress which requires the assent of two of the great departments of the government, the Executive and Legislative. . . .

The Acts of 1795 and 1807 did not, and could not, under the Constitution, confer on the President the power of declaring war against a State of this Union, or of deciding that war existed, and upon that ground authorize the capture and confiscation of the property of every citizen of the State whenever it was found on the waters. The laws of war . . . convert every citizen of the hostile State into a public enemy, and treat him accordingly, whatever may have been his previous conduct. This great power over the business and property of the citizen is reserved to the Legislative Department by the express words of the Constitution. It cannot be delegated or surrendered to the Executive. Congress alone can determine whether war exists or should be declared. . . .

I am compelled to the conclusion that no civil war existed between this Government and the States in insurrection until recognized by the Act of Congress 13th July, 1861; that the President does not possess the power under the Constitution to declare war or recognize its existence within the meaning of the law of nations, which carries with it belligerent rights, and thus change the country and all its citizens from a state of peace to a state of war; that this power belongs exclusively to the Congress of the United States and consequently, that the President had no power to set on foot a blockade under the law of nations.[33]

The opinions of Grier and Nelson represented opposing constitutional theories about who might initiate war under the Constitution. But notwithstanding any constitutional shortcomings of his position, Lincoln continued to direct the war. He issued the Emancipation Proclamation of January 1, 1863, under his authority as commander in chief, and his authority to do so was never challenged before the Court.

MERRYMAN AND MILLIGAN

Article I, Section 9, of the Constitution states: "The Privilege of the Writ of Habeas Corpus shall not be suspended, unless when in Cases of Rebellion or Invasion the public Safety may require it." Under this clause Lincoln suspended the privilege of the writ in sections of the country where military forces attempted to prevent southern sympathizers from disrupting transportation and communications systems. The wartime suspension of habeas corpus was challenged as early as 1861 by none other than the chief justice of the United States. Lincoln, however, continued to suspend habeas corpus during the war. In March 1863 Congress authorized the suspension of the privilege by the president at his discretion.

Early Challenge

In 1861 Chief Justice Taney, holding circuit court in Baltimore, ordered federal military officers to justify their detention of John Merryman, a civilian southern sympathizer detained in a military prison for his part in burning railroad bridges near Baltimore, and to show cause why Merryman should not be released for proceedings in a civilian court.[34] Citing Lincoln's suspension order, the military commander refused to respond.

Taney regarded the officer's refusal as a violation of proper judicial procedure. He wrote an opinion that lectured the president on his duty to faithfully execute the laws. Failure to support the proceedings of the court, Taney remarked, amounted to usurpation of civilian authority and the substitution of military government.[35] Taney warned:

[T]he people of the United States are no longer living under a government of laws, but every citizen holds life, liberty and property at the will and pleasure of the army officer in whose military district he may happen to be found.[36]

To southern sympathizers the *Merryman* case became a symbol of oppression. Merryman eventually was handed over to civilian authorities and indicted for treason.

The question remained unresolved: did the president have the power to order civilians tried by military tribunals in regions outside the war zone where civil courts remained open? The administration argued that military trials were necessary because the civilian court and peacetime procedures were inadequate to deal with the problem of organized rebellion.

In 1864 the Court refused to address the question in the case of Clement L. Vallandigham, a "Copperhead"—a northerner who sympathized with the Confederate cause—and a former Democratic representative from Ohio who denounced Lincoln's war policy in speeches. Vallandigham was arrested and tried by a military commission.

The Supreme Court refused to hear Vallandigham's appeal of his conviction. Justice Wayne wrote that the Court "cannot without disregarding its frequent decisions and interpretation of the Constitution in respect to its judicial power . . . review or pronounce any opinion upon the proceedings of a military commission."[37]

But after the war, the Court took on that issue and resolved it—against the president.

The Milligan Case

In 1864 L. P. Milligan was tried by a military commission in Indiana and convicted of conspiracy. He was sentenced to die for his part in a plot to release and arm rebel prisoners and march them into Missouri and Kentucky to cooperate in an invasion of Indiana.

President Andrew Johnson commuted Milligan's sentence to life in prison. Milligan, nevertheless, came to the Supreme Court to challenge his trial and conviction. In 1866 the Court unanimously ordered his release, holding that the president had no power to require civilians to be tried by military courts in an area where regular courts continued to function.

Justice Davis, Lincoln's own nominee to the Court, wrote the opinion, condemning Lincoln's use of military tribunals in areas where the civil courts remained open. The Court divided 5–4 on

The constitutionality of the arrest and trial of these five southern sympathizers, charged with treason by military authorities, was settled by the Supreme Court in *Ex parte Milligan* (1866). *Clockwise from top:* William A. Bowles, Andrew Humphreys, Stephen Horsey, H. Heffren, and Lambdin P. Milligan.

whether Congress had the power to authorize military trials under such circumstances. The decision established that martial law must be confined to "the theater of active military operations."[38] Davis's opinion, issued in December 1866, after the war emergency had passed, and eight months after the decision itself was announced, held that:

The Constitution of the United States is a law for rulers and people, equally in war and in peace, and covers with the shield of its protection all classes of men, at all times and under all circumstances. No doctrine, involving more pernicious consequences, was ever invented by the wit of man than that any of its provisions can be suspended during any of the great exigencies of government. . . . Martial law cannot arise from a threatened invasion. The necessity must be actual and present; the invasion real, such as effectually closes the courts. . . . Martial rule can never exist where the courts are open, and in the proper and unobstructed exercise of their jurisdiction. It is also confined to the locality of actual war.[39]

The assumption of broad presidential powers in a wartime emergency ended—temporarily—with Lincoln's death and the end of the war.

President Wilson and World War

As a professor at Princeton University, Woodrow Wilson minimized the presidential role in the constitutional system.[40] Moreover, as Wilson's biographer has observed, Wilson did not concern himself with foreign affairs in the years prior to his election as president because "he did not think they were important enough to warrant any diversion from the mainstream of his thought."[41]

President-elect Wilson changed his mind. A month before taking office, Wilson asserted that the chief executive "must be prime minister, and he is the spokesman of the nation in everything."[42]

Wilson's terms as president brought the broadest assertion of presidential powers up to that time. During the world war, Congress cooperated with Wilson and delegated vast authority to the president for the conduct of the war. Legislative sanction of extraordinary presidential actions insulated Wilson's war policy—at home and abroad—from judicial review.

Even before World War I, Wilson ordered U.S. troops to pursue Mexican bandits across the border into Mexico. American troops engaged Mexican regulars in a sporadic border war during Mexico's revolution and subsequent search for stable and democratic government.[43]

As the war in Europe engulfed the United States, and American troops entered the conflict in 1917, Wilson sought and obtained from Congress broad delegations of power to prepare for war and to mobilize the home front.[44] During the war, Wilson managed the nation's economy by delegating power to a series of war management and war production boards created to coordinate domestic production and supply. "It is not an army that we must shape and train for war," Wilson explained, "it is a nation."[45]

Wilson commandeered plants and mines; he requisitioned supplies, fixed prices, seized and operated the nation's transportation and communications networks, and managed the production and distribution of food. The Council of National Defense, an umbrella agency created by Wilson, administered the economy during the war. Wall Street broker Bernard Baruch, appointed by Wilson to head the War Industries Board, became the nation's virtual economic dictator. The board had no statutory authority; Wilson simply created it under his authority as commander in chief.[46]

Wilson's exercise of the war power went unchallenged by the Supreme Court, in part because Wilson had obtained prior congressional approval for all his actions. Issues that raised constitutional questions, moreover, reached the Court only after the armistice, when they were no longer urgent. All three branches of the government seemed to assume that the broad powers exercised by Lincoln during the Civil War carried over for use in foreign wars.

The delegation of legislative power by Congress to the president reached unprecedented heights during World War I. Many statutes simply stated their general objectives and left it to the president to interpret the goals and administer the measures he felt necessary to achieve them. When the Senate attempted to form a watchdog committee to oversee management of the war, Wilson opposed the measure as a check on his leadership. The House then killed the proposal.[47]

The closest the Court came to questioning executive war power during World War I came with its 1921 decision declaring part of the Lever Food Control Act unconstitutional. The Lever Act provided for federal control of the distribution and production of food and the marketing of fuel. The bill subjected the nation's economy to whatever regulations the president mandated to guarantee Allied victory. It authorized the president to license the manufacture and distribution of food and to seize factories and mines to ensure continued production of defense-related commodities. Section 4 of the act made it a criminal offense to charge excessive prices for commodities.[48] The Court invalidated that section of the law because it set no ascertainable standard of guilt and failed to define unjust or unreasonable prices. The Court found that Section 4 was, therefore, in conflict with the constitutional guarantees of due process of law and of adequate notice to persons accused of crimes of the nature and cause of the charge against them.[49]

President Roosevelt and Total War

The concept of expanded presidential powers in wartime, tested in the crisis of civil war and sanctioned by Congress in World War I, underwent further expansion during the twelve years of Franklin Roosevelt's tenure in the White House. In his March 4, 1933, inaugural speech Roosevelt said he would ask Congress, "for the one remaining instrument to meet the crisis—broad Executive power to wage a war against the emergency as great as the power that would be given me if we were in fact invaded by a foreign foe."[50]

The emergency was the Great Depression. Roosevelt's New Deal legislative program sought to meet economic disaster with emergency measures similar to those employed by Lincoln and Wilson in wartime. The Supreme Court, however, was far more reluctant to sanction these measures than those taken in military crises. (See "The Court and the Roosevelt Revolution," pp. 248–252.)

The rise of fascist dictators in Germany and Italy and the expansion of the Japanese empire into China and Southeast Asia changed the focus of the nation from economic recovery to foreign aggression abroad. Although the Neutrality Acts of 1935, 1936, and 1937 required the president to avoid negotiations that might involve the nation in another war, Roosevelt in these years claimed broad executive powers as commander in chief to deal with belligerent nations. The president's personal diplomacy committed the United States to a "neutrality" weighted in favor of Anglo-American interests in Europe against the plans of conquest pursued by Germany, Italy, and by Japan in the Far East.[51]

The Supreme Court supported Roosevelt's use of broad powers in the area of foreign policy—and, after war came, of the war power. It recognized the "plenary and exclusive" power of the president in foreign affairs and sanctioned the president's use of the executive agreement, as well as treaties, to make binding foreign policy commitments on behalf of the United States.[52] (See "The 'Sole Negotiator,'" p. 211.)

The president declared a limited national emergency in May 1939 and an unlimited emergency in May 1941. These declarations, though questioned by the Senate at the time, made available to Roosevelt statutory authority to wield extraordinary presidential powers. Roosevelt set out his own theory to justify the exercise of unusual power in the war crisis in a September 7, 1942, message to Congress. The message demanded repeal of certain provisions contained in the Emergency Price Control Act of 1942. (Congress subsequently amended the law to meet the president's objections.)

I ask the Congress to take this action by the first of October. Inaction on your part by that date will leave me with an inescapable responsibility to the people of this country to see to it that the war effort is no longer imperilled by threat of economic chaos.

In the event that the Congress should fail to act, and act adequately, I shall accept the responsibility and I will act. . . .

The President has the powers, under the Constitution and under Congressional acts, to take measures necessary to avert a disaster which would interfere with the winning of the war.

. . . the American people can be sure that I will use my powers with a full sense of my responsibility to the Constitution and to my country. The American people can also be sure that I shall not hesitate to use every power vested in me to accomplish the defeat of our enemies in any part of the world where our own safety demands such defeat.

When the war is won, the powers under which I act automatically revert to the people—to whom they belong.[53]

DELEGATED POWER

Woodrow Wilson's management of the economy during World War I had eroded reservations about the constitutionality of a broad federal war power. During World War II, Congress again delegated vast federal powers to the president to prosecute the war. Roosevelt's war management program caused hardly a stir of protest on constitutional grounds. Congress and the president developed a working partnership to win the war. What prevented confrontation between Roosevelt and the legislative and judicial branches was the assumption that war powers exercised by Lincoln and Wilson carried over to the new emergency.

Roosevelt created a vast number of new administrative agencies responsible to him to conduct the war. By 1945 there were twenty-nine separate agencies grouped under the Office of Emergency Management alone.

The most significant Court challenge to the delegation of power during World War II was to the Emergency Price Control Act of January 30, 1942. The law directed the Office of Price Administration (OPA) to set price ceilings on rents and consumer goods and to ration some products in short supply. Albert Yakus, Benjamin Rottenberg, and B. Rottenberg, Incorporated,

In his September 7, 1942, message to Congress, President Franklin D. Roosevelt claimed broad executive powers to "avert a disaster which would interfere with the winning of the war." The Supreme Court supported Roosevelt's exercise of unusual powers during the war crisis, recognizing the exclusive power of the president in foreign affairs and upholding the constitutionality of laws and government agencies established for the successful prosecution of the war effort.

were convicted of selling beef at wholesale prices above the maximum prescribed by the OPA. These wholesalers challenged their conviction, arguing that the Emergency Price Control Act was an unconstitutional delegation of legislative power by Congress to the executive.

The Supreme Court upheld the price control act in 1944.[54] In contrast to its rejection of earlier New Deal measures, the Court declared this grant of power valid because it contained precise standards to confine the administrator's regulations and orders within fixed limits. Moreover, the Court stated, judicial review offered sufficient remedy for transgression of those limits.

In a dissenting opinion, Justice Owen J. Roberts registered his concern over Congress's delegation of power to the executive branch. Roberts posed the following question: Could Congress suspend any part of the Constitution in wartime? Then he continued:

My view is that it may not suspend any of the provisions of the instrument. What any of the branches of government do in war must find warrant in the charter and not in its nullification, either directly or stealthily by evasion and equivocation. But if the court puts its decision on the war power I think it should say so. The citizens of this country will then know that in war the function of legislation may be surrendered to an autocrat whose "judgment" will constitute the law; and that his judgment will be enforced by federal officials pursuant to civil judgments, and criminal punishments will be imposed by courts as matters of routine.[55]

In an opinion delivered the same day as the *Yakus* decision, the Court upheld rent control powers of the OPA.[56] Justice William O. Douglas's opinion justified this delegation of power to the OPA administrator as a necessary wartime measure:

We need not determine what constitutional limits there are to price fixing legislation. Congress was dealing here with conditions created by

activities resulting from a great war effort. . . . A nation which can demand the lives of its men and women in the waging of that war is under no constitutional necessity of providing a system of price control on the domestic front which will assure each landlord a "fair return" on his property.[57]

In 1947 the Court upheld a similar rent control law as justified by the reduction in residential housing available to veterans demobilized at the end of the war. Again writing for the Court, Douglas observed, however, that the Court would not approve indefinite extension of wartime controls into peacetime, "to treat all the wounds which war inflicts on our society."[58]

The Supreme Court never upheld challenges to the authority of other wartime agencies or to the authority of the 101 government corporations created by the president and engaged in production, insurance, transportation, banking, housing, and other lines of business related to successful prosecution of the war effort.

Furthermore, the Court upheld the power of the president to apply sanctions to individuals, labor unions, and industries that refused to comply with wartime guidelines. These sanctions had no statutory basis. A retail fuel distributor who admitted violating fuel rationing orders challenged these sanctions. In his case the Court ruled that where rationing supported the war effort, presidential sanctions forcing compliance with rationing guidelines were constitutional.[59]

MILITARY TRIALS

In 1942 the Court backed the president's power to set up military commissions to try persons who have committed military crimes but who are not members of the armed forces of the United States. This decision came in the case of *Ex parte Quirin*.[60]

President Roosevelt set up a military commission in 1942 to try eight Nazi saboteurs captured after they entered the United States clandestinely from a German submarine. The military commission tried the saboteurs for offenses against the laws of war. Although the president's proclamation creating the commission specifically denied the eight saboteurs access to American courts, their lawyers obtained a writ of habeas corpus that contended the president lacked statutory and constitutional authority to order trial by military commission, that they had been denied constitutional guarantees extended to persons charged with criminal offenses, and that they should have been tried in civilian courts.

The Court convened a special term to hear the case argued July 29–30, 1942. On July 31 the Court ruled that such constitutional requirements did not apply to trials held by military commissions for those who entered U.S. territory as belligerents. It was not necessary for the commander in chief to set up military commissions because Congress had authorized military commissions to try offenders against the laws of war. Therefore, the president's action was more broadly based than Lincoln's use of military commissions, struck down in 1866. (See "The Milligan Case," pp. 198–199.)

Ex parte Quirin also established the authority of civil courts to review a military commission's jurisdiction to try certain persons.[61]

RELOCATION PROGRAM

By Executive Order No. 1066, issued February 19, 1941, President Franklin Roosevelt placed Japanese-Americans living on the West Coast under rigid curfew laws and restricted their movements day and night. A congressional resolution of March 21, 1942, supported the president's action. Roosevelt subsequently ordered the removal of all Japanese from the coastal region for the duration of the war as a measure of protection against sabotage by persons of Japanese ancestry.

Instituted under the powers of the commander in chief, the removal program made no distinction between citizens and aliens. Japanese-Americans suffered great economic and psychological distress as the plan was hastily implemented. By the spring of 1942, more than 100,000 Japanese-Americans had been relocated in internment camps by the War Relocation Authority. Seventy thousand American citizens of Japanese ancestry were detained in camps for periods up to four years, subjected to forcible confinement, and then resettled in areas away from the Pacific coast.[62]

The constitutionality of the curfew, exclusion, and relocation programs came before the Supreme Court in three cases decided in 1943 and 1944. The effect of all three decisions was to uphold this extraordinary exercise of the war power by Congress and the president.

Curfew Case

In June 1943 the Court, in Hirabayashi v. United States, unanimously upheld the curfew order as applied to U.S. citizens as "within the boundaries of the war power." The Court's opinion, written by Chief Justice Harlan Fiske Stone, made clear, however, that the Court was not considering "whether the President, acting alone, could lawfully have made the curfew order."[63]

Because Congress had ratified Roosevelt's executive order by statute, the question became that of "the constitutional power of the national government through the joint action of Congress and the executive to impose this restriction as an emergency war measure." The Court held that the curfew order was within that jointly exercised power.[64]

Exclusion, Detention

Eighteen months later, in December 1944, the Court upheld the exclusion of Japanese-Americans from their West Coast homes. The vote was 6–3 in the case of Korematsu v. United States. The majority relied heavily upon the reasoning in Hirabayashi in concluding that it was not outside the power of Congress and the executive, acting together, to impose this exclusion.[65]

The same day, however, the Court granted a writ of habeas corpus to Mitsuye Endo, a Japanese-American girl, freeing her from one of the detention centers. These centers were intended as "interim places of residence" for persons whose loyalty was being ascertained. After one was determined to be loyal, the intent was that loyal persons be resettled outside the centers.

Endo's loyalty had been determined, but she had not been released from the center. The Court ordered her release. Without ruling on the constitutionality of the relocation program, the Court held that "whatever power the War Relocation Authority may have to detain other classes of citizens, it has no authority to subject citizens who are concededly loyal to its leave procedures."[66]

"The authority to detain a citizen or grant him a conditional release as protection against espionage or sabotage is exhausted at least when his loyalty is conceded," wrote Justice Douglas for the Court.[67]

The challenge of total war pointed up the tension between the idea of constitutional government and the demands of military policy and national security. Effective conduct of the war raised cries of executive dictatorship as it had in 1861 and 1917. But so long as the presidential war powers rested on the twin foundations of statutory authority and the prerogatives of the commander in chief, they seemed safe from constitutional challenge.

(More than forty years later, the government's treatment of Japanese-Americans during World War II would be revisited in Washington. In 1988 Congress passed and President Reagan signed legislation offering a formal apology on behalf of the nation to Japanese-Americans held in U.S. camps during the war and promising the estimated sixty thousand surviving internees $20,000 each. The payments were to be spread over ten years, but estimates of the original number of claimants was about eighteen thousand too low and Congress did not appropriate enough money for the program. In 1992, after four years of con-

In 1944 the Supreme Court upheld the constitutionality of interning Japanese-Americans in detention centers as a military necessity during World War II

tinued controversy over U.S. reparations, the federal fund was expanded to compensate all seventy-eight thousand estimated claimants.)

Postwar Powers

Between 1945 and 1947 postwar differences between the United States and the Soviet Union brought on the cold war, a state of permanent international crisis and half-war that shaped presidential policy making for three decades. Superpower rivalries, and this permanent state of ideological war, permitted President Harry S. Truman and his successors to retain control of policy making in the postwar era. Congress placed few obstacles in the way of presidential formulation of cold war strategy.

Truman had virtually a free hand in the development of that policy. The Truman Doctrine, the Marshall Plan, and "containment" of communism met only token resistance in Congress.

When, six months after communists took control of the mainland of China, communist North Korea invaded South Korea, Truman acted decisively—and unilaterally. On June 27, 1950, he announced that American air and naval forces would help South Korea repel the invasion from the north. Truman claimed authority for his actions from the United Nations Security Council vote that condemned North Korea's action and the June 27 resolution that urged UN members to assist South Korea.[68] The United States, however, had never signed an agreement to assign American military forces to the security council for such "police actions."

The decision to commit U.S. forces brought some criticism in the Senate of this abuse of the war power. The House, howev-er, broke into applause when it received official news of the president's action.

THE STEEL SEIZURE CASE

The first modern rebuff to presidential war powers was administered by the Court to President Truman in the *Steel Seizure* case of 1952. The idea of broad emergency powers in time of cold war as well as hot war met Court opposition when Truman took over the nation's steel mills to prevent a strike and ensure continued steel production for the war in Korea. Six members of the Court held Truman's seizure an unconstitutional usurpation of powers and ordered the mills returned to private hands.[69]

Truman's seizure order cited no statutory authority for the action. The president's directive stated simply that the action was taken under his powers as commander in chief and in accordance with the Constitution and the laws of the United States.

Although a majority of the Court agreed that the president had by this action overstepped constitutional boundaries that separated legislative and executive powers, they did not rule out the possibility that such seizures might be legal if done under statutory authority.[70]

Justice Hugo L. Black's brief opinion for the Court rejected the proposition that either the president's powers as commander in chief or some inherent executive prerogative powers authorized the seizure:

Even though "theater of war" be an expanding concept, we cannot with faithfulness to our constitutional system hold that the Commander in Chief of the Armed Forces has the ultimate power as such to take possession of private property in order to keep labor disputes from stop-

WARTIME SEIZURE POWER

Presidents since Woodrow Wilson have seized industrial plants to prevent interruption of production during wartime. The term "government seizure" means that the government assumes temporary custody of the property. People responsible for management of the plant or industry continue to operate it. Seizures have been regarded as an effective way to break a stalemate in stalled labor-management contract negotiations to prevent production interruptions in vital industries during a national emergency.

President Franklin D. Roosevelt ordered some two thousand regular army troops to prevent disruption of production at the North American Aviation Plant in Los Angeles, which had been struck June 5, 1941. The president's executive order said that it was necessary to send troops to ensure continued production of aircraft while labor and management negotiated an end to the walk-out over wages. The government retained control until July 2, 1941.

The strike was called less than ten days after Roosevelt had proclaimed an unlimited national emergency urging employers and employees to cooperate as war approached.[1]

No specific statute authorized the president to seize plants in a labor dispute. The Selective Service Act provided for seizure of plants when they refused to obey government orders to manufacture necessary arms and supplies.

Attorney General Robert H. Jackson's legal opinion justifying the seizure order derived the president's power from the "aggregate" of executive powers set out in the Constitution and federal statutes. Jackson said that the president had the inherent constitutional duty "to exert his civil and military as well as his moral authority to keep the defense effort of the United States a going concern."[2] In 1943 Congress enacted the War Labor Disputes Act, authorizing presidential seizures of plants involved in a labor dispute.

The single wartime court test of the seizure power proved inconclusive. After a three-year struggle between Montgomery Ward and Company and the War Labor Board, the president in 1944 ordered the company's property seized to prevent a work stoppage. A federal district court ruled that the company engaged in "distribution," not "production." The president has no general war power to seize the property, the court said.

An appeals court interpreted "production" in broader terms and reversed the lower court. The Supreme Court accepted the case, then dismissed it as moot when the army returned the property to company control.[3]

1. Bennett M. Rich, *The Presidents and Civil Disorder* (Washington, D.C.: Brookings, 1941), 177–183.
2. Ibid., 184.
3. *Montgomery Ward & Co. v. United States*, 326 U.S. 690 (1944).

ping production. This is a job for the Nation's lawmakers, not for its military authorities.[71]

In a concurring opinion, Justice Robert H. Jackson wrote that the commander in chief clause

is sometimes advanced as support for any presidential action, internal or external, involving use of force, the idea being that it vests power to do anything, anywhere, that can be done with an army or navy. . . . But no doctrine that the court could promulgate would seem to me more sinister and alarming than that a President . . . can vastly enlarge his mastery over the internal affairs of the country by his own commitment of the nation's armed forces to some foreign venture. . . . There are indications that the Constitution did not contemplate that the title Commander-in-Chief of the Army and Navy will constitute him also Commander-in-Chief of the country, its industries and its inhabitants. He has no monopoly of "war powers," whatever they are. While Congress cannot deprive the President of the command of the army and navy, only Congress can provide him an army and navy to command. . . .

That military powers of the Commander-in-Chief were not to supercede representative government of internal affairs seems obvious from the Constitution and from elementary American history. . . . Congress, not the Executive, should control utilization of the war power as an instrument of domestic policy.[72]

Three members of the Court dissented, arguing that the president possessed broad executive powers to take such action in the state of emergency created by the Korean War.[73] Chief Justice Fred M. Vinson's dissenting opinion, joined by Justices Stanley F. Reed and Sherman Minton, was a pragmatic argument in support of the president's action, drawing upon histor-

ical precedents and emphasizing the gravity of the threat presented by a steel strike during the Korean conflict.

The dissenters relied primarily on the general executive power, not the commander in chief clause:

Those who suggest that this is a case involving extraordinary powers should be mindful that these are extraordinary times. . . .

The broad executive power granted by Article II to an officer on duty 365 days a year cannot, it is said, be invoked to avert disaster. Instead, the President must confine himself to sending a message to Congress recommending action. Under this messenger-boy concept of the Office, the President cannot even act to preserve legislative programs from destruction so that Congress will have something left to act upon. There is no judicial finding that the executive action was unwarranted because there was in fact no basis for the President's finding of the existence of an emergency, for, under this view, the gravity of the emergency and the immediacy of the threatened disaster are considered irrelevant as a matter of law. . . . Presidents have been in the past, and any man worthy of the Office should be in the future, free to take at least interim action necessary to execute legislative programs essential to survival of the Nation.[74]

CHINA, CUBA, AND VIETNAM

Presidents after Truman received similar congressional carte blanche for their foreign policy decisions as the state of permanent crisis continued into the 1950s and 1960s.

Congress in January 1955 authorized President Dwight D. Eisenhower to use force if necessary to defend Chiang Kai-shek's government on Taiwan against the threat of attack from mainland China.

COMMANDER IN THE FIELD, GOVERNOR AT HOME

Within the broad sweep of the power of the commander in chief to conduct war fall a myriad of related duties and powers.

FIELD DECISIONS

First among these is the authority to make command decisions for field operations. Presidents generally have delegated that power to the generals—although Abraham Lincoln, for example, ordered Gen. George McClellan to make a general advance in 1862 to bolster morale and to carry the war into the enemy's territory.

President Woodrow Wilson settled a command controversy that erupted on the Western Front in 1918. Franklin D. Roosevelt personally participated in the decisions that directed the strategy of World War II, the outcome of the war, and postwar territorial divisions.

President Harry S. Truman ordered the atomic bombs dropped at Hiroshima and Nagasaki, and Presidents Lyndon B. Johnson and Richard Nixon selected or approved targets to be hit by air strikes during the Vietnam conflict.

Exercise of constitutional authority as commander in chief extends to all decision-making powers accorded any supreme military commander under international law.

MILITARY JUSTICE

The commander in chief governs the creation of military commissions and tribunals in territories occupied by U.S. forces and fixes the limits of their jurisdiction absent congressional limits on this power. The president's authority also endures after hostilities have ceased.[1]

The commander in chief is the ultimate arbiter of all matters involving the enforcement of rules and regulations related to courts martial,[2] including the amendment of the rules during war.[3] However, the president may dismiss an officer in peacetime only as part of a sentence following court martial.

The Supreme Court has never limited the president's wartime dismissal power. The president may displace an officer in the military service by appointing someone else in his place with the advice and consent of the Senate.[4] He may not make additions to the list of military grades and ranks established by Congress.

CONDUCT OF WAR

In the conduct of war the president may use secret agents to secure information,[5] he may authorize trade with the enemy if Congress approves,[6] and he may compel the aid of citizens and friendly aliens in theaters of military operations.

He may negotiate an armistice to end the fighting and set conditions for the armistice that affect the terms of the subsequent peace agreement.[7]

The president may authorize the occupation of a region or a nation and provide government administration for it,[8] but he cannot annex a region without the approval of Congress.[9]

CONTROL OF PROPERTY

In time of war, the commander in chief may requisition property for military use—an act that incurs the obligation of the United States to give "just compensation."[10] The Court has upheld broad presidential power to use or "take" private property for federal use in wartime. But the government is obligated by the Fifth Amendment to pay "just compensation" to the owners of private property converted or condemned for public use in wartime.[11] Moreover, property taken, but not used, obligates the government to pay compensation.[12]

The president has the power to declare someone an enemy and to order his property seized,[13] and that authority extends to the property of friendly aliens as well as to enemy aliens.[14]

While the concept of "just compensation" applies to citizens and friendly aliens, no such guarantee extends to alien enemies, nor is there an obligation on the part of the government to respond to suits by enemy aliens for return of seized properties.[15]

In addition, the president may, under the war power, fix prices, nullify private contracts,[16] and forbid, regulate, and control the use of foods and malt liquors.[17]

1. *Madsen v. Kinsella*, 343 U.S. 341 at 348 (1952); *Johnson v. Eisentrager*, 399 U.S. 763 at 789 (1950).

2. *Swaim v. United States*, 165 U.S. 553 (1897).

3. *Ex parte Quirin*, 317 U.S. 1 at 28–29 (1942).

4. *Mullan v. United States*, 140 U.S. 240 (1891); *Wallace v. United States*, 257 U.S. 541 (1922).

5. *Totten v. United States*, 92 U.S. 105 (1876).

6. *Hamilton v. Dillon*, 21 Wall. 73 (1875); *Haver v. Yaker*, 9 Wall. 32 (1869).

7. Protocol of August 12, 1898 (stated in McKinley's Second Annual Message) in Fred L. Israel, ed., *The State of the Union Messages of the Presidents 1790–1966*, 3 vols. (New York: Chelsea House, Robert Hector Publishers, 1966), II: 1848–1896; Wilson's Address to Congress (Fourteen Points), in Henry S. Commager, ed., *Documents of American History*, 7th ed. (New York: Appleton-Century-Crofts, 1962), 137–144.

8. *Santiago v. Nogueras*, 214 U.S. 260 (1909); *Dooley v. United States*, 192 U.S. 222 at 230–231 (1901).

9. *Fleming v. Page*, 9 How. 603 at 615 (1850).

10. *Mitchell v. Harmony*, 13 How. 115 (1852); *United States v. Russell*, 13 Wall. 623 (1869).

11. *Davis v. Newton Coal Co.*, 267 U.S. 292 (1925).

12. *International Paper Co. v. United States*, 282 U.S. 399 at 406 (1931); *United States v. Caltex (Philippines) Inc.*, 344 U.S. 149 (1952).

13. *Central Union Trust v. Garvan*, 254 U.S. 554 (1921).

14. *Silesian American Corp. v. Clark*, 332 U.S. 469 (1947).

15. *Clark v. Uebersee-Finanz-Korp.*, 332 U.S. 480 at 484–486 (1947).

16. *Addy v. United States; Ford v. United States*, 264 U.S. 239 at 244–246 (1924).

17. *Starr v. Campbell*, 208 U.S. 527 (1908); *United States v. Standard Brewery Co.*, 251 U.S. 210 (1920).

In March 1956 Eisenhower sought and received congressional authorization to act to block communist aggression in the Middle East. Sixteen months later, he sent Marines to Lebanon to prevent an outbreak of fighting between warring factions there.[75]

President John F. Kennedy obtained a joint congressional resolution on October 3, 1962, authorizing him to use force if necessary to prevent the spread of communism in the Western Hemisphere. The resolution followed discovery of a Soviet-supported missile capability in Cuba, ninety miles from the Florida coast. President Kennedy's decision to "quarantine" Cuba to prevent the landing of Soviet ships laden with missiles and equipment brought the world to the brink of nuclear war.[76]

As the long war in Southeast Asia began to involve the United States more and more, President Lyndon B. Johnson in 1964 sought and received from Congress passage of the Gulf of Tonkin Resolution that read, in part:

. . . the United States is . . . prepared, as the President determines, to take all necessary steps, including the use of armed force, to assist any member or protocol state of the Southeast Asia Collective Defense Treaty requesting defense of its freedom.[77]

Johnson asked Congress to pass the resolution after North Vietnamese patrol boats reportedly attacked U.S. destroyers on patrol in the Gulf of Tonkin. The vote in support of the Southeast Asia Resolution (Tonkin Gulf) was 88–2 in the Senate and 416–0 in the House. Johnson relied on that expression of congressional support, and the broad language of the document, to wage the war in Vietnam.[78]

Military appropriations for defense, approved by Congress, continued to be regarded by some as signaling approval of the president's policies. As in the cases of Lincoln and Wilson, it seemed likely that Presidents Eisenhower, Kennedy, and Johnson would have taken the same actions even without the authorizing resolutions.

Vietnam and the War Powers Debate

The longest undeclared war in U.S. history, costing well over $100 billion and 360,000 American dead and wounded, drew to a close January 23, 1973, with the signing of a cease-fire agreement in Paris.

The fullest expression of legal justification for the Vietnam War came from the State Department's legal adviser, Leonard Meeker, in a memorandum submitted March 11, 1966, to the Senate Committee on Foreign Relations.[79] Meeker argued that the Framers of the Constitution intended the president to be free to repel sudden attacks without prior congressional sanction, even though in the modern era that attack might occur halfway around the globe. Meeker's memorandum identified 125 historical precedents of congressionally unauthorized executive use of military force.[80] The precedents, however, were mostly minor skirmishes that involved a minimum amount of force or actual fighting: landings to protect citizens, enforcement of laws against piracy, Indian skirmishes, the occupation of Caribbean states (usually to prevent political instability, economic collapse, or European intervention).

Meeker argued that the Tonkin Gulf Resolution and the SEATO Treaty authorized Johnson to act to defend Southeast Asia against communism. Making perhaps his most telling political point, Meeker noted the large majorities by which Congress had approved the Tonkin Gulf Resolution and its continuing support of the war through appropriation of funds.[81]

Federal courts were asked repeatedly during the late 1960s and early 1970s to hold that American involvement in the war in Southeast Asia was unconstitutional because Congress had never declared war there.

The Supreme Court, however, steadily declined to hear cases that raised this issue.[82] The Court's refusal was based on the view that war was a political question. *(See box, Court, Congress, and Cambodia, p. 136, in Chapter 4.)*

Nixon and the War Powers

Even after President Richard Nixon signed the Tonkin Gulf repealer measure January 12, 1971, he continued the war in Vietnam under the aegis of the powers of the commander in chief.

The Nixon administration emphasized that Congress was ratifying its policy by approving appropriations for it and declared that the war presented political questions beyond the purviews of judicial scrutiny.[83] Nixon officials emphasized the "merger" theory of war powers, pointing out the progressive blurring of the constitutional distinction between Congress's war power and the president's commander in chief role. Distinctions between the power to declare wars and the power to conduct them were invidious, proponents of the theory argued; the nation was in the strongest position when the president and Congress acted in unison. Therefore, Congress should support the president's policies through appropriations with a minimum of dissent so long as the president, in turn, informed the Congress of his political and military decisions on a regular basis.[84] The clear result of this theory was a virtual monopoly of the war power by the president.

Acting on this theory, Nixon, beginning in 1969, authorized secret American air raids in neutral Cambodia without informing Congress. The following year he ordered American forces into Cambodia to destroy supply centers and staging areas used by North Vietnam for its operations in the South.

In 1972 the president, acting on his own initiative, directed the mining of North Vietnamese ports to forestall the flow of arms to guerrilla and regular forces in South Vietnam, a decision that risked collisions with Russian and Chinese supply vessels. In 1973, attempting to force North Vietnam to make a truce, Nixon ordered carpet bombing of Hanoi and Haiphong. Nixon neither sought nor obtained explicit congressional approval for any of his policies with respect to Vietnam and, when the truce was signed, the 1973 Paris Accords had been negotiated by the president's men without congressional participation.[85]

War Powers Act of 1973

In response to the disregard of its prerogatives by Nixon and his predecessors, Congress on November 7, 1973, passed the War Powers Act over Nixon's veto.[86]

The act authorized the president to undertake limited military action in the absence of a declaration of war. Within forty-eight hours of such action, the law directed the president to make a report in writing to Congress. Military action and troop deployment were limited to sixty days, renewable for an additional thirty days to effect the safe removal of troops. At any

President George Bush shares a meal with troops stationed in the Persian Gulf. In January 1991 Bush asked for and received congressional support for "Operation Desert Storm," the U.S. military operation that drove Iraqi forces out of Kuwait.

time during the sixty-day period, the law stipulated, Congress could order the immediate removal of forces by concurrent resolution, not subject to presidential veto.[87] The legislative veto provision was effectively nullified by the Court's decision in *Immigration and Naturalization Service v. Chadha* (1983), but Congress had not, by 1996, replaced it.

While the act appeared to limit presidential discretion, critics pointed out that it could be interpreted as expanding the president's war-making ability. A blank check to commit troops any-

where, at any time, subject only to a sixty-day to ninety-day limit, indefinitely renewable, appeared to critics as an invitation to havoc or holocaust. Moreover, precisely how Congress could reverse presidential commitment of troops once deployed was never spelled out.[88]

In the early 1980s a group of representatives went to court to sue President Ronald Reagan for violating the War Powers Act by sending military personnel to El Salvador. A federal district judge dismissed the suit in 1982, saying it was up to Congress,

---

THE PRESIDENT, THE GOVERNORS, AND THE NATIONAL GUARD

The Supreme Court in 1990 affirmed the sweep of federal power over the states' National Guard units, upholding a law in which Congress had expressly eliminated the requirement that governors consent before their states' units were called up and sent out of the country. The case that tested this question was brought by Minnesota governor Rudy Perpich, who objected to members of the Minnesota National Guard being put on active duty and sent to Honduras for joint exercises with that country's military.

The call-up and subsequent activity of the National Guard was authorized by a 1986 law allowing the president to dispatch the reservists without the governors' consent. The law was added as part of a defense authorization act after several governors objected on political grounds to units going to Pentagon-sponsored training exercises in Central America.

The provision—called the Montgomery amendment after its sponsor, Rep. G. V. "Sonny" Montgomery, D-Miss.—amended the Armed Forces Reserve Act of 1952, which had required a governor's consent before a National Guard unit could be called to active duty. The new law barred a governor from blocking the participation of a state National Guard unit in a training exercise because of the location or purpose of the exercise.

Perpich contended that the law intruded on states' control over the National Guard under the Constitution's militia clauses. Under

Article I, Section 8, Congress has the power to "provide for calling forth the Militia to execute the Laws of the Union, suppress Insurrections and repel Invasions." A second clause gives Congress power to govern the militia while "employed in the Service of the United States, reserving to the States respectively, the Appointment of the Officers, and the Authority of training the Militia according to the discipline prescribed by Congress."

Making quite clear that federal power is supreme in the area of military affairs, the Supreme Court in June 1990 ruled unanimously that the president has the power to order National Guard units to training missions outside the United States without the approval of governors. Writing for the Court in *Perpich v. Department of Defense*, Justice John Paul Stevens said the 1986 law did not infringe on state powers and was valid.[1]

Stevens wrote:

[T]he members of the National Guard of Minnesota who are ordered into federal service with the National Guard of the United States lose their status as members of the state militia during their period of active duty. . . . If the discipline required for effective service in the Armed Forces of a global power requires training in distant lands, or distant skies, Congress has the authority to provide it.[2]

1. *Perpich v. Department of Defense*, 496 U.S. 334 (1990).
2. Id. at 347, 350–351.

not the courts, to decide whether Reagan's action violated the law. The Supreme Court refused to review the decision.[89]

Similarly, in late 1990, as the Bush administration and Congress braced for a possible war in the Persian Gulf, a group of representatives filed a lawsuit seeking a preliminary injunction to prevent President Bush from ordering U.S. troops in the gulf into offensive combat without prior authorization from Congress. In arguments in federal district court, the members of Congress said the Constitution's war powers clause dictated that Congress debate and vote in favor of a formal declaration of war before U.S. troops could be used to drive Iraqi forces from Kuwait. In response, the Justice Department said Article II gave the president the ultimate authority in foreign affairs as commander in chief. A federal judge refused to issue an injunction, saying that the case was not ripe because only 10 percent of Congress was seeking relief rather than a majority.[90] The judge said it would be premature and presumptuous to issue a decision on the question.

On the same day, another federal judge issued a decision more in keeping with the courts' traditional reluctance to become embroiled in war-making disputes.[91] The judge held that the courts could not decide whether Bush needed congressional permission to go to war because it was a political question beyond the judicial realm. The judge dismissed a complaint by a member of the National Guard who protested serving in the gulf until Bush received congressional authorization.

In January 1991, the legal issue became moot when Bush decided to request—and Congress approved—a resolution authorizing use of U.S. military to force Iraq out of Kuwait.

THE COURT'S ROLE

While the Supreme Court's rulings have served to enlarge the scope of the executive's war power rather than to narrow it, the possibility remains that some court, convinced of the unconstitutionality of a president's course of action, could and would order him to desist.

But the Supreme Court has generally adhered to the view which Justice Robert H. Jackson set out in the 1952 *Steel Seizure* case:

We should not use this occasion to circumscribe, much less to contract, the lawful role of the President as Commander-in-Chief. I should indulge the widest latitude of interpretation to sustain his exclusive function to command the instruments of national force, at least when turned against the outside world for the security of our society. But when it is turned inward, not because of rebellion but because of a lawful economic struggle . . . it should have no such indulgence. His command power is not such an absolute . . . but is subject to limitations consistent with a constitutional Republic whose law and policy-making branch is a representative Congress. The purpose of lodging dual titles in one man was to insure that the civilian would control the military, not to enable the military to subordinate the presidential office. No penance would ever expiate the sin against free government of holding that a President can escape control of executive powers by law through assuming his military role.[92]

The Architect of Foreign Policy

The Constitution grants the president the power to make treaties and to receive and appoint ambassadors. In addition to the foreign policy powers asserted by the president as commander in chief, these specific grants of power are the source of the president's authority to conduct the nation's foreign relations and shape its foreign policy.

The treaty-making power has been the more significant grant, and it has been interpreted by the Supreme Court as a broad base for the president's power over foreign policy. The Court's traditional view on this matter was foreshadowed by Rep. John Marshall's speech on the floor of the House in 1800, defending President John Adams's unilateral decision to return a British fugitive to British authorities.

Marshall declared:

The President is the sole organ of the nation in its external relations, and its sole representative with foreign nations. Of consequence, the demand of a foreign nation can only be made on him. He possesses the whole executive power.[1]

The Constitution, as in the grant of war powers, divided the power over foreign affairs. The Founding Fathers desired a strong executive but not another English monarch. They brought Congress into the treaty-making process. The president was to initiate policy and make treaties with other nations, but he had to obtain the consent of two-thirds of the Senate for ratification of a treaty.

The internal tension established in the Constitution with respect to foreign relations powers provided a check on the president. Congress was granted other powers related to foreign relations: notably, the appropriations power; the authority to raise, maintain, and regulate the armed forces; and the power "to declare War, grant Letters of Marque and Reprisal, and make rules concerning Captures on Land and Water."

Alexander Hamilton noted the reciprocal nature of the treaty-making power when he observed that "The power of making treaties . . . seems therefore to form a distinct department and to belong, properly neither to the legislative nor to the executive."[2]

The debate over control of foreign policy began at the Constitutional Convention, when the Founding Fathers pondered the merits of lodging the foreign relations power almost exclusively in the hands of the chief executive.[3]

In 1793 Hamilton and James Madison engaged in an exchange of views over the executive prerogative in foreign affairs prompted by the debate over America's neutrality in the wars of the French Revolution.

Hamilton, as "Pacificus," defended President George Washington's Neutrality Proclamation and his unilateral promulgation of it. Foreign policy was an executive function, Hamilton declared. Congress had the power to declare war, but the president had the power to make treaties and preserve peace until Congress declared war. Hamilton noted, "it belongs to the 'executive power' to do whatever else the law of nations, co-operating with the treaties of the country, enjoin in the intercourse of the United States with foreign powers."[4] Hamilton conceded that executive policy might influence the decision of Congress, but he insisted that each branch of government was free to perform its assigned duties, according to its view of the matter.

At Thomas Jefferson's instigation, Madison responded to Hamilton's defense of executive prerogative. Under the pseudonym "Helvidius," Madison defended the congressional initiative in foreign affairs. He compared Hamilton's assertions of presidential independence to the royal prerogative of British monarchs and asserted that Congress, too, could decide when matters of national policy led to war. Deliberations over grave matters of war and peace could not be foreclosed by the president's decisions, Madison said. What would be the result if Congress declared war and the president proclaimed neutrality? he asked.[5]

The question never received a formal reply from Hamilton, but in 1794 Congress passed the first neutrality act superseding the president's proclamation. This act established a congressional role in declarations of neutrality. Even Jefferson had already conceded, however, that the role of Congress in the negotiation of treaties and in the conduct of diplomacy was limited. In 1790 he observed that "[t]he transaction of business with foreign nations is Executive altogether."[6]

The Supreme Court has sustained the "sole organ" principle upholding the president's preeminence in the conduct of foreign relations, and it has checked challenges to the president's treaty-making power by the states and by the Senate while affirming the president's exclusive role. But the Court has refused to hear other cases that challenged the president's conduct of foreign affairs on the grounds that the issue was political in nature and therefore beyond the realm of judicial determination.

"A Divided Power"

The Supreme Court has extended to the president broad discretionary powers in foreign affairs even while it limited or denied the president the same latitude in the exercise of power related to domestic affairs.

As E. S. Corwin has observed, in the field of foreign affairs "[t]he power to determine the substantive content of American policy is a divided power, with the lion's share falling, usually, though by no means always, to the president."[7] Other government actors in the policy process are the states, the Court, and Congress.

THE STATES' ROLE

One of the first foreign policy matters settled by the Supreme Court was the question of the states' role in foreign affairs. The source of the foreign affairs power was debated in 1795 by Justices William Paterson and James Iredell. Iredell wrote that sovereignty belonged to the states in foreign affairs prior to ratification of the Constitution; with ratification, that sovereignty passed to the national government from the states.

Paterson disagreed. Sovereignty never belonged to the separate states, he argued; the power to conduct foreign relations passed to the national government as an inheritance of power from the Continental Congress.[8] Paterson's view of an inherent foreign affairs power was expanded by the 1936 *Curtiss-Wright* decision.[9]

The outcome of the Court's argument in 1795, however, was a flat denial to the states of any control over or role in foreign policy matters. The treaty-making power was not affected by the doctrine of "dual federalism" reserving undelegated powers to the states.

In *Ware v. Hylton* (1796) a war law passed by Virginia during the Revolution provided that British-owned property be sequestered and individual debts owed to British citizens be paid to a designated state official. But the 1783 peace treaty permitted British subjects to sue in state courts to collect debts owed them prior to the Revolution.

The year after the Iredell-Paterson debate, the Supreme Court ruled that the treaty provision nullified the state law. Powers reserved to the states by the Tenth Amendment did not include any powers in the field of foreign relations. Justice Samuel Chase observed:

A treaty cannot be the Supreme law of the land, that is of all the United States, if any act of a State Legislature can stand in its way. . . . It is the declared will of the people of the United States that every treaty made, by the authority of the United States shall be superior to the Constitution and laws of any individual state.[10]

Exclusive federal control over foreign relations and the treaty-making power was again asserted by the Court in an 1840 case. The state of Vermont had decided to comply with Canada's request to return a fugitive Canadian murderer. Writing for the Court, Chief Justice Roger B. Taney denied the state authorities' power to return the prisoner because the United States government had no extradition treaty with Great Britain. Taney wrote:

It was one of the main objects of our Constitution to make us, so far as regarded our foreign relations, one people and one nation; and to cut off all communications between foreign governments and the several State authorities.[11]

Justice William O. Douglas reiterated this view in a 1942 opinion.

Power over external affairs is not shared by the States; it is vested in the national government exclusively. . . . And the policies of the States become wholly irrelevant to judicial inquiry when the United States, acting within its constitutional sphere, seeks enforcement of its foreign policy in the courts.[12]

THE SUPREME COURT'S ROLE

In the field of foreign policy, the Supreme Court often has invoked the "political question" doctrine to avoid head-on collisions with the president. The doctrine rests on the separation of powers theory—that the Supreme Court exercises the judicial power and leaves political, or policy, questions to Congress and the president.

Chief Justice John Marshall in 1829 explained the rule in one of the first cases in which it was applied. The Court refused to rule on a boundary dispute between Spain and the United States.

In a controversy between two nations concerning national boundary, it is scarcely possible that the courts of either should refuse to abide by the measures adopted by its own government. There being no common tribunal to decide between them, each determines for itself on its own rights, and if they cannot adjust their differences peaceably, the right remains with the strongest. The judiciary is not that department of the government to which the assertion of its interests against foreign powers is confided. . . . A question like this respecting the boundaries of nations, is . . . more a political than a legal question.[13]

Subsequent Court rulings increased the list of political questions. The Court either supported the decision of the political departments or refused to judge them. These political questions include: presidential decisions about the status of belligerents under international law;[14] the determination of when negotiated treaties had been ratified by another signatory nation;[15] decisions as to the recognition and treatment of de jure and de facto governments;[16] judgments about accredited diplomatic representatives to the United States;[17] the length of military occupations under treaty terms;[18] the effective date of treaties;[19] and when tacit consent renewal of lapsed treaties was permissible.[20]

In the landmark political question decision of *Baker v. Carr* (1962), Justice William J. Brennan Jr. provided a concise statement of the Court's criteria for considering matters that concern foreign relations:

There are sweeping statements to the effect that all questions touching foreign relations are political questions. . . . Yet it is error to suppose that every case or controversy which touches foreign relations lies beyond judicial cognizance. Our cases in this field show a discriminating analysis of the particular question posed, in terms of the history of its management by the political branches, of its susceptibility to judicial handling in the light of its nature and posture in the specific case, and of the possible consequences of judicial action.[21]

THE SENATE'S ROLE

While the Constitution divides the war powers fairly evenly between Congress and the executive, the only explicit foreign policy power it grants to Congress is the Senate's power to approve treaties the president has negotiated.

The Constitution does not say so, but the Senate traditionally has claimed, and the Supreme Court upheld, the right to amend and modify treaties submitted for its approval. *(See "Treaty Powers," pp. 139–140, in Chapter 4.)*

In 1901 the Court defined a valid treaty and the Senate's role in making it:

Obviously the treaty must contain the whole contract between the parties, and the power of the Senate is limited to a ratification of such terms as have already been agreed upon between the President, acting for the United States, and the commissioners of the other contracting power. The Senate has no right to ratify the treaty and introduce new terms into it, which shall be obligatory upon the other power, although it may refuse its ratification, or make such ratification conditional upon the adoption of amendments to the treaty.[22]

THE "SOLE NEGOTIATOR"

The logical result of the Court's restrictive view of the roles left for the states, for the Court itself, and even for the Senate in foreign affairs was its 1936 decision that the president was the "sole negotiator" of foreign policy. Improbable as it may seem, a war between Paraguay and Bolivia in 1932 was the catalyst for that broad ruling from the Court undergirding the president's primary role in foreign affairs.[23]

Both sides in the war depended upon outside military suppliers. American arms manufacturers, facing a depressed economy at home, exported weapons to the belligerents. Revulsion against the war, isolationist sentiment at home, and pressure from Great Britain and the League of Nations caused the United States to act to end the arms trade.

Congress on May 24, 1934, approved a joint resolution that authorized President Franklin D. Roosevelt to embargo the arms shipments if, in his judgment, an embargo would contribute to ending the war.[24] The resolution provided for fines and imprisonment, or both, for those who violated the embargo. Roosevelt signed the resolution into law May 28, 1934.[25] The resolution in no way restricted or directed his discretion in instituting the embargo.

Roosevelt soon declared an embargo in effect. Curtiss-Wright Export Corporation and two other companies subsequently were convicted of selling aircraft machine guns to Bolivia in violation of the embargo. They challenged the constitutionality of the resolution, arguing that it was an improper delegation of congressional power to the president. The Court already had evinced sympathy for such challenges, striking down several major New Deal initiatives in 1925 on that basis.[26] *(See "The Court and the Roosevelt Revolution," pp. 248–252.)*

But the Court upheld the embargo resolution. The vote was 7–1. Justice Harlan Fiske Stone took no part in the case. Justice James C. McReynolds dissented.

Justice George Sutherland's majority opinion upheld sweeping executive powers in foreign affairs. Sutherland distinguished between "external" and "internal" powers of the federal government—foreign policy and domestic policy. Based on his reading of the historical evidence and on his own previous studies of the foreign affairs power, Sutherland concluded that the source of national authority in foreign relations was the British crown, not the separate states. This source placed the foreign affairs power on an extraconstitutional footing different from that of the internal powers, which passed from the states to the federal government.[27]

Sutherland's opinion elaborated on the theory of external sovereignty argued in 1795 by Justice William Paterson. Sutherland wrote:

The broad statement that the federal government can exercise no powers except those specifically enumerated in the Constitution, and such implied powers as are necessary and proper to carry into effect the enumerated powers, is categorically true only in respect of our internal affairs. In that field, the primary purpose of the Constitution was to carve from the general mass of legislative powers then possessed by the states such positions as it was thought desirable to vest in the federal government, leaving those not included in the enumeration still in the states. . . . That this doctrine applies only to powers which the state had is self-evident. And since the states severally never possessed international powers, such powers could not have been carved from the mass of state powers but obviously were transmitted to the United States from some other source. . . .

As a result of separation from Great Britain by the colonies, acting as a unit, the powers of external sovereignty passed from the Crown not to the colonies severally, but to the colonies in their collective and corporate capacity as the United States of America. . . . Rulers come and go; governments and forms of government change; but sovereignty survives. A political society cannot endure without a supreme will somewhere. Sovereignty is never held in suspense. When, therefore, the external sovereignty of Great Britain in respect of the colonies ceased, it passed to the Union. . . . It results that the investment of the federal government with the powers of external sovereignty did not depend upon the affirmative grants of the Constitution. The powers to declare and wage war, to conclude peace, to make treaties, to maintain diplomatic relations with other sovereignties, if they had never been mentioned in the Constitution, would have vested in the federal government as necessary concomitants of nationality.[28]

Sutherland then, echoing John Marshall's phrases, asserted that the president has the major role in foreign affairs.

The President alone has the power to speak as a representative of the nation. He makes treaties with the advice and consent of the Senate; but he alone negotiates. Into the field of negotiation the Senate cannot intrude; and Congress is powerless to invade it. . . .

It is important to bear in mind that we are here dealing not alone with an authority vested in the President by an exertion of legislative power, but with such an authority plus the very delicate, plenary and exclusive power of the President as the sole organ of the federal government in the field of international relations—a power which does not require as a basis for its exercise an act of Congress, but which . . . must be exercised in subordination to the applicable provisions of the Constitution.[29]

Delegation of power to the president in the foreign affairs field, therefore, was not to be judged by the same standards as delegation of power over domestic matters.

When the President is to be authorized by legislation to act in respect of a matter intended to affect a situation in foreign territory, the legislator properly bears in mind the important consideration that the form of the President's action—or, indeed whether he shall act at all—may well depend, among other things, upon the nature of . . . confidential information which he has or may thereafter receive. . . . This consideration . . . discloses the unwisdom of requiring Congress in this field of governmental power to lay down narrowly definite standards by which the President is to be governed.[30]

Although the United States had negotiated treaties that promised immigrants free entry into the country, Congress in the 1800s passed laws taxing their admission. In 1884 the Court declared such taxes valid. Justice Samuel F. Miller stated in the *Head Money Cases* that "a treaty made by the United States with any foreign nation . . . is subject to such acts as Congress may pass."

The Treaty Power: Its Effects and Its Limits

Treaties—their effect, their relationship to conflicting laws, to the Constitution, and to the allocation of power between the states and the federal government—have been the subject of numerous Supreme Court rulings.

In 1829 Chief Justice John Marshall discussed the nature and the force of a treaty:

A treaty is in its nature a contract between two nations, not a Legislative Act. It does not generally effect, of itself, the object to be accomplished, especially so far as its operation is infraterritorial; but is carried into execution by the sovereign power of the respective parties to the instrument.

In the United States a different principle is established. Our Constitution declares a treaty to be the law of the land. It is, consequently, to be regarded in courts of justice as equivalent to an Act of the Legislature, whenever it operates of itself without the aid of any legislative provision. But when the terms of the stipulation import a contract—when either of the parties engages to perform a particular act—the treaty addresses itself to the political, not the judicial department; and the Legislature must execute the contract before it can become a rule for the court.[31]

The distinction that Marshall set out—between a self-executing treaty and a non-self-executing treaty, which requires legislative action—survives to the present. A self-executing treaty requires no legislation to put it into effect. For example, treaties that defined the rights of aliens in the United States would be self-implementing once approved by the Senate and would bind the courts to enforce their terms.

A non-self-executing treaty, on the other hand, does not take effect until implemented through legislation approved by the political departments of the government and would not be enforced by the courts until then.

Neither a treaty nor a statute has intrinsic superiority, and the more recent will prevail. In the case of a non-self-executing treaty, however, congressional acts take precedence. Justice Samuel F. Miller stated the rule in the *Head Money Cases* (1884): "a treaty made by the United States with any foreign nation . . . is subject to such acts as Congress may pass for its enforcement, modification, or repeal."[32]

Despite earlier treaties with several nations that guaranteed free admission of immigrants to the United States, the Court upheld a law that placed a tax on immigrants. The majority opinion defined a valid treaty and its relationship to acts of Congress:

A treaty is primarily a compact between independent nations. It depends for the enforcement of its provisions on the interest and the honor of the governments which are parties to it. If these fail, its infraction becomes the subject of international negotiations and reclamations, so far as the injured party chooses to seek redress, which may in the end be enforced by actual war. It is obvious that with all this the judicial courts have nothing to do and can give no redress. But a treaty may also contain provisions which confer certain rights upon citizens or subjects of one of the nations residing in the territorial limits of the other, which partake of the nature of municipal law, and which are capable of enforcement as between private parties in the courts of the country. . . .

A treaty, then, is a law of the land as an act of Congress is, whenever its provisions prescribe a rule by which the rights of the private citizen or subject may be determined. And when such rights are of a nature to be enforced in a court of justice, that court resorts to the treaty for a rule of decision for the case as it would to a statute.[33]

A treaty, the Court has held, may shift regulation of a matter from state to federal control, thereby giving Congress new powers it would not possess without the treaty. In 1916 the United States, Britain, and Canada signed a treaty to protect migratory birds by limiting hunting seasons and by other measures. The treaty stipulated that both the United States and Canada would seek domestic legislation to put the law into effect.

Two previous acts of Congress regulating migratory bird hunting had been struck down in lower federal courts, which found them an unconstitutional extension of federal power into an area reserved to the states by the Tenth Amendment. The 1916 treaty was implemented by a 1918 law that regulated the hunting of migratory birds and authorized the secretary of agriculture to administer the rules.[34]

Missouri challenged the law. But the Court upheld it as necessary to carry treaty provisions into effect. The plenary nature of the federal treaty-making power, said the Court, was sufficient to grant Congress control over matters otherwise ascribed to the states.

The effect of the ruling in *Missouri v. Holland* was to hold that ratification of a treaty could give Congress powers it would not otherwise have. Justice Oliver Wendell Holmes's opinion viewed the treaty power broadly:

To answer this question it is not enough to refer to the Tenth Amendment, reserving the powers not delegated to the United States, because by Article II, § 2, the power to make treaties is delegated expressly, and by Article VI treaties made under authority of the United States, along with the Constitution and the laws of the United States made in pursuance thereof, are declared the supreme law of the land. If the treaty is valid there can be no dispute about the validity of the statute under Article I, § 8, as a necessary and proper means to execute the powers of the Government. . . .

It is said that a treaty cannot be valid if it infringes the Constitution, that there are limits, therefore, to the treaty making power, and that one such limit is that what an act of Congress could not do unaided, in derogation of the powers reserved to the States, a treaty cannot do. An earlier act of Congress that attempted by itself and not in pursuance of a treaty to regulate the killing of migratory birds within the States had been held bad in the District Court. . . . Those decisions were supported by arguments that migratory birds were owned by the States in their sovereign capacity for the benefit of their people, and that . . . this control was one that Congress had no power to displace. The same argument is supposed to apply now with equal force.

Whether the two cases were decided rightly or not they cannot be accepted as a test of the treaty power. Acts of Congress are the supreme law of the land only when made in pursuance of the Constitution, while treaties are declared to be so when made under the authority of the United States. . . . We do not mean to imply that there are no qualifications to the treaty making power; but they must be ascertained in an different way. It is obvious that there may be matters of the sharpest exigency for the national well-being that an act of Congress could not deal with but that a treaty followed by such an act could and it is not lightly to be assumed that, in matters requiring national action, "a power which must belong to and somewhere reside in every civilized government" is not to be found. . . . The treaty in question does not

contravene any prohibitory world to be found in the Constitution. The only question is whether it is forbidden by some invisible radiation from the general terms of the Tenth Amendment. . . .

Here a national interest of very nearly the first magnitude is involved. It can be protected only by national action in concert with that of another power. The subject-matter is only transitorily within the state and has no permanent habitat therein. But for the treaty and the statute there soon might be no birds for any power to deal with. We see nothing in the Constitution that compels the government to sit by while a food supply is cut off and the protectors of our forests and our crops are destroyed. It is not sufficient to rely upon the States.[35]

TERMINATION OF TREATIES

The Court has held that the termination of treaties, even those terminable on notice, requires an act of Congress. Legislative repeal of a treaty, however, may violate international obligations undertaken in the treaty provisions. In that case, as previously noted, the Court has said the matter

becomes the subject of international negotiations and reclamations, so far as the injured party chooses to seek redress, which may in the end be enforced by actual war. It is obvious that with all this the judicial courts have nothing to do and can give no redress.[36]

The Court affirmed its support of congressional power to repeal treaties in 1899 when it held that:

Congress by legislation and so far as the people and authorities of the United States are concerned, could abrogate a treaty made between this country and another country which had been negotiated by the President and approved by the Senate.[37]

An act of Congress has been held to have superseded a conflicting provision of a prior treaty. Although the Court has never declared a treaty unconstitutional, it has voided an executive agreement with Canada that conflicted with extant legislation.[38]

Generally, legislative practice and executive opinion support the view that terminating international pacts belongs, as a prerogative of sovereignty, to Congress. But the president, in his function of interpreting treaties prior to their enforcement, may find that a treaty has been breached and may decide that a treaty is no longer binding on the United States. The Court has stipulated that treaties may be abrogated by agreement between the contracting parties, by the treaty provisions, by congressional repeal, by the president, and by the president and the Senate acting jointly.[39] In 1979 the Court sidestepped a challenge to President Jimmy Carter's unilateral abrogation of a mutual defense treaty with Taiwan, a consequence of Carter's recognition of the Chinese government in Beijing. As a result, there is now political—if not legal—precedent for this type of action by a president.[40]

CONSTITUTIONAL LIMITS

In 1889 the Court discussed the unlimited nature of the treaty power—but made clear that a treaty could be found unconstitutional. The Court wrote:

That the treaty power of the United States extends to all proper subjects of negotiation between our government and the governments of other nations, is clear. . . . The treaty power, as expressed in the Constitution, is in terms unlimited except by those restraints which are found

INTERPRETING A TREATY LITERALLY

The abduction of a Mexican citizen, reportedly at the direction of U.S. officials, led to an unusual legal dispute over an extradition treaty in 1992. The Mexican allegedly had taken part in the grisly murder of an undercover federal drug agent.

Humberto Alvarez-Machain was abducted in 1990 from his home in Guadalajara and flown by private plane to Texas, where U.S. federal agents arrested him. He was indicted for participating in the kidnapping and murder of Drug Enforcement Administration special agent Enrique Camarena-Salazar and a Mexican pilot working with Camarena, Alfredo Zavala-Avelar. The defendant, a medical doctor, was accused of joining in the drug agent's murder by prolonging the agent's life with drugs so that others could torture and interrogate him. Widely reported in the United States, the crime came to represent part of the abomination of illegal drug trafficking.

But lower courts dismissed the indictment against Alvarez-Machain, saying his abduction violated the 1978 Extradition Treaty between the United States and Mexico. In June 1992, the Supreme Court by a 6–3 vote reversed and said Alvarez-Machain could be tried here. The Court read the treaty literally and observed, "The Treaty says nothing about the obligations of the United States and Mexico to refrain from forcible abductions of people from the territory of the other nation, or the consequence under the Treaty if such an abduction occurs."[1]

Writing for the majority, Chief Justice William H. Rehnquist said, "Mexico has protested the abduction of respondent through diplomatic notes, and the decision of whether respondent should be returned to Mexico, as a matter outside of the Treaty, is a matter for the Executive Branch."[2]

He relied in *United States v. Alvarez-Machain* on a pair of 1886 cases: *United States v. Rauscher,* in which the Court held that an individual brought to the United States under an extradition treaty must be tried according to the provisions of the treaty, and *Ker v. Illinois,* in which the Court upheld the larceny conviction of a man who had been abducted in Lima, Peru to face his charges in an Illinois court.[3]

The Court said the Alvarez-Machain case more aptly compared to *Ker,* because the defendant's seizure was not according to the terms of a treaty. The majority downplayed the fact that in *Ker,* the U.S. government did not participate in the abduction and Peru did not object to the man's prosecution.

While the U.S.-Mexico treaty gives the two countries the option of either extraditing the individuals in question or keeping them in their own country for prosecution, Rehnquist said the treaty

does not purport to specify the only way in which one country may gain custody of a national of the other country for the purposes of prosecution. . . . The history of negotiation and practice under the Treaty also fails to show that abductions outside of the Treaty constitute a violation of the Treaty. As the Solicitor General notes, the Mexican government was made aware, as early as 1906, of the Ker doctrine, and the United States' position that it applied to forcible abductions made outside of the terms of the United States-Mexico extradition treaty.[4]

Rehnquist was joined by Justices Byron R. White, Antonin Scalia, Anthony M. Kennedy, David H. Souter, and Clarence Thomas. Dissenting were Justices Harry A. Blackmun, John Paul Stevens, and Sandra Day O'Connor. In a statement written by Stevens, they said the treaty with Mexico was a comprehensive document containing twenty-three articles and designed to cover the entire subject of extradition.

Stevens said the Court's opinion

fails to differentiate between the conduct of private citizens, which does not violate any treaty obligation, and conduct expressly authorized by the Executive Branch of the Government, which unquestionably constitutes a flagrant violation of international law, and in my opinion, also constitutes a breach of our treaty obligations. . . . [T]he desire for revenge exerts a kind of hydraulic pressure before which even well settled principles of law will bend, but it is precisely at such moments that we should remember and be guided by our duty to render judgment evenly and dispassionately according to law.[5]

1. *United States v. Alvarez-Machain* 112 S. Ct. 2188 (1992).
2. Id.
3. *United States v. Rauscher,* 119 U.S. 407 (1886), *Ker v. Illinois,* 119 U.S. 436 (1886).
4. *United States v. Alvarez-Machain,* 112 S. Ct. 2188 (1992).
5. Id.

in that instrument against the action of the government or of its departments, and those arising from the nature of the government itself and of that of the States. It would not be contended that it extends so far as to authorize what the Constitution forbids, or a change in the character of the government or in that of one of the States, or a cession of any portion of the territory of the latter, without its consent.[41]

The Court has never held a treaty unconstitutional, but in 1957 it made clear the continuing validity of the view that the treaty power is subject to the limits set by the Constitution. Writing for the Court in the case of *Reid v. Covert,* Justice Hugo L. Black stated,

no agreement with a foreign nation can confer power on the Congress, or on any other branch of government, which is free from the re-

straints of the Constitution. . . . It would be manifestly contrary to the objectives of those who created the Constitution . . . let alone alien to our entire constitutional history and tradition—to construe Article VI [the supremacy clause] as permitting the United States to exercise power under an international agreement without observing constitutional prohibitions. . . .

The prohibitions of the Constitution were designed to apply to all branches of the National Government and they cannot be nullified by the Executive and the Senate combined.

There is nothing new or unique about what we say here. This Court has regularly and uniformly recognized the supremacy of the Constitution over a treaty. . . . This Court has also repeatedly taken the position that an Act of Congress, which must comply with the Constitution, is on a full parity with a treaty, and that when a statute which is subsequent in time is inconsistent with a treaty, the statute to the extent of conflict renders the treaty null. It would be completely anomalous to say that a treaty need not comply with the Constitution when such an agreement can be overridden by a statute that must conform to that instrument.

There is nothing in *State of Missouri v. Holland* . . . which is contrary to the position taken here. There the Court carefully noted that the treaty involved was not inconsistent with any specific provision of the Constitution. The Court was concerned with the Tenth Amendment which reserves to the States or the people all power not delegated to the National Government. To the extent that the United States can validly make treaties, the people and the States have delegated their power to the National Government and the Tenth Amendment is no barrier.[42]

The Use of Executive Agreements

"Every time we open a new privy, we have to have an executive agreement," Secretary of State John Foster Dulles facetiously told a Senate subcommittee in 1953.[43] Dulles exaggerated the problem but underscored the growing preference by presidents to negotiate executive agreements rather than submit treaties for Senate approval. Presidents can negotiate executive agreements personally and have the advantage of greater control by avoiding Senate debate and delays as in treaty ratification.

In that hearing Dulles estimated that the United States had entered into roughly ten thousand executive agreements in connection with the North Atlantic Treaty Organization (NATO) alone.[44]

Of the large number of such agreements, however, only a small percentage rested only upon the president's powers in foreign relations or as commander in chief. Many of the agreements, authorized in advance by Congress, rested in addition upon congressional statutes or Senate-ratified treaty provisions.[45] Therefore, executive agreements can be divided into two types: those authorized by Congress and those made on presidential initiative.

AUTHORIZED AGREEMENTS

Authorized agreements have been made on a wide variety of matters early and often in the nation's history. Congress authorized the executive branch to enter into negotiations when the United States needed to borrow money from foreign countries, and when it appropriated money to pay tribute to the pirates to prevent attacks on shipping.[46] Moreover, Texas, Hawaii, and Samoa became U.S. possessions by executive agreements approved by congressional resolution.[47] Similar broad grants of

RECOGNITION AND NONRECOGNITION

The power of recognition of foreign governments or the reverse side of the coin—nonrecognition—has been an important tool in the president's conduct of foreign relations. This power has been derived from the Constitution's statement that the executive "shall receive ambassadors and other public ministers."

Although the president occasionally has sought the cooperation of Congress in recognizing nations, the act of recognition is a presidential function. Presidential power to determine which nation held sovereign jurisdiction over a region has been sustained by the Court. In *Williams v. Suffolk Ins. Co.* (1839), the Court refused to consider a challenge to President Martin Van Buren's decision not to recognize Argentina's claim of sovereignty over the Falkland Islands.

The opinion defined the narrow purview of the Court's scrutiny where executive and/or "political" questions were involved:

When the executive branch of the government, which is charged with our foreign relations, shall . . . assume a fact in regard to the sovereignty of any island or country, it is conclusive on the judicial department. . . . And in this view, it is not material to inquire, nor is it the province of the court to determine, whether the executive be right or wrong. It is enough to know, that in the exercise of his constitutional functions, he had decided the question. Having done this . . . it is obligatory on the people and government of the Union.[1]

An 1897 Senate Foreign Relations Committee report on the subject of recognition concluded that "the executive branch is the sole mouthpiece of the nation in communication with foreign sovereignties."[2]

The practice of refusing to recognize governments has been largely a political decision vested in the executive branch and unchallenged by the courts.

President Woodrow Wilson decided not to recognize the de facto government of Mexico's provisional president Huerta in 1913—an act that hastened Huerta's downfall a year later.[3] Wilson used the nonrecognition policy with considerable discretion, and American presidents in the twentieth century followed suit.

Every president between Wilson and Franklin D. Roosevelt had refused to recognize the Union of Soviet Socialist Republics, until Roosevelt's policy reversal in 1933.[4] President Herbert C. Hoover followed the nonrecognition principle with respect to the Japanese puppet government (Manchukuo) in Manchuria in 1932.[5]

And every president from Harry S. Truman to Lyndon B. Johnson refused to recognize the communist government of mainland China until President Richard Nixon's de facto recognition in 1972. In 1995 President Bill Clinton recognized Vietnam, urged in part by U.S. business interests that saw rich potential in Vietnam's oil reserves and economic development. A year earlier President Clinton, with the legally unnecessary but politically important endorsement of the Senate, had formally ended eighteen years of trade sanctions against Vietnam, sanctions that had been imposed at the conclusion of the U.S. war in Southeast Asia.

1. *Williams v. Suffolk Ins. Co.*, 13 Pet. 414 at 419–420 (1839).
2. Senate Doc., No. 56, 54th Cong., 2d sess. (1897), 20–22.
3. Samuel E. Morison, Henry Steele Commager, and William E. Leuchtenburg, *The Growth of the American Republic*, 2 vols. (New York: Oxford University Press, 1969), II: 354.
4. *The Constitution of the United States of America, Analysis and Interpretation* (Washington, D.C.: U.S. Government Printing Office, 1973), 544.
5. Ibid.

authority through congressional approval of executive agreements underlie the president's power to lower tariff barriers and ease restrictions on international trade.

The Lend-Lease Act of March 11, 1941, granted Franklin Roosevelt the power to enter into executive agreements to manufacture in government arsenals or "otherwise procure" defense articles and "to sell, transfer, exchange, lease, and lend those war materials to the governments of any country deemed vital to the defense of the United States."[48]

Another form of congressional authorization of presidential agreements was the United Nations Participation Act of December 20, 1945, which permitted the president to negotiate a series of agreements with the UN Security Council providing for the number and types of armed forces to be made available to the council for the purpose of maintaining peace and international security.[49]

Presidents also have negotiated agreements with other nations about the status of forces stationed on foreign soil. These agreements usually afforded American military personnel and their dependents a qualified privilege of trial by United States courts martial while within the jurisdiction of another country.

PRESIDENTIAL INITIATIVES

In 1817 President James Monroe agreed with Great Britain to limit arms on the Great Lakes. Executive treaty-making, accomplished by an exchange of notes approved by the Senate, took place without an exchange of ratifications.[50] Indian raids along the border between Mexico and the United States led to a series of agreements (1882–1896) that permitted troops of both nations to cross the international border in pursuit of marauding Indians. Presidents took these actions under their commander in chief powers, and the Court in 1902 found "probable" justification for the agreements.

While no act of Congress authorizes the department to permit the introduction of foreign troops, the power to give such permission without legislative assent was probably assumed to exist from the authority of the President as commander in chief.[51]

Four justices in dissent, however, said that such acts by the president required treaty or statutory sanction.

President William McKinley ended the Spanish-American War by such an agreement, sent troops to China in the face of the Boxer Rebellion, and signed a Boxer Indemnity Protocol, along with other European powers—without Senate approval.[52] Secretary of State John Hay agreed to the substance of the "open door" notes that guaranteed Chinese sovereignty and called a halt to the establishment of "spheres of influence" in China.[53] President Theodore Roosevelt initialed what amounted to a secret treaty between Japan and the United States that recognized Japan's military protectorate in Korea, as well as agreements that dealt with Japanese immigration and the balance of power in the Pacific.[54]

Woodrow Wilson's secretary of state, Robert Lansing, exchanged letters with Japan that recognized that nation's "special

---

BANNING THE BOAT PEOPLE

The relatively unfettered power of the president to use the Coast Guard to stop and return unwanted visitors beyond the territorial waters of the United States was underscored by a Supreme Court ruling in 1993.

In the case of *Sale v. Haitian Centers Council Inc.* (113 S. Ct. 2549, 1993), the Court was asked to invalidate the "interdiction policy" toward Haitian refugees seeking to come to the United States by boat. This policy had been adopted by President George Bush and was continued by President Bill Clinton.

To deter Haitians from making the dangerous journey from their homeland to the United States in small, unseaworthy boats, Bush and Clinton ordered the Coast Guard to stop those boats on the high seas and return them to Haiti, without any hearing or other opportunity for them to argue their case that they should be allowed to enter the United States.

This policy was challenged as violating refugee protection provisions of U.S. immigration law and a 1951 treaty, the United Nations Convention on the Status of Refugees. Two federal appeals courts heard this challenge and they divided on the issue. When the Supreme Court reviewed the matter, it voted 8–1 to uphold the policy, saying that neither the law nor the treaty applied outside U.S. borders. Only Justice Harry A. Blackmun dissented.

---

interests" in China in return for Japanese recognition of the "open door" policy.[55]

Franklin Roosevelt's use of executive agreements made that procedure a primary instrument for attaining his foreign policy objectives and nearly replaced the treaty-making power in its effect. He recognized the Soviet Union by an exchange of notes in 1933, and, in the fall of 1940, an executive agreement that provided for hemisphere defense in the event of an attack changed U.S. policy from neutrality to a state of quasi-belligerency with the Axis powers.

The Hull-Lothian agreement of September 2, 1940, authorized the exchange of destroyers for bases.[56] A 1941 agreement with the Danish foreign minister, entered into after Nazi Germany occupied Denmark, permitted the United States to occupy Greenland for defense purposes.[57] The agreements at Cairo, Tehran, Yalta, and Potsdam outlined the contours of the postwar peace.[58]

COLD WAR AGREEMENTS

Treaty making reemerged for a time in the cold war era in the form of multinational defense pacts such as the North Atlantic Treaty Organization (NATO), Southeast Asia Treaty Organization (SEATO), Central Treaty Organization (CENTO), and the United Nations Charter itself.

But executive agreements remained a primary instrument of foreign policy. In 1956 congressional concern about the proliferation of commitments by executive agreement emerged in a Senate bill that would have required the president to submit all such agreements for Senate perusal within sixty days. The House took no action on the measure.[59]

A 1969–1970 study of executive agreements by the Senate Foreign Relations Subcommittee on Security Agreements and Commitments Abroad uncovered many secret agreements made during the 1960s with a variety of countries including Ethiopia, Spain, Laos, Thailand, and South Korea.

A 1971 agreement made by the Nixon administration with Portugal for the use of an air base in the Azores and an agreement with Bahrain for naval base facilities on the Persian Gulf stirred the Senate to pass a "sense of the Senate" resolution to the effect that both agreements should have been submitted to the Senate for approval as treaties.[60] In 1972 the Senate voted to cut off funds but the House failed to act on the matter.

THE COURT AND EXECUTIVE AGREEMENTS

During the Roosevelt administration, the Supreme Court upheld the executive agreement as a valid exercise of presidential power. In *United States v. Belmont* the Court held that the presidential decision to recognize the Soviet Union in 1933, and the executive agreement that gave effect to that policy, constituted a valid international compact. Moreover, the Court noted, such agreement, without Senate approval, had the effect of a treaty and overruled conflicting state laws. Justice Sutherland, author of the *Curtiss-Wright* opinion earlier in the term, delivered the Court's opinion:

The recognition, establishment of diplomatic relations, the assignment, and agreements with respect thereto, were all parts of one transaction, resulting in an international compact between the two governments. That the negotiations, acceptance of the assignment and agreements and understandings in respect thereof were within the competence of the President may not be doubted. Governmental power over external affairs is not distributed, but is vested exclusively in the national government. And in respect of what was done here, the Executive had authority to speak as the sole organ of that government. . . .[61]

. . . [A]n international compact as this was, is not always a treaty which requires the participation of the Senate. There are many such compacts, of which a protocol, a modus vivendi, a postal convention, and agreements like that now under consideration are illustrations.[62]

In 1942—in a decision reminiscent of its 1796 decision in *Ware v. Hylton* first affirming the supremacy of a federal treaty over state law—the Court reaffirmed the force and validity of executive arguments. The case was *United States v. Pink*.

The 1933 executive agreement that extended diplomatic recognition to the Soviet Union provided that after settlement of U.S. claims against Russian-owned companies, the assets that remained would be returned to the Soviet Union. New York

State, however, went to court to prevent the return of the remaining assets of an insurance company with New York offices.

The Court upheld the terms of the executive agreement against the state's claims. The majority held that the terms of the agreement bound the state just as if they were treaty provisions, because the president possessed the power to remove obstacles to diplomatic recognition. It was, Justice Douglas said,

a modest implied power of the President who is the "sole organ of the Federal Government in the field of international relations." . . . It was the judgment of the political department that full recognition of the Soviet Government required the settlement of outstanding problems including the claims of our nationals. . . . We would usurp the executive function if we held that the decision was not final and conclusive in the courts.[63]

With respect to state power in the field of foreign affairs or the conflict of state laws with international agreements, Douglas affirmed the long-standing rule that

state law must yield when it is inconsistent with, or impairs the policy or provisions of, a treaty or of an international compact or agreement. . . . The power of a State to refuse enforcement of rights based on foreign law which runs counter to the public policy of the forum . . . must give way before the superior Federal policy evidenced by a treaty or international compact or agreement.[64]

No state had the power to modify an international agreement or to reject part of a policy that underpinned the broader diplomatic policy of recognition of a foreign government, in this case the Soviet Union, wrote Douglas. Such an exercise of state power would be a "dangerous invasion of Federal authority" that "would tend to disturb that equilibrium in our foreign relations which the political departments of our national government had diligently endeavoured to establish."[65]

Pink was cited by the Court almost forty years later when it upheld, in a lengthy opinion, President Carter's executive agreement resulting in freedom for fifty-two American hostages held by Iran for more than fourteen months. In *Dames & Moore v. Regan* the Court unanimously upheld Carter's multiple actions and agreements that constituted the financial arrangement necessary to free the hostages.[66]

Central to the opinion, written by Justice William H. Rehnquist, was evidence, presented in a variety of ways, that Congress had approved fully of the use of executive agreements to settle individual claims. "We do not decide that the President possesses plenary power to settle claims, even as against foreign governmental entities," he wrote. "But where, as here, the settlement of claims had been determined to be a necessary incident to the resolution of a major foreign policy dispute between our country and another, and where, as here, we can conclude that Congress acquiesced in the President's action, we are not prepared to say that the President lacks the power to settle such claims."[67]

The President as Executive

"The executive Power shall be vested in a President of the United States of America," begins Article II. But the Constitution quickly follows this sweeping statement of power with a correspondingly broad responsibility: the president is obligated to "take Care that the Laws be faithfully executed."

Presidents, justices, and scholars have disagreed over the import of the executive power provision. Is it a broad grant of inherent executive authority, adding to the enumerated powers that follow? Or is it simply a designation of office, adding nothing in substantive power?

In practice, the provision has been interpreted as granting presidents virtually all power necessary for management of the executive branch in the public interest. Even William Howard Taft, who adopted the conservative view—that the president's powers were limited to those spelled out in the Constitution or clearly included within those express powers—acted as president on the broader interpretation of executive power.[1]

Not only did pragmatic necessity bolster the broad view of executive power, but those who adopted it also found support for it in the "decision of 1789," the discussion by the First Congress of the specific powers of the executive. *(See box, The "Decision of 1789," p. 222.)*

The "take care" clause blended the Founding Fathers' distrust of concentrated power with the practical necessity of vesting administrative and enforcement authority in the president. This provision clearly rendered the president subordinate to the laws to be administered.

Through precedent and practice the "faithful execution" clause has come to incorporate a broad series of powers that range from the administrative interpretation of acts of Congress to the declaration of martial law in times of civil disorder or national emergency. The Court generally has granted the president broad discretion to act under this clause.

The Court also has viewed this clause as early acknowledgment of the executive's need to carry out many duties through subordinates. The clause does not direct the executive to faithfully execute the laws, but only to take care that the laws are faithfully executed, a clearly supervisory function.

As early as 1839 the Court set out the general rule that the duties and obligations placed on the president by law could be carried out by subordinates. The case arose under an 1823 law stating that public money could not be disbursed by officers of the United States except at the president's discretion. The Court in the case of *Wilcox v. McConnel* ruled that the chief executive "speaks and acts through the heads of the several departments in relation to subjects which appertain to their respective duties."[2]

Four years later the Court wrote:

The President's duty in general requires his superintendence of the administration; yet this duty cannot require of him to become the ad-ministrative officer of every department and bureau, or to perform in person the numerous details incident to services which, nevertheless, he is, in a correct sense, by the Constitution and laws required and expected to perform. This cannot be, 1st. Because, if it were practicable, it would be to absorb the duties and responsibilities of the various departments of the government in the personal action of the one chief executive officer. It cannot be, for the stronger reason, that it is impracticable—nay, impossible.[3]

The Appointment Power

The president's power to appoint and remove subordinate officials was a necessary complement to the power to manage the executive branch. Members of the president's administration are responsible for carrying out the duties of the office they have been selected to fill and to serve the president who appointed them.

Article II, Section 2, provides that the president

shall nominate, and by, and with the advice and consent of the Senate, shall appoint ambassadors, other public ministers and consuls, judges of the Supreme Court, and all other officers of the United States, whose appointments are not herein otherwise provided for, and which shall be established by law; but the Congress may by law vest the appointment of such inferior officers, as they think proper, in the Presidents alone, in the courts of law, or in the heads of departments.

The clause provided four methods of appointment: presidential appointments with Senate confirmation, presidential appointments without Senate confirmation, appointments by courts of law, and appointments by heads of departments. Congress exercises no power to appoint executive officers, although it may set qualifications for offices established by statute. Congressional requirements usually have pertained to citizenship, grade, residence, age, political affiliation, and professional competence.

The appointment power of the president has been exercised in conformance with a blend of historical precedents, custom, constitutional requirements, and statutory provisions established by Congress.

Congress has narrowed the range of officers over whom the president has the discretionary appointment power. The creation of the Civil Service Commission (now the Office of Personnel Management) and the steady addition of positions to the professional civil service list has reduced the scope of the president's exercise of the appointment power. Moreover, the establishment of a professional foreign service and the enumeration of the list of diplomatic posts available for presidential appointments also narrowed the president's range of appointments.

There have been relatively few Supreme Court decisions concerning the appointment power, and the decisions that have been made, from *Marbury v. Madison* on, have controlled the president's power to appoint and limited his discretionary power to remove officials. But two major modern rulings concerning the separation of powers, *Bowsher v. Synar* and *Morrison v. Olson,* have turned in large part on the power to appoint and remove officials.

The most famous decision made by Chief Justice John Marshall, and perhaps the most famous in the Court's history, began as a relatively unimportant controversy over a presidential appointment.

William Marbury sought delivery of his commission of appointment as a justice of the peace. In addition to the political significance of the case in constitutional history as the means by which the Marshall Court established the principle of judicial review, *Marbury v. Madison* had something to say about the appointment process.[4]

The Court held that Marbury should have received his commission, which had been duly signed and sealed, but not delivered. But, Marshall held, the Court lacked the power to issue the order commanding Secretary of State James Madison to deliver it. The effect of *Marbury* was that, in making appointments, the

"Midnight appointee" William Marbury, whose suit against James Madison led to a landmark Supreme Court case in 1803. John Marshall's opinion in *Marbury v. Madison* established the Court's authority to review the constitutionality of acts of Congress.

president was under no enforceable obligation to deliver a commission, even after the nominee was confirmed by the Senate.

CONFIRMATION AND COURTESY

Senate consent to executive appointments was a unique innovation incorporated into the Constitution. The original idea of Senate participation in the selection, as well as confirmation, of nominees never materialized, however. President George Washington collided with the Senate over approval of an Indian treaty and subsequently refused to consult the Senate on appointment matters, except to send up nominations for approval. Senate consent to an executive appointment came to mean simply that a majority of the Senate approved the president's nomination.

Presidents customarily have consulted individual senators of their own political party on matters of appointments related to their home states. But policy and political considerations often take precedence over the practice of senatorial courtesy, and failure of the president to extend this courtesy to the appropriate senators usually has not alone resulted in a nominee's rejection.

Once the Senate has approved a nominee, it cannot reverse its decision, but earlier Senate rules permitted a move for reconsideration and recall of a confirmation resolution within two days after its passage. In December 1930 President Herbert C.

DIPLOMATIC APPOINTMENTS

With establishment of the Foreign Service, Congress reduced the discretionary appointment power with respect to diplomatic posts.

The president completely controlled the appointment and removal of diplomatic ministers during the first sixty-five years of the nation's history. All matters of grade, rank, and compensation were left to presidential discretion during this period.

One example of the breadth of this power came in 1814. President James Madison, with the Senate in recess, appointed three commissioners to negotiate with the British to end the War of 1812. Opponents in Congress argued that the offices had not been created by statute; hence no vacancies existed to allow the president to appoint peace commissioners.

Madison responded that there were two classes of offices under the Constitution. One included the range of posts created by law to manage the government; the second related to foreign affairs and were diplomatic posts, completely under presidential control and not subject to congressional scrutiny or prior approval. Congress protested, but took no action. The peace made by these commissioners ended the war.[1]

In 1955 Congress created an official list of envoys and ministers in the public service with salary and rank specified for each post. Today, foreign service appointments are nominally made by the president, but they are governed by the Foreign Service Act of 1946.

The president retains the right and power to appoint ambassadors-at-large as personal emissaries for specific foreign missions without Senate consultation or approval. Such appointments are not regarded as regular ambassadorial or ministerial appointments by Congress or the Supreme Court.[2]

1. *U.S. Constitution, Analysis and Interpretation* (Washington, D.C.: U.S. Government Printing Office, 1973), 520.
2. Ibid.

Hoover nominated George O. Smith as chairman of the Federal Power Commission. The Senate, in executive session on December 20, confirmed Smith and ordered the resolution of confirmation sent to the president. Later that same day, the Senate adjourned until January 5, 1931. The president, notified of Smith's confirmation, delivered the commission of appointment, and Smith took office. On January 5, when the Senate was next in session, it voted to reconsider Smith's nomination. A month later it voted again and did not confirm it.

President Hoover refused to return the confirmation resolution as requested by the Senate, describing this maneuver as a congressional effort to exercise the power of removal. The Senate then took the matter to court to test Smith's right to continue in office. When the matter came to the Supreme Court, it upheld Smith's right to the post on the grounds that Senate precedent did not support the Senate's reconsideration of a confirmation action, after the nominee assumed the duties of the office.[5]

RECESS APPOINTMENTS

The Constitution authorizes the president to fill vacant offices during a Senate recess. *Recess* is here held to mean periods longer than a holiday observance or a brief and temporary adjournment. It states:

The President shall have Power to fill up all Vacancies that may happen during the Recess of the Senate, by granting Commissions which shall expire at the End of their next Session.

If the vacancy occurs with the Senate in session, the president may fill the office with an ad interim appointment, if such an appointment is provided for by the statute creating the position.

A recess appointee, however, may not receive the salary of the office until confirmed by the Senate. This practice has prevented the president from using recess appointments to keep people in office whom the Senate would refuse to confirm.[6]

The Removal Power

The Constitution says nothing about the president's power to remove from office the officials he has appointed with the advice and consent of the Senate, although Article II provides for congressional impeachment and removal of some of these officers. The president's power to remove derives from the power to appoint and from the debate concerning the executive power in the First Congress in 1789.

In the first major modern Supreme Court ruling on the removal power, Chief Justice William Howard Taft, the only former president to head the Court, traced the origins of the power back to that debate—on the bill creating the Department of Foreign Affairs. *(See box, The "Decision of 1789," p. 222.)*

Taft concluded that the removal power was understood in the "decision of 1789" to exist as a complement of the president's power to appoint.

It is very clear from this history that the exact question which the House voted upon was whether it should recognize and declare the

William Howard Taft, the only former president to serve on the Supreme Court, wrote the opinion in *Myers v. United States* (1926) establishing that the president has the sole power to remove executive branch officers.

power of the President under the Constitution to remove the Secretary of Foreign Affairs without the advice and consent of the Senate. That was what the vote was taken for . . . there is not the slightest doubt, after an examination of the record, that the vote was, and was intended to be, a legislative declaration that the power to remove officers appointed by the President and the Senate vested in the President alone.[7]

Despite that early decision, there has been much debate over this aspect of executive power. "Controversy pertaining to the scope and limits of the President's power of removal fills a thick chapter of our political and judicial history," wrote Justice Felix Frankfurter in 1958.[8]

President Andrew Jackson asserted the executive's right to remove officials as an essential element of his power to control the personnel within his department. When he removed his secretary of the Treasury for failure to comply with a directive to remove government deposits from the Bank of the United States, the Senate condemned Jackson's removal of the secretary as an assumption of power "not conferred by the Constitution and laws, but in derogation of both."

Jackson responded with a protest message to the Senate in which he asserted that the executive's removal power was a direct corollary of his responsibility to oversee faithful execution of the laws:

The whole executive power being invested in the President, who is responsible for its exercise, it is a necessary consequence that he should have a right to employ agents of his own choice to aid him in the performance of his duties, and to discharge them when he is no longer willing to be responsible for their acts.[9]

By 1839 the Court acknowledged that, as a practical matter, the president alone exercised the removal power. Although it was clear the president and the Senate together had the power to remove officers appointed and confirmed by them, "it was very early adopted as the practical construction of the Constitution that this power was vested in the President alone," wrote the Court.[10]

The first major challenge by Congress to this executive power came with the Tenure of Office Act of March 2, 1867, enacted amid the conflict between Congress and President Andrew Johnson over Reconstruction. The measure provided that any civil officer appointed by the president with the advice and consent of the Senate could be removed only with Senate approval. The law stripped President Johnson and future presidents of the discretionary removal power. Johnson protested the law and removed his secretary of war without complying with its provisions. That action became one of the factors in the impeachment attempt against him. Modified during the administration of Ulysses S. Grant, the law was repealed in 1887 without any judicial ruling on its constitutionality.

Few presidents were as conscious of the prerogatives of the executive as Woodrow Wilson. A 1919 act of Congress created an executive budget bureau under the president's direction. The legislation established the office of comptroller general and an assistant comptroller of the United States who were to head an independent accounting department. The two officers were to be appointed by the president and confirmed by the Senate to serve during "good behavior." They were to be removed from office only by concurrent resolution of Congress on the grounds of inefficiency, neglect of duty, or malfeasance in office.

Wilson favored the idea of a budget bureau but vetoed the measure, objecting that the removal procedure violated the Constitution because it denied the president the power to remove officials he had appointed to office. He explained that he regarded "the power of removal from office as an essential incident to the appointing power," and so could not "escape the conclusion that the vesting of this power of removal in the Congress is unconstitutional."[11]

President Warren G. Harding subsequently signed a similar bill, the Budget and Accounting Act, on June 10, 1921.[12]

THE CASE OF THE RECALCITRANT POSTMASTER

President Wilson fired a postmaster and brought about the first major Supreme Court decision on the removal power. The ruling, in *Myers v. United States,* was handed down in 1926, after Wilson and Myers, the postmaster, both had died. It seemed to grant the president an unlimited power to remove all officers he appointed except judges.

In 1876 Congress had passed a law making removal of postmasters subject to Senate consent. President Wilson removed Myers without Senate consent. Myers and his heirs sued, challenging the validity of the removal in light of the 1876 law. The Court upheld the dismissal, ruling that Congress could not properly limit the executive's removal power in this way.

The opinion of Chief Justice Taft rested heavily on the "decision of 1789"—the decisions made by the First Congress as it passed measures creating the machinery of the executive department. Those early decisions, Taft noted, "have always been regarded . . . as of the greatest weight in the interpretation of the fundamental instrument."[13]

Taft discussed the removal power as it was considered in these sessions:

Mr. Madison and his associates in the discussion in the House dwelt at length upon the necessity there was for construing article 2 to give the President the sole power of removal in his responsibility for the conduct of the executive branch, and enforced this by emphasizing his duty expressly declared in the third section of the article to "take care that the laws be faithfully executed.". . .

The vesting of the executive power in the President was essentially a grant of the power to execute the laws. But the President alone and unaided could not execute the laws. He must execute them by the assistance of subordinates. This view has since been repeatedly affirmed by this court. . . . As he is charged specifically to take care that they be faithfully executed, the reasonable implication, even in the absence of express words, was that as part of his executive power he should select those who were to act for him under his direction in the execution of the laws. The further implication must be, in the absence of any express limitation respecting removals, that as his selection of administrative officers is essential to the execution of the laws by him, so must be his power of removing those for whom he cannot continue to be responsible. . . .

. . . A veto by the Senate—a part of the legislative branch of the government—upon removals is a much greater limitation upon the executive branch, and a much more serious blending of the legislative with the executive, than a rejection of a proposed appointment. It is not to be implied. The rejection of a nominee of the President for a particular office does not greatly embarrass him in the conscientious discharge of his high duties in the selection of those who are to aid him, because the President usually has an ample field from which to select for office, according to his preference, competent and capable men. The Senate has full power to reject newly proposed appointees whenever the President shall remove the incumbents. Such a check enables the Senate to prevent the filling of offices with bad or incompetent men, or with those against whom there is tenable objection.

The power to prevent the removal of an officer who has served under the President is different from the authority to consent to or reject his appointment. When a nomination is made, it may be presumed that the Senate is, or may become, as well advised as to the fitness of the nominee as the President, but in the nature of things the defects in ability or intelligence or loyalty in the administration of the laws of one who has served as an officer under the President are facts as to which the President, or his trusted subordinates, must be better informed than the Senate, and the power to remove him may therefore be regarded as confined for very sound and practical reasons, to the governmental authority which has administrative control. . . .

. . . Mr. Madison and his associates pointed out with great force the unreasonable character of the view that the convention intended, without express provision, to give to Congress or the Senate, in case of political or other differences, the means of thwarting the executive in the exercise of his great powers and, in the bearing of his great responsibility by fastening upon him, as subordinate executive officers, men who by their inefficient service under him, by their lack of loyalty to the service, or by their different views of policy might make his taking care that the laws be faithfully executed most difficult or impossible.

Made responsible under the Constitution for the effective enforcement of the law, the President needs as an indispensable aid to meet it the disciplinary influence upon those who act under him of a reserve power of removal. . . . Each head of a department is and must be the President's alter ego in the matters of that department where the President is required by law to exercise authority.

In all such cases, the discretion to be exercised is that of the President in determining the national public interest and in directing the action to be taken by his executive subordinates to protect it. In this field his cabinet officers must do his will. He must place in each member of his official family, and his chief executive subordinates, implicit faith. The moment that he loses confidence in the intelligence, ability, judgment, or loyalty of any one of them, he must have the power to remove him without delay. To require him to file charges and submit them to the consideration of the Senate might make impossible that unity and coordination in executive administration essential to effective action.[14]

The Court saw no reason why Congress should be allowed to limit the president's removal of postmasters. Taft wrote:

There is nothing in the Constitution which permits a distinction between the removal of a head of a department or a bureau, when he discharges a political duty of the President or exercises his discretion, and the removal of executive officers engaged in the discharge of their other normal duties. The imperative reason requiring an unrestricted power to remove the most important of his subordinates in their most important duties must therefore control the interpretation of the Constitution as to all appointed by him.[15]

Taft's opinion seemed to extend the president's removal power even to officers appointed to independent regulatory commissions:

[T]here may be duties of a quasi-judicial character imposed on executive officers and members of executive tribunals whose decisions after hearing affect interests of individuals, the discharge of which the President cannot in a particular case properly influence or control. But even in such a case he may consider the decision after its rendition as a reason for removing the officer, on the ground that the discretion regularly entrusted to that officer by statute has not been on the whole intelligently or wisely exercised. Otherwise he does not discharge his own constitutional duty of seeing that the laws be faithfully executed.[16]

Justices James C. McReynolds, Louis D. Brandeis, and Oliver Wendell Holmes Jr. dissented from the *Myers* ruling. They viewed the 1876 law as a legitimate exercise of congressional authority to impose statutory limits on grants of power. In a separate opinion, McReynolds emphasized that the office in question was that of a postmaster—an inferior and civil position created by Congress.

The Constitution empowers the President to appoint ambassadors, other public ministers, consuls, judges of the Supreme Court and superior officers, and no statute can interfere therein. But Congress may authorize both appointment and removal of all inferior officers without regard to the President's wishes—even in direct opposition to them. This important distinction must not be overlooked. And consid-

---

THE "DECISION OF 1789"

One of the major tasks facing the First Congress in 1789 was to set up the machinery needed to run the government. The Constitution provided the framework, but the legislative measures adopted by Congress supplied the structure and organization for each of the branches.

Chief Justice William Howard Taft explained in the Court's 1926 opinion in *Myers v. United States* why the Court gave such weight to the "decision of 1789" concerning the president's removal power.

We have devoted much space to this discussion and decision of the question of the presidential power of removal in the First Congress, not because a congressional conclusion on a constitutional issue is conclusive, but first because of our agreement with the reasons upon which it was avowedly based, second because this was the decision of the First Congress on a question of primary importance in the organization of the government made within two years after the Constitutional Convention and within a much shorter time after its ratification, and third because that Congress numbered among its leaders those who had been members of the convention. It must necessarily constitute a precedent upon which many future laws supplying the machinery of the new government would be based and, if erroneous, would be likely to evoke dissent and departure in future Congresses. It would come at once before the executive branch of the government for compliance and might well be brought before the judicial branch for a test of its validity. As we shall see, it was soon accepted as a final decision of the question by all branches of the government.

The decision of 1789 related to a bill proposed by James Madison to establish an executive department of foreign affairs. It provided that the principal officer was "to be removed from office by the President of the United States." Debate over the removal clause led to a change in wording so that the bill finally read, "whenever the principal officer shall be removed by the President of the United States."

Taft's exhaustive analysis of the decision of 1789 in *Myers* led to the majority's conclusion that this change reflected the understanding of the First Congress that the president had the sole power to remove executive branch officers.

SOURCE: *Myers v. United States*, 272 U.S. 52 at 136–137 (1926).

---

eration of the complete control which Congress may exercise over inferior officers is enough to show the hollowness of the suggestion that a right to remove them may be inferred from the President's duty to "take care that the laws be faithfully executed." He cannot appoint any inferior officer, however humble, without legislative authorization; but such officers are essential to execution of the laws. Congress may provide as many or as few of them as it likes. It may place all of them beyond the President's control; but this would not suspend his duty concerning faithful execution of the laws. Removals, however important, are not so necessary as appointments.[17]

Brandeis wrote: "Power to remove . . . a high political officer might conceivably be deemed indispensable to democratic government and, hence, inherent in the President. But power to remove an inferior administrative officer . . . cannot conceivably be deemed an essential of government."[18]

Holmes called the majority's arguments "a spider's web inadequate to control the dominant facts." He noted that the postmaster's position was

an office that owes its existence to Congress and that Congress may abolish tomorrow. Its duration and the pay attached to it while it lasts depend on Congress alone. Congress alone confers on the President the power to appoint to it and at any time may transfer the power to other hands. . . . The duty of the President to see that the laws be executed is a duty that does not go beyond the law or require him to achieve more than Congress sees fit to leave within his power.[19]

A few years later the Court adopted the dissenters' focus to limit the removal power asserted in *Myers*.

THE CASE OF THE FEDERAL TRADE COMMISSIONER

Nine years after the *Myers* ruling the Court narrowed the scope of the president's removal power to include only "all purely executive offices." The Court explicitly rejected the president's claim to inherent power to remove members of regulatory agencies.

William E. Humphrey was appointed to the Federal Trade Commission (FTC) by President Calvin Coolidge and reappointed by President Hoover. When Franklin D. Roosevelt became president, he wanted to replace the conservative Humphrey with a moderate Republican. Roosevelt sought Humphrey's resignation, denied him a personal interview to discuss the matter, and then decided to view a later communication from Humphrey as a resignation letter which Roosevelt made effective October 7, 1933.

Humphrey challenged the president's action. He denied any intention to resign and claimed the president had violated the Constitution and the terms of the act that created the FTC. The FTC was an independent quasi-judicial body protected from political removal by the terms of its enabling statute. Members of the FTC were given seven-year terms by the act, with removal from office by the president limited to cause such as inefficiency, neglect of duty, or malfeasance in office. Roosevelt never claimed any wrongdoing on Humphrey's part. Humphrey sued for his salary, but died during court proceedings; his executor pursued the litigation, now entitled *Humphrey's Executor v. United States*.[20]

The Decision

On May 27, 1935, the "Black Monday" of the Court's battle with President Roosevelt over New Deal legislation, the Court ruled unanimously for Humphrey's executor—and against Roosevelt. Justice George Sutherland stated for the Court that because the Federal Trade Commission was both a quasi-judicial and quasi-legislative body, it was not subject to the unlimited and absolute executive power of removal. The Court not only denied the president power to remove members of independent regulatory agencies but also implied that other officers who per-

formed functions not wholly executive in character might not be subject to executive removal.

Sutherland's opinion distinguished between the duties of a postmaster, such as Myers, and the responsibilities of a member of the FTC:

The office of a postmaster is so essentially unlike the office now involved that the decision in the *Myers* case cannot be accepted as controlling our decision here. A postmaster is an executive officer restricted to the performance of executive functions. He is charged with no duty at all related to either the legislative or judicial power. The actual decision in the *Myers* case finds support in the theory that such an officer is merely one of the units in the executive department, and, hence, inherently subject to the exclusive and illimitable power of removal by the Chief Executive, whose subordinate and aide he is.[21]

The Court discarded Taft's *dicta* in *Myers,* stating that

the necessary reach of the decision goes far enough to include all purely executive officers. It goes no farther. . . . Much less does it include an officer who occupies no place in the executive department and who exercises no part of the executive power vested by the Constitution in the President.[22]

Sutherland then explained that the absolute executive removal power extended only to those officers whose functions are purely executive and that "illimitable power of removal is not possessed by the President" over FTC commissioners.

The authority of Congress, in creating quasi-legislative or quasi-judicial agencies, to require them to act independently of executive control cannot well be doubted; and that authority includes . . . power to fix the period during which they shall continue in office, and to forbid their removal except for cause in the meantime. For it is quite evident that one who holds his office only during the pleasure of another cannot be depended upon to maintain an attitude of independence against the latter's will.[23]

The Court thus claimed for Congress the power to set the terms of office and conditions of removal for those offices whose functions were an amalgam of executive, legislative, and judicial functions. The Court thereby limited the executive removal power, declaring that the extent of that power depended upon the "nature of the office" involved.

The fundamental necessity of maintaining each of the three general departments of government entirely free from the control or coercive influence, direct or indirect, of either of the others, has often been stressed and is hardly open to serious question. . . . The sound application of a principle that makes one master in his own house precludes him from imposing his control in the house of another. . . .

The power of removal here claimed for the President falls within this principle, since its coercive influence threatens the independence of a commission, which is not only wholly disconnected from the executive department, but which, as already fully appears, was created by Congress as a means of carrying into operation legislative and judicial powers, and as an agency of the legislative and judicial departments. . . . Whether the power of the president to remove an officer shall prevail over the authority of Congress to condition the power by fixing a definite term and precluding a removal except for cause, will depend upon the character of the office; the *Myers* decision, affirming the power of the President alone to make the removal, is confined to purely executive officers; and as to officers of the kind here under consideration, we hold that no removal can be made during the prescribed term for which the officer is appointed, except for one or more of the causes named in the applicable statute.[24]

In Humphrey's case, Justice Felix Frankfurter wrote more than twenty years later, the Court

drew a sharp line of cleavage between officials who were part of the Executive establishment and were thus removable by virtue of the President's constitutional powers, and those who are members of a body "to exercise its judgment without the leave or hindrance of any other official or any department of the government," . . . as to whom a power of removal exists only if Congress may fairly be said to have conferred it. This sharp differentiation derives from the difference in functions between those who are part of the Executive establishment and those whose tasks require absolute freedom from executive interference.[25]

The Morgan Case

The *Humphrey* decision, however, did not prevent President Roosevelt from removing someone from an office for which Congress had not set terms of removal.

In 1938 Dr. E. A. Morgan, chairman of the Tennessee Valley Authority (TVA), relied on the *Humphrey* ruling in challenging his removal by the president. A federal appeals court ruled that the TVA act did not limit the president's exercise of the removal power. Because the action by the president promoted the smooth functioning of the TVA, the court viewed the removal as within the president's duty to see that the laws were faithfully executed. The Supreme Court declined to review that decision.[26]

THE CASE OF THE WAR CLAIMS COMMISSIONER

In the *Humphrey's Executor* decision the Court seemed to rule that Congress must specify the terms and conditions of removal before courts would limit the executive power of removal. However, a case decided twenty-three years later extended the *Humphrey* doctrine to limit the president's power to remove quasi-judicial officers even where no specific statutory language set out the terms of their removal. The Court thus reinforced the "nature of the office" approach to this question.

President Harry S. Truman had appointed three Democrats to the War Claims Commission, established to settle certain types of claims that grew out of World War II. The commission was to go out of business after it settled all claims. The law made no provision for removal of commissioners. When President Dwight D. Eisenhower took office in 1953, he wanted to name three Republicans to the commission and so requested the resignations of the three Democratic members. They refused, and Eisenhower removed them.

One of the commissioners named Wiener sued for his salary in the U.S. Court of Claims, arguing that his removal was illegal. The court agreed that his duties had been quasi-judicial, but denied Wiener's claim, relying on the fact that the statute creating the commission had not limited the executive's power to remove its members.[27] The *Humphrey* ruling did not apply, the court decided, because here there was no explicit statutory explication of the removal procedure for a claims commissioner.[28]

The Supreme Court, with Justice Frankfurter writing the

opinion, ruled unanimously for Wiener. The Court noted the similarity of facts in this case with the facts in *Humphrey*:

We start with one certainty. The problem of the President's power to remove members of agencies entrusted with duties of the kind with which the War Claims Commission was charged was within the lively knowledge of Congress. Few contests between Congress and the President have so recurringly had the attention of Congress as that pertaining to the power of removal. . . .

. . . The ground of President Eisenhower's removal of petitioner was precisely the same as President Roosevelt's removal of Humphrey. Both Presidents desired to have Commissioners, one on the Federal Trade Commission, the other on the War Claims Commission, "of my own selection." They wanted these Commissioners to be their men. The terms of removal in the two cases are identic [sic] and express the assumption that the agencies of which the two Commissioners were members were subject in the discharge of their duties to the control of the Executive. An analysis of the Federal Trade Commission Act left this Court in no doubt that such was not the conception of Congress in creating the Federal Trade Commission. The terms of the War Claims Act of 1948 leave no doubt that such was not the conception of Congress regarding the War Claims Commission.[29]

Frankfurter, after analyzing the law, concluded that Congress did not intend that the commissioners be subject to the threat of presidential removal.

If, as one must take for granted, the War Claims Act precluded the President from influencing the Commission in passing on a particular claim, *a fortiori* must it be inferred that Congress did not wish to have hang over the Commission the Damocles' sword of removal by the President for no reason other than that he preferred to have on that Commission men of his own choosing.

For such is this case. . . . Judging the matter in all the nakedness in which it is presented, namely, the claim that the President could remove a member of an adjudicatory body like the War Claims Commission merely because he wanted his own appointees on such a Commission, we are compelled to conclude that no such power is given to the President directly by the Constitution, and none is impliedly conferred upon him by statute simply because Congress said nothing about it. The philosophy of *Humphrey's Executor,* in its explicit language as well as its implication, precludes such a claim.[30]

THE COMPTROLLER AND THE PROSECUTOR

When the Supreme Court in 1986 held unconstitutional major provisions of the Balanced Budget and Emergency Deficit Control Act of 1985, much of its reasoning turned on the question of who could remove the nation's comptroller general. Two years later another question of separation of powers turned on the power to appoint an independent counsel to investigate charges of wrongdoing by top executive branch officials.

The deficit control act, popularly known as Gramm-Rudman-Hollings for its Senate sponsors, gave the comptroller general authority to dictate to the president where the executive branch must reduce its spending. That provision was its flaw, the Court held.

The comptroller general, who heads the General Accounting Office, the investigatory and auditing arm of Congress, is appointed by the president but is subject to removal only by Congress, not the president. The lower court that first heard the case of *Bowsher v. Synar* found that Congress, by retaining the power to remove the comptroller, placed the office firmly in the legislative branch, not the executive. The Supreme Court agreed, 7–2.

Citing *Myers, Humphrey's Executor,* and "the decision of 1789," Chief Justice Warren E. Burger wrote:

Congress cannot reserve for itself the power of removal of an officer charged with the execution of the laws except by impeachment. To permit the execution of the laws to be vested in an officer answerable only to Congress would, in practical terms, reserve in Congress control over the execution of the laws. . . . The structure of the Constitution does not permit Congress to execute the laws; it follows that Congress cannot grant to an officer under its control what it does not possess.[31]

Linking this reasoning with the *Chadha* decision, Burger continued:

To permit an officer controlled by Congress to execute the laws would be, in essence, to permit a congressional veto. Congress could simply remove, or threaten to remove, an officer for executing the laws in any fashion found to be unsatisfactory to Congress. This kind of congressional control over the execution of the laws, *Chadha* makes clear, is constitutionally impermissible.[32]

The executive branch won the day on the Gramm-Rudman-Hollings issue, but lost a major separation of powers case two years later when the Court upheld the unusual arrangement that Congress had set up for the appointment of an independent prosecutor, when charges of high-level wrongdoing warranted it. The Independent Counsel Act of 1978, part of the Ethics in Government Act of that year, set up a complex process for appointing such a counsel: judges, not anyone in the executive branch, appointed this official. The counsel was, however, subject to removal by the attorney general for good cause.

Three high-ranking officers in the Justice Department, under investigation by an independent counsel, challenged this arrangement as a violation of the separation of powers. They argued that the way in which the counsel was appointed interfered unduly with the functions of the chief executive. They lost the first round, won the second, and lost again, 7–1, in the Supreme Court.[33]

Writing for the Court in *Morrison v. Olson,* Chief Justice William H. Rehnquist explained that the majority found the independent counsel an "inferior" officer within the language of the Constitution that permits Congress to decide who can appoint someone to that post. "We do not mean to say that Congress' power to provide for interbranch appointments of 'inferior officers' is unlimited," he wrote. But in this situation,

Congress, of course, was concerned when it created the office of independent counsel with the conflicts of interest that could arise in situations when the Executive Branch is called upon to investigate its own high-ranking officers. If it were to remove the appointing authority from the Executive Branch, the most logical place to put it was in the Judicial Branch.[34]

Citing *Bowsher, Myers, Humphrey's Executor,* and *Wiener,* Rehnquist addressed the question of whether the Independent Prosecutor Act impermissibly interfered with the president's exercise of his constitutional functions. The Court decided it did

not. By requiring that there must be good cause before an attorney general removed a special prosecutor, the law guaranteed the counsel a necessary measure of independence, the Court held. At the same time, this requirement did not interfere with the president's ability to ensure the faithful execution of the laws.

Executive Discretion

Is the president's power to see that the laws are faithfully executed limited simply to carrying out the letter of the laws enacted by Congress? Or does the president have power to act, beyond or in conflict with those laws, if he thinks the public interest demands it?

In general, Court decisions in the twentieth century have tended to adopt the more expansive view, a view enhanced by the increasing practice of Congress of delegating power to the executive branch.

TO PROTECT A JUSTICE

One of the Court's first rulings on this overall question of executive power occurred in 1890 in one of the more bizarre cases ever to come before it. Despite the absence of any authorizing statute, the Court upheld the power of the president to provide federal protection for a Supreme Court justice whose life was threatened in the course of his judicial duties.

Sarah Althea Terry and her husband David, angry over a decision against their claim to an estate, threatened to kill Justice Stephen J. Field, who had led the panel of judges ruling against them. In response to these threats, the attorney general ordered federal marshals to protect Field. While he was in California on judicial business, Field was attacked by David Terry. Deputy Marshal Neagle, who was protecting Field, shot Terry and killed him. California tried to hold Neagle and charge him with murder under state law. *(See box, Circuit Riding: Burdens and Hazards, p. 819, in Chapter 17.)*

The Supreme Court ruled that California could not try Neagle, because the killing had occurred in the course of his duties under federal law—even though there was no federal law authorizing him to protect the justice. The Court ordered Neagle released from state custody.

Writing for the Court, Justice Samuel F. Miller asked:

Is this duty [to take care that the laws be faithfully executed] limited to the enforcement of Acts of Congress or of treaties of the United States according to their express terms, or does it include the rights, duties and obligations growing out of the Constitution itself, our international relations, and all the protection implied by the nature of the government under the Constitution?[35]

The Court's answer came as it implicitly adopted the latter view:

In the view we take of the Constitution of the United States, any obligation fairly and properly inferable from that instrument, or any duty of the marshal to be derived from the general scope of his duties under the laws of the United States, is "a law.". . . It would be a great reproach

When David S. Terry threatened to kill Justice Stephen J. Field, the attorney general ordered an armed federal marshal, David Neagle, to protect Field during his circuit court travels in California. In a railroad station restaurant, Terry accosted Field and slapped him. Thinking Terry was armed, Neagle shot him and was charged with murder. Neagle contended that the state could not try him for actions taken in the course of duties carried out under federal law. The Supreme Court heard the case, absent Field, in 1890 and ordered Neagle's release.

to the system of government of the United States, declared to be within its sphere sovereign and supreme, if there is found within the domain of its powers no means of protecting the judges, in the conscientious and faithful discharge of their duties, from the malice and hatred of those upon whom their judgments may operate unfavorably.[36]

TO PROTECT THE PUBLIC INTEREST

This broad view of presidential power was reaffirmed by the Court in 1915, with its decision in the case of the *United States v. Midwest Oil Co.* By law, all public lands containing minerals were declared open to occupation, exploration, and purchase by citizens. In 1909, however, President William Howard Taft withdrew from further public use some three million acres in public lands containing oil deposits in order to preserve oil supplies for the navy.

This withdrawal was challenged by citizens who had subsequently explored and discovered oil on these lands; they cited the law declaring all such lands open to citizen exploration. But the Court upheld the president's prerogative to withdraw the lands from private acquisition.

Justice Joseph R. Lamar cited historical precedent as the basis for upholding the president's action:

[The president] . . . has, during the past eighty years, without express statutory—but under the claim of power to do so—made a multitude of Executive orders which operated to withdraw public land that would otherwise have been open to private acquisition. They affected every kind of land—mineral and nonmineral. . . .

The President was in a position to know when the public interest required particular portions of the people's lands to be withdrawn from entry or relocation; his action inflicted no wrong upon any private citizen, and being subject to disaffirmance by Congress, could occasion no harm to the interest of the public at large. Congress did not repudiate the power claimed or the withdrawal orders made. On the contrary, it uniformly and repeatedly acquiesced in the practice. . . .

. . . Government is a practical affair, intended for practical men.

Both officers, lawmakers and citizens naturally adjust themselves to any long-continued action of the Executive Department, on the presumptions that unauthorized acts would not have been allowed to be so often repeated as to crystallize into a regular practice.[37]

Delegation of Power

Congress vastly expanded the president's discretionary power in the twentieth century by delegating an increasing amount of authority to the office. The process began at the end of the last century.

In 1890 Congress provided for the duty-free admission of certain imported items, but gave the president the authority to impose duties on these items if the country of origin began to impose unreasonable duties on American-made goods. In 1892 the Court, ruling in *Field v. Clark,* upheld this congressional delegation of power: Congress furnished a remedy and authorized the president to decide when it should be applied. The Court held that this delegation did not violate the separation of powers or result in executive lawmaking.[38]

In 1891 Congress authorized the president to set aside public lands in any state or territory as forest reservations. A subsequent statute authorized the secretary of agriculture to administer these lands and to make rules governing their use and occupancy. Violations of the rules were punishable by fines or imprisonment or both. This delegated power was challenged as unconstitutional.

The Court upheld the president's authority, stating that

the authority to make administrative rules is not a delegation of legislative power, nor are such rules raised from an administrative level to a legislative character because the violation thereof is punishable as a public offense.[39]

Not until 1935 did the Court invalidate a statute on the grounds that it constituted an improper delegation of power from Congress to the president. The ruling was followed with several in that term and the next that found New Deal legislation unconstitutional for this reason. (See "The Court and the Roosevelt Revolution," pp. 248–252.)

But after its turnabout on the New Deal in 1937, the Court also returned to its generally approving view of congressional delegation, a view that has prevailed for nearly sixty years.

If the Court's rulings in *Neagle* and *Midwest Oil* and its general inclination to back congressional delegation of power to the executive seemed to imply that there were no limits on the scope of the inherent powers a president could claim, that impression was dramatically corrected in 1952. A divided Court flatly rejected President Harry S. Truman's claim of inherent power to seize the nation's steel mills in order to avoid disruption of steel production and possible disruption of supplies to military forces in Korea. The executive order directing seizure of the mills explained that a work stoppage would jeopardize national defense. (See "The Steel Seizure Case," pp. 203–204.)

Congress had decided against giving the president such seizure power in the Taft-Hartley Act, passed in 1947; Truman chose to ignore other provisions of that law that might have been useful in the circumstances, relying instead on a broad view of inherent presidential power.

For the majority, Justice Hugo L. Black wrote that the president was improperly "making" the law he wished to execute.

In the framework of our Constitution, the President's power to see that the laws are faithfully executed refutes the idea that he is to be a lawmaker. The Constitution limits his function in the lawmaking process to the recommending of laws he thinks wise and the vetoing of laws he thinks bad.[40]

In a concurring opinion, Justice Robert H. Jackson commented:

Loose and irresponsible use of adjectives colors all non-legal and much legal discussion of presidential powers. "Inherent" powers, "implied" powers, "incidental" powers, "plenary" powers, "war" powers and "emergency" powers are used, often interchangeably and without fixed or ascertainable meanings.

The vagueness and generality of the clauses that set forth presidential powers afford a plausible basis for pressures within and without an administration for action beyond that supported by those whose responsibility it is to defend his actions in court.[41]

Executives and Emergencies

The preservation of peace and order in the community is a requirement for successful execution of the laws. Disregard or disobedience of the laws may require the president to act to preserve the peace and restore order in the community.

Since 1792 presidents have possessed statutory authority to use troops to quell disorder when, in their judgment, the disorder hinders the execution of the laws. Ever since the case of *Martin v. Mott,* decided in 1827, the Supreme Court has steadily backed the president's authority to decide when and if an emergency exists that requires the use of federal troops.

Justice Joseph Story's opinion in that case limited the exercise of the power to times of actual invasion or imminent danger thereof, but affirmed the president's authority "to decide whether the exigency has arisen." Moreover, Story wrote, the decision "belongs exclusively to the president, and . . . his decision is conclusive upon all other persons."[42]

Chief Justice Roger B. Taney reaffirmed the president's authority in such matters in *Luther v. Borden.* Explaining that the president's decision to use troops to keep order was beyond the authority of judges to question, he wrote:

Judicial power presupposes an established government capable of enacting laws and enforcing their execution. . . . The acceptance of the judicial office is a recognition of the authority of the government from which it is derived.[43]

In emergencies, the president may employ several means short of calling out federal troops. President Thomas Jefferson used the *posse comitatus* (a body of persons summoned to assist in the preservation of public peace) to enforce the embargo imposed during the conflict with Britain. President Franklin Pierce's attorney general ruled that federal marshals could command citizens' aid to enforce the Fugitive Slave Act of 1850. During the "bleeding Kansas" episode in the pre–Civil War strife over slavery in the territories, Pierce placed military forces in a posse to prevent further bloodshed. The most extraordinary posse was the group of seventy-five thousand volunteers summoned by Lincoln to suppress the "civil disorder" in 1861.

President Dwight D. Eisenhower invoked the same provision when he dispatched troops to Little Rock, Arkansas, to enforce court-ordered desegregation at a high school. Eisenhower's actions in this case set a modern precedent for executive support of judicial decisions, in contrast to President Andrew Jackson's stance in the *Cherokee Indian Cases* 125 years earlier, of leaving the Court to fend for itself when a state ignored a Court decision.[44]

Presidents also have used troops to quell labor strikes and attendant civil disorders that threatened the public safety or disrupted services and functions under federal jurisdiction. One of the most hotly contested assertions of presidential power arose after a strike against the Pullman railroad car company in 1894 paralyzed rail traffic west of Chicago. Workers at the Pullman car works went on strike because of a wage reduction order. Members of the American Railway Union, with the support of its president, Eugene V. Debs, carried out a secondary boycott against the Pullman company by refusing to service Pullman sleeping cars attached to trains.

Violence threatened, and President Grover Cleveland dispatched federal troops to Chicago to preserve peace. He ordered the U.S. attorney in the city to seek an order halting the Debs boycott on the basis that the strike crippled interstate commerce and interfered with delivery of the mail.

Debs and his associates ignored the court order. They were arrested, convicted of contempt, and sentenced to prison. Debs then petitioned the Supreme Court for a writ of habeas corpus. He challenged his detention as illegal.

Affirming broad executive power to deal with such emergen-

President Grover Cleveland's suppression of the Pullman Railroad Strike of 1894 is an example of presidential enforcement authority. Here, a meat train leaves the Chicago stockyards under escort of U.S. Cavalry.

cies the Court refused to issue the writ, thereby upholding Debs's conviction. For the Court, Justice David J. Brewer wrote:

The entire strength of the nation may be used to enforce in any part of the land the full and free exercise of all national powers and the security of all rights entrusted by the Constitution to its care. The strong arm of the national government may be put forth to brush away all obstructions to the freedom of interstate commerce or the transportation of the mails. If the emergency arises, the army of the nation, and all its militia, are at the service of the nation to compel obedience to its laws. . . .

. . . whenever the wrongs complained of are such as affect the public at large, and are in respect of matters which by the Constitution are entrusted to the care of the nation, and concerning which the nation owes the duty to all the citizens of securing to them their common rights, then the mere fact that the government has no pecuniary interest in the controversy is not sufficient to exclude it from the courts.[45]

Even after Congress restricted the use of injunctions against unions the restrictions were not held to forbid government-sought orders to seize and operate mines in the face of a strike, nor did it forbid mine operators from getting court orders preventing government seizures.[46]

The Power to Veto and to Pardon

The Constitution equips the president with two means of nullifying particular actions of the other branches of the government: the veto and the pardon.

By use of the veto, a president may kill a measure that Congress has already approved. A veto spells death for a bill, unless each chamber can muster a two-thirds vote in its favor to override the veto.

This quasi-legislative device has developed from an infrequently used tool wielded only against unconstitutional or defective laws into a policy weapon often used in the political struggles between the White House and Congress over the proper shape of legislation.

The pardon power permits the president to reduce sentences, remit penalties, or entirely exempt individuals and classes of persons from sentences imposed by the courts. The only express limitation on the pardon power is that persons impeached may not be pardoned.

This power has been sparingly exercised, and generally, occasions of its use draw little public notice.

The Veto Power

President Franklin D. Roosevelt, who vetoed more bills than any other president, is said to have told his aides on more than one occasion, "Give me a bill that I can veto," as a reminder to Congress that every bill that it approves faces possible rejection by the president.[1] While measures occasionally are challenged before the Supreme Court, every bill has to pass political muster in the Oval Office.

Article I of the Constitution provides that the president may veto a bill by returning it to the house of its origin unsigned and accompanied by a statement of objections to the measure. The veto kills the bill unless it is overridden by a two-thirds majority vote of the members of each house.

Perhaps because the Congress and the White House generally accept the politically determined outcome of veto battles, the Supreme Court has never been called upon to judge the validity of a direct veto.

But Article I also provides the following:

If any bill shall not be returned by the President within ten days (Sundays excepted) after it shall have been presented to him, the same shall be a law, in like manner as if he had signed it, unless the Congress by their adjournment prevent its return, in which case it shall not be a law.

The section permits a bill to become a law without the president's signature, presumably a measure the president disapproves of but finds it impolitic to veto.

With Congress adjourned, however, the president's failure to sign a bill constitutes an absolute "pocket" veto over the measure because Congress has no opportunity to override the veto. The Supreme Court's only significant decisions on the veto power have attempted to clarify the conditions under which a pocket veto can be used.

Alexander Hamilton considered the "qualified negative" of the veto a shield against encroachment on executive power by the legislative branch and a barrier to hasty enactment of "improper laws."[2] Hamilton viewed the veto power as a means of improving the spirit of cooperation between the president and the Congress, producing further reflection on measures. He argued that the qualified veto was less harsh than an absolute veto. Hamilton declared that the Framers

have pursued a mean in this business [the veto power], which will both facilitate the exercise of the power vested in this respect in the executive magistrate, and make its efficacy to depend on the sense of a considerable part of the legislative body. . . . A direct and categorical negative has something in the appearance of it more harsh, and more apt to irritate, than the mere suggestion of argumentative objections to be approved or disapproved by those to whom they are addressed.[3]

Use of the veto power has varied greatly from president to president. The first six presidents vetoed only ten measures in their entire administrations, usually on constitutional grounds or because of technical flaws in the legislation. Andrew Jackson, however, began to use the veto as a political device to defeat measures he opposed as a matter of political principle, although he vetoed only twelve measures in eight years. In the entire period up to the Civil War, only fifty-two bills were vetoed, and no presidential veto was overridden until 1866.

President Andrew Johnson used the veto in his battle with Radical Republicans in Congress over control of Reconstruction. Johnson's vetoes were overridden fifteen times.

Eight presidents never cast any vetoes, although the most recent of these was President James A. Garfield. During the late nineteenth century, many presidential vetoes were cast to block private bills and "pork barrel" legislation.

Presidents Grover Cleveland and Franklin D. Roosevelt cast the most vetoes. Roosevelt cast 631 negatives and Cleveland 584. Many of Cleveland's vetoes pertained to private bills that awarded individuals pensions or other government benefits.

The New Deal and World War II broadened the scope of legislative activity and brought greater complexity to government legislation, which resulted in a greater number of vetoes cast on substantive legislative measures. Until Roosevelt vetoed a revenue bill it had been assumed that tax measures were exempt from presidential veto.

In all, presidents vetoed 2,524 measures between 1789 and 1995, with all but fifty-eight of the vetoes cast after 1860. The direct veto had been used 1,459 times, the pocket veto 1,065. Only 105 times in that period did Congress override a veto.[4]

The Pocket Veto

The Supreme Court's major ruling on the veto power came in 1929 as it attempted to clarify the Constitution's intent with respect to the president's use of the pocket veto.

In the *Pocket Veto* case of 1929, the Court ruled that a bill must be returned to a sitting chamber of Congress and cannot be "returned" to an officer of the chamber during a recess period. Thus, the pocket veto could be used any time the chamber of a bill's origin was not in session on the tenth day following submission of the bill to the chief executive. Subsequent rulings, however, have undercut both points. The executive branch and Congress still remain at odds over what constitutes a congressional adjournment and permits the use of this veto.

THE *POCKET VETO* CASE

The first time the Court considered the pocket veto, it upheld it, finding that it was appropriate for President Calvin Coolidge to use the pocket veto to kill a bill passed just before a four-month congressional recess. The bill, which gave certain Indian tribes the right to file claims in the U.S. Court of Claims, was sent to Coolidge for his signature on June 24, 1926.

When the first session of the Sixty-ninth Congress adjourned nine days later, on July 3, Coolidge had neither signed nor returned the bill. He subsequently took no action on the measure and assumed he had pocket-vetoed it. Congress did not reconvene until December, when the second session began.

Certain Indian tribes in Washington State sought to file claims under the measure, arguing that it had become law without the president's signature because Coolidge had not vetoed it. They argued that a pocket veto could only be used between Congresses, when there was no Congress in existence. The word *adjournment* they read to mean only the final adjournment of a Congress, not simply an adjournment between sessions.

Furthermore, they argued, the "ten days" allowed the president to consider and sign or return legislation meant ten legislative, not calendar, days. Under this interpretation, the ten-day period for this particular bill would have run from June 24 until December 1926.[5]

The Supreme Court rejected those arguments, holding that a pocket veto could properly be used between sessions of Congress. The Court concluded that adjournment included interim adjournments. Justice Edward T. Sanford wrote the Court's opinion in which he described the president's exercise of the pocket veto power.

The Constitution in giving the President a qualified negative over legislation—commonly called a veto—entrusts him with an authority and imposes upon him an obligation that are of the highest importance, in the execution of which it is made his duty not only to sign bills that he approves in order that they may become law, but to return bills that he disapproves, with his objections, in order that they may be reconsidered by Congress. The faithful and effective exercise of this momentous duty necessarily requires time in which the President may carefully examine and consider a bill and determine, after due deliberation, whether he should approve or disapprove it, and if he disap-

proves it, formulate his objections for the consideration of Congress. To that end a specified time is given, after the bill has been presented to him, in which he may examine its provisions and either approve it or return it, not approved, for reconsideration. . . . The power thus conferred upon the President cannot be narrowed or cut down by Congress, nor the time within which it is to be exercised lessened, directly or indirectly. And it is just as essential a part of the constitutional provisions, guarding against ill-considered and unwise legislation, that the President, on his part, should have the full time allowed him for determining whether he should approve or disapprove a bill, and if disapproved, for adequately formulating the objections that should be considered by Congress, as it is that Congress, on its part, should have an opportunity to repass the bill over his objections.[6]

Justice Sanford noted that the failure of the bill in question to become law could not "properly be ascribed to the disapproval of the President—who presumably would have returned it before the adjournment if there had been sufficient time in which to complete his consideration and take such action but is attributable solely to the action of Congress in adjourning before the time allowed the President for returning the bill that expired."[7] Moreover, the term *days* meant calendar and not legislative days:

The word "days," when not qualified, means in ordinary and common usage calendar days. This is obviously the meaning in which it is used in the constitutional provision, and is emphasized by the fact that "Sundays" are excepted.[8]

On the question of "adjournment," Sanford wrote:

We think under the constitutional provision the determinative question in reference to an "adjournment" is not whether it is a final adjournment of Congress or an interim adjournment, such as the adjournment of the first session, but whether it is one that "prevents" the President from returning the bill to the House in which it originated within the time allowed. It is clear, we understand, it is not questioned, that since the President may return a bill at any time within the allotted period, he is prevented from returning it, within the meaning of the constitutional provision if by reason of the adjournment it is impossible for him to return it to the House in which it originated on the last day of that period. . . .

We find no substantial basis for the suggestion that although the House in which the bill originated is not in session the bill may nevertheless be returned, consistently with the constitutional mandate, by delivering it, with the President's objections, to an officer or agent of the House, for subsequent delivery to the House when it resumes its sittings at the next session, with the same force and effect as if the bill had been returned to the House on the day it was delivered to such officer or agent. Aside from the fact that Congress has never enacted any statute authorizing any officer or agent of either House to receive for it bills returned by the President during its adjournment, and that there is no rule to that effect in either House, the delivery of the bill to such office or agent, even if authorized by Congress itself, would not comply with the constitutional mandate. . . . In short it was plainly the object of the constitutional provision that there should be a timely return of the bill, which should not only be a matter of official record . . . but should enable Congress to proceed immediately with its reconsideration; and that the return of the bill should be an actual and public return to the House itself, and not a fictitious return by a delivery of the bill to some individual which could be given a retroactive effect at a later date when the time for the return of the bill to the House had expired.[9]

THE *WRIGHT* CASE

Within a decade, the broad sweep of the Court's ruling in the *Pocket Veto* case was limited by a later Court decision. In *Wright v. United States* (1938) the Court held that during a short recess of one chamber—the one to which a vetoed bill must be returned—an official of that chamber could receive a veto message to deliver to the chamber after the recess. Therefore, a pocket veto could not be used in those circumstances.[10]

In that case, the Court said that the statement in the *Pocket Veto* ruling that a bill must be returned to a sitting chamber "should not be construed so narrowly as to demand that the President must select a precise moment when the House is within the walls of its chambers and that a return is absolutely impossible during a recess however temporary."[11]

It has now become a routine practice for the House and Senate to appoint their clerk or secretary to receive messages from the president during a recess.

THE NIXON POCKET VETOES

After a period of peace in the pocket veto area, President Richard Nixon revived the controversy by pocket-vetoing a bill during the six-day Christmas recess in 1970. In a challenge to his action brought by Sen. Edward M. Kennedy, D-Mass., a federal court of appeals held the veto invalid because the recess was not long enough to prevent Nixon from returning the bill to Congress with a direct veto message.

Two years later another Nixon pocket veto was held invalid by a federal appeals court, which pointed out that Congress had appointed officials to receive veto messages during the time that the two chambers were not in session.

And Kennedy went to court again after President Gerald R. Ford pocket-vetoed a bill passed just before a break between sessions. Once again an appeals court held that pocket vetoes could not be used except after adjournment sine die—unless Congress recesses without leaving agents appointed to receive presidential messages.[12]

President Ronald Reagan sparked a new round in this debate by declaring that the pocket veto was usable any time Congress recessed for longer than three days. During a brief recess, he pocket-vetoed a bill barring aid to El Salvador. This action was challenged by thirty-three House members who won an appeals court ruling reaffirming the limit on pocket vetoes to periods following the final adjournment of a Congress.

The administration appealed the case of *Burke v. Barnes* to the Supreme Court, which raised hopes that it would finally give a definitive answer to this question—and then dashed them by finding the dispute moot and leaving the lower court decision in place and the issue still unresolved.[13]

The Power to Grant Pardons and Reprieves

With the single exception of persons impeached, the Constitution gives the president the unlimited power "to grant Reprieves and Pardons for Offenses against the United States."

THE POWER TO SIGN BILLS

For 150 years presidents went to Capitol Hill on the last day of the legislative session in order to sign all approved bills by the end of the congressional session.

The custom was based in part on the belief that all legislative power, including the president's power to sign legislation, expired with the end of a session. It meant, however, that certain bills received only hasty consideration by the president.[1]

Near the conclusion of the June 1920 congressional session President Woodrow Wilson asked the attorney general to determine if bills might be constitutionally approved within the ten days following adjournment. The attorney general reported affirmatively, and Wilson accordingly signed bills into law during this period after an interim adjournment.[2]

At the end of the final 1931 congressional session, President Herbert C. Hoover, on the advice of his attorney general, began the practice of signing measures after final adjournment.[3] On March 5, 1931, the day after Congress adjourned, Hoover signed a bill.[4] The question of its validity resulted in a Supreme Court decision upholding the president's action. The Court cited

the fundamental purpose of the constitutional provision to provide appropriate opportunity for the President to consider the bills presented to him. The importance of maintaining that opportunity unimpaired increases as bills multiply.[5]

The Court noted that in the week prior to adjournment 269 bills were sent to the president, of which 184 reached his desk on the last day of the session.[6] The Court found no reason why the time for the president's consideration of bills should be cut short because Congress had adjourned.

No public interest would be conserved by the requirement of hurried and inconsiderate examination of bills in the closing hours of a session, with the result that bills may be approved which on further consideration would be disapproved.[7]

The Court has not decided, however, whether bills passed less than ten days before the end of a president's term may be approved or vetoed by an incoming president. *Dicta* in the 1932 case suggested that the incoming president would not approve such a bill because it was not submitted to him, but to the previous president. President Harry S. Truman, however, signed bills sent to the White House before President Franklin D. Roosevelt's death. His authority to do so was not challenged.

1. Carl B. Swisher, *American Constitutional Development*, 2d ed. (Cambridge, Mass.: Houghton Mifflin, 1954), 785.
2. Ibid., 786.
3. Ibid.
4. *Edwards v. United States*, 286 U.S. 482 at 493 (1932).
5. Id.
6. Id.
7. Id.

A pardon is an exemption from sentence and guilt; a reprieve is the suspension of a sentence or other legally imposed penalties for a temporary period.

The Supreme Court has supported the president's discretion to exercise the pardon power against all challenges. A pardon may be full or partial, absolute or conditional, or general. The president may attach conditions to a pardon, the Court has held, so long as they are not contrary to the Constitution or federal laws.[14]

Although acceptance of a pardon is generally considered a necessary act, conditional pardons—and commutations—have been upheld against challenge by the person pardoned. The effect of a full pardon, the Court has held, is to end the punishment and blot out the guilt "so that in the eyes of the law the offender is as innocent as if he had never committed the offence."[15]

The early view of the pardon power was set out by Chief Justice John Marshall, who defined a pardon as an act of grace. But a century later, the individual act of mercy had become, as well, in the words of Justice Oliver Wendell Holmes Jr., "part of the Constitutional scheme."[16]

Presidents have issued pardons and granted amnesty—a general pardon to groups or communities—since President Washington issued a general amnesty to the western Pennsylvania "whiskey rebels" in 1795.

The most famous pardon in American history to date was that granted by President Ford on September 8, 1974, to his predecessor, former president Nixon, who had resigned the presidency amid allegations of his involvement in crimes related to the Watergate cover-up.

The pardon was "full, free and absolute . . . for all offenses against the United States which he . . . has committed or may have committed" as president.[17] Nixon accepted the pardon with a statement describing it as a "compassionate act." *(See box, Nixon Pardon Proclamation, p. 234.)*

The Framers of the Constitution granted the president of the United States a pardon power similar to that exercised by British monarchs.[18] Alexander Hamilton, writing in *The Federalist Papers,* advocated that the use of this power be unfettered.

Humanity and good policy conspire to dictate that the benign prerogative of pardoning should be as little as possible fettered or embarrassed. The criminal code of every country partakes so much of necessary severity, that without an easy access to exceptions in favor of unfortunate guilt, justice would wear a countenance too sanguinary and cruel.[19]

ACCEPTANCE

In one of the Court's first rulings on the pardon power, Chief Justice Marshall stated that acceptance of a pardon by the recipient was a necessary condition of its taking effect. In the case of *United States v. Wilson,* decided in 1833, Marshall wrote:

A pardon is an act of grace, proceeding from the power entrusted with the execution of the laws, which exempts the individual, on whom it is bestowed, from the punishment the law inflicts for a crime he has committed. It is the private, though official act of the executive magistrate, delivered to the individual for whose benefit it is intended, and not communicated officially to the court. . . . A pardon is a deed, to the validity of which delivery is essential, and delivery is not complete without acceptance. It may then be rejected by the person to whom it is tendered; and if it be rejected, we have discovered no power in a court to force it on him. A pardon may be conditional, and the condi-

tion may be more objectionable than the punishment inflicted by the judgment.[20]

This opinion reflected the common-law tradition, which viewed the sovereign's pardon as an act of grace—and the common English practice that a pardon or commutation was often granted on the condition that the convicted felon move to another place.

In 1915 the Court reaffirmed Marshall's view of the need for acceptance of a pardon. The decision came in the case of *Burdick v. United States.*[21]

George Burdick, city editor of the *New York Tribune,* refused to testify before a federal grand jury investigating customs fraud, saying that his testimony would tend to incriminate him. President Woodrow Wilson then offered Burdick a full and unconditional pardon in connection with any matters he might be questioned about.

Burdick refused the pardon, refused again to testify, and was imprisoned for contempt. But a unanimous Supreme Court upheld his right to reject the pardon, citing Marshall's 1833 opinion.

Justice Joseph McKenna, writing for the Court, explained the risk of implied guilt in the granting of pardons to individuals who, although not convicted of a crime, nevertheless accepted a pardon:

[T]he grace of a pardon . . . may be only in pretense or seeming . . . involving consequences of even greater disgrace than those from which it purports to relieve. Circumstances may be made to bring innocence under the penalties of the law. If so brought, escape by confession of guilt implied in the acceptance of a pardon may be rejected.[22]

THE EFFECT OF A PARDON

The leading case defining the effect of a presidential pardon came just after the Civil War. The case involved one of the nation's leading attorneys, southerner Augustus H. Garland, and an 1865 act of Congress that required all attorneys who wished to practice in the Supreme Court and other federal courts to take an oath that declared that they had not aided the Confederate cause by word or deed.[23]

Garland had practiced before the Supreme Court prior to the war. When Arkansas, his home state, joined the Confederacy, he followed the state and served in the Confederate congress. Under the "test oath" requirement imposed by the 1865 law, Garland was forever disqualified from resuming his legal practice before the federal courts.

In July 1865, however, Garland received a full pardon from President Andrew Johnson for all offenses committed, direct or implied, in the Civil War. Garland cited the pardon and asked for permission to practice in federal court, although he was still unable, due to his service to the Confederacy, to take the test oath.

Garland argued that the disqualifying act of Congress, so far as it affected him, was unconstitutional and void as a bill of attainder prohibited by the Constitution. Beyond that, he argued that even if the act was constitutional, the pardon released him from compliance with its provisions.[24]

After the Civil War Congress imposed a "test oath" on persons wishing to practice law in federal courts, which required them to affirm their loyalty—past and present—to the Union. In 1867 the Supreme Court found the test oath unconstitutional in *Ex parte Garland*.

"The Benign Prerogative of Mercy"

The Supreme Court ruled for Garland on both points. For the first time, in the case of *Ex parte Garland*, it struck down an act of Congress by the narrow margin of 5 to 4. The majority found the test oath law unconstitutional as a bill of attainder and an ex post facto law. *(See box, Specific Constitutional Limits on Congressional Powers, p. 84, in Chapter 4.)*

But even if the law were valid, wrote Justice Stephen J. Field for the majority, the pardon placed Garland "beyond the reach of punishment of any kind" for his Civil War role. "It is not within the constitutional power of Congress thus to inflict punishment beyond the reach of executive clemency," Field wrote.[25]

Field then examined the presidential pardon power and its effect on the recipient and on Congress.

The power thus conferred is unlimited, with the exception stated [impeachment]. It extends to every offence known to the law, and may be exercised at any time after its commission, either before legal proceedings are taken, or during their pendency, or after conviction and judgement. This power of the President is not subject to legislative control. Congress can neither limit the effect of his pardon, nor exclude from its exercise any class of offenders. The benign prerogative of mercy reposed in him cannot be fettered by any legislative restrictions.[26]

Having established the unlimited nature of the president's pardoning power, Field discussed the effect of a presidential pardon on the recipient:

A pardon reaches both the punishment prescribed for the offense and the guilt of the offender; and when the pardon is full, it releases the punishment and blots out of existence the guilt, [so that in the eyes of the law the offender is as innocent as if he had never committed the offence.] If granted before conviction, it prevents any of the penalties and disabilities consequent upon conviction from attaching; if granted after conviction, it removes the penalties and disabilities, and restores him to all his civil rights; it makes him, as it were, a new man, and gives him a new credit and capacity.[27]

In Dissent

The dissenters, in an opinion written by Justice Samuel F. Miller, focused on the initial question of the constitutionality of the disqualifying law: whether it was an ex post facto law and whether Congress could pass laws to ensure the character and loyalty of the nation's lawyers. They found the law a proper exercise of congressional power, and disagreed that the pardon put Garland beyond its reach:

The right to practice law in the courts . . . is a privilege granted by the law . . . not an absolute right . . . the presidential pardon relieves the party from all the penalties, or in other words, from all the punishment, which the law inflicted for his offence. But it relieves him from nothing more. If the oath required as a condition to practising law is not a punishment, as I think I have shown it is not, then the pardon of the President has no effect in releasing him from the requirement to take it. If it is a qualification which Congress had a right to prescribe as necessary to an attorney, then the President, cannot, by pardon or otherwise, dispense with the law requiring such qualification.

This is not only the plain rule as between the legislative and executive departments of the government, but it is the declaration of common sense. The man who, by counterfeiting, by theft, by murder, or by treason, is rendered unfit to exercise the functions of an attorney or counselor-at-law, may be saved by the executive pardon from the penitentiary or the gallows, but is not thereby restored to the qualifications which are essential to admission to the bar. No doubt it will be found that very many persons among those who cannot take this oath, deserved to be relieved from the prohibition of the law; but this in no wise depends upon the act of the President in giving or refusing a pardon. It remains to the legislative power alone to prescribe under what circumstances this relief shall be extended.[28]

The Court thus allowed former Confederates to resume the practice of law in the nation's federal courts. The decision produced a furor in the North and led to legislative efforts to reform the Court. Reacting to the ruling, Congress considered barring all ex-Confederates from the practice of law, but the bill

NIXON PARDON PROCLAMATION

Following is the text of the proclamation by which President Gerald R. Ford, September 8, 1974, pardoned former president Richard Nixon:

Richard Nixon became the thirty-seventh President of the United States on January 20, 1969, and was re-elected in 1972 for a second term by the electors of forty-nine of the fifty states. His term in office continued until his resignation on August 9, 1974.

Pursuant to resolutions of the House of Representatives, its Committee on the Judiciary conducted an inquiry and investigation on the impeachment of the President extending over more than eight months. The hearings of the committee and its deliberations, which received wide national publicity over television, radio, and in printed media, resulted in votes adverse to Richard Nixon on recommended articles of impeachment.

As a result of certain acts or omissions occurring before his resignation from the office of President, Richard Nixon has become liable to possible indictment and trial for offenses against the United States. Whether or not he shall be so prosecuted depends on findings of the appropriate grand jury and on the discretion of the authorized prosecutor. Should an indictment ensue, the accused shall then be entitled to a fair trial by an impartial jury, as guaranteed to every individual by the Constitution.

It is believed that a trial of Richard Nixon, if it became necessary, could not fairly begin until a year or more has elapsed. In the meantime, the tranquility to which this nation has been restored by the events of recent weeks could be irreparably lost by the prospects of bringing to trial a former President of the United States. The prospects of such trial will cause prolonged and divisive debate over the propriety of exposing to further punishment and degradation a man who has already paid the unprecedented penalty of relinquishing the highest elective office in the United States.

Now, therefore, I, Gerald R. Ford, President of the United States, pursuant to the pardon power conferred upon me by Article II, Section 2, of the Constitution, have granted and by these presents do grant a full, free, and absolute pardon unto Richard Nixon for all offenses against the United States which he, Richard Nixon, has committed or may have committed or taken part in during the period from January 20, 1969, through August 9, 1974.

In witness whereof, I have hereunto set my hand this 8th day of September in the year of Our Lord Nineteen Hundred Seventy-Four, and of the Independence of the United States of America the 199th.

was not approved. Garland later became attorney general of the United States, during the administration of President Grover Cleveland.

Broad, But Not Perpetual

Despite the broad effect of a pardon on a person convicted of or under investigation for a crime, the Court has held that a pardon cannot protect an individual who is convicted of a second, postpardon crime.

A New York court tried and convicted a person whose first federal offense had been pardoned. The court nevertheless took the fact of a prior conviction into consideration in determining the penalty for the second offense. The convicted individual

challenged consideration of that factor, but the Supreme Court warned that it was incorrect to think

that a pardon would operate to limit the power of the United States in punishing crimes against its authority to provide for taking into consideration past offenses committed by the accused as a circumstance of aggravation even though for such past offenses there had been a pardon granted.[29]

The Court has held that a pardon restores a convict's competency as a witness in a court of law. The justices found that the disability resulted from the conviction and that the pardon obliterated the effect of the conviction and therefore restored the person's competency to testify.[30]

Undoing the Past

A pardon, however, cannot make amends for the past, the Court has held. It cannot afford compensation for time spent in prison, nor does it restore property rights that have been legally vested in others. The leading case on this aspect of the effects of a presidential pardon arose, like *Ex parte Garland*, out of the Civil War.

The property of a man who served with the Confederacy was condemned and sold for his "treason." After the general pardon issued to ex-Confederates in 1868 by President Andrew Johnson, the former owner of the property sued for the proceeds of the sale. The Court denied his claim and declared that a pardon cannot

make amends for the past. It affords no relief for what has been suffered by the offender in his person by imprisonment, forced labor, or otherwise; it does not give compensation for what has been done or suffered, nor does it impose upon the government any obligation to give it. The offense being established by judicial proceedings, that which has been done or suffered when they were in force is presumed to have been rightly done and justly suffered, and no satisfaction for it can be required. . . . Neither does the pardon affect any rights which have vested in others directly by the execution of the judgment for the offense, or which have been acquired by others whilst that judgment was in force. If, for example, by the judgment a sale of the offender's property has been had, the purchaser will hold the property notwithstanding the subsequent pardon. . . . The rights of the parties have become vested, and are as complete as if they were acquired in any other legal way. So, also, if the proceeds have been paid into the treasury, the right to them has so far become vested in the United States that they can only be secured to the former owner of the property through an act of Congress. Moneys once in the treasury can only be withdrawn by an appropriation by law. However large, therefore, may be the power of pardon possessed by the President, and however extended may be its application, there is this limit to it, as there is to all his powers, it cannot touch moneys in the Treasury of the United States, except expressly authorized by Act of Congress.[31]

CONDITIONS AND COMMUTATIONS

The questions posed by conditional pardons came before the Court after President Abraham Lincoln, on December 8, 1863, offered pardons to all Confederates who swore allegiance to the Constitution and the Union. Lincoln's pardon offer, if accepted, would have granted former Confederates the right to restoration of their property taken during the war.

In *United States v. Klein*, decided in 1872, the Court upheld the president's right to offer pardon and property restoration in exchange for allegiance.

It was competent for the President to annex to his offer of pardon any conditions or qualifications he should see fit; but after those conditions and qualifications had been satisfied, the pardon and its connected promises took full effect.[32]

Congress had tried, through legislation, to block the property restoration effect of this pardon. The Court rejected that effort:

To the Executive alone is intrusted the power of pardon; and it is granted without limit. Pardon includes amnesty. It blots out the offense pardoned and removes all its penal consequences. It may be granted on conditions. In these particular pardons, that no doubt might exist as to their character, restoration of property was expressly pledged; and the pardon was granted on condition that the person who availed himself of it should take and keep a prescribed oath.

Now, it is clear that the Legislature cannot change the effect of such a pardon any more than the Executive can change a law.[33]

Commutation Challenges

In a series of cases involving the president's exercise of his pardon power to commute—reduce—sentences, the Court has held that this aspect of the power may be exercised without the recipient's consent.

William Wells, convicted of murder, was to be hanged on April 23, 1852. On execution day, President Millard Fillmore granted him a conditional pardon, commuting his sentence to life in prison. Wells accepted the pardon, but challenged the condition as illegal, seeking his release from prison through a writ of habeas corpus. His attorneys argued to the Supreme Court that

a President granting such a pardon assumes a power not conferred by the Constitution—that he legislates a new punishment into existence, and sentences the convict to suffer it; in this way violating the legislative and judicial power of the government, it being the power of the first to enact laws for the punishment of offences . . . and that of the judiciary, to sentence . . . according to them.[34]

The Court in 1856 rejected this argument, upheld the president's power to commute a sentence without the recipient's consent, and concluded:

it may be said, [that] . . . the condition, when accepted, becomes a substitute for the sentence of the court . . . [and] is substantially the exercise of a new power. But this is not so, for the power to offer a condition, without ability to enforce its acceptance, when accepted by the convict, is the substitution, by himself, of a lesser punishment than the law has imposed upon him, and he cannot complain if the law executes the choice he has made.[35]

In subsequent cases, the Court has declared that the president's prerogative includes the power to remit fines, penalties, and forfeitures and to pardon contempt of court.[36]

Biddle v. Perovich

Seventy years later, the Court reaffirmed its holding in the *Wells* case, ruling that a president could commute a death sentence entirely without the recipient's consent.

Vuco Perovich, convicted of murder in Alaska in 1905 and sentenced to be hanged, received a commuted sentence of life imprisonment from President William Howard Taft in 1909. Authorities moved Perovich to a state penitentiary and then, some years later, to the federal prison at Leavenworth, Kansas. Perovich twice applied unsuccessfully for a pardon.

He then applied for release through a writ of habeas corpus, arguing that his removal from an Alaskan jail to a federal penitentiary and the president's commutation of his death sentence were effected without his consent and without legal authority.

Perovich's attorney urged the Supreme Court to hold that a sentence could not be commuted without consent. The Court rejected that argument, and ruled that consent was not required for commutation of sentence. "When we come to the commutation of death to imprisonment for life," wrote Justice Oliver Wendell Holmes Jr., "it is hard to see how consent has much to do with the effect of the president's action. Supposing that Perovich did not accept the change, he could not have got himself hanged against the Executive order."[37] Justice Holmes then set out the modern Court's view of the presidential pardon power:

A pardon in our days is not a private act of grace from an individual happening to possess power. It is part of the Constitutional scheme. When granted it is the determination of the ultimate authority that the public welfare will be better served by inflicting less than what the judgment fixed. . . . Just as the original punishment would be imposed without regard to the prisoner's consent and in the teeth of his will, whether he liked it or not, the public welfare, not his consent, determines what shall be done. So far as a pardon legitimately cuts down a penalty, it affects the judgment imposing it.[38]

Schick v. Reed

In 1974 the Court for the third time rejected a challenge to the power of commutation. President Dwight D. Eisenhower commuted the death sentence of a child murderer to life in prison without possibility of parole, a sentence not at that time authorized by law for the crime of murder.

After serving twenty years, the prisoner sued to require the parole board to consider him eligible for parole on the basis that he had served the equivalent to a "life" sentence, and, furthermore, that the death penalty had in the interim been outlawed by a Supreme Court decision of 1972.[39] Schick, the prisoner, argued that he had made a "bad bargain" in exchanging a death sentence for life in prison without opportunity for parole.

The Supreme Court held that the conditional commutation of his sentence was lawful and that intervening events had not undermined its validity.[40] Writing for the Court, Chief Justice Warren E. Burger explained:

A fair reading of the history of the English pardoning power, from which our Art. II, § 2, derives, of the language of that section itself, and of the unbroken practice since 1790 compels the conclusion that the power flows from the Constitution alone, and not from any legislative enactments, and that it cannot be modified, abridged, or diminished by the Congress. Additionally, considerations of public policy and humanitarian impulses support an interpretation of that power so as to permit the attachment of any condition which does not otherwise offend the Constitution. The plain purpose of the broad power conferred . . . was to allow plenary authority in the President to "forgive" the convicted person in part or entirely, to reduce a penalty in terms of a specified number of years, or to alter it with conditions which are in themselves constitutionally unobjectionable. . . . We therefore hold that the pardoning power is an enumerated power of the Constitution and its limitations, if any, must be found in the Constitution itself.[41]

Three justices, however, questioned the "extra-legal nature of the Executive action." Justice Thurgood Marshall, writing for Justices William O. Douglas and William J. Brennan Jr., argued that "in commuting a sentence the Chief Executive is not imbued with the constitutional power to create unauthorized punishments."[42]

Privilege and Immunity

The Constitution makes no mention of executive immunity or executive privilege, yet they are important aspects of presidential power. These two concepts, both of which are invoked to protect the presidency from undue interference by other branches, have evolved from the system of separated powers, the constitutional design of three coordinate branches, each protected from coercion by the others.

Executive immunity shields the chief executive against judicial interference with presidential policy making. Once effected, a policy may be reviewed by a court for its results, but a court cannot order the president to take, or refrain from taking, any particular policy action.

And yet the president is not immune from all challenge to his actions. Article II, Section 4, provides that the other political branch—Congress—may impeach and remove a president from office if it finds him guilty of "Treason, Bribery or other high Crimes and Misdemeanors." The question is unresolved whether a sitting president might be charged and prosecuted for crimes in any court other than a court of impeachment. Once impeached, however, the Constitution is explicit in making the point that an official is then "liable and subject to Indictment, Trial, Judgment and Punishment, according to Law."

Executive privilege, on the other hand, generally has been asserted as the president's prerogative to withhold information, documents, and the testimony of his aides from public or congressional scrutiny. Congress has never fully accepted the principle, although it has been asserted and practiced by presidents since George Washington.

Presidents find the basis for this claim in the separation of powers principle, vaguely stated at the beginning of Article II—"The executive power shall be vested in a President of the United States of America"—and their responsibility to "take care that the laws be faithfully executed."

The Court's rulings on executive privilege have acknowledged the existence of a limited privilege as necessary to protect the national security and the conduct of diplomatic negotiations. The Court, however, has denied emphatically any absolute privilege to withhold information under all circumstances.

Executive Immunity

The turmoil of Reconstruction and the troubled presidency of Andrew Johnson provided the backdrop for the leading Supreme Court decision on the immunity of the president, as an official and an individual, from judicial interference with the conduct of his office.

In 1866 the Court—in *Ex parte Milligan*—had declared that Lincoln had exceeded his authority in setting up Civil War military commissions outside the war zone. This ruling gave the South reason to hope that the Court would also strike down the congressional program of Reconstruction outlined in the Reconstruction Act of 1867. *(See "The Milligan Case," pp. 198–199.)*

Mississippi came to the Supreme Court asking the justices to order the president to stop carrying out the Reconstruction program. The state challenged both the constitutionality of the laws upon which it was based and the president's authority to carry them out.[1]

In *Marbury v. Madison* the Court had held that a court with jurisdiction could issue a writ to order the president to perform a ministerial duty, a duty as to which he had little discretion.[2] But Mississippi was asking the Court to exercise its authority to restrain the president's enforcement of an act of Congress.

The Court rejected the state's request. Chief Justice Salmon P. Chase wrote the Court's opinion, which distinguished between the ministerial duties of a president and his general responsibility for seeing that the laws were faithfully executed. Ministerial acts, wrote Chase, could be subject to court orders, but acts involving political discretion were beyond judicial reach.

When a court issued an injunction against a political act, it interfered with the operation of the political branches and risked a collision between the judicial and political departments. There were practical reasons to avoid such collisions, explained Chief Justice Chase:

If the President refuse obedience, it is needless to observe that the Court is without power to enforce its process. If, on the other hand, the President complies . . . and refuses to execute the acts of Congress, is it not clear that a collision may occur between the executive and legislative departments. . . ? May not the House of Representatives impeach the President for such refusal? And in that case could this Court interfere in behalf of the President, thus endangered by compliance with its mandate. . . ?

A ministerial duty . . . is one in respect to which nothing is left to discretion. It is a simple, definite duty, arising under conditions admitted or proved to exist, and imposed by law. . . .

Very different is the duty of the President in the exercise of the power to see that the laws are faithfully executed. . . . The duty thus imposed on the President is in no just sense ministerial. It is purely executive and political.

An attempt on the part of the Judicial Department of the Government to enforce the performance of such duties by the President might be justly characterized, in the language of Chief Justice Marshall, as "an absurd and excessive extravagance."

It is true that in the instance before us the interposition of the court is not sought to enforce action by the Executive under constitutional legislation, but to restrain such action under legislation alleged to be unconstitutional. But we are unable to perceive that this circumstance takes the case out of the general principles which forbid judicial interference with the exercise of executive discretion. . . .

The Congress is the Legislative Department of the Government; the President is the Executive Department. Neither can be restrained in its action by the Judicial Department; though the acts of both, when performed, are, in proper cases, subject to its cognizance.[3]

Mississippi suggested that the injunctive relief sought might be issued against Johnson as a private citizen if the office of the president was beyond the reach of such an order. But Chase declared that no such distinction could be entertained in the case:

[I]t is plain that relief as against the execution of an Act of Congress by Andrew Johnson, is relief against its execution by the President. A bill praying an injunction against the execution of an act of Congress by the incumbent of the presidential office cannot be received, whether it describes him as President or as citizen of a State.[4]

The Court dismissed Georgia's subsequent effort to prevent enforcement of the Reconstruction acts by Secretary of War Edwin M. Stanton and General Ulysses S. Grant.[5] The Court refused to issue to these presidential subordinates the order it would not issue to the president. The suit involved political questions and political rights, the Court said, and the issue lay beyond the Court's jurisdiction.[6] The rights involved were not personal or property rights, the Court observed, but "the rights of sovereignty, of political jurisdiction, of government, of corporate existence as a State, with all its constitutional powers and privileges."[7]

Thus, held the Court, once the president moves into the realm of policy and politics, the Court cannot compel him to act or prevent him from acting. Once completed, however, the Court may consider a challenge to the results of the president's policies and at that point may review and disallow those policies. But the president's subordinates may be ordered by a court not to carry out a threatened illegal act that would lead to irreparable damage. Those subordinates also may be commanded by a court to carry out some ministerial duty required by law.

In *Kendall v. United States* the Court in 1838 held that the postmaster general could be ordered by a court to pay an account due without breaching the powers and prerogatives of the president. Justice Smith Thompson's majority opinion discussed the president's discretionary powers, their derivation, and exercise:

The theory of the constitution undoubtedly is, that the great powers of the government are divided into separate departments; and so far as these powers derived from the constitution, the departments may be regarded as independent of each other. But beyond that, all are subject to regulations by law, touching the discharge of the duties required to be performed. The executive power is vested in a president; and so far as his powers are derived from the constitution, he is beyond the reach of any other department. . . . But it by no means follows, that every officer in every branch of that department is under the exclusive direction of the president. Such a principle, we apprehend, is not, and certainly cannot be claimed by the president. There are certain political duties imposed upon many officers in the executive department, the discharge of which is under direction of the president. But it would be an alarming doctrine, that congress cannot impose upon any executive officer any duty they may think proper, which is not repugnant to any rights secured and protected by the constitution; and in such cases, the duty and responsibility grow out of and are subject to the control of the law, and not to the direction of the president.[8]

The Court rejected the argument that the postmaster general, a presidential cabinet officer, was under the sole direction of the president. That principle, wrote the Court,

if carried out in its results to all cases falling within it, would [result in] . . . clothing the President with a power entirely to control legislation of Congress, and paralyze the administration of justice.

To contend that the obligation imposed on the President to see the laws faithfully executed implies a power to forbid their execution, is a novel construction of the Constitution, and entirely inadmissible.[9]

Subsequent rulings by the Court have held that subordinate executive officers may be held personally liable for damages wrought by acts in excess of their authority.[10] But some executive immunity protects them from liability for reasonable actions taken in good faith in the performance of their duties.[11] *(See box, The Sovereign's Immunity, p. 271, in Chapter 6.)*

In 1982 the Court granted the president absolute immunity from personal liability as a result of injuries or losses caused by official actions.

A. Ernest Fitzgerald lost his air force job during the Nixon administration, as reprisal, he contended, for revealing to Congress cost overruns on air force contracts. He sued President Richard Nixon and other top executive branch officers for causing him to lose his job. When the case came to the Supreme Court, Fitzgerald lost, 5–4. By that time, Nixon was no longer president, but the immunity for his actions as president remained.

This absolute immunity, wrote Justice Lewis F. Powell Jr., is "a functionally mandated incident of the president's unique office, rooted in the constitutional tradition of the separation of powers and supported by our history."[12]

"Because of the singular importance of the President's duties, diversion of his energies by concern with private lawsuits would raise unique risks to the effective functioning of government," Powell continued in *Nixon v. Fitzgerald.* If a president were vulnerable personally to lawsuits, it "could distract a President from his public duties, to the detriment not only of the President and his office, but also the Nation that the Presidency was designed to serve."[13]

Although this immunity encompassed actions within the "outer perimeter" of the president's official responsibility, it "will not leave the Nation without sufficient protection against misconduct on the part of the chief executive," Powell concluded, mentioning the constitutional remedy of impeachment, constant scrutiny by the press, vigilant oversight by Congress, as well as the desire to earn reelection, to maintain prestige, and to preserve a proper historical reputation.[14]

Justices Harry A. Blackmun, William J. Brennan Jr., Thurgood Marshall, and Byron R. White dissented.

In a companion case decided the same day, *Harlow v. Fitzgerald,* the Court held that the president's close aides did not enjoy such absolute liability from these suits. Instead, Powell wrote, they had a qualified immunity that protected them unless their actions, upon which the claims against them are based, violated clearly established statutory or constitutional rights of which a reasonable person would have been aware.[15]

Executive Privilege

Presidents, acknowledging that Congress has the right to inquire into executive branch matters, have from time to time claimed executive privilege to withhold information from Congress.

These claims, however, have been exceptions to the general rule of compliance with congressional requests for such information. As one investigator has written, in "virtually every incident . . . prior to the Civil War, presidents complied substantially with congressional requests, withholding information only if specifically authorized to do so by Congress."[16]

Since 1954 the incidence of claims of privilege has risen sharply, resulting in a number of Supreme Court pronouncements on the subject. Until 1974 the legal basis for the privilege was much debated. Attorneys general and others seeking to justify a claim of privilege relied heavily on historical precedents of presidential refusals to provide requested information.[17] The precedents, however, often provided ambiguous support for the privilege.

One writer, after investigating the precedents cited, concluded that, contrary to presidential claims, "Congress prevailed, and got precisely what it sought to get" in most cases.[18] Raoul Berger, author of a book on the question, called executive privilege a "constitutional myth."[19]

In 1974, however, in the case of *United States v. Nixon*, the Supreme Court for the first time placed a constitutional foundation under the privilege.[20] Upholding a limited privilege, the assertion of which must be justified in each case by the executive, the Court rejected President Nixon's particular claim of absolute privilege to withhold information. Yet in so doing, the Court provided a fortified basis for future presidential claims of privilege.

PRESIDENTS AND PRIVILEGE

The phrase *executive privilege* did not come into use until 1958 when Justice Stanley F. Reed used it in an opinion.[21] But the practice described by the phrase began much earlier. President Washington only once denied Congress access to papers, refusing to allow the House to see papers related to negotiation of the controversial Jay Treaty. Washington based his refusal on the fact that the House lacked power under the Constitution to demand treaty-related documents. Washington acknowledged the right of the Senate to have access to those papers.[22]

Chief Justice John Marshall, writing for the Court in *Marbury v. Madison,* implicitly acknowledged a basis for some executive privilege:

By the Constitution of the United States, the President is invested with certain important political powers, in the exercise of which he is to use his own discretion, and is accountable only to his country in his political character and to his own conscience.[23]

Marshall, however, saw limits to the president's prerogative of secrecy:

Questions in their nature political, or which are, by the Constitution and the laws, submitted to the executive, can never be made in this court.

But, if this be not such a question; if, so far from being an intrusion into the secrets of the cabinet . . . if it be no intermeddling with a sub-

The Supreme Court's decision in *United States v. Nixon* (1974) cost President Richard Nixon his job but provided a lot of work for editorial cartoonists across the country.

ject over which the executive can be considered as having exercised any control; what is there in the exalted station of the officer, which shall bar a citizen from asserting, in a court of justice, his legal rights, or shall forbid a court to listen to the claim, or to issue a mandamus directing the performance of a duty, not depending on executive discretion, but on particular acts of congress, and the general principles of law?[24]

President Thomas Jefferson, contrary to popular misconception, complied partially when the House requested information from him about the Aaron Burr conspiracy. Jefferson provided the information, withholding the names of individuals mentioned in parts of a letter requested, saying that the names were not pertinent to the House inquiry.

During Burr's 1807 treason trial, Jefferson was subpoenaed to appear, and declined to do so, but he eventually produced the letter sought by Burr's counsel. The presiding judge, John Marshall, again recognized a limited privilege protecting state secrets, but said that the court would weigh the need for secrecy against the need of the accused for the document sought in order that he might have a fair trial.[25]

President Andrew Jackson in 1835 rejected a Senate request for a list of charges against Surveyor-General Gideon Fitz in connection with fraudulent land sales.[26] Presidents John Tyler, James K. Polk, and Franklin Pierce all withheld information demanded by Congress.

THE COURT AND THE PRIVILEGE

Early in the twentieth century the Court acknowledged that heads of executive departments could raise claims of executive privilege with respect to court-ordered demands for records of the department or the testimony of department employees.[27]

In 1927 the Court held that executive privilege did not protect the executive branch from legitimate legislative investigation. In *McGrain v. Daugherty* the Court upheld the right of the Senate to inquire into the failure of President Warren G. Harding's attorney general to prosecute major figures in the Teapot Dome scandal.[28] (*See details of the case, pp. 164–165, in Chapter 4.*)

National Security

In 1948 the Court acknowledged that there were areas of executive power—military and national security matters in particular—about which the president might properly refuse to disclose all facts relative to a decision. The case involved a challenge to the president's decision to award certain foreign air travel routes to one company while denying them to a competitor.[29] In the opinion, Justice Robert H. Jackson wrote:

The President, both as Commander-in-Chief and as the Nation's organ for foreign affairs, has available intelligence services whose reports neither are nor ought to be published to the world. It would be intolerable that courts, without the relevant information, should review and perhaps nullify actions of the Executive taken on information properly held secret. . . . But even if courts could require full disclosure, the very nature of executive decisions as to foreign policy is political, not judicial. Such decisions are wholly confided by our Constitution to the political departments of the government, Executive and Legislative. They are delicate, complex, and involve large elements of prophecy. They are and should be undertaken only by those directly responsible to the people, whose welfare they advance or imperil. They are decisions of a kind for which the Judiciary has neither aptitude, facilities nor responsibility and have long been held to belong to the domain of political power not subject to judicial intrusion or inquiry.[30]

A Judicial Role

Five years later the Court asserted a judicial role in assessing claims of executive privilege asserted to protect military or national security secrets. The decision in *United States v. Reynolds* set out guidelines for judging such claims.[31]

The widow of a civilian pilot killed in a plane crash during a test of secret military equipment sought copies of investigative reports of the accident. The secretary of the air force refused, claiming that the reports were privileged documents.

The Supreme Court accepted that claim, but in doing so declared that in each case of this sort "the court itself must determine whether the circumstances are appropriate for the claim of privilege."[32]

Chief Justice Fred M. Vinson continued:

In each case, the showing of necessity which is made will determine how far the court should probe in satisfying itself that the occasion for invoking the privilege is appropriate. Where there is a strong showing of necessity, the claim of privilege should not be lightly accepted, but even the most compelling necessity cannot overcome the claim of privilege if the court is ultimately satisfied that military secrets are at stake.[33]

The Modern Privilege

Executive claims of an absolute privilege to withhold information accelerated after 1954, a Library of Congress study reported in 1973. In 1954 President Dwight D. Eisenhower wrote Defense Secretary Charles Wilson advising him to direct his subordinates not to testify about certain matters during the much publicized Army-McCarthy hearings.[34]

In the course of that investigation by the Senate Permanent Subcommittee on Investigations, Chairman Joseph R. McCarthy, R-Wis. (1947–1957), insisted that John Adams, counsel for the army, tell the subcommittee about a meeting held in the attorney general's office with high-level White House staff members.[35]

In response, Adams submitted to the subcommittee copies of a letter from Eisenhower to Wilson invoking executive privilege with respect to testimony by executive department officials. The letter included copies of a memorandum that listed historical precedents of prior successful claims of executive privilege. Eisenhower's letter "became the major authority cited for exercise of 'executive privilege' to refuse information to the Congress for the next seven years," reported the Library of Congress.[36]

President John F. Kennedy refused a special Senate subcommittee's request for the identity of individuals assigned to edit speeches of military leaders. Kennedy directed Secretary of Defense Robert S. McNamara and all personnel under his jurisdiction not to comply with the committee's request. Such refusals of information, Kennedy said, would not be automatic. "Each case must be judged on its own merits," the president maintained.[37] Kennedy reaffirmed that position in an exchange of correspondence with Rep. John E. Moss, D-Calif. (1933–1979): "Executive privilege can be invoked only by the President and will not be used without specific Presidential approval."[38]

President Lyndon B. Johnson assured Moss that "the claim of 'executive privilege' will continue to be made only by the President."[39] Moss later received a similar declaration from President Nixon, who issued a memorandum to the heads of all executive departments and agencies stating the policy that "executive privilege will not be used without specific Presidential approval."[40]

The memorandum required that requests to invoke executive privilege in answer to an inquiry from Congress go to the attorney general. If he and the department head agreed the privilege should not be invoked, Congress would receive the information. If either or both wished, the issue would be submitted to the president. Despite these specific declarations, some executive branch officials during the Nixon administration did claim "executive privilege" without presidential approval.[41]

The Supreme Court denied the president's claim of executive privilege in the 1971 *Pentagon Papers* decision. The Court held that President Nixon had not satisfied the heavy burden of proof required to enjoin publication of classified material allegedly injurious to national security.[42]

In 1973 the Supreme Court ruled that federal courts lacked power to review executive branch classification decisions that exempted materials from disclosure under the 1966 Freedom of Information Act. Congress subsequently amended the law to allow courts to review classification decisions.[43]

UNITED STATES V. NIXON

The most significant Supreme Court decision concerning claims of executive privilege came in 1974 and resulted in the resignation of President Nixon. The Court rebuffed Nixon's claim of an absolute privilege to reject judicial demands for information, holding that Nixon must surrender to the Watergate special prosecutor subpoenaed tapes of White House conversations between the president and his aides.

The tapes were required for use as evidence in the criminal trial of former White House aides charged with attempting to obstruct justice by covering up White House involvement in the 1972 break-in at the Democratic National Committee headquarters in the Watergate office building.

Special Prosecutor Leon Jaworski in April 1974 obtained a subpoena ordering delivery of certain tapes, memoranda, and papers related to specific meetings of the president with particular White House aides. The president's counsel moved to quash the subpoena, formally claiming executive privilege as a defense against compliance. The district court denied all motions and ordered the president to deliver the requested materials.

Nixon appealed to the Supreme Court, which heard arguments July 8 in the cases of *United States v. Nixon, Nixon v. United States.* On July 24, with Chief Justice Warren E. Burger speaking for a unanimous Court, the justices rejected Nixon's claim of privilege. Burger discussed the derivation of executive privilege:

Whatever the nature of the privilege of confidentiality of presidential communications in the exercise of Art. II powers the privilege can be said to derive from the supremacy of each branch within its own assigned area of constitutional duties. Certain powers and privileges flow from the nature of the enumerated powers; the protection of the confidentiality of presidential communications has similar constitutional underpinnings.[44]

The Court then observed that

neither the doctrine of separation of powers, nor the need for confidentiality of high level communications, without more, can sustain an absolute, unqualified presidential privilege of immunity from judicial process under all circumstances. The President's need for complete candor and objectivity from advisers calls for great deference from the courts. However, when the privilege depends solely on the broad undifferentiated claim of public interest in the confidentiality of such conversations, a confrontation with other values arises. Absent a claim of need to protect military, diplomatic or sensitive national security secrets, we find it difficult to accept the argument that even the very important interest in confidentiality of presidential communications is significantly diminished by protection of such material for in camera inspection with all the protection that a district court will be obliged to provide.

The impediment that an absolute, unqualified privilege would place in the way of the primary constitutional duty of the Judicial Branch to do justice in criminal prosecutions would plainly conflict with the function of the courts under Art. III. In designing the structure of our Government and dividing and allocating the sovereign power among three coequal branches, the Framers of the Constitution sought to provide a comprehensive system, but the separate powers were not intended to operate with absolute independence. . . .

To read the Art. II powers of the President as providing an absolute privilege as against a subpoena essential to enforcement of criminal statutes on no more than a generalized claim of the public interest in confidentiality of nonmilitary and nondiplomatic discussions would upset the constitutional balance of "a workable government" and gravely impair the role of the courts under Art. III.[45]

In rejecting this particular claim of privilege, however, the Court for the first time acknowledged a constitutional basis for executive privilege:

A President and those who assist him must be free to explore alternatives in the process of shaping policies and making decisions and to do so in a way many would be unwilling to express except privately. These are the considerations justifying a presumptive privilege for presidential communications. The privilege is fundamental to the operation of government and inextricably rooted in the separation of powers under the Constitution. . . .

Nowhere in the Constitution . . . is there any explicit reference to a privilege of confidentiality, yet to the extent this interest relates to the effective discharge of a President's powers, it is constitutionally based.[46]

In this case the claim of an absolute privilege failed when weighed against the requirements of evidence in a criminal proceeding. Burger observed:

No case of the Court . . . has extended this high degree of deference to a President's generalized interest in confidentiality. . . .

In this case we must weigh the importance of the general privilege of confidentiality of presidential communications in performance of his responsibilities against the inroads of such a privilege on the fair administration of criminal justice. The interest in preserving confidentiality is weighty indeed and entitled to great respect. However we cannot conclude that advisers will be moved to temper the candor of their remarks by the infrequent occasions of disclosure because of the possibility that such conversations will be called for in the context of a criminal prosecution. . . .

A President's acknowledged need for confidentiality in the communications of his office is general in nature, whereas the constitutional need for production of relevant evidence in a criminal proceeding is specific and central to the fair adjudication of a particular criminal case in the administration of justice. Without access to specific facts a criminal prosecution may be totally frustrated. The President's broad interest in confidentiality of communications will not be vitiated by disclosure of a limited number of conversations preliminarily shown to have some bearing on the pending criminal cases.

We conclude that when the ground for asserting privilege as to subpoenaed materials sought for use in a criminal trial is based only on the generalized interest in confidentiality, it cannot prevail over the fundamental demands of due process of law in the fair administration of criminal justice. The generalized assertion of privilege must yield to the demonstrated, specific need for evidence in a pending criminal trial.[47]

THE NIXON PAPERS

In 1977 the Supreme Court rejected a second Nixon claim of executive privilege to restrict access to the records of his administration. Against such a claim, the Court upheld a 1974 act of Congress that placed the records, tapes, and papers of the Nixon administration in federal custody.[48]

Presidents historically have retained control of their papers and governed both their use and public access to them. But the unusual circumstances surrounding Nixon's departure from office moved Congress to depart from that custom.[49] Nixon's attorneys argued that by removing control of the papers from the former president, Congress had infringed upon presidential prerogative and had opened the way for wide disclosure of privileged matters.

The Supreme Court majority rejected that argument. Justice Brennan wrote for the Court that the president's challenge to the act on these grounds rested on "an archaic view of the separation of powers as requiring three airtight departments of government."[50]

Executive privilege would not be violated by government archivists' screening the papers any more than had federal judge John Sirica's private review of the White House tapes used as evidence in the Watergate cover-up trials, Brennan said. The archivists'

screening constitutes a very limited intrusion by personnel in the Executive Branch sensitive to executive concerns. These very personnel have performed the identical task in each of the presidential libraries without any suggestion that such activity has in any way interfered with executive confidentiality. . . . Nor should the American people's ability to reconstruct and come to terms with their history be truncated by an analysis of Presidential privilege that focuses only on the needs of the present.[51]

Chief Justice Burger and Justice William H. Rehnquist dissented. Burger argued that the law would severely affect the conduct of executive branch business. The law, Burger stated, would be

a "ghost" at future White House conferences with conferees choosing their words more cautiously because of the enlarged prospect of compelled disclosure to others.[52]

Justice Rehnquist warned that the Court's decision "will daily stand as a veritable sword of Damocles over every succeeding President and his advisers."[53]

The Supreme Court weighed Nixon's claim of privilege against the need to preserve intact the records of his administration. The majority as well as the dissenters recognized the existence of a limited privilege but in this instance found the countervailing necessity of the public's right to know to outweigh Nixon's claim.

Among the most dramatic chapters in American history are those that relate the collision between a president and the Supreme Court. Infrequent though they are, these confrontations span the nation's history.

Some of these clashes have been personal as well as political, as in the case of fellow Virginians Thomas Jefferson and John Marshall. Others have resulted from the efforts of presidents—Abraham Lincoln, Franklin D. Roosevelt and Harry S. Truman—to use extraordinary powers in extraordinary times.

In some of these episodes the president emerges the victor; in others the Court prevails in the constitutional battle. But in all of them, the shape of the system is altered—as are the powers of the Court and the executive to deal with future crises.

Jefferson Versus Marshall

The long conflict between the administration of President Thomas Jefferson and the Federalist-dominated Supreme Court led by John Marshall had its roots in the politics of Virginia and in the national debate between Democratic-Republicans and Federalists over the proper stance for the United States during the European wars following the French Revolution. In the remainder of this section, the Democratic-Republicans are referred to as the Republicans.

President Washington's 1793 proclamation of neutrality effectively terminated the French-American alliance of 1778.[1] Opponents of the policy saw it as evidence of the partiality of the Washington administration to Great Britain. The Jeffersonians feared that this Federalist stance would enmesh the United States in Britain's imperial enterprises.[2]

The political conflict was heightened further by the moves taken by the Federalists, during the Quasi-War with France (1798–1800), to put the nation on a war footing. During that undeclared maritime conflict, Congress passed the controversial Sedition Acts, intended to silence editors and pamphleteers who attacked President John Adams's administration and the defense measures he supported. During the Quasi-War crisis some twenty-five persons were arrested for seditious libel under the terms of the Sedition Act.[3] Most of them were Republican editors. Ten were convicted for violations of the act.

One response to the Alien and Sedition Acts came in the form of resolutions adopted by the legislatures of Kentucky and Virginia. The resolutions, drafted by Jefferson and James Madison, protested what they perceived to be a dangerous usurpation of power by the central government.[4]

THE "REVOLUTION" OF 1800

Jefferson saw his defeat of Adams for the presidency in 1800 and the transfer of power from one political group to another as a revolution. But the revolution was incomplete. Federalist judges were firmly in control of the fledgling federal courts. And perhaps the most enduring legacy the Federalists left President Jefferson was the new chief justice of the United States—John Marshall.[5]

On January 20, 1801, six weeks before the end of his term, Adams nominated Marshall, then secretary of state, to head the Supreme Court. The post had been vacant since September 1800 when Oliver Ellsworth resigned.

Adams had first nominated, and the Senate approved, John Jay, who had been the nation's first chief justice, but he declined the post, grumbling about ill health and the rigors of riding circuit. Adams also had considered Justice William Cushing for the position, but Cushing was sixty-eight years old, and he had declined appointment as chief justice in 1796. Justice William Paterson, another promising and younger candidate, was considered but dropped because the president's rival within Federalist ranks, Alexander Hamilton, supported Paterson's candidacy. Moreover, as Cushing was Paterson's senior on the High Court, it would appear that Adams slighted Cushing in making the appointment.[6]

Marshall's appointment was opposed in the Senate by members unhappy that Paterson was not nominated, but he was confirmed January 27 in the waning days of the Adams presidency. Marshall received his commission as chief justice on February 4, 1801, and took his seat on the bench over which he would preside for thirty-four years.[7]

Marshall's legal and judicial experience was meager. He had been a successful lawyer in Richmond after only a few months' education at William and Mary College.[8] His mission to France as one of the three American ministers in the abortive XYZ mission won him a reputation in international law. He had served as a Federalist representative in the House from Virginia's Richmond district, staunchly supporting President Adams's policies, and then had become Adams's secretary of state.[9]

Marshall's appointment rankled Jefferson. The two Virginians had been on opposite sides of the political fence since the Revolution. Although third cousins, the two men had a mutual antagonism that probably dated to Jefferson's term as governor of Virginia in 1780 when he had been forced to flee the capital by the approach of the British army. Marshall had served in the revolutionary army, and his war experiences undoubtedly bred contempt for Jefferson's failure to face the enemy.[10]

In one of his first official acts as chief justice, Marshall administered the oath of office to President Jefferson. While Jefferson's inaugural speech was conciliatory, he moved within the year to repeal the newly enacted Judiciary Act of 1801 passed by the "lame-duck" Federalist Congress as a judicial reform measure.

THE JUDICIARY ACT OF 1801

The 1801 act was an admirable piece of legislation, but its passage was ill-timed. The House passed the law January 20, 1801—the day of Marshall's nomination—without a single Republican vote. The Senate approved it February 7, and Adams signed the bill on February 13. The law added new circuit judgeships, removed the requirement that Supreme Court justices ride circuit, and reduced the number of justices from six to five by stating that the next vacancy would not be filled.

Adams appointed sixteen new circuit court justices to fill the new posts, as well as a number of marshals and justices of the peace, whose posts were also created by the 1801 act. In his last full month in office, Adams appointed 217 individuals to public office—of whom 93 were legal or judicial officers.[11]

The Judiciary Act of 1801 was repealed March 31, 1802. An act passed in April restored the number of seats on the Supreme Court to six, fixed one annual term for the Court instead of two, and set up six circuits, each presided over by a Supreme Court justice who would continue to ride circuit.[12]

MARBURY V. MADISON

In the rush of business at the end of the Adams administration, Secretary of State Marshall failed to see to the delivery of several commissions of appointment. William Marbury, one of Adams's "midnight appointments" as justice of the peace for the District of Columbia, was among those who did not receive his commission, which Adams had signed and Marshall had sealed. Secretary of State Madison, acting under President Jefferson's orders, refused to deliver the commission at Marbury's request.[13]

Marbury then asked the Supreme Court to order Madison to deliver the commission. At its February 1803 session, the Court ruled on Marbury's application for the order. In a historic opinion by Marshall, the Court held itself powerless to issue such an order, declared part of the Judiciary Act of 1789 unconstitutional, and lectured Jefferson on the proper performance of his duties.[14] Marshall's opinion was a bold and politically astute attack on Jefferson and his administration.

The chief justice expounded upon Marbury's vested right to the commission and reminded the president he was not above the law:

The commission being signed, the subsequent duty of the secretary of state is prescribed by law, and to be guided by the will of the president. He is to affix the seal of the United States to the commission, and is to record it.

This is not a proceeding which may be varied, if the judgment of the executive shall suggest one more eligible; but is a precise course accurately marked out by law, and is to be strictly pursued. It is the duty of the secretary of state to conform to the law, and in this he is an officer of the United States, bound to obey the laws. He acts, in this respect, . . . under the authority of law and not by the instruction of the president. It is a ministerial act which the law enjoins on a particular officer for a particular purpose.[15]

Marshall protected the Court against the charge that it sought to aggrandize power by finding that the Court lacked jurisdiction to issue the writ. By so doing, the Court for the first time exercised the power to strike down an act of Congress as unconstitutional.

That aspect of *Marbury* did not receive as much attention at the time as the Court's lecture to Jefferson.[16] Judicial review had been regarded by many as a necessary adjunct of the constitutional system. The Court had earlier assumed that it had this power.[17] (See "Marbury v. Madison," pp. 76–79, in Chapter 4.)

This decision was as close as the Court and the Jefferson administration came to an institutional collision. But neither Jefferson nor Marshall ceased their efforts to undercut the prestige and power of the other, and of the branches they headed.

IMPEACHMENT: A POLITICAL WEAPON

Jefferson, convinced by *Marbury* that stronger measures were needed to blunt the Court's influence under Marshall, turned to the only way provided by the Constitution to remove judges from office: impeachment for high crimes and misdemeanors. Conviction after impeachment and trial in the Senate required removal from office.

The Jeffersonians interpreted "high crimes and misdemeanors" broadly to allow impeachment for political acts. Their strategy was to use the impeachment process to remove federal judges from the bench for "crimes" such as ethical lapses and irresponsible political statements.

New Hampshire district court judge John Pickering was impeached, convicted, and removed from office in proceedings begun in February 1803. Jefferson sent a message to the House accompanied by evidence that Pickering was a hopelessly insane drunkard. For the previous three years his behavior on the bench had been irrational and irresponsible. The House impeached Pickering, and the Senate tried him in March 1804.

The Senate convicted Pickering by a 19–7 vote along strict party lines and removed him from office. The impeachment of Pickering settled nothing with respect to the nature of impeachments brought against rational judges whose major crime was political opposition to Jeffersonian principles.

The main issue was Republican use of the impeachment process to remove politically obnoxious Federalist judges. Flawed precedent aside, with Pickering impeached and removed, Republicans went after bigger game.[18]

THE IMPEACHMENT OF JUSTICE SAMUEL CHASE

Republican leaders agreed that Justice Samuel Chase was an excellent impeachment target.[19] He had campaigned for Adams while on the Supreme Court bench, tried and convicted a group of rebels of treason in Pennsylvania for their part in opposing a new tax law (1799–1800), made political harangues from the bench to grand juries, and personally conducted the trial of Republican editor James Thomson Callendar under the Sedition Act.[20] Chase left no doubts about his staunch Federalism; in Republican minds he forfeited any claim to judicial impartiality on the bench.

Moreover, the time was ripe for a counterattack against the

judiciary. Republicans still seethed over the lecture Marshall gave Jefferson in *Marbury v. Madison*. With John Randolph of Virginia guiding Republican forces, the House appointed a committee to inquire into Chase's conduct in January 1804. The House voted March 12 to impeach Chase on a strict party-line vote (73–32).[21]

The first seven articles of impeachment recounted Chase's "oppressive" conduct in the trials under the Sedition Act. The last article referred to an address by Chase characterized as an inflammatory diatribe designed to excite unrest against the government of the United States. The charges referred to Chase's outspoken criticism of Republican policies at the state and national levels.[22]

Vice President Aaron Burr, fresh from his duel with Alexander Hamilton, presided over the Senate trial that began in February 1805. Chase's attorneys maintained that an impeachable offense must be one indictable under law. It was clear to observers and participants alike that the independence of the federal judiciary was on trial. Removal of Chase would spur further Republican assaults on the bench.[23] The vote in the Senate fell short of the necessary two-thirds majority on any of the impeachment articles, and Chase remained on the bench.

Chase's impeachment and trial set a precedent of strict construction of the impeachment clause and bolstered the judiciary's claim of independence from political tampering. The failure of the Chase impeachment was a source of political embarrassment to Jefferson.

The Jeffersonians abandoned the idea of removing federalist judges by impeachment. Federal judges, as a result of the trial, for a time exhibited greater restraint in their conduct and refrained from political lectures while on the bench.

BURR TRIAL

Vice President Burr had presided over the trial of Justice Chase. In August 1807 Burr was the defendant, tried for treason in a dramatic trial that saw the chief justice of the United States collide again with President Jefferson. Marshall heard the case as judge of the United States circuit court for Virginia, but the antagonism between Jefferson and Marshall, and the tenacity with which Jefferson attempted to orchestrate Burr's conviction produced a trial with unmistakable political and personal overtones.[24]

Aaron Burr lost his political power base in New York when he refused to step aside and let Jefferson assume the presidency in the disputed election of 1800. Jefferson won the office after a compromise among the electors assured Jefferson enough electoral votes to win. Burr's failure to acknowledge Jefferson as the legitimate winner in 1800 earned Burr Jefferson's everlasting animosity.

Burr's attempts to recoup his political fortunes led him into a protracted political struggle with Hamilton that ended with the duel that cost Hamilton his life and Burr all chances of regaining legitimate political power.[25] Burr went west to revive his political fortunes and assembled a small force of men at Blenner-hassett Island in the upper Ohio River. The men and equipment moved down the Mississippi River to New Orleans.[26]

Burr's plans for the band of adventurers have remained obscure, but rumors circulated that Burr intended to separate the Southwest from the Union. At first unconcerned, Jefferson in 1806 issued an order for Burr's arrest. Burr fled but was captured and returned to Richmond for trial.[27]

Marshall's rulings as presiding judge thwarted Jefferson's hopes that Burr would be convicted. The chief justice had no affection for Burr, but he refused to permit the court to be stampeded into a conviction simply because Burr was an unpopular and unscrupulous individual.[28]

Marshall ruled first on Burr's request to obtain from Jefferson, by subpoena, certain letters Burr claimed he needed to provide an adequate defense.[29] Burr's evidentiary claim turned the trial into a polite but intense confrontation between the chief justice and the president. Marshall ruled that the evidence sought was germane to the case and issued a subpoena seeking delivery of certain letters to the court in Richmond. The president refused to comply with the subpoena. Jefferson declined to make an appearance at court or to furnish the documents without certain portions deleted,[30] but he did say that transcripts of portions of the letters would be turned over to the court if the material was required. The case turned on other issues, and the subpoena and confrontation faded away. The exchanges between Jefferson and Marshall were outwardly polite and solicitous of cooperation, but they masked the inner tension of the combatants.

The main issue in the case was Marshall's definition of treason. Burr's attorneys maintained that treason consisted of an actual "levying of war" against the United States. They drew a distinction between the act of war and the advising of it.[31]

The prosecution relied on a broader definition of treason found in English common law that reviewed all who contemplated treason as engaging in the act itself. They argued that Burr was guilty because he advised assembling an armed force and moving it down river to New Orleans.[32]

Marshall ruled that because the prosecution failed to produce two witnesses to the act of treason, or to the procurement of men and arms for the expedition, it had not met the burden of proving the charge of treason.[33] *(See box, Treason, p. 418, in Chapter 9.)*

Following Marshall's ruling, the jury found "that Aaron Burr is not proved to be guilty under this indictment by any evidence submitted to us. We therefore find him not guilty."[34]

Antagonism between Marshall and the executive branch subsided when Jefferson retired in 1809. The election of Madison, the appointment of several Republicans to the Court, the changing nature of national issues, and the demise of Federalism reduced the grounds of antagonism between the Court and the president.

Neither Jefferson nor Marshall "won" the series of confrontations between them.

Both men maintained the integrity of their departments.

Jefferson managed to chastise the judiciary through the threat of impeachment, and Marshall raised the prestige of the Court and maintained the independence of the judiciary.

Jackson, the Court, and the Indians

Andrew Jackson—whose determination to play a strong executive role laid the foundations for the modern concept of presidential power—clashed indirectly with the Supreme Court and claimed for the executive an independent role in constitutional interpretation.

In vetoing the bill to recharter the Second Bank of the United States, Jackson denied that the Supreme Court alone was the ultimate arbiter of constitutional questions. Jackson asserted that the president too might exercise an independent judgment separate from the Court and Congress in matters of policy:

The Congress, the Executive, and the Court must each for itself be guided by its own opinion of the Constitution. Each public officer who takes an oath to support the Constitution swears that he will support it as he understands it, and not as it is understood by others. . . . The opinion of the judges has no more authority over Congress than the opinion of Congress has over the judges, and on that point the President is independent of both. The authority of the Supreme Court must not, therefore, be permitted to control the Congress or the Executive when acting in their legislative capacities, but to have only such influence as the force of their reasoning may deserve.[35]

The theory had its impractical side. If there was no final decision about the constitutionality of a statute, how would serious controversies be resolved? Jackson was vague in his response and frequently settled matters by sheer force of will, bolstered by his general popularity.[36]

Constitutional conflict between the president and the Court threatened to break into open warfare in the early 1830s when the Supreme Court steadfastly rejected the efforts of the state of Georgia to assert its jurisdiction over Cherokee Indians living on Indian land within its boundaries. The Cherokees had become settled farmers on this land, adopted a constitution, developed an alphabet, and proclaimed themselves an independent state. But Georgia, anxious to expel the Indians and open their land for settlement, extended state authority over the region in 1829, declared Indian law nullified by state law, and passed measures designed to permit seizure of the Indian lands.[37]

Asserting its newly claimed sovereignty over the region, the Georgia courts convicted a Cherokee named Corn Tassel of murder.[38] The Supreme Court granted Corn Tassel permission to contest his conviction; the basis for his challenge was that Georgia had no jurisdiction over Indians and their territory. The state ignored the Court's action and executed Corn Tassel on December 24, 1830, before the Court could hear his case.[39]

The Supreme Court, faced with such defiance, could do nothing to enforce its authority. President Jackson, sympathetic to the state, did nothing. Subsequently, the Cherokees asked the Supreme Court to restrain Georgia from enforcing its laws over the Indians. Acting as an independent nation, the Cherokees filed their request as an original case before the Court. The Court dismissed the suit, ruling that Indian tribes were not foreign nations, but "domestic dependent nations" under the sovereignty and dominion of the United States.[40]

In still another case, decided in 1832, however, the Court ruled against Georgia's claim to jurisdiction over the Cherokees.[41] A missionary among the Indians refused to pay a state license fee required of white persons living in Indian territory. Challenging the fee as unconstitutional state interference in Indian matters, the missionary took his case to the Court, which agreed with him, denying the state power to enforce the fee requirement and ordering him released from prison. The state declared it would resist enforcement of the Court's ruling.[42]

President Jackson refused to act. The Supreme Court was powerless to enforce its own ruling. Jackson is alleged to have said: "Well, John Marshall has made his decision, now let him enforce it." *(See box, Did Jackson Really Say That? p. 247.)*

For a few months, the stalemate held. Then Georgia's precedent was followed by South Carolina, which declared that it had the power to nullify—through nonenforcement—the controversial tariff act of 1832.[43] That threat prompted Jackson to issue a vigorous rebuttal, asserting federal authority against a state challenge to enforcement of federal law.[44] Jackson's strong stand against nullification cooled the conflict between Georgia and the Court. The state realized that Jackson could not continue to support Georgia's defiance while condemning South Carolina for similar action. *(See "Repeal and Resistance," pp. 320–321, in Chapter 7.)*

Lincoln Versus Taney

Chief Justice Roger B. Taney helped elect Abraham Lincoln president in 1860. The Supreme Court's 1857 decision in the controversial Dred Scott case—in which Taney wrote the major opinion—split the Democratic party into northern and southern wings over the issue of slavery. That schism gave Lincoln, a Republican, the victory over the northern Democrat Stephen A. Douglas and two southern candidates, John C. Breckinridge and John Bell.

In the Dred Scott case, the Court held that Congress lacked the power to ban the expansion of slavery into the territories. Lincoln's opposition to this ruling brought him to national prominence in 1858. Running against Douglas for a Senate seat, Lincoln aired his opposition to the decision in a series of seven head-to-head debates on slavery around the state of Illinois. *(See "Dred Scott's Case," p. 145, in Chapter 4.)*

Lincoln promised to do all he could to have the ruling overturned and, as president, he asserted the chief executive's right to a solution as equal to that of the Court. In his first inaugural address, Lincoln declared:

[I]f the policy of the Government upon vital questions affecting the whole people, is to be irrevocably fixed by decisions of the Supreme Court, the instant they are made in ordinary litigation between parties in personal actions, the people will have ceased to be their own rulers, having to that extent practically resigned their government into the hands of that imminent tribunal.[45]

Against this backdrop of confrontation, the old Jacksonian Democrat Taney and the new Republican president locked horns over Lincoln's suspension of the privilege of the writ of habeas corpus during the Civil War. Their antagonism intensified with the war. Six weeks after the outbreak of the war at Fort Sumter, Taney challenged Lincoln's decision to suspend the privilege of the writ.

John Merryman was arrested by Union soldiers in Maryland and charged with aiding Baltimore secessionists. Imprisoned by the military at Fort McHenry, Merryman obtained a writ of habeas corpus challenging his detention. Prison officials refused to comply with the writ, which ordered Merryman's release, citing Lincoln's proclamation suspending the writ when public safety was threatened.[46]

Chief Justice Taney, acting as a circuit judge, issued a contempt citation against the fort commander and demanded the appearance of Merryman at circuit court proceedings in Baltimore. The military commander prevented the writ from being served and refused to surrender Merryman. Taney then wrote an opinion holding suspension of the writ unconstitutional.[47] Taney lectured President Lincoln on his duty to enforce the law:

I can see no ground whatever for supposing that the President in any emergency or in any state of things can authorize the suspension of the privilege of the writ of habeas corpus, or arrest a citizen except in aid of the judicial power. He certainly does not faithfully execute the laws if he takes upon himself legislative power by suspending the writ of habeas corpus—and the judicial power, also, by arresting and imprisoning a person without the process of law.[48]

Lincoln responded to the Taney opinion in his July 4, 1861, message to Congress, in which he maintained his theory that wartime emergency measures superseded constitutional niceties.[49]

During the next two years, Lincoln, through Secretary of War Edwin M. Stanton, instituted censorship, military arrest and trial, and continued to suspend or ignore habeas corpus requirements in the cases of individuals suspected of aiding the Confederate cause.[50]

The State Department directed arrests through an elaborate network of secret servicemen, federal marshals, and military authorities. Hundreds of people were arrested without being told why. The suspension of habeas corpus enabled authorities to hold them without sufficient evidence or legal action until the emergency that led to the arrest passed. Military officers disregarded judicial orders for the release of prisoners. Legal clashes between civil and military authorities were frequent during the war, but the military—backed by the president—held the upper hand.[51]

In 1862 the administration turned control of arrests over to the War Department. Lincoln declared that all persons resisting the draft or discouraging military enlistments were subject to court martial. Thousands of citizens suspected of disloyalty were arrested, imprisoned, and then released without trial after the particular emergency passed.[52] Lincoln elaborated his theory of presidential leadership in an 1863 letter to Erastus Corning.

DID JACKSON REALLY SAY THAT?

Historical research indicates that Andrew Jackson probably never made the remark attributed to him for decades after the crisis between Georgia and the Supreme Court over the Cherokee Indians in 1832.[1] When the Court, led by Chief Justice John Marshall, ruled that Georgia had no jurisdiction over the Cherokees and their lands that lay within the state, Jackson allegedly commented: "Well, John Marshall has made his decision, now let him enforce it."

The words reflected Jackson's views, but, like the story of George Washington and the cherry tree, Jackson's remarks probably were invented by folklorists to enhance the reputation of a famous man.

The remark was attributed by American journalist and newspaperman Horace Greeley in 1864 to Jackson's reported conversation with Rep. George N. Briggs of Massachusetts.[2] No writer before Greeley had reported it.

The remark reappeared in William G. Sumner's *Life of Andrew Jackson* (1899) and was reprinted by others. John Spencer Bassett, Jackson's biographer, wrote in 1910 that the remark was "a popular tradition. . . . It is not sure that the words were actually uttered, but it is certain, from Jackson's view and temperament, that they might have been spoken."[3]

1. Joseph C. Burke, "The Cherokee Cases: A Study in Law, Politics and Morality," *Stanford Law Review* 21: 500–531.

2. Horace Greeley, *American Conflict: A History of the Great Rebellion in the United States of America, 1860–1865*, 2 vols. (Westport, Conn.: Greenwood Press, 1969 reprint of 1894 ed.), I: 106.

3. John S. Bassett, *Life of Andrew Jackson*, 2 vols. in 1 (Hamden, Conn.: Shoe String Press, 1967 reprint of 1931 ed.), II: 688–692.

Thoroughly imbued with a reverence for the guaranteed rights of individuals, I was slow to adopt the strong measures which by degrees I have been forced to regard as being within the exceptions of the Constitution and as indispensable to the public safety. . . . I concede that the class of arrests complained of can be constitutional only when in cases of rebellion or invasion the public safety may require them; and I insist that in such cases they are constitutional wherever the public safety does require them, as well as in places in which they may prevent the rebellion extending as in those where it may already be prevailing.[53]

Beneath the legal arguments, the clash between Taney and Lincoln rested on differences of opinion about the importance of preserving the Union. Lincoln believed it paramount. The federal government in such an emergency could exercise powers that required the temporary sacrifice of civil liberties and civil procedures. Taney considered the bloodshed and the extraconstitutional actions necessary to preserve the Union a greater disaster than dissolution.[54]

Taney died October 12, 1864. Two years later in the case of *Ex parte Milligan*, the Court vindicated his stance in *Merryman* and ruled the president's use of military tribunals outside the war zone unconstitutional.[55]

Lincoln appointed his secretary of the Treasury, Salmon P. Chase, chief justice in Taney's place. In 1870 it was Chief Justice

Chase, however, who wrote the Court's opinion in the first *Legal Tender* case, declaring the Lincoln administration's Legal Tender Acts, which authorized the use of paper money during the war, unconstitutional.

The Court and the Roosevelt Revolution

The stock market crash of 1929 and the ensuing Great Depression were economic crises of proportions unprecedented in American history. But President Herbert C. Hoover was philosophically unable to view the depression as more than an economic "adjustment period"; he continued optimistically to predict that the economy would correct itself. Many business leaders believed Hoover, preaching confidently that prosperity was just around the corner. But the dream of recovery became an American nightmare.

Unemployment reached twelve million, industrial production toppled to less than half of 1929 levels, and by 1933 the entire banking network of the nation was on the verge of collapse.[56] Economic crisis precipitated social crisis. And social discontent found its expression in a major political upheaval.

Hoover did not believe in broad governmental relief or social reform programs. His abiding faith in "rugged individualism" and limited government prevented his espousal of any full-scale economic recovery measures. His constitutional conservatism rejected any suggestion that federal power might be expanded to deal with the crisis.

It was not surprising that Hoover was repudiated at the polls in 1932. Democratic candidate Franklin D. Roosevelt, former governor of New York, was elected president by an impressive margin.

THE "HUNDRED DAYS"

Roosevelt took office in March 1933; large Democratic majorities controlled both houses of Congress. In his inaugural address, Roosevelt made clear his view of the economic crisis as a national emergency in which he would exercise "broad executive power to wage a war against the emergency as great as the power that would be given me if we were in fact invaded by a foreign foe."[57]

The new president called a special session of Congress that convened March 9, 1933. In the next hundred days, Congress, led by Roosevelt and his "Brain Trust," attacked the depression on all fronts.

Relief Programs

The Emergency Banking Act of March 9, 1933, retroactively sanctioned a "bank holiday." Roosevelt had earlier closed all the nation's banks and suspended all gold exports and foreign exchange operations. The bill also called for surrender of all gold and gold certificates to the Treasury to be exchanged for an equal amount of other currency.

The purpose of the act was to halt the hoarding of currency and to set the stage for a mild inflationary devaluation of the money supply. The banking measures, the Gold Reserve Act of 1934, and the congressional resolution of June 5, 1933, took gold out of circulation, reduced the gold content of the dollar, and canceled the "gold clause" in private contracts that stipulated that a fixed amount of a debt be paid in gold.[58]

The most important agricultural relief measure of the New Deal was the Agricultural Adjustment Act (AAA) of May 12, 1933. The purpose of the AAA was to restore agricultural prices to prewar (1914) levels—reducing farm production by retiring acreage from use.

The AAA provided for an agreement between farmers and the federal government that the farmer would plant fewer acres and in return would receive better prices for his goods—prices bolstered by a government subsidy.[59] The whole program was financed through a tax on processors of each affected commodity.

New Deal efforts to restore industrial production and reduce unemployment operated on a theory of limited industrial self-government. The program attempted to bring about cooperation between large and small manufacturing concerns and their employees.

The National Industrial Recovery Act (NIRA) of June 16, 1933, established "codes of fair competition" for wages, prices, and trade practices. The codes, drafted by representatives of business and trade groups, were submitted for approval to the president, who was empowered to prescribe the codes. Once approved, the codes became the standard of commercial practice in a particular industry, with violations punishable as violations of the Federal Trade Commission Act.

In addition, the NIRA stipulated that labor had the right to organize workers for collective bargaining.[60]

An act of May 18, 1933, created the Tennessee Valley Authority (TVA), a government corporation authorized to construct dams and reservoirs as part of a development project for the Tennessee Valley region. The entire project included flood control, reforestation, and agricultural and industrial projects. TVA also produced fertilizer, explosives, and, eventually, electric power.

The Constitutional Base

This emergency relief and recovery program had its constitutional basis in emergency executive powers and the power of Congress to provide for the general welfare and to regulate interstate commerce. It was the most far-reaching assertion to date of national leadership.

The need for immediate action eliminated the usual procedures of lengthy debate and deliberation. Roosevelt's Brain Trust hammered out the legislation in conference with the president and representatives of affected interest groups. Once drafted, the bills were presented to Congress as "must" legislation, and Congress generally responded with alacrity.

NEW DEAL AND OLD COURT

The extraordinary exercise of legislative and executive power reflected and authorized by the New Deal legislation was certain to be tested in the Supreme Court. Several of the major cases that came to the Court in the next three years were, in fact, test cases, brought by the administration itself.

The Supreme Court of 1933, however, was not a body that could be expected to be receptive to revolutionary uses of federal power. Six of the justices had sat on the bench since the pre-depression 1920s—or earlier. Four of them were staunch conservatives: Taft nominee Willis Van Devanter, Wilson choice James C. McReynolds, and two Harding nominees, George Sutherland and Pierce Butler. Two other justices—Louis D. Brandeis and Harlan Fiske Stone—had been appointed by Wilson and Coolidge, respectively, and tended to take more liberal views on questions of federal power. The three newest members of the Court were all Hoover nominees—Chief Justice Charles Evans Hughes and Associate Justices Benjamin N. Cardozo and Owen J. Roberts.

Hughes, a former associate justice, governor of New York, presidential nominee, and secretary of state, had been considered a liberal earlier in his career, but had acquired a more conservative reputation as his fame and fortune increased. He was named chief justice in 1930, to succeed Chief Justice William Howard Taft.

Roberts, a successful Republican attorney from Pennsylvania, had been named to the Court in the same year. Hoover, noting Roberts's progressive reputation, considered him a liberal appointment.[61] Cardozo, a liberal and well-regarded legal scholar and judge, had been appointed by Hoover in 1932.

Hopeful Signs

In 1934 the Court seemed to hint that it would take a favorable attitude toward the "emergency" exercise of extraordinary power in the New Deal statutes. In January of that year, the Court upheld, against constitutional challenge, a state moratorium law.[62]

Chief Justice Hughes explained that although emergencies did not create power they did empower government to act in ways that might be considered unconstitutional in normal circumstances. The vote in the case, however, was 5–4. The dissenters were Sutherland, Van Devanter, McReynolds, and Butler.

Two months later, by an identical vote, the Court upheld a state law creating a board empowered to fix minimum and maximum prices for milk.[63] In the majority opinion, Roberts wrote that the states possessed the power to decide and adopt whatever reasonable economic policy toward business promoted the public welfare.

But the hopes raised by these rulings were shattered by important decisions announced in the next two Court terms.

The "Hot Oil" Case

Between January 1935 and June 1936 the Supreme Court ruled against the administration in eight out of ten major cases involving New Deal statutes. The Court upheld only the emergency monetary legislation of 1933 and the creation of the Tennessee Valley Authority.[64]

The first blow came on January 7, 1935. In *Panama Refining Co. v. Ryan,* the so-called hot oil case, the Court held unconstitutional the portion of the National Industrial Recovery Act that provided for a code to govern the production of oil and petroleum products. With only Cardozo dissenting, the Court held that the contested portion unlawfully delegated legislative power to the president.[65]

Four months later, on May 6, the Railroad Retirement Act was struck down. The Court ruled that Congress had exceeded the scope of its power to regulate interstate commerce when it approved the creation of an industrywide pension system. The vote was 5–4; Roberts sided with the conservatives. Chief Justice Hughes, dissenting with Brandeis, Cardozo, and Stone, scolded the majority for placing such "an unwarranted limitation upon the commerce clause of the Constitution."[66]

"Black Monday"

The most devastating single day of this period, however, came on "Black Monday," May 27, 1935. In unanimous decisions the Court struck to the heart of President Roosevelt's concept of presidential power.

The Court struck down a federal farm mortgage relief act, finding it unfair to creditors.[67] Then in *Schechter Poultry Corp. v. United States* the Court held the main portion of the National Industrial Recovery Act unconstitutional.[68] In a third blow to the power of the executive, the Court held that the president lacked any inherent power to remove members of the Federal Trade Commission from their posts.[69] *(See "The Case of the Federal Trade Commissioner," pp. 223–224.)*

The most crushing was the NIRA ruling. Rejection of that recovery plan threatened nullification of the entire New Deal economy program. The NIRA had encouraged the creation of industrywide, presidentially approved codes of competition, eventually adopted to govern almost every service trade and industry. But its critics saw the NIRA as government interference in matters that should be left to private enterprise. Even before the Court heard the *Schechter* case, difficulties with implementing the NIRA had convinced the administration that a major overhaul of the program was needed.[70]

Despite it shortcomings, however, the NIRA had provided needed action in time of crisis. Psychologically, it had worked to restore confidence among the American people—in themselves and in the economy, although by 1935 there was also clear evidence that the codes were sometimes used by business to promote their interests at the expense of the public.

Schechter was picked as a test case by the administration, which acknowledged it was not the best vehicle for ascertaining the validity of the NIRA program.[71] It focused on the fair trade provisions affecting the poultry industry. The Schechter brothers of Brooklyn had been convicted of violating both fair trade and the labor provisions of the poultry industry's code.[72]

When the Supreme Court ruled on the matter, it found unanimously that the NIRA was an unconstitutional delegation of legislative power to the president, allowing him to approve the codes for each industry, which then had the force of law.

Furthermore, wrote Chief Justice Hughes for the majority, allowing trade and industry groups to make the codes in the first place amounted to delegation of the legislative authority to private citizens.[73]

Roosevelt assessed the implications of the Black Monday decisions in a press conference on May 31:

Is the United States going to decide . . . that their Federal Government shall in the future have no right under any implied or any court-approved power to enter into a solution of a national economic problem, but that national economic problems must be decided only by the States? . . . We thought we were solving it, and now it has been thrown right straight in our faces. We have been relegated to the horse-and-buggy definition of interstate commerce.[74]

States' Rights Rulings

The year 1936 began with still another blow to the New Deal. On January 6, the Court struck down the Agricultural Adjustment Act as an unconstitutional invasion of states' rights. The Court divided 6–3 on the question, and the divisions were bitter.[75] Roberts and Chief Justice Hughes voted with the conservatives; Stone, Brandeis, and Cardozo dissented.

Writing for the majority in *United States v. Butler,* Justice Roberts set out the view that agriculture was a matter reserved to state, not federal, regulation. The AAA program was an improper use of congressional authority to regulate agriculture, the majority held. The processing tax it imposed was a penalty to force compliance with the AAA acreage reduction program—an impermissible objective and thus an impermissible use of the taxing power.

In May 1936 the Court struck again. The Bituminous Coal Conservation Act was held an unconstitutional invasion of states' rights. The law, also called the Guffey Act, set up a commission to adopt codes to regulate production in various regions and levied a tax on coal that was partially refunded to operators abiding by the code. It also guaranteed collective bargaining rights in the industry.[76]

Mining, like agriculture, was a matter for states to regulate, wrote Justice Sutherland for the majority in *Carter v. Carter Coal Co.* The tax in this case, as in *Butler,* was a means to an impermissible end and therefore must fall. Congress had overreached its proper power.[77]

A week later, the Court struck down the Municipal Bankruptcy Act—again as an invasion of the rights of states. The vote in *Ashton v. Cameron County District* was 5–4. Hughes, Cardozo, Brandeis, and Stone dissented.

Writing for the majority, Justice McReynolds held that the law permitting subdivisions of the states to file for bankruptcy to readjust their debt obligations was unconstitutional, an impermissible extension of federal power.[78] The dissenters responded that the voluntary municipal bankruptcy petitions to which the state consented were not an invasion of state sovereignty.[79]

The Roosevelt recovery and reform programs launched in the first hundred days did extend federal authority over matters left previously to state authority. The shift in the balance between state and federal power seemed to many to threaten to erode the structure of the Union. Such critics supported the Court's strict construction and dual federalism doctrines to counterbalance the New Deal's challenge to the traditional arrangements of power.

COUNTERATTACK

If the justices of the Supreme Court read the election results in November 1936, they received a clear message that Roosevelt had overwhelming popular support in his attempt to combat the depression and its effects. In the 1936 presidential election a moderate economic recovery blended with a sense of pragmatic purpose, Roosevelt's personal charm, and his expressed concern for the "little man" won over the mildly reform-minded Alfred E. Landon, the Republican standard-bearer. Landon's only issue was Roosevelt; even the Republicans had to admit the necessity of many New Deal reforms.[80] Landon carried Maine and Vermont. Roosevelt carried all the other states.

The Court's opposition to a program and a president with such an overwhelming mandate began to produce a public view of the Court as an obstacle to reform. Members of Congress recommended that Congress curtail the Court's jurisdiction. Sen. Joseph O'Mahoney, D-Wyo. (1934–1953, 1954–1956), proposed that the Court be required to have a two-thirds majority vote when it declared acts of Congress unconstitutional. Sen. Burton K. Wheeler, D-Mont. (1923–1947), proposed a constitutional amendment that permitted Congress to override a Court decision by a two-thirds vote of both houses.[81]

But the thrust of the counterattack came from Roosevelt. In his second inaugural speech he urged all agencies of the government to cooperate in advancing the common good.[82]

The Plan

On February 5, 1937, Roosevelt sent Congress a message that proposed a judicial "reorganization." The measure would have increased the number of Supreme Court justices to as many as fifteen, creating one new seat for each justice who, upon reaching the age of seventy, declined to retire.[83] In other words, for every justice age seventy or over the president could appoint another one up to a maximum of six.

The measure also called for other changes: the addition of a total of fifty new judges for all federal courts; a rule that appeals on constitutional matters move directly to the Supreme Court; a requirement that government attorneys be heard before any court granted an injunction against enforcement of an act of Congress in cases where the act's constitutional status was questioned; and assignment of district judges to congested areas to relieve the backlog and expedite business.[84]

Roosevelt presented the plan as a bill to relieve the justices' workload. In his message he explained that the Court's work was "handicapped by insufficient personnel" and by the presence of old judges unable to perform their duties. As Roosevelt put it, "little by little, new facts became blurred through old

Justices James C. McReynolds, Willis Van Devanter, George Sutherland, and Pierce Butler were nicknamed the "Four Horsemen," a double allusion to the Four Horsemen of the Apocalypse and Notre Dame's defensive team, because of their persistent opposition to Franklin D. Roosevelt's New Deal legislation. This 1937 cartoon presents one view of Roosevelt's attempt to weaken the conservative bloc's power by trying to persuade Congress to allow him to appoint up to six new justices to the Supreme Court.

glasses fitted, as it were, for the needs of another generation."[85]

It was not a characteristic Roosevelt message. It lacked simplicity and clarity. The proposals were too technical and too confusing for easy public comprehension. And the president's purpose was only slightly concealed. It was a "Court-packing" scheme to get liberal Roosevelt-appointed justices on the bench to reverse its anti–New Deal stance.

Public Reaction

Roosevelt, however, had miscalculated public reaction to such a proposal. He had not prepared the public or obtained the advice of Senate leaders before introducing the measure.[86] The message, and the remedy suggested, reflected the president's sense of desperate frustration with the Court's performance. With a number of important measures pending before the Court, the president felt impelled to make certain the New Deal would not be further obstructed by the Court. As Robert Jackson would later write, "The Court seemed to have declared the mortality table unconstitutional and a nation was waiting for the President to move."[87]

The plan touched off a widespread and bitter debate in Congress and in the nation. Harold Ickes, Roosevelt's secretary of the interior, noted that no other single measure "has caused the spilling of so much printer's ink or led to so many fervent discussions. The President has a first class fight on his hands. Prac-

tically all of the newspapers are against him. . . . But the worst of it is that some of the progressives in Congress and outside are lining up with the reactionaries."[88]

At a Democratic victory dinner March 4, 1937, Roosevelt assailed the Court for rendering the nation powerless to deal with the problems of economic recovery.[89] In a radio "fireside chat" broadcast a few days later Roosevelt told the American people that the Court had

cast doubts on the ability of the elected Congress to protect us against catastrophe by meeting squarely our modern social and economic conditions. . . . This plan will save our National Constitution from hardening of the judicial arteries.[90]

But the idea of tampering with the Supreme Court met vigorous public opposition. The public still regarded the nine-member Court as the guardian of the Constitution, aloof from politics. The proposal to increase the Court's membership was criticized as perverting the Constitution and destroying judicial integrity and independence.[91]

The Court-plan fight split the Democrats in Congress. By early March Senator Wheeler, a New Dealer, was leading the fight against the bill, whose supporters in the Senate were led by Carter Glass, D-Va. (1920–1946), Joseph Robinson, D-Ark. (1913–1937), and Edward Burk, D-Neb. (1935–1941).[92]

The Republican minority, content to let Democrats fight among themselves over the merits of the plan, remained in the background.

During hearings on the bill by the Senate Judiciary Committee, Senator Wheeler made public a letter from Chief Justice Hughes that denied every assertion the president had made with respect to the Court's workload and performance. An increase in the number of justices, wrote Hughes, would actually delay the Court's work by prolonging deliberation on each case.

Justice Brandeis, convinced that Roosevelt's plan threatened the separation of powers doctrine under the Constitution, added his signature to the letter. Hughes had told Wheeler that in the interest of saving time he had not obtained the signatures of the other justices to the letter. Hughes's remark left Wheeler with the impression that the letter reflected the unanimous opinion of the Court. Later research revealed, however, that Justice Stone would not have supported Hughes or signed the letter.[93] However, publication of the Hughes-Brandeis letter damaged chances for passage of the reorganization plan.

A COURT REVERSAL

The Court itself dealt the death blow to the Court-packing plan with a series of decisions announced between late March and late May 1937 upholding New Deal measures.

On March 29, by a 5–4 vote, the Court upheld a state minimum wage law for women—nearly identical to a state law struck down ten months earlier, also by a 5–4 vote.[94] The same day, the Court unanimously upheld a revised farm mortgage moratorium act—repassed by Congress after its predecessor was unanimously voided by the Court in 1935.[95]

On April 12, again by a 5–4 vote, the Court upheld the National Labor Relations Act.[96] And on May 24, by votes of 5–4 and 7–2, the Court upheld both the unemployment compensation and the old-age benefits of the Social Security Act.[97]

In each case where the vote was 5–4, Justice Roberts—now in favor of New Deal statutes—cast the deciding vote, abandoning the four conservatives with whom he had voted in previous terms to join Chief Justice Hughes and the three more liberal justices.

Justice Roberts's "switch in time" was long assumed to be a direct response to the Court-packing threat. The case indicating his shift was the minimum wage ruling. When the Court in June 1936 struck down New York State's minimum wage law—citing a 1923 precedent—Roberts had voted with the conservatives to form the five-man majority against the law. They found it an unconstitutional infringement on the freedom of contract.[98] In December 1936 a similar case from Washington State, *West Coast Hotel v. Parrish,* was argued before the Court.[99]

On December 19 the justices voted in conference on that case. Justice Harlan Fiske Stone was absent. The Court divided 4–4—with Roberts this time voting to uphold the law. The justices decided to await Stone's return and his vote. On February 6, the day after Roosevelt sent his "judicial reorganization" message to Congress, Stone voted. As he had done in the New York case, he voted to uphold the minimum wage law. The Court was now on its own private record, 5–4, to uphold the law. The decision was announced on March 29 after the Court-packing battle was under way—but Roberts's switch had occurred long before.

The story of Roberts's switch did not emerge until later. At the time it was widely assumed to show the impact of the president's threat. Felix Frankfurter later obtained from Roberts a memorandum outlining the events related above that made clear that Roberts's decision had preceded the Court-packing threat.[100]

Other developments also spelled defeat for the plan. The Supreme Court Retirement Act approved by Roosevelt in March 1937 permitted justices to retire without resigning, retaining pension and other benefits, at age 70. Justice Willis Van Devanter, a New Deal foe, announced May 18 that he would retire at the end of the term, giving Roosevelt his first opportunity to appoint someone to the Court.

Sen. "Joe" Robinson, the majority leader in the Senate floor fight on behalf of the Roosevelt plan, died of a heart attack July 14. The Senate recommitted the Court-packing bill to the Judiciary Committee July 22.[101] The administration later accepted a watered-down reorganization measure that reformed lower court procedure but included no provision for additional justices on the Supreme Court. Roosevelt signed the bill August 26.[102]

Roosevelt's victory was not without its costs. His proposal and the battle that ensued opened a break in Democratic party ranks that took years to heal. After 1938 a conservative congressional coalition composed of southern Democrats and Republicans blocked New Deal measures with repeated regularity.[103]

Roosevelt made four appointments to the Court between 1937 and 1940. Sen. Hugo L. Black replaced Van Devanter in 1937. Stanley F. Reed replaced George Sutherland in 1938. Roosevelt's longtime friend Felix Frankfurter took Cardozo's place in 1939, and Justice William O. Douglas was appointed after Brandeis retired in 1939.

After 1937 the Supreme Court launched a revolution of its own. It repudiated the dual federalism concept that federal power was limited by states' rights. In cases involving labor relations, manufacturing, agriculture, and the spending power, the Court espoused a broad concept of federal power.

The Court gradually repudiated the earlier limits it had imposed on the commerce power. In the 1941 decision in *United States v. Darby,* the Court approved federal wage and hour standards prescribed in the Fair Labor Standards Act. In 1939, with its decision in *Mulford v. Smith,* the Court upheld the second Agricultural Adjustment Act. And soon the limitation on federal spending imposed in *Butler* also was swept away.[104] *(See "Wages and Hours," pp. 110–111, in Chapter 4; see also details of Steward Machine Co. v. Davis and Helvering v. Davis, p. 128, in Chapter 4.)*

Truman Versus the Court

Late in his second term, President Harry S. Truman collided with the Supreme Court. The issue was his decision to seize and operate the nation's steel mills in order to avoid a strike that would disrupt production and, Truman felt, jeopardize the U.S. war effort in Korea.

The result was a ruling in which the Court declared a halt to the steady expansion of "emergency" executive power that began in the days of the Great Depression and accelerated during World War II.

The decision was announced June 2, 1953. The vote was 6–3. Of the four justices named to the Court by Truman, two voted to uphold the president's action and two opposed it.

THE SEIZURE ORDER

The United Steel Workers of America announced an industrywide strike to begin April 9, 1952.[105] Bargaining sessions to avert the strike through negotiation, encouraged by the efforts of the Wage Stabilization Board (WSB), ended in failure when the plant operators rejected a WSB wage-settlement formula.[106]

On April 8 Truman issued an executive order to Secretary of Commerce Charles Sawyer directing him to seize and operate the nation's steel mills. The order cited the state of national emergency proclaimed December 16, 1950—after the Chinese invasion of Korea—and the necessity to maintain uninterrupted steel production during the war. Truman explained his action as a proper exercise of general executive authority granted by Article II, as well as his more specific power as commander in chief.[107]

Truman's advisers calculated that a halt in steel production would endanger the lives of men on the battlefield by reducing supplies of guns and ammunition. They forecast that shortages in steel would limit aircraft production, power plant construction, shipbuilding, and atomic weapons research.

The steel companies attacked the order as unconstitutional and went to court, obtaining an injunction in the District of Columbia restraining Sawyer from carrying out the seizure order.[108] The court of appeals then stayed the district court injunction, and the case moved to the Supreme Court for consideration of the constitutional challenge to the president's seizure power.

THE DECISION

The case of *Youngstown Sheet and Tube Co. v. Sawyer* was argued May 12–13, 1952. Three weeks later on June 2 the Court ruled 6–3 against Truman. In an opinion written by Justice Black, the majority held that the president's seizure of the steel mills was an unconstitutional exercise of power.

The Court rejected the theory of executive prerogative implicit in Truman's order. The president lacked statutory authority for the seizure, Black wrote, and neither the commander in chief power nor any inherent executive prerogative provided authority for it.

The executive order was invalid, the Court held, because it attempted to make law although the Constitution limited the president "to the recommending of laws he thinks wise and the vetoing of laws he thinks bad." Black relied on the legislative history of the 1947 Labor-Management Relations (Taft-Hartley) Act, in which Congress had decided against authorizing the president to seize strikebound industrial plants. *(See "The Steel Seizure Case," pp. 203–204.)*

All five other members of the majority wrote concurring opinions.

Justices Harold H. Burton and Felix Frankfurter thought the president should have invoked the Taft-Hartley Act provisions for a cooling-off period. They declared that in light of Congress's rejection of such a seizure authority in that act, Truman's order contradicted "the clear will of Congress."[109]

Justice Tom C. Clark agreed that the president had, in this instance, violated procedures set out by Congress for the settlement of strikes.[110] Justice Douglas wrote that Court sanction of Truman's seizure would have expanded Article II of the Constitution to "suit the political conveniences of the present emergency."[111]

Chief Justice Fred M. Vinson, joined by Justices Reed and Sherman Minton, dissented, emphasizing the nature of the national emergency and the discretionary power of the president in times of crisis. Vinson found the president's action supportive of congressional intention in that the seizure was for the purpose of ensuring steel for weapons to conduct a congressionally supported war in Korea. Vinson's dissent was a pragmatic argument that accepted the view of an expanded executive prerogative as a fact of constitutional life in the twentieth century.[112]

One cartoonist's view of the Court's decision in the *Steel Seizure Case,* June 3, 1952.

Truman later wrote:

[T]he Supreme Court's decision . . . was a deep disappointment to me. I think Chief Justice Vinson's dissenting opinion hit the nail right on the head, and I am sure that someday his view will come to be recognized as the correct one.[113]

The administration decided not to attempt a settlement. The following week Truman sought legislative authorization for the seizure. Congress refused.

The strike lasted fifty-three days, ending July 24. Six hundred thousand steel workers and twenty-five thousand iron-ore workers had been idled seven weeks. Losses in wages and production were estimated at $2 billion.

Truman claimed that military shortages in certain types of ammunition were experienced in the summer and fall of 1952 as a result of the loss in steel production occasioned by the strike and the Court's refusal to sanction his handling of it.[114]

Truman's *Memoirs* gave his view of the Court's action and presidential powers:

It is not very realistic for the justices to say that comprehensive powers shall be available to the President only when a war has been declared or when the country has been invaded. We live in an age when hostilities begin without polite exchanges of diplomatic notes. There are no longer sharp distinctions between combatants and noncombatants. . . . Nor can we separate the economic facts from the problems of defense and security. . . . The President, who is Commander-in-Chief and who represents the interests of all the people, must [be] able to act at all times to meet any sudden threat to the nation's security. A wise President will always work with Congress, but when Congress fails to act or is unable to act in a crisis, the President, under the Constitution, must use his powers to safeguard the nation.[115]

Nixon, Watergate, and the Court

Richard Nixon campaigned for the presidency in 1968 as an anti-Court candidate, promising that, if elected, he would by his appointments change the Court from one that "coddled" criminals to one that was more responsive to the problems and needs of law enforcement officers.

Nixon was elected and, in his first term, placed four new members on the Court: Chief Justice Warren E. Burger and Justices Harry A. Blackmun, Lewis F. Powell Jr., and William H. Rehnquist, all chosen for their conservative views on questions of law and order.

But in the most ironic of circumstances, Nixon in 1974 found himself before the Court arguing that he had the right to withhold evidence sought by a prosecutor for use in a criminal trial. The Court's response was negative. After an initial silence, Nixon accepted the Court's decision. Two weeks later—realizing the significance of that evidence for his own reputation and his fate in an ongoing impeachment inquiry—Nixon resigned the presidency.

Nixon's resignation mooted the impeachment proceedings, which had begun as a result of Nixon's response to the investigation of the so-called Watergate scandal. The burglary of the Democratic National Committee's headquarters offices in the Washington, D.C., Watergate complex in mid-1972, and the attempted cover-up of White House involvement in the affair, was the immediate source of Nixon's troubles. But it was by no means the only matter that brought him into collision with the Supreme Court.

During his years in office, Nixon's claims of broad executive prerogative to act in the interests of national security, to refuse to spend congressionally provided funds, or to withhold information brought him before the Court. In five of the six cases involving Nixon's claims, the Court ruled against him.

PENTAGON PAPERS

In June 1971 the *New York Times* and the *Washington Post* began publication of articles based on a top-secret Defense Department analysis of the U.S. role in the war in Southeast Asia.

Both newspapers had obtained copies of the classified document. The Nixon administration, criticized for its conduct of the war, attempted to block publication of the articles. Administration attorneys argued that publication would result in a diplomatic imbroglio and would damage the nation's security.[116]

Attorney General John N. Mitchell first asked the newspapers to halt publication. Both refused. Mitchell then obtained an injunction from a federal court in New York ordering the *Times* to halt publication of the articles, but a federal court in the District of Columbia refused to grant a similar order against the *Post*. Both cases were appealed to the Supreme Court.

The Nixon administration argued that national security interests justified such "prior restraint" of publication; the *Times*

and the *Post* responded that such a curb on the freedom of the press violated the First Amendment.

On June 30, 1971, the Court ruled 6–3 against the Nixon administration. The majority held that the government had failed to meet the heavy burden of justifying prior restraint based on the claim that publication would damage national security. The Court allowed publication of the articles to continue.[117]

The Court did not deny that there might be circumstances in which such a restraint might be justified; they simply held that it had not been justified here.[118] *(See mention of the case, p. 240.)*

WIRETAPPING

A year later, the Nixon administration again lost a national security argument before the Court. Only since 1968 had Congress provided statutory authority for the use of wiretaps or electronic surveillance by law enforcement officers. To minimize the invasion of individual rights that could result, Congress required that every wiretap or electronic surveillance be approved by a federal judge, who would issue a warrant approving the action. This provision was part of the Omnibus Crime Control and Safe Streets Act of 1968.[119]

The Nixon administration claimed, however, that the court approval and warrant requirement did not apply to its use of wiretaps to keep track of the activities of domestic groups suspected of subversive activities. These wiretaps were legal, administration lawyers argued, as "a reasonable exercise of the President's power . . . to protect the national security."[120]

By a 6–2 vote the Supreme Court in 1972 rejected that claim of inherent power.

In domestic security matters, wrote Justice Powell, the "convergence of First and Fourth Amendment values" requires strict observance of constitutional safeguards. "[U]nreviewed executive discretion," he warned, "may yield too readily to pressure to obtain incriminating evidence and overlook potential invasions of privacy and protected speech."[121]

IMPOUNDMENT

When Congress earmarked funds for programs the president wished to curtail, Nixon simply refused to spend the money. This assertion of the power to impound funds gave Nixon the equivalent of an item veto over congressional appropriations bills, a seemingly unchallengeable mechanism to block any program involving federal expenditures.

Nixon was not the first chief executive to try this tool. Presidents Jefferson, Grant, and Franklin Roosevelt had impounded funds, and the procedure had been used as an instrument of fiscal policy by Presidents Truman, Eisenhower, and Kennedy.[122]

But legislative authority for impoundment could be derived from the language of the authorizing statute in most previous impoundment incidents. Furthermore, if the money impounded was for defense projects, the president could also argue that, as commander in chief, he had authority to withhold spending for such programs.

JUSTICES FROM THE CABINET

Thirty-three justices of the Supreme Court—including ten chief justices—served as executive branch officials either before or after their appointment to the Court. Eighteen held cabinet-level posts—nine of them were attorneys general—and another eight served in other posts in the Department of Justice.

Four men, Roger B. Taney, Levi Woodbury, William H. Moody, and William Howard Taft, held more than one cabinet post. Taft held more high executive branch posts than any other justice. He is the only man to serve both as president and chief justice of the United States.

The following table lists the justices, the major executive branch positions they held, and their years of service.

Justice	Position	Court Service
John Jay*	Secretary for foreign affairs under the Articles of Confederation, 1784–1789; U.S. diplomat, 1794–1795	1789–1795
John Marshall*	Envoy to France, 1797–1798; secretary of state, 1818–1823	1801–1835
Smith Thompson	Secretary of the Navy, 1818–1823	1823–1843
Gabriel Duvall	Comptroller of the Treasury, 1802–1811	1812–1835
John McLean	Postmaster general, 1823–1829	1829–1861
Roger B. Taney*	Attorney general, 1831–1833; secretary of the Treasury, 1833–1834	1836–1864
Levi Woodbury	Secretary of the Navy, 1831–1834; secretary of the Treasury, 1834–1841	1845–1851
Nathan Clifford	Attorney general, 1846–1848	1858–1881
Salmon P. Chase*	Secretary of the Treasury, 1861–1864	1864–1873
Lucius Q. C. Lamar	Secretary of the interior, 1885–1888	1888–1893
Joseph McKenna	Attorney general, 1897–1898	1898–1925
William H. Moody	Secretary of the Navy, 1902–1904; attorney general, 1904–1906	1906–1910
Charles E. Hughes*	Secretary of state, 1921–1925	1910–1926; 1930–1941
Willis Van Devanter	Counsel, Interior Department, 1897–1903	1910–1937
James McReynolds	Attorney general, 1913–1914	1914–1941
William H. Taft*	U.S. solicitor general, 1890–1892; secretary of war, 1904–1908; president, 1908–1912	1921–1930
Edward T. Sanford	Assistant attorney general, 1907–1908	1923–1930
Harlan F. Stone*	Attorney general, 1924–1925	1925–1946
Owen J. Roberts	Prosecuting attorney, Teapot Dome scandal, 1924	1930–1945
Stanley Reed	Solicitor general, 1935–1938	1938–1957
William O. Douglas	Chairman, Securities and Exchange Commission, 1937–1939	1939–1975
Frank Murphy	Attorney general, 1938–1940	1940–1949
James F. Byrnes	Secretary of state, 1945–1947	1941–1942
Robert H. Jackson	Solicitor general, 1938–1939; attorney general, 1940–1941	1941–1954
Fred M. Vinson*	Secretary of the Treasury, 1945–1946	1946–1953
Tom C. Clark	Attorney general, 1945–1949	1949–1967
Byron R. White	Deputy attorney general, 1961–1962	1962–1993
Arthur J. Goldberg	Secretary of labor, 1961–1962	1962–1963
Abe Fortas	Under secretary of interior, 1942–1946	1965–1969
Thurgood Marshall	Solicitor general, 1964–1967	1967–1991
Warren E. Burger*	Assistant attorney general, 1953–1955	1969–1986
William H. Rehnquist*	Assistant attorney general, 1969–1971	1971–
Clarence Thomas	Assistant secretary of education, 1981–1982; chairman, Equal Employment Opportunity Commission, 1982–1990	1991–

* Denotes chief justice.

SOURCES: Leon Friedman, Fred L. Israel, eds., *The Justices of the United States Supreme Court 1789–1969, Their Lives and Major Opinions,* 5 vols. (New York and London: Chelsea House, 1969, 1978); William F. Swindler, *Court and Constitution in the Twentieth Century,* 2 vols. (Indianapolis and New York: Bobbs-Merrill, 1969, 1970); *American Leaders 1789–1994* (Washington, D.C.: Congressional Quarterly, 1994).

Nixon, however, used impoundment more frequently than his predecessors. Between 1969 and 1973, he impounded more than $15 billion in funds intended for more than one hundred programs. Those affected included pollution control, housing, public education, and other social programs.

On January 31, 1973, Nixon asserted the president's

constitutional right . . . to impound funds and that is, not to spend money, when the spending of money would mean either increasing prices or increasing taxes for all the people, that right is absolutely clear.[123]

But when one particular impoundment of billions in funds authorized for distribution to states under the Water Pollution Control Act of 1972 came before the Supreme Court, the Court rejected Nixon's claim of a constitutional power to impound these funds.

The ruling came six months after Nixon had left office. On February 19, 1975, the Court held unanimously that Nixon had exceeded his authority when he refused to allocate those water pollution funds to the states. The wording of the 1972 act, wrote Justice Byron R. White, left the president no power to withhold the funds. The decision did not set limits for the president's impoundment power generally, but its implication was that Nixon's claim of such a power was a shaky one.[124]

WATERGATE AND THE WHITE HOUSE TAPES

The most dramatic of confrontations between court and chief executive came between Nixon and the Supreme Court in July 1974. The decision cost Nixon his office. In July 1973 a witness before the Senate Select Committee on Presidential Campaign Activities revealed that, through secret recording devices, many of President Nixon's conversations with his staff had been recorded on tape.

This subpoena *duces tecum* (a writ to produce documents or other evidence) was issued by the first special prosecutor July 23, 1973. It ordered President Richard Nixon or his subordinates to appear before the grand jury and to bring tapes relevant to the Watergate investigation.

At the time of the revelation, the Watergate affair and alleged White House involvement in it were under investigation by the select committee, a federal grand jury, and a Watergate special prosecution force led by Archibald Cox.

The disclosure of the taping system set off a year-long battle for certain White House tapes. The tug-of-war eventually brought Nixon's lawyers to the Supreme Court, defending his right to withhold this evidence.

Special Prosecutor Cox quickly obtained a subpoena for certain tapes that he wished to use as evidence to the grand jury. Nixon refused to comply, setting off a legal battle that culminated in the "Saturday Night Massacre" of late October 1973. The "massacre," resulting from Cox's refusal to stop his efforts to obtain the tapes, included Cox's firing and the resignations of Attorney General Elliot Richardson and his deputy, William Ruckelshaus, both of whom chose to resign rather than follow Nixon's order to fire Cox. Cox eventually was fired by Solicitor General Robert Bork.

The public outcry over Nixon's actions in this episode forced him to turn over some of the subpoenaed tapes—and led to the initiation of a House impeachment inquiry into the president's conduct.[125]

In March 1974, as the House Judiciary Committee's impeachment investigation was getting under way, former attorney general John N. Mitchell, former presidential assistants John D. Ehrlichman and H. R. (Bob) Haldeman, and four other former Nixon aides were indicted for conspiracy to defraud the United States and to obstruct justice. The charges related to their efforts to cover up White House involvement in the Watergate affair.

In mid-April the new special prosecutor, Leon Jaworski, obtained a subpoena ordering Nixon to hand over additional taped conversations for use as evidence in the trial of Mitchell and the others. Nixon's lawyers moved to quash the subpoena. Judge John J. Sirica of the U.S. District Court for the District of Columbia refused and denied the motion. Late in the Supreme Court term, the case moved onto its docket, and the Court decided to review the matter promptly.[126]

In an extraordinary summer argument session, the cases of *United States v. Nixon, Nixon v. United States* were argued on July 8, 1974. *(See details of the cases, p. 241.)*

The Court ruled July 24. By an 8–0 vote, it rejected Nixon's claim of an absolute executive privilege to withhold the evidence sought by the special prosecutor. Chief Justice Warren E. Burger, Nixon's own choice to head the Court, wrote the opinion. Only Justice Rehnquist, who had served in the Justice Department under Mitchell before moving to the Court, did not participate in the case.

Nixon, the Court said, must surrender the tapes. The president was at the western White House in California when the decision came. For a few hours there was no word of his reaction. Then came a statement that the president accepted the decision.

That evening the House Judiciary Committee began nationally televised debates on the charges against Nixon. Within the week, it had approved three articles of impeachment.[127] Two weeks later on August 9 Nixon resigned the post of the presidency.[128]

STILL MORE TAPES

Resignation did not end Nixon's battles before the Supreme Court. Soon thereafter, Nixon and the head of the General Services Administration reached an agreement concerning control of and access to the tapes and papers of the Nixon administration. As had been the case with other former presidents, Nixon was to have control of those materials.

But Congress, sensitive to the unusual circumstances surrounding Nixon's departure from office, passed a law—the Presidential Recordings and Materials Preservation Act—placing those materials in federal custody.[129] Nixon immediately went to court, challenging the law as violating a long list of rights and privileges—including the separation of powers, executive privilege, the right of privacy, First Amendment freedom of expression, the Fourth Amendment's protection against unreasonable search and seizure, the right to equal protection under the law, and the constitutional ban on bills of attainder—laws passed to punish individuals.[130]

On June 28, 1977, the Court upheld the law by a 7–2 vote. The majority opinion, written by Justice William J. Brennan Jr., acknowledged that the law might infringe on some of Nixon's rights. But the Court then weighed the damage done to the former president as an individual against the public interest in preserving the Nixon materials intact and concluded that the latter outweighed Nixon's claim.

Still another Nixon tapes case was yet to be decided by the Supreme Court. In 1978 Nixon finally won the last of these cases. On April 18, 1978, by a 5–4 vote, the Court granted Nixon's request that lower courts not be allowed to permit broadcasters to copy the White House tapes used as evidence in the trial of Mitchell, Haldeman, and Ehrlichman. The broadcasters were seeking to market the tapes commercially. The Court ruled that such access need not be granted immediately—especially since the 1974 act concerning the tapes and other Nixon materials did set up procedures for public access to those items at some future date.[131]

NOTES

INTRODUCTION (PP. 191–193)

1. *Youngstown Sheet and Tube Co. v. Sawyer,* 343 U.S. 579 at 653 (1952).
2. *Youngstown Sheet and Tube Co. v. Sawyer,* 343 U.S. 579 (1952); *United States v. Nixon,* 418 U.S. 683 (1974).
3. *Youngstown Sheet and Tube Co. v. Sawyer,* 343 U.S. 579 at 646–647 (1952).
4. George E. Reedy, *The Twilight of the Presidency* (New York: New American Library, 1970), 4.
5. Louis Koenig, *The Chief Executive,* 5th ed. (San Diego: Harcourt Brace Jovanovich, 1986), 12–13.
6. *Youngstown Sheet and Tube Co. v. Sawyer,* 343 U.S. 579 at 653–654 (1952).
7. William Howard Taft, *Our Chief Magistrate and His Powers* (New York: Columbia University Press, 1916), 144.

8. Theodore Roosevelt, *An Autobiography* (New York: Macmillan, 1920), 406.
9. John Locke, *Second Treatise of Government,* with an Introduction by Charles L. Sherman (New York: Appleton-Century-Crofts, 1937), 109.
10. *Youngstown Sheet and Tube Co. v. Sawyer,* 343 U.S. 579 at 635–636 (1952).
11. *United States v. Curtiss-Wright Export Corporation,* 299 U.S. 304 (1936).
12. Laurence H. Tribe, *God Save This Honorable Court* (New York: Random House, 1985), 50, 74–75.
13. Charles Warren, *The Supreme Court in United States History,* rev. ed., 2 vols. (Boston: Little, Brown, 1922, 1926), I: 2.

THE COMMANDER IN CHIEF (PP. 194–208)

1. *Youngstown Sheet and Tube Co. v. Sawyer,* 343 U.S. 579 at 641 (1952).
2. *The Federalist Papers,* with an Introduction by Clinton Rossiter (New York: New American Library, Mentor Books, 1961), No. 61, 417–418.
3. Ibid., No. 74, 447.
4. Louis Koenig, *The Chief Executive,* 5th ed. (San Diego: Harcourt Brace Jovanovich, 1986), 23–31.
5. C. Herman Pritchett, *The American Constitution* (New York: McGraw-Hill, 1959), 344.
6. Arthur M. Schlesinger Jr., *The Imperial Presidency* (New York: Popular Library, 1973), 68–69.
7. James D. Richardson, ed., *Messages and Papers of the Presidents,* 20 vols. (New York: Bureau of National Literature, 1897), VII: 3225–3226.
8. Edward S. Corwin with Randall W. Bland et al., *The President, Offices and Powers, 1787–1984,* 5th rev. ed. (New York: New York University Press, 1984), 270–278.
9. Glendon A. Schubert, *The Presidency in the Courts* (Minneapolis: University of Minnesota Press, 1957), 286–290.
10. Ibid., 287
11. Clinton Rossiter, *The Supreme Court and the Commander in Chief* (Ithaca, N.Y.: Cornell University Press, 1951), 126.
12. Louis Fisher, *Presidential War Power* (Lawrence: University Press of Kansas, 1995), xi.
13. Ibid., xii–xiii.
14. *Talbot v. Seeman,* 1 Cr. 1 (1801); *Bas v. Tingy,* 4 Dall. 37 (1800).
15. *Martin v. Mott,* 12 Wheat. 19 (1827).
16. Id. at 29.
17. Id. at 31–32.
18. *Fleming v. Page,* 9 How. 603 at 615 (1850).
19. Richard W. Leopold, *The Growth of American Foreign Policy* (New York: Knopf, 1962), 96–98.
20. W. Taylor Reveley III, "Presidential War-Making: Constitutional Prerogative or Usurpation?" *Virginia Law Review* 55: 1258n–1259n.
21. Samuel Eliot Morison, Henry Steele Commager, and William E. Leuchtenburg, *The Growth of the American Republic,* 2 vols. (New York: Oxford University Press, 1969), I: 550–551.
22. *Congressional Globe,* 30th Cong., 1st sess. 95 (1848).
23. Leopold, *American Foreign Policy,* 150–152, 180–188, 212.
24. Ibid.
25. Ibid., 215–218.
26. Ibid., 316–321.
27. Corwin, *The President,* 264–265.
28. Richardson, ed., *Messages and Papers of the Presidents,* VII: 3225–3226.
29. Carl B. Swisher, *American Constitutional Development,* 2d ed. (Cambridge, Mass.: Houghton Mifflin, 1954), 29.
30. Elisabeth Joan Doyle, "The Conduct of the War, 1861," in *Congress Investigates 1792–1974,* ed. Arthur M. Schlesinger Jr. and Roger Bruns (New York: Chelsea House, 1975), 72.
31. *The Prize Cases,* 2 Bl. 635 (1863).
32. Id. at 668–669.

33. Id. at 688–689, 690, 693, 698.

34. Carl B. Swisher, *History of the Supreme Court of the United States: Vol. V, The Taney Period, 1836–1864* (New York: Macmillan, 1974), 844–846.

35. Ibid., 847–850.

36. *Ex parte Merryman,* 17 Fed. Cas. (No. 9487) (C.C.D. Md. 1861), quoted in *Documents of American History,* 7th ed., ed. Henry Steele Commager (New York: Appleton-Century-Crofts, 1963), 402.

37. *Ex parte Vallandigham,* 1 Wall. 243 (1864).

38. *Ex parte Milligan,* 4 Wall. 2 at 127 (1866).

39. Id. at 120–121, 126–127.

40. Woodrow Wilson, *Congressional Government* (Boston: Houghton Mifflin, 1885).

41. Arthur Link, *Wilson, the Diplomatist: A Look at His Major Foreign Policies* (New York: Watts, Franklin, 1965), 5–11.

42. Morison, Commager, Leuchtenburg, *The Growth of the American Republic,* II: 337.

43. Ibid. at 349, 353–357.

44. Alfred H. Kelly and Winfred A. Harbison, *The American Constitution: Its Origin and Development,* 7th ed. (New York: Norton, 1991), 626.

45. Morison, Commager, Leuchtenburg, *The Growth of the American Republic,* II: 337.

46. Corwin, *The President,* 272, 502.

47. Ibid., 235.

48. *United States Statutes at Large,* Vol. XL, 276ff.

49. *United States v. L. Cohen Grocery Co.,* 255 U.S. 81 at 81–82 (1921).

50. *The Public Papers and Addresses of Franklin D. Roosevelt,* 5 vols. (New York: Random House, 1938), II: 15.

51. Morison, Commager, Leuchtenburg, *The Growth of the American Republic,* II: 538–539.

52. *United States v. Curtiss-Wright Export Corp.,* 299 U.S. 304 (1936); *United States v. Belmont,* 310 U.S. 324 (1937); *United States v. Pink,* 315 U.S. 203 (1942).

53. 88 *Congressional Record* (1942), 7044.

54. *Yakus v. United States,* 321 U.S. 414 (1944).

55. Id. at 459–460.

56. *Bowles v. Willingham,* 321 U.S. 504 (1944).

57. Id. at 519.

58. *Woods v. Cloyd W. Miller Co.,* 333 U.S. 138 (1948).

59. *Steuart & Bros. Inc. v. Bowles,* 322 U.S. 398 at 405–406 (1944).

60. *Ex parte Quirin,* 317 U.S. 1 (1942).

61. Id. at 46, 48.

62. James M. Burns, *Roosevelt: The Soldier of Freedom* (New York: Harcourt Brace Jovanovich, 1970), 214–217, 266–268. See also *United States v. Hohri,* 482 U.S. 64 (1987).

63. *Hirabayashi v. United States,* 320 U.S. 81 at 103 (1043).

64. Id. at 92.

65. *Korematsu v. United States,* 323 U.S. 214 (1944).

66. *Ex parte Endo,* 323 U.S. 283 at 297 (1944).

67. Id. at 302.

68. "Authority of the President to Repel the Attack in Korea," 23 *State Department Bulletin* (1950), 173.

69. *Youngstown Sheet and Tube Co. v. Sawyer,* 343 U.S. 579 at 641 (1942).

70. Id. at 585–587.

71. Id. at 587.

72. Id. at 641–644.

73. Id. at 667–668.

74. Id. at 668, 708–709.

75. Dwight D. Eisenhower, *Waging Peace, 1956–1961* (Garden City, N.Y.: Doubleday, 1965), 272–273.

76. *Public Papers of the Presidents, John F. Kennedy, 1962* (Washington, D.C.: U S. Government Printing Office, 1963), 806–815.

77. PL-88-408, 78 *Statutes* 384; *Public Papers of the Presidents, Lyndon B. Johnson, 1963–1964,* 2 vols. (Washington, D.C.: U.S. Government Printing Office, 1965), I: 926–932, 946–947.

78. Lyndon B. Johnson, *The Vantage Point, Perspectives on the Presidency, 1963–1969* (New York: Holt, Rinehart, and Winston, 1971), 112–119.

79. Leonard Meeker, "The Legality of United States' Participation in the Defense of Vietnam," 54 *State Department Bulletin* (1966), 474.

80. Ibid., 484–489.

81. Ibid., 485–486.

82. *Mora v. McNamara,* 387 F. 2d 862 (D.C. Cir.) cert. denied, 389 U.S. 934 (1967); *Luftig v. McNamara,* 373 F. 2d 664 (D.C. Cir.) cert. denied, 387 U.S. 945 (1967); *United States v. Mitchell,* 369 F. 2d 323 (2d Cir. 1966) cert. denied, 386 U.S. 972 (1967); *Velvel v. Johnson,* 287 F. Supp. 846 (D. Kan. 1968).

83. Francis D. Wormuth, "The Nixon Theory of the War Power: A Critique," *California Law Review* 60: 624.

84. *Hearings on U.S. Commitments to Foreign Powers Before the Senate Committee on Foreign Relations,* 90th Cong., 1st sess. (1967), 108, 140–154.

85. Kelly and Harbison, *The American Constitution,* 1016.

86. *Congressional Quarterly's Guide to Congress,* 4th ed. (Washington, D.C.: Congressional Quarterly, 1991), 204–209.

87. Ibid.

88. Louis W. Koenig, *The Chief Executive,* 5th ed. (San Diego: Harcourt Brace Jovanovich, 1986), 210.

89. *Crockett v. Reagan,* 558 F. Supp 893 (D.D.C., 1982; cert. denied, 467 U.S. 1251 (1984); see Louis Fisher, *Constitutional Dialogues* (Princeton, N.J.: Princeton University Press, 1988), 32–33.

90. *CQ Almanac 1990* (Washington, D.C.: Congressional Quarterly, 1991), 739; *Dellums v. Bush,* 752 F. Supp. 1141 (1990).

91. *Ange v. Bush,* 752 F. Supp. 509 (1990).

92. *Youngstown Sheet and Tube Co. v. Sawyer,* 343 U.S. 579 at 645–646 (1952).

THE ARCHITECT OF FOREIGN POLICY
(PP. 209–217)

1. *United States Congress, Debates and Proceedings, First Congress, First Session, March 3, 1789 to Eighteenth Congress, First Session, May 27, 1824. [Annals of Congress].* 42 vols., (Washington, D.C.: Gales and Seaton, 1834–1856), X: 596, 613–614 (1800).

2. *The Federalist Papers,* with an Introduction by Clinton Rossiter (New York: New American Library, Mentor Books, 1961), No. 75, 450–451.

3. Max Farrand, ed., *The Records of the Federal Convention of 1787,* rev. ed. (New Haven, Conn.: Yale University Press, 1937), II: 183.

4. "Pacificus," Nos. 1, 3, in John C. Hamilton, ed., *Works of Alexander Hamilton,* 7 vols. (New York: John F. Trow, 1851), VII: 76, 82–83.

5. Gailiard Hunt, ed., *The Writings of James Madison,* 9 vols. (New York: Putnam's, 1900–1910), VI: 128–188.

6. Paul L. Ford, ed., *The Writings of Thomas Jefferson,* 10 vols. (New York: Putnam's, 1892–1899), V: 161–162.

7. Edward S. Corwin, *The Constitution and What It Means Today* (Princeton, N.J.: Princeton University Press, 1958), 171.

8. *Penhallow v. Doane,* 3 Dall. 54 at 80–83 (1795).

9. *United States v. Curtiss-Wright Export Corp.,* 299 U.S. 304 (1936).

10. *Ware v. Hylton,* 3 Dall. 199 at 236–237 (1796).

11. *Holmes v. Jennison,* 14 Pet. 540 at 575 (1840).

12. *United States v. Pink,* 315 U.S. 203 at 233–234 (1942).

13. *Foster v. Neilson,* 2 Pet. 253 at 307, 309 (1829).

14. *United States v. Palmer,* 3 Wheat. 610 (1818).

15. *Doe v. Braden,* 16 How. 635 at 657 (1853).

16. *Jones v. United States,* 137 U.S. 202 (1890); *Oetjen v. Central Leather Co.,* 246 U.S. 297 (1918).

17. *In re Baiz,* 135 U.S. 403 (1890).

18. *Neely v. Henkel,* 180 U.S. 109 (1901).

19. *Terlinden v. Ames,* 184 U.S. 270 (1902).

20. *Charlton v. Kelly,* 229 U.S. 447 (1913).

21. *Baker v. Carr,* 369 U.S. 186 at 212 (1962).

22. *Fourteen Diamond Rings v. United States,* 183 U.S. 176 at 183 (1901).

23. *United States v. Curtiss-Wright Export Corp.,* 299 U.S. 304 (1936).

24. Charles A. Lofgren, "United States v. Curtiss-Wright: An Historical Assessment," *Yale Law Journal* 83 (November 1973): 1–13.

25. 48 Stat. 1744 (1934).

26. *Schechter Poultry Corp. v. United States,* 295 U.S. 495 (1935); *Carter v. Carter Coal Co.,* 298 U.S. 238 (1936); *Panama Refining Co. v. Ryan,* 293 U.S. 288 (1935).

27. George Sutherland, *Constitutional Power and World Affairs,* (New York: Columbia University Press, 1919), 25–47, 116–126.

28. *United States v. Curtiss-Wright Export Corp.,* 299 U.S. 304 at 315–318 (1936).

29. Id. at 319–320.

30. Id. at 321–322.

31. *Foster v. Neilson,* 2 Pet. 253 at 314 (1829).

32. *Head Money Cases,* 112 U.S. 580 at 598 (1884).

33. Id. at 598–599.

34. Migratory Bird Treaty Act, July 3, 1918, c. 183, 40 Stat. 755.

35. *Missouri v. Holland,* 252 U.S. 416 at 432–435 (1920).

36. *Head Money Cases,* 112 U.S. 580 at 598–599 (1884).

37. *La Abra Silver Mining Co. v. United States,* 175 U.S. 423 at 460 (1899).

38. *Whitney v. Robertson,* 124 U.S. 190 (1888); *United States v. Guy W. Capps Inc.,* 348 U.S. 296 (1955).

39. *Charlton v. Kelly,* 229 U.S. 447 (1913); *Bas v. Tingy,* 4 Dall. 37 (1800); *Head Money Cases,* 112 U.S. 580 (1884).

40. *Goldwater v. Carter,* 444 U.S. 996 (1979).

41. *Geofroy v. Riggs,* 133 U.S. 258 at 266–267 (1889).

42. *Reid v. Covert,* 354 U.S. 1 at 16–18 (1957).

43. Hearings on S.J. Res. 1 and S.J. Res. 43 Before a Subcommittee of the Senate Judiciary Committee, 83d Cong., 1st sess. (1953), 877.

44. Ibid.

45. *The Constitution of the United States of America, Analysis and Interpretation* (Washington, D.C.: U.S. Government Printing Office, 1973), 506.

46. Wallace McClure, *International Executive Agreements: Democratic Procedure Under the Constitution of the United States* (New York: AMS Press, 1941), 41.

47. Ibid., 62–70.

48. Henry S. Commager, ed., *Documents of American History,* 7th ed. (New York: Appleton-Century-Crofts, 1962), 449–450.

49. "A Decade of American Foreign Policy," Senate Doc., No. 123, 81st Cong., 1st sess. (1950), 126.

50. *The Constitution of the United States, Analysis and Interpretation,* 512.

51. *Tucker v. Alexandroff,* 183 U.S. 424 at 435, 467 (1902).

52. Samuel B. Crandall, *Treaties: Their Making and Enforcement,* 2d ed. (New York: Columbia University Press, 1916), 103–104.

53. Samuel E. Morison, Henry S. Commager, and William E. Leuchtenburg, *The Growth of the American Republic,* 2 vols. (New York: Oxford University Press, 1969), II: 261–264.

54. McClure, *International Executive Agreements,* 96–97.

55. Commager, *Documents of American History,* 45, 52–53, 133–134.

56. McClure, *International Executive Agreements,* 391–393.

57. 4 *State Department Bulletin* (1941), 443.

58. "A Decade of American Foreign Policy, Basic Documents, 1941–1949," Senate Doc., No. 123, Part 1, 81st Cong., 1st sess. (1950).

59. Arthur M. Schlesinger Jr., *The Imperial Presidency* (New York: Popular Library, 1973, 1974), 299–300.

60. *CQ Almanac 1972* (Washington, D.C.: Congressional Quarterly, 1972), 279–280, 435.

61. *United States v. Belmont,* 310 U.S. 324 at 330 (1936).

62. Id. at 330–331.

63. *United States v. Pink,* 315 U.S. 203 at 229–230 (1942).

64. Id. at 230–231.

65. Id. at 233.

66. *Dames & Moore v. Regan,* 453 U.S. 654 (1981).

67. Id. at 688.

THE PRESIDENT AS EXECUTIVE (PP. 218–228)

1. *Myers v. United States,* 272 U.S. 52 (1926).

2. *Wilcox v. McConnel,* 13 Pet. 498 at 513 (1839).

3. *Williams v. United States,* 1 How. 290 at 197 (1843).

4. *Marbury v. Madison,* 1 Cr. 137 (1803).

5. *United States v. Smith,* 286 U.S. 6 (1932).

6. C. Herman Pritchett, *The American Constitution* (New York: McGraw-Hill, 1959), 319.

7. *Myers v. United States,* 272 U.S. 52 at 114 (1926).

8. *Wiener v. United States,* 357 U.S. 349 at 351 (1958).

9. James D. Richardson, ed., *Messages and Papers of the Presidents,* 20 vols. (New York: Bureau of National Literature, 1897), III: 1304.

10. *Ex parte Hennen,* 13 Pet. 230 at 257–259 (1839).

11. Carl B. Swisher, *American Constitutional Development,* 2d ed. (Cambridge, Mass.: Houghton Mifflin, 1954), 742.

12. Ibid. at 743.

13. *Myers v. United States,* 272 U.S. 52 at 174–175 (1926).

14. Id. at 117, 121–122, 130–134.

15. Id. at 134.

16. Id. at 135.

17. Id. at 192–193.

18. Id. at 247.

19. Id. at 177.

20. *Humphrey's Executor v. United States,* 295 U.S. 602 at 618–619 (1935).

21. Id. at 627.

22. Id. at 627–628.

23. Id. at 629.

24. Id. at 629–632.

25. *Wiener v. United States,* 357 U.S. 349 at 353 (1958).

26. *Morgan v. TVA,* 312 U.S. 701 (1941), cert. denied; C. Herman Pritchett, *The Tennessee Valley Authority: A Study in Public Administration* (Chapel Hill: University of North Carolina Press, 1943), 203–216.

27. *Wiener v. United States,* 357 U.S. 349 (1958).

28. Id. at 352.

29. Id. at 353, 354.

30. Id. at 356.

31. *Bowsher v. Synar,* 478 U.S. 714 at 726 (1986).

32. Id. at 726–727.

33. *Morrison v. Olson,* 487 U.S. 654 (1988).

34. Id. at 675–676, 677.

35. *In re Neagle,* 135 U.S. 1 at 64 (1890).

36. Id. at 59.

37. *United States v. Midwest Oil Co.,* 236 U.S. 459 at 469, 472–473 (1915).

38. *Field v. Clark,* 143 U.S. 649 (1892).

39. *United States v. Grimaud,* 220 U.S. 506 at 521 (1911).

40. *Youngstown Sheet and Tube Co. v. Sawyer,* 343 U.S. 579 at 587 (1952).

41. Id. at 646–647.

42. *Martin v. Mott,* 12 Wheat. 19 at 28 (1827).

43. *Luther v. Borden,* 7 How. 1 at 40 (1849).

44. *Cherokee Indian Cases,* 5 Pet. 1 (1831).

45. *In re Debs,* 158 U.S. 564 at 582, 584, 586 (1895).

46. *Youngstown Sheet and Tube Co. v. Sawyer,* 343 U.S. 579 (1952); *United States v. United Mine Workers,* 330 U.S. 258 (1947).

THE POWER TO VETO AND TO PARDON (PP. 229–236)

1. Louis Koenig, *The Chief Executive,* 5th. ed. (San Diego: Harcourt Brace Jovanovich, 1986), 162.

2. *The Federalist Papers,* with an Introduction by Clinton Rossiter (New York: New American Library, Mentor Books, 1961), No. 73, 442.

3. Ibid., 445.

4. Michael Nelson, ed., *Congressional Quarterly's Guide to the Presidency,* 2d ed. (Washington, D.C.: Congressional Quarterly, 1996), 553.

5. *Okanogan Indians et al. v. United States (The Pocket Veto Case),* 279 U.S. 655 (1929).

6. Id. at 677–679.

7. Id. at 678–679.

8. Id. at 679–680.

9. Id. at 680–681, 683–685.

10. *Wright v. United States*, 302 U.S. 583 (1938).

11. Id. at 594.

12. *CQ Almanac 1970* (Washington, D.C.: Congressional Quarterly, 1971), 592–593.

13. *Burke v. Barnes*, 479 U.S. 361 (1987).

14. *United States v. Klein*, 13 Wall. 128 (1872).

15. *Ex parte Garland*, 4 Wall. 333 at 380–381 (1867).

16. *United States v. Wilson*, 7 Pet. 150 (1833); *Biddle v. Perovich*, 274 U.S. 480 at 486 (1927).

17. *Historic Documents of 1974* (Washington, D.C.: Congressional Quarterly, 1975), 816–817.

18. Edward S. Corwin with Randall W. Bland et al., *The President: Offices and Powers*, 5th rev. ed. (New York: New York University Press, 1984), 180–181.

19. *The Federalist Papers*, No. 74, p. 447.

20. *United States v. Wilson*, 7 Pet. 150 at 160–161 (1833).

21. *Burdick v. United States*, 236 U.S. 79 (1915).

22. Id. at 90–91.

23. Charles Warren, *The Supreme Court in United States History*, rev. ed., 2 vols. (Boston: Little, Brown, 1922, 1926), II: 450–451.

24. *Ex parte Garland*, 4 Wall. 333 at 374–376 (1866).

25. Id. at 381.

26. Id. at 380.

27. Id. at 380–381.

28. Id. at 396–397.

29. *Carlesi v. New York*, 233 U.S. 51 at 59 (1914).

30. *Boyd v. United States*, 142 U.S. 450 (1892).

31. *Knote v. United States*, 95 U.S. 149 at 153–154 (1877).

32. *United States v. Klein*, 13 Wall. 128 at 142 (1872).

33. Id. at 147–148.

34. *Ex parte Wells*, 18 How. 307 at 307–309 (1856).

35. Id. at 314–315.

36. *The Laura*, 114 U.S. 411 (1885); *Illinois Central R.R. v. Bosworth*, 133 U.S. 92 (1890); *Ex parte Grossman*, 267 U.S. 87 (1925).

37. *Biddle v. Perovich*, 274 U.S. 480 at 487 (1927).

38. Id. at 485–486.

39. *Furman v. Georgia, Jackson v. Georgia, Branch v. Texas*, 408 U.S. 238 (1972).

40. *Schick v. Reed*, 419 U.S. 256 (1974).

41. Id. at 266–267.

42. Id. at 274.

PRIVILEGE AND IMMUNITY (PP. 237–242)

1. *Mississippi v. Johnson*, 4 Wall. 475 (1867).

2. *Marbury v. Madison*, 1 Cr. 137 (1803).

3. *Mississippi v. Johnson*, 4 Wall. 475 at 500–501, 498–499 (1867).

4. Id. at 501.

5. *Georgia v. Stanton*, 6 Wall. 50 (1868).

6. Id. at 77.

7. Ibid.

8. *Kendall v. United States ex. rel. Stokes*, 12 Pet. 524 at 609–610, 613 (1838).

9. Id. at 613.

10. *Little v. Bareme*, 2 Cr. 170 (1804); *United States v. Lee*, 106 U.S. 196 (1882); *Bivens v. Six Unknown Named Agents of the Federal Bureau of Narcotics*, 403 U.S. 388 (1971).

11. *Barr v. Mateo*, 360 U.S. 564 (1959); *Butz v. Economou*, 438 U.S. 478 (1978).

12. *Nixon v. Fitzgerald*, 457 U.S. 731 at 749 (1982).

13. Id. at 751–753.

14. Id. at 757–758.

15. *Harlow v. Fitzgerald*, 457 U.S. 800 (1982).

16. Norman Dorson and Richard Shattuck, "Executive Privilege, the Congress and the Court," *Ohio State Law Journal* 35: 13.

17. Herman Wollkinson, "Demand of Congressional Committees for Executive Papers," *Federal Bar Journal* 10: 103–150; Robert Kramer and Herman Marcuse, "Executive Privilege—A Study of the Period 1953–1960," *George Washington Law Review* 29: 623–718, 827–916; Irving Younger, "Congressional Investigations and Executive Secrecy: A Study in Separation of Powers," *University of Pittsburgh Law Review* 20: 757, 773.

18. J. Russell Wiggins, "Government Operations and the Public's Right to Know," *Federal Bar Journal*, XIX: 76.

19. Raoul Berger, *Executive Privilege: A Constitutional Myth* (Cambridge: Harvard University Press, 1974), 1.

20. *United States v. Nixon*, 418 U.S. 683 (1974).

21. *Kaiser Aluminum & Chem. Co. v. United States*, 157 F. Supp. 937, 943 (Ct. Cl. 1958).

22. Berger, *Executive Privilege*, 178–179, 232–233.

23. *Marbury v. Madison*, 1 Cr. 138 at 165–166 (1803).

24. Id. at 170.

25. Berger, *Executive Privilege*, 179–181, 187–194.

26. Id. at 181.

27. *Boske v. Comingore*, 177 U.S. 459 (1900); *United States ex rel. Touhy v. Ragan, Warden, et al.*, 340 U.S. 462 (1951).

28. *McGrain v. Daugherty*, 273 U.S. 135 (1927).

29. *Chicago & Southern Airlines v. Waterman S.S. Co.*, 333 U.S. 103, 105 (1948).

30. Id. at 111.

31. *United States v. Reynolds*, 345 U.S. 1 at 11 (1953).

32. Id.

33. Id.

34. "The Present Limits of Executive Privilege," Study Prepared by the Government and General Research Division of the Library of Congress, *Congressional Record*, H. 2243-46 (March 28, 1973). Cited as LC Study.

35. Ibid.

36. Eisenhower to Secretary of Defense, May 17, 1954, *Public Papers of the Presidents, Dwight D. Eisenhower, 1954* (Washington, D.C.: U.S. Government Printing Office, 1960), 483–485.

37. U.S. Congress, Senate, Committee on Armed Services, Special Preparedness Subcommittee, *Military Cold War and Speech Review Policies, Hearings*, 87th Cong., 2d sess. (Washington, D.C.: U.S. Government Printing Office, 1962), 508–509.

38. Ibid.

39. Johnson to the Hon. John E. Moss, April 2, 1965. *Public Papers of the Presidents, Lyndon B. Johnson, 1965*, 2 vols. (Washington, D.C.: U.S. Government Printing Office, 1966), II: 376.

40. U.S. Congress, Senate, Committee on the Judiciary, Subcommittee on the Separation of Powers, *Executive Privilege: The Withholding of Information by the Executive, Hearings*, 92d Cong., 1st sess. (Washington, D.C.: U.S. Government Printing Office, 1971), 2.

41. LC Study, *Congressional Record*, H. 2243-46 (March 28, 1973).

42. *New York Times Co. v. United States, United States v. Washington Post*, 403 U.S. 713 (1971).

43. *Environmental Protection Agency v. Mink*, 410 U.S. 73 (1973); *Congress and the Nation*, Vol. IV (Washington, D.C.: Congressional Quarterly, 1977), 805–806.

44. *United States v. Nixon, Nixon v. United States*, 418 U.S. 683 at 705–706 (1974).

45. Id. at 706–707.

46. Id. at 708, 711.

47. Id. at 711–713.

48. *Nixon v. Administrator, General Services Administration*, 433 U.S. 425 (1977).

49. Id. at 433–435.

50. Id. at 443.

51. Id. at 451–452.

52. Id. at 520.

53. Id. at 545.

CONFRONTATION: THE PRESIDENT VERSUS THE COURT (PP. 243–257)

1. Samuel F. Bemis, *A Diplomatic History of the United States* (New York: Holt, 1936), 95–100.

2. Samuel E. Morison, Henry S. Commager, and William E. Leuchtenburg, *The Growth of the American Republic*, 2 vols. (New York: Oxford University Press, 1969), I: 218–319.

3. James M. Smith, *Freedom's Fetters: The Alien and Sedition Laws and American Civil Liberties* (Ithaca, N.Y.: Cornell University Press, 1956).

4. Frank M. Anderson, "Contemporary Opinion of the Virginia and Kentucky Resolutions," *American Historical Review* V: 45–63, 225–252; Adrienne Koch, *Jefferson and Madison, The Great Collaboration* (New York: Knopf, 1950).

5. Eugene P. Link, *Democratic-Republican Societies* (New York: Octagon Books, 1965); Noble E. Cunningham Jr., *The Jeffersonian Republicans: The Formation of Party Organization, 1789–1801* (Chapel Hill: University of North Carolina Press, 1957); Alexander DeConde, *The Quasi-War: The Politics and Diplomacy of the Undeclared War with France, 1797–1801* (New York: Scribner's, 1966).

6. Donald O. Dewey, *Marshall versus Jefferson: The Political Background of Marbury v. Madison* (New York: Knopf, 1970), 3–4.

7. Ibid., 5–8.

8. Leonard Baker, *John Marshall: A Life in Law* (New York: Macmillan, 1974), 61.

9. William Stinchcombe, "The Diplomacy of the WXYZ Affair," *William and Mary Quarterly*, 3d series, XXXIV: 590–617.

10. Dewey, *Marshall versus Jefferson*, 31.

11. Erwin C. Surrency, "The Judiciary Act of 1801," *American Journal of Legal History* 2: 53–65; Kathryn Turner, "Federalist Policy and the Judiciary Act of 1801," *William and Mary Quarterly* XXII: 3–32; Dewey, *Marshall versus Jefferson*, 55, 58–59.

12. Dewey, *Marshall versus Jefferson*, 68–69; Richard E. Ellis, *The Jeffersonian Crisis: Courts and Politics in the Young Republic* (New York: Oxford University Press, 1971), 45, 50–51.

13. *Marbury v. Madison*, 1 Cr. 137 at 138–139 (1803).

14. Id. at 173.

15. Id. at 158.

16. Dewey, *Marshall versus Jefferson*, 135–141.

17. See *Holmes v. Walton* (New Jersey, 1780); *Trevett v. Weeden* (Rhode Island, 1786); *Bayard v. Singleton* (North Carolina, 1787); *Ware v. Hylton*, 3 Dall. 199 (1796).

18. Dewey, *Marshall versus Jefferson*, 141; Ellis, *The Jeffersonian Crisis*, 72–73, 76.

19. Baker, *John Marshall*, 148; Richard B. Lillich, "The Chase Impeachment," *American Journal of Legal History* 4 (1960): 49–72.

20. Baker, *John Marshall*, 418–419; Dewey, *Marshall versus Jefferson*, 148–149.

21. Ellis, *The Jeffersonian Crisis*, 81.

22. Charles Warren, *The Supreme Court in United States History*, 2 vols. (Boston: Little, Brown, 1922), I: 236–237.

23. Ibid.

24. Leonard Levy, *Jefferson and Civil Liberties: The Darker Side* (New York: Quadrangle, 1973).

25. Baker, *John Marshall*, 452–453.

26. Thomas P. Abernathy, *The Burr Conspiracy* (New York: Oxford University Press, 1954).

27. "The Deposition of William Eaton, Esq.," in *Ex parte Bollman, Ex parte Swartout*, 4 Cr. 75 Appendix A at 463–466 (1807).

28. Baker, *John Marshall*, 452–453.

29. Dewey, *Marshall versus Jefferson*, 162–163.

30. *United States v. Burr*, 25 Fed. Cas. 187 (No. 14,694) (1807).

31. Raoul Berger, *Executive Privilege: A Constitutional Myth* (Cambridge: Harvard University Press, 1974), 193.

32. Bradley Chapin, *The American Law of Treason: Revolutionary and Early National Origins* (Seattle: University of Washington Press, 1964).

33. Baker, *John Marshall*, 464–465, 513.

34. Ibid., 514–515.

35. James D. Richardson, ed., *Messages and Papers of the Presidents*, 20 vols. (New York: Bureau of National Literature, 1897), III: 1145.

36. Morison, Commager, and Leuchtenburg, *The Growth of the American Republic*, I: 419–423; John W. Ward, *Andrew Jackson: Symbol for an Age* (New York: Oxford University Press, 1962).

37. Warren, *The Supreme Court in United States History*, I: 730–731.

38. *Johnson v. McIntosh*, 8 Wheat. 543 (1823); Warren, *The Supreme Court in United States History*, I: 732–733.

39. Ibid., 733–734.

40. *Cherokee Nation v. Georgia*, 5 Pet. 1 (1831).

41. *Worcester v. Georgia*, 6 Pet. 515 (1832).

42. Warren, *The Supreme Court in United States History*, I: 754.

43. Morison, Commager, and Leuchtenburg, *The Growth of the American Republic*, I: 438–442.

44. Richardson, *Messages and Papers of the Presidents*, III: 1203–1204.

45. Ibid., VII: 3210.

46. *Ex parte Merryman*, Fed. Cas. (No. 9847); Carl B. Swisher, *American Constitutional Development*, 2d ed. (Cambridge, Mass.: Houghton Mifflin, 1954), 279.

47. Ibid., 280–281.

48. *Ex parte Merryman* in *Documents of American History*, 7th ed., ed. Henry S. Commager (New York: Appleton-Century-Crofts, 1963), 398–401.

49. Richardson, *Messages and Papers of the Presidents*, VII: 3225–3226.

50. Carl B. Swisher, *History of the Supreme Court of the United States, Vol. V: The Taney Period, 1836–64* (New York: Macmillan, 1971), 852–853.

51. Warren, *The Supreme Court in United States History*, II: 372–373.

52. Richardson, *Messages and Papers of the Presidents*, VII: 3303–3305.

53. Lincoln to Erastus Corning, June 12, 1863, in *The Complete Works of Abraham Lincoln*, 12 vols., ed. John C. Nicolay and John Hay (New York: Francis D. Tandy, 1905–1934), VIII: 298–314.

54. Alfred H. Kelly and Winfred A. Harbison, *The American Constitution*, 7th ed. (New York: Norton, 1991), 413.

55. *Ex parte Milligan*, 4 Wall. 2 (1866).

56. Morison, Commager, and Leuchtenburg, *The Growth of the American Republic*, II: 485–487, 502–503.

57. Samuel I. Rosenman, comp., *The Public Papers and Addresses of Franklin D. Roosevelt*, 5 vols. (New York: Random House, 1938), II: 15.

58. William F. Swindler, *Court and Constitution in the 20th Century*, 2 vols. (Indianapolis and New York: Bobbs-Merrill, 1970), II: 20–21; Morison, Commager, and Leuchtenburg, *The Growth of the American Republic*, II: 484–489.

59. Swisher, *American Constitutional Development*, 848–859; Commager, *Documents of American History*, 242–246.

60. Swindler, *Court and Constitution in the 20th Century*, II: 23–24; *U.S. Statutes at Large*, Vol. XLVIII, 195.

61. Robert H. Jackson, *The Struggle for Judicial Supremacy: A Study of a Crisis in American Power Politics* (New York: Random House, 1941), 83–84; Swisher, *American Constitutional Development*, 920–921.

62. *Home Building and Loan Association v. Blaisdell*, 290 U.S. 398 (1934).

63. *Nebbia v. New York*, 291 U.S. 502 (1934).

64. *Norman v. The Baltimore and Ohio Railroad Co.*, 294 U.S. 240 (1935); *John N. Perry v. United States*, 294 U.S. 330 (1935); *Ashwander et al. v. Tennessee Valley Authority*, 297 U.S. 288 (1936).

65. *Panama Refining Co. v. Ryan*, 293 U.S. 388 (1935); *Amazon Petroleum Corp. v. Ryan*, 293 U.S. 389 (1935).

66. *Railroad Retirement Board v. Alton*, 295 U.S. 330 (1935).

67. *Louisville Bank v. Radford*, 295 U.S. 555 (1935).

68. *Schechter Poultry Corp. v. United States*, 295 U.S. 495 (1935).

69. *Humphrey's Executor v. United States*, 295 U.S. 602 (1935).

70. Jackson, *The Struggle for Judicial Supremacy*, 12.

71. Ibid., 113.

72. Ibid.

73. *Schechter Poultry Corp. v. United States*, 295 U.S. 495 at 536–539, 541–542 (1935).

74. Rosenman, *The Public Papers and Addresses of Franklin D. Roosevelt,* IV: 215, 221.

75. *United States v. Butler,* 297 U.S. 1 (1936).

76. *Carter v. Carter Coal Co.,* 298 U.S. 238 (1936).

77. Id. at 288–289, 303.

78. *Ashton v. Cameron County District,* 298 U.S. 513 (1936).

79. Id. at 542–543.

80. Swindler, *Court and Constitution in the 20th Century,* II: 56.

81. Kelly and Harbison, *The American Constitution,* 714.

82. Rosenman, *The Public Papers and Addresses of Franklin D. Roosevelt,* V: 635–636, 638–639, 641–642.

83. "Reform of the Federal Judiciary," 75th Cong., 1st sess., Sen. Report No. 711.

84. Commager, *Documents of American History,* 382–383.

85. "Recommendation to Reorganize Judicial Branch," 75th Cong., 1st sess., HR Doc. No. 142.

86. Harold L. Ickes, *The Secret Diary of Harold L. Ickes,* 3 vols. (New York: Simon and Schuster, 1954), II: 7.

87. Jackson, *The Struggle for Judicial Supremacy,* 187.

88. Ickes, *Diary,* II: 74–75.

89. Ibid., 88–89.

90. "Address by the President of the United States," March 9, 1937, in Commager, *Documents of American History,* 383–387.

91. Ickes, *Diary,* II: 74–75, 93, 104, 109, 115, 251; Swindler, *Court and Constitution in the 20th Century,* 68–71.

92. Ickes, *Diary,* II: 70, 98, 100, 103, 105–106, 251, 424.

93. Swindler, *Court and Constitution in the 20th Century,* 71–73.

94. *West Coast Hotel Co. v. Parrish,* 300 U.S. 379 at 390 (1937).

95. *Wright v. Vinton Branch,* 300 U.S. 440 (1937).

96. *N.L.R.B. v. Jones & Laughlin Steel Corp.,* 301 U.S. 1 (1937).

97. *Steward Machine Co. v. Davis,* 301 U.S. 548 (1937); *Helvering v. Davis,* 307 U.S. 619 (1937).

98. *Morehead v. New York ex rel. Tipaldo,* 298 U.S. 587 (1936).

99. *West Coast Hotel v. Parrish,* 300 U.S. 379 (1937).

100. Max Freedman, ann., *Roosevelt and Frankfurter: Their Correspondence, 1928–1945* (Boston: Little, Brown, 1967), 392–395.

101. "Judiciary Reform Act of 1937, August 24, 1937," in Commager, *Documents of American History,* 391–393; Jackson, *The Struggle for Judicial Supremacy,* 192–193; Ickes, *Diary,* II: 144, 152–153, 170–172.

102. Kelly and Harbison, *The American Constitution,* 718.

103. James T. Patterson, *Congressional Conservatism and the New Deal: The Growth of the Conservative Coalition in Congress, 1933–1939* (Lexington: University of Kentucky Press, 1967).

104. *United States v. Darby,* 312 U.S. 100 (1941); *Mulford v. Smith,* 307 U.S. 38 (1939).

105. Harry S. Truman, *Memoirs,* 2 vols. (Garden City, N.Y.: Doubleday, 1956), II: 465–467.

106. Ibid., 468.

107. Ibid., 471–472.

108. Ibid., 469–470.

109. *Youngstown Sheet and Tube Co. v. Sawyer,* 343 U.S. 579 at 609 (1952).

110. Id. at 662.

111. Id. at 632.

112. Id.

113. Truman, *Memoirs,* II: 428.

114. Ibid., 477.

115. Ibid., 478.

116. *New York Times Co. v. United States; United States v. The Washington Post,* 403 U.S. 713 (1971).

117. Id. at 714–715.

118. Id. at 724–725.

119. 82 *United States Statutes at Large,* 198 ff., PL 90-351.

120. *United States v. United States District Court,* 407 U.S. 297 at 301 (1972).

121. Id. at 317.

122. Kelly and Harbison, *The American Constitution,* 1020–1021.

123. *Nixon, The Fifth Year of His Presidency* (Washington, D.C.: Congressional Quarterly, 1974), 153-A.

124. *Train v. City of New York,* 420 U.S. 35 (1975); *Train v. Campaign Clean Water,* 420 U.S. 136 (1975).

125. *Watergate: Chronology of a Crisis* (Washington, D.C.: Congressional Quarterly, 1975), 191–194, 220, 224–225, 293–294, 297, 341–345, 353–362.

126. Ibid., 535–537, 600–648.

127. Ibid., 689–692, 711–723, 734–742.

128. Ibid., 754–756.

129. PL 93-526 (1974); *Congress and the Nation,* Vol. IV (Washington, D.C.: Congressional Quarterly, 1977), 952.

130. *Nixon v. Administrator, General Services Administration,* 433 U.S. 425 (1977).

131. *Nixon v. Warner Communications Inc. et al.,* 453 U.S. 589 (1978).

CHAPTER 6

The Court and Judicial Power: Article III

DURING ITS FIRST TWELVE YEARS as a nation, the United States had neither a Supreme Court nor any federal system of courts.

The lack of a federal court system seemed to many a major factor contributing to the "national humiliation" the young nation suffered during the period of its government under the Articles of Confederation.[1]

Article III of the Constitution of 1789 remedied the deficiency with two concise provisions. The first provided that "[t]he judicial power of the United States, shall be vested in one Supreme Court," and whatever inferior federal courts Congress "from time to time" saw fit to establish. The second set out the types of cases and controversies that should be considered by a federal—rather than a state—tribunal.

Among the most articulate of the advocates of a federal judiciary was Alexander Hamilton. In *The Federalist Papers* he argued that an independent system of national courts was "peculiarly essential" in a limited government like that set up by the Constitution. The limits that the Constitution devised to curtail the power of Congress, he wrote, "can be preserved in practice no other way than through the medium of courts of justice, whose duty it must be to declare all acts contrary to the manifest tenor of the Constitution void. Without this, all the reservations of particular rights or privileges would amount to nothing."[2] National power required national courts. Hamilton wrote,

[I]f it be possible at any rate to construct a federal government capable of regulating the common concerns and preserving the general tranquility . . . [i]t must stand in need of no intermediate legislations, but must itself be empowered to employ the arm of the ordinary magistrate to execute its own resolutions. The majesty of the national authority must be manifested through the medium of the courts of justice.[3]

Despite his high hopes for the contribution a national judiciary would make to national power and stability, Hamilton recognized that "the judiciary is beyond comparison the weakest of the three departments . . . it is in continual jeopardy of being over-powered, awed, or influenced by its coordinate branches."[4]

Congress filled in the skeletal structure of national judicial power with the Judiciary Act of 1789 and subsequent statutes. But it was left chiefly to the Supreme Court to define the jurisdiction of the federal courts—itself included—with precision, and to guide the use of the powers of the federal judiciary. With every decision it has issued since its initial term, the Supreme Court has shaped the power of the federal courts.

The federal judicial power is limited. It extends only to certain types of cases and controversies. And its arsenal is small. Therefore, it has been necessary that its authority be exercised with care and restraint.

Federal judicial power grew slowly through the interaction of the courts, the president, who appoints members, and Congress, which exerts statutory control over much of the jurisdiction and most of the powers of the federal courts.

Questions of jurisdiction, proper remedies, abstention, and comity seem technical matters to many—often overlooked by those who find more interest in the substantive issues resolved by the court. But it is the resolution of these seemingly esoteric matters that governs the breadth of access, and the scope of the remedy, that is available to those who seek redress in the federal courts.

Overall, the Supreme Court has carefully circumscribed its powers, its jurisdiction, and those of the lower federal courts. Felix Frankfurter, writing in the 1920s, described this self-limitation as possibly "the most significant aspect of judicial action in the American constitutional scheme." Such self-denial, he wrote, was "the expression of an energizing philosophy of the distribution of governmental powers. For a court to hold that decision does not belong to it, is merely to recognize that a problem calls for the exercise of initiative and experimentation possessed only by political processes."[5]

By exercising self-restraint, the Court has clearly demonstrated its awareness of the prerogatives of its coordinate branches—Congress and the executive—and of the states. As Justice Lewis F. Powell Jr. has written:

Repeated and essentially head-on confrontations between the life-tenured branch and the representative branches of the government will not, in the long run, be beneficial to either. The public confidence essential to the former and the vitality critical to the latter may well erode if we do not exercise self-restraint in the utilization of our power to negate the actions of the other branches.[6]

This concern has infused the Court's dealing with questions of jurisdiction and judicial review, requests for orders halting state proceedings or mandating federal action, access to writs of habeas corpus, and political matters. In two notable periods—just before the Civil War and during the New Deal—the Court abandoned caution in such matters and deliberately collided with Congress and the executive. For this assertiveness, it was severely criticized.

For all its limits—constitutional, statutory, and self-imposed—the federal judiciary possesses extraordinary power. Indeed, wrote Charles Grove Haines early in this century, "the distinguishing characteristic of the American system of government is the extraordinary power and position of the judiciary."

Haines continued:

The practice of all departments of government to defer to the courts and abide by their decisions, when in a suit between private parties, the majority of justices hold that in their opinion a statute or executive order is unconstitutional and therefore null and void, is the most significant feature of constitutional law in the United States.[7]

Haines wrote that assessment in 1932—before the New Deal confrontation of Congress, the Court, and the president, before the revolution in civil rights accelerated by Court decisions, before the *Steel Seizure Case*, and before the Watergate ruling that drove a president from office.

But these events reinforced his general assessment of modern judicial power. As another constitutional scholar, Alexander Bickel, wrote more recently: Hamilton's least dangerous branch of the American government has become "the most extraordinarily powerful court of law the world has ever known."[8]

Judicial power is of no use to a court that lacks jurisdiction. Unless a court has jurisdiction over the persons or issues in a dispute, its power cannot reach the matter. Jurisdiction has been described as the vessel into which judicial power may be poured, the prerequisite to the exercise of judicial power.[1]

In 1869 Chief Justice Salmon P. Chase explained:

Without jurisdiction the court cannot proceed at all in any cause. Jurisdiction is the power to declare the law, and when it ceases to exist, the only function remaining to the court is that of announcing the fact and dismissing the cause.[2]

All federal courts are courts of limited jurisdiction, in contrast to state courts, which are presumed to have jurisdiction over a case, unless jurisdiction is disproved.

Most questions of federal jurisdiction affect the distribution of power between the states and the federal government. "Expansion of the jurisdiction of the federal courts," one scholar has reminded us, "diminishes the power of the states."[3]

Constitutional Possibilities and Political Realities

Article III, Section 2, of the Constitution outlines a broad area for the exercise of federal judicial power:

The Judicial Power shall extend to all Cases, in Law and Equity, arising under this Constitution, the Laws of the United States, and Treaties made, or which shall be made, under their Authority;—to all cases affecting Ambassadors, other public Ministers and Consuls;—to all Cases of admiralty and maritime Jurisdiction;—to Controversies to which the United States shall be a party;—to Controversies between two or more States;—between Citizens of different States;—between Citizens of the same State claiming Lands under Grants of different States, and between a State, or the Citizens thereof, and foreign States, Citizens, or Subjects.

This general grant of jurisdiction divides into two categories: cases that merit federal consideration because of their subject matter—a claim or question arising under the Constitution, federal statutes or treaties, or admiralty or maritime law—and cases that merit federal attention because of the parties involved—the United States, a state, citizens of different states, and representatives of foreign countries.

Article III gave the Supreme Court original jurisdiction over two of the latter category of cases. The Court has the right to hear cases initially, before any other court, if they involve ambassadors or other foreign diplomats, or if they involve states.

With those exceptions, the Constitution granted Congress the power of determining how much of the broad area outlined in Article III actually came within the jurisdiction of the federal courts.

The Supreme Court clearly has kept in mind the language of Article III giving Congress complete control over the existence and jurisdiction of all federal courts below the Supreme Court

itself. "[T]he judicial power of the United States," stated the Court in 1845, is "dependent for its distribution and organization, and for the modes of its exercise, entirely upon the action of Congress," with some exceptions related to the high court itself.[4]

Twenty years later the Court reiterated that point: "[T]wo things are necessary to create jurisdiction. . . . The Constitution must have given to the court the capacity to take it, and an Act of Congress must have supplied it."[5]

Congress moved quickly to exercise this power. The First Congress enacted the Judiciary Act of 1789. It set up a system of lower federal courts (district courts and circuit courts with limited jurisdiction), spelled out the appellate jurisdiction of the Supreme Court, and gave the Court the power to review state court rulings rejecting federal claims.[6] *(See text of Judiciary Act of 1789, pp. 979–984, Vol. II.)* The 1789 act made clear that most cases would be resolved in state courts. Federal district courts were to hear admiralty and maritime matters; circuit courts would hear cases involving disputes between residents of different states, the United States and aliens, and where more than $500 was at stake. Circuit courts also had some limited "federal question" jurisdiction concurrent with state courts, as well as some jurisdiction to hear appeals from district court rulings.

The Supreme Court acquiesced in this congressional limitation of federal jurisdiction. Writing a 1799 decision holding federal courts without jurisdiction over a particular case, Chief Justice Oliver Ellsworth—himself one of the authors of the Judiciary Act—declared that "[a] circuit court . . . is of limited jurisdiction and has cognizance, not of cases generally, but only of a few specially circumstanced."[7]

Underscoring that point, Justice Samuel Chase added a footnote:

The notion has frequently been entertained that the federal courts derive their judicial power immediately from the constitution; but the political truth is, that the disposal of the judicial power (except in a few specified instances) belongs to Congress. If Congress has given the power to this court, we possess it, not otherwise; and if Congress has not given the power to us or to any other court, it still remains at the legislative disposal. Besides, Congress is not bound . . . to enlarge the jurisdiction of the federal courts, to every subject, in every form, which the constitution might warrant.[8]

A MATTER OF SUBJECT

Although Article III clearly envisioned that federal courts would have the final word on cases raising claims under the Constitution, federal laws, and treaties, it was eighty years before Congress granted such jurisdiction to those courts. Until then, most federal questions were resolved in state courts, subject to review—if the federal claim were denied—by the Supreme Court.

The 1789 act did grant the Supreme Court the power to con-

THE JURISDICTIONAL AMOUNT

To keep trivial matters out of the federal courts, Congress throughout the nation's history, has set a "jurisdictional amount"—a dollar figure for the minimum amount that must be in controversy before most cases can enter the federal judicial system.

In 1789 the amount was set at $500. In 1887 the figure was quadrupled to $2,000. The next increase was in 1911 to $3,000—where it remained until 1958, when Congress raised it to $10,000. In 1988, it was increased to $50,000.

From 1789 until 1925 there was also a jurisdictional amount—of varying levels—required for appeal to the Supreme Court in certain cases. Since 1925 there has been no such requirement.

In the 1970s the main categories of cases affected by the jurisdictional amount requirement were diversity cases and some federal question cases.

In many modern statutes, Congress has granted federal courts jurisdiction over cases without regard to the amount of money involved. Among the areas in which this requirement for federal jurisdiction is waived by statute are admiralty and maritime cases, bankruptcy matters, and cases arising under acts of Congress regulating commerce; patent, trademark, and copyright cases; internal revenue, customs duty, and postal matters; most civil rights cases and elections disputes; and cases to which the United States is a party.

SOURCE: Charles Alan Wright, *The Law of Federal Courts*, 4th ed. (St. Paul, Minn.: West Publishing, 1983), 176–208.

sider the constitutionality of state laws—when state courts rejected federally based challenges to them. But the act said nothing about any power of the Court to review acts of Congress for their constitutional validity. The Court simply assumed that power early in its history. *(See "Review Acts of Congress," pp. 277–279.)*

Federal Questions

In 1875 Congress granted lower federal courts virtually the entire federal question jurisdiction outlined in Article III.

For the first time, all cases arising under the Constitution, federal laws, or treaties could be initiated in federal district courts.

Professors Felix Frankfurter and James M. Landis, half a century later, described the 1875 act as revolutionary:

From 1789 down to the Civil War the lower federal courts were, in the main, designed as protection to citizens litigating outside of their own states and thereby exposed to the threatened prejudice of unfriendly tribunals. Barring admiralty jurisdiction, the federal courts were subsidiary courts. The Act of 1875 marks a revolution in their function. . . . These courts ceased to be restricted tribunals of fair dealing between citizens of different states and became the primary and powerful reliances for vindicating every right given by the Constitution, the laws and treaties of the United States. Thereafter, any suit asserting such a right could be begun in federal courts; any such action begun in state court could be removed to the federal courts for disposition.[9]

No subsequent jurisdictional statute has so greatly enlarged the jurisdiction of the federal courts. But as Congress has enacted laws reaching into areas heretofore left to state control, federal question jurisdiction has become a larger and larger category.

The new statutes have brought particular expansion of this category of federal cases to labor law and civil rights law.

Under the Judiciary Act of 1789, jurisdiction over admiralty and maritime matters was assigned to federal district courts. The Brooklyn Bridge can be seen in the background of this 1887 view of New York Harbor.

Admiralty and Maritime Law

"Like the Constitution itself," wrote Frankfurter and Landis, the Judiciary Act of 1789 "was a response to the practical problems and controversies of our early history."[10]

To its contemporaries, the admiralty and maritime jurisdiction of federal district courts did not appear the limited area it does to modern interpretation. Instead, it reflected a fact of life:

Trade requires dependable laws and courts. Maritime commerce was then the jugular vein of the Thirteen States. The need for a body of law applicable throughout the nation was recognized by every shade of opinion in the Constitutional Convention.[11]

And so, to ensure that a uniform body of admiralty and maritime law would develop, Congress vested jurisdiction over all such cases in the federal district courts. Although the Supreme Court initially adopted a narrow definition of the waters covered by the grant, it eventually expanded its view to include virtually all navigable and potentially navigable waterways within the country.[12] *(See box, The Coastal Licensing Act, p. 93, in Chapter 4.)*

A QUESTION OF PARTY

To preserve national sovereignty, to provide a neutral forum, and to ensure federal control of foreign relations, the Constitution gave federal courts jurisdiction over cases in which the United States itself was a party, in cases between states and between citizens of different states, and in cases involving representatives of foreign governments.

United States Versus . . .

Because of the protection of sovereign immunity, most cases involving the United States are initiated by the federal government. *(See box, The Sovereign's Immunity, p. 271.)*

When the United States comes into the federal courts as a plaintiff, however, it must satisfy the same requirements as any other party seeking to file a federal suit. It must demonstrate a real interest that is seriously threatened in a manner susceptible of judicial resolution.

The Court, however, has made clear that such an interest need not be simply one of property or monetary concern: "The obligations which it [the United States] is under to promote the interest of all, and to prevent the wrongdoing of one resulting in injury to the general welfare, is often of itself sufficient to give it a standing in court."[13] *(See "Standing to Sue," pp. 300–302.)*

Cases brought by the United States against a state are adjudicated in federal court. The first such case before the Supreme Court arrived in 1890—with no challenge from the state to Supreme Court jurisdiction. Two years later, however, when the United States sued Texas in the Supreme Court, Texas argued that such federal jurisdiction was an infringement of its sovereignty.

The Supreme Court quickly disposed of that argument: when Texas entered the Union, it had acquiesced in the provisions of Article III extending federal judicial power to all cases arising under the Constitution, federal laws, or treaties, without regard to the parties involved; and to all controversies in which the United States was a party, without regard to the subject of the dispute; and granting the Supreme Court original jurisdiction over cases in which states were parties.[14]

The Court does not automatically take jurisdiction of all such cases. It has refused those in which it appeared that the matter at issue was only a difference of opinion and not an actual collision of interests between state and national government.[15]

State Versus State

The Supreme Court has original and exclusive jurisdiction over cases between states. *(See "Interstate Relations," pp. 381–383, in Chapter 7.)*

As in the case of suits brought by the United States, the Court does not necessarily agree to accept jurisdiction over all interstate cases. Refusing to consider a tax-based dispute between Massachusetts and Missouri in 1939 the Court explained:

To constitute . . . a [justiciable] controversy, it must appear that the complaining State has suffered a wrong through the action of the other State, furnishing ground for judicial redress, or is asserting a right against the other State which is susceptible of judicial enforcement according to the accepted principles of the common law or equity systems of jurisprudence. . . . In the exercise of our original jurisdiction so as truly to fulfill the constitutional purpose we not only must look to the nature of the interest of the complaining state—the essential quality of the right asserted—but we must also inquire whether recourse to that jurisdiction . . . is necessary for the State's protection.[16]

Citizen Versus State

Taking the language of Article III literally, the Supreme Court—in its first major decision, issued in 1793—overrode claims of state immunity from suits brought without the state's consent, and it held that citizens of one state could sue another state in federal court, even over the state's objection.[17] Within five years the decision in *Chisholm v. Georgia* was overruled by ratification of the Eleventh Amendment, which narrowed federal jurisdiction to cases initiated by a state against citizens of another state or initiated by those citizens against the state with its consent. *(See details of Chisholm v. Georgia, pp. 316–317, in Chapter 7.)*

The Supreme Court has original, but not exclusive, jurisdiction over such cases. Only civil cases between states and nonresidents may come into federal court under this provision; states may not use federal courts to enforce state criminal laws against nonresidents.[18] And the Court has held that a state's suit against its own citizens is outside the scope of federal judicial power and can be initiated only in state courts.[19]

Furthermore, when the state is allowed to come into federal court to sue a nonresident—often a corporation—the Supreme Court has required that the state be defending its own interest or the general welfare of its population—not simply the private interest of some individual resident of the state.[20]

Citizen Versus Citizen

"A . . . powerful influence behind the demand for federal courts was due to the friction between individual states which came to the surface after the danger of the common enemy had disappeared," wrote Professors Frankfurter and Landis. "In one respect it gave rise to lively suspicions and hostilities by the citizens of one state toward those of another as well as toward aliens. This fear of parochial prejudice, dealing unjustly with litigants from other states and foreign countries, undermined the sense of security necessary for commercial intercourse."[21]

To ensure a neutral forum for the resolution of disputes between citizens of different states, Congress concurred with the grant of jurisdiction in Article III, giving the new circuit courts authority to hear such "diversity" cases.

The Supreme Court generally has required "complete diversity" of residence, ruling in 1806 that if diversity was the basis for federal jurisdiction over a case, no party on one side of a case could be a citizen of the same state as any party on the other side.[22] In certain types of cases, the Court has held that Congress can waive this strict interpretation of the diversity of residence requirement.[23]

A few years after the Court announced in 1806 the strict application of the diversity requirement, it applied a corollary to make it more difficult for persons challenging corporate actions to move their cases into federal courts by citing diversity of residence.

In 1810 the Court held that such a case could come into federal court only if all a corporation's stockholders were citizens of a state other than that of the plaintiff.[24] As a result, there was very little corporate litigation in federal courts until 1844, when the Supreme Court overruled itself and decided that, for purposes of determining diversity jurisdiction, a corporation would be assumed to be a citizen of the state in which it was chartered.

This assumption was subsequently replaced by one that viewed all of a corporation's stockholders as citizens of the state of its incorporation.[25] This "developing doctrine of corporate citizenship," noted Frankfurter and Landis, "enormously extended" the reach of federal diversity jurisdiction.[26]

One primary limitation on diversity cases is the "jurisdictional amount" imposed by law for federal jurisdiction. Initially $500, this amount has been increased over time and in 1996 was $50,000. Cases between residents of different states involving less than $50,000 are heard by state courts. (Certain types of cases—such as divorce and custody cases—generally are left to state courts regardless of the amount of money involved.)[27] *(See box, The Jurisdictional Amount, p. 264.)*

Since 1890 efforts have been made to abolish federal diversity jurisdiction as an anachronism that simply burdens the federal courts. These efforts have been consistently unsuccessful.

The jurisdiction of federal courts over cases in which citizens of the same states claimed land under grants from different states quickly became obsolete.

THE RIGHT TO REMOVE CASES FROM STATE

With the expansion of federal jurisdiction, Congress also has enlarged the right of persons charged initially in state courts to "remove" or transfer those cases into federal courts for trial and final resolution. The Judiciary Act of 1789, which left most matters to state courts, provided a limited right of removal from state to federal courts in civil suits involving aliens, diversity of residence or of land grant sources, and involving more than $500.

In 1815 Congress provided a similar right of removal in all cases involving federal customs officials—and, in 1833, involving federal revenue officials.

The Civil War brought further expansion of this right—to include all persons sued in state courts for actions under federal authority during the war. The Supreme Court upheld the validity of these removal statutes in 1868:

It is the right and the duty of the National Government to have its constitution and laws interpreted and applied by its own judicial tribunals. In cases arising under them, properly brought before it, this court is the final arbiter.

Without such a provision for removal, state courts could punish federal officials for carrying out federal law or policy. A government without the power to protect such an official, wrote the Court, "would be one of pitiable weakness, and would wholly fail to meet the ends which the framers of the Constitution had in view."[1]

Twelve years later the Court upheld the right of a federal revenue officer, charged with murder for killing a man who was defending an illegal still, to have his trial take place in federal, not state courts.

"If, whenever and wherever a case arises under the Constitution and laws or treaties of the United States, the National Government cannot take control of it," wrote Justice William Strong for the Court, "whether it be civil or criminal, in any stage of its progress, [the National Government's] judicial power is, at least, temporarily silenced, instead of being at all times supreme."[2]

The Court viewed the power of Congress to enact removal statutes as part of its power to enact all laws necessary and proper to carry into effect the enumerated powers granted it and the federal courts by the Constitution. As Congress enlarged the

Foreign Relations

To ensure that control of foreign relations remained unmistakably in the hands of national—not local and state—authorities, the Constitution granted the federal courts power to hear all cases between a state or American citizens and a foreign state or its citizens or subjects, and all cases involving ambassadors, public ministers, or consuls.

After the Supreme Court made clear that a foreign nation, like a state, could be sued in federal court only if it gave its con-

INTO FEDERAL COURT

"federal question" jurisdiction of the federal courts after the Civil War, it also expanded the right of removal. That right remains firmly established. The defendant in any civil case that could have been initiated in federal court may transfer the case to a federal court. A federal official sued or prosecuted in state court for official acts may remove his case into federal court. And a defendant in any case, civil or criminal, who can show that he is denied, or is unable to enforce, his constitutional civil rights in a state court may have his case transferred into federal court.

Concerned about how the removal of such "civil rights" cases might affect federal-state relationships, the Court has allowed them to be removed only when a defendant has presented convincing evidence that he will be denied his federally ensured rights if brought to trial in a state court. Two pairs of cases, in 1880 and again in 1966, illustrate this caution on the part of the Court.

The first "civil rights" removal provision was part of the Civil Rights Act of 1866. On March 1, 1880, the Supreme Court ruled in a pair of cases concerning this right of removal and demonstrated the strict scrutiny it gave such requests.

1880 RULINGS

Taylor Strauder, a black man charged with murder in West Virginia, was allowed to remove his case for trial from state to federal courts because he could point to a state law that excluded blacks from jury duty. The Court found this law persuasive evidence that he would, by state action, be denied his equal rights during a state trial.[3]

But Burwell and Lee Reynolds, two black brothers charged with murder in Virginia, were not so lucky. Their claim was similar to Strauder's, but they could cite no state law excluding blacks from the juries of the state. They could only point to the fact that there was no black on the jury that had indicted them or the one empaneled to try them. This was evidence, they argued, of strong community prejudice that would operate to deny them equal rights. Taking a narrow view of state action, the Court refused to allow removal of the Reynolds's trial to federal courts.[4]

For the next eighty years the Supreme Court had no occasion to rule on the scope of this right because there was no law providing for appeal of a federal judge's refusal to allow removal of a case from state court.

1966 RULINGS

In one of its first modern statements on the right of removal, the Supreme Court—in another pair of cases—renewed its insistence upon a careful application of the removal law.

Civil rights demonstrators were charged with trespass under Georgia law for attempting to exercise their right of equal access to public accommodations, which had been secured by the Civil Rights Act of 1964. The demonstrators sought to remove their trials to federal court, and the Supreme Court granted that request.[5] But on the same day in 1966 the Supreme Court refused to allow removal of a case in which civil rights demonstrators were charged under Mississippi law with obstructing the streets and otherwise disrupting the peace of the town of Greenwood.[6]

The situations in Georgia and in Mississippi, in the Court's view, were different. The Georgia demonstrators were exercising a right granted by federal law. But no federal law gave the Mississippi demonstrators the right "to obstruct a public street, to contribute to the delinquency of a minor, to drive an automobile without a license, or to bite a policeman."[7]

Justice Potter Stewart stated the Court's view of the authority granted under the civil rights removal statute of 1866. The law

does not require and does not permit the judges of the federal courts to put their brethren of the state judiciary on trial. Under . . . [the law] the vindication of the defendant's federal rights is left to the state courts except in the rare situations where it can be clearly predicted by reason of the operation of a pervasive and explicit state or federal law that those rights will inevitably be denied by the very act of bringing the defendant to trial in the state court.[8]

Congress could enlarge the conditions under which civil rights cases could be transferred from state to federal courts, Stewart wrote, but "if changes are to be made in the long-settled interpretation of the provisions of this century-old removal statute, it is for Congress and not for this Court to make them."[9]

1. *Nashville v. Cooper*, 6 Wall. 247 at 253 (1868).
2. *Tennessee v. Davis*, 100 U.S. 257 at 266 (1880).
3. *Strauder v. West Virginia*, 100 U.S. 303 (1880).
4. *Virginia v. Rives*, 100 U.S. 313 (1880).
5. *Georgia v. Rachel*, 384 U.S. 780 (1966).
6. *City of Greenwood, Miss. v. Peacock*, 384 U.S. 808 (1966).
7. Id. at 826–827.
8. Id. at 828.
9. Id. at 833–834.

sent to the suit, few such suits arose.[28] A century later the Court further narrowed this category of cases, ruling that a state could not be sued by a foreign nation without the state's consent.[29]

For more than a century, it has been firmly established that a foreign nation may come into federal court with a civil claim, just as a citizen or domestic corporation may. In 1871 the Supreme Court had "not the slightest difficulty" in upholding the right of Emperor Napoleon III to sue in federal court for damages caused to a French ship that had collided with an American vessel. "A foreign sovereign, as well as any other foreign person, who has a demand of a civil nature against any person here, may prosecute it in our courts. To deny him this privilege would manifest a want of comity and friendly feeling."[30] The privilege survives for all nations recognized by and at peace with the United States.[31]

Federal jurisdiction over cases involving ambassadors, public ministers, and consuls extends only to foreign officials in the United States, not to U.S. officials accredited to foreign governments.[32] Because diplomatic immunity protects most high-ranking figures from lawsuits, most cases involve consuls or suits brought by diplomatic personnel against U.S. citizens. The Supreme Court has granted state courts jurisdiction over some cases involving consular officials, particularly if the subject of the case, like domestic relations, is one normally left to the states. But in so doing, the Court indicated that Congress could require that all such cases be heard in federal courts.[33]

Supreme Court Jurisdiction

The Constitution grants the Supreme Court original jurisdiction in "all cases affecting Ambassadors, other public Ministers and Consuls, and those in which a State shall be a Party." These cases may be heard initially by the Supreme Court. This original jurisdiction may be exclusive or concurrent, shared with other federal courts or with state courts.

Cases brought under its original jurisdiction comprise a very small portion of the modern Court's caseload—and most of those cases involve interstate controversies. Only a very few original cases have been brought involving foreign diplomats.

Congress may not expand or curtail the Court's original jurisdiction. Those restrictions were established by the Court in its 1803 decision in *Marbury v. Madison*. The act of Congress the Court found unconstitutional in *Marbury* was a provision of the Judiciary Act of 1789. The thirteenth section of the act authorized the Court to issue writs of mandamus to federal officials; the Court viewed this provision as an expansion of the original jurisdiction granted to it by the Constitution and therefore unconstitutional. Congress lacked the power to amend that grant, reasoned Marshall.

It has been insisted . . . that as the original grant of jurisdiction to the Supreme and inferior courts, is general and the clause, assigning original jurisdiction to the Supreme Court, contains no negative or restrictive words, the power remains to the legislature, to assign original jurisdiction to that court in other cases than those specified in the article . . . provided those cases belong to the judicial power of the United States.

If it had been intended to leave it in the discretion of the legislature to apportion the judicial power between the supreme and inferior courts . . . it would certainly have been useless to have proceeded further than to have defined the judicial power, and the tribunals in which it should be vested. The subsequent part of the section [of Article III assigning original jurisdiction to the Supreme Court] is mere surplusage, is entirely without meaning, if such is to be the construction. . . . It cannot be presumed that any clause in the constitution is intended to be without effect; and, therefore, such a construction is inadmissible.[34]

Congress, however, has successfully asserted the power to decide whether the Court's original jurisdiction over certain matters is exclusive or concurrent with the jurisdiction of other courts. In 1789 the Judiciary Act gave the Court exclusive jurisdiction over all civil suits between a state and the United States or between two states; suits between a state and an individual might be heard in other courts and only later before the

Supreme Court. In addition, the 1789 act gave the Court exclusive jurisdiction over all suits against ambassadors, public ministers, or their domestics, but not over all cases brought by ambassadors or public ministers, nor over all cases involving consuls.

The reasoning behind this division of original jurisdiction was set out by the Supreme Court a century later. The purpose of the grant of original jurisdiction, explained Chief Justice Morrison Waite, was

to open and keep open the highest court of the Nation, for the determination, in the first instance, of suits involving a State or a diplomatic or commercial representative of a foreign government. So much was due to the rank and dignity of those for whom the provision was made; but to compel a State to resort to this one tribunal for the redress of all its grievances or to deprive an ambassador, public minister or consul of the privilege of suing in any court he chose having jurisdiction . . . would be, in many cases, to convert what was intended as a favor into a burden.[35]

Therefore, continued Waite, "Congress took care to provide that no suit should be brought against an ambassador or other public minister except in the Supreme Court, but that he might sue in any court he chose that was open to him." And, he continued, the same approach gave a state the right—any time it was sued by the United States or another state—to have its case heard originally by the Supreme Court. It could choose to bring its own cases against individuals, however, in any court it chose.[36]

Exercise of the Court's original jurisdiction is not mandatory. Just before the Civil War, Kentucky came to the Court asking for an order directing the governor of Ohio to return a fugitive free black man indicted in Kentucky for helping a slave to escape. The Court reaffirmed its jurisdiction over such a case—and then declined to issue the requested order.[37]

Several decades later the Court declared it would not exercise its original jurisdiction over criminal cases between states and citizens of other states.

Wisconsin came to the Supreme Court in 1887 seeking assistance in enforcing penalties that state courts had assessed against an out-of-state corporation. The Supreme Court declined to take original jurisdiction over the case. Justice Horace Gray explained:

[T]he mere fact that a State is the plaintiff is not a conclusive test that the controversy is one in which this court is authorized to grant relief against another State or her citizens. . . . [T]his court has declined to take jurisdiction of suits between States to compel the performance of obligations which, if the States had been independent nations, could not have been enforced judicially, but only through the political departments of their governments.

The penal laws of a country do not reach beyond its own territory, except when extended by express treaty or statute to offenses committed abroad by its own citizens; and they must be administered in its own courts only, and cannot be enforced by the courts of another country. . . .

[T]he jurisdiction conferred by the Constitution upon this court, in cases to which a State is a party, is limited to controversies of a civil nature.[38]

THE SOVEREIGN'S IMMUNITY

The United States cannot be sued in federal court unless Congress expressly authorizes such lawsuits.

This legal doctrine is a corollary of the theory that the king could do no wrong. It has been applied, wrote a Supreme Court justice, "by our courts as vigorously as it had been on behalf of the crown."[1]

This immunity was recognized by the Court as early as 1834. Chief Justice John Marshall stated in that year that "the party who institutes such suit [against the United States] must bring his case within the authority of some act of Congress, or the Court cannot exercise jurisdiction over it." Subsequently, the Court held the federal government immune even from suits seeking recompense for damages or injuries inflicted by its agents or employees.[2]

In 1940 the Supreme Court explained that "the reasons for this immunity partake somewhat of dignity and decorum, somewhat of practical administration, somewhat of the political desirability of an impregnable legal citadel where government as distinct from its functionaries may operate undisturbed by the demands of litigants." However, the Court continued, "[a] sense of justice has brought a progressive relaxation by legislative enactments of the rigor of the immunity rule."[3]

This relaxation, through acts of Congress waiving immunity, actually began with a Supreme Court decision in the 1882 case of *United States v. Lee*.[4] George Lee, a son of Robert E. Lee, sued to recover his family home, Arlington, which had been seized by federal officials acting under presidential order and was being used as a cemetery and a fort. The government claimed that such a suit could not be brought because of sovereign immunity.

The Supreme Court, in a 5–4 decision, disagreed and rejected the defense of sovereign immunity. When it was claimed that a federal officer was holding property illegally, a federal court could take jurisdiction to hear out the claim, held the Court. The doctrine of sovereign immunity, wrote Justice Samuel F. Miller for the majority, was "not permitted to interfere with the judicial enforcement of the established rights of plaintiffs, when the United States is not a defendant or necessary party to the suit."[5]

The use of the sovereign immunity defense in such a case, continued Miller, "seems to be opposed to all the principles upon which the rights of the citizen, when brought in collision with the acts of the Government, must be determined. In such cases there is no safety for the citizen, except in the protection of the judicial tribunals,

for rights which have been invaded by the officers of the Government, professing to act in its name."[6]

Miller continued:

No man in this country is so high that he is above the law. No officer of the law may set that law at defiance, with impunity. All the officers of the Government, from the highest to the lowest, are creatures of the law and are bound to obey it.

It is the only supreme power in our system of government, and every man who, by accepting office, participates in its functions, is only the more strongly bound to submit to that supremacy, and to observe the limitations which it imposes upon the exercise of the authority which it gives.[7]

Five years later, in 1887, Congress passed the Tucker Act, specifically granting to the Court of Claims (now the U.S. Claims Court) and federal district courts jurisdiction over cases such as *United States v. Lee*.

In 1946 Congress approved the Federal Tort Claims Act, waiving the government's immunity from certain personal injury claims against government employees or contractors.

Cases against federal officials generally fall into four categories, Justice Felix Frankfurter once explained. First, there are cases in which a person seeks a share of government property. Second, there are those which seek to compel the exercise of official authority. Neither of these is usually allowed to survive in the face of a defense of sovereign immunity.

Third, there are cases in which a person sues a government official because he is threatened or injured by that official's action taken under an allegedly unconstitutional law or in excess of his legal authority. These cases are usually allowed to proceed.[8]

And finally, there are cases in which an official is charged with inflicting some common-law injury on another and seeks to invoke sovereign immunity by citing the law or the command of his superior as authority for his action. The Court has allowed some such cases to proceed, and it has found that sovereign immunity blocks others.[9]

1. *Feres v. United States*, 340 U.S. 135 at 139 (1950).
2. *United States v. Clarke*, 8 Pet. 436 at 444 (1834); *Gibbons v. United States*, 8 Wall. 269 (1869).
3. *United States v. Shaw*, 309 U.S. 495 at 500–501 (1940).
4. *United States v. Lee*, 106 U.S. 196 (1882).
5. Id. at 207–208.
6. Id. at 218–219.
7. Id. at 220.
8. See *Butz v. Economou*, 438 U.S. 478 (1978).
9. *Larson v. Domestic & Foreign Corp.*, 337 U.S. 682 at 705 (1949).

APPELLATE JURISDICTION

In all other cases falling within the scope of federal judicial power—aside from those placed in the Court's original jurisdiction by the Constitution—Article III grants the Court appellate jurisdiction "both as to Law and Fact, with such Exceptions, and under such Regulations as the Congress shall make." Congress quickly accepted the invitation to make exceptions and regulations concerning the high court's jurisdiction over appeals from lower courts.

The Judiciary Act of 1789 granted the Court jurisdiction over appeals from the decisions of the circuit courts in civil cases, so

long as more than $2,000 was at stake. Not until 1889 did the Supreme Court have the jurisdiction to hear appeals in criminal cases.

In addition, the famous Section 25 of the Judiciary Act granted the Supreme Court authority to take appeals from rulings of high state courts upholding state laws or state actions against challenge that they are in conflict with the U.S. Constitution, federal laws, or treaties.

The Supreme Court has always concurred in the assertion of congressional power over its appellate jurisdiction.[39] In 1866 the Court declared:

A FEDERAL COMMON LAW?

When federal judges, dealing with diversity cases, resolve matters normally dealt with by state courts and state law, what law do they apply? This question resulted in one of the most remarkable turnabouts in Supreme Court history, in which the Court not only overturned a century-old precedent, but also declared that precedent-setting ruling unconstitutional.

The Judiciary Act of 1789 provided that "the laws of the several states" should in general "be regarded as the rules of decision in trials at common law" in applicable cases in federal courts. "No issue in the whole field of federal jurisprudence has been more difficult than determining the meaning of this statute," wrote one scholar. "The central question has been whether the decisions of state courts are 'laws of the several states' within the meaning of the statute, and thus of controlling effect in some situations at least in the federal courts."[1]

In 1842 the Supreme Court, in *Swift v. Tyson*, stated that the "laws of the several states" applied in diversity cases by federal courts included only the written statutes of the states—not the common law or interpretation of the statutes set out by the decisions of state courts.[2]

The apparent basis for the ruling, Carl Swisher wrote, was the belief of the justices that state courts would follow the federal courts' interpretation of the common law, resulting in uniform application among the states. But, he noted, "the strategy failed. . . . State courts continued to follow in their own interpretations, with the result that state courts and federal courts . . . were handing down different interpretations" of the same law.[3]

In 1938 the Supreme Court took the opportunity presented by a diversity case and overruled *Swift v. Tyson*. Furthermore, the Court declared its earlier ruling unconstitutional. The Constitution, the Court said in *Erie Railroad Co. v. Tompkins*, required that the law in diversity cases be the law of the applicable state—both its written laws and the decisions of its courts. The most essential uniformity was consistency of interpretation and application of a state's laws within its limits by federal as well as state courts.[4] "There is no federal general common law," stated the Court.[5]

1. Charles Alan Wright, *The Law of Federal Courts,* 4th ed. (St. Paul, Minn.: West Publishing, 1983), 347.
2. *Swift v. Tyson,* 16 Pet. 1 (1842).
3. Carl B. Swisher, *American Constitutional Development,* 2d ed. (Cambridge: Houghton Mifflin, 1954), 980.
4. *Erie Railroad Co. v. Tompkins,* 304 U.S. 64 (1938).
5. Id. at 78.

Court and the nation three years later. In 1867 Congress expanded the availability of the writ of habeas corpus to persons who felt they were illegally detained by state or federal authority. The 1867 act allowed federal judges to issue such a writ in "all cases where any person may be restrained of his or her liberty, in violation of the Constitution or of any treaty or law of the United States." The purpose of the postwar law was to provide protection from state prosecution and detention for federal officials enforcing Reconstruction laws in the South.

Ironically, the first major test of the law came as a result of its use by William McCardle, a southern editor who had been charged by a military tribunal with impeding Reconstruction through his newspaper articles. McCardle came to the Supreme Court seeking a writ of habeas corpus ordering the military authorities to release him. He contended that the military commission had no jurisdiction to try him because he was a civilian. It was widely believed, according to histories of the time, that the Court would avail itself of this opportunity to declare the Reconstruction Acts unconstitutional.[41]

The first question under consideration in the McCardle case, argued and decided in February 1868, was whether the Supreme Court had jurisdiction to hear an appeal of a lower court's refusal to issue the writ.

The unanimous Supreme Court held that it did. Describing the 1867 act, it said:

This legislation is of the most comprehensive character. It brings within the habeas corpus jurisdiction of every court and of every judge every possible case of privation of liberty contrary to the National Constitution, treaties, or laws. It is impossible to widen this jurisdiction.

And it is to this jurisdiction that the system of appeals is applied. From decisions of a judge or of a district court appeals lie to the Circuit Court, and from the judgment of the Circuit Court to this court. . . . Every question of substance which the Circuit Court could decide upon the return of the habeas corpus . . . may be revised here on appeal from its final judgment.[42]

March 1868 was an eventful month. From March 2 until March 9 the Supreme Court heard arguments on the merits of McCardle's appeal for a writ of habeas corpus. Three days into the arguments, Chief Justice Salmon P. Chase left the high court bench for the chair of the presiding official in the Senate impeachment trial of President Andrew Johnson.

On March 12 Congress acted to prevent the Court's possible use of the McCardle case to strike down the Reconstruction Acts. As a rider to a revenue bill, Congress added a provision repealing the portion of the 1867 Habeas Corpus Act extending the Supreme Court's appellate jurisdiction over cases arising under it. Despite his own difficult position, President Johnson vetoed the bill March 25. It was repassed over his veto two days later.[43]

A week later, on April 2, the Supreme Court agreed to hear further arguments in the McCardle case, now focusing on the impact of the repeal on the case already argued. The Court then delayed matters further by postponing these arguments until its

The original jurisdiction of this court, and its power to receive appellate jurisdiction, are created and defined by the Constitution; and the Legislative Department of the Government can enlarge neither one nor the other. But it is for Congress to determine how far, within the limits of the capacity of this court to take, appellate jurisdiction shall be given, and when conferred, it can be exercised only to the extent and in the manner prescribed by law. In these respects, it is wholly the creature of legislation.[40]

The full truth of this statement was brought home to the

next term, a move much protested by at least two of the justices.

In May President Johnson was acquitted by one vote in the Senate.

In March 1869 the Court heard the postponed arguments; on April 12, 1869, it held that Congress had eliminated the Court's jurisdiction over the case. Chief Justice Chase spoke for the Court; there was no dissenting opinion.

The provision of the Act of 1867, affirming the appellate jurisdiction of this court in cases of habeas corpus, is expressly repealed. It is hardly possible to imagine a plainer instance of positive exception.

We are not at liberty to inquire into the motives of the Legislature. We can only examine into its power under the Constitution; and the power to make exceptions to the appellate jurisdiction of this court is given by express words.

What, then, is the effect of the repealing Act upon the case before us? We cannot doubt as to this. Without jurisdiction the court cannot proceed at all in any cause. . . .

It is quite clear, therefore, that this court cannot proceed to pronounce judgment in this case, for it has no longer jurisdiction of the appeal; and judicial duty is not less fitly performed by declining ungranted jurisdiction than in exercising firmly that which the Constitution and the laws confer.[44]

Later in the year Chase would comment, in another opinion, that such a repeal of jurisdiction was "unusual and hardly to be justified except upon some imperious public exigency."[45]

Carl Swisher has pointed out that passage of this legislation was, to date, "the only instance in American history in which Congress has rushed to withdraw the appellate jurisdiction of the Supreme Court for the purpose of preventing a decision on the constitutionality of a particular law."[46] (The Supreme Court's appellate jurisdiction in cases of habeas corpus was restored in 1885.)

But as Charles L. Black Jr. stated, the McCardle case "marks the extent of the vulnerability of the Judiciary to congressional control, and hence underlines the significance of Congress' never (except for this case and perhaps one or two other ambiguous and minor instances) having tried to employ this power to hamper judicial review even of its own acts."[47] (See "Pressures on the Institution," pp. 717–725, in Chapter 13, Vol. II.)

THE MODERN SYSTEM OF APPEALS

During the nation's first century the Supreme Court was virtually the only federal appeals court. The circuit and district courts functioned as trial courts. The Supreme Court therefore was obliged to rule on all appeals brought from the rulings of those lower courts—as well as on those brought under the Judiciary Act of 1789 from state courts.

And, wrote Professors Frankfurter and Landis,

for a hundred years the range of Supreme Court litigation remained practically unchanged. The same types of cases which in 1789 the framers of the Judiciary Act had designated for review by the Supreme Court continued to come before it till 1891. Despite the vast transformation of thirteen seaboard colonies into a great nation, with all that this implied in the growth of judicial business and the emergence of new controversies of vast proportions, a heavy stream of petty litigation reached the Supreme Court.[48]

Especially after the Civil War, the number of cases flowing to the Supreme Court began to swell. First in 1891 and then most notably in 1925, Congress gave the Supreme Court the power to select the most important of these cases for review and to refuse to review others.

There are two primary routes to Supreme Court review of the decision of an inferior court. The first is through the "writs of right"—first the writ of error issued to state courts under the 1789 act and then the appeal still in use today. If the Court finds that it has jurisdiction over an appeal, it is obligated to decide the issues it raises. The second is through the writ of certiorari—a discretionary writ issued by the Supreme Court to a lower court ordering it to forward the record of the case. In the twentieth century the overwhelming majority of the cases coming to the Court have been transferred from the appeals route to the discretionary certiorari route, giving the Court great control over its docket.

The Circuit Court of Appeals

This process of giving the Supreme Court more control over its docket began in 1891 with creation by Congress of a new level of federal courts, between the circuit and district courts on the one hand and the Supreme Court on the other. These new courts—circuit courts of appeals—were to hear all appeals from decisions of the district and circuit courts. Their word was to be final in almost all diversity, admiralty, patent, revenue, and noncapital criminal cases. (In 1911 Congress abolished the old circuit courts.)

The Circuit Court of Appeals Act of 1891 provided for Supreme Court review of such cases, after their decision by the appeals courts, only if the appeals court judges certified a case to the high court—or if the Supreme Court decided to grant review through issuing a writ of certiorari. Still granted a right to appeal to the Supreme Court were parties to cases involving constitutional questions, matters of treaty law, jurisdictional questions, capital crimes, and conflicting laws.

A Broader Jurisdiction

Early in the twentieth century Congress twice found it necessary to enlarge the Court's appellate jurisdiction.

In 1907 the Criminal Appeals Act granted the government the right to appeal directly to the Supreme Court a federal judge's ruling dismissing an indictment, so long as the defendant's trial had not begun before dismissal of the charges. This statute remedied an omission in the 1891 act, which, the Court had ruled in 1892, left the government without this right.[49]

Thus, if a federal judge dismissed an indictment, finding the law on which it was based unconstitutional, no appeal of that ruling was possible under the 1891 act. The prosecution was terminated. After a federal district judge blocked the Roosevelt administration's prosecution of the Beef Trust in this manner, Congress acted to remedy the deficiency in the law.[50]

In 1914 Congress enlarged the power of the Supreme Court to review state court decisions. In 1911 the New York Court of

THE DUTY TO DECIDE

In 1821 Chief Justice John Marshall set out, in clear and certain terms, his view of the Supreme Court's duty to decide all cases that properly fall within its jurisdiction. As history would show, such an approach was deceptively simple; the Court would many times disagree on whether a matter was properly before it and was appropriate for decision.

Marshall wrote:

It is most true that this Court will not take jurisdiction if it should not: but it is equally true, that it must take jurisdiction if it should. The judiciary cannot, as the legislature may, avoid a measure because it approaches the confines of the constitution. We cannot pass it by because it is doubtful. With whatever doubts, with whatever difficulties, a case may be attended, we must decide it, if it be brought before us. We have no more right to decline the exercise of jurisdiction which is given, than to usurp that which is not given. The one or the other would be treason to the constitution. [*Cohens v. Virginia,* 6 Wheat. 264 at 404 (1821)]

Appeals had held that state's workmen's compensation law—the nation's first—unconstitutional under the state and federal constitutions. Because the Supreme Court could review only state court rulings in which the state court denied a federal challenge to a state law, or held a federal law invalid, this ruling was outside the scope of judicial review.

Congress therefore authorized the Court to review—through issuing a writ of certiorari—rulings of a high state court upholding, as well as denying, a federal right or challenge.[51] Later Congress made review of all state court rulings on federal questions subject to Supreme Court discretion—except those where a state court held a federal treaty, law, or action invalid or upheld a state law or action against federal challenge.[52] Review in those categories of cases remained obligatory.

The cases coming to the Supreme Court continued to increase in numbers. As early as 1909, President William Howard Taft urged Congress to curtail the appellate jurisdiction of the Court to confine it to statutory and constitutional questions.

The "Judges Bill"

After Taft became chief justice in 1921, his campaign for reform shifted into high gear. The result was passage in 1925 of a new judiciary act, often known as the "judges bill" because the original legislation was drafted by members of the Supreme Court.[53]

Under the Judiciary Act of 1925, the Supreme Court retains over federal cases a broad right of review, usually exercised at the Court's discretion. The act made the circuit courts of appeals, well-established after three decades, the last word on most

cases they decided. (*See text of Judiciary Act of 1925, pp. 979–984, Vol. II.*)

The only cases in which there was an appeal of right from an appeals court ruling were those in which the appeals court held a state law invalid under the Constitution, federal laws, or federal treaties. In such cases, review by the Supreme Court was limited to the federal question involved. In all other cases, Supreme Court review of appeals court decisions was available only through the issuance of a writ of certiorari—over which the Court had complete discretion.[54]

Under the 1925 act—and for half a century after that—the right of direct appeal to the Supreme Court from district court decisions remained available in cases decided under antitrust or interstate commerce laws; appeals by the United States under the Criminal Appeals Act; suits to halt enforcement of state laws or other official state actions; and suits designed to halt enforcement of Interstate Commerce Commission orders.

During the 1970s, these direct appeal routes were all redirected by Congress through the courts of appeals.

From state courts, only two types of cases retained a right of direct appeal to the Supreme Court under the 1925 act—those in which a state law was upheld against a federally based challenge and those in which a federal law or treaty was held invalid.

The Court's power to review state court rulings, however, remained, as always, quite limited in contrast to its broad power to review federal court decisions. The Court could review only such cases in which substantial federal questions were raised and in which state courts had rendered final judgment.

In 1988, after years of urging from the Court, Congress eliminated virtually all of the Court's remaining mandatory jurisdiction for cases. The legislation removed obligatory review of decisions striking down acts of Congress, appeals court decisions striking down state laws as unconstitutional, and final judgments of state supreme courts questioning the validity of a federal law or treaty. The Court retained mandatory review of decisions of three-judge district courts (for example, involving reapportionment and voting rights).

At the end of the twentieth century, the Judiciary Act of 1925 stood with the acts of 1789 and 1891 as one of the great organizational statutes in the history of the federal judiciary. For the most part, Chief Justice Taft's hopes for the accomplishments of the new law seem to have been achieved. In late 1925 he wrote in the *Yale Law Journal:*

The sound theory of the new Act is that litigants have their rights sufficiently protected by the courts of first instance, and by one review in an intermediate appellate federal court. The function of the Supreme Court is conceived to be, not the remedying of a particular litigant's wrong, but the consideration of those cases whose decision involves principles, the application of which are of wide public and governmental interest.[55]

Federal Judicial Power

Once it is clear that a court has jurisdiction over a case, the scope of judicial power determines what the court may do about the dispute before it. Judicial power was defined by Supreme Court Justice Samuel Miller late in the nineteenth century as "the power of a court to decide and pronounce a judgment and carry it into effect."[1]

Federal judicial power includes the power of judicial review—the power to measure the acts of Congress, the actions of the executive, and the laws and practices of the states against the Constitution and to invalidate those that conflict with the requirements of that basic national charter.

In addition, the courts have the power to enforce their judgments through the use of writs, to punish persons for contempt, and to make rules governing the judicial process and admission to the bar.

Judicial Review

"If men were angels, no government would be necessary," wrote James Madison in *The Federalist Papers*.

He continued:

If angels were to govern men, neither external nor internal controls on government would be necessary. In framing a government which is to be administered by men over men, the great difficulty lies in this: you must first enable the government to control the governed; and in the next place, oblige it to control itself.[2]

The power of judicial review is one of the major self-control mechanisms of the American system of government. Judicial review—especially as exercised over acts of Congress—is a uniquely American concept. The Constitution makes no mention of this power, but many of those who drafted its language made clear their belief that the Supreme Court must have this power. The Court soon assumed its existence and—within fifteen years of the framing of the Constitution—exercised it to establish its validity in practice.

And not only does this power operate as a constant admonition to Congress—and the states, who first felt the full force of its workings—but also to the executive. One hundred and seventy-one years after the Supreme Court struck down the first act of Congress, it cited that ruling as it informed a president that he too must comply with the law, even at the cost of disgrace and resignation from office.[3]

The origins of judicial review are obscure. During the colonial period, the Privy Council in London had the power to review and nullify acts of the colonial assemblies. During the revolutionary period, state courts exercised the power to strike down laws found to violate state constitutions, although such rulings usually provoked considerable controversy.[4]

The Constitutional Convention apparently did not discuss judicial review. It did, however, consider and reject a proposal set forth by James Madison that would have lodged the veto power in a council composed of members of the executive and judicial branches. In the debate on this proposal, some members of the convention expressed their belief that "the Judges in their proper official character . . . have a negative on the laws"—and so should not be given the chance to impose "a double negative."[5]

A long and scholarly debate developed over the legitimacy of the power of judicial review as assumed and exercised by the Supreme Court. Some scholars argued that the Framers assumed the courts would exercise this power; others found its assumption clear usurpation. As one legal scholar noted several decades ago, by the twentieth century the debate had become irrelevant in light of the long tradition of national acquiescence in the exercise of this power within the U.S. system.[6]

REVIEW OF STATE ACTS

Clearly granted to the Supreme Court, however, was the power to review and reverse certain state court decisions. From 1789 until the Civil War, this aspect of judicial review was the most vigorously exercised, debated, protested, and resisted. *(See "Judicial Review and the States," pp. 316–321, in Chapter 7.)*

The Judiciary Act of 1789, of which Oliver Ellsworth was the chief sponsor, expressly granted the Supreme Court the power to review and reverse or affirm the final rulings of state courts upholding a state law against a challenge that it was in conflict with the U.S. Constitution, federal laws, or a federal treaty.

This provision, Section 25 of the act, was viewed as implementing the supremacy clause—the portion of the Constitution that states that the Constitution, federal laws, and federal treaties are the supreme law of the land. (Congress in 1914 expanded this aspect of judicial review further, allowing the Supreme Court to review state court decisions finding state laws invalid because they conflicted with the Constitution, federal laws, or federal treaties. See *"A Broader Jurisdiction,"* pp. 273–274.)

Section 25 was highly controversial—especially after the Court, in 1810, began exercising this power to hold certain state laws unconstitutional. Twice, in 1816 and 1821, the Court firmly rejected state challenges to Section 25 as unconstitutional. First, Justice Joseph Story in *Martin v. Hunter's Lessee* and, second, Chief Justice John Marshall in *Cohens v. Virginia* defended the Court's power over such state rulings as essential to preserve national sovereignty.[7] *(See details of these two cases, pp. 319–320, in Chapter 7.)*

Despite innumerable proposals that Congress abolish or curtail this aspect of judicial review, Congress has not given its final approval to any such measure. Part of the reason that this power has survived may lie in the restraint with which it has been exercised by the Court. *(See "Judicial Restraint," pp. 297–306.)*

After Section 25 was amended in 1867, it appeared that Con-

JUDICIAL REVIEW: SUPREME COURT OR SUPERLEGISLATURE?

In its second century the Supreme Court more often wielded its power of judicial review to overturn acts of Congress and state legislatures. Its critics repeatedly charged that the Court was acting as a superlegislature, engaging in "judicial legislation" and substituting its judgment for those of elected representatives. One of the justices most critical of this development was John Marshall Harlan, who dissented from the 1895 decision voiding the peacetime income tax:

Is the judiciary to supervise the action of the legislative branch of the government upon questions of public policy? Are they to override the will of the people, as expressed by their chosen servants, because, in their judgment, the particular means employed by Congress in execution of the powers conferred by the Constitution are not the best that could have been devised, or are not absolutely necessary to accomplish the objects for which the government was established? . . .

The vast powers committed to the present government may be abused, and taxes may be imposed by Congress which the public necessities do not in fact require, or which may be forbidden by a wise policy. But the remedy for such abuses is to be found at the ballot-box, and in a wholesome public opinion which the representatives of the people will not long, if at all, disregard.[1]

Ten years later Justice Harlan was joined by Justice Oliver Wendell Holmes Jr. in dissent, as the Court struck down New York's law setting maximum hours for bakers. Harlan wrote: "Whether or not this be wise legislation, it is not the province of the court to inquire. Under our system of government, the courts are not concerned with the wisdom or policy of legislation."[2] Justice Holmes elaborated:

This case is decided upon an economic theory which a large part of the country does not entertain. If it were a question whether I agreed with that theory, I should desire to study it further and long before making up my mind. But I do not conceive that to be my duty, because I strongly believe that my agreement or disagreement has nothing to do with the right of a majority to embody their opinions in law. It is settled by various decisions of this court that state constitutions and state laws may regulate life in many ways which we as legislators might think as injudicious, or, if you like as tyrannical as this. . . .

But a constitution is not intended to embody a particular economic theory, whether of paternalism . . . or of laissez faire. It is made for people of fundamentally different views, and the accident of our finding certain opinions natural and familiar or novel and even shocking ought not to conclude our judgment upon the question whether statutes embodying them conflict with the Constitution of the United States.[3]

"THE PROPER ADMINISTRATION OF JUSTICE"

Chief Justice William Howard Taft led the Court during the 1920s, a period when the Court invalidated more legislation than it had in the half century preceding it. Taft easily accepted the idea that the Court did, in fact, "make" law. He dismissed the idea that judges should try to ascertain and apply "the exact intention of those who established the Constitution." People with that view did not understand "the proper administration of justice."[4] In 1913 he wrote:

Frequently, new conditions arise which those who were responsible for the written law could not have had in view, and to which existing common law principles have never before been applied, and it becomes necessary for the Court to make applications of both. . . . [Such an application] is not the exercise of legislative power . . . [but] the exercise of a sound judicial discretion in supplementing the provisions of constitutions and laws and custom, which are necessarily incomplete or lacking in detail essential to their proper application, especially to new facts and situations constantly arising. . . . Indeed it is one of the highest and most useful functions that courts have to perform in making a government of law practical and uniformly just.[5]

As might be expected, justices serving with Taft took issue with his view. Among them was Louis D. Brandeis. When the Court held invalid a state law setting standard sizes for loaves of bread, Brandeis wrote:

It is not our function to weigh evidence. Put at its highest, our function is to determine . . . whether the measure enacted in the exercise of an unquestioned police power and of a character inherently unobjectionable, transcends the bounds of reason. That is, whether the provision as applied is so clearly arbitrary or capricious that legislators acting reasonably could not have believed it to be necessary or appropriate for the public welfare.

To decide, as a fact, that the prohibition of excess weights "is not necessary for the protection of the purchasers" and that it "subjects bakers and sellers of bread" to heavy burdens, is in my opinion, an exercise of the powers of a super-legislature—not the performance of the constitutional function of judicial review.[6]

The Court majority that so consistently struck down New Deal legislation in the 1930s was not insensitive to charges that it was imposing its own will—on Congress, the president, and the American people. In *United States v. Butler* (1936) Justice Owen J. Roberts, whose vote during this period often meant the difference between the Court's declaring a statute valid or invalid, sought to answer these charges by minimizing the Court's role:

It is sometimes said that the court assumes a power to overrule or control the action of the people's representatives. This is a misconception. . . . When an act of Congress is appropriately challenged in the courts as not conforming to the constitutional mandate, the judicial branch of Government has only one duty—to lay the article of the Constitution which is in-

gress, by omitting a restrictive sentence, had granted the Court—when reviewing state court decisions—the power to review all the issues in such cases, not simply the federal issue that justified its review in the first place. But the Court in 1875 refused to interpret the 1867 amendment as expanding its power in this direction.[8] In 1945 Justice Robert H. Jackson described the traditional approach in reviewing state court rulings:

This Court from the time of its foundation has adhered to the principle that it will not review judgments of state courts that rest on adequate and independent state grounds. . . . The reason is so obvious that it has rarely been thought to warrant statement. It is found in the partitioning of power between the state and federal judicial systems and in the limitations of our own jurisdiction. Our only power over state judgments is to correct them to the extent that they incorrectly adjudge federal rights.[9]

voked beside the statute which is challenged and to decide whether the latter squares with the former. . . . The only power [the judiciary] has, if such it may be called, is the power of judgment. This court neither approves nor condemns any legislative policy.[7]

Roberts's claim did not go unanswered. In a strong dissent, Justice Harlan Fiske Stone said that the majority in *Butler* had assumed the very power Roberts said the Court did not have: the power to judge the wisdom of the statute and not its constitutionality. There were two guiding principles for the judiciary to follow, Stone said:

One is that courts are concerned only with the power to enact statutes, not with their wisdom. The other is that while unconstitutional exercise of power by the executive and legislative branches . . . is subject to judicial restraint, the only check upon our own exercise of power is our own sense of self-restraint. For the removal of unwise laws from the statute books appeal lies not to the courts but to the ballot and to the processes of democratic government. . . . The present levy is held invalid, not for any want of power in Congress to lay such a tax . . . but because the use to which its proceeds are put is disapproved.[8]

Justice Benjamin N. Cardozo, another of Roberts's colleagues, had earlier written critically of judges who took the approach Roberts outlined:

Their notion of their duty is to match the colors of the case at hand against the colors of many sample cases spread out upon their desk. The sample nearest the shade supplies the applicable rule. But, of course, no system of living law can be evolved by such a process, and no judge of a high court, worthy of his office, views the function of his place so narrowly. If that were all there was to our calling, there would be little of intellectual interest about it. The man who had the best card index would also be the wisest judge. It is when the colors do not match . . . that the serious business of the judge begins.[9]

In the years following resolution of the New Deal crisis—political, economic, and judicial—the debate over "judicial legislation" intensified as the Court extended its scrutiny into the area of controversial state laws and practices affecting individual rights and freedoms.

"A GENERAL HAVEN FOR REFORM MOVEMENTS"

The Court in the early 1960s moved into legislative malapportionment, ordering states to redraw their legislative districts to make them more equal in population. Chief Justice Earl Warren defended the Court's involvement in a matter traditionally left entirely to legislative power.

We are told that the matter of apportioning representation in a state legislature is a complex and many-faceted one. We are advised that States can rationally consider factors other than population in apportioning legislative representation. We are admonished not to restrict the power of the States to impose differing views as to political philosophy on their citizens. We are cautioned about the dangers of entering into political thickets and mathematical quagmires. Our answer is this: a denial of constitutionally protected rights demands judicial protection; our oath and our office require no less of us.[10]

This assertion was vigorously rebutted in 1964 by the second justice named John Marshall Harlan:

What is done today deepens my conviction that judicial entry into this realm is profoundly ill-advised and constitutionally impermissible.

. . . I believe that the vitality of our political system, on which in the last analysis all else depends, is weakened by reliance on the judiciary for political reform; in time a complacent body politic may result.

These decisions also cut deeply into the fabric of our federalism. . . .

Finally, these decisions give support to a current mistaken view of the Constitution and the constitutional function of this Court. This view, in a nutshell, is that every major social ill in this country can find its cure in some constitutional "principle," and that this Court should "take the lead" in promoting reform when other branches of government fail to act.

The Constitution is not a panacea for every blot upon the public welfare, nor should this Court, ordained as a judicial body, be thought of as a general haven for reform movements. The Constitution is an instrument of government, fundamental to which is the premise that in a diffusion of governmental authority lies the greatest promise that this Nation will realize liberty for all its citizens.

This Court, limited in function in accordance with that premise, does not serve its high purpose when it exceeds its authority, even to satisfy justified impatience with the slow workings of the political process.[11]

1. *Pollock v. Farmers' Loan & Trust Co.*, 158 U.S. 601 at 679–680 (1895).

2. *Lochner v. New York*, 198 U.S. 45 at 69 (1905).

3. Id. at 75–76.

4. Alpheus T. Mason, *The Supreme Court from Taft to Warren* (Baton Rouge: Louisiana State University Press, 1958), 46, citing William Howard Taft, *Popular Government: Its Essence, Its Permanence, Its Perils* (New Haven: Yale University Press, 1913), 222–223.

5. Ibid.

6. *Burns Baking Company v. Bryan*, 264 U.S. 504 at 533–534 (1923).

7. *United States v. Butler*, 297 U.S. 1 at 62–63 (1936).

8. Id. at 78–79.

9. Benjamin N. Cardozo, "The Nature of the Judicial Process" in *Selected Writings*, ed. Margaret E. Hall (New York: Fallon, 1947), 113.

10. *Reynolds v. Sims*, 377 U.S. 533 at 566 (1964).

11. Id. at 624–625.

REVIEW OF ACTS OF CONGRESS

The first case challenging the validity of an act of Congress came to the Supreme Court in 1796. Both sides in the matter—a tax question—simply assumed that the Supreme Court could strike down the act. The Court upheld it.[10]

Five years later, just before the end of President John Adams's term in office, Adams named William Marbury a justice of the peace for the District of Columbia. Although Marbury was confirmed and his commission duly signed by Adams, Secretary of State John Marshall failed to deliver the commission before Adams left office. President Thomas Jefferson, Adams's successor, declined to deliver the commission.

Marbury, with former attorney general Charles Lee as his attorney, came to the Supreme Court late in the year. They asked the justices to issue a writ of mandamus ordering James Madison, Jefferson's secretary of state, to deliver the commission. (*Mandamus* means "we command.") In response, the Court directed Madison to show cause why they should not issue such an order. Arguments in the case were set for the next term, then scheduled to begin in June 1802.

Congress, however, repealed the law providing for a June Court term and replaced it with one providing that the next term would begin in February. As a result, the Court did not meet for fourteen months, during which Marbury's request remained pending.[11]

Finally the case was argued, and on February 24, 1803, the unanimous decision was announced. The Court refused to issue the order Marbury requested. The refusal came despite its finding, announced by Chief Justice John Marshall, that Marbury had a legal right to his commission, that failure to deliver the commission violated that right, and that a writ of mandamus was the proper remedy for such a situation.

The Court refused to issue a writ of mandamus because, it said, it lacked the power to issue one: the law that purported to authorize it to issue such orders was unconstitutional. Section 13 of the Judiciary Act of 1789 specifically authorized the Supreme Court "to issue writs of *mandamus* in cases warranted by the principles and usages of law, to any courts appointed or persons holding office, under the authority of the United States." Citing this provision, Marbury had come directly to the Supreme Court with his request.

With reasoning more notable for its conclusion than its clarity, Marshall found that this provision expanded the Court's original jurisdiction.

It is the essential criterion of appellate jurisdiction, that it revises and corrects the proceedings in a cause already instituted, and does not create that cause. Although, therefore, a mandamus may be directed to courts, yet to issue such a writ to an officer for the delivery of a paper, is in effect the same as to sustain an original action for that paper, and, therefore, seems not to belong to appellate, but to original jurisdiction.[12]

Congress, continued the Court, had no power to modify its original jurisdiction, and so this grant of authority was unconstitutional. The Court asserted its power:

It is emphatically the province and duty of the judicial department to say what the law is. . . .

. . . if a law be in opposition to the constitution; if both the law and the constitution apply to a particular case, so that the court must either decide that case conformably to the law, disregarding the constitution; or conformably to the constitution, disregarding the law; the court must determine which of these conflicting rules governs the case. This is of the very essence of judicial duty.

If then, the courts are to regard the constitution, and the constitution is superior to any ordinary act of the legislature, the constitution, and not such ordinary act, must govern the case to which they both apply.[13]

To rule to the contrary, Chief Justice Marshall said,

would subvert the very foundation of all written constitutions. It would declare that an act which, according to the principles and theory of our government, is entirely void, is yet, in practice, completely oblig-

atory. It would declare that if the legislature shall do what is expressly forbidden, such act, notwithstanding . . . is in reality effectual. It would be giving to the legislature a practical and real omnipotence, with the same breath which professes to restrict their powers within narrow limits. It is prescribing limits, and declaring that those limits may be passed with pleasure.

. . . [I]t thus reduces to nothing what we have deemed the greatest improvement on political institutions, a written constitution."[14]

Defining the Constitution

With that decision, and the firm establishment of the power of the Court to nullify unconstitutional acts of Congress, the Supreme Court changed the meaning of the word *constitution*. Prior to the founding of the United States, the word referred not to a written basic law but simply to the principles observed in the operation of the government. Every government had some constitution, but not every government was bound by its constitution as a supreme law.[15]

With *Marbury v. Madison* the Supreme Court became the effective instrument for enforcing the supremacy of the U.S. Constitution.

Criticism of judicial review, led after *Marbury* by none other than President Jefferson, continued. However, as Charles Evans Hughes noted in 1928: "The reasoning of Chief Justice Marshall's opinion has never been answered. . . . The doctrine of judicial review . . . practically is as much a part of our system of government as the judicial office itself."[16]

Adding another perspective, Charles P. Curtis has written that John Marshall "snatched from the majority and offered to our courts, the function of rendering our political decencies and aspirations into immanent law. What we owe to Marshall is the opportunity he gave us of combining a reign of conscience with a republic."[17]

The Power Exercised

For the first century of the nation's history, the Supreme Court exercised the power of judicial review primarily to enhance national power by striking down state laws and upholding acts of Congress challenged as infringing upon states' rights.

As one scholar wrote, the Marshall Court wielded the power of judicial review "to place its stamp of approval upon the idea of the Constitution as an instrument of expanding national power."[18]

Not until 1857—fifty-four years after *Marbury*—was a second act of Congress declared unconstitutional by the Supreme Court.

In the infamous Dred Scott case, the Court held that the Missouri Compromise was unconstitutional because Congress lacked the power to exclude slavery from the territories. That decision, which contributed to intensification of the debate over slavery and its eventual explosion in civil war, also inflicted severe damage upon the Court. Hughes later would describe the case as the first of three of the Court's "self-inflicted wounds . . . a public calamity."[19] *(See details of Scott v. Sandford, pp. 143–146, in Chapter 4.)*

Fifteen years after the Dred Scott decision, the Court dealt itself the second such injury. It first struck down—and fifteen months later reversed itself to uphold—the acts of Congress making paper money legal tender in payment of debts incurred before the passage of the acts.[20] *(See "First Legal Tender Decision" and "Second Legal Tender Decision," pp. 129–132, in Chapter 4.)*

In the following century—from 1870 through 1970—the pace of judicial invalidation of congressional acts quickened. By mid-1996, 133 acts of Congress had been struck down, in whole or in part, by the Supreme Court. This number did not include all the laws affected by the Court's ruling on the legislative veto. *(See "Acts of Congress Held Unconstitutional," pp. 1102–1113, Vol. II.)*

As the Court exercised its power of judicial review more frequently, it found itself more and more the center of controversy. Proposals to curb the power of judicial review proliferated. But as one legal scholar wrote in 1956, such proposals "have been directed mainly, if not always, not against the existence of the power but against the manner or the finality of its exercise."[21]

And the judicial consensus in 1996 seemed to be the same as that set out in 1928 by Hughes, a man who had served on the Court, had left to run for president, and later returned to the Court as chief justice:

The dual system of government implies the maintenance of the constitutional restrictions of the powers of Congress as well as of those of the States. The existence of the function of the Supreme Court is a constant monition to Congress. A judicial, as distinguished from a mere political, solution of the questions arising from time to time has its advantages.[22]

The Power to Issue Writs

The Judiciary Act of 1789 authorized all federal courts to issue all writs "which may be necessary for the exercise of their respective jurisdictions, and agreeable to the principles and usages of law." That provision, slightly reworded, remains the general statutory authority for federal courts to issue orders to carry out their decisions.[23]

Most significant and most controversial of the writs generally employed by the federal courts is the "Great Writ"—the writ of habeas corpus. When issued, it requires government officials to justify their decision to hold a person in custody over his or her objection. This writ has been described with many superlatives as "the best and only sufficient defense of personal freedom."[24]

Other writs used by the courts have included the writ of error, used until early in the twentieth century to notify a state court that the Supreme Court was to review one of its rulings; the writ of certiorari, now the most common notice to a lower or state court that the Supreme Court has granted review of its decision; and the writ of mandamus, the writ involved in *Marbury v. Madison.*

A federal court, the Supreme Court has said, may use all these "auxiliary writs as aids in the performance of its duties, when the use of such historic aids is calculated in its sound judgment to achieve the ends of justice entrusted to it."[25]

HABEAS CORPUS

First in importance of the writs available to the federal courts is the writ of habeas corpus. An integral part of the nation's English heritage, this writ is used by a court to inquire into the reasons for a person's detention by government authority. Loosely translated from the Latin, it means "you have the body." A writ orders the government to produce the prisoner—the corpus or the body—so that the prisoner may make his case to a court.

Habeas corpus, the Court has noted, "has time and again played a central role in national crises, wherein the claims of order and of liberty clash most acutely." The Court continued:

Although in form the Great Writ is simply a mode of procedure, its history is inextricably intertwined with the growth of fundamental rights of personal liberty. For its function has been to provide a prompt and efficacious remedy for whatever society deems to be intolerable restraints. Its root principle is that in a civilized society, government must always be accountable to the judiciary for a man's imprisonment: if the imprisonment cannot be shown to conform with the fundamental requirements of law, the individual is entitled to his immediate release.[26]

Since the nation's founding, the use of the writ of habeas corpus by the federal courts has gradually expanded it into a major instrument for the reform of federal and state criminal procedures.[27]

Federal courts have broad discretion in determining when the issuance of this writ is appropriate to order release of a prisoner. But the Supreme Court has emphasized that "[d]ischarge from conviction through habeas corpus is not an act of judicial clemency, but a protection against illegal custody."[28]

There is no time limit within which a prisoner must seek a writ of habeas corpus as a remedy for errors at his trial.[29] It may be issued to military or civilian authorities.[30]

Release through the writ should not be sought as a substitute for appeal of a conviction. "Mere convenience cannot justify use of the writ as a substitute for an appeal," wrote Justice Felix Frankfurter in 1942. "But dry formalism should not sterilize procedural resources which Congress has made available to the federal courts."[31]

The Supreme Court has declared that the power of federal courts to issue this writ must be given by written law—as it always has been.

Despite its antiquity, this assertion is open to debate in light of the express statement in the Constitution forbidding suspension of the privilege of the writ except when the public safety demands it.[32]

The Court also has maintained that proceedings begun by a petition for this writ are entirely separate from the question of a defendant's guilt or innocence, and thus are no substitute for a direct appeal of a conviction. The writ has been used in modern times to challenge a lack of jurisdiction of the sentencing court or to charge constitutional error, which, if proved, makes the entire detention illegal, regardless of the guilt of the person detained.[33]

Restricted Use

For most of the nineteenth century, the use of the writ of habeas corpus by federal courts was strictly limited by two factors. First, the Supreme Court viewed the writ as properly used only to challenge the jurisdiction of the sentencing court. In 1830 the Court declared that the inquiry sparked by a request for this writ began and ended with the question of jurisdiction. If a person was detained under the judgment of a court with jurisdiction over him and his case, his detention was lawful.[34]

Second, the Court faithfully observed the statutory restriction of the federal use of the writ to question the detention of federal prisoners only. In 1845 the Court refused to issue such a writ to state officials, even though the state prisoner seeking the writ argued that his state jailers were blocking all his efforts to appeal to the Supreme Court.[35]

Small exceptions to this limitation were approved by Congress in 1833 and 1842 when it extended the use of habeas corpus to order state officials to release federal officers imprisoned for enforcing federal laws, and to order state officials to release foreign nationals detained by a state in violation of a treaty.

Despite these restrictions, in the pre-Civil War period some individuals did use a request for a writ of habeas corpus, coupled with a writ of certiorari, as a clumsy method of invoking the appellate jurisdiction of the Supreme Court. A few prisoners using this device were successful in obtaining their release.[36]

The Beginning of Expansion

In 1867 there began a century of expansion of the federal right to release from government custody through the writ of habeas corpus. In that year Congress ended the restriction of this right to federal prisoners.

Intending to prevent state imprisonment of federal officials engaged in Reconstruction programs, Congress authorized federal courts "to grant writs of habeas corpus in all cases where any person may be restrained of his or her liberty in violation of the Constitution, or of any treaty or law of the United States." The 1867 act also provided for review by the Supreme Court of lower court rulings denying habeas corpus relief to persons seeking it under this law.

Almost before the ink was dry on the statute, the case of *Ex parte McCardle* was argued before the Supreme Court, and Congress—fearful of a ruling that would invalidate the Reconstruction Acts—repealed this expansion of the Supreme Court's appellate jurisdiction.[37] *(See details of Ex parte McCardle, pp. 272–273.)*

But despite this backward step, the basic expansion of the federal use of the writ remained intact. Lower federal courts could now use the writ to release state prisoners detained in violation of their federal rights.

And the Supreme Court soon made clear that the 1868 repeal affected only the 1867 enlargement of its appellate jurisdiction. The Court's preexisting jurisdiction over questions of habeas corpus relief—although procedurally cumbersome—was still valid. This point was made late in 1869 in *Ex parte Yerger.*

Edward Yerger, a civilian, was held by military authorities in Mississippi after his conviction by a military commission for killing an army major. A lower federal court granted his petition for a writ of habeas corpus, reviewed the reasons for his detention, and found it proper. The Supreme Court agreed to review that decision and affirmed its jurisdiction to issue an "original" writ of habeas corpus under the Judiciary Act of 1789.[38]

In 1885 Congress restored the jurisdiction of the Supreme Court to consider direct appeals from circuit court rulings denying habeas corpus relief. But before the 1885 legislation, in a set of cases decided in 1880, the Court used the "original" writ to consider situations in which persons accused of violating civil rights laws sought release through habeas corpus, arguing that the laws under which they were convicted were not constitutional. In each case, the Court denied the writ and upheld the challenged law.[39]

Returning to the jurisdictional view of the writ, the Supreme Court based its power to act upon the reasoning that if the law was in fact unconstitutional, then the court that convicted the prisoner lacked jurisdiction to detain him—and so the writ should be issued to order his release. The Court explained that questions concerning the constitutionality of the law under which an indictment is brought or a conviction obtained affect the foundation of the entire proceeding:

An unconstitutional law is void, and is as no law. An offense created by it is not a crime. A conviction under it is not merely erroneous, but is illegal and void, and cannot be a legal cause of imprisonment.[40]

Nine years later, after Congress had restored its jurisdiction over lower court denials of habeas corpus relief to persons alleging that they were detained in violation of their federal rights, the Court found a logical link between the jurisdictional basis for such relief and the new rights-based grounds for the writ.

It is difficult to see why a conviction and punishment under an unconstitutional law is more violative of a person's constitutional rights, than an unconstitutional conviction and punishment under a valid law. In the first case, it is that the court has no authority to take cognizance of the case; but in the other it has no authority to render judgment against the defendant.[41]

The Modern Writ

Although Congress in its 1867 expansion of the right to habeas corpus clearly contemplated federal intervention in state matters, for half a century after the act there were few collisions of state and federal power in this area. This lack of conflict resulted from the narrow definition of federal rights, the Court's continuing limited view of the issues properly raised by a petition for habeas corpus relief, and the fact that most of the Bill of Rights was not applied to protect persons against state action.

As the Court expanded the category of federally protected rights, and applied the guarantees of the first eight amendments to the states, the use of the writ to challenge and overturn state convictions became more frequent and more controversial.

The modern federal use of the writ of habeas corpus to question detention of state prisoners can be traced to the Court's 1915 decision in *Frank v. Mangum.* This ruling signaled an end to the Court's traditional view that so long as a sentencing court had jurisdiction to impose the challenged sentence, the Supreme Court would not inquire further into the legality of a person's confinement.

In *Frank v. Mangum* the Court refused to order the release of a man convicted of murder by a state court, even though he alleged that he had been denied a fair trial because the court was dominated by a mob. But in its opinion, written by Justice Mahlon Pitney, the Court enlarged its traditional view of the responsibility of a federal court to examine state convictions.

First, the Court indicated its belief that a court with jurisdiction over a case could lose jurisdiction if it allowed events to deny a defendant his federal rights.

Second, the Court held that the 1867 Habeas Corpus Act gave state prisoners the right to "a judicial inquiry in a court of the United States into the very truth and substance of causes of his detention," even if that required the federal court "to look behind and beyond the record of his conviction."[42]

But the Court denied habeas corpus relief in this case because the defendant's claim of mob domination had been reviewed fully—and rejected—by a state appeals court. Eight years later the Court granted a similar plea. In *Moore v. Dempsey* the Court, speaking through Justice Oliver Wendell Holmes Jr., declared that

if the case is that the whole proceeding is a mask—that counsel, jury and judge were swept to the fatal end by an irresistible wave of public passion, and that the State Courts failed to correct the wrong, neither perfection in the machinery for correction nor the possibility that the trial court and counsel saw no other way of avoiding an immediate outbreak of the mob can prevent this Court from securing to the petitioners their constitutional rights.[43]

And in 1942 the Court finally acknowledged that habeas corpus relief involved far more than jurisdictional issues.

[T]he use of the writ in the federal courts to test the constitutional validity of a conviction for crime is not restricted to those cases where the judgment of conviction is void for want of jurisdiction of the trial court to render it. It extends also to those exceptional cases where the conviction has been in disregard of the constitutional rights of the accused and where the writ is the only effective means of preserving his rights.[44]

Subsequently, the Court has broadened the power of federal courts, when considering state prisoners' petitions for habeas corpus, to redetermine matters already considered and resolved by state courts. In 1953 the Court held that federal courts could rehear such a prisoner's claims "on the merits, facts or law" to be certain that his federal rights had been protected.[45]

Ten years later the Court in *Townsend v. Sain* ruled that although a federal judge might defer to a state court's reliable findings of fact, where the facts remained in dispute, the federal judge should rehear the relevant evidence if there was not a "full and fair evidentiary hearing" on the prisoner's claim in a state court, either at the time of his trial or in subsequent proceedings. Furthermore, the Court made clear in that decision that a federal judge should not defer to a state judge's findings of law: "It is the district judge's duty," stated the Court, "to apply the applicable federal law . . . independently."[46]

Exhausting State Remedies

To prevent unnecessary collisions between state and federal authority through the exercise of this expanded power of habeas corpus, the Supreme Court adopted the general rule that federal courts should await completion of state proceedings before ordering release of a state prisoner on habeas corpus.

In 1885 the Court refused to order the release, before trial, of a state prisoner who sought a writ of habeas corpus from federal court. In its decision in *Ex parte Royall*, the Court affirmed the power of the federal courts to issue such a pretrial writ, but it urged discretion in the use of that power in the interest of comity and preservation of the balance between state and federal power.[47]

This rule, slowly enlarged on a case-by-case basis, became the "exhaustion requirement" set out in a 1944 ruling:

Ordinarily an application for habeas corpus by one detained under a state court judgment of conviction for crime will be entertained by a federal court only after all state remedies available, including all appellate remedies in the state courts and in this court by appeal or writ of certiorari, have been exhausted.[48]

Four years later, when the Judicial Code was revised, this requirement was included.

In 1950 the Court reaffirmed that this rule meant that a direct challenge to a state conviction should be taken all the way to the Supreme Court before a prisoner could then begin a collateral attack on his conviction by seeking a writ of habeas corpus from federal district court. In its opinion the Court set out the reasoning upon which such a requirement was based:

Since the states have the major responsibility for the maintenance of law and order within their borders, the dignity and importance of their

---

STATE COURTS AND HABEAS CORPUS

State courts have the power to issue writs of habeas corpus, but federal supremacy places one major restraint on their use of the Great Writ. State judges may not use it to require release of persons held in federal custody.

In the years preceding the Civil War, considerable resistance arose in abolitionist states to federal enforcement of the Federal Fugitive Slave Act. In Wisconsin, after newspaper editor Sherman Booth was convicted for helping fugitive slaves escape, state courts ordered his federal jailers to release him, issuing a writ of habeas corpus to them for this purpose.

In 1859 the Supreme Court made clear that such an order exceeded the bounds of state power in the federal system. Federal supremacy, the Court held in *Ableman v. Booth*, meant that state courts could not use the writ to order release of federal prisoners.[1] *(See box, A Clash of Courts: The Fugitive Slave Law, p. 375.)*

More than half a century later the Court modified this ban slightly. With the consent of the United States, state courts could use the writ to direct federal officials to present a federal prisoner to state court for trial on state charges.[2]

1. *Ableman v. Booth*, 21 How. 506 (1859).
2. *Ponzi v. Fessenden*, 258 U.S. 254 (1922); *Smith v. Hooey*, 393 U.S. 374 (1969).

role as guardians of the administration of criminal justice merits review of their acts by this Court before a prisoner, as a matter of routine, may seek release . . . in the district courts of the United States. It is this Court's conviction that orderly federal procedure under our dual system of government demands that the state's highest court should ordinarily be subject to reversal only by this Court and that a state's system for the administration of justice should be condemned as constitutionally inadequate only by this Court.[49]

Three years later the Court was more succinct: "A failure to use a state's available remedy, in the absence of some interference or incapacity . . . bars federal habeas corpus."[50]

Exceptions to the Rule

Although the Court had always left open the possibility that it would not enforce the exhaustion requirement in exceptional circumstances, federal courts until 1963 were quite consistent in requiring adherence to the rule.[51] But in that year the Supreme Court ruled in *Fay v. Noia* that a state prisoner's failure to appeal his conviction did not necessarily bar him forever from obtaining habeas corpus relief from a federal court.[52]

Charles Noia and two other men were convicted in 1942 of killing a Brooklyn storekeeper. All three were sentenced to life imprisonment in Sing Sing. The other two men unsuccessfully appealed their convictions; Noia did not. Eventually, the other two won release on federal habeas corpus, after a federal judge agreed that their detention was unconstitutional because they had been convicted on the basis of confessions coerced from them.

Despite identical circumstances concerning his confession and conviction, Noia was denied release on habeas corpus because he had not exhausted state remedies by appealing his conviction. Noia could not rectify the situation, for his right to appeal had terminated when he did not file an appeal within thirty days after conviction.

By a 6–3 vote the Supreme Court ordered Noia's release, despite his failure to appeal. Writing for the majority, Justice William J. Brennan Jr. declared that it was just this sort of situation, which "affront[ed] . . . the conscience of a civilized society," for which habeas corpus relief was intended. "If the States withhold effective remedy, the federal courts have the power and the duty to provide it."[53]

The exhaustion requirement meant, wrote Justice Brennan, only that a state prisoner could not obtain federal habeas corpus relief unless he had first tried all state remedies still available. Because Noia's right to appeal had expired, his failure to avail himself of it did not foreclose habeas corpus relief.

When a federal court was applying this rule to deny relief to a state prisoner, wrote Brennan, it must be certain that a person who had failed to exhaust his state remedies had done so deliberately, that he "understandingly and knowingly forewent the privilege of seeking to vindicate his federal claims in the state courts, whether for strategic, tactical, or any other reasons that can fairly be described as the deliberate by-passing of state procedures."[54]

Noia's choice not to appeal in 1942, when appeal could have resulted in a new trial and death sentence, could not realistically be viewed as his "considered choice," wrote Brennan, and so should not be held to bar him from habeas corpus relief in federal courts.[55]

The Court in *Fay v. Noia* also overruled its 1950 decision that required a person to appeal his or her conviction all the way to the Supreme Court before seeking federal habeas corpus relief. That requirement, held the Court in 1963, placed an unnecessary burden on the prisoner and the Court.[56]

Restricting the Writ of Habeas Corpus

In the 1970s the Supreme Court began to narrow the impact of *Fay v. Noia*. A prisoner's claim that illegally obtained evidence had been improperly used to convict him could not serve as a basis for federal habeas corpus relief so long as the state had provided him an opportunity for "full and fair litigation" of that claim at an earlier time.[57]

The Court also narrowed availability of federal habeas corpus relief through a stricter application of the exhaustion requirement. The Court abandoned the "deliberate bypass" standard of *Fay v. Noia,* under which state prisoners who had not deliberately bypassed their right to assert their federal claim ear-

The Court under Chief Justice William H. Rehnquist has restricted the availability of federal habeas corpus relief. Rehnquist has been an outspoken critic of the death penalty appeals process, which in many cases allowed condemned inmates to delay their execution through protracted petitions for habeas corpus.

lier could obtain federal habeas corpus review. In its place it adopted, first for federal prisoners and then for state prisoners seeking this relief, a new standard: an earlier failure to assert a federal claim would bar habeas corpus relief unless the prisoner could show *both* good reason for the earlier omission *and* actual prejudice to his case as a result of the claimed violation of his federal right.[58]

William H. Rehnquist, who became chief justice in 1986, outspokenly criticized the death penalty appeals process, which allowed condemned inmates to delay their execution through protracted petitions for habeas corpus and other appeals. Rehnquist persuaded his colleagues to limit an inmate's access to successive petitions and thus bring finality to the process.

One of the first and most important restrictions imposed by the Rehnquist Court on the "Great Writ" came with its decision in the 1989 case of *Teague v. Lane*.[59] Frank Dean Teague, a black man, was convicted of attempted murder in 1982 by an all-white jury. During trial and on appeal, he objected to the prosecutor's use of peremptory strikes to eliminate black jurors. He said the prosecutor's action denied him the right to be tried by a jury that was representative of the community. Teague lost initial appeals, but while he was continuing to contest his case, the Supreme Court ruled in a separate dispute, the 1986 case of *Batson v. Kentucky*, that defendants may challenge race bias in peremptory strikes.

Teague argued that he should receive the benefit of the *Batson* decision. No, ruled the Supreme Court in February 1989: new constitutional rules of criminal procedure would not be applied retroactively unless the new rule affects the fundamental fairness of a trial. That very high standard was not met by a challenge to jury composition. Sandra Day O'Connor wrote the opinion, joined by Chief Justice Rehnquist and Justices Antonin Scalia, Anthony M. Kennedy, and, for the most part, Byron R. White. William J. Brennan Jr., Thurgood Marshall, Harry A. Blackmun, and John Paul Stevens dissented.

Justice O'Connor said Teague's "conviction became final two and a half years prior to *Batson*, thus depriving petitioner of any benefit from the rule announced in that case."[60] The opinion drew a sharp dissenting statement from Brennan:

Out of an exaggerated concern for treating similarly situated habeas petitioners the same, the [O'Connor opinion] would for the first time preclude the federal courts from considering on collateral review a vast range of important constitutional challenges; where those challenges have merit, it would bar the vindication of personal constitutional rights and deny society a check against further violations until the same claim is presented on direct review.[61]

In 1990 the Court refined *Teague* and continued to narrow avenues for prisoners' petitions. It ruled that a trial judge's good faith interpretation of legal principles at the time of a conviction could stand even when later rulings in other cases contradicted the judge's interpretation.[62] It held that a defendant could not challenge his conviction based on a new constitutional rule that a state court could not reasonably have predicted.[63] It also said that a defendant is not entitled to federal habeas corpus relief based on a new court ruling in another case unless the principle of the new case is "fundamental to the integrity of the criminal proceeding."[64]

In 1991 the Court further narrowed *Fay v. Noia* (1963) and said a death row inmate may not file a habeas corpus petition in federal court if he failed to abide by state court procedural rules.[65] The convicted murderer in this case, *Coleman v. Thompson,* missed a deadline for filing an appeal at the state level by three days. O'Connor wrote the opinion.

Justice Brennan had been succeeded in the fall of 1990 by David H. Souter, who voted with Rehnquist, White, O'Connor, Scalia, and Kennedy in the majority. Blackmun, Marshall, and Stevens dissented.

Also in 1991 the same six-justice majority said death row prisoners should be allowed (barring extraordinary circumstances) only one round of federal court review through petitions for habeas corpus, after state court appeals are exhausted.[66] The Court in this case, *McCleskey v. Zant,* said a prisoner may file a second habeas corpus petition only if good reason exists for not having raised the new constitutional error on the first round. The prisoner is also required to show that he suffered "actual prejudice" from the error he asserts. Under earlier Court rulings, second and subsequent habeas corpus petitions were dismissed out of hand only if a prisoner deliberately withheld grounds for appeal (possibly to raise the arguments in later petitions and prolong the process).

In 1992 the Court reversed *Townsend v. Sain* (1963) and said federal courts no longer were required to hold a hearing to weigh evidence based on the claim that important facts had not been adequately presented in state court. Under the new standard of *Keeney v. Tamayo-Reyes,* a federal judge must hold a hearing only when a prisoner asserted a credible claim of "factual innocence."[67] In the majority were Chief Justice Rehnquist, and Justices White (who wrote the opinion), Scalia, Souter, and Thomas. Justices O'Connor, Blackmun, Stevens, and Kennedy dissented.

The majority stressed that it is up to state courts, not federal courts, to resolve factual issues. It said that a prisoner is entitled to an evidentiary hearing in federal court only if he can show "cause" for his failure to develop the facts in state proceedings and actual "prejudice" resulting from the failure. The "cause and prejudice" standard is very difficult for a defendant to meet.

In 1996 Congress placed new obstacles in the way of state prisoners seeking review of their sentences in federal court, and the legislation was immediately challenged as effectively suspending the writ of habeas corpus.[68] The provision at issue in *Felker v. Turpin,* the first case testing the Antiterrorism and Effective Death Penalty Act, required prisoners filing second or successive petitions to first obtain permission from a court of appeals. The law set a tough standard for whether the petition would be heard and barred any appeal to the Supreme Court of the court of appeals' decision to hear or not to hear the case.

The Court unanimously upheld the provision of the law, finding that it neither breached the Court's jurisdiction nor constituted an impermissible "suspension" of the writ. Writing for the Court, Chief Justice Rehnquist observed that while the law established new criteria for consideration of habeas corpus petitions, the statute did not affect the Court's authority to hear cases brought as original writs of habeas corpus.

WRITS OF MANDAMUS

"The remedy of *mandamus* is a drastic one," the Supreme Court has written, "to be invoked only in extraordinary situations."[69]

The writ of mandamus is a court order to a government official requiring him to take some action related to his post. The writ may be peremptory—an absolute and unqualified command. Or it may be an alternative command, giving the individual to whom it is addressed the opportunity to show cause to the court why he should not comply with its order. Companion to the mandamus is the writ of prohibition, which bars a government official or lower court from taking certain action, instead of ordering action.

In modern times, the Supreme Court actually issues very few writs of mandamus, even when it finds the person seeking them entitled to such an order. It customarily rules that the party is entitled to that remedy, but withholds the issuance of the writ assuming that the official or the lower court will now act in conformity with that ruling.[70]

Early in its history, with its decision in *Marbury v. Madison*, the Supreme Court made clear that this writ was to be used only in cases over which the issuing court already had jurisdiction. The Court held that Marbury was entitled to his commission and that a writ of mandamus was the proper remedy for the situation, but it refused to issue that order to Secretary of State Madison. The reason for the Court's refusal was its finding that it lacked original jurisdiction over the case, which involved neither a state nor a foreign minister.[71] *(See details of Marbury v. Madison, pp. 76–79, in Chapter 4, and p. 277 in this chapter.)*

Subsequent rulings reinforced this requirement, but as the jurisdiction of the federal courts has been expanded, so have the types of cases in which the writ of mandamus may be used.

The separation of powers has limited the issuance of these writs from federal courts to federal executive officials. Not until 1838 did the Supreme Court rule that any lower federal court could issue such a writ to a federal official in the executive branch.[72]

In *Marbury* the Court distinguished between the types of action that a court might order an executive branch official to take and those in which the separation of powers forbids judicial interference. Only ministerial acts, wrote Chief Justice John Marshall, could be the subject of writs of mandamus:

Where the head of a department acts in a case, in which executive discretion is to be exercised; in which he is the mere organ of executive will . . . any application to a court to control, in any respect, his conduct, would be rejected. . . .

But where he is directed by law to do a certain act affecting the absolute rights of individuals, in the performance of which he is not

placed under the particular direction of the President, and the performance of which the President cannot lawfully forbid . . . in such cases, it is not perceived on what ground the courts . . . are further excused from the duty of giving judgment that right be done to an injured individual.[73]

When the Court, in 1838, upheld the issuance of a writ of mandamus to the postmaster general, it made clear that it so ruled because the action ordered was "a precise, definite act, purely ministerial, and about which the Postmaster-General had no discretion whatever."[74]

The extraordinary nature of these writs in the federal system has been further underscored by the Court's insistence that such writs be issued only to persons who lack any other legal remedy. As early as 1803 and as recently as 1976, the Court has reiterated this point:

As a means of implementing the rule that the writ will issue only in extraordinary circumstances, we have set forth various conditions for its issuance . . . [including that] the party seeking issuance of the writ have no other adequate means to attain the relief he desires . . . and that he satisfy "the burden of showing that [his] right to issuance of the writ is 'clear and indisputable.'"[75]

It is a general rule within the federal judicial system that only final judgments are reviewable by a higher court. Intermediate rulings should not be reviewed until the trial or proceeding has concluded in a final judgment. In keeping with this policy, the Supreme Court has resisted most efforts by parties to obtain a writ of mandamus to review or undo an interim, or interlocutory, ruling of a lower court. The Court also has steadfastly insisted, since early in its history, that the writ of mandamus is not to be used as a substitute for a direct appeal from a ruling.[76] In 1943 the Court affirmed this last point with particular emphasis:

Mandamus, prohibition and injunction against judges are drastic and extraordinary remedies. . . . These remedies should be resorted to only where appeal is a clearly inadequate remedy. We are unwilling to utilize them as a substitute for appeals. As extraordinary remedies, they are reserved for really extraordinary cases.[77]

The most frequent modern use of writs of mandamus is by an appellate court to confine a lower court "to a lawful exercise of its prescribed jurisdiction," or to compel it "to exercise its authority when it is its duty to do so."[78] These writs, the Court has made clear, are "meant to be used only in the exceptional case where there is clear abuse of discretion or 'usurpation of judicial power.'"[79]

Most such orders are issued by the court immediately superior to the receiving court, but the Supreme Court possesses the power to issue a writ directly to a district court "where a question of public importance is involved or where the question is of such a nature that it is peculiarly appropriate that such action by this court should be taken."[80] The Supreme Court also has the power to issue the writ to a state court, so long as the case involved is within the appellate jurisdiction of the Supreme Court.[81]

Although the decision to issue or deny the request for such a writ is left to the discretion of the court to whom the request is addressed, the Supreme Court has not hesitated to overturn what it considers unnecessary use of this writ. The Court has held that the writ of mandamus should not be used to order a trial judge to reinstate certain pleas, because his decision to dismiss them could be reviewed on appeal.[82]

On the other hand, the Court has upheld the use of the writ to override trial judges' decisions to appoint a special master to hear a case, to deny a jury trial, and to reverse a federal judge's decision that in order to avoid delay in hearing a case, it should be tried in state, not federal, court.[83]

INJUNCTIONS

Complementing the affirmative function of the writ of mandamus is the negative function of the injunction—an order directing someone to halt a course of action that will cause irreparable injury to another, for which no adequate recompense can be made by a subsequent lawsuit.

Injunctions are issued under the equity power of the federal courts—their general responsibility to ensure fairness and justice—rather than under their more specific jurisdiction over matters arising from the Constitution and laws.

Injunctions may be temporary, simply preserving the status quo pending final resolution of the issues in a dispute, or they may be permanent bans on certain courses of action. A federal judge may issue a preliminary or temporary injunction even before deciding whether he or she has jurisdiction over a case. The order must be obeyed until it is reversed or lifted.[84]

Some consider the power to issue injunctions, as well as the other writs, to be inherent in the nature of the federal courts, but the Supreme Court traditionally has held that Congress must authorize the federal courts to issue such orders. Since 1789 Congress has provided such statutory authority and has steadily exercised its power to limit the circumstances in which federal courts may issue injunctions. The Judiciary Act of 1789 made clear that equity suits were to be brought only when no legal remedy existed to resolve a dispute.

More specific limitations followed quickly. In 1793 Congress forbade the courts to use injunctions to stay state court proceedings. The Anti-Injunction Act, which set out the fundamental policy of federal noninterference with state judicial proceedings, remains in effect today.

In 1867 Congress forbade federal courts to use injunctions to interfere with the assessment or collection of federal taxes. One result of this ban: the landmark case of *Pollock v. Farmers' Loan & Trust Co.*(1895), which challenged the constitutionality of the peacetime income tax, was actually a suit seeking an injunction directing a bank *not* to pay its federal income taxes.[85]

The extensive use of the injunction by federal courts sympathetic to the efforts of property owners and employers to curtail the activities of organized labor brought the enactment of laws in 1914 and 1932 limiting such "government by injunction." *(See box, "Government by Injunction," this page.)*

In similar fashion, Congress in 1910 and 1937 required that

"GOVERNMENT BY INJUNCTION"

In the early days of organized labor in the United States, federal courts were so receptive to the requests of employers to issue injunctions against boycotts, picketing, and other now-legitimate union activity, that this unity of judiciary and management came to be termed "government by injunction."[1] *(See "Antitrust and Labor," pp. 101–103, in Chapter 4.)*

Congress in 1914 attempted to restrict this use of federal injunctive power.

Included in the Clayton Act, enacted that year, were provisions forbidding the issuance of federal injunctions in labor disputes unless necessary to prevent irreparable injury to property, and providing a limited right to a jury trial for persons charged with contempt for disobeying federal injunctions.

But the Supreme Court, with two 1921 decisions, interpreted the Clayton Act restriction into ineffectiveness. It upheld, as still appropriate, injunctions against a union—rather than against particular employees—and against a variety of "unlawful" labor activities.[2]

A more successful effort to limit government by injunction came in 1932 with passage of the Norris-LaGuardia Act. That act prohibited issuance of injunctions by federal courts in labor disputes except after a hearing and findings that the order was necessary to prevent substantial and irreparable injury, the result of unlawful acts; and that the injury inflicted by granting the injunction was outweighed by the injury that would result if it were not granted.

Some questions were raised about the power of Congress to impose such a limit on the equity jurisdiction of the federal courts.

But in 1938 the Supreme Court upheld this restriction. Writing for the Court, Justice Owen J. Roberts stated that "[t]here can be no question of the power of Congress thus to define and limit the jurisdiction of the inferior courts of the United States."[3]

The Supreme Court has held that this restriction does not foreclose federal injunctions to halt a strike by a union against mines being operated by the government.[4]

And the Court has also upheld the provision of the Taft-Hartley Act that granted federal courts jurisdiction to issue such an injunction against a strike when the court found that the strike affected an entire industry or substantial part of it and, if allowed to continue, would potentially threaten the nation's health or safety.[5]

1. Carl B. Swisher, *American Constitutional Development*, 2d ed. (Cambridge: Houghton Mifflin, 1954), 806–812; *In re Debs*, 158 U.S. 564 (1895); *Gompers v. Buck's Stove & Range Co.*, 221 U.S. 417 (1911).

2. *Duplex Printing Press v. Deering*, 254 U.S. 443 (1921); *American Steel Foundries v. Tri-City Central Trades Council*, 257 U.S. 184 (1921).

3. *Lauf v. E. G. Shinner & Co.*, 303 U.S. 323 at 330 (1938).

4. *United States v. United Mine Workers*, 330 U.S. 258 (1947).

5. *United Steelworkers of America v. United States*, 361 U.S. 39 (1959).

injunctions halting enforcement of state laws or acts of Congress challenged as unconstitutional be granted only by panels of three federal judges, not by a single federal judge. Appeals from the decisions of these panels could be taken directly to the Supreme Court. These provisions were repealed in 1976.

In the 1930s Congress further restricted the use of federal injunctions to interfere with state affairs, forbidding their use to halt the collection or enforcement of public utility rates fixed by state order or the collection of state or local taxes. These bans were not effective in situations where no adequate state remedy was available to persons protesting the rates or the taxes.

During World War II Congress again demonstrated its power to limit the use of this remedy by the courts. It provided that only one court in the country could enjoin rules or orders issued by the Office of Price Administration. The Supreme Court upheld even this limitation on injunctive relief.[86]

The Other Branches

The question of the Supreme Court's power—or that of any other federal court—to use the injunction to halt the proceedings of either Congress or the executive branch arose soon after the Civil War and was quickly and decisively settled.

When Mississippi came to the Court seeking an injunction ordering President Andrew Johnson, as an official or as an individual, to cease enforcing the allegedly unconstitutional Reconstruction Acts, the Court held that it lacked the power to issue such an order. The Court reasoned that this request fell under the same general principles set out in the mandamus cases of *Marbury v. Madison* and *Kendall v. United States ex rel. Stokes,* which "forbid judicial interference with the exercise of executive discretion." Only purely ministerial duties of executive officials were subject to such orders.[87]

In his opinion in *Mississippi v. Johnson* Chief Justice Salmon P. Chase provided a succinct statement of the Court's view of the impropriety of its enjoining the operations of either of the other coordinate branches:

The Congress is the Legislative Department of the Government; the President is the Executive Department. Neither can be restrained in its action by the Judicial Department; though the acts of both, when performed, are, in proper cases, subject to its cognizance.[88]

This ruling, however, did not prevent federal courts from exercising the power to enjoin federal officials from enforcing an unconstitutional act of Congress, an action that fell into the ministerial category. The courts assumed this power long before any statutory authorization could be found for it, but an authorization was provided in the 1937 statute requiring that such injunctions be issued by three-judge panels.

Federal Courts and State Power

Few problems regarding the exercise of federal judicial power have been more persistent than those resulting from the power of federal judges to enjoin state officials and halt state proceedings.

It was to that clearly evident point of friction that Congress spoke in 1793 when it passed the Anti-Injunction Act, a nearly complete ban on such federal interference in state affairs. In recent decades the Court has supplemented the statute with the judicial doctrine of abstention, the rule that federal courts should normally deny requests to halt state enforcement of state laws.

Although its rationale is lost in history, the language of the Anti-Injunction Act is clear: federal courts should not use injunctions to stay proceedings in state courts unless Congress approves such use of these writs.

The modern version of the law, revised in 1948, states:

A court of the United States may not grant an injunction to stay proceedings in a state court except as expressly authorized by Act of Congress, or where necessary in aid of its jurisdiction or to protect or effectuate its judgments.

Through the years the Court has found express exception to this ban in a number of federal laws, including removal statutes, those giving federal courts jurisdiction over farm mortgages, federal habeas corpus statutes, and federal price control laws.[89]

Furthermore, the Court found implicit exceptions to this ban that allow it to permit federal courts to halt state court proceedings when necessary to protect jurisdiction of the federal court over a case or to prevent relitigation in state courts of issues already resolved in federal court.[90] (In 1941 the Court appeared to abandon this last exception, but seven years later, when the anti-injunction statute was rewritten, this exception was reinstated as proper.[91])

Subsequently, the Court has found additional exceptions to the ban in cases brought by the United States and in cases brought under the civil rights law that authorizes individuals to sue for damages in federal court when they have been deprived of a constitutional right by someone acting under color of state law.[92]

The Anti-Injunction Act applies only when a federal court is asked to halt an ongoing state court proceeding. It does not affect the power of federal courts to order state officers to stop enforcing unconstitutional state laws. This latter aspect of federal judicial power was recognized by the Supreme Court as early as 1824.[93] And since its 1908 decision in *Ex parte Young*, federal judges may issue such injunctions to state officials even before the challenged law is actually ruled invalid.[94]

But to curtail instances of clear federal intervention in state business, the Court has required that individuals exhaust their state legislative and administrative remedies before seeking a federal injunction of this sort.[95] And in 1910 Congress limited the power to issue such injunctions to three-judge panels, denying it to a single federal judge acting alone.

The exercise of this power has been tempered by concern for preserving the balance of the federal system. As Justice William J. Brennan Jr. wrote in 1965:

[T]he Court has recognized that federal interference with a State's good-faith administration of its criminal laws is peculiarly inconsistent with our federal framework. It is generally to be assumed that state courts and prosecutors will observe constitutional limitations . . . and that the mere possibility of erroneous initial application of constitutional standards will usually not amount to the irreparable injury necessary to justify a disruption of orderly state proceedings.[96]

To win such an injunction a defendant must show a threat of irreparable injury "both great and immediate," substantially more than simply that attendant upon any criminal prosecution or enforcement of the laws.[97]

In a series of rulings in the 1940s, the Court reinforced this requirement with a new doctrine of abstention. Under this approach to federal injunctive power, federal judges were generally to refrain from enjoining state officials until state courts had full opportunity to consider the challenged law or practice and revise or interpret it to remove the constitutional problem.[98] The Court applied the doctrine to requests both that federal judges halt ongoing state court proceedings and that they halt enforcement of challenged state laws by forbidding any future prosecutions under them.

But the civil rights revolution of the following decades strained this doctrine and resulted in several exceptions to the Court's rule. In 1963 the Court ruled that when a civil rights case involved no question of state law sufficient to resolve the dispute, there was no need to require the people bringing the case to exhaust state remedies before seeking a federal injunction.[99] Two years later the Court held that there was no reason for federal courts to defer to state proceedings in a case where no possible reinterpretation of state law could bring the challenged provisions within constitutional bounds.[100]

Still another—and even more significant—exception to the abstention doctrine was the apparent result of the Supreme Court's 1965 decision in *Dombrowski v. Pfister*. The Court ruled that abstention was inappropriate in cases in which state laws were "justifiably attacked on their face as abridging free expression or as applied for the purpose of discouraging protected activities."[101]

James A. Dombrowski, executive director of a civil rights group, the Southern Conference Educational Fund, and several of his associates had been arrested in 1963 by Louisiana officials and charged with violating that state's laws against subversive activities and communist propaganda. The charges were dropped, but state officials continued to threaten Dombrowski with prosecution. Charging that the threats were part of the state's campaign to discourage civil rights activity, and that the state laws under which the charges had been brought against him violated his First Amendment rights, Dombrowski sought a federal injunction against the alleged harassment.

The Anti-Injunction Act did not apply because there were no pending state court proceedings. But the three-judge panel hearing Dombrowski's request found this an appropriate case for abstention—to give state courts an opportunity to interpret the challenged laws to bring them into line with the First Amendment.

The Supreme Court, by a vote of 5–2, overturned that ruling. Abstention served no legitimate purpose in such a case, held the majority, especially in the face of the clear "chilling effect" that

prosecution under the challenged laws would have on the First Amendment freedoms involved.

Many, including a number of federal judges, saw this ruling as broadening the permissible use of federal injunctions to halt or forestall state criminal prosecutions. The decision seemed to allow such orders in cases in which a state law on its face was so vague or so broad as to collide with the First Amendment—even if the particular case involved no showing of bad faith or harassment on the part of state officials, or any other clear threat of irreparable injury.

This interpretation of *Dombrowski* was short-lived. In a set of five cases decided in 1971, the Supreme Court reaffirmed the basic requirement that before an injunction is issued, there must be a showing of threatened irreparable injury. In cases involving ongoing prosecutions, "the normal thing to do when federal courts are asked to enjoin pending proceedings in state courts is not to issue such injunctions," said the Court in *Younger v. Harris*.[102] This was one of the five decisions handed down together.[103]

Justice Hugo L. Black, who had not participated in the *Dom-*

INJUNCTIONS AND FREE SPEECH

In one of the Court's most recent rulings involving the power of federal judges to issue injunctions, the Court weighed the injunction power of the courts against the free speech interests of individuals.

The Justices permitted judges to establish "buffer zones" to keep antiabortion protesters from blocking access to abortion clinics but warned judges that they cannot restrict more speech than necessary to safeguard access. The vote was 6–3: Chief Justice William H. Rehnquist was joined in the majority by Justices Harry A. Blackmun, John Paul Stevens, Sandra Day O'Connor, David H. Souter, and Ruth Bader Ginsburg. Dissenting were Justices Antonin Scalia, Anthony M. Kennedy, and Clarence Thomas.

The 1994 ruling in *Madsen v. Women's Health Center* upheld portions of a Florida state judge's injunction limiting demonstrations around a health clinic in Melbourne, Florida.

Writing for the Court, Rehnquist rejected the protesters' arguments that the injunction should be subject to the highest level of judicial review—"strict scrutiny"—because it singled out antiabortion views. Instead, Rehnquist said, the injunction was "content neutral" and could be upheld if it "burdens no more speech than necessary to serve a significant government interest."[1] Rehnquist listed "a woman's freedom to seek lawful medical counseling or counseling services in connection with her pregnancy" as one of the interests that would justify "an appropriately tailored injunction."[2] On that basis he upheld a thirty-six-foot buffer zone around most of the clinic and a broad noise ban during hours when abortions were performed.

1. *Madsen v. Women's Health Center*, 114 S. Ct. 2516 (1994).
2. Id.

The Court in *Pennzoil Company v. Texaco Inc.* (1987) ruled that federal judges should not have become involved in an ongoing state case between two oil companies.

browski decision although a member of the Court at the time, wrote the Court's opinions. Only Justice William O. Douglas dissented in *Younger,* although several other justices took issue with the application of the abstention doctrine in one of the other cases decided that day.

In each case the Court reversed a lower court's decision to enjoin state prosecution based on a law challenged as violating the First Amendment. "[T]he existence of a 'chilling effect,' even in the area of First Amendment rights," wrote Justice Black, "has never been considered a sufficient basis, in and of itself, for prohibiting state action."[104] In his view, *Dombrowski* permitted an injunction because of a clear threat of irreparable injury from a possible prosecution, not because the law at issue was alleged to violate the First Amendment. In these cases the Court found no such threat, no showing of bad faith or harassment sufficient to justify an immediate injunction.

The Court in *Younger v. Harris* did not base its ruling on the Anti-Injunction Act but on the broader notion of the "comity" necessary to preserve the federal system. Comity, Black explained, was simply "a proper respect for state functions."[105]

In a series of rulings following *Younger,* the Court, by nar-

rowing margins, has extended the doctrine of nonintervention to limit federal injunctions halting state criminal proceedings begun *after* the injunction was requested, and to curtail their use to intervene in some state civil proceedings.[106] In each case the Court has based the extensions of the *Younger* rule on the general principle of comity rather than on any statutory prohibition.

One of the Court's invocations of the *Younger v. Harris* doctrine came in 1987 in *Pennzoil Company v. Texaco Inc.* The Court was unanimous in holding that federal judges were wrong to become involved in an ongoing state case between the two oil companies. The result of the ruling was to remove a shield that the federal courts had imposed to protect Texaco from having to post a bond of more than $10 billion in order to appeal a damage award that Pennzoil had won.

Writing for the Court, Justice Lewis F. Powell Jr. reemphasized that in all but the most extreme cases, federal judges should refrain from interfering in ongoing state litigation. "Proper respect for the ability of state courts," Powell wrote, requires that federal courts stay their hands in such cases.

Comity, he said, requires federal courts to abstain from becoming involved "not only when the pending state proceedings are criminal, but also when certain civil proceedings are pending, if the State's interests in the proceedings are so important that exercise of the federal judicial power would disregard the comity between the states and the federal government."[107]

DECLARATORY JUDGMENTS

A milder and less intrusive judicial remedy than the injunction is the declaratory judgment. In such a ruling a federal court simply declares conclusively the rights and obligations of the parties in dispute. No coercive or consequential order is necessarily attached to the declaration, although the judgment may be accompanied by, or may serve as the basis for, an injunction.

Because neither the Supreme Court nor other federal courts may issue advisory opinions, the Court initially wavered in its view of the propriety of declaratory judgments. The Court faced the issue after a number of states adopted laws early in the twentieth century authorizing their courts to issue such judgments. When some cases decided in this way found their way to the Supreme Court, the question of the Court's jurisdiction over them arose. Were they actual "cases and controversies" as required by the Constitution? *(See "Cases and Controversies," pp. 297–300.)*

In 1928 the answer seemed to be no. But five years later, in an apparent change of mind, the Court took jurisdiction over a case requesting a declaratory judgment.[108]

Congress effectively resolved any remaining doubts with passage of the Federal Declaratory Judgment Act of 1934, specifically authorizing the issuance of such judgments by federal courts in "cases of actual controversy." The Supreme Court upheld the constitutionality of the law three years later.

By confining the use of declaratory judgments to actual controversies, wrote Chief Justice Charles Evans Hughes, the act simply provided a new procedural remedy for the courts to use in cases already within their jurisdiction.[109]

Nevertheless, the line between declaratory judgments and advisory opinions is a thin one. In 1941 the Court wrote:

The difference between an abstract question and a "controversy" contemplated by the Declaratory Judgment Act is necessarily one of degree, and it would be difficult, if it would be possible, to fashion a precise test for determining in every case whether there is such a controversy. Basically, the question in each case is whether the facts alleged, under all the circumstances, show that there is a substantial controversy, between parties having adverse legal interests, of sufficient immediacy and reality to warrant the issuance of a declaratory judgment.[110]

Although it has insisted that "case or controversy" requirements are applied just as strictly to cases seeking declaratory judgments as to other cases, the Supreme Court has hesitated to approve resolution of major constitutional questions through such judgments. In 1961 it refused a doctor's request for a declaratory judgment that Connecticut's law against all contraceptive devices was unconstitutional. Four years later the Court reversed the doctor's conviction for violating that law and held the statute unconstitutional.[111]

"The Declaratory Judgment Act was an authorization, not a command," the Court has stated. "It gave the federal courts competence to make a declaration of rights; it did not impose a duty to do so."[112] Federal courts thus have broad discretion in deciding whether to grant requests for such judgments. The judgment is available as a remedy in all civil cases except those involving federal taxes, an area Congress excluded in 1935.

Unlike the injunction, a declaratory judgment may be issued even though another adequate remedy for the dispute exists, and even though there are other pending state or federal suits concerning the same matter—although the latter circumstance may bring stricter standards into play on the decision whether to grant the judgment. Yet the Supreme Court has limited the use of declaratory judgments, particularly when its use would leave a state law unenforceable.

The law barring injunctions against state taxes makes no mention of declaratory judgments, but in 1943 the Court applied the abstention doctrine to preclude use of this remedy in such cases as well.[113]

Is a showing of threatened irreparable injury necessary to justify a declaratory judgment against a law under which the person seeking the judgment is being prosecuted or threatened with prosecution? The Court has waffled on this point, but the answer appears to be that such a threat must be demonstrated only if the judgment would disrupt ongoing state proceedings. Otherwise, there is no need to prove such possible injury.

Following its seeming relaxation of the abstention doctrine in cases where injunctions were sought against state laws challenged as violating the First Amendment, the Court in 1967 appeared to adopt a broader view of the power of federal judges to issue declaratory judgments against such laws as well.

In a New York case, *Zwickler v. Koota*, the Court ruled that federal judges had a duty to hear constitutional challenges to state laws. "[E]scape from that duty is not permissible," it said, "merely because state courts also have the solemn responsibility" of protecting constitutional rights.

The Court held that the abstention doctrine allowed escape from this duty only in special circumstances. Injunctions and declaratory judgments were not twin remedies, ruled the Court: when a plaintiff in a single case requested both, the factors in favor and against each remedy should be weighed separately by the judge.[114]

INJURY STANDARD

When a declaratory judgment was sought to halt an ongoing state criminal prosecution, only a clear threat of immediate and irreparable injury justified its issuance, the Court made clear in 1971.

The same standard required for an injunction applied, explained Justice Black, because "ordinarily a declaratory judgment will result in precisely the same interference with and disruption of state proceedings that the long-standing policy limiting injunctions was designed to avoid."[115]

But the Court subsequently held that there need be no demonstration of irreparable injury to justify a declaratory judgment against a state law, if no prosecution under that law is pending against the person seeking the judgment.[116] When there is no ongoing state proceeding that a judgment would disrupt,

---

"MILDER MEDICINE"

Declaratory judgments, wrote Justice William J. Brennan Jr. in 1974, were plainly intended by Congress "as an alternative to the strong medicine of the injunction," particularly when the medicine is to be administered to state officials. Justice William H. Rehnquist chimed in: "A declaratory judgment is simply a statement of rights, not a binding order."[1]

Earlier, in a 1971 dissenting opinion, Brennan, joined by Justices Byron R. White and Thurgood Marshall, had outlined the differences between these two forms of judicial relief:

The effects of injunctive and declaratory relief in their impact on the administration of a State's criminal laws are very different. . . . An injunction barring enforcement of a criminal statute against particular conduct immunizes that conduct from prosecution under the statute. A broad injunction against all enforcement of a statute paralyzes the State's enforcement machinery: the statute is rendered a nullity. A declaratory judgment, on the other hand, is merely a declaration of legal status and rights; it neither mandates nor prohibits state action. . . .

What is clear . . . is that even though a declaratory judgment has "the force and effect of a final judgment," . . . it is a much milder form of relief than an injunction. Though it may be persuasive, it is not ultimately coercive; non-compliance with it may be inappropriate, but is not contempt.[2]

1. *Steffel v. Thompson*, 415 U.S. 452 at 466, 482 (1974).
2. *Perez v. Ledesma*, 401 U.S. 82 at 124, 125–126 (1971).

"considerations of equity, comity, and federalism have little vitality," the Court stated in 1974; therefore, the individual's right to have his federal claim considered in a federal court is paramount.[117] "Requiring the federal courts totally to step aside when no state criminal prosecution is pending against the federal plaintiff would turn federalism on its head," wrote Justice Brennan for a unanimous Court.[118]

The Court also has rejected the argument that if there is no pending state prosecution under a challenged law against the person bringing the challenge, there is no real "case or controversy." So long as a genuine threat of enforcement of such a law exists, there is a case or controversy falling within federal jurisdiction.[119]

The Contempt Power

To maintain decorum within the courtroom and to enforce obedience to its orders, courts possess the inherent power to punish persons for contempt. Contempt may be civil or criminal, depending upon the action involved and the purpose of the penalty imposed. A judge may punish individuals summarily for contempts committed in his or her presence. In recent years, however, the Supreme Court has used the due process guarantee to impose procedural restraints on the exercise of this judicial power.

The contempt power was reinforced by the Judiciary Act of 1789, which authorized the new federal courts "to punish by fine or imprisonment, at the[ir] discretion . . . all contempts of authority in any cause or hearing before the same."

As early as 1821, the Supreme Court urged restraint in the exercise of this power, cautioning courts to use "the least possible power adequate to the end proposed."[120] At least one judge, James H. Peck, disregarded this advice. In 1830 he was impeached for using the contempt power to disbar and imprison a man who had published an article criticizing one of his opinions.

Peck was acquitted, but the event resulted in an 1831 statute that limited the use of the contempt power to punishing, by fine or imprisonment, three types of offenses: "the misbehavior of any person in their presence, or so near thereto as to obstruct the administration of justice, the misbehavior of any of the officers of said courts in their official transactions, and the disobedience or resistance by any such officer, or by any party, juror, witness, or other person, to any lawful writ, process, order, rule, decree, or command of the said courts."

In 1874, with its decision in *Ex parte Robinson*, the Court upheld the limitations imposed upon the use of the contempt power by the 1831 law. It reversed the disbarment of an attorney found to be guilty of contempt of court for actions outside the presence of the judge. The Court held that the 1831 law limited not only the types of misconduct punishable as contempt but also the penalties that might be imposed. Disbarment was not among them.[121]

CONTUMACIOUS CONDUCT

The essential characteristic of contempt is obstructiveness, blocking the proper judicial functions of the court. Little question has been raised about judicial power to maintain peace within the courtroom through the use of the contempt power.

As the Court declared in 1888:

[I]t is a settled doctrine . . . that for direct contempts committed in the face of the court . . . the offender may, in its discretion, be instantly apprehended and immediately imprisoned, without trial or issue, and

---

ENFORCEMENT POWERS

Beyond the power of contempt, federal courts have little equipment with which to enforce their rulings. This is particularly true of the Supreme Court. As Justice Samuel F. Miller wrote in 1890:

[I]n the division of the powers of government between the three great departments, executive, legislative and judicial, the judicial is the weakest for the purposes of self-protection and for the enforcement of the powers which it exercises. The ministerial officers through whom its commands must be executed are marshals of the United States, and belong emphatically to the Executive Department of the government. They are appointed by the President, with the advice and consent of the Senate. They are removable from office at his pleasure. They are subjected by Act of Congress to the supervision and control of the Department of Justice, in the hands of one of the cabinet officers of the President, and their compensation is provided by Acts of Congress. The same may be said of the district attorneys of the United States, who prosecute and defend the claims of the government in the courts.[1]

"The court's only effective power is the power to persuade," Henry J. Abraham wrote in 1968, and at times that power has failed. Although the writ of mandamus is available to compel federal officials to carry out some duties, the Court has been reluctant to use it against lower federal court judges, who have been among the most notable resisters to decisions of the higher court.[2]

Early in the twentieth century, one remarkable case arose in which the Supreme Court itself exercised the contempt power to punish a person who had deliberately disregarded its order—with tragic consequences. A man named Johnson, sentenced to death by a state court in Tennessee, convinced the Supreme Court to hear his challenge to his conviction. In granting his request for review, the Court issued an order staying his execution.

Despite that order, Johnson was taken from jail and lynched. Sheriff Shipp, who had custody over Johnson, was charged by the attorney general with conspiring in the death. Shipp was found guilty of contempt of the Supreme Court, a verdict which resulted in a brief imprisonment.[3] The Supreme Court acted in this case through a commissioner appointed to take testimony.[4]

1. *In re Neagle*, 135 U.S. 1 at 63 (1890).
2. Henry J. Abraham, *The Judicial Process*, 2d ed. (New York: Oxford University Press, 1968), 231; see also 225–231, 338–340; and Stephen T. Early, *Constitutional Courts of the United States* (Totowa, N.J.: Littlefield, Adams, 1977), 64–69, 156–160.
3. *United States v. Shipp*, 203 U.S. 563 (1906).
4. Henry M. Hart Jr. and Herbert Wechsler, *The Federal Courts and the Federal System* (Brooklyn, N.Y.: Foundation Press, 1953), 421.

without other proof than its actual knowledge of what occurred; . . . such power, although arbitrary in its nature and liable to abuse, is absolutely essential to the protection of the courts in the discharge of their functions. Without it, judicial tribunals would be at the mercy of the disorderly and the violent, who respect neither the laws . . . nor the officers charged with the duty of administering them.[122]

In 1970 the Supreme Court affirmed the power of a judge to keep peace in his courtroom, even at the cost of having a defendant bound and gagged or physically removed from the room.[123]

Direct disobedience to a court order is perhaps the most frequent conduct outside the courtroom penalized as contempt. Affirming the contempt conviction of labor leader Eugene Debs for such disobedience in 1895, the Court wrote:

The power of a court to make an order carries with it the equal power to punish for a disobedience of that order, and the inquiry as to the question of disobedience has been, from time immemorial, the special function of the court.[124]

Willful disregard of a court order may be both civil and criminal contempt, the Court has ruled.[125]

"THE VICINITY OF THE COURT"

Generally, the Supreme Court has viewed the 1831 act as allowing use of the contempt power only to punish conduct actually impeding a trial or other judicial proceeding. In 1918 the Court strayed from its usual practice. In *Toledo Newspaper Co. v. United States* the Court, 5–2, upheld a contempt citation against a newspaper for publishing articles and cartoons about a railway rate dispute pending in court. The judge viewed the articles as intended to provoke public resistance to his eventual order and to intimidate him. For the first time, the Court approved the use of the power to punish conduct that simply tended to obstruct the courts in carrying out their duty.[126]

Two decades later the Court reversed this ruling and returned to the strict construction of the contempt power as defined by the 1831 law. In *Nye v. United States* the Court reversed the contempt convictions of persons who had successfully used liquor and other methods of persuasion—miles from the courtroom—to convince a plaintiff to drop his case. These actions were reprehensible, stated the Court, but were punishable under other laws. The phrase used in the 1831 law—allowing courts to punish misconduct "in their presence or so near thereto as to obstruct the administration of justice"—meant that the conduct should be geographically near the courtroom or it should not be punished as contempt, held the Court. The conduct in this case, although it did obstruct justice, "was not misbehavior in the vicinity of the court disrupting to quiet and order or actually interrupting the court in the conduct of its business."[127]

The Obstinate Witness

The Fifth Amendment guarantees witnesses before courts or grand juries the right to refuse to incriminate themselves. But no other privilege allows persons simply to refuse to answer proper questions addressed to them in those forums. Furthermore, once a witness is granted immunity from prosecution for crimes revealed by his testimony, his privilege of silence ends altogether. False testimony, however, is prosecutable as perjury—whether given by an immunized witness or not.

In 1919, in *Ex parte Hudgings,* the Supreme Court held that a witness committing perjury should not be held in contempt as a penalty for his false testimony unless the perjury was clearly an obstructive tactic. "[I]n order to punish perjury . . . as a contempt," wrote Chief Justice Edward D. White for the Court, "there must be added to the essential elements of perjury under the general law the further element of obstruction to the court in the performance of its duty."[128]

But the Court has backed the use of the contempt power to punish obstinate witnesses who simply refused, for reasons other than self-incrimination, to respond to certain questions. In 1958 Justice Felix Frankfurter commented:

Whatever differences the potentially drastic power of courts to punish for contempt may have evoked, a doubt has never been uttered that stubborn disobedience of the duty to answer relevant inquiries in a judicial proceeding brings into force the power of the federal courts to punish for contempt.[129]

In 1975 the Court in *United States v. Wilson* upheld the use of the summary contempt power to punish an immunized trial witness who persisted in his refusal to respond to questions. Such "intentional obstructions of court proceedings," held the Court, could destroy a prosecution. "In an ongoing trial with the judge, jurors, counsel, and witnesses all waiting," wrote Chief Justice Warren Burger, the summary contempt power is "an appropriate remedial tool to discourage witnesses from contumacious refusals to comply with lawful orders essential to prevent a breakdown of the proceedings."[130]

Although grand jury witnesses who refuse to answer questions despite a grant of immunity may be cited for contempt, such punishment may not be summary; it may be imposed only after a hearing at which the accused witness is allowed to defend himself against the charge. This 1965 holding in *Harris v. United States* overruled a 1959 decision allowing summary punishment of grand jury witnesses in this situation.[131]

Attorneys and Fugitives

Lawyers—as officers of the Court—have received their share of contempt citations.

In 1952 the Supreme Court upheld the contempt citations and convictions of the defense attorneys for eleven Communist Party leaders convicted of violating the Smith Act. Lower court judges reviewing the attorneys' actions during the trial described their conduct as "wilfully obstructive," "abominable," and "outrageous, . . . conduct of a kind which no lawyer owes his client, which cannot ever be justified."[132] *(See details of this 1952 case, Sacher v. United States, p. 295.)*

But the Court continues to insist that the element of obstruction be clear before a contempt conviction can be properly imposed. In 1962 the Court reversed the contempt conviction of an attorney penalized simply for asserting his right to ask questions until he was stopped by a court official.[133]

THE COURT: SUPERVISOR OF FEDERAL COURTS, THE FEDERAL BAR, AND FEDERAL PROCEDURE

By virtue of its position at the apex of the nation's judiciary, the Supreme Court exerts broad supervisory power over the administration of justice in the federal courts.

This responsibility is multifaceted. Among its elements are the Court's power to review the functioning of the lower courts, to propose rules of procedure governing processes in the federal courts, and to oversee the admission, conduct, and expulsion of members of the federal bar.

All federal courts have an inherent power to supervise their officers, the conduct of litigants, witnesses, attorneys, and jurors, and to protect property within their custody.[1]

To help them resolve certain issues, the Supreme Court and other federal courts are empowered to appoint persons of special skills. For example, the Supreme Court may appoint special masters to hear evidence and recommend judgment in original cases involving complex factual matters such as boundary locations. The rationale for the use of special personnel was set out by Justice Louis D. Brandeis in 1920:

Courts have (at least in the absence of legislation to the contrary) inherent power to provide themselves with appropriate instruments required for the performance of their duties . . . [including] authority to appoint persons unconnected with the court to aid judges in the performance of specific judicial duties, as they may arise.[2]

GENERAL SUPERVISION

The Court's general supervisory power over lower federal courts is exercised randomly and sporadically through its decisions reviewing their actions—approving some and rebuking others.

The Court at times has taken the opportunity to go beyond the decision required to resolve a particular dispute and prescribed or clarified rules of procedure.

An example of this mode of exercising the supervisory power is the 1966 Supreme Court decision in *Cheff v. Schnackenberg*.[3] While upholding the lower court's refusal of a jury trial to the plaintiff in that case, the Court ruled, in its supervisory role, that anyone sentenced by a federal judge to more than six months in prison for contempt should be given a jury trial.

Several years earlier the Court exercised its supervisory power to reduce a contempt sentence, after the sentencing court had ignored Supreme Court suggestions that a reduction was necessary.[4]

"The Supreme Court's review power," wrote one student of the judicial system, "is probably its most extensively used method for instructing the lower courts in the constitutional or statutory law and procedural niceties they are to apply. Processes of appeal and reversal are parts—most important parts—of the internal control mechanism of the constitutional court system."[5]

"Judicial supervision of the administration of criminal justice in the federal courts," wrote Justice Felix Frankfurter in 1943, "implies the duty of establishing and maintaining civilized standards of procedure and evidence."[6] Frankfurter indicated his belief that such standards might be considerably stiffer than those required by the Constitution itself.

RULE-MAKING POWER

The Judiciary Act of 1789 authorized all federal courts to make rules for the orderly conduct of their business. In addition, Congress has enacted "process acts" to specify certain forms and procedures for use in the federal courts.[7]

In 1825 the Supreme Court sustained the power of Congress to make procedural rules for the federal courts and to delegate considerable responsibility for drafting such rules to the courts themselves.[8] The Court in the ensuing century set out various rules applying to different types of lawsuits, but not until the 1930s was there a uniform set of rules governing procedures in all federal courts.[9]

In 1933 Congress authorized the Supreme Court to propose rules governing postverdict proceedings in all federal criminal cases. The following year it granted similar authority to the Court to propose rules of civil procedure, subject to veto by Congress. And in 1940 Congress gave the Court authority to propose rules governing criminal case procedures prior to a verdict.

Using advisory committees of distinguished attorneys and legal scholars and judges, the Supreme Court proposed, and Congress approved, the Federal Rules of Civil Procedure, which took effect in 1938, and the Federal Rules of Criminal Procedure, which took effect in 1946. Both have been subsequently amended through this same process of committee drafting, Supreme Court recommendation, and congressional examination and approval.[10]

OVERSEEING THE BAR

It is well settled, declared Chief Justice Roger B. Taney in 1857, "that it rests exclusively with the court to determine who is qualified to become one of its officers, as an attorney and a counselor, and for what cause he ought to be removed. That power, however, is not an arbitrary and despotic one, to be exercised at the pleasure of the court, or from passion, prejudice, or personal hostility; but it is the duty of the court to exercise and regulate it by a sound and just judicial discretion, whereby the rights and independence of the bar may be as scrupulously guarded and maintained by the court, as the rights and dignity of the court itself."[11]

Ten years later the Court invalidated an act of Congress imposing a test oath requirement upon all attorneys wishing to practice before federal courts. Congress may set statutory qualifications for admission to the bar, the Court held in that ruling in *Ex parte Garland*, but those qualifications are subject to judicial review and disallowance.

Writing for the majority in this case, Justice Stephen Field elaborated upon the federal courts' responsibility for admission to the bar:

The order of admission is the judgment of the court that the parties possess the requisite qualifications as attorneys and counselors, and are entitled to appear as such and conduct causes therein. From its entry the parties become officers of the court, and are responsible to it for professional misconduct. They hold their office only during good behavior and can only be deprived of it for misconduct ascertained and declared by the judgment of the court after opportunity to be heard has been afforded. . . . Their admission or their exclusion is not the exercise of a mere ministerial power. It is the exercise of judicial power. . . .

The attorney and counselor being, by the solemn judicial act of the court, clothed with his office, does not hold it as a matter of grace and favor. The right which it confers upon him to appear for suitors, and to argue causes, is something more than a mere indulgence, revocable at the pleasure of the court, or at the command of the Legislature. It is a right of which he can only be deprived by the judgment of the court, for moral or professional delinquency.[12]

In modern times the Court has ruled on questions of state bar qualifications and disqualifications. It has held that alienage alone is insufficient reason to deny someone admission to a state bar, but has allowed state bar officials to exclude conscientious objectors and individuals refusing to answer questions concerning possible membership in the Communist Party.[13]

Delving into First Amendment issues in recent years, the Court has held that lawyers may be prohibited from making extrajudicial statements to the press that present a "substantial likelihood of materially prejudicing a trial."[14] The Court also has upheld a bar rule preventing lawyers from sending letters of solicitation to accident victims and their relatives for thirty days after an incident.[15]

1. U.S. Congress, Library of Congress, Congressional Reference Service, *The Constitution of the United States of America: Analysis and Interpretation* (Washington, D.C.: U.S. Government Printing Office, 1973), 583–584.

2. *Ex parte Peterson*, 253 U.S. 300 at 312 (1920).

3. *Cheff v. Schnackenberg*, 384 U.S. 373 at 380 (1966).

4. *Yates v. United States*, 356 U.S. 363 at 366 (1958).

5. Stephen T. Early Jr., *Constitutional Courts of the United States* (Totowa, N.J.: Littlefield, Adams, 1977), 149; see also 149–156.

6. *McNabb v. United States*, 318 U.S. 332 at 340 (1943).

7. Julius Goebel Jr., *History of the Supreme Court of the United States*: Vol. I, *Antecedents and Beginnings to 1801* (New York: MacMillan Publishing, 1971), 509–551.

8. *Wayman v. Southard*, 10 Wheat. 1 (1825).

9. Henry M. Hart Jr. and Herbert Wechsler, *The Federal Courts and the Federal System* (Brooklyn, N.Y.: Foundation Press, 1953), 577–611.

10. Charles Alan Wright, *The Law of Federal Courts*, 4th ed. (St. Paul, Minn.: West Publishing, 1983), 402–403.

11. *Ex parte Secombe*, 19 How. 9 at 13 (1857).

12. *Ex parte Garland*, 4 Wall. 333 at 378–379 (1867); see also *Ex parte Robinson*, 19 Wall. 505 (1874).

13. *In re Griffiths*, 413 U.S. 717 (1973); *Konigsberg v. California*, 366 U.S. 36 (1961) and 353 U.S. 252 (1957); *In re Summers*, 325 U.S. 561 (1945).

14. *Gentile v. State Bar of Nevada*, 501 U.S. 1030 (1991).

15. *Florida Bar v. Went for It Inc.*, 115 S. Ct. 2371 (1995).

The Court also has upheld the use of the contempt power of federal judges to punish—by additional prison terms—persons convicted of a crime who absconded and were fugitives from justice for a period of years before surrendering to serve the sentences for those crimes.[134]

CIVIL AND CRIMINAL CONTEMPT

Contempt may be civil or criminal in nature. As the justices have had many occasions to acknowledge, it is sometimes difficult to distinguish between the two. The test developed by the Court—and used consistently since 1911—focuses upon the character and purpose of the penalty imposed. In *Gompers v. Buck's Stove and Range Co.* the Court declared that if the penalty "is for civil contempt the punishment is remedial, and for the benefit of the complainant [generally the other party to a case]. But if it is for criminal contempt the sentence is punitive, to vindicate the authority of the court."[135]

Justice Joseph R. Lamar continued:

[I]mprisonment for civil contempt is ordered where the defendant has refused to do an affirmative act required by the provisions of an order. . . . Imprisonment in such cases . . . is intended to be remedial by coercing the defendant to do what he had refused to do. . . .

For example: if a defendant should refuse to pay alimony . . . he could be committed until he complied with the order. Unless there

United Mine Workers of America and its president, John L. Lewis *(above),* were convicted of contempt for disobeying a court order forbidding a strike. The Supreme Court upheld the conviction in *United States v. United Mine Workers* (1947).

"'THE LEAST POSSIBLE POWER'"

Intervening in a tense, long-standing battle between the city of Yonkers, New York, and the federal government over segregated housing, the Supreme Court in 1990 reiterated the strict standard of care that judges must employ in using the contempt power.

The Court held, 5–4, that a federal district judge abused his power when he imposed contempt fines against city officials who failed to put in place a court-ordered plan to desegregate housing in the city. The Court said that the fines levied against the individual officials were not a proper exercise of judicial power. Upholding the much larger fines against the city, totaling more than $800,000, the Court said that the lower court should have waited a reasonable time to see if that fine was sufficient to win compliance with his order before levying the fines against the individual officials.

Chief Justice William H. Rehnquist acknowledged that stiff monetary penalties were sometimes necessary to enforce court orders. Fining legislators, however, is an extreme step because it "effects a much greater perversion of the normal legislative process than does the imposition of fines on the city." He continued: fining legislators "is designed to cause them to vote, not with a view to the interest of their constituents or of the city, but with a view solely to their own personal interests."

Spallone v. United States, Chema v. United States, Longo v. United States, 493 U.S. 265 at 279, 280 (1990).

---

were special elements of contumacy, the refusal to pay . . . is treated as being rather in resistance to the opposite party than in contempt of the court.[136]

Citing the often-quoted statement that a person imprisoned for civil contempt carries the keys of the prison in his pocket, Justice Lamar pointed out that such a person "can end the sentence and discharge himself at any moment by doing what he had previously refused to do."[137]

Criminal contempt, on the other hand, results when

the defendant does that which he has been commanded not to do, the disobedience is a thing accomplished. Imprisonment cannot undo or remedy what has been done, nor afford any compensation for the pecuniary injury caused by the disobedience. If the sentence is limited to imprisonment for a definite period, the defendant . . . cannot shorten the term by promising not to repeat the offense. Such imprisonment operates . . . solely as punishment.[138]

Summarizing the test, one can say that civil contempt consists of the refusal to act as the court commands, a disobedience punished by imprisonment until the person obeys; criminal contempt consists of doing the forbidden and being punished for a definite term.

In 1925 the Supreme Court reinforced the distinction between civil and criminal contempt, ruling that the president's power of pardon extended to allow pardons of persons convicted of criminal—but not of civil—contempt.[139]

In 1947 the Supreme Court muddied somewhat the distinction between civil and criminal contempt by ruling that the same action could be both—and by upholding the conviction of the United Mine Workers of America and its president, John L. Lewis, on both types of contempt as a result of his and the union's disobedience of a court order forbidding a strike. "Common sense," wrote Chief Justice Fred M. Vinson, "would recognize that conduct can amount to both civil and criminal contempt. The same acts may justify a court in resorting to coercive and to punitive measures."[140]

The distinction was illuminated again in one small portion of the decision. Lewis and the union argued that the order they had disobeyed was invalid, a violation of statutory restrictions on the use of injunctions in labor disputes. *(See box, "Government by Injunction," p. 285.)*

The Supreme Court found the injunction valid but declared that even if it had been illegally issued, it was to be obeyed—on pain of contempt—until it was reversed "by orderly and proper proceedings." If the injunction had been found invalid, Vinson explained, the civil contempt citation would be set aside because any duty to obey the order had vanished. But the criminal contempt conviction—punishment for disobedience to an outstanding and unreversed court order—would remain in effect.[141]

The Court in 1966 ruled that individuals imprisoned for contempt, after refusing to answer grand jury questions despite a grant of immunity, were being penalized for civil contempt. Whether the contempt is civil or criminal depends on the character of the disobedience and the purpose of the penalty. Their disobedience, wrote Justice Tom Clark, was in refusing to do what the court ordered, and their punishment was "for the obvious purpose of compelling the witnesses to obey the orders to testify," and whenever they did so, they would be released.[142]

In 1994 the Court unanimously rejected a $52 million contempt-of-court fine imposed on the United Mine Workers, ruling that the penalty was too serious to be applied without a jury trial.[143] A state judge in Virginia had imposed the fine after finding the union in contempt of court for violating an injunction intended to prevent violence in a 1989 coal strike. The Virginia supreme court said the fine was a proper sanction for civil contempt because it was intended to force compliance with the injunction, not to punish the union. But the U.S. Supreme Court disagreed, 9–0. Ruling in *United Mine Workers v. Bagwell*, it said the fine could not be regarded as a civil penalty because it was not intended to compensate a private party, the alleged contempt did not occur in the judge's presence, and the conduct involved a broad range of activities instead of a single, discrete act.

A SUMMARY POWER

"A contempt proceeding," stated the Court in 1904, "is *sui generis*"—a unique type of judicial process.[144] One aspect of this uniqueness is the fact that contempt has traditionally been a summary power—that is, a judge could, on the spot, hold someone in contempt and impose punishment without a trial before a jury or many of the other procedural safeguards guaranteed by the Bill of Rights.

The summary nature of this power is directly related to its original purpose—to enable a judge to maintain order in the courtroom. As the Supreme Court, quoting a lower court, wrote in an 1888 ruling:

The judicial eye witnessed the act and the judicial mind comprehended all the circumstances of aggravation, provocation or mitigation; and the fact being thus judicially established, it only remained for the judicial arm to inflict proper punishment.[145]

A few years later, in upholding the use of the contempt power to punish disobedience of a court order, the Supreme Court rejected the suggestion that a person charged with contempt of the orders of one court or one judge should be sentenced by another judge. "To submit the question of disobedience to another tribunal, be it a jury or another court, would operate to deprive the proceedings of half its efficiency," stated the Court.[146]

AN UNBIASED JUDGE

But by 1925 the Supreme Court began to apply some of the elements of the due process guarantee to contempt proceedings. The Court recommended that when a judge became so personally involved with an allegedly contemptuous course of behavior that he lacked the necessary neutrality to be fair in imposing a sentence, he should turn the matter over to a colleague. In the case of *Cooke v. United States*, Chief Justice William Howard Taft wrote for the majority:

[W]here conditions do not make it impracticable, or where the delay may not injure public or private right, a judge called upon to act in a case of contempt by personal attack upon him, may, without flinching from his duty properly ask that one of his fellow judges take his place.[147]

Nevertheless, the Court continued to defer to the discretion of the trial judge in most situations. The most notable example of this judicial deference came in 1952 in *Sacher v. United States* when the Court upheld as proper the criminal contempt citations imposed by federal judge Harold Medina upon the attorneys who had, during a long and controversial trial before him, defended eleven men accused of violating the Smith Act in their roles as leaders of the U.S. Communist Party.

Noting that Medina waited until after the trial to cite and sentence them for contempt, the attorneys challenged the summary nature of the contempt proceedings and argued that Medina should have referred the contempt charges to another judge for hearing and sentencing.

Justice Robert H. Jackson set out the reasoning behind the decision to uphold Medina's actions:

It is almost inevitable that any contempt of a court committed in the presence of the judge during a trial will be an offense against his dignity and authority. At a trial the court is so much the judge and the judge so much the court that the two terms are used interchangeably. . . . It

cannot be that summary punishment is only for such minor contempts as leave the judge indifferent and may be evaded by adding hectoring, abusive and defiant conduct toward the judge as an individual. Such an interpretation would nullify, in practice, the power it purports to grant.[148]

But just two years later, in a less highly publicized case, *Offutt v. United States*, the Court held that a judge who had become involved in a wrangle with a defense attorney presenting a case before him should have sent contempt charges against that attorney to another judge for resolution.

Justice Felix Frankfurter, who had dissented from the ruling upholding Medina's actions, wrote for the Court:

The pith of this rather extraordinary power to punish without the formalities required by the Bill of Rights for the prosecution of federal crimes generally, is that the necessities of the administration of justice require such summary dealing with obstructions to it. It is a mode of vindicating the majesty of law, in its active manifestation, against obstruction and outrage. The power thus entrusted to a judge is wholly unrelated to his personal sensibilities, be they tender or rugged. But judges also are human, and may . . . quite unwittingly identify offense to self with obstruction to law. Accordingly, this Court has deemed it important that district judges guard against this easy confusion by not sitting themselves in judgment upon misconduct of counsel where the contempt charged is entangled with the judge's personal feeling against the lawyer.[149]

A unanimous Court reaffirmed this holding in 1971.[150]

THE RIGHT TO TRIAL

As early as the nineteenth century, the Supreme Court began to place some limits on the summary nature of the contempt power, requiring the use of normal adversary procedures to deal with contempts occurring out of the presence of the court. In 1946 the new rules of federal criminal procedure allowed summary punishment only of conduct seen or heard by the judge and "committed in the actual presence of the court."

All other criminal contempt was to be prosecuted separately, after notice, with a hearing at which a defense to the charge could be presented, and opportunity for release on bail. Furthermore, the rule stated that if the contempt involved "disrespect to or criticism of a judge, that judge is disqualified from presiding at the trial or hearing except with the defendant's consent."

This was not a sudden change. The Court had taken the opportunity in earlier cases to state that the presumption of innocence applied in criminal contempt cases, that guilt must be proven beyond a reasonable doubt, that a person charged with contempt could not be compelled to be a witness against himself, and that persons accused of contempt other than that occurring in open court should be advised of the charges and should have an opportunity to present a defense against them with the aid of counsel and to call witnesses.[151]

But in a long and unbroken line of cases, the Court insisted that persons charged with contempt did not have the right to a trial by jury—except in such unusual cases as those in which Congress by law provided that right.[152] The Sixth Amendment states that "in all criminal prosecutions the accused shall enjoy the right to a speedy and public trial, by an impartial jury." The Court's position was simply that criminal contempt was not a crime in the sense of this amendment and thus its guarantee did not apply.

Citing long lines of precedents, the Court in 1958, 1960, and 1964 reaffirmed its position: there was no constitutional right to a jury trial for persons charged with contempt.[153] Then, almost in passing, the Court in 1966 announced that federal courts could not sentence persons to more than six months in prison for criminal contempt unless they had been tried by a jury—or had waived their right to such a trial.[154]

The Court's turnabout came in the case of Paul Cheff, who did not benefit because his contempt sentence was for six months—no longer. The Court did not base its statement imposing the jury trial requirement upon a constitutional basis but upon its power to supervise the conduct of lower federal courts. *(See box, The Court: Supervisor of Federal Courts, the Federal Bar, and Federal Procedure, pp. 292–293.)*

Two years later, however, the Court placed the requirement of a jury trial for serious criminal contempt charges upon a constitutional basis. On the same day that it extended the Sixth Amendment right to a jury trial to state proceedings in *Duncan v. Louisiana*, the Court ruled that state courts, like federal ones, must accord the right to a jury trial to persons charged with serious criminal contempts.[155]

Writing for the seven-man majority in *Bloom v. Illinois* (1968), Justice Byron R. White explained:

Our deliberations have convinced us . . . that serious criminal contempts are so nearly like other serious crimes that they are subject to the jury trial provisions of the Constitution, now binding on the states. . . .

Criminal contempt is a crime in the ordinary sense; it is a violation of the law, a public wrong which is punishable by fine or imprisonment or both. . . .

Indeed, in contempt cases an even more compelling argument can be made for providing a right to jury trial as a protection against the arbitrary exercise of official power. Contemptuous conduct, though a public wrong, often strikes at the most vulnerable and human qualities of a judge's temperament. Even when the contempt is not a direct insult to the court or the judge, it frequently represents a rejection of judicial authority, or an interference with the judicial process or with the duties of officers of the court.[156]

White cited the Court's 1895 statement in *In re Debs* that contempt proceedings would be less efficient if they were conducted before a court other than that which was the object of the contempt. The modern Court, he wrote, disagreed:

In our judgment, when serious punishment for contempt is contemplated, rejecting a demand for jury trial cannot be squared with the Constitution or justified by considerations of efficiency or the desirability of vindicating the authority of the court. . . . Perhaps to some extent we sacrifice efficiency, expedition, and economy, but the choice in favor of jury trial has been made, and retained, in the Constitution.[157]

Six years later a more closely divided Court, 5–4, affirmed this extension of the right to a jury trial in contempt cases. Due process, the Court held in 1974, required that persons whose aggregate criminal contempt sentences were more than six months should have a jury trial on the contempt charges against them.[158]

But in 1996 the Court ruled that no right exists to a jury trial when a defendant is prosecuted for multiple "petty" offenses, even if the aggregate sentence might exceed six months in prison. The Court distinguished the decision from its 1974 ruling, saying that in the earlier dispute it was not clear whether the legislature considered the offense (criminal contempt) petty or serious because it did not set a specific penalty. In the new case, however, Congress had established a six-month maximum penalty for the crime, obstructing the mail, placing the offense in the "petty" category.[159]

Political and constitutional necessity require the federal courts—limited both in power and in jurisdiction—to exercise their authority with restraint. The Supreme Court has recognized this truth from its earliest years. As one scholar noted, "[N]early all of the specific limitations which are said to govern the exercise of judicial review have been announced by the Supreme Court itself."[1]

The rules, principles, and doctrines that compose this posture of restraint have evolved as the Court has said yes to some cases and no to others. They usually develop from the "threshold questions"—the seemingly technical issues that the Court must resolve before moving on to the "merits," or the substance, of the controversy. The elements of restraint on the power of the Court are given sometimes overlapping labels—"case or controversy" requirement, advisory opinion, "mootness," "friendly" suits, test cases, "standing to sue," precedent and *stare decisis*, "political questions," and comity.

Those who follow debates over judicial activism and judicial restraint may be surprised to learn that even during "activist" periods of Supreme Court history the rules have rarely changed. Only their application has varied.

Justices often differ on whether a case is moot, whether a litigant has standing, or whether a question is "political," but few have advocated discarding any of those standards. In his concurring opinion in *Ashwander v Tennessee Valley Authority* (1936), Justice Louis D. Brandeis set out some of these rules in a classic exposition of judicial restraint.

The justice—to summarize the Brandeis rules—said that the Court avoided deciding many constitutional questions by adhering to the rules that:

• It would not consider the constitutionality of legislation in friendly, nonadversary cases.

• It would not decide any constitutional question before a decision on such matter was necessary.

• It would not set out any constitutional rule broader than warranted by the facts in the particular case before it.

• It would resolve a dispute on a nonconstitutional basis rather than a constitutional basis, if possible.

• It would not consider a challenge to a law's validity brought by someone who fails to demonstrate that he has been injured by the law or by someone who had benefited from the law.

• When an act of Congress was challenged as invalid, the Court would be certain there was no possible interpretation under which the law would be found constitutional before striking it down as unconstitutional.[2] *(See box, Justice Brandeis and Rules of Restraint, p. 298.)*

These rules, as Chief Justice Earl Warren and others have taken pains to point out, are neither absolute nor purely constitutional. In them, the Court has blended political reality, policy considerations, and constitutional elements into a posture of judicial restraint, which the Court applies as it wishes from case to case. Therefore, it is quite possible to find major decisions of the Court that count as exceptions to every one of Brandeis's rules—as well as to others he did not mention.

Cases and Controversies

The single most basic restriction on the work of the federal courts is the requirement that they decide only cases or controversies. Article III, Section 2, states that federal judicial power extends to certain types of "cases" and certain "controversies." As interpreted by the Supreme Court, those words limit the power of federal courts to resolving disputes between adversary parties whose legal rights and interests are truly in collision, a collision for which federal courts may have a remedy.

A controversy, to qualify, Chief Justice Charles Evans Hughes once explained,

must be definite and concrete, touching the legal relations of parties having adverse legal interests. . . . It must be a real and substantial controversy admitting of specific relief through a decree of a conclusive character, as distinguished from an opinion advising what the law would be upon a hypothetical state of facts.[3]

In the words of Justice Felix Frankfurter, real cases and controversies have "that clear concreteness provided when a question emerges precisely framed and necessary for decision from a clash of adversary argument exploring every aspect of a multifaced situation embracing conflicting and demanding interests."[4]

A more modern term to describe a case or controversy properly before the court is "justiciable." Chief Justice Warren in 1968 described this concept and its link to the "case or controversy" doctrine. *(See box, The Tip of an Iceberg, p. 299.)*

ADVISORY OPINIONS

One of the earliest corollaries developed by the Court from the Constitution's use of "case" and "controversy" was its firm decision that neither it nor lower federal courts would give advisory opinions—that is, speak not to resolve an actual conflict but simply to give advice on abstract issues or hypothetical situations.

In 1793 the justices of the Supreme Court politely refused to answer a set of questions submitted to them by Secretary of State Thomas Jefferson, on behalf of President George Washington, concerning neutrality and the Court's interpretation of several major treaties with Britain and France.[5] The Court indicated in correspondence that it found the issuance of advisory opinions contrary to the basic separation of powers and functions in the federal government.

More than a century later the Court reaffirmed this stance with its decision in 1911 in *Muskrat v. United States.*[6]

Congress, desiring to determine the constitutionality of cer-

JUSTICE BRANDEIS AND RULES OF RESTRAINT

In a concurring opinion in *Ashwander v. Tennessee Valley Authority* (1936), Justice Louis D. Brandeis delineated a set of Court-formulated rules useful in avoiding constitutional decisions. The portion of his opinion setting forth those rules follows:

The Court developed, for its own governance in the cases confessedly within its jurisdiction, a series of rules under which it has avoided passing upon a large part of all the constitutional questions pressed upon it for decision. They are:

1. The Court will not pass upon the constitutionality of legislation in a friendly, non-adversary, proceeding, declining because to decide such questions "is legitimate only in the last resort, and as a necessity in the determination of real, earnest and vital controversy between individuals. It never was the thought that, by means of a friendly suit, a party beaten in the legislature could transfer to the courts an inquiry as to the constitutionality of the legislative act." *Chicago & Grand Trunk Ry v. Wellman*, 143 U.S. 339, 345. Compare *Lord v. Veazie*, 8 How. 251; *Atherton Mills v. Johnston*, 259 U.S. 13, 15.

2. The Court will not "anticipate a question of constitutional law in advance of the necessity of deciding it." *Liverpool, N.Y. & P.S.S. Co. v. Emigration Commissioners*, 113 U.S. 33, 39;[1] *Abrams v. Van Schaick*, 293 U.S. 188; *Wilshire Oil Co. v. United States*, 295 U.S. 100. "It is not the habit of the Court to decide questions of a constitutional nature unless absolutely necessary to a decision of the case." *Burton v. United States*, 196 U.S. 283, 295.

3. The Court will not "formulate a rule of constitutional law broader than is required by the precise facts to which it is to be applied." *Liverpool, N.Y. & P.S.S. Co. v. Emigration Commissioners, supra.* Compare *Hammond v. Schappi Bus Line*, 275 U.S. 164, 169–172.

4. The Court will not pass upon a constitutional question although properly presented by the record, if there is also present some other ground upon which the case may be disposed of. This rule has found most varied application. Thus, if a case can be decided on either of two grounds, one involving a constitutional question, the other a question of statutory construction or general law, the Court will decide only the latter. *Siler v. Louisville & Nashville R. Co.*, 213 U.S. 175, 191; *Light v. United States*, 220 U.S. 523, 538. Appeals from the highest court of a state challenging its decision of a question under the Federal Constitution are frequently dismissed be-

cause the judgment can be sustained on an independent state ground. *Berea College v. Kentucky*, 211 U.S. 45, 53.

5. The Court will not pass upon the validity of a statute upon complaint of one who fails to show that he is injured by its operation.[2] *Tyler v. The Judges*, 179 U.S. 405; *Hendrick v. Maryland*, 235 U.S. 610, 621. Among the many applications of this rule, none is more striking than the denial of the right of challenge to one who lacks a personal or property right. Thus, the challenge by a public official interested only in the performance of his official duty will not be entertained. *Columbus & Greenville Ry. v. Miller*, 283 U.S. 96, 99–100. In *Fairchild v. Hughes*, 258 U.S. 126, the Court affirmed the dismissal of a suit brought by a citizen who sought to have the Nineteenth Amendment declared unconstitutional. In *Massachusetts v. Mellon*, 262 U.S. 447, the challenge of the federal Maternity Act was not entertained although made by the Commonwealth on behalf of all its citizens.

6. The Court will not pass upon the constitutionality of a statute at the instance of one who has availed himself of its benefits.[3] *Great Falls Mfg. Co. v. Attorney General*, 124 U.S. 581; *Wall v. Parrot Silver & Copper Co.*, 244 U.S. 407, 411–412; *St. Louis Malleable Casting Co. v. Prendergast Construction Co.*, 260 U.S. 469.

7. "When the validity of an act of the Congress is drawn in question, and even if a serious doubt of constitutionality is raised, it is a cardinal principle that this Court will first ascertain whether a construction of the statute is fairly possible by which the question may be avoided." *Crowell v. Benson*, 285 U.S. 22, 62.[4]

1. E.g., *Ex parte Randolph*, 20 Fed. Cas. No. 11,558, pp. 242, 254; *Charles River Bridge v. Warren Bridge*, 11 Pet. 420, 553; *Trade-Mark Cases*, 100 U.S. 82, 96; *Arizona v. California*, 283 U.S. 423, 462–464.

2. E.g., *Hatch v. Reardon*, 204 U.S. 152, 160–161; *Corporation Commission v. Lowe*, 281 U.S. 431, 438; *Heald v. District of Columbia*, 259 U.S. 114, 123; *Sprout v. South Bend*, 277 U.S. 163, 167; *Concordia Fire Insurance Co. v. Illinois*, 292 U.S. 535, 547.

3. Compare *Electric Co. v. Dow*, 166 U.S. 489; *Pierce v. Somerset Ry.*, 171 U.S. 641, 648; *Leonard v. Vicksburg, S. & P. R. Co.*, 198 U.S. 416, 422.

4. E.g., *United States v. Delaware & Hudson Co.*, 213 U.S. 366, 407–408; *United States v. Jin Fuey Moy*, 241 U.S. 394, 401; *Baender v. Barnett*, 255 U.S. 224; *Texas v. Eastern Texas R. Co.*, 258 U.S. 204, 217; *Panama R. Co. v. Johnson*, 264 U.S. 375, 390; *Linder v. United States*, 268 U.S. 5, 17–18; *Missouri Pacific R. Co. v. Boone*, 270 U.S. 466, 471–472; *Richmond Screw Anchor Co. v. United States*, 275 U.S. 331, 346; *Blodgett v. Holden*, 275 U.S. 142, 148; *Lucas v. Alexander*, 279 U.S. 573, 577; *Interstate Commerce Comm'n v. Oregon-Washington R. & N. Co.*, 288 U.S. 14, 40.

tain laws it had passed concerning Indian lands, authorized certain Indians to sue the United States to obtain a Supreme Court ruling on the question. When the case reached the Court in 1911, the Court dismissed it as outside its power because no actual dispute existed: all parties to the case were in reality working together to ascertain the constitutionality of the law, not to resolve any actual conflict between legal rights or concrete interests.

Justice William R. Day wrote for the Court that a judgment in such a case would be "no more than an expression of opinion upon the validity of the acts in question." That was not the function of the Supreme Court.[7]

When the use of declaratory judgments by lower courts was begun a few years later, one of the main questions raised by this new remedy was whether it was appropriate for use by federal courts, given the case or controversy requirement of federal jurisdiction. *(See "Declaratory Judgments," p. 288–289.)*

MOOTNESS

A second corollary of this requirement is the rule that the Court will not decide a case when circumstances are sufficiently altered by time or events to remove the dispute or conflict of interests. Such cases are then dead, or "moot": for purposes of federal jurisdiction, they no longer exist. There is nothing left for the Court to resolve; a judgment would have no effect beyond a mere expression of opinion.

The Court has long defined its function in this way—"to decide actual controversies by a judgment which can be carried into effect, and not to give opinions upon moot questions or abstract propositions, or to declare principles or rules of law which cannot affect the matter in issue in the case before it."[8]

In 1974 Marco DeFunis came to the Court charging that he had been denied admission to a state university law school in order that his place in the class might be given, under an affirmative action program, to a less-qualified minority applicant. DeFunis, in the course of his lawsuit, had obtained a court order directing the school to admit him. By the time his case was argued before the Supreme Court, he was in his final year of law school. The Court—in the spring that he would graduate—held the case moot: whatever their decision, it would not have affected DeFunis, who was to graduate regardless.[9]

In a controversial application of this tenet of judicial restraint, the Court in 1983 overturned a court order barring Los Angeles police from using choke holds on suspects except in unusual circumstances. The Court in *City of Los Angeles v. Lyons* held that the individual bringing the case—although he had been subjected to this potentially fatal type of hold after he was stopped by police for a traffic violation—could not obtain this court order without showing that the choke hold would be used against him in the future.[10]

MOOTNESS RULE EXCEPTIONS

The Court has developed a number of exceptions to the rigid application of this rule. In criminal cases where the defendant has served out his sentence, the Court still finds his case viable if there is the possibility he will continue to suffer adverse legal consequences as a result of the conviction he is challenging.[11] A similar rule applies in civil cases if the challenged judgment or situation may continue to have an adverse effect on the plaintiff.

Such an exception also exists for conduct and situations that are necessarily of short duration, "capable of repetition, yet evading review" if the mootness rule is strictly applied. An example of the application of this "capable of repetition" exception is the 1973 abortion decision in *Doe v. Bolton, Roe v. Wade*. The plaintiffs in the cases challenging state laws against abortions included pregnant women. Given the predictable nine-month term of a pregnancy, and the less predictable and usually slower term of a constitutional case making its way to the Supreme Court, it was no surprise that the women were no longer pregnant when the case arrived at the Supreme Court.

But the Court, 7–2, rejected the argument that the end of these pregnancies made the case moot. This, wrote Justice Harry A. Blackmun for the Court, was a clear situation in which a condition "capable of repetition" might never win Supreme Court review if the standard of mootness were applied rigidly.[12]

Election cases, those challenging the application of certain election law requirements, provide another example of cases where the actual dispute may end—after an election is held—yet the problem remains.[13]

"FRIENDLY" SUITS AND TEST CASES

Taken at face value, the Court's insistence on actual cases and disputes involving clearly colliding legal interests precludes its ruling in any "friendly" suits—those in which there is no real or substantial controversy, but each side agrees to pursue the suit in order to attain a mutually desired judicial resolution. In 1850 Chief Justice Roger B. Taney minced no words when he spoke

---

THE TIP OF AN ICEBERG

The concept of justiciability—the characteristic that makes a case appropriate for review—was described by Chief Justice Earl Warren in 1968. He linked the concept to the Court's self-imposed rules implementing the "case and controversy" doctrine:

The jurisdiction of federal courts is defined and limited by Article III of the Constitution. In terms relevant to the question for decision in this case, the judicial power of federal courts is constitutionally restricted to "cases" and "controversies." As is so often the situation in constitutional adjudication, those two words have an iceberg quality, containing beneath their surface simplicity submerged complexities which go to the very heart of our constitutional form of government. Embodied in the words "cases" and "controversies" are two complementary but somewhat different limitations. In part those words limit the business of the federal courts to questions presented in an adversary context and in a form historically viewed as capable of resolution through the judicial process. And in part those words define the role assigned to the judiciary in a tripartite allocation of power to assure that federal courts will not intrude into areas committed to the other branches of government. Justiciability is the term of art employed to give expression to this dual limitation placed upon federal courts by the case-and-controversy doctrine.

Justiciability is itself a concept of uncertain meaning and scope. Its reach is illustrated by the various grounds upon which questions sought to be adjudicated in federal courts have been held not to be justiciable. Thus no justiciable controversy is presented when the parties seek adjudication of only a political question, when the parties are asking for an advisory opinion, when the question sought to be adjudicated has been mooted by subsequent developments, and when there is no standing to maintain the action.

SOURCE: *Flast v. Cohen*, 392 U.S. 83 at 94–95 (1968).

---

for the Court to dismiss such a case. He found such collusion "contempt of the court, and highly reprehensible."[14]

The classic statement on friendly suits came in 1892 when the Court backed up a state court's refusal to declare unconstitutional a state law regulating railroad fares. Writing the Court's opinion, Justice David J. Brewer explained:

The theory upon which, apparently, this suit was brought is that parties have an appeal from the Legislature to the courts; and that the latter are given an immediate and general supervision of the constitutionality of the acts of the former. Such is not true. Whenever, in pursuance of an honest and actual antagonistic assertion of rights by one individual against another, there is presented a question involving the validity of any Act of any Legislature, state or federal, and the decision necessarily rests on the competency of the Legislature to so enact, the court must, in the exercise of its solemn duties, determine whether the Act be constitutional or not; but such an exercise of power is the ultimate and supreme function of courts. It is legitimate only in the last resort, and as a necessity in the determination of real, earnest, and vital controversy between individuals. It never was the thought that, by means of a friendly suit, a party beaten in the Legislature could transfer to the courts an inquiry as to the constitutionality of the legislative Act.[15]

Yet some of the landmark decisions in the Court's history have come in friendly cases, arranged because both sides were interested in obtaining a final judicial determination of a question. Perhaps the first was the tax case, *Hylton v. United States*, decided in 1796. The government paid the attorneys for both sides to get the case taken all the way to the Supreme Court.[16]

Among other major cases that could have been rejected as friendly suits are *Fletcher v. Peck* (1810), *Dred Scott v. Sandford* (1857), and—only a few years after Justice Brewer's ringing statement—*Pollock v. Farmers' Loan and Trust Co.* (1895).[17] In the last case, brought by a stockholder in a bank seeking an order directing the bank not to pay certain federal income taxes—a result the bank was happy to encourage—the Court held the peacetime federal income tax unconstitutional. Justice Brewer made no comment on the "friendly" nature of the suit. *(See details of Fletcher v. Peck, pp. 322–323, in Chapter 7; Dred Scott v. Sandford, pp. 143–147, in Chapter 4; and Pollock v. Farmers' Loan and Trust Co., pp. 118–121, in Chapter 4.)*

Another example came in 1936, when the Court struck down a major New Deal statute in *Carter v. Carter Coal Co.*, which was brought by the president of the company against the company and the other officers, among whom was his own father.[18] *(See details of this case, pp. 107–108, in Chapter 4.)*

In the same vein, although the Court has refused to rule on some obviously concocted test cases like *Muskrat,* it does not dismiss cases simply because they have been selected by the administration or some pressure group as the proper vehicle to test a law. The Court's decision to hear or dismiss such a test case usually turns on whether it presents an actual conflict of legal rights susceptible of judicial resolution.

"Standing to Sue"

Not only must there be an actual legal dispute to justify a federal case, but it may be brought only by persons directly involved in or affected by the dispute. The question of whether a person has a sufficient interest at stake in such a dispute is described as a question of legal "standing." Such questions serve "on occasion, as a short-hand expression for all the various elements of justiciability," Chief Justice Warren once commented.[19]

To bring a federal suit, a person must have "such a personal stake in the outcome of the controversy as to assure that concrete adverseness which sharpens the presentation of issues upon which the court so largely depends for illumination of difficult constitutional questions."[20]

In most cases involving private disputes, the injury or interest asserted is clear beyond question. Issues of legal standing, therefore, tend to generate more discussion and debate when they arise in cases in which laws or other government action are challenged as unconstitutional; in these cases, the relationship between the plaintiff and the challenged action is more remote than it is in cases involving private disputes.

Perhaps the best illustration of the way in which the Court has addressed the issue of standing to sue is provided by several of the "taxpayer" suits decided over the last half-century. The first was actually a pair of cases in 1923: *Massachusetts v. Mellon,*

Frothingham v. Mellon

The state of Massachusetts and Mrs. Frothingham, a federal taxpayer, came to the Supreme Court challenging as unconstitutional the use of federal grants-in-aid to states for maternal and child health programs. Massachusetts argued that such federal aid invaded the powers reserved to the states by the Tenth Amendment; Mrs. Frothingham asserted in addition that such an improper use of her tax money effectively deprived her of her property without due process of law as guaranteed by the Fifth Amendment.

The Supreme Court refused to address those constitutional arguments, finding that neither the state nor the taxpayer had standing to bring the cases in the first place. Writing for the Court, Justice George Sutherland found the question posed by Massachusetts to be "political, and not judicial in character" and thus outside the Court's jurisdiction.[21] In addition, Mrs. Frothingham's interest in the use of federal revenues was "comparatively minute and indeterminable" and the effect of federal payments from those funds upon her future tax burden "so remote, fluctuating, and uncertain," that she lacked an adequate personal interest in the situation to bring the federal challenge.[22] (The Court did note, however, that local taxpayers often had sufficient interest at stake to bring justiciable cases challenging local expenditures.[23])

Sutherland explained the Court's reasoning concerning federal taxpayer suits:

The administration of any statute, likely to produce additional taxation to be imposed upon a vast number of taxpayers, the extent of whose several liability is indefinite and constantly changing, is essentially a matter of public and not of individual concern. If one taxpayer may champion and litigate such a cause, then every other taxpayer may do the same . . . in respect of every other appropriation act and statute whose administration requires the outlay of public money, and whose validity may be questioned. The bare suggestion of such a result, with its attendant inconveniences, goes far to sustain the conclusion which we have reached, that a suit of this character cannot be maintained.[24]

In conclusion, Sutherland reiterated the Court's view that its power to review the validity of acts of Congress was not a general one, but was properly invoked "only when the justification for some direct injury suffered or threatened, presenting a justiciable issue, is made to rest upon such an act." The person invoking the exercise of this aspect of federal judicial power, declared the Court, "must be able to show not only that the statute is invalid, but that he has sustained or is immediately in danger of sustaining some direct injury as the result of its enforcement, and not merely that he suffers in some indefinite way in common with people generally."[25]

Until 1968 the Court's ruling in *Frothingham v. Mellon* was interpreted to bar virtually all taxpayer efforts to challenge the constitutionality of a federal law, unless the taxpayer could show some additional personal stake in its enforcement.

In 1968, however, the Court modified this rule with its decision in *Flast v. Cohen.* Mrs. Flast, a federal taxpayer, sued Secre-

JUDICIAL IMMUNITY

One restraint to which judges are not vulnerable in their exercise of judicial power is the threat of civil damage suits. Judges may not be sued for their official actions, no matter how erroneous or injurious these acts may be. That rule has been the policy of the federal judicial system throughout its history, proclaimed most firmly by the Supreme Court in an 1872 decision involving the judge who presided over the trial of one of the men accused of the murder of Abraham Lincoln.

In *Bradley v. Fisher* Justice Stephen Field wrote:

it is a general principle of the highest importance to the proper administration of justice that a judicial officer, in exercising the authority vested in him, shall be free to act upon his own convictions, without apprehension of personal consequence to himself. Liability to answer to everyone who might feel himself aggrieved by the action of the judge, would be inconsistent with the possession of this freedom, and would destroy that independence without which no judiciary can be either respectable or useful.[1]

Furthermore, stated the Court, this immunity was not breached even if the judicial actions protested were taken in bad faith.

The purity of their motives cannot in this way be the subject of judicial inquiry. . . . If civil actions could be maintained . . . against the judge, because the losing party should see fit to allege in his complaint that the acts of the judge were done with partiality, or maliciously, or corruptly, the protection essential to judicial independence would be entirely swept away. Few persons sufficiently irritated to institute an action against a judge for his judicial acts would hesitate to ascribe any character to the acts which would be essential to the maintenance of the action.[2]

The only situation in which such cases might be allowed was one in which the challenged acts were taken to affect a matter over which the judge had no jurisdiction.

"[F]or malice or corruption in their action whilst exercising their judicial functions within the general scope of their jurisdiction," the Court concluded, "judges . . . can only be reached by public prosecution in the form of impeachment, or in such other form as may be specially prescribed."[3]

The complete protection of this immunity was affirmed by the Court in a 1967 ruling. The justices held this immunity unaffected by the federal civil rights law that allows damage suits to be brought against anyone who deprives another person of his civil rights while acting under "color of law." And in a 1978 decision the Court held that this immunity protected a state judge from a damage suit resulting from his allowing a teen-ager to be sterilized without her knowledge or consent.[4]

Judges, however, enjoy no such immunity from prosecution under the criminal laws if they commit a crime or engage in other illegal action outside their judicial office.[5]

The Constitution stipulates that the compensation paid to judges shall not be reduced during their time in office. Using this provision as the basis for their holding, the Supreme Court in 1920 ruled that a federal judge appointed to his post before passage of the federal income tax law could not be forced to pay income taxes because to do so would unconstitutionally reduce his salary. Five years later the Court extended this immunity to judges appointed after the income tax law took effect.[6]

But this exemption was short-lived. Congress in 1932 expressly applied the income tax to the salaries of judges taking office after mid-1932. And in 1939 the Court upheld the 1932 law and overruled its 1920 decision, stating that to require judges to pay a nondiscriminatory federal income tax was "merely to recognize that judges are also citizens, and that their particular function in government does not generate an immunity from sharing with their fellow citizens the material burden of the government whose Constitution and laws they are charged with administering."[7]

1. *Bradley v. Fisher*, 13 Wall. 335 at 347 (1872).
2. Id. at 347, 348.
3. Id. at 354.
4. *Pierson v. Ray*, 386 U.S. 547 (1967); *Stump v. Sparkman*, 435 U.S. 349 (1978).
5. *Forrester v. White*, 484 U.S. 219 (1988).
6. *Evans v. Gore*, 253 U.S. 245 (1920); *Miles v. Graham*, 268 U.S. 501 (1925).
7. *O'Malley v. Woodrough*, 307 U.S. 277 at 282 (1939).

tary of Health, Education, and Welfare Wilbur J. Cohen to halt the use of federal funds under the Elementary and Secondary Education Act of 1965 to aid pupils in parochial, as well as public, schools. This use of her tax monies, argued Mrs. Flast, violated the First Amendment ban on establishment of religion and on government efforts to impede the free exercise of religion.

A three-judge federal panel dismissed her case, citing *Frothingham v. Mellon*. But the Supreme Court reversed the decision, ruling that a federal taxpayer does have standing to bring constitutional challenges to federal spending and taxing programs when he alleges that they conflict with constitutional provisions restricting the taxing and spending power of Congress. A federal taxpayer, wrote Chief Justice Warren, "may or may not have the requisite personal stake in the outcome, depending upon the circumstances of the particular case. Therefore, we find no absolute bar in Article III to suits of federal taxpayers challenging

allegedly unconstitutional federal taxing and spending programs."[26]

To prove the "requisite personal stake," wrote Warren, a taxpayer must establish a logical connection, or nexus, between his taxpayer status and the claim he brought to the Court. In this case, Mrs. Flast had done so, and so the lower federal court should go on to consider the substance of her challenge. The establishment of this connection assured that a taxpayer was not simply seeking "to employ a federal court as a forum in which to air his generalized grievances about the conduct of government or the allocation of power in the Federal System," Warren continued. That was still an impermissible use of the federal courts.[27]

That particular portion of the *Flast* opinion was cited frequently by the Court in the 1970s, as it made clear that, despite *Flast*, there was still a standing requirement for federal cases.

A WRONG, BUT NO RIGHT

Unless a person can assert a federally protected right or interest that has been injured or threatened with injury, he or she lacks the essential element of a federal case.

The Latin maxim *damnum absque injuria* describes the situation: there is loss, but no injury sufficient to provide a basis for judicial remedy.

In 1938 such a situation was before the Court in the case of *Alabama Power Company v. Ickes* (302 U.S. 464). The privately owned company came into federal court seeking to halt federal grants to cities within its service area. The grants were to enable the cities to set up their own utility systems as competitors to the private system. The company argued that such grants were unlawful and asserted, as the necessary injury, the loss of business it would suffer from such competition.

The Supreme Court dismissed the case. The company had no protected legal or equitable right to operate free of competition, and so it had no standing to challenge the validity of the grants. The Court wrote that if the company's business was destroyed or curtailed, "it will be by lawful competition from which no legal wrong results." What the company sought to claim, continued the Court, was "damage to something it does not possess—namely, a right to be immune from lawful municipal competition." (at 480)

In 1974, with the decision in *United States v. Richardson,* the Court held that a taxpayer did not have standing to challenge the secrecy of the Central Intelligence Agency's budget, a secrecy he alleged to be in direct conflict with the Constitution. Writing for the Court, Chief Justice Warren E. Burger explained that this was not a challenge to the power to tax or to spend—the only sort of taxpayer challenge that *Flast* had addressed—but rather to the laws concerning the CIA. Furthermore, he wrote, William Richardson did not allege that as a taxpayer he was suffering any particular concrete injury as a result of this secrecy.[28]

A concurring opinion by Justice Lewis F. Powell Jr. noted the lowering of standing requirements over the three preceding decades, through statutes granting standing to bring certain cases and through Court rulings such as *Flast v. Cohen* and *Baker v. Carr,* which allowed voters to challenge state malapportionment.[29] Despite these developments, wrote Powell, "the Court has not broken with the traditional requirement that, in the absence of a specific statutory grant of the right of review, a plaintiff must allege some particularized injury that sets him apart from the man on the street.[30] This point was emphasized by a series of rulings in which the Court held that persons lacked standing to challenge military surveillance programs, the membership of some members of Congress in the armed forces reserves, municipal zoning ordinances, and the tax-exempt status of certain hospitals.[31]

One area in which the modern Court has clearly enlarged

access to the federal judiciary is in the categories of interests that may be asserted by citizens and taxpayers in federal cases. The asserted interest may be economic, constitutional, aesthetic, conservationist, or recreational. It still must be personal, rather than general, although in certain voting rights and environmental cases that requirement, too, has been applied flexibly.[32]

Toward the end of the twentieth century, the Court seemed to tighten standing requirements somewhat. In the 1992 environmental case of *Lujan v. Defenders of Wildlife,* the Court insisted that there be demonstrated injury to the parties bringing the lawsuit before standing was granted. And in the 1995 voting rights case *United States v. Hays* the Court said that white voters could not challenge the creation of a black-majority voting rights district unless they were resident in the district or could otherwise demonstrate a clear and direct interest.[33]

Although the Court generally has insisted that a plaintiff be arguing his own interest as the primary one—not that of a third party—there have been notable exceptions to that rule.[34] As early as 1915, the Court allowed alien *employees* to challenge a state law requiring *employers* to hire four times as many residents as aliens.[35] A decade later the Court allowed a religious organization that operated a parochial school to challenge a state law penalizing parents who did not send their children to public schools.[36]

In situations where it appears unlikely that the people most directly affected by the challenged law will be able to bring their own legal protest to the Court, the justices generally have allowed others to make the challenge. Such was apparently the reasoning behind several cases in which white plaintiffs challenged laws restricting the rights of blacks to live or buy property in certain neighborhoods.[37] And in some recent cases, the Court has allowed doctors to challenge laws restricting the advice or treatment they may give their patients.[38]

Organizations whose members are injured by government action may assert the interest of their members in seeking judicial review, but the Court has made clear that there must be injury—as well as an interest—in such cases.[39]

States, acting as *parens patriae,* are allowed to bring some federal suits in behalf of their citizens, challenging acts that are injurious to the health or welfare of the entire population. *Massachusetts v. Mellon,* however, made clear that such *parens patriae* suits may not be brought against the federal government.[40]

Political Questions

In his classic discussion of judicial power in the Court's opinion in *Marbury v. Madison,* Chief Justice John Marshall declared:

The province of the court, is, solely, to decide on the rights of individuals, not to inquire how the executive, or executive officers, perform duties in which they have a discretion. Questions in their nature political, or which are, by the constitution and laws, submitted to the executive, can never be made in this court.[41]

Since that time, the Court has employed the "political question" doctrine as a convenient device for avoiding head-on collisions with Congress, the president, or the states on matters ranging from foreign relations to malapportioned congressional districts.

The attributes of this doctrine are quite variable. One modern justice has observed that they "in various settings, diverge, combine, appear and disappear in seeming disorderliness."[42] Several decades earlier a scholar suggested that expediency was indeed the chief determinant of "political questions."[43]

The Constitution provides that the United States shall guarantee to every state a republican form of government. When the question of enforcing that guarantee came to the Supreme Court in 1849, the Court made clear that this was indeed a political question. *Luther v. Borden* involved two competing groups, each asserting that it was the lawful government of Rhode Island. In the Court's opinion Chief Justice Taney stated firmly that "it rests with Congress to decide what government is the established one in a state."[44] Taney continued:

when the senators and representatives of a State are admitted into the councils of the Union, the authority of the government under which they are appointed, as well as its republican character, is recognized by the proper constitutional authority. And its decision is binding on every other department of the government, and could not be questioned in a judicial tribunal.[45]

In the same case the Court displayed a similar deference to the decision of the president, as authorized by law, to call out the militia of a state to suppress an insurrection there.[46]

The Court has remained quite consistent in applying the political question doctrine to refuse cases in which individuals attempt to use this "guaranty" provision of the Constitution as a basis for challenging state government or state action.[47] Tennessee was unsuccessful, however, when it attempted to use this line of precedents to shield its state legislative apportionment statute from judicial review in *Baker v. Carr.*[48]

The Court generally has left questions of foreign policy and foreign affairs to the political branches. In 1829 the Court refused to settle an international border question, stating that it was not the role of the judiciary to assert national interests against foreign powers.[49] Throughout its history the Court has steadily reaffirmed that point, based firmly on its view that in foreign affairs the nation should speak with a single voice.[50] *(See "The States' Role," p. 210, in Chapter 5.)*

In similar fashion, the Court has used the political question doctrine to refuse to intervene in questions of legislative process or procedure, including issues concerning constitutional amendments. It has left the resolution of those matters to Congress or the states.[51]

The exception to that general practice has come in cases raising questions of basic constitutional standards—such as the power of Congress over certain subjects or the propriety of a chamber's excluding a member who meets the constitutional qualifications and has been duly elected—or in matters such as the *Pocket Veto Case* where the political branches deadlock on an issue.[52] *(See "Qualifications," p. 171, in Chapter 4; details of Pocket Veto Case, p. 230, in Chapter 5.)*

For most of the nation's history, the Court also viewed challenges to state decisions allocating population among electoral districts as a political question outside the realm of judicial consideration. In 1946 Justice Felix Frankfurter reiterated this view, making clear that it was based on practical political considerations.

Nothing is clearer than that this controversy [over malapportionment of Illinois congressional districts] concerns matters that bring courts into immediate and active relations with party contests. From the determination of such issues this Court has traditionally held aloof. It is hostile to a democratic system to involve the judiciary in the politics of the people.[53]

Twenty-six years later the Court overturned that ruling and held that its earlier refusal to intervene in apportionment matters was based on an overbroad view of the political question doctrine. The decision was *Baker v. Carr,* in which the Court held that challenges to malapportionment of state legislatures *were* justiciable questions.

After reviewing the line of political question cases, Justice William J. Brennan Jr. stated for the majority that

It is the relationship between the judiciary and the coordinate branches of the Federal Government, and not the federal judiciary's relationship to the States, which gives rise to the "political question." . . .

. . . The nonjusticiability of a political question is primarily a function of the separation of powers.[54]

The basic question of fairness at the heart of the lawsuit that had begun *Baker v. Carr,* Brennan concluded for the Court, was constitutional, not political, and was well within the jurisdiction of the Court. Simply "the presence of a matter affecting state government does not [in and of itself] render the case nonjusticiable."[55]

Writing in 1936, C. Gordon Post described the political question doctrine as a judicial concession founded "in the inadequacy of the judiciary itself." He continued:

If the court found it better to limit its jurisdiction, to restrict its power of review, it was not because of the doctrine of the separation of powers or because of a lack of rules, but because of expediency. If the court left certain questions pertaining to foreign relations in the hands of the political departments, it was because in our foreign relations a unified front is sensible, practical and expedient. If the court placed the question of whether a state . . . possessed or did not possess a republican form of government within the jurisdiction of the political departments, it was because of very practical considerations. If the court was fully conscious that its mandate could not, or would not, be enforced in the particular case, obviously it was more expedient to leave the matter to the political departments exclusively. In general, judicial review or not, the court has found it more expedient to leave the decision of certain questions to governmental bodies more appropriately adapted to decide them.[56]

The Role of Precedent

Supreme Court decisions are final (unless, that is, Congress overrules them by statute, Congress and the states amend the

Constitution to reverse the Court, or the Court itself decides to overturn precedent).

The doctrine of *stare decisis*—"let the decision stand"— binds the Court to adhere to the decisions of an earlier day. This rule of precedent, wrote one scholar, is linked to "the idea that our law and judicial decisions have a historical continuity—as opposed to a system by which courts might endeavor to render justice in each case anew, as though each case constituted a problem unto itself, in no way related to any previous problems which courts have disposed of."[57]

The doctrine has a very practical basis: the need for stability in law. As Justice Louis D. Brandeis once wrote: "in most matters it is more important that the applicable rule of law be settled than that it be settled right."[58]

And Justice William O. Douglas, no advocate of slavish adherence to precedent, wrote:

Stare decisis provides some moorings so that men may trade and arrange their affairs with confidence. *Stare decisis* serves to take the capricious element out of law and to give stability to a society. It is a strong tie which the future has to the past.[59]

But the application of precedent is not as simple as it might appear. Robert K. Carr explained:

In actual practice, two cases are rarely, if ever, exactly alike. . . . Thus a judge may have wide discretion in deciding in a given case to follow either precedent A or precedent B, both of which seem to have considerable bearing on the case but which, unfortunately, are completely contradictory to one another.[60]

In more than one hundred situations, from 1810 to the present, the Court has made exception to the doctrine of *stare decisis* and overruled an earlier decision. Century-old precedents have fallen, as have those barely a year old.[61]

In 1810 the Court in *Hudson and Smith v. Guestier* overruled an 1808 decision concerning the jurisdiction of a foreign power over vessels offshore. Chief Justice John Marshall disagreed with the Court's decision to overrule the earlier holding.

Only two other decisions were overruled by the Court during Marshall's tenure as chief justice, and only four were reversed by the Court during the chief justiceship of his successor, Roger B. Taney.[62]

After the Civil War, changing conditions and changing Court personnel placed increasing strain on the reverence for precedent. In 1870 the Court held the Legal Tender Acts unconstitutional; a year later, with two new members, it reversed itself and upheld the same laws.[63] *(See details of two Legal Tender Cases, Hepburn v. Griswold and Knox v. Lee, pp. 129–132, in Chapter 4.)*

Twenty-five years later the Court found the statute authorizing a peacetime income tax unconstitutional; it revised a century-old definition of "direct taxes" and ignored previous rulings that would seem to dictate that the Court should uphold the tax laws.[64] This 1895 ruling was eventually reversed by adoption of the Sixteenth Amendment in 1913. *(See details of Pollock v. Farmers' Loan and Trust Co., pp. 118–121, in Chapter 4.)*

The Supreme Court of the twentieth century clearly has felt free to overrule its previous decisions; more than three out of

The doctrine of *stare decisis,* binding the Court to adhere to its previous decisions, has contributed to the stability of the American legal system. The Court of the twentieth century has felt free to depart from this doctrine, reasoning that modern conditions and circumstances call for new interpretations of the Constitution.

four of the Court's self-reversals have come since 1900. The Court's reversals on child labor, minimum wage and maximum hour laws, New Deal legislation, and state flag salute laws are among the major chapters in modern Supreme Court history.

As its actions have made clear, the modern Court views *stare decisis* as "a principle of policy and not a mechanical formula of adherence to the latest decision, however recent and questionable, when such adherence involves collision with a prior doctrine more embracing in its scope, intrinsically sounder, and verified by experience."[65]

The modern Court also tends to apply the doctrine more faithfully to questions of statutory law than to constitutional issues. As Justice Stanley Reed explained for the Court in 1944:

we are not unmindful of the desirability of continuity of decision in constitutional questions. However, when convinced of former error, this Court has never felt constrained to follow precedent. In constitutional questions, where correction depends upon amendment, and not upon legislative action this Court throughout its history has freely exercised its power to re-examine the basis of its constitutional decisions. This has long been accepted practice, and this practice has continued to this day.[66]

The rule of precedent is also made more flexible by the Court's practice of "distinguishing" a new case from a precedent that would seem to be controlling, pointing out factors that

PRECEDENT AND PUBLIC ACCEPTANCE

The importance of adhering to precedent and the Court's need for public acceptance of its decisions, in order for them to have real effect, were emphasized in 1992 when the Supreme Court reaffirmed the central holding of *Roe v. Wade,* the 1973 decision that made abortion legal. The Court must speak in a way that enables people to accept its decisions as grounded and shaped by principle, not the political winds of the day, said Justices Sandra Day O'Connor, Anthony M. Kennedy, and David H. Souter. Following is an excerpt from their opinion in *Planned Parenthood of Southeastern Pennsylvania v. Casey. (See details of the case, p. 689, in Chapter 12.)*

Our analysis would not be complete . . . without explaining why overruling *Roe's* central holding would not only reach an unjustified result under principles of *stare decisis,* but would seriously weaken the Court's capacity to exercise the judicial power and to function as the Supreme Court of a Nation dedicated to the rule of law. To understand why this would be so it is necessary to understand the source of this Court's authority, the conditions necessary for its preservation, and its relationship to the country's understanding of itself as a constitutional Republic.

The root of American governmental power is revealed most clearly in the instance of the power conferred by the Constitution upon the Judiciary of the United States and specifically upon this Court. As Americans of each succeeding generation are rightly told, the Court cannot buy support for its decisions by spending money and, except to a minor degree, it cannot independently coerce obedience to its decrees. The Court's power lies, rather, in its legitimacy, a product of substance and perception that shows itself in the people's acceptance of the Judiciary as fit to determine what the Nation's law means and to declare what it demands.

The underlying substance of this legitimacy is of course the warrant for the Court's decisions in the Constitution and the lesser sources of legal principle on which the Court draws. That substance is expressed in the Court's opinions, and our contemporary understanding is such that a decision without principled justification would be no judicial act at all. But even when justification is furnished by apposite legal principle, something more is required. Because not every conscientious claim of principled justification will be accepted as such, the justification claimed must be beyond dispute. The Court must take care to speak and act in ways that allow people to accept its decisions on the terms the Court claims for them, as grounded truly in principle, not as compromises with social and political pressures having, as such, no bearing on the principled choices that the Court is obliged to make. Thus, the Court's legitimacy depends on making legally principled decisions under circumstances in which their principled character is sufficiently plausible to be accepted by the Nation. (505 U.S. 833)

Quite the opposite in terms of social conditions happened in 1992, when the Court decided not to overturn *Roe v. Wade,* the landmark ruling that made abortion legal nationwide. In a closely divided decision in *Planned Parenthood of Southeastern Pennsylvania v. Casey,* a plurality of justices articulated their view of precedent.[68] The three controlling justices, Sandra Day O'Connor, Anthony M. Kennedy, and David H. Souter, wrote:

The obligation to follow precedent begins with necessity, and a contrary necessity marks its outer limit. . . . Indeed, the very concept of the rule of law underlying our own Constitution requires such continuity over time that a respect for precedent is, by definition, indispensable. At the other extreme, a different necessity would make itself felt if a prior judicial ruling should come to be seen so clearly as error that its enforcement was for that very reason doomed. . . .[69] *(See box, Precedent and Public Acceptance, this page.)*

The rule of precedent, preserving stability and continuity, creates a certain predictability in the law as proclaimed by the Supreme Court. But the exceptions to that rule, the departures from the doctrine of *stare decisis,* are one method by which the Court adapts the Constitution to new circumstances and new conditions.[70]

The Demands of Comity

The existence of dual judicial systems in the United States—state courts and federal courts—imposes certain peculiar restraints upon the conduct of the federal judiciary. Law enforcement remains primarily the responsibility of state officials; yet the final word on questions of federal law and federal rights is left to the federal courts. The operations of such a dual system require continuing adjustment.

Federal judges have several powerful instruments to wield against improper state action: the writ of habeas corpus to order release of a state prisoner detained in violation of his constitutional rights; the injunction to halt improper state proceedings; and the declaratory judgment to hold a state law unconstitutional, invalid, and unenforceable.

When state action is challenged by persons who ask a federal judge to intervene in state matters, the Supreme Court often counsels restraint, citing the demands of "comity." Comity, wrote E. S. Corwin, is "a self-imposed rule of judicial morality, whereby independent tribunals of concurrent or coordinate jurisdiction exercise a mutual restraint in order to prevent interference with each other and to avoid collisions of authority."[71]

More simply, Justice Hugo L. Black wrote in 1971, comity is "a proper respect for state functions, a recognition of the fact that the entire country is made up of a Union of separate state governments, and a continuance of the belief that the National Government will fare best if the States and their institutions are left free to perform their separate functions in their separate ways."[72]

Black, years earlier a local police judge, continued:

This, perhaps for lack of a better and clearer way to describe it, is referred to by many as "Our Federalism." . . . The concept does not mean blind deference to "States' Rights" any more than it means centraliza-

make the two situations different, and justifying a different result. A precedent can eventually be distinguished into complete uniqueness—and utter uselessness. This sort of erosion took place during the late 1930s and 1940s with regard to the Court's 1896 decision in *Plessy v. Ferguson,* allowing "separate, but equal" facilities for blacks and whites. By the time the Court in 1954 officially overruled *Plessy,* the decision's value as a precedent had long been destroyed.[67]

tion of control over every important issue in our National Government and its courts. . . . What the concept does represent is a system in which there is sensitivity to the legitimate interest of both State and National Governments, and in which the National Government, anxious though it may be to vindicate and protect federal rights and federal interests, always endeavors to do so in ways that will not unduly interfere with the legitimate activities of the States.[73]

The demands of comity have produced at least two corollary rules—the requirement that individuals who challenge state actions in federal courts first "exhaust" all possible state remedies for their complaint, and the "abstention" doctrine, which requires federal judges to refrain from acting or asserting federal jurisdiction over a matter within state hands until the state courts have had a full opportunity to correct the situation at issue.

The application of these rules by the Supreme Court has led to much debate on and off the bench, particularly since the Court has applied most of the procedural guarantees of the Bill of Rights to state court proceedings. In the 1960s the Supreme Court tended to find or create new exceptions to these rules of restraint. Under more conservative leadership since then, the Court has tended to narrow such exceptions. The process of adjustment continues.

NOTES

INTRODUCTION (PP. 263–264)

1. *The Federalist Papers*, with an Introduction by Clinton Rossiter (New York: New American Library, Mentor Books, 1961), No. 15, 106–107.
2. Ibid., No. 78, 466.
3. Ibid., No. 16, 116.
4. Ibid., No. 78, 465–466.
5. Felix Frankfurter, *The Commerce Clause Under Marshall, Taney and Waite* (Chapel Hill: University of North Carolina Press, 1927), 95–96.
6. *United States v. Richardson*, 418 U.S. 166 at 188 (1974).
7. Charles G. Haines, *The American Doctrine of Judicial Supremacy* (Berkeley: University of California Press, 1932), 23–24.
8. Alexander M. Bickel, *The Least Dangerous Branch* (Indianapolis: Bobbs-Merrill, 1962), 1.

FEDERAL JURISDICTION (PP. 265–274)

1. 291 F. 940 (7th Cir. 1923), revised by *Michaelson v. United States*, 266 U.S. 42 (1924).
2. *Ex parte McCardle*, 7 Wall. 506 at 514 (1869).
3. Charles Alan Wright, *Handbook of the Law of Federal Courts*, 2d ed. (St. Paul: West Publishing, 1970), 2.
4. *Cary v. Curtis*, 3 How. 236 at 245 (1845).
5. *Nashville v. Cooper*, 6 Wall. 247 at 252 (1868).
6. See Felix Frankfurter and James M. Landis, *The Business of the Supreme Court: A Study in the Federal Judicial System* (New York: Macmillan, 1928), 1–14; see also Julius Goebel Jr., *History of the Supreme Court of the United States: Vol. I, Antecedents and Beginnings to 1801* (New York: Macmillan, 1971), 457–508.
7. *Turner v. Bank of North America*, 4 Dall. 8 at 11 (1799).
8. Id. at 10.
9. Frankfurter and Landis, *The Business of the Supreme Court*, 64–64.
10. Ibid., 6–7.
11. Ibid.
12. *The Thomas Jefferson*, 10 Wheat. 428 (1825); *The Genessee Chief*, 12 How. 443 (1851); *United States v. Appalachian Power Co.*, 311 U.S. 377 (1940).

13. *In re Debs*, 158 U.S. 564 at 584 (1895).
14. *United States v. Texas*, 143 U.S. 621 (1892).
15. *United States v. West Virginia*, 295 U.S. 463 (1935).
16. *Massachusetts v. Missouri*, 308 U.S. 1 at 15, 18 (1939).
17. *Chisholm v. Georgia*, 2 Dall. 419 (1793).
18. *Wisconsin v. Pelican Insurance Co.*, 127 U.S. 265 (1888).
19. *California v. Southern Pacific Railway Co.*, 157 U.S. 220 (1895).
20. *Georgia v. Tennessee Copper Co.*, 206 U.S. 230 (1907); *Georgia v. Pennsylvania R. Co.*, 324 U.S. 439 (1945).
21. Frankfurter and Landis, *The Business of the Supreme Court*, 8–9.
22. *Strawbridge v. Curtiss*, 3 Cr. 267 (1806).
23. *State Farm, Fire & Casualty Co. v. Tashire*, 386 U.S. 523 (1967).
24. *Bank of the United States v. Deveaux*, 5 Cr. 61 (1809).
25. *Louisville RR v. Letson*, 2 How. 497 (1844); *Marshall v. Baltimore and Ohio R. Co.*, 16 How. 314 (1854); *Muller v. Dows*, 94 U.S. 444 (1877).
26. Frankfurter and Landis, *The Business of the Supreme Court*, 65, 89; see also Wright, *Handbook*, 89.
27. Wright, *Handbook*, 84–85; *Ex parte Burrus*, 136 U.S. 586 (1890); *Barber v. Barber*, 21 How. 582 (1858).
28. *The Schooner Exchange v. McFaddon*, 7 Cr. 116 at 145 (1812).
29. *Monaco v. Mississippi*, 292 U.S. 313 (1934).
30. *The Ship Sapphire v. Napoleon III*, 11 Wall. 164 at 167 (1871).
31. *Pfizer Inc. v. Government of India*, 434 U.S. 308 (1978).
32. *Ex parte Gruber*, 269 U.S. 302 (1925).
33. *Popovici v. Agler*, 280 U.S. 289 (1930).
34. *Marbury v. Madison*, 1 Cr. 137 at 174 (1803).
35. *Ames v. Kansas*, 111 U.S. 449 at 464 (1884).
36. Id. at 464–465.
37. *Kentucky v. Dennison*, 24 How. 66 (1861).
38. *Wisconsin v. Pelican Insurance Co.*, 127 U.S. 265 at 287, 288, 289–290, 297 (1888).
39. *Wiscart v. Dauchy*, 3 Dall. 321 at 327 (1796); *Durousseau v. United States*, 6 Cr. 307 at 314 (1810).
40. *Daniels v. Chicago & Rock Island Railroad Co.*, 3 Wall. 250 at 254 (1866).
41. Carl B. Swisher, *American Constitutional Development*, 2d ed. (Cambridge: Houghton Mifflin, 1954), 324.
42. *Ex parte McCardle*, 6 Wall. 318 at 325–326, 327 (1868).
43. Charles Warren, *The Supreme Court in United States History*, 2 vols. (Boston: Little, Brown, 1922, 1926), II: 474–485.
44. *Ex parte McCardle*, 7 Wall. 506 at 514, 515 (1869).
45. *Ex parte Yerger*, 8 Wall. 85 at 104 (1869).
46. Swisher, *American Constitutional Development*, 325.
47. Charles L. Black Jr., *Perspectives in Constitutional Law* (Englewood Cliffs, N.J.: Prentice-Hall, 1963), 13.
48. Frankfurter and Landis, *The Business of the Supreme Court*, 299.
49. *United States v. Sanges*, 144 U.S. 310 (1892).
50. Frankfurter and Landis, *The Business of the Supreme Court*, 113–119.
51. Ibid., 193–198.
52. Ibid., 211.
53. Ibid., 255–286.
54. Wright, *Handbook*, 477.
55. William Howard Taft, "The Jurisdiction of the Supreme Court Under the Act of February 13, 1925," *Yale Law Journal* (November 1925): 2, cited in *The Supreme Court from Taft to Warren* by Alpheus T. Mason (Baton Rouge: Louisiana State University Press, 1958), 222, n. 83.

FEDERAL JUDICIAL POWER (PP. 275–296)

1. Samuel F. Miller, *Lectures on the Constitution* (Albany, N.Y.: Banks and Brothers, 1891), 314.
2. *The Federalist Papers*, with an Introduction by Clinton Rossiter (New York: New American Library, Mentor Books, 1961), No. 51, 322.
3. *United States v. Nixon*, 418 U.S. 683 at 705 (1974).
4. Robert K. Carr, *The Supreme Court and Judicial Review* (New York: Farrar & Rinehart, 1942), 43.

5. Ibid., 45, citing Max Farrand, *The Records of the Federal Convention of 1787* (New Haven, Conn.: Yale University Press, 1911), II: 73.

6. Thomas Reed Powell, *Vagaries and Varieties in Constitutional Interpretation* (New York: Columbia University Press, 1956; reprint ed. New York: AMS Press, 1967), 20.

7. *Martin v. Hunter's Lessee*, 1 Wheat. 304 (1816); *Cohens v. Virginia*, 6 Wheat. 264 (1821).

8. *Murdock v. Memphis*, 20 Wall. 590 (1875).

9. *Herb v. Pitcairn*, 324 U.S. 117 at 125–126 (1945).

10. *United States v. Hylton*, 3 Dall. 171 (1796).

11. Charles Warren, *The Supreme Court in United States History*, 2 vols. (Boston: Little, Brown, 1922, 1926), II: 222–223.

12. *Marbury v. Madison*, 1 Cr. 137 at 175–176 (1803).

13. Id. at 177–178.

14. Id. at 178.

15. Carl B. Swisher, *American Constitutional Development*, 2d ed. (Cambridge: Houghton Mifflin, 1954), 10.

16. Charles G. Haines, *The American Doctrine of Judicial Supremacy* (Berkeley: University of California Press, 1932), 202–203; Charles Evans Hughes, *The Supreme Court of the United States* (New York: Columbia University Press, 1928), 87–89.

17. Charles P. Curtis, "Review and Majority Rule," in *Supreme Court and Supreme Law*, ed. Edmond Cahn (New York: Simon and Schuster, 1971), 198.

18. Carr, *The Supreme Court and Judicial Review*, 71.

19. Hughes, *The Supreme Court*, 50–51.

20. *Hepburn v. Griswold*, 8 Wall. 603 (1870); *Knox v. Lee*, 12 Wall. 457 (1871).

21. Powell, *Vagaries and Varieties*, 18.

22. Hughes, *The Supreme Court*, 95–96.

23. The current version of that provision—referred to as the All Writs Act—grants federal courts power to issue "all writs necessary or appropriate in aid of their respective jurisdictions and agreeable to the usages and principles of law." 28 U.S.C. 1651(a).

24. *Ex parte Yerger*, 8 Wall. 85 at 95 (1869).

25. *Adams v. United States ex rel. McCann*, 317 U.S. 269 at 273 (1942).

26. *Fay v. Noia*, 372 U.S. 391 at 401–402 (1963).

27. U.S. Congress, Library of Congress, Congressional Reference Service, *The Constitution of the United States of America: Analysis and Interpretation* (Washington, D.C.: U.S. Government Printing Office, 1973), 617–618.

28. *Brown v. Allen*, 344 U.S. 443 at 465 (1953).

29. *United States v. Smith*, 331 U.S. 469 at 475 (1947).

30. *Gusik v. Schilder*, 339 U.S. 977 (1950).

31. *Adams v. United States ex rel. McCann*, 317 U.S. 269 at 274 (1942).

32. Library of Congress, *The Constitution*, 616–617.

33. *Ex parte Bollman*, 4 Cr. 75 at 101 (1807).

34. *Ex parte Watkins*, 3 Pet. 193 at 202 (1830).

35. *Ex parte Dorr*, 3 How. 104 at 105 (1845).

36. Charles Fairman, *History of the Supreme Court of the United States*: vol. VI, *Reconstruction and Reunion, 1864–1888, Part One* (New York: MacMillan, 1971), 443–447.

37. Ibid., 451; *Ex parte McCardle*, 7 Wall. 506 (1869).

38. *Ex parte Yerger*, 8 Wall. 85 (1869).

39. *Ex parte Virginia*, 100 U.S. 339 (1880); *Ex parte Clarke*, 100 U.S. 399 (1880); *Ex parte Siebold*, 100 U.S. 371 (1880).

40. *Ex parte Siebold*, 100 U.S. 371 at 376–377 (1880).

41. *Ex parte Nielsen*, 131 U.S. 176 at 183–184 (1889).

42. *Frank v. Mangum*, 237 U.S. 309 at 327, 331 (1915).

43. *Moore v. Dempsey*, 261 U.S. 86 at 91 (1923); see also *Hawk v. Olson*, 326 U.S. 271 at 276 (1945).

44. *Waley v. Johnston*, 316 U.S. 101 at 104–105 (1942).

45. *Brown v. Allen*, 344 U.S. 443 at 464–465 (1953).

46. *Townsend v. Sain*, 372 U.S. 293 at 312, 318 (1963).

47. *Ex parte Royall*, 117 U.S. 241 (1886).

48. *Ex parte Hawk*, 321 U.S. 114 at 116–117 (1944); see also *Darr v. Burford*, 339 U.S. 200 at 217 (1950).

49. *Darr v. Burford*, 339 U.S. 200 at 217 (1950).

50. *Brown v. Allen*, 344 U.S. 443 at 487 (1953).

51. *Darr v. Burford*, 339 U.S. 200 at 210, 216 (1950).

52. *Fay v. Noia*, 372 U.S. 391 (1963).

53. Id. at 441.

54. Id. at 438–439.

55. Id. at 440.

56. Id. at 435–437.

57. *Stone v. Powell*, 428 U.S. 465 (1976).

58. *Davis v. United States*, 411 U.S. 233 (1973); *Francis v. Henderson*, 425 U.S. 536 (1976); *Wainwright v. Sykes*, 433 U.S. 72 (1977); *Rose v. Lundy*, 455 U.S. 509 (1982); *Engle v. Isaac*, 456 U.S. 107 (1982).

59. *Teague v. Lane*, 489 U.S. 255 (1989).

60. Id.

61. Id.

62. *Saffle v. Parks*, 494 U.S. 484 (1990).

63. *Butler v. McKellar*, 494 U.S. 407 (1990).

64. *Sawyer v. Smith*, 497 U.S. 227 (1990).

65. *Coleman v. Thompson*, 501 U.S. 722 (1991).

66. *McCleskey v. Zant*, 499 U.S. 467 (1991).

67. *Keeney v. Tamayo-Reyes*, 504 U.S. 1 (1992).

68. *Felker v. Turpin*, ____ U.S. ____ (1996).

69. *Kerr v. United States District Court*, 426 U.S. 394 at 402 (1976).

70. *United States v. Haley*, 371 U.S. 18 (1962); *Deen v. Hickman*, 358 U.S. 57 (1958).

71. *Marbury v. Madison*, 1 Cr. 137 (1803).

72. *McIntire v. Wood*, 7 Cr. 504 (1813); *McClung v. Silliman*, 6 Wheat. 598 (1821); *Kendall v. Stokes*, 12 Pet. 524 at 624 (1838).

73. *Marbury v. Madison*, 1 Cr. 137 at 170–171 (1803).

74. *Kendall v. United States ex rel. Stokes*, 12 Pet. 524 at 613 (1838).

75. *Kerr v. United States District Court*, 426 U.S. 394 at 403 (1976); see also *Marbury v. Madison*, 1 Cr. 137 at 169 (1803); *United States v. Duell*, 172 U.S. 576 at 582 (1899); *Ex parte Republic of Peru*, 318 U.S. 578 at 584 (1943).

76. *The Bank of Columbia v. Sweeny*, 1 Pet. 567 at 569 (1828).

77. *Ex parte Fahey*, 332 U.S. 258 at 259–260 (1947); see also *Parr v. United States*, 351 U.S. 513 at 520 (1956); *Roche v. Evaporated Milk Association*, 319 U.S. 21 at 26, 29 (1943).

78. *Ex parte Republic of Peru*, 318 U.S. 578 at 583 (1943).

79. *Bankers Life & Casualty v. Holland*, 346 U.S. 379 at 383 (1953).

80. *Ex parte United States*, 287 U.S. 241 at 248–249 (1932).

81. *Deen v. Hickman*, 358 U.S. 57 (1958).

82. *Roche v. Evaporated Milk Association*, 319 U.S. 21 (1943).

83. *La Buy v. Howes Leather*, 352 U.S. 249 (1957); *Beacon Theatres Inc. v. Westover*, 359 U.S. 500 (1959); *Thermtron Products v. Hermansdorfer*, 423 U.S. 336 (1976).

84. *United States v. United Mine Workers*, 330 U.S. 258 (1947).

85. *Pollock v. Farmers' Loan & Trust Co.*, 158 U.S. 601 (1895).

86. *Lockerty v. Phillips*, 319 U.S. 182 (1943).

87. *Mississippi v. Johnson*, 4 Wall. 475 at 498–499 (1867).

88. Id. at 500.

89. See *Mitchum v. Foster*, 407 U.S. 225 at 234–235 (1972).

90. Id. at 235–236.

91. *Toucey v. New York Life Insurance Co.*, 314 U.S. 118 at 139 (1941).

92. *Leiter Minerals v. United States*, 352 U.S. 220 (1957); *Mitchum v. Foster*, 407 U.S. 225 (1972).

93. *Osborn v. Bank of the United States*, 9 Wheat. 738 (1824).

94. *Ex parte Young*, 209 U.S. 123 (1908).

95. *Prentis v. Atlantic Coast Line Co.*, 211 U.S. 210 (1908).

96. *Dombrowski v. Pfister*, 380 U.S. 479 at 484–485 (1965).

97. *Fenner v. Boykin*, 271 U.S. 240 at 244 (1926).

98. *Beal v. Missouri Pacific R.R. Co.*, 312 U.S. 45 (1941); *Railroad Commission of Texas v. Pullman Co.*, 312 U.S. 496 (1941); *Douglas v. City of Jeannette*, 319 U.S. 157 (1943).

99. *McNeese v. Board of Education for Community Unit School District*, 373 U.S. 668 (1963).

100. *Harman v. Forssenius*, 380 U.S. 528 at 534–535 (1965).

101. *Dombrowski v. Pfister*, 380 U.S. 479 at 489–490 (1965).

102. *Younger v. Harris*, 401 U.S. 37 at 45 (1971).

103. *Younger v. Harris*, 401 U.S. 37 (1971); *Samuels v. Mackell, Fernandez v. Mackell*, 401 U.S. 66 (1971); *Byrne v. Karalexis*, 401 U.S. 216 (1971); *Perez v. Ledesma*, 401 U.S. 82 (1971); *Dyson v. Stein*, 401 U.S. 200 (1971).

104. *Younger v. Harris*, 401 U.S. 37 at 51 (1971).

105. Id. at 44; *Imperial County v. Munoz*, 449 U.S. 54 (1980); *Deakins v. Monaghan*, 484 U.S. 193 (1988).

106. *Hicks v. Miranda*, 422 U.S. 332 (1975); *Huffman v. Pursue Ltd.*, 420 U.S. 592 (1975); *Trainor v. Hernandez*, 431 U.S. 434 (1976); *Juidice v. Vail*, 430 U.S. 327 (1976).

107. *Pennzoil Company v. Texaco Inc.*, 481 U.S. 1 at 14, 11 (1987).

108. *Willing v. Chicago Auditorium Association*, 277 U.S. 274 at 289 (1928); *Nashville, Chicago & St. Louis Railway Company v. Wallace*, 288 U.S. 249 at 264 (1933).

109. *Aetna Life Insurance Co. v. Haworth*, 300 U.S. 227 (1937).

110. *Maryland Casualty Co. v. Pacific Coal & Oil Co.*, 312 U.S. 270 at 273 (1941); *Alabama State Federation of Labor v. McAdory*, 325 U.S. 450 at 461 (1945).

111. *Poe v. Ullman*, 367 U.S. 497 (1961); *Griswold v. Connecticut*, 381 U.S. 479 (1965).

112. *Public Affairs Associates v. Rickover*, 369 U.S. 111 at 112 (1962); *Brillhart v. Excess Insurance Co.*, 316 U.S. 491 at 494 (1942).

113. *Great Lakes Dredge and Dock Co. v. Huffman*, 319 U.S. 293 (1943).

114. *Zwickler v. Koota*, 389 U.S. 241 at 254, 248 (1967).

115. *Samuels v. Mackell*, 401 U.S. 66 at 72 (1971).

116. *Steffel v. Thompson*, 415 U.S. 452 (1974); *Ellis v. Dyson*, 421 U.S. 426 (1975).

117. *Steffel v. Thompson*, 415 U.S. 452 at 462 (1974).

118. Id. at 472.

119. *Lake Carriers Association v. MacMullan*, 406 U.S. 498 (1972); *Steffel v. Thompson*, 415 U.S. 452 (1974); *Ellis v. Dyson*, 421 U.S. 426 (1975).

120. *Anderson v. Dunn*, 6 Wheat. 204 at 231 (1821).

121. *Ex parte Robinson*, 19 Wall. 505 (1874).

122. *Ex parte Terry*, 128 U.S. 289 at 313 (1888).

123. *Illinois v. Allen*, 397 U.S. 337 (1970).

124. *In re Debs*, 158 U.S. 564 at 594–595 (1895).

125. *United States v. United Mine Workers*, 330 U.S. 258 (1947).

126. *Toledo Newspaper Co. v. United States*, 247 U.S. 402 (1918).

127. *Nye v. United States*, 313 U.S. 33 at 52 (1941).

128. *Ex parte Hudgings*, 249 U.S. 378 at 383 (1919); see also *In re Michael*, 326 U.S. 224 (1945).

129. *Brown v. United States*, 356 U.S. 148 at 153 (1958).

130. *United States v. Wilson*, 421 U.S. 309 at 315–316, 319 (1975).

131. *Harris v. United States*, 382 U.S. 162 (1965), overruling *Brown v. United States*, 359 U.S. 41 (1959).

132. *Sacher v. United States*, 343 U.S. 1 at 3 (1952).

133. *In re McConnell*, 370 U.S. 230 (1962).

134. *Green v. United States*, 356 U.S. 165 (1958).

135. *Gompers v. Buck's Stove and Range Co.*, 221 U.S. 418 at 441 (1911).

136. Id. at 442.

137. Id.

138. Id. at 442–443.

139. *Ex parte Grossman*, 267 U.S. 87 (1925).

140. *United States v. United Mine Workers*, 330 U.S. 258 at 300 (1947).

141. Id. at 295.

142. *Shillitani v. United States, Pappadio v. United States*, 384 U.S. 364 at 368 (1966).

143. *United Mine Workers v. Bagwell*, 114 S. Ct. 2552 (1994).

144. *Bessette v. W. B. Conkey*, 194 U.S. 324 at 326 (1904).

145. *Ex parte Terry*, 128 U.S. 289 at 312 (1888).

146. *In re Debs*, 158 U.S. 564 at 595 (1895).

147. *Cooke v. United States*, 267 U.S. 517 at 539 (1925).

148. *Sacher v. United States*, 343 U.S. 1 at 12 (1952).

149. *Offutt v. United States*, 348 U.S. 11 at 14 (1954).

150. *Mayberry v. Pennsylvania*, 400 U.S. 455 (1971).

151. *Michaelson v. United States*, 266 U.S. 42 at 66 (1924); *Cooke v. United States*, 267 U.S. 517 at 537 (1925).

152. The Clayton Act of 1914 provides a jury trial for persons charged with contempt for disobeying court orders, when their disobedient conduct also constitutes a crime under other state or federal law; some limited right to jury trial for contempt was provided by portions of the Civil Rights Acts of 1957 and 1964.

153. *Green v. United States*, 356 U.S. 165 (1958); *Levine v. United States*, 362 U.S. 610 (1960); *United States v. Barnett*, 376 U.S. 681 (1964).

154. *Cheff v. Schnackenberg*, 384 U.S. 373 (1966).

155. *Duncan v. Louisiana*, 391 U.S. 145 (1968); *Bloom v. Illinois*, 391 U.S. 194 (1968).

156. *Bloom v. Illinois*, 391 U.S. 194 at 198, 201, 202 (1968).

157. Id. at 208, 209.

158. *Codispoti v. Pennsylvania*, 418 U.S. 506 (1974).

159. *Lewis v. United States*, ____ U.S. ____ (1996).

JUDICIAL RESTRAINT (PP. 297–306)

1. Robert K. Carr, *The Supreme Court and Judicial Review* (New York: Farrar & Rinehart, 1942), 185.

2. *Ashwander v. Tennessee Valley Authority*, 297 U.S. 288 at 346–348 (1936).

3. *Aetna Life Insurance Company v. Haworth*, 300 U.S. 227 at 240–241 (1937).

4. *United States v. Fruehauf*, 365 U.S. 146 at 157 (1961).

5. Alexander M. Bickel, *The Least Dangerous Branch* (Indianapolis: Bobbs-Merrill, 1962), 113–114; Charles Warren, *The Supreme Court in United States History*, 2 vols. (Boston: Little, Brown, 1922, 1926), I: 110–111.

6. *Muskrat v. United States*, 219 U.S. 346 (1911).

7. Id. at 362.

8. *Mills v. Green*, 159 U.S. 651 at 653 (1895); see also *California v. San Pablo & Tulare Railroad Company*, 149 U.S. 308 at 314 (1893).

9. *DeFunis v. Odegaard*, 416 U.S. 312 (1974).

10. *City of Los Angeles v. Lyons*, 461 U.S. 95 (1983).

11. *Sibron v. New York*, 392 U.S. 40 (1968); *Benton v. Maryland* 395 U.S. 784 (1969).

12. *Roe v. Wade, Doe v. Bolton*, 410 U.S. 113, 179 (1973); *Southern Pacific Terminal Co. v. Interstate Commerce Commission*, 219 U.S. 498 at 515 (1911).

13. *Moore v. Ogilvie*, 394 U.S. 814 (1969).

14. *Lord v. Veazie*, 8 How. 251 at 255 (1850).

15. *Chicago & Grand Trunk Railway Co. v. Wellman*, 143 U.S. 339 at 344–345 (1892).

16. *Hylton v. United States*, 3 Dall. 171 (1796).

17. *Fletcher v. Peck*, 6 Cr. 87 (1810); *Dred Scott v. Sandford*, 19 How. 393 (1857); *Pollock v. Farmers' Loan and Trust Co.* 157 U.S. 429, 158 U.S. 601 (1895).

18. *Carter v. Carter Coal Company*, 298 U.S. 238 (1936).

19. *Flast v. Cohen*, 392 U.S. 83 at 99 (1968).

20. *Baker v. Carr*, 369 U.S. 186 at 204 (1962).

21. *Massachusetts v. Mellon, Frothingham v. Mellon*, 262 U.S. 447 at 483 (1923).

22. Id. at 487.

23. See *Everson v. Board of Education*, 330 U.S. 1 (1947); *Doremus v. Board of Education*, 342 U.S. 429 (1952); *Engel v. Vitale*, 370 U.S. 421 (1962).

24. *Frothingham v. Mellon*, 262 U.S. 447 at 487 (1923).

25. Id. at 488.

26. *Flast v. Cohen*, 392 U.S. 83 at 101 (1968).

27. Id. at 106.

28. *United States v. Richardson*, 418 U.S. 166 at 175, 177 (1974).

29. *Baker v. Carr*, 369 U.S. 186 (1962).

30. *United States v. Richardson*, 418 U.S. 166 at 193 (1974).

31. *Laird v. Tatum*, 408 U.S. 1 (1972); *Schlesinger v. Reservists Committee to Stop the War*, 418 U.S. 208 (1974); *Warth v. Seldin*, 422 U.S. 490 (1975); *Simon v. Eastern Kentucky Welfare Rights Organization*, 426 U.S. 26 (1976).

32. *Association of Data Processing Organizations v. Camp,* 397 U.S. 150 at 154 (1970); *Sierra Club v. Morton,* 405 U.S. 727 at 738–739 (1972); *United States v. Richardson,* 418 U.S. 166 at 193–194 (1974); *Baker v. Carr,* 369 U.S. 186 (1962); *United States v. SCRAP,* 412 U.S. 669 (1973).

33. *Lujan v. Defenders of Wildlife,* 504 U.S. 555 (1992); *United States v. Hays,* 115 S. Ct. 2431 (1995).

34. *Tileston v. Ullman,* 318 U.S. 44 (1943); *United States v. Raines,* 362 U.S. 17 at 20–24 (1960).

35. *Truax v. Raich,* 239 U.S. 33 (1915).

36. *Pierce v. Society of Sisters,* 268 U.S. 510 (1925).

37. *Buchanan v. Warley,* 245 U.S. 60 (1917); *Barrows v. Jackson* 346 U.S. 249 (1953). But also see *Allen v. Wright,* 468 U.S. 737 (1984).

38. *Griswold v. Connecticut,* 381 U.S. 479 (1965); *Doe v. Bolton,* 410 U.S. 179 (1973); *Singleton v. Wulff,* 428 U.S. 106 (1976).

39. *Joint Anti-Fascist Committee v. McGrath,* 341 U.S. 123 (1951); *NAACP v. Alabama ex rel. Patterson,* 357 U.S. 449 (1958); *NAACP v. Button,* 371 U.S. 415 (1963); *Sierra Club v. Morton,* 405 U.S. 727 at 739 (1972).

40. *Missouri v. Illinois,* 180 U.S. 208 (1901); *Georgia v. Tennessee Copper Company,* 206 U.S. 230 (1907); *Pennsylvania v. West Virginia,* 262 U.S. 553 (1923); *Georgia v. Pennsylvania R. Co.,* 324 U.S. 439 (1945); *Massachusetts v. Mellon,* 262 U.S. 447 (1923).

41. *Marbury v. Madison,* 1 Cr. 137 at 170 (1803).

42. *Baker v. Carr,* 369 U.S. 186 at 210 (1962).

43. C. Gordon Post, *Supreme Court and Political Questions* (Baltimore: Johns Hopkins University Press, 1936; reprint ed. New York: Da Capo Press, 1969), 130.

44. *Luther v. Borden,* 7 How. 1 at 42 (1849).

45. Id.

46. Id. at 43; see also *Martin v. Mott,* 12 Wheat. 19 (1827).

47. *Pacific States Telephone and Telegraph v. Oregon,* 223 U.S. 118 (1912).

48. *Baker v. Carr,* 369 U.S. 186 at 209–210 (1962).

49. *Foster v. Neilson,* 2 Pet. 253 at 307 (1829).

50. *Oetjen v. Central Leather Co.,* 246 U.S. 297 at 302 (1918); *United States v. Curtiss-Wright Export Corporation,* 299 U.S. 304 (1936).

51. *Hawke v. Smith,* 253 U.S. 221 (1920); *Coleman v. Miller,* 307 U.S. 433 (1939); *Powell v. McCormack,* 395 U.S. 486 (1969).

52. *Pocket Veto Case,* 279 U.S. 655 (1929).

53. *Colegrove v. Green,* 328 U.S. 549 at 553–554 (1946).

54. *Baker v. Carr,* 369 U.S. 186 at 210 (1962).

55. Id. at 232.

56. Post, *Supreme Court and Political Questions,* 129–130.

57. Carr, *Supreme Court and Judicial Review,* 18–19.

58. *Burnet v. Coronado Oil & Gas Company,* 285 U.S. 393 at 406 (1932).

59. William O. Douglas, "Stare Decisis," *The Record* of the Association of the Bar of the City of New York, IV (1949), 152–179, reprinted in *The Supreme Court: Views from Inside,* ed. Alan F. Westin (New York: W. W. Norton, 1961), 123.

60. Carr, *Supreme Court and Judicial Review,* 18–19.

61. Albert P. Blaustein and Andrew H. Field, "'Overruling' Opinions in the Supreme Court," *Michigan Law Review* 47 (December 1958): 151–194, reprinted in Robert Scigliano, ed., *The Courts: A Reader in the Judicial Process* (Boston: Little, Brown, 1962), 393–408.

62. *Hudson and Smith v. Guestier,* 6 Cr. 281 (1810), overruling *Rose v. Himely,* 4 Cr. 241 (1808); Blaustein and Field, "'Overruling' Opinions," 397.

63. *Knox v. Lee,* 12 Wall. 457 (1871), overruling *Hepburn v. Griswold,* 8 Wall. 603 (1870).

64. *Pollock v. Farmers' Loan and Trust Co.,* 157 U.S. 601 (1895).

65. *Helvering v. Hallock,* 309 U.S. 106 at 119 (1940).

66. *Smith v. Allwright,* 321 U.S. 649 at 665–666 (1944), overruling *Grovey v. Townsend,* 295 U.S. 45 (1935).

67. Blaustein and Field, "'Overruling' Opinions," 395.

68. *Planned Parenthood of Southeastern Pennsylvania v. Casey,* 505 U.S. 833 (1992).

69. Id.

70. Loren P. Beth, *The Constitution, Politics and the Supreme Court* (New York: Harper & Row, 1962), 49.

71. Edward S. Corwin, ed., *The Constitution of the United States of America: Analysis and Interpretation* (Washington, D.C.: U.S. Government Printing Office, 1953), 626.

72. *Younger v. Harris,* 401 U.S. 37 at 441 (1971).

73. Id.

CHAPTER 7

The Court and the States

*I*ndestructible HARDLY SEEMED THE WORD—four years after the end of the nation's bloody civil war—for either the Union or the states. Yet that is exactly what the chief justice of the United States wrote in 1869: "The Constitution looks to an indestructible Union, composed of indestructible States." The declaration came as the Court ruled that the states lacked the power to secede. In the Court's view, the confederate states had never left the Union.[1]

This brave assertion notwithstanding, the survival of the Union had been far from certain for the preceding eighty years. States' rights, interposition, nullification, and civil war had all placed the fragile fabric of national unity under intense strain.

The indestructibility of the states has been called into serious question many times since 1869. As the national government gained in strength and power, the states' existence as viable governmental units has at times seemed quite precarious.

The Constitution, written to create the national government, imposes substantial and severe limitations upon the powers and activities of the states. Yet it assumes their continued operation as effective units of local government. Gradually, as called upon to interpret the meaning of the Constitution, the Supreme Court has defined the limits upon state powers. Time and again it has struck down state action as in conflict with the Constitution or federal law. This function of the Court was particularly significant during the period from the founding of the nation to the Civil War.

But, as Professor Charles Black has pointed out, the Court has affirmed the powers of the states even as it has set their limits.

The states have had to be fenced in, saving their dignity; this is obvious in the nature of the case, and was explicitly provided for in the Constitution and amendments. But the line that marks the limit of their power is necessarily the line that marks the area within which their actions are legitimate.[2]

THE NATIONAL PERIOD

"The general government, though limited as to its objects, is supreme with respect to those objects," wrote Chief Justice John Marshall in 1821.

With the ample powers confided to this supreme government are connected many express and important limitations on the sovereignty of the states. The powers of the Union, on the great subjects of war, peace, and commerce . . . are in themselves limitations of the sovereignty of the states.[3]

The success of the Union was by no means a certainty. The confederation that preceded it was a failure: the central government was too weak; the states, too strong.

Overriding all other questions during the nation's first century was the simple one: would the nation survive? The threat was not from outside, but from within. Would centrifugal force—the states' insistence on retaining power that should belong to the national government—splinter the Union?

On the eve of the Civil War, Chief Justice Roger B. Taney wrote: "The Constitution was not formed merely to guard the States against danger from foreign nations, but mainly to secure union and harmony at home; for if this object could be attained, there would be but little danger from abroad."[4]

Until the conflict between states' rights and national power moved onto the battlefields of the Civil War, much of it was focused in the small courtrooms that served as early homes to the U.S. Supreme Court. As Charles Warren, historian of the Court's first century, explains:

The success of the new government depended on the existence of a supreme tribunal, free from local political bias or prejudice, vested with power to give an interpretation to federal laws and treaties which should be uniform throughout the land, to confine the federal authority to its legitimate field of operation, and to control state aggression on the federal domain.[5]

Two of the nation's greatest statesmen, both Virginians, led the national debate of the early decades over the respective rights and powers of the states and the national government. Speaking for the states was Thomas Jefferson, the third president of the United States. Speaking for national supremacy was John Marshall, its fourth chief justice.

Three years before Jefferson and Marshall moved into the White House and the Supreme Court chambers, respectively, Jefferson set out his view of the relationship of state to federal power in the Kentucky Resolutions, written to protest congressional enactment of the Alien and Sedition Acts. His view of this relationship contrasted sharply with the "supreme government" view set out by Marshall in 1821.

The states, wrote Jefferson, "constituted a general government for special purposes, delegated to that government certain definite powers, reserving, each state to itself, the residuary mass of right to their own self-government . . . Whensoever the general government assumed undelegated powers, its acts are unauthoritative, void and of no force."[6]

By Jefferson's death in 1826, it was clear that Marshall's views, not his, had prevailed. The states were operating under clear and

THE NATURE OF THE UNION

Four years after the Civil War ended, the Supreme Court—in deciding *Texas v. White*—considered and discussed the meaning of "state" and the nature of the Union.

During the Civil War, the Confederate government of Texas had sold off some of the U.S. bonds in its possession to one George W. White and other purchasers, in return for medical and other needed supplies. After the war, the new government of Texas sued White and the other purchasers to recover title to the bonds. The case was argued before the Supreme Court in February 1869 and was decided on April 12, 1869. The Court ruled that Texas could recover title to the bonds, because the actions of the Confederate government were not binding.[1]

Because this case was brought to the Court by Texas under the Constitution's grant of original jurisdiction over a case brought by a state, the Court first considered the status of the state of Texas. Had it, by its secession and participation in the rebellion against national authority, rendered itself ineligible to bring such suits?

The answer was no. And in the process of reaching that answer, Chief Justice Salmon P. Chase discussed "the correct idea of a State" and its relationship to the Union:

The word "state" . . . describes sometimes a people or community of individuals united more or less closely in political relations, inhabiting temporarily or permanently the same country; often it denotes only the country or territorial region, inhabited by such a community; not unfrequently it is applied to the government under which the people live; at other times it represents the combined idea of people, territory, and government.

It is not difficult to see that in all these senses the primary conception is that of a people or community. The people, in whatever territory dwelling, either temporarily or permanently, and whether organized under a regular government, or united by looser or less definite relations, constitute the State.

This is undoubtedly the fundamental idea upon which the republican institutions of our own country are established. . . .

In the Constitution the term "state" most frequently expresses the combined idea just noticed of people, territory and government. A State, in the ordinary sense of the Constitution, is a political community of free citizens, occupying a territory of defined boundaries, and organized under a government sanctioned and limited by a written constitution, and established by the consent of the governed. It is the union of such States, under a common constitution, which forms the distinct and greater political unit, which that Constitution designates as the United States, and makes of the people and States which compose it one people and one country.[2]

Chase then recited the steps Texas took upon seceding:

In all respects, so far as the object could be accomplished by ordinances of the Convention, by Acts of the Legislature, and by votes of the citizens, the relations of Texas to the Union were broken up. . . . Did Texas, in consequence of these Acts, cease to be a State? Or, if not, did the State cease to be a member of the Union? . . .

The Union of the States never was a purely artificial and arbitrary relation. It began among the Colonies, and grew out of common origin, mutual sympathies, kindred principles, similar interests and geographical relations. It was confirmed and strengthened by the necessities of war, and received definite form, and character, and sanction from the Articles of Confederation. By these the Union was solemnly declared to "be perpetual." And when these articles were found to be inadequate . . . the Constitution was ordained "to form a more perfect Union." It is difficult to convey the idea of indissoluble unity more clearly. . . . What can be indissoluble if a perpetual Union, made more perfect, is not?

But the perpetuity and indissolubility of the Union by no means implies the loss of distinct and individual existence, or of the right of self-government by the States. . . . [W]e have already had occasion to remark . . . that "without the States in union, there could be no such political body as the United States." . . . [I]t may be not unreasonably said that the preservation of the States, and the maintenance of their governments are as much within the design and care of the Constitution as the preservation of the Union and the maintenance of the National Government. The Constitution, in all its provisions, looks to an indestructible Union, composed of indestructible States.

When, therefore, Texas became one of the United States, she entered into a [sic] indissoluble relation. All the obligations of perpetual union, and all the guaranties of republican government in the Union, attached at once to the State. The Act which consummated her admission into the Union was something more than a compact; it was the incorporation of a new member into the political body. And it was final.[3]

1. *Texas v. White,* 7 Wall. 700 (1869).
2. Id. at 720–721.
3. Id. at 724, 725, 726.

definite constitutional restraints applied firmly by the Supreme Court. The laws of ten states had been struck down by the Court because they were in conflict with federal treaties, impaired the obligation of contracts, or interfered too far with the broadly construed powers of Congress.

Six months before his death, Jefferson conceded defeat, as he wrote to a friend:

I see, as you do . . . the rapid strides with which the Federal branch of our Government is advancing towards the usurpation of all the rights reserved to the States, and the consolidation in itself of all powers, foreign and domestic; and that too by constructions which, if legitimate, leave no limits to their power. . . .

Under the power to regulate commerce, they assume indefinitely that also over agriculture and manufactures. . . . Under the authority to establish postroads, they claim that of cutting down mountains for the construction of roads, of digging canals, and, aided by a little sophistry on the words "general welfare," a right to do, not only the acts to effect that which are sufficiently enumerated and permitted, but whatsoever they shall think or pretend will be for the general welfare.[7]

The process of subordination of state power to national power that Jefferson deplored slowed in the decades following his death and that of Marshall in 1835. Chief Justice Taney, Marshall's successor, held views much more congenial to Jefferson's.

During his tenure, the Court left undisturbed the basic principles of national supremacy set out by the seminal rulings of the Marshall Court. Within that framework, however, the Taney Court found room for broad state powers—the power to govern its land, its people, and its resources, to ensure the public health, and to preserve the public welfare. The rulings recognizing this "police power" survived as good law and strong precedent long after the Taney Court's decision in the Dred Scott case was overturned, first by war and then by the Fourteenth Amendment.

PRESERVING THE STATES

In the Reconstruction era the Supreme Court protected the southern states from the "reforms" in the status of blacks desired by some in Congress. But in so doing, the Court delayed for a century the movement of blacks toward equality.

The first such ruling came in the *Slaughterhouse Cases* of 1873. From that point on the Court steadily limited the list of rights protected by the Fourteenth Amendment against state infringement. Much of the postwar civil rights legislation was narrowly construed or invalidated altogether as unconstitutional.

Half a century later, a scholar wrote that had this set of cases been decided otherwise,

the States would have largely lost their autonomy and become, as political entities, only of historical interest. If every civil right possessed by a citizen of a State was to receive the protection of the National Judiciary, and if every case involving such a right was to be subject to its review, the States would be placed in a hopelessly subordinate position. . . . The boundary lines between the States and the National Government would be practically abolished.[8]

Yet even as this was written, the Supreme Court was beginning to extend national protection to the rights of individuals threatened by state action.

PROTECTING PROPERTY

In contrast to its post–Civil War reluctance to extend federal control over the state's treatment of the individual, the Court did not hesitate to extend federal protection over property threatened by overly vigorous assertion of the state's police powers. After a brief fling with state regulation in the 1870s and 1880s, the Court settled into a laissez-faire posture from which it wielded the Fourteenth Amendment's due process guarantee to control state regulatory efforts. As the contract clause faded out of use in this fashion, the due process guarantee was wielded more and more.

And using the Tenth Amendment's concept of powers reserved to the states—and therefore, the Court reasoned, denied to the national government—the Court likewise struck down federal regulatory laws as intruding upon the rights of the states. A twilight zone was created, a no-man's land, where regulation could not be effectively imposed by either state or national authority.

The Great Depression and the New Deal—and the new social and economic realities they created—brought a dramatic end to this period. The Court widened the field for state regulation, even as it upheld the extension of federal power deeper than ever into the domain of the states.

Since 1937, explains one scholar, "the Court's function is more like that of a traffic cop—to see that our multiple legisla-

---

:o:

JIM CROW LAW.

UPHELD BY THE UNITED STATES SUPREME COURT.

Statute Within the Competency of the Louisiana Legislature and Railroads—Must Furnish Separate Cars for Whites and Blacks.

Washington, May 18.—The Supreme Court today in an opinion read by Justice Brown, sustained the constitutionality of the law in Louisiana requiring the railroads of that State to provide separate cars for white and colored passengers. There was no interstate commerce feature in the case for the railroad upon which the incident occurred giving rise to case—Plessey vs. Ferguson—East Louisiana railroad, was and is operated wholly within the State, to the laws of Congress of many of the States. The opinion states that by the analogy of the laws of Congress, and of many of states requiring establishment of separate schools for children of two races and other similar laws, the statute in question was within competency of Louisiana Legislature, exercising the police power of the State. The judgment of the Supreme Court of State upholding law was therefore upheld.

Mr. Justice Harlan announced a very vigorous dissent saying that he saw nothing but mischief in all such laws. In his view of the case, no power in the land had right to regulate the enjoyment of civil rights upon the basis of race. It would be just as reasonable and proper, he said, for states to pass laws requiring separate cars to be furnished for Catholic and Protestants, or for descendants of those of Teutonic race and those of Latin race.

The Court in *Plessy v. Ferguson* (1892) upheld Louisiana's Jim Crow laws requiring separate railroad cars for white and colored passengers. *Plessy v. Ferguson* established the "separate but equal" doctrine that permitted legal segregation to flourish for the next sixty years. The Warren Court unanimously abandoned the doctrine in *Brown v. Board of Education* (1954), declaring racial segregation unconstitutional and setting off a reaction in the southern states comparable in intensity only to the hostility of the previous century's debate over slavery.

tures, in their many activities, do not collide, to make sure that the road is kept free for national power, which, under the rules laid down in 1789, has the right of way."[9]

PROTECTING INDIVIDUALS

As the Court relinquished as no longer necessary its role as guardian of property and commerce against state interference, it began to assert the role of protector of individuals against state action. As written, the Bill of Rights protects people only against action by the federal government. Early in the nation's history, the Court refused to extend those protections to those threatened by state action.

But in the mid-1920s, the Court began using the Fourteenth Amendment's guarantee of due process to protect certain of those individual rights against infringement by the state. First Amendment freedoms of expression were the first to win such protection, followed by due process rights of fair trial and fair treatment for persons suspected or accused of crimes. Then, at mid-century, that amendment's equal protection guarantee came into use as the effective guarantee of individual rights its authors had intended it to be.

Using the equal protection clause as its measure, the Court struck down state laws requiring racial segregation in public schools, public transportation, and public accommodations, setting off a civil rights revolution that continues today. Black citizens were not the only beneficiaries of equal protection rulings; during the second half of the twentieth century, the Court found a similar rationale useful for discarding laws that discriminated against women and aliens as well.

Just as the Court's landmark rulings of the Marshall era establishing national supremacy over state rights were met with resistance from the states, so too were the Court's rulings under Chief Justice Earl Warren. The Court's decision decreeing an end to public school segregation set off a reaction in the southern states comparable in intensity only to the hostility of the previous century's debate over slavery. The antagonism was further inflamed by the Supreme Court's interference with matters previously left entirely to the states—the drawing of electoral district lines and the treatment of criminal suspects. An "Impeach Earl Warren" movement grew up, motivated by a variety of reasons.

TOWARD A HEALTHY BALANCE

Just as Marshall's nationalism was moderated by Taney's sensitivity to state concerns, so Warren's tenure was followed by that of two chief justices, Warren E. Burger and William H. Rehnquist, both of whom gave more weight to a state's right and need to operate with flexibility within the federal system.

In 1971 Justice Hugo L. Black—who came to the Court of 1937 as a liberal southern senator and Franklin D. Roosevelt's first appointment to the bench—sounded this theme for the Court of the 1970s as he described what he called "Our Federalism":

a proper respect for state functions, a recognition of the fact that the entire country is made up of a Union of separate state governments,

and a continuance of the belief that the National Government will fare best if the States and their institutions are left free to perform their separate functions in their separate ways.[10]

Through the 1970s the Court was more sensitive to the needs of the states. No decision raised the hopes of state officials higher than the Court's 1976 ruling in *National League of Cities v. Usery*. By a 5–4 vote the Court struck down an act of Congress that had imposed federal minimum wage and overtime rules on state employees.

The majority—Chief Justice Burger and Justices Rehnquist, Potter Stewart, Harry A. Blackmun, and Lewis F. Powell Jr.—seemed to breathe new life into the constitutional language reserving power to the states. In Rehnquist's words, it declared that "there are attributes of sovereignty attaching to every state government which may not be impaired by Congress not because Congress may lack an affirmative grant of legislative authority to reach the matter, but because the Constitution prohibits it from exercising the authority in that manner."[11]

But the Court soon reneged on the promise of greater state autonomy implicit in this decision, overruling it in 1985 by the margin of a single vote. Justice Blackmun wrote the Court's opinion in *Garcia v. San Antonio Metropolitan Transit Authority,* acknowledging that he had changed his mind since *National League of Cities.*[12]

Joined by the 1976 dissenters—William J. Brennan Jr., Byron R. White, Thurgood Marshall, and John Paul Stevens—Blackmun declared that states must rely on the political process, not the Constitution, to protect them from such intrusions on internal affairs.

Of course we continue to recognize that the States occupy a special and specific position in our constitutional system. . . . But the principal and basic limit on the federal commerce power is that inherent in all congressional action—the built-in restraints that our system provides through state participation in federal government action. The political process ensures that laws that unduly burden the States will not be promulgated.[13]

Scholars who looked at the matter from the state's point of view were quick to take issue with the Court's rationale. "*Garcia* rests on erroneous assumptions about the ways in which the nation's political process actually works," wrote University of Virginia law professor A. E. Dick Howard. Blackmun's assumptions, Howard continued, "have two dimensions. One is institutional—that the states play a major role in structuring the national government. The other is political—that the nature of the process (especially in Congress) permits adequate focus on the states' interests as states."

"Neither branch of the argument reflects reality," Howard concluded.[14]

A year after the *Garcia* ruling, Rehnquist succeeded Burger as chief justice. The guiding principle of his decisions, wrote University of Delaware political science professor Sue Davis, is federalism: "Protecting the states from what he perceives to be undesirable federal intrusion is so central to Rehnquist's decision making that he has adopted those tools of constitutional interpretation which are most useful in accomplishing his goal."[15]

With the strength of his own convictions on this point, Rehnquist began to have some success in persuading his colleagues to share his view of the need to protect state prerogatives more vigorously. In 1995 he won a significant victory when the Court struck down a federal law banning guns at local schools, saying it reached too far into local affairs. For the first time in sixty years, the Court found that Congress, in passing a law regulating personal conduct, had overreached its commerce clause power.[16]

Rehnquist wrote in *United States v. Lopez:* "Just as the separation and independence of the coordinate branches of the Federal Government serves to prevent the accumulation of excessive power in any one branch, a healthy balance of power between the States and the Federal Government will reduce the risk of tyranny and abuse from either front."[17]

That same year the Court, with Rehnquist in dissent, struck down states' limits on the number of terms their representatives served in Congress.[18] The only justice to be in the majority in both of these cases, Anthony M. Kennedy, seemed to agree with Rehnquist that the goal was a healthy balance between state and federal power: "That the states may not invade the sphere of federal sovereignty is as incontestable, in my view, as the corollary proposition that the federal government must be held within the boundaries of its own power when it intrudes upon matters reserved to the states."[19]

"I do not think that the United States would come to an end if we lost our power to declare an Act of Congress void," said Justice Oliver Wendell Holmes Jr. "I do think the Union would be imperilled if we could not make that declaration as to the laws of the several states."[1]

Although the landmark assertion of judicial review over acts of Congress in *Marbury v. Madison* (1803) was left unused, uncontested, and undisturbed for more than half a century after its announcement, the history of the Court from its first term to the Civil War is a narrative of continuing controversy over the assertion of its statutory power to review state laws and the decisions of state courts.

During that time, "the chief conflicts arose over the court's decisions restricting the limits of state authority and not over those restricting the limits of congressional power. Discontent with its actions on the latter subject arose, *not* because the court held an Act of Congress unconstitutional, but rather because it refused to do so."[2]

Sources of Power

Article III of the Constitution grants the federal courts jurisdiction over all controversies between states, those in which the United States is a party, controversies between a state and the citizens of another state, and between a state and foreign states, their citizens, or subjects.

The Judiciary Act of 1789 expressly gave the Court the power to review state court rulings involving federal issues or claims. *(See box, Judicial Review and State Courts, this page.)*

RESISTANCE: *CHISHOLM V. GEORGIA*

No sooner had the Court handed down its first major decision than the states made clear their resistance to the assertion of federal judicial power. Within five years a new amendment had become part of the Constitution, overruling the Court's decision.

The case of *Chisholm v. Georgia* arose when two South Carolinians sued Georgia in the Supreme Court, invoking the jurisdiction granted to the Court by Article III. As executors of the estate of a man to whom money was owed by persons whose property the state of Georgia confiscated during the war, the South Carolinians asked Georgia to pay the debt. The state of Georgia refused to appear before the Supreme Court, denying its authority to hear cases in which a state was the defendant.

Finding clear authority for such suits in Article III, the Court on February 18, 1793, upheld the right of citizens of one state to bring a suit against another state in the Supreme Court. Chief Justice John Jay delivered the majority opinion. Only Justice James Iredell disagreed.[3]

Jay took note of the fact that Georgia was at that very time

"prosecuting an action in this court against two citizens of South Carolina," while disclaiming the correlative right. Jay commented:

That rule is said to be a bad one, which does not work both ways; the citizens of Georgia are content with a right of suing citizens of other states; but are not content that citizens of other states should have a right to sue them.[4]

To buttress his ruling in support of the Court's jurisdiction, Jay said he had no precedents to refer to, but, he explained:

The extension of the judiciary power of the United States to such controversies appears to me to be wise, because it is honest, and because it is useful . . . because it leaves not even the most obscure an [sic] friendless citizen without means of obtaining justice from a neighboring state; because it obviates occasions of quarrels between states on account of the claims of their respective citizens; because it recognizes and strongly rests on this great moral truth, that justice is the same whether due from one man or a million, or from a million to one man.[5]

This decision, reports historian Charles Warren, "fell upon the country with a profound shock. . . . The vesting of any such jurisdiction over sovereign states had been expressly disclaimed . . . by the great defenders of the constitution, during the days of the contest over its adoption."[6]

The day after the *Chisholm* ruling, a proposed constitutional amendment to override the decision was introduced in the House of Representatives. State pride was injured, but more

---

JUDICIAL REVIEW AND STATE COURTS

Unlike the power of the Supreme Court to review acts of Congress to measure their constitutionality, the authority of the Court to review acts of state courts is explicitly granted by law—by Section 25 of the Judiciary Act of 1789.

That act provided:

That a final judgment or decree in any suit, in the highest court of law or equity of a State in which a decision in the suit could be had, where is drawn in question the validity of a treaty or statute of, or an authority exercised under the United States, and the decision is against their validity;

or where is drawn in question the validity of a statute of, or an authority exercised under any State, on the ground of their being repugnant to the constitutions, treaties or laws of the United States, and the decision is in favour of such their validity,

or where is drawn in question the construction of any clause of the constitution, or of a treaty, or statute of, or commission held under the United States, and the decision is against the title, right, privilege or exemption specifically set up or claimed by either party under such clause of the said Constitution, treaty, statute or commission, may be re-examined and reversed or affirmed in the Supreme Court of the United States.

than that was at issue. Already in delicate financial condition after the Revolution, the states feared fiscal disaster if suits such as that upheld in *Chisholm* were brought to recover property confiscated during the war.

Georgia reacted dramatically. The Georgia House approved a measure declaring that whoever carried out the Supreme Court's decision would be "guilty of felony and shall suffer death, with benefit of clergy, by being hanged." The bill did not become law.[7]

The following year the U.S. House and Senate approved the proposed amendment.[8] On January 8, 1798, the Eleventh Amendment was formally added to the Constitution. It states:

The Judicial power of the United States shall not be construed to extend to any suit of equity, commenced or prosecuted against one of the United States by Citizens of another State, or by Citizens or Subjects of any Foreign State.

Chisholm v. Georgia was overruled. The states had won the first battle.

The Supreme Court acquiesced. Within a month of ratification, the Court dismissed a suit against the state of Virginia by citizens of another state, citing the amendment in support of its statement that it had no jurisdiction over the matter.[9] *(For further discussion of the Eleventh Amendment, see pp. 337–339.)*

SUPREMACY: *WARE V. HYLTON*

Similar facts—but a much longer effective life—characterized the Court's next major decision, which again involved a clear question of state rights.

Article VI of the Constitution asserts national supremacy, stating that the Constitution, federal laws, and treaties are the supreme law of the land and all conflicting state laws or constitutions are invalid.

The peace treaty with Britain, which ended the Revolutionary War, provided that neither nation would raise any legal obstacle to the recovery of debts due from its citizens to those of the other nation. Large sums of money were affected by this provision. One scholar estimates that in Virginia alone as much as $2 million was owed to British subjects.[10] Like many other states, Virginia had confiscated the property of British loyalists during the Revolution. And state law had provided that people owing money to British subjects could satisfy their obligation by making payments to the state.

After the treaty was signed, British creditors came into federal court to sue Virginia debtors for payment of their obligations. Defending the debtors and the state was John Marshall. He argued only this one case before the Supreme Court—and he lost.[11]

Early in 1796 the Court ruled against the debtors, against the state, and for the British creditors. The debts must be paid, it held in *Ware v. Hylton*.[12] The state had a moral obligation to return the payments made during the war, but whether it did so, the debtors were still liable.

National supremacy was affirmed. "Here is a treaty," wrote Justice William Cushing, "the supreme law, which overrules all state laws upon the subject to all intents and purposes; and that makes the difference."[13]

RESISTANCE: *UNITED STATES V. JUDGE PETERS*

For almost fifteen years after *Ware v. Hylton,* the Court—by a cautious approach to the use of its authority to review state court actions—avoided collisions with state power. But in 1809 it found itself head to head with the state of Pennsylvania.

The controversy that culminated in 1809 had begun during the Revolutionary War when Gideon Olmstead and his companions seized a British ship as a prize of war. The ship was sold as a prize vessel, and the proceeds became the object of a tug-of-war between Olmstead and the state of Pennsylvania.

In 1803 a federal judge—Richard Peters—ordered that the money be paid to Olmstead. Instead of complying, the state legislature ordered it placed in the state treasury. Until that time, it had been in the personal custody of the state treasurer, a man named David Rittenhouse.

Apparently deterred by the legislature's action, Judge Peters did not actually issue the order directing payment to Olmstead. Finally, in 1808 the eighty-two-year-old Olmstead asked the Supreme Court to direct Peters to issue the order. The state of Pennsylvania responded that such a suit could not be brought in federal court because of the Eleventh Amendment denial of federal jurisdiction over suits brought by citizens against a state.

The Supreme Court on February 20, 1809, issued Olmstead's requested order. The Court found it necessary to grant his request, explained Chief Justice Marshall, to preserve national supremacy:

If the legislatures of the several states may, at will, annul the judgments of the courts of the United States, and destroy the rights acquired under those judgments, the constitution itself becomes a solemn mockery, and the nation is deprived of the means of enforcing its laws by the instrumentality of its own tribunals.[14]

On the Eleventh Amendment defense raised by the state, the Court found that it did not apply to this situation simply because the state was not the defendant.

The Supreme Court decision did not settle the matter. The governor of Pennsylvania declared he would use the militia to prevent enforcement of its order, which Judge Peters finally issued on March 24. When the federal marshal attempted to deliver the order to the two women who were executors of the now-deceased Rittenhouse's estate, he was met by the state militia. The marshal called out a posse of two thousand men. A federal grand jury indicted the militia commander and ordered his arrest for resisting federal law.

The governor asked President James Madison to intervene. Madison declined. The legislature then capitulated, removing the militia, appropriating the money due Olmstead, and making the payment, thus ending the long quarrel.[15]

SUPREMACY

The Constitution is quite clear on what happens when a state law conflicts with a federal law. Article VI states that the laws of the United States "shall be the supreme Law of the Land; . . . any Thing in the Constitution or Laws of any state to the Contrary notwithstanding." As Justice John Paul Stevens wrote in 1992, "[S]ince our decision in *McCulloch v. Maryland* (1819), it has been settled that state law that conflicts with federal law is 'without effect.'"[1]

Case by case, that clarity begins to blur. The Court strikes down state laws when valid federal statutes dominate the field or explicitly bar the state action. Closer cases arise when federal law does not specifically detail its impact on state law, or when federal legislation addresses only part of a field, with regulation that does not make clear that it leaves no room for the states to act.

Today's preemption standard has evolved over the last half century.[2] Stevens summarized in the 1992 case of *Cipollone v. Liggett Group:*

Consideration of issues arising under the Supremacy Clause starts with the assumption that the historic police powers of the States are not to be superseded by . . . Federal Act unless that is the clear and manifest purpose of Congress. Accordingly, the purpose of Congress is the ultimate touchstone of pre-emption analysis. Congress' intent may be explicitly stated in the statute's language or implicitly contained in its structure and purpose. In the absence of an express congressional command, state law is pre-empted if that law actually conflicts with federal law, or if federal law so thoroughly occupies a legislative field as to make reasonable the inference that Congress left no room for the States to supplement it.[3]

Writing for a seven-justice majority, Stevens added that the express preemption provisions of a law dictate the scope of its preemption: "Congress' enactment of a provision defining the preemp-

tive reach of a statute implies that matters beyond that reach are not preempted."[4]

In that 1992 case the Court said the Federal Cigarette Labeling and Advertising Act did not preempt lawsuits based on express warranty, intentional fraud, misrepresentation, or conspiracy. The ruling permitted people to sue under state tort law cigarette manufacturers who lied about the dangers of smoking or otherwise misrepresented their products. Cigarette companies had argued that the federal labeling law preempted state liability claims. But the Court said the federal statute superseded only state laws requiring particular warnings on cigarette labels or in cigarette advertising.

In another 1992 case the Court ruled that the federal Airline Deregulation Act of 1978 precluded states from regulating advertising of airline fares.[5] But three years later the Court allowed travelers to sue in state court for breach of contract over changes in frequent-flier benefits.[6] The Court also held in 1995 that the National Traffic and Motor Vehicle Safety Act did not preclude common-law tort lawsuits against truck companies for failure to install antilock brakes, noting in its opinion that while *Cipollone* suggested that an express preemption clause forecloses implied preemption, that suggestion was not a hard and fast rule.[7]

1. *Cipollone v. Liggett Group*, 112 S. Ct. 2608 (1992), quoting from McCulloch v. Maryland, 4 Wheat. 316 (1819).
2. *Rice v. Santa Fe Elevator Corp.*, 331 U.S. 218 (1947).
3. *Cipollone.*
4. Id.
5. *Morales v. Trans World Airlines*, 112 S. Ct. 2031 (1992)
6. *American Airlines v. Wolens*, 115 S. Ct. 817 (1995).
7. *Freightliner Corp. v. Myrick*, 115 S. Ct. 1483 (1995); See also *Medtronic Inc. v. Lohr*, ____ U.S. ____ (1996).

Challenge to Power

The Judiciary Act of 1789 left to the state courts all cases arising within the states, even if they involved some federal question. But to ensure that constitutional principles and federal law were uniformly applied, the act granted, in such cases, the right of appeal to the Supreme Court. The provision granting this right was the much debated Section 25. *(See box, Judicial Review and State Courts, p. 316.)*

Section 25 authorized the Supreme Court to reexamine and reverse or affirm the final judgment of the highest court in a state when the state court decided a case involving the Constitution, federal laws, or federal treaties and resolved the matter against the federal claim.

In 1914 Congress expanded the scope of this power of review by allowing the Supreme Court to review state court decisions upholding—as well as those denying—a federal claim. *(See "A Broader Jurisdiction," pp. 273–274, in Chapter 6.)*

"In view of the extreme jealousy shown by the States from the outset towards the Federal government, it is a singular fact

in our history that this Section was in force 24 years before any State resented its existence or attempted to controvert the right of Congress to enact it," wrote Charles Warren.[16]

When the challenge came, in 1816, it came from Virginia, Marshall's home state. The state court that posed the challenge and denied the power of the Supreme Court to review its decisions was led by Judge Spencer Roane, a close friend of Thomas Jefferson and, it is said, the man who would have been chief justice instead of John Marshall had Oliver Ellsworth resigned the post a few months later and Jefferson, not Adams, been president.[17]

Like *Chisholm* and *Ware*, the facts of this case involved land belonging to British subjects, which Virginia had confiscated and then granted to new owners. Lord Fairfax owned land in Virginia, which he willed at his death in 1781 to his nephew, Denny Martin, a British subject. Virginia law not only denied the right of aliens to inherit land within its boundaries, but also it claimed that it had confiscated the estate during the Revolution and subsequently granted portions to other owners, including one David Hunter. Eventually, some of this contested land was purchased by John Marshall's brother—and perhaps even the chief justice himself. At any rate, Marshall did not take part in the Court's considerations of this case.

First titled *Hunter v. Fairfax's Devisee*, the case came to court in 1796, but it was postponed due to the death of Hunter's attorney.[18] Almost fifteen years passed before a Virginia court upheld Hunter's claim, and the Fairfax heirs moved the matter back to the Supreme Court, where it was argued in 1812 under the name *Fairfax's Devisee v. Hunter's Lessee*.

In 1813 the Court ruled for the British heirs. The vote was 3–1, with Justice William Johnson dissenting and two justices—Marshall being one—not taking part in the case. Justice Joseph Story wrote a forceful opinion, holding that aliens could inherit land in Virginia, state law to the contrary. Therefore, Denny Martin held title to the disputed lands, and the state could not grant title to them to anyone else. The Court ordered the Virginia court to issue an order to this effect, settling the case in Martin's favor.[19]

Resentful of the ruling and of the damage inflicted by Story's opinion upon the state's confiscation and inheritance laws, the state court refused to follow the Supreme Court's directive. Instead, it decided to consider the question of the constitutionality of the Supreme Court's claimed power to consider the case at all: was Section 25 of the Judiciary Act constitutional?

Late in 1815 the state court held the section invalid, declaring that the Supreme Court could not constitutionally review state court rulings, and thus it would not obey the Court's order:

The appellate power of the Supreme Court of the United States does not extend to this Court, under a sound construction of the Constitution. . . . So much of the Twenty-fifth Section of the Act . . . to establish the Judicial Courts of the United States as extends the appellate jurisdiction of the Supreme Court to this court, is not in pursuance of the Constitution.

And back went the matter to the Supreme Court.

Again Marshall did not consider the case, now known as *Martin v. Hunter's Lessee*.

Within three months of the state court challenge, the Supreme Court responded with a sweeping affirmance of the validity of Section 25. In its opinion issued on March 29, 1816, the Court stated:

[T]he appellate power of the United States does extend to cases pending in the state courts; and . . . the 25th section of the judiciary act, which authorizes the exercise of this jurisdiction in the specified cases, by a writ of error, is supported by the letter and spirit of constitution. We find no clause in that instrument which limits this power; and we dare not interpose a limitation where the people have not been disposed to create one.[20]

Justice Story, author of the Court's opinion, took the opportunity to deliver a ringing defense of national supremacy:

The constitution of the United States was ordained and established, not by the states in their sovereign capacities, but emphatically, as the preamble of the constitution declares, by "the people of the United States." There can be no doubt that it was competent to the people to invest the general government with all the powers which they might deem proper and necessary; to extend or restrain these powers accord-

ing to their own good pleasure, and to give them a paramount and supreme authority. As little doubt can there be that the people had a right to prohibit to the states the exercise of any powers which were, in their judgment, incompatible with the objects of the general compact; to make the powers of the state governments, in given cases, subordinate to those of the nation.[21]

Examining Article III "creating and defining the judicial power of the United States," Story pointed out that

[i]t is the case, then, and not the court, that gives the jurisdiction [to federal courts]. If the judicial power extends to the case, it will be in vain to search in the letter of the Constitution for any qualification as to the tribunal where it depends.[22]

The Constitution, he continued:

is crowded with provisions which restrain or annul the sovereignty of the states. . . . When, therefore, the states are stripped of some of the highest attributes of sovereignty, and the same are given to the United States; when the legislatures of the states are, in some respects, under the control of Congress, and in every case are, under the constitution, bound by the paramount authority of the United States; it is certainly difficult to support the argument that the appellate power over the decisions of state courts is contrary to the genius of our institutions. The courts of the United States can, without question, revise the proceedings of the executive and legislative authorities of the states, and if they are found to be contrary to the constitution, may declare them to be of no legal validity. Surely the exercise of the same right over judicial tribunals is not a higher or more dangerous act of sovereign power.[23]

And further, wrote Justice Story:

. . . [a] motive of another kind, perfectly compatible with the most sincere respect for state tribunals, might induce the grant of appellate power over the decisions. That motive is the importance, and even the necessity of uniformity of decisions throughout the whole United States, upon all subjects within the purview of the constitution. Judges of equal learning and integrity, in different states, might differently interpret a statute, or a treaty of the United States, or even the constitution itself. If there were no revising authority to control these jarring and discordant judgments, and harmonize them into uniformity, the laws, the treaties, and the constitution of the United States would be different in different states, and might, perhaps, never have precisely the same construction, obligation, or efficacy, in any two states. The public mischiefs that would attend such a state of things would be truly deplorable . . . the [Supreme Court's] appellate jurisdiction must continue to be the only adequate remedy for such evils.[24]

A SECOND CHALLENGE

Despite the firmness of the Court's decision in *Martin v. Hunter's Lessee*, the Virginia court of appeals, led by Roane, continued to resist the Supreme Court's authority to review its rulings.

A second collision between the two judicial bodies came just five years after the first. This time Chief Justice Marshall participated. The Court again affirmed its power of reviewing state court actions, and the matter was settled.

Although state law forbade the sale of out-of-state lottery tickets in Virginia, two people named P. J. and M. J. Cohen sold tickets in Virginia to a congressionally authorized lottery in the District of Columbia. They were convicted of violating the Virginia law. But they appealed their conviction to the Supreme Court, arguing that the Virginia law must fall before the conflicting—and overriding—federal law authorizing the lottery and the sale of tickets.

Virginia's response was to argue that the case should be dismissed because the Supreme Court lacked jurisdiction over it. Arguing the state's case was Philip P. Barbour, who later became a member of the Supreme Court.

On March 3, 1821, the Court again rejected this argument, holding that it was founded upon a mistaken view of the relationship of the state and federal judicial systems. Writing for the Court, Chief Justice Marshall rejected the idea that these systems were totally separate and independent, like those of different sovereign nations.

That the United States form, for many, and for most important purposes, a single nation, has not yet been denied. In war, we are one people. In making peace, we are one people. In all commercial regulations, we are one and the same people. In many other respects, the American people are one; and the government which is alone capable of controlling and managing their interests in all these respects, is the government of the Union. It is their government, and in that character they have no other. America has chosen to be, in many respects, and to many purposes, a nation; and for all these purposes, her government is complete; to all these objects, it is competent. The people have declared, that in the exercise of all powers given for these objects it is supreme. It can, then, in effecting these objects, legitimately control all individuals or governments within the American territory. The constitution and laws of a state, so far as they are repugnant to the constitution and laws of the United States, are absolutely void. These states are constituent parts of the United States. They are members of one great empire—for some purposes sovereign, for some purposes subordinate.

In a government so constituted, is it unreasonable that the judicial power should be competent to give efficacy to the constitutional laws of the legislature? That department can decide on the validity of the constitution or law of a state, if it be repugnant to the constitution or to a law of the United States. Is it unreasonable that it should also be empowered to decide on the judgment of a state tribunal enforcing such unconstitutional law? . . . We think it is not.[25]

To hold that the Supreme Court lacked jurisdiction over this and similar cases, Marshall wrote, would have "mischievous consequences."

It would prostrate, it has been said, the government and its laws at the feet of every state in the Union. And would not this be its effect? What power of the government could be executed by its own means, in any state disposed to resist its execution? . . . Each member will possess a veto on the will of the whole. . . .[26]

No government ought to be so defective in its organization as not to contain within itself the means of securing the execution of its own laws against other dangers than those which occur every day. Courts of justice are the means most usually employed; and it is reasonable to expect that a government should repose on its own courts, rather than on others. There is certainly nothing in the circumstances under which our constitution was formed; nothing in the history of the times, which would justify the opinion that the confidence reposed in the states was so implicit as to leave in them and their tribunals the power of resisting, or defeating, in the form of law, the legitimate measures of the Union.[27]

The Eleventh Amendment had no application here, the Court held, because this case was initiated by the state, not the Cohens.

After this resounding decision on the question of jurisdiction, the Court's ruling on the merits of the case—against the Cohens and in favor of the state—was merely a postscript. In approving the District of Columbia lottery, the Court held, Congress had not intended to authorize the sale of tickets in a state forbidding such a transaction.[28]

REPEAL AND RESISTANCE

The decade following the Supreme Court's decision in *Cohens v. Virginia* saw the states' battle against judicial review shift to forums other than the Supreme Court.

In Congress there was a series of efforts to repeal Section 25 or otherwise terminate the Court's jurisdiction over state court rulings. It was proposed that the Senate become the court of appeals for all cases involving the states—or that a certain number of the justices, above a simple majority, be required to agree in any decision on the validity of a state law. None succeeded.

Perhaps the most celebrated clash of the Court and state power followed the decisions affirming judicial review. During Andrew Jackson's first term in the White House, the Court collided with the state of Georgia and Jackson—unlike Madison in the Olmstead case—was on the side of the state.

The Cherokee Indians occupied land within the boundaries of Georgia. The state attempted to assert control over the Indians and these lands with a series of increasingly stringent laws passed during the 1820s. Finally, the Cherokees—acting as an independent nation—filed a request with the Supreme Court, under its original jurisdiction, for an order directing the state to stop enforcing these laws.

Not only did the state of Georgia fail to appear to defend against this request, but even before it was ruled upon, the governor and legislature executed an Indian convicted of murder under the contested laws. The execution was carried out in direct defiance of a Supreme Court notice to the state that it was going to review the murder conviction in light of the challenge to the laws.[29]

In March 1831 the Court denied the Cherokees' request, holding that its original jurisdiction did not extend to such a suit because the Cherokees were not a foreign state. "If it be true that wrongs have been inflicted, and that still greater are to be apprehended," wrote Chief Justice Marshall, "this is not the tribunal which can redress the past or prevent the future."[30]

A second challenge to these laws quickly arrived before the Court. Georgia law required white persons living in Indian territory to obtain a state license. Two missionaries, Samuel Worcester and Elizur Butler refused, and were convicted of violating the law and sentenced to four years at hard labor.

They appealed to the Supreme Court, which issued a writ of error to the state court, notifying it to send the record of the case to Washington for review. The order was ignored. The case was argued February 20, 1832, without the appearance of counsel for the state.

On March 3 the Court ruled. Federal jurisdiction over the Cherokees was exclusive; therefore, the state had no power to pass any laws affecting them. The missionaries' convictions were reversed because the laws under which they were charged were void. Worcester and Butler should be released, said the Court.[31] But it did not actually issue the order directing release before it adjourned its term two weeks later, leaving the matter suspended until its new term in 1833.

There was reason for the Court to delay. President Jackson was known to side with the state. Often-repeated but unsubstantiated reports quoted him as saying: "Well, John Marshall has made his decision, now let him enforce it." Whether Jackson made such a statement, his failure to act bore out the sentiment.

Justice Story wrote a friend the week of the ruling:

Georgia is full of anger and violence. What she will do it is difficult to say. Probably she will resist the execution of our judgment, and if she does, I do not believe the President will interfere. . . . The rumor is, that he has told the Georgians he will do nothing. . . . The Court has done its duty. Let the Nation now do theirs. If we have a Government, let its command be obeyed; if we have not, it is as well to know it at once, and to look to consequences.[32]

As the year wore on, Chief Justice Marshall became increasingly pessimistic about the standoff. He wrote to Story:

I yield slowly and reluctantly to the conviction that our Constitution cannot last. I had supposed that North of the Potomack a firm and solid government competent to the security of rational liberty might be preserved. Even that now seems doubtful. The case of the South seems to me to be desperate. Our opinions are incompatible with a united government even among ourselves. The Union has been prolonged thus far by miracles. I fear they cannot continue.[33]

But they did continue, for a while. Events made it politically impossible for Jackson to continue to give even tacit support to Georgia's defiance of the Court. Late in 1832 South Carolina, protesting a new tariff law and other intrusions upon state's rights, approved the Nullification Ordinance. It asserted the right of a state to disregard and thereby nullify federal laws it viewed as unconstitutional. The ordinance forbade any appeal to the Supreme Court from state courts in cases involving the ordinance or any federal law.

President Jackson responded by describing the nullification theory as treason. Firmly planted on the side of federal power,

he could hardly continue to sanction Georgia's disobedience to the Court's ruling in the missionary case.

Realizing that political fact of life, the governor of Georgia pardoned Worcester and Butler in 1833; they subsequently dropped their case.

TAXES, SLAVES, AND WAR

State resistance to federal judicial power did not end with the Cherokee controversy. Ohio courts refused for a matter of years in the 1850s to carry out a Supreme Court ruling on a tax matter. Also in the 1850s the supreme court of California held Section 25 of the Judiciary Act invalid—but its legislature ordered the judges to comply with the federal law. And in the years just before the Civil War, a great struggle between state and federal judicial power took place in Wisconsin over the trial of an abolitionist for violating the Federal Fugitive Slave Act.[34] (See box, A Clash of Courts, p. 375.)

The Civil War, Justice Robert H. Jackson wrote years later, practically ended state resistance to the Supreme Court's power to review state laws and state court decisions. Yet after the Civil War the pace of that use of judicial review accelerated. From 1789 to 1863 only thirty-eight state or local laws had been held unconstitutional by the Supreme Court. In the two dozen years from 1864 to 1888 the Court struck down ninety-nine laws, but in the two dozen between 1914 and 1938 the pace tripled as the Court invalidated more than three hundred laws.

Nonetheless, in 1941 Jackson wrote:

It is now an accepted part of our constitutional doctrine that conflicts between state legislation and the federal Constitution are to be resolved by the Supreme Court and, had it not been, it is difficult to see how the Union could have survived.[35]

Strong state and public reaction to the Court's rulings in the last half of the century—on questions of civil rights, criminal law, individual rights, and state prerogatives—would nonetheless continue.

Yet even as the Court struck down hundreds of state and local laws between 1964 and 1995, the fierce opposition of some states to some of these rulings did not produce anything approaching a successful drive against the institution of judicial review.

The States and the Economy

For the first 150 years of its history, the Supreme Court exerted its greatest influence on the states of the Union through its decisions on matters of economic interest. In case after case—as the justices construed the contract clause, the commerce clause, and defined the state's power of taxation—the Court determined the relationship of state to federal power.

"Certainly," wrote Thomas Reed Powell in the midtwentieth century, "the commerce powers of the nation and the state raise the most perennial and persistent problems of constitutional federalism."[1] The commerce clause, wrote Felix Frankfurter in 1937, "has throughout the Court's history been the chief source of its adjudications regarding federalism."[2]

Anticipating the creation of a national economy, the Constitution granted the federal government the power to regulate interstate and foreign commerce. Supplementing that grant, the Constitution forbade states without congressional consent to tax imports or exports or to impose tonnage duties on incoming ships.

To guarantee the stability of commercial transactions and to protect property against legislative encroachment, the Framers of the Constitution included in that document a prohibition on passage of state laws impairing the obligation of contracts. Further, they added language forbidding states to coin money, issue bills of credit, or make changes in the legal tender.

Each of these constitutional restrictions on state powers over commerce received its initial interpretation during the tenure of John Marshall as chief justice from 1801 to 1835. The net impact of these rulings, particularly those interpreting the commerce clause itself, was to establish the Court's power to limit state authority. As Frankfurter wrote: "Marshall's use of the commerce clause . . . gave momentum to the doctrine that state authority must be subject to such limitations as the Court finds it necessary to apply for the protection of the national community."[3]

New York saw its steamboat monopoly fall before the Court's broad interpretation of the federal power over commerce. Georgia became the first state to have a law declared unconstitutional, when its effort to repeal a corruptly obtained land grant collided with the contract clause. Maryland was rebuked by the Court for taxing vendors of foreign goods. And Missouri was told firmly that it could not issue state loan certificates without violating the Constitution's ban on state issuance of bills of credit.

Once these limits were well established, the Court seemed willing to acknowledge that, within the structure of federal supremacy, states retained certain basic powers with which to regulate commerce within their borders.

This broad reserved power, most often called the police power, received the stamp of judicial approval in the 1830s and serves to modern times as a firm basis for a wide variety of state actions to protect its citizens, its public health and morals, and its natural resources.

"Because the 'police power' is a response to the dynamic aspects of society," wrote Frankfurter, "it has eluded attempts at definition. But precisely because it is such a response, it is one of the most fertile doctrinal sources for striking an accommodation between local interests and the demands of the commerce clause."[4]

During the laissez-faire period of the late nineteenth and early twentieth centuries, the justices viewed many of the state laws enacted in exercise of this police power as too vigorous, particularly in their impact on the use of private property. In the due process clause of the Fourteenth Amendment, the conservative Court found a useful instrument to counter such laws, many of which fell before the Court's finding that they deprived businessmen of their property without due process of law.

The New Deal—and the economic depression that precipitated it—wrote a conclusion to that period in the Court's history. Since 1937 the Court has been more tolerant of state regulation of business even as it has upheld the extension of federal power into areas of the economy formerly left entirely to state control. As Powell wrote, the modern Court tends to sanction state actions when they interfere with the national economy only so far as is necessary to protect community interests.[5]

The Obligation of Contracts

From the nation's founding to the Civil War, the contract clause served as one of the most effective instruments for establishing federal control over state actions. One scholar wrote:

The cases of *Fletcher v. Peck* and *Dartmouth College v. Woodward* formed the beginning of an extensive series of restrictions upon state legislation, made possible through the fact that many laws may be attacked on the ground of infringement of property rights. . . . The [Court's early] decisions aligned on the side of nationalism the economic interests of corporate organizations.[6]

LAND GRANTS

In 1810 the Court for the first time struck down a state law as unconstitutional. In *Fletcher v. Peck* the Court ruled that grants made by a state legislature cannot be repealed without violating the constitutional prohibition on impairment of contract obligations.

In 1795 the Georgia legislature granted some 35 million acres of land along the Yazoo River to four land speculator companies. The price—for what is now most of the states of Alabama and Mississippi—was $500,000. And approval of the grant was facilitated by the promise of the speculators to many legislators that they would share in the land thus granted.

Chagrined by the obvious bribery, the new legislature elected after the grant revoked it in 1796 and declared all claims result-ing from it void. But the land companies already had resold much of the land to innocent purchasers, who now held ques-tionable titles.

A long debate began. Pointing to the corruption that attend-ed the 1795 land grant, Georgia argued that the titles held under it were worthless. The purchasers argued that the state legisla-ture did not have the power to nullify their rights.

Because many of the purchasers lived in New England, the case quickly became a federal problem. After several years of discussion in Congress, the matter moved into the federal courts. One of the attorneys arguing the case before the Supreme Court was Joseph Story, a thirty-year-old Massachu-setts attorney. Within two years he would sit on the Supreme Court bench, the youngest nominee in its history.

On March 16, 1810, the Court ruled. The original land grant was a valid contract; Georgia could not annul the titles granted under it—such an attempt ran headlong into the ban on state action impairing the obligation of contracts.

The Court would not inquire into the motives behind ap-proval of the 1795 land grant. Marshall wrote:

That corruption should find its way into the governments of our in-fant republics, and contaminate the very source of legislation, or that impure motives should contribute to the passage of law, or the forma-tion of a legislative contract, are circumstances most deeply to be de-plored.[7]

[But if] the title be plainly deduced from a legislative act, which the legislature might constitutionally pass, if the act be clothed with all the requisite forms of a law, a court . . . cannot sustain a suit . . . founded on the allegation that the act is a nullity, in consequence of the impure motives which influenced certain members of the legislature which passed the law.[8]

Marshall explored the implications of upholding Georgia's right to repeal the grant:

[S]uch powerful objections to a legislative grant . . . may not again ex-ist, yet the principle, on which alone this rescinding act is to be sup-ported, may be applied to every case in which it shall be the will of any legislature to apply it. The principle is this: that a legislature may, by its own act, devest [sic] the vested estate of any man whatever, for reasons which shall, by itself, be deemed sufficient."[9]

The Court rejected that principle. The Court agreed that one legislature could repeal any general legislation passed by a for-mer legislature. Yet the new legislature could not undo any ac-tion taken under the repealed law: "The past cannot be recalled by the most absolute power."[10]

"When, then, a law is in its nature a contract, when absolute rights have vested under that contract, a repeal of the law can-not devest those rights."[11]

TAX EXEMPTIONS

Two years later the Court extended its interpretation of the contract clause as a restraint on the tendency of state legislators to change their minds. In the case of *New Jersey v. Wilson* in 1812,

the Court refused to allow a state to modify or revoke a clear contractual grant of exemption from taxes.[12]

The colonial legislature of New Jersey had granted certain lands to the Delaware Indians. Included in the grant was an ex-emption from taxation for the lands held by the Indians. After the Indians sold this land to other owners, the state tried to tax it. The new owners challenged the tax as a violation of the con-tract in the original grant—and they won.

As the Supreme Court noted, the state could have limited the tax exemption to the period when the land belonged to the In-dians, but it had placed no such condition upon the exemption. Therefore, the exemption passed with title to the land, and efforts to repeal or ignore it impaired the original obligation.

Eighteen years later the Court made clear that no tax exemp-tion could ever be assumed to be a part of a contract, grant, or charter. In *Providence Bank v. Billings* the Court held that "[a]ny privileges which may exempt it [a corporation] from the bur-thens common to individuals do not flow necessarily from the charter, but must be expressed in it, or they do not exist."[13]

The power to tax could indeed be used as a means of de-stroying a business—and thereby impairing a contract, Chief Justice Marshall conceded, "but the Constitution of the United States was not intended to furnish the corrective for every abuse of power which may be committed by the State governments. The interest, wisdom and justice of the representative body, and its relations with its constituents, furnish the only security where there is no express contract against unjust and excessive taxation, as well as against unwise legislation generally   [A]n incorporated bank, unless its charter shall express the exemp-tion, is no more exempted from taxation than an unincorporat-ed company would be, carrying on the same business."[14]

In 1854 the state of Ohio brought this question back before the justices, leading to the first Supreme Court ruling finding a portion of a state's constitution unconstitutional. The state bank of Ohio was chartered under a law that provided that the bank would pay a certain percentage of its profits to the state in lieu of taxes. Subsequently, the state legislature passed a law pro-viding for a tax on banks and assessed one branch of the state bank $1,266.63 as its share of the new tax.

The bank refused to pay, arguing that the state's effort to im-pose this new tax on it impaired the contract of the original charter.[15]

The Court upheld the bank's exemption from taxes. Justice John McLean wrote the majority opinion. The charter was per-fectly clear, he wrote.

Nothing is left to inference. . . . The payment was to be in lieu of all taxes to which the Company or stockholders would otherwise be sub-ject. This is the full measure of taxation on the Bank. It is in the place of any other tax which, had it not been for this stipulation, might have been imposed on the Company or stockholders.[16]

Every valuable privilege given by the charter . . . is a contract which cannot be changed by the Legislature, where the power to do so is not reserved in the charter. . . . A municipal corporation . . . may be changed at the will of the Legislature. Such is a public corporation, used for public purposes. But a bank, where the stock is owned by individuals, is a private corporation.[17]

A state, in granting privileges to a bank . . . exercises its sovereignty, and for a public purpose, of which it is the exclusive judge. Under such circumstances, a contract made for a specific tax, as in the case before us, is binding. . . . Having the power to make the contract, and rights becoming vested under it, it can no more be disregarded nor set aside by a subsequent Legislature, than a grant for land.[18]

Still determined to tax the bank, Ohio amended its state constitution to provide for such a tax. Back came the issue to the Supreme Court. Once again, in 1856, the Court reiterated its holding that the effort to tax the bank impermissibly impaired the obligation of the original agreement with the bank. Justice James M. Wayne wrote for the Court:

A change of constitution cannot release a state from contracts made under a constitution which permits them to be made. . . . The moral obligations never die. If broken by states and nations, though the terms of reproach are not the same with which we are accustomed to designate the faithlessness of individuals, the violation of justice is not the less.[19]

PRIVATE CORPORATE CHARTERS

Fletcher v. Peck extended to agreements involving the state the protection of a clause many had thought protected only agreements between two private parties. Nine years later the Court further extended that protection to shield private corporate charters against alteration or repeal.

The extension came in the landmark *Dartmouth College v. Woodward,* decided in 1819. Dartmouth College in New Hampshire originally was set up by a royal charter. After the formation of the Union, the agreement with the king became an agreement with the state. In 1816 the state legislature passed several laws amending the college's charter to convert it into a university, to enlarge the number of its trustees, and otherwise to revise the means and purpose of its operations.

The trustees of the college resisted, charging that these amendments impaired the obligation of the contract implicit in the original charter. In 1818 the case came to the Supreme Court, with the famous advocate Daniel Webster arguing the college's case. The state defended the changes in the charter by contending that the school was a public corporation subject to such legislative action.

Webster was convincing. In 1819 the Court ruled for the college, finding the amendments an unconstitutional impairment of the contract obligation. Chief Justice Marshall wrote the Court's opinion.

Simply assuming a much-debated point, Marshall stated that the charter incorporating the private college was a contract within the protection of the Constitution:

It is a contract made on a valuable consideration. It is a contract for the security and disposition of property. It is a contract, on faith of which real and personal estate has been conveyed to the corporation. It is then a contract within the letter of the constitution, and within its spirit also.[20]

Dartmouth College's trustees, who had lost control of the renamed Dartmouth University, sued William H. Woodward, the college secretary, pictured here. The Supreme Court decided that the school's original charter was a contract that the Constitution forbade the state legislature to arbitrarily change.

Marshall conceded that this application of the contract clause probably never occurred to the men who wrote it into the Constitution: "It is more than possible that the preservation of rights of this description was not particularly in the view of the framers of the constitution when the clause under consideration was introduced into that instrument."[21]

But the chief justice found no good reason to except these contracts from constitutional protection.

It is probable that no man ever was, and that no man ever will be, the founder of a college, believing at the time that an act of incorporation constitutes no security for the institution; believing that it is immediately to be deemed a public institution, whose funds are to be governed and applied, not by the will of the donor, but by the will of the legislature. All such gifts are made in the . . . hope, that the charity will flow forever in the channel which the givers have marked out for it. If every man finds in his own bosom strong evidence of the universality of this sentiment, there can be but little reason to imagine that the framers of our constitution were strangers to it, and that, feeling the necessity and policy of giving permanence and security to contracts, of withdrawing them from the influence of legislative bodies, whose fluctuating policy, and repeated interferences, produced the most perplexing and injurious embarrassments, they still deemed it necessary to leave these contracts subject to those interferences.[22]

In his concurring opinion, Justice Joseph Story made clear the avenue by which states could retain the power to make modifications in such charters without violating the Constitution. "If the legislature mean to claim such an authority, it must be reserved in the grant," Story wrote.[23] And most charters granted by the states since that time have contained language reserving to the state the power to repeal or modify them.

For the half-century following the *Dartmouth College* decision, the contract clause produced more litigation than any other part of the Constitution. Charles Warren, historian of the Court during this period, wrote that this ruling came at a "peculiarly opportune" time:

[B]usiness corporations were for the first time becoming a factor in the commerce of the country, and railroad and insurance corporations were, within the next fifteen years, about to become a prominent field for capital. The assurance to investors that rights granted by state legislatures were henceforth to be secure against popular or partisan vacillation, and capricious, political or fraudulent change of legislative policy, greatly encouraged the development of corporate business.[24]

BANKRUPTCY LAWS

Using the contract clause to strike down state insolvency laws, the Supreme Court threw much of the nation into chaos during the 1820s. Two weeks after the *Dartmouth College* decision, the Court held New York's insolvency law invalid as impairing the obligation of contracts. The law freed debtors and discharged them from liability for all previous debts, once they surrendered their remaining property to the state.

Although it was unclear at the time and contributed to the misimpression that all state insolvency laws would be held unconstitutional, the decision of the Court was based on the fact that the New York law freed a debtor from liability for debts contracted *before* the law passed, and thus impaired the obligation of those existing "contracts."

In the opinion Chief Justice Marshall stated that the constitutional power of Congress to pass a uniform bankruptcy law did not, by its mere existence, deny states the power to pass such laws. Until Congress exercised that power, he wrote, states could pass bankruptcy and insolvency laws so long as they did not violate the contract clause.[25]

Eight years later, in 1827, the Court cleared up the confusion on this matter, ruling that state laws discharging debts contracted *after* the laws' passage did not violate the contract clause. Argued in 1824 and reargued in 1827, this case, entitled *Ogden v. Saunders,* divided the justices, 4–3, and for the only time in his long career as chief justice, John Marshall was on the losing side in a constitutional case.[26]

The Court upheld a new version of the New York insolvency law, with Justice Bushrod Washington setting out his often-quoted opinion on how the Supreme Court should approach cases challenging a state law:

It is but a decent respect due to the wisdom, the integrity, and the patriotism of the legislative body, by which any law is passed, to presume in favor of its validity, until its violation of the constitution is proved beyond all reasonable doubt.[27]

Marshall, joined in dissent by Justices Story and Gabriel Duvall, argued that the contract clause forbade any legislative impairment of future as well as existing contracts. The majority's view, Marshall warned, could be used to construe that clause "into an inanimate, inoperative, unmeaning" provision.[28]

With its rejection of this viewpoint, the Court for the first time placed a limit on the protection of the contract clause. This decision concluded the Court's expansion of the contract clause as a curb on the powers of the state legislatures.

During the same term the Court upheld the decision of the Rhode Island legislature to abolish imprisonment as a punishment for debtors. This modification of the remedy for defaulting on contracts did not impair the obligation imposed by the contract, held the Court, even though it applied to debtors already in default at the time of its passage.[29] In the first state bankruptcy case, Chief Justice Marshall had written that "without imparing [*sic*] the obligation of the contract, the remedy may certainly be modified. . . . Imprisonment is no part of the contract, and simply to release the prisoner does not impair its obligation."[30]

But the Court made clear that a state could go too far in modifying the remedy provided for enforcing debt obligations. In 1843 it held invalid—under the contract clause—an Illinois law that so altered the remedies for default on mortgages that it effectively impaired the obligation involved.[31]

THE PUBLIC INTEREST

Having made clear its insistence upon state respect of contract obligations, the Court in the 1830s began to open loopholes in the protection that the contract clause provided to property rights.

Certain state powers were inalienable, the Court held; they could not be simply contracted away, even if the state wished to do so. Primary among them were a state's power of eminent domain and its police power. The relationship of these powers to contract obligations was set out by the Court in three nineteenth century cases.

The Power of Eminent Domain

The case that began this narrowing of the contract clause protection was argued in Marshall's last years and then set for reargument. It was finally decided by the Court in 1837, during the first term of Chief Justice Roger B. Taney. For some, the decision in *Charles River Bridge v. Warren Bridge* marks the shift from the Marshall Court to the Taney Court.

In 1785 the Massachusetts legislature chartered a company to build a bridge across the Charles River to Boston, to operate it, and to collect tolls from passengers. The Charles River Bridge quickly became profitable; tolls were collected long after its costs were recovered.

Decades later, in 1828, the legislature chartered another company to build a second bridge across the Charles. Located near the first bridge, the Warren Bridge would be a toll way only until

The monopoly of this chartered toll bridge, built in the 1780s to link Boston with Cambridge, Massachusetts, was later challenged by builders of a rival bridge. The result was the landmark Supreme Court decision *Charles River Bridge v. Warren Bridge* (1837). The owners of the Charles River Bridge claimed that their state charter gave them exclusive right to traffic across the river, but the Court ruled that the state had the authority to approve construction of a second bridge because it was in the public interest.

its costs were paid—or for six years, whichever was shorter—and then it would be a free bridge.

Realizing that its business would disappear once it was in competition with a free bridge, the Charles River Bridge Company challenged the law authorizing the second bridge. This law, the company said, impaired the contract in its charter and destroyed the value of its franchise by preventing it from earning the tolls it was authorized to collect.

By the time the case was decided in 1837, the new Warren Bridge was not only built, but was paid for and operating on a toll-free basis. And the Charles River Bridge Company lost its case before the Court. The vote was 4–3.

"[I]n grants by the public nothing passes by implication," wrote Chief Justice Taney for the Court. Without an explicit grant of exclusive privilege in the original bridge company charter, none was assumed to exist to limit the state's power to authorize construction of another bridge.[32]

Taney said the same rule applied in this case that Marshall had applied in the 1830 decision in *Providence Bank v. Billings*: the Court would not read into a bank charter an implied grant of privilege against the state. *(See details of Providence Bank v. Billings, p. 323.)*

The state power in question in the bridge case was no less vital than the taxing power, wrote Taney. He elaborated:

The object and end of all government is to promote the happiness and prosperity of the community by which it is established, and it can never be assumed that the government intended to diminish its power of accomplishing the end for which it was created.

And in a country like ours, free, active and enterprising, continually advancing in numbers and wealth; new channels of communication are daily found necessary, both for travel and trade, and are essential to the comfort, convenience and prosperity of the people. A State ought never to be presumed to surrender this power, because, like the taxing power, the whole community have an interest in preserving it undiminished.

And when a corporation alleges that a State has surrendered for seventy years its power of improvement and public accommodation, in a great and important line of travel, along which a vast number of its citizens must daily pass; the community have a right to insist . . . "that its abandonment ought not to be presumed, in a case in which the deliberate purpose of the State to abandon it does not appear."

The continued existence of a government would be of no great value, if by implications and presumptions, it was disarmed of the powers necessary to accomplish the ends of its creation, and the functions it was designed to perform, transferred to the hands of privileged corporations. . . .

While the rights of private property are sacredly guarded, we must not forget that the community also have rights, and that the happiness and well being of every citizen depends on their faithful preservation. . . .

The whole community are interested in this inquiry, and they have a right to require that the power of promoting their comfort and convenience, and of advancing the public prosperity, by providing safe, convenient, and cheap ways for the transportation of produce, and the purposes of travel, shall not be construed to have been surrendered or diminished by the State, unless it shall appear by plain words that it was intended to be done.[33]

Considering the implications of the Charles River Bridge claim, Taney noted that turnpikes—like the toll bridge—had in many areas been rendered useless by the coming of the railroad. If the Court approved the Charles River Bridge claim, he warned:

[Y]ou will soon find the old turnpike corporations awakening from their sleep, and calling upon this court to put down the improvements which have taken their place. . . . We shall be thrown back to the improvements of the last century, and obliged to stand still until the claims of the old turnpike corporations shall be satisfied, and they shall consent to permit these States to avail themselves of the lights of modern science.[34]

The broad power of eminent domain gained further recognition a few years after the *Charles River Bridge* decision, as a result of the Court's resolution of a quarrel between the owners of a toll bridge and the town of Brattleboro, Vermont.

The owners of the toll bridge had been granted a century-long franchise to build and operate the bridge. But after the state authorized the building of highways, the town of Brattleboro ran a free highway right across the toll bridge, converting it into a free bridge. Although they were compensated by the state, the bridge owners protested that this impaired their charter and the contract obligation it contained.

In 1848 the Supreme Court rejected this claim, upholding a broad state power of eminent domain paramount to contract rights. Justice Peter V. Daniel wrote the Court's opinion:

[I]n every political sovereign community there inheres necessarily the right and the duty of guarding its own existence, and of protecting and promoting the interests and welfare of the community at large. . . . This power, denominated "eminent domain" of the State, is, as its name imports, paramount to all private rights vested under the government, and these last are, by necessary implication, held in subordination to this power, and must yield in every instance to its proper exercise.

The Constitution of the United States . . . can, by no rational interpretation, be brought to conflict with this attribute in the States; there is no express delegation of it by the Constitution; and it would imply an incredible fatuity in the States, to ascribe to them the intention to relinquish the power of self-government and self-preservation.[35]

The validity of this ruling was reemphasized eighty years later, when the Court ruled that a state retained the power of eminent domain even in the face of its express agreement to surrender it—and could thus exercise it properly in a way in which it had contracted to forego.[36]

The Police Power

In 1880, with the Court's decision in *Stone v. Mississippi*, the police power joined the power of eminent domain on the list of inalienable powers that a state could not surrender permanently.

The "carpetbagger" legislature of Mississippi had chartered a state lottery corporation, the Mississippi Agricultural, Educational and Manufacturing Aid Society. As soon as a new legislature was in power, Mississippi amended its constitution to ban lotteries from the state. The state then sued the society for existing in violation of this prohibition. The society responded with the argument that the state ban was invalid because it impaired the contract obligation of the society's charter.

The Court ruled against the lottery. In a brief but weighty opinion, Chief Justice Morrison R. Waite announced the decision of the unanimous Court:

All agree that the Legislature cannot bargain away the police power of a State. . . . Many attempts have been made in this court and elsewhere to define the police power, but never with entire success. . . . No one denies, however, that it extends to all matters affecting the public health or the public morals. . . . No Legislature can bargain away the public health or the public morals. . . . The supervision of both these subjects of governmental power is continuing in its nature, and they are to be dealt with as the special exigencies of the moment may require. Government is organized with a view to their preservation, and cannot divest [sic] itself of the power to provide for them. . . .

Anyone, therefore, who accepts a lottery charter, does so with the implied understanding that the People, in their sovereign capacity . . . may resume it at any time when the public good shall require.[37]

REMEDIES AND OBLIGATIONS

The climax in the use of the contract clause as a curb on state legislation came just after the Civil War. In the eight years from 1865 to 1873 there were twenty cases in which state laws or actions were held invalid as in conflict with the contract clause. After this point, the combined effect of the eminent domain and police power exceptions to the clause's protection for property began to reduce its restraining force.[38]

The due process clause, for a time, took the place of the contract clause as a shield for property rights. The Court linked the two with its statement—in the 1897 case of *Allgeyer v. Louisiana*—that the right to make contracts was an element of the liberty guarantee by the due process clause.[39] This "freedom of contract" would be used for several decades by the Court to curtail state efforts to regulate wages, hours, and working conditions. (*See "Wages and Hours," pp. 340–343.*)

The last major contract clause ruling came during the depression. Since that time, the contract clause has become no more than "a tail to the due process of law kite . . . a fifth wheel to the Constitutional law coach."[40]

In 1933 the Minnesota legislature responded to the plight of the many people unable to meet mortgage payments during the depression, and it passed a mortgage moratorium act. The law allowed postponement of foreclosure sales and extension of the period during which the property might be retained and redeemed by the defaulting mortgagor. The law was clearly temporary, set to expire May 1, 1935.

One mortgage holder, Home Building & Loan Association, challenged the law as impairing the obligation of contract contained in the mortgage.

By a vote of 5–4, the Supreme Court upheld the law, emphasizing the emergency conditions that justified its passage. Chief Justice Charles Evans Hughes wrote the opinion in *Home Building & Loan Association v. Blaisdell*:

Emergency does not create power. Emergency does not increase granted power or remove or diminish the restrictions imposed upon power. . . . But while emergency does not create power, emergency may furnish the occasion for the exercise of power.

The prohibition in the contract clause "is not an absolute one," Hughes continued, "and is not to be read with literal exactness like a mathematical formula."[41]

The majority, in Hughes's words, declared:

[T]he state . . . continues to possess authority to safeguard the vital interests of its people. It does not matter that legislation appropriate to that end "has the result of modifying or abrogating contracts already in effect." . . . Not only are existing laws read into contracts in order to fix obligations as between the parties, but the reservation of essential attributes of sovereign power is also read into contracts as a postulate of the legal order. The policy of protecting contracts against impairment presupposes the maintenance of a government by virtue of which contractual relations are worthwhile,—a government which retains adequate authority to secure the peace and good order of society. This principle of harmonizing the constitutional prohibition with the necessary residuum of state power has had progressive recognition in the decisions of this court.[42]

In light of the rulings in *Charles River Bridge v. Warren Bridge, West River Bridge v. Dix, Stone v. Mississippi* and their progeny, Hughes found it untenable to argue that the contract clause prevented "limited and temporary interpositions with respect to the enforcement of contracts if made necessary by a great public calamity such as fire, flood, or earthquake."

Hughes continued:

The reservation of state power appropriate to such extraordinary conditions may be deemed to be as much a part of all contracts as is the reservation of state power to protect the public interest in the other situations to which we have referred. And if state power exists to give temporary relief from the enforcement of contracts in the presence of disasters due to physical causes such as fire, flood, or earthquake, that power cannot be said to be nonexistent when the urgent public need demanding such relief is produced by other and economic causes. . . .

Where, in earlier days, it was thought that only the concerns of individuals . . . were involved, and that those of the state itself were touched only remotely, it has later been found that the fundamental interests of the state are directly affected; and that the question is no longer merely that of one party to a contract as against another, but of the use of reasonable means to safeguard the economic structure upon which the good of all depends.[43]

Making clear the significance of the emergency and temporary nature of the legislation upheld in *Blaisdell*, the Court struck down similar but more sweeping laws from other states.[44]

This seemed to end the long line of contract clause cases decided by the Court. Edward S. Corwin explains: "Until after the Civil War the 'obligation of contracts' clause was the principal source of cases challenging the validity of state legislation. Today the clause is much less important. But," he adds, "it would be premature to issue the clause's death certificate."[45]

Sounding a similar note, Justice Potter Stewart in 1978 wrote that "the Contract Clause remains part of the Constitution. It is not a dead letter." Stewart wrote the Court's opinion striking down part of a state pension law as it was applied to increase the liability and obligations of employers who had pension agreements with their employees in force when the law was passed.[46] The previous term the Court had applied the contract clause to hold that the legislatures of New Jersey and New York had acted unconstitutionally when they changed the terms under which bonds were issued by the Port Authority of New York and New Jersey.[47]

The Control of Commerce

"The spirit of enterprise, which characterizes the commercial part of America, has left no occasion of displaying itself unimproved," wrote Alexander Hamilton in *The Federalist Papers*. "It is not at all probable that this unbridled spirit would pay much respect to those regulations of trade by which particular states might endeavor to secure exclusive benefits to their own citizens. The infractions of these regulations on one side, the efforts to prevent and repeal them, on the other, would naturally lead to outrages, and these to reprisals and war."

Later Hamilton would carry his warning further, predicting that without a strong federal power to regulate interstate and foreign commerce, the United States might soon become like the German Empire "in continual trammels from the multiplicity of the duties which the several princes and states exact upon the merchandises passing through their territories."[48]

Hamilton would not have been surprised to hear Justice Felix Frankfurter say, some 175 years later, that "with us, the commerce clause is perhaps the most fruitful and important means for asserting authority against the particularism of State policy."[49]

Unlike the contract clause, which is clearly a restriction on state action, the commerce clause in Article I, Section 8, makes no mention of state powers. It simply gives Congress the power "to regulate commerce with foreign nations, and among the several states, and with the Indian tribes."

Even as the twentieth century was coming to a close, Congress's reliance on its commerce power for ever-deepening involvement in state affairs continued to be a source of controversy in the nation. The justices themselves were sharply divided. A five-justice majority warned in the 1995 case of *United States v. Lopez* that the dual system of government necessarily limits interstate commerce power lest that power be used to destroy the distinction between what is national and what is local.

THE STEAMBOAT MONOPOLY

From the states' perspective, the restrictive force of this clause was brought home with the Court's first ruling on this grant of power to Congress. The decision came in 1824 with *Gibbons v. Ogden*, the case of the New York steamboat monopoly.

Since 1798 Robert R. Livingston and Robert Fulton had held a grant from the New York legislature of the exclusive right to run steamboats in the state's waters. In 1811 Livingston and Fulton secured a similar monopoly for steamship transportation near New Orleans, the young nation's other great port besides New York.

The monopoly was a source of aggravation to other states, which passed laws excluding the Livingston-Fulton boats from their waters while granting a monopoly for their state to another company. Instead of unifying the states, steamboat transportation appeared to be dividing them further. Arguing this case before the Court, Attorney General William Wirt described the situation as one in which New York was almost at war with Ohio, Connecticut, and New Jersey.[50]

In 1807 genius inventor Robert Fulton put a steam engine in the *Clermont,* pictured here, and proved that boats could be powered by something other than wind and manpower. New York State granted Fulton and his partner Robert Livingston a monopoly to operate steamboats on the Hudson River. The monopoly was contested, and the resulting case, *Gibbons v. Ogden,* became an important test of Congress's right to regulate interstate commerce.

Aaron Ogden, former New Jersey governor, operated steamboats in New York under license from the monopoly. But Thomas Gibbons, his former partner, was competing with Ogden—and the monopoly—by running steamboats between New York and New Jersey. Although Gibbons was not licensed by the monopoly, his ships were licensed under the federal law governing the coasting trade.

Ogden obtained an order from the New York courts directing Gibbons to stop his competing business. Gibbons took the case to the Supreme Court.

For five days in February 1824 the case was argued before the justices. Daniel Webster argued along with Wirt for the antimonopoly side.

On March 2 the Court announced its decision. It struck down the monopoly because it was in conflict with the broad federal power to regulate interstate commerce. The Court rejected a narrow definition of commerce. Speaking for the Court, Chief Justice Marshall defined commerce as intercourse—not simply traffic, or buying and selling alone. And commerce included navigation, the particular subject at issue here. Marshall explained: "The power over commerce, including navigation, was one of the primary objects for which the people of America adopted their government, and must have been contemplated in forming it."[51]

And this federal power did not cease to exist at state borders, continued Marshall.

Commerce among the states cannot stop at the external boundary line of each state, but may be introduced into the interior. . . . The power of Congress, then, comprehends navigation within the limits of every state in the Union; so far as that navigation may be, in any manner, connected with "commerce with foreign nations, or among the several states, or with the Indian tribes."[52]

New York's effort to confine the use of its waters to the monopoly's ships and deny use to vessels such as Gibbons's, which were licensed under the federal coasting law, collided with federal regulation of commerce and so must fall. The Court held:

The nullity of any act, inconsistent with the constitution, is produced by the declaration that the constitution is the supreme law. The appropriate application of that part of the clause . . . is to such acts of the state legislature as do not transcend their powers, but though enacted in the execution of acknowledged state powers, interfere with, or are contrary to the laws of Congress, made in pursuance of the constitution. . . . In every such case, the act of Congress . . . is supreme; and the law of the state, though enacted in the exercise of powers not controverted, must yield to it.[53]

Much has been written about the significance of this decision. Felix Frankfurter, later to sit on the Supreme Court, wrote that the theme Marshall first sounded in *Gibbons v. Ogden* became the focal point of the constitutional system—"the doctrine that the commerce clause, by its own force, and without national legislation, puts it into the power of the Court to place limits upon state authority."

"Marshall's use of the commerce clause," he continued, "gave momentum to the doctrine that state authority must be subject to such limitations as the Court finds it necessary to apply for the protection of the national community."[54]

In addition to its impact on the nation's constitutional development, the ruling had considerable effect on the Union's economic development; as other observers have noted:

Steamboat navigation, freed from the restraint of state-created monopolies . . . increased at an astonishing rate. Within a few years steam railroads, encouraged by the freedom of interstate commerce from state restraints, were to begin a practical revolution of internal transportation. The importance of national control of commerce in the rapid economic development is almost incalculable. For many years after 1824 Congress enacted but few important regulatory measures, and commerce was thus free to develop without serious monopolistic or governmental restraint.[55]

Another scholar emphasized the latter point, noting:

Like most of the important cases decided by Chief Justice Marshall, [*Gibbons v. Ogden*] involved, not the assertion of the power of the federal government over interstate commerce, but acted rather as a prohibition against state activity. Apart from granting coasting licenses, the federal government was not interested in the commerce involved. The decision was an act in defense of laissez-faire, rather than of positive federal control.[56]

AN EXCLUSIVE POWER?

For thirty years after the *Gibbons* ruling, the nation would be preoccupied with the debate over whether the power of Congress to regulate commerce was exclusive—or whether the states retained some concurrent authority in that area.

Underlying this debate was the simmering issue of slavery. Charles Warren wrote:

[T]hroughout the long years when the question of the extent of the Federal power over commerce was being tested in numerous cases in the Court, that question was, in the minds of Southerners, simply coincident with the question of the extent of the Federal power over slavery. So the long-continued controversy as to whether Congress had exclusive or concurrent jurisdiction over commerce was not a conflict between theories of government, or between Nationalism and State-Rights, or between differing legal construction of the Constitution, but was simply the naked issue of State or Federal control of slavery. It was little wonder, therefore, that the Judges of the Court prior to the Civil War displayed great hesitation in deciding this momentous controversy.[57]

The particular question left hanging by *Gibbons* was whether the existence of federal power to regulate navigation left the states entirely powerless in that area. In the 1829 case of *Willson v. Blackbird Creek Marsh Co.*, the Court held that the states did retain some power over navigation within their borders—at least so long as Congress had not acted to regulate it.

As allowed under state law, the Blackbird Creek Marsh Company built a dam on the creek of that name in Delaware. The operators of a federally licensed sloop, irritated by the obstruction, rammed and broke the dam. The dam company won a damage judgment in state court against the ship owners, who then appealed to the Supreme Court, arguing that the dam and the authorizing state law were impermissible infringements upon the federal power over navigation.

The mere existence of federal power to regulate navigation on such creeks—if not exercised—did not foreclose state action to regulate such matters, held the Court, particularly if the objectives of state action were, as in this case, to preserve the value of property and to enhance the public health. "Measures calculated to produce these objects, provided they do not come into collision with the powers of the general government, are undoubtedly within those which are reserved to the States," wrote Chief Justice Marshall.[58]

The *Willson* decision paved the way for formulation of the concept of the state police power during the era of Chief Justice Taney. That concept served as a useful implement for carving out an area within which state regulation of commerce was permissible. (*See "The Police Power," pp. 336–343.*)

For two decades after *Willson*, however, neither the Court nor the country found it easy to ascertain the line between permissible and impermissible state regulation affecting commerce. The Court's decisions grew more and more unpredictable.

In *Mayor of New York v. Miln* (1837) the Court upheld a New York law that required reports to be filed on all passengers arriving on ships in the city's port. Although the law was challenged as an invasion of the federal power over foreign commerce, the Court found no such intrusion. Instead, the justices viewed the law, which intended to minimize the possibility of the immigrant passengers becoming public charges, as a proper exercise of the state police power not in conflict with federal authority.[59]

Four years later, when the question of a state's power to forbid the importation of slaves came to the Court, the justices sidestepped a decision on that issue. But all the justices expressed their personal opinions, revealing "almost complete chaos of interpretation."[60]

In 1847 the Court decided the *License Cases,* in which it upheld the right of states to require that all sales of alcohol within the state be licensed, even the sales of imported alcohol. Again the Court held such a requirement a valid exercise of the police power. But the six justices wrote nine opinions, none of which could be characterized as a majority's view. The decision provided little guidance for future state action.[61]

And two years later, with a similar multiplicity of opinions, the Court struck down New York and Massachusetts laws taxing all alien passengers arriving in their ports. The Court divided 5–4. Once again there was no opinion that could be identified as having the support of a majority of the justices.[62]

These *Passenger Cases* were argued three times before the Court finally decided them in 1849. When they were decided, each justice read his own opinion, a process consuming seven hours.[63]

The numerical majority, led by Justice John McLean, found the taxes a direct infringement of the exclusive federal power over interstate and foreign commerce. The dissenters, led by Chief Justice Taney, viewed the states as having a concurrent power with Congress and saw the tax laws as a proper use of state police power.

"YES, AND NO"

At last in 1852, almost three decades after *Gibbons v. Ogden,* the Court managed to formulate its divergent opinions into some sort of rule to determine whether states could exercise any regulatory authority over matters of interstate and foreign commerce. The case, *Cooley v. Board of Wardens of the Port of Philadelphia,* turned on the question of whether the state of Pennsylvania could require vessels entering the port of Philadelphia to take on a pilot to enter, or, if they refused, to pay a certain fee. Aaron B. Cooley had refused to take on a pilot or pay the fee, challenging the requirement as an infringement by the state on exclusive federal power over matters of commerce such as pilotage. But Congress in 1789 had enacted a law that said pilots should continue to be regulated by state law until such time as Congress acted to impose a uniform system of regulation on them.

The Court upheld Pennsylvania's pilot requirement. Writing the opinion was the most junior justice, Benjamin R. Curtis, a forty-one-year-old Boston attorney in his first term on the Court. Curtis explained that the Court found the state law permissible because Congress clearly had intended state regulation of this matter to continue, because Congress had not passed any superseding legislation concerning pilotage, and because the subject was in fact one better dealt with by local regulation.

In explaining this last point, Curtis set out what came to be known as the "Cooley rule," used to distinguish matters of exclusive federal control under the commerce power from those where a concurrent federal and state power existed.

The grant of commercial power to Congress does not contain any terms which expressly exclude the States from exercising an authority over its subject matter. If they are excluded, it must be because the nature of the power, thus granted to Congress, requires that a similar authority should not exist in the States. . . .

Now, the power to regulate commerce embraces a vast field, containing not only many, but exceedingly various subjects, quite unlike in their nature; some imperatively demanding a single uniform rule, operating equally on the commerce of the United States in every port; and some, like the subject now in question, as imperatively demanding that diversity, which alone can meet the local necessities of navigation.

Either absolutely to affirm, or deny, that the nature of this power requires exclusive legislation by Congress, is to lose sight of the nature of the subjects of this power, and to assert concerning all of them, what is really applicable but to a part. Whatever subjects of this power are in their nature national, or admit only of one uniform system, or plan of regulation, may justly be said to be of such a nature as to require exclusive legislation by Congress. That this cannot be affirmed of laws for the regulation of pilots and pilotage is plain. . . . [A]lthough Congress has legislated on this subject, its legislation manifests an intention . . . not to regulate this subject, but to leave its regulation to the several States.[64]

A century later one constitutional scholar would describe the *Cooley* decision this way:

To the question whether the power of Congress is exclusive, Mr. Justice Curtis took a great step forward by answering, "Yes, and no." This is the wisest initial answer to give to many questions that embrace such a variety and diversity of issues that no single answer can possibly be suitable for all.[65]

The line-drawing process that the *Cooley* rule demanded was a difficult one. During the same term when the rule was announced, the Court held that Virginia had impermissibly built a bridge across the Ohio River, and infringed on the federal power to regulate interstate commerce. The bridge was too low for some boats to pass under. Although the facts of the case seemed similar, except in scale, to those of the Blackbird Creek decision, the Court decided against the state.

By licensing ships under the coasting law to navigate the Ohio River, held the Court, Congress clearly had asserted its authority over traffic there. In the earlier case, it was doubtful whether federal power had been extended over small creeks. "No state law can hinder or obstruct the free use of a license granted under an Act of Congress," wrote Justice McLean for the Court.[66]

Congress overrode this decision. By passing a law authorizing the already-built bridge, it removed any objection to its existence as in conflict with congressional power. This was the first time that Congress directly blocked the effect of a Court decision. In 1856 the Court reviewed and upheld this act as within the power of Congress to regulate navigation.[67]

NATIONAL CONCERNS

Railroad rates and immigration were two subjects to which the Court applied the *Cooley* rule and found them to fall within the category of issues requiring exclusive federal regulation.

Immigration

Immigration had been an issue in the *Miln* case of 1837 and again in the *Passenger Cases* of 1849. In the former, the Court had upheld a state requirement of reports on all incoming alien passengers; in the latter, it had struck down state taxes on all incoming aliens.

By the 1870s immigration clearly had become a matter of national concern. In 1876 the Court voided New York, Louisiana, and California laws that attempted to regulate immigration—and reduce the burden it might place on state finances—by requiring the owners of every ship bringing immigrants into the state to give bond for each alien. In the New York case the bond was $300 a passenger; payment could be waived by payment of a $1.50-per-person tax within twenty-four hours of landing. The states defended these laws as "a suitable regulation" to protect their cities and towns "from the expense of supporting persons who are paupers or diseased, or helpless women and children, coming from foreign countries."

But the Supreme Court saw these laws as merely imposing a tax on the privilege of landing passengers in the state. That was impermissible interference with federal power over foreign commerce. Writing for the Court, Justice Samuel Miller explained that the transportation of persons from foreign lands to this country had become foreign commerce, the regulation of which was exclusively reserved to Congress. Over such a subject, the state could not exercise its police power:

[T]he matter of these statutes may be and ought to be the subject of a uniform system or plan. The laws which govern the right to land passengers in the United States from other countries ought to be the same in New York, Boston, New Orleans and San Francisco. . . . [T]his whole subject has been confided to Congress by the Constitution.[68]

Emphasizing this point again in the companion California case, Justice Miller wrote:

The passage of laws which concern the admission of citizens and subjects of foreign nations to our shore belongs to Congress, and not to the states. . . . If it be otherwise, a single state can, at her pleasure, embroil us in disastrous quarrels with other nations.[69]

One result of these decisions was the passage by Congress, in 1882, of the nation's first general law governing immigration.

Railroad Rates

By the Civil War, commerce was moving across country by rail as well as water. Reflecting this shift, many of the Court's postwar commerce clause rulings focused on the efforts of states to regulate the railroads.

For a time the Court flirted with state regulation of railroad rates. But as the rail networks expanded across the United States, it became clear that the intrastate operations of an interstate railroad was hardly the subject for local regulation. In 1886 the Court issued a decision to that effect, and the following year Congress created the Interstate Commerce Commission.

In many states it was pressure from farmers that resulted in the passage of state laws regulating railroad rates. A secret order called the National Grange won passage of a number of laws regulating how much railroads could charge farmers to carry their produce to market. In like fashion, some states passed laws to regulate rates that grain elevator companies could charge to store the farmers' grain.

In 1877 the Supreme Court appeared to sanction state regulation of these businesses with its decision in a set of cases involving both railroad and grain elevator rate regulation. These decisions are referred to as the *Granger Cases,* or by the title of the grain elevator case, *Munn v. Illinois.*[70]

Acknowledging that these matters fell within the purview of federal power, the Court nevertheless upheld the state laws. Writing in the Wisconsin railroad rate case, Chief Justice Morrison R. Waite stated:

Until Congress acts in reference to the relations of this Company to interstate commerce, it is certainly within the power of Wisconsin to regulate its fares, etc., so far as they are of domestic concern. With the people of Wisconsin, this Company has domestic relations. Incidentally, these may reach beyond the State. But certainly, until Congress undertakes to legislate for those who are without the State, Wisconsin

may provide for those within, even though it may indirectly affect those without.[71]

To limit the implications of the grant of this power to the states, the Court devised the criteria of "public interest" with which to distinguish those businesses that might be subject to state regulation from those that could not be. Chief Justice Waite outlined the rationale:

Property does become clothed with a public interest when used in a manner to make it of public consequence and affect the community at large. When, therefore, one devotes his property to a use in which the public has an interest, he, in effect, grants to the public an interest in that use, and must submit to be controlled by the public for the common good, to the extent of the interest he has thus created.[72]

State regulation of grain elevators survived for several decades, upheld by the Court again in 1892.[73]

But state power to regulate railroad rates was soon sharply curtailed. In 1886—less than a decade after the *Granger Cases*—the Supreme Court held that if a railroad was part of an interstate network, states could not regulate its rates, even for the intrastate portion of a trip.[74] Speaking for the Court, Justice Miller wrote:

It cannot be too strongly insisted upon, that the right of continuous transportation from one end of the country to the other is essential in modern times to that freedom of commerce from the restraints which the States might choose to impose upon it, that the commerce clause was intended to secure. This clause . . . was among the most important of the subjects which prompted the formation of the Constitution. . . .

SPEED LIMITS, MUD FLAPS, AND BRAKES

Although the Court removed the subject of railroad rates from state control before the end of the nineteenth century, it left the states some authority to regulate interstate traffic to protect the public safety. In a series of cases, the Court upheld as permissible such regulation so long as it does not unduly burden interstate commerce. Since World War II, however, the Court has been much less tolerant of such state regulation.

In judging the validity of these state laws, the Court usually weighs the benefits produced by the regulation against the burden it imposes on the regulated vehicles.

As early as 1910, the Court upheld Georgia's speed limit for interstate trains, but later it struck down Georgia's requirement that trains slow down at all grade crossings. The effect of the latter requirement was to double the travel time of some trains that passed one crossing per minute.[1]

In the Motor Carrier Act of 1935, Congress left to the state the regulation of the size and weight of interstate motor vehicles traveling through its territory. Subsequently, the Court upheld South Carolina's limits on the size of trucks and trailers, even though they were substantially stricter than those of adjoining states.[2]

In 1945 the Court struck down Arizona's law restricting the length of railroad trains operating within the state. Although Congress had not regulated that subject, the Court held that the limits

placed by the law were so in conflict with the railroad industry's usual train length that they burdened commerce and did not sufficiently benefit the public safety to be justified.[3]

In general, the Court has held that states have more control over the highways than over the railroads within their boundaries. In 1959 the Court said Illinois burdened commerce by requiring that trucks passing through the state have a certain kind of rear-fender mudguard different from the usual mudflap, which Illinois declared illegal.[4] And in 1978 the Court struck down Wisconsin's ban on double-trailer trucks. The Court held that the state did not provide any proof that the ban enhanced the safety of highway traffic, and so its law must fall as an undue burden on interstate commerce. Three years later the Court similarly struck down an Iowa statute that prohibited the use of certain large trucks.[5] In 1983 Congress passed legislation requiring states to allow twin-trailer trucks to use interstate highways. Congress in later legislation allowed exceptions if a state could justify them as required for safety.

1. *Southern Railway Co. v. King,* 217 U.S. 524 (1910); *Seaboard Air Line R. Co. v. Blackwell,* 244 U.S. 310 (1917).
2. *South Carolina Highway Department v. Barnwell Brothers,* 303 U.S. 177 (1938).
3. *Southern Pacific Co. v. Arizona,* 325 U.S. 761 (1945).
4. *Bibb v. Navajo Freight Lines,* 359 U.S. 520 (1959).
5. *Raymond Motor Transportation Inc. v. Rice,* 434 U.S. 429 (1978); *Kassel v. Consolidated Freightways Corp.,* 450 U.S. 662 (1981).

In the *Granger Cases* (1877) the Supreme Court endorsed state regulation of railroads. Less than a decade later, in 1886, the Court held that if a railroad was part of an inter-state network, states could not regulate its rates, even for the intrastate portion of a trip.

And it would be a very feeble and almost useless provision, but poorly adapted to secure the entire freedom of commerce among the States which was deemed essential to a more perfect union by the framers . . . if, at every stage of the transportation of goods and chattels through the country, the State within whose limits a part of this transportation must be done could impose regulations concerning the price, compensation, or taxation, or any other restrictive regulation interfering with and seriously embarrassing this commerce. . . .[75]

[I]t is not, and never has been, the deliberate opinion of a majority of this Court that a statute of a State which attempts to regulate the fares and charges by railroad companies within its limits, for a transportation which constitutes a part of commerce among the States, is a valid law. . . .[76]

As restricted to a transportation which begins and ends within the limits of the State, it may be very just and equitable, and it certainly is the province of the State Legislature to determine that question. But when it is attempted to apply to transportation through an entire series of States a principle of this kind, and each one . . . shall attempt to establish its own rates of transportation . . . the deleterious influence upon the freedom of commerce among the States and upon the transit of goods through those States cannot be overestimated. That this species of regulation is one which must be, if established at all, of a general and national character, and cannot be safely and wisely remitted to local rules and local regulations, we think it is clear.[77]

The next year Congress enacted the long-pending legislation to create the Interstate Commerce Commission, the primary mission of which was the regulation of interstate railroad systems. States were still able to regulate purely intrastate railroad rates and to exercise their police power to regulate other aspects of railroad operations, under judicial supervision to ensure that the states did not burden interstate commerce or deny the railroad due process of law.

With passage of the Interstate Commerce Act, Congress began to extend affirmative federal control over commerce. The period in which most of the Supreme Court's commerce clause

rulings viewed the clause chiefly as a limit on state power came to an end. The exercise of federal power in this area brought a whole new set of commerce clause issues to the Court, phrased in terms of national, not state, authority. *(See "Congress, Commerce, and the Railroads," pp. 94–98, in Chapter 4.)*

LOCAL CONCERNS

But if the Court saw it necessary to remove the issues of immigration and railroad regulation from state control, it by no means left the states bereft of power over economic matters. Between the Civil War and the New Deal, the Court held that insurance, liquor, manufacturing, segregation, agriculture, and child labor were all matters of strictly local concern. After the first years of the New Deal, the line between local and national matters—preserved chiefly through the doctrine of dual federalism—became indistinct and of relatively little importance. *(See "The State as Sovereign," pp. 366–380.)*

Insurance

In 1869 the Court held that the business of insurance regulation should be left to the states. The justices upheld a Virginia law requiring out-of-state insurance companies to obtain a state license and post bond with the state before doing business there. This was a proper local law governing local transactions, held the Court in the case of *Paul v. Virginia.*[78]

And this decision remained the law for seventy-five years. During World War II, several fire insurance companies were indicted under federal antitrust law. Insurance, they argued in their defense, was outside the category of "commerce," the subject of the Sherman Antitrust Act under which the charges were brought. The government contested this claim, and the Supreme Court rejected the insurers' argument.

The Court upheld the indictment in 1944 and in so doing brought insurance within the definition of commerce subject to federal regulation. Writing for the Court, Justice Hugo L. Black said:

No commercial enterprise of any kind which conducts its activities across state lines has been held to be wholly beyond the regulatory power of Congress under the Commerce Clause. We cannot make an exception of the business of insurance.[79]

In all cases in which the Court has relied upon the proposition that "the business of insurance is not commerce," its attention was focused on the validity of state statutes—the extent to which the Commerce Clause automatically deprived states of the power to regulate the insurance business. Since Congress had at no time attempted to control the insurance business, invalidation of the state statutes would practically have been equivalent to granting insurance companies engaged in interstate activities a blanket license to operate without legal restraint.[80]

Congress, however, quickly handed this subject back to the state legislatures. In 1945 it passed the McCarran-Ferguson Act exempting the insurance business from the reach of all but a few major federal antitrust and labor laws. In 1946 the Supreme Court upheld this action.[81] The 1945 law would remain controversial for the next fifty years. Although proposals continually were introduced in Congress for the statute's repeal, none succeeded.

Manufacturing

By defining commerce to exclude manufacturing or production, the Supreme Court effectively placed a number of issues beyond federal reach and within state control.

In 1888 the Court upheld an Iowa law that forbade the manufacture of liquor in Iowa for sale outside the state as well as in the state. Writing for the Court, Justice Lucius Quintus Cincinnatus Lamar proclaimed this distinction between production and commerce:

No distinction is more popular to the common mind, or more clearly expressed in economic and political literature, than that between manufactures and commerce. Manufacture is transformation—the fashioning of raw materials into a change of form for use. The functions of commerce are different. The buying and selling and the transportation incidental thereto constitute commerce; and the regulation of commerce in the constitutional sense embraces the regulation at least of such transportation. . . .

If it be held that the term includes the regulation of all such manufactures as are intended to be the subject of commercial transactions in the future, it is impossible to deny that it would also include all productive industries that contemplate the same thing. The result would be that Congress would be invested, to the exclusion of the States, with the power to regulate, not only manufacture, but also agriculture, horticulture, stock raising, domestic fisheries, mining—in short, every branch of human industry. . . .

The power being vested in Congress and denied to the States, it would follow as an inevitable result that the duty would devolve on Congress to regulate all of these delicate, multiform, and vital interests—interests which in their nature are, and must be, local in all the details of their successful management.[82]

It does not follow that, because the products of a domestic manufacture may ultimately become the subjects of interstate commerce, . . . the legislation of the State respecting such manufacture is an attempt-

---

GARBAGE AND COMMERCE

"All objects of interstate trade merit Commerce Clause protection; none is excluded by definition at the outset," stated the Supreme Court in 1978, including garbage within that constitutional protection.[1]

By a 7–2 vote the Court struck down—as an infringement of federal power to regulate commerce—a New Jersey law forbidding the importation of solid or liquid waste originated or collected out of state. Justice Potter Stewart wrote the Court's opinion; Justice William H. Rehnquist and Chief Justice Warren E. Burger dissented.

New Jersey, whose landfills had for years been used by the cities of Philadelphia and New York as depositories for their garbage, sought to preserve the remaining landfill space within its boundaries for dumping its own garbage. But the Court found that the state had chosen a constitutionally impermissible means of achieving that end. Stewart wrote:

[W]hatever New Jersey's ultimate purpose, it may not be accomplished by discriminating against articles of commerce coming from outside the State unless there is some reason, apart from their origin, to treat them differently.[2]

[This law] falls squarely within the area that the Commerce Clause puts off-limits to state regulation. On its face, it imposes on out-of-state commercial interests the full burden of conserving the State's remaining landfill space. . . . What is crucial is the attempt by one State to isolate itself from a problem common to many by erecting a barrier against the movement of interstate trade.[3]

The Court has continued to value garbage as part of commerce. In 1992 it struck down a Michigan law that allowed county officials to stop private landfill operators from accepting solid waste from outside the county.[4] The Court also rejected surcharges imposed by some states on out-of-state waste.[5] Then in 1994 it denied local governments the power to require that all trash generated within their borders be processed locally.[6]

1. *Philadelphia v. New Jersey,* 437 U.S. 617 (1978).
2. Id. at 626–627.
3. Id. at 628.
4. *Fort Gratiot Landfill Inc. v. Michigan Department of Natural Resources,* 112 S. Ct. 2019 (1992).
5. *Chemical Waste Management Inc. V. Hunt,* 112 S. Ct. 2009 (1992), *Oregon Waste Systems Inc. v. Department of Environmental Quality,* ____ U.S. ____ (1994).
6. *C&A Carbone Inc. v. Town of Clarkstown,* 114 S. Ct. 1677 (1994).

---

ed exercise of the power of commerce exclusively conferred upon Congress.[83]

Seven years later the distinction used in the liquor case to uphold state regulation was exercised again—this time to preclude federal regulation. In the *Sugar Trust* case of 1895, the Court held that the Sherman Antitrust Act, enacted under the federal commerce power, could not be used as a basis for prosecuting sugar manufacturers.

Wrote Chief Justice Melville W. Fuller:

Commerce succeeds to manufacture, and is not a part of it. The power to regulate commerce is the power to prescribe the rule by which commerce shall be governed, and is a power independent of the power to suppress monopoly.[84]

The relief of the citizens of each state from the burden of monopoly was left with the states to deal with, and this court has recognized their possession of that power even to the extent of holding that an employment or business carried on by private individuals, when it becomes a matter of such public interest and importance as to create a common charge or burden upon the citizen; in other words, when it becomes a practical monopoly, to which the citizen is compelled to resort . . . is subject to regulation by state legislative power. . . .

It is vital that the independence of the commercial power and of the police power, and the delimitation between them, however sometimes perplexing, should always be recognized and observed, for while the one furnishes the strongest bond of union, the other is essential to the preservation of the autonomy of the states as required by our dual form of government.[85]

In subsequent similar decisions, the Court held mining, lumbering, fishing, farming, the production of oil, and the generation of electric power to be outside the scope of the federal commerce power and hence within the scope of state regulation.[86]

Although the Court did not directly overrule these particular decisions separating manufacture and commerce, in the late 1930s it simply abandoned the distinction, upholding federal laws that regulated manufacturing, such as the National Labor Relations Act.[87] Similarly, it upheld the Agricultural Adjustment Act of 1938, setting marketing quotas for farm products. This, the Court reasoned, regulated farm production at the point where it entered interstate commerce, the marketing warehouse. The justices dismissed the argument that not all products regulated were sold in interstate commerce.[88]

And three years later the Court upheld the application of these quotas to a farmer who grew wheat, in excess of his quota, but only for use on his own farm. Despite the lack of any clear connection between the excess wheat on this farm and interstate commerce, the Court sustained the reach of federal power. Justice Robert H. Jackson explained the Court's rationale: if the price of wheat rose high enough, the farmer would be induced to put his wheat into interstate commerce—and if he did not, he would use it for his own purposes and therefore not buy wheat in interstate commerce that he otherwise would need to buy. "Home-grown wheat in this sense competes with wheat in commerce," Jackson said.[89]

At the same time, the Court continued to sanction state regulation of production. A few months after the farmer's wheat decision, the Court upheld California's detailed system for regulating raisin production and marketing, even to the point of controlling the flow of raisins into interstate commerce to maintain a certain price level.[90]

Segregation

Late in the nineteenth century, the Court used the *Cooley* rule to deny Louisiana the power to prohibit racial discrimination while granting Mississippi the authority to enforce it.

When Josephine DeCuir, "a person of color," boarded *The Governor Allen,* a Mississippi River steamboat, to travel from New Orleans to another point in Louisiana, she sought a seat in the cabin set aside for white persons. Denied entrance, she subsequently sued the steamboat owners for violating an 1869 state law forbidding racial discrimination on common carriers.

The state courts found that this law affected interstate commerce and thus was invalid. On appeal, the Supreme Court in 1878 declared itself bound by this finding of the state courts and ruled against DeCuir and against the law. Under the *Cooley* rule the justices held that equal access to steamboat accommodations was a matter for national regulation. State regulation of such matters, if it affected interstate commerce, burdened interstate commerce.

Chief Justice Waite explained:

If each State was at liberty to regulate the conduct of carriers while within its jurisdiction, the confusion likely to follow could not but be productive of great inconvenience and unnecessary hardship. Each State could provide for its own passengers and regulate the transportation of its own freight, regardless of the interests of others. Nay more, it could prescribe the rules by which the carrier must be governed within the State in respect to passengers and property brought from without. On one side of the river . . . he might be required to observe one set of rules, and on the other another. Commerce cannot flourish in the midst of such embarrassments.[91]

If the public good requires such legislation [decreeing equal access], it must come from Congress and not from the States.[92]

Just twelve years later, however, the Court upheld a Mississippi law requiring railroads doing business in the state to provide separate accommodations for black and white passengers. In this case, unlike the *DeCuir* case, the state court held that this law applied solely to intrastate railroad operations, and in accord with that finding the Supreme Court in 1890 held it no burden on interstate commerce.[93]

In dissent, Justice John Marshall Harlan found Chief Justice Waite's comments in the earlier case "entirely pertinent to the case before us. . . . It is difficult to understand how a state enactment, requiring the separation of the white and black races on interstate carriers of passengers, is a regulation of commerce among the States, while a similar enactment forbidding such separation is not."[94]

In 1896, in the famous *Plessy v. Ferguson* decision, the Court upheld "separate but equal" accommodations on common carriers again—this time against challenge as a violation of the Fourteenth Amendment. Harlan dissented.[95]

It was fifty-six years before the Court reversed its 1890 ruling allowing Mississippi to require railroads to segregate passengers. In 1946 the Court declared that "seating arrangements for the different races in interstate motor travel require a single uniform rule to promote and protect national travel." Hence the justices struck down a Virginia law requiring black passengers to ride in the rear of interstate buses, and it reversed the conviction of Irene Morgan who had refused to move to comply with the law.[96]

The end to tolerance of local segregation of any segment of interstate transportation came in the mid-1950s with an Interstate Commerce Commission rule terminating racial segregation on all interstate trains and buses and in all public waiting rooms in railway and bus stations. In 1956 the Supreme Court affirmed a lower court's ruling striking down such segregation in intrastate transportation as a violation of the Fourteenth Amendment.[97]

Child Labor

Perhaps the most extreme of the Court's cases reserving areas of the economy for strictly state or local supervision were its child labor rulings of 1918 and 1922. The Court overturned the efforts of Congress to prohibit child labor.

These rulings depended upon the dichotomy between manufacturing and commerce—and upon the Tenth Amendment reservation of powers to the states and the accompanying doctrine of dual federalism, the idea that the state governments and the national government operated within neatly defined and separated domains, within which each was supreme.

The first child labor case was that of *Hammer v. Dagenhart.* Congress had attempted to forbid factories, quarries, or mines employing children under fourteen years of age from using the channels of interstate commerce for their products. The act, held the Court, intruded too far upon state concerns. Justice William R. Day wrote for the majority:

Over interstate transportation . . . the regulatory power of Congress is ample, but the production of articles, intended for interstate commerce, is a matter of local regulation. . . .

There is no power vested in Congress to require the states to exercise their police power to prevent possible unfair competition. . . .

The grant of power to Congress . . . was to enable it to regulate such commerce, and not to give it authority to control the states in their exercise of the police power over local trade and manufacture.

The grant of authority over a purely federal matter was not intended to destroy the local power always existing and carefully reserved to the states in the Tenth Amendment to the Constitution.[98]

. . . [I]f Congress can thus regulate matters entrusted to local authority by prohibition of the movement of commodities in interstate commerce, all freedom of commerce will be at an end, and the power of the states over local matters may be eliminated, and thus our system of government practically destroyed.[99]

In candid dissent, Justice Oliver Wendell Holmes Jr. declared:

The Act does not meddle with anything belonging to the states. They may regulate their internal affairs and their domestic commerce as they like. But when they seek to send their products across the State line they are no longer within their rights. If there were no Constitution and no Congress their power to cross the line would depend upon their neighbors. Under the Constitution such commerce belongs not to the States but to Congress to regulate. It may carry out its views of public policy whatever indirect effect they may have on the activities of the States.[100]

Four years later the Court struck down a second congressional effort to discourage child labor—this time through the use of the taxing power. Chief Justice William Howard Taft, speaking for the majority in *Bailey v. Drexel Furniture Co.,* set out the same objections that Day had voiced:

Grant the validity of this law, and all that Congress would need to do hereafter, in seeking to take over to its control any one of the great number of subjects of public interest, jurisdiction of which the states

have never parted with, and which are reserved to them by the 10th Amendment, would be to enact a detailed measure of complete regulation of the subject and enforce it by a so-called tax. . . . To give such magic to the word "tax" would be to break down all constitutional limitation of Congress and completely wipe out the sovereignty of the states.[101]

These two rulings stood until 1941, when the Court overruled *Hammer v. Dagenhart* and discarded the doctrine of dual federalism; the Court upheld the Fair Labor Standards Act, which, among other provisions, prohibited child labor. The case bringing this landmark opinion was *United States v. Darby.*

Writing for the Court, Justice Harlan Fiske Stone declared that

[s]uch regulation is not a forbidden invasion of state power merely because either its motive or its consequence is to restrict the use of articles of commerce within the states of destination. . . . Whatever their motive and purpose, regulations of commerce which do not infringe some institutional prohibition are within the plenary power conferred on Congress by the Commerce Clause. . . .

The power of Congress over interstate commerce . . . extends to the activities intrastate which so affect interstate commerce or the exercise of the power of Congress over it as to make regulation of them appropriate means to the attainment of a legitimate end, the exercise of the granted power of Congress to regulate interstate commerce.[102]

A Changing Answer

A century after Justice Curtis formulated the *Cooley* rule to bring some clarity into the confusion of the exclusive and concurrent commerce power debate, the answer to the questions that debate posed still seemed to be "Yes, and No." As Thomas Reed Powell wrote in the mid-1950s:

Once it was thought that the test of what states may do is what the nation may not do, or that the test of what the states may not do is what the nation may do, but the criteria are no longer so clear cut as that. The involutions of state power must be considered with a greater particularity than can be compressed into a formula.[103]

The Police Power

Early in the nation's history, the Court began to recognize a state police power, which is the power to govern its people and to regulate the use of its land to ensure the public welfare.

The police power, in effect, grants the states some power to affect interstate commerce. Legal scholar Thomas Reed Powell wrote:

By this judicial invention there is no constitutional division between concurrent and exclusive power over commerce. The power of Congress is concurrent with that of the states; the power of the states is concurrent with that of Congress. The exercise of state power, however, is subject to several restrictions. It must not impose regulation in conflict with regulations of Congress. It must not, even in the absence of conflict, impose regulations if Congress, by what it has done, is deemed to have "occupied the entire field."[104]

Oddly enough, the first recognition by the Court of this power came even as Chief Justice Marshall was asserting the sweeping federal power over commerce. In the opinion resolving the case of *Gibbons v. Ogden,* Marshall acknowledged the power of a state "to regulate its police, its domestic trade, and to govern its own citizens." This power, he continued, might even enable the state to legislate—concurrently with Congress—on the subject of navigation.

And earlier in the opinion, he had mentioned the state's power to require inspection of items departing the state before they entered into the stream of interstate or foreign commerce. Inspection laws, Marshall wrote, "form a portion of that immense mass of legislation which embraces everything within the territory of a state not surrendered to the general government. . . . Inspection laws, quarantine laws, health laws of every description, as well as laws for regulating the internal commerce of a state, and those which respect turnpike-roads, ferries, etc. are component parts of this mass."[105]

Five years later in *Willson v. Blackbird Creek Marsh Co.,* Marshall appeared to base the Court's approval of a state-built dam across a small creek upon the power of the state to act to preserve property values and enhance the public health.[106]

But it was during the tenure of Chief Justice Roger B. Taney that the Court first fully enunciated the concept of police power. In the opinion of the Court in the case of *Charles River Bridge v. Warren Bridge,* Taney spoke of the importance of protecting the states' "power over their own internal police and improvement, which is so necessary to their well being and prosperity."[107]

Within the same month in 1837 as the *Charles River Bridge* decision, the Court ruled in *The Mayor of New York v. Miln,* giving its first extended exposition of the police power.

In an effort to lighten the burden immigration placed upon its port city, New York law required the master of any ship arriving in New York Harbor from outside the state to report to the mayor the birthplace, previous residence, age, and occupation of every passenger. George Miln, owner of the ship *Emily,* did not comply and was sued by the state for the penalties he incurred. In his defense, Miln argued that the state law was invalid, that it regulated foreign commerce and navigation in conflict with federal power over those areas.

The Supreme Court rejected that defense. Writing for the majority, Justice Philip Barbour stated that

the [challenged] act is not a regulation of commerce, but of police, and . . . being thus considered, it was passed in the exercise of a power which rightfully belonged to the States. . . . It is apparent . . . that the object of the Legislature was to prevent New York from being burdened by an influx of persons brought thither in ships . . . and for that purpose a report was required . . . that the necessary steps might be taken by the city authorities to prevent them from becoming chargeable as paupers.[108]

Gibbons v. Ogden did not control the decision because this case concerned regulation of state territory, not of navigation, wrote Justice Barbour. And here there was no colliding federal law, he continued; so even under the reasoning of *Gibbons v. Ogden* the New York law could stand. Barbour wrote for the majority:

But we do not place our opinion on this ground. We choose rather to

---

THE "PERILS" OF COLORED OLEO

To the modern view, one of the oddest sets of police power laws and accompanying Supreme Court decisions involved the efforts of states to protect their citizens from the "perils" of colored oleo.

Ostensibly to protect the public health and to prevent fraud (the selling of oleo as butter), Pennsylvania banned the sale of colored oleomargarine within the state. In 1888 the Supreme Court held the ban a reasonable exercise of the state police power.[1]

Six years later, the original package doctrine notwithstanding, the Court upheld a Massachusetts law that forbade the sale of imported margarine in the original package, if the margarine was colored to resemble butter. Due to the risk of fraud, the Court found this a different question from that resolved in *Leisy v. Hardin.* In that decision the Court ruled against a state ban on the sale of imported liquor in the original package.[2] *(See details of Leisy v. Hardin, p. 339.)*

Subsequent rulings modified the scope of state power over colored margarine, but in 1902 Congress passed a law providing that oleomargarine was subject to state regulation upon arrival within the limits of the state.

1. *Powell v. Pennsylvania,* 127 U.S. 678 (1888).
2. *Plumley v. Massachusetts,* 155 U.S. 461 (1894).

---

plant ourselves on what we consider impregnable positions. They are these: That a State has the same undeniable and unlimited jurisdiction over all persons and things within its territorial limits, as any foreign nation, where that jurisdiction is not surrendered or restrained by the Constitution of the United States. That, by virtue of this, it is not only the right, but the bounden and solemn duty of a State, to advance the safety, happiness and prosperity of its people, and to provide for its general welfare, by any and every act of legislation which it may deem to be conducive to these ends; where the power over the particular subject, or the manner of its exercise is not surrendered or restrained, in the manner just stated. That all those powers which relate to merely municipal legislation, or what may, perhaps, more properly be called internal police, are not thus surrendered or restrained; and that, consequently, in relation to these, the authority of a State is complete, unqualified and exclusive.

In regard to the particular subject of this case, the Court held that the power exercised was encompassed in the recognized power of a state to pass and enforce inspection and quarantine laws, which operated directly upon items in interstate and foreign commerce, delaying and sometimes even destroying them.

We think it as competent and as necessary for a State to provide precautionary measures against the moral pestilence of paupers, vagabonds, and possibly convicts, as it is to guard against the physical pestilence which may arise from unsound and infectious articles imported, or from a ship, the crew of which may be laboring under an infectious disease.[109]

The significance of the development of this concept by the Supreme Court under Chief Justice Taney—and of the underlying doctrine of dual federalism as a limit on federal power—has been described by Alpheus T. Mason and William M. Beaney:

[I]n the context of his times, state police power was the only available weapon with which government could face the pressing problems of the day. In a period in which the national government was not yet prepared to deal realistically with economic and social problems, national supremacy had the effect of posing the unexercised commerce power of Congress, or the contract clause, as barriers to any governmental action. Taney's dual federalism . . . enabled the state to deal experimentally with problems that the national government would not face until another half-century had elapsed. Thus Marshall and Taney left as legacies two official conceptions of federalism [national supremacy and duel federalism] that succeeding justices were free to apply as their inclinations or the needs of the time dictated.[110]

The police power has been employed for a variety of ends: to control entry to the state, to protect the public health and public morals, to ensure public safety, to regulate business, and to regulate working conditions. The Court has by no means approved all of the uses to which the states have put the police power. A number fell as interfering with the federal power to regulate commerce; others fell as interfering with the freedom of contract or the liberty of property. But the police power has served as a broad basis for state efforts to control economic and business matters for the public good.

CONTROL OF ENTRY

After *Miln* recognized some state power to control the entry of individuals, the Court in 1839 indicated that states possessed a correlative power to exclude out-of-state corporations from doing business within their boundaries. In that ruling, however, in *Bank of Augusta v. Earle,* the Court held that it would be assumed—absent clear evidence to the contrary—that a state gave its consent to the conduct of business by an out-of-state corporation.[111]

Although the right to exclude a foreign corporation obviously included the right to place conditions on such an entity's conduct of business within the state, the Court some four decades later made clear that a state could not exercise this power to place an undue burden on an out-of-state corporation wishing to engage in interstate commerce within the state. The decision in *Pensacola Telegraph Co. v. Western Union* (1877) made clear, notes one commentator, that the state's power to exclude foreign corporations was subject to "the overriding force of a congressional license to carry on interstate commerce," in this case, communication by telegraphic messages.[112]

In the 1841 case of *Groves v. Slaughter* the Court managed to sidestep a decision on the question of the state's power to ban the entry of out-of-state slaves—although the justices took the opportunity to air quite diverse personal views on the matter.[113]

And in the *Passenger Cases* of 1849 the Court held, by a narrow margin, that the federal commerce power clearly limited the state's power to control the entry of people. Striking down state laws taxing entering aliens, the Court, in the words of Justice John McLean, held that

the police power of the State cannot draw within its jurisdiction objects which lie beyond it. It meets the commercial power of the Union in dealing with subjects under the protection of that power, yet it can only be exercised under peculiar emergencies and to a limited extent. In guarding the safety, the health, and morals of its citizens, a State is restricted to appropriate and constitutional means.

In dissent, Chief Justice Taney and his colleagues argued that "the several States have a right to remove from among their people, and to prevent from entering the State, any person, or class or description of persons, whom it may deem dangerous or injurious to the interests and welfare of its citizens.[114]

But the majority's view in the *Passenger Cases* has prevailed to modern times. In 1876 the Court held that control of immigration from abroad was a matter exempt from state regulation and entrusted exclusively to Congress. And in 1941 it struck down—as an obstruction of interstate commerce—a California law that penalized persons bringing poor people into the state to live.[115]

PUBLIC HEALTH AND MORALS

Perhaps the acknowledged objective of the police power is the protection of the public health, the focus of the quarantine and inspection laws about which Chief Justice Marshall commented in *Gibbons v. Ogden* (1824).

When the Court in 1847 upheld state laws licensing the sale of alcohol, one of the few points upon which the justices could agree was the paramount responsibility of the state to use the police power to protect its public health and to preserve public morals. Justice McLean set forth his views:

The acknowledged police power of a State extends often to the destruction of property. A nuisance may be abated. . . . Merchandise from a port where a contagious disease prevails, being liable to communicate the disease, may be excluded; and in extreme cases, it may be thrown into the sea. This comes in direct conflict with the regulation of commerce; and yet no one doubts the local power. It is a power essential to self-preservation. . . . It is, indeed, the law of nature, and is possessed by man in his individual capacity. He may resist that which does him harm, whether he be assailed by an assassin, or approached by poison. And it is the settled construction of every regulation of commerce, that, under the sanction of its general laws, no person can introduce into a community malignant diseases, or anything which contaminates its morals, or endangers its safety. . . . From the explosive nature of gunpowder, a city may exclude it. Now this is an article of commerce, and is not known to carry infectious disease; yet to guard against a contingent injury, a city may prohibit its introduction.

When in the appropriate exercise of these federal and State powers, contingently and incidentally the lines of action run into each other; if the State power be necessary to the preservation of the morals, the health, or safety of the community, it must be maintained.[116]

No better illustration of the complexities of applying the police power for the purpose of safeguarding public health and morals can be provided than the *License Cases.* Begun in 1847 and extending well into the twentieth century, these rulings concerned state power to regulate all aspects of intoxicating liquors. In 1874 the Court upheld Iowa's prohibition of the sale of liquor, even that owned at the time of the law's passage.[117] In

With the enactment of the Twenty-first Amendment repealing Prohibition, the states were granted power to regulate all aspects of alcohol control. The Supreme Court has construed the power granted by the amendment broadly.

1887 the Court upheld a Kansas law that forbade both the manufacture and sale of intoxicating liquor. But Justice John Marshall Harlan, writing for the Court, made clear that the police power was not without limits:

If . . . a statute purporting to have been enacted to protect the public health, the public morals, or the public safety, has no real or substantial relation to those objects, or is a palpable invasion of rights secured by the fundamental law, it is the duty of the courts to so adjudge. . . .

[But in this case, we] cannot shut out of view the fact, within the knowledge of all, that the public health, the public morals, and the public safety, may be endangered by the general use of intoxicating drinks; nor the fact, established by statistics accessible to everyone, that the idleness, disorder, pauperism, and crime existing in the country are, in some degree at least, traceable to this evil. If, therefore, a State deems the absolute prohibition of the manufacture and sale, within her limits, of intoxicating liquors for other than medical, scientific and manufacturing purposes, to be necessary to the peace and security of society, the courts cannot, without usurping legislative functions, override the will of the people as thus expressed by their chosen representatives.[118]

The following year the Court upheld a state's ban on the manufacture of liquor in the state for export but struck down a ban on the importation of liquor into that state. The ban on importation, the Court held, interfered with interstate commerce.[119]

And two years later the Court further weakened state power over the importation of liquor by holding that a state could not forbid the first sale of such liquor in its original package. This ruling was based on the doctrine—first announced by Chief Justice John Marshall in the 1827 case of *Brown v. Maryland*— that as long as an imported product remained in the package in which it had entered the state, it was beyond state regulation or taxation.[120]

Iowa had banned the sale of imported liquor in any package. The firm of Gus. Leisy & Co., a Peoria, Illinois, brewer, shipped liquor to Keokuk, Iowa, where it was seized by A. J. Hardin, a law enforcement officer. Leisy challenged Iowa's ban on the first sale of imported liquor as infringing upon the federally protected flow of interstate commerce. The Court agreed with Leisy and struck down that portion of the law.

Writing for the Court, Chief Justice Melville W. Fuller stated:

Up to that point of time [after the first sale in the original package], we hold that, in the absence of congressional permission to do so, the State had no power to interfere by seizure, or any other action, in prohibition of importation and sale by the foreign nonresident importer. Whatever our individual views may be, as to the deleterious or dangerous qualities of particular articles, we cannot hold that any articles which Congress recognizes as subjects of interstate commerce are not such, or . . . can be controlled by state laws amounting to regulations, while they retain that character.[121]

Fuller's opinion invited Congress to act. In 1890, the year of the decision, Congress approved the Wilson Act, stripping imported liquor of the protection of interstate commerce—or the original package. The law stated that upon arrival in a state, intoxicating liquors were subject to whatever police power laws the state wished to pass, just as if the liquor had been produced in the state and not imported. In 1891 the Supreme Court approved the act.[122]

Congress subsequently acted to place alcohol control even more completely under state authority. The Webb-Kenyon Act of 1913 forbade the shipment of liquor into any state where its use or sale would violate state law. In 1917 the Court upheld state power under this law to forbid the entry of intoxicating liquor.[123]

The addition to the Constitution in 1933 of the Twenty-first

To help stabilize the market, the New York Milk Control Board fixed the price of a quart of milk at nine cents. When Leo Nebbia, pictured here, the owner of a grocery store, sold two quarts of milk and a loaf of bread for eighteen cents, the state convicted him of violating the board's order. In 1934 the Supreme Court rejected Nebbia's claim that the order violated his constitutional rights, ruling that it was a valid exercise of state power.

Amendment (repeal of Prohibition) placed the matter entirely under state control. Section 2 states that "the transportation or importation into any State, Territory, or possession of the United States for delivery or use therein of intoxicating liquors, in violation of the laws thereof, is hereby prohibited." The Court has construed the power granted by this amendment broadly, holding only that states may not forbid the sale of liquor on federal property, that Congress may continue to regulate the importation of liquor from abroad, and that a state may only place reasonable restrictions on the passage of liquor through its territory.[124]

"PUBLIC INTEREST" REGULATION

From its 1877 decision in *Munn v. Illinois* until 1934, the Supreme Court used the doctrine of the "public interest" as its standard for determining the types of businesses that states might properly regulate. Businesses that appeared to the justices to be "clothed with a public interest" might be regulated; others that lacked this characteristic were to remain free of state control.

Explaining the logic of this standard, Chief Justice Morrison R. Waite wrote in *Munn v. Illinois* that under the police power "the government regulates the conduct of its citizens one towards another, and the manner in which each shall use his own property, when such regulation becomes necessary for the public good. . . . Property does become clothed with a public interest when used in a manner to make it of public consequence, and affect the community at large."[125]

Although the "public interest" doctrine survived for half a century, as a standard for decisions by courts or state legislatures, it never acquired any clear meaning. The Court held that

bakeries, meatpackers, ticket-scalpers, employment agencies, gas stations, and ice vendors were not businesses "clothed with a public interest" but railroads, public utilities, grain elevators, stockyards, fire insurance companies, and tobacco warehouses were.[126]

In 1934 the Court abandoned this rationale for state regulation with its decision in *Nebbia v. New York*. New York, it said, could set the acceptable range of prices to be charged for milk within the state. States could regulate virtually any business for the public good, held the Court, so long as the regulation was reasonable and effected through appropriate means. Discarding the *Munn* approach, Justice Owen J. Roberts wrote for the majority:

It is clear there is no closed class or category of businesses affected with a public interest. . . . The function of courts . . . is to determine in each case whether circumstances vindicate the challenged regulation as a reasonable exertion of governmental authority or condemn it as arbitrary or discriminatory. . . . The phrase "affected with a public interest" can, in the nature of things, mean no more than that an industry, for adequate reason, is subject to control for the public good. . . . [T]here can be no doubt that upon proper occasion and by appropriate measures the state may regulate a business in any of its aspects. . . .

The Constitution does not secure to any one liberty to conduct his business in such fashion as to inflict injury upon the public at large, or upon any substantial group of the people. Price control, like any other form of regulation, is unconstitutional only if arbitrary, discriminatory, or demonstrably irrelevant to the policy the legislature is free to adopt, and hence an unnecessary and unwarranted interference with individual liberty.[127]

WAGES AND HOURS

As the Court found the contract clause a less and less useful instrument to counter the increasingly vigorous assertions of the police power to regulate property or business, it began to use the Fourteenth Amendment's due process clause in its place. The Supreme Court moved into a period of laissez-faire rulings, finding that there were some areas of business that neither federal nor state power could reach.

As a companion to this philosophy, the Court began espousing the doctrine of "freedom of contract"—a part of the liberty protected by the Fourteenth Amendment. Thus armed, the Court for decades dealt unkindly with the efforts of states to control the hours, and later the wages, of workers within their jurisdiction.

The first of these laws considered fully by the Supreme Court—in 1898—was upheld. Utah limited to eight hours a day the period that miners could work in underground mines except in an emergency. This law was challenged as denying both the worker and the employer their freedom of contract.

In *Holden v. Hardy* the Court rejected the challenge and found the law a proper exercise of the police power by the state to protect its citizens' health by limiting the amount of time they spent in admittedly hazardous and unhealthy conditions.[128]

Bakery Workers: Lochner

Seven years later, however, health considerations did not weigh so heavily when the Court considered and struck down New York's law limiting the hours that bakery employees might work. The Court found the law an infringement of the liberty of contract without due process of law. Justice Rufus Peckham wrote for the majority in *Lochner v. New York:*

Clean and wholesome bread does not depend upon whether the baker works but ten hours per day or only sixty hours a week. The limitation of the hours of labor does not come within the police power on that ground.

It is a question of which of two powers or rights shall prevail—the power of the state to legislate or the right of the individual to liberty of person and freedom of contract. . . . We think the limit of the police power has been reached and passed in this case. There is . . . no reasonable foundation for holding this to be necessary or appropriate as a health law to safeguard the public health. . . . We think that there can be no fair doubt that the trade of a baker, in and of itself, is not an unhealthy one to that degree which would authorize the legislature to interfere with the right to labor, and with the right of free contract on the part of the individual, either as employer or employee.

[If the Court upheld this law] no trade, no occupation, no mode of earning one's living, could escape this all-pervading power, and the acts of the legislature in limiting the hours of labor in all employments would be valid, although such limitation might seriously cripple the ability of the laborer to support himself and his family. . . .

Statutes of the nature of that under review, limiting the hours in which grown and intelligent men may labor to earn their living, are mere meddlesome interferences with the rights of the individual, and they are not saved from condemnation by the claim that they are passed in the exercise of the police power and upon the subject of the health of the individual whose rights are interfered with, unless there be some fair ground . . . to say that there is material danger to the public health, or to the health of the employees, if the hours of labor are not curtailed.[129]

Laundry Women: Muller

The vote in *Lochner* was 5–4. And the narrowness of that balance came into focus three years later, when the Court—in *Muller v. Oregon* (1908)—upheld Oregon's law setting a maximum ten-hour day for women working in laundries. Arguing this case for Oregon was Louis D. Brandeis, later to become one of the Court's most famous justices. In *Muller,* he used what came to be called a "Brandeis brief," a brief heavily buttressed with sociological and statistical information intended to support the legal argument. The Court, in its opinion, paid a rare compliment to Brandeis by mentioning his brief and him by name. The information was apparently convincing. The Court upheld the law unanimously.[130]

Where the hazards of the occupation had distinguished *Hardy* from *Lochner,* sex apparently made the difference between *Lochner* and *Muller.* State regulation of working hours for women was seen as valid because women were thought to be

When Oregon imposed a sixty-hour maximum work week for women, laundry owner Curt Muller (with arms folded) argued that the law violated his rights. In 1908 a unanimous Supreme Court upheld the validity of state maximum working hour laws, accepting sociological arguments about the effects of long hours on women's health.

physically less strong than men, and longer working hours were considered likely to impair their childbearing function.

Ten years later, in 1917, the Court upheld still another maximum hours law from Oregon—this one setting the ten-hour day as the maximum for all industrial workers. The vote was 5–3; Justice Brandeis, counsel when these cases began, did not take part in the ruling.

The Court made little effort to explain why it upheld this law, when it had struck down the New York law in *Lochner*. The opinion in *Bunting v. Oregon* indicated that the Court had given the benefit of the doubt to the law.

It is enough for our decision if the legislation under review was passed in the exercise of an admitted power of government. . . . There is a contention made that the law . . . is not either necessary or useful "for the preservation of the health of employees. . . ." The record contains no facts to support the contention.[131]

This ruling established the right of states to limit the hours of work for men and women in almost all occupations, free of challenge under the due process clause, so long as the standard imposed had some clear relationship to the society's health and safety.

Wages of Women, Children

But *Lochner* was not altogether dead; it soon reappeared as the Court began striking down state and federal efforts to regulate wages. In 1923 the Court invalidated a law enacted by Congress for the District of Columbia that set a minimum wage for women and children workers.

In *Adkins v. Children's Hospital* the vote was 5–3; Brandeis again did not participate. The opinion was written by Justice George Sutherland, who had been named to the Court in 1922. Felix Frankfurter, then an attorney for the parties supporting the law, filed a long Brandeis brief demonstrating the unhappy effects of substandard wages on women. Although Frankfurter would later become a member of the Court, the majority here found his statistics of little relevance to the validity of the law.

This was "simply and exclusively a price-fixing law," wrote Sutherland, "confined to adult women . . . who are legally as capable of contracting for themselves as men." A law could not prescribe the proper wage to preserve the health and moral character of a woman, he said. And it was lopsided, requiring an employer to pay a worker a certain amount regardless of whether the employer found the worker that valuable.

"A statute which prescribes payment . . . solely with relation to circumstances apart from the contract of employment, the business affected by it and the work done under it," Sutherland concluded, "is so clearly the product of a naked, arbitrary exercise of power that it cannot be allowed to stand under the Constitution."[132]

In dissent, Chief Justice William Howard Taft expressed his surprise at the revival of the doctrine of freedom of contract, saying that he thought *Lochner* had been overruled after *Muller* and *Bunting*.

Also in dissent, Justice Oliver Wendell Holmes Jr. wrote:

This statute does not compel anybody to pay anything. It simply forbids employment at rates below those fixed as the minimum requirement of health and right living. It is safe to assume that women will not be employed at even the lowest wages allowed unless they earn them, or unless the employer's business can sustain the burden. In short, the law in its character and operation is like hundreds of so-called police laws that have been upheld.[133]

Holmes said he did not understand "the principle on which the power to fix a minimum for the wages of women can be denied by those who admit the power to fix a maximum for their hours of work. . . . I perceive no difference in the kind or degree of interference with liberty . . . between one case and the other."[134]

The Court remained adamant. Fourteen years after *Adkins*, the Court struck down a New York minimum wage law for women and children. The vote was 5–4, resolving the case of *Morehead v. New York ex rel. Tipaldo* against the state. The four justices still serving who had formed the *Adkins* majority were joined by Justice Owen J. Roberts, who had been appointed to the Court after the earlier ruling. This decision was announced in the spring of 1936.

Writing for the majority, Justice Pierce Butler declared any minimum wage law a violation of due process: "[T]he state is without power by any form of legislation to prohibit, change or nullify contracts between employers and adult women workers as to the amount of wage to be paid."[135]

The dissenters—Chief Justice Charles Evans Hughes and Justices Brandeis, Benjamin Cardozo, and Harlan Fiske Stone—viewed the matter as of broader concern to the community. Justice Stone wrote:

We have had opportunity to perceive more clearly that a wage insufficient to support the worker does not visit its consequences upon him alone; that it may affect profoundly the entire economic structure of society and, in any case, that it casts on every tax payer, and on government itself, the burden of solving the problems of poverty, subsistence, health and morals of large numbers in the community. Because of their nature and extent, these are public problems. A generation ago they were for the individual to solve; today they are the burden of the nation.[136]

Within a year the Court had reversed itself and overruled *Adkins*. In 1937, in the midst of the Court-packing fight, the Court, 5–4, upheld Washington State's law setting minimum wages for women and children workers. Elsie Parrish, a chambermaid, had sued the hotel for which she worked to recover the difference between her pay and the minimum wage, under the state law, of $14.50 a week. The West Coast Hotel Company used *Adkins* as its defense.

Justice Roberts, who had voted against the New York law, joined the dissenters from that case to form a majority upholding the Washington law in the decision known as *West Coast Hotel Co. v. Parrish*.

Chief Justice Hughes wrote the opinion:

What can be closer to the public interest than the health of women and their protection from unscrupulous and overreaching employers? And if the protection of women is a legitimate end of the exercise of state power, how can it be said that the requirement of the payment of a minimum wage fairly fixed in order to meet the very necessities of existence is not an admissible means to that end? . . . The Legislature had the right to consider that its minimum wage requirements would be an important aid in carrying out its policy of protection. The adoption of similar requirements by many states evidences a deep-seated conviction both as to the presence of the evil and as to the means adapted to check it. Legislative response to that conviction cannot be regarded as arbitrary or capricious and that is all we have to decide. Even if the wisdom of the policy be regarded as debatable and its effects uncertain, still the Legislature is entitled to its judgment.[137]

Recent economic experience, wrote Hughes, required the Court to take a broader view of the purposes for which states might exercise their police power. The theory of the freedom of contract, upon which *Lochner* had been based, was defective when applied to situations where the contracting parties were clearly not of equal bargaining power.

The exploitation of a class of workers who are in an unequal position with respect to bargaining power and are thus relatively defenseless against the denial of a living wage is not only detrimental to their health and well being but casts a direct burden for their support upon the community. What these workers lose in wages the taxpayers are called upon to pay. The bare cost of living must be met. . . . The community is not bound to provide what is in effect a subsidy for unconscionable employers. The community may direct its law-making power to correct the abuse which springs from their selfish disregard of the public interest.[138]

Fair Labor Standards Act

Within a year, federal power had been extended into this area so recently opened to state regulation. Congress in 1938 approved the Fair Labor Standards Act, setting minimum wage and maximum hour standards for businesses using the facilities of interstate commerce.

The act provided criminal penalties for violating these standards, and a lumber company president named Fred W. Darby was indicted for such offenses. His case became a test of the constitutionality of the act. In the 1941 decision in *United States v. Darby,* the Court upheld the federal authority under the commerce power to impose such standards.[139]

Congress later extended the protection of these standards through amendments to the act. In 1966 it included the employees of state hospitals, schools, and institutions. Two years later, in *Maryland v. Wirtz,* the Court upheld this extension against challenge from the states that it encroached too far on their internal affairs.[140]

In 1974 Congress went even further to eliminate the traditional exemption for state government employees from the minimum wage and overtime standards of the act. In 1976 the Supreme Court overruled *Maryland v. Wirtz* and held the 1974 changes in the act unconstitutional. Congress had intruded too far into the internal affairs of the states, held the Court, 5–4: "[B]oth the minimum wage and the maximum hour provisions will impermissibly interfere with the integral governmental functions" of the states.[141]

This time the states' exemption was short-lived. In 1985 the

A TAX ON EXPORTS

The Supreme Court has had relatively few opportunities to elaborate on the application of the export-import clause of the Constitution to exports. By far most of the rulings on this ban on state taxes have dealt with state efforts to tax imported goods.

But in 1860 the Court considered—and struck down—California's attempt to impose a stamp tax on bills of lading of gold to be taken out of the state. Writing for the Court, Chief Justice Roger B. Taney found little difference between this tax and the license law voided by the Court in *Brown v. Maryland,* its first ruling on the clause.

"A bill of lading . . . is invariably associated with every cargo of merchandise exported to a foreign country, and consequently a duty upon that is, in substance and effect, a duty on the article exported," Taney wrote. "And if the law of California is constitutional, then every cargo of every description exported from the United States may be made to pay an export duty to the State, provided the tax is imposed in the form of a tax on the bill of lading, and this in direct opposition to the plain and express prohibition in the Constitution."[1]

In subsequent cases interpreting this clause with respect to exports, however, the Court has generally attempted to preserve the state's right to tax an item so long as it appears possible that the item will not actually leave the state.

But when it is clear that the items are being shipped out of the state, that dooms a state or local tax. In *Xerox Corp. v. County of Harris, Texas,* the Court struck down a Texas law on items held in a customs-bonded warehouse prior to shipment abroad.[2]

1. *Almy v. California,* 24 How. 169 at 174 (1860).
2. *Xerox Corp. v. County of Harris, Texas,* 459 U.S. 145 (1982).

Court, again 5–4, overruled its 1976 holding and approved the application of federal minimum wage and maximum hour standards to employees of state and local governments.[142]

The Taxing of Commerce

The Constitution imposes two limitations upon the state's power to raise revenue through taxes. The first is implicit in the commerce clause; the second is an explicit ban upon state duties on imports or exports, or state-imposed tonnage duties, unless Congress should consent to such state taxes.

Most of the Court's interpretation of the taxing powers of the states has been inextricably entwined with the Court's developing view of the commerce clause. Justice Felix Frankfurter wrote in 1946:

The power of the state to tax and the limitations upon that power imposed by the commerce clause have necessitated a long continuous process of judicial adjustment. The need for such adjustment is inherent in a federal government like ours, where the same transaction has aspects that may concern the interests and involve the authority of both the central government and the constituent states. . . . To attempt to harmonize all that has been said in the past would neither clarify what has gone before nor guide the future. Suffice it to say that especially in this field opinions must be read in the setting of the particular case and as the product of preoccupation with their special facts.[143]

This approach is less than satisfactory for many judges and legislators who attempt to gauge the proper reach of state taxes. "This case-by-case approach," noted Justice Byron R. White twenty years after Frankfurter wrote, "has left much 'room for controversy and confusion and little in the way of precise guides to the States in the exercise of their indispensable power of taxation.'"[144]

A CONCURRENT POWER

There is a major difference between the commerce and the taxing powers in a constitutional sense: the taxing power may be exercised concurrently by the state and federal governments, and the commerce power may not be.

In *Gibbons v. Ogden* Chief Justice Marshall discussed the distinction:

Although many of the powers formerly exercised by the states, are transferred to the government of the Union, yet the state governments remain, and constitute a most important part of our system. The power of taxation is indispensable to their existence, and is a power which, in its own nature, is capable of residing in, and being exercised by, different authorities at the same time. . . .

Congress is authorized to lay and collect taxes, etc., to pay the debts, and provide for the common defense and general welfare of the United States. This does not interfere with the power of the states to tax for the support of their own governments; nor is the exercise of that power by the states an exercise of any portion of the power that is granted to the United States. In imposing taxes for state purposes, they are not doing what Congress is empowered to do. Congress is not empowered to tax for those purposes which are within the exclusive province of the states. When, then, each government exercises the power of taxation, neither is exercising the power of the other.[145]

A LIMITED POWER

But even before Marshall wrote these words, the Court—in its first major ruling affecting the state's power to tax, *McCulloch v. Maryland*—had made clear the limit that federal power placed upon that exercise of state sovereignty.

The tax question involved the power of the state of Maryland to tax a branch of the Bank of the United States, located in Baltimore. The tax was instituted by the state as an antibank move, intended to curtail the issuance of bank notes by the bank. Such a use of the state taxing power was improper, held the Court, a violation of the Constitution's provision that federal law is supreme over the states.

Marshall explained:

[T]he Constitution and the laws made in pursuance thereof are supreme; . . . they control the constitution and laws of the respective states, and cannot be controlled by them. . . .

[T]he power to tax involves the power to destroy; . . . the power to destroy may defeat and render useless the power to create; . . . there is a plain repugnance, in conferring on one government a power to control the constitutional measures of another, which other, with respect to those very measures, is declared to be supreme.[146]

Marshall then described the consequences of allowing such a tax:

If the states may tax one instrument, employed by the government in the execution of its powers, they may tax any and every other instrument. They may tax the mail; they may tax the mint; they may tax patent rights; they may tax the papers of the custom-house; they may tax judicial process; they may tax all the means employed by the government, to an excess which would defeat all the ends of government. This was not intended by the American people. They did not design to make their government dependent on the states.[147]

Limiting the sweep of the ruling, Marshall concluded:

This opinion does not deprive the states of any resources which they originally possessed. It does not extend to a tax paid by the real property of the bank, in common with other real property within the state, nor to a tax imposed on the interest which the citizens of Maryland may hold in this institution, in common with other property of the same description throughout the State. But this is a tax on the operations of the Bank, and is, consequently, a tax on the operation of an instrument employed by the government of the Union to carry its powers into execution. Such a tax must be unconstitutional.[148]

TAXING IMPORTS

Within eight years Maryland—and its use of the tax power—was back before the Supreme Court. Its lawyer was Roger B. Taney. The case was *Brown v. Maryland.*

The purpose of the constitutional ban on state taxes on imports and exports was to prevent discrimination against imports and against states within the interior of the country. State taxes could be used to make imported goods more expensive than similar domestic goods. And if coastal states were allowed to tax incoming goods passing on to other states, they could impose a considerable burden on the citizens of those interior states.

Maryland law required persons who sold imported goods to purchase licenses. The law was challenged as violating the ban on import taxes and as interfering with the federal regulation of interstate and foreign commerce.

The Court agreed with the challenge on both points. The license requirement was basically an indirect tax on imports. Chief Justice Marshall wrote:

The constitutional prohibition on the states to lay a duty on imports . . . may certainly come in conflict with their acknowledged power to tax persons and property within their territory. The power, and the restriction on it, though quite distinguishable when they do not approach each other, may yet, like the intervening colors between white and black, approach so nearly as to perplex the understanding. . . .

It is sufficient for the present to say, generally, that when the importer has so acted upon the thing imported that it has become incorporated and mixed up with the mass of property in the country, it has, perhaps, lost its distinctive character as an import, and has become subject to the taxing power of the state; but while remaining the property of the importer, in his warehouse, in the original form or package in which it was imported, a tax upon it is too plainly a duty on imports to escape the prohibition in the constitution. . . .

This indictment is against the importer, for selling a package of dry goods in the form in which it was imported, without a license. This state of things is changed if he sells them, or otherwise mixes them with the general property of the state, by breaking up his packages, and traveling with them as an itinerant peddler. In the first case, the tax intercepts the import, as an import, on its way to become incorporated with the general mass of property, and denies it the privilege of becoming so incorporated until it shall have contributed to the revenue of the state.[149]

With the ruling in *Brown v. Maryland,* wrote Felix Frankfurter more than a century later, Chief Justice Marshall "gave powerful practical application to the possibilities intimated in *Gibbons v. Ogden.* Imminent in the commerce clause were severe limitations upon the power of the states to tax as well as to regulate commerce."[150] And the "original package" doctrine that Marshall first set out in this case would stand for decades as a valid limit on the exercise of state tax and police powers.

In *Brown v. Maryland* Marshall concluded: "[W]e suppose the principles laid down in this case . . . apply equally to importations from a sister state," as well as to importation of goods from foreign countries.[151]

Forty-two years later auctioneer L. P. Woodruff cited this comment in his challenge to the sales tax Mobile, Alabama, placed on goods he brought into the state and sold, in their original package, at auction. Woodruff claimed that under *Brown v. Maryland* the tax was in violation of the export-import clause.[152]

Not so, held the Supreme Court in 1869, dismissing Marshall's comment and limiting the prohibition on state import taxes to imports from foreign countries. Justice Samuel Miller, writing for the Court, explained the effect such a broad exemption from state taxes would have:

The merchant of Chicago who buys his goods in New York and sells at wholesale in the original packages, may have his millions employed in trade for half a lifetime and escape all state, county, and city taxes: for all that he is worth is invested in goods which he claims to be protected as imports from New York. Neither the State nor the city which protects his life and property can make him contribute a dollar to support its government, improve its thoroughfares or educate its children.[153]

Two points were thus settled by the decision in *Woodruff v. Parham:* the state power to tax goods imported from other states is not hindered by the export-import clause, and once interstate transportation of those goods has ended, a state may tax them, even in their original package.

So the protection of the original package—against state taxes—terminated earlier for goods from other states than for goods from other countries. The point was reaffirmed in the Court's 1885 decision in *Brown v. Houston.* The Court held that Louisiana could tax coal from Pennsylvania even while it was on the barges in which it had entered the state.[154]

And for two hundred years the Supreme Court steadfastly rejected all state efforts to tax imported foreign goods so long as those goods retained their character as imports. In 1872 the Court refused to allow a state to tax such goods—even just as property like any other within the state. Adolph Low of San Francisco, an importer, was assessed a state property tax upon some $10,000 worth of French champagne he had imported and

had stored in its original package, awaiting sale. The tax on the champagne also fell upon all other personal and real property in the state, based upon its value.

Low came to the Supreme Court, arguing that this tax violated the ban of the export-import clause. He won his case. The Court struck down the tax with its decision in the case of *Low v. Austin.*

Brown v. Maryland (1827) and the original package doctrine governed this case. Justice Stephen Field wrote:

In that case it was also held that the authority given to import, necessarily carried with it a right to sell the goods in the form and condition, that is, in the bale or package, in which they were imported; and that the exaction of a license tax for permission to sell in such case was not only invalid as being in conflict with the constitutional prohibition . . . but also as an interference with the power of Congress to regulate commerce with foreign nations.[155]

It made no difference that the tax did not fall directly upon imports as a class, but simply upon the whole category of citizen-owned property. The original package doctrine still prevented their taxation.

The question is not as to the extent of the tax, or its equality with respect to taxes on other property, but as to the power of the State to levy any tax. . . . Imports, therefore, whilst retaining their distinctive character as such, must be treated as being without the jurisdiction of the taxing power of the State.[156]

The Court subsequently extended this principle even further, holding that a state could not tax imports brought into a state for the importer's own use.[157]

In 1976 *Low v. Austin* was overruled. The Court held that a state could assess a value-based property tax upon imported tires stored in a warehouse awaiting sale. *Low v. Austin* had been based upon a misinterpretation of *Brown v. Maryland,* explained Justice William J. Brennan Jr. for the Court. Such a nondiscriminatory tax was not the type the Constitution or *Brown v. Maryland* prohibited:

Such an exaction, unlike discriminatory state taxation against imported goods as imports, was not regarded as an impediment that severely hampered commerce or constituted a form of tribute by seaboard States to the disadvantage of the interior States. It is obvious that such nondiscriminatory property taxation can have no impact whatsoever on the Federal Government's exclusive regulation of foreign commerce. . . .

Unlike imposts and duties, which are essentially taxes on the commercial privilege of bringing goods into a country, such property taxes are taxes by which a State apportions the cost of such services as police and fire protection among the beneficiaries according to their respective wealth; there is no reason why an importer should not bear his share of these costs along with his competitors handling only domestic goods. The Import-Export Clause clearly prohibits state taxation based on the foreign origin of the imported goods, but it cannot be read to accord imported goods preferential treatment that permits escape from uniform taxes imposed without regard to foreign origin for services which the State supplies.[158]

A decade later the Court reiterated this point in a case involving local property taxes in North Carolina on imported tobacco, which was being aged in warehouses before it was made into cigarettes to be sold in the United States. The Court unanimously permitted the taxes, saying that states may tax such imported goods so long as the tax is clearly not a duty and the goods are no longer "in transit" from their foreign point of origin.[159]

COMMERCE AND TAXES

The classic description of the intricate and ever-shifting relationship between the national power to regulate interstate commerce to keep it flowing and the desire of the states to tax such commerce was delivered by Justice Tom C. Clark in the 1959 case of *Northwestern States Portland Cement Co. v. Minnesota*:

Commerce between the States having grown up like Topsy, the Congress meanwhile not having undertaken to regulate taxation of it, and the States having understandably persisted in their efforts to get some return for the substantial benefits they have afforded it, there is little wonder that there has been no end of cases testing out state tax levies.

The resulting judicial application of constitutional principles to specific state statutes leaves much room for controversy and confusion and little in the way of precise guides to the States in the exercise of their indispensable power of taxation. This Court alone has handed down some three hundred full-dress opinions. . . . [T]he decisions have been "not always clear . . . consistent or reconcilable. . . ." From the quagmire there emerge, however, some firm peaks of decision which remain unquestioned.

[The commerce clause] requires that interstate commerce shall be free from any direct restrictions or impositions by the States [including any burdens imposed by state taxes]. Nor may a State impose a tax which discriminates against interstate commerce either by providing a direct commercial advantage to local business . . . or by subjecting interstate commerce to the burden of "multiple taxation."[160]

Railroad Cases

The application of these principles to the questions raised by state taxes on commerce is best illustrated by three sets of cases: the railroad cases, the "privilege" cases, and the so-called "peddlers and drummers" cases of the late nineteenth century.

The first cases involve railroads and the effort of Pennsylvania to tax the Philadelphia & Reading Railroad. Pennsylvania imposed a tonnage tax on freight the railroad moved through the state. And it imposed a tax on the gross receipts of the company.

On March 3, 1873, the Supreme Court ruled in two cases, each challenging one of these taxes as in conflict with the commerce clause.

The Court struck down the tonnage tax for being in conflict with the requirement that interstate commerce be unimpeded by the states. Writing for the Court, Justice William Strong declared:

It is of national importance that over that subject [transportation of people or products through a state or from one state to another] there should be but one regulating power, for if one State can directly tax persons or property passing through it, or tax them indirectly by levying a tax upon their transportation, every other may, and thus commercial intercourse between States remote from each other may be destroyed. The produce of Western States may thus be effectually excluded from Eastern markets, for though it might bear the imposition of a single tax, it would be crushed under the load of many. It was to guard against the possibility of such commercial embarrassments, no doubt, that the power of regulating commerce among other States was conferred upon the Federal Government.[161]

But on the same day, the Court upheld Pennsylvania's tax upon the gross receipts of the railroad even though some of those receipts obviously resulted from interstate commerce.

Again Justice Strong wrote the opinion, starting from the proposition that

every tax upon personal property or upon occupations, business or franchises, affects more or less the subjects and the operations of commerce. Yet it is not everything that affects commerce that amounts to a regulation of it, within the meaning of the Constitution. We think it may safely be asserted that the States have authority to tax the estate, real and personal, of all their corporations, including carrying companies, precisely as they may tax similar property when belonging to natural persons, and to the same extent. . . . A power to tax to this extent may be essential to the healthy existence of the state governments and the Federal Constitution ought not to be so construed as to impair, much less destroy, anything that is necessary to their efficient existence.

Strong then proceeded to apply a version of the "original package" doctrine to the issue:

While it must be conceded that a tax upon interstate transportation is invalid, there seems to be no stronger reason for denying the power of a State to tax the fruits of such transportation after they have become intermingled with the general property of the carrier, than there is for denying her power to tax goods which have been imported, after their original packages have been broken, and after they have been mixed with the mass of personal property in the country.[162]

The Court said a state could not tax goods still moving in interstate commerce but could tax them—even in their original package—once the interstate movement ended. How, then, does one define an interstate journey's beginning and end?

The general principles developed by the Court hold that interstate commerce begins once an item is surrendered to a common carrier for transportation or otherwise begins its journey out of the state. The journey—and the protection of interstate commerce—ends when the items arrive at their destination, usually defined as in the possession of the person to whom they are sent. Temporary and unexpected interruptions in the journey do not terminate the protection of the commerce clause against state taxation, but a true break in the journey may allow a state to tax items in commerce.

Following the decision upholding Pennsylvania's gross receipts tax as applied to railroads, the Court has dealt with a variety of state efforts to tax interstate corporations doing business within the state. The Court generally has upheld both net income and gross receipts taxes so long as they are fairly apportioned to reflect the share of the company's overall business done in the state and to accord with the services and protection provided by the state to the company.[163]

In the 1980s and 1990s the Court steadily upheld against corporate challenges state taxes imposed on interstate and international corporations using the "worldwide unitary" method of taxation. The Court held that this method, when properly implemented, produced a tax that violated neither the guarantee of due process nor the federal power to regulate interstate and foreign commerce.[164]

"Privilege" Cases

The second set of cases illustrating the Court's effort to apply the commerce clause requirement carefully but not too strictly to state taxation involves the question of state taxes on "the privilege of doing interstate business."

In the 1869 case of *Paul v. Virginia*, the Court held that Virginia could impose conditions upon its grant to an out-of-state insurance company of the right to do business in the state. Virginia's law required the company to obtain a license and to deposit security bonds of $30,000 to $50,000 with the state treasurer.[165]

But when Kentucky sought to enforce its law requiring out-of-state express companies to obtain a state license before carrying on business in the state, the United States Express Company protested that this requirement was an infringement of the federal power to regulate commerce. The case came to the Supreme Court in 1890 and was decided—against the state—in 1891.

"To carry on interstate commerce is not a franchise or a privilege granted by the State," wrote Justice Joseph P. Bradley, "it is a right which every citizen of the United States is entitled to exercise under the Constitution and laws of the United States." A state could not use a license tax to exclude or burden corporations engaged in interstate commerce. Distinguishing the *Paul* decision, Bradley wrote: "The case is entirely different from that of foreign corporations seeking to do a business which does not belong to the regulating power of Congress." Insurance, the Court had held in *Paul v. Virginia*, was not subject to that congressional power. (See "Insurance," pp. 333–334.)

And the Court rejected any defense of the Kentucky law as an exercise of the police power: "[I]t does not follow that everything which the Legislature of a State may deem essential for the good order of society and the well being of its citizens can be set up against the exclusive power of Congress to regulate the operations of foreign and interstate commerce."[166]

For almost a century, with increasing confusion and diminishing effect, the Court adhered to this rule. As constitutional scholar Carl B. Swisher wrote:

The question whether state taxes bore so heavily upon interstate commerce as to be an unconstitutional burden arose perennially. If a generalization is to be made at all, it is perhaps to the effect that the principles involved became less clear with the passing years, and the decisions rested more obviously upon the beliefs of the Court as to what in each case would best serve the public welfare. The lines of the original-package doctrine . . . became increasingly blurred as decisions dealt with such matters as natural gas and electricity which only in a highly figurative sense could be thought of as in packages at all. The principle that state control began when the article shipped in interstate commerce came to rest in the state was likewise blurred because of the fact that so many of the items of interstate commerce could not be thought of as coming to rest. The absence of a clear line marking the taxing jurisdiction of the state resulted, not from any particular line of decisions of the Supreme Court, but from the nature of commerce itself and the nature of the federal system.[167]

By 1977 the Supreme Court realized that the prohibition on taxes on "the privilege of doing interstate business" had become little more than a formalism, "a trap for the unwary draftsman" who failed to choose other phrases for the state tax law.

In that year the Court discarded its opposition to all taxes described in this way and adopted the practical approach already in evidence in most of its modern rulings on state tax. Rejecting the challenge of an interstate motor carrier to a Mississippi tax, Justice Harry A. Blackmun explained the Court's decision in *Complete Auto Transit Inc. v. Brady*. Citing several of the other recent state tax cases, he noted that they "considered not the formal language of the tax statute, but rather the practical effect, and have sustained a tax against Commerce Clause challenge when the tax is applied to an activity with a substantial nexus with the taxing state, is fairly apportioned, does not discriminate against interstate commerce and is fairly related to the services provided by the State.

[The modern Court] consistently has indicated that 'interstate commerce may be made to pay its way,' and has moved toward a standard of permissibility of state taxation based upon its actual effect rather than legal terminology."[168]

In this case, finding that the challenged tax resulted in no effect forbidden by the commerce clause, the Court upheld it. The full measure of this about-face by the Court was illustrated the following year, in 1978, when the Court approved a Washington State tax on stevedoring virtually identical to one it had twice held an unconstitutional burden on interstate commerce.[169]

Business Across Borders

The third set of cases begins with the "peddlers and drummers" decisions of the late nineteenth century. They illustrate the intricate nature of the task of deciding when a state tax discriminates against interstate commerce and when it does not.

Peddlers traveled through the country during the nineteenth century, carrying with them the goods they sold. Drummers, on the other hand, carried only samples, taking orders from their customers for future delivery. The distinction became significant when states tried to tax the peddlers and the drummers and were challenged in this effort as interfering with interstate commerce. The Court's decisions came in the cases of *Welton v. Missouri* and *Robbins v. Shelby County Taxing District*.

M. M. Welton was a peddler in Missouri; he sold sewing machines produced in another state. In 1876 the Supreme Court held that Missouri could not require Welton to obtain a license for his peddling, because the law imposing that requirement affected only persons selling out-of-state goods and so discriminated against interstate commerce in violation of the commerce clause. The commerce clause protects a commodity, "even after it has entered the State, from any burdens imposed by reason of its foreign origin," wrote Justice Stephen Field.[170]

Four years later, however, the Court upheld Tennessee's requirement that all peddlers of sewing machines obtain licenses. That requirement applied to an agent of a Connecticut-based manufacturer. Justice Noah Swayne wrote for the Court:

In all cases of this class, it is a test question whether there is any discrimination in favor of the State or of the citizens of the State which enacted the law. Wherever there is, such discrimination is fatal. . . . In the case before us, the statute . . . makes no such discrimination. It applies alike to sewing machines manufactured in the State and out of it. The exaction is not an unusual or unreasonable one. The State, putting all such machines upon the same footing . . . had an unquestionable right to impose the burden.[171]

Seven years later, however, the Court held that the commerce clause forbade states to place any sort of license requirement or tax on drummers, who take orders in one state for future deliveries of goods from another state. These deliveries are interstate commerce, held the Court, and thus are not subject to state taxes.

Sabine Robbins sold stationery by displaying samples and taking orders in Memphis, Tennessee. The stationery came from Ohio. Tennessee law required all such "drummers" to obtain a license, whether they were employed by in-state or out-of-state firms. Robbins failed to comply and was fined. He challenged his fine by arguing that the drummers' license was an improper interference with interstate commerce.

The Supreme Court, in 1887, agreed. Writing for the majority, Justice Joseph Bradley held that "to tax the sale of such [out-of-state] goods, or the offer to sell them, before they are brought into the State . . . seems to us clearly a tax on interstate commerce itself." The fact that the license requirement applied also to the persons who sold in-state goods was irrelevant.

Interstate commerce cannot be taxed at all, even though the same amount of tax should be laid on domestic commerce. . . . The negotiation of sales of goods which are in another State, for the purpose of introducing them into the State in which the negotiation is made, is interstate commerce.

This particular license tax discriminated against out-of-state businesses that had little alternative to this mode of selling, while in-state businesses could simply open stores in the state where they had their offices anyway. "This kind of taxation is usually imposed at the instance and solicitation of domestic dealers, as a means of protecting them from foreign competition," Bradley wrote.

If this sort of tax were upheld, he concluded, "[T]he confusion into which the commerce of the country would be thrown . . . would be but a repetition of the disorder which prevailed under the Articles of Confederation."[172]

The principle from the *Robbins* case was later extended to protect mail-order businesses from state taxes, particularly the sales taxes increasingly adopted by states. Those taxes affected only local sales, not those from out-of-state merchants.

In an effort to impose an equal tax burden on sales from out-of-state sources, states developed a "use tax," a tax on the in-state use of an item acquired from an out-of-state seller. This tax

---

COINS, CURRENCY, AND CREDIT

The Constitution flatly forbids states to coin money, issue bills of credit, or make any changes in the legal tender. As Justice John McLean commented once: "Here is an act inhibited in terms so precise that they cannot be mistaken. They are susceptible of but one construction."[1]

In light of such clarity, it is not surprising that the Supreme Court has ruled on these prohibitions only a few times in its history. And most of the rulings have dealt with the prohibition on state issuance of bills of credit.

In 1830 the Court ruled that the ban foreclosed a state from issuing loan certificates.[2] Seven years later, however, it found that the ban did not extend to preclude a state-chartered bank from issuing notes, even if the state owned all the bank's stock.[3]

But the leeway that this ruling appeared to afford the states in this area was sharply curtailed just after the Civil War, when the Court held that the national power over the currency was broad enough to sanction the use of the taxing power of Congress to drive state bank notes out of circulation altogether.[4]

1. *Briscoe v. Bank of Kentucky,* 11 Pet. 257 at 318 (1837).
2. *Craig v. Missouri,* 4 Pet. 410 (1830).
3. *Briscoe v. Bank of Kentucky,* 11 Pet. 257 (1837).
4. *Veazie Bank v. Fenno,* 8 Wall. 533 (1869).

---

was equivalent to the "sales tax" imposed on the in-state purchase of a similar item.

The "use tax" was quickly challenged as in conflict with the commerce clause. But the Supreme Court in 1937 found it nondiscriminatory and therefore permissible. Writing for the Court in *Henneford v. Silas Mason Co.,* Justice Benjamin Cardozo explained that the tax was incurred after any interstate commerce had ceased, that the tax did not hamper commerce or discriminate against interstate commerce. "When the account is made up, the stranger from afar is subject to no greater burdens as a consequence of ownership than the dweller within the gates. The one pays upon one activity or incident, and the other upon another, but the sum is the same when the reckoning is closed."[173]

Subsequently, the Court held that a state imposing a use tax may require the out-of-state seller to collect it, so long as there is a sufficient connection between the state and the out-of-state seller to support imposition of this duty. The connection can be the fact that the seller has local agents in the taxing state, that a mail-order company has retail outlets in the taxing state, or even that a company that runs a mail-order business has offices within the taxing state that solicit advertising for a magazine also published by the mail-order company.[174]

But the basic principle of *Welton* and *Robbins* survives as the effective guide for state taxation in this area. In 1977 the Court cited *Welton* when it struck down a New York tax that burdened stock transactions taking place on out-of-state stock exchanges, not the New York Stock Exchange or the New York–based American Stock Exchange. Writing for the Court, Justice Byron R. White noted that the consequence of the New York tax was that "the flow of securities sales is diverted from the most economically efficient channels and directed to New York. This diversion of interstate commerce and diminution of free competition in securities sales are wholly inconsistent with the free trade purpose of the Commerce Clause."[175]

Five years later the Court said states may not force out-of-state catalog companies that do not have a "substantial nexus" with a state to pay taxes.[176] The 1992 case arose after North Dakota sought to require Quill Corp., a mail-order house with neither outlets nor sales representatives in North Dakota, to collect and pay taxes on goods purchased for use in the state. While the Court agreed with North Dakota that the taxes imposed did not violate due process, the Court said a company would have to have a greater physical presence in the state to meet the requirements of the commerce clause.

Many of the state tax cases the Court heard in the past quarter century sprang from states' new approaches to modern budget dilemmas. One important case of the era, however, grew out of citizens' concerns over escalating taxes.

California voters in 1978 adopted Proposition 13, which im-posed strict limits on real property taxes. The approach allowed longtime owners to pay less in taxes than did newer owners of comparable property. A new owner challenged the scheme as a violation of the equal protection clause.

The Court upheld the state law—Proposition 13—by a vote of 8–1 in *Nordlinger v. Hahn* (1992). The justices said having lower taxes on longtime property owners rationally furthers legitimate state interests, notably in neighborhood preservation and stability. Further, the Court said a state may conclude that a new owner does not have the same reliance interest warranting protection against higher taxes as does a longtime owner. The latter already has bought and does not have the option of deciding not to purchase a home if taxes become prohibitively high.[177]

Writing for the Court, Harry A. Blackmun noted that the justices traditionally have given great deference to the democratic process of taxation. "Certainly, California's grand experiment appears to vest benefits in a broad, powerful, and entrenched segment of society, and, as the Court of Appeal surmised, ordinary democratic processes may be unlikely to prompt its reconsideration or repeal. Yet, many wise and well-intentioned laws suffer from the same malady. [The tax law] is not palpably arbitrary, and we must decline petitioner's request to upset the will of the people of California."[178]

On its face, the Constitution imposes few restraints on how a state deals with an individual. Early in its history, the Supreme Court ruled that the guarantees of individual rights in the first ten amendments, the Bill of Rights, did not apply directly to the states—a ruling the Court has yet to overturn.

Although the Court addressed the issue of slavery in a variety of ways, it never did so as a human rights question. Slaves were property.

Even after the addition of the Thirteenth, Fourteenth, and Fifteenth Amendments to the Constitution, the Supreme Court refused for decades to interpret them in a way that would expand the list of civil rights protected against state action. Citing the doctrine of reserved state powers, the Court held that most civil rights questions still remained within the purview of the states.

Not until the twentieth century did the Court begin to employ the Fourteenth Amendment's guarantees of due process and equal protection to apply to state actions the most fundamental of the guarantees of the Bill of Rights. The revolution thus begun is still continuing.

The Constitution

The Constitution forbade states or the federal government to pass any bill of attainder or ex post facto law. Until the twentieth century, these were the only explicit constitutional provisions interpreted by the Supreme Court to restrain state actions affecting the individual.

An ex post facto law is one that operates retroactively to make an earlier action invalid, illegal, or criminal. A bill of attainder, in English law, was an act of Parliament declaring a person guilty of treason, sentencing him to die, and confiscating his property. In American law, a bill of attainder has simply come to mean any measure that punishes an individual without a trial.

There is some evidence that those who wrote the ban on ex post facto laws into the Constitution intended it to protect property as well as persons, to apply to civil as well as criminal laws. But the Supreme Court—in its first ruling on this portion of the Constitution—nullified such intent. Rejecting the contention of a person named Calder that a state law nullifying his title to certain property was in conflict with this provision, the Court held that the ban on ex post facto laws applied only to criminal legislation.

Writing for the Court, Justice Samuel Chase set out its views:

I do not think it [the prohibition] was inserted to secure the citizen in his private rights, of either property or contracts . . . the restriction not to pass any ex post facto law, was to secure the person of the subject from injury, or punishment, in consequence of such law.

I do not consider any law ex post facto, within the prohibition, that mollifies the rigor of the criminal law; but only those that create, or ag-

gravate the crime; or increase the punishment; or change the rules of evidence, for the purpose of conviction.[1]

It is the view of some scholars that the later rulings of the Marshall Court, which interpreted broadly the protection of the contract clause for property rights against legislative amendment or nullification, were an effort to regain the protection for property lost through this narrow interpretation of the ex post facto clause.[2]

In later rulings on this language, the Court has held that it does not forbid a state to make any retroactive changes in its trial procedure and rules of evidence. The Court has simply limited those changes that may be applied to the trials of persons who committed crimes before the change to those that work to the advantage of the defendant. In a pair of cases decided in 1898, the Court, for example, held that a state could alter the rules of evidence to allow the admission of additional evidence, in cases already set for trial before the change because that was simply a change in procedures, but that it could not reduce the size of a jury for the trial of crimes already committed, because it was easier to convince fewer jurors to convict.[3]

In a more recent ruling, the Supreme Court in 1977 refused to use this clause to invalidate a death sentence imposed upon a man convicted of murder. He had argued that it should operate to nullify his sentence because the capital punishment law in operation at the time of the murders was subsequently declared unconstitutional and invalid—and he was sentenced under a new law passed after that Court decision.

By a 6–3 vote the Court rejected his claim, holding that the change from the old law to the new one was simply procedural and that in fact the new law worked more to the benefit of the defendant.[4] Also in 1977 the Court held that Congress had not violated this ban when it took the papers and tapes of the Nixon administration out of the custody of former president Richard Nixon and placed them under government control.[5]

The first broad application of the bills of attainder ban, along with the ex post facto prohibition, came soon after the Civil War. A number of states and Congress enacted laws requiring persons who wished to engage in a variety of activities to take "test oaths" to ensure their loyalty to the Union.

In Missouri the test oath requirement was particularly severe. Before any person could vote, run for or hold office, practice law, teach, hold property in trust for a religious organization, or serve as a clergyman, he was required to take a sweeping oath that he had always been loyal to the United States and that he had never, by act or word, given any aid or support to any enemy. The effect of the law was to exclude from those activities anyone who had even voiced sympathy with the Confederacy.

John A. Cummings, a Catholic priest, refused to be sworn and was convicted and sentenced for acting as a priest without

GUN CONTROL

The constitutional validity of gun control laws is a constant topic of debate among legislators and the public, but the scope of the relevant constitutional language has never been fully tested at the Supreme Court.

The Second Amendment says, "A well regulated Militia, being necessary to the security of a free State, the right of the people to keep and bear Arms, shall not be infringed." Legal scholars disagree over whose right to bear arms the amendment protects. The prevailing view among lower courts is that the Second Amendment was intended to prevent federal interference with a state-sponsored militia, comparable to the modern-day National Guard, rather than to protect an individual's right to own a gun.

In 1886 the Court ruled that the amendment did not apply to the states and in the only case interpreting the amendment in this century, the Supreme Court in 1939 rejected a challenge to a federal law that made it a crime to transport sawed-off shotguns across state lines.[1] By an 8–0 vote, the Court spurned arguments that the law infringed the reserved powers of the states and violated the Second Amendment. Justice James C. McReynolds wrote:

In the absence of any evidence tending to show that possession or use of a shotgun having a barrel of less than eighteen inches in length at this time has some reasonable relationship to the preservation or efficiency of a well regulated militia, we cannot say that the Second Amendment guarantees the right to keep and bear such an instrument. Certainly it is not within judicial notice that this weapon is any part of the ordinary military equipment or that its use could contribute to the common defense."[2]

1. *Presser v. Illinois*, 116 U.S. 252 (1886); and *United States v. Miller*, 307 U.S. 174 (1939).

2. *United States v. Miller*, 307 U.S. 174 at 178 (1939).

taking the oath. He challenged the requirement as a violation of the constitutional prohibitions on bills of attainder and ex post facto laws.

The Court agreed with his challenge on both points. In an opinion written by Justice Stephen Field, it declared:

We admit . . . that among the rights reserved to the States is the right of each State to determine the qualifications for office, and the conditions upon which its citizens may exercise their various callings and pursuits within its jurisdiction. . . . But it by no means follows that, under the form of creating a qualification or attaching a condition, the States can, in effect, inflict a punishment for a past act which was not punishable at the time it was committed.

The disabilities imposed by Missouri upon persons who did not take the oath certainly could be considered punishments, Field wrote. The state could not constitutionally pass a law that declared Cummings personally, or all clergymen, guilty of any crime, and, likewise, it could not pass a law *assuming* such guilt, Field continued.

The Constitution deals with substance, not shadows. Its inhibition was leveled at the thing, not the name. It intended that the rights of the citizen would be secure against deprivation for past conduct by legislative enactment, under any form, however disguised.[6]

The Court also held the federal test oath invalid.[7]

In subsequent rulings the Court has relaxed somewhat its opposition to after-the-fact disqualifications of persons for certain actions. It has held that a state's police power—as applied to protect the public health—justified its forbidding a person convicted of a felony to resume the practice of medicine. And it has upheld the right of a state to exclude convicted felons from holding certain labor union offices. The Court also has permitted states to require their public employees to take loyalty oaths, so long as the oaths are narrowly drawn and carefully applied.[8]

The Court, however, refused to apply any of the provisions of the Bill of Rights to state action. In paving its streets, the city of Baltimore disrupted the course of certain streams, which then dumped debris and gravel into Baltimore Harbor around the wharf owned by a man named John Barron. As a result the value of Barron's wharf was destroyed; the water around it had been made too shallow for vessels to approach to off-load at the wharf.

Barron sued the city of Baltimore and took his case to the Supreme Court, arguing that the Fifth Amendment guarantee against the government's taking private property for public use without just compensation required the city to compensate him for his loss.

Barron lost again at the Supreme Court. Chief Justice John Marshall, in the Court's opinion, said: "These amendments contain no expression indicating an intention to apply them to the State governments. This Court cannot so apply them."[9]

The Civil War Amendments

Few stranger chapters can be found in the history of the Court than the story of the way in which the justices, after the Civil War, read the Thirteenth, Fourteenth, and Fifteenth Amendments to the Constitution. The Court's interpretation was so narrow that it frustrated almost entirely the intentions of the men who drafted them and worked for their incorporation into the Constitution. The amendments' sponsors intended to extend federal protection to citizens against state action infringing the rights already protected by the Bill of Rights against federal action. The Court rejected this interpretation for decades.

SERVITUDE AND DISCRIMINATION

"Neither slavery nor involuntary servitude, except as a punishment for crime whereof the party shall have been duly convicted, shall exist within the United States, or any place subject to their jurisdiction," reads the Thirteenth Amendment, abolishing slavery and authorizing Congress to pass legislation enforcing that ban. Although it conceded that this amendment empowered Congress to pass laws to abolish "all badges and incidents of slavery," the Court in the *Civil Rights Cases* of 1883 refused to view racial discrimination as a "badge of slavery."

Writing for the Court, Justice Joseph Bradley stated:

Congress did not assume, under the authority given by the 13th Amendment, to adjust what may be called the social rights of men and races in the community; but only to declare and vindicate those

When Louisiana granted the Crescent City Live Stock Landing and Slaughter House Company a twenty-five year monopoly on live-stock-butchering in New Orleans, it forced every butcher to use the facility and to pay for the use. The butchers sued, basing their 1873 case before the Supreme Court on the Fourteenth Amendment, which forbids states to pass laws that "abridge the privileges or immunities" of U.S. citizens. The Court upheld the Louisiana law.

fundamental rights which appertain to the essence of citizenship, and the enjoyment or deprivation of which constitutes the essential distinction between freedom and slavery. . . . It would be running the slavery argument into the ground, to make it apply to every act of discrimination which a person may see fit to make as to the guests he will entertain, or as to the people he will take into his coach or cab or car, or admit to his concert or theater, or deal with in other matters of intercourse or business.[10]

Early in the twentieth century the Court did cite this amendment to strike down state peonage laws, which required a person who defaulted on a contract either to go to jail or to go to work for his creditor to "work off" his default.[11]

The Court, however, has recognized a number of established exceptions to the "involuntary servitude" banned by the Thirteenth Amendment—among them work for the state on state roads, jury duty, and compulsory military service.[12]

PRIVILEGES AND IMMUNITIES

"All persons born or naturalized in the United States, and subject to the jurisdiction thereof, are citizens of the United States and of the State wherein they reside," states the first section of the Fourteenth Amendment, overruling the Court's holding in *Dred Scott v. Sandford* that blacks were not citizens.

The same section of the amendment, clearly directed against state action, also declares, "No State shall make or enforce any law which shall abridge the privileges or immunities of citizens of the United States; nor shall any State deprive any person of life, liberty, or property, without due process of law; nor deny to any person within its jurisdiction the equal protection of the laws."

Adopted in 1868, this amendment contained four other sections, only one of which—giving Congress the authority to pass appropriate enforcing laws—is pertinent here.

During congressional consideration of the Fourteenth Amendment, advocates of the measure in both chambers made clear their belief that it would extend federal protection for a broad range of basic rights, including those guaranteed by the Bill of Rights, to persons denied the rights by state action.[13]

Slaughterhouse Cases

Five years after the amendment was ratified, the Supreme Court ruled that it did *not* give citizens the full protection of the Bill of Rights against actions by the states.

Oddly enough, it was butchers, not black men, bringing these landmark cases. New Orleans butchers charged that the state of Louisiana had violated the Fourteenth Amendment by granting to one company the exclusive right to operate a slaughterhouse in the city. This monopoly, the butchers charged, deprived them of their right to carry on their business, a right included among the privileges and immunities guaranteed by the first section of the amendment. The cases were known collectively as the *Slaughterhouse Cases.*[14]

The monopoly was granted in 1869; the case reached the Supreme Court the next year. It was argued in 1872 and then reargued in 1873. Representing the butchers was former justice John A. Campbell of Alabama, who had left the Court when his state seceded from the Union. He placed the burden of his argument on the privileges and immunities section of the amendment, although reference was made to the due process and equal protection guarantees as well.

On April 14, 1873—eight years after the end of the Civil War—the Court issued its opinion. The vote was 5–4; the majority opinion was written by Justice Samuel F. Miller. Dissenting were Chief Justice Salmon P. Chase and Justices Stephen Field, Noah Swayne, and Joseph Bradley.

The monopoly was granted by the state in the exercise of its police power, wrote Miller. It did not forbid the protesting butchers to practice their trade—it merely required them to do so at a particular slaughterhouse. By law, all other slaughterhouses in the area were to be closed.

Considering the citizenship section of the amendment,

Miller made an important distinction: "It is quite clear, then, that there is a citizenship of the United States and a citizenship of a State, which are distinct from each other and which depend upon different characteristics or circumstances in the individual."

Moving on to the next portion of the amendment, Miller continued:

Of the privileges and immunities of the citizens of the United States, and of the privileges and immunities of the citizens of the State, and what they respectively are, we will presently consider; but we wish to state here that it is only the former which are placed by this clause under the protection of the Federal Constitution, and that the latter, whatever they may be, are not intended to have any additional protection by this paragraph of the Amendment.[15]

With the exception of the Constitution's language forbidding states to pass ex post facto laws, bills of attainder, and laws impairing the obligation of contract, Miller wrote,

the entire domain of the privileges and immunities of citizens of the States lay within the constitutional and legislative power of the States, and without that of the Federal Government. Was it the purpose of the 14th Amendment . . . to transfer the security and protection of all the civil rights which we have mentioned, from the States to the Federal Government? And where it is declared that Congress shall have the power to enforce that article, was it intended to bring within the power of Congress the entire domain of civil rights heretofore belonging exclusively to the States?

All this and more must follow, if the proposition of the plaintiffs . . . [the butchers] be sound. . . . [S]uch a construction . . . would constitute this Court a perpetual censor upon all legislation of the States, on the civil rights of their own citizens, with authority to nullify such as it did not approve as consistent with those rights, as they existed at the time of the adoption of this amendment. . . .

We are convinced that no such results were intended by the Congress which proposed these Amendments, nor by the Legislatures of the States, which ratified them."

Thus, the butchers' challenge to the monopoly failed, for "the privileges and immunities relied on in the argument are those which belong to citizens of the States as such, and . . . are left to the state governments for security and protection, and not by this article placed under the special care of the Federal Government."

"The argument has not been much pressed in these cases that the defendants' charter deprives the plaintiffs of their property without due process of law, or that it denies to them the equal protection of the law," added Miller. However, he noted that "under no construction of that provision that we have ever seen, or any that we deem admissible, can the restraint imposed by the State of Louisiana upon the exercise of their trade by the butchers of New Orleans be held to be a deprivation of property within the meaning of that provision."[16]

In dissent, Justice Field argued that the Fourteenth Amendment did extend protection to citizens against the deprivation of their common rights by state legislation.

The fundamental rights, privileges and immunities which belong to him as a free man and a free citizen, now belong to him as a citizen of the United States, and are not dependent upon his citizenship of any State. . . . They do not derive their existence from its legislation, and cannot be destroyed by its power.

To hold the majority's view, confining this protection to the privileges and immunities specifically or implicitly set out as belonging to U.S. citizens, rendered this portion of the amendment "a vain and idle enactment, which accomplished nothing, and most unnecessarily excited Congress and the people on its passage. With privileges and immunities thus designated no State could ever have interfered by its laws, and no new constitutional provision was required to inhibit such interference. . . . But if the Amendment refers to the natural and inalienable rights which belong to all citizens, the inhibition has a profound significance and consequence."[17]

Not surprisingly, the Fourteenth Amendment so interpreted provided little protection for any of the disadvantaged groups who sought its shelter during the next half-century—blacks, women, aliens, and criminal defendants.

Civil Rights Cases

In the opinion in the *Slaughterhouse Cases* Justice Miller stated his doubts that "any action of a State not directed by way of discrimination against the negroes as a class, or on account of their race, will ever be held to come within the purview of this [equal protection] provision. It is so clearly a provision for that race and that emergency."[18]

Yet, ten years later, in its decision in the *Civil Rights Cases* of 1883, the Court so narrowly interpreted the amendment's protection for black citizens that even Justice Miller's limited view of the equal protection clause seemed too broad. And during those years the Court struck down a number of the laws Congress had passed—under the power granted by the Civil War amendments—to enforce those amendments. This narrowing process consisted of two elements: a limited category of federally protected rights and an insistence that the Fourteenth Amendment reached only state, not private, action.[19]

In the *Civil Rights Cases* the Court struck down the Civil Rights Act of 1875 as beyond the power granted to Congress by the enforcing section of the Fourteenth Amendment. That act made it a crime to deny equal access and enjoyment of public accommodations to black persons. There were five such cases grouped under the rubric of the *Civil Rights Cases* and decided together by the Court: *United States v. Stanley* from Kansas, *United States v. Ryan* from California, *United States v. Nichols* from Missouri, *United States v. Singleton* from New York, and *Robinson v. Memphis and Charleston Railroad Co.* from Tennessee.

In the *Stanley* and *Nichols* cases, the defendants were charged with refusing to allow blacks equal access to inns and hotels; in the *Ryan* and *Singleton* cases, the defendants had refused to allow black people to sit in a certain part of theaters in San Francisco and in New York; and the *Robinson* case resulted from a railroad conductor's refusal to allow a black woman to ride in the "ladies'" car on the train.

The Court voted 8–1 to strike down the Civil Rights Act. Writing for the majority, Justice Bradley found the reason simple: the Fourteenth Amendment forbade state action, not "individual invasion of individual rights." Bradley continued:

It does not invest Congress with power to legislate upon subjects which are within the domain of state legislation; but to provide modes of relief against state legislation or state action. . . . It does not authorize Congress to create a code of municipal law for the regulation of private rights; but to provide modes of redress against the operation of state laws, and the action of state officers executive or judicial, when these are subversive of the fundamental rights specified in the Amendment.

Such legislation [as Congress is authorized to pass] cannot properly cover the whole domain of rights. . . . That would be to establish a code of municipal law regulative of all private rights between man and man in society. It would be to make Congress take the place of the State Legislatures, and to supersede them. . . . [T]he legislation which Congress is authorized to adopt in this behalf is not general legislation upon the rights of the citizen, but corrective legislation, that is, such as may be necessary and proper for counteracting such laws as the States may adopt or enforce. . . .

In this connection it is proper to state that civil rights, such as are guarantied [sic] by the Constitution against state aggression, cannot be impaired by the wrongful acts of individuals, unsupported by state authority. . . . The wrongful act of an individual, unsupported by any such authority, is simply a private wrong, or a crime of that individual, an invasion of the rights of the injured party, it is true, whether they affect his person, his property or his reputation; but if not sanctioned in some way by the State, or not done under state authority, his rights remain in full force and may presumably be vindicated by resort to the laws of the State for redress.[20]

In dissent, Justice John Marshall Harlan lamented:

Constitutional provisions, adopted in the interest of liberty, and for the purpose of securing, through national legislation, if need be, rights inhering in a state of freedom and belonging to American citizenship, have been so construed as to defeat the ends the people desired to accomplish, which they attempted to accomplish, and which they supposed they had accomplished by changes in their fundamental law.

Harlan viewed Congress as authorized under both the Thirteenth and Fourteenth Amendments to pass legislation barring private racial discrimination.

If, then, exemption from discrimination, in respect of civil rights, is a new constitutional right . . . and I do not see how this can now be questioned . . . why may not the Nation, by means of its own legislation of a primary direct character, guard, protect and enforce that right? It is a right and privilege which the nation conferred.[21]

Harlan's dissent had no effect on his colleagues. Thirteen years later he would again dissent alone, as the Court in the famous and since overruled case of *Plessy v. Ferguson* held state-imposed racial segregation no violation of the rights guaranteed to citizens by the Fourteenth Amendment. The majority found such segregation on railway cars a proper and reasonable exercise of the state police power.

Writing for the Court, Justice Henry B. Brown stated, "The object of the amendment was undoubtedly to enforce the absolute equality of the two races before the law, but in the nature of things, it could not have been intended to abolish distinctions based upon color, or to enforce social, as distinguished from political, equality."

Brown rejected the "assumption that the enforced separation of the two races stamps the colored race with a badge of inferiority." He continued:

If this be so, it is not by reason of anything found in the act, but solely because the colored race chooses to put that construction upon it. . . . The [plaintiff's] argument also assumes that social prejudices may be overcome by legislation, and that equal rights cannot be secured to the negro except by an enforced commingling of the two races. We cannot accept this proposition. If the two races are to meet on terms of social equality, it must be the result of natural affinities, a mutual appreciation of each other's merits and a voluntary consent of individuals.[22]

For sixty years *Plessy* would stand to allow states to enforce "separate but equal" rules, despite the Fourteenth Amendment's command of equal protection.

Not only did black citizens find little aid in the Court's view of the Fourteenth Amendment, but the same plight also afflicted women. In 1873 the Court refused to apply the Fourteenth Amendment's privileges and immunities clause to require a state to license a woman to practice law in its courts.[23] And two years later it ruled that a state did not deny a woman privileges and immunities guaranteed by the Fourteenth Amendment by refusing to allow her to vote.[24]

Charles Warren comments that by 1875, the year of this ruling, "it now became evident that the privileges and immunities clause of the Amendment, as construed by the Court, afforded slight protection to an individual and no protection to a corporation, affected by oppressive state legislation.[25]

State laws discriminating against aliens also were not doomed by the Fourteenth Amendment. In only one ruling during the late nineteenth century did the Court strike down any municipal ordinance or state law as denying aliens equal protection of the law.[26]

And the Fourteenth Amendment was of no aid to criminal defendants in state courts. In 1884 the Court refused to use the Fourteenth Amendment's due process guarantee to require that a state, in prosecuting someone for a capital crime, first obtain a grand jury indictment.[27]

THE RIGHT TO VOTE

"The right of citizens of the United States to vote shall not be denied or abridged by the United States or by any State on account of race, color, or previous condition of servitude," states the first section of the Fifteenth Amendment. The second section gives Congress the power to enforce that ban.

This constitutional protection also diminished during the postwar years. The Supreme Court, in 1876, handed down a pair of decisions that effectively nullified the 1870 law Congress had passed to enforce the guarantee of the right to vote.

"Exemption from Discrimination"

Adhering closely to the wording of the amendment, the Court in *United States v. Reese* struck down the parts of the law that provided punishment for state election officials who refused to accept or count black votes or who otherwise obstructed citizens from voting. The Court held that the penalties covered a broader range of behavior than that proscribed by the amendment, and hence must fall.

"The Fifteenth Amendment does not confer the right of suffrage upon anyone," wrote Chief Justice Morrison Waite for the Court. But, Waite continued, the "Amendment has invested the citizens of the United States with a new constitutional right which is within the protecting power of Congress. That right is exemption from discrimination in the exercise of the elective franchise on account of race, color or previous condition of servitude."

But the law at issue was too broad, covering actions outside the jurisdiction of Congress as well as those within. Therefore, it must be struck down: "Within its legitimate sphere, Congress is supreme and beyond the control of the courts; but if it steps outside of its constitutional limitation . . . the courts . . . must annul its encroachments upon the reserved power of the States and the people."[28]

The same day—March 27, 1876—the Court issued its opinion in *United States v. Cruikshank* in which the 1870 act had been used to bring charges against several people for violent and fraudulent actions to keep blacks from exercising a number of constitutional rights—among them the right of assembly, the right to petition for redress of grievances, the right to bear arms, and the right to vote. Again, the Court held that these actions were outside federal jurisdiction, that the rights allegedly interfered with were not federally protected rights, and that Congress could not prescribe punishment for those who violated them.

"The Government of the United States," wrote Chief Justice Waite,

is one of delegated powers alone. Its authority is defined and limited by the Constitution. All powers not granted to it by that instrument are reserved to the States or the people. No rights can be acquired under the Constitution or laws of the United States, except such as the Government of the United States has the authority to grant or secure. All that cannot be so granted or secured are left under the protection of the States.

The Fourteenth Amendment, the Chief Justice continued, "adds nothing to the rights of one citizen as against another. It simply furnishes an additional guarantee against any encroachment by the States upon the fundamental rights which belong to every citizen as a member of society."

Again, Waite made the point announced in *Reese:*

The right to vote in the States comes from the States; but the right of exemption from the prohibited discrimination comes from the United States. The first has not been granted or secured by the Constitution of the United States; but the last has been.

In this case there was no explicit charge that the fraud and violence that occurred had been intended to prevent blacks from voting on account of their race. "It does not appear," said Waite, "that it was their intent to interfere with any right granted or secured by the Constitution or laws of the United States." Although "[w]e may suspect that 'race' was the cause of the hostility; . . . it is not so averred."[29]

But the Court did not entirely undercut the force of the Fifteenth Amendment. In 1884 it upheld the convictions of several members of the Ku Klux Klan who had beaten up a black man to keep him from voting in federal elections. These convictions were obtained under the portions of the 1870 enforcement law that remained in effect after the Court's 1876 rulings in *Reese* and *Cruikshank.*

"If this government is anything more than a mere aggregation of delegated agents of other States and governments, each of which is superior to the General Government, it must have the power to protect the elections on which its existence depends from violence and corruption," wrote Justice Samuel Miller for the Court in *Ex parte Yarbrough* (1884).

In some circumstances, Miller continued, the Fifteenth Amendment did grant blacks the right to vote, "and Congress had the power to protect and enforce that right."[30]

Circumvention

Ex parte Yarbrough and federal enforcement power notwithstanding, the southern states adopted and used a number of devices that successfully kept most blacks from voting for about a century after the Civil War. Judicial action to outlaw these devices was belated.

The first such device to fall was the "grandfather" clause, setting some literacy or other standard that prospective voters must meet—unless they or their father or grandfather had been a registered voter in the years before adoption of the Fifteenth Amendment. In 1915 the Supreme Court struck down such a clause implemented by the state of Oklahoma, finding it a clear violation of the amendment.

Oklahoma then required all persons who had not voted in the 1914 election to register within two weeks in order to become voters. In 1939 the Court held this requirement also in violation of the amendment.[31]

The "white primary" was used effectively to disenfranchise blacks until the Court in 1944 held the "white primary" impermissible as a violation of the equal protection guarantee and the Fifteenth Amendment.[32]

In 1898 the Court held that neither poll taxes nor a literacy test violated the amendment, and as recently as 1960 the Supreme Court upheld a North Carolina literacy requirement for voters.[33] However, in 1964 the adoption of the Twenty-fourth Amendment forbade the use of poll taxes in federal elections, and in 1966 the Supreme Court held a state's poll tax for state elections a denial of equal protection.[34] Four years later the Court upheld a 1970 act of Congress suspending all use of literacy tests. Such a ban was a proper implementation of the Fifteenth Amendment, held the Court.[35]

And even before it moved into the general "political thicket" of reapportionment, the Court in 1960 struck down the racial gerrymandering of electoral districts as a violation of the Fifteenth Amendment guarantee.[36] (See "The Racial Gerrymander," pp. 512–513, in Chapter 10.)

After Joseph Lochner, the owner of a bakery located in Utica, New York, was convicted of violating a state maximum hour work law, he asked the Supreme Court to strike it down as violative of his constitutional rights. In *Lochner v. New York* (1905) the justices agreed. The majority found that the law impermissibly interfered with the right of employers to enter into contracts with their employees.

The Guarantee of Due Process

It was doubly ironic that the first extended use of the due process clause by the Supreme Court was to protect business against regulation by the state. This portion of the Fourteenth Amendment, which was enacted to protect individuals, was thereby turned into a shield for property. And the provision first tested before the Court in an unsuccessful effort to claim its protection for the right to carry on business would, by the end of the nineteenth century, take the place of the contract clause as business's most effective weapon against state regulation.

The first decision signaling this development appeared to be a defeat for propertied interests. In the 1897 case of *Allgeyer v. Louisiana,* the Court held that due process protected a citizen's right to do business with out-of-state as well as in-state insurance companies.

But in writing the Court's opinion, Justice Rufus Peckham set out for the first time from the bench the theory that the liberty protected by the due process guarantee of the Fourteenth Amendment included the right to make contracts, free of state interference.

Liberty, wrote Peckham, includes "not only the right of the citizen to be free from the merely physical restraint of his person . . . but the term is deemed to embrace the right of the citizen to be free in the enjoyment of all his faculties; to be free to use them in all lawful ways; to live and work where he will; to earn his livelihood by any lawful calling; to pursue any livelihood or avocation, and for that purpose to enter into all contracts which may be proper, necessary and essential to his carrying out to a successful conclusion the purposes above mentioned."[37]

Within that year the Court held that due process required a

state to compensate the owner of property taken for public use—by requiring a railroad to pay for crossing facilities and flagmen.[38] And in 1898 the Court held that courts should review the railroad rates set by state commissions to ensure that they did not deprive the railroad company of due process by failing to provide a fair return on its investment.[39]

From these precedents, the Court had little philosophical distance to travel to its 1905 ruling in *Lochner v. New York,* invalidating New York's maximum hours law for bakers as violating the freedom of contract and, hence, due process. *Lochner* was the first in a long series of rulings in which the Court used this theory to strike down state efforts to set maximum hours or minimum wages for workers. *(See "Bakery Workers: Lochner," p. 341.)*

This use of due process—to examine and test the constitutional validity of the substance of a law, not simply the procedures it provides—is called "substantive due process." The effect of its use during the early twentieth century is described by one scholar:

From the standpoint of the development of the federal system, the rise of substantive due process meant two things: one, that a national agency—the Supreme Court—was to decide (in many instances) what the states could and could not do; it thus meant a diminution of state autonomy. Second, to the extent that the Court used substantive due process to frustrate state attempts to regulate business, there would be more pressure exerted by nonbusiness interests for the national government to act, thus accelerating the march to Washington and the accretion of power in the hands of federal officials.

The conservative justices who espoused this use of substantive due process were "unwitting nationalists in the battle over the nature of the federal system."[40]

The Court continued to employ this approach—and the theory of freedom of contract—until the New Deal was well under way.

The Quiet Revolution

The first crack in the Court's refusal to apply the Bill of Rights to protect individuals against state action came quietly and with little argument. In 1925 the Court was considering Benjamin Gitlow's argument that his right to due process of law—and his First Amendment freedom of expression—were violated by the state of New York. Gitlow, a member of the Socialist Party, was indicted for publishing and distributing al-

legedly subversive documents. The charges were based on New York's criminal anarchy law, which forbade the use of language or the distribution of publications advocating the forcible overthrow of organized government.

Gitlow argued that this law also violated the due process guarantee because under it the state could punish someone for speaking his thoughts, without any evidence that concrete or substantive evil was likely to result from his words.

His argument simply assumed that the "liberty" protected by the Fourteenth Amendment's due process clause included the First Amendment guarantees of freedom of speech and of the press.

The Court upheld Gitlow's prosecution, finding the state law

THE STATE AND PRIVACY

A right of personal privacy, which protects the individual from the interference of the state, emerged as the basis for several Supreme Court decisions beginning in the 1960s. But this trend slowed in the 1980s, particularly after William H. Rehnquist, who has not acknowledged any such constitutional right, became chief justice.

The Court over the decades has struggled with the constitutional foundation for the right to privacy. Nevertheless, a majority of the justices has accepted that right and agreed that because of that right, it should strike down state laws prohibiting the use of contraceptives, criminalizing abortions, and criminalizing the mere possession of obscene material.

"We deal with a right of privacy older than the Bill of Rights," wrote Justice William O. Douglas when the Supreme Court struck down a Connecticut law forbidding the use—or counseling of the use—of contraceptives by anyone in the state.[1] Also suggested as the basis for this holding and this right were the due process guarantee of the Fourteenth Amendment, the "penumbra" of the privacy interests protected by the First, Third, Fourth, and Fifth Amendments, and the Ninth Amendment's statement that the enumeration of rights in the Constitution is not complete and exclusive and that other rights are "retained by the people."

In 1969 the Court held that a state could not forbid the possession of obscene material. The holding was based in part upon the fundamental First Amendment right "to receive information and ideas, regardless of their social worth," but also upon the "right to be free, except in very limited circumstances, from unwanted governmental intrusions into one's privacy." The state had no right to control the content of a person's thoughts, held the Court.[2]

And in the most controversial of the privacy-related rulings, the Court in 1973 used the right of privacy as the basis for its holding that states could not stand in the way of a woman who decided, early in a pregnancy, to terminate it through an abortion.[3]

Writing the Court's opinion in *Roe v. Wade*, Justice Harry A. Blackmun took note of the conflicting views on the foundation of the right and declared firmly that "[t]his right of privacy, whether it be founded in the Fourteenth Amendment's concept of personal liberty and restrictions upon state action, as we feel it is, or . . . in

the Ninth Amendment's reservation of rights to the people, is broad enough to encompass a woman's decision whether or not to terminate her pregnancy." The Court also recognized the right and interest of the state to regulate the factors or conditions governing the decision as pregnancy progressed toward the time at which a live child could be born and live outside the mother.

In 1989 the Court, 5–4, cut back sharply on the scope of the woman's right to privacy in having an abortion. It upheld a Missouri law that placed definite restrictions on that decision. The Court's primary opinion, written by Rehnquist, did not mention the right of privacy.[4] But in 1992, as the Court upheld additional state abortion regulations from Pennsylvania, it reaffirmed the core of *Roe v. Wade* allowing women a fundamental right to end an unwanted pregnancy.[5] The affirmation of *Roe* came on another bitter 5–4 vote—the outcome controlled by an unusual joint opinion by Justices Sandra Day O'Connor, Anthony M. Kennedy, and David H. Souter.

The separate privacy issue of homosexual rights first came to the Court in 1986. Again divided 5–4, the justices reversed a lower court's finding that the right of privacy protected private, consensual homosexual activity from being forbidden or punished by the state. Writing for the Court, Justice Byron R. White said that whatever constitutional right of privacy existed, and he—like Rehnquist—was dubious that one did, it did not protect the right to engage in homosexual conduct.[6]

A decade later when the Court invalidated a Colorado constitutional amendment prohibiting local gay-rights laws, the majority relied on equal protection grounds and did not cite *Bowers v. Hardwick* at all, raising questions about the long-term validity of the 1986 ruling.[7] *(See the discussion of the rights of homosexuals, pp. 693–695, in Chapter 12.)*

1. *Griswold v. Connecticut*, 381 U.S. 479 at 486 (1965).
2. *Stanley v. Georgia*, 394 U.S. 557 (1969)
3. *Roe v. Wade, Doe v. Bolton*, 410 U.S. 113 at 153 (1973).
4. *Webster v. Reproductive Health Services*, 492 U.S. 490 (1989).
5. *Planned Parenthood of Southeastern Pennsylvania v. Casey*, 505 U.S. 833 (1992).
6. *Bowers v. Hardwick*, 478 U.S. 186 (1986).
7. *Romer v. Evans*, ____ U.S. ____ (1996).

not in conflict with the due process guarantee. But in its opinion, written by conservative justice Edward Terry Sanford, the Court merely assumed that Gitlow was correct: the Fourteenth Amendment due process clause *did* apply the First Amendment's protections to persons threatened by state action.

"For present purposes," wrote Sanford, "we may and do assume that freedom of speech and of the press—which are protected by the 1st Amendment from abridgment by Congress—are among the fundamental personal rights and 'liberties' protected by the due process clause of the 14th Amendment from impairment by the states. . . ."[41] However, the Court held, the New York law did not violate those rights.

The door was thus opened to the gradual, case-by-case process of the following decades, as the Court would use the due process guarantee of the Fourteenth Amendment to apply to the states those protections of the Bill of Rights it found to be fundamental. Six years later, in the case of *Stromberg v. California* (1931), the Court for the first time struck down a state law as violating freedom of speech.[42]

The beneficiary of the ruling was Yetta Stromberg, a young woman who conducted a daily flag salute ceremony in a Young Communist League children's camp; the flags involved were those of Soviet Russia and the Communist Party. She was convicted of violating California's "red-flag" law, which forbade the display of a red flag for propaganda or protest purposes. The law denied Stromberg the freedom for political expression and discussion, wrote Chief Justice Charles Evans Hughes, finding it too broad to withstand challenge under the now-applicable First Amendment standards.

Freedom of the press also was now protected against state action. In 1931 the Court invalidated, for the first time, a state law as infringing on freedom of the press. Struck down by the Court was a Minnesota law that allowed a newspaper or magazine publishing scandalous, malicious, defamatory, or obscene material to be "padlocked" as a nuisance by an injunction. If the newspaper were published despite the injunction, the publisher could be convicted of contempt of court. The padlocking would end only if the judge approving it was convinced that the publication would be unobjectionable in the future.[43]

In 1934 the Court held that freedom of religion was protected against state action by the due process guarantee. In the particular case decided, the Court held that although the guarantee did apply, a state university did not abridge a student's freedom of religion by requiring him to take military drill.[44]

Three years later freedom of assembly was granted the same protection when the Court overturned the conviction of a Communist Party member for conducting a party meeting.[45]

And in 1947 the Court made clear that not only the First Amendment freedoms but also the First Amendment guarantee against establishment of religion was protected by due process.[46] Again the Court held that this guarantee was not infringed upon by a school board policy of reimbursing parents for the costs of transporting their children to school, parochial as well as public. This was the first in a long and complicated series of

rulings as the Court has worked to determine what forms of state aid might be constitutionally provided to church-related schools. (*See details of Everson v. Board of Education, pp. 490–492, in Chapter 9.*)

The Court then expanded the reach of the First Amendment protection against state action to encompass the expression of ideas in handbills, meetings, and demonstrations and participation in patriotic programs. (*See "Public Speech and Public Safety," pp. 427–435, in Chapter 9.*)

In 1938 the Court held that a city could not require everyone who wished to distribute any publication in the city—by hand or otherwise—to obtain written permission to do so. Overturning the conviction of a Jehovah's Witness for failing to obtain such permission, the Court held the ordinance a violation of the freedom of the press, a freedom that included "every sort of publication which affords a vehicle of information and opinion."[47]

In 1939 the justices held that a city could regulate but not absolutely deny the use of public parks, roads, and buildings to organizations wishing to use them for meetings and other forms of communication.[48]

Jehovah's Witnesses are taught that saluting a flag is contrary to the teachings of the Bible. The conflict between this teaching and the requirement of many public schools that children daily salute the U.S. flag came to the Court in the case of the *Minersville School District v. Gobitis*.

With its decision in this case, announced in 1940, the Court appeared to halt its expansion of First Amendment protection against state action. By an 8–1 vote, the Court rejected the argument that the flag salute requirement abridged the freedom of religion guaranteed to the children of Jehovah's Witnesses.[49]

But only three years later—in the middle of World War II—the Court reversed itself. In *West Virginia Board of Education v. Barnette* the Court ruled that the state could not compel children to participate in a patriotic ceremony when to do so violated their religious beliefs.

Justice Robert H. Jackson wrote for the Court:

If there is any fixed star in our constitutional constellation, it is that no official . . . can prescribe what shall be orthodox in politics, nationalism, religion or other matters. . . . We think the action of the local authorities in compelling the flag salute and pledge transcends constitutional limitations on their power and invades the sphere of intellect and spirit which it is the purpose of the First Amendment . . . to reserve from all official control.[50]

FAIR CRIMINAL PROCEDURES

After the Court began to extend First Amendment protections against state action, pressure began to build for a similar extension of other guarantees in the Bill of Rights, in particular those intended to protect persons charged with crimes.

Right to Counsel

In 1932 the Court began this process. The right first extended was the right to counsel, guaranteed in federal cases by the Sixth Amendment. The case was that of the black "Scottsboro boys" charged with raping two white women on a freight train passing through Alabama. Taken off the train and jailed in Scottsboro, the black men were never asked whether they wished to have the aid of lawyers, and the first case came to trial with no defense attorney present. Lawyers eventually did act as defense counsel; the defendants were convicted.

The Supreme Court reversed their convictions, holding in *Powell v. Alabama* that the denial of the right to the effective aid of legal counsel was, in the circumstances of this case, a denial of due process under the Fourteenth Amendment. Writing for the Court, Justice George Sutherland declared:

[I]n a capital case, where the defendant is unable to employ counsel, and is incapable adequately of making his own defense because of ignorance, feeblemindedness, illiteracy, or the like, it is the duty of the court, whether requested or not, to assign counsel for him as a necessary requisite of due process of law; and that duty is not discharged by an assignment at such a time or under such circumstances as to preclude the giving of effective aid in the preparation and trial of the case. To hold otherwise would be to ignore the fundamental postulate . . . "that there are certain immutable principles of justice which inhere in the very idea of free government which no member of the Union may disregard."[51]

Ten years later the Court limited the effect of this holding by ruling in *Betts v. Brady* that "[t]he due process clause of the Fourteenth Amendment does not incorporate, as such, the specific guarantees found in the Sixth Amendment although a denial by a state of rights or privileges specifically embodied in that . . . may . . . operate, in a given case, to deprive a litigant of due process of law." Thus the justices refused to require that the state must always furnish counsel to a defendant charged with a crime and unable to employ his own lawyer.[52]

But thirty-one years after *Powell,* in 1963, the Supreme Court overruled *Betts v. Brady* and held that the Sixth Amendment right to counsel was incorporated in the due process clause and that every defendant in a state criminal trial, just as in a federal trial, was guaranteed representation by counsel whom he employed or who was appointed for him by the court. This ruling came in *Gideon v. Wainwright.*[53] *(See details of Powell v. Alabama, Betts v. Brady, and Gideon v. Wainwright, pp. 599–602, in Chapter 11.)*

Judge and Jury

Early in the century the Court extended to state courts the requirement that a person tried for a crime be tried by an impartial judge. In 1927 the Court struck down an Ohio law that allowed a city's mayor to try bootleggers and to put half the fines assessed and collected into the city coffers.

"It certainly violates the Fourteenth Amendment," wrote Chief Justice William Howard Taft, "and deprives a defendant in a criminal case of due process of law, to subject his liberty or property to the judgment of a court the judge of which has a direct, personal, substantial pecuniary interest in reaching a conclusion against him."[54]

Although it was not until 1968 that the right to a jury trial was extended to state criminal defendants, the Court held

decades earlier that if a jury was provided, it must be fairly chosen. In 1923 the Court ruled that five black men convicted in Arkansas of murdering a white man were denied due process because of the atmosphere in which their jury was selected and their trial conducted.

And in another case arising out of the prosecution of the Scottsboro boys, the Court reversed their convictions after a second trial. Due process had been denied them, the Court said, because blacks had been excluded from the juries that indicted and tried them. Subsequently, the Court ruled that indictments of blacks by grand juries from which blacks were excluded were invalid.[55]

In two decisions in 1876 and 1900 the Court held that the Fourteenth Amendment did not require states to provide jury trials to individuals accused of crimes, although the Sixth Amendment provided such a guarantee for those charged with federal crimes. In 1968, in *Duncan v. Louisiana,* the Court reversed those earlier rulings and extended the jury trial guarantee to state criminal defendants.[56] *(See "State Trials," pp. 564–565, in Chapter 11.)*

Earlier, in 1965, the Court had applied still another element of the fair trial guarantee to state courts—the right to confront witnesses against oneself.[57]

Fifth Amendment Protections

Few constitutional guarantees have generated as much controversy as the Fifth Amendment right not to be forced to incriminate oneself.

One aspect of this right is the right to remain silent when accused, and to refuse to testify in one's own defense. In 1908 the Court held that this privilege was not protected in state proceedings by the due process guarantee. The Court declined to forbid a state judge to comment on a defendant's silence.[58]

More than fifty years later, in 1964, the Court overruled that holding. In *Malloy v. Hogan* the justices extended the Fifth Amendment protection to persons charged with state crimes. The following year the Court held it unfair for a judge or prosecutor to comment adversely during a trial upon a defendant's failure to testify in his or her own behalf.[59]

As early as 1936 the Court began to use the Fifth Amendment to forbid the use of forced confessions in state trials. That year the Court reversed the murder convictions of three blacks because they were based in part upon confessions extracted from them through torture, a clear denial of due process.[60]

Malloy v. Hogan and *Gideon v. Wainwright* were combined by the Court into a foundation for two of its most criticized rulings of the 1960s. In *Escobedo v. Illinois* the Court ruled that a confession of murder could not be used against Danny Escobedo because it was obtained after intensive police interrogation during which the accused was denied his request to see a lawyer. The confession, therefore, was obtained in clear violation of his constitutional right to counsel and could not properly be used against him, held the Court.[61]

Two years later, with its decision in *Miranda v. Arizona,* the

Court kindled further controversy. Applying this "exclusionary rule" against illegally or unconstitutionally obtained evidence, the Court held that confessions could not be used as evidence if they were obtained from suspects interrogated by police without being advised of their rights to remain silent and to obtain legal counsel.

In *Miranda* the Court required that police inform individuals who were held in custody of their right to remain silent, of the fact that anything they said could be used against them in court, and of their right to have assistance of counsel before and during interrogation, even if they could not afford to hire an attorney themselves.[62]

Law enforcement officials charged that such decisions made their tasks impossible. Congress considered acting to reverse the rulings, and the decisions were criticized again and again during the 1968 presidential campaign.

A less controversial portion of the Fifth Amendment protects people against being tried twice for the same action by the same sovereign. Because the federal system includes two systems of justice, one state and one national, everyone is subject to both criminal jurisdictions and may—without violating this guarantee—be tried by both for crimes arising from the same actions.[63]

Not until 1969 did the Court extend the guarantee against double jeopardy to protect defendants from being tried twice by a state for the same actions. Thirty-two years earlier the Court had held that this guarantee did not protect state defendants. In *Palko v. Connecticut* (1937) Justice Benjamin Cardozo explained why the Court viewed some of the guarantees of the Bill of Rights as applicable to the states while others were not. Certain rights, like the right to a jury trial, were valuable, he wrote, yet "they are not of the very essence of a scheme of ordered liberty. To abolish them is not to violate a 'principle of justice so rooted in the traditions and conscience of our people as to be ranked as fundamental.'"

Other rights, which are applied to the states through the Fourteenth Amendment, are of such importance, wrote Cardozo, "that neither liberty nor justice would exist if they were sacrificed. . . . This is true, for illustration, of freedom of thought and speech."

In 1969 the Court overruled this holding to the extent it restricted the double jeopardy guarantee to federal defendants. In *Benton v. Maryland* the Court held that this guarantee was indeed fundamental to the American system of justice.[64] *(See "Double Jeopardy," pp. 605–607, in Chapter 11.)*

Unreasonable Search and Seizure

The Fourth Amendment protects citizens from searches and seizures that are unreasonable. In 1949 a Colorado abortionist challenged his conviction because it was based on records seized from his office by officers acting without a warrant. The Supreme Court stated that the Fourth Amendment freedom from unreasonable searches was a necessary part of the concept of "ordered liberty"—to which Cardozo had referred in *Palko*—

and thus was protected by the Fourteenth Amendment against state action.[65]

As early as 1914 the Court had held that evidence obtained in searches violating the Fourth Amendment could not be used in federal courts.[66] But in this 1949 state case, the Court did not forbid the use of evidence even if it was unconstitutionally obtained.

In 1961 the Court reversed this stance and excluded illegally obtained evidence from use at state trials as well as federal ones. In the Court's opinion in *Mapp v. Ohio*, Justice Tom C. Clark explained:

The ignoble shortcut to conviction left open to the State [by the Court's failure to apply the exclusionary rule earlier] tends to destroy the entire system of constitutional restraints on which the liberties of the people rest. Having once recognized that the right to privacy embodied in the Fourth Amendment is enforceable against the States, and that the right to be secure against rude invasions of privacy by state officers is, therefore, constitutional in origin, we can no longer permit that right to remain an empty promise.[67]

The Fourth Amendment forbids only *unreasonable* searches and seizures. A long line of cases raises the question of what is *reasonable* in various circumstances. In 1963 the Court held that the same standards were to be used to judge the reasonableness of searches and seizures by state as by federal officers.[68] Subsequently, the Court has upheld as reasonable "stop-and-frisk" searches by police, searches of the area within reach of a recently arrested suspect, and certain car searches—all without warrants.[69] *(See "Search and Seizure," pp. 573–588, in Chapter 11.)*

Cruel Punishment

The Eighth Amendment forbids cruel and unusual punishment.

In a bizarre Louisiana case, Willie Francis, a convicted murderer, prepared for his death by electrocution, sat in the portable electric chair, heard the switch pulled—and nothing happened. The chair failed to function. Francis was then returned to his cell to await repair of the chair and a second "execution." In the meantime, he challenged this "sentence" as cruel and unusual punishment.

The Supreme Court assumed, but did not actually rule, that the Eighth Amendment applied to the states. But even if the standard applied, the justices found that it had not been violated in Francis's case.[70]

In 1962 the Court directly applied this prohibition to the states. It struck down a California law that made drug addiction a crime.[71]

During the 1970s the Court considered two sets of cases challenging the death penalty as cruel and unusual—and unconstitutional—punishment. In the first set, decided in 1972, the Court effectively invalidated all existing capital punishment laws by holding that the procedures they provided to guide judges and juries imposing the death sentence violated due process. The procedures left so much discretion to the judge or jury imposing the sentence, held the Court, that the result was a system under which receiving a death sentence was as arbitrary and irrational as being struck by lightning.[72]

Four years later the Court held that death, in and of itself, was not an unconstitutionally cruel and unusual punishment for those convicted of first-degree murder. But it did strike down laws that made death the mandatory sentence for someone convicted of first-degree murder. The due process guarantee, the Court held, required individualized consideration of a crime and the criminal, before such a final sentence was imposed.[73]

Other state penalties also have been measured by the Court against the ban on cruel and unusual punishment, and the Court has found it difficult to resolve some of those questions. In 1980 it voted 5–4 to permit a state to impose a mandatory life sentence upon a man convicted of three relatively petty nonviolent crimes; but three years later the Court, again 5–4, reversed its earlier holding. In *Solem v. Helm* the Court held that South Dakota violated this ban by imposing a life sentence without parole on a man convicted on seven separate occasions of nonviolent felonies.[74]

Juvenile Rights

The Court also has extended certain of the guarantees of the Bill of Rights to juvenile court proceedings. They include the right of a juvenile to be notified of charges against him, to have the aid of counsel, to confront witnesses against him, to be informed of his right to remain silent, and to be found guilty—or delinquent—beyond a reasonable doubt.

The Court has refused, however, to extend the right to a jury trial to juvenile court proceedings, which by their nature are less formal than regular criminal court proceedings. To require a jury trial, the Court reasoned, would unnecessarily rigidify and formalize the operations of the juvenile courts. In one of its more recent rulings concerning state powers to deal with juveniles accused of crimes, the Court upheld New York's law permitting pretrial detention of juveniles when there is a high risk they may commit serious crimes before trial.[75]

THE GUARANTEE OF EQUAL PROTECTION

For the first seventy years after it became a part of the Constitution, the Fourteenth Amendment's guarantee of equal protection of the laws seemed useless. Despite it, the Court steadfastly upheld the "separate but equal" segregation codes of the southern states. And in only one of the first ten cases brought under this provision, did a challenge to a state law succeed.[76]

Not until 1938 did the Court begin reexamining segregation laws with an eye to the equality they were supposed to preserve. Not until the civil rights revolution of the 1950s and 1960s did the equal protection clause take on the meaning its authors had intended.

Voting Rights

The right to vote—for which the Court had provided only narrow federal protection under the Fifteenth Amendment—was brought within the protection of the Fourteenth Amendment by a series of rulings culminating in the Court's famous "one person, one vote" edict of 1964.

White Primaries. But before the Court addressed directly the issue of malapportionment, it confronted one of the most effective antiblack electoral devices—the white primary.

In a campaign spending case decided in 1921, the Court appeared to limit federal regulation of elections to the final general election of an officer, excluding any regulation of primary contests.[77] With this understanding, many states in the South felt free to forbid blacks to vote in Democratic primaries, which in most of the South were the actual election because little or no Republican opposition to a Democratic nominee ever surfaced.

The first time that such a white primary law came to the Court, in 1927, the Court struck it down as a clear violation of the equal protection guarantee.[78] Texas, the state involved in that case, next passed a law empowering the state's political parties to set the qualifications for primary voters; the Democratic Party then exercised that power to exclude blacks from eligibility as primary voters. In 1932 the Court held that law unconstitutional. The party had acted as the agent of the state, it held, and thus the party's action fell under the equal protection clause with which it clearly conflicted.[79]

Persisting in its effort to keep black voters from participating in its electoral processes, the Texas Democratic Party then voted to confine party membership to whites. Because there was no connection to the state in this case, the Supreme Court upheld that exclusion in its decision in *Grovey v. Townsend* in 1935.[80]

But this form of discrimination did not survive much longer. In 1941 the Court held that primary elections were, in many states, an integral part of the process of electing members of Congress. Therefore, Congress had the authority to regulate such primaries. Three years later, with the case of *Smith v. Allwright,* the Court reversed *Grovey.* It redefined state action to include political parties that followed state regulation of primary elections and thereby became state agencies, in that respect. Racial discrimination by political parties in primary voting came under the ban of the Fifteenth Amendment.[81] (See "White Primaries," pp. 509–511, in Chapter 10.)

Poll Taxes and Literacy Tests. In the late nineteenth century the Court had upheld the use of a poll tax and an "understanding" or literacy test to screen out incompetent persons who wished to vote. In 1964, after such devices had been abandoned by most states, the Twenty-fourth Amendment was added to the Constitution to prohibit the use of poll taxes to abridge the right to vote in federal elections. And in 1966 the Court struck down poll tax requirements for state elections, finding them a violation of the equal protection guarantee.[82]

Voting Rights Act. The continuing success of many southern states in keeping black citizens from voting moved Congress during the 1950s and 1960s to enact progressively stronger civil rights laws authorizing federal action to counter such obstruction. By 1965, however, the lack of success of these new laws—coupled with the brutal response in the South to black demonstrations for equal rights—made it clear that Congress must act forcefully.

The result was the Voting Rights Act of 1965, which prohibited the use of any test or device as a qualification for voting in any state where less than half the voting age population was registered—or voted—at the time of the 1964 presidential election. That test applied the act to six southern states and a number of counties in other states. South Carolina, one of the affected states, immediately challenged the act as a violation of the Tenth Amendment, which reserves to the states any powers not delegated to the United States—in this case the power to set voter qualifications. A three-judge federal court agreed with the state, but the Supreme Court did not. The justices upheld the law as an appropriate exercise of congressional power to enforce the Fifteenth Amendment.[83]

Reapportionment Revolution

The most far-reaching extension of Supreme Court power into state affairs mandated by the Court under Chief Justice Earl Warren came with its reapportionment rulings. In 1962 the Court ended years of abstention from the sensitive political issue of redistricting and reapportionment and agreed to assess the fairness of congressional and state legislative district lines.

Only sixteen years earlier, in the case of *Colegrove v. Green,* the Court had refused to intervene in such matters, despite enormous disparity in population between state electoral districts. Justice Felix Frankfurter had explained:

From the determination of such issues this Court has traditionally held aloof. It is hostile to a democratic system to involve the judiciary in the politics of the people. . . .Courts ought not to enter this political thicket. The remedy for unfairness in districting is to secure State legislatures that will apportion properly, or to invoke the ample powers of Congress.[84]

But less than twenty years later the Court reversed that holding to rule that challenges to the fairness of the apportionment of state legislatures were, in fact, proper matters for the federal courts to resolve.

In the landmark case *Baker v. Carr,* the Court directed a lower federal court to hear the challenge of certain Tennessee voters that the malapportionment of the state legislature denied them equal protection of laws under the Fourteenth Amendment. At that time the Tennessee legislature had not been reapportioned for more than sixty years, during which there had been substantial shifts in population, chiefly from rural to urban areas.

Writing for the Court, Justice William J. Brennan Jr. reviewed the history of the "political question" doctrine of judicial restraint. He concluded that the equal protection claim here did not require decision of any truly political question and that the case was not removed from the purview of federal courts by the fact that it affected state government. "The right asserted is within the reach of judicial protection under the Fourteenth Amendment," he stated.[85]

"One Person, One Vote" Rule. The following year the Court struck down Georgia's county unit system of electing state offi-

cials and set out the guidelines for the fair apportionment of legislative representation:

Once the geographical unit for which a representative is to be chosen is designated, all who participate in the election are to have an equal vote—whatever their race, whatever their sex, whatever their occupation, whatever their income and wherever their home may be in that geographical unit. This is required by the Equal Protection Clause of the Fourteenth Amendment.

Writing for the Court in this case, Justice William O. Douglas concluded with the statement:

The conception of political equality from the Declaration of Independence, to Lincoln's Gettysburg Address, to the Fifteenth, Seventeenth, and Nineteenth Amendments can mean only one thing—one person, one vote.[86]

The following year this standard was applied by the Court to require congressional redistricting and state legislative reapportionment.[87]

Although in subsequent cases the Court set the strict rule of mathematical equality for newly drawn districts, it relaxed that standard in 1973 for state legislative districts. It approved the creation of districts that were "as nearly of equal population as practicable" and allowed some legitimately based divergence from strict equality.[88] *(See "State Districts: More Leeway," pp. 526–531, in Chapter 10.)*

Political and Racial Gerrymandering. The Court in 1986 opened the door to a whole new set of decisions dealing with political gerrymanders. In a case from Indiana, *Davis v. Bandemer,* the Court responded to a challenge by the state's Democrats to a map of state legislative districts drawn by Republicans. For the first time the Court held that political gerrymanders were subject to review by the federal courts—even if they met the "one person, one vote" test.[89]

Seven years later, in a critical decision leading to more reapportionment litigation, the Court ruled that white voters could challenge irregularly shaped "majority-minority" districts that apparently were drawn only to separate voters by race. Such districts were created in many states to enhance the political power of traditionally underrepresented constituencies. But the five-justice majority in *Shaw v. Reno* said racial gerrymanders in "majority-minority" districts may exacerbate the very patterns of racial bloc voting that they were intended to counteract.[90] *(See details of this case, pp. 529–530.)*

Housing, Schools, and Marriage

Even before the Court began to wield the equal protection clause in behalf of voters, it began to use it to strike down the racial segregation that had come to characterize so many parts of American life after the Civil War.

As early as 1917 the Court made its first move against housing segregation. In that year it struck down a Louisville, Kentucky, residential segregation ordinance as an unconstitutional interference with the right of a property owner to sell his real estate to whomever he pleased.

But what could not be accomplished legally by city action

could be achieved by private agreement, and so "restrictive covenants" flourished. A purchaser accepting a contract or title with such a covenant agreed not to sell the real estate to a black person. This maneuver was clearly private action, unreachable under the Fourteenth Amendment, according to the *Civil Rights Cases* decision. Yet in 1948 the Court effectively circumvented the "private action" limitation by holding that any state action to enforce such a covenant would violate the Fourteenth Amendment.[91]

In subsequent rulings the Court held that state voters could not amend their constitution to restrict the efforts of state or local government to end racial discrimination, nor could they require that all fair housing laws be approved by referendum. Where discrimination is not clearly based on race, however, the Court has hesitated to strike down such voter-approval requirements or to overturn local decisions concerning housing.[92]

Early in the twentieth century the Court extended its tolerance of segregation, signaled by the "separate but equal" holding of *Plessy v. Ferguson,* to schools. It upheld a Kentucky law that forbade colleges to teach whites and blacks at the same time and in the same place.[93]

School segregation began to come under scrutiny by the Supreme Court in the 1930s, beginning at the graduate school level. In 1938 the Court held that a state providing graduate education in law to white students must, under the equal protection guarantee, offer substantially similar education to black state residents. The Court rejected the state's offer to pay a black student's tuition in an out-of-state law school. The state was obligated, held the Court in *Missouri ex rel. Gaines v. Canada,* to provide equal protection within its own borders.

Chief Justice Charles Evans Hughes wrote:

That obligation is imposed by the Constitution upon the States severally as governmental entities,—each responsible for its own laws establishing the rights and duties of persons within its borders. It is an obligation the burden of which cannot be cast by one State upon another. . . . That separate responsibility of each State within its own sphere is of the essence of statehood.[94]

This holding was reaffirmed in 1948. And in 1950 the Court struck down one state university's practice of making a black graduate student sit at special seats and tables in classrooms, the cafeteria, and the library.[95]

On the same day as the latter ruling, the Court ordered the University of Texas Law School to admit a qualified black student. The newly created "black" law school in the state did not provide equal opportunity for a legal education, held the Court. A qualified black student had a constitutional right to a state-provided legal education equal to that offered to qualified white students, the justices stated in *Sweatt v. Painter.*[96]

Then, in 1954, the Court extended this principle to elementary and secondary education with the famous decisions known as *Brown v. Board of Education of Topeka.*[97] The "separate but equal" doctrine as applied to public schools was ruled a clear denial of equal protection of the laws. *Plessy v. Ferguson* was overruled.

The southern states reacted belligerently. The following year, in the second *Brown* decision, the Court required states to move with "all deliberate speed" to carry out the mandate to end public school segregation.[98]

Implementation was slow and painful, continuing for decades after the ruling. In a long line of follow-up rulings, the Court steadfastly rejected state and local efforts to obstruct or circumvent its requirements and made clear that it would sanction substantial changes in and costs to a school system as the price for carrying out the edict of *Brown.* Although *Brown,* decided upon an equal protection basis, dealt with states where segregated schools had been required by law, the Court did not hesitate to require an end to public school segregation in states that had not had such laws.[99]

And in still another use of the equal protection clause to end state discrimination, the Court in 1967 held that the Fourteenth Amendment guarantee was violated by a state law that prohibited the intermarriage of persons of different races.[100]

Rich and Poor

The Court has been more reluctant to strike down discrimination based on economic status than that based on race. In 1973, for example, it refused to invalidate the property tax–based systems through which most states finance their public schools. Texas's financing system had been challenged as denying equal protection to students who lived in poorer districts where the property tax produced less revenue. "The consideration and initiation of fundamental reforms with respect to state taxation and education are matters reserved for the legislative process of the different states," wrote Justice Lewis F. Powell Jr. for the Court, refusing to intervene.[101]

But the Court has held that the equal protection guarantee forbids states to deny divorces to people too poor to pay the usual court fees, or to require poor people to stay in prison to "work off" a fine they cannot pay while people who can pay the fine are released earlier, even when convicted of the same offense.

A state must provide a poor defendant a free transcript of his trial when such is necessary for him to appeal his conviction, and it must provide legal counsel to all persons charged with any offense for which they are imprisoned and who cannot afford to pay their own attorney.[102]

The Rights of Aliens

The only successful equal protection challenge among the first cases brought to the Supreme Court in the decade after the Fourteenth Amendment was added to the Constitution involved the rights of aliens. Yick Wo, a Chinese resident of San Francisco, was denied the license necessary to run a laundry in the city, as were all other Chinese laundry operators. Although the license requirement was superficially nondiscriminatory, it obviously was enforced in such a way as to deny equal protection. The Supreme Court struck it down in 1886.[103]

The Court, out of respect for the state's right to control property and resources within its territory, has upheld state laws requiring that all persons working on its public works projects be citizens, and denying to aliens (who were ineligible to become citizens) the right to acquire certain state land. But the Court has never given a state carte blanche to discriminate against lawfully admitted aliens.[104]

In 1915 the Court used the equal protection guarantee to void an Arizona law requiring that employers hire four citizens for every alien they employed.[105]

And in 1948 the Court struck down a California law that denied aliens ineligible for citizenship the right to obtain the licenses necessary to earn a living as commercial fishermen. The guarantee of equal protection, stated the Court, meant that "all persons lawfully in this country shall abide 'in any state' on an equality of legal privileges with all citizens under nondiscriminatory law." A state could not deny aliens the right to earn a living in the same way citizens did.[106]

The same year another California law fell before an equal protection challenge from aliens. That law—intended to prevent alien parents from buying land through their native-born citizen children—forbade ineligible aliens to pay for land being sold to a citizen.[107]

In the 1970s the Court further expanded the rights of aliens, even, in some cases, to receive benefits provided by a state. The Court held that states could not deny resident aliens welfare benefits, the right to practice law in the state, or the right to be considered for state civil service jobs. In 1977 the Court held that a state could not exclude resident aliens from eligibility for state scholarships, and in 1982 it said a state could not deny illegal alien children a free public education. Conversely, in 1978 and 1979, the Court upheld New York laws requiring state police officers and public school teachers to be citizens.[108] *(See "The Modern Standard," pp. 671–672, in Chapter 12.)*

The Rights of Women

Women as a class have been the least successful of the plaintiffs under the equal protection clause. As noted earlier, their efforts to use other portions of the Fourteenth Amendment to challenge state refusals to admit women to the practice of law or to register women to vote were rejected by the Court in the nineteenth century. *(See "'Romantic' Paternalism," pp. 677–678, in Chapter 12.)*

In 1904 the Court not only rejected an equal protection challenge to a state law forbidding women to work in saloons, but went on to hold that a state could by law bar women from even entering such places. As recently as 1948, the Court again upheld a state law forbidding women to work as barmaids, unless they were married to or the child of the bar owner.[109]

Sex was simply considered a valid reason for state discrimination. In 1961 the Court upheld a Florida law that "exempted" women from jury duty on the basis of their function as "the center of home and family life."[110]

Ten years later, however, the Court began to apply the equal protection test more strictly against state laws that discriminated simply on the basis of sex. In a case involving the appointment of an executor for a deceased child, the Court struck down an Idaho law that gave preference to male relatives over female relatives in selecting among equally qualified executors. "To give mandatory preference to members of either sex over members of the other, merely to accomplish the elimination of hearing on the merits, is to make the very kind of arbitrary legislative choice forbidden by the Equal Protection Clause," wrote Chief Justice Warren E. Burger for the Court.[111]

And four years later the Court overruled its 1961 decision concerning women and jury duty, holding that state laws exempting women from jury duty violated the requirement that a jury be drawn from a fair cross-section of the community. Such a general exclusion of women from the group eligible for jury duty was not rational, held the Court.[112]

Also in 1975 the Court overturned a Utah law that set different ages at which men and women were considered adults. In 1976 it struck down an Oklahoma law setting different drinking ages for men and women, and in 1977 an Alabama law which, by setting minimum height and weight requirements for prison guards, effectively denied such jobs to most women in the state.[113]

But the Court did not, in its important sex bias rulings of the last decades of the twentieth century, adopt the stiff standard for testing sex discrimination by states that it used to judge race discrimination. States merely had to prove that laws discriminating on the basis of sex were reasonable and related to the achievement of important governmental goals. But a law discriminating on the basis of race would be held constitutional only if it was found necessary to serve a compelling state interest.

Further, the Court still maintained some vestiges of the view that women should be protected. In 1974, with Justice Douglas, a liberal, writing the opinion, the Court upheld a Florida law giving widows—but not widowers—a special property tax exemption.[114] And in 1977, after striking down the height and weight requirements for prison guards, the Court nevertheless upheld a state regulation excluding women from certain prison guard jobs, holding that their sex made them vulnerable to attack in all-male prisons and thus disqualified them for the job of preserving security there.[115]

The Court also was reluctant to make states revise their disability insurance programs to include coverage for pregnant women unable to work for a time during or after pregnancy and childbirth. The decision to exclude women in this category from coverage of an otherwise comprehensive plan was upheld by the Court as rational in light of the state's fiscal objectives.[116]

In the late twentieth century this area of the law was still evolving. Justice Ruth Bader Ginsburg, who as a lawyer had urged the Court to be more aggressive in its scrutiny of sex classifications, wrote in 1994, "[E]ven under the Court's equal protection jurisprudence, which requires 'an exceedingly persuasive justification,' it remains an open question whether 'classifications based upon gender are inherently suspect.'"[117]

In 1996 Ginsburg was the author of a decision against the men-only admissions policy of the state-funded Virginia Military Institute. Although Bader used "intermediate," rather than "strict," scrutiny—which was likely to win support from a majority of justices—she again emphasized that a state must show an "exceedingly persuasive justification" for any classification based on sex.[118]

The State as Sovereign

With the firm establishment of the Court's power of judicial review of state action, of Congress's broad power over interstate and foreign commerce, and of the application of many of the provisions of the Bill of Rights to state action, what rights or powers do the states have left?

The Constitution provides a partial answer. The Tenth Amendment declares that the powers not given to the federal government by the Constitution nor removed from the arsenal of the states by the Constitution are reserved for the states and the people. The Eleventh Amendment grants states freedom from being unwillingly hauled into federal court by citizens having nonconstitutional complaints.

And the Court itself, while ever maintaining the framework of federal supremacy, has affirmed a variety of powers for the states—the power over elections, the powers of their courts, the broad police power over their land and people, the power to tax, and the power to form compacts with other states for the resolution of matters of mutual concern.

The well-founded fear of the original thirteen states that a strong national government would limit their own power and sovereignty was a major obstacle to ratification of the Constitution. James Madison wrote in *The Federalist Papers* to calm such fears:

The powers delegated by the proposed Constitution to the federal government are few and defined. Those which are to remain in the State governments are numerous and indefinite. The former will be exercised principally on external objects, as war, peace, negotiation, and foreign commerce; with which last the power of taxation will, for the most part, be connected. The powers reserved to the several States will extend to all the objects which, in the ordinary course of affairs, concern the lives, liberties, and properties of the people, and the internal order, improvement and prosperity of the State.[1]

Reserved State Powers

To write this view into the Constitution, the first Congress approved the Tenth Amendment, which states: "The powers not delegated to the United States by the Constitution, nor prohibited by it to the States, are reserved to the States respectively, or to the people."

In an action that would gain significance with the years, Congress, before approving this provision, rejected an amendment that would have inserted the word "expressly" before the word "delegated." Such an insertion, if approved, would have severely limited—or altogether prevented—any expansion of national power through the doctrine of implied powers.

Until well into the twentieth century, the Tenth Amendment was wielded, with varying degrees of success, to curtail federal power, particularly federal power over the economy in areas claimed to be reserved for state regulation. The subjects thus "reserved" ranged from child labor to farm production.

But the first effort to use the Tenth Amendment to curtail federal power was a distinct failure. Maryland based its challenge to the Second Bank of the United States upon the argument that the Constitution did not grant Congress the power to create corporations and that the Tenth Amendment thereby reserved such power to the states. Furthermore, the state argued that the power of taxation, except for taxes on imports and exports, was reserved to the state, giving Maryland the right to tax the bank if Congress had the right to create it.

Speaking for the Court, Chief Justice John Marshall in 1819 firmly rejected both prongs of the state's argument—and the concept that the Tenth Amendment provided the states with an instrument to limit national power. "[T]he states have no power, by taxation or otherwise, to retard, impede, burden, or in any manner control the operations of the constitutional laws enacted by Congress to carry into execution the powers vested in the general government," Marshall wrote. And the absence of the word "expressly" from the amendment left it up to the Court to decide if a particular power had been granted the national government—a decision to be made in light of its interpretation of the constitutional system as a whole.[2]

Five years later, in 1824, Marshall felt it necessary, in concluding his opinion in the New York steamboat case, to issue a further warning against a broad interpretation of the Tenth Amendment:

Powerful and ingenious minds, taking as postulates, that the powers expressly granted to the government of the Union are to be contracted . . . into the narrowest possible compass, and that the original powers of the States are retained, if any possible construction will retain them, may . . . explain away the constitution . . . and leave it a magnificent structure indeed, to look at, but totally unfit for use.[3]

"DUAL FEDERALISM"

During the tenure of Marshall's successor, Chief Justice Roger B. Taney, Tenth Amendment arguments received a friendlier hearing, and the Court began to develop the concept of "dual federalism." In this view, the respective domains of state and federal government are neatly defined: each government is sovereign and supreme within its own sphere, and the enumerated powers of the central government are limited by the reserved powers of the state.

During its laissez-faire period in the early part of the twentieth century, the Court used the Tenth Amendment to limit federal power, even while it used the concept of due process to limit state power to regulate property, thus creating a "twilight zone" within the economy where no effective regulation existed. During this period the Court wielded the Tenth Amendment to restrict the reach of the federal antitrust laws, to nullify federal efforts to limit or prohibit child labor, and to strike down major New Deal programs such as those intended to regulate agriculture, to aid bankrupt cities, and to restore order in the coal industry.[4]

In the child labor and agriculture cases, in particular, the Court did what the first Congress had refused to do and in effect inserted the word "expressly" into the Tenth Amendment to qualify the enumerated powers of the federal government.

Justice Owen J. Roberts wrote in 1936:

From the accepted doctrine that the United States is a government of delegated powers, it follows that those not expressly granted or reasonably to be implied from such as are conferred, are reserved to the states or to the people. To forestall any suggestion to the contrary, the Tenth Amendment was adopted. The same proposition, otherwise stated, is that powers not granted are prohibited.[5]

The Court was not consistent in its application of the reserved powers doctrine. During the early part of the century, it rejected Tenth Amendment challenges to the exercise of the federal police power over lotteries, prostitution, colored oleo, and the repeal of Prohibition.[6]

But its insistence on Tenth Amendment restrictions on national power in the 1930s provoked President Franklin D. Roosevelt's "Court-packing" plan, and soon the dual federalism concept and the reserved powers doctrine both were discarded by the Court's majority. In 1937 the Court rebuffed a Tenth Amendment challenge to the Social Security Act as intruding upon the powers of the states. In its opinion, Justice Benjamin Cardozo acknowledged that changing economic and political facts made it necessary now for the national government to assume functions once considered the proper responsibility of state and local authority. The Court subsequently approved new versions of the agriculture, coal, and bankruptcy legislation it had struck down just a few years earlier as intruding upon the reserved powers of the states.[7]

"COOPERATIVE FEDERALISM"

In 1941 the Court formally interred the Tenth Amendment with its decision in *United States v. Darby Lumber Co.* upholding the Fair Labor Standards Act which, among other provisions, prohibited child labor. Finding the act constitutional as it extended federal regulation over working conditions in virtually all major sectors of the economy, Justice Harlan Fiske Stone wrote:

Our conclusion is unaffected by the Tenth Amendment. . . . The amendment states but a truism that all is retained which has not been surrendered. There is nothing in the history of its adoption to suggest that it was more than declaratory of the relationship between national and state governments as it had been established by the Constitution before the amendment or that its purpose was other than to allay fears that the new national government might seek to exercise powers not granted, and that the states might not be able to exercise fully their reserved powers. . . . From the beginning and for many years the amendment has been construed as not depriving the national government of authority to resort to all means for the exercise of a granted power which are appropriate and plainly adapted to the permitted end.[8]

Dual federalism was replaced by cooperative federalism. The Court abandoned the effort of neatly defining the boundaries of state and federal power over matters of mutual interest. Instead it began to sanction an overlapping system of complementary state and federal regulation.

Liability to Lawsuits

The states were stunned by the Supreme Court's first major ruling. In 1793 the Court held that a state could be hauled into federal court, without its consent, if it was sued by the citizens of another state. In response, Congress approved and the states ratified the Eleventh Amendment to overrule that decision in *Chisholm v. Georgia;* the new amendment was in place by 1798.[9] (*See details of this case, pp. 316–317.*)

As added to the Constitution, the Eleventh Amendment denied federal jurisdiction over any "suit in law or equity" brought against a state by citizens of another state or of a foreign state. The amendment did not expressly forbid federal courts from taking jurisdiction over suits brought against a state by its own citizens, but the Supreme Court in 1890 held that the amendment did bar such suits. Later the Court also held the amendment to forbid suits brought by a foreign nation against a state.[10] The amendment did not forbid suits against a state brought under the Constitution, an omission that became significant only in the twentieth century.[11]

STATES' PROTECTION NARROWED

The Supreme Court has narrowed the protection that the Eleventh Amendment provides to the states. The first shrinkage occurred in 1824, when the Court held that this immunity did not protect a state official who was acting under an unconstitutional state law or who was exceeding his properly granted authority. This ruling was announced in the case of *Osborn v. Bank of the United States.*[12]

Half a century later the bar imposed by the Eleventh Amendment appeared to deny any federal remedy to citizens holding bonds repudiated by the financially strained southern states. In frustration, some groups began to demand repeal of the Eleventh Amendment.[13]

The Supreme Court, however, resolved the impasse. In an 1885 case involving the bond situation in Virginia, the Court allowed suits against state officials who were carrying out an unconstitutional law or otherwise exceeding their proper authority. In such circumstances, held the Court, the official acts as an individual and can be sued as such. The Eleventh Amendment did not bar such suits.

In that and later rulings the Court has reasoned that the amendment was intended to forbid the use of the courts by citizens seeking to compel a state to take some affirmative action or to exercise its authority in some nonministerial and discretionary matter.[14]

In subsequent cases the Court also has held that the Eleventh Amendment provides no protection for state officials who damage property or injure persons in deliberate and negligent disregard of state law or individual rights.[15] That point was

ACTS VOIDED AS HEDGING STATE POWERS

Of the 135 acts of Congress struck down by the Supreme Court during the past two hundred years, many were found invalid because Congress had reached too far into matters that were left to the states to regulate. Among the laws so invalidated were:

• The Gun-Free School Zones Act of 1990, which banned the possession of guns within 1,000 feet of local public schools. (*United States v. Lopez*, 115 S. Ct. 1624, 1995)

• The Low-Level Radioactive Waste Policy Amendments Act of 1985 insofar as it required a state that failed to provide for disposal of radioactive waste generated within its borders to become the legal owner of the waste and assume liability for any injuries caused by it. (*New York v. United States*, 488 U.S. 1041, 1992)

• The Fair Labor Standards Act as amended to extend minimum wage and overtime provisions to employees of state and local governments. (*National League of Cities v. Usery*, 426 U.S. 833, 1976)

• The Voting Rights Act Amendments of 1970 insofar as they reduced to eighteen the voting age for state and local elections as well as federal elections. This change subsequently was made through the Twenty-sixth Amendment. (*Oregon v. Mitchell*, 400 U.S. 112, 1970)

• The first Municipal Bankruptcy Act of the New Deal, which provided for the readjustment of municipal indebtedness. The Court later approved a revised version of this law. (*Ashton v. Cameron County District*, 298 U.S. 513, 1936)

• The Home Owners' Loan Act of the New Deal insofar as it provided for the conversion of state building and loan associations into federal associations. (*Hopkins Savings Assn. v. Cleary*, 296 U.S. 315, 1935)

• The first Bituminous Coal Conservation Act to regulate the mining industry, a matter left to that time entirely to the states. The Court later approved a revised coal industry regulation law. (*Carter v. Carter Coal Company*, 298 U.S. 238, 1936)

• The New Deal's first Agricultural Adjustment Act regulating agricultural production, a matter left heretofore entirely to the states. The Court later approved a new Agricultural Adjustment Act. (*United States v. Butler*, 297 U.S. 1, 1936)

• The Futures Trading Act, which taxed sales of grain for future delivery, a matter not in interstate commerce, according to the Court. (*Hill v. Wallace*, 259 U.S. 44, 1922)

• The Child Labor Tax Act of 1919 and the Child Labor Law of 1916, both of which sought to prohibit the employment of children under a certain age in factories or mills. (*Bailey v. Drexel Furniture Co.*, 259 U.S. 20, 1922; *Hammer v. Dagenhart*, 247 U.S. 251, 1918)

• The Federal Corrupt Practices Act insofar as it limited the spending of a senatorial candidate in a primary campaign. This ruling, limiting federal power over elections to the general elections alone, was later overruled. (*Newberry v. United States*, 256 U.S. 232, 1921)

• The Oklahoma Enabling Act, which conditioned the admission of Oklahoma to the Union in part on the requirement that its state capital should not be moved before 1913. Such a decision was left to the discretion of other states, held the Court, and to impose that condition upon a state's admission to the Union placed it on an unequal footing with the other states. (*Coyle v. Smith*, 221 U.S. 559, 1911)

• The Federal Employers' Liability Act, which regulated the liability of common carriers operating intrastate as well as interstate. The Court later upheld a similar law applying only to interstate carriers. (*The Employers' Liability Cases*, 207 U.S. 463, 1908)

• The Immigration Act of 1907 insofar as it penalized the harboring of a prostitute who was an alien. The Court held that once aliens are admitted to the country, control over such matters passed to the states. (*Keller v. United States*, 213 U.S. 138, 1909)

• The Civil Rights Act of 1875 insofar as it penalized individuals who denied equal access to blacks seeking entry to public accommodations. (*The Civil Rights Cases*, 109 U.S. 3, 1883)

• The original trademark law applying to trademarks for exclusive use within the United States, which, the Court found, applied to intrastate as well as interstate commerce. (*The Trademark Cases*, 100 U.S. 82, 1879)

• The Internal Revenue Act of 1867 insofar as it banned the sale of illuminating oil within a state if it was flammable at too low a temperature. This was simply a police regulation, held the Court, and should be left to state officials. (*United States v. DeWitt*, 9 Wall. 41, 1870)

In the late nineteenth century, the Court also held that the federal income tax law was void insofar as it applied to the salaries of state officials and that a city—as an agent of the state—was exempt from federal taxes on the interest paid on municipal bonds. This first ruling was later overturned by the Court. (*Collector v. Day*, 11 Wall. 113, 1871; *United States v. Baltimore & O. R. Co.*, 17 Wall. 322, 1873)

In certain areas Congress may not delegate power to the states. In *Knickerbocker Ice Co. v. Stewart* in 1920, the Court held that Congress could not delegate to states the power of setting maritime workers' rights and remedies, in terms of workmen's compensation, for on-the-job injuries. This delegation, held the Court, defeated the need—and the constitutional intention—of a uniform maritime law.

A second effort of Congress to achieve the same end was struck down in 1924. (*Knickerbocker Ice Co. v. Stewart*, 253 U.S. 149, 1920; *Washington v. Dawson & Co.*, 264 U.S. 219, 1924)

---

reaffirmed in a 1974 case brought against state officials by the parents of children killed during an antiwar demonstration. The Court stated: "The Eleventh Amendment provides no shield for a state official confronted by a claim that he had deprived another of a federal right under color of state law."[16]

HALTING STATE ACTION

Questions of the immunity of a sovereign state from the compulsion of court orders again arise when a federal court is asked to halt enforcement of a state law that allegedly violates the constitutional rights of citizens.

Since 1908 the Supreme Court has allowed federal judges to grant such requests, temporarily enjoining the enforcement of a state law until its constitutional validity is ruled upon. Subsequent to that ruling in *Ex parte Young* Congress required that such orders be issued, not by a single federal judge, but by a panel of three judges.[17]

Such orders may operate only prospectively, that is, they may halt only future actions under a challenged law; in general, they may not require a state to remedy injuries already inflicted by actions under such a law.[18] However, the Court held in 1976 that Congress could by law—as an exercise of its power to enforce the guarantees of the Fourteenth Amendment—set aside immunity from retroactive relief and require states to make remedial payments to victims of state discrimination, in this particular case, state employees.[19]

And in 1978 the Court upheld as a proper exercise of federal judicial power an award of attorneys' fees from the state to prison inmates who had brought a successful suit challenging state prison conditions as unconstitutional. When a state refuses to comply with a federal court order, Justice John Paul Stevens wrote for the Court in that case, such a financial penalty might well be the most effective way to ensure compliance: "The principles of federalism that inform Eleventh Amendment doctrine surely do not require federal courts to enforce their decrees only by sending high state officials to jail."

Furthermore, Stevens noted, court costs had been awarded against states since at least the middle of the nineteenth century. The Eleventh Amendment had never, he said, been viewed as forbidding those awards.[20]

In 1996 the Court reinvigorated the Eleventh Amendment and state sovereign immunity by striking down a portion of the Indian Gaming Regulatory Act of 1988 that allowed tribes to sue states in federal court. The act, passed under the Indian Commerce Clause, required states to negotiate in good faith with a tribe seeking to run gambling activities on a reservation in the state. Tribes could sue a state in federal court to force negotiations of a gaming compact.

By 5–4 the Court ruled that the Eleventh Amendment prevents Congress from authorizing lawsuits against states under the Indian Commerce Clause. The opinion by Chief Justice William H. Rehnquist hemmed in the power of Congress to create a private right of action based on a claim that a state has violated a federal right.[21]

Rehnquist said constitutional limits on federal jurisdiction transcend congressional authority in this situation. He was joined by Justices Sandra Day O'Connor, Antonin Scalia, Anthony M. Kennedy, and Clarence Thomas. *Seminole Tribe of Florida v. Florida* directly overruled only one case, a 1989 opinion holding that the interstate commerce clause gave Congress the power to abrogate state sovereign immunity. That decision said the power to regulate interstate commerce would be ineffective without matching authority to make states liable for damages.[22]

But dissenting justices in the Indian gambling case—John Paul Stevens, David Souter, Ruth Bader Ginsburg, and Stephen G. Breyer—said the Court's action marked a shift away from history. Souter, who took the unusual step of reading portions of his statement from the bench declared: "The Court today holds for the first time since the founding of the Republic that Congress has no authority to subject a state to the jurisdiction of a federal court at the behest of an individual asserting a federal right."[23] He said such action "flies in the face of" the Constitution. His opinion was joined by Ginsburg and Breyer.

Separately, Stevens wrote that the ramifications could prevent Congress from allowing lawsuits by individuals when states do not follow federal regulation in other areas, notably environmental law and copyright and patent law.

Political Powers

In no area of state affairs has the Supreme Court been more reluctant to intervene than in questions of state political power. This reluctance to involve itself in political questions was evident as early as the Court's decision in the 1849 case of *Luther v. Borden.*[24]

The case arose under Article IV of the Constitution, which provides that "[T]he United States shall guarantee to every State in this Union a republican form of government." The dispute involved two competing groups claiming to be the legitimate government of the state of Rhode Island. The Court refused to resolve this "political question," holding that enforcement of the constitutional guarantee was a matter for Congress, not the courts.

On the basis of this same "political question" doctrine, the Court in 1912 declined to decide whether Oregon—by adopting the direct legislative devices of the initiative and the referendum—had destroyed its republican form of government and thus its own lawful authority. The Court held that Congress, by seating the U.S. senators and House members from Oregon, had sanctioned these changes in the character of the state government.[25]

ELECTORAL DISTRICTS

The Constitution, besides providing that "the times, places and manner of holding elections for Senators and Representatives, shall be prescribed in each state by the legislature thereof," grants Congress some power to regulate the subject.

Congress first exercised this authority in 1842, requiring states to divide themselves into districts for the election of House members. Subsequent laws also required that these districts be compact—that is, not gerrymandered. But after a 1929 act omitted that requirement, the Court ruled in 1932 that without such statutory authority, it could not act to correct a state's gerrymandered districts.[26]

Until 1962 the Court held steadfastly to the position that malapportionment of legislative districts was a "political question," not for the courts to resolve. But to leave this matter to the legislators elected from those very districts was clearly to prevent any

Although debate over whether the terms of members of Congress should be limited is as old as the Constitution, the legal issue did not arrive at the Supreme Court until the mid-1990s. The term limits movement had exploded onto the national political scene as supporters won ballot initiatives or gained term-limit laws in twenty-three states from 1990 to 1995. Opposition grew to "business as usual" in Washington, and the slogan of the day was "throw the bums out."

The Court case concerned a 1992 amendment to the Arkansas Constitution that barred the state's members of Congress from appearing on the ballot after a certain number of terms, three for members of the U.S. House and two for U.S. senators. Arguing for term limits, state officials and national term-limit activists said the nation's Founders envisioned a Congress of citizen legislators. Incumbency with its modern-day perquisites including incomparable name recognition and ability to raise money created lawmakers who lost touch with the people, they said.

Arkansas' term limits law was challenged by Bobbie Hill, a former president of the state's League of Women Voters. Hill and other opponents of term limits cited Article I of the Constitution, which sets out only three qualifications for federal office: age, citizenship, and residency. No other qualifications could be imposed, they said. If voters wanted to limit the tenure of their representatives, they could do so by voting them out of office.

Advocates of term limits, however, also found support in Article I, in the clause giving states the power to regulate the "times, places and manner" of holding elections for members of Congress.

When the Court announced its opinion in *U.S. Term Limits Inc. v. Thornton* in May 1995, it was by a surprisingly narrow 5–4 vote. Justice John Paul Stevens, a liberal Republican who was in his twentieth year on the Court, wrote the opinion, joined by Justices Anthony M. Kennedy, David H. Souter, Ruth Bader Ginsburg, and Stephen G. Breyer. Justice Clarence Thomas wrote the dissenting opinion, joined by Chief Justice William H. Rehnquist and Justices Sandra Day O'Connor and Antonin Scalia.

The people may choose whom they wish to govern them, said

Skip Cook, left, and Tim Jacob of Arkansans for Governmental Reform spoke at a news conference on a 1992 ballot measure to limit the terms of the members of the Arkansas congressional delegation. Voters approved the measure, Amendment 73, in November 1992 by a 3–2 margin. Two years later, the Supreme Court struck down the Arkansas law in *U.S. Term Limits Inc. v. Thornton.*

the Court. Justice Stevens wrote: "Allowing individual States to adopt their own qualifications for congressional service would be inconsistent with the Framers' vision of a uniform National Legislature representing the people of the United States. If the qualifications set forth in the text of the Constitution are to be changed, that text must be amended."[1]

The Court relied on its 1969 ruling in *Powell v. McCormack* that even Congress lacked the power to add to or alter the qualifications of its members. After Rep. Adam Clayton Powell, a veteran Democratic lawmaker from New York City, won reelection in 1966 despite a conviction for criminal contempt and a record of misuse of public funds, the House of Representatives voted to "exclude" him. Powell sued. The Supreme Court ultimately agreed that the House action was illegal, ruling by 8–1 that neither chamber of Congress can add to the qualifications for membership listed in the Constitution.

Stevens said the fundamental ideas behind the decision in *Powell* were "that the opportunity to be elected was open to all" and "that sovereignty confers on the people the right to choose freely their representatives to the National Government."[2]

Directly addressing the question of state authority in this area, Stevens wrote, "[W]e conclude that the power to add qualifications is not within the 'original powers' of the States, and thus is not reserved to the States by the Tenth Amendment. Second, even if States possessed some original power in this area, we conclude that the Framers intended the Constitution to be the exclusive source of qualifications for members of Congress, and that the Framers thereby 'divested' States of any power to add qualifications."[3]

Fearing that the diverse interests of the states would undermine the national government, the Framers tried to minimize the possibility of state interference with federal elections, the majority observed. It noted that the Framers unanimously had rejected a proposal to add term limits to the Constitution.

Concluding, Stevens wrote, "We are . . . firmly convinced that allowing the several States to adopt term limits for congressional service would effect a fundamental change in the constitutional framework. Any such change must come not by legislation adopted either by Congress or by an individual State, but rather—as have other important changes in the electoral process—through the Amendment procedures set forth in Article V."[4]

In his dissent, Thomas observed that he found it ironic that the majority "defends the right of the people of Arkansas to 'choose whom they please to govern them' by invalidating a provision that won nearly 60% of the votes cast in a direct election."[5] The dissenters assumed that states have such power over federal elections unless the Constitution explicitly states otherwise. Thomas said, "I take it to be established . . . that the people of Arkansas do enjoy 're-served' powers over the selection of their representatives in Congress. . . . Whatever one might think of the wisdom of this arrangement, we may not override the decision of the people of Arkansas unless something in the Federal Constitution deprives them of the power to enact such measures."[6]

1. *U.S. Term Limits Inc. v. Thornton,* 115 S. Ct. 1842 (1995).
2. Id.
3. Id.
4. Id.
5. Id.
6. Id.

improvement in the situation. In 1962 the Court discarded this "political question" response to the problem with its decision in *Baker v. Carr*. Using the Fourteenth Amendment's equal protection guarantee as the basis for its intervention, the Court entered the "political thicket" and ordered states to draw new congressional and state legislative district lines to ensure the equality of votes cast within the state.[27]

These rulings resulted in a long line of Supreme Court cases concerning implementation of the "one person, one vote" rule. And in 1973, while maintaining the standard of strict mathematical equality for congressional districts, the Court relaxed that standard slightly for state legislative districts. Some deviation might be justified, wrote Justice William H. Rehnquist for the Court. He cited a statement from an earlier reapportionment ruling: "So long as the divergences from a strict population standard are based on legitimate consideration incident to the effectuation of a rational state policy, some deviations from the equal population principle are constitutionally permissible with respect to the apportionment of seats" in the state legislature.[28]

That double standard (strict for congressional districts, lenient for state legislative districts) was illustrated vividly on June 22, 1983, when the Court issued two decisions concerning apportionment. In *Karcher v. Daggett* the Court, 5–4, struck down New Jersey's congressional redistricting plan because the state had not justified the less than 1 percent variation between the most populous and least populous districts.[29]

And the same day, by a very different 5–4 vote, the Court upheld Wyoming's requirement that each county have at least one representative in its state House, even though the result was an 89 percent population variance between the smallest county and the largest. The variance was permissible, the Court said, in light of the state's interest in making sure that each county had its own representative.[30]

PRIMARIES, VOTER QUALIFICATIONS

Until 1941 the control of primary elections was left entirely to the states. This tradition was reinforced by a Supreme Court ruling in 1921 that appeared to read the Constitution's references to "elections" to mean only the general election, not preliminary contests.[31]

But in 1941 that interpretation was overturned by the Court, which held that in states where primary elections were an integral part of the process of electing members of Congress, congressional power to regulate elections extended over them.[32]

States have long been conceded the power to set qualifications for voters, but the national government—chiefly through the amending process—possesses the power to declare certain qualifications unreasonable. That power was exercised in the Fifteenth, Nineteenth, and Twenty-sixth Amendments, forbidding states to deny the right to vote because of race, sex, or age—so long as the prospective voter is at least eighteen years of age. State challenges to this means of expanding the electorate were disposed of by the Court in 1922 with the dismissal of Tennessee's argument that its political autonomy had been destroyed by the Nineteenth Amendment, which added many new voters to its electorate without its consent.[33]

And in 1970 the Supreme Court ruled that Congress by statute can lower the voting age only for federal elections—not for state and local ones. That ruling led to the approval and ratification of the Twenty-sixth Amendment, which lowered the voting age to eighteen for all elections. In that same decision, the Court upheld an act of Congress that restricted residence requirements to thirty days for presidential elections and forbade the use of literacy tests in all elections.[34]

The most comprehensive federal scheme of regulation for the conduct of elections by states was approved by Congress in the Voting Rights Act of 1965, legislation enacted in response to the continuing efforts of some parts of the South to deny qualified black residents the right to vote. The act authorized federal supervision of elections in those areas, forbade the affected states to use any literacy test or similar device to qualify voters, and required federal approval of any change in their voting laws, practices, or procedures.

The states of South Carolina and New York (affected because of a provision concerning tests for non-English-speaking voters) challenged the law as an invasion of the reserved rights of the states to set voter qualifications. The Supreme Court rejected this argument and upheld the law: "As against the reserved powers of the States, Congress may use any rational means to effectuate the constitutional prohibition of racial discrimination in voting."[35]

The Supreme Court in modern times also has struck down state election laws that made it unreasonably difficult for third parties to win a place on a ballot, required excessively high filing fees for candidates, set unreasonable primary registration requirements and long residency requirements for voters, or required political parties to hold "closed" primaries in which only one party could vote.[36]

One of the Court's recent rulings on state power over elections, *U.S. Term Limits v. Thornton* (1995), has become one of the most famous decisions of the decade. Entering the heated battle over term limits for members of Congress, the Court in 1995 said states could not deny incumbents access to the ballot in order to limit their tenure. *(See box, p. 514, in Chapter 10.)*

The Taxing Power

Apart from the commerce clause, the Court has imposed three other limiting principles upon the state's power to raise money through taxes: (1) the tax must be imposed on persons or property or activities within its own jurisdiction; (2) the tax must be for public purposes; and (3) the tax cannot fall directly upon the federal government.

A series of post–Civil War rulings established the first principle.[37] The second was settled by the Court's 1875 decision in *Loan Association v. Topeka*. The Court struck down a Kansas law authorizing a tax to pay for city bonds issued to assist a private bridge-building corporation. Writing for the Court, Justice Samuel Miller was candid in condemning such an action:

To lay, with one hand, the power of the government on the property of the citizen, and with the other to bestow it upon favored individuals to aid private enterprises and build up private fortunes, is none the less a robbery because it is done under the forms of law and is called taxation.[38]

And the third principle, set out emphatically by Chief Justice John Marshall in the 1819 ruling in *McCulloch v. Maryland,* denies states the right to use taxes to hinder the operations of the federal government.[39]

After settling the question of the state's power to tax the Bank of the United States, the Court in 1829 issued the first in a series of rulings protecting government securities from state taxation. State taxes on federal stock, bonds, and even national bank shares, without congressional consent, impermissibly interfere with the federal power to borrow, a power expressly granted by the Constitution, held the Court.[40]

In 1886 the Court for the first time ruled that a state may not tax federally owned real estate, a holding that has been expanded to include most federally owned property.[41]

INTERGOVERNMENTAL IMMUNITY

In announcing the Court's decision in *McCulloch v. Maryland,* Chief Justice Marshall asserted that "the power to tax involves the power to destroy."[42] This statement became the basis for a long, involved series of rulings in which the Court—for a time—granted to federal and state governments and their officials immunity, each from taxation by the other.

The first of these rulings came in 1842 in *Dobbins v. Erie County.*[43] The Court held that a state could not tax the income of federal revenue officers without impermissibly interfering with federal functions. Years later the Court granted a corresponding immunity to state officials with its ruling in *Collector v. Day,* striking down a federal tax on the salary of a state judge.[44]

In 1895 the Court granted state and municipal bonds—and the interest they generated—immunity from federal taxation similar to that already enjoyed by national securities from state taxes. This was part of the Court's income tax ruling in *Pollock v. Farmers' Loan & Trust Co.*[45] Some limit on this immunity—for state governments—was recognized in 1905, when the Court held that only governmental functions of state governments were immune from federal taxes. Therefore, it upheld the imposition of federal taxes on the state-run liquor business in South Carolina.[46]

Notwithstanding this decision, the Court continued to elaborate on the intergovernmental tax immunity question for three more decades. It struck down a federal tax on motorcycles that were to be sold to a city police department.[47] Also falling as impermissible were state taxes on income from federally granted copyrights and patents, on gasoline sold to the federal govern-

ment, and on income from leases of public lands.[48] But the end of this body of rulings was in sight even as some of these last decisions were announced late in the 1920s. In dissent from the gasoline tax case, Justice Oliver Wendell Holmes Jr. met Marshall's assertion head-on and declared: "The power to tax is not the power to destroy while this court sits."[49]

DILUTED IMMUNITY

Beginning with reversal of the copyright royalties income case in 1932, the Court dropped its effort to preserve this immunity in such extended form. In the 1938 decision in *Helvering v. Gerhardt* and the 1939 ruling in *Graves v. New York ex rel. O'Keefe,* the Court overruled *Dobbins* and *Collector.*[50]

The immunity granted to state officials in *Collector,* explained Justice Harlan Fiske Stone in the *Helvering* opinion, "was sustained only because it was one deemed necessary to protect the states from destruction by federal taxation of those governmental functions which they were exercising when the Constitution was adopted and which were essential to their continued existence." Such immunity is not justified "where the tax laid upon individuals affects the state only as the burden is passed on to it by the taxpayer."[51]

The last remaining significant example of state immunity from federal taxes—the immunity granted the interest paid on municipal bonds—was erased, as a constitutional matter, by the Court in 1988. With its 7–1 ruling in *South Carolina v. Baker,* the Court made clear that nothing in the Constitution limited federal power to tax state government. Repeating the reasoning set out in the *Garcia* case three years earlier, Justice William J. Brennan Jr. wrote that such immunity, if granted, was to be won through the political process, not invoked as a constitutional matter.[52]

Federal immunity from state taxes protects the property, institutions, and activities of the federal government, but it no longer extends to persons merely doing business with the federal government—even if state taxes are passed on as higher costs to the federal government.[53]

Early in its exposition of the Constitution's prohibition on state action impairing the obligation of contracts, the Court applied this contract clause to the state's power to grant and revoke exemptions from state taxes. Unless a reservation of state right to modify or nullify such a grant of exemption is included in the granting agreement, the contract clause forbids a state to rescind or modify such an exemption. The major impact of these holdings is simply to guarantee that states include reservation clauses in such grants.[54] *(See "Tax Exemptions," pp. 323–324.)*

The Police Power

Broadest of the powers reserved to the states is the police power—the authority of the state to govern its citizens, its land, and its resources, and to restrict individual freedom to protect

FISH BUT NOT ALL FOWL

Under the police power, states have broad authority over fish and game and can prohibit, allow, or license hunting and fishing within their borders. In one of the more peculiar chapters in federal-state relations, the national government used the treaty power to take the subject of migratory birds out of state control.

Spurred by conservationists' concern, Congress in 1913 enacted a law strictly regulating the killing of birds that migrated from state to state. Several federal courts held this law invalid, dealing with a subject Congress had no power to control.

But before any Supreme Court ruling was obtained on the matter, the United States in 1916 signed a treaty with Canada providing for the protection of migratory birds. Using the treaty as the basis for its action, Congress in 1918 enacted a new migratory bird protection law.

The state of Missouri challenged the law as an invasion of the rights reserved to the states. But the Court upheld the law on the basis that the treaty had removed the subject of migratory birds from state to federal jurisdiction. (*Missouri v. Holland,* 252 U.S. 416 (1920)

or promote the public good. Most of the Supreme Court's rulings on this power concern its impact on foreign or interstate commerce. Yet states exercise their police power in a multitude of ways that affect only matters within their borders.

One use of the police power is illustrated by Louisiana's grant of a slaughterhouse monopoly, which later was upheld in the 1873 ruling in the *Slaughterhouse Cases.* The Court upheld the monopoly against a constitutional challenge, finding it a proper exercise of the police power. Justice Miller acknowledged, for the Court, that this power "is, and must be from its very nature, incapable of any very exact definition or limitation. Upon it depends the security of social order, the life and health of the citizen, the comfort of an existence in a thickly populated community, the enjoyment of private and social life, and the beneficial use of property."[55]

And in an earlier judicial description of the power, Justice Philip Barbour explained that under it a state had "the same undeniable and unlimited jurisdiction over all persons and things within its territorial limits, as any foreign nation, where . . . not . . . restrained by the Constitution."[56]

The Supreme Court considers this internal use of the police power only when it is challenged as violating some constitutional right. When a state comes to the Court to defend its use of this power against such a challenge, the Court usually adopts a balancing approach, weighing the benefits the law provides against the constitutional cost.

The Court in these decisions has recognized that the states have wide latitude to act to protect their natural resources from damage or diversion, to protect property values and the general quality of life in an area by the use of zoning requirements, and

to protect the public health and morals through quarantine and health and even some censorship laws.

ENVIRONMENTAL PROTECTION

"It is a fair and reasonable demand on the part of a sovereign," wrote Justice Holmes in one of the first state environmental cases before the Court, "that the air over its territory should not be polluted on a great scale." And so in 1907 the Court upheld Georgia's successful effort to win a court order directing a Tennessee copper company to stop its outpouring of sulphurous fumes that were destroying all vegetation in the vicinity in both states.[57]

The following year the Court upheld New Jersey's right to prohibit diversion of water from its streams to New York. And in 1922 the justices, at the request of Wyoming, ordered Colorado to stop its diversion of the Laramie River.[58]

This principle has its limits. In 1923 the Court refused to allow West Virginia to retain within the state and for its own use all the natural gas produced there. But the Court has approved state laws prohibiting the waste of its natural resources by companies exploiting them.[59]

And when Congress began enacting national environmental protection measures, the Court continued to uphold nonconflicting state legislation. In 1973 the Court upheld Florida's water pollution law as complementary to federal legislation concerning oil spills in navigable waters. The Court reasoned that Congress had not preempted all state regulation of such matters and that the state could exercise its police power over maritime activities concurrently with the federal government. Five years later, however, the Court struck down Washington State's laws setting standards for the size and type of oil tankers permitted in Puget Sound, finding that they conflicted with federal law and the intent of Congress to set uniform national standards for such ships.[60]

In the same vein the Court in 1990 said standards set by the Federal Energy Regulatory Commission for water flows in streams diverted by hydraulic power plants preempt tougher state regulations.[61] Two years later it ruled that states cannot impose licensing and training requirements on hazardous-waste-site operators that are stricter than regulations under the Occupational Safety and Health Act.[62] In both cases the Court said federal law was clearly intended to preempt state regulation. *(See box, "Supremacy," p. 318.)*

Occasionally, Congress's efforts to protect the environment have been curtailed to avoid impinging on state sovereignty. The Court in 1992 struck down part of a federal law intended to make states responsible for the low-level radioactive waste they generate. A principal section of that law made any state that failed to provide for the disposal of the waste generated within its borders the legal owner of the waste, liable for any injuries it caused. Such a penalty, the Court held, violates the Tenth Amendment guarantee of state sovereignty by usurping states' legislative processes and compelling them to enforce a federal regulatory scheme.[63]

ZONING

The validity of the state's power—through zoning ordinances—to govern land use was recognized by the Court early in the twentieth century. In 1915 it upheld a city's prohibition of brickmaking in a certain area, although the effect of the ban was virtually to put one brickmaker out of business. The brickmaker challenged the ban as a due process violation, but the Court did not agree.[64]

Two years later it did strike down the housing segregation ordinance of Louisville, Kentucky, which forbade blacks and whites to live in areas inhabited predominantly by members of the other race. This restriction, held the Court, interfered too far with the right of property, effectively denying individuals the right to sell to black purchasers.[65]

In 1926 came the landmark zoning ruling when the Court, 6–3, upheld a city ordinance that excluded apartment houses from certain residential neighborhoods. This limitation was challenged in *Euclid v. Ambler Realty Co.* as a due process violation of the individual's freedom to put his property to whatever use he desired. The Court heard the case argued twice. In the Court's opinion upholding the restriction, Justice George Sutherland said changing conditions justified regulations that, half a century earlier, "probably would have been rejected as arbitrary." The ordinance, he said, was a justifiable use of the police power to prevent a form of local nuisance:

A nuisance may be merely a right thing in the wrong place—like a pig in the parlor instead of the barnyard. If the validity of the legislative classification for zoning purposes be fairly debatable, the legislative judgment must be allowed to control.

In this case, the city had decided that apartment houses created disadvantages for homeowners in an area, "interfering by their height and bulk with the free circulation of air and monopolizing the rays of the sun which otherwise would fall upon the smaller homes, and bringing . . . the disturbing noises incident to increased traffic and business . . . depriving children of the privilege of quiet and open spaces for play." And that value judgment would be allowed to stand.[66]

With this approach the Court consistently rebuffed challenges to zoning ordinances. In 1954 the Court upheld the use of the federal police power in a slum-clearance project intended to result in a more attractive community. Justice William O. Douglas wrote that "[i]t is within the power of the legislature to determine that the community should be beautiful as well as healthy, spacious as well as clean, well-balanced as well as carefully patrolled."

And twenty years later Douglas spoke for the Court as it upheld a zoning ordinance adopted by the village of Belle Terre, New York, that restricted occupancy of its homes to single families, excluding groups of more than two unrelated persons.

The regimes of boarding houses, fraternity houses, and the like present urban problems. More people occupy a given space; more cars rather continuously pass by; more cars are parked; noise travels with crowds.

A quiet place where yards are wide, people few, and motor vehicles restricted are legitimate guidelines in a land use project addressed to family needs. . . . The police power is not confined to elimination of filth, stench, and unhealthy places. It is ample to lay out zones where family values, youth values, and the blessings of quiet seclusion, and clean air make the area a sanctuary for people.[67]

The Court subsequently upheld Detroit's use of zoning power to require that adult movie theaters and adult bookstores be dispersed within the city.[68] And it sustained—against an equal protection challenge—a suburb's refusal to modify its zoning requirements for one area to allow the construction there of a racially integrated low-income housing complex.[69] Finding New York's historic preservation law an exercise of power analogous to zoning laws, the Court upheld it in 1978 against a property owner's challenge that it constituted a governmental "taking" of property without just compensation.[70]

The Court has set some limits on the exercise of this police power. Just two years after the *Euclid* decision, the Court rejected a Seattle ordinance that required the written consent of property owners in a neighborhood before a home for the aged could be built there. The justices found it unlikely that the home for the elderly could result in any injury, inconvenience, or annoyance to the community.[71]

And in 1977 the Court struck down a village ordinance that denied a grandmother the right to live in the same household with her sons and grandsons. The vote was 5–4. Writing for the majority, Justice Lewis F. Powell Jr. declared that the challenged ordinance "slice[d] deeply into the family itself . . . select[ing] certain categories of relatives who may live together and declar[ing] that others may not. . . . When a city undertakes such intrusive regulation of the family, neither *Belle Terre* nor *Euclid* governs; the usual judicial deference to the legislature is inappropriate."[72]

After dancing around the issue for years, the Court in 1987 raised warning signs for states and localities using their zoning power to curtail the power of landowners to decide how to use their land. In two cases decided separately, but both from California, the Court made clear that in some cases property owners would have a claim against the regulating bodies for just compensation—if the regulation so curtailed their use of the land that it effectively took its value away from them.[73]

In 1994 the Court further limited the power of local governments to force landowners to permit public use of their property as a condition of new development or construction on the site. In a 5–4 ruling the Court held that municipalities have the burden of showing a connection and a "rough proportionality" between conditions imposed on the development permit and any claimed harm to the public from the development. Without such justification, a municipality's action could amount to "an uncompensated taking of property" in violation of the Fifth Amendment. The decision in *Dolan v. City of Tigard* cleared the way for the family owners of an Oregon hardware store to challenge a requirement that they provide land for flood control and a bike path before expanding the store.[74]

A CLASH OF COURTS: THE FUGITIVE SLAVE LAW

During the turbulent decade before the outbreak of the Civil War, the controversial Federal Fugitive Slave Act set off an extended tug-of-war between federal and state judicial power, centering around one Sherman Booth, an abolitionist newspaper editor.

In 1854 Booth, a resident of Milwaukee, Wisconsin, was arrested there and charged with violating the law by helping a fugitive slave escape from a deputy federal marshal. Because there was no federal prison in the area, Booth was confined after his arrest in a local jail.

From there he sought the aid of a state supreme court judge, who—like most people in Wisconsin—was not in sympathy with slavery or the federal law requiring the return of runaway slaves. The state judge issued a writ of habeas corpus to the federal marshal, Stephen Ableman, holding Booth. He then declared the federal fugitive slave law unconstitutional and ordered Booth's release. Ableman complied, but after the order was upheld by the full state supreme court, he asked the U.S. Supreme Court to review the case. *(Ableman v. Booth)*

Before the Court heard arguments in the case, federal and state authorities clashed again. In 1855 Booth was indicted by a federal grand jury for violating the Federal Fugitive Slave Act. He was tried, convicted, and sentenced to spend one month in prison and to pay a $1,000 fine.

Three days after being sentenced, Booth again appealed to the Wisconsin courts for relief. The following day the court issued a writ of habeas corpus. It subsequently decided that Booth's imprisonment was illegal and ordered his release. He was set free, and the attorney general of the United States took the case to the Supreme Court. *(United States v. Booth)*

The Court did not resolve the matter until 1859, but when the decision came it was a vigorous assertion of national judicial supremacy. In writing the opinion, Chief Justice Roger B. Taney noted that it was the first time the state courts had tried to assert their supremacy over federal courts in cases arising under the Constitution and U.S. laws.

That assertion was soundly rejected by a unanimous Court.

It would seem to be hardly necessary to do more than to state the result to which these decisions of the state courts must inevitably lead. . . . [N]o one will suppose that a government which has now lasted nearly seventy years, enforcing its laws by its own tribunals, and preserving the union of the States, could have lasted a single year, or fulfilled the high trusts committed to it, if the offenses against its laws could not have been punished without the consent of the State in which the culprit was found. . . .

[A]lthough the State of Wisconsin is sovereign within its territorial limits to certain extent, yet that sovereignty is limited and restricted by the Constitution of the United States. And the powers of the General Government, and of the State, although both exist and are exercised within the same territorial limits, are yet separate and distinct sovereignties, acting separately and independently of each other, within their respective spheres. And the sphere of action appropriated to the United States is as far beyond the reach of the judicial process issued by a state judge or a state court, as if the line of division was traced by landmarks and monuments visible to the eye.

(Ableman v. Booth, United States v. Booth, 21 How. 506 at 514–516, 1859)

PORNOGRAPHY

The recurring problem of obscenity has called into play a wide variety of state and city police power laws and regulations intended to prohibit or curtail the distribution of offensive, sexually oriented films, books, and magazines within communities. This exercise of the police power has come before the Court in a long series of cases in which the persons whose activities are banned or restricted argue that the state is impermissibly infringing upon their First Amendment freedoms.

Although it approved state censorship of movies as early as 1915, the Court reversed this holding in 1952 and brought movies within the protection of the First Amendment.[75]

Subsequently, the Court held that obscene material is not protected against state action by the First Amendment. But while working to formulate a useful definition of obscenity, the Court has dealt with challenges to obscenity laws of states and companion city regulations on a case-by-case basis. The primary concern of the Court has been to ensure that state and local anti-obscenity efforts do not sweep so broadly that they curtail forms of expression protected by the First Amendment.[76]

The Court has moved carefully. It has refused to deny states all power of censorship, but it has set out some guidelines for censorship laws to follow.[77] It has allowed state courts to halt the sale of indecent materials so long as there is a speedy hearing to determine if in fact the objectionable materials are obscene. It has struck down state grants of broad authority to police to seize any items they consider obscene; it has struck down state laws making it a crime to possess obscene books for sale; and it has overturned official efforts to curtail distribution of particular magazines and books.[78]

In 1973 the Court reaffirmed state power to regulate obscene material. In that decision the Court set out new guidelines for the definition of obscenity, giving added weight to local community standards. Since 1973, however, the Court has made it clear that jury decisions on obscenity are subject to judicial review, that anti-obscenity ordinances must be carefully drafted, and that objective national standards must be used in determining whether an allegedly obscene book or film has any scientific, literary, or artistic value.[79]

Reviewing an Indiana public indecency statute that outlawed nude dancing, the Court in 1991 acknowledged that nude dancing could have some expressive value entitling it to protection under the First Amendment, but a majority said community interests in safety and morality were overriding. Writing for the five-justice majority in *Barnes v. Glen Theatre*, Chief Justice William H. Rehnquist said, "The traditional police power of the states is defined as the authority to provide for the public health, safety, and morals, and we have upheld such a basis for legislation."[80]

PUBLIC HEALTH

The most drastic exercises of the police power upheld by the Court have come under its use to protect the public health. In 1905 the Court rejected a man's challenge to the compulsory vaccination ordinance adopted by the city of Cambridge, Massachusetts, to protect its people against smallpox. Justice John Marshall Harlan wrote the Court's opinion rejecting the challenge to this requirement as depriving a citizen of his personal liberty without due process of law:

Upon the principle of self-defense, of paramount necessity, a community has the right to protect itself against an epidemic of disease which threatens the safety of its members. . . . [I]n every well-ordered society charged with the duty of conserving the safety of its members the rights of the individual in respect of his liberty may at times, under the pressure of great dangers be subject to such restraint . . . as the safety of the general public may demand.[81]

Twenty-two years later the Court applied this rationale to justify Virginia's decision, under state law, to sterilize Carrie Buck, a mentally defective woman with a "feeble-minded" mother and a "feeble-minded" child. The Court held that the sterilization was not a deprivation of rights without due process. Justice Holmes wrote:

[T]he principle that sustains compulsory vaccination is broad enough to cover cutting the Fallopian tubes.

We have seen more than once that the public welfare may call upon the best citizens for their lives. It would be strange if it could not call upon those who already sap the strength of the State for these lesser sacrifices . . . in order to prevent our being swamped with incompetence. . . . Three generations of imbeciles are enough.[82]

Although this case has not been directly overruled, it was effectively nullified by the Court in 1942, when the justices struck down a similar Oklahoma law.[83]

The Judicial Power

Federal judicial power clearly curtails the power of state courts. Most significant of these restraints is the Supreme Court's power to review the rulings of state courts on federal claims and questions. Initially granted by Congress in 1789, contested in the 1809 controversy with Gideon Olmstead, and challenged by Virginia in 1816 and 1821, the power was ringingly upheld by the Court in *Martin v. Hunter's Lessee* and *Cohens v. Virginia*. (See "Judicial Review and the States," pp. 316–321, in Chapter 7.)

Once the power of the Supreme Court to have the last word on any federal question was made certain, however, the Court seemed quite willing, for decades, to leave large categories of litigation to the state courts. Until the mid-nineteenth century, almost all corporate and criminal litigation—as well as much admiralty litigation—was left to state courts.

In 1810 the Court ruled that federal jurisdiction did not include cases brought by or against a corporation unless all the corporate stockholders lived in a state other than that of the opposing party. Historian Charles Warren states:

As a result of this decision the reports of the Supreme Court and of the Circuit Courts during the first forty years thereafter reveal an almost complete absence of cases in which corporations (other than banking and insurance) were litigants; and the development of a body of corporation law by the Federal Courts was postponed to a late date in their history.[84]

Thirty-five years later the Court effectively reversed itself on this point, holding that a corporation was assumed to be a citizen of the state in which it was chartered. Therefore, any suit brought by or against a citizen of another state was properly within federal jurisdiction because of the diversity of citizenship.[85]

In the same term that it decided *Martin v. Hunter's Lessee*, the Court ruled that federal courts lacked any criminal jurisdiction except that created by passage of federal laws declaring certain crimes to be federal ones.[86]

Until the mid-nineteenth century much of admiralty law was left to state courts, despite the Judiciary Act's explicit grant of admiralty jurisdiction to federal district courts. In 1825 the Supreme Court adopted a narrow definition of federal admiralty jurisdiction, limited to waters affected by the ebb and flow of the tides. This ruling left most of the nation's inland waterways under state control.[87]

As steamboat traffic and barge traffic increased, the Court reconsidered that definition and reversed it in 1851. Chief Justice Roger B. Taney was frank about the impact of economic reality upon the Court's opinion: "[T]he conviction that this definition of admiralty powers was narrower than the Constitution contemplated, has been growing stronger every day with the growing commerce on the lakes and navigable rivers of the western States."

The Court ruled that federal admiralty courts had jurisdiction over all public navigable waters upon which interstate or foreign commerce was carried.

Fifteen years later the Court completed the removal of such matters from state courts, asserting exclusive federal jurisdiction over admiralty cases. States could still pass laws providing remedies in maritime accidents, but they could be enforced only in federal courts. This decision removed an "immense class of cases" from the state courts, reported Warren.[88]

In 1880 the Court ruled that state election judges charged with supervising elections of state and congressional officers were properly charged with violating federal civil rights laws by stuffing the ballot box, also a violation of state law.[89]

During the early years of the nation's existence, the federal government frankly depended on state courts to enforce some federal laws such as the Fugitive Slave Act of 1793 and the Embargo Acts of Thomas Jefferson's administration. Local hostility to the intent of some of these laws caused a cessation of this practice, but the Court in this century has twice affirmed federal power to require states to enforce federal laws.[90]

INTERFERENCE

Even after the establishment of the power of judicial review, questions steadily recurred of interference by state courts in federal matters and federal courts in state court matters. The Court ruled that state courts could not enjoin the judgment of a federal court or order a federal official to perform some duty by issuing a writ of mandamus; that states could not regulate the processes of federal courts; that a state court's interpretation of state laws was not binding on federal courts.[91] The last holding was substantially modified in 1938, after almost a century. The Supreme Court then held that in the absence of an applicable and controlling federal law or constitutional provision, federal courts should apply the appropriate state law to a situation before it.[92]

The Court also has ruled that a federal court may not take property out of state court custody, and that a state may not seize property attached by a federal court.[93]

Since its landmark 1859 ruling in *Ableman v. Booth*, the Court has steadfastly denied to state courts the power to order federal officials to release a person they hold in custody. *(See box, A Clash of Courts: The Fugitive Slave Law, p. 375.)*

But federal courts retain the power to issue a writ of habeas corpus to state officials ordering the release of a person held in custody in violation of his constitutional rights. The Judiciary Act of 1789 authorized federal courts to issue writs of habeas corpus as necessary "in the exercise of their respective jurisdictions," but until after the Civil War that writ could be used only to order the release of federal, not state, prisoners.

In 1867 Congress expanded the habeas corpus power to allow use of the writ to order the release of any person held "in violation of the Constitution or of any treaty or law of the United States."

The expansion of habeas corpus gave a new instrument to state prisoners who felt that their conviction had been obtained in a way that violated their constitutional rights. The Supreme Court generally has required, however, that before a state prisoner uses this means of challenging his conviction in federal court, he exhaust all possible avenues to challenge the conviction within the state court system. In the 1960s and 1970s the Supreme Court was divided over how strictly to apply this "exhaustion of remedies" requirement. In 1963 the Court held that a prisoner who missed the opportunity to raise federally based challenges to his conviction in state courts was not foreclosed by that failure from requesting a federal court to issue a writ of habeas corpus.[94]

In subsequent years, however, the Court returned to its insistence on compliance with all state requirements before moving into the federal courts. In a 1977 ruling denying habeas corpus relief to a Florida prisoner who had failed to raise his constitutional claim at the proper time in state courts, Justice William H. Rehnquist spoke of the need for ensuring that the state trial was the "'main event,' so to speak, rather than a tryout on the road for what will later be the determinative federal habeas hearing."[95] Then in 1991 the Court said a prisoner could not file a habeas corpus petition in state court if he had failed to abide by state court procedural rules.[96]

ANTITRUST IMMUNITY AND STATE ECONOMY

Recognizing that "the states are sovereign, save only as Congress may constitutionally subtract from their authority," the Supreme Court in 1943 held that the Sherman Antitrust Act of 1890 was not intended to prevent states from adopting policies or programs that restrained competition in some portion of the state's economy.

The ruling came in *Parker v. Brown* in which California's raisin marketing program—which clearly operated to limit competition among raisin growers—was challenged as in conflict with federal antitrust and agricultural laws. The Court upheld the state's program.

Chief Justice Harlan Fiske Stone explained the reasoning behind its finding that states were immune from the federal antitrust law:

We find nothing in the language of the Sherman Act or in its history which suggests that its purpose was to restrain a state or its officers or agents from activities directed by its legislature. In a dual system of government in which, under the Constitution, the states are sovereign, save only as Congress may constitutionally subtract from their authority, an unexpressed purpose to nullify a state's control over its officers and agents is not lightly to be attributed to Congress.

The Sherman Act makes no mention of the state as such, and gives no hint that it was intended to restrain state action or official action directed by a state. . . . There is no suggestion of a purpose to restrain state action in the Act's legislative history. The sponsor of the bill which was ultimately enacted as the Sherman Act declared that it prevented only "business combinations." . . .

True, a state does not give immunity to those who violated the Sherman Act by authorizing them to violate it, or by declaring that their action is lawful . . . and we have no question of the state . . . becoming a participant in a private agreement or combination by others for restraint of trade. . . . Here the state command . . . is not rendered unlawful by the Sherman Act since . . . it must be taken to be a prohibition of individual and not state action. . . .

The state in adopting and enforcing the prorate program made no contract or agreement and entered into no conspiracy in restraint of trade or to establish monopoly but, as sovereign, imposed the restraint as an act of government which the Sherman Act did not undertake to prohibit.[1]

Twenty-five years later, in 1978, the Court held that this immunity did not extend to cities, unless their anticompetitive conduct was undertaken in carrying out state policy to replace competition with regulation or monopoly.[2]

1. *Parker v. Brown*, 317 U.S. 341 at 350–352 (1943).
2. *City of Lafayette, La. v. Louisiana Power & Light Co.*, 435 U.S. 389 (1978).

INJUNCTIONS

Another exercise of federal power over state court proceedings is the use of the injunction, issued by a federal judge, ordering state officials to stop enforcing a state law, or ordering state judicial proceedings to halt. In 1793 Congress unconditionally forbade such federal interference with state court proceedings. But since that time several exceptions have been made to the ban. Federal courts may interfere in this way (1) when authorized by Congress, (2) when necessary to protect their own jurisdiction, and (3) to carry out their judgments.

In 1908 the Supreme Court added an exception with its ruling in *Ex parte Young*. There it held that a person about to be tried in state court could obtain a federal order halting the trial if he could show that he would suffer irreparable damage if tried.[97]

Amid the tense civil rights conflicts of the 1960s, the Court appeared to broaden this exception to allow federal judges to halt state court proceedings when defendants claimed that the state laws under which they were charged violated their First Amendment freedom of expression. In a particular case decided by the Court in 1965, *Dombrowski v. Pfister*, the Court held that such a threat existed and that it was a proper use of federal power to halt the enforcement of the challenged law until it was determined valid or invalid.[98]

Defendants prosecuted under state laws subject to this sort of First Amendment challenge took full advantage of the ruling, producing a wave of petitions to federal courts and a resulting flood of federal injunctions to halt enforcement of such state laws. In 1971 the Court curtailed this trend. "[T]he normal thing to do when federal courts are asked to enjoin pending proceedings in state courts is not to issue such injunctions," wrote Justice Hugo L. Black. Black explained that federal courts should abstain from interference in state business unless there was an immediate threat of irreparable injury resulting from continuation of the trial or enforcement of the law, unless the challenged law was flagrantly unconstitutional, or unless there had been official disregard of the law.[99]

The policy of federal abstention was based upon "the notion of 'comity,'" wrote Black. He continued to define the notion:

. . . a proper respect for state functions, a recognition of the fact that the entire country is made up of a Union of separate state governments, and a continuance of the belief that the National Government will fare best if the States and their institutions are left free to perform their separate functions in their separate ways. This, perhaps for lack of a better and clearer way to describe it, is referred to by many as "Our Federalism.". . . The concept does not mean blind deference to "States' Rights" any more than it means centralization of control over every important issue in our National Government and its courts. The Framers rejected both these courses. What the concept does represent is a system in which there is sensitivity to the legitimate interests of both State and National Governments, and in which the National Government, anxious though it may be to vindicate and protect federal rights and federal interests, always endeavors to do so in ways that will not unduly interfere with the legitimate activities of the States.[100]

NO FOREIGN AFFAIRS!

The Constitution strictly forbade states to involve themselves in foreign affairs. It prohibited the formation of treaties, alliances, confederations; it required the consent of Congress for states to tax imports, exports, or freight brought into their ports; it forbade states to maintain troops or ships of war in peacetime or to conclude any agreement or compact with a foreign power; and it prohibited states from engaging in war unless they were invaded or otherwise in imminent danger.

These provisions left relatively little need for interpretation by the Supreme Court. One of the Court's first rulings made quite clear the supremacy of federal treaties over conflicting state laws.[1] And in 1920 the Court affirmed the power of a treaty to remove from state jurisdiction a subject, in this case migratory birds, normally left to its control.[2] *(See box, Fish, But Not All Fowl, p. 373.)*

In 1840 the Court held that the Constitution's ban on states making treaties denied a state the power even to return a fugitive to a foreign state.[3]

One small crack in the Court's opposition to state laws involving matters of foreign import appeared just after World War I, when the Court upheld state espionage laws as a proper exercise of state police power.[4]

But several decades later, in 1956, the Court overturned that holding, ruling that the Smith Act of 1940, a national sedition act, had preempted all state power over espionage and sedition.[5] *(See box, The Court and State Sedition Laws, p. 541, in Chapter 10.)*

1. *Ware v. Hylton*, 3 Dall. 199 (1796).
2. *Missouri v. Holland*, 252 U.S. 416 (1920).
3. *Holmes v. Jennison*, 14 Pet. 540 (1840).
4. *Gilbert v. Minnesota*, 254 U.S. 325 (1920).
5. *Pennsylvania v. Nelson*, 350 U.S. 497 (1956).

The Power to Govern

Although the Supreme Court ruled firmly—after the end of the Civil War—that states have no power to secede from the Union, the Court has left to the states a certain area of freedom concerning the conduct of their internal government.[101]

In the nineteenth century the Court upheld the state's power to move a county seat or to reduce the pay of its officers. Both actions were challenged as violating the contract clause.[102]

A twenty-year tug-of-war followed Congress's decision in the 1960s to extend federal minimum wage and overtime requirements to some state employees. The Court first upheld this action as proper but later struck it down as undue federal interference in state business.[103] Justice Rehnquist wrote that the Constitution protected states from such federal interference with their traditional governmental functions. But after almost a decade of trying to separate out those functions from nontraditional ones in which Congress could interfere, the Court gave

"Punitive damages are a powerful weapon. Imposed wisely and with restraint, they have the potential to advance legitimate state interests. Imposed indiscriminately, however, they have a devastating potential for harm."[1] With those words Justice Sandra Day O'Connor summarized in 1991 the tension that focused the Court's attention again and again in the 1980s and 1990s on the question of state laws and procedures governing the award of punitive damages in civil suits.

An underlying issue was whether the state's jury procedures violated the federal guarantee of due process. Even as these cases were argued and decided, state legislatures and Congress were struggling to overhaul the nation's civil justice system, under attack for what some felt were far too many frivolous lawsuits and a great number of indiscriminate jury awards. The challenge for lawmakers and justices alike was to reconcile the needs to punish reprehensible conduct and to ensure that awards were fair, based on some objective standard rather than just jurors' personal predilections.

While the Court's decisions in these cases generated no simple rules for assessing whether an award was excessive, by 1996 a majority of the Court agreed that damages "grossly out of proportion to the severity of the offense" should not be permitted.

In its first rulings on this issue, however, the Court rejected several challenges to particularly large awards.

In 1989 the justices ruled that the Eighth Amendment's prohibition on excessive fines did not apply to punitive-damage awards in civil cases. The Court by a 7–2 vote upheld a $6 million jury award—more than 100 times the amount of actual damages involved—to a Vermont waste disposal firm that a competitor had tried to run out of business.[2] Justices O'Connor and John Paul Stevens dissented. Some of the justices in the majority suggested that a defendant could base a challenge to such an award on the Fourteenth Amendment's due process guarantee.

But two years later, when just such a challenge came to the Court in the case of *Pacific Mutual Life Insurance Co. v. Haslip*, the Court rebuffed that argument and said, 7–1, that juries have broad discretion to set punitive damages even if the resulting awards are greatly disproportionate to the injury suffered.[3]

Writing for the majority in that case, Justice Harry A. Blackmun explained that the Court could not draw a "mathematical bright line between the constitutionally acceptable and the constitutionally unacceptable that would fit every case. We can say, however, that general concerns of reasonableness and adequate guidance from the court . . properly enter into the constitutional calculus."[4] Blackmun said the Alabama jury, which had awarded an insurance fraud victim more than $1 million, had been properly instructed that punitive damages were to punish the defendant and deter future wrongdoing, not to compensate the victim. Only O'Connor dissented.

In 1993 the Court again refused to rely on the due process guarantee to set strict guidelines for juries.[5] The justices upheld a West Virginia jury's award of $10 million in punitive damages against a Texas corporation in a dispute over oil and gas drilling rights. The defendant, TXO Production Corp., argued the award was grossly excessive when compared to the jury's award of $19,000 in compensatory damages. The six justices who rejected TXO's due process complaint (Stevens, William H. Rehnquist, Blackmun, Anthony M.

Kennedy, Antonin Scalia, and Clarence Thomas) produced three opinions that took different approaches to reviewing punitive damages. The dissenting justices (O'Connor, Byron R. White, and David Souter) called the award "monstrous" and faulted the majority for failing to provide "a single guidepost" for lower courts to use in reviewing punitive damages.

The following year the Court, 7–2, struck down as a denial of due process a provision of Oregon's constitution that forbade courts to review the size of a punitive damage award unless there was "no evidence" to support the verdict. No other state had such a restriction, but the Court's action was heartening to business groups who contended juries were targeting unpopular defendants. The Oregon jury had awarded $735,000 in compensatory damages and $5 million in punitive damages to a man injured in an accident involving a Honda all-terrain vehicle.[6] Justices Ruth Bader Ginsburg and Rehnquist dissented.

In 1996 the Court for the first time invalidated a jury award as unconstitutionally excessive.[7]

Ira Gore Jr., a Birmingham, Alabama, physician, had sued BMW of North America Inc. after discovering that his new black sedan had been partly repainted before it was sold. The car was marred by acid rain as it was shipped from Germany to a U.S. distributor; BMW's policy was not to disclose repairs worth 3 percent or less of a car's retail price. A jury awarded Gore $4 million as punishment to BMW for fraud and breach of contract for failing to disclose the refinishing. A state court reduced it to $2 million on appeal, still about 500 times the amount of actual damage to the car.

The Court ruled for BMW, 5–4, saying the Fourteenth Amendment's due process clause prohibits awards that are "grossly out of proportion to the severity of the offense."

"Elementary notions of fairness enshrined in our constitutional jurisprudence dictate that a person receive fair notice not only of the conduct that will subject him to punishment but also of the severity of the penalty that a state may impose," wrote Stevens for the majority.[8] He set out three factors for determining whether an award breaches due process: the reprehensibility of the conduct; the harm suffered by the victim; and a comparison between the award and potential civil penalties authorized or imposed in comparable cases.

Stevens was joined by O'Connor, Kennedy, Souter, and Breyer. Rehnquist, Scalia, Thomas, and Ginsburg dissented. Scalia, who wrote for himself and Thomas, said, "One might understand the Court's eagerness to enter this field, rather than leave it with the state legislatures, if it had something useful to say. In fact, however, its opinion provides virtually no guidance to legislatures."[9] Ginsburg, for herself and Rehnquist, criticized the court for "unnecessarily and unwisely ventur[ing] into territory traditionally within the states' domain."[10]

1. *Pacific Mutual Life Insurance Co. v. Haslip*, 499 U.S. 1 at 42 (1991).
2. *Browning-Ferris Industries of Vermont v. Kelco Disposal*, 492 U.S. 257 (1989).
3. *Pacific Mutual Life Insurance Co. v. Haslip*, 499 U.S. 1 (1991).
4. Id. at 18.
5. *TXO Production Corp. v. Alliance Resources*, 113 S. Ct. 2711 (1993).
6. *Honda Motor Co. Ltd. v. Oberg*, 114 S. Ct. 2331 (1994).
7. *BMW of North America v. Gore*, ____ U.S. ____ (1996).
8. Id.
9. Id.
10. Id.

up. In 1985 it returned to its original position that it was proper for Congress to require state governments to pay their employees in line with federal minimum wage and overtime law.[104]

The power of state and local governments to hire, fire, and retire individuals is, of course, constrained by the Constitution's guarantees of individual rights. In two decisions in the late twentieth century, the Court made that clear, applying the First Amendment to forbid states to base hiring, firing, and promotion decisions on party affiliation.[105] But in a third case the Court rejected a challenge, grounded in federal anti-age-discrimination law, to Missouri's mandatory retirement provision for judges who reached the age of seventy. The Court said that a state's authority to set qualifications for important officials lies "at the heart of representative government."[106]

Interstate Relations

Interstate relations, a matter given little thought by the average citizen in the late twentieth century, evoked great concern from the men who wrote the Constitution. The Confederation—the first effort to unite the former colonies into one nation—had failed. As the Framers labored at the constitutional convention, they were well aware of the situation that Charles Warren would later describe:

[T]he differences between the States—economic, social, religious, commercial—were in some instances as great as the differences between many of the nations of Europe today; and out of these differences arose materially hostile and discriminating state legislation. . . . Pierce Butler of South Carolina said, in the Federal Convention, that he considered the interests of the Southern States and of the Eastern States "to be as different as the interests of Russia and Turkey."[1]

To facilitate smooth relationships between the newly linked states, the Constitution adopted some of the principles of international relations and converted them into provisions governing the relationships of the states.

And so Article IV requires each state to give "full faith and credit" to the public acts of the other states, to grant all citizens of all states certain privileges and immunities, and to surrender a fugitive to the state where he is sought.

And although the Constitution denies states the sovereign right to make treaties or alliances, it did give some recognition to the potential usefulness of interstate agreements by providing, in Article I, that states could—with congressional consent—enter into compacts with each other.

Article IV, Section 1, Clause 1, states: "Full faith and credit shall be given in each state to the public acts, records, and judicial proceedings of every other state." Congress is authorized by the Constitution to provide for the implementation of this provision, and it did so in laws passed in 1790 and 1804.

The meaning of the full faith and credit clause is simple: one state must treat the final judgment of the courts of another state as conclusive, settling the issues raised by the case. In 1813 the Supreme Court rejected the argument that the clause meant only that one state's judgment should be considered as important evidence when a second state's courts considered the same facts and the same question.[2]

However, the judgment of one state can be enforced or implemented in a second state only through that state's courts—where the second state, if opposed to the judgment, can usually block enforcement.

Furthermore, the first state's judgment can be challenged in the second state with the claim that the first state court did not have jurisdiction over the matter decided, or otherwise disregarded necessary technical points. Most modern cases arising under the full faith and credit clause involve questions of jurisdiction—especially called into play in cases when a divorce is granted to a temporary resident of a state. Most states now, however, recognize divorces granted in other states.[3]

This requirement affects only civil matters, not criminal cases. One state does not enforce the criminal laws of another, chiefly because a person has the right to be tried for a crime in the place where the crime was committed—and the courts of other jurisdictions have no right to try him.[4]

E. S. Corwin wrote of the full faith and credit clause:

There are few clauses of the Constitution, the literal possibilities of which have been so little developed. Congress has the power under the clause to decree the effect that the statutes of one State shall have in other States . . . power to enact standards whereby uniformity of State legislation may be secured as to almost any matter with which interstate recognition of private rights would be useful and valuable.

But Congress has exercised this power very little.[5]

"The citizens of each state shall be entitled to all privileges and immunities of citizens in the several states," declares the Constitution in Article IV, Section 2, leaving open the definition of "privileges and immunities."

The primary purpose of this requirement, wrote Justice Samuel Miller a century after its adoption, was to require states to treat the citizens of other states in the same way as their own,

to declare to the several States, that whatever those rights, as you grant or establish them to your own citizens, or as you limit or qualify, or impose restrictions on their exercise, the same, neither more nor less, shall be the measure of the rights of citizens of other states [when they are] within your jurisdiction.[6]

As to the definition of privileges and immunities, Miller referred to the case of *Corfield v. Coryell*, decided in 1823 by Justice Bushrod Washington, sitting as a circuit judge. Washington held that despite this clause, New Jersey could forbid out-of-state persons from gathering oysters in New Jersey. The privileges and immunities that New Jersey—and other states—were bound to grant all states' citizens were more general ones, such as the right to be protected by the government, the right to property, the right to travel through or live in a state other than the state of one's usual residence, the right to bring lawsuits.

In 1869 the Court held that the privileges and immunities clause did not protect corporations from discriminatory treatment by states other than those where they were chartered. And the Court has allowed states to distinguish in some areas between residents and nonresidents, upholding reasonable residency requirements and reasonably different nonresident license fees for people who wish to obtain fish and game licenses, business licenses, the right to practice a profession, to vote in state elections, or to run for state office.[7]

The modern Court, however, has looked with increasing disfavor at state or city actions giving preference to local residents in the job market—whether it be in oil and gas development, public works, or the practice of law.[8]

A state may not tax nonresidents (with a commuter's tax for example) if no comparable tax is imposed on its residents.[9] A state may not make medical services that are legal for its residents, such as abortions, illegal for nonresidents to obtain within its borders.[10] Nor may a state impose on goods brought from outside the state higher taxes than on in-state purchases, even if the difference is small.[11]

To offset the fact that states are not required to enforce each other's criminal laws, Article IV states that "[a] person charged in any state with treason, felony, or other crime, who shall flee from justice, and be found in another state, shall, on demand of the executive authority of the state from which he fled, be delivered up, to be removed to the state having jurisdiction of the crime."

For more than a century, however, the Supreme Court effectively nullified this requirement. The Court in 1861 held that this clause imposed a moral obligation on the governor of Ohio to surrender a fugitive to Kentucky, where he had been indicted for helping a slave to escape. But the Court then ruled that the national government, whether through the courts or other means, could not compel the surrender of this fugitive. Such federal coercion of state officials would be unconstitutional, it held in *Kentucky v. Dennison*.[12]

The resulting ineffectiveness of this clause has been somewhat offset by the enactment of a federal law making it a crime to flee from state to state to avoid prosecution and the adoption, by most states, of a uniform extradition act.

In 1987 the Court discarded *Kentucky v. Dennison*, declaring it "the product of another time." *Dennison*, it said, reflected a relationship between states and the federal government that "is fundamentally incompatible with more than a century of constitutional development." In *Puerto Rico v. Branstad* the Court held that federal courts could indeed act to compel the surrender of an extradited fugitive. In a declaration with meaning that rippled far beyond the subject of extradition, Justice Thurgood Marshall declared, "The fundamental premise of the holding in *Dennison*—'that the states and the Federal Government in all circumstances must be viewed as coequal sovereigns'—is not representative of the law today.'"[13]

Although Article I, Section 10, declares that "no state shall, without the consent of Congress, . . . enter into any Agreement or Compact with another state," the Supreme Court has never invalidated any compact on the basis that it lacked congressional approval.

The Court adopted a relaxed approach to this requirement of congressional consent when it ruled in 1893 that Congress, by its silence, had given its approval to a compact settling a boundary dispute between Virginia and Tennessee.[14] Writing in that case, Justice Stephen Field interpreted the requirement of formal congressional consent to apply only to "the formation of any combination tending to the increase of political power in the States, which may encroach upon or impair the supremacy of the United States or interfere with their rightful management of particular subjects placed under their entire control."[15]

And so compacts that do not tend to increase the power of the states vis-à-vis that of the national government or otherwise infringe on national prerogatives are assumed—in the absence of congressional action to the contrary—to have the requisite consent.

Since New York and New Jersey resolved their long-standing dispute over New York Harbor in the 1830s with a compact, ending their pending case before the Supreme Court, many states have found compacts useful means of resolving mutual problems—from boundaries to resource conservation to pollution control. In one of the Court's modern rulings on the compact clause, it upheld—as valid without express congressional consent—the MultiState Tax Compact in which more than a dozen states joined to improve their methods of taxing interstate corporations.[16]

The Court also strengthened the usefulness of compacts when it ruled in 1951 that once a state has adopted a compact, and the approval of Congress is granted or assumed, the state cannot unilaterally withdraw from it.[17]

When, despite these facilitating provisions of the Constitution, two states find themselves suing each other, it is the exclusive function of the Supreme Court to hear the case. This power of the Court to settle disputes between states of the Union, at odds as states, is a unique characteristic of the American judicial system.

Addressing the centennial celebration of the Supreme Court in 1889 Justice Stephen Field explained:

Controversies between different States of the world respecting their boundaries, rights of soil, and jurisdiction have been the fruitful source of irritation between their people, and not infrequently of blood conflicts. . . .

Between the States in this country, under the Articles of Confederation, there were also numerous conflicts as to boundaries and consequent rights. . . . [But] by the judicial article of the Constitution, all such controversies are withdrawn from the arbitrament of war to the arbitrament of law.[18]

Article III specifically extends federal judicial power to controversies between two or more states. But it was decades before the Court settled such a controversy on its merits. The first case between states—New York and Connecticut—arrived at the Court in 1799 but was dismissed before it was decided.[19]

Thirty years later the state of New Jersey brought to the Court its quarrel with New York over control of the port of New York. New York refused to acknowledge the Supreme Court's jurisdiction over the dispute. Chief Justice John Marshall firmly rejected the state's claim of immunity from the Court's reach in such a matter, but the states then resolved their problems by compact, ending their case before the Court. The compact adopted was the ancestor of the agreement establishing the Port of New York Authority.[20]

In 1846—after the case had been before it for eight years—the Court settled its first boundary dispute between states. At issue was 150 square miles claimed by both Rhode Island and Massachusetts. Once again, before the Court could get to the merits of the dispute, it was obliged to assert its authority to decide such interstate matters, an authority disputed by Massachusetts. The Court reaffirmed that authority—and then decided the case in favor of Massachusetts.[21]

Missouri and Iowa almost went to war with each other over some two thousand square miles of contested territory, each state calling out its militia, before the Supreme Court decided the case in favor of Iowa in 1850. With its decision the Court placed the territory in a free state rather than a slave state, no small issue at the time.[22]

The settlement of the dispute drew favorable notice in Congress, where a senator commented:

In Europe armies run [boundary] lines and they run them with bayonets and cannon. They are marked with ruin and devastation. In our country, they are run by an order of the Court. They are run by an unarmed surveyor with his chain and his compass, and the monuments which he puts down are not monuments of devastation but peaceable ones.[23]

Only months before the onset of the Civil War, the Supreme Court's power over interstate matters was acknowledged by the submission to the Court of a boundary dispute between the states of Alabama and Georgia.[24]

After the war, boundary disputes multiplied, many involving changes in the courses of the rivers or channels that had marked an original boundary. But by that period in history, the Court's authority to resolve such matters was so generally accepted that they came naturally to the justices for settlement.

And the variety of interstate issues coming to the Court increased greatly. The classic postwar interstate case was between Virginia and West Virginia. Upon becoming a separate state, West Virginia had agreed to assume a certain portion of Virginia's state debt. Soon after the end of the war, Virginia opened negotiations with West Virginia for payment of the money, but West Virginia resisted. In 1906 Virginia brought the matter to the Supreme Court, which declared that it did have jurisdiction over this sort of interstate dispute and that West Virginia—by 1915—owed Virginia some $12 million.

West Virginia still refused to pay. Virginia asked the Supreme Court to order the West Virginia legislature to impose a tax to raise the money to pay the debt. Realizing that if it granted this unprecedented request, it might well be met with resistance from West Virginia, the Court delayed. The justices scheduled arguments on the question of how they might enforce such an order.

West Virginia finally agreed to pay the debt, without the necessity of an order from the Supreme Court, and enacted a bond issue that did pay it off.[25]

Earlier, the Court had held that South Dakota, which owned North Carolina bonds, not only could sue North Carolina to recover money due, but also could foreclose, if need be, on the security pledged to back the bonds.[26]

In the long series of water-related disputes that began with that between New York and New Jersey in 1829, the Court has been quite willing to hear states argue their points but hesitant to order one state to act—or cease acting—without strong proof by the complaining state of the need for such a judicial decree.

Early in the twentieth century, the Court heard Missouri argue, in defense of its citizens' health, that Illinois should be ordered to halt its diversion of sewage into the Mississippi River, because it was thereby exposing the citizens of Missouri to the risk of typhoid. The Court did not issue such an order, holding that Missouri had not proved its case.[27]

Similarly, the Court heard Kansas argue for an order halting Colorado's diversion of the Arkansas River, but it held in 1907 that Kansas had not presented sufficient evidence to support issuance of the order. Fifteen years later, in 1922, the Court did grant Wyoming an injunction halting Colorado's diversion of the Laramie River.[28] Through the end of the twentieth century, disputes over water rights continued to be a staple of the Court's calendar. The justices often were called in to interpret water-use agreements, river boundaries, and flow allocations to states.

NOTES

INTRODUCTION (PP. 311–315)

1. *Texas v. White*, 7 Wall. 700 at 725 (1869).
2. Charles Lund Black, *The People and the Court* (New York: Macmillan, 1960), 143.
3. *Cohens v. Virginia*, 6 Wheat. 264 at 382 (1821).
4. *Ableman v. Booth*, 21 How. 506 at 517 (1859).
5. Charles Warren, *The Supreme Court in United States History*, rev. ed., 2 vols. (Boston: Little, Brown, 1922, 1926), I: 5–6.
6. C. Herman Pritchett, *The American Constitution*, 3d ed. (New York: McGraw-Hill, 1977), 46.
7. Letter to William B. Giles, December 26, 1825, cited in Warren, *The Supreme Court in United States History*, I: 620–621.
8. Warren, *The Supreme Court in United States History*, II: 547–548.
9. Alpheus T. Mason, *The Supreme Court from Taft to Warren* (Baton Rouge: Louisiana State University Press, 1958), 167.
10. *Younger v. Harris*, 401 U.S. 37 at 44 (1971).
11. *National League of Cities v. Usery*, 426 U.S. 833 at 845 (1976).
12. *Garcia v. San Antonio Metropolitan Transit Authority*, 469 U.S. 528 (1985).
13. Id.
14. A. E. Dick Howard, "Federalism at the Bicentennial," in *Federalism: Studies in History, Law and Policy*, ed. Harry N. Scheiber (Berkeley: University of California Press, 1988).
15. Sue Davis, *Justice Rehnquist and the Constitution* (Princeton, N.J.: Princeton University Press, 1989), 204.
16. *United States v. Lopez*, 115 S. Ct. 1624 (1995).
17. Id.
18. *U.S. Term Limits v. Thornton*, 115 S. Ct. 1842 (1995).
19. Id.

JUDICIAL REVIEW AND THE STATES (PP. 316–321)

1. Oliver Wendell Holmes Jr., *Collected Legal Papers* (New York: Harcourt Brace, 1920), 295–296; Address, February 15, 1913, to Harvard Law School Association of New York.
2. Charles Warren, *The Supreme Court in United States History*, rev. ed., 2 vols. (Boston: Little, Brown, 1922, 1926), I: 5.
3. *Chisholm v. Georgia*, 2 Dall. 419 (1793).
4. Id. at 473.
5. Id. at 478–479.
6. Warren, *The Supreme Court in United States History*, I: 96.
7. Ibid., 99–101.
8. The vote in the Senate was 23–2; in the House, 81–9. Ibid., 101.
9. Ibid., 102.
10. Ibid., 144.

11. Ibid., 145–146.

12. *Ware v. Hylton,* 3 Dall. 199 (1796).

13. Id. at 283.

14. *United States v. Judge Peters,* 5 Cr. 115 at 136 (1809).

15. Warren, *The Supreme Court in United States History,* I: 374–387; Charles G. Haines, *American Doctrine of Judicial Supremacy,* 2d ed. (Berkeley: University of California Press, 1932), 290–292.

16. Warren, *The Supreme Court in United States History,* I: 443.

17. Carl B. Swisher, *American Constitutional Development,* 2d ed. (Cambridge: Houghton Mifflin, 1954), 108.

18. *Hunter v. Fairfax's Devisee,* 3 Dall. 305 (1796).

19. *Fairfax's Devisee v. Hunter's Lessee,* 7 Cr. 602 (1813).

20. *Martin v. Hunter's Lessee,* 1 Wheat. 304 at 351 (1816).

21. Id. at 324–325.

22. Id. at 338.

23. Id. at 343–344.

24. Id. at 347–348; further details, see Warren, *The Supreme Court in United States History,* I: 442–453.

25. *Cohens v. Virginia,* 6 Wheat. 264 at 413–415 (1821).

26. Id. at 385.

27. Id. at 387–388.

28. Warren, *The Supreme Court in United States History,* I: 547–564.

29. Ibid., 729–779.

30. *Cherokee Nation v. State of Georgia,* 5 Pet. 1 at 20 (1831).

31. *Worcester v. Georgia,* 6 Pet. 515 (1832).

32. Warren, *The Supreme Court in United States History,* I: 757, citing *Life and Letters of Joseph Story* (1851), II: 83, 86.

33. Ibid., I: 769, citing Massachusetts Historical Society Proceedings, 2d series, XIV.

34. Warren, *The Supreme Court in United States History,* II: 256–260.

35. Robert H. Jackson, *The Struggle for Judicial Supremacy,* (New York: Knopf, 1941), 17.

THE STATES AND THE ECONOMY (PP. 322–349)

1. Thomas Reed Powell, *Vagaries and Varieties in Constitutional Interpretation* (New York: AMS Press, 1967), 85.

2. Felix Frankfurter, *The Commerce Clause under Marshall, Taney and Waite* (Chapel Hill: University of North Carolina Press, 1937), 66–67.

3. Ibid., 18–19.

4. Ibid., 27.

5. Powell, *Vagaries and Varieties,* 176.

6. Charles G. Haines, *American Doctrine of Judicial Supremacy,* 2d ed. (Berkeley: University of California Press, 1932), 313–314.

7. *Fletcher v. Peck,* 6 Cr. 87 at 130 (1810).

8. Id. at 131.

9. Id. at 134.

10. Id. at 135.

11. Id.

12. *New Jersey v. Wilson,* 7 Cr. 164 (1812).

13. *The Providence Bank v. Billings,* 4 Pet. 514 at 562 (1830).

14. Id. at 563.

15. *Piqua Branch of the State Bank of Ohio v. Knoop,* 16 How. 369 (1854).

16. Id. at 378.

17. Id. at 380.

18. Id. at 389.

19. *Dodge v. Woolsey,* 18 How. 331 at 360 (1856); see Charles Warren, *The Supreme Court in United States History,* 2 vols. (Boston: Little, Brown, 1922, 1926), II: 250–255.

20. *Dartmouth College v. Woodward,* 4 Wheat. 519 at 644 (1819).

21. Id.

22. Id. at 647–648.

23. Id. at 712.

24. Warren, *The Supreme Court in United States History,* I: 491.

25. *Sturges v. Crowninshield,* 4 Wheat. 122 (1819).

26. *Ogden v. Saunders,* 12 Wheat. 213 (1827).

27. Id. at 270.

28. Id. at 339.

29. *Mason v. Haile,* 12 Wheat. 370 (1827).

30. *Sturges v. Crowninshield,* 4 Wheat. 122 at 201 (1819).

31. *Bronson v. Kinzie,* 1 How. 311 (1843).

32. *Charles River Bridge v. Warren Bridge,* 11 Pet. 420 at 546 (1837).

33. Id. at 547–550.

34. Id. at 552–553.

35. *West River Bridge Co. v. Dix.,* 6 How. 530 at 531–532 (1848).

36. *Pennsylvania Hospital v. Philadelphia,* 245 U.S. 20 (1917).

37. *Stone v. Mississippi,* 101 U.S. 814 at 1079 (1880).

38. Library of Congress, *The Constitution of the United States of America: Analysis and Interpretation* (Washington, D.C.: U.S. Government Printing Office, 1964), 409–410.

39. *Allgeyer v. Louisiana,* 165 U.S. 578 (1897).

40. Library of Congress, *The Constitution,* 410.

41. *Home Building & Loan Association v. Blaisdell,* 290 U.S. 398 at 425–426, 428 (1934).

42. Id. at 434–435.

43. Id. at 439–440.

44. *W. B. Worthen Co. v. Thomas,* 292 U.S. 426 (1934); *Worthen Co. v. Kavanaugh,* 295 U.S. 56 (1935).

45. Edward S. Corwin, *The Constitution and What It Means Today,* 14th ed. (Princeton, N.J.: Princeton University Press, 1978), 140.

46. *Allied Structural Steel Co. v. Spannaus,* 438 U.S. 234 at 241 (1978).

47. *United States Trust Co. v. New Jersey,* 431 U.S. 1 (1977).

48. *The Federalist Papers,* with an Introduction by Clinton Rossiter (New York: New American Library, Mentor Books, 1961), No. 7, 63; No. 22, 145.

49. Felix Frankfurter, "Some Observations on the Nature of the Judicial Process of Supreme Court Litigation." *Proceedings of the American Philosophical Society* 98 (1954): 233, reprinted in *The Supreme Court: Views from Inside,* ed. Alan F. Westin (New York: Norton, 1961), 39.

50. Warren, *The Supreme Court in United States History,* I: 598.

51. *Gibbons v. Ogden,* 9 Wheat. at 189–190 (1824).

52. Id. at 194, 196.

53. Id. at 210–211.

54. Frankfurter, *The Commerce Clause,* 18–19.

55. Alfred H. Kelly and Winfred A. Harbison, *The American Constitution: Its Origins and Development,* 7th ed. (New York: Norton, 1991), 296.

56. Carl B. Swisher, *American Constitutional Development,* 2d ed. (Cambridge: Houghton Mifflin, 1954), 193.

57. Warren, *The Supreme Court in United States History,* II: 627–628.

58. *Willson v. Blackbird Creek Marsh Co.,* 2 Pet. 245 at 251 (1829).

59. *Mayor of New York v. Miln,* 11 Pet. 102 (1837).

60. *Groves v. Slaughter,* 15 Pet. 449 (1841); see Swisher, *American Constitutional Development,* 198.

61. *Thurlow v. Massachusetts, Fletcher v. Rhode Island, Peirce v. New Hampshire,* 5 How. 504 (1847).

62. *Smith v. Turner, Norris v. Boston,* 7 How. 283 (1849).

63. Warren, *The Supreme Court in United States History,* II: 178.

64. *Cooley v. Board of Wardens of the Port of Philadelphia,* 12 How. 299 at 318–320 (1852).

65. Powell, *Vagaries and Varieties,* 152.

66. *Pennsylvania v. Wheeling & Belmont Bridge Co.,* 13 How. 518 at 566 (1852).

67. Warren, *The Supreme Court in United States History,* II: 236.

68. *Henderson v. Wickham, Commissioners of Immigration v. The North German Lloyd, Chy Lung v. Freeman,* 92 U.S. 259, 275 at 273 (1876).

69. Id. at 280.

70. *Chicago, Burlington & Quincy Railroad Co. v. Iowa,* 94 U.S. 155; *The Chicago, Milwaukee & St. Paul Railroad Co. v. Ackley,* 94 U.S. 179; *Peik v. Chicago & Northwestern Railway Co.,* 94 U.S. 164; *The Winona & St. Peter Railroad Co. v. Blake,* 94 U.S. 180; *Stone v. Wisconsin,* 94 U.S. 181; *Munn v. Illinois,* 94 U.S. 113 (1877).

71. *Peik v. Chicago & Northwestern Railway Co.*, 94 U.S. 164 at 178 (1877).

72. *Munn v. Illinois*, 94 U.S. 113 at 126 (1877).

73. *Budd v. New York*, 143 U.S. 517 (1892).

74. *Wabash, St. Louis & Pacific Railway Co. v. Illinois*, 118 U.S. 557 (1886).

75. Id. at 573.

76. Id. at 575.

77. Id. at 577.

78. *Paul v. Virginia*, 8 Wall. 168 (1869).

79. *United States v. Southeastern Underwriters Association*, 322 U.S. 533 at 553 (1944).

80. Id. at 544.

81. *Prudential Insurance Co. v. Benjamin, Robertson v. California*, 328 U.S. 408 (1946).

82. *Kidd v. Pearson*, 128 U.S. 1 at 20, 21 (1888).

83. Id. at 22–23.

84. *United States v. E. C. Knight Co.*, 156 U.S. 1 at 12 (1895).

85. Id. at 11, 13.

86. *Oliver Iron Mining Co. v. Lord*, 262 U.S. 172 (1923); *Coe v. Errol*, 116 U.S. 517 (1886); *Champlin Refining Co. v. Corporation Commission*, 286 U.S. 210 (1932); *Utah Power & Light v. Pfost*, 286 U.S. 165 (1932).

87. *National Labor Relations Board v. Jones & Laughlin Steel Corp.*, 301 U.S. 1 (1937).

88. *Mulford v. Smith*, 307 U.S. 38 (1939).

89. *Wickard v. Filburn*, 317 U.S. 111 at 128 (1942).

90. *Parker v. Brown*, 317 U.S. 341 (1942).

91. *Hall v. DeCuir*, 95 U.S. 485 at 489 (1878).

92. Id. at 490.

93. *Louisville, New Orleans & Texas Railway Company v. Mississippi*, 133 U.S. 587 (1890).

94. Id. at 594.

95. *Plessy v. Ferguson*, 163 U.S. 537 (1896).

96. *Morgan v. Virginia*, 328 U.S. 373 (1946).

97. *Gayle v. Browder*, 352 U.S. 903 (1956).

98. *Hammer v. Dagenhart*, 247 U.S. 251 at 272–274 (1918).

99. Id. at 276–277.

100. Id. at 281.

101. *Bailey v. Drexel Furniture Co.*, 259 U.S. 20 at 38 (1922).

102. *United States v. Darby*, 312 U.S. 100 at 114, 115, 118 (1941).

103. Powell, *Vagaries and Varieties*, 85.

104. Ibid., 162–163.

105. *Gibbons v. Ogden*, 9 Wheat. 1 at 208, 203 (1824).

106. *Willson v. Blackbird Creek Marsh Co.*, 2 Pet. 245 (1829).

107. *Charles River Bridge v. Warren Bridge*, 11. Pet. 420 at 552 (1837).

108. *Mayor of New York v. Miln*, 11 Pet. 102 at 132–133 (1837).

109. Id. at 139, 142.

110. Alpheus T. Mason and William M. Beaney, *The Supreme Court in a Free Society* (Englewood Cliffs, N.J.: Prentice–Hall, 1959), 82.

111. *Bank of Augusta v. Earle*, 13 Pet. 519 (1839).

112. Frankfurter, *The Commerce Clause*, 106; *Pensacola Telegraph Co. v. Western Union*, 96 U.S. 1 (1877).

113. *Groves v. Slaughter*, 15 Pet. 449 (1841).

114. *Smith v. Turner, Norris v. Boston*, 7 How. 283 at 408, 467 (1849).

115. *Edwards v. California*, 314 U.S. 160 (1941).

116. *Thurlow v. Massachusetts, Fletcher v. Rhode Island, Peirce v. New Hampshire*, 5 How. 504 at 589–590, 592 (1847).

117. *Bartemeyer v. Iowa*, 18 Wall. 129 (1874).

118. *Mugler v. Kansas*, 123 U.S. 623 at 691–692 (1887).

119. *Kidd v. Pearson*, 128 U.S. 1 (1888); *Bowman v. Chicago & Northwestern Railroad Co.*, 125 U.S. 465 (1888).

120. *Leisy v. Hardin*, 135 U.S. 100 (1890); *Brown v. Maryland*, 12 Wheat. 419 (1827).

121. *Leisy v. Hardin*, 135 U.S. 100 at 124–125 (1890).

122. *In re Rahrer*, 140 U.S. 545 (1891).

123. *Clark Distilling Co. v. Western Maryland Railway*, 242 U.S. 311 (1917).

124. *Collins v. Yosemite Park and Curry Co.*, 304 U.S. 518 (1938); *James &*

Co. v. Margenthau, 307 U.S. 171 (1939); *Duckworth v. Arkansas*, 314 U.S. 390 (1941); *Carter v. Virginia*, 321 U.S. 131 (1944).

125. *Munn v. Illinois*, 94 U.S. 113 at 125–126 (1877).

126. *Burns Baking Co. v. Bryan*, 264 U.S. 504 (1924); *Wolff Packing Co. v. Industrial Court*, 262 U.S. 522 (1923); *Tyson and Brother v. Banton*, 273 U.S. 418 (1927); *Ribnik v. McBride*, 277 U.S. 350 (1928); *Williams v. Standard Oil Co.*, 278 U.S. 235 (1929); *New State Ice Co. v. Liebmann*, 285 U.S. 262 (1932); *Cotting v. Kansas City Stock Yards Co.*, 183 U.S. 79 (1901); *Townsend v. Yeomans*, 301 U.S. 441 (1937); *German Alliance Ins. Co. v. Lewis*, 233 U.S. 389 (1914).

127. *Nebbia v. New York*, 291 U.S. 502 at 536–537, 539 (1934).

128. *Holden v. Hardy*, 169 U.S. 366 (1898).

129. *Lochner v. New York*, 198 U.S. 45 at 57–58, 59, 61 (1905).

130. *Muller v. Oregon*, 208 U.S. 412 (1908).

131. *Bunting v. Oregon*, 243 U.S. 426 at 438, 439 (1917).

132. *Adkins v. Children's Hospital*, 261 U.S. 525 at 554, 559 (1923).

133. Id. at 562.

134. Id. at 570, 569.

135. *Morehead v. New York ex rel. Tipaldo*, 298 U.S. 587 at 611 (1936).

136. Id. at 635.

137. *West Coast Hotel v. Parrish*, 300 U.S. 379 at 398 (1937).

138. Id. at 399, 400.

139. *United States v. Darby*, 312 U.S. 100 (1941).

140. *Maryland v. Wirtz*, 392 U.S. 183 (1968).

141. *National League of Cities v. Usery*, 426 U.S. 833 at 851 (1976).

142. *Garcia v. San Antonio Metropolitan Transit Authority*, 469 U.S. 528 (1985).

143. *Freeman v. Hewit*, 329 U.S. 249 at 251 (1946).

144. *Boston Stock Exchange v. State Tax Commission*, 429 U.S. 318 at 329 (1977), quoting Justice Tom C. Clark in *Northwestern States Portland Cement Co. v. Minnesota*, 358 U.S. 450, 457 (1959).

145. *Gibbons v. Ogden*, 9 Wheat. 1 at 199 (1824).

146. *McCulloch v. Maryland*, 4 Wheat. 316 at 426, 431 (1819).

147. Id. at 432.

148. Id. at 436–437.

149. *Brown v. Maryland*, 12 Wheat. 419 at 441–442, 443 (1827).

150. Frankfurter, *The Commerce Clause*, 149.

151. *Brown v. Maryland*, 12 Wheat. 419 at 449 (1827).

152. *Woodruff v. Parham*, 8 Wall. 123 (1869).

153. Id. at 137.

154. *Brown v. Houston*, 114 U.S. 622 (1885).

155. *Low v. Austin*, 13 Wall. 29 at 33 (1872).

156. Id. at 34–35.

157. *Hooven & Allison Co. v. Evatt*, 324 U.S. 652 (1945).

158. *Michelin Tire Corp. v. Wages*, 423 U.S. 276 at 286 (1976); see also *Limbach v. The Hooven & Allison Co.*, 466 U.S. 353 (1984).

159. *R. J. Reynolds v. Durham County, N.C.*, 479 U.S. 130 (1986).

160. *Northwestern States Portland Cement Co. v. Minnesota*, 358 U.S. 450 at 457–458 (1959).

161. *State Freight Tax Case, Philadelphia & Reading RR v. Pennsylvania*, 15 Wall. 232 at 280 (1873).

162. *State Tax on Railroad Gross Receipts, Philadelphia & Reading RR Co. v. Pennsylvania*, 15 Wall. 284 at 293, 295 (1873).

163. *Coe v. Errol*, 116 U.S. 517 (1886); *General Oil v. Crain*, 209 U.S. 211 (1908); *Western Union Telegraph Co. v. Massachusetts*, 125 U.S. 530 (1888); *Hans Rees' Sons v. North Carolina*, 283 U.S. 123 (1931); *United States Glue Co. v. Oak Creek*, 247 U.S. 321 (1918); *Maine v. Grand Trunk Railway Co.*, 142 U.S. 217 (1891); *Wisconsin v. J. C. Penney Co.*, 311 U.S. 432 (1940); *General Motors Corp. v. Washington*, 377 U.S. 436 (1964); *Northwestern States Portland Cement Co. v. Minnesota*, 358 U.S. 450 (1959).

164. *Mobil v. Vermont*, 445 U.S. 425 (1980); *Exxon v. Wisconsin*, 447 U.S. 207 (1980); *ASARCO v. Idaho State Tax Commission*, 458 U.S. 307 (1982); *F. W. Woolworth Co. v. Taxation and Revenue Department of New Mexico*, 458 U.S. 354 (1982); *Container Corporation of America v. Franchise Tax Board*, 463 U.S. 159 (1983); *Shell Oil Co. v. Iowa Department of Revenue*,

____ U.S. ____ (1989); *Barclays Bank PLC v. Franchise Tax Board of California*, 114 S. Ct. 2268 (1994).

165. *Paul v. Virginia*, 8 Wall. 168 (1869).

166. *Crutcher v. Kentucky*, 141 U.S. 47 at 57, 59, 60 (1891).

167. Swisher, *American Constitutional Development*, 844.

168. *Complete Auto Transit Inc. v. Brady*, 430 U.S. 274 (1977).

169. *Department of Revenue of the State of Washington v. Association of Washington Stevedoring Companies*, 435 U.S. 734 (1978); *Western and Southern Life Insurance Co. v. State Board of Equalization of California*, 451 U.S. 648 (1981); *D. H. Holmes Co. Ltd. v. McNamara*, 486 U.S. 24 (1988); *Goldberg v. Sweet*, ____ U.S. ____ (1989).

170. *Welton v. Missouri*, 91 U.S. 275 at 282 (1876).

171. *Howe Machine Co. v. Gage*, 100 U.S. 676 at 679 (1880).

172. *Robbins v. Shelby County Taxing District*, 120 U.S. 489 at 497–499 (1887).

173. *Henneford v. Silas Mason Co.*, 300 U.S. 577 at 584 (1937).

174. *Felt & Tarrant Co. v. Gallagher*, 306 U.S. 62 (1939); *Nelson v. Sears, Roebuck & Co.*, 312 U.S. 359 (1941); *Nelson v. Montgomery Ward & Co.*, 312 U.S. 373 (1941); *Scripto v. Carson*, 362 U.S. 207 (1960); *National Geographic Society v. California Board of Equalization*, 430 U.S. 551 (1977).

175. *Boston Stock Exchange v. State Tax Commission*, 429 U.S. 318 at 336 (1977); see also *Maryland v. Louisiana*, 452 U.S. 456 (1981); *Commonwealth Edison v. Montana*, 453 U.S. 609 (1981); *Armco Inc. v. Hardesty*, 467 U.S. 638 (1984); *Bacchus Imports Ltd. v. Dias*, 468 U.S. 263 (1984); *Tyler Pipe Industries v. Washington State Department of Revenue*, 483 U.S. 232 (1987); *American Trucking Associations v. Scheiner*, 483 U.S. 266 (1987); *New Energy Company of Indiana v. Limbach*, 486 U.S. 269 (1988).

176. *Quill Corp. v. North Dakota*, 504 U.S. 298 (1992).

177. *Nordlinger v. Hahn*, 112 S. Ct. 2326 (1992).

178. Id.

THE STATE AND THE INDIVIDUAL (PP. 350–365)

1. *Calder v. Bull*, 3 Dall. 386 at 390, 391 (1798).

2. Alpheus T. Mason and William M. Beaney, *The Supreme Court in a Free Society* (Englewood Cliffs, N.J.: Prentice–Hall, 1959), 197.

3. *Thompson v. Missouri*, 171 U.S. 380 (1898); *Thompson v. Utah*, 170 U.S. 343 (1898).

4. *Dobbert v. Florida*, 432 U.S. 282 (1977).

5. *Nixon v. Administrator of General Services*, 433 U.S. 425 (1977).

6. *Cummings v. Missouri*, 4 Wall. 277 at 319, 325 (1867).

7. *Ex parte Garland*, 4 Wall. 333 (1867).

8. *Hawker v. New York*, 170 U.S. 189 (1898); *DeVeau v. Braisted*, 363 U.S. 144 (1960); *Garner v. Board of Public Works*, 341 U.S. 716 (1951); *Cole v. Richardson*, 405 U.S. 676 (1972); *Elfbrandt v. Russell*, 384 U.S. 11 (1966).

9. *Barron v. Baltimore*, 7 Pet. 243 at 250 (1833).

10. *The Civil Rights Cases*, 109 U.S. 3 at 22, 24–25 (1883).

11. *Bailey v. Alabama*, 219 U.S. 219 (1911).

12. *Butler v. Perry*, 240 U.S. 328 (1916); *Arver v. United States (Selective Draft Law Cases)*, 245 U.S. 366 (1918).

13. Carl B. Swisher, *American Constitutional Development*, 2d ed. (Cambridge, Mass.: Houghton Mifflin, 1954), 330–333, citing 36 *Congressional Globe*, 1089–1090, 2542, 2765–2766, and 44 *Congressional Globe*, Appendix 84.

14. *The Butchers' Benevolent Association of New Orleans v. The Crescent City Livestock Landing and Slaughterhouse Company, Esteben v. Louisiana (The Slaughterhouse Cases)*, 16 Wall. 36 (1873).

15. Id. at 74.

16. Id. at 77–78, 80–81.

17. Id. at 95–96.

18. Id. at 81.

19. *United States v. Reese*, 92 U.S. 214 (1876); *United States v. Cruikshank*, 92 U.S. 542 (1876); *United States v. Harris*, 106 U.S. 629 (1883).

20. *The Civil Rights Cases*, 109 U.S. 3 at 11, 13–14, 17 (1883).

21. Id. at 26, 50.

22. *Plessy v. Ferguson*, 163 U.S. 537 at 544, 551 (1896).

23. *Bradwell v. The State*, 16 Wall. 130 (1873).

24. *Minor v. Happerset*, 21 Wall. 162 (1875).

25. Charles Warren, *The Supreme Court in United States History*, rev. ed., 2 vols. (Boston: Little, Brown, 1922, 1926), II: 567.

26. *Yick Wo v. Hopkins*, 118 U.S. 356 (1886).

27. *Hurtado v. California*, 110 U.S. 516 (1884).

28. *United States v. Reese*, 92 U.S. 214 at 217–218, 221 (1876).

29. *United States v. Cruikshank*, 92 U.S. 542 at 551, 554, 546 (1876).

30. *Ex parte Yarbrough*, 110 U.S. 651 at 657–658, 665 (1884).

31. *Guinn v. United States*, 238 U.S. 347 (1915); *Lane v. Wilson*, 307 U.S. 368 (1939).

32. *United States v. Classic*, 313 U.S. 299 (1941); *Smith v. Allwright*, 321 U.S. 649 (1944).

33. *Williams v. Mississippi*, 170 U.S. 213 (1898); *Lassiter v. Northampton County Board of Elections*, 360 U.S. 45 (1960).

34. *Harper v. Virginia State Board of Elections*, 383 U.S. 663 (1966).

35. *Oregon v. Mitchell, Texas v. Mitchell, United States v. Idaho, United States v. Arizona*, 400 U.S. 112 (1970).

36. *Gomillion v. Lightfoot*, 364 U.S. 339 (1960).

37. *Allgeyer v. Louisiana*, 165 U.S. 578 at 589 (1897).

38. *Chicago, Burlington & Quincy Railroad Co. v. Chicago*, 166 U.S. 226 (1897).

39. *Smyth v. Ames*, 169 U.S. 466 (1898).

40. Loren P. Beth, *The Development of the American Constitution: 1877–1917* (New York: Harper and Row, 1971), 67–68.

41. *Gitlow v. New York*, 268 U.S. 652 at 666 (1925).

42. *Stromberg v. California*, 283 U.S. 359 (1931).

43. *Near v. Minnesota*, 283 U.S. 697 (1931).

44. *Hamilton v. Board of Regents*, 293 U.S. 245 (1934).

45. *De Jonge v. Oregon*, 299 U.S. 353 (1937).

46. *Everson v. Board of Education*, 330 U.S. 1 (1947).

47. *Lovell v. Griffin*, 303 U.S. 444 (1938); *Cantwell v. Connecticut*, 310 U.S. 296 (1940).

48. *Hague v. CIO*, 307 U.S. 496 (1939).

49. *Minersville School District v. Gobitis*, 310 U.S. 586 (1940).

50. *West Virginia State Board of Education v. Barnette*, 319 U.S. 624 at 642 (1943).

51. *Powell v. Alabama*, 287 U.S. 45 at 71–72 (1932).

52. *Betts v. Brady*, 316 U.S. 455 at 461–462 (1942).

53. *Gideon v. Wainwright*, 372 U.S. 335 (1963).

54. *Tumey v. Ohio*, 273 U.S. 510 at 523 (1927).

55. *Moore v. Dempsey*, 261 U.S. 86 (1923); *Norris v. Alabama*, 294 U.S. 587 (1935); *Smith v. Texas*, 311 U.S. 128 (1940).

56. *Walker v. Sauvinet*, 92 U.S. 90 (1876); *Maxwell v. Dow*, 176 U.S. 581 (1900); *Duncan v. Louisiana*, 391 U.S. 145 (1968).

57. *Pointer v. Texas*, 380 U.S. 400 (1965).

58. *Twining v. New Jersey*, 211 U.S. 78 (1908).

59. *Malloy v. Hogan*, 378 U.S. 1 (1964); *Griffin v. California*, 380 U.S. 609 (1965).

60. *Brown v. Mississippi*, 297 U.S. 278 (1936).

61. *Escobedo v. Illinois*, 378 U.S. 478 (1964).

62. *Miranda v. Arizona*, 384 U.S. 436 (1966).

63. *United States v. Lanza*, 260 U.S. 377 (1922).

64. *Palko v. Connecticut*, 302 U.S. 319 at 325–326 (1937); *Benton v. Maryland*, 395 U.S. 784 (1969).

65. *Wolf v. Colorado*, 338 U.S. 25 (1949).

66. *Weeks v. United States*, 232 U.S. 383 (1914).

67. *Mapp v. Ohio*, 367 U.S. 643 at 660 (1961).

68. *Ker v. California*, 374 U.S. 23 (1963).

69. *Terry v. Ohio*, 392 U.S. 1 (1968); *Chimel v. California*, 395 U.S. 752 (1969); *Schneckloth v. Bustamonte*, 412 U.S. 218 (1973); *Cady v. Dombrowski*, 413 U.S. 433 (1973); *Gustafson v. Florida, United States v. Robinson*, 414 U.S. 218 (1973); *Cardwell v. Lewis*, 417 U.S. 583 (1974); *South Dakota v. Opperman*, 428 U.S. 364 (1976).

70. *Louisiana ex. rel. Francis v. Resweber*, 329 U.S. 459 (1947).

71. *Robinson v. California*, 370 U.S. 660 (1962).

72. *Furman v. Georgia*, 408 U.S. 238 (1972).

73. *Gregg v. Georgia*, 428 U.S. 153 (1976); *Woodson v. North Carolina, Roberts v. Louisiana*, 428 U.S. 280, 325 (1976).

74. *Rummel v. Estelle*, 445 U.S. 263 (1980); *Solem v. Helm*, 463 U.S. 277 (1983).

75. *In re Gault*, 387 U.S. 1 (1967). See also *Schall v. Martin, Abrams v. Martin*, 467 U.S. 253 (1984); *In re Winship*, 397 U.S. 358 (1970); *McKeiver v. Pennsylvania*, 403 U.S. 528 (1971).

76. *Yick Wo v. Hopkins*, 118 U.S. 356 (1886); Warren, *The Supreme Court in United States History*, II: 596.

77. *Newberry v. United States*, 256 U.S. 232 (1921).

78. *Nixon v. Herndon*, 273 U.S. 536 (1927).

79. *Nixon v. Condon*, 286 U.S. 73 (1932).

80. *Grovey v. Townsend*, 295 U.S. 45 (1935).

81. *United States v. Classic*, 313 U.S. 45 (1941); *Smith v. Allwright*, 321 U.S. 649 (1944).

82. *Harper v. Virginia Board of Elections*, 383 U.S. 663 (1966).

83. *South Carolina v. Katzenbach*, 393 U.S. 301 (1966).

84. *Colegrove v. Green*, 328 U.S. 549 at 553–554, 556 (1946).

85. *Baker v. Carr*, 369 U.S. 186 at 237 (1962).

86. *Gray v. Sanders*, 372 U.S. 368 at 379, 381 (1963).

87. *Reynolds v. Sims*, 377 U.S. 533 (1964); *Wesberry v. Sanders*, 376 U.S. 1 (1964).

88. *Kirkpatrick v. Preisler*, 394 U.S. 526 (1969); *Mahan v. Howell*, 410 U.S. 315 (1973).

89. *Davis v. Bandemer*, 478 U.S. 109 (1986).

90. *Shaw v. Reno*, 509 U.S. 630 (1993).

91. *Buchanan v. Warley*, 245 U.S. 601 (1917); *Shelley v. Kraemer*, 334 U.S. 1 (1948).

92. *Reitman v. Mulkey*, 387 U.S. 369 (1967); *Hunter v. Erickson*, 393 U.S. 385 (1969); *James v. Valtierra*, 402 U.S. 137 (1971); *Village of Arlington Heights v. Metropolitan Housing Development Corp.*, 429 U.S. 252 (1977).

93. *Berea College v. Kentucky*, 211 U.S. 45 (1908).

94. *Missouri ex rel. Gaines v. Canada*, 305 U.S. 337 at 350 (1938).

95. *Sipuel v. University of Oklahoma*, 332 U.S. 631 (1948); *McLaurin v. Oklahoma State Regents*, 339 U.S. 637 (1950).

96. *Sweatt v. Painter*, 339 U.S. 629 (1950).

97. *Brown v. Board of Education of Topeka*, 347 U.S. 483 (1954).

98. *Brown v. Board of Education of Topeka* (II), 349 U.S. 294 (1955).

99. *Cooper v. Aaron*, 358 U.S. 1 (1958); *Griffin v. School Board*, 377 U.S. 218 (1964); *Green v. County School Board*, 391 U.S. 430 (1968); *Swann v. Charlotte-Mecklenburg Board of Education*, 402 U.S. 1 (1971); *Keyes v. Denver School District #1*, 413 U.S. 921 (1973).

100. *Loving v. Virginia*, 388 U.S. 1 (1967).

101. *San Antonio Independent School District v. Rodriguez*, 411 U.S. 1 (1973).

102. *Boddie v. Connecticut*, 401 U.S. 371 (1971); *Williams v. Illinois*, 399 U.S. 235 (1970); *Griffin v. Illinois*, 351 U.S. 12 (1955); *Argersinger v. Hamlin*, 407 U.S. 25 (1972).

103. *Yick Wo v. Hopkins*, 118 U.S. 356 (1886).

104. *Heim v. McCall*, 239 U.S. 175 (1915); *Terrace v. Thompson*, 263 U.S. 197 (1923).

105. *Truax v. Raich*, 239 U.S. 33 (1915).

106. *Takahashi v. Fish & Game Commission*, 334 U.S. 410 (1948).

107. *Oyama v. California*, 332 U.S. 633 (1948).

108. *Graham v. Richardson*, 403 U.S. 365 (1971); *In re Griffiths*, 413 U.S. 717 (1973); *Sugarman v. Dougall*, 413 U.S. 634 (1973); *Nyquist v. Mauclet*, 422 U.S. 1 (1977); *Plyler v. Doe*, 457 U.S. 202 (1982); *Foley v. Connelie*, 435 U.S. 291 (1978); *Ambach v. Norwick*, 441 U.S. 68 (1979).

109. *Cronin v. Adams*, 192 U.S. 108 (1904); *Goesaert v. Cleary*, 335 U.S. 465 (1948).

110. *Hoyt v. Florida*, 368 U.S. 57 (1961).

111. *Reed v. Reed*, 404 U.S. 71 (1971).

112. *Taylor v. Louisiana*, 419 U.S. 522 (1975).

113. *Stanton v. Stanton*, 421 U.S. 7 (1975); *Craig v. Boren*, 429 U.S. 190 (1976); *Dothard v. Rawlinson*, 433 U.S. 321 (1977).

114. *Kahn v. Shevin*, 416 U.S. 351 (1974).

115. *Dothard v. Rawlinson*, 433 U.S. 321 (1977).

116. *Geduldig v. Aiello*, 417 U.S. 484 (1974).

117. *Harris v. Forklift Systems Inc.*, 510 U.S. 17 (1994). Justice Ginsburg is quoting from *Kirchberg v. Feenstra*, 450 U.S. 455, 461 (1982).

118. *United States v. Virginia*, _____ U.S. _____ (1996).

THE STATE AS SOVEREIGN (PP. 366–380)

1. *The Federalist Papers*, with an Introduction by Clinton Rossiter (New York: New American Library, Mentor Books, 1961), No. 45, 292–293.

2. *McCulloch v. Maryland*, 4 Wheat. 316 at 436 (1819).

3. *Gibbons v. Ogden*, 9 Wheat. 1 at 222 (1824).

4. *United States v. E. C. Knight*, 156 U.S. 1 (1895); *Hammer v. Dagenhart*, 247 U.S. 251 (1918); *Bailey v. Drexel Furniture Co.*, 259 U.S. 20 (1922); *United States v. Butler*, 297 U.S. 1 (1936); *Ashton v. Cameron County*, 298 U.S. 513 (1936); *Carter v. Carter Coal Co.*, 298 U.S. 238 (1936).

5. *United States v. Butler*, 297 U.S. 1 at 68 (1936).

6. *Champion v. Ames*, 188 U.S. 321 (1903); *McCray v. United States*, 195 U.S. 27 (1904); *Rhode Island v. Palmer*, 253 U.S. 350 (1920); *Hoke v. United States*, 227 U.S. 308 (1913).

7. *Steward Machine Co. v. Davis*, 301 U.S. 548 (1937); *Mulford v. Smith*, 307 U.S. 38 (1939); *Sunshine Anthracite Coal Co. v. Adkins*, 310 U.S. 381 (1940); *Chicot County Drainage District v. Baxter State Bank*, 308 U.S. 371 (1940).

8. *United States v. Darby Lumber Co.*, 312 U.S. 100 at 123–125 (1941).

9. *Chisholm v. Georgia*, 2 Dall. 419 (1793).

10. *Hans v. Louisiana*, 134 U.S. 1 (1890); *Monaco v. Mississippi*, 292 U.S. 313 (1934).

11. Thomas Reed Powell, *Vagaries and Varieties in Constitutional Interpretation* (New York: AMS Press, 1967), 19.

12. *Osborn v. Bank of the United States*, 9 Wheat. 738 (1824).

13. Charles Warren, *The Supreme Court in United States History*, rev. ed., 2 vols. (Boston: Little, Brown, 1922, 1926), II: 665.

14. *Poindexter v. Greenhow*, 114 U.S. 270 (1885).

15. *Johnson v. Lankford*, 245 U.S. 541 (1918).

16. *Scheuer v. Rhodes*, 416 U.S. 233 at 237 (1974).

17. *Ex parte Young*, 209 U.S. 123 (1908). In 1976 Congress eliminated this requirement, returning to the situation in which a single federal judge may issue an injunction to halt enforcement of an allegedly unconstitutional state law. *Congress and the Nation*, Vol. 4 (Washington, D.C.: Congressional Quarterly, 1977), 616.

18. *Edelman v. Jordan*, 415 U.S. 651 (1974).

19. *Fitzpatrick v. Bitzer*, 427 U.S. 445 (1976).

20. *Hutto v. Finney*, 437 U.S. 678, 691, 695 (1978).

21. *Seminole Tribe of Florida v. Florida*, _____ U.S. _____ (1996).

22. *Pennsylvania v. Union Gas Co.*, 491 U.S. 1 (1989).

23. *Seminole Tribe of Florida v. Florida*, _____ U.S. _____ (1996).

24. *Luther v. Borden*, 7 How. 1 (1849).

25. *Pacific States Telephone & Telegraph Co. v. Oregon*, 223 U.S. 118 (1912).

26. *Wood v. Broom*, 287 U.S. 1 (1932).

27. *Colegrove v. Green*, 328 U.S. 549 (1946); *Baker v. Carr*, 369 U.S. 186 (1962); *Wesberry v. Sanders*, 376 U.S. 1 (1964); *Reynolds v. Sims*, 377 U.S. 533 (1964); *Davis v. Bandemer*, 478 U.S. 109 (1986).

28. *Mahan v. Howell*, 410 U.S. 315 (1973).

29. *Karcher v. Daggett*, 462 U.S. 725 (1983).

30. *Brown v. Thomson*, 462 U.S. 835 (1983).

31. *Newberry v. United States*, 256 U.S. 232 (1921).

32. *United States v. Classic*, 313 U.S. 299 (1941).

33. *Leser v. Garnett*, 258 U.S. 130 (1922).

34. *Oregon v. Mitchell, Texas v. Mitchell, United States v. Idaho, United States v. Arizona*, 400 U.S. 112 (1970).

35. *South Carolina v. Katzenbach*, 383 U.S. 301 at 324 (1966); *Katzenbach v. Morgan*, 384 U.S. 641 (1966).

36. *Williams v. Rhodes*, 393 U.S. 23 (1968); *Bullock v. Carter*, 405 U.S. 134 (1972); *Lubin v. Panish*, 415 U.S. 709 (1974); *Kusper v. Pontikes*, 414 U.S. 51 (1973); *Dunn v. Blumstein*, 405 U.S. 330 (1972); *Tashjian v. Republican Party of Connecticut*, 479 U.S. 208 (1986); *Munro v. Socialist Workers Party*, 479 U.S. 189 (1986).

37. Warren, *The Supreme Court in United States History*, II: 69.

38. *Loan Association v. Topeka*, 20 Wall. 655 (1875).

39. *McCulloch v. Maryland*, 4 Wheat. 316 (1819).

40. *Weston v. City Council of Charleston*, 2 Pet. 449 (1829); *Bank of Commerce v. New York*, 2 Bl. 620, 635 (1863); *Bank Tax Cases*, 2 Wall. 200 (1865).

41. *Van Brocklin v. Tennessee*, 117 U.S. 151 (1886).

42. *McCulloch v. Maryland*, 4 Wheat. 316 at 431 (1819).

43. *Dobbins v. Erie County*, 16 Pet. 435 (1842).

44. *Collector v. Day*, 11 Wall. 113 (1871).

45. *Pollock v. Farmers' Loan & Trust Co.*, 158 U.S. 601 (1895).

46. *South Carolina v. United States*, 199 U.S. 437 (1905).

47. *Indian Motorcycle Co. v. United States*, 283 U.S. 570 (1931).

48. *Long v. Rockwood*, 277 U.S. 142 (1928); *Panhandle Oil Co. v. Mississippi*, 277 U.S. 218 (1928); *Gillespie v. Oklahoma*, 257 U.S. 501 (1922).

49. *Panhandle Oil Co. v. Mississippi*, 277 U.S. 218 at 223 (1928).

50. *Fox Film Corp. v. Doyal*, 286 U.S. 123 (1932); *Helvering v. Gerhardt*, 304 U.S. 405 (1938); *Graves v. New York ex. rel. O'Keefe*, 306 U.S. 466 (1939).

51. *Helvering v. Gerhardt*, 304 U.S. 405 at 414, 419–420 (1938).

52. *South Carolina v. Baker*, 485 U.S. 505 (1988).

53. *United States v. Allegheny County*, 322 U.S. 174 (1944); *Alabama v. King & Boozer*, 314 U.S. 1 (1941). See also *United States v. New Mexico*, 455 U.S. 720 (1982); *Washington v. United States*, 460 U.S. 536 (1983); *Rockford Life Insurance Co. v. Illinois Department of Revenue*, 482 U.S. 182 (1987).

54. *New Jersey v. Wilson*, 7 Cr. 164 (1810); *The Providence Bank v. Billings*, 4 Pet. 514 (1830).

55. *The Slaughterhouse Cases*, 16 Wall. 36 at 62 (1873).

56. *Mayor of New York v. Miln*, 11 Pet. 102 at 139 (1837).

57. *Georgia v. Tennessee Copper Co.*, 206 U.S. 230 at 238 (1907).

58. *Hudson Water Co. v. McCarter*, 209 U.S. 349 (1908); *Wyoming v. Colorado*, 259 U.S. 419 (1922).

59. *Pennsylvania v. West Virginia*, 262 U.S. 553 (1923); *Bandini Petroleum Co. v. Superior Court*, 284 U.S. 1 (1931); *Champlin Refining Co. v. Commission*, 286 U.S. 210 (1932).

60. *Askew v. American Waterways Operators Inc.*, 411 U.S. 325 (1973); *Ray v. Atlantic Richfield Co.*, 435 U.S. 151 (1978).

61. *California v. Federal Energy Regulatory Commission*, ____ U.S. ____ (1990).

62. *Gade v. National Solid Wastes Management Association*, 505 U.S. 88 (1992).

63. *New York v. United States*, 488 U.S. 1041 (1992).

64. *Hadacheck v. Los Angeles*, 239 U.S. 394 (1915).

65. *Buchanan v. Warley*, 245 U.S. 60 (1917).

66. *Euclid v. Ambler Realty Co.*, 272 U.S. 365 at 387, 388, 394 (1926).

67. *Berman v. Parker*, 348 U.S. 26 at 33 (1954); *Village of Belle Terre v. Boraas*, 416 U.S. 1 at 9 (1974).

68. *Young v. American Mini Theatres Inc.*, 427 U.S. 50 (1976); *City of Renton v. Playtime Theatres Inc.*, 475 U.S. 41 (1986).

69. *Village of Arlington Heights v. Metropolitan Housing Development Corp.*, 429 U.S. 252 (1977).

70. *Penn Central Transportation Co. v. New York City*, 438 U.S. 104 (1978).

71. *Washington ex rel. Seattle Trust Co. v. Roberge*, 278 U.S. 116 (1928).

72. *Moore v. City of East Cleveland*, 431 U.S. 494 at 498–499 (1977).

73. *Agins v. Tiburon*, 477 U.S. 255 (1980); *San Diego Gas and Electric Co. v. San Diego*, 450 U.S. 621 (1981); *First English Evangelical Church v. Los Angeles County*, 482 U.S. 304 (1987); *Nollan v. California Coastal Commission*, 483 U.S. 825 (1987).

74. *Dolan v. City of Tigard*, 114 S. Ct. 2309 (1994).

75. *Mutual Film Corp. v. Industrial Commission*, 236 U.S. 230 (1915); *Burstyn v. Wilson*, 343 U.S. 495 (1952).

76. *Roth v. United States*, 354 U.S. 476 (1957).

77. *Times Film Corp. v. Chicago*, 365 U.S. 43 (1961); *Freedman v. Maryland*, 380 U.S. 51 (1965).

78. *Kingsley Books v. Brown*, 354 U.S. 436 (1957); *Smith v. California*, 361 U.S. 147 (1959); *Marcus v. Search Warrant*, 376 U.S. 717 (1961); *Bantam Books Inc. v. Sullivan*, 372 U.S. 58 (1963).

79. *Miller v. California*, 413 U.S. 15 (1973); *Jenkins v. Georgia*, 418 U.S. 152 (1974); *Erznoznik v. City of Jacksonville*, 422 U.S. 205 (1975); *Pope v. Illinois*, 481 U.S. 497 (1987). See also *New York v. Ferber*, 458 U.S. 747 (1982); *Brockett v. Spokane Arcades*, 472 U.S. 491 (1985).

80. *Barnes v. Glen Theatre*, 501 U.S. 560 (1991).

81. *Jacobson v. Massachusetts*, 197 U.S. 11 at 27, 29 (1905).

82. *Buck v. Bell*, 274 U.S. 200 at 207 (1927).

83. *Skinner v. Oklahoma*, 316 U.S. 535 (1942).

84. Warren, *The Supreme Court in United States History*, I: 391.

85. *Bank of the United States v. Deveaux*, 5 Cr. 61 (1810); *Louisville Railroad v. Letson*, 2 How. 497 (1845).

86. *United States v. Hudson and Goodwin*, 7 Cr. 32 (1812); *United States v. Coolidge*, 1 Wheat. 415 (1816).

87. *The Thomas Jefferson*, 10 Wheat. 428 (1825).

88. *The Propeller Genessee Chief v. Fitzhugh*, 12 How. 443 at 451 (1851); *The Moses Taylor, The Hine v. Trevor*, 4 Wall. 411, 555 (1866); Warren, *The Supreme Court in United States History*, II: 415.

89. *Ex parte Siebold*, 100 U.S. 371 (1880).

90. *Second Employers' Liability Cases*, 223 U.S. 1 (1912); *Testa v. Katz*, 330 U.S. 386 (1947).

91. *McKim v. Voorhees*, 7 Cr. 279 (1812); *McClung v. Silliman*, 6 Wheat. 598 (1821); *Wayman v. Southard*, 10 Wheat. 1 (1825); *Swift v. Tyson*, 16 Pet. 1 (1842); *Martin v. Waddell's Lessee*, 16 Pet. 367 (1842).

92. *Erie Railroad Co. v. Tompkins*, 304 U.S. 64 (1938).

93. *Peck v. Jenness*, 7 How. 612 (1848); *Taylor v. Carryl*, 20 How. 583 (1858); *Freeman v. Howe*, 24 How. 450 (1861).

94. *Fay v. Noia*, 372 U.S. 391 (1963).

95. *Wainwright v. Sykes*, 433 U.S. 72 at 90 (1977).

96. *Coleman v. Thompson*, 501 U.S. 722 (1991).

97. *Ex parte Young*, 209 U.S. 123 (1908).

98. *Dombrowski v. Pfister*, 380 U.S. 479 (1965).

99. *Younger v. Harris*, 401 U.S. 37 at 45 (1971).

100. Id. at 44; *Pennzoil Co. v. Texaco Inc.*, 481 U.S. 1 (1987).

101. *Texas v. White*, 7 Wall. 700 (1869).

102. *Newton v. Commissioners*, 100 U.S. 548 (1880); *Butler v. Pennsylvania*, 10 How. 402 (1851).

103. *Maryland v. Wirtz*, 392 U.S. 183 (1968); *National League of Cities v. Usery*, 426 U.S. 833 at 845, 851 (1976).

104. *Garcia v. San Antonio Metropolitan Transit Authority*, 469 U.S. 528 (1985).

105. *Elrod v. Burns*, 427 U.S. 347 (1976); and *Rutan v. Republican Party of Illinois*, 497 U.S. 62 (1990). See also *O'Hare Truck Service v. Northlake*, ____ U.S. ____ (1996); *Board of County Commissioners, Wabaunsee County v. Umbehr*, ____ U.S. ____ (1996).

106. *Gregory v. Ashcroft*, 501 U.S. 452 (1991).

INTERSTATE RELATIONS (PP. 381–383)

1. Charles Warren, *The Supreme Court and Sovereign States*, (Princeton, N.J.: Princeton University Press, 1924), 9.

2. *Mills v. Duryee*, 7 Cr. 481 (1813).

3. *Atherton v. Atherton*, 181 U.S. 155 (1901); *Haddock v. Haddock*, 201 U.S. 562 (1906); *Williams v. North Carolina*, 317 U.S. 387 (1942) and 325 U.S. 226 (1945); *Sherrer v. Sherrer*, 334 U.S. 343 (1948).

4. *Huntington v. Attrile*, 146 U.S. 657 (1892).

5. Edward S. Corwin, *The Constitution and What It Means Today*, 14th ed. (Princeton, N.J.: Princeton University Press, 1978), 166.

6. *The Slaughterhouse Cases*, 16 Wall. 36 at 77 (1873).

7. *Paul v. Virginia*, 8 Wall. 168 (1869); *McCready v. Virginia*, 94 U.S. 391 (1877); *Toomer v. Witsell*, 334 U.S. 385 (1948); *LaTourette v. McMaster*, 248

U.S. 465 (1919); *Blake v. McClung,* 172 U.S. 239 (1898); *Baldwin v. Montana Fish & Game Commission,* 436 U.S. 371 (1978).

8. *Hicklin v. Orbeck,* 437 U.S. 518 (1978); *United Building and Construction Trades Council of Camden County v. Mayor and Council of City of Camden,* 465 U.S. 208 (1984); *Supreme Court of New Hampshire v. Piper,* 470 U.S. 274 (1985).

9. *Ward v. Maryland,* 12 Wall. 418 (1871); *Travis v. Yale and Towne Mfg. Co.,* 252 U.S. 60 (1920); *Austin v. New Hampshire,* 420 U.S. 656 (1975).

10. *Doe v. Bolton,* 410 U.S. 179 (1973).

11. *Associated Industries of Missouri v. Lohman,* ____ U.S. ____ (1994).

12. *Kentucky v. Dennison,* 24 How. 66 (1861).

13. *Puerto Rico v. Branstad,* 483 U.S. 219 (1987).

14. *Virginia v. Tennessee,* 148 U.S. 503 (1893).

15. Id. at 517–518.

16. *United States Steel Corp. v. MultiState Tax Commission,* 434 U.S. 452 (1978).

17. *West Virginia ex rel. Dyer v. Sims,* 341 U.S. 22 (1951).

18. Hampton L. Carson, *The Supreme Court of the United States: Its History* (Philadelphia: A. R. Keller, 1892), 708.

19. Warren, *The Supreme Court and Sovereign States,* 38–39.

20. *New Jersey v. New York,* 3 Pet. 461 (1830); also 5 Pet. 284 (1831); 6 Pet. 323 (1832).

21. *Rhode Island v. Massachusetts,* 4 How. 591 (1846).

22. *Missouri v. Iowa,* 7 How. 660 (1849) and 10 How. 1 (1850).

23. Charles Warren, *The Supreme Court in United States History,* 2 vols. (Boston: Little, Brown, 1922, 1926), II: 298.

24. *Alabama v. Georgia,* 23 How. 509 (1860).

25. *Virginia v. West Virginia,* 238 U.S. 202 (1915), 241 U.S. 531 (1916), and 246 U.S. 565 (1918).

26. *South Dakota v. North Carolina,* 192 U.S. 286 (1904).

27. *Missouri v. Illinois,* 180 U.S. 208 (1901).

28. *Kansas v. Colorado,* 206 U.S. 46 (1907); *Wyoming v. Colorado,* 259 U.S. 419 (1922).

The Court and the Individual

CHAPTER 8

The Court and the Individual

THE SUPREME COURT'S role as guardian of the rights and liberties of the individual is a new one, a responsibility assumed in the twentieth century.

For most of its history, the Court had little to say about the Constitution's guarantees of individual freedom. Preoccupied with defining the relationship of nation to state, state to state, and government to business, the Court found little occasion and less reason to deal with individual rights.

Indeed, until the twentieth century there was no broad constitutional basis for the assertion of individual rights against government action.

The Constitution itself contains few provisions touching individual rights; and those few have been infrequently invoked. The Bill of Rights operated solely against federal action until adoption of the Fourteenth Amendment in 1868.

That amendment's guarantees of the privileges and immunities of U.S. citizens, due process of law, and equal protection were designed to extend the protection of the Bill of Rights to individuals threatened by state action.

But not until half a century after its ratification was the purpose of this amendment in any way fulfilled. In the 1920s the Court finally began to read its guarantees as its authors had intended.

In the 1960s the promises of due process and equal protection were construed to apply most of the guarantees of the Bill of Rights to the states. In the closing decades of the twentieth century, questions of individual rights versus government authority consumed more and more of the Court's time and became its most controversial and pressing business.

A Narrow Base: 1789–1865

The Supreme Court deals with cases that arise under the Constitution and the laws of the United States.

Only half a dozen sentences in the original Constitution deal directly with matters of individual rights. The Constitution does forbid suspension of the privilege of the writ of habeas corpus except in time of public emergency.[1] And it prohibits the passage of bills of attainder or ex post facto laws.[2] For almost all crimes, the Constitution requires jury trials in the state where the crime was committed;[3] it defines the crime of treason, sets the standard of evidence, and limits the penalty for that crime.[4] And it provides for extradition of fugitives[5] and forbids religious tests for federal officeholders.[6]

THE DEMAND FOR GUARANTEES

Not surprisingly, many persons active in the formulation of the new government—with all-too-fresh memories of governmental oppression—found the lack of more comprehensive guarantees of individual rights a serious deficiency. Historian Charles Warren described the situation:

Men on all sides contended that, while the first object of a Constitution was to establish a government, its second object, equally important, must be to protect the people against the government. That was something which all history and all human experience had taught.

The first thing that most of the colonies had done, on separating from Great Britain, had been to assure to the people a Bill of Rights, safeguarding against state legislative despotism those human rights which they regarded as fundamental. Having protected themselves by specific restrictions on the power of their state legislatures, the people of this country were in no mood to set up and accept a new national government, without similar checks and restraints. As soon as the proposed Constitution was published, the demand for a national Bill of Rights was heard on all sides.[7]

Practical concerns motivated this demand. Warren wrote:

They were thinking of facts, not theories. They had lived through bitter years, when they had seen governments, both royal and state, trample on the human rights which they and their ancestors in the colonies and in England had fought so hard to secure. In the seven years prior to the signing of the federal Constitution, they had seen the legislatures of four states . . . deprive their citizens of the right to jury trial in civil cases. They had seen the state legislatures . . . pass bills of attainder sentencing men to death or banishment without a criminal trial by jury. They had seen the legislatures of nearly all the states deprive persons of their property without due process, by the passage of laws allowing tender of worthless paper and other property in payment of debts and of judgments. They had seen a Massachusetts legislature impair the freedom of the press by confiscatory taxation. They had seen the royal government quarter troops on the inhabitants in time of peace and deny to the people the right of assembly and of petition. They had seen the King's officials search their houses without lawful warrants. They knew that what government had done in the past, government might attempt in the future, whether its ruling power should be royal, state, or national—king, governor, legislature, or Congress. And they determined that, in America, such ruling power should be definitely curbed at the outset. There should be no uncontrolled power in the government of American citizens. Rightly had Jefferson said, "an elective despotism was not the government we fought for."[8]

Thus, a number of the states that ratified the Constitution did so only with the assurance that a top priority of the First Congress would be the approval of a Bill of Rights to be added to the Constitution.

THE BILL OF RIGHTS

In June 1789 James Madison of Virginia introduced a dozen proposed constitutional amendments in the First Congress, a Bill of Rights generally modeled after existing state bills of rights. Congress approved the amendments in September 1791, and ten of them took effect in December after ratification by the requisite number of states.[9]

These amendments are called the Bill of Rights. As Chief Justice Earl Warren noted, its provisions do not guarantee novel rights, but do "summarize in a striking and effective manner the personal and public liberties which Americans [of that time] . . . regarded as their due and as being properly beyond the reach of any government."[10]

The Bill of Rights was conceived to protect the individual against the government. Chief Justice Warren continued:

The men of our First Congress . . . knew . . . that whatever form it may assume, government is potentially as dangerous a thing as it is a necessary one. They knew that power must be lodged somewhere to prevent anarchy within and conquest from without, but that this power could be abused to the detriment of their liberties.[11]

The guarantees perform an affirmative as well as a negative function, Zechariah Chafee Jr. points out:

They fix a certain point to halt the government abruptly with a "thus far and no farther"; but long before that point is reached they urge upon every official of the three branches of the state a constant regard for certain declared fundamental policies of American life.[12]

The first of these amendments protects freedom of thought and belief. It forbids Congress to restrict freedom of religion, speech, the press, peaceable assembly, and petition.

The Second Amendment ensures the right of the states to maintain militia and, in connection with that state right, the right of the people to keep and bear arms. The Third Amendment restricts government power to quarter soldiers in people's homes. Neither has been the subject of many cases before the federal courts.[13]

The Fourth Amendment protects the individual's right to be secure in his person, house, papers, and effects against unreasonable searches or seizures. This security is ensured by requiring that searches and arrests be authorized by warrants issued only if there is probable cause for the action and when the person to be arrested or the place to be searched and the objects sought are precisely described.

The Fifth Amendment requires indictment of all persons charged in civilian proceedings with capital or otherwise serious crimes. It forbids trying a person twice for the same offense or compelling a person to incriminate himself. It states that no one should be deprived of life, liberty, or property without due process of law, and it protects private property against being taken for public use without just compensation.

The Sixth Amendment sets out certain requirements for criminal trials, guaranteeing a speedy and public jury trial for all persons accused of crime, with an impartial jury selected from the area of the crime. The defendant is further guaranteed the right to be notified of the charge against him, to confront witnesses testifying against him, to compel witnesses to come to testify in his favor, and to have the aid of an attorney in his defense.

The Seventh Amendment provides for a jury trial in all common law suits involving more than $20.

The Eighth Amendment forbids excessive bail, excessive fines, and cruel and unusual punishment.

The Ninth and Tenth Amendments do not guarantee specific rights. The Ninth declares that the mention in the Constitution of certain rights should not be interpreted as denying or disparaging other rights retained by the people. The Tenth reserves to the states, or to the people, all powers not delegated by the Constitution to the national government nor prohibited by the Constitution to the states.

THE JUDICIAL ROLE

James Madison, father of these amendments, expected the federal courts to play a major role in implementing their guarantees. "Independent tribunals of justice will consider themselves in a peculiar manner the guardians of those rights; they [the courts] will be an impenetrable bulwark against every assumption of power in the Legislative or Executive; they will naturally be led to resist every encroachment upon rights expressly stipulated for in the Constitution by the declaration of rights," he told his fellow members of Congress.[14]

But the Supreme Court itself had little occasion to apply these promises in its first 130 years.

The Alien and Sedition Acts of 1798—severe infringements of the rights and liberties of the individual, particularly those protected by the First Amendment—were never challenged before the High Court. The acts expired early in 1801. (It is worth noting, however, that most of the early members of the Court, in their roles as circuit judges, presided over trials of persons charged with sedition and displayed no disinclination to enforce that law.)[15]

Slavery, despite the prolonged national debate it engendered, was never dealt with by the Court as a matter of individual rights. The few pronouncements by the Court on the issue demonstrate clearly that the justices saw it as a matter of property rights, not human rights. *(See box, The Court and the Issue of Slavery, pp. 396–397.)*

In 1833 the Court ruled that the Bill of Rights provided no protection against state action but only against federal authority.

Barron v. Baltimore arose when the owner of a wharf in Baltimore, Maryland, challenged city action that seriously impaired the value of his property by creating shoals and shallows around it. Barron argued that this was a "taking" of his property without just compensation, in violation of the Fifth Amendment.[16]

When Barron's case came before the Supreme Court, Chief Justice John Marshall found the question it posed to be "of great importance, but not of much difficulty." Marshall described Barron's argument: the Fifth Amendment "being in favor of the liberty of the citizen ought to be so construed as to restrain the legislative power of a State, as well as that of the United States."[17]

That argument could not prevail, however, continued the chief justice. The Bill of Rights was adopted to secure individual rights against the "apprehended encroachments of the general government—not against those of the local governments."[18] The Court could find no indication that Congress intended the Bill of Rights to safeguard the individual against state action, and it would not undertake such an extension of those provisions on its own. Marshall concluded:

Had Congress engaged in the extraordinary occupation of improving the constitutions of the several States by affording the people additional protection from the exercise of power by their own governments in matters which concerned themselves alone, they would have declared this purpose in plain and intelligible language.[19]

Barron v. Baltimore stands to this day, unreversed in its precise finding—that the first Congress, in approving the Bill of Rights, did not intend these amendments to protect the individual against state action but only against action by federal authorities.

The Civil War Amendments

After the Civil War Congress added three new amendments to the Constitution. The language of these additions seemed to overturn the restrictions *Barron v. Baltimore* placed on the guarantees of the Bill of Rights.

The Thirteenth Amendment, adopted in 1865, abolished slavery and involuntary servitude, except for persons sentenced to such service as punishment for crime. It authorizes Congress to pass laws to enforce this guarantee.

The Fifteenth Amendment, adopted in 1870, forbids state or federal authorities to deny or abridge the right of U.S. citizens to vote because of race, color, or previous condition of servitude. It, too, authorized Congress to pass legislation enforcing its prohibition.

The Fourteenth Amendment, the most complex and most litigated of the three, was adopted in 1868. It declares that all persons born or naturalized in the United States are citizens. This is the Constitution's only definition of citizenship.

In addition, the amendment forbids states to abridge any privilege or immunity of U.S. citizens, to deprive any person of life, liberty, or property without due process of law, or to deny to any person the equal protection of the law.

These guarantees are undergirded by a grant of power to Congress to enforce them through legislation. They have been the foundation of the modern revolution in civil rights and criminal procedure, although for decades after their addition to the Constitution they seemed almost useless as protection for individual rights.

THE INTENT OF CONGRESS

The privileges and immunities, due process, and equal protection clauses were intended by their author, Rep. John A. Bing-ham, R-Ohio (1855–1863, 1865–1873), to extend the guarantees of the Bill of Rights against state action. Bingham thought that the privileges and immunities section of the Fourteenth Amendment would be the chief vehicle for this extension.

In 1871 Bingham explained his view of this portion of the amendment, in response to a query from a fellow member of the House. He stated that "the privileges and immunities of citizens of the United States . . . are chiefly defined in the first eight amendments to the Constitution. . . . These eight articles . . . were never limitations upon the power of the States, until made so by the Fourteenth Amendment."[20]

During Senate consideration of the amendment, the chief Senate spokesman in behalf of the proposal had stated that "the great object of the first section of this amendment is . . . to restrain the power of the States and compel them at all times to respect these great fundamental guarantees."[21]

During the process of ratification, however, the other sections of the amendment—concerning apportionment of representatives among the states, the holding of federal posts by persons who had forsaken such offices to support the rebellious states, and the validity of the public debt—were given far more attention than Section 1.

FRUSTRATION OF THE PROMISE

Almost a century would pass before the hopes explicit in the adoption of the Thirteenth, Fourteenth, and Fifteenth Amendments were fulfilled. In large part, the frustration of their promises was the work of the Court.

Partly in response to waning public enthusiasm for Reconstruction, partly out of concern for healing the wounds of war, partly because the nation had not developed its sensitivity to issues of individual rights, the Court in the postwar decades severely curtailed the operation of the Civil War amendments to protect individual citizens.

The restrictive interpretation of these amendments came in two lines of rulings. In the first, the Court defined narrowly the privileges and immunities, due process, and equal protection clauses of the Fourteenth Amendment, and the similar substantive phrases of the Thirteenth and Fifteenth Amendments. In the second, the Court confined rigidly the enforcement power these three amendments granted Congress.

Early in the 1870s the Supreme Court first indicated its limited view of the effect of these amendments. The privileges and immunities of U.S. citizenship were a brief list, the Court ruled in the *Slaughterhouse Cases,* and did not include, for example, the right to vote.[22] The Thirteenth Amendment did no more than abolish the institution of slavery, the Court ruled in *United States v. Reese.* Nor did the Fifteenth Amendment grant to anyone a federal right to vote, only the right to exercise the state-granted franchise free of racial discrimination, the justices held in *United States v. Cruikshank.*[23]

A decade later the Court held in *Hurtado v. California* that the due process guarantee did not extend the specific protections of the Bill of Rights against state action.[24] And in the well-

THE COURT AND THE ISSUE OF SLAVERY . . . A QUESTION OF LEGALITY, NOT MORALITY

The issue of slavery came to the Supreme Court in its first decades only as a question of international or commercial law or of states' rights and federal power, not as a human rights issue. Not until after the Civil War did the status of the nation's blacks become a question of individual rights rather than property rights.

As the United States celebrated the bicentennial of the Constitution in 1987, Justice Thurgood Marshall reminded the nation that "when the Founding Fathers used the phrase 'We the People' in 1797, they did not have in mind the majority of America's citizens." At the time of the founding of the nation, the phrase included neither blacks nor women.

The Framers, said Marshall, "could not have imagined, nor would they have accepted, that the document they were drafting would one day be construed by a Supreme Court to which had been appointed a woman and a descendant of an African slave."

Marshall pointed out that "the record of the Framers' debates on the slave question is especially clear: the Southern states acceded to the demands of the New England states for giving Congress broad power to regulate commerce, in exchange for the right to continue the slave trade."[1]

Slavery had a continuing impact upon pre–Civil War constitutional history. As Carl B. Swisher explained:

Concern for the preservation of slavery furnished the driving power back of theories of state rights and of limitation upon the power of the federal government which for many decades hampered the expansion of federal power. Concern for the protection of slavery entered into the interpretation of the commerce clause . . . of clauses having to do with the rights of citizenship, and of other important constitutional provisions. The clash of interest between slavery and non-slavery groups brought on the crisis of a civil war which threatened the complete destruction of the American constitutional system.[2]

Historian Charles Warren also viewed the slavery issue as underlying the early debate over the scope of the commerce power:

[T]hroughout the long years when the question of the extent of the federal power over commerce was being tested in numerous cases in the court, that question was, in the minds of Southerners, simply coincident with the question of the extent of the Federal power over slavery.[3]

The Court gave firm support to federal power over the subject of fugitive slaves. At the same time, it left as much as possible to the states the question of the status of slaves who had spent time in both slave and free areas.

The Court's divergence from this position—in the Dred Scott case of 1857—added fuel to the conflagration that ignited civil war.

INTERNATIONAL LAW

In the first case involving slavery decided by the Court, the justices held that the slave trade, even though illegal in the United States by 1825, was not illegal under international law. The case involved slaves who arrived in the United States after being removed from a vessel captured by an American warship.

Chief Justice John Marshall made clear in his opinion that the legality of the situation alone, not its morality, was before the Court. He wrote:

In examining claims of this momentous importance; claims in which the sacred rights of liberty and of property come in conflict with each other . . . this Court must not yield to feelings which might seduce it from the path of duty, but must obey the mandates of the law. . . . Whatever might be the answer of a moralist to this question, a jurist must search for its legal solution in those principles of action which are sanctioned by the usages, the national acts, and the general assent of that portion of the world of which he considers himself as a part.[4]

COMMERCIAL LAW

Four years later the Court ruled that a slave who died in an abortive rescue attempt after a steamboat fire was a passenger, not freight, for purposes of his owners' damage suit against the vessels involved. "A slave has volition, and has feelings which cannot be entirely disregarded," wrote Chief Justice Marshall.

"He cannot be stowed away as a common package. . . . The carrier has not, and cannot have, the same absolute control over him that he has over inanimate matter. In the nature of things, and in

---

known 1896 ruling in *Plessy v. Ferguson,* the Court found no denial of equal protection in the requirement of segregated public facilities for blacks and whites.[25]

Furthermore, the Court refused to acknowledge that the enforcement clauses of these amendments significantly enlarged federal power to protect individual rights. The enforcement power granted to Congress to implement these provisions was rigidly confined by state prerogatives.

Congress enacted a number of major statutes to enforce the Thirteenth, Fourteenth, and Fifteenth Amendments. By the end of the century, most of their provisions had either been declared invalid by the Court, repealed directly, or rendered obsolete by subsequent legislation.[26] Charles Warren, writing in the 1920s, described the effect of the Civil War amendments upon the na-

tion's black citizens, as a result of these Supreme Court decisions:

The first section of the 14th Amendment is a prohibitory measure, and the prohibitions operate against the states only, and not against acts of private persons; the fifth section only gives Congress power, by general legislation, to enforce these prohibitions, and Congress may, within bounds, provide the modes of redress against individuals when a State has violated the prohibitions; and though Congress cannot act directly against the states, Congress may regulate the method of appeal to United States courts by any persons whose right under the Amendment has been affected by action of the states. As to the 15th Amendment, though theoretically it is capable of being enforced to a certain extent by direct congressional action, Congress has, in fact, taken few steps toward such enforcement; and only a few acts of a state or of a state officer have been found by the courts to violate it. Meanwhile, the southern states, by constitutional and statutory provisions, which have

his character, he resembles a passenger, and not a package of goods."[5]

In 1841 the Court was faced with a case challenging Mississippi's ban on the importation of slaves. But the justices found a way to decide the case without ruling directly on the importation ban.[6]

FUGITIVE SLAVE LAWS

As the tension between slave and free states built, and the operations of the underground railway accelerated, an increasing number of cases challenged the federal fugitive slave law, enacted in 1793 to govern the return of fugitive slaves from one state to another.

In 1842 the Court affirmed the exclusive power of Congress to regulate these disputes. The justices struck down a Pennsylvania law providing that before a fugitive was returned to his alleged owner or the owner's representative, a hearing should be held before a magistrate to determine the validity of the claim to the supposed fugitive slave.[7]

Six years later the Court reaffirmed the validity of the federal fugitive slave law and specifically disclaimed any power to resolve the moral dilemma it posed.

[S]ome notice should be taken of the argument, urging on us a disregard of the Constitution and the act of Congress in respect to this subject, on account of the supposed inexpediency and invalidity of all laws recognizing slavery or any right of property in man. But that is a political question, settled by each state for itself; and the federal power over it is limited and regulated by the people of the states in the Constitution itself, as one of its sacred compromises, and which we possess no authority as a judicial body to modify or overrule.[8]

On the eve of the Civil War, the Court resolved the most famous of the fugitive slave cases, *Ableman v. Booth.* Sherman Booth, an abolitionist editor, was prosecuted under the federal fugitive slave law for helping a fugitive slave to escape. The state courts of Wisconsin, Booth's residence, repeatedly issued writs of habeas corpus, ordering federal authorities to release Booth from custody, on the grounds that the federal fugitive slave law was unconstitutional.

The Court in March 1859 resoundingly defended the freedom of federal courts from such state interference—and upheld Booth's conviction.[9]

SLAVE OR FREE?

The Court in 1850 was asked to decide what effect residence in a free state or territory had on the status of a slave. This first case on the matter was resolved with restraint and without incident.

The individuals involved were slaves in Kentucky who worked for a time in the free state of Ohio but returned to Kentucky to live. The Court held that their status depended on the state where they were residing. No constitutional provision controlled state action on this matter, it held.[10]

The Court reached a similar conclusion seven years later in the landmark case of *Dred Scott v. Sandford,* but unfortunately it did not stop there.

Dred Scott, the alleged slave, brought the case on his own behalf. By holding that Scott's status was determined by the law of the state in which he resided—the slave state of Missouri—the Court also held that he could not bring the suit, as a slave, and thus it had no jurisdiction over the matter at all. The Court then held that slaves were not citizens and that Congress lacked the power to exclude slavery from the territories.[11]

Slavery became an issue to be resolved only on the battlefield; the Supreme Court did not speak again on the subject.

1. Thurgood Marshall, speech at the annual seminar of the San Francisco Patent and Trademark Law Association, May 6, 1987.
2. Carl B. Swisher, *American Constitutional Development,* 2d ed. (Cambridge, Mass.: Houghton Mifflin, 1954), 230.
3. Charles Warren, *The Supreme Court in United States History,* 2 vols. (Boston: Little, Brown, 1922, 1926), I: 627.
4. *The Antelope,* 10 Wheat. 66 at 114, 121 (1825).
5. *Boyce v. Anderson,* 2 Pet. 150 at 154–155 (1829).
6. *Groves v. Slaughter,* 15 Pet. 449 (1841).
7. *Prigg v. Pennsylvania,* 16 Pet. 539 (1842).
8. *Jones v. Van Zandt,* 5 How. 215 at 231 (1848).
9. *Ableman v. Booth,* 21 How. 506 (1859).
10. *Strader v. Graham,* 10 How. 82 (1851).
11. *Dred Scott v. Sandford,* 19 How. 393 (1857).

been in general upheld by the court, have found methods of limiting the negro right to vote.[27]

Early in the twentieth century, one student of these Court rulings declared that the enforcement acts were struck down because "they were in fact out of joint with the times. They did not square with public consciousness, either North or South. They belonged . . . to a more arbitrary period. They fitted a condition of war, not of peace, and suggested autocracy, rather than a democracy!"[28]

But eventually the Court's narrow view of these amendments gave way to a more expansive one, and these amendments provided the groundwork for the modern revolution in civil and criminal rights.

Congress made possible this shift in federal judicial concern by expanding the class of persons who could ask a federal court to issue a writ of habeas corpus ordering their release from custody. This new law allowed persons detained by state officials to win their release if they could show that their detention was in violation of their constitutional rights. In 1875 Congress enlarged the jurisdiction of the federal courts and expanded the categories of cases they could hear; it gave them the right to hear all cases arising under the Constitution or federal laws. Several years later Congress further expanded Supreme Court jurisdiction, authorizing the Court to hear appeals in criminal cases.

PROPERTY, NOT PEOPLE

In one of the most ironic chapters in Supreme Court history, these new powers and guarantees were for half a century wield-

CELEBRATION AT BALTIMORE ON MAY 19th 1870.

Lithograph commemorating the celebration in Baltimore of the enactment of the Fifteenth Amendment. Featured are likenesses of prominent supporters of the amendment. *Top, left to right:* President Ulysses S. Grant, Vice President Schuyler Colfax, President Abraham Lincoln, abolitionist martyr John Brown, and Baltimore jurist Hugh Lennox Bond. *Bottom, left to right:* abolitionist Frederick Douglass and Mississippi senator Hiram R. Revels.

ed much more effectively to protect property than to protect persons.

Developing the doctrine of substantive due process, the Court found the Fourteenth Amendment a useful tool for striking down a wide range of "progressive" state laws—ranging from those setting minimum wages and maximum hours for working men and women to consumer-oriented measures concerning weights and measures of items produced for sale.

Only a few isolated cases kept alive the hope that the Court would eventually exercise its authority to protect the individual against the government.

In 1886 the Court held that the equal protection clause assured aliens the right to run laundries in San Francisco free of discriminatory application of licensing requirements by city officials.[29]

The same year the Court held that the Fourth and Fifth Amendments provided absolute protection from federal seizure for an individual's private papers.[30] Twenty-eight years later—

in 1914—the Court provided for enforcement of this protection through an "exclusionary rule"—declaring that persons from whom federal agents took evidence illegally had the right to demand that the evidence be excluded from use in federal court.[31]

In 1915 the Court invoked the Fourteenth Amendment to strike down state laws restricting the right of aliens to work.[32] The Court also held that the Fifteenth Amendment was violated by Oklahoma's use of a grandfather clause that effectively required all blacks—and only blacks—to take a literacy test before being qualified to vote.[33]

World War I brought the most restrictive set of federal laws concerning speech and the press since 1798. Challenged as violating the First Amendment, these laws were upheld by the Court, but the cases posing these questions to the Court were the first steps in the still-continuing process of shaping the standards by which to judge the government's actions restricting individual freedom.

BROADENING PROTECTION

However, the Bill of Rights still operated only against federal, not state, action. Because state authorities exert far more impact upon the everyday lives of individual citizens than do their federal counterparts, this left most citizens inadequately protected against arbitrary, coercive, and unfair state government action.

The Court's 1925 ruling in *Gitlow v. New York* marked the waning of this view and the beginning of the expansion of federal protection for individual rights. Benjamin Gitlow, a left-wing socialist, was indicted for violating New York's criminal anarchy law by publishing and distributing subversive documents. The material at issue was a "Left Wing Manifesto" calling for class revolution and the organization of a proletariat state to suppress the bourgeoisie. He came to the Supreme Court arguing that the state law was unconstitutional, denying him his rights of free speech and free press, guaranteed by the First Amendment.[34]

The Court upheld the law, but in so doing, the majority stated that it now assumed "that freedom of speech and of the press—which are protected by the First Amendment from abridgment by Congress—are among the fundamental personal rights and 'liberties' protected by the due process clause of the Fourteenth Amendment from impairment by the states."[35]

With that decision the Court began reading into the due process guarantee many of the specific rights and liberties set out in the Bill of Rights.

This process, variously described as the incorporation or absorption of the Bill of Rights into the Fourteenth Amendment, continued for a half a century. By the mid-1970s, the Court had extended the Bill of Rights at last to the point that Representative Bingham had intended a century earlier, when Congress approved Section 1 of the Fourteenth Amendment.

The first rights absorbed into the due process clause and thus protected against state action were those set out in the First Amendment. In 1931 the Court for the first time struck down state laws as infringing on the freedom to speak and the freedom of the press.[36] In 1934 it assumed that freedom of religion was likewise protected against state infringement.[37] And in 1937 the Court held the right of peaceable assembly to be so protected.[38]

The Court also began in the 1930s to enforce the equal protection guarantee against racial discrimination by state officials—and to use the due process clause to require fundamental fairness in state dealings with criminal suspects. The groundwork for revolution was laid.

A DOUBLE STANDARD

As the federal courts, led by the Supreme Court, began to assume the role intended for them by Madison and the drafters of the Fourteenth Amendment, the Court indicated that it would apply a stricter standard to laws challenged as infringing on individual rights than it used for those attacked as abridging economic rights.

In *United States v. Carolene Products Co.*, decided in 1938, the Court upheld a federal law barring interstate shipment of certain types of skimmed milk.[39] This ruling reflected the Court's shift away from disapproval of all such interstate regulation as interfering too much with states' rights and the free flow of commerce.

Writing for the majority, Justice Harlan Fiske Stone said that the Court would now uphold economic regulation against a constitutional challenge so long as the regulation had a rational basis.[40]

And in a footnote to that statement, the famous Footnote Four, Stone suggested that "[t]here may be narrower scope for operation of the presumption of constitutionality when legislation appears on its face to be within a specific prohibition of the Constitution, such as those of the first ten Amendments."[41] *(See box, "Footnote Four," p. 400.)*

This meant, Justice Robert H. Jackson said several years later, that the "presumption of validity which attaches in general to legislative acts is frankly reversed in the case of interferences with free speech and free assembly."[42] He explained the reasoning behind this double standard:

Ordinarily, legislation whose basis in economic wisdom is uncertain can be redressed by the processes of the ballot box or the pressures of opinion. But when the channels of opinion or of peaceful persuasion are corrupted or clogged, these political correctives can no longer be relied on, and the democratic system is threatened at its most vital point. In that event the Court, by intervening, restores the processes of democratic government; it does not disrupt them.[43]

Freedom for Ideas

The First Amendment protects against government suppression the unrestricted exchange of ideas. The guarantees of freedom for speech, press, and religion have been "first" in several ways—the first listed in the Bill of Rights and the first of those amendments to be fully applied against state action.

Furthermore, many argue, this amendment is in fact first in importance among the Constitution's guarantees of individual rights. Such a "preferred position" is linked to the function of these freedoms in maintaining an environment that fosters responsive democratic government.

In 1937 Chief Justice Charles Evans Hughes explained:

The greater the importance of safeguarding the community from incitement to the overthrow of our institutions by force and violence, the more imperative is the need to preserve inviolate the constitutional rights of free speech, free press and free assembly in order to maintain the opportunity for free political discussion, to the end that government may be responsive to the will of the people and that changes, if desired, may be obtained by peaceful means. Therein lies the security of the Republic, the very foundation of constitutional government.[44]

A CHARTER FOR GOVERNMENT

Eight years later Justice Wiley B. Rutledge brought together the Court's acknowledgment of its new role with respect to the rights of the individual, the view of the First Amendment free-

"FOOTNOTE FOUR"

In a footnote to its decision in *United States v. Carolene Products Co.,* the Court in 1938 foreshadowed its shift in concern from economic to individual rights:

4. There may be narrower scope for operation of the presumption of constitutionality when legislation appears on its face to be within a specific prohibition of the Constitution, such as those of the first ten Amendments, which are deemed equally specific when held to be embraced within the Fourteenth. See Stromberg v. California, 283 U.S. 359, 369, 370, 51 S.Ct. 532, 535, 536, 75 L.Ed. 1117, 73 A.L.R. 1484; Lovell v. Griffin, 303 U.S. 444, 58 S.Ct. 666, 82 L.Ed. 949, decided March 28, 1938.

It is unnecessary to consider now whether legislation which restricts those political processes which can ordinarily be expected to bring about repeal of undesirable legislation, is to be subjected to more exacting judicial scrutiny under the general prohibitions of the Fourteenth Amendment than are most other types of legislation. On restrictions upon the right to vote, see Nixon v. Herndon, 273 U.S. 536, 47 S.Ct. 446, 71 L.Ed. 984, 88 A.L.R. 458; on restraints upon the dissemination of information, see Near v. Minnesota, 283 U.S. 697, 713-714, 718-720, 722, 51 S.Ct. 625, 630, 632, 633, 75 L.Ed. 1357; Grosjean v. American Press Co., 297 U.S. 233, 56 S.Ct. 444, 80 L.Ed. 660; Lovell v. Griffin, supra; on interferences with political organizations, see Stromberg v. California, supra, 283 U.S. 359, 369, 51 S.Ct. 532, 535, 75 L.Ed. 1117, 73 A.L.R. 1484; Fiske v. Kansas, 274 U.S. 380, 47 S.Ct. 655, 71 L.Ed. 1108; Whitney v. California, 274 U.S. 357, 373-378, 47 S.Ct. 641, 647, 649, 71 L.Ed. 1095; Herndon v. Lowry, 301 U.S. 242, 57 S.Ct. 732, 81 L.Ed. 1066; and see Holmes, J. in Gitlow v. New York, 268 U.S. 652, 673, 45 S.Ct. 625, 69 L.Ed. 1138; as to prohibition of peaceable assembly, see De Jonge v. Oregon, 299 U.S. 353, 365, 57 S.Ct. 255, 260, 81 L.Ed. 278.

Nor need we enquire whether similar considerations enter into the review of statutes directed at particular religious, Pierce v. Society of Sisters, 268 U.S. 510, 45 S.Ct. 571, 69 L.Ed. 1070, 39 A.L.R. 468, or national, Meyer v. Nebraska, 262 U.S. 390, 43 S.Ct. 625, 67 L.Ed. 1042, 29 A.L.R. 1446; Bartels v. Iowa, 262 U.S. 404, 43 S.Ct. 628, 67 L.Ed. 1047; Farrington v. Tokushige, 273 U.S. 284, 47 S.Ct. 406, 71 L.Ed. 646, or racial minorities. Nixon v. Herndon, supra; Nixon v. Condon, supra: whether prejudice against discrete and insular minorities may be a special condition which tends seriously to curtail the operation of these political processes ordinarily to be relied upon to protect minorities, and which may call for a correspondingly more searching judicial inquiry. Compare McCulloch v. Maryland, 4 Wheat. 316, 428, 4 L.Ed. 579; South Carolina State Highway Department v. Barnwell Bros., 303 U.S. 177, 58 S.Ct. 510, 82 L.Ed. 734, decided February 14, 1938, note 2, and cases cited.

doms as "preferred," and the stricter test for laws challenged as violating that freedom:

The case confronts us again with the duty our system places on this Court to say where the individual's freedom ends and the State's power begins. Choice on that border, now as always delicate, is perhaps more so where the usual presumption supporting legislation is balanced by the preferred place given in our scheme to the great, the indispensable democratic freedoms secured by the First Amendment. . . . That priority gives these liberties a sanctity and a sanction not permitting dubious intrusions. And it is the character of the right, not of the limitation, which determines what standard governs the choice. . . .

For these reasons any attempt to restrict those liberties must be justified by clear public interest, threatened not doubtfully or remotely, but by clear and present danger. The rational connection between the remedy provided and the evil to be curbed, which in other contexts might support legislation against attack on due process grounds, will not suffice. These rights rest on firmer foundation.[45]

"The First Amendment," added Justice Rutledge later in his opinion, "is a charter for government, not for an institution of learning."[46]

Concurring, Justice Jackson wrote:

[I]t cannot be the duty, because it is not the right, of the state to protect the public against false doctrine. The very purpose of the First Amendment is to foreclose public authority from assuming a guardianship of the public mind through regulating the press, speech and religion. In this field every person must be his own watchman for truth, because the forefathers did not trust any government to separate the true from the false for us. . . .

This liberty was not protected because the forefathers expected its use would always be agreeable to those in authority or that its exercise would always be wise, temperate, or useful to society.

As I read their intentions, this liberty was protected because they knew of no other way by which free men could conduct representative democracy.[47]

In 1979 Justice William J. Brennan Jr. discussed the way in which the First Amendment operates to "foster the values of democratic self-government":

The First Amendment bars the State from imposing upon its citizens an authoritative vision of truth. It forbids the State from interfering with the communicative processes through which its citizens exercise and prepare to exercise their rights of self-government. And the Amendment shields those who would censure the State or expose its abuses.[48]

NO ABSOLUTE RIGHT

But neither the intrinsic importance of free expression nor its "societal function" enshrines in the First Amendment an absolute ban on all official restrictions on speech, the press, assembly, or religion.

The collective good—the nation's security or the public's safety—warrants some restriction on the individual's freedom to speak, to publish, to gather in groups, and to exercise his or her religious beliefs. The task of the Court has been to balance the community's interest against the individual's rights, to determine when order and safety demand that limits be set to individual freedom.

Wartime, the cold war, and the civil rights era all caused the Supreme Court to work to reconcile these competing concerns. The Court's course has been uneven: it has discarded "tests" for determining permissible government constraints almost as soon as it has developed them.

The often mentioned "clear and present danger" test, although little used by the modern Court, nevertheless stands as a symbol of the basic position still held by the Court on free speech questions: only for very good reason may the government suppress speech—and the Court will evaluate the reasons.

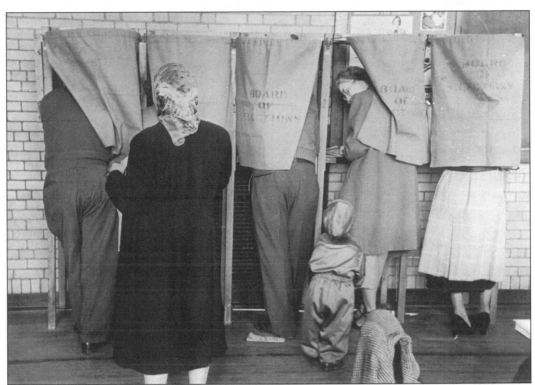

The Court's narrow interpretation of the privileges and immunities clause of the Fourteenth Amendment, articulated in *Minor v. Happersett* (1875), stood in the way of women's suffrage. By passing the Nineteenth Amendment, in 1920, Congress removed all obstacles to a woman's right to vote.

Freedom of the press has come more and more frequently before the Court since 1960. The Court has steadfastly rejected all prior restraints upon publication—most dramatically in the Pentagon Papers case of 1971. And although it has rejected efforts by the news media to expand the protection of the First Amendment into special privileges for the press, it has extended new protection to the news media from libel suits brought by public officials or public figures.

Freedom of religion, a guarantee reflecting the original purpose of many of the nation's earliest settlers, has been at issue in some of the Court's most controversial modern rulings. While it has generally upheld laws enacted to enhance the public welfare against challenges that they incidentally curtail the freedom to exercise one's religious beliefs, the Court has turned strict scrutiny on laws challenged as violating the amendment's ban on the establishment of religion. Such scrutiny has resulted in decisions rejecting state efforts to require or allow devotional exercises in public schools or to use public funds to aid parochial schools.

Political Rights

For the first 130 years of American history, the privilege of political participation was strictly limited. Until well into the twentieth century, the right to vote was the prerogative of the adult white man, and often only of those adult white men who could pay a poll tax, pass a literacy test, or meet other qualifications.

The Constitution barely mentions the right to vote; and there is no mention at all of the right to have that vote counted equally with others nor of the protected freedom of political association. Yet during the twentieth century these rights have won judicial recognition and protection. By 1975 the right to vote belonged to all citizens eighteen years of age and older, regardless of sex or race.

Since 1962, when the Court abandoned its traditional aloofness from the issue of electoral districting, the right to have one's vote count as equal to those of other city or state residents has become firmly established. As it has implemented that right, the Court has redistributed the balance of political power in every state of the Union.

Unrestricted political association—the freedom to associate with others who share one's political views—has been recognized as an individual and institutional right.

Although the Court during the peak of the cold war upheld state and federal programs and statutes curtailing the exercise of this freedom, the modern Court considers this freedom to be the core value the First Amendment was intended to protect.

THE SUFFRAGE

Congress, not the Court, has led in expansion of the suffrage. Three constitutional amendments were required to lower the barriers of race, sex, and age.

Indeed, it was the Court's narrow view of the privileges, immunities, and rights protected by the Civil War amendments that necessitated adoption of the Nineteenth Amendment to enfranchise women[49] and that rendered the Fifteenth Amendment a hollow promise for most of a century.[50]

Government officers and clerks loading a police ambulance with literature seized at the Communist Party headquarters in Cambridge, Massachusetts, in 1919. The Court upheld the validity of antisubversion laws through World War II and during much of the subsequent cold war, but in the late 1950s set strict standards by which such laws could be enforced.

After the Civil War, despite the clear language of the Fourteenth and Fifteenth Amendments, the Supreme Court continued to defer to state power to set voter qualifications, steadily upholding a variety of devices used to exclude blacks from voting. In the twentieth century the Court slowly asserted itself and began to strike down the most blatant of these mechanisms—the grandfather clause in 1915 and the white primary in 1927 and again in 1944.[51]

But it was left for Congress to take the lead, as it did in the 1960s, abolishing poll tax requirements through a constitutional amendment, suspending literacy tests, and imposing federal control over the electoral machinery of states with high minority population and low voter registration or participation.

The Court's role—although secondary—was crucial. A century earlier the Court had undercut similar efforts by Congress to guarantee the right to vote against racial discrimination, by adopting a constricted view of the power of Congress to enforce the constitutional amendments adopted in the wake of the Civil War.

In the 1960s the Court gave full backing to the exercise of unprecedented federal power to guarantee civil rights to the nation's blacks. The most aggressive and effective of the major civil rights statutes was the Voting Rights Act of 1965, which superimposed federal power and machinery upon the electoral processes of states that had long denied blacks the right to vote.

In 1966 the Court upheld the law against every point of a multifaceted constitutional challenge by the affected states.[52] Within five years of enactment, more than one million blacks had been newly registered to vote.

REDISTRICTING REVOLUTION

In stark contrast with the Court's early reluctance to enforce the clear ban of the Fifteenth Amendment was its unexpected plunge into the subject of legislative redistricting and malapportionment of legislative power.

After decades of declaring such issues "political" and unsuitable for judicial resolution, the Court in 1962 reconsidered. In *Baker v. Carr* the Court announced its reversal, holding that constitutionally based challenges to the malapportionment of state legislative bodies were "federal questions" that federal courts might properly consider.[53] Although the Court in 1962 went no further than that declaration, *Baker v. Carr* set off a judicial revolution that is still reverberating.

The following year the justices declared that the Fourteenth Amendment's guarantee of equal protection—when applied to voting rights—meant "one person, one vote."[54] Each vote cast in an electoral district in a state or in a city should be of equal weight with every other. The application of this rule to federal and state electoral divisions revolutionized the political base of every legislative body of any significance in the nation.

BELIEFS AND ASSOCIATION

Out of the unlikely context of the antisubversive and anti–civil rights laws of the 1950s and 1960s, the protected freedom of political association won judicial affirmation.

In addition to its constitutional basis in the First Amendment, the right of association has a clear practical basis: no point of view can win recognition in the increasingly complex American society without organized backing.

War slowed the progress of this right toward acknowledged constitutional status. During World War II and the subsequent cold war, Congress and state legislatures sought to protect the nation against subversion with laws and programs that declared a belief in communism or a similar political system and affiliation with such a system criminal, tantamount to treason.

As it had during the Civil War and World War I, the Court reflected its sensitivity to the national mood with decisions upholding the validity of these antisubversive devices. The Court backed the power of Congress to enact laws that effectively made illegal participation in Communist Party activities by anyone aware of the party's aims. The Court seemed to sanction the use of guilt by association as a basis for depriving or denying persons jobs. Yet within a few years of these rulings, the Court began to circumscribe the methods by which such laws could be enforced. Enforcement became so difficult that, in many instances, it was altogether abandoned.

In one line of rulings beginning in 1957, the Court set out strict standards of proof for government efforts to prosecute persons who were members of the U.S. Communist Party. Simple association could not properly serve as the basis for denying a person a job, firing him, depriving him of his U.S. passport, or refusing him admission to the bar, held the Court.[55]

Almost simultaneously, in another series of decisions, the Court began to give full recognition to the right of association. These rulings, most of which dealt with civil rights activists, soon influenced the Court's view of legislation penalizing simple membership in "subversive" organizations.[56]

By 1967 the right had gained clear constitutional status. As Justice Byron R. White wrote:

The right of association is not mentioned in the Constitution. It is a judicial construct appended to the First Amendment rights to speak freely, to assemble, and to petition for redress of grievances. While the right of association has deep roots in history and is supported by the inescapable necessity for group action in a republic as large and complex as ours, it has only recently blossomed as the controlling factor in constitutional litigation; its contours as yet lack delineation.[57]

In the past quarter century the Court has further defined those contours as it applied the right of association to curtail the exercise of state power over radical student groups, national political party delegations, independent candidates, and party-switching voters. The Court held that this freedom shielded some government workers from being fired or denied promotion because they belonged to the "wrong" political party. It steadfastly refused, however, to allow private clubs to invoke this right to protect their discriminatory practices.

Equality Before the Law

The Fourteenth Amendment's promise of equal protection of the laws was intended, said one of its key advocates, Sen. Jacob M. Howard, R-Mich. (1862–1871), to give "to the humblest, the poorest, the most despised of the race, the same rights and the same protection before the law as it gives to the most powerful, the most wealthy, or the most haughty."[58]

Not until well past the middle of the next century, however, was the protection of this guarantee actually extended to the nation's black citizens, to aliens, to women, the poor, and the illegitimate. And even then, the extension was less than complete.

At first, the Supreme Court seemed in accord with the intent of this portion of the Fourteenth Amendment. The equal protection clause, wrote Justice Samuel F. Miller in 1873, was clearly meant to guarantee equal treatment of blacks. He expressed doubt "whether any action of a State not directed by way of discrimination against the negroes as a class . . . will ever be held to come within the purview of this provision."[59]

Six years later the Court used the equal protection clause to strike down a state law excluding blacks from jury duty. The equal protection guarantee, declared the Court, meant that "the law in the States shall be the same for the black as for the white; that all persons, whether colored or white, shall stand equal before the laws of the States."[60]

But this declaration soon eroded into superficiality. In 1883—with its rulings in the *Civil Rights Cases*—the Court held that the Fourteenth Amendment applied only to state, not individual, action; that individual discrimination did not violate the Thirteenth Amendment; and that Congress could act only to remedy discrimination by a state, not to prevent it before it occurred.[61]

In 1896 the Court in *Plessy v. Ferguson* held reasonable Louisiana's requirement of "equal but separate" accommodations for black and white passengers on railway trains.[62] This ruling, wrote one commentator, left the Fourteenth Amendment's guarantees "virtually nonexistent except as a bulwark of the rights of corporations."[63]

Plessy was the logical outcome of a conservative view of the power of the law. In the majority opinion, written by Justice Henry B. Brown, the Court declared:

If the two races are to meet upon terms of social equality, it must be the result of natural affinities, a mutual appreciation of each other's merits and a voluntary consent of individuals. . . . Legislation is powerless to eradicate racial instincts or to abolish distinctions based upon physical differences, and the attempt to do so can only result in accentuating the difficulties of the present situation. If the civil and political rights of both races be equal one cannot be inferior to the other civilly or politically. If one race be inferior to the other socially, the Constitution of the United States cannot put them upon the same plane.[64]

Business interests, generally more able than individuals to present their views to the Court in the late nineteenth and early twentieth century, did not hesitate to use the equal protection clause as a basis from which to challenge state taxes, police regulations, and labor laws.

They too met with no more than a modicum of success. The Court adopted rationality as the test for such challenges and would uphold all such laws so long as they had a reasonable basis. Nevertheless, businessmen persisted, and economic cases accounted for the vast majority of equal protection questions before the Court until 1960.[65]

THE MODERN VIEW

On the seventieth anniversary of its adoption—in 1938—the Fourteenth Amendment began to take on new strength in its intended role as protector of individual rights. In the first of a line of rulings that would erode the declaration of *Plessy v. Ferguson* into uselessness, the Supreme Court in 1938 held that a state that maintained no "black" law school violated the equal protection promise when it refused to admit a black resident to its "white" state law school, just because of his race.[66]

Six years later, even as the Court upheld the war power of the federal government to remove Japanese-Americans from their West Coast homes, the justices signaled their waning tolerance for laws using racial classifications. In the Court's opinion in *Korematsu v. United States*, the majority stated that "all legal restrictions which curtail the civil rights of a single racial group are immediately suspect" as violations of the Fourteenth Amendment's guarantee of equal protection. Such laws were subject to "the most rigid scrutiny," declared the Court. "Pressing public necessity may sometimes justify the existence of such restrictions; racial antagonism never can."[67]

Led by the National Association for the Advancement of Colored People and its legal defense fund, civil rights groups quickly accepted this clear judicial invitation to challenge the segregation that pervaded American life. In several subsequent cases decided in the late 1940s, the justices indicated their increasing skepticism as to whether separate facilities could ever be truly equal.

Finally, in its ruling in *Brown v. Board of Education*, the Court in 1954 abandoned the "separate but equal" doctrine and held state segregation of public schools unconstitutional.[68] Eighty-six years after adoption of the Fourteenth Amendment, the Court at last set the nation on the road to fulfilling the promise of equal protection.

Although the Court mandated a change in the nation's direction, progress was slow. In the 1960s the frustration of the nation's blacks erupted in protests, boycotts, sit ins, and demonstrations. The reaction was often violent.

The compound of protest and reaction sparked congressional action. In 1964 Congress passed the most comprehensive civil rights measure since Reconstruction. The Civil Rights Act of 1964 translated the guarantee of equal protection into a statutory requirement of equal opportunity in employment and equal access to public facilities for blacks and whites.

Historian Irving Brant wrote that the 1964 act brought to fruition "all that a once-aroused nation had attempted" in adopting the Fourteenth Amendment.[69] The act was immediately challenged as unconstitutional and just as quickly upheld by a unanimous Supreme Court.[70]

In 1968 Congress approved a federal Fair Housing Act. The Court reinforced its provisions with a broadened interpretation of the Civil Rights Act of 1866, which guaranteed similar rights of equal treatment to blacks and whites seeking to sell, buy, or rent housing.[71]

THE EXPANDING GUARANTEE

In the last quarter of the twentieth century, the Supreme Court faced a range of "second-generation" questions raised by the national effort to ensure equal treatment for blacks and whites. The justices wrestled with the problem of defining proper remedies for past discrimination. White plaintiffs charged that employers engaged in "reverse discrimination"—penalizing innocent members of the majority group in order to compensate minority group members for past unfairness. Mindful of history, however, the Court generally condoned "affirmative action" to make up for past discrimination. But in the closing years of the twentieth century, the Court began to question the continuing appropriateness of programs that favored racial minorities. Ruling in favor of a white highway contractor who challenged a decision awarding a contract to a Hispanic firm instead of his, the Court said policies based on race must undergo the strictest judicial scrutiny to ensure that no individual's right to equal protection of the laws had been infringed.[72]

The protection of the Fourteenth Amendment's guarantee of equality before the law was broadened as the Court brought aliens and women within its scope. In 1971 the Court formally declared alienage, like race, to be in all circumstances a suspect classification upon which to base laws. Absent a compelling state justification, such laws would be held invalid.[73]

Women as a class fared less well. The Court has not yet declared sex a suspect classification in all circumstances. But in 1971 the Court for the first time nullified a state law because it violated the equal protection guarantee by treating men and women differently without a sufficient justification.[74] Since then the Court has struck down a variety of federal regulations and state laws for this same reason. It generally employs the rule that classification by gender must serve important governmental objectives, and be substantially related to achieving those objectives, in order to be upheld.

Fundamental Fairness

The Constitution twice promises the individual that government will not deprive him of life, liberty, or property without due process of law.

Neither of these guarantees—in the Fifth and Fourteenth Amendments—protects absolutely against loss of life, liberty, or property. They simply assure the individual that this deprivation will occur only after the government has adhered to certain standard, approved procedures.

But what is due process for the person faced with a sentence of death, or life in prison, or loss of property?

The Supreme Court has spent more than a century answering that question. The first time it considered the matter, it noted that the phrase "due process" probably meant no more to those who wrote it into the Bill of Rights than simply "by the law of the land"—that is, by accepted legal procedures.[75]

From that matter-of-fact origin, however, the guarantee of due process has expanded into the basic constitutional assurance to the individual that the government will deal fairly with him, even when it suspects or charges him with serious crimes.

The close relationship between procedure and substance, particularly in the nation's judicial system, was pointed out by Justice Rutledge in 1947. "At times," he wrote, "the way in which courts perform their function becomes as important as what they do in the result. In some respects matters of procedure constitute the very essence of ordered liberty under the Constitution."[76]

Despite the many landmark due process decisions that dot the history of the Supreme Court in the twentieth century, the definition of due process remains incomplete. Justice Felix Frankfurter explained why:

Due process of law . . . conveys neither formal nor fixed nor narrow requirements. It is the compendious expression for all those rights which the courts must enforce because they are basic to our free society. But basic rights do not become petrified as of any one time, even though, as a matter of human experience, some may not too rhetorically be called eternal verities. It is of the very nature of a free society to advance in its standards of what is deemed reasonable and right. Representing as it does a living principle, due process is not confined within a permanent catalogue of what may at a given time be deemed the limits or the essentials of fundamental rights.[77]

Frankfurter wrote that in 1949. In the following two decades the Court expanded the meaning of due process to include virtually all the specific guarantees of the Bill of Rights.

THE LONG DEBATE

The original due process guarantee is contained in the Fifth Amendment. But *Barron v. Baltimore* made plain that its reach was limited to federal action.

The Fourteenth Amendment, added in 1868, included a similar guarantee, specifically directed against state action. But in one of history's odd turnabouts, this provision was used at first by the Court as a means of dismantling state economic regulation. At the same time, the justices were refusing to read into the due process clause any requirement that states use the indictment process for persons charged with capital crimes, or that they provide twelve-man juries to try persons charged with seri-

ous crimes, or that they observe the privilege against compelled self-incrimination.[78]

For a century after 1868, the Court and legal scholars argued over whether or not the Fourteenth Amendment's due process guarantee "incorporated" or "absorbed" the Bill of Rights—making each particular guarantee applicable against state action. As the debate continued from decision to decision, it tended to obscure the growing consensus among the justices that due process meant more than "by the law of the land"—that it indeed represented a promise of fundamental fairness. Frankfurter described it as "representing a profound attitude of fairness between man and man, and more particularly between the individual and the government."[79] Eventually, this consensus rendered the "incorporation" debate moot.

A fundamentally conservative Court in the 1920s began the enlargement of due process. Inherent in the concept of due process, that Court declared, were the guarantees that one's trial would be free from mob domination, that the judge would be impartial, that the jury would be representative of the community, and that one should have the effective aid of an attorney.[80] These guarantees the Court first recognized as essential in particular cases—where the crimes were serious and the defendant young, ignorant, or a member of a minority group.

In the 1930s the Court began to apply constitutional standards to the evidence used by state prosecutors. Confessions extracted by torture could not fairly be used against the persons so forced to incriminate themselves, held the Court—decades before it formally extended the Fifth Amendment privilege against compelled self-incrimination to state defendants.[81]

In the 1940s the Court simply assumed that the ban on cruel and unusual punishment applied to the states as well as the federal government.[82] It held that the Fourth Amendment guarantee of personal security against unreasonable search and seizure applied against state action, but it declined to require state judges to exclude evidence seized in violation of that guarantee.[83]

THE DUE PROCESS REVOLUTION

The decade of the 1960s saw the most rapid expansion of the meaning of due process. Led by Chief Justice Warren, the Supreme Court firmly applied the guarantees of the Fourth, Fifth, Sixth, and Eighth Amendments against state action.

Right by right, the Court read into the Constitution greater protection for criminal defendants. In 1960 the Court forbade federal agents to use evidence seized illegally by state agents. In 1961 it required the exclusion of illegally obtained evidence from state trials.[84]

Since 1938 all federal defendants had been guaranteed the aid of an attorney. In 1963 the Supreme Court finally closed the gap between the right of state and federal defendants in that regard. The Court declared that all persons charged with serious crimes in state court were assured the aid of an attorney, who would be appointed by the court and paid by the state if necessary.[85]

Rejecting "the notion that the Fourteenth Amendment applies to the states only a 'watered-down subjective version of the Bill of Rights,'" the Court in 1964 held that state suspects, like federal suspects, are protected against being forced to incriminate themselves.[86] In 1965 the Court held that this privilege also barred adverse comment, by judge or prosecutor, on a defendant's failure to testify in his own defense.[87] Also that year, the Court held that due process required states to provide a defendant with the opportunity to confront and crossexamine persons who testified against him.[88]

In 1967 the Court held that states were obliged to provide a speedy trial to criminal defendants.[89] In 1968 it added the requirements of a jury trial for all persons charged by the state with serious crimes.[90] Then, on the last day of Chief Justice Warren's tenure, the Court in 1969 applied the ban on double jeopardy to state criminal proceedings.[91]

State interference with personal privacy came under equal scrutiny in the 1960s. The Court in 1965 said a couple's use of contraceptives is protected by the due process guarantee of the Fourteenth Amendment, as well as by the "penumbra" of privacy interests covered by the First, Third, Fourth, and Fifth Amendments, and the Ninth Amendment's reservation of rights to the people. Then in a singularly controversial decision, *Roe v. Wade,* the Court ruled in 1973 that the Constitution also ensures a woman's right to abortion.[92]

The Court—and the public—would be torn for decades over the breadth of constitutional protections for abortion. In 1992 the Court narrowly affirmed *Roe v. Wade.* A plurality of justices whose position on the issue had not been clear previously, Sandra Day O'Connor, Anthony M. Kennedy, and David H. Souter, jointly wrote in *Planned Parenthood of Southeastern Pennsylvania v. Casey,* "Our law affords constitutional protection to personal decisions relating to marriage, procreation, contraception, family relationships, child rearing, and education. . . . These matters involving the most intimate and personal choices a person may make in a lifetime, choices central to personal dignity and autonomy, are central to the liberty protected by the Fourteenth Amendment. At the heart of liberty is the right to define one's own concept of existence, of meaning, of the universe, and of the mystery of human life. Beliefs about these matters could not define the attributes of personhood were they formed under compulsion of the State."[93]

By the closing years of the twentieth century, the Bill of Rights had at last been nationalized. And the due process guarantee of the Fourteenth Amendment had been expanded to protect an individual's liberty to choose, when confronted with the most personal dilemmas of life and death. But the interpretation of individual rights is a continuing one, as a look at the decisions of any recent term will show. In the words of Justice Frankfurter "'due process,' unlike some legal rules, is not a technical conception with a fixed content. . . . Due process is not a mechanical instrument. It is not a yardstick. It is a process. It is a delicate process of adjustment."[94]

NOTES

1. Article I, Section 9, Clause 2.
2. Article I, Section 9, Clause 3.
3. Article III, Section 2, Clause 3.
4. Article III, Section 3.
5. Article IV, Section 2, Clause 2.
6. Article VI, Section 3.
7. Charles Warren, *Congress, the Constitution and the Supreme Court* (Boston: Little, Brown, 1925), 79–80.
8. Ibid., 81–82.
9. Irving Brant, *The Bill of Rights* (Indianapolis: Bobbs-Merrill, 1965), 42–67; Julius Goebel Jr., *History of the Supreme Court of the United States,* Vol. I: *Antecedents and Beginnings to 1801* (New York: Macmillan, 1971), 413–456.
10. Henry M. Christman, ed., *The Public Papers of Chief Justice Earl Warren* (New York: Simon and Schuster, 1959), 70.
11. Ibid.
12. Zechariah Chafee Jr., *Free Speech in the United States* (Cambridge: Harvard University Press, 1941; reprint ed., New York: Atheneum, 1969), 6–7.
13. Brant, *Bill of Rights,* 486; see also Goebel, *Antecedents and Beginnings,* 633–651.
14. Brant, *Bill of Rights,* 49–50.
15. Ibid., 314; see also Goebel, *Antecedents and Beginnings,* 633–651.
16. *Barron v. Baltimore,* 7 Pet. 243 (1833).
17. Id. at 247.
18. Id. at 250.
19. Ibid.
20. Brant, *Bill of Rights,* 333; see also Carl B. Swisher, *American Constitutional Development,* 2d ed. (Cambridge, Mass.: Houghton Mifflin, 1954), 331.
21. Brant, *Bill of Rights,* 336.
22. *Slaughterhouse Cases,* 16 Wall. 36 (1873); *Minor v. Happersett,* 21 Wall. 162 (1875).
23. *United States v. Reese,* 92 U.S. 214 (1876); *United States v. Cruikshank,* 92 U.S. 542 (1876).
24. *Hurtado v. California,* 110 U.S. 516 (1884).
25. *Plessy v. Ferguson,* 163 U.S. 537 (1896).
26. Charles Warren, *The Supreme Court in United States History,* 2 vols. (Boston: Little, Brown, 1922, 1926), II: 618.
27. Ibid., 617.
28. William W. Davis, *The Federal Enforcement Acts,* Studies on Southern History and Politics (1914), cited in Warren, *The Supreme Court in United States History,* II: 618.
29. *Yick Wo v. Hopkins,* 118 U.S. 356 (1886).
30. *Boyd v. United States,* 116 U.S. 616 (1886).
31. *Weeks v. United States,* 232 U.S. 383 (1914).
32. *Truax v. Raich,* 239 U.S. 33 (1915).
33. *Guinn v. United States,* 238 U.S. 347 (1915).
34. *Gitlow v. New York,* 268 U.S. 652 (1925).
35. Id. at 666.
36. *Stromberg v. California,* 283 U.S. 359 (1931); *Near v. Minnesota,* 283 U.S. 697 (1931).
37. *Hamilton v. Board of Regents,* 293 U.S. 245 (1934).
38. *DeJonge v. Oregon,* 299 U.S. 353 (1937).
39. *United States v. Carolene Products Co.,* 304 U.S. 144 (1938).
40. Id. at 152.
41. Ibid.
42. Robert H. Jackson, *The Struggle for Judicial Supremacy* (New York: Random House, Vintage Books, 1941), 284–285.
43. Ibid.
44. *DeJonge v. Oregon,* 299 U.S. 353 at 365 (1937).
45. *Thomas v. Collins,* 323 U.S. 516 at 529–530 (1945).
46. Id. at 537.
47. Id. at 545–546.

48. *Herbert v. Lando,* 441 U.S. 153 (1979).

49. *Minor v. Happersett,* 21 Wall. 162 (1875).

50. *United States v. Reese* (1876) 92 U.S. 214 (1876); *United States v. Cruikshank,* 92 U.S. 542 (1876).

51. *Guinn v. United States,* 238 U.S. 347 (1915); *Nixon v. Herndon,* 273 U.S. 536 (1927); *Smith v. Allwright,* 321 U.S. 649 (1944).

52. *South Carolina v. Katzenbach,* 383 U.S. 301 (1966).

53. *Baker v. Carr,* 369 U.S. 186 (1962).

54. *Gray v. Sanders,* 372 U.S. 368 (1963).

55. *Yates v. United States,* 354 U.S. 298; *Scales v. United States,* 367 U.S. 203 (1961); *Noto v. United States,* 367 U.S. 290 (1961); *Elfbrandt v. Russell,* 384 U.S. 11 (1966); *Aptheker v. Secretary of State,* 378 U.S. 500 (1964); *Schware v. Board of Bar Examiners,* 353 U.S. 232 (1957); *Keyishian v. Board of Regents,* 385 U.S. 589 (1967); *United States v. Robel,* 389 U.S. 258 (1967).

56. *National Association for the Advancement of Colored People (NAACP) v. Alabama,* 357 U.S. 449 (1958); *NAACP v. Button,* 371 U.S. 415 (1963).

57. *United States v. Robel,* 389 U.S. 258 at 282–283 (1967).

58. Brant, *Bill of Rights,* 337.

59. *Slaughterhouse Cases,* 16 Wall. 36 at 81 (1873).

60. *Strauder v. West Virginia,* 100 U.S. 303 at 307 (1880).

61. *Civil Rights Cases,* 100 U.S. 3 (1883).

62. *Plessy v. Ferguson,* 163 U.S. 537 (1896).

63. Brant, *Bill of Rights,* 367.

64. *Plessy v. Ferguson,* 163 U.S. 537 at 551–552 (1896).

65. Robert J. Harris, *The Quest for Equality* (Baton Rouge: Louisiana State University Press, 1960), 59; cited by C. Herman Pritchett, *The American Constitution,* 2d ed. (New York: McGraw-Hill, 1968), 682.

66. *Missouri ex rel. Gaines v. Canada,* 305 U.S. 337 (1938).

67. *Korematsu v. United States,* 323 U.S. 214 at 216 (1944).

68. *Brown v. Board of Education,* 347 U.S. 483 (1954).

69. Brant, *Bill of Rights,* 377.

70. *Heart of Atlanta Motel v. United States,* 379 U.S. 241 (1964).

71. *Jones v. Alfred H. Mayer Co.,* 392 U.S. 409 (1968).

72. *Adarand Constructors Inc. v. Peña,* 115 s. ct. 2097 (1995).

73. *Graham v. Richardson,* 403 U.S. 365 (1971).

74. *Reed v. Reed,* 404 U.S. 71 (1971).

75. *Murray's Lessee v. Hoboken Land & Improvement Co.,* 18 How. 272 (1856).

76. *United States v. United Mine Workers,* 330 U.S. 258 at 342 (1947).

77. *Wolf v. Colorado,* 338 U.S. 25 at 27 (1949).

78. *Hurtado v. California,* 110 U.S. 516 (1884); *Maxwell v. Dow,* 176 U.S. 581 (1900); *Twining v. New Jersey,* 211 U.S. 78 (1908).

79. *Joint Anti-Fascist Refugee Committee v. McGrath,* 341 U.S. 123 at 162 (1951).

80. *Moore v. Dempsey,* 261 U.S. 86 (1923); *Tumey v. Ohio,* 273 U.S. 510 (1927); *Norris v. Alabama,* 294 U.S. 587 (1935); *Powell v. Alabama,* 287 U.S. 45 (1932).

81. *Brown v. Mississippi,* 297 U.S. 278 (1936).

82. *Louisiana ex rel. Francis v. Resweber,* 329 U.S. 459 (1947).

83. *Wolf v. Colorado,* 338 U.S. 25 (1949).

84. *Elkins v. United States,* 364 U.S. 206 (1960); *Mapp v. Ohio,* 367 U.S. 643 (1961).

85. *Gideon v. Wainwright,* 372 U.S. 335 (1963).

86. *Malloy v. Hogan,* 378 U.S. 1 at 10–11 (1964).

87. *Griffin v. California,* 380 U.S. 609 (1965).

88. *Pointer v. Texas,* 380 U.S. 400 (1965).

89. *Klopfer v. North Carolina,* 386 U.S. 213 (1967).

90. *Duncan v. Louisiana,* 391 U.S. 145 (1968).

91. *Benton v. Maryland,* 395 U.S. 784 (1969).

92. *Griswold v. Connecticut,* 381 U.S. 479 (1965); *Roe v. Wade,* 410 U.S. 113 (1973).

93. *Planned Parenthood of Southeastern Pennsylvania v. Casey,* 505 U.S. 833 (1992).

94. *Joint Anti-Fascist Refugee Committee v. McGrath,* 341 U.S. 123 at 163 (1951).

CHAPTER 9

Freedom for Ideas: The Right to Believe, to Speak, to Assemble, to Petition, to Publish, and to Practice

O F ALL THE LIBERTIES GUARANTEED by the Bill of Rights, the freedoms of the First Amendment are the most widely cherished. Won through revolution, the freedoms of speech, press, religion, peaceable assembly, and petition are values fundamental to the American ideals of individual freedom and representative self-government.

The guarantee of freedom for the individual's expression of ideas and opinions reflects a belief in the worth of each person. So, too, does the decision to entrust the government of society to the will of its members.

The "First Amendment protects two kinds of interests on free speech," wrote Professor Zechariah Chafee Jr. "There is an individual interest, the need of many men to express their opinions on matters vital to them if life is to be worth living, and a social interest in the attainment of truth, so that the country may not only adopt the wisest course of action but carry it out in the wisest way."[1]

The two freedoms are inextricably bound together. Professor Thomas I. Emerson observed that freedom of individual expression is essential to preserve a stable community in the face of ever-changing political, economic, and social circumstances and to maintain "the precarious balance between healthy cleavage and necessary consensus."[2]

Suppression of free expression, on the other hand, endangers both the development and liberty of the individual and the sta-

Freedom of individual expression, including the right to speak one's mind without fear of repression, has been crucial to the success of representative government in the United States.

bility of representative government. In the words of constitutional historian Thomas M. Cooley,

Repression of full and free discussion is dangerous in any government resting upon the will of the people. The people cannot fail to believe that they are deprived of rights, and will be certain to become discontented, when their discussion of public measures is sought to be circumscribed by the judgment of others upon their temperance or fairness. They must be left at liberty to speak with the freedom which the magnitude of the supposed wrongs appears in their minds to demand; and if they exceed all the proper bounds of moderation, the consolation must be, that the evil likely to spring from the violent discussion will probably be less, and its correction by public sentiment more speedy, than if the terrors of the law were brought to bear to prevent the discussion.[3]

Justice Louis D. Brandeis explained this relationship:

Those who won our independence believed that the final end of the State was to make men free to develop their faculties; and that in its government the deliberative forces should prevail over the arbitrary. They valued liberty both as an end and as a means. They believed liberty to be the secret of happiness and courage to be the secret of liberty. They believed that freedom to think as you will and to speak as you think are means indispensable to the discovery and spread of political truth; that without free speech and assembly discussion would be futile; that with them, discussion affords ordinarily adequate protection against the dissemination of noxious doctrine; that the greatest menace to freedom is an inert people; that public discussion is a political duty; and that this should be a fundamental principle of the American government. They recognized the risks to which all human institutions are subject. But they knew that order cannot be secured merely through fear of punishment for its infraction; that it is hazardous to discourage thought, hope and imagination; that fear breeds repression; that repression breeds hate; that hate menaces stable government; that the path of safety lies in the opportunity to discuss freely supposed grievances and proposed remedies; and that the fitting remedy for evil counsels is good ones. Believing in the power of reason as applied through public discussion, they eschewed silence coerced by law—the argument of force in its worst form. Recognizing the occasional tyrannies of governing majorities, they amended the Constitution so that free speech and assembly should be guaranteed.[4]

THE FIRST AMENDMENT

The First Amendment states: "Congress shall make no law respecting an establishment of religion, or prohibiting the free exercise thereof; or abridging the freedom of speech, or of the press; or the right of the people peaceably to assemble, and to petition the Government for a redress of grievances." Given the fundamental character of these rights, it seems somewhat ironic that they were not enumerated in the main body of the Constitution. In that document the Framers sought to prevent federal infringement of certain crucial personal rights by specifically prohibiting Congress to enact ex post facto laws and bills of attainder or to require religious oaths from government officers. The Framers also limited suspension of the writ of habeas corpus.

The Constitution's authors were apparently convinced, however, that the limited powers given the central government and their division among three separate and coequal branches of government were sufficient guarantees against abuse of the freedoms of belief and expression. Many of the Framers also thought any enumeration of individual rights was bound to be incomplete and would imply that those freedoms not listed were not protected.

Participants in the state ratifying conventions were unsatisfied with these explanations. Some of the colonies agreed to ratify the Constitution only on the condition that these and other critical rights—such as indictment and trial by jury—be added. The First Congress approved twelve amendments and submitted them to the states in the fall of 1789. Two of these—dealing with apportionment of U.S. representatives and compensation of members of Congress—were not ratified at the time. The other ten were made part of the Constitution late in 1791.

No Absolute Rights

For nearly 130 years, the Supreme Court had very little occasion to review or interpret the First Amendment. Seven years after its ratification, however, Congress, fearing war with France, curtailed speech and press by passing the Sedition Act of 1798. The law proved so unpopular that it precipitated the fall of the Federalist Party that sponsored it and was allowed to expire before constitutional challenges to it reached the Supreme Court.

In the late 1800s the Court reviewed a pair of federal territorial laws outlawing polygamy, which were challenged as abridging the free exercise of religion. The Court held polygamy a crime that could not be justified as a religious practice. The laws against it therefore did not violate the First Amendment.

Not until World War I, when Congress enacted new sedition and espionage acts, was the Supreme Court forced to consider whether the First Amendment's prohibition against federal interference with speech, press, religion, and assembly was absolute or whether certain emergencies might limit its protection.

In a series of nine cases testing the constitutionality of these two wartime laws, the Supreme Court made clear that the guarantees of free speech and press were not absolute. The justices, however, disagreed on the point at which government might curb exercise of these freedoms.

Rights and the States

At the same time, the Court began to consider whether the First Amendment prohibited state as well as federal abridgment of its guarantees. The First Amendment explicitly prohibits only Congress from abridging its guaranteed freedoms.

In *Barron v. Baltimore* (1833), the Court ruled that the Bill of Rights restricted only the federal government and not the states.[5] In 1868 the Fourteenth Amendment was added to the Constitution, forbidding the states to deprive anyone of "liberty" without due process of law. By 1890 the Court had defined liberty to include economic and property rights, but personal liberties remained outside the Court's view of the Fourteenth Amendment. As historians Alpheus T. Mason and William M. Beaney observed, "This illogical position could not long endure."[6]

Application of First Amendment strictures to state action traces to the minority opinion in the case of *Gilbert v. Minnesota* in 1920. Justice Brandeis, dissenting, said he could not believe "that the liberty guaranteed by the Fourteenth Amendment includes only liberty to acquire and enjoy property."[7]

Nonetheless, as late as 1922 a majority of the Court still declared: "[T]he Constitution of the United States imposes upon the States no obligation to confer upon those within their jurisdiction . . . the right of free speech."[8] In 1923, however, the Court began to include personal freedoms in the definition of liberty protected by the Fourteenth Amendment. Liberty, the majority wrote in *Meyer v. Nebraska,*

denotes not merely freedom from bodily restraint but also the right of the individual to contract, to engage in any of the common occupations of life, to acquire useful knowledge, to marry, establish a home and bring up children, to worship God according to the dictates of his own conscience, and generally to enjoy those privileges long recognized at common law as essential to the orderly pursuit of happiness by free men.[9]

Two years later with little explanation the Court changed its position: the First Amendment guarantees of free speech and free press were applicable to the states. This view is expressed, almost as an aside, in *Gitlow v. New York* (1925):

For present purposes we may and do assume that freedom of speech and of the press—which are protected by the First Amendment from abridgment by Congress—are among the fundamental personal rights and "liberties" protected by the due process clause of the Fourteenth Amendment from impairment by the States.[10]

That same year the Court moved toward including religious liberty within this protection when it struck down an Oregon law requiring all children to attend public schools. In *Pierce v. Society of Sisters* (1925) the Court said that the right of parents to rear their children included the right to send those children to private and parochial schools.[11]

But it was fifteen more years before the Court explicitly applied the First Amendment ban on governmental interference with free exercise of religion to the states. In 1940 in *Cantwell v. Connecticut,* the Court declared that the Fourteenth Amendment "has rendered the legislatures of the states as incompetent as Congress to enact" such restrictions. The states were specifically barred from passing any laws respecting establishment of religion by the 1947 ruling in *Everson v. Board of Education.*[12]

In 1931 the Supreme Court, for the first time, struck down a state law as an unconstitutional prior restraint on the press. This action came in *Near v. Minnesota.* Six years later the Court held that the freedom of assembly was guaranteed against state infringement by the First and Fourteenth Amendments. In the case of *DeJonge v. Oregon,* the Court held the right of peaceful assembly to be as fundamental as the rights of free speech and press and therefore equally entitled to protection from restriction by the states.

The right of assembly, the Court wrote, "is one that cannot be denied without violating those fundamental principles of liberty and justice which lie at the base of all civil and political institutions, principles which the Fourteenth Amendment embodies in the general terms of its due process clause."[13]

GOVERNMENT RESTRAINTS

Government has restrained the exercise of First Amendment free speech and free press rights in two ways: (1) suppression of the utterance before it is spoken or published and (2) punishment of the person who made the offending utterance.

Prohibition of prior restraints—censorship, severe taxation, and licensing systems, for example—is particularly vital to ensure freedom of the press. The English legal commentator Sir William Blackstone thought that liberty of the press lay entirely in allowing "no previous restraints upon publications and not in freedom from censure for criminal matter when published."[14]

But the First Amendment has been interpreted by the Supreme Court to limit subsequent punishment as well as prior restraint. Cooley wrote,

[t]he mere exemption from previous restraints cannot be all that is secured by the constitutional provisions, inasmuch as of words to be uttered orally there can be no previous censorship, and the liberty of the press might be rendered a mockery and a delusion, and the phrase itself a byword, if, while every man was at liberty to publish what he pleased, the public authorities might nevertheless punish him for harmless publications. . . . The evils to be prevented were not the censorship of the press merely, but any action of the government by means of which it might prevent such free and general discussion of public matters as seems absolutely essential to prepare the people for an intelligent exercise of their rights as citizens.[15]

Although the First Amendment is stated absolutely—"Congress shall make no law . . ."—few contend that the amendment is an absolute ban on governmental restriction of the amendment's guarantees. Most justices and constitutional scholars distinguish between pure expression and expression that is in itself conduct or that incites conduct. The first, with a few exceptions, is absolutely protected against governmental infringement; the second is not. Although the Court was speaking specifically of the freedom of religion, its explanation of this distinction in *Cantwell v. Connecticut* (1940) may be applied to all First Amendment freedoms: "[T]he Amendment embraces two concepts—freedom to believe and freedom to act. The first is absolute but, in the nature of things the second cannot be. Conduct remains subject to regulation for the protection of society."[16]

Unprotected Speech

Some forms of expression that fall outside protection of the First Amendment are fairly obvious. Few would apply First Amendment protection to a person who counsels murder or, as Justice Oliver Wendell Holmes Jr. said, to a "man falsely shouting fire in a theater and causing a panic." Few would argue that publishers are free to print deliberately false and defamatory material about public or private individuals. The outer bounds of First Amendment protection are not fixed. The Supreme Court initially held commercial speech—speech proposing a financial transaction—to be outside the amendment's reach. In a line of rulings beginning in 1975, the Court has reversed that position. The Court has held that the First Amendment protects commercial advertising, but it has emphasized that the protection is less than that accorded political and other noncommercial speech.

The Court once ruled that libelous statements were unprotected. It has since held false and defamatory statements about public officials and figures protected unless actual malice is proved. Obscenity is still outside the scope of First Amendment protection, but even there the standards for determining what is obscene and what is not have undergone significant change in recent decades, bringing additional material under protection.

Speech and Conduct

Commercial speech, libel, and obscene material are examples of pure expression. What has proved difficult for the Court to determine with consistency is the precise point at which expression becomes conduct that breaches the bounds of First Amendment protection and becomes subject to government restraint and regulation.

Assume, for example, that a man is making an intemperate speech on a controversial issue on a public street corner. Does the First Amendment protect him against punishment for any consequences his speech might have? If not, must the government wait to stop the speech until his listeners take action either against the speaker or the object of his speech? May it stop him at the point that it thinks his words will lead to a breach of the peace? Or can the government, knowing from past experience that the speaker is a rabble-rouser, prevent him from speaking at all?

Finding an answer to these questions is made more difficult by the emotional response generated by many forms of expression. As Justice Robert H. Jackson once observed, the "freedom to differ is not limited to things that do not matter much."[17]

The voicing of a popular opinion held by a majority rarely raises any First Amendment challenge. It is the unpopular opinion and minority position on matters of crucial concern that are most likely to draw hostility and hatred from the majority upon whose good will the rights of the minority depend. And if the unpopular opinion is perceived as a threat to a way of life or a form of government, it may prompt the majority to petition the government to repress the expression. Such suppression is just what the First Amendment was designed to curb, explained Justice Holmes in a dissenting opinion:

Persecution for the expression of opinions seems to me perfectly logical. . . . But when men have realized that time has upset many fighting faiths, they may come to believe even more than they believe the very foundations of their own conduct that the ultimate good desired is better reached by free trade in ideas—that the best test of truth is the power of the thought to get itself accepted in the competition of the market, and that truth is the only ground upon which their wishes safely can be carried out. That at any rate is the theory of our Constitution.[18]

THE TASK OF BALANCING

The Supreme Court's job has been to balance the scales so that personal rights are restricted only so much as needed to preserve an organized and orderly society. This has not been an easy task, for some justices give more weight to certain factors in the equation than others. If, for instance, a judge believes the preservation of First Amendment rights to be worth more than the tranquility of the established society, the judge may require the society to show that the expression places it in some grave and immediate jeopardy. If, on the other hand, the judge gives the need for an orderly society the same or greater weight than the need for free expression, even a small degree of disruption may be enough for him to justify governmental restraint of the threatening idea.

The Absolute Position

Very few justices have believed that the First Amendment is absolute, that the government may under no circumstances restrict the exercise of free speech, press, religion, or assembly.

Justice Hugo L. Black was one who held this view. "[T]he Amendment provides in simple words that Congress shall make no law . . . abridging freedom of speech or of the press," he wrote in one case. "I read 'no law abridging' to mean no law abridging."[19]

Black elaborated on this in a 1961 dissent:

I believe that the First Amendment's unequivocal command that there shall be no abridgment of the rights of free speech and assembly shows that the men who drafted our Bill of Rights did all the "balancing" that was to be done in this field. . . . [T]he very object of adopting the First Amendment, as well as the other provisions of the Bill of Rights, was to put the freedoms protected there completely out of the area of any congressional control that may be attempted through the exercise of precisely those powers that are now being used to "balance" the Bill of Rights out of existence.[20]

Black's view of the First Amendment meant that he would extend its protection to obscenities and libel. But even Black placed certain kinds of expression outside the reach of the First Amendment. In 1949 he wrote an opinion holding that a particular instance of picketing was so intertwined with illegal labor practices that it lost any First Amendment protection it might otherwise have. And in two cases in the mid-1960s, Black contended that civil rights demonstrations were not protected if they occurred in inappropriate places. (*See details of Brown v. Louisiana and Adderly v. Florida, p. 437.*)

Preferred Position

If First Amendment rights generally have not been viewed as absolute, most justices still accord them a preferred position when weighed against competing rights and interests. This preferred position arises from the judicial belief that preservation of these rights is so essential to the maintenance of democratic values as to warrant special judicial consideration.

Justice Benjamin N. Cardozo first voiced this view from the bench in a 1937 case. He suggested that because the freedom of "thought and speech . . . is the matrix, the indispensable condition, of nearly every other form of freedom," First Amendment rights are on a "different plane of social and moral values" than the other rights and freedoms guaranteed by the Bill of Rights.[21]

Cardozo's statement was followed in 1938 by a broad hint that the Court might apply stricter standards to test the validity of laws restricting First Amendment rights than it did in cases involving property and economic rights. Traditionally the Court deferred to legislative judgment in enacting statutes levying taxes and regulating business. So long as there was a reasonable basis for the regulation, the Court would presume it constitutional.

But in the famous *Carolene Products* footnote, Justice Harlan Fiske Stone wrote that "[T]here may be a narrower scope for operation of the presumption of constitutionality when legislation appears on its face to be within a specific prohibition of the Constitution, such as those of the first ten amendments."[22] (*Text of footnote, p. 400.*)

The following year all but one member of the Court endorsed the premise implicit in that footnote. "Mere legislative preferences or beliefs respecting matters of public convenience may . . . be insufficient to justify such [regulation] as diminishes the exercise of rights [of freedom of speech and press] so vital to the maintenance of democratic institutions," the majority wrote. Furthermore, it was the duty of the courts "to weigh the circumstances and to appraise the substantiality of the reasons advanced" to support regulation of First Amendment rights rather than to defer to legislative judgment.[23]

This special treatment of the First Amendment came to be known as the "preferred position," a phrase first used by Stone, then chief justice, in a dissent in *Jones v. Opelika* (1942). The first use by a majority came in the decision that overturned *Jones*. In *Murdock v. Pennsylvania* (1943) the majority flatly stated that "[f]reedom of press, freedom of speech, freedom of religion are in a preferred position."[24]

The fullest elaboration of this attitude came in the 1945 case of *Thomas v. Collins*. Justice Wiley B. Rutledge wrote that it was the Court's duty

to say where the individual's freedom ends and the State's power begins. Choice on that border, now as always delicate, is perhaps more so where the usual presumption supporting legislation is balanced by the preferred place given in our scheme to the great, the indispensable democratic freedoms secured by the First Amendment. . . . That priority gives these liberties a sanctity and a sanction not permitting dubious intrusions. . . .

. . . [A]ny attempt to restrict those liberties must be justified by clear public interest, threatened not doubtfully or remotely, but by clear and present danger. The rational connection between the remedy provided and the evil to be curbed, which in other contexts might support legislation against attack on due process grounds, will not suffice. These rights rest on firmer foundation. Accordingly, whatever occasion would restrain orderly discussion and persuasion, at appropriate time and place, must have clear support in public danger, actual or impending. Only the gravest abuses, endangering paramount interests, give occasion for permissible limitation.[25]

Use of the phrase "preferred position" faded away, but the concept recurs. The Court considers statutes that limit First Amendment rights highly suspect, requiring close judicial attention and compelling justification for their existence. Chief Justice Warren E. Burger stated that consensus in 1978:

Deference to a legislative finding cannot limit judicial inquiry when First Amendment rights are at stake. . . . A legislature appropriately inquires into and may declare the reasons impelling legislative action but the judicial function commands analysis of whether the specific conduct charged falls within the reach of the statute and if so whether the legislation is consonant with the Constitution. Were it otherwise, the scope of freedom of speech and of the press would be subject to legislative definition and the function of the First Amendment as a check on legislative power would be nullified.[26]

A few justices opposed the preferred position concept. Chief among these was Felix Frankfurter, a vigorous advocate of judicial restraint. In 1949 he characterized the preferred position approach to the First Amendment as "a mischievous phrase, if it carries the thought, which it may subtly imply, that any law touching communication is infected with presumptive invalidity."[27]

When he balanced First Amendment rights against competing interests, Frankfurter placed great weight on legislative judgment. Two years later he wrote:

Free speech cases are not an exception to the principle that we are not legislators, that direct policy making is not our province. How best to reconcile competing interests is the business of legislatures, and the balance they strike is a judgment not to be displaced by ours, but to be respected unless outside the pale of fair judgment.[28]

THE SEARCH FOR A STANDARD

The Supreme Court has never held the freedoms of speech, press, religion, and assembly to be absolute. Although it has written specific rules for determining whether speech is obscene or libelous, the Court has been unable to settle on a general standard for determining at what point a form of expression becomes sufficiently threatening to society to justify its being regulated or otherwise restrained by government.

Clear and Present Danger

The first time the Supreme Court ruled directly on the extent to which government might limit speech, Justice Oliver Wendell Holmes Jr. proposed the "clear and present danger" test as the standard for such regulation. The case, *Schenck v. United States* (1919), was the first of several challenging convictions under the World War I espionage and sedition acts that made it a federal crime to obstruct the U.S. war effort.

Writing for a unanimous Court, Holmes said:

The question in every case is whether the words are used in such circumstances and are of such a nature as to create a clear and present danger that they will bring about the substantive evils that Congress has a right to prevent. It is a question of proximity and degree.[29]

In the eyes of the justices, the fact that the country was engaged in a war made Schenck's efforts to obstruct recruitment a clear and present danger punishable under federal law. *(See details of the case, p. 417.)*

Eight months later a majority of the Court moved away from the clear and present danger standard toward what became known as the "bad tendency" test. This test held that government may punish any speech that tends to interfere with the successful prosecution of a war effort, no matter how remote in time or unlikely the effect of the interference might be. The majority applied the bad tendency test in several cases.[30] But in 1937 it renewed reliance on the clear and present danger doctrine.

The case concerned a black communist who went to Georgia to solicit members for the Communist Party and to encourage black Georgians to demand equal rights with whites. He was convicted under a state law because a trial court found that his speeches and documents had a dangerous tendency to incite insurrection.

A majority of the Court overturned the conviction on the ground that the speech and documents did not threaten "a clear and present danger of forcible obstruction of a particular state function."[31] *(See details of Herndon v. Lowry, p. 426.)*

Until 1937 the Court had considered free speech questions primarily in the context of seditious speech—utterances that threatened the viability of the established governing and economic system.

After 1937 the Court began to review more cases weighing the constitutional guarantee of free speech against state limitations designed to preserve public peace. In these cases it frequently employed the clear and present danger test. Thus in 1940 the Court held that a state could not constitutionally punish a person for peacefully picketing an employer with whom he had a labor dispute.[32]

In another 1940 case the Court overturned the conviction of a Jehovah's Witness for breach of the peace. His verbal attack on other religions highly incensed two passersby who had consented to listen to it. In the absence of a definitive statute making such conduct a clear and present danger to a substantial interest of the state, the Court said the situation had threatened no "clear and present menace to public peace and order."[33] *(See details of Cantwell v. Connecticut, p. 428.)* It soon became apparent that the justices could seldom reach a consensus on whether a danger was "clear and present." In 1949 a majority of the Court held that the clear and present danger to public order was not threatened by a speaker whose speech in a private hall sparked a near-riot by several hundred protesters gathered outside the hall. But in 1951 the Court upheld the conviction of a speaker whose utterances caused one listener to threaten to stop the speaker from continuing his remarks. Here the Court majority held that a clear and present danger of greater disorder warranted restraint of the speaker.[34]

The widely held fear that the American system of government was in danger of subversion by communists led to enactment of a federal law outlawing membership in the Communist Party and the advocacy of the violent overthrow of the established government. *(See "Freedom of Political Association," pp. 532–554, in Chapter 10.)* The question whether this act was an unconstitutional infringement on free speech came to the Supreme Court in the 1951 case of *Dennis v. United States.* A majority of the Court upheld the federal law, using a substantially revised version of the clear and present danger test. The justices read the traditional rule as being applicable only when the probability of success of the intended dangerous effect was imminent.

Chief Justice Fred M. Vinson, however, found this an inadequate protection from subversive activity that included advocacy of the future overthrow of the government by force. The clear and present danger test must be reinterpreted, he wrote in his dissent: "In each case [courts] must ask whether the gravity of the 'evil' discounted by its improbability, justified such invasion of free speech as is necessary to avoid the danger."[35]

With this restatement, the original meaning of the clear and present danger test appeared to be lost. The doctrine was little used after the 1957 case of *Yates v. United States.*[36]

The Balancing Doctrine

The test was replaced for a time by the so-called balancing doctrine in which the Court weighed the value of preserving free speech against the value of preserving whatever governmental interest that speech might adversely affect. This standard first appeared in a 1950 decision sustaining a federal law that denied the protection of the National Labor Relations Act to any union whose officers failed to swear that they were not communists and did not believe in the violent overthrow of the government.

The majority found that the law's primary purpose was to prevent a union official from using his power to force a strike to advance the communist cause. In the Court's view this law limited speech only incidentally. It found application of the clear and present danger test inappropriate and turned instead to the balancing test:

When particular conduct is regulated in the interest of public order, and the regulation results in an indirect, conditional, partial abridgment of speech, the duty of the courts is to determine which of these two conflicting interests demands the greater protection under the particular circumstances presented.[37]

Throughout the cold war period (roughly the late 1940s to the late 1980s), the Court employed the balancing test to determine the validity of numerous state and federal laws restricting the speech and actions of individuals associated with the Communist Party and other allegedly subversive organizations.[38]

When the Court was asked to weigh the interest of a state in obtaining the membership lists of a state branch of the National Association for the Advancement of Colored People (NAACP) against the members' right to privacy in association, it balanced the scales in favor of the right of association. The Court did not apply the balancing test to other 1960s civil rights cases involving picketing and demonstrations. In 1967 the Court specifically rejected the use of that test in a national security case.[39]

The Court disposed of some of the cold war cases by using the "incitement test," which distinguished between advocacy of unlawful conduct (such as the violent overthrow of the government) as abstract doctrine, and advocacy that actually incited action. The first was protected by the First Amendment; the second was not.[40]

Alternative Approaches

Recognizing the inadequacy of these substantive tests, the Court now relies on several standards that focus on the challenged statute rather than on the conduct or speech it regulates. The three standards most frequently employed are "statutory vagueness," "facial overbreadth," and the "least restrictive means" test. They are based on the premise that laws imposing restrictions that are too broad might inhibit some persons from exercising their constitutionally protected freedoms.

An overly broad statute restricts forms of expression that are protected as well as those that are not. Under the least restrictive means test, government may restrain expression only as much as necessary to achieve its purpose: "[E]ven though the governmental purpose be legitimate and substantial, that purpose cannot be pursued by means that broadly stifle fundamental personal liberties when the end can more narrowly be achieved."[41]

Statutes deficient in any of these respects may be challenged by persons whose speech may in fact be properly punished by the state under the law.

The contemporary Court's scrutiny of government's limits on speech has generally yielded ample freedom for ideas. In 1990, when the Court struck down a federal statute prohibiting flag burning, Justice Brennan wrote, "If there is a bedrock principle underlying the First Amendment, it is that the government may not prohibit the expression of an idea simply because society finds the idea itself offensive or disagreeable."[42]

Freedom of Speech

Speech is the basic vehicle for communicating ideas, thoughts, and beliefs. The right to speak freely is necessary to the free flow of ideas that is considered so crucial to the success of representative government in the United States. This belief spurred the people of the new nation to add to the Constitution a prohibition on government action "abridging" the freedom of speech.

Although the First Amendment states its protection absolutely, few contend that the right it protects is without limit. And there are forms of speech that merit no First Amendment protection, such as libel and obscenity.

The Supreme Court's cases repeatedly come down to two recurring questions: What is protected speech and when may such speech be curbed?

The Court approaches speech that stands alone in a manner different from speech that is accompanied by a course of conduct, such as picketing. Verbal expression of thought and opinion, whether spoken calmly in the privacy of one's home or delivered passionately in a soapbox harangue, is the purest form of speech.

Constitutional historian C. Herman Pritchett has observed that the "distinctive qualities of pure speech are that it relies for effect only on the power of the ideas or emotions that are communicated by speech and that usually the audience is a voluntary one which chooses to listen to the speaker's message."[1]

Because it does not interfere with or inconvenience others, pure speech is subject to the least amount of government control. The Court, however, recognizes the right of government to curb pure speech that threatens the national security or public safety. It also acknowledges that government has a right to regulate pure speech that does interfere with others.

The broadest official restrictions on pure speech have come during times of war when the Court has upheld federal and state controls on seditious and subversive speech. It has sustained punishment of nonseditious speech that stimulates a violent and hostile reaction by those who hear it. But because the Court considers the varying circumstances attending each free speech case, it has been unable to develop and apply consistently a standard for determining when the threat to national security or public safety warrants a restriction on or punishment of the speech.

Certain forms of pure speech and expression fall outside the protection of the First Amendment because they are not essential to communication of ideas and have little social value. "Fighting words"—public insults calculated to elicit a violent response—fall into this category, as does obscenity. Here again, however, the Court has had great difficulty settling on a standard by which to define the obscene.

Initially the Court placed speech that advertised products and services outside the protection of the First Amendment. Since 1975, however, the Court has recognized that advertisements convey ideas and information of substantial value to the public and so has brought commercial speech under First Amendment coverage.

Expression that makes a symbolic statement has been considered pure speech by the Court. The justices have upheld the right of students to wear armbands and to fly the flag upside down in symbolic protest of the Vietnam War. Although such symbolism may make itself felt on an involuntary audience, it relies for effect, like pure speech, primarily on evocation of an idea or emotion.

The Court has also held, however, that symbolic speech, like pure speech, may be so intertwined with conduct that the state may regulate both.

When speech is combined with conduct—usually parading, demonstrating, or picketing—the Court is more open to government regulation. Pritchett wrote that "speech plus" involves:

physical movement of the participants, who rely less upon the persuasive influence of speech to achieve their purposes and more upon the public impact of assembling, marching and patrolling. Their purpose is to bring a point of view—by signs, slogans, singing or their mere presence—to the attention of the widest possible public, including those uninterested or even hostile.[2]

The Court has upheld the right of persons to engage in speech plus conduct, but at the same time it has accorded government the right to regulate the conduct aspect to ensure public safety and order. Such regulation must be precisely drawn and applied in a nondiscriminatory fashion. The government also must have a legitimate and substantial interest to justify the regulation, and the regulation must restrict the speech aspect as little as possible.

One area of speech plus conduct—picketing—has been held by the Court to have almost no First Amendment protection. Although the Court at first ruled that the information conveyed to the public by labor picketing merited some degree of First Amendment protection, later decisions have virtually reversed this holding. Peaceful labor picketing is protected under federal labor law, however.

The Court has established that government has limited power to prevent public property from being used for public speech and assembly. It has made an exception, however, of property, such as a jailyard, that is dedicated to specific uses making it an inappropriate public forum.

Because it bars only government action abridging speech, the First Amendment generally does not affect speech that occurs on private property. Here, too, there are exceptions. The First Amendment does apply to privately owned company towns that provide all services to its residents that a municipally owned town would. But the owners of private property dedicated to specific public purposes—a shopping mall, for example—may restrict speech on their property that is not directly related to its public use.

Seditious Speech and National Security

Just seven years after ratification of the First Amendment, the Federalist-dominated Congress passed the Sedition Act of 1798. This act set stiff penalties for false, scandalous, or malicious writings about the president, either chamber of Congress, or the government, if published with intent to defame any of them, excite hatred against them, stir up sedition, or aid foreign countries hostile to the United States.

The Republicans charged that it abridged the freedoms of speech and press, but no challenge got to the Supreme Court before the act expired. Although only twenty-five people were arrested and ten convicted under the act, it was extremely unpopular and is credited with bringing about the demise of the Federalist Party. Upon taking office in 1801, Republican Thomas Jefferson pardoned all those convicted under it, and several years later Congress refunded their fines with interest.

Although martial law imposed in some areas during the Civil War substantially curtailed freedoms of speech and press, the constitutionality of these actions was never presented to the Court, and it was not until after the United States entered World War I in 1917 that Congress again passed legislation restricting free speech and free press.

ESPIONAGE AND SEDITION

The Espionage Act of 1917 made it a crime to make false statements with the intent to interfere with the operation of the armed forces or to cause insubordination, disloyalty, or mutiny in the armed forces or to obstruct recruiting and enlistment efforts.

The Sedition Act of 1918, passed the year World War I ended, made it a crime to say or do anything to obstruct the sale of government war bonds; or to utter, print, write, or publish anything intended to cause contempt and scorn for the government of the United States, the Constitution, the flag, or the uniform of the armed forces; or to say or write anything urging interference with defense production. The act also made it a crime to advocate, teach, defend, or suggest engaging in any of that conduct proscribed by the law.

Challenges to these two laws reached the Supreme Court in 1919 and 1920. They presented the Court with its first opportunity to define the protection afforded by the First Amendment. Was the right of free speech absolute, or could its exercise be restrained? If the latter, under what circumstances and to what extent?

The Court's answer to the first question was that the right was not absolute. Under certain circumstances Congress could forbid and punish speech it considered seditious. In those early cases, the Court never seriously examined the federal acts themselves, as it later would scrutinize state laws curbing free speech. Instead, the Court deferred to the congressional judgment that the speech and conduct prohibited by the laws would be detrimental to the success of the war effort.

The Court did not speak as easily or as firmly to the question of acceptable limits on free speech. Although the first postwar

The Sedition Act, which made it a crime to criticize the U.S. government or its leaders, became law in 1798 and was repealed in 1801. Of the twenty-five people arrested under the act, one was Rep. Matthew Lyon of Vermont, shown in this contemporary cartoon attacking a fellow member of Congress.

decisions were unanimous, the Court quickly divided on this point. A substantial majority took the view that speech and publications that tended to bring about evils that Congress wished to prevent could be punished. The proofs required to show that speakers or publishers intended their remarks to have evil effects were not particularly strict. In balancing preservation of First Amendment rights against preservation of existing government policies, the Court found the latter interest to have greater weight.

Justices Oliver Wendell Holmes Jr. and Louis D. Brandeis were an eloquent minority. They held that, to be restricted, speech or publication must raise an immediate danger that its intended effect would damage the war effort. They would require that intent to achieve this effect be proved more by evidence than inference.

The Schenck Case

The first of six major seditious speech cases was *Schenck v. United States* (1919). The secretary of the Socialist Party, Charles Schenck, and others were convicted of conspiring to cause insubordination in the armed forces and to obstruct recruiting and enlistment. Schenck printed and distributed fifteen thousand leaflets opposing the recently passed Selective Service law; many were mailed to draftees.

Justice Holmes, who wrote the unanimous opinion affirming Schenck's conviction, described the leaflet's message: "In impassioned language it intimated that conscription was despotism in its worst form and a monstrous wrong against humanity in the interest of Wall Street's chosen few." The leaflet urged its readers to oppose the draft.

Again in Holmes's words, the pamphlet

described the arguments on the other side [in favor of the draft] as coming from cunning politicians and a mercenary capitalist press, and even silent consent to the conscription law as helping to support an infamous conspiracy. It denied the power to send our citizens away to foreign shores to shoot up the people of other lands, and added that words could not express the condemnation such cold-blooded ruthlessness deserves . . . winding up, "You must do your share to maintain, support and uphold the rights of the people of this country."[3]

At his trial Schenck did not deny that the intended effect of this circular was to persuade people to resist conscription. But he argued that such expression was protected by the First Amendment.

The Court, however, rejected this contention. "We admit that in many places and in ordinary times the defendants in saying all that was said in the circular would have been within their constitutional rights," Holmes wrote. "But the character of every act depends upon the circumstances in which it is done."[4]

Holmes then framed what became known as the "clear and present danger" doctrine. If words raised a clear and present danger of bringing about the evils that Congress had the constitutional authority to prevent, the First Amendment protections of free speech and press must give way and the words could be punished. *(See "Clear and Present Danger," pp. 413–414.)*

In Holmes's view, Schenck's words, printed during wartime and with the admitted intent to persuade men to refuse induction, presented such a clear and present danger. "When a nation is at war," he wrote, "many things that might be said in time of peace are such a hindrance to its effort that their utterance will not be endured so long as men fight and that no Court could regard them as protected by any constitutional right."[5]

It made no difference that Schenck and his compatriots had not succeeded in obstructing recruitment. "The statute . . . punishes conspiracies to obstruct as well as actual obstruction," Holmes concluded. "If the act (speaking or circulating a paper), its tendency and the intent with which it is done are the same, we perceive no ground for saying that success alone warrants making the act a crime."[6]

The Frohwerk Case

The next two cases, decided on the same day a week after the *Schenck* decision, also unanimously affirmed convictions under the espionage and sedition laws. But in both cases, the evidence showing intent to create a clear and present danger was less convincing than in *Schenck*.

In *Frohwerk v. United States* (1919), Justice Holmes indicated that the defendant might well have been acquitted had more evidence been presented. Frohwerk had placed in a German-language newspaper twelve articles that the government considered attempts to cause disloyalty and insubordination among the armed forces.

Writing the opinion, Holmes said there was little in the language of the articles to distinguish them from the language Schenck used in his leaflets. But from the trial record, the Court was unable to determine whether the circumstances surrounding the publishing and distribution of the articles were such that no clear and present danger was raised:

It may be that all this might be said or written even in time of war in circumstances that would not make it a crime. We do not lose our right to condemn either measures or men because the Country is at war. It does not appear that there was any special effort to reach men who were subject to the draft. . . . But we must take the case on the record as it is, and on that record it is impossible to say that it might not have been found that the circulation of the paper was in quarters where a little breath would be enough to kindle a flame and that the fact was known and relied upon by those who sent the paper out.[7]

The Debs Case

In the second case decided that day in 1919, the Court upheld the conviction of Socialist Eugene V. Debs for violating the espionage act by a speech he gave in Canton, Ohio. The government alleged the speech was intended to interfere with recruiting and to incite insubordination in the armed forces.

Debs's speech was primarily about socialism. He discussed its growing popularity and predicted its eventual success. However, he also spoke in support of several people serving sentences for violations of the espionage and sedition acts, saying of one that if she was guilty, then so was he. He made statements such as, "You need to know that you are fit for something better than slavery and cannon fodder" and "You have your lives to lose; you certainly ought to have the right to declare war if you consider a war necessary." On this evidence, a trial jury convicted Debs.

The Supreme Court affirmed the conviction. Based on these statements, wrote Holmes, a jury could reasonably conclude that Debs was opposed "not only [to] war in general but this war, and that the opposition was so expressed that its natural and intended effect would be to obstruct recruiting."[8]

The Court then considered whether Debs actually intended his speech to have this effect and decided that he did. Here Holmes looked at evidence showing that just before speaking, Debs endorsed the view that U.S. involvement in World War I was unjustifiable and should be opposed by all means.[9]

The Abrams Case

Eight months later, in November 1919, the Court issued its first divided decision in a seditious speech case. *Abrams v. Unit-*

In *Abrams v. United States* (1919) the Court upheld the conviction on espionage charges of Russian emigrés Samuel Lipman, Hyman Lychowsky, Mollie Steimer, and Jacob Abrams. They had thrown leaflets from the windows and roofs of New York City buildings calling for weapons workers to strike.

TREASON

Article III, Section 3, of the Constitution specifically defines treason against the United States as consisting "only in levying War against them, or in adhering to their Enemies, giving them Aid and Comfort. No Person shall be convicted of Treason unless on the Testimony of two Witnesses to the same overt Act, or on Confession in open Court."

The Supreme Court has reviewed only three charges of treason, all arising from World War II incidents. Two of these decisions left interpretation of part of the law in some doubt; the third added little to the discussion.

The case of *Cramer v. United States* (1945) concerned a German-born laborer, Anthony Cramer, who became a U.S. citizen in 1936. Six years later Cramer befriended two German saboteurs who had landed in the United States to sabotage the American war effort. He met twice with them in public places and held some money in safekeeping for one of them.

Cramer was charged with giving aid and comfort to the enemy, but the Supreme Court held, 5–4, that Cramer's traitorous intent had not been proved and that eating and drinking with the enemy did not establish guilt.[1]

The 1947 case of *Haupt v. United States* grew out of the same incident. Hans Max Haupt was the father of one of the saboteurs and was convicted of giving aid and comfort to the enemy after he sheltered his son, helped him try to find employment, and bought him an automobile. Sustaining the conviction, 8–1, the Court held that sheltering the enemy was an overt act that gave aid and comfort and there was no further need to prove that Haupt had traitorous intent when he took in his son.[2]

In the third case, *Kawakita v. United States* (1952), the Court held that charges of treason could be brought against an American citizen who had committed a treasonous act against the United States in a foreign country.[3]

1. *Cramer v. United States,* 325 U.S. 1 (1945).
2. *Haupt v. United States,* 330 U.S. 631 (1947).
3. *Kawakita v. United States,* 343 U.S. 717 (1952).

---

ed States concerned the convictions of five Russian-born immigrants for writing, publishing, and distributing in New York City two allegedly seditious pamphlets criticizing the U.S. government for sending troops into Russia in 1918.

One of the pamphlets described President Woodrow Wilson as a coward and a hypocrite, implying that the real reason for sending troops to Russia was not to protect supplies for use in the war against Germany but to aid those fighting takeover of Russia by Communist revolutionaries. The pamphlet also described capitalism as the "one enemy of the workers."

The second pamphlet, printed in Yiddish, warned workers in munitions factories that their products would be used to kill Russians as well as Germans. It called for a general strike. The five immigrants distributed some of these pamphlets by tossing them from a window; others were circulated secretly around the city. The five were each sentenced to twenty years imprisonment.

A seven-justice majority upheld the convictions. Justice John H. Clarke, writing for the majority, quickly dismissed the direct free speech issue by citing the *Schenck* and *Frohwerk* cases as precedents. The only question the Court need answer, Clarke said, was whether there was sufficient evidence presented to the jury to sustain its guilty verdict.

Clarke quoted sections of the two pamphlets—the evidence in the case—and from these excerpts concluded:

the plain purpose of their propaganda was to excite, at the supreme crisis of war, disaffection, sedition, riots, and, as they hoped, revolution, in this country for the purpose of embarrassing and if possible defeating the military plans of the [U.S.] Government in Europe. . . . Thus it is clear not only that some evidence but that much persuasive evidence was before the jury tending to prove that the defendants were guilty as charged.[10]

This reasoning strayed too far from the clear and present danger test to win the concurrence of Holmes and Brandeis. Holmes agreed with the majority that the five defendants had advocated a general strike and curtailment of war materials production, but he questioned whether their intent to hinder the war effort had been proved.

Holmes further contended that the espionage and sedition acts required conviction of a speaker only if it was proved that he intended his speech to have the criminal effect proscribed by the law and that the speech must produce or be intended to produce a "clear and imminent danger that it will bring about forthwith certain substantive evils that the United States constitutionally may seek to prevent."

Continuing, he wrote:

But as against dangers peculiar to war . . . the principle of the right to free speech is always the same. It is only the present danger of immediate evil or an intent to bring it about that warrants Congress in setting a limit to the expression of opinion where private rights are not concerned. Congress certainly cannot forbid all effort to change the mind of the country. Now nobody can suppose that the surreptitious publishing of a silly leaflet by an unknown man, without more, would present any immediate danger that its opinions would hinder the success of the government arms or have any appreciable tendency to do so.[11]

Only the Yiddish pamphlet criticizing the U.S. intervention in Russia could afford "even a foundation" for the government's charge, Holmes said.

The Schaefer Case

In the next case the Court majority moved even farther away from Holmes's clear and present danger test. *Schaefer v. United States* (1920) arose after five officers of a German-language newspaper in Philadelphia were convicted of publishing false news items with the intent to promote Germany's success in the war and hamper recruiting efforts.

The articles, generally unfavorable to the U.S. war effort, were reprinted from other publications, but the paper's officers had either added to or omitted parts of the original text. One article was found objectionable by the trial court solely because one word had been mistranslated so that "bread lines" read "bread riots."

Six of the justices voted to reverse the convictions of two of the men but sustained the convictions of the other three. Speaking through Justice Joseph McKenna, the majority said it had no doubt that the statements were deliberately falsified, "the purpose being to represent that the war was not demanded by the people but was the result of the machinations of executive power."[12]

Nor, said the majority, was it unreasonable for a jury to conclude that the additions and omissions were made with the intent that the reprinted articles would have the effect alleged. To readers, McKenna wrote, the articles' "derisive contempt may have been truly descriptive of American feebleness and inability to combat Germany's prowess, and thereby [may have served] to chill and check the ardency of patriotism."[13]

Furthermore, the majority held that there was no need to show that the articles presented an immediate danger but only that they tended to have a bad effect. Were the articles, McKenna asked,

the mere expression of peevish discontent, aimless, vapid and innocuous? We cannot so conclude. We must take them at their word, as the jury did, and ascribe to them a more active and sinister purpose. They were the publications of a newspaper, deliberately prepared, systematic, always of the same trend, more specific in some instances, it may be, than in others. Their effect or the persons affected could not be shown, nor was it necessary. The tendency of the articles and their efficacy were enough for offense . . . and to have required more would have made the law useless. It was passed in precaution. The incidence of its violation might not be immediately seen, evil appearing only in disaster, the result of disloyalty engendered and the spirit of mutiny.[14]

Holmes and Brandeis would have acquitted all five defendants on the ground that the articles did not raise a clear and present danger to the government's war efforts. Of one of the reprints, Brandeis wrote:

It is not apparent on a reading of this article . . . how it could rationally be held to tend even remotely or indirectly to obstruct recruiting. But . . . the test to be applied . . . is not the remote or possible effect. There must be the clear and present danger. Certainly men judging in calmness and with this test presented to them could not reasonably have said that this coarse and heavy humor immediately threatened the success of recruiting.[15]

Brandeis not only chided the majority for failing to apply the test in its review of the case but criticized the lower courts for failing to offer the test to the jury as the standard to be used. Instead, the jury had been instructed to convict if they found that any of the articles would diminish "our will to win" the war.

Brandeis concluded with a strong warning against restricting free speech too readily:

To hold that such harmless additions to or omissions from news items and such impotent expressions of editorial opinion, as were shown here, can afford the basis even of a prosecution will doubtless discourage criticism of the policies of the Government. To hold that such publications can be suppressed as false reports, subjects to new perils the constitutional liberty of the press

. . . Nor will this grave danger end with the passing of the war. The constitutional right of free speech has been declared to be the same in peace and in war. In peace, too, men may differ widely as to what loyalty to our country demands; and an intolerant majority, swayed by passion or by fear, may be prone in the future, as it has often been in the past, to stamp as disloyal opinions with which it disagrees. Convictions such as these, besides abridging freedom of speech, threaten freedom of thought and of belief.[16]

Justice Clarke also dissented, but not on free speech grounds.

The Pierce Case

The final major case in this series centered on a pamphlet entitled "The Price We Pay," written by an eminent Episcopal clergyman and published by the Socialist Party.

A federal district judge in Baltimore acquitted several persons accused of violating the espionage act by distributing the

The right of an individual to associate with others who share similar beliefs and aspirations is not explicitly granted by the Constitution or the Bill of Rights. But the Supreme Court has found this right to be implicit within the First Amendment freedoms of speech and assembly and in the concept of liberty protected by the Fourteenth Amendment.

Judicial recognition of this right is of recent vintage. In 1927 a majority of the justices upheld the conviction of a woman for violating California's criminal syndicalism law by associating with people in an organization that advocated overthrow of the government by unlawful means.[1]

In 1928 the Court upheld conviction of a Ku Klux Klan officer who disobeyed a New York statute that required certain organizations to file membership lists with the state. The Court held the statute a proper exercise of the state's police power.[2]

A distaste for implying guilt by association underlay the Court's decision in *DeJonge v. Oregon* (1937), reversing Dirk DeJonge's conviction for conducting a public meeting under the auspices of the Communist Party.

The Court distinguished between the party's illegal intent to overthrow the U.S. government and the protected right of a party member to speak and assemble for lawful purposes.[3] *(See details of the case, pp. 425–426.)*

This right was sorely tested during the cold war years, when Americans saw their national security threatened by communist subversion.

Laws intended to protect the nation against communist subversion were repeatedly challenged with the claim that political associations were constitutionally protected. Although this contention won a few adherents on the Court, the justices did not base any of their rulings on a right of association during this period. *(See further discussion, pp. 534–552.)*

THE NAACP CASES

The civil rights movement late in the 1950s won judicial recognition of a constitutionally protected right of association.

The issue was membership in the National Association for the Advancement of Colored People (NAACP). Several southern states, incensed by the association's influential role in the civil rights movement, tried to prevent the NAACP from continuing its activities within their borders.

The NAACP challenged these measures. Not only did the Supreme Court strike them down, but in so doing it found in the First and Fourteenth Amendments an implicit right of association that stood on an equal plane with the explicitly guaranteed freedoms of speech, press, assembly, and religion.

Disclosure of Membership. The first case arose in Alabama. Like many other states, Alabama required all out-of-state corpora-

tions to register with the state before doing business there. Although local branches of the NAACP had operated in Alabama since 1915, it had never registered, nor had the state indicated it should do so.

In 1956 the state attorney general, charging the NAACP with failure to register, won a temporary restraining order prohibiting the organization from working in the state. The attorney general also requested, and the state court ordered, that the NAACP turn over certain records, including lists of all its Alabama members.

The NAACP eventually produced all the records requested except the membership lists. The state court held the organization in contempt, fining it $100,000.

The Supreme Court unanimously reversed the contempt conviction with its decision in the case of *NAACP v. Alabama ex rel. Patterson* (1958). Justice John Marshall Harlan wrote the Court opinion:

Effective advocacy of both public and private points of view, particularly controversial ones, is undeniably enhanced by group association, as this Court has more than once recognized by remarking upon the close nexus between the freedoms of speech and assembly. . . . It is beyond debate that freedom to engage in association for the advancement of beliefs and ideas is an inseparable aspect of the "liberty" assured by the Due Process Clause of the Fourteenth Amendment.[4]

Furthermore, Justice Harlan said, the right of association also entails the right to privacy in that association. "It is hardly a novel perception that compelled disclosure of affiliation with groups engaged in advocacy may constitute [an] effective . . . restraint on freedom of association."[5]

Turning to the NAACP case, he observed that the association had offered unrebutted evidence that previous public disclosures of its membership had resulted in economic reprisal, loss of employment, and physical violence to members. The Court held that Alabama had not presented a sufficient reason to justify an infringement of this protected right.

The reversal of the contempt citation was not the end of this particular story, however. The Court sent the case back to the state court for a decision on whether the NAACP had violated Alabama law by failing to register. The state court forbade the NAACP to operate in Alabama.[6] The Supreme Court reversed the decision in 1964.[7]

TEACHERS' ASSOCIATIONS

In 1960 the Court struck down an even more subtle attempt to discourage membership in the NAACP.

Arkansas law required teachers in state-supported schools to file affidavits listing all the organizations they had belonged to or contributed to within the past five years. It was widely understood that this law was aimed at exposing teachers who belonged to the NAACP.

The case of *Shelton v. Tucker* (1960) came to the Court after teachers whose contracts were not renewed because they refused to comply with the statute charged that the law violated their rights to personal, academic, and associational liberties.

For the majority Justice Potter Stewart wrote there was no question that a state might, in an appropriate investigation of the fitness and competence of its teachers, consider their associational ties. However, the law's "comprehensive interference with associational freedom goes far beyond what might be justified in the exercise of the State's legitimate inquiry into the fitness and competency of its teachers," he wrote.[8] The law was struck down.

LITIGATION AND SOLICITATION

Using a different method, Virginia in 1956 amended its regulations governing ethical conduct of attorneys. The newly amended rules forbade solicitation of clients by an agent of an organization that litigates a case in which it is not a party and has no pecuniary interest.

Litigation aid, including advising persons that they might have a claim, was one of the primary methods the NAACP used in its work for racial equality. The organization sued to stop enforcement of Virginia's new rule, arguing that it infringed its right to associate to help persons seek redress for violations of their rights.

The Supreme Court held 6–3 in *NAACP v. Button* (1963) that Virginia's statute impermissibly infringed on the right of association. That opinion, written by Justice William J. Brennan Jr., extended the concept of expression to a point not previously reached by the Court.[9]

Brennan wrote:

[A]bstract discussion is not the only species of communication which the Constitution protects: the First Amendment also protects vigorous advocacy, certainly of lawful ends, against government intrusion. . . . In the context of NAACP objectives, litigation is not a technique of resolving private differences; it is a means for achieving the lawful objective of equality of treatment by all government . . . for the members of the Negro community in this country. It is thus a form of political expression. . . . And under the conditions of modern government, litigation may well be the sole practicable avenue open to a minority to petition for redress of grievances.

We need not, in order to find constitutional protection for the kind of cooperative, organizational activity disclosed by this record, whereby Negroes seek through lawful means to achieve legitimate political ends, subsume such activity under a narrow, literal conception of freedom of speech, petition or assembly. For there is no longer any doubt that the First and Fourteenth Amendments protect certain forms of orderly group activity.[10]

The majority held Virginia's statute impermissibly vague, risking the "gravest danger of smothering all discussion looking to the eventual institution of litigation" on behalf of minority group members. Furthermore, the Court held, the state had not shown a sufficiently compelling reason for restricting this right to associate.[11]

Fifteen years later the Court reaffirmed *Button*, declaring that "collective activity undertaken to obtain meaningful access to the courts is a fundamental right within the protection of the First Amendment."[12]

The final NAACP case in this series arose after a committee established by the Florida legislature to investigate communist activity in the state obtained information that some former or present Communist Party members might be members of the Florida NAACP.

The committee called as a witness the president of the Miami branch of the NAACP and asked him to verify this information. He refused and was convicted of contempt. The Court overturned his contempt conviction by a 5–4 vote in *Gibson v. Florida Legislative Investigating Committee* (1963).[13]

ASSOCIATIONAL RIGHTS: AN EVOLVING VIEW

In the 1980s the Court began to define more carefully the scope of the First Amendment's protection for various relationships. This definition came as the Court rebuffed efforts by large "clubs"—the U.S. Jaycees and the Rotary Club International—to invoke the freedom of association to shield their all-male clubs from pressure to admit women.[14] Both decisions were unanimously against the club's argument.

In these decisions the Court distinguished between a freedom of intimate association—the right to enter into and carry on private relationships—and a freedom of expressive association—the right to associate with others of a like mind in order to further a particular goal.

The first aspect of freedom was involved in neither club case; to the extent the second was infringed in either, the Court held, it was outweighed by society's interest in equal treatment of women and men.

1. *Whitney v. California*, 274 U.S. 357 (1927).
2. *Bryant v. Zimmerman*, 278 U.S. 63 (1928).
3. *DeJonge v. Oregon*, 299 U.S. 353 (1937).
4. *NAACP v. Alabama ex rel. Patterson*, 357 U.S. 449 at 460–461 (1958).
5. Id. at 461.
6. *NAACP v. Alabama ex rel. Patterson*, 360 U.S. 240 (1959); *NAACP v. Gallion*, 368 U.S. 16 (1961).
7. *NAACP v. Alabama ex rel. Flowers*, 377 U.S. 288 (1964); see also *Louisiana ex rel. Gremillion v. NAACP*, 366 U.S. 293 (1961); *Bates v. City of Little Rock*, 361 U.S. 516 (1960).
8. *Shelton v. Tucker*, 464 U.S. 479 at 490 (1960).
9. Thomas I. Emerson, *The System of Freedom of Expression* (New York: Random House, Vintage Books, 1970), 429.
10. *NAACP v. Button*, 371 U.S. 415 at 429–430 (1963).
11. Id. at 434.
12. *In re Primus*, 436 U.S. 412 at 426 (1978), quoting *United Transportation Union v. Michigan Bar*, 401 U.S. 576 at 585 (1971).
13. *Gibson v. Florida Legislative Investigating Committee*, 372 U.S. 539 (1963).
14. *Roberts v. U.S. Jaycees*, 468 U.S. 609 (1984); *Board of Directors of Rotary International v. Rotary Club of Duarte*, 481 U.S. 537 (1987); see also *New York State Club Assn. v. City of New York*, 487 U.S. 1 (1988).

pamphlet in that city. The judge found that the booklet was an attempt to recruit persons to the Socialist Party and its philosophy and not an attempt to persuade them to interfere with the war effort.

However, an Albany, New York, judge and jury found the latter to be true. Consequently, several persons who distributed the pamphlet in Albany were convicted of conspiring to attempt to cause insubordination in the armed forces. They appealed to the Supreme Court on the ground that the government failed to show intent to cause insubordination or to prove that distribution of the pamphlet created a clear and present danger that insubordination would result.

Seven justices upheld the convictions in *Pierce v. United States* (1920). A jury could conclude that several of the statements were false, the majority reasoned, and that the distributors knew them to be false or distributed them without any regard for whether the statements were false or not. Among those statements the Court majority thought a jury might consider false were the following:

"Into your homes the recruiting officers are coming. They will take your sons of military age and impress them into the army. . . . And still the recruiting officers will come; seizing age after age, mounting up to the elder ones and taking the younger ones as they grow to soldier size."

"The Attorney General of the United States is so busy sending to prison men who do not stand up when the Star Spangled Banner is played, that he has no time to protect the food supply from gamblers."

"Our entry into [the war] was determined by the certainty that if the allies do not win, J. P. Morgan's loans to the allies will be repudiated, and those American investors who bit on his promises would be hooked."

A jury would also be warranted in concluding that such statements, when circulated, would have a tendency to cause insubordination and that that was the intent of the distributors. Even if a jury was not agreed on the probable effect of the pamphlet, said Justice Mahlon Pitney,

at least the jury fairly might believe that, under the circumstances existing, it would have a tendency to cause insubordination, disloyalty and refusal of duty in the military and naval forces. . . . Evidently it was intended, as the jury found, to interfere with the conscription and recruitment services; to cause men eligible for the service to evade the draft; to bring home to them, and especially to their parents, sisters, wives, and sweethearts, a sense of impending personal loss, calculated to discourage the young men from entering the service.[17]

Holmes and Brandeis dissented in an opinion written by Brandeis. They disagreed that the statements cited by the majority were false. The first, regarding recruiting, was eventually proved true. The second, concerning the attorney general, was false if taken literally but was clearly meant to suggest that the attorney general could spend his time in better ways than prosecuting people for allegedly seditious statements. The third, regarding the reason for U.S. entry into the war, was an expression of opinion rather than fact. To buttress this last statement, Brandeis noted that some members of Congress found the loans instrumental in the government's decision to enter the war. Brandeis then said:

To hold that a jury may make punishable statements of conclusions or of opinion, like those here involved, by declaring them to be statements of facts and to be false would practically deny members of small political parties freedom of criticism and of discussion in times when feelings run high and the questions involved are deemed fundamental.[18]

Furthermore, Brandeis continued, even if the statements were false, the government offered no proof showing that the men who distributed the pamphlet knew they were false. Nor was there any proof that the pamphlet intended to dampen military morale. The defendants did not even distribute the pamphlet to military men, Brandeis observed. And finally, he said, there was no indication that distribution of "The Price We Pay" raised a clear and present danger of causing insubordination.

Brandeis again concluded his dissent with a warning that the Court majority had placed the guarantee of free speech in a precarious position:

The fundamental right of free men to strive for better conditions through new legislation and new institutions will not be preserved, if efforts to secure it by argument to fellow citizens may be construed as criminal incitement to disobey the existing law—merely, because the argument presented seems to those exercising judicial power to be unfair in its portrayal of existing evils, mistaken in its assumptions, unsound in reasoning or intemperate in language.[19]

The Hartzel Case

Distance in time from actual combat brought calmer voices to the debate on seditious speech. The 1918 sedition law was repealed in 1921, and many of those convicted of violating it, including Debs, were ultimately pardoned or had their sentences reduced.

The Espionage Act was still in force when the United States entered World War II in 1941. The Supreme Court reviewed only one conviction under it. The case concerned a man who printed and sent out several articles urging in hostile and intemperate language that the white race stop fighting each other and band together to war against the yellow races.

The question in *Hartzel v. United States* (1944) was not whether what Hartzel said fell within the reach of the federal law, but whether there was enough evidence to sustain his conviction, the same question prominent in the World War I cases of *Pierce, Schaefer,* and *Abrams.* A five-justice majority concluded that the government had not proved beyond a reasonable doubt that Hartzel had intended his statements to incite insubordination in the armed forces.[20]

STATE SEDITION LAWS

From time to time in U.S. history, states have perceived their internal security to be threatened by radical political forces and, like the federal government, they have sought to minimize those threats by restricting the exercise of free speech, free press, and free assembly.

The first round of such state laws was enacted after President William McKinley was assassinated in 1901 by a professed anarchist. The model for these criminal anarchy laws—and for the federal Smith Act of 1940—was New York's 1902 law that defined criminal anarchy as "the doctrine that organized government should be overthrown by force or violence, or by assassination of the executive head or any of the executive officials of government, or by any unlawful means." The law made it a felony for anyone to advocate criminal anarchy by speech or by printing and distributing any material advocating or teaching it.

Following the communist revolution of 1917 and World War I, which ended the next year, thirty-three states enacted peacetime sedition or criminal syndicalism statutes. Similar to but broader than the criminal anarchy laws, these statutes made it unlawful to advocate, teach, or aid the commission of a crime, sabotage, or other unlawful act of violence in order to bring about political change or a change in industrial ownership. These laws also made it unlawful to organize or knowingly become a member of an organization that advocated criminal syndicalism.

The Supreme Court initially sustained the constitutionality and application of these laws, but by the late 1930s it began to reverse convictions in lower courts, holding either that the law was too vague or broad or that it had been applied to persons whose advocacy of overthrow of the government presented no immediate threat.

During the cold war years, states focused exclusively on preventing communist infiltration of government. Many required public employees to swear that they did not advocate forceful overthrow of the government. Persons refusing to take such oaths were liable to dismissal; those who lied were subject to prosecution for perjury.

At first the Court sustained convictions under these laws, but as the threat of infiltration receded, the Court began to find several of the loyalty oath statutes unconstitutionally vague. In some instances, the Court found their application violated due process requirements. *(See "Federal Loyalty Programs," pp. 544–546, in Chapter 10.)*

By the late 1960s the fear that communists would destroy the established order was replaced by concern that the public peace was in jeopardy from civil rights activists, antiwar protesters, and members of the so-called New Left. Once again, several states turned to their criminal anarchy and syndicalism laws to restrain the disturbing speech that came from dissident elements of the society. In its first review of this latest application of a criminal syndicalism law, however, the Court cast doubt on the validity of all such laws. The First Amendment protected the advocacy of forceful overthrow of the government, the Court said, unless that advocacy actually incited someone to undertake such action.

The Gitlow Case

The first of these state sedition laws to be tested in the Supreme Court was New York's criminal anarchy law.

Benjamin Gitlow, a member of the left wing of the Socialist Party, was convicted under the law for printing and distributing

Benjamin Gitlow and William Z. Foster, Communist Workers' Party candidates for president and vice president in 1928, at Madison Square Garden. Three years earlier the Supreme Court had upheld Gitlow's conviction for publishing an article calling for workers to overthrow capitalism and the government by force.

some sixteen thousand copies of the "Left Wing Manifesto." This tract repudiated the moderate stance of the main body of the Socialist Party and called for the overthrow of the democratic state by *"class action* of the proletariat *in any form* having as its objective the conquest of the power of the state." It also urged the proletariat to "organize its own state *for the coercion and suppression of the bourgeoisie.*"

Gitlow appealed his conviction to the Supreme Court on the ground that the statute unconstitutionally restricted his rights of free speech and free press by condemning certain classes of speech without considering whether they presented a clear and present danger of bringing about the evil that the state had the right to prevent.

Gitlow won one of his arguments. The First Amendment explicitly prohibited only Congress, and not the states, from restricting free speech. Gitlow argued, however, that the First Amendment rights of free speech and free press were implicit in the concept of liberty guaranteed by the Fourteenth Amendment. The Court agreed, almost casually, with this contention. (*See mention of this case, p. 410.*)

But a majority of the Court nonetheless sustained the conviction in *Gitlow v. New York* (1925). The majority opinion, written by Justice Edward T. Sanford, first held that Gitlow's manifesto fell within the speech proscribed by the law. It was neither abstract doctrine nor the "mere prediction that industrial disturbances and revolutionary mass strikes will result spontaneously in an inevitable process of evolution in the economic system."[21] Instead, the manifesto urged mass strikes for the purpose of fomenting industrial disturbance and revolutionary action to overthrow the organized government.

The Court next held that the state was within its police power when it punished "those who abuse this freedom [of expression] by utterances inimical to the public welfare, tending to corrupt public morals, incite to crime, or disturb the public peace."[22]

The state need not show that such utterances created a clear and present danger of inciting overthrow of the government but only that they tended to have that effect. Sanford explained:

That utterances inciting to the overthrow of organized government by unlawful means present a sufficient danger of substantive evil to bring their punishment within the range of legislative discretion is clear. Such utterances, by their very nature, involve danger to the public peace and to the security of the State. They threaten breaches of the peace and ultimate revolution. And the immediate danger is none the less real and substantial, because the effect of a given utterance cannot be accurately foreseen. The State cannot reasonably be required to measure the danger from every such utterance in the nice balance of a jeweler's scale. A single revolutionary spark may kindle a fire that, smouldering for a time, may burst into a sweeping and destructive conflagration. It cannot be said that the state is acting arbitrarily or unreasonably when in the exercise of its judgment as to the measures necessary to protect the public peace and safety, it seeks to extinguish the spark without waiting until it has enkindled the flame or blazed into the conflagration. It cannot reasonably be required to defer the adoption of measures for its own peace and safety until the revolutionary utterances lead to actual disturbances of the public peace or imminent and immediate danger of its own destruction; but it may, in the exercise of its judgment, suppress the threatened danger in its incipiency.[23]

Having upheld the authority of the state to determine that a certain class of speech presented a danger, the majority then refused to consider whether the First Amendment protected specific utterances falling within that class.

The majority's reasoning was different from the Court's traditional approach to convictions under federal sedition laws, which condemned certain kinds of actions. Under those laws, speech was unprotected only if the government could prove that the circumstances in which it was uttered made it the equivalent of the proscribed action.

Justices Holmes and Brandeis dissented, arguing that the clear and present danger test should be applied to state, as well as to federal, statutes restricting the right of free speech. In Gitlow's case, wrote Holmes,

there was no present danger of an attempt to overthrow the government by force on the part of the admittedly small minority who shared [Gitlow's] views. It is said that this manifesto was more than a theory, that it was an incitement. Every idea is an incitement. It offers itself for belief and if believed it is acted on unless some other belief outweighs it or some failure of energy stifles the movement at its birth. The only difference between the expression of an opinion and an incitement in the narrower sense is the speaker's enthusiasm for the result. Eloquence may set fire to reason. But whatever may be thought of the redundant discourse before us it had no chance of starting a present conflagration. If in the long run the beliefs expressed in proletarian dictatorship are destined to be accepted by the dominant forces of the community, the only meaning of free speech is that they should be given their chance and have their way.[24]

The Whitney Case

California's criminal syndicalism statute was the next state sedition law tested in the Supreme Court. Anita Whitney, a niece of former Supreme Court justice Stephen J. Field, participated in a convention establishing the California branch of the new Communist Labor Party.

At the convention, Whitney advocated adoption of a resolution dedicating the party to seek political change through the ballot, but this proposition was rejected in favor of a resolution urging revolutionary class struggle as the means to overthrow capitalism. Despite her defeat, Whitney continued to participate in the convention and the party. Whitney testified that she had no intention of helping to create an unlawful organization, but she was convicted of violating the California law prohibiting organization and participation in groups advocating criminal syndicalism.

The Supreme Court unanimously sustained her conviction. After holding that the state law was not unconstitutionally vague, Justice Sanford said the majority saw little to distinguish Whitney's actions from Gitlow's manifesto. In fact, Whitney's actions in assembling with others to form a group advocating forceful overthrow of the government posed an even greater danger to the state. Sanford wrote:

The essence of the offense denounced by the Act is the combining with others in an association for the accomplishment of the desired ends through the advocacy and use of criminal and unlawful methods. It partakes of the nature of a criminal conspiracy. . . . That such united and joint action involves even greater danger to the public peace and security than the isolated utterances and acts of individuals is clear. We cannot hold that, as here applied, the Act is an unreasonable or arbitrary exercise of the police power of the State, unwarrantedly infringing any right of free speech, assembly or association, or that those persons are protected from punishment by the due process clause who abuse such rights by joining and furthering an organization thus menacing the peace and welfare of the state.[25]

Although Justices Holmes and Brandeis concurred with the majority, their separate opinion written by Brandeis sounded more like a dissent. Under the California statute, Brandeis wrote,

[t]he mere act of assisting in forming a society for teaching syndicalism, of becoming a member of it, or of assembly with others for that purpose is given the dynamic quality of crime. There is guilt although the society may not contemplate immediate promulgation of the doctrine. Thus the accused is to be punished, not for contempt, incitement or conspiracy, but for a step in preparation, which, if it threatens the public order at all, does so only remotely. The novelty in the prohibition introduced is that the statute aims, not at the practice of criminal syndicalism, nor even directly at the preaching of it, but at association with those who propose to preach it.[26]

Brandeis did not deny that the freedom of assembly, like the freedoms of speech and press, could be restricted by the state, but he again insisted that the restriction be permitted only if the assembly presented a clear and present danger of resulting in the intended evil. The danger must be imminent and serious, he wrote; fear of danger is not enough to restrict the First Amendment freedoms:

To justify suppression of free speech there must be reasonable ground to fear that serious evil will result if free speech is practiced. There must be reasonable ground to believe that the danger apprehended is imminent. There must be reasonable ground to believe that the evil to be prevented is a serious one. Every denunciation of existing law tends in some measure to increase the probability that there will be violation of it. Condonation of a breach enhances the probability. Expressions of approval add to the probability. Propagation of the criminal state of mind by teaching syndicalism increases it. Advocacy of law-breaking heightens it still further. But even advocacy of violation, however reprehensible morally, is not a justification for denying free speech where the advocacy falls short of incitement and there is nothing to indicate that the advocacy would be immediately acted on. The wide difference between advocacy and incitement, between preparation and attempt, between assembling and conspiracy, must be borne in mind. In order to support a finding of clear and present danger it must be shown either that immediate serious violence was to be expected or was advocated, or that the past conduct furnished reason to believe that such advocacy was then contemplated. . . .

. . . The fact that speech is likely to result in some violence or in destruction of property is not enough to justify its suppression. There

must be the probability of serious injury to the State. Among free men, the deterrents ordinarily to be applied to prevent crime are education and punishment for violations of the law, not abridgment of the rights of free speech and assembly.[27]

Although they believed that under these standards the California law improperly restricted Whitney's rights of free speech and assembly, Brandeis and Holmes felt compelled to concur in Whitney's conviction for technical reasons. A few months later California's governor pardoned Whitney, with reasons that echoed Brandeis's opinion.

The Fiske Case

The same day that it decided *Whitney,* the Supreme Court for the first time reversed a conviction for violating a state criminal syndicalism act.

In *Fiske v. Kansas* (1927) the Court for the first time held that the First Amendment guarantee of free speech had been violated by the conviction of Fiske, an organizer for International Workers of the World (IWW). The only evidence introduced at trial to show the unlawful nature of the organization was the IWW preamble, which read in part: "Between these two classes a struggle must go on until the workers of the world organize as a class, take possession of the earth and the machinery of production, and abolish the wage system."

The trial jury apparently assumed that this class struggle would involve the violent overthrow of the government, which would make the IWW and participation in it unlawful under the Kansas statute. But the Supreme Court reversed, seeing no evidence showing that the IWW actually advocated violence or other criminal acts to bring about political and industrial change.[28]

The Fiske decision was a turning point. The Court heard three more major cases testing the constitutionality of state criminal syndicalism laws as applied in particular circumstances. In all three, the Court reversed convictions for violating these laws.

The DeJonge Case

Two of these cases came to the Court in 1937, ten years after *Fiske. DeJonge v. Oregon* arose after DeJonge was convicted for conducting a public meeting under Communist Party auspices. DeJonge maintained he was innocent because he had not advocated or taught any criminal doctrine at the meeting but merely discussed issues of public concern. The state courts, however, interpreted the statute to make criminal any participation in any meeting sponsored by an organization that advocated at any time the forceful overthrow of the established government.

The Court unanimously reversed DeJonge's conviction, holding that the state's interpretation of the statute was unnecessarily restrictive of the rights of free speech and assembly. In one of the Court's first expositions on the right of assembly, Chief Justice Charles Evans Hughes wrote that peaceable assembly for lawful discussion cannot be made a crime. The holding of meetings for peaceable political action cannot be proscribed. Those who assist in the conduct of such meetings cannot be branded as criminals on that score. The question, if the rights of free speech and peaceable assembly are to be preserved, is not as to the auspices under which the meeting is held but as to its purpose; not as to the relations of the speakers, but whether their utterances transcend the bounds of the freedom of speech which the Constitution protects. If the persons assembling have committed crimes elsewhere, if they have formed or are engaged in a conspiracy against the public peace and order, they may be prosecuted for their conspiracy or other violation of valid laws. But it is a different matter when the State, instead of prosecuting them for such offense, seizes upon mere participation in a peaceable assembly and a lawful public discussion as the basis for a criminal charge.[29]

The Herndon Case

In a second case decided in 1937, *Herndon v. Lowry,* a majority of the Court abandoned the "bad tendency" test adopted in *Gitlow* in favor of something more like the clear and present danger standard.

Herndon, a black organizer, was sent to Atlanta to recruit members for the Communist Party. He held three meetings and signed up a few members. He had with him membership blanks, literature on the Communist Party, and a booklet entitled "The Communist Position on the Negro Question." This booklet called for self-determination for blacks living in the southern "black belt." The booklet envisioned a black-dominated government separate from the rest of the United States. To achieve this goal, the tract advocated strikes, boycotts, and a revolutionary power struggle against the white ruling class.

Herndon was arrested and convicted of violating a Georgia law that made it unlawful for anyone to attempt to persuade anyone else to participate in an insurrection against the organized government. Herndon appealed his conviction on the grounds that he had said or done nothing to create any immediate danger of an insurrection.

A five-justice majority agreed, holding the state statute too vague and too broad. The state needed to show more than that Herndon's words and actions might tend to incite others to insurrection at some future time. Justice Owen J. Roberts wrote:

The power of a state to abridge freedom of speech and of assembly is the exception rather than the rule and penalizing even of utterances of a defined character must find its justification in a reasonable apprehension of danger to organized government. The judgment of the legislature is not unfettered. The limitation upon individual liberty must have appropriate relation to the safety of the state.[30]

The majority did not accept the state court's view that Herndon was guilty if he intended an insurrection to occur "at any time within which he might reasonably expect his influence to continue to be directly operative in causing such action by those whom he sought to induce." This view left a jury without any precise standard for measuring guilt, Roberts said, and could conceivably allow a jury to convict a person simply because it disagreed with his opinion:

The statute, as construed and applied, amounts merely to a dragnet which may enmesh anyone who agitates for a change of government if a jury can be persuaded that he ought to have foreseen his words would have some effect in the future conduct of others. No reasonably ascertainable standard of guilt is prescribed. So vague and indeterminate are the boundaries thus set to the freedom of speech and assembly that the law necessarily violates the guarantee of liberty embodied in the Fourteenth amendment.[31]

The four dissenters would have used the bad tendency test to uphold the conviction. They said Herndon's possession of the booklets on black self-determination showed that he intended to distribute them. He had not denied that intention, they noted. They also said it was apparent that by endorsing the self-determination plan, Herndon was advocating insurrection. "Proposing these measures was nothing short of advising a resort to force and violence, for all know that such measures could not be effected otherwise," they wrote.[32]

The Brandenburg Case

State criminal syndicalism laws reemerged in the late 1960s as states sought ways to restrain civil rights and antiwar activists. The Court, however, in a 1969 *per curiam* opinion called into question the continuing validity of most criminal syndicalism laws.

In the case of *Brandenburg v. Ohio,* the Court extended the *Herndon* decision by setting out what has been called the "incitement" test. This standard distinguishes between advocacy of the use of force as an abstract doctrine, which is protected by the First Amendment, and actual incitement to use force, which is not protected.

Clarence Brandenburg, the leader of a Ku Klux Klan group, invited a newsman and photographer to film a Klan rally. Parts of the film were subsequently broadcast both locally and nationally. They showed Brandenburg declaring that "if our President, our Congress, our Supreme Court, continues to suppress the white Caucasian race, it's possible that there might have to be some revengance [*sic*] taken." As a result of the speech shown on the film, Brandenburg was convicted of violating Ohio's criminal syndicalism act.

The Supreme Court reversed the conviction in an unsigned opinion. It observed that the *Brandenburg* case was similar to *Whitney.*

Both had assembled with others in a group that advocated unlawful means to change the political order. Although the Court sustained Whitney's conviction in 1927,

later decisions have fashioned the principle that the constitutional guarantees of free speech and free press do not permit a State to forbid or proscribe advocacy of the use of force or of law violation except where such advocacy is directed to inciting or producing imminent lawless action and is likely to incite or produce such action. . . . Measured by this test, Ohio's Criminal Syndicalism Act cannot be sustained.[33]

The Court also overturned *Whitney.*

The Ku Klux Klan marches in Washington, D.C., 1926. In *Brandenburg v. Ohio* (1969), which concerned the Klan, the Supreme Court held that it is unconstitutional to punish a person who advocates violence as a means of accomplishing political reform.

Public Speech and Public Safety

Speech that threatens the community peace and order is far more prevalent than speech that jeopardizes the national security.

The Supreme Court's role in community peace cases has been much the same as its role in national security cases—to find the balance among the right of an individual to make a public speech, the right of listeners to assemble to hear that speech, and the obligation of the state to maintain public order, safety, and tranquility.

If the incident involves only verbal or symbolic expression, the balance tips in favor of the right to speak. Government may place no restraint on or punish such speech unless it threatens or actually harms public safety, the Court has held.

Because the Court examines the individual circumstances of each case, the point at which speech becomes an incitement or a threat to the welfare of the community varies considerably and the Court has been unable to devise a general standard for determining the point at which First Amendment protection must give way to government restriction.

Government cannot place any prior restraints on speech, but it can legally regulate the time, place, and manner of speech that is likely to interfere with other rightful uses of public property—especially speech that is combined with potentially disruptive conduct such as parading or demonstrating. These regulations must be precisely drawn to restrict speech only as much as is necessary, and they must be applied and enforced in a nondiscriminatory manner.

PERMITS AND PRIOR RESTRAINT

Until the Supreme Court applied the First Amendment to the states, it conceded to municipalities absolute authority to regulate and even to prohibit speech on public property. In 1897 the Court sustained the validity of a Boston ordinance prohibiting public speeches on Boston Common without a permit from the mayor. The Supreme Court endorsed the holding of the Massachusetts Supreme Court, which, in an opinion written by Oliver Wendell Holmes Jr., declared that a legislature

as representative of the public . . . may and does exercise control over the use which the public may make of such places. . . . For the legislature absolutely or constitutionally to forbid public speaking in a highway or public park is no more an infringement of the rights of a member of the public than for the owner of a private house to forbid it in his house.[34]

Some forty years passed before the Court was obliged to rule again on this question. By that time, it had decided that the First Amendment acted as a bar against state infringement of free speech. In line with that view, cases claiming that government was abridging free speech were getting special scrutiny.

The case of *Hague v. C.I.O.* (1939) arose out of Jersey City, New Jersey, mayor Frank Hague's opposition to attempts to organize workers in the city into closed-shop unions. To discourage these organizing efforts, Hague harassed members of the Committee for Industrial Organization (C.I.O.), searching them when they entered the city, arresting them for distributing union literature, and forcibly throwing some of them out of the city. He also refused to grant any member of the union the permit required by city ordinance before a public speech could be made on public property. The C.I.O. brought suit to stop Hague from enforcing this statute.

The Supreme Court granted the injunction against continued enforcement of the ordinance. Writing for two members of the majority, Justice Roberts said that the right to speak and assemble in public was a privilege and immunity of national citizenship that states and cities could not abridge:

Wherever the title of streets and parks may rest, they have immemorially been held in trust for the use of the public and, time out of mind, have been used for purposes of assembly, communicating thoughts between citizens, and discussing public questions. Such use of the streets and public places has, from ancient times, been a part of the privileges, immunities, rights and liberties of citizens. The privilege of a citizen of the United States to use the streets and parks for communication of views on national questions may be regulated in the interest of all; it is not absolute, but relative, and must be exercised in subordination to the general comfort and convenience, and in consonance with peace and good order; but it must not, in the guise of regulation, be abridged or denied.[35]

In a concurring opinion, Justices Harlan Fiske Stone and Stanley F. Reed viewed the rights of free speech and assembly as included not in the privileges and immunities clause of the Fourteenth Amendment but in that amendment's prohibition against state deprivation of personal liberty without due process of law. Under the due process guarantee, these rights were secured to all persons in the United States and not just to citizens. This broader view was eventually accepted by a majority of the Court.

In the *Hague* case, Roberts indicated that states and cities might regulate certain aspects of public speaking. In 1941 the Court elaborated on this, holding that the time, manner, and place of public speeches or other forms of expression could be regulated so long as the regulation was precisely and narrowly drawn and applied neutrally to all speakers and demonstrators.[36] *(See details of Cox v. New Hampshire, p. 436.)*

Disturbing the Peace

Having established in *Hague* the right of individuals to communicate ideas in public places, the Court was quickly faced with the question whether the First Amendment protected speech that sparked a breach of the peace.

Speech to Passersby. The first case raising this issue concerned a Jehovah's Witness named Jesse Cantwell. Seeking converts to his faith in New Haven, Connecticut, in 1938, Cantwell stopped two men on a sidewalk and asked if he could play a phonograph record for them. They agreed, and he played "Enemies," which attacked organized religion in general and Catholicism in particular. The two men, both Catholics, were offended and told Cantwell to go away. There was no violence or other disturbance. Nonetheless, Cantwell was convicted of inciting others to a breach of the peace.

The Supreme Court reversed the conviction in *Cantwell v. Connecticut* (1940), finding the breach-of-the-peace ordinance too vague as applied to Cantwell:

The offense known as breach of the peace embraces a great variety of conduct destroying or menacing public order and tranquility. It includes not only violent acts but acts and words likely to produce violence in others. No one would have the hardihood to suggest that the principle of freedom of speech sanctions incitement to riot or that religious liberty connotes the privilege to exhort others to physical attack upon those belonging to another sect. When clear and present danger of riot, disorder, interference with traffic upon the public streets, or other immediate threat to public safety, peace or order, appears, the power of the State to prevent or punish is obvious. Equally obvious is it that a State may not unduly suppress free communication of views, religious or other, under the guise of conserving desirable conditions. Here we have a situation analogous to a conviction under a statute sweeping in a great variety of conduct under a general and indefinite characterization, and leaving to the executive and judicial branches too wide a discretion in its application.[37]

Looking at the facts of the situation, the Court said it found "no assault or threatening of bodily harm, no truculent bearing, no intentional discourtesy, no personal abuse." Absent a statute narrowly drawn to define and punish the conduct Cantwell engaged in, his conduct, the Court said, "raised no such clear and present menace to public peace and order as to render him liable" under the general breach-of-the-peace statute.[38]

Near Riot. The next breach-of-the-peace case required the Court to decide to what extent the First Amendment protected speech that provoked a near riot.

Terminiello was a defrocked Catholic priest who in 1946 spoke at a private meeting in Chicago sponsored by the Christian Veterans of America. In his speech Terminiello virulently attacked Jews, blacks, and the Roosevelt administration but did not urge his five hundred listeners to take any specific action.

While he spoke, some one thousand protesters gathered outside the hall, shouting, throwing rocks through windows, and trying to break into the meeting. The police restrained the mob with difficulty. As a result of the disturbance, Terminiello was arrested for and convicted of disorderly conduct under an ordinance that made it illegal for anyone to aid in a "breach of the peace or a diversion tending to a breach of the peace."

The Supreme Court reversed Terminiello's conviction by a vote of 5 to 4 but without reaching the constitutional issues involved. Instead, the majority held that the trial judge had improperly instructed the jury when he defined a breach of the peace as speech that "stirs the public to anger, invites dispute, brings about a condition of unrest, or creates a disturbance." Some parts of this instruction, the majority felt, would punish speech protected by the First Amendment, and since it was not apparent under which part the jury had convicted Terminiello, the conviction must fall.

Justice William O. Douglas explained the majority position in *Terminiello v. Chicago* (1949):

[A] function of free speech under our system of government is to invite dispute. It may indeed best serve its high purpose when it induces a condition of unrest, creates dissatisfaction with conditions as they are, or even stirs people to anger. Speech is often provocative and challenging. It may strike at prejudices and preconceptions and have profound unsettling effects as it presses for acceptance of an idea. That is why freedom of speech, though not absolute, . . . is nevertheless protected against censorship or punishment, unless shown likely to produce a clear and present danger of a serious substantive evil that rises far above public inconvenience, annoyance or unrest. . . . There is no room under our Constitution for a more restrictive view. For the alternative would lead to standardization of ideas either by legislatures, courts, or dominant political or community groups.[39]

Chief Justice Fred M. Vinson dissented, contending that Terminiello's speech consisted of "fighting words" that are outside the protection of the First Amendment. *(See box, Fighting Words and Hate Crimes, pp. 430–431.)*

In a separate dissent joined by Justices Felix Frankfurter and Harold H. Burton, Justice Robert H. Jackson maintained that Terminiello's speech created a "clear and present danger" that a riot would ensue and that the authorities were entitled to act to preserve the public peace "at least so long as danger to public order is not invoked in bad faith, as a cover for censorship or suppression." The choice [for the courts], Jackson wrote,

is not between order and liberty. It is between liberty with order and anarchy without either. There is danger that, if the court does not temper its doctrinaire logic with a little practical wisdom, it will convert the constitutional Bill of Rights into a suicide pact.[40]

Street Meeting. Two years later the Supreme Court drew closer to Jackson's position when it affirmed the breach-of-the-peace conviction of a student whose street corner speech seemed much less threatening to public order than Terminiello's. The different conclusions in these two cases illustrate the difficulty the Court has had in settling on a general standard by which to determine when speech oversteps the bounds of First Amendment protection. *(See "The Search for a Standard," pp. 413–414.)*

Irving Feiner spoke at an open-air gathering in Syracuse, New York, inviting listeners to attend a meeting that evening of the Progressive Party. In the course of his speech, Feiner made insulting remarks about President Harry S. Truman, the American Legion, and the mayor of Syracuse. He also urged blacks to fight for equal rights. Someone complained to the police, who sent two officers to investigate. The crowd was restless, and some passersby were jostled and forced into the street. Finally one listener told the officers that if they did not stop Feiner, he would. The police then asked Feiner to stop speaking. When he refused they arrested him for breach of the peace.

The six justices voting to sustain the conviction in *Feiner v. New York* (1951) found that the police had acted not to suppress speech but to preserve public order. Chief Justice Vinson wrote:

We are well aware that the ordinary murmurings and objections of a hostile audience cannot be allowed to silence a speaker, and are also mindful of the possible danger of giving overzealous police officials complete discretion to break up otherwise lawful public meetings. . . . But we are not faced here with such a situation. It is one thing to say that the police cannot be used as an instrument for the oppression of unpopular views, and another to say that, when as here the speaker passes the bounds of argument or persuasion and undertakes incitement to riot, they are powerless to prevent a breach of the peace.[41]

In dissent, Justice Hugo L. Black said that the majority's deci-

sion in effect made the police censors of public speech. Instead, the duty of the police should be to protect the speaker in the exercise of his First Amendment rights, even if that necessitates the arrest of those who would interfere, he said. Justices Douglas and Sherman Minton also dissented.

Prior Restraint

In contrast with its difficulty in defining the point at which speech loses its First Amendment protection, the Court has steadfastly rejected state efforts to place prior restraints on speech. In 1931 the Court held that an injunction against continued publication of a newspaper was an unconstitutional prior restraint of the press.[42] In 1940 it held that a statute permitting city officials to determine what was a religious cause and what was not amounted to an unconstitutional restraint on the free exercise of religion.[43] But not until 1945 did the Court overturn a state statute as an improper prior restraint on speech.

Union Organizer. The case of *Thomas v. Collins* arose after Thomas, a union organizer, refused to apply for the organizer's permit required by Texas law. The state issued an injunction to stop Thomas from soliciting for union members. He made a speech advocating union membership anyway and was convicted of contempt. He appealed to the Supreme Court, which voted 5–4 to overturn his contempt conviction.

Elaborating on the reasoning behind the Court's earlier permit decisions, Justice Wiley B. Rutledge said it was clear that the injunction against soliciting restrained Thomas's right to speak and the rights of the workers to assemble to hear him. The statute prohibiting solicitation without a permit was so imprecise that it in essence forbade "any language which conveys, or reasonably could be found to convey, the meaning of invitation." Rutledge continued, "How one might 'laud unionism,' as the State and the State Supreme Court concede Thomas was free to do, yet in these circumstances not imply an invitation, is hard to conceive."[44]

Consequently, the law operated to require Thomas to obtain a permit in order to make a public speech. This was incompatible with the First Amendment, Rutledge said.

If the exercise of the rights of free speech and assembly cannot be made a crime, we do not think this can be accomplished by the device of requiring previous registration as a condition for exercising them and making such a condition the foundation for restraining in advance their exercise.[45]

The dissenters would have affirmed Thomas's conviction. Justice Roberts contended that the contempt conviction was based not on Thomas's speech but on his explicit solicitation of workers to join the union in violation of the order not to solicit without a permit. The dissenters thought the registration requirement was well within the powers of the state to regulate business transactions.

Street Speaker. A solid majority of the Court struck down as an unconstitutional prior restraint a permit system applied in *Kunz v. New York*, decided the same day in 1951 as *Feiner*.

New York City had an ordinance that barred worship services

FIGHTING WORDS AND HATE CRIMES

"Fighting words," words so insulting that they provoke violence from the person they are addressed to, are generally unprotected by the First Amendment guarantee of free speech. However, laws criminalizing "hate speech," which targets persons because of their race or religion, have run afoul of the First Amendment.

The Supreme Court first addressed the issue of "fighting words" in the 1942 case of *Chaplinsky v. New Hampshire.* Chaplinsky, a Jehovah's Witness, provoked a public disturbance when he publicly assailed another religion as "a racket," and called a police officer "a God damned racketeer" and "a damned Fascist." He was convicted of violating a state statute making it a crime to call another person "offensive and derisive names" in public.

The Supreme Court sustained the conviction, upholding the statute against a challenge that it violated the guarantee of free speech. "[R]esort to epithets or to personal abuse is not in any proper sense communication of information or opinion safeguarded by the Constitution," the unanimous Court declared:

Allowing the broadest scope to the language and purpose of the . . . Amendment, it is well understood that the right of free speech is not absolute at all times and under all circumstances. There are certain well-defined and narrowly limited classes of speech, the prevention and punishment of which has never been thought to raise any Constitutional problem. These include the lewd and obscene, the profane, the libelous, and the insulting or "fighting" words—those which by their very utterance inflict injury or tend to incite an immediate breach of the peace. It has been well observed that such utterances are no essential part of any exposition of ideas, and are of such slight social value as a step to truth that any benefit that may be derived from them is clearly outweighed by the social interest in order and morality.[1]

But the Court in *Chaplinsky* was willing to uphold the statute only because the state court had narrowly construed its language to apply to fighting words and no other speech.

The Supreme Court has continued to insist that statutes penalizing fighting words be narrowly drawn and strictly interpreted. In 1972 the Court affirmed the reversal of a Georgia man's conviction for calling a police officer a "son of a bitch" and threatening the officer with physical abuse. The Supreme Court concluded that the state court's interpretation of the statute was too broad, making it applicable to protected speech as well as to fighting words.[2]

In 1971 the Court ruled that a state may not punish as a crime the public display of an offensive word, used as an expression of legitimate protest and not resulting in a breach of the peace. In protest of the Vietnam War, Paul Cohen wore into a Los Angeles courthouse a jacket inscribed with the slogan "Fuck the Draft." He was arrested and convicted under a state breach-of-the-peace law making "offensive conduct" a crime. Writing for the majority in *Cohen v. California* (1971), Justice John Marshall Harlan described the offending slogan not as conduct but as speech expressing a political viewpoint. Such expression is entitled to First Amendment protection, Harlan said, unless it provoked or intended to provoke a breach of the peace.

The state cannot properly prohibit public display of the offending expletive, Harlan continued. For if a state had the power to outlaw public use of one word, he wrote, it could outlaw the use of other words and such action would run "a substantial risk of suppressing ideas in the process. Indeed, governments might soon seize upon the censorship of particular words as a convenient guise for banning the expression of unpopular views."[3]

The Court later held that the Federal Communications Commission could regulate the times at which radio and television may broadcast offensive words.[4] *(See "Content and Context," p. 474.)*

During the 1980s, verbal and physical attacks on victims who were chosen because of their race, religion, ethnic origin, or sexual orientation spurred enactment of numerous laws forbidding such "hate speech" and "hate crimes." In the early 1990s, two of these

---

on public streets without a permit. Carl J. Kunz, an ordained Baptist minister, had been granted a permit for one year but his application for renewal was rejected because his vituperative denunciations of Catholics and Jews had created public disturbances. When Kunz spoke without the permit, he was convicted and fined ten dollars. He appealed his conviction to the Supreme Court, which overturned it by an 8–1 vote. Writing for the majority, Chief Justice Vinson rejected as too arbitrary the New York court's rationale that the permit had been revoked "for good reasons." He said:

We have here . . . an ordinance which gives an administrative official discretionary power to control in advance the right of citizens to speak on religious matters on the streets of New York. As such, the ordinance is clearly invalid as a prior restraint on the exercise of First Amendment rights.[46]

In lone dissent, Justice Jackson contended that Kunz's speeches were filled with "fighting words," the kind of verbal abuses and insults that were likely to incite violent response and that city officials were entitled to restrain. "The question . . . is not whether New York could, if it tried, silence Kunz, but whether it must place its streets at his service to hurl insults at the passer-by," Jackson said.[47]

SYMBOLIC SPEECH

Symbolic speech, the expression of ideas and beliefs through symbols rather than words, has generally been held protected by the First Amendment. The Supreme Court first dealt with the issue of symbolic speech in 1931 when it found California's "red flag" law unconstitutional. The statute made it a crime to raise a red flag as a symbol of opposition to organized government, or as "an invitation . . . to anarchistic action, or as an aid to propaganda that is of a seditious character." A state jury convicted Yetta Stromberg of raising a reproduction of the Soviet flag every morning at a children's summer camp, but it did not say which part of the law she violated.

The Supreme Court held that the first clause of the statute was an unconstitutional restriction of free speech because the flying of any banner symbolizing advocacy of a change in gov-

laws were challenged before the Supreme Court as violations of free speech rights.

The first case, decided in 1992, arose after three white teenagers in St. Paul, Minnesota, put up and burned a makeshift cross in the yard of a black family. The crudely made cross recalled the racist symbol of the Ku Klux Klan. The youths were charged under an ordinance prohibiting the display of a symbol that one knows "arouses anger, alarm or resentment in others on the basis of race, color, creed, religion or gender." The justices struck down the ordinance, saying it unconstitutionally singled out specific types of "hate speech" for criminal punishment. Although the judgment was unanimous, the justices split sharply in their rationale. A five-justice majority in an opinion penned by Justice Antonin Scalia said, "content-based regulations are presumptively invalid." Government may not ban speech "based on hostility—or favoritism—toward the underlying message expressed."[5]

Scalia said that if a municipality wants to outlaw a particular kind of speech that would be considered "fighting words," it must outlaw all fighting words, not just race-, religion-, or gender-based epithets. Government, he continued, cannot treat various conducts differently within a category of prohibited speech. "Thus, the government may proscribe libel; but it may not make the further content discrimination of proscribing only libel critical of the government," he said.

Dissenting justices, led by Byron R. White, called the majority's method "a simplistic, all-or-nothing-at-all approach" to the First Amendment. But they joined the judgment of the Court, finding the ordinance too sweeping; "[a]lthough the ordinance reaches conduct that is unprotected [by the First Amendment], it also makes criminal expressive conduct that causes only hurt feelings, offense, or resentment, and is protected by the First Amendment."

The second ruling, a year later, upheld a law that required enhanced penalties for crimes committed because of prejudice. That case began when a group of black youths beat a white teenager in Kenosha, Wisconsin. The assailants, angry after having watched a movie about the abuse of blacks, spotted the white youth as he was walking along a street. "There goes a white boy," yelled one of them. "Go get him." The white teenager was beaten into unconsciousness. The young man who led the attack was charged under Wisconsin's hate crime law, which allowed judges to add up to five years to the sentence of a defendant who "intentionally selects" his victim on the basis of race, religion, ethnic origin, disability, or sexual orientation. After the leader was convicted of aggravated battery, the judge imposed the maximum two-year sentence for the offense and an additional two years under the hate crime law.

The Supreme Court unanimously upheld the sentence. Chief Justice Rehnquist wrote that judges traditionally have been permitted to consider "a wide variety of factors" in sentencing a defendant, including the motive for the crime. Courts cannot consider a defendant's abstract beliefs, he said, but they can take racial bias or other prejudice into account when that is part of the motive for the offense. Wisconsin lawmakers passed the measure, he said, because "bias-inspired conduct . . . is thought to inflict greater individual and societal harm. . . . The State's desire to redress these perceived harms provides an adequate explanation for its penalty-enhancement provisions over and above mere disagreement with offenders' belief or biases."[6]

1. *Chaplinsky v. New Hampshire,* 315 U.S. 568 at 571, 572 (1942).
2. *Gooding v. Wilson,* 405 U.S. 518 (1972); see also *Lewis v. City of New Orleans,* 415 U.S. 130 (1974).
3. *Cohen v. California,* 403 U.S. 15 at 26 (1971).
4. *Federal Communications Commission v. Pacifica Foundation,* 438 U.S. 726 (1978).
5. *R.A.V. v. City of St. Paul,* 505 U.S. 377 (1992).
6. *Wisconsin v. Mitchell,* 508 U.S. 476 (1993).

ernment through peaceful means could be penalized. Such punishment would violate the right of free speech. Because it was possible that the jury had believed Stromberg guilty of violating only this clause of the law, its unconstitutionality rendered her conviction a denial of due process. Chief Justice Charles Evans Hughes wrote:

The maintenance of the opportunity for free political discussion to the end that government may be responsive to the will of the people and that changes may be obtained by lawful means, an opportunity essential to the security of the Republic, is a fundamental principle of our constitutional system. A statute which upon its face, and as authoritatively construed, is so vague and indefinite as to permit the punishment of the fair use of this opportunity is repugnant to the guaranty of liberty contained in the Fourteenth Amendment.[48]

Saluting the Flag

The fullest exposition of symbolism as a form of communication protected by the First Amendment came in the Court's decision in the second wartime "flag salute" case. The Court ruled that states could not compel schoolchildren to pledge allegiance to the American flag. (*See details of case, pp. 483–484.*)

For the majority in *West Virginia State Board of Education v. Barnette* (1943), Justice Jackson wrote:

There is no doubt that, in connection with the pledges, the flag salute is a form of utterance. Symbolism is a primitive but effective way of communicating ideas. The use of an emblem or flag to symbolize some system, idea, institution, or personality, is a short cut from mind to mind. Causes and nations, political parties, lodges and ecclesiastical groups seek to knit the loyalty of their followings to a flag or banner, a color or design. The State announces rank, function, and authority through crowns and maces, uniforms and black robes, the church speaks through the Cross, the Crucifix, the altar and shrine, and clerical raiment. Symbols of State often convey political ideas just as religious symbols come to convey theological ones. Associated with many of these symbols are appropriate gestures of acceptance or respect: a salute, a bowed or bared head, a bended knee. A person gets from a symbol the meaning he puts into it, and what is one man's comfort and inspiration is another's jest and scorn.[49]

The First Amendment, Jackson said, no more permitted a state to compel allegiance to a symbol of the organized govern-

LOUD SOUNDS AND FREE SPEECH

Does a city impermissibly interfere with freedom of speech by regulating the use of loudspeakers and other amplification devices? Over the years the Court's position has changed several times.

The Court first considered the question in *Saia v. New York* (1948). A Lockport, New York, ordinance prohibited the use of sound equipment without permission from the chief of police. Samuel Saia, a Jehovah's Witness, obtained a permit to amplify religious lectures in a public park. Because some people complained about the noise, Saia's permit was not renewed. He spoke with the loudspeaker anyway and was arrested and convicted of violating the ordinance. He countered that the ordinance violated his right to free speech.

The Court, 5–4, struck down the ordinance because it set no standards for granting or denying permits. Justice William O. Douglas explained:

The present ordinance would be a dangerous weapon if it were allowed to get a hold on our public life. . . . Any abuses which loud-speakers create can be controlled by narrowly drawn statutes. When a city allows an official to ban them in his uncontrolled discretion, it sanctions a device for suppression of free communication of ideas.[1]

In dissent Justice Felix Frankfurter insisted that a city has a right to regulate the use of sound amplification to protect the privacy of other users of the park. "Surely there is not a constitutional right to force unwilling people to listen," he said.[2] In a separate dissent Justice Robert H. Jackson drew a distinction between speech and amplification of speech. Regulating amplification, even prohibiting it altogether, in no way interfered with the freedom of speech itself, he said.

Just a year later, however, the four dissenters in *Saia* and Chief Justice Fred M. Vinson joined together to sustain a Trenton, New Jersey, ordinance prohibiting the use on all public streets of any sound equipment that emitted "loud and raucous noise."

This language might have been interpreted as barring all use of sound equipment in city streets, but a three-justice plurality in *Kovacs v. Cooper* (1949), for whom Justice Stanley F. Reed spoke, distinguished between "loud and raucous noise" and other sounds that might come from amplifying systems.

Reed agreed that "[a]bsolute prohibition within municipal limits of all sound amplification, even though reasonably regulated in place, time and volume, is undesirable and probably unconstitutional as an unreasonable interference with normal activities." But regulation of noise was permissible. The ordinance in no way re-stricts "communication of ideas or discussion of issues by the human voice, by newspapers, by pamphlets."[3]

Justice Hugo L. Black in dissent disagreed with Reed's interpretation of the ordinance, contending that it prohibited all sound amplification. This repudiation of *Saia*, he wrote, was "a dangerous and unjustifiable breach in the constitutional barriers designed to insure freedom of expression."[4]

In 1952 the Court majority held that individuals do not have an absolute right to privacy in public places. A private transit company in the District of Columbia piped music, occasionally interspersed with commercials, into its streetcars. Despite a challenge from passengers that the practice violated their right to privacy, the programming was approved by the local public utilities commission.

The Court held that courts had no authority to interfere with such a decision by the commission so long as it was arrived at through proper procedures. Justice Douglas dissented, calling the programming "a form of coercion to make people listen."[5]

The Court's definitive answer came in 1989 in *Ward v. Rock Against Racism*. The Court, 6–3, upheld New York City's regulation requiring all performers at its band shell in Central Park to use the sound amplification system and sound technician provided by the city.

"Music, as a form of expression and communication, is protected under the First Amendment," Justice Anthony M. Kennedy wrote, and the city's regulation did not violate that protection. The regulation was justified by the city's substantial interest in protecting its citizens from unwelcome noise; it was reasonable; and it was narrowly tailored to accomplish its purpose.

The lower court had invalidated the regulation, holding it was not the least restrictive means of attaining the city's objective. The Supreme Court held that was an unnecessary additional criterion. "A regulation of the time, place or manner of protected speech must be narrowly tailored to serve the government's legitimate content-neutral interests, but . . . it need not be the least restrictive or least intrusive means of doing so."[6]

1. *Saia v. New York*, 334 U.S. 558 at 562 (1948).
2. Id. at 563.
3. *Kovacs v. Cooper*, 336 U.S. 77 at 8 –82, 89 (1949).
4. Id. at 101–102.
5. *Public Utilities Commission of the District of Columbia v. Pollak*, 343 U.S. 451 at 468 (1952).
6. *Ward v. Rock Against Racism*, 491 U.S. 781(1989).

ment than it permitted the state to punish someone who used a symbol to express peaceful opposition to organized government.

Sit-In Demonstrations

Another form of symbolic speech reviewed by the Supreme Court was the student sit-in of the early 1960s. To protest racial discrimination in public accommodations, blacks requested service at "whites only" lunch counters and remained there quietly until ejected or arrested.

At least one justice believed that these sit-ins were a form of expression guaranteed constitutional protection under some circumstances. In a concurring opinion in *Garner v. Louisiana* (1961), Justice John Marshall Harlan wrote that a sit-in was

as much a part of the "free trade in ideas" . . . as is verbal expression, more commonly thought of as "speech." It, like speech, appeals to good sense and to "the power of reason as applied through public discussion" . . . just as much, if not more than, a public oration delivered from a soapbox at a street corner. This Court has never limited the right to speak . . . to mere verbal expression.[50]

The Court avoided answering the question whether the First

and Fourteenth Amendments protected the protesters from conviction for trespassing on private property.[51] But two decades later the Court held that civil rights demonstrators who boycotted the shops of white merchants could not be assessed damages for economic losses. Such a sustained, nonviolent boycott, the Court held in *NAACP v. Claiborne Hardware Co.,* was protected by the First Amendment. Violence, however, was not protected and those who practiced it could be held liable for the damages inflicted.[52]

Antiwar Protests

The unpopularity of the Vietnam War generated several symbolic speech cases. In *United States v. O'Brien* (1968), the Supreme Court refused to view draft card burning, an expression of protest to the war and the draft, as symbolic speech protected by the First Amendment. "We cannot accept the view that an apparently limitless variety of conduct can be labeled 'speech' whenever the person engaging in the conduct intends thereby to express an idea," the majority said. Even if that view were adopted, the majority continued, the First Amendment would not protect draft card burning:

This Court has held that when "speech" and "nonspeech" elements are combined in the same course of conduct, a sufficiently important governmental interest in regulating the nonspeech element can justify incidental limitations on First Amendment freedoms.[53]

Here, the majority said, Congress had a substantial interest in maintaining the draft registration system as part of its duty to raise and maintain armies. (Almost thirty years later in quite a different context, the Court cited this idea of a substantial public interest that permits some restriction on freedom of expression when it upheld a state law that forbade nude dancing.[54])

In another case during the Vietnam War, *Tinker v. Des Moines School District* (1969), the Supreme Court ruled that

A RIGHT TO BE SILENT

The First Amendment guarantees individuals the right to speak freely. The Supreme Court also has held that this guarantee includes a right to remain silent. In other words, the state may not coerce or compel a person to state a position or belief he or she does not voluntarily endorse.

Among the most dramatic examples of this right are the two 1940 cases arising from the refusal of children of Jehovah's Witnesses to salute the American flag in school. In their view, pledging allegiance to the flag violated their religious belief that they should not worship graven images.

The first time the Court considered this matter it held that the flag salute requirement did not violate religious freedom; three years later the Court reversed itself to rule that compulsory flag salutes did abridge the freedom guaranteed by the First Amendment for speech and religious belief.[1] *(See details of cases, pp. 481–484.)*

More recently, the Court held that First Amendment freedom includes the right to refuse to carry a state-required ideological message on your car license plates.

George Maynard was convicted of a misdemeanor for obscuring the motto on his New Hampshire license plate, which read "Live Free or Die." A member of the Jehovah Witnesses, he protested the motto on religious and moral grounds.

Affirming a lower court's reversal of Maynard's conviction, the Supreme Court said, "[T]he right of freedom of thought protected by the First Amendment against state action includes both the right to speak freely and the right to refrain from speaking at all."[2]

1. *Minersville School District v. Gobitis,* 310 U.S. 586 (1940), overruled by *West Virginia State Board of Education v. Barnette,* 319 U.S. 624 (1943).
2. *Wooley v. Maynard,* 430 U.S. 705 at 714 (1977).

On March 31, 1966, David O'Brien and three other antiwar protesters demonstrated their opposition to U.S. military action in Vietnam by burning their draft cards on the steps of the South Boston courthouse. Their convictions for violating the Selective Service Act were affirmed in *United States v. O'Brien.*

school officials improperly suspended students for wearing black armbands in symbolic protest of the war. The officials said they based the suspensions on their fear that the armbands might create a disturbance among the students. The majority wrote that

undifferentiated fear or apprehension of disturbance is not enough to overcome the right to freedom of expression. . . . In order for the State in the person of school officials to justify prohibition of a particular expression of opinion, it must be able to show that its action was caused by something more than a mere desire to avoid the discomfort and unpleasantness that always accompany an unpopular viewpoint.[55]

In yet another form of protest against the Vietnam War, an actor wore an army uniform while he and others performed a protest play on a sidewalk outside an army induction center in Houston. The play depicted U.S. soldiers killing Vietnamese women and children. The actor was arrested and convicted of violating a federal law that made it a crime to wear an official military uniform in a theatrical production unfavorable to the armed forces.

The Supreme Court unanimously overturned that conviction in *Schacht v. United States* (1970), concluding that the wearing of the uniform was part of the actor's speech. "An actor, like everyone else in our country enjoys a constitutional right to freedom of speech, including the right openly to criticize the Government during a dramatic performance," the Court said.[56]

Protest and the Flag

The Supreme Court in five modern cases (one in 1969, two in 1974, one in 1989, and one in 1990) reversed the convictions of persons who used the American flag to symbolize opposition to government policy and the course of public events.

Street v. New York (1969) concerned a man who protested the shooting of civil rights activist James Meredith by publicly burning a flag while declaring: "If they did that to Meredith, we don't need an American flag." He was convicted under a New York law that made it illegal to mutilate a flag or to cast contempt upon it either by words or conduct. Overturning the conviction, the Supreme Court said the statute as applied to Street was too broad because it permitted the punishment of his words, which were protected by the First and Fourteenth Amendments.[57]

In *Smith v. Goguen* (1974), the Court overturned the conviction of a man who wore a small flag on the seat of his pants. The Massachusetts statute, which made contemptuous treatment of the flag a crime, was unconstitutionally vague, the Court said, because it "fails to draw reasonably clear lines between the kinds of non-ceremonial treatment [of the flag] that are criminal and those that are not."[58]

In the third case, the Supreme Court directly confronted the question whether using the flag for protest was expression protected by the First Amendment. *Spence v. Washington* (1974) arose when a student flew a flag, on which he had superimposed a peace symbol, upside down from his apartment window. The student was protesting the U.S. invasion of Cambodia and the

shooting of four student protesters at Kent State University. He was arrested and convicted for violating a Washington statute prohibiting defacement of the flag.

In a *per curiam* opinion, the Court majority overturned the conviction, holding that the student's conduct was a form of symbolic speech protected under the First Amendment. The majority wrote:

[T]here can be little doubt that appellant communicated through the use of symbols. . . . [This communication] was a pointed expression of anguish by appellant about the then-current domestic and foreign affairs of his government. An intent to convey a particularized message was present, and in the surrounding circumstances the likelihood was great that the message would be understood by those who viewed it.[59]

Because the communication was protected by the First Amendment, the majority continued, the state could punish the communication only if it clashed with some substantial interest of the state. But there was no evidence that the flag caused a breach of the peace, and the possibility that some passersby might be offended by the message was not sufficient to warrant restraint of speech.

In 1989 the Court set off a storm of protest and demands for a constitutional amendment when it agreed with a lower court's reversal of Gregory Johnson's conviction for burning an American flag at the Republican National Convention in Dallas in 1984. Johnson was protesting the policies of Ronald Reagan's administration.

Citing the Court's rulings in *Street, Goguen,* and *Spence,* Justice William J. Brennan Jr. declared:

Texas attempts to convince us that even if its interest in preserving the flag's symbolic role does not allow it to prohibit words or some expressive conduct critical of the flag, it does permit it to forbid the outright destruction of the flag. . . . Texas' focus on the precise nature of Johnson's expression, moreover, misses the point of our prior decisions: their enduring lesson, that the Government may not prohibit expression simply because it disagrees with the message, is not dependent on the particular mode in which one chooses to express an idea.

"We do not consecrate the flag by punishing its desecration, for in doing so we dilute the freedom that this cherished emblem represents," he wrote in conclusion.[60]

Within weeks Congress attempted to reverse the Court by passing the Flag Protection Act, which would have subjected to arrest anyone who "knowingly mutilates, defaces, physically defiles, burns, maintains on the floor or ground, or tramples upon any flag."

But the same five-justice majority in *Texas v. Johnson* struck down the 1989 flag law in June 1990. Brennan, again writing for the majority, said, "Although Congress cast the Flag Protection Act in somewhat broader terms than the Texas statute at issue in Johnson, the act still suffers from the same fundamental flaw: it suppresses expression out of concern for its likely communicative impact."[61]

Protest in 1990 of the Persian Gulf War led to a Court ruling limiting the authority of cities to prohibit residents from displaying signs on their own lawns. The unanimous 1994 decision

Gregory Johnson, who has a record of flag burning, holds the American flag while another protester sets it alight. In 1989 the Supreme Court ruled that the conviction of Johnson for burning a flag during a demonstration in Dallas violated his First Amendment rights.

struck down an ordinance enacted by Ladue, Missouri, to minimize "visual clutter" by prohibiting most signs on residential property. A community activist who put up signs in her yard and window opposing the Persian Gulf War challenged the ordinance as a violation of her free speech rights. In a broadly worded decision, Justice John Paul Stevens said the ordinance "almost completely foreclosed a venerable means of communication that is both unique and important."[62]

The Freedom of Assembly

At first the Supreme Court considered the right to peaceable assembly to be a privilege and immunity of national citizenship guaranteed by the Fourteenth Amendment. In the 1876 case of *United States v. Cruikshank,* the Court said:

The right of the people peaceably to assemble for the purpose of petitioning Congress for a redress of grievances, or for any thing else connected with the powers or the duties of the national government, is an attribute of national citizenship, and, as such, under the protection of, and guaranteed by, the United States. The very idea of a government,

republican in form, implies a right on the part of its citizens to meet peaceably for consultation in respect to public affairs and to petition for a redress of grievances.[63]

It was more than sixty years before the Court again addressed the issue of the right of assembly. In the 1937 case of *De Jonge v. Oregon,* a majority of the Court recognized, first, that the right of assembly was on an equal status with the rights of free speech and free press, and, second, that it was applicable to the states through the due process clause of the Fourteenth Amendment.

The meaning of this First Amendment protection was simple, the Court said, "peaceable assembly for lawful discussion cannot be made a crime."[64] *(See details of DeJonge case, p. 425.)*

THE RIGHT OF PETITION

The First Amendment right "to petition the Government for a redress of grievances" has its origins in the Magna Carta, the medieval English charter of political and civil liberties.

One of the earliest exercises of the right in the United States occurred in the 1830s when Congress received scores of petitions seeking abolition of slavery in the District of Columbia. The right of petition was later invoked by the unemployed petitioners of Jacob S. Coxey's Ohio army of 1894, the bonus marchers in 1932, and participants in the Poor People's Campaign of 1968.

Petitioners are not restricted to seeking redress of grievances only from Congress. They may petition administrative agencies and the courts.

Application of the First Amendment to the states through the due process clause of the Fourteenth Amendment has also ensured citizens the right to make their views known to state governments.

Nor is petition of government limited solely to seeking a redress of grievances: petitioners may seek benefits. Individuals, citizen groups, and corporations all lobby government to persuade it to adopt policies that will benefit their particular interests.

The major decision defining lobbyists' right to petition came in 1954, when the Court upheld the authority of Congress to require certain lobbyists to register.[1]

Then in 1980 the Court ruled that the right of petition is not infringed by military regulations that require the approval of the base commander before military personnel may send a petition to members of Congress.[2] This right, however, does not protect those who exercise it from being sued for libel for what they include in their petition, the Court decided in 1985.[3] Also that year the Court held that the ten dollar limit on what a veteran can pay an attorney for representation in pursuing claims with the Veterans Administration did not abridge the veteran's right effectively to petition the government for redress.[4]

1. *United States v. Harriss,* 347 U.S. 612 (1954).
2. *Brown v. Glines,* 444 U.S. 348 (1980).
3. *McDonald v. Smith,* 472 U.S. 479 (1985).
4. *Walters v. National Association of Radiation Survivors,* 473 U.S. 305 (1985).

Two years later in the case of *Hague v. C.I.O.*, a plurality of three justices again held that the right of peaceable assembly was protected by the privileges and immunities clause of the Fourteenth Amendment. Two other justices found this right included in the "liberty" guaranteed by the Fourteenth Amendment due process clause. It is this latter view that has prevailed.[65] *(See details of Hague case, pp. 427–428.)*

PARADES AND DEMONSTRATIONS

The right peacefully to parade or demonstrate to make known one's views or to support or oppose an issue of public policy is based on the twin guarantees of the rights of free speech and free assembly. But because parading and demonstrating involve conduct that might interfere with the ability of other members of the public to use the same public places, they have always been considered subject to greater regulation than exercises of pure speech and assembly.

To preserve the freedoms of speech and assembly, the Supreme Court has insisted that parade and demonstration regulations be precisely worded and applied in nondiscriminatory fashion. To preserve the public welfare, the Court has held that not all public places are appropriate sites for public protests.

Time, Place, and Manner

The primary precedent on parades and demonstrations was the 1941 case of *Cox v. New Hampshire*. Cox was one of sixty-eight Jehovah's Witnesses convicted of parading without a permit. He challenged the statute as an improper infringement on his rights of free speech and assembly, but the Supreme Court rejected his argument in a unanimous decision. As construed and applied, the ordinance did not allow denial of permits, the Court said, because the views of the paraders might be unpopular; the ordinance was intended only to ensure that paraders would not unduly interfere with others using the streets. Chief Justice Hughes explained:

If a municipality has authority to control the use of its public streets for parades and processions, as it undoubtedly has, it cannot be denied authority to give consideration, without unfair discrimination, to time, place and manner in relation to the other proper uses of the streets.[66]

Half a century later the Court again spoke to this point, declaring in a 1992 ruling that parade regulations must be neutral and not give unbridled discretion to a local official. A Forsyth County, Georgia, ordinance required organizers of a parade to pay up to $1,000 for police protection. The Court ruled 5–4 that this ordinance violated the First Amendment because it allowed a county administrator to set an excessive fee. The ordinance lacked definite standards to guide the administrator, the Court said, noting that the administrator could decide not to assess the fee and was not required to provide an explanation for action taken.[67]

Three years later the Court held unanimously that parade organizers cannot be required by state law to include participants with whom they disagree. Boston veterans wanted to exclude marchers whose main purpose was to proclaim their ho-

mosexual identity. When a parade is privately organized, the Court said, it is a form of private expression protected by the First Amendment's guarantee of free speech.[68]

Civil Rights Protests

Cases arising out of the civil rights movement of the late 1950s and 1960s gave the Court the opportunity to explore more fully the extent of First Amendment protection for peaceable demonstrations and protests.

In a series of cases arising out of nonviolent demonstrations in southern states, the Supreme Court ruled that peaceful protests conducted according to valid regulations on public property designated for general use were protected by the First Amendment. But peaceful protests on public property reserved for specific purposes might not be protected.

Breach of Peace. The first case in this series arose in Columbia, South Carolina, where in early 1961 some 180 black high school and college students marched to the state capitol grounds to protest discrimination. Between two hundred and three hundred people gathered to watch the peaceful demonstration.

Although there was no threat of violence or other disturbance, the police grew concerned that trouble might flare up and so ordered the demonstrators to disperse within fifteen

Mass demonstrations were an important element in the civil rights movement during the 1960s. A huge crowd attended a 1963 demonstration in front of the Lincoln Memorial.

minutes. The students refused, were arrested, and subsequently convicted of breach of the peace.

The Supreme Court overturned the convictions in *Edwards v. South Carolina* (1963).[69] The Court accepted the state courts' finding that the students' conduct constituted a breach of the peace under state law. But the justices held that the state law was unconstitutionally broad because it penalized the exercise of free speech, assembly, and petition for redress of grievances "in their most pristine and classic form."

Justice Potter Stewart wrote for the Court:

These petitioners were convicted of an offense so generalized as to be, in the words of the South Carolina Supreme Court, "not susceptible of exact definition." And they were convicted upon evidence which showed no more than that the opinions which they were peaceably expressing were sufficiently opposed to the views of the majority of the community to attract a crowd and necessitate police protection.[70]

Recalling that the majority in *Terminiello v. Chicago* (1949) had held provocative and unsettling speech to be constitutionally protected, Stewart declared that "the Fourteenth Amendment does not permit a State to make criminal the peaceful expression of unpopular views."[71]

In lone dissent Justice Tom C. Clark would have upheld the convictions because the police were trying to preserve the peace and did not intend to suppress speech.

Similar circumstances attended the arrest and conviction of the Reverend B. Elton Cox for breach of the peace in Baton Rouge, Louisiana. In 1961 Cox led some two thousand black college students in a two-and-one-half block march from the state capitol to a courthouse where twenty-three other students were in jail for their attempts to integrate whites-only lunch counters.

Prior to the march, police officials asked Cox to abandon the demonstration, but he refused. The march was orderly. Once at the courthouse, Cox and the students complied with police instructions to stay on the sidewalk.

Between one hundred and three hundred white onlookers watched the students wave picket signs and sing patriotic and religious songs. Cox then spoke to explain the reasons for the demonstration. At its conclusion, he urged the marchers to seek service at the lunch counters.

At this point the sheriff ordered the demonstrators to disperse. Soon afterwards the police fired a tear gas canister into the crowd and the demonstrators left the area.

Cox was arrested and convicted of disturbing the peace. The Supreme Court, 7–2, set aside his conviction in *Cox v. Louisiana* (1965). As in *Edwards,* the majority found Louisiana's breach-of-the-peace statute unconstitutionally broad in scope because it penalized persons who were lawfully exercising their rights of free speech, assembly, and petition.[72]

Courthouse Picketing. In a second case arising from Cox's protest that day in 1961, the Court, 5–4, overturned his conviction for violating a Louisiana statute prohibiting picketing or parading "in or near" a courthouse.[73] The Court sustained the validity of the statute, as justified by the state interest protecting

the administration of justice from outside influence. The statute was precisely drawn so that it did not restrict the rights of free speech and assembly but instead regulated conduct which, though entwined with speech and assembly, was not constitutionally protected.

But the Court also held that the term "near" was so vague that it was not unreasonable for Cox to rely on the interpretation of the police as to how close they might come to the courthouse. By specifically confining the demonstration to a particular segment of the sidewalk, the police had in effect given permission for the demonstration to take place at that particular place. Thus the statute had been applied improperly to convict Cox.

Library Protest. The following year the Court overturned the breach-of-the-peace convictions of five black men who staged a peaceful and orderly protest against racial segregation by refusing to leave a library reserved for white use.

The Court held this demonstration to be constitutionally protected in the case of *Brown v. Louisiana* (1966). The First Amendment freedoms

embrace appropriate types of action which certainly include the right in a peaceable and orderly manner to protest by silent and reproachful presence, in a place where the protestant has every right to be, the unconstitutional segregation of public facilities.[74]

In dissent Justice Black maintained that the First Amendment did not "guarantee to any person the right to use someone else's property, even that owned by the government and dedicated to other purposes, as a stage to express dissident ideas."[75]

Jailhouse Demonstration. Justice Black's views won the adherence of a majority in a case decided later in 1966. *Adderly v. Florida* arose after blacks demonstrated at a county jail to protest the arrests of several students who had tried to integrate a segregated theater. The demonstrators were convicted of criminal trespass.

Writing the opinion for the five-justice majority, Black acknowledged that the jail, like the capitol grounds in *Edwards,* was public property, but there the similarities ended. "Traditionally, state capitol grounds are open to the public. Jails, built for security purposes, are not," he said. Black continued:

The State, no less than a private owner of property, has power to preserve the property under its control for the use to which it is lawfully dedicated. For this reason there is no merit to the [demonstrators'] argument that they had a constitutional right to stay on the property over the jail custodian's objections, because this "area chosen for the peaceful civil rights demonstration was not only 'reasonable' but also particularly appropriate. . . ." Such an argument has as its major unarticulated premise the assumption that people who want to propagandize protests or views have a constitutional right to do so whenever and however and wherever they please. That concept of constitutional law was vigorously and forthrightly rejected in [previous cases]. . . . We reject it again.[76]

For the four dissenters, Justice Douglas said the Court was effectively negating *Edwards* and *Cox.* Douglas wrote:

The jailhouse, like an executive mansion, a legislative chamber, a courthouse, or the statehouse itself . . . is one of the seats of government, whether it be the Tower of London, the Bastille, or a small county jail. And when it houses political prisoners or those who many think are unjustly held, it is an obvious center for protest. . . . Conventional methods of petitioning may be, and often have been, shut off to large groups of our citizens. . . . Those who do not control television and radio, those who cannot afford to advertise in newspapers or circulate elaborate pamphlets may have only a more limited type of access to public officials. Their methods should not be condemned as tactics of obstruction and harassment as long as the assembly and petition are peaceable, as these were.[77]

Residential Area. In 1969 the Court upheld the right of peaceful demonstrators to parade in a residential neighborhood on the public sidewalks near Chicago mayor Richard Daley's home. The demonstrators advocated desegregation of Chicago public schools. White residents grew threatening, and, to ward off potential violence, police asked the marchers to disperse. They refused and were arrested. Five were convicted of disorderly conduct.

In a unanimous decision in *Gregory v. City of Chicago,* the Supreme Court overturned the convictions. Because there was no evidence that the marchers' conduct had been disorderly, the Court said the convictions violated due process. The Court also said that the "march, if peaceful and orderly, falls well within the sphere of conduct protected by the First Amendment."[78]

Almost twenty years later, however, the Court in *Frisby v. Schultz,* upheld Brookfield, Wisconsin's, ordinance forbidding picketing of an individual residence. The Court found the ordinance narrowly tailored enough to preserve residential privacy while leaving open alternative methods of expression. "The First Amendment permits the government to prohibit offensive speech as intrusive when the 'captive' audience cannot avoid the objectionable speech," wrote Justice Sandra Day O'Connor for the Court.[79]

Boycotts and Sleep-Ins. In *NAACP v. Claiborne Hardware Co.,* the Court unanimously ruled that a nonviolent boycott in 1966 by civil rights demonstrators, intended to curtail business at the shops of white merchants in Port Gibson, Mississippi, was speech and conduct protected by the First Amendment. Damages for economic losses suffered as a result of the boycott could not be assessed against those who merely participated in it.

Violence, the Court explained, was not protected activity, and a state court could assess damages against those responsible for such violence, but that liability must reflect the individual's participation in violence and could not be lodged against anyone simply because he or she was part of the boycott group.

The following year the Court struck down as unconstitutional a federal law barring all demonstrations on the sidewalks adjacent to its own building on Capitol Hill in Washington, D.C.[80]

Then in 1984 came the case of *Clark v. Community for Creative Non-Violence.* This group, protesting the Reagan administration's treatment of the nation's poor and homeless, challenged the administration's ban on camping in certain national parks. When applied to Lafayette Park across from the White House, site of a variety of periodic and ongoing demonstrations, the challengers argued, this ban violated the First Amendment freedom of expression.

The Court, 7–2, upheld the ban—which defined camping as sleeping overnight—as a reasonable restriction on the time, place, and manner in which First Amendment rights could be exercised.[81]

Abortion Protests. In 1994 the Court ruled that judges may establish "buffer zones" preventing antiabortion protesters from getting too close to clinics where abortions are performed. Writing for the majority, Chief Justice William H. Rehnquist was careful to say that judges cannot restrict "more speech than necessary" to protect access to the clinics. When an injunction restricting protest is "content-neutral," it can be permitted so long as it "burdens no more speech than necessary to serve a significant government interest." Rehnquist said "a woman's freedom to seek lawful medical counseling or counseling services in connection with her pregnancy" is such an interest to justify a narrowly tailored injunction.[82]

LABOR PICKETING

The question of how much protection the First Amendment affords labor picketing has troubled the Supreme Court. Picketing conveys a message to the public about the issues in labor disputes and is therefore a form of expression. But unlike other sorts of parades and demonstrations, picketing also uses economic pressure and coercion to bring about better working conditions and, as conduct, can be regulated by government.

Permissible Pickets

Initially courts considered all labor picketing illegal. As labor unions grew in power and acceptability, however, that view began to change. In a 1921 decision the Supreme Court permitted a union to post one picket at each entrance and exit of a factory for the purpose of explaining a union grievance against the employer. Although the First Amendment issue of free speech was not directly raised in this case, the Court acknowledged that "[w]e are a social people and the accosting by one of another in an inoffensive way and an offer by one to communicate and discuss information with a view to influence the other's action are not regarded as aggression or a violation of the other's rights."[83]

In a 1937 decision the Court moved closer to the First Amendment question. In *Senn v. Tile Layers Union,* it upheld a Wisconsin statute permitting peaceful picketing against a challenge that such picketing constituted a "taking" of the employer's property without due process of law guaranteed by the Fourteenth Amendment. "Clearly, the means which the state authorizes—picketing and publicity—are not prohibited by the Fourteenth Amendment. Members of a union might . . . make known the facts of a labor dispute, for freedom of speech is guaranteed by the Federal Constitution," Justice Brandeis wrote for a slim majority.[84]

Full Protection

Three years later in 1940 a substantial majority of the Court drew industrial picketing under the protective wing of the First Amendment. In *Thornhill v. Alabama* (1940) Byron Thornhill appealed his conviction under an Alabama law that forbade

The Court has struggled with the question of how much protection the First Amendment affords labor picketing. While recognizing picketing as a form of expression, the Court has stopped short of granting it unlimited First Amendment protection.

picketing. He argued that the statute violated his rights of free speech, assembly, and petition for redress of grievances.

Speaking through Justice Frank Murphy, eight justices held the statute invalid. "In the circumstances of our times the dissemination of information concerning the facts of a labor dispute must be regarded as within that area of free discussion that is guaranteed by the Constitution," Murphy wrote.[85]

The picketing did not lose its First Amendment protection just because it might result in some degree of economic coercion, Murphy explained.

It may be that effective exercise of the means of advancing public knowledge may persuade some of those reached to refrain from entering into advantageous relations with the business establishment which is the scene of the dispute. Every expression of opinion . . . has the potentiality of inducing action in the interests of one rather than another group in society. But the group in power at any moment may not impose penal sanctions on peaceful and truthful discussion of matters of public interest merely on a showing that others may thereby be persuaded to take action inconsistent with its interests.[86]

The following year, 1941, the Court in *AFL v. Swing* relied on *Thornhill*. A state policy limiting picketing to cases where union members had a dispute with their employer was ruled an unconstitutional infringement of the First Amendment guarantee of free speech. The Court said the state could not forbid organizational picketing by unions hoping to persuade nonunion workers to join.[87]

Prior Restraint of Violence

In another case decided the same day as *AFL v. Swing,* the Court indicated that the First Amendment did not foreclose pri-

or restraint of picketing in the interest of public safety. By a 6–3 vote, the majority upheld an injunction forbidding a union of milk wagon drivers to engage in picketing because their past picketing had resulted in violence. Justice Frankfurter wrote the opinion for the majority in *Milk Wagon Drivers Union v. Meadowmoor Dairies Inc.* (1941).

"Peaceful picketing is the workingman's means of communication," said Frankfurter, but the First Amendment does not protect "utterance in a context of violence" that becomes "part of an instrument of force." Under the circumstances of the case, he continued, "it could justifiably be concluded that the momentum of fear generated by past violence would survive even though future picketing might be wholly peaceful."[88]

Third-Party Picketing

In 1942 the Court delivered two conflicting decisions on the permissibility of picketing of persons not directly involved in a labor dispute.

In the case of *Bakery and Pastry Drivers v. Wohl,* the Court lifted an injunction against a union of bakery truck drivers who had picketed bakeries and groceries using nonunion drivers in order to induce the nonunion drivers to give some of their work to union drivers. The Court majority observed that the mobility and "middle-man" status of the nonunion drivers separated them from the public. Therefore picketing those who did business with them was "the only way to make views, admittedly accurate and peaceful, known."[89]

But in a second case decided the same day, *Carpenters and Joiners Union v. Ritter's Cafe,* the Court sustained an injunction

PUBLIC SPEECH ON PRIVATE PROPERTY . . . THE FIRST AMENDMENT RESTRICTED

The First Amendment prohibits only government action abridging the freedom of speech. Most First Amendment cases thus involve situations in which speech occurs or is abridged in a public forum or on public property.

Some private property is dedicated to public use, however, and there the question arises whether the property owner becomes subject to the First Amendment prohibition. If that is so, then a private owner may no more restrict exercise of First Amendment freedoms on his property than may a government.

THE COMPANY TOWN

The Court first confronted this issue in the 1946 case of *Marsh v. Alabama*. Chickasaw, Alabama, a suburb of Mobile, was wholly owned by a private corporation. A Jehovah's Witness, Grace Marsh, passed out handbills on a Chickasaw street in violation of a regulation forbidding such distribution. She challenged her subsequent arrest and conviction, claiming that her First Amendment rights had been infringed.

A majority of the Supreme Court agreed. Save for its private ownership, wrote Justice Hugo L. Black, Chickasaw had all the characteristics of any other American town. And its residents had the same interest as residents of municipally owned towns in keeping channels of communication open. "There is no more reason for depriving these people of the liberties guaranteed by the First and Fourteenth Amendments than there is for curtailing these freedoms with respect to any other citizens," Black said.[1]

PICKETING AND PRIVATE MALLS - I

In 1968 the Court relied on *Marsh v. Alabama* when it forbade the owner of a private shopping mall to prohibit union picketing of a store in the mall. A nonunion supermarket in a privately owned mall near Altoona, Pennsylvania, was picketed by members of a food employees union who wished to point out that the supermarket did not employ union workers or abide by union pay and work-

ing condition requirements. The owners of the store and the shopping center won an injunction forbidding picketing in the mall and its private parking lots.

By a 6–3 vote, the Supreme Court declared the injunction invalid in *Amalgamated Food Employees Union Local 590 v. Logan Valley Plaza* (1968). Noting the similarities between the shopping center and the business district in the company town involved in *Marsh*, Justice Thurgood Marshall observed that the general public had unrestricted access to the mall and that it served as the functional equivalent of a town business district.

These circumstances, the majority said, rendered the mall public for purposes of the First Amendment, and consequently its owners could not invoke state trespass laws to prohibit picketing that advanced the communication of ideas. Marshall noted the narrowness of the ruling:

All we decide here is that because the shopping center serves as the community business block "and is freely accessible and open to the people in the area and those passing through" . . . the State may not delegate the power, through the use of its trespass laws, wholly to exclude those members of the public wishing to exercise their First Amendment rights on the premises in a manner and for a purpose generally consonant with the use to which the property is actually put.[2]

Justice Black dissented, contending that the majority erred in its reliance on *Marsh* as a precedent. *Marsh* held that the First Amendment applied when the private property had taken on *all* of the aspects of a town, he said, adding:

I can find nothing in Marsh which indicates that if one of these features is present, e.g., a business district, this is sufficient for the Court to confiscate a part of an owner's private property and give its use to people who want to picket on it.[3]

HANDBILL PROTESTS IN SHOPPING CENTERS

Within four years a majority of the Court qualified the ruling in *Logan Valley Plaza*, holding that owners of a private shopping mall

against a carpenters' union, forbidding it to picket a cafe owned by a man whose nearby house was being built by a nonunion contractor. The five-justice majority noted that the union's real complaint was with the contractor and concluded:

As a means of communication of the facts of a labor dispute, peaceful picketing may be a phase of the constitutional right of free utterance. But recognition of peaceful picketing as an exercise of free speech does not imply that the state must be without power to confine the sphere of communication to that directly related to the dispute.[90]

The conclusion of the two holdings seemed to be that a third party to a labor dispute could be picketed only if the union had no other means to make its views effectively known.

In both these cases the majority recognized that industrial picketing, in Justice William O. Douglas's words,

is more than free speech, since it involves patrol of a particular locality and since the very presence of a picket line may induce action of one

kind or another, quite irrespective of the nature of the ideas which are being disseminated. Hence those aspects of picketing make it the subject of restrictive regulation.[91]

Illegal Conduct

The Court moved another step away from *Thornhill* in 1949. Picketing as "conduct" may in some circumstances be so intertwined with illegal labor practices that states may prohibit it, held a unanimous Court in *Giboney v. Empire Storage and Ice Co.*

A Missouri court issued an injunction against a union of ice drivers who had picketed an ice company in order to persuade the company to refuse to sell ice to nonunion drivers. Other unions had observed the picket line, and the company's sales fell by 85 percent. If the company had entered into the proposed union agreement, however, it would have violated Missouri's

could prohibit the distribution of leaflets unrelated to business conducted in the mall.

The circumstances in *Lloyd Corporation, Ltd. v. Tanner* (1972) were similar to those in *Marsh* with one major difference. The Lloyd Center was not a company town but a privately owned and operated shopping mall that prohibited the circulation of handbills. Inside the mall, several people attempted to distribute handbills inviting the general public to attend a meeting to protest the Vietnam War. When asked to desist, they did, but then brought suit charging they had been denied their right to free speech.

By a 5–4 vote the Supreme Court rejected the charge. Writing for the majority, Justice Lewis F. Powell Jr. held that although the shopping mall served the public it still maintained its private character:

The invitation is to come to the Center to do business with the tenants. . . . There is no open-ended invitation to the public to use the Center for any and all purposes, however incompatible with the interests of both the stores and the shoppers whom they serve. . . . This Court has never held that a trespasser or an uninvited guest may exercise general rights of free speech on property privately owned and used nondiscriminatorily for private purposes only.[4]

Writing for the dissenters, Justice Marshall saw nothing to distinguish this case from the Court's holdings in *Marsh* and *Logan Valley Plaza.*

PICKETING AND PRIVATE MALLS - II

In 1976 the Court moved a step closer to divesting speech on private property used for specific public purposes of any First Amendment protection. But a majority of the Court still refused to overturn the *Logan Valley Plaza* decision, leaving the issue unsettled.

Hudgens v. National Labor Relations Board arose after striking employees of a shoe company warehouse decided also to picket the company's retail stores. One of these was situated in a shopping mall whose owners threatened to have the pickets arrested for trespassing if they did not desist. The pickets withdrew but challenged

the owners' threat as an unfair labor practice under the National Labor Relations Act.

Before answering that question, the Supreme Court majority felt it necessary to determine whether the picketing was entitled to any First Amendment protection. A majority concluded it was not.

Three of the members of the majority held that the *Lloyd* decision had in effect overruled the *Logan Valley Plaza* decision and that, consequently, uninvited speech on private property was not protected.

The three other justices comprising the majority did not believe that the *Logan Valley Plaza* decision had been overruled. But they distinguished between the pickets in that case who conveyed information about the operation of a store actually located in the mall and the pickets in *Hudgens* who tried to convey information about a warehouse located away from the mall.

Justices Marshall and William J. Brennan Jr. dissented. Marshall insisted that when an owner of a private shopping mall invited the public onto his property to conduct business he gave up a degree of privacy to the interests of the public. One public interest was "communicating with one another on subjects relating to businesses that occupy" the shopping center. "As far as these groups are concerned," said Marshall, "the shopping center owner has assumed the traditional role of the state in its control of historical First Amendment forums."[5]

Just four years later, however, the Court seemed to move again on this question, holding unanimously that a state could require the owner of a shopping mall to permit students to collect signatures on a petition to Congress within his mall.[6]

1. *Marsh v. Alabama,* 326 U.S. 501 at 508–509 (1946); see also *Tucker v. Texas,* 326 U.S. 517 (1946).

2. *Amalgamated Food Employees Union Local 590 v. Logan Valley Plaza,* 391 U.S. 308 at 319–320 (1968).

3. Id. at 332.

4. *Lloyd Corporation, Ltd. v. Tanner,* 407 U.S. 551 at 564–565, 568 (1972).

5. *Hudgens v. National Labor Relations Board,* 424 U.S. 507 at 543 (1976).

6. *PruneYard Shopping Center v. Robins,* 447 U.S. 74 (1980).

restraint of trade law. The union contended that because its picketing publicized the facts about the labor dispute, the picketing was entitled to First Amendment protection. The Supreme Court rejected this thesis. In an opinion written by Justice Black, the Court found that the picketing was an integral part of conduct that violated a valid state law and was therefore not protected by the First Amendment. Black wrote: "It has never been deemed an abridgment of freedom of speech or press to make a course of conduct illegal merely because the conduct was in part initiated, evidenced or carried out by means of language."[92]

State Regulation

In a series of cases beginning with *Giboney* and continuing with three decisions in 1950, the Court effectively reversed

Thornhill, making clear that the expressive aspects of picketing did not protect it from state regulation and prohibition. If the purpose of the picketing could be construed as contrary to state statute or policy, the Court would hold a state-imposed injunction valid.

The first of the 1950 cases blended the aspects of industrial picketing and civil rights demonstrations. In *Hughes v. Superior Court of California,* the Court upheld an injunction forbidding picketing by blacks trying to force a grocer to hire a certain percentage of black employees. Although no state law prohibited racial hiring quotas, the California judge who issued the injunction held the picketing inimical to the state's policy of supporting nondiscrimination.[93]

In two other cases decided the same day, the Court upheld injunctions against picketing aimed at forcing an employer to pressure his employees to choose the picketing union as their bargaining representative, and against picketing to compel a family business with no employees to operate by union standards.[94]

In the 1953 case of *Local Plumbers Union #10 v. Graham,* the Court again held that the speech aspects of picketing did not protect it from regulation. The union claimed that the picketing simply announced to the public that the picketed employer hired nonunion workers, but the Supreme Court found that the major purpose of the picketing was to force the employer to replace his nonunion employees with union workers, action that would violate the state's "right-to-work" law.[95]

In 1957 the Court upheld an injunction against unions engaged in picketing of a nonunion gravel pit. Such picketing violated a state law making it an unfair labor practice to force an employer "to interfere with any of his employees in the enjoyment of their legal rights." Writing for the majority in *International Brotherhood of Teamsters, Local 695 v. Vogt,* Justice Frankfurter reviewed the cases decided by the Court since the *Thornhill* finding that picketing was protected by the First Amendment. *Thornhill* was still valid, he said, because "[s]tate courts, no more than state legislatures, can enact blanket prohibitions against picketing." But, he added, the cases decided since then had

established a broad field in which a state, in enforcing some public policy, whether of its criminal or its civil law, and whether announced by its legislature or its courts, could constitutionally enjoin peaceful picketing aimed at preventing effectuation of that policy.[96]

For the three dissenters, Justice Douglas said that the majority had completely abandoned *Thornhill.* Douglas urged the Court to return to the proposition that the First Amendment protects from state restriction all picketing that is not violent or a part of illegal conduct:

[W]here, as here, there is no rioting, no mass picketing, no violence, no disorder, no fisticuffs, no coercion—indeed nothing but speech, the principles announced in Thornhill . . . should give the advocacy of one side of a dispute First Amendment protection.[97]

In 1968 the Court held that the First Amendment forbade a state to delegate to the owner of a shopping mall the power to restrict labor picketing of a store in the mall. But the continuing validity of this decision has since been called into question, and the decision in the *Vogt* case stands as the Court's position on labor picketing's relation to the First Amendment.[98] *(See box, Public Speech on Private Property, pp. 440–441.)*

SOLICITING AND CANVASSING

Door-to-door noncommercial solicitation of a neighborhood by persons seeking financial and moral support for their religious, political, or civic cause squarely sets the freedoms of speech, press, and religion against the right of privacy in one's home. Must the right to disseminate ideas give way to privacy, or does privacy yield to the uninvited dissemination of ideas?

Professor Zechariah Chafee Jr. argued that privacy may be the value more worthy of preservation:

Of all the methods of spreading unpopular ideas . . . [solicitation] seems the least entitled to extensive [First Amendment] protection. The possibilities of persuasion are slight compared with the certainties of annoyance. Great as is the value of exposing citizens to novel views, home is one place where a man ought to be able to shut himself up in his own ideas if he desires.[99]

But the Supreme Court has generally held in solicitation cases that freedom of ideas takes precedence over privacy. To protect their citizens from annoyance, governments may regulate the time and manner of solicitation, and to protect the public from fraud or crime, governments may require solicitors to identify themselves. But such regulations must be narrowly drawn and precisely defined to avoid infringing First Amendment rights.

One of the first solicitation ordinances to fall under Supreme Court scrutiny was a Connecticut statute that prohibited solicitation of money or services without the approval of the secretary of the local public welfare office. The secretary had the discretion to determine if the solicitation was in behalf of a *bona fide* religion or charitable cause. The Supreme Court struck down the statute in *Cantwell v. Connecticut* (1940):

Without doubt a State may protect its citizens from fraudulent solicitation by requiring a stranger in the community, before permitting him publicly to solicit funds for any purpose, to establish his identity and his authority to act for the cause which he purports to represent. The State is likewise free to regulate the time and manner of solicitation generally, in the interest of public safety, peace, comfort or convenience. But to condition the solicitation of aid for the perpetuation of religious views or systems upon a license, the grant of which rests in the exercise of a determination by state authority as to what is a religious cause, is to lay a forbidden burden upon the exercise of liberty protected by the Constitution.[100]

Although continuing to uphold the authority of a town to require solicitors to meet identification requirements, the Court in 1976 ruled a New Jersey town ordinance too vague to meet First Amendment standards, and in 1980 it held invalid an Illinois village's ordinance denying the right to solicit funds door-to-door to any group that spent more than a certain percentage on administrative costs. That, the Court said, was an undue infringement upon free speech.[101] This point was subsequently reaffirmed when the Court struck down Maryland and North Carolina laws regulating the professional solicitation of funds.[102]

Membership Solicitations

A Texas law required all labor union organizers to register with the state before soliciting union members there. To test the statute, union organizer R. J. Thomas announced that he would solicit members without registering.

A Texas court issued an order restraining Thomas from addressing an organizing rally without the proper credentials, but he defied the order and was subsequently convicted of contempt. Thomas challenged the registration requirement as violating his right of free speech. The Supreme Court agreed.

MONEY AND POLITICAL SPEECH

When legislators limit the amount anyone can contribute to a candidate or a political campaign or the amount a candidate may spend, they restrict free speech.

After avoiding the issue for years, the Supreme Court in 1976 struck down limits that Congress had imposed on campaign spending.[1] Similar limits upon campaign contributions, however, were upheld. Both provisions were part of the Federal Election Campaign Act of 1974. "A restriction on the amount of money a person or group can spend on political communication during a campaign necessarily reduces the quantity of expression," declared the Court, "by restricting the number of issues discussed, the depth of their exploration and the size of the audience reached. . . . [V]irtually every means of communicating ideas in today's mass society requires the expenditure of money."[2] Acknowledging that the contribution limits also curtailed free speech, the Court found them justified by the government's interest in preventing corruption.

In 1981 a divided Court again upheld contribution limits, in particular a limit of $5,000 per year that an individual or unincorporated association could contribute to a political action committee. But four years later the Court struck down the federal law limiting to $1,000 the amount that a political action committee could spend independently to promote or prevent the election of publicly funded presidential candidates.[3] Justice William H. Rehnquist said that this limit curtailed freedom of speech in the same way as "allowing a speaker in a public hall to express his views while denying him the use of an amplifying system."

In 1978 the Court made clear that corporations also have a right to free speech. Striking down a state law that forbade corporations to spend money to influence voters' decisions on referendum issues, Justice Lewis F. Powell Jr. wrote:

If the speakers here were not corporations, no one would suggest that the State could silence their proposed speech. It is the type of speech indispensable to decisionmaking in a democracy, and this is no less true because the speech comes from a corporation rather than an individual. The inherent worth of the speech in terms of its capacity for informing the public does not depend upon the identity of the source, whether corporation, association, union or individual.[4]

In 1981 the Court struck down a city ordinance limiting to $250 the amount a citizen could contribute to a group taking a position on a ballot issue. This decision reaffirmed a citizen's right to contribute as much as he or she wishes to such a debate.[5] Seven years later the justices unanimously struck down Colorado's law making it a crime to pay persons to circulate petitions to get an issue on the ballot. That, the Court said, violated the First Amendment's protection for political speech.[6] The Court said the law limited the number of voices communicating a political message and diminished the chances of placing an issue on the ballot.

In another case that began in Colorado but involved federal limits on how much political parties could spend on congressional races, the Supreme Court in 1996 ruled that party expenditures cannot be limited when they are made independently of a candidate. By a 7–2 vote, the Court struck down federal limits on "independent expenditures" by political parties on behalf of candidates. The justices fragmented in their reasoning, with no approach commanding a majority. The ruling also skirted the larger question of whether all party spending limits infringe the constitutional guarantee of freedom of speech.[7]

1. *Buckley v. Valeo*, 424 U.S. 1 (1976); see also *United States v. CIO*, 335 U.S. 106 (1948); *United States v. United Auto Workers*, 352 U.S. 567 (1957); *Pipefitters v. United States*, 407 U.S. 385 (1972).

2. *Buckley v. Valeo*, 424 U.S. 1 at 19 (1976).

3. *California Medical Association v. Federal Election Commission*, 453 U.S. 182 (1981); *Federal Election Commission v. National Conservative Political Action Committee*, 470 U.S. 480 (1985); see also *Federal Election Commission v. Massachusetts Citizens for Life*, 479 U.S. 238 (1986).

4. *First National Bank of Boston v. Bellotti*, 435 U.S. 765 at 777 (1978).

5. *Citizens Against Rent Control/Coalition for Fair Housing v. City of Berkeley*, 454 U.S. 290 (1981).

6. *Meyer v. Grant*, 486 U.S. 414 (1988).

7. *Colorado Republican Party v. Federal Election Commission*, _____ U.S._____ (1996).

In the 1945 case of *Thomas v. Collins*, the Court held that the First Amendment clearly protected a speech made to solicit persons for membership in a lawful organization:

That there was restriction upon Thomas' right to speak and the right of the workers to hear what he had to say, there can be no doubt. The threat of the restraining order, backed by the power of contempt, and of arrest for crime, hung over every word. . . . We think a requirement that one must register before he undertakes to make a public speech to enlist support for a lawful movement is quite incompatible with the requirements of the First Amendment.[103]

Doorbells

In 1943 the Court in the case of *Martin v. Struthers* struck down a Struthers, Ohio, ordinance that prohibited all distributors of handbills or other advertisements from knocking on doors or ringing bells to ensure that residents would receive the flyer.

Ignoring this ordinance, a Jehovah's Witness distributed a flyer, which advertised a religious meeting, in a neighborhood where many of the residents were night workers and consequently slept in the daytime. He was arrested and defended himself with the claim that the ordinance was unconstitutional.

The Court agreed by a 5–4 vote. "While door to door distributors of literature may be either a nuisance or a blind for criminal activities, they may also be useful members of society engaged in dissemination of ideas," wrote Justice Black. He enumerated causes that depended on door-to-door solicitation for their success, observing that this form of dissemination of ideas "is essential to the poorly financed causes of little people." The First Amendment prohibited the community from substituting its judgment for that of an individual in determining whether the individual may receive information.

In dissent Justice Reed maintained that the ordinance did not violate any First Amendment right but simply respected a homeowner's privacy:

No ideas are being suppressed. No censorship is involved. The freedom to teach or preach by word or book is unabridged, save only the right to call a householder to the door of his house to receive the summoner's message.[104]

Airport Solicitations

In 1992 the Court, divided 6–3, said airports may forbid individuals and groups to solicit money in air terminals. The case was brought by the Krishnas, a religious group that disseminates religious literature and solicits funds in public places. The group challenged regulations by the Port Authority of New York and New Jersey, which operated three major airports in the New York City area. Airports, the Court ruled, are not traditional forums for public speech, so a solicitations ban need only be reasonable to be upheld. Solicitation may disrupt business by slowing the path of those who are approached for money or who change their paths to avoid being solicited, the justices said. In a separate decision involving the same parties, the Court ruled that the airport authority's ban on the mere distribution of literature in the terminals was invalid.[105]

COMMERCIAL SPEECH

The Supreme Court originally held that commercial speech—advertising or any speech that proposes a commercial transaction—was unprotected by the First Amendment and therefore subject to regulation and even prohibition by the states. But in a series of decisions in the 1970s, the Court changed its view. Finding that commercial speech provides information to which the consuming public has a right, the Court struck down state and local prohibitions of certain advertisements. The Court, however, continued to emphasize that commercial advertising is subject to regulation to prevent false, deceptive, and misleading information.

The result has been a hodgepodge of rulings and inconsistently applied standards for assessing advertising, leading one federal appeals court judge, Alex Kozinski of California, to observe: "The commercial speech doctrine is the stepchild of First Amendment jurisprudence. Liberals don't much like commercial speech because it's commercial; conservatives mistrust it because it's speech. Yet, in a free market economy, the ability to give and receive information about commercial matters may be as important, sometimes more important" than noncommercial expression.[106]

Unprotected Speech

Commercial speech was first discussed by the Court in *Schneider v. Irvington* (1939). The majority ruled that the First Amendment prohibited a city from requiring a person soliciting for religious causes to first obtain permission from city officials. However, the Court cautioned that it was not ruling on whether such a condition would be unconstitutional if applied to commercial solicitation and canvassing.[107]

Schneider was followed by the Court's unanimous opinion in *Valentine v. Chrestensen* (1942), the case that became the early precedent on commercial speech. Here the Court held that the First Amendment did not protect commercial handbills even if one side of a handbill contained a statement protesting the ordinance banning the circulation of commercial handbills:

This Court has unequivocally held that the streets are proper places for the exercise of the freedom of communicating information and disseminating opinion and that, though the states and municipalities may appropriately regulate the privilege in the public interest, they may not unduly burden or proscribe its employment in these public thoroughfares. We are equally clear that the Constitution imposes no such restraint on government as respects purely commercial advertising. Whether, and to what extent, one may promote or pursue a gainful occupation in the streets, to what extent such activity shall be adjudged a derogation of the public right of the user, are matters for legislative judgment.[108]

In a 1951 case salesmen of nationally known magazines claimed that freedom of the press was infringed by ordinances prohibiting door-to-door solicitation for subscriptions without prior consent of the homeowners. The Court rejected the claim. "We agree that the fact that periodicals are sold does not put them beyond the protection of the First Amendment. The selling, however, brings into the transaction a commercial feature," the Court wrote.[109]

Communication of Information

This commercial feature was enough to allow states to bar door-to-door solicitation, but it was not enough to deprive a paid political advertisement of all First Amendment protection. In the landmark libel case of *New York Times v. Sullivan* (1964), the Court held that an advertisement seeking support for the civil rights movement

was not a commercial advertisement in the sense in which the word was used in Chrestensen. It communicated information, expressed opinion, recited grievances, protested claimed abuses, and sought financial support on behalf of a movement whose existence and objectives are matters of the highest public interest. . . . That the *Times* was paid for publishing this advertisement is as immaterial in this connection as is the fact that newspapers and books are sold. . . . Any other conclusion would discourage newspapers from carrying "editorial advertisements" of this type.[110]

This reasoning in the *Times* case was used more than a decade later. In 1975 the Court held that Virginia violated the First Amendment when it punished a local newspaper editor for printing an advertisement concerning the availability of legal abortions in New York. The advertisement did more than propose a commercial transaction, the Court said in *Bigelow v. Virginia*. It conveyed information not only to women who might be interested in seeking an abortion but to people interested in the general issue of whether abortions should be legalized.[111]

The Consumer's Right

The following year, in *Virginia State Board of Pharmacy v. Virginia Citizens Consumer Council Inc.,* the Court majority abandoned its distinction between advertising that publicly conveyed important information and thereby merited some First Amendment protection and advertising that did not.

Agreeing with a lower court that Virginia could not constitu-

PUBLIC EMPLOYEES

Although public employees have the same First Amendment right to speak freely as other Americans, the way they exercise that right may affect or be affected by the fact that they work for the government.

The First Amendment does not protect public employees from dismissal as a result of their complaints about their working conditions or supervisors, the Court held, 5–4, in 1983. In the case of *Connick v. Myers*, the Court said that nothing in the First Amendment requires a public employer to tolerate action that he feels will undermine his authority or the operation of his office.

That same year the Court held that a federal employee demoted for criticizing his agency had rights under the law to claim remedies for such unconstitutional action and therefore did not have the right to bring a damage suit against his employer to protest the demotion.[1]

The Court in *Rankin v. McPherson* (1987) upheld the First Amendment rights of a state police officer. A Texas constable violated those rights when he fired a deputy in 1981 for commenting, "if they go for him again, I hope they get him." The deputy was referring to President Ronald Reagan, who had just been shot but not killed.[2]

Justice Harry A. Blackmun explained that as long as a public employee is not in a confidential, policy-making, or public-contact role, the danger to the agency's successful function from that employee's private speech is minimal. At some point, he wrote, "such concerns are so removed from the effective function of the public employer that they cannot prevail over the free speech rights of the public employee. This is such a case."

The vote was close on this one: 5–4. The dissenters—Chief Justice William H. Rehnquist and Justices Byron R. White, Sandra Day O'Connor, and Antonin Scalia—maintained that "no law enforcement agency is required by the First Amendment to permit one of its employees to 'ride with the cops and cheer for the robbers.'"

In 1994, more than a decade after *Myers,* the Court gave public employees limited procedural rights against being fired for comments they make. The 7–2 ruling in *Waters v. Churchill* forbade the discharge of a government employee because of something the worker said unless the employer has a "reasonable belief" that the comments were disruptive or unrelated to matters of "public concern." The Court was splintered in its rationale, and a majority did not agree on procedures for employers to use before firing employees because of their comments or criticism.[3]

Then in a closely watched 1995 case, the Court struck down a federal law that barred most executive branch workers from earning outside income by giving speeches and writing articles. The honoraria ban had the commendable purpose of preventing influence buying and the appearance of impropriety among government workers. But it had the unconstitutional consequence of restricting the free-speech rights of government workers.

The justices, 6–3, ruled the ban unconstitutional because it applied when neither the subject of a freelance piece nor the person paying for it had any link to the worker's official duties. Writing for the Court, Justice John Paul Stevens emphasized that a ban on payment is effectively a ban on free speech: "Publishers compensate authors because compensation provides a significant incentive toward more expression."[4]

1. *Connick v. Myers,* 461 U.S. 138 (1983); *Bush v. Lucas,* 462 U.S. 367 (1983).
2. *Rankin v. McPherson,* 483 U.S. 378.
3. *Waters v. Churchill,* _____ U.S. _____ (1994).
4. *United States v. National Treasury Employees Union,* 115 S. Ct. 1003 (1995).

---

tionally forbid pharmacists to advertise the prices of prescription drugs, the Court wrote:

> Advertising, however tasteless and excessive it sometimes may seem, is nonetheless dissemination of information as to who is producing and selling what product, for what reason, and at what price. So long as we preserve a predominantly free enterprise economy, the allocation of our resources in large measure will be made through numerous private economic decisions. It is a matter of public interest that those decisions, in the aggregate, be intelligent and well informed. To this end, the free flow of commercial information is indispensable. . . . And if it is indispensable to the proper allocation of resources in a free enterprise system, it is also indispensable to the formation of intelligent opinions as to how that system ought to be regulated or altered. Therefore, even if the First Amendment were thought to be primarily an instrument to enlighten public decisionmaking in a democracy, we could not say that the free flow of information does not serve that goal.[112]

In other words, the ability to obtain drug price information assists consumers in making a multitude of economic decisions, small and large.

In subsequent cases the Court used this reasoning to rule that a state could not prohibit advertisement of contraceptives, advertisement of prices for routine legal services, or the posting of "For Sale" and "Sold" signs in private yards.[113] Using traditional First Amendment tests, the Court found that the right of the public to the commercial information outweighed any interest the government had in suppressing that information.

Since the 1970s, the Court has recognized a corporate right of free speech, first acknowledged in the political arena, and often entwined with commercial speech. *(See box, Money and Political Speech, p. 443.)*

Lawyers' advertising has been the backdrop for several rulings. The Court in 1977 ruled that lawyers could not be stopped from advertising the price of "routine legal services." But the Court has held that the First Amendment was not violated by a state bar's disciplinary action against an attorney who solicited clients in person, for pecuniary gain, under circumstances that posed dangers of fraud, undue influence, and intimidation—all of which was conduct the Court thought the state had a right to prevent.[114] The Court has since ruled that states may regulate advertising by attorneys only to ensure that it is not deceptive or misleading.[115]

Modifying its stance slightly in 1995, a 5–4 majority upheld a Florida regulation that prohibited lawyers from soliciting accident victims by mail for thirty days after an accident.[116] In two other cases, the Court said states may not prohibit lawyers from truthfully advertising themselves as certified public accountants or bar accountants from personally soliciting new clients.[117]

A Question of Government Interests

The prevailing standard for assessing government regulation of commercial speech traces to a 1980 case in which the Court reviewed a New York regulation that banned promotional advertising by an electrical utility. The Court said whether commercial speech will be protected turns on both the nature of the expression and the governmental interest served by the regulation. The Court concluded that a state cannot ban all promotional advertising by a utility—even in light of the state's legitimate interest in energy conservation.[118]

Justice Lewis F. Powell Jr. wrote in that case involving Central Hudson Gas & Electric Corp.:

In commercial speech cases . . . a four-part analysis has developed. At the outset, we must determine whether the expression is protected by the First Amendment. For commercial speech to come within that provision, it at least must concern lawful activity and not be misleading. Next, we ask whether the asserted governmental interest is substantial. If both inquiries yield positive answers, we must determine whether the regulation directly advances the governmental interest asserted, and whether it is not more extensive than is necessary to serve that interest.[119]

The Court in 1980 also held that a state cannot forbid a utility to send out statements of its views on controversial matters of public policy as inserts in customer bills. Six years later it also said that the state cannot force a utility to send out inserts carrying messages with which the company does not agree.[120]

The Court has been more deferential to government regulation of products or activities deemed harmful. It permitted Puerto Rico to ban advertising of gambling within its borders, even though gambling is legal there.[121]

A decade later the Court struck down a Rhode Island ban on the advertisement of retail liquor prices.[122] While the justices were fragmented in their reasoning and did not overturn the 1986 ruling, a majority nonetheless were critical of any government restrictions on truthful, nonmisleading advertising. Justice Stevens, who wrote the principal opinion, said at one point, joined by Justices Kennedy, Souter, and Ginsburg, that regulations that entirely suppress commercial speech for some purpose other than consumer protection must be reviewed with "special care." Joined at another point by Kennedy, Thomas, and Ginsburg, Stevens emphasized that a state cannot justify a ban on advertising related to drinking, smoking, or other possibly harmful activities by a paternalistic impulse to protect its citizens.

FEDERAL MONEY AND FREE SPEECH

The issue was abortion counseling, but the Supreme Court's ruling carried a broader message: if the government is going to pay for a program, it can attach conditions—even ones that curtail the right of free speech.

In the 1991 case of *Rust v. Sullivan*, a five-justice majority upheld congressional language that forbade workers at clinics that received federal funds to advise pregnant women about abortion. The Court said Title X of the Public Health Service Act of 1970 barred not only abortions but also abortion counseling.

Chief Justice William H. Rehnquist wrote the opinion and was joined by Justices Byron R. White, Antonin Scalia, Anthony M. Kennedy, and David H. Souter. In dissent were Justices Harry A. Blackmun, Thurgood Marshall, John Paul Stevens, and Sandra Day O'Connor.

In Title X of the Public Health Service Act, Congress stipulated that no federal funds could be used in "programs where abortion is a method of family planning." The act was passed three years before *Roe v. Wade*, the landmark 1973 ruling that legalized abortions.

During the 1980s, the Reagan administration, consistent with its effort to stem abortions, invoked Title X language to stop abortion counseling at federally funded clinics. The Bush administration continued the practice, and Planned Parenthood and the state and city of New York sued in protest. They contended the statute was written to deny the use of federal money for abortions. They also alleged that the regulations breached the First Amendment rights of physicians and interfered with a woman's right to privacy.

The Supreme Court in *Rust v. Sullivan* rejected both lines of attack. On the First Amendment question, Rehnquist had this to say: "The employees' freedom of expression is limited during the time they actually work for the project; but this limitation is a consequence of their decision to accept employment in a project" the government has financed.[1]

"The government may validly choose to fund childbirth over abortion . . . and . . . 'implement that judgment by the allocation of public funds,'" Rehnquist continued.[2] He said government has no constitutional duty to subsidize an activity because it is constitutionally protected, be it free speech or privacy.

In his dissent, Blackmun maintained that the regulations "impose viewpoint-based restrictions upon protected speech and are aimed at a woman's decision whether to continue or terminate her pregnancy. In both respects, they implicate core constitutional values."[3]

1. *Rust v. Sullivan*, 500 U.S. 173 at 199 (1991).
2. Id. at 201.
3. Id. at 205.

Freedom of the Press

Much of the significance of free speech would be lost if speech could not be freely printed and circulated. Not only is it virtually impossible for individuals to disseminate their views on public matters without help from the press—including, in modern times, the broadcast media, cable television, and on-line information systems—but it is also impossible for individuals otherwise to procure for themselves the information they need to make informed judgments on the conduct of government and other matters of public concern.

Thomas Jefferson spelled out the importance of this informing function in 1787, when he criticized omission of a free press guarantee from the Constitution. Writing from France, where he had been during the Constitutional Convention, Jefferson said:

The people are the only censors of their governors; and even their errors will tend to keep these to the true principles of their institution. To punish these errors too severely would be to suppress the only safeguard of the public liberty. The way to prevent these irregular interpositions of the people is to give them full information of their affairs thru the channel of the public papers, & to contrive that those papers should penetrate the whole mass of the people. The basis of our government being the opinion of the people, the very first object should be to keep that right; and were it left to me to decide whether we should have a government without newspapers or newspapers without a government, I should not hesitate for a moment to prefer the latter.[1]

Nearly two hundred years later Justice Lewis F. Powell Jr. stated the same case for a free press in the context of modern communications:

An informed public depends on accurate and effective reporting by the news media. No individual can obtain for himself the information needed for the intelligent discharge of his political responsibilities. For most citizens the prospect of personal familiarity with newsworthy events is hopelessly unrealistic. In seeking out the news the press therefore acts as an agent of the public at large. It is the means by which the people receive that free flow of information and ideas essential to intelligent self-government. By enabling the public to assert meaningful control over the political process, the press performs a crucial function in effecting the societal purpose of the First Amendment.[2]

The First Amendment is premised on the view that its societal purpose can be achieved only if publishers are free to determine for themselves what they will print. Although the First Amendment is usually thought of in terms of individual freedom, the societal value of a free press is what the Supreme Court has stressed in its decisions.

At the least, the guarantee of freedom of the press means freedom from prior restraint or censorship. At the most, the guarantee also means that governments may not punish the press for what it publishes.

As is true of many other constitutional guarantees, however, only a few justices have taken this absolute view of free press. Most justices have viewed freedom of the press as subject to certain restrictions.

Restrictions and Restraints

The Supreme Court has struck down a number of laws as prior restraints on the press. This list includes statutes that forbade continued publication of malicious criticisms of government officials, prohibited circulation of noncommercial handbills, or placed a discriminatory tax on some newspapers.

In 1971 the Supreme Court rejected a request by the Nixon administration to stop publication of the *Pentagon Papers,* articles about U.S. involvement in Vietnam that were based on classified information. The Court said the government had failed to show sufficient justification for restraining continued publication of the documents. But in that case and others the Court has strongly implied that prior restraints might be permissible under certain extreme circumstances. The Court also has upheld the right of government to regulate certain aspects of publishing, including labor and business practices and the manner and place of distribution of circulars and handbills. These regulations may operate from time to time as prior restraints on the press.

The Court has not guarded the press quite so rigorously against subsequent punishment as against prior restraint. During World War I it upheld the convictions of several persons for publication of articles the Court found in violation of the Espionage Act of 1917 and the Sedition Act of 1918. *(See "Espionage and Sedition," pp. 416–422.)*

Libel, the printed defamation of an individual, was long thought by the Court to be outside the protection of the First Amendment. But in the 1960s the Court began to reverse this posture, extending publishers considerable protection against libel suits brought by public officials and public figures. The Court has held that the First Amendment affords less protection from libel suits brought by private individuals, and little if any when the case does not involve a matter of public concern.

A corollary question faced by the Court is whether the First Amendment protects the press against claims that published articles or broadcast reports have impermissibly interfered with individual privacy. In the few cases it has decided involving this issue, the Court has ruled against the privacy claims unless the claimants could prove that the publisher acted with actual malice or displayed reckless disregard for the truth of the report.

The Court still considers obscene publications to be outside the protection of the First Amendment and subject both to prior restraint and subsequent punishment. The justices, however, have great difficulty in defining what is obscene, and the standard, which has been changed many times, continues to evolve as societal mores change.

In the mid-twentieth century freedom of the press has collided upon occasion with the right to impartial and fair administration of justice. Comprehensive reporting of the workings of the justice system is crucial to its fair administration. But news reports—especially of sensational crimes—may injure a defendant's rights by prejudicing the community against him.

Gag rules are one response of trial judges to this situation. With these rules a trial court restricts the information the press may report about a trial. In 1976 the Court reviewed such a gag order and found it an unconstitutional prior restraint. But the Court has upheld several contempt citations against reporters who defied court-ordered gag rules.

To protect a defendant's right to a fair trial, some judges have excluded the press and the public from pretrial hearings. In 1979 the Supreme Court upheld such an exclusion order, but in 1980 the Court read the First Amendment to guarantee both the press and the public the right to attend trials.

Does the role of the press in a representative government entitle reporters to special access to sources? The Supreme Court has ruled against journalists' arguments that the First Amendment gives them special privileges. Gag rules are just one aspect of this access question. Another aspect—access to prisons to view conditions and interview inmates—has been answered negatively by a majority of the Court.

Confidentiality is a more troubling area. Can reporters be required to divulge their news sources to court officials and other law enforcement officers investigating alleged criminal activities? Reporters contend that their relationship with news sources should be privileged just as are the relationships between doctor and patient, lawyer and client, and husband and wife. But the Court has so far rejected this argument, holding that a reporter has no more constitutional right to withhold information that might help resolve a crime than does an ordinary citizen.

In another ruling disappointing to the press, the Court held that the First Amendment does not require police to use subpoenas instead of search warrants when it seeks evidence of a crime from newspaper offices and files. Congress responded to that ruling by passing a law in 1980 imposing the subpoena requirement.

Prior Restraint: Censorship

Of the effect of censorship on the press, Professor Thomas I. Emerson wrote:

A system of prior restraint is in many ways more inhibiting than a system of subsequent punishment: It is likely to bring under government scrutiny a far wider range of expression; it shuts off communication before it takes place; suppression by a stroke of the pen is more likely to be applied than suppression through a criminal process; the procedures do not require attention to the safeguards of the criminal process; the system allows less opportunity for public appraisal and criticism; the dynamics of the system drive toward excesses, as the history of all censorship shows.[3]

It was a history of excesses that impelled the Founders to add the free press guarantee to the First Amendment. Prior restraint of the press had been widely practiced—and sharply attacked—

in England. Both church and state authorities there had imposed a licensing system on the press from the development of the printing press in the fifteenth century until 1695, when the licensing laws were finally repealed. Indirect censorship through heavy taxation also was common.

Several of the colonies also attempted to censor the press, but these efforts were unpopular and short-lived.

Consequently, when the guarantee of freedom of the press was written it was widely assumed to mean freedom from prior restraint. And, in fact, few prior restraints have been imposed on the press throughout U.S. history.

PUBLIC NUISANCE

Not until 1931 did the Supreme Court review a case of prior restraint of the press. *Near v. Minnesota* concerned a state law that prohibited, as a public nuisance, publication of malicious, scandalous, and defamatory newspapers, magazines, and other publications. The truth of the defamatory allegations was a defense only if the allegations were made with good motive and for justifiable ends.

In 1927 the county attorney for Hennepin County sought an injunction under this statute. The attorney wanted to halt publication of a weekly periodical that had charged that county officials were derelict in their duties regarding a Jewish gangster who ran gambling, bootlegging, and racketeering operations in Minneapolis. The articles charged that the police chief was in collusion with the gangster, that a member of the grand jury investigating the rackets was sympathetic to the gangster, and that the county attorney seeking the injunction had failed to take adequate measures to stop the vice operations. The publication was clearly a scandal sheet, and its managers seemed prejudiced against Jews.

A state court issued a temporary injunction forbidding continued publication of the newspaper. At the ensuing trial it was concluded that the paper had violated the state statute, and a permanent injunction forbidding further publication of the paper was issued. At every opportunity, J. M. Near, the manager of the paper, raised the argument that the law as applied to his paper violated his rights under the Fourteenth Amendment. When the state supreme court affirmed the order for the permanent injunction, Near appealed to the Supreme Court.

By a 5–4 vote the Supreme Court lifted the injunction, holding that the Minnesota statute was an unconstitutional prior restraint on the press in violation of the First and Fourteenth Amendments.

Admittedly, the statute did not operate exactly like the old English licensing laws that required editors to submit all articles to government censors for approval prior to publication, wrote Chief Justice Charles Evans Hughes for the majority. But "if we cut through mere details of procedure," he continued,

the operation and effect of the statute in substance is that public authorities may bring the owner or publisher of a newspaper or periodical before a judge upon a charge of conducting a business of publishing scandalous and defamatory matter—in particular that the matter

The only known photograph of *Saturday Press* editor Jay Near appeared April 19, 1936, in the *Minneapolis Tribune*. Near's successful appeal to the Supreme Court in 1931 marked the first time the Court enforced the First Amendment's guarantee of freedom of the press to strike a state law that imposed a prior restraint on a newspaper.

consists of charges against public officers of official dereliction—and unless the owner or publisher is able and disposed to bring competent evidence to satisfy the judge that the charges are true and are published with good motives and for justifiable ends, his newspaper or periodical is suppressed and further publication is made punishable as a contempt. This is of the essence of censorship.[4]

Acknowledging that freedom of the press from prior restraint was not absolute, Hughes suggested four exceptional situations in which government censorship might be permissible: publication of crucial war information such as the number and location of troops, obscene publications, publications inciting "acts of violence" against the community or violent overthrow of the government, and publications that invade "private rights."

The nature of these exceptions, none of which applied in the pending case, placed "in a strong light the general conception that liberty of the press . . . has meant, principally although not exclusively, immunity from prior restraints or censorship," Hughes wrote.[5]

The passage of time had not lessened the necessity for that immunity, he continued.

While reckless assaults upon public men, and efforts to bring obloquy upon those who are endeavoring faithfully to discharge official duties, exert a baleful influence and deserve the severest condemnation in public opinion, it cannot be said that this abuse is greater, and it is believed to be less, than that which characterized the period in which our institutions took shape. Meanwhile, the administration of government has become more complex, the opportunities for malfeasance and corruption have multiplied, crime has grown to most serious proportions, and the danger of its protection by unfaithful officials and of the impairment of the fundamental security of life and property by criminal alliances and neglect, emphasizes the primary need of a vigilant and courageous press, especially in great cities. The fact that the liberty of the press may be abused by miscreant purveyors of scandal does not make any the less necessary the immunity of the press from previous restraint in dealing with official misconduct. Subsequent punishment for such abuses as may exist is the appropriate remedy, consistent with constitutional privilege.[6]

Hughes said the Minnesota statute could not be justified on the grounds that a publisher might avoid its penalties by showing that the defamatory material was true and printed with good motives and for justifiable ends. This would place the legislature in the position of deciding what were good motives and justifiable ends and thus "be but a step to a complete system of censorship."[7]

Nor was the statute justified because it was intended to prevent scandals that might disturb the public peace and even provoke assaults and the commission of other crimes. "Charges of reprehensible conduct, and in particular of official malfeasance, unquestionably create a public scandal," Hughes wrote, "but the theory of the constitutional guaranty is that even a more serious public evil would be caused by authority to prevent publication."[8]

The four dissenters, in an opinion written by Justice Pierce Butler, contended that the Minnesota law did not "operate as a *previous* restraint . . . within the proper meaning of that phrase." The restraint occurred only after publication of articles adjudged to constitute a public nuisance and served only to pro-

---

THE PRESS AS BUSINESS

When the Court in 1936 struck down certain state taxes on the press as an unconstitutional prior restraint, Justice George Sutherland made clear that the First Amendment does not immunize newspapers from payment of ordinary business taxes.[1] The First Amendment also does not exempt the press from compliance with general laws regulating business and labor relations.

"The publisher of a newspaper has no special immunity from the application of general laws," the Court said in 1937, ruling that the National Labor Relations Act applied to the press.[2] It also held that the press must abide by federal minimum wage and maximum hour standards.[3]

The Court also has held that the press is subject to antitrust laws. In *Associated Press v. United States* (1945), Justice Hugo L. Black said that antitrust laws were vital to preservation of a free press:

The First Amendment, far from providing an argument against application of the Sherman Act, here provides powerful reasons to the contrary. That Amendment rests on the assumption that the widest possible dissemination of information from diverse and antagonistic sources is essential to the welfare of the public, that a free press is a condition of a free society. Surely a command that the government itself shall not impede the free flow of ideas does not afford nongovernment combinations a refuge if they impose restraints upon that constitutionally guaranteed freedom. Freedom to publish means freedom for all and not for some. Freedom to publish is guaranteed . . . but freedom to combine to keep others from publishing is not.[4]

1. *Grosjean v. American Press Company*, 297 U.S. 233 (1936).
2. *Associated Press v. National Labor Relations Board*, 301 U.S. 103 at 132 (1937).
3. *Oklahoma Press Publishing Co. v. Walling*, 327 U.S. 186 (1946).
4. *Associated Press v. United States*, 326 U.S. 1 at 20 (1945). See also *Lorain Journal Co. v. United States*, 342 U.S. 143 (1951); *United States v. Radio Corporation of America*, 358 U.S. 334 (1959); *Citizen Publishing Company v. United States*, 394 U.S. 131 (1969); *United States v. Greater Buffalo Press Inc.*, 402 U.S. 549 (1971).

hibit further illegal publications of the same kind. "There is nothing in the statute purporting to prohibit publications that have not been adjudged to constitute a nuisance," Butler said.[9]

Furthermore, the dissenters thought the threat of subsequent punishment inadequate to protect against this sort of evil. Libel laws are ineffective against false and malicious assaults printed by "insolvent publishers who may have purpose and sufficient capacity to contrive to put into effect a scheme . . . for oppression, blackmail or extortion."[10]

Sixty years later the Court invoked *Near* when it struck down a New York State law that denied criminals the right to any proceeds from any book or article written about their crimes; the law redirected those moneys to a victims' fund. In the case of *Simon & Schuster Inc. v. Members of New York State Crime Victims Board*, the Court held that this "Son-of-Sam" law was too broad in its sweep and thereby violated the First Amendment. Justice O'Connor explained in her opinion that the so-called Son-of-Sam laws are named for a 1977 serial killer in New York, David Berkowitz, who was known popularly as Son of Sam and whose story was worth a substantial amount of money to publishers.

Justice Anthony Kennedy summarized the Court's view in his concurring opinion: "Here a law is directed to speech alone where the speech in question is not obscene, not defamatory, not words tantamount to an act otherwise criminal, not an impairment of some other constitutional right, not an incitement to lawless action, and not calculated or likely to bring about imminent harm the State has the substantive power to prevent. No further inquiry is necessary to reject the State's argument that the statute should be upheld."[11]

RESTRICTIVE TAXATION

The Supreme Court prohibited the use of a more traditional kind of prior restraint in the 1936 case *Grosjean v. American Press Co.*

The Louisiana legislature under the direction of Governor Huey Long placed a state tax of 2 percent on the gross receipts of newspapers that sold advertisements and had circulation in excess of twenty thousand per week. The tax was promoted as a tax on the privilege of doing business, but it had been calculated to affect only nine big city newspapers opposed to the Long regime. The papers immediately sought an injunction in federal district court to stop enforcement of the law on the grounds that the tax violated freedom of the press and, because smaller newspapers were exempt, denied them equal protection.

The federal district court issued the injunction, and a unanimous Supreme Court affirmed that decision solely on First Amendment grounds. The tax "operates as a restraint in a double sense," wrote Justice George Sutherland. "First, its effect is to curtail the amount of revenue realized from advertising, and, second, its direct tendency is to restrict circulation."[12]

Sutherland then reviewed the history of restrictive taxation of the press. The British Parliament had frequently imposed so-called "taxes on knowledge" to suppress criticism of the government. Despite strong opposition, these stamp taxes persisted until 1855.

VENDING RIGHTS

The First Amendment protects the right of newspaper publishers to sell their papers on sidewalk racks, even though the sidewalks are public property, the Court held in the 1988 case of *Lakewood v. Plain Dealer Publishing Co.*[1]

By the narrowest of margins, 4–3, the Court struck down an ordinance enacted by the town of Lakewood, Ohio, which gave the mayor almost total discretion to grant or deny vending rack permits to the *Cleveland Plain Dealer*.

Lakewood and other cities may regulate or license newspaper racks, said Justice William J. Brennan Jr. in the opinion announcing the decision. But they must do so by using neutral criteria to ensure that the decision to grant a license is not based on the content or the point-of-view of the newspaper seeking a license.

Lakewood's procedure left so much discretion to the mayor that it raised a "real and substantial threat of . . . censorship," Brennan said. "It is not difficult to visualize a newspaper . . . feeling significant pressure to endorse the incumbent mayor, . . . or to refrain from criticizing him, in order to receive a favorable and speedy disposition" of its application for a permit to sell papers in sidewalk boxes.

Justices Byron R. White, John Paul Stevens, and Sandra Day O'Connor dissented. Neither Chief Justice William H. Rehnquist nor Justice Anthony Kennedy participated.

In 1993 the Court struck down a Cincinnati ordinance that said newsracks on public property could not be used to distribute commercial handbills; the ordinance, however, permitted newspapers to be sold from sidewalk vending machines.[2] Writing for a six-justice majority, Justice Stevens said the city had failed to show a "reasonable fit" between the ordinance and its interest in "the safety and attractive appearance of its streets and sidewalks."

The dissenting justices, Rehnquist, White, and Clarence Thomas, argued that the city's selective ban on commercial newsracks was permitted by the lower degree of constitutional protection for commercial speech. (*See "Commercial Speech," pp. 444–446.*)

1. *Lakewood v. Plain Dealer Publishing Co.*, 486 U.S. 750 (1988).
2. *City of Cincinnati v. Discovery Network*, 507 U.S. 410 (1993).

Massachusetts in 1785 and 1786 imposed both a stamp tax and an advertising tax on newspapers and magazines, but hostility to the taxes was so strong that they were quickly repealed. Given this background, Sutherland said, the Framers of the First Amendment must have meant to prohibit the imposition of such taxes. He continued:

The predominant purpose of the grant of immunity here invoked was to preserve an untrammeled press as a vital source of public information. The newspapers, magazines and other journals of the country, it is safe to say, have shed and continue to shed, more light on the public and business affairs of the nation than any other instrumentality of publicity; and since informed public opinion is the most potent of all restraints upon misgovernment, the suppression or abridgement of the publicity afforded by a free press cannot be regarded otherwise than with grave concern. The tax here involved is bad not because it takes money from the pockets of the . . . [newspapers]. If that were all, a wholly different question would be presented. It is bad because, in the light of its history and of its present setting, it is seen to be a deliberate and calculated device in the guise of a tax to limit the circulation of information to which the public is entitled in virtue of the constitutional guaranties: A free press stands as one of the great interpreters between the government and the people. To allow it to be fettered is to fetter ourselves.[13]

HANDBILLS

The Supreme Court has always considered handbills, leaflets, circulars, and other types of flyers containing an individual or group opinion on public issues to be a part of the press entitled to First Amendment protection.

Chief Justice Hughes voiced this principle in 1938:

The liberty of the press is not confined to newspapers and periodicals. It necessarily embraces pamphlets and leaflets. These indeed have been historic weapons in the defense of liberty, as the pamphlets of Thomas Paine and others in our own history abundantly attest. The press in its historic connotation comprehends every sort of publication which affords a vehicle of information and opinion.[14]

Consequently, the Court has been unsympathetic to efforts of municipalities to restrict distribution of handbills on public property. The arguments that some restriction is necessary to protect the public from fraud or to keep the streets clean have not been considered sufficient to justify the resulting infringement on the freedoms of speech and press. The Court has only limited distribution of noncommercial handbills when distribution has occurred on private property dedicated to specific public purposes. *(See box, Public Speech on Private Property, pp. 440–441.)*

The Lovell Case

The first test of a city ordinance controlling distribution of handbills came in the 1938 case of *Lovell v. Griffin*. Alma Lovell, a Jehovah's Witness, distributed religious tracts in Griffin, Georgia, in violation of an ordinance that prohibited circulation of literature without written permission. The Court struck down the ordinance as a prior restraint on the press. Chief Justice Hughes wrote:

THE COMMAND TO PUBLISH

Freedom of the press means that government may not stop the press from printing nor command it to print. The Supreme Court has found only one exception to the rule that government may not dictate the form or content of what the press prints: gender-based advertisements for help.

THE "HELP-WANTED" CASE

In 1973 the Court upheld a government order to a newspaper forbidding it to place help-wanted advertisements under columns labeled "Jobs—Male Interest" and "Jobs—Female Interest" in violation of an ordinance that prohibited discrimination by sex in employment. The Court reached that decision in *Pittsburgh Press Co. v. Pittsburgh Commission on Human Relations* by a 5–4 vote.

The majority explained that the help-wanted ads were commercial speech unprotected by the First Amendment and that the column heads added by the newspaper were indistinguishable from that speech. *(See "Commercial Speech," pp. 444–446.)* Even if commercial speech merited First Amendment protection, the majority said, illegal commercial speech did not:

The advertisements, as embroidered by their placement, signaled that the advertisers were likely to show an illegal sex preference in their hiring decisions. Any First Amendment interest which might be served by advertising an ordinary commercial proposal and which might arguably outweigh the governmental interest supporting the regulation is altogether absent when the commercial activity itself is illegal and the restriction on advertising is incidental to a valid limitation on economic activity.[1]

THE RIGHT OF REPLY

In a decision handed down the following year, the Court emphasized the narrowness of the *Pittsburgh Press* holding when it struck down a Florida statute that required newspapers to grant political candidates equal space to reply to the paper's criticism of their public records.

Writing for a unanimous Court in *Miami Herald Publishing Co. v. Tornillo* (1974), Chief Justice Warren E. Burger carefully reviewed the arguments in favor of the law, while acknowledging that the diminishing number of newspapers and the concentration of media ownership meant that frequently only one view of an issue was published.

"Chains of newspapers, national newspapers, national wire and news services, and one-newspaper towns are the dominant features of a press that has become noncompetitive and enormously powerful and influential in its capacity to manipulate popular opinion and change the course of events," he wrote.[2]

But a governmental command to print specific information collides with the freedom of the press guaranteed by the First Amendment, he said, and under the decisions of the Court

any such compulsion to publish that which "'reason' tells them should not be published" is unconstitutional. A responsible press is an undoubtedly desirable goal, but press responsibility is not mandated by the Constitution and like many other virtues it cannot be legislated.[3]

In conclusion, Burger wrote:

A newspaper is more than a passive receptacle or conduit for news, comment and advertising. The choice of material to go into a newspaper, and the decisions made as to limitations on the size and content of the paper, and treatment of public issues and public officials—whether fair or unfair—constitute the exercise of editorial control and judgment. It has yet to be demonstrated how governmental regulation of this crucial process can be exercised consistent with First Amendment guarantees of a free press as they have evolved to this time.[4]

1. *Pittsburgh Press Co. v. Pittsburgh Commission on Human Relations*, 413 U.S. 376 at 389 (1973).
2. *Miami Herald Publishing Co. v. Tornillo*, 418 U.S. 241 at 249 (1974).
3. Id. at 256.
4. Id. at 258.

OBSCENITY: AN ELUSIVE DEFINITION . . . AND A CHANGING STANDARD

The Supreme Court has never considered obscenity to be protected by the First Amendment. Obscenity is one category of expression that is unprotected because it is "no essential part of any exposition of ideas, and of . . . slight social value as a step to truth."[1]

But to place obscenity outside the protection of the First Amendment does not end the matter. It only shifts the focus of judicial effort to the problem of defining what is obscene.

The problem has proved frustrating. The only criterion the Court has consistently agreed upon is that to be obscene, material must deal with sex. Blasphemous or sacrilegious expression is not considered obscene, nor, generally, are scatological profanities. Violence has been found obscene only when linked with sex.

As Justice John Marshall Harlan explained when the Court ruled that the phrase "Fuck the Draft" on a jacket worn in a courthouse was not obscene: "Whatever else may be necessary to give rise to the States' broader power to prohibit obscene expression, such expression must be, in some significant way, erotic."[2]

Most state laws restricting the dissemination of obscene materials date back to the Victorian era. The earliest standard for obscenity, stated by a British court in *Regina v. Hicklin* (1868), was "whether the tendency of the matter charged as obscenity is to deprave and corrupt those whose minds are open to such immoral influences and into whose hands a publication of this sort may fall."[3]

As Thomas I. Emerson observed, the *Hicklin* test "brought within the ban of the obscenity statutes any publication containing isolated passages that the courts felt would tend to exert an immoral influence on susceptible persons."[4]

By the 1930s that standard was being rejected as too rigid. In 1934 appeals court judge Augustus Hand proposed a new standard:

While any construction of the statute that will fit all cases is difficult, we believe that the proper test of whether a given book is obscene is in its dominant effect. In applying this test, relevancy of the objectionable parts to the theme, the established reputation of the work in the estimation of approved critics, if the book is modern, and the verdict of the past, if it is ancient, are persuasive pieces of evidence; for works of art are not likely to sustain a high position with no better warrant for their existence than their obscene content.[5]

THE *ROTH* STANDARD

The Supreme Court did not express any opinion on a definition of obscenity until 1957 when, in one ruling, it considered both a federal and state obscenity law. *Roth v. United States* concerned a federal statute making it a crime to mail materials that were "obscene, lewd, lascivious or filthy." *Alberts v. California* concerned a state law making it illegal to publish, sell, distribute, or advertise any "obscene or

indecent" material. The majority relied heavily on Judge Hand's test in drawing up what became known as the *"Roth* standard."

Obscene matter, declared the Court, has no First Amendment protection. Justice William J. Brennan Jr. wrote:

All ideas having even the slightest redeeming social importance—unorthodox ideas, controversial ideas, even ideas hateful to the prevailing climate of opinion—have the full protection of the guaranties, unless excludable because they encroach upon the limited area of more important interests. But implicit in the history of the First Amendment is the rejection of obscenity as utterly without redeeming social importance.[6]

Brennan then proposed a definition of obscenity:

[S]ex and obscenity are not synonymous. Obscene material is material which deals with sex in a manner appealing to prurient interest. The portrayal of sex, e.g., in art, literature, and scientific works is not itself sufficient reason to deny material the constitutional protection of freedom of speech and press. . . . It is therefore vital that the standards for judging obscenity safeguard the protection of freedom of speech and press for material which does not treat sex in a manner appealing to prurient interest.[7]

The standard for making this determination, Brennan said, was "whether to the average person, applying contemporary standards, the dominant theme of the material taken as a whole appeals to the prurient interest."[8]

Finding that the trial courts in *Roth* and *Albert* had applied this standard to hold the material in question obscene, the majority upheld convictions under both the federal and state laws.

After *Roth* the Court grew increasingly fragmented on what makes material obscene. In a 1962 case, *Manual Enterprises v. Day,* Justice Harlan held that, to be obscene, material must not only appeal to prurient interest but also be patently offensive. That is, he wrote, obscene materials are those "so offensive on their face as to affront current community standards of decency."[9] Because the case involved a federal obscenity statute, Harlan thought the community and the standards of decency should be national in scope.

Two years later in *Jacobellis v. Ohio* (1964), Justice Brennan added the requirement that the materials in question must be found "utterly without redeeming social importance."[10] Justice Stewart added in a concurrence in *Jacobellis* that while obscenity is hard to define, "I know it when I see it."[11]

The height of confusion over a definition of obscenity was reached one day in 1966 when the Court, deciding three cases, issued fourteen separate opinions. In one case the Court ruled that the book *Fanny Hill* was not obscene. The threefold test to be applied was that the dominant theme of the book must appeal to

---

The ordinance prohibits the distribution of literature of any kind at any time, at any place, and in any manner without a permit from the City Manager. . . . Whatever the motive which induced its adoption, its character is such that it strikes at the very foundation of the freedom of the press by subjecting it to license and censorship.[15]

The Handbill Cases

In cases considered together in 1939, the Court struck down four ordinances seeking to regulate handbill circulation. The

first of these cases, *Schneider v. Irvington,* again involved a Jehovah's Witness who was convicted of canvassing and distributing religious tracts without the required permit. The Court held that the ordinance, as in *Lovell,* left too much to official discretion.

In the other three cases the Court held unconstitutional ordinances that prohibited all distribution of handbills on public streets.[16]

ctrlρ

prurient interest, that the book must be found patently offensive when judged by contemporary community standards, and that it must be found utterly without redeeming social value. Because the trial court had found that the book might have "some minimal literary value," it was not obscene.[12]

In the second case the Court came up with the "pandering" test: material that might not be obscene on its own merits might become so if it was placed "against a background of commercial exploitation of erotica solely for the sake of their prurient appeal."[13]

Then the Court retreated, indicating in a 1967 *per curiam* opinion in *Redrup v. New York* that it would sustain obscenity convictions only to protect juveniles or unwilling adults from exposure to obscene materials or in cases of pandering.[14]

THE *MILLER* STANDARD

In 1973, for the first time since the 1957 *Roth* decision, a slim majority of the Court endorsed a standard for determining what was obscene. This new standard gave governments at all levels much more latitude to ban obscene materials than did the *Roth* test.

Writing for the five-justice majority in *Miller v. California*, Chief Justice Warren E. Burger held that states could regulate

works which depict or describe sexual conduct. That conduct must be specifically defined by the applicable state law, as written or authoritatively construed. A state offense must also be limited to works which, taken as a whole, appeal to the prurient interest in sex, which portray sexual conduct in a patently offensive way, and which, taken as a whole, do not have serious literary, artistic, political or scientific value.[15]

Under this standard, Burger said, the majority intended to exclude only hard-core materials from First Amendment protection.

As a guideline, he suggested that such materials were those that included "patently offensive representations or descriptions of ultimate sexual acts, normal or perverted, actual or simulated" and "patently offensive representations or descriptions of masturbation, excretory functions, and lewd exhibition of the genitals."[16]

The majority specifically rejected the *Jacobellis* test that to be obscene, materials must be "utterly without redeeming social value." It also rejected the idea that the community standard must be national in scope. "It is neither realistic nor constitutionally sound to read the First Amendment as requiring that the people of Maine or Mississippi accept public depiction of conduct found tolerable in Las Vegas or New York City," Burger wrote.[17]

The majority stressed that First Amendment values would be adequately protected by this standard. Burger noted that appellate courts had the authority to "conduct an independent review of constitutional claims when necessary."[18]

The Court did just that when it overturned a Georgia jury's finding that the movie "Carnal Knowledge" was obscene. Holding that local juries did not have "unbridled discretion" to determine what is patently offensive, the Court in *Jenkins v. Georgia* (1974) found nothing in the movie that fit its *Miller* standards for what might constitute hard-core obscenity.[19] Subsequently, the Court upheld state laws prohibiting the promotion of sexual performances by children but struck down a state law banning material just because it incited lust. That covered material that did no more than "arouse 'good, old-fashioned, healthy' interest in sex."[20]

In 1982 the Court held that the First Amendment limited the power of public school officials to take books off the library shelves because some parents found the contents objectionable.[21]

But four years later the Court held that the First Amendment was not abridged when school officials suspended a student for a lewd speech at a school assembly. "It is a highly appropriate function of public school education to prohibit the use of vulgar and offensive terms in public discourse," the Court declared.[22]

In *Pope v. Illinois* (1987) the Court revisited the *Miller* test for "literary, artistic, political, or scientific value." The Court declared that local community standards should not be used in deciding whether an allegedly obscene book or film has any such value. Instead, an objective, national standard should be used, with the overriding question being whether a reasonable person would find value in the material, taken as a whole.[23]

1. *Chaplinsky v. New Hampshire*, 315 U.S. 568 at 572 (1942).
2. *Cohen v. California*, 403 U.S. 15 at 20 (1971).
3. *Regina v. Hicklin*, L.R. 3 Q.B. 360 at 371 (1868), quoted in Thomas I. Emerson, *The System of Freedom of Expression* (New York: Random House, Vintage Books, 1970), 469.
4. Emerson, *System*, 469.
5. *United States v. One Book Entitled "Ulysses,"* 72 F.2d. 705 at 708 (2d Cir. 1934).
6. *Roth v. United States, Alberts v. California*, 354 U.S. 476 at 484 (1957).
7. Id. at 487–488.   8. Id. at 489.
9. *Manual Enterprises v. Day*, 370 U.S. 478 at 482 (1962).
10. *Jacobellis v. Ohio*, 378 U.S. 184 at 191 (1964).
11. Id. at 197.
12. *A Book Named "John Cleland's Memoirs of a Woman of Pleasure" [Fanny Hill] v. Attorney General of Massachusetts*, 383 U.S. 413 at 419 (1966).
13. *Ginzburg v. United States*, 383 U.S. 463 at 466 (1966); the third case was *Mishkin v. New York*, 383 U.S. 502 (1966).
14. *Redrup v. New York*, 386 U.S. 767 (1967).
15. *Miller v. California*, 413 U.S. 15 at 24 (1973).
16. Id. at 25.   17. Id. at 32.
18. Id. at 25.
19. *Jenkins v. Georgia*, 418 U.S. 153 (1974).
20. *New York v. Ferber*, 458 U.S. 747 (1982); *Brockett v. Spokane Arcades, Eikenberry v. J-R Distributors*, 472 U.S. 491 (1985).
21. *Board of Education, Island Trees Union Free School District #26 v. Pico*, 457 U.S. 853 (1982).
22. *Bethel School District No. 403 v. Fraser*, 478 U.S. 675 (1986).
23. *Pope v. Illinois*, 481 U.S. 497 (1987).

In *Schneider*, Justice Owen J. Roberts attempted to explain how a city might properly regulate circulation of handbills:

Municipal authorities, as trustees for the public, have the duty to keep their communities' streets open and available for movement of people and property, the primary purpose to which the streets are dedicated. So long as legislation to this end does not abridge the constitutional liberty of one rightfully upon the street to impart information through speech or the distribution of literature, it may lawfully regulate the conduct of those using the streets. For example, a person could not exercise this liberty by taking his stand in the middle of a crowded street, contrary to traffic regulations, and maintain his position to the stoppage of all traffic; a group of distributors could not insist upon a constitutional right to form a cordon across the street and to allow no pedestrian to pass who did not accept a tendered leaflet; nor does the guarantee of freedom of speech or of the press deprive a municipality of power to enact regulations against throwing literature broadcast in the streets. Prohibition of such conduct would not abridge the constitutional liberty since such activity bears no necessary relationship to the freedom to speak, write, print or distribute information or opinion.[17]

The desire to prevent litter was not a sufficient reason to limit circulation of handbills, the Court held. Cities could prevent litter by other methods.

Responding to the argument that cities should be permitted to prohibit the dissemination of handbills in public streets so long as other public places were available for distribution, Roberts wrote that "one is not to have the exercise of his liberty of expression in appropriate places abridged on the plea that it may be exercised in some other place."[18]

Anonymous Handbills

In 1960 the Supreme Court struck down a Los Angeles ordinance that required all handbills to include the name and address of the person preparing, sponsoring, or distributing them. "There can be no doubt that such an identification requirement would tend to restrict freedom to distribute information and thereby freedom of expression," wrote Justice Hugo L. Black in *Talley v. California*.[19] Throughout history, he observed, persecuted groups and sects have had to resort to anonymous criticism of oppressive practices to avoid further persecutions.

Three justices dissented, maintaining that the Court should weigh the state's interest in preventing fraud against the individual's claimed rights.

In another decision on the side of pamphleteers, *McIntyre v. Ohio Elections Commission* (1995), the Court invalidated an Ohio prohibition on anonymous campaign literature. The Court said that part of an individual's freedom of speech is the freedom to remain anonymous. The vote was 7–2, and Justice John Paul Stevens, writing for the majority, praised the U.S. tradition of pamphleteering: "Under our Constitution, anonymous pamphleteering is not a pernicious, fraudulent practice, but an honorable tradition of advocacy and of dissent. Anonymity is a shield from the tyranny of the majority."[20]

Injunctions

In a 1971 case, *Organization for a Better Austin v. Keefe*, the Supreme Court ruled that a temporary injunction against the publication of certain handbills was an unconstitutional abridgment of the freedoms of speech and press. An organization that sought to maintain the racial make-up of its neighborhood grew upset with the tactics real estate agent Keefe used to induce whites to sell their homes to blacks. After Keefe denied the allegations and refused to cooperate with the association, it began to circulate handbills in Keefe's neighborhood describing what it considered to be his unsavory real estate activities. Keefe then sought and was granted the injunction.

The Supreme Court held that "the injunction, so far as it imposes prior restraint on speech and publication, constitutes an impermissible restraint on First Amendment rights." The aim of the organization in circulating the handbills—namely, to coerce Keefe into cooperation with it—was "not fundamentally differ-

ent from the function of a newspaper," the majority said. Nor could the injunction be justified as protecting Keefe's privacy. Keefe was "not attempting to stop the flow of information into his own household, but to the public."[21]

ELECTION-DAY EDITORIALS

The basic need to protect free discussion of government lay at the heart of the Court's 1966 decision to strike down an Alabama statute that made it a crime to solicit votes on election day.

A newspaper editor who printed an editorial on election day urging his readers to vote a certain way on a ballot proposition was convicted under this law. A statute setting criminal penalties "for publishing editorials such as the one here silences the press at a time when it can be most effective," wrote Justice Black for the majority in *Mills v. Alabama*. "It is difficult to conceive of a more obvious and flagrant abridgment of the constitutionally guaranteed freedom of the press."[22]

THE *PENTAGON PAPERS*

Publication in June 1971 of articles based upon a classified history of U.S. involvement in Vietnam precipitated an unprecedented confrontation between the U.S. government and the press.

The forty-seven-volume, seven-thousand-page history, which soon became known as the "Pentagon Papers," covered the Truman, Eisenhower, Kennedy, and Johnson administrations. It indicated that the U.S. government was more involved in the Vietnamese civil war at almost every stage than U.S. officials had ever publicly admitted.

Copies of the *Pentagon Papers* were made available to the press by Daniel Ellsberg, an analyst who had helped prepare the history and then had become an antiwar activist.

The *New York Times* was the first newspaper to publish articles based on the papers; the first installment appeared in its June 13, 1971, edition. The following day, after the second installment appeared, the Justice Department asked the *Times* to return the documents and to halt publication of the series. The articles, they said, would cause "irreparable injury to the defense interests of the U.S." The *Times* refused to comply.

On June 15 U.S. District Court judge Murray I. Gurfein granted the temporary restraining order requested by the Justice Department against the *Times*. He put the order in effect until he could hold hearings on the government's request for a permanent injunction.

After the hearings, Gurfein ruled June 19 that the government was not entitled to a permanent injunction against publication by the *Times* of further articles. But Judge Irving R. Kaufman of the U.S. Court of Appeals immediately granted a restraining order against the *Times*, at the Justice Department's request, to permit the government to appeal Judge Gurfein's decision. The appeals court June 23 returned the case to the lower court for further secret hearings, and it extended until June 25 a restraining order against the *Times*. The *Times* on June 24 petitioned the Supreme Court to review the order by the Court of Appeals.

The government also sought to restrain the *Washington Post*, which had published its first *Pentagon Papers* article June 18, from further publications. The *Post* case arrived at the Supreme Court through an involved succession of hearings and temporary restraining orders similar to those in the *Times* case. However, both the district court and the court of appeals in Washington refused the Justice Department's request for a permanent injunction against the *Post*. The government appealed on June 24.

The Court heard arguments on June 26 and announced its decision four days later. By a 6–3 vote, the Court June 30 ruled that the government had failed to meet "the heavy burden of showing justification" for restraining further publications of the *Pentagon Papers*.[23]

Each of the nine justices wrote a separate opinion. Taken together, these opinions covered the wide range of sentiment that exists when a First Amendment right must be weighed against national security claims.

The Majority

In separate concurring opinions Justices Black and William O. Douglas maintained that freedom of the press was absolute and could not be abridged by the government under any circumstances.

"[E]very moment's continuance of the injunctions against these newspapers amounts to a flagrant, indefensible, and continuing violation of the First Amendment," Black asserted in the last opinion he wrote before his retirement. "Both the history and language of the First Amendment support the view that the press must be left free to publish news, whatever the source, without censorship, injunctions or prior restraints."[24]

Douglas wrote: "The First Amendment provides that 'Congress shall make no law . . . abridging the freedom of speech or of the press.' That leaves, in my view, no room for governmental restraint on the press."[25]

Justice William J. Brennan Jr. thought the government might properly restrain the press in certain clear emergencies. But the circumstances of this case did not present such an emergency, Brennan said, and there should have been no injunctive restraint. The government sought the injunction on the grounds that the publication "could," "might," or "may" damage national security, Brennan said. "But the First Amendment tolerates absolutely no prior judicial restraints of the press predicated upon surmise or conjecture that untoward consequences may result."[26]

Justices Potter Stewart and Byron R. White both thought that prior restraints might be permissible under certain conditions and that disclosure of some of the information in the *Pentagon Papers* might be harmful to national interests. "But I cannot say that disclosure of any of them [the papers] will surely result in direct, immediate, and irreparable damage to our Nation or its people," concluded Stewart. "That being so, there can under the

First Amendment be but one judicial resolution of the issues before us."[27]

White said he concurred with the majority "only because of the concededly extraordinary protection against prior restraints enjoyed by the press under our constitutional system." The government's position, White said, is that the necessity to preserve national security is so great that the president is entitled to an injunction against publication of a newspaper story whenever he can convince a court that the information to be revealed threatens "grave and irreparable" injury to the public interest; and the injunction should issue whether or not . . . publication would be lawful . . . and regardless of the circumstances by which the newspaper came into possession of the information.

At least in the absence of legislation by Congress . . . I am quite unable to agree that the inherent powers of the Executive and the courts reach so far as to authorize remedies having such a sweeping potential for inhibiting publications by the press.[28]

PRIOR RESTRAINT OF OBSCENITY

In *Near v. Minnesota* (1931) the Supreme Court indicated that obscenity was one form of expression that might be subject to prior restraint.

Twenty-six years later a majority of five justices upheld, against a challenge of unconstitutional prior restraint, a New York statute that allowed public officials to seek injunctions against the sale of obscene publications.

Contrary to the discussion in *Near*, the majority indicated that the First Amendment might protect even obscene publications from licensing or censorship before publication. But this challenged statute was not such a prior restraint. Instead, the majority said, it "studiously withholds restraint upon matters not already published and not yet found to be offensive." As such it was a valid means "for the seizure and destruction of the instruments of ascertained wrongdoing."[1]

In another 5–4 decision, the Court upheld a Chicago ordinance that prohibited public showings of movies found to be obscene. In *Times Film Corp. v. City of Chicago* (1961), the majority held that the doctrine of prior restraint was not absolute and that the censorship procedure was a valid means for controlling the dissemination of obscene movies. In dissent Chief Justice Earl Warren said the majority decision "gives formal sanction to censorship in its purest and most far-reaching form."[2]

In 1965 the Court limited the impact of this decision by prescribing strict rules authorities must follow when censoring films. The burden of proving the film obscene falls on the censor, who must license it quickly or seek a restraining order in court. Furthermore, the process must "assure a prompt final judicial decision." The Court has been consistent in enforcing these procedural safeguards.[3]

1. *Kingsley Books v. Brown*, 354 U.S. 436 at 445, 444 (1957).
2. *Times Film Corp. v. City of Chicago*, 365 U.S. 43 at 55 (1961).
3. *Freedman v. Maryland*, 380 U.S. 51 at 59 (1965); see also *Southeastern Promotions, Ltd. v. Conrad*, 420 U.S. 546 (1975); *Roaden v. Kentucky*, 413 U.S. 496 (1973).

The critical factor for Justice Thurgood Marshall was that Congress had twice refused to give the president authority to prohibit publications disclosing matters of national security or to make such disclosures criminal. It would be a violation of the doctrine of separation of powers, Marshall said,

for this Court to use its power of contempt to prevent behavior that Congress has specifically declined to prohibit. . . . The Constitution provides that Congress shall make laws, the President execute laws, and courts interpret law. . . . It did not provide for government by injunction in which the courts and the Executive can "make law" without regard to the action of Congress.[29]

The Dissenters

Chief Justice Warren E. Burger and Justices John Marshall Harlan and Harry A. Blackmun dissented. All three lamented the haste with which the cases had been decided. Holding that the press did not enjoy absolute protection from prior restraint, Burger said that the exception which might permit restraint "may be lurking in these cases and would have been flushed had they been properly considered in the trial courts, free from unwarranted deadlines and frenetic pressures."[30]

Burger also thought the newspapers had been derelict in their duty to report the discovery of stolen property or secret government documents. That duty "rests on taxi drivers, Justices and the *New York Times*," he said.[31]

Justice Harlan listed a number of questions that he said should and would have been considered if the cases had been deliberated more fully. On the merits of the cases, the judiciary should not "redetermine for itself the probable impact of disclosure on the national security."[32]

Therefore, Harlan would have sent the cases back to the lower courts for further proceedings, during which time he would have permitted the temporary restraining orders to remain in effect. Harlan said he could "not believe that the doctrine prohibiting prior restraints reaches to the point of preventing courts from maintaining the *status quo* long enough to act responsibly in matters of such national importance."[33]

In his dissent, Justice Blackmun wrote:

The First Amendment, after all, is only one part of the entire Constitution. Article II . . . vests in the Executive Branch primary power over the conduct of foreign affairs. . . . Each provision of the Constitution is important and I cannot subscribe to a doctrine of unlimited absolutism for the First Amendment at the cost of downgrading other provisions. . . . What is needed here is a weighing, upon properly developed standards, of the broad right of the press to print and of the very narrow right of the government to prevent.[34]

The three dissenters and Stewart and White from the majority indicated that they believed the newspapers might be subject to criminal penalties for publishing classified government documents. But the question never arose. The government's prosecution of Ellsberg for espionage, theft, and conspiracy for leaking the papers was dismissed because of government misconduct. (Four members of a secret White House investigative team burglarized the office of Ellsberg's psychiatrist in an effort to find Ellsberg's records, presumably to use against him in the *Pentagon Papers* case.) The government brought no further prosecutions.

Subsequent Punishment: Libel

Libel occurs when something printed or broadcast defames the character or reputation of an individual. The effort to punish publishers for printing defamatory statements can be traced back to England, where state and church authorities suppressed criticism of their policies, calling it sedition.

It is not certain whether the First Amendment guarantee of a free press was intended to prohibit Congress from enacting similar seditious libel laws. Whatever the case, the Federalist-dominated Congress enacted a libel law in 1789, but it proved extremely unpopular and was allowed to expire. Although the validity of the law was never tested, later justices assumed it was unconstitutional.[35]

In any event, Congress has never again enacted a law making general criticism of government officials and their conduct unlawful. It is now well accepted that criticism of government policies and officials is protected by the First Amendment, although specific types of criticism may be punishable. The Sedition Act of 1918, for example, set penalties for interfering with the war effort, and the Smith Act of 1940 punished those who conspired to advocate overthrow of the government. Both types of conduct are considered outside the protection of the First Amendment.

CIVIL LIBEL

When anyone is libeled, the question arises as to the proper balance between the need for open discussion of public issues and personalities and the need of individuals for protection against false, irresponsible, and malicious publications.

Certain public figures—judges, legislators, and executive officials—enjoy absolute immunity from libel suits. Certain professionals, such as doctors and lawyers, enjoy a more limited or qualified immunity, but publishers historically have been liable to damage suits.

Libelous publications include those that charge that an individual is guilty of a criminal offense, carries a dread disease such as leprosy or AIDS (acquired immune deficiency syndrome), is incompetent in his or her profession or, if a public official, is guilty of misconduct.

In the United States, truth is a defense to libel. But truth can be expensive to prove. And when the truth involves a matter of judgment, as in a political opinion, it may be impossible to prove. Placing this burden of proof on publishers can lead to self-censorship, a hesitancy to print information about public officials and others influential in public life. Such self-censorship impairs the societal function of the press in a democratic system.

Cognizant of this restrictive impact, several states early in the twentieth century began to enact laws protecting publishers

FREEDOM TO CIRCULATE

"Liberty of circulating is as essential to that freedom [of the press] as liberty of publishing; indeed, without the circulation, the publication would be of little value," the Supreme Court said as early as 1878.[1]

But in that case and others, the Court nonetheless upheld the right of Congress to prohibit the use of the mails to circulate materials considered injurious to public morals.

Circulation through the mails of publications espousing unpopular political opinions and doctrines also has been restricted. During the two world wars the government permitted the postmaster general to withdraw second-class mailing privileges from publications that violated the espionage laws.

In 1921 the Court upheld this delegation of authority when it sustained the postmaster general's withdrawal of second-class mail rates from the Socialist newspaper *Milwaukee Leader* without directly addressing the First Amendment questions implied in the case.[2]

The Court appeared more willing to protect publications that clearly posed no threat to national security. In 1946 it ruled that the postmaster general had exceeded his authority when he withdrew second-class mail privileges from *Esquire* magazine because he determined the magazine's contents fell outside the matter eligible for the special mailing rates. The Court said that Congress had authorized the postmaster general to decide only whether publications contained "information of a public character, literature or art" and not "whether the contents meet some standard of the public good or welfare."[3]

The Court also extended some protection to dissident publications in 1965 when it struck down a 1962 federal statute permitting the postmaster general to deliver "Communist political propaganda" only at the recipient's specific request.[4]

Because obscenity has no First Amendment protection, the Court has consistently sustained federal statutes restricting its dissemination. In 1957 the Court upheld a law prohibiting the mailing of obscene materials, and in 1970 it sustained a federal statute allowing individuals to request the post office not to deliver them obscene materials.[5]

In other cases the Supreme Court has upheld the right of Congress to bar the importation of obscene matter and to prohibit the transport of such matter by common carrier through interstate commerce.[6] But in 1983 the Court unanimously struck down a federal law barring the mailing of unsolicited ads for contraceptives.[7]

1. *Ex parte Jackson*, 96 U.S. 727 at 733 (1878); see also *In re Rapier*, 143 U.S. 110 (1892).
2. *United States ex rel. Milwaukee Social Democratic Publishing Co. v. Burleson*, 255 U.S. 407 (1921).
3. *Hannegan v. Esquire*, 327 U.S. 146 at 158–159 (1946).
4. *Lamont v. Postmaster General*, 381 U.S. 301 (1965).
5. *Roth v. United States*, 354 U.S. 476 (1957); *Rowan v. Post Office Department*, 397 U.S. 728 (1970).
6. *United States v. Thirty-seven Photographs*, 402 U.S. 363 (1971); *United States v. 12 200-Ft. Reels of Super 8mm. Film*, 413 U.S. 123 (1973); *United States v. Orito*, 413 U.S. 139 (1973).
7. *Bolger v. Youngs Drug Products Corp.*, 463 U.S. 60 (1983).

from libel suits in all cases except those where the publisher printed the charges in actual malice. The seminal decision came from the Kansas Supreme Court in the 1908 case of *Coleman v. MacLennan* in which a political candidate sued a newspaper publisher for libel:

[W]here an article is published and circulated among voters for the . . . purpose of giving what the defendant believes to be truthful information concerning a candidate for public office, and for the purpose of enabling such voters to cast their ballots more intelligently, and the whole thing is done in good faith, and without malice, the article is privileged, although the principal matters contained in the article may be untrue in fact and derogatory to the character of the plaintiff, and in such a case the burden is on the plaintiff to show actual malice in the publication of the article.[36]

To protect the communication of information relevant to public affairs, the U.S. Supreme Court—fifty years later—adopted this "actual malice" rule for libel suits brought against publishers by public officials and other personalities in the public eye.

Now libel cases involving anyone of public note immediately pull the First Amendment into play. But the Court in 1985 reminded the country that the First Amendment provides no shield against damage awards in a libel case that involves only private parties and no "matter of public concern."

"We have long recognized that not all speech is of equal First Amendment importance," wrote Justice Powell for the Court in *Dun & Bradstreet Inc. v. Greenmoss Builders Inc.* "It is speech on 'matters of public concern' that is 'at the heart of the First Amendment's protection.'"[37]

NEW YORK TIMES V. SULLIVAN

The Supreme Court revised the rules for libel in the case of *New York Times Co. v. Sullivan* (1964).

L. B. Sullivan was an elected commissioner of the city of Montgomery, Alabama, responsible for the police department. He sued the *New York Times* and four black clergymen—Ralph D. Abernathy, Fred L. Shuttlesworth, S. S. Seay Sr., and J. E. Lowery—for libel as a result of an advertisement the clergymen had placed in the newspaper on March 29, 1960.

The advertisement, entitled "Heed Their Rising Voices," called attention to the fledgling struggle for civil rights in the South and appealed for funds to support the black student movement, the "struggle for the right-to-vote," and the legal defense of civil rights leader Dr. Martin Luther King Jr., who had been indicted for perjury in Montgomery.

The advertisement recounted the violence with which the civil rights movement had been met. Sullivan's libel suit was based on two paragraphs that read:

In Montgomery, Alabama, after students sang "My Country, 'Tis of Thee" on the State Capitol steps, their leaders were expelled from school, and truckloads of police armed with shotguns and tear-gas ringed the Alabama State College Campus. When the entire student body protested to state authorities by refusing to re-register, their dining hall was padlocked in an attempt to starve them into submission. . . .

GROUP LIBEL

From time to time states have sought to quell racial and religious intolerance and unrest by enacting group libel laws—laws that make it illegal for anyone to defame groups of people. Such laws clearly restrain the freedom of the press to discuss public issues concerning particular groups. But in the only case it has heard on the validity of group libel laws, the Supreme Court sustained it, holding that the First Amendment offered no protection for such statements.

The case of *Beauharnais v. Illinois* (1952) concerned a man who headed an organization called the White Circle League. He distributed on Chicago streets leaflets making clearly racist statements about blacks and calling on the mayor and city council to protect white residents and neighborhoods against harassment by blacks.

Beauharnais was convicted of violating an Illinois group libel statute that made it illegal to publish anything defamatory or derogatory about "a class of citizens of any race, color, creed or religion."

He appealed his conviction, but the Supreme Court sustained it by a 5–4 vote.

For the majority, Justice Felix Frankfurter observed that it would be libelous to accuse an individual falsely of being a rapist or robber. And, he said, "if an utterance directed at an individual may be the object of criminal sanctions, we cannot deny to a State power to punish the same utterance directed at a defined group" unless the state had acted arbitrarily when it passed its group libel law.[1]

Frankfurter mentioned the First Amendment only at the end of his opinion, holding it irrelevant to this case on the basis of the Court's earlier *dicta* that the First Amendment afforded no protection for libel.

In a separate dissenting opinion, Justice William O. Douglas wrote:

Today a white man stands convicted for protesting in unseemly language against our decisions invalidating restrictive covenants. Tomorrow a negro will be hailed before a court for denouncing lynch law in heated terms. . . . Intemperate speech is a distinctive characteristic of man. Hot-heads blow off and release destructive energy in the process. . . . So it has been from the beginning; and so it will be throughout time. The Framers of the Constitution knew human nature as well as we do.[2]

The viability of the *Beauharnais* decision as a precedent has been called into question by the Court's later decisions that both civil and criminal libels are within the scope of the First Amendment protections, but the Court has not reconsidered the 1952 decision.[3]

1. *Beauharnais v. Illinois,* 343 U.S. 250 at 258 (1952).
2. Id. at 286–287.
3. See *The New York Times Co. v. Sullivan,* 376 U.S. 254 (1964); *Garrison v. Louisiana,* 379 U.S. 64 (1964); *Ashton v. Kentucky,* 384 U.S. 195 (1966).

Again and again the Southern violators have answered Dr. King's peaceful protests with intimidation and violence. They have bombed his home almost killing his wife and child. They have assaulted his person. They have arrested him seven times—for "speeding," "loitering" and similar "offenses." And now they have charged him with "perjury"—a felony under which they could imprison him for ten years.[38]

The advertisement did not refer to Sullivan personally, but Sullivan contended that the references to police included him. He also contended that because arrests are usually made by police, the "they" in "They have arrested" referred to him, and that the "they" who made the arrests were equated with the "they" who bombed King's home and assaulted him.

The two paragraphs contained errors. The students sang the national anthem, not "My Country, 'Tis of Thee." Several students were expelled from the school for demanding service at an all-white lunch counter, but not for leading the demonstration at the capitol. Police were deployed near the campus, but they did not "ring" it. Students protested the expulsions by boycotting classes for a day, not by refusing to re-register. The campus dining room was never padlocked; the only students denied access to it were those who did not have meal tickets. King had been arrested four times, not seven times.

The suit was tried under Alabama libel law, and Sullivan was awarded damages of $500,000. Other plaintiffs brought suits against the *Times* seeking damages totaling $5.6 million.

The *Times* appealed the decision to the Supreme Court, which unanimously reversed it. Writing for six justices, Justice Brennan dismissed the Court's earlier *dicta* viewing all libel as outside the protection of the First Amendment. "None of . . . [those] cases sustained the use of libel laws to impose sanctions upon expression critical of the official conduct of public officials," he said.

"[L]ibel can claim no talismanic immunity from constitutional limitations. It must be measured by standards that satisfy the First Amendment."[39]

At the outset Brennan distinguished the civil rights advertisement from the kind of commercial speech the Court still held unprotected. The ad, he explained, primarily communicated information about a public issue of great concern. *(See "Commercial Speech," pp. 444–446.)*

Reviewing the role of a free press in a democratic society, Brennan said:

we consider this case against the background of a profound national commitment to the principle that debate on public issues should be uninhibited, robust, and wide-open, and that it may well include vehement, caustic, and sometimes unpleasantly sharp attacks on government and public officials. . . . The present advertisement, as an expression of grievance and protest on one of the major public issues of our time, would seem clearly to qualify for the constitutional protection. The question is whether it forfeits that protection by the falsity of some of its factual statements and by its alleged defamation of . . . [Sullivan].[40]

The courts, said Brennan, have recognized that "erroneous statement is inevitable in free debate, and that it must be pro-

The purpose of this ad was to publicize and raise money for the cause of civil rights. Commissioner L. B. Sullivan of Montgomery, Alabama, claimed the ad libeled him. In deciding against Sullivan, the Supreme Court established a new standard for libel suits.

tected if the freedoms of expression are to have the 'breathing space' that they 'need . . . to survive.'"[41]

This was true of speech about public officials as well as public issues, Brennan noted:

A rule compelling the critic of official conduct to guarantee the truth of all his factual assertions—and to do so on pain of libel judgments virtually unlimited in amount—leads to a comparable "self-censorship." . . . Under such a rule, would-be critics of official conduct may be deterred from voicing their criticism, even though it is believed to be true and even though it is in fact true, because of doubt whether it can be proved in court or fear of the expense of having to do so. . . . The rule thus dampens the vigor and limits the variety of public debate. It is inconsistent with the First and Fourteenth Amendments.[42]

Drawing heavily on *Coleman v. MacLennan,* Brennan then set out the standard for determining whether defamatory statements about public officials were protected by the First Amendment:

The constitutional guarantees require, we think, a federal rule that prohibits a public official from recovering damages for a defamatory falsehood relating to his official conduct unless he proves that the statement was made with 'actual malice'—that is, with knowledge that it was false or with reckless disregard of whether it was false or not.[43]

This oft-relied upon standard became known as the *New York Times* rule or actual malice rule.

In applying that rule to the circumstances of the *Sullivan* case, the Court discovered no evidence that the individual clergymen knew their statements to be false or were reckless in that regard. Although the *Times* had information in its news files that would have corrected some of the errors contained in the advertisement, the Court did not find that the *Times* personnel had acted with any actual malice. The evidence against the *Times,* said Brennan, "supports at most a finding of negligence in failing to discover the misstatements, and is constitutionally insufficient to show the recklessness that is required for a finding of actual malice."[44]

Concurring, Justice Black, joined by Justice Douglas, contended that the First and Fourteenth Amendments prevented a state from ever awarding libel damages to public officials for false statements made about their public conduct. The newspaper and the individual clergymen "had an absolute, unconditional constitutional right to publish in the *Times* advertisement their criticisms of the Montgomery agencies and officials," he wrote.[45]

In another concurring opinion, Justice Arthur J. Goldberg, again joined by Douglas, held that the First Amendment provided an absolute right to criticize the public conduct of public officials. He also questioned how much protection the "actual malice" rule would afford publishers. Can "freedom of speech which all agree is constitutionally protected . . . be effectively safeguarded by a rule allowing the imposition of liability upon a jury's evaluation of the speaker's state of mind?" he asked.[46]

In a series of subsequent decisions, the Court elaborated on its *New York Times* rule. In *Garrison v. Louisiana* (1964), the Court ruled that the actual malice rule limited state power to impose criminal as well as civil sanctions against persons criti-

---

PERFORMANCE, PUBLICITY, AND THE PRESS

In August 1972 an Ohio television station filmed, without the performer's consent, the entire fifteen-second act of Hugo Zacchini, a "human cannonball" whose "act" consisted of being shot from a cannon into a net two hundred feet away.

After the station showed the film clip on its nightly news program as an item of interest, Zacchini sued, charging that the television station had appropriated his right to control publicity concerning his performance.

The Ohio Supreme Court ruled in favor of the television station. Unless Zacchini showed that the station intentionally meant to harm him or to use the film for some private purpose, its airing of Zacchini's act was protected by the First and Fourteenth Amendments, the court held.

By a 5–4 vote, the Supreme Court overturned that ruling with its decision in *Zacchini v. Scripps-Howard Broadcasting Co.* (1977).

"Wherever the line in particular situations is to be drawn between media reports that are protected and those that are not, we are quite sure that the First and Fourteenth Amendments do not immunize the media when they broadcast a performer's entire act without his consent," wrote Justice Byron R. White for the majority. "The Constitution no more prevents a State from requiring . . . [the station] to compensate petitioner for broadcasting his act on television than it would privilege . . . [the station] to film and broadcast a copyrighted dramatic work without liability to the copyright owner."

Three of the dissenters held that the broadcast was privileged under the First and Fourteenth Amendments. The film was a simple report on a newsworthy event and shown as part of an ordinary daily news report. The broadcast was therefore no more than a "routine example of the press fulfilling the informing function so vital to our system." (433 U.S. 562 at 574–575, 580, 1977)

---

cizing the official conduct of public officials. In 1968 the Court ruled that to prove reckless disregard for the truth or falsity of the allegedly libelous statement there must be "sufficient evidence to permit the conclusion that the defendant in fact entertained serious doubts as to the truth of his publications."[47]

In the 1979 case of *Herbert v. Lando,* the Court by a 6–3 vote rejected a television producer's claim that the First Amendment protected him from having to answer questions about the editorial process of a certain story. The Court held that the *New York Times* actual malice standard required inquiry into the editorial process—the prepublication thoughts, conclusions, and conversations of editors and reporters—by persons who charge they have been libeled by the product of that process.

The Court said that nothing in the First Amendment restricted a person alleging libel from obtaining the evidence necessary to prove actual malice under the *New York Times* rule. To the contrary, *New York Times v. Sullivan*

and its progeny made it essential to proving liability that plaintiffs [alleging libel] focus on the conduct and state of mind of the defendant [publishers]. To be liable, the alleged defamer of public officials or of public figures must know or have reason to suspect that his publication is false. In other cases [brought by private individuals] proof of some kind of fault, negligence perhaps, is essential to recovery. Inevitably, unless liability is to be completely foreclosed, the thoughts and editorial processes of the alleged defamer would be open to examination.[48]

Since *Herbert v. Lando,* the Court has been seriously divided in determining against what category of person the *New York Times* rule operates. All the justices agreed that public officials and public figures must show actual malice to win damages.

After a brief period when the Court seemed to apply the actual malice standard to suits brought by private individuals involving matters of public concern, it now allows states to set less stringent standards of proof for private citizens alleging libel.

PUBLIC OFFICIALS

Two years after *New York Times Co. v. Sullivan,* the Court further defined the category of public officials. In the case of *Rosenblatt v. Baer,* a former supervisor of a county ski resort sued a newspaper columnist for an allegedly libelous statement about his management of the recreation area. Without being instructed to use the *New York Times* rule, the jury found in favor of the supervisor. The Supreme Court reversed, but the justices in the majority disagreed on their reasons.

Justice Brennan, who wrote the formal Court opinion in which only two other justices concurred, put in context the issue of freedom of the press:

There is, first, a strong interest in debate on public issues, and second, a strong interest in debate about those persons who are in a position significantly to influence the resolution of those issues. Criticism of government is at the very center of the constitutionally protected area of free discussion. Criticism of those responsible for government operations must be free, lest criticism of government itself be penalized.

He then defined "public officials":

It is clear, therefore, that the "public official" designation applies at the very least to those among the hierarchy of government employees who have, or appear to the public to have, substantial responsibility for or control over the conduct of governmental affairs. . . . Where a position in government has such apparent importance that the public has an independent interest in the qualifications and performance of the person who holds it, beyond the general public interest in the qualifications and performance of all government employees, both elements we identified in *New York Times* are present and the *New York Times* malice standards apply.[49]

Although this has come to be the accepted definition of "public official," a majority of the Court did not initially endorse it. Justice Tom C. Clark concurred in the judgment without an opinion. Justice Douglas concurred, but thought the question should turn on whether the alleged libel involved a public issue rather than a public official. Justice Stewart also agreed with the judgment but cautioned that the actual malice rule should be applied only "where a State's law of defamation has been unconstitutionally converted into a law of seditious libel."[50]

Justice Harlan concurred with the judgment but disagreed with part of Brennan's opinion. Justice Black concurred, maintaining that the First and Fourteenth Amendments forbade all libel judgments against newspaper comment on public issues. Justice Abe Fortas dissented for technical reasons.

The Court was considerably more unified in 1971 when it ruled that candidates for public office were public officials and that the *New York Times* rule protected publishers from libel charges resulting from their decision to print information on the criminal records of these persons.[51]

PUBLIC FIGURES

The wide diversity of views on the applicability of the actual malice rule was again evident in two 1967 decisions in which the Court applied the *New York Times* rule to persons who were not public officials but were nonetheless in the public eye.

The first of these cases, *Curtis Publishing Co. v. Butts,* concerned a libel action brought by former University of Georgia athletic director Wallace Butts against the *Saturday Evening Post,* which was owned by the Curtis Publishing Company.

The *Post* had printed a story in which it alleged that Butts had "fixed" a football game by revealing his team's offensive and defensive plays to the opposing coach, Paul Bryant of the University of Alabama.

At his trial, completed before the Supreme Court issued its malice rule in *New York Times Co. v. Sullivan,* Butts admitted talking to Bryant but said he had revealed nothing of value to him. Butts was supported by expert witnesses, and there was substantial evidence that the *Post* investigation of the allegation had been gravely inadequate. The jury found in Butts's favor and the final award was $480,000. After the *New York Times* rule was issued, the publishing company asked for another trial, which the state courts denied.

The second case, *Associated Press v. Walker,* concerned an allegedly libelous eyewitness-news report that former general Edwin A. Walker had led rioters against federal marshals at the University of Mississippi. The marshals were trying to maintain order during turmoil over the enrollment of a black student, James Meredith.

Walker, who had commanded federal troops guarding black students who tried to enter a Little Rock, Arkansas, high school in 1958, was awarded $500,000 in compensatory damages. The Supreme Court unanimously reversed the award in Walker's case but by a 5–4 vote upheld the award of damages to Butts.[52]

All of the justices agreed that both Butts and Walker were public figures, but four of the justices would not have applied the actual malice rule to their cases. Three of the remaining five justices would have applied the actual malice rule, and the other two maintained that freedom of the press absolutely protects publishers from libel suits.

Court's Opinion

Justice Harlan, joined by Justices Clark, Stewart, and Fortas, concluded that Butts and Walker were "public figures." (Chief

THE PRESS AND PERSONAL PRIVACY

Freedom of the press might be justifiably curtailed, wrote Chief Justice Charles Evan Hughes in *Near v. Minnesota* (1931), to prevent the invasion of "private rights." *(Near ruling, p. 448.)*

The Court has not yet addressed the specific question whether government may prevent publication of articles that invade a person's privacy, but it has considered whether publications may be punished for such invasions of personal privacy.

Time Inc. v. Hill (1967) brought to the Court a claim of privacy by a family held hostage in their Pennsylvania home in 1952 by three escaped convicts. The convicts treated the family politely and released them unharmed.

A 1953 book entitled *The Desperate Hours* recounted a story similar to the Hill family's experience, but the convicts in the story, unlike those in the actual event, treated their captives violently. The novel was made into a play and later a film. In an article on the play, *Life* magazine sent actors to the former Hill house where they were photographed acting scenes from the play. The article characterized the play as a reenactment of the Hill incident.

Hill sued the magazine under a New York right of privacy statute that made it a misdemeanor for anyone to use without consent another's name for commercial purposes. The jury found in favor of Hill, and the state appeals courts affirmed.

The Supreme Court reversed, 6–3.[1] The Hill family was newsworthy, albeit involuntarily, wrote Justice William J. Brennan Jr. for the majority. The New York law permitted newsworthy persons to recover if they could show that the article was fictionalized. But, said Brennan, the actual malice standard set out in *New York Times Co. v. Sullivan* (1964) must be applied to this case even though private individuals were involved.[2] Brennan wrote:

The guarantees for speech and press are not the preserve of political expression or comment upon public affairs, essential as those are to healthy government. One need only pick up any newspaper or magazine to comprehend the vast range of published matter which exposes persons to public view, both private citizens and public officials. Exposure of the self to others in varying degrees is a concomitant of life in a civilized community. The risk of this exposure is an essential incident of a society which places a primary value on freedom of speech and of press. . . . We have no doubt that the subject of the *Life* article . . . is a matter of public interest. . . . Erroneous statement is no less inevitable in such a case than in the case of comment upon public affairs, and in both, if innocent or merely negligent, ". . . it must be protected if the freedoms of expression are to have the 'breathing space' that they need . . . 'to survive'. . . ."

. . . We create a grave risk of serious impairment of the indispensable service of a free press in a free society if we saddle the press with the impossible burden of verifying to a certainty the facts associated in news articles with a person's name, picture or portrait, particularly . . . [in] nondefamatory matter.[3]

Because the jury had not been instructed that it could award damages to the Hills only if it found the article had been published

with actual malice, the majority sent the case back to the lower courts.

However, in the next case, *Cantrell v. Forest City Publishing Co.* (1974), the Court found that a jury had been justified in finding that false statements had been printed with reckless disregard for the truth.

The case concerned a published report on the family of a man who had been killed in a bridge collapse. Among the admitted misrepresentations in the article were "quotes" from the man's widow, who had not been interviewed. This was a "calculated falsehood," the majority said, portraying the Cantrell family "in a false light through knowing or reckless untruth."[4]

In *Cox Broadcasting Corporation v. Cohn* (1975), the Court struck down a Georgia law making it illegal to broadcast the name of rape victims. The father of a girl who had died as a result of an assault and rape sued a television station for reporting his daughter's name in two of their news reports. The reporter testified that he had obtained the name of the victim at an open court hearing at which five of the suspects pleaded guilty.

The Court said that the First Amendment does not allow states to "impose sanctions for the publication of truthful information contained in official court records open to public inspection." The majority wrote:

If there are privacy interests to be protected in judicial proceedings, the States must respond by means which avoid public documentation or other exposure of private information. Their political institutions must weigh the interests in privacy with the interests of the public to know and of the press to publish.[5]

In 1979 a unanimous Court struck down a state law that forbade newspapers, but not other forms of the press, from reporting the names of juveniles involved in criminal proceedings.[6]

A decade later, in *The Florida Star v. B. J. F.*, the Court held that the First Amendment protected a newspaper from being sued for damages because it published the name of a rape victim when state law barred such disclosure. The paper had obtained the name from a publicly released police report.

"We do not hold that a state may never punish publication of the name of a victim of a sexual offense," Justice Thurgood Marshall wrote for the Court. "We hold only that where a newspaper publishes truthful information which it has lawfully obtained, punishment may lawfully be imposed, if at all, only when narrowly tailored to a state interest of the highest order."[7]

1. *Time Inc. v. Hill*, 385 U.S. 374 (1967).
2. *The New York Times Co. v. Sullivan*, 376 U.S. 254 (1964).
3. *Time Inc. v. Hill*, 385 U.S. 374 at 388, 389 passim (1967).
4. *Cantrell v. Forest City Publishing Co.*, 419 U.S. 245 at 253 (1974).
5. *Cox Broadcasting Corp. v. Cohn*, 420 U.S. 469 at 495, 496 (1975).
6. *Smith v. Daily Mail Publishing Co.*, 443 U.S. 97 (1979).
7. *The Florida Star v. B. J. F.*, 491 U.S. 524 (1989).

Justice Earl Warren, the fifth member of the majority, agreed with Harlan's result but not with his reasoning.)

"Butts may have attained that status by position alone and Walker by his purposeful activity amounting to a thrusting of his personality into the 'vortex' of an important public contro-

versy," Harlan said. Both men "commanded sufficient public interest and had sufficient access to the means of counter-argument to be able to 'expose through discussion the falsehood and fallacies' of the defamatory statements."[53]

But those four justices would apply a rule less strict than actual malice in libel cases brought by such public figures. Harlan wrote,

a "public figure" who is not a public official may also recover damages for a defamatory falsehood whose substance makes substantial danger to reputation apparent, on a showing of highly unreasonable conduct constituting an extreme departure from the standards of investigation and reporting ordinarily adhered to by reasonable publishers.[54]

Using this standard, Harlan found that the *Post* had failed to exercise elementary journalistic precautions to determine if the allegation against Butts was true. The libel award to Butts must be sustained. But the award to Walker must be overturned, Harlan said, because nothing in the evidence suggests a "departure from accepted publishing standards."[55]

The remaining five justices agreed with Chief Justice Warren that public figures must prove actual malice under the *New York Times* rule to win libel damages. Applying that rule, it was evident that Walker had not proved actual malice, Warren said. But in Butts's case, the conduct of the *Saturday Evening Post* showed the "degree of reckless disregard for the truth" that constituted actual malice under the rule.

Narrowing the Definition

In 1979 the Supreme Court sharply narrowed the public figure category. In its decisions in the cases of *Wolston v. Reader's Digest Association Inc.* and *Hutchinson v. Proxmire,* the justices held that two men who had been involuntarily thrust into the public eye were not public figures and could recover libel damages without proving actual malice in the publications charged.

Ilya Wolston was convicted of contempt in 1958 for refusing to appear and testify before a grand jury investigating Soviet espionage attempts. Ronald Hutchinson, a scientist, found himself in the public eye after his research—paid for in part with federal funds—was the target of a "Golden Fleece" award from Sen. William Proxmire, D-Wis. (1957–1988), who described the research as a waste of tax moneys. Neither Wolston nor Hutchinson, held the Court, was a public figure as a result of this publicity.

The vote in the *Wolston* case was 8–1. Only Justice Brennan dissented. Justice William H. Rehnquist explained that the majority felt that "[a] private individual is not automatically transformed into a public figure just by becoming involved in or associated with a matter that attracts public attention."

"A libel defendant must show more than mere newsworthiness [on the part of the person charging libel] to justify application of the demanding burden of *New York Times*" wrote Rehnquist.[56]

Moving away from definition and toward procedural safeguards, the Court in 1984 ruled that federal appeal courts reviewing libel awards won by public figures must take a new look at the evidence to see if it proved actual malice. Two years later the Court held that judges should summarily dismiss libel charges brought by a public figure unless they find clear and convincing evidence of actual malice in the challenged article.

And in 1988 the Court denied damages for emotional distress to a public figure who did not prove actual malice.[57]

OPINION AND PRIVILEGE

In a case involving the publication of commentary rather than straight news, the Court ruled unanimously in 1990 that statements of opinion do not enjoy a special privilege under the First Amendment and are within the reach of state libel law. Chief Justice Rehnquist wrote for the Court that free speech concerns must be balanced by society's interest in preventing attacks on reputation and defamation.[58]

The dispute arose after a newspaper columnist insinuated in an article that a high school wrestling coach had perjured himself at a judicial hearing. The hearing concerned a melee that had erupted during a wrestling match. The Ohio Supreme Court said the article contained "constitutionally protected opinion." Reversing, the Supreme Court said there is no "wholesale defamation exemption" for opinion. Labeling a column "opinion," Rehnquist explained, does not remove the implication that the writing is factual.

PRIVATE INDIVIDUALS

In *Rosenbloom v. Metromedia Inc.* (1971), the Court considered for the first time whether private individuals must prove actual malice to win damages for libel.

George Rosenbloom, a distributor of nudist magazines, was arrested in a police crackdown on pornography. A local radio station reported that Rosenbloom had been arrested for possession of obscene literature. After he was acquitted of criminal obscenity charges, Rosenbloom sued the radio station for libel. A jury awarded him $750,000, but an appeals court reversed on the grounds that the jury should have been required to apply the *New York Times* actual malice standard to the case.

In the 5–3 decision affirming the appeals court, the Supreme Court splintered into four groups. Chief Justice Burger and Justices Brennan and Blackmun agreed that the actual malice rule should be applied to all discussion of public issues, even discussion including defamatory statements about private individuals. The First Amendment protects discussion of public issues, Brennan said, and an issue does not become less public

merely because a private individual is involved. . . . The public's primary interest is in the event; the public focus is on the conduct of the participant and the content, effect, and significance of the conduct, not the participant's prior anonymity or notoriety.[59]

Justice Black concurred, maintaining that the guarantee of a free press protected publishers against all libel suits. Justice White also concurred, holding that the *New York Times* rule protected newspapers that praised public officials—in this case the police who undertook the pornography investigation—and criticized their adversaries.

In dissent, Justices Marshall, Stewart, and Harlan said they would not apply the actual malice rule to libel cases involving private individuals. Douglas did not participate.

The Gertz Decision

Three years later the Court shifted, adopting the *Rosenbloom* dissenters' position that the actual malice rule did not apply in libel cases brought by private individuals. Five justices endorsed this view in *Gertz v. Robert Welch Inc.* (1974).

Attorney Elmer Gertz sued a Chicago policeman in behalf of the family of a youth killed by the officer. *American Opinion,* the journal of the John Birch Society, printed an article characterizing Gertz as a "Leninist" with a criminal record who was part of a Communist conspiracy to discredit local police. Charging that the allegations were false, Gertz sued the journal for damages.

The jury awarded him $50,000, but the trial court overruled the jury. Citing *Rosenbloom,* the court said that the First Amendment protected publishers from libel suits in connection with discussions of public interest even if they defamed private individuals unless the individual could prove actual malice on the part of the publisher.

The Supreme Court reversed, 5–4.

The majority included the two newest members of the Court, Powell and Rehnquist, who had succeeded Justices Black and Harlan late in 1971. Voting with them were *Rosenbloom* dissenters Marshall and Stewart and, with reservations, Justice Blackmun.

The *New York Times* rule is not appropriate in libel cases involving private individuals, wrote Justice Powell for the majority. Private citizens lack the access of public officials and public figures to "channels of effective communication" to combat allegations about their conduct, he observed. Furthermore, private individuals, unlike public officials and figures, have not voluntarily subjected themselves to public scrutiny.

A private person, Powell wrote,

has relinquished no part of his interest in the protection of his own good name, and consequently he has a more compelling call on the courts for redress of injury inflicted by defamatory falsehood. Thus, private individuals are not only more vulnerable to injury than public officials and public figures; they are also more deserving of recovery.[60]

Therefore, Powell continued, "[S]o long as they do not impose liability without fault, the States may define for themselves the appropriate standard of liability for a publisher or broadcaster of defamatory falsehood injurious to a private individual."[61]

To avoid self-censorship, Powell cautioned, the liability of publications to private-person libel suits must be limited. Therefore, private individuals who proved, for example, only that a publisher had been negligent when he printed false defamatory statements could recover damages only for the actual injury to his reputation. Punitive or presumed damages could be awarded only on a showing that actual malice, as defined by the *New York Times* rule, was intended, Powell held.

Turning to the case at hand, Powell maintained that Gertz was a private individual despite his active participation in community and professional affairs:

Absent clear evidence of general fame or notoriety in the community, and pervasive involvement in the affairs of society, an individual should not be deemed a public personality for all aspects of his life. It is preferable to reduce the public-figure question to a more meaningful context by looking to the nature and extent of an individual's participation in the particular controversy giving rise to the defamation.[62]

The majority sent the case back for a new trial. The jury should not have been allowed to award damages without a finding of fault on the part of *American Opinion.* The majority also said that the trial court had erred in holding that the actual malice standard should be applied.

The dissenting justices, Chief Justice Burger and Justice Brennan, joined by Justice Douglas, maintained that discussions of public interest, including those touching private persons, should be protected by the actual malice rule. Justice White also dissented, claiming that the majority opinion made it almost impossible for private individuals to defend their reputations successfully.

The Time Decision

The Court reaffirmed the principles of *Gertz* in *Time Inc. v. Firestone* (1976). The cause of the libel suit occurred nearly a decade earlier. On December 22, 1967, *Time* magazine carried an item in its "Milestones" section announcing the divorce of Russell A. Firestone Jr., heir to the tire fortune, from his third wife, Mary Alice Sullivan. In that item the magazine wrote: "The 17-month intermittent trial produced enough testimony of extramarital adventures on both sides, said the judge, 'to make Dr. Freud's hair curl.'"

This report, as *Time* was soon to discover, was less than accurate. Although Firestone's suit for divorce had charged his wife with adultery and extreme cruelty, the judge in granting him the divorce did not specify that those charges were the grounds upon which the divorce was granted.

CONFIDENTIAL PROCEEDINGS

A state may not fine a newspaper for printing a true report of confidential proceedings of a state commission considering disciplinary action against a sitting state judge. This was the Supreme Court's unanimous holding in *Landmark Communications Inc. v. Virginia* (435 U.S. 829, 1978).

After the Norfolk *Virginian-Pilot* printed an accurate report of an inquiry by the state judicial review commission into the conduct of a sitting judge named in the article, the newspaper was indicted, tried, convicted, and fined $500 for violating state law by breaching the confidentiality of the commission's proceedings.

The state justified the law as necessary to protect public confidence in the judicial process, to protect the reputation of judges, and to protect persons who bring complaints to the commission. The Court held that those interests justified the law protecting the confidentiality of proceedings before the commission, but they did not justify imposing criminal penalties on news media, uninvolved in the commission's proceedings, who breached that confidentiality.

When *Time* refused to retract the item, the former Mrs. Firestone sued the magazine for libel. She won a $100,000 damage judgment. *Time* appealed, claiming that Mrs. Firestone was a public figure and therefore must prove actual malice to win the suit. The magazine also argued that reports of court proceedings are of sufficient public interest that they cannot be the basis for libel judgments—even if erroneous or false and defamatory—unless it is proved that they were published maliciously.

The Supreme Court, in a mixed victory for Mrs. Firestone, rejected both of the arguments by *Time* and sent the case back to Florida courts to determine whether *Time* had been negligent or was otherwise at fault.

Writing for the majority, Justice Rehnquist stated that Mrs. Firestone was not a public figure despite her involvement in the sensational divorce case. She "did not assume any role of especial prominence in the affairs of society . . . and she did not thrust herself to the forefront of any particular public controversy in order to influence the resolution of the issues involved in it."[63]

Gertz established that the actual malice rule did not apply to cases brought by private individuals. Rehnquist also noted that in *Gertz* the justices rejected use of the actual malice rule for reports of court proceedings. The public interest in such reports, he added, was sufficiently protected under a 1975 decision forbidding the states to allow the media to be sued for reporting true information available to the public in official court records. (*See box, The Press and Personal Privacy, p. 462.*)

Justice White dissented, saying that the libel award to Mrs. Firestone should be upheld. Justice Brennan also dissented, arguing that the First Amendment protected *Time* for reporting of public judicial proceedings unless actual malice was proved. The third dissenter, Justice Marshall, thought Mrs. Firestone was a public figure and that the *New York Times* actual malice rule should therefore apply to protect *Time*.

In 1979 the Court again upheld *Gertz*, ruling that private individuals who were placed in the public eye involuntarily were not "public figures" and did not have to prove actual malice under the *New York Times* rule in order to bring a successful libel suit. But seven years later the Court seemed to rebalance this equation somewhat, holding that private persons who sue for libel must prove both the falsity of the challenged report as well as fault of the media before they can recover damages.[64]

QUESTIONABLE QUOTES,
SENSITIVE SOURCES

Two high-profile cases involving the methods used by reporters came to the Court in 1991: *Masson v. New Yorker* and *Cohen v. Cowles Media Co.*

The first case arose from the writings of *New Yorker* reporter Janet Malcolm about Jeffrey Masson, a psychoanalyst who was fired from his job as projects director of the Sigmund Freud Archives after disputing some of Freud's theories. Masson challenged some of the direct quotations attributed to him in the stories, saying they were fabricated. Many of the quotes made

him sound boastful and, in one of the more damning quotes, Malcolm wrote that Masson said he was considered an "intellectual gigolo," a phrase he said he never used. Masson sued for libel.[65]

By 7–2, the Court ruled that fabricated quotes may be libelous if they are published with knowledge of falsity or convey a meaning different from what the speaker actually said. Justice Anthony M. Kennedy, writing for the majority, said that a jury should decide whether Malcolm acted with knowledge of falsity or reckless disregard for the truth of the passages in question. In general, quotation marks signify a verbatim reproduction, Kennedy noted. He then explained that the common law of libel does not concern itself with slight inaccuracies; it concentrates instead on issues of truth.

The second dispute arose from a Minnesota gubernatorial race. A political consultant offered reporters negative information about a candidate in return for a promise of confidentiality. After two newspapers printed the source's name, the consultant was fired from his job. He then sued the newspapers, alleging breach of contract and fraudulent misrepresentation.

The Supreme Court ruled 5–4 that the First Amendment does not shield the news media from lawsuits if they break promises of confidentiality to sources. A state doctrine of promissory estoppel, which protects people who rely to their detriment on promises from others, applied to all citizens' daily transactions, Justice White wrote for the majority.[66]

In deciding that the First Amendment does not bar action for a broken contract, White said any resulting constraint on truthful reporting "is no more than the incidental, and constitutionally insignificant, consequence of applying to the press a generally applicable law that requires those who make certain kinds of promises to keep them."[67]

A Free Press Versus the Right to a Fair Trial

At times the First Amendment guarantee of freedom of the press collides with the Sixth Amendment guarantee of trial by an impartial jury. As Justice Clark wrote in 1966:

A responsible press has always been regarded as the handmaiden of effective judicial administration, especially in the criminal field. . . . The press does not simply publish information about trials, but guards against the miscarriage of justice by subjecting the police, prosecutors, and judicial processes to extensive public scrutiny and criticism.[68]

In this way the public may assure itself that justice is attained, to the benefit both of society and of the individual defendant.

The conflict between the freedom of the press and the right to a fair trial arises from the Constitution's promise that a defendant shall be judged by an impartial jury solely on evidence produced in court, and that both judge and jury shall be free from outside influence. But in cases concerning prominent people or sensational crimes, pretrial publicity can so saturate a community that the pool of unbiased potential jurors is significantly diminished. News accounts and editorials may influence jurors and judges while a case is pending. The question then is what, if any, restrictions on the free press are constitutionally permissible to ensure a fair trial.

CONTEMPT OF COURT

The Supreme Court has had little tolerance for efforts by judges to restrict criticism of their official conduct. From time to time judges have held in contempt publishers, editors, and writers who have criticized them—while a case was still pending—for the way they have handled it.

The argument in support of such punishment is that public criticism of a judge might influence or coerce him to rule in a way that will maintain the good will of the publisher and the community at large at the expense of the parties in the case.

Federal Courts

The potential for judicial abuse of the contempt power prompted Congress in 1831 to enact a law forbidding the use of contempt citations to punish misbehavior other than that which occurred in court "or so near thereto as to obstruct the administration of justice." In 1918 the Supreme Court allowed the use of the contempt power to curtail a newspaper's criticisms of a judge's conduct in a pending case.[69]

In 1941, however, the Court overruled that decision, holding that the phrase "so near thereto" meant only physical proximity. Thus, federal law as presently construed gives published criticisms of federal judicial conduct absolute protection from summary contempt proceedings.[70]

State Courts

In 1907 the Court sustained a contempt citation against a newspaper publisher for publishing articles and a cartoon critical of a state court's actions on pending cases.

If the court determines that a critical publication tends to interfere with the fair administration of justice, wrote Justice Oliver Wendell Holmes Jr., then the publisher may be punished. "When a case is finished, the courts are subject to the same criticism as other people, but the propriety and necessity of preventing interference with the court of justice by premature statement, argument or intimidation hardly can be denied," he said.[71]

Since 1925, and the application to the states as well as the federal government of the First Amendment guarantees of free speech and press, the Court has not sustained any contempt citation issued by a judge against a newspaper critical of his actions on a pending case. The leading decision in this area is *Bridges v. California* (1941), in which the Court overturned, 5–4, contempt rulings against a labor leader and an anti-union Los Angeles newspaper.

While a motion for a new trial was pending in a dispute between two competing longshoremen's unions, Bridges, the president of one of the unions, sent a telegram to the U.S. secretary of labor describing as outrageous the judge's initial decision favoring the competing union. Bridges threatened to strike the entire Pacific coast if the original decision were allowed to stand. The telegram was reprinted in several California newspapers.

A companion case to *Bridges, Times-Mirror Co. v. Superior Court of California* involved a *Los Angeles Times* editorial that urged a trial judge to give severe sentences to two union members found guilty of beating up nonunion truck drivers.

Writing for the five-justice majority overturning the contempt citation against the newspaper, Justice Black said that punishment for contempt improperly restricted freedom of the press. If the contempt citations were allowed to stand, Black said,

anyone who might wish to give public expression to his views on a pending case involving no matter what problem of public interest, just at the time his audience would be most receptive, would be as effectively discouraged as if a deliberate statutory scheme of censorship had been adopted.[72]

Such a restriction would be permissible only if the criticism raised a clear and present danger that a substantive evil would result, Black continued. The only dangers cited by the court in this case were that the articles might result in disrespect for the court and unfair administration of justice. Black dismissed the first of these rationales:

The assumption that respect for the judiciary can be won by shielding judges from published criticism wrongly appraises the character of American public opinion. For it is a prized American privilege to speak one's mind, although not always with perfect good taste, on all public institutions. And an enforced silence, however limited, solely in the name of preserving the dignity of the bench, would probably engender resentment, suspicion, and contempt much more than it would enhance respect.[73]

The Court also did not find any evidence that the articles in question created a clear and present danger of interfering with the fair administration of justice. The judge in the *Los Angeles Times* case was likely to know that a lenient sentence for the two union members would result in criticism from the paper. "To regard it [the editorial], therefore, as in itself of substantial influence upon the course of justice would be to impute to judges a lack of firmness, wisdom, or honor, which we cannot accept as a major premise," Black wrote.[74]

Likewise, the judge in the *Bridges* case was likely to realize that his decision might result in a labor strike. "If he was not intimidated by the facts themselves," Black said, "we do not believe that the most explicit statement of them could have sidetracked the course of justice."[75]

Speaking for the dissenters, Justice Felix Frankfurter said the judges were within their rights to punish comments that had a "reasonable tendency" to interfere with the impartial dispensation of justice. Frankfurter wrote:

Freedom of expression can hardly carry implications that nullify the guarantees of impartial trials. And since courts are the ultimate resorts for vindicating the Bill of Rights, a state may surely authorize appropriate historic means [the contempt power] to assure that the process for such vindication be not wrenched from its rational tracks into the more primitive melee of passion and pressure. The need is great that courts be criticized, but just as great that they be allowed to do their duty.[76]

In *Pennekamp v. Florida* (1946), the Court reaffirmed its opinion that editorial comment on judicial handling of a pending case did not present a clear and present danger of interfering with the fair administration of justice and was therefore not punishable. "In the borderline instances where it is difficult to say upon which side the alleged offense falls, we think the specific freedom of public comment should weigh heavily against a possible tendency to influence pending cases," the Court said.[77]

The following year the Court in *Craig v. Harney* (1947) overturned a contempt citation for articles that gave an unfair and inaccurate account of a trial. The majority found that neither the articles nor a critical editorial constituted "an imminent and serious threat to the ability of the court to give fair consideration" to the pending case.[78]

Although the Court almost totally abandoned use of the clear and present danger test in other contexts during the 1950s, it reaffirmed the use of that test in contempt cases in 1962. *(See "The Search for a Standard," pp. 413–414.)*

In *Wood v. Georgia* the Court reversed the contempt citation of a county sheriff who denounced a county judge's order to a grand jury to investigate rumors of purchased votes and other corrupting practices as a "political attempt to intimidate" black voters. The lower court held that the sheriff's criticism, publicized in several news accounts, created a clear and present danger of influencing the grand jury. The Supreme Court disagreed, observing that the lower courts had made no attempt to show how the criticism created "a substantive evil actually designed to impede the course of justice."[79]

PRETRIAL PUBLICITY

The press contempt cases concerned criticism of judges and their conduct. Another frequent threat to the fair administration of justice is posed by publications that cast defendants in such a bad light that their rights to fair treatment are jeopardized. In those instances the Court has held that trial courts should take regulatory actions to protect the right to a fair trial with the least possible restriction on a free press.

Defense attorneys frequently claim that news reports are so inflammatory and pervasive as to deny their clients due process. The Supreme Court rejected such a claim in the 1951 case of *Stroble v. California,* noting that the publicity had receded six weeks before the trial, that the defendant had not requested a change of venue, and that his publicized confession was voluntary and placed in evidence in open trial.[80]

In 1959 the Court overturned a federal conviction because jurors had been exposed through news accounts to information that was not admitted in evidence at the trial.[81]

Two years later in *Irvin v. Dowd,* the Supreme Court for the first time reversed a state conviction on grounds that pretrial publicity had denied the defendant due process.

Irvin had been arrested and indicted for one of six murders committed in and around Evansville, Indiana. Shortly after his arrest, the police sent out press releases saying that he had confessed to all six crimes. The news media covered the crimes and the confession extensively; it also reported on previous crimes in which Irvin had been implicated.

Irvin's attorney won a change of venue to a neighboring rural county, but that area was just as saturated by the same news reports. A request for a second change of venue was denied.

The pervasiveness of the news reports was evident during jury selection. Of the 420 potential jurors asked, 370 said that they had some opinion about Irvin's guilt. Eight of the 12 jurors selected said they thought he was guilty even before the trial began.

Given these circumstances, a unanimous Court found that the jury did not meet the constitutional standard of impartiality. But Justice Clark, who wrote the opinion, cautioned that it was not necessary for jurors to

be totally ignorant of the facts and issues involved. In these days of swift, widespread and diverse methods of communication, an important case can be expected to arouse the interest of the public in the vicinity, and scarcely any of those best qualified to serve as jurors will not have formed some impression or opinion as to the merits of the case. This is particularly true in criminal cases. To hold that the mere existence of any preconceived notion as to the guilt or innocence of an accused, without more, is sufficient to rebut the presumption of a prospective juror's impartiality would be to establish impossible standards.[82]

The following year a narrow majority of the Court held that pretrial publicity had not denied Teamsters Union president David D. Beck a fair trial on charges of grand larceny. The adverse publicity, stemming largely from a U.S. Senate investigation, had been diluted by time and by the presence of other labor leaders also under investigation, and both the grand jury and petit jury had been carefully questioned to avoid selection of those unduly influenced by media reports, the majority said.[83]

But in *Rideau v. Louisiana* (1963), the Court held that a murder defendant whose filmed confession was broadcast and seen by three jurors had been denied due process when his effort to win a change of venue was rejected. Clark dissented. There was no evidence, he argued, that the telecast confession had indelibly marked the minds of the jurors.[84]

CONDUCT OF TRIAL

The very presence of working news reporters in and near a courtroom during the course of a trial may also jeopardize its fairness. In 1965 the Court had little trouble holding in *Estes v. Texas* that the presence of television cameras, radio microphones, and newspaper photographers at the pretrial hearing and trial of financier Billie Sol Estes denied Estes his right to a fair trial.

"[V]ideotapes of these hearings clearly illustrate that the picture presented was not one of that judicial serenity and calm to which petitioner was entitled," the Court said.[85]

Dr. Sam Sheppard in September 1966 with his son and second wife. The Court decided that negative pretrial publicity had influenced the outcome of Sheppard's trial and overturned his conviction.

Two years later the Supreme Court in *Sheppard v. Maxwell* (1966) laid out some ground rules to ensure fair trials with minimal restriction on the operation of a free press.

The Sheppard Case

The 1954 bludgeon murder of a pregnant woman in her suburban Cleveland home and the subsequent arrest, trial, and conviction of her husband, Dr. Sam Sheppard, for that murder excited some of the most intense and sensational press coverage the country had witnessed.

Pretrial publicity as much as proclaimed Sheppard's guilt. Reporters had access to witnesses during the trial itself and frequently published information damaging to Sheppard that could have come only from the prosecuting attorneys. Some of this information was never introduced as evidence. Reporters in the courtroom were seated only a few feet from the jury and from Sheppard and his counsel who were constantly besieged by reporters and photographers as they entered and left the courtroom.

"The fact is that bedlam reigned at the courthouse during the trial and newsmen took over practically the entire courtroom," said the Supreme Court, overturning Sheppard's conviction by an 8–1 vote. "The carnival atmosphere at trial could easily have been avoided since the courtroom and courthouse premises are subject to control of the court," the majority wrote. "[T]he presence of the press at judicial proceedings must be limited when it is apparent that the accused might otherwise be prejudiced or disadvantaged."[86]

Change of venue and postponement of the trial until publicity dies down would be proper if pretrial publicity threatens the fair administration of justice, the Court said. Once the trial has begun, the judge may limit the number of reporters permitted in the courtroom and place strict controls on their conduct while there. Witnesses and jurors should be isolated from the press, and the jury may be sequestered to prevent it from being influenced by trial coverage.

The majority also indicated that the judge should have acted to prevent officials from releasing certain information to the press:

[T]he trial court might well have proscribed extrajudicial statements by any lawyer, party, witness or court official which divulged prejudicial matters, such as the refusal of Sheppard to submit to an interrogation or take any lie detector tests; any statement made by Sheppard to officials; the identity of prospective witnesses or their probable testimony; any belief in guilt or innocence; or like statements concerning the merits of the case. . . .

Being advised of the great public interest in the case, the mass coverage of the press, and the potential prejudicial impact of publicity, the court could also have requested the appropriate city and county officials to promulgate a regulation with respect to dissemination of information about the case by their employees. In addition, reporters who wrote or broadcast prejudicial stories could have been warned as to the impropriety of publishing material not introduced in the proceedings. . . . In this manner, Sheppard's right to a trial free from outside interference would have been given added protection without corresponding curtailment of the news media.[87]

Gag Rules

So-called gag rules bar the press by judicial order from publishing articles containing certain types of information about pending court cases. Refusal to comply with the order may result in being held in contempt of court.

After *Sheppard*, which said a gag rule was needed to ensure the defendant in that case of a fair trial, trial judges began to use

INMATES AND FREE SPEECH

Prison rules limiting inmate communications with persons outside the walls must be measured against the First Amendment, held a unanimous Supreme Court in *Procunier v. Martinez* (1974). The justices thus invalidated California regulations allowing prison mailroom officials wide discretion to censor letters to or from inmates.

The traditional "hands-off" policy of the federal courts toward prison regulations is rooted in a realistic appreciation of the fact that "the problems of prisons . . . are complex and intractable, and . . . not readily susceptible of resolution by decree," Justice Lewis F. Powell Jr. explained.[1]

However, he continued, "[w]hen a prison regulation or practice offends a fundamental constitutional guarantee, federal courts will discharge their duty to protect constitutional rights. . . . This is such a case."[2]

The Court recognized that censorship of inmate mail jeopardized the First Amendment rights of those free persons who wished to communicate with prisoners.

But it also acknowledged that the government had a legitimate interest in maintaining order in penal institutions, an interest that might justify the imposition of certain restraints on inmate correspondence.

To determine whether a censorship regulation constituted an impermissible restraint on First Amendment liberties, the Court set out a two-part test: the regulation must further a substantial government interest—not simply the suppression of criticism or other expression—and the restraint on speech "must be no greater than is necessary or essential to the protection of the particular governmental interest involved."[3]

The Court also held that the inmate and author must be informed of the censorship of a particular letter.

Later in the year the Court held that states were under no First Amendment obligation to permit prisoners to have face-to-face interviews with news reporters. An inmate's First Amendment rights might legitimately be constrained by security, rehabilitative, and discipline considerations, the Court said in *Procunier v. Hillery* (1974).

Referring to *Martinez*, the Court pointed to the mail as one alternative means inmates had of communicating with persons outside the prison.[4]

In 1987 the Court in *Turner v. Safley* announced a standard against which such prison regulations could be measured. If the regulation was reasonably related to legitimate penological interests, said the Court, it would be upheld.

The justices then used the *Turner* standard to strike down a state prison rule forbidding most inmate marriages—but upheld, 5–4, a regulation that bars most correspondence between inmates.[5]

1. *Procunier v. Martinez*, 416 U.S. 396 at 404–405 (1974).
2. Id. at 405–406.
3. Id. at 413.
4. *Procunier v. Hillery*, 417 U.S. 817 (1974).
5. *Turner v. Safley*, 482 U.S. 78 (1987).

such orders. Gag rules are clearly a prior restraint on publication, and their constitutionality has been challenged repeatedly by the press.

In the Court's first full-scale review of a gag rule, all nine justices held the challenged order an unconstitutional prior restraint on the press. Only three justices, however, said that all gag rules were unconstitutional. Four felt they might be permissible under some circumstances. The remaining two justices indicated their inclination to agree that all gag rules were unconstitutional.

In the small town of Sutherland, Nebraska, in October 1975, six members of a family were murdered. Police arrested Erwin Charles Simants, who was charged with the crimes. Because of the nature of the crimes and the location—a rural area with a relatively small number of potential jurors—the judge issued a gag order on the day of the preliminary hearing. Although that hearing took place in open court, the press was forbidden to report any of the testimony given or the evidence presented. The order remained in effect until the jury was chosen.

Writing the Court's opinion in *Nebraska Press Association v. Stuart* (1976), Chief Justice Burger said that the judge could have used less drastic means than the gag order to ensure that excessive publicity did not make it impossible to assemble an unbiased jury and conduct a fair trial.

"[P]rior restraints on speech and publication are the most serious and the least tolerable infringement on First Amendment rights," Burger wrote. "A prior restraint . . . has an immediate and irreversible sanction. If it can be said that a threat of criminal or civil sanctions after publication 'chills' speech, prior restraint 'freezes' it at least for the time."[88] *(See "Prior Restraint: Censorship," pp. 448–456.)*

Furthermore, said Burger, the right to report evidence given in an open courtroom is a settled principle. "[O]nce a public hearing had been held, what transpired there could not be subject to prior restraint."[89]

But the chief justice refused to rule out the possibility that the circumstances of some particular case might justify imposition of a gag rule. "This Court has frequently denied that First Amendment rights are absolute and has consistently rejected the proposition that a prior restraint can never be employed."[90]

"The right to a fair trial by a jury of one's peers is unquestionably one of the most precious and sacred safeguards enshrined in the Bill of Rights," wrote Justice Brennan in a concurring opinion joined by Justices Marshall and Stewart.

But, Brennan added, "I would hold . . . that resort to prior restraints on the freedom of the press is a constitutionally impermissible method for enforcing that right." Judges have less drastic means of ensuring fair trials than by prohibiting press "discussion of public affairs."[91] Eight years later in 1984, however, the Court upheld a state court order restraining the publication of information about a religious organization obtained through pretrial discovery that took place under court order.[92]

Lawyers' extrajudicial statements to the press became an issue for the Court in 1991. By a 5–4 vote, the Court ruled in *Gen-*

tile v. State Bar of Nevada that the free speech rights of lawyers may be curtailed if their comments present "substantial likelihood of material prejudice" during a trial. The opinion by Chief Justice Rehnquist rejected a higher "clear and present danger standard."[93]

Access and Confidentiality

In a very practical sense, the public delegates to the press the job of gathering, sifting, and reporting the news that shapes its political, economic, and social views of the world. As surrogate for the public, the press attends and reports on events that the vast majority of the public does not or cannot attend.

The news gathering process has been the subject of several Supreme Court cases as the justices have considered whether the First Amendment guarantees the press special access to or special protection for its news sources. The Court generally has refused to adopt such an expansive view of the First Amendment freedom, although the one exception to that view came when the press linked arms with the general public to argue for access to criminal trials.

In 1979 the Court in *Gannett Co. Inc. v. DePasquale* rejected the newspaper chain's claim that it had a constitutional right, under the First and the Sixth Amendments, to attend a pretrial hearing on suppression of evidence in a murder case.

By a vote of 5–4, the Court held that the judge in the case had properly granted the request of the defendants to exclude the press and public from the hearing. Upholding the judge's action were Chief Justice Burger, Justices Stewart, Powell, Rehnquist, and John Paul Stevens. Dissenting were Justices Blackmun, Brennan, White, and Marshall.

The majority based its decision wholly on the Sixth Amendment, reading it literally and finding that it guaranteed the right to a *public* trial only to the person *charged* with crime, not to the public or the press. In this case the defendants had requested that the pretrial hearing be closed; the judge had granted that request.

Justice Stewart pointed out that closing such a hearing was "often one of the most effective methods that a trial judge can employ to attempt to insure that the fairness of a trial will not be jeopardized by the dissemination of such [prejudicial] information throughout the community before the trial itself has even begun."[94]

Within a year the Court had effectively reversed itself. By 7–1, the Court in *Richmond Newspapers Inc. v. Commonwealth of Virginia* (1980) recognized that both press and public had a First Amendment right of access to trials and pretrial hearings. Justice Rehnquist dissented; Powell did not participate.

In some situations, wrote Chief Justice Burger for the Court, it might be necessary—to ensure a fair trial—to limit access to that trial. But if a judge found such limitations necessary, they must be clearly set out to support his finding that closure of the trial was necessary to preserve some overriding interest.[95]

This trend continued to a surprising climax the following year in *Chandler v. Florida*. Nothing in the Constitution—neither in the due process clause nor the guarantee of a fair trial—precluded a state from permitting television cameras in a courtroom to broadcast trial proceedings, the Court ruled.[96]

When the press asks for special access to institutions and persons not generally available to the public, it almost always gets a judicial cold shoulder. Twice the Supreme Court has confronted such a request. On both occasions, the Court held that the press had no greater access to such institutions than that enjoyed by the general public.

In 1974 the Court heard two companion cases—*Saxbe v. Washington Post Co.* and *Pell v. Procunier*—that weighed the right of reporters to gather news within the prison system against society's interest in secure prisons. In both the Court sustained, 5–4, prison regulations that bar interviews by reporters with inmates they request by name to see.[97]

The regulations prohibiting face-to-face interviews were apparently written to curtail the so-called "big wheel" phenomenon, in which the influence of certain inmates is so enhanced by publicity that disruption and disciplinary problems result.

Justice Stewart, writing for the majority, held that prison officials were justified in adopting the ban on interviews to minimize disruptive behavior. The ban did not mean that reporters had no access to the prisons, he stressed. Reporters could communicate with specific inmates through the mail. Furthermore, both the California and federal prison systems permitted reporters to visit prisons and to talk with inmates they met in the course of their supervised tour, or with inmates selected by prison officials.

But nothing in the First or Fourteenth Amendments requires "government to afford the press special access to information not shared by members of the public generally," wrote Stewart.[98]

In a dissenting opinion joined by two other justices, Justice Powell saw the ban on interviews as "impermissibly restrain[ing] the ability of the press to perform its constitutionally established function of informing the people on the conduct of their government."[99]

Elaborating on this point, Powell said the government had no legitimate interest in withholding the information reporters might gather in personal interviews:

Quite to the contrary, federal prisons are public institutions. The administration of these institutions, the effectiveness of their rehabilitative programs, the conditions of confinement they maintain, and the experiences of the individuals incarcerated therein are all matters of legitimate societal interest and concern. Respondents [the reporters] do not assert a right to force disclosure of confidential information or to invade in any way the decision-making process of governmental officials. Neither do they seek to question any inmate who does not wish to be interviewed. They only seek to be free of an exceptionless prohibition against a method of newsgathering that is essential to effective reporting in the prison context.[100]

In 1978 the Court, 4–3, reaffirmed its holding that reporters have no right to greater access to institutions and persons than the general public has.

A federal judge six years earlier found conditions in an Alameda County, California, jail to be so shocking as to constitute cruel and unusual punishment. As a result, television station KQED sought access to the prison to interview inmates and film conditions there.

The county sheriff agreed to begin monthly scheduled tours of the prison open to the press and general public but prohibited the use of cameras or sound equipment as well as interviews with inmates. KQED then won an order from a federal judge directing the sheriff to grant the press wider access, to allow the interviews and the use of sound and camera equipment. The sheriff appealed in the case of *Houchins v. KQED Inc.*

Neither the First nor Fourteenth Amendment mandates "a right of access to government information or sources of information within the government's control," wrote Chief Justice Burger, announcing the decision in an opinion only two other justices joined. The First Amendment does not guarantee access to information but only the freedom to communicate information once acquired. "[U]ntil the political branches decree otherwise, as they are free to do, the media has no special right of access to the Alameda County Jail different from or greater than that accorded the public generally," Burger wrote.[101]

The fourth member of the majority, Justice Stewart, agreed only that the order was too broad. The three dissenters—Justices Brennan, Stevens, and Powell—argued that "information-gathering is entitled to some measure of constitutional protection . . . not for the private benefit of those who might qualify as representatives of the 'press' but to insure that the citizens are fully informed regarding matters of public interest."[102]

PROTECTING CONFIDENTIALITY

Does the First Amendment allow reporters to withhold information from the government to protect a news source? Members of the press contend that the threat of exposure will discourage those news sources who, for a variety of reasons, agree to provide information to reporters only if they are assured confidentiality. Not only will the individual reporter's effectiveness be damaged by forced disclosure, they contend, but the public will also suffer, losing information that it is entitled to have. For these reasons they argue that the First Amendment protects the confidentiality of news sources, even if the sources reveal to the reporter information about crimes.

Several states have laws shielding reporters from demands of grand juries, courts, and other investigating bodies for confidential or unpublished information they have collected. But the Supreme Court has refused to recognize a constitutional privilege of journalists to refuse to answer legitimate inquiries from law enforcement officers.

Grand Jury Investigations

In 1972 the Court decided three cases in which reporters challenged grand jury subpoenas for confidential information. These cases concerned:

- Paul M. Branzburg, an investigative reporter for the Louisville *Courier-Journal* who wrote several articles based on personal observations of drug users whom he had promised not to identify. He was then subpoenaed by a grand jury to testify on what he had observed.
- Paul Pappas, a television newsman who was allowed to visit a Black Panthers headquarters during a period of civil unrest on the condition that he not report what he saw. He later was subpoenaed to testify about that visit.
- Earl Caldwell, a black reporter for the *New York Times* who gained the confidence of Black Panthers in the San Francisco area and wrote several articles about them. He was then called to testify before a grand jury about alleged criminal activity among the Panthers.

State courts in *Branzburg* and *Pappas* ruled that the reporters must provide the information sought to the grand juries. The two reporters appealed.

In *Caldwell* a federal court of appeals, reversing a lower court, held that freedom of the press protected Caldwell not only from testifying but even from appearing before the grand jury. The Justice Department appealed this ruling to the Supreme Court.

By 5–4 the Supreme Court sustained the state courts in *Branzburg v. Hayes* and *In re Pappas*, and reversed the appeals court in *United States v. Caldwell*. "Until now the only testimonial privilege for unofficial witnesses that is rooted in the Federal Constitution is the Fifth Amendment privilege against self-incrimination," wrote Justice White for the majority in one opinion that addressed all three cases. "We are asked to create another by interpreting the First Amendment to grant newsmen a testimonial privilege that other citizens do not enjoy. This we decline to do."[103]

The majority denied that any infringement of First Amendment rights was involved in these cases:

We do not question the significance of free speech, press or assembly to the country's welfare. Nor is it suggested that news gathering does not qualify for First Amendment protection; without some protection for seeking out the news, freedom of the press could be eviscerated. But this case involves no intrusions upon speech or assembly, no prior restraint or restriction on what the press may publish and no express or implied command that the press publish what it prefers to withhold. No exaction or tax for the privilege of publishing, and no penalty, civil or criminal, related to the content of published material is at issue here. The use of confidential sources by the press is not forbidden or restricted; reporters remain free to seek news from any source by means within the law. No attempt is made to require the press to publish its sources of information or indiscriminately to disclose them on request.[104]

White observed that the First Amendment did not protect the press from obeying other valid laws such as labor and antitrust regulations. The authority of grand juries to subpoena witnesses was vital to their task. "Fair and effective law enforcement aimed at providing security for the person and property of the individual is a fundamental function of government," he wrote, "and the grand jury plays an important constitutionally mandated role in this process."[105] On the record, said the Court, it found that the public interest in law enforcement and in ensuring effective grand jury proceedings outweighed the uncertain burden on newsgathering that might result from insisting that reporters, like other citizens, respond to relevant questions put to them in the course of a valid grand jury investigation or criminal trial.

The majority thought that potential exposure would affect few of a reporter's confidential news sources. "Only where news sources themselves are implicated in crime or possess information relevant to the grand jury's task need they or the reporter be concerned about grand jury subpoenas," White wrote. Nor can we "seriously entertain the notion that the First Amendment protects a newsman's agreement to conceal the criminal conduct of his source . . . on the theory that it is better to write about crime than to do something about it," he said.[106]

The majority's "crabbed view of the First Amendment reflects a disturbing insensitivity to the critical role of an independent press in our society," wrote Justice Stewart in a dissent that Justices Marshall and Brennan joined. The majority decision "invites state and federal authorities to undermine the historic independence of the press by attempting to annex the journalistic profession as an investigative arm of government."[107]

Stewart contended that a reporter had a constitutional right to maintain a confidential relationship with news sources. The right to publish must include the right to gather news, he said, and that right in turn must include a right to confidentiality. A reporter's immunity to grand jury probes is not a personal right but the right of the public to maintain an access to information of public concern, Stewart said.[108]

Stewart did not believe the immunity was absolute. Weighed against other constitutional rights, First Amendment rights must be given a preferred position, he said, and government must show a compelling reason for restricting them. He suggested that a reporter be required to appear before a grand jury only if the government can

(1) show that there is probable cause to believe that the newsman has information which is clearly relevant to a specific probable violation of law; (2) demonstrate that the information sought cannot be obtained by alternative means less destructive of First Amendment rights; and (3) demonstrate a compelling and overriding interest in the information.[109]

Justice Douglas also dissented, holding that the First Amendment immunized reporters from grand jury investigations unless they were implicated in a crime.

Newsroom Searches

The Supreme Court sanctioned a different threat to confidentiality when it ruled in *Zurcher v. The Stanford Daily* (1978) that the First Amendment does not protect newspaper offices from warranted police searches for information or evidence.

The lineup of the justices was almost identical to that in the three "newsman's privilege" cases of 1972. Justice Brennan did not participate; Justice Stevens dissented as had Justice Douglas (whom Stevens succeeded) in the earlier cases. By 5–3, the Court rejected the argument of the nation's press that police should use subpoenas, not search warrants, to obtain information or evidence from news files, at least so long as the reporter or newspaper was not suspected of any involvement in criminal activity.

A subpoena is a less intrusive means for obtaining evidence than is a search by police armed with a warrant. The subpoena requires a person to search his own home, office, or files for certain specified items. The search warrant authorizes police, unannounced, to enter a home or office by force if necessary to search for the particular material the warrant describes.

Furthermore, a person faced with a search warrant has no opportunity to contest the search before it takes place. But a person subpoenaed to produce information may move to quash the subpoena.

The case arose from a 1971 police search of the offices of the *Stanford Daily,* the campus newspaper of Stanford University. The search occurred after conflict between police and demonstrators at Stanford University Hospital resulted in injury to nine police officers. Police obtained a warrant to search the files, wastebaskets, desks, and photo laboratories at the *Daily* offices; the object of the fruitless search was evidence of the identity of the demonstrators responsible for the police injuries.

The Supreme Court majority declared that the men who wrote the Fourth Amendment were well aware of the conflict between the government and the press, and if they had felt that special procedures were needed when the government wanted information in the possession of the press, they would have said so.

The First Amendment guarantee of a free press that can gather, analyze, and publish news without governmental interference is sufficiently protected by the Fourth Amendment requirement that searches be reasonable and that warrants be issued by neutral magistrates, wrote Justice White for the majority. He continued:

Properly administered, the preconditions for a warrant—probable cause, specificity with respect to the place to be searched and the things to be seized, and overall reasonableness—should afford sufficient protection against the harms that are assertedly threatened by warrants for searching newspaper offices.[110]

Magistrates could ensure that the search not interfere with publication—and that the warrant be specific enough to prevent officers from rummaging in newspaper files or intruding into editorial decisions. White also said the majority was no more persuaded than it had been in 1972 "that confidential sources will disappear and that the press will suppress news because of fears of warranted searches."[111]

In his dissent Justice Stewart, joined by Justice Marshall, found it

self-evident that police searches of newspaper offices burden the freedom of the press. . . . [I]t cannot be denied that confidential information may be exposed to the eyes of police officers who execute a search warrant by rummaging through the files, cabinets, desks and wastebaskets of a newsroom. Since the indisputable effect of such searches will thus be to prevent a newsman from being able to promise confidentiality to his potential sources, it seems obvious to me that a journalist's access to information, and thus the public's, will thereby be impaired. . . . The end result, wholly inimical to the First Amendment, will be a diminishing flow of potentially important information to the public.[112]

Justice Stevens also disagreed with the majority, arguing that documentary evidence in the possession of an innocent third party should be sought by subpoena rather than search warrant.

THE FREEDOM TO BROADCAST

The modern expansion of the "press" to include radio and television broadcasters generated a new set of First Amendment issues.

Because the number of broadcast frequencies is limited, the government has found it necessary to allocate access to them through a licensing system. With regard to print media, such a system would be considered prior restraint in violation of free speech and free press. But as the Supreme Court noted in 1969, "[w]ithout government control the . . . [broadcast media] would be of little use because of the cacophony of competing voices, none of which could be clearly and predictably heard."[113]

The Court has sustained the right of the Federal Communications Commission (FCC) to determine who receives broadcast licenses, but it has emphasized that such determinations must be made on neutral principles that do not favor one broadcaster over another because of the particular views espoused. As early as 1943 the Court wrote that "Congress did not authorize the Commission to choose among applicants upon the basis of their political, economic or social views or upon any other capricious basis."[114]

The Fairness Doctrine

The unique nature of the broadcast media does not place it altogether outside the protection of the First Amendment. But the freedom guaranteed to those who wish to broadcast is a different variety, subject to different requirements.

For almost forty years the FCC required broadcasters to give individuals whose views or records were attacked on the air an opportunity to respond. The commission, to protect what it viewed as the public's right to hear a fair presentation of both sides of a dispute, also required broadcasters who editorialized to offer persons with opposing views the right of reply. This policy was known as the fairness doctrine.

In *Red Lion Broadcasting Co. v. Federal Communications Commission* (1969), broadcasters challenged the fairness doctrine as a violation of their First Amendment rights to determine the content of broadcasts without governmental interference. The Supreme Court unanimously rejected this argument. "Where there are substantially more individuals who want to broadcast than there are frequencies to allocate, it is idle to posit an unabridgeable First Amendment right to broadcast comparable to the right of every individual to speak, write, or publish," wrote Justice White for the majority.[115]

The First Amendment right of viewers and listeners to diverse viewpoints on matters of political, economic, and social concern is paramount to the rights of broadcasters, White argued:

A license permits broadcasting, but the licensee has no constitutional right to be the one who holds the license or to monopolize a radio frequency to the exclusion of his fellow citizens. There is nothing in the First Amendment which prevents the Government from requiring a licensee to share his frequency with others and to conduct himself as a proxy or fiduciary with obligations to present those views and voices which are representative of his community and which would otherwise, by necessity, be barred from the airwaves.[116]

The Right of Access

Conversely, the Supreme Court has ruled that radio and television stations are not required by the First Amendment's guarantee to sell time to all individuals and groups who wish to expound their views on public issues across the airwaves. The Court announced this decision in *Columbia Broadcasting System v. Democratic National Committee* (1973) by a 7–2 vote.

Six of the justices, led by Chief Justice Burger, held that while the fairness doctrine did require broadcasters to provide a right of reply to opposing views, Congress had firmly rejected the idea that all persons wishing to air their views should have access to broadcast facilities. The fairness doctrine makes the broadcaster responsible for adequate coverage of public issues in a manner that fairly reflects different viewpoints, the six agreed, but since every viewpoint cannot be aired, Congress and the FCC have appropriately left it to the broadcaster to exercise journalistic discretion in selecting those that present a fair picture of the issue.

Five of the six justices saw the basic question as "not whether there is to be discussion of controversial issues of public importance in the broadcast media, but rather who shall determine what issues are to be discussed by whom, and when."[117] Providing a right of access to the airwaves would work chiefly to benefit persons who could afford to buy the time, and these persons could not be held accountable for fairness, they said.

Justice Douglas agreed with the outcome of the majority's reasoning but went beyond its opinion to contend that the First Amendment actually prohibited the government from requiring broadcasters to accept such paid editorial advertisements. Broadcasters, Douglas wrote, are entitled to the same protection under the guarantee of a free press that newspapers receive.

Justices Brennan and Marshall dissented. By approving the broadcasters' policy of refusing to sell such air time, the government was abridging the right of its citizens to free speech, they wrote.

The public's First Amendment interest "in the reception of a full spectrum of views presented in a vigorous and uninhibited manner on controversial issues of public importance" was thwarted by a policy of refusing paid editorials, Brennan argued. That refusal was government action clearly violating the First Amendment ban, he explained, noting as his reasons the public nature of the airwaves, the preferred status given to broadcasters to whom the government granted the right to use a certain frequency, the extensive government regulation of broadcast programming, and FCC approval of the challenged policy. Such a policy gave broadcasters nearly exclusive control over the "selection of issues and viewpoints to be covered, the manner of presentation, and, perhaps most important, who shall speak." The fairness doctrine was insufficient to ensure this necessary wide-open exchange of views, said Brennan.[118]

Another side of this issue came to the Court in 1984, when the justices in *FCC v. League of Women Voters of California* struck down a federal law barring editorials on public radio and television programs that received federal grants. This curtailed precisely the sort of speech the Framers meant to protect, wrote Brennan.[119]

President Ronald Reagan opposed the fairness doctrine and he appointed to the FCC commissioners who agreed with him. After the Court declined to review a lower court ruling that the FCC could abandon this doctrine without congressional approval, the FCC voted 4–0 in August 1987 to discard it.[120]

Content and Context

In 1978 the Court upheld against a First Amendment challenge the FCC's power to limit the hours during which radio stations may broadcast material that, although offensive to many listeners, is not obscene.

About two o'clock one afternoon, a New York radio station owned by the Pacifica Foundation aired a recorded monologue by humorist George Carlin. Entitled "Filthy Words," the monologue satirized society's attitude toward certain words, in particular seven that are usually barred from use on the air. In the monologue, Carlin lists the seven "dirty words" (shit, piss, fuck, cunt, cocksucker, motherfucker, and tits) and then uses them in various forms throughout the recording.

After receiving a parent's complaint that his young son had heard the monologue, the FCC issued an order to the station restricting the hours during which such an "offensive" program could be broadcast. Pacifica challenged the order, arguing that the FCC was regulating the content of a program in violation of the guarantee of free speech.

"No such absolute rule [forbidding government regulation of content] is mandated by the Constitution," said Justice John Paul Stevens for the majority of five. "[B]oth the content and the context of speech are critical elements of First Amendment analysis." While "some uses of even the most offensive words are unquestionably protected" by the First Amendment, "the constitutional protection accorded to . . . such patently offensive . . . language [as used in the monologue] need not be the same in every context. . . . Words that are commonplace in one setting are shocking in another," he said.[121]

The context of the broadcast justified the FCC's regulation, the majority concluded. Because the broadcast media has established a "uniquely pervasive presence," offensive material that is broadcast reaches people in the privacy of their homes "where the individual's right to be let alone plainly outweighs the First Amendment rights of an intruder." Furthermore, the broadcast was "uniquely accessible to children," and the Court has held that speech otherwise protected might be regulated to protect the welfare of children.[122] Four justices dissented.

Cross-Media Ownership and Cable Television

The Supreme Court upheld in 1978 the authority of the FCC to decree an end to common ownership of a community's single newspaper and its only radio or television station.

The commission has broad power "to regulate broadcasting in the 'public interest,'" wrote Justice Marshall for the unanimous Court. The FCC issued its order to encourage diversity of ownership that could possibly result in diversity of viewpoints aired within a community. This was a valid public interest and a rational means of reaching that goal, Marshall said in *Federal Communications Commission v. National Citizens Committee for Broadcasting.*[123]

The Court in 1994 extended to cable television First Amendment protections comparable to those enjoyed by print media. Writing for the majority in *Turner Broadcasting System v. Federal Communications Commission,* Justice Anthony M. Kennedy said cable television is not subject to the kind of regulations imposed on broadcasters because the rationale for that regulation, the scarcity of radio and television channels, does not apply. Seven other justices joined that portion of the opinion. The Court ruling, however, did not address a constitutional challenge in the same case to a 1992 law requiring cable systems to carry local broadcast programs. In returning the conflict to a lower court for review, the majority said the "must carry" rules were content-neutral and could be judged under the intermediate level of scrutiny. Kennedy led five justices in concluding that the rules were not designed to favor or disadvantage speech of any particular content, but rather to protect broadcast television from potential unfair competition by cable systems.[124]

In 1996 the Court again struggled with free speech protections for cable television, this time with an eye toward ensuring that children are not exposed to sexually explicit programming. The Court's splintered opinion and fractured reasoning (no approach commanded a majority) revealed the difficulty of legal questions involving indecency as well as the evolving cable industry. The case concerned three sections of the 1992 cable law restricting indecent programming. The Court, 7–2, upheld sections of the act permitting cable operators to refuse indecent shows on "leased access channels," which are bought and controlled by independent programmers. But the Court, 5–4, struck down a section allowing cable companies to refuse to air indecent programming on "public access channels," those required by local governments. The justices also invalidated, 6–3, a section requiring cable operators to place indecent "leased access" programming on a blocked channel that could be seen only by a subscriber's written request. The majority said that method of regulation was too restrictive.[125]

Freedom of Religion

It is unthinkable to most Americans that Congress or the president could or would dictate what religious beliefs individuals must hold and what church, if any, they must attend. The freedom to believe as one chooses, or not to believe at all, is as basic to the concept of American democracy as the rights of free speech and press.

The First Amendment's guarantees of free exercise of religion and separation of church and state were the direct products of colonial experience. Many of the colonies were established by settlers fleeing from religious persecution, primarily in Anglican-dominated England.

Some of the colonialists were themselves intolerant, persecuting those whose religious beliefs and practices were different from their own. Several colonies forbade Catholics and/or non-Christians to hold certain offices and jobs. For a time, there was a state religion in some of the colonies. Others, however, notably Rhode Island, Pennsylvania, and Delaware, tolerated religious diversity.[1]

By the time of the American Revolution, belief in religious toleration was well established, and, when the First Amendment was written in 1789, it was religious freedom that led the list of rights Congress was forbidden to abridge. As Justice Joseph Story wrote in his commentaries on the Constitution:

It was under a solemn consciousness of the dangers from ecclesiastical ambition, the bigotry of spiritual pride, and the intolerance of sects, thus exemplified in our domestic as well as in foreign annals, that it was deemed advisable to exclude from the national government all power to act upon the subject.[2]

The Supreme Court has never viewed either of the religion clauses—"Congress shall make no law respecting an establishment of religion, or prohibiting the free exercise thereof"—as absolute.

Freedom to *believe* is absolute, but freedom to *practice* that belief may be circumscribed by government under certain conditions. Government may not directly aid religion, but secular programs that indirectly benefit religious institutions may be permissible.

The Court's task has been to ensure that government remains neutral toward religion. As Chief Justice Warren E. Burger explained in 1970:

The course of constitutional neutrality in this area cannot be an absolutely straight line; rigidity could well defeat the basic purpose of these provisions, which is to insure that no religion be sponsored or favored, none commanded and none inhibited. The general principle deducible from the First Amendment and all that has been said by the Court is this: that we will not tolerate either governmentally established religion or governmental interference with religion. Short of those expressly proscribed governmental acts there is room for play in the joints productive of a benevolent neutrality which will permit religious exercise to exist without sponsorship and without interference.

Each value judgment under the Religion Clauses must therefore turn on whether particular acts in question are intended to establish or interfere with religious beliefs and practices or have the effect of doing so. Adherence to the policy of neutrality that derives from an accommodation of the Establishment and Free Exercise Clauses has prevented the kind of involvement that would tip the balance toward government control of churches or governmental restraint on religious practice.[3]

To maintain this neutrality, the Court has developed general tests that it applies to the circumstances of each case invoking the religion clauses. These tests, or sets of standards, have not been uniformly applied by the Court.

But generally, if a law allegedly interferes with the free exercise of religion, the Court will first examine the statute to see if it carefully describes the conduct that may be restricted. The statute may not be vague or too broad, nor may it leave too much to the discretion of the officials administering it. It may not discriminate on the basis of religion.

If the statute is carefully drawn and its purpose and effect are to achieve a secular goal, such as setting the time and place of open-air religious meetings to minimize disruption to other members of the public, the restriction likely will be permitted, even if it occasionally restricts a religious exercise. When an action indirectly restricts religious liberty, government must show that it has a compelling reason for taking the action and that no means less restrictive of religious freedom could have accomplished the same secular goal.

If government action is alleged to constitute establishment of religion, the government can successfully defend it only by showing that both the purpose and effect of the action are secular and not intended to aid religion; that the government involvement with religion required by the challenged action is not excessive; and that it does not require continued governmental surveillance of the religious institutions affected.

Civil libertarians have protested that the contemporary Court has applied these general rules far too leniently, allowing undue restriction of religious exercise, on the one hand, and increasing state involvement in religious affairs, on the other. But overall, most observers agree the Court has held onto the Framers' mandate of separation of state and religious domain.

Marvin E. Frankel, a former federal judge and Columbia University law professor, has reviewed the last half century of Supreme Court decisions in the area of religious liberty. In his book published in 1994, he concluded: "[D]espite the appearance of petty inquisitors from time to time, the pressure for orthodoxy in religious conceptions has never prevailed in America. There can be no heresy here. Or blasphemy. We are all free to believe as we please. And none of us is entitled to force beliefs on others. Above all, no person and no church is brigaded with the power of the state or condemned to be coerced by the state in matters of conscience."[4]

The Free Exercise of Religion

Freedom of religion is inextricably bound up with the other freedoms guaranteed by the First Amendment. Without the freedoms of speech and press, the expression and circulation of religious beliefs and doctrines would be impossible. Without the freedoms of assembly and association, the right to participate with others in public and private religious worship would be curtailed.

Before and after the Court held in 1940 that the Fourteenth Amendment protected the free exercise of religion from restriction by the states, it resolved many cases challenging state infringements on religious liberty by relying on the freedoms of speech and press.

The Court held in *Lovell v. Griffin* (1938) that a municipal prohibition against distribution of handbills without a permit was an unconstitutional prior restraint on freedom of the press; at issue in this particular case was the right of a Jehovah's Witness to pass out religious circulars. And in *Kunz v. New York* (1951), the Court held that arbitrary denial of a public speech permit to a Baptist minister was a violation of the rights of free speech and assembly as well as of religious liberty.[5] *(See details of Lovell case, pp. 451–452; Kunz case, pp. 429–430, 479.)*

As a result of this close relationship, the Supreme Court uses many of the same tests developed in the context of restrictions on free speech and press to determine if government has impermissibly restricted free exercise of religion.

In general the Supreme Court has ruled that states and the federal government may restrict the free exercise of religion if the exercise involves fraud or other criminal activity and there is no other means of protecting the public. Government also may restrict religious practices that threaten public peace and order but only if the restriction is nondiscriminatory, narrowly drawn, and precisely applied.

In some circumstances, the Court has upheld the right of government to compel an individual to take action contrary to his or her religious belief. As the rule was stated late in the 1970s, such a compulsory law will stand against a First Amendment challenge if its primary purpose and effect are to advance a valid secular goal and if the means chosen are calculated to have the least possible restrictive effect on free exercise of religion.

RELIGION AND CRIME

In its first direct pronouncement on the First Amendment's protection for the free exercise of religion, the Supreme Court held in 1879 that polygamy was a crime, not a religious practice. *Reynolds v. United States* brought before the Court a Mormon's challenge to the constitutionality of the federal law that barred plural marriages in Utah territory.

Observing that bigamy and polygamy were considered punishable offenses in every state, the Court found "it . . . impossible to believe that the constitutional guaranty of religious freedom was intended to prohibit legislation in respect to this most important feature of social life."[6]

Eleven years later the Court elaborated on this reasoning when it upheld an Idaho territorial statute denying the vote to bigamists, polygamists, and those who advocated plural marriages.

In *Davis v. Beason* (1890), the Court for the first time distinguished between protected belief and unprotected conduct:

It was never intended or supposed that the [First] Amendment could be evoked as a protection against legislation for the punishment of acts inimical to the peace, good order and morals of society. With man's relations to his Maker and the obligations he may think they impose, and the manner in which an expression shall be made by him of his belief on those subjects, no interference can be permitted provided always the laws of society designed to secure its peace and prosperity, and the morals of its people, are not interfered with. However free the exercise of religion may be, it must be subordinate to the criminal laws of the country, passed with reference to actions regarded by general consent as properly the subjects of punitive legislation.[7]

Justice Stephen J. Field, who wrote the Court's opinion, concluded succinctly: "Crime is not the less odious because sanctioned by what any particular sect may designate as religion."[8]

Fraud

States and municipalities, wishing to protect their citizens from fraud, occasionally have restricted religious groups' freedom to solicit funds to maintain the religion.

In *Cantwell v. Connecticut* (1940), the Court laid out the type of restriction that might be permitted:

Nothing we have said is intended even remotely to imply that, under the cloak of religion, persons may, with impunity, commit fraud upon the public. . . . Even the exercise of religion may be at some slight inconvenience in order that a State may protect its citizens from injury. Without doubt a State may protect its citizens from fraudulent solicitation by requiring a stranger in the community . . . to establish his identity and his authority to act for the cause which he purports to represent. The State is likewise free to regulate the time and manner of solicitation generally, in the interest of public safety, peace, comfort or convenience.[9]

In *Martin v. City of Struthers* (1943), the Court held that the possibility that some persons might use house-to-house solicitations as opportunities to commit crimes did not warrant an ordinance prohibiting all solicitors from ringing doorbells to summon the occupants of the house. The Court said that the municipality must find a way of preventing crime that was less restrictive of those persons soliciting for sincere causes.[10] *(See details of this case, pp. 443–444.)*

Only once has the Supreme Court dealt with the question whether a movement designated as religious by its founders was actually fraudulent.

Guy Ballard, the leader of the "I Am" movement in the mid-1940s, at one point had approximately three million followers. He and two relatives claimed that their spiritual teachings had been dictated by God, that Jesus had personally appeared to them, and that they could cure both curable and incurable diseases. They were indicted by the federal government for mail fraud.

The sole question before the Supreme Court in *United States v. Ballard* (1944) was whether the trial jury had been properly instructed that it need not determine whether the Ballards' beliefs were true but only whether the Ballards believed them to be true.

A majority of the Court found the instruction proper. Religious freedom, wrote Justice William O. Douglas,

embraces the right to maintain theories of life and of death and of the hereafter which are rank heresy to followers of the orthodox faiths. Heresy trials are foreign to our Constitution. Men may believe what they cannot prove. They may not be put to the proof of their religious doctrines or beliefs. . . . The religious views espoused by respondents might seem incredible, if not preposterous, to most people. But if those doctrines are subject to trial before a jury charged with finding their truth or falsity, then the same can be done with the religious beliefs of any sect.[11]

Chief Justice Harlan Fiske Stone dissented, saying that a jury could properly be instructed to determine whether the representations were true or false. Stone said he saw no reason why the government could not submit evidence, for instance, showing that Ballard had never cured anyone of a disease. Justice Robert H. Jackson also dissented, on the grounds that the case should have been dismissed altogether. *(See box, Religion: An Evolving Definition, this page.)*

Laws that make employment of children under a certain age a crime have been upheld against claims that they impinge on religious liberty.

In 1944 the Court sustained a Massachusetts statute that prohibited girls younger than eighteen from selling newspapers on the streets. The law had been applied to forbid a nine-year-old Jehovah's Witness from distributing religious literature. The state's interest in protecting children from the harmful effects of child labor "is not nullified merely because the parent grounds his claim to control the child's course of conduct on religion or conscience," the Court wrote in *Prince v. Massachusetts*.[12]

RELIGION: AN EVOLVING DEFINITION

As the nation's tolerance for religious diversity has broadened, so has the Supreme Court's definition of beliefs it considers religious and therefore entitled to First Amendment protection.

Originally the Court considered religion only in the traditional Judeo-Christian sense, which demanded belief in a divine being. "The term 'religion' has reference to one's views of his relations to his Creator, and the obligations they impose of reverence for his being and character, and of obedience to his will," the Court said in the 1890 case of *Davis v. Beason*.[1]

This view prevailed in 1931, when Chief Justice Charles Evans Hughes wrote that "[t]he essence of religion is belief in a relation to God involving duties superior to those arising from any human relation."[2] This definition guided Congress in 1948 when it tried to define the belief one must hold to qualify for exemption from military service as a conscientious objector. *(See box, Religion and War, p. 482.)*

In the 1940s the Court began to move toward a more expansive interpretation of "religion," accepting beliefs that were neither orthodox nor theistically based. In 1943 Justice Felix Frankfurter quoted with approval the words of federal judge Augustus Hand in a case earlier that year:

It is unnecessary to attempt a definition of religion; the content of the term is found in the history of the human race and is incapable of compression into a few words. Religious belief arises from a sense of the inadequacy of reason as a means of relating the individual to his fellow men and to his universe. . . . [I]t may justly be regarded as a response of the individual to an inward mentor, call it conscience or God, that is for many persons at the present time the equivalent of what has always been thought a religious impulse.[3]

The following year Justice William O. Douglas, speaking for the Court majority, said that the free exercise of religion "embraces the right to maintain theories of life and of death and of the hereafter which are rank heresy to followers of the orthodox faiths."[4] In 1953 Douglas wrote that "it is no business of courts to say that which is religious practice or activity for one group is not religion under the protection of the First Amendment."[5]

As one commentator noted, these decisions made clear that "the classification of a belief as religion does not depend upon the tenets of its creed."[6]

The breadth of the Court's modern definition of religion was perhaps most clearly stated in its 1961 decision in *Torcaso v. Watkins*:

neither a State nor the federal government can constitutionally force a person "to profess a belief or disbelief in any religion." Neither can constitutionally pass laws nor impose requirements which aid all religions as against non-believers, and neither can aid those religions based on a belief in the existence of God as against those religions founded on different beliefs.[7]

In 1965 the Court reaffirmed its *Torcaso* judgment, viewing as religious any sincere and meaningful belief that occupies a place in the possessor's life parallel to the place God holds in the faith of an orthodox believer.

The Court expanded this definition in 1970 to include moral and ethical beliefs held with the strength of traditional religious convictions.[8]

1. *Davis v. Beason*, 133 U.S. 333 at 342 (1890).
2. *United States v. Macintosh*, 283 U.S. 605 at 633–634 (1931).
3. *United States v. Kauten*, 133 P. 2d 703 at 708 (1943), quoted by Justice Felix Frankfurter, dissenting, in *West Virginia State Board of Education v. Barnette*, 319 U.S. 624 at 658–659 (1943).
4. *United States v. Ballard*, 322 U.S. 78 at 86 (1944).
5. *Fowler v. Rhode Island*, 345 U.S. 67 at 70 (1953).
6. "Toward a Constitutional Definition of Religion," *Harvard Law Review* 91 (March 1978) 5: 1056.
7. *Torcaso v. Watkins*, 367 U.S. 488 at 495 (1961).
8. *United States v. Seeger*, 380 U.S. 163 at 166 (1965); *Welsh v. United States*, 398 U.S. 333 (1970).

Drugs and Sacrifice

A state must prove that it has a "compelling interest" in enforcing a law that infringes on religious practices, the Court ruled in 1963. In 1990 the Court significantly narrowed that standard and its generous view of the free exercise clause.[13] The 1990 case, *Employment Division v. Smith*, involved the sacramental use of the drug peyote.

The ruling unleashed a torrent of criticism against the Court, and Congress in 1993 passed legislation reversing the effects of *Smith. (See details of Sherbert v. Verner, p. 484.)*

Two Oregonians were fired from their jobs with a private drug rehabilitation program because they took peyote at a Native American church ceremony. Peyote, a cactus that contains the hallucinogen mescaline, is a traditional element of Native American religious ceremonies. Oregon law subjected anyone who used the drug to criminal penalties, making no exception, as some laws do, for its sacramental use. The workers were then denied state unemployment compensation on the grounds that they had been discharged for criminal behavior.

The Supreme Court not only upheld the denial of benefits, but also declared that states may outlaw all use of peyote without violating the guarantee of free exercise of religion. A five-justice majority, led by Justice Antonin Scalia, said no constitutional violation occurs when a criminal law that applies generally to all people has the incidental effect of infringing on religious exercise for some.

The vote in the case was 5–4. Scalia was joined by Chief Justice William H. Rehnquist, Byron R. White, John Paul Stevens, and Anthony M. Kennedy. Justices Harry A. Blackmun, William J. Brennan Jr., Thurgood Marshall, and Sandra Day O'Connor dissented.

(O'Connor sought to keep the stricter constitutional standard but joined the majority to uphold the denial of benefits, saying the state of Oregon had convincingly argued that its interest in drug control was compelling and outweighed the law's burden on religious practice.)

In 1993, after extensive lobbying by religious and civil liberty groups, Congress passed the Religious Freedom Restoration Act. This legislation was intended to reverse the *Smith* ruling by making it more difficult for states to enforce laws that incidentally affected some people's freedom to exercise their religion. The law says government may burden a person's exercise of religion only if it demonstrates that the regulation furthers a compelling governmental interest and is the least restrictive means of furthering that compelling governmental interest.[14]

In a separate case the Court in 1993 unanimously struck down a city's ban on ritual animal sacrifices, saying that it interfered with the free exercise of an Afro-Cuban religion. The justices said the city of Hialeah, Florida, had improperly targeted followers of the Santeria religion. The ban against animal killing was not generally applied, the justices noted. Rather, the ban was only on ritual sacrifice and, as such, infringed only on the Santerians' exercise.[15] The Court observed that although the ordi-

Santeria priest Rigoberto Zamora cooks the lamb and goat he sacrificed in a religious ritual the previous day. Zamora and other members of his church celebrated the Supreme Court's decision striking down city attempts to prohibit animal sacrifices in religious worship.

nances at issue ostensibly sought to protect public health or prevent cruelty to animals, they applied only to "ritual sacrifice" and not to other killings, such as those by hunters.

RELIGION AND SOCIAL ORDER

At times, society's need for order and tranquility may be strong enough to warrant restriction of religious liberty. But the Supreme Court has made it clear that such restrictions must be narrowly drawn and uniformly applied.

The conflict between public order and religious liberty was first raised in *Cantwell v. Connecticut* (1940). Jesse Cantwell, a Jehovah's Witness, played a recording that attacked the Catholic church. Two passersby who were Catholic heard it. When they indicated their displeasure with the message, he stopped the record and moved on. The next day he was arrested for breach of the peace.

The Supreme Court overturned the conviction, finding the statute defining breach of the peace too broad, "sweeping in a great variety of conduct under a general and indefinite characterization." This vagueness left too much discretion to officials charged with applying it.

Cantwell had not started a riot or caused anyone else to take action that amounted to a breach of the peace, the majority said. He therefore raised no "clear and present menace to public peace and order as to render him liable to conviction of the common law offense in question."[16] *(See details of this case, p. 428.)*

Permits

In *Cantwell* the Court struck down a statute that forbade solicitation for religious causes without a permit because the law allowed a state official discretion to withhold permits if he did not think the cause was a religious one. "[T]o condition the solicitation of aid for the perpetuation of religious views or systems upon a license, the grant of which rests in the exercise of a determination by state authority as to what is a religious cause, is to lay a forbidden burden upon the exercise of [religious] liberty," the Court wrote.[17] Permit systems requiring speakers, demonstrators, and paraders to seek a license before undertaking their activity were valid only if narrowly drawn and precisely applied.

In *Cox v. New Hampshire* (1941) the Court upheld conviction of a group of Jehovah's Witnesses who paraded without obtaining the required permit. The Court said the statute was not enacted or applied with intent to restrict religious freedom. Rather, it was intended simply to determine the time, manner, and place of parades so as to minimize public disruption and disorder. Such a precisely drawn and applied statute did not unconstitutionally impinge on religious liberty.[18] *(See details of this case, p. 436.)*

In *Kunz v. New York* (1951) the Court reversed the conviction of a Baptist minister who continued to give highly inflammatory public street sermons even though his permit to speak on the streets had not been renewed because earlier speeches had caused disorder.

The Court said that "an ordinance which gives an administrative official discretionary power to control in advance the right of citizens to speak on religious matters on the streets . . . is clearly invalid as a prior restraint on the exercise of First Amendment rights."[19] *(See case details, pp. 429–430.)*

In another 1951 case the Supreme Court ruled that a city could not deny a permit for a public meeting to a group whose religious views it disapproved. Jehovah's Witnesses had applied for a permit to hold a religious meeting in Havre de Grace, Maryland.

The permit was denied after officials questioned the Witnesses about their religious beliefs. The Witnesses held their meeting despite the permit denial and were arrested for disorderly conduct.

The Supreme Court reversed their convictions in *Niemotko v. Maryland* (1951). Denial of a permit to one religious group when permits had been granted to other religious meetings amounted to a denial of equal protection, the Court said.[20]

Two years later the Court reversed the conviction of a Jehovah's Witness who spoke at an open-air meeting in violation of a Pawtucket, Rhode Island, ordinance prohibiting religious addresses in public parks.

During the trial, the state admitted that it had allowed ministers of other churches to deliver sermons at church services held in public parks. The Court ruled that such unequal treatment constituted an improper establishment of religion. "To call the words which one minister speaks to his congregation a sermon, immune from regulation, and the words of another minister an address, subject to regulation, is merely an indirect way of preferring one religion over another," the Court said in *Fowler v. Rhode Island* (1953).[21]

License Fees

The validity of license fees imposed on peddlers was challenged by Jehovah's Witnesses who contested the application of the fees to Witnesses who sold religious literature from door to door.

At first review the Court sustained the license fees. In *Jones v. Opelika* (1942), a five-justice majority ruled that the solicitations were more commercial than religious:

When proponents of religious or social theories use the ordinary commercial methods of sales of articles to raise propaganda funds, it is a natural and proper exercise of the power of the state to charge reasonable fees for the privilege of canvassing. Careful as we may and should be to protect the freedoms safeguarded by the Bill of Rights, it is difficult to see in such enactments a shadow of prohibition of the exercise of religion or of abridgement of the freedom of speech or the press. It is prohibition and unjustifiable abridgement which is interdicted, not taxation.[22]

The following year Justice James F. Byrnes, who had voted with the majority, resigned and was replaced by Wiley B. Rutledge, a liberal. The Court decided to consider the license fee issue a second time, and this time struck it down, again 5–4.

The case generating the reversal concerned a Jeannette, Pennsylvania, ordinance that placed a tax of $1.50 a day on the privilege of door-to-door solicitation. It also required all persons taking orders for or delivering goods door-to-door to obtain a license from the city.

Without obtaining such a license, Jehovah's Witnesses went from house to house in the town soliciting new members. They requested "contributions" of specific amounts from persons showing an interest in their books and pamphlets but on occasion gave the literature free of charge to residents who were unable to pay. Arrested and convicted of violating the ordinance, the Witnesses claimed it unconstitutionally restricted their religious liberty.

"A state may not impose a charge for the enjoyment of a right granted by the federal constitution," the five-justice majority said in *Murdock v. Pennsylvania* (1943), overruling the Court's decision the year before in *Jones v. Opelika*.

The majority held that because Jehovah's Witnesses believe that each Witness is a minister ordained by God to preach the gospel, the license fee constituted a tax on the free exercise of religion. Soliciting new adherents by personal visitation and the sale of religious tracts was an evangelical activity that "occupies the same high estate under the First Amendment as do worship in the churches and preaching from the pulpits," wrote Justice William O. Douglas for the Court.[23]

Unlike the majority in *Opelika*, this majority did not hold that the commercial aspects of religious solicitation deprived it of its First Amendment protection:

[T]he mere fact that the religious literature is "sold" by itinerant preachers rather than "donated" does not transform evangelism into a commercial enterprise. If it did, then the passing of the collection plate in church would make the church service a commercial project. The constitutional rights of those spreading their religious beliefs through

JEHOVAH'S WITNESSES: DEFINERS OF FREEDOM

The broad interpretation of the First Amendment guarantee of the free exercise of religion has evolved almost solely in connection with one of the most reviled religious sects in American history. "Probably no sect since the early days of the Mormon Church has been as much a thorn in the communal side and as much a victim of communal hate and persecution as Jehovah's Witnesses," wrote commentator Leo Pfeffer.[1]

Jehovah's Witnesses were originally followers of Charles T. Russell, a Presbyterian who grew disillusioned with all existing religious organizations and began to fashion a new religion in the late 1860s and early 1870s.

His followers, known as Russellites, adopted the name Jehovah's Witnesses after Joseph F. Rutherford succeeded Russell in 1931 as leader of the group. In 1884 the sect established the Watchtower Bible and Tract Society to print and disseminate religious literature distributed by the Witnesses.

In 1931 the Witnesses described their mission:

As Jehovah's Witnesses our sole and only purpose is to be entirely obedient to his commandments; to make known that he is the only true and almighty God; that his Word is true and that his name is entitled to all honor and glory; that Christ is God's King, whom he has placed upon his throne of authority; that his kingdom is now come, and in obedience to the Lord's commandments we must now declare this good news as a testimony or witness to the nations and to inform the rulers and the people of and concerning Satan's cruel and oppressive organization, and particularly with reference to Christendom, which is the most wicked part of that visible organization, which great act will be quickly followed by Christ the King's bringing to the obedient peoples of the earth peace and prosperity, liberty and health, happiness and everlasting life; that God's kingdom is the hope of the world and there is no other, and that this message must be delivered by those who are identified as Jehovah's Witnesses.[2]

To carry this message across the country, the Witnesses organized Watchtower Campaigns in the 1930s and 1940s. Each house in a town would be visited by a Witness.

If the occupants were willing, the Witness would give them literature, usually for a monetary contribution, and play a phonograph record. The gist of the message was that organized religions, the Roman Catholic church in particular, were "rackets."

A typical publication, entitled *Enemies*, claimed that

the greatest racket ever invented and practiced is that of religion. The most cruel and seductive public enemy is that which employs religion to carry on the racket, and by which means the people are deceived and the name of Almighty God is reproached. There are numerous systems of religion, but the most subtle, fraudulent and injurious to humankind is that which is generally labeled the "Christian religion," because it has the appearance of a worshipful devotion to the Supreme Being, and thereby easily misleads many honest and sincere persons.[3]

In a chapter entitled "Song of the Harlot," the booklet says in part: "Referring now to the foregoing scriptural definition of harlot: what religious system exactly fits the prophecies recorded in God's Word? There is but one answer, and that is, the Roman Catholic Church."[4]

Understandably, the Witnesses were not popular in many communities. On more than one occasion members of the sect met with violence from those affronted by their views.

Several communities enacted laws to curb the activities of the Witnesses, and it was these laws that the Witnesses challenged in court.

According to constitutional historian Robert F. Cushman, members of the sect have brought some thirty major cases testing the principles of religious freedom to the Supreme Court beginning in 1938. In most of those cases, the Court ruled in their favor.[5]

The first case brought by the Witnesses was *Lovell v. Griffin* (1938), in which the Court held that religious handbills were entitled to protection of freedom of the press.

In another important case, *Cantwell v. Connecticut* (1940), the Court held, first, that the Fourteenth Amendment prohibited abridgment by the states of the free exercise of religion; second, that public officials did not have the authority to determine that some causes were religious and others were not; and third, that a breach-of-the-peace law as applied to a Jehovah's Witness whose message angered two passersby was overbroad and vague and therefore unconstitutional.[6]

In other significant decisions the Court has upheld the right of Witnesses to solicit from door to door and to ring home-owners' doorbells, to refuse to salute the flag, and to be exempt from peddler's fees on sales of their literature.[7]

1. Leo Pfeffer, *Church, State and Freedom*, rev. ed. (Boston: Beacon Press, 1967), 650; Pfeffer and Justice Robert H. Jackson's dissenting opinion in *Douglas v. City of Jeannette*, 319 U.S. 157 (1943) served as the main sources for this information.
2. Quoted by Pfeffer, *Church, State and Freedom*, 651.
3. Quoted by Justice Jackson, *Douglas v. City of Jeannette*, 319 U.S. 157 at 171 (1943).
4. Ibid.
5. Robert F. Cushman, *Cases in Civil Liberties*, 2d ed. (Englewood Cliffs, N.J.: Prentice-Hall, 1976), 305.
6. *Lovell v. Griffin*, 303 U.S. 444 (1938); *Cantwell v. Connecticut*, 310 U.S. 296 (1940).
7. *Martin v. City of Struthers*, 319 U.S. 141 (1943); *West Virginia State Board of Education v. Barnette*, 319 U.S. 624 (1943), overruling *Minersville School District v. Gobitis*, 310 U.S. 586 (1940); *Murdock v. Pennsylvania*, 319 U.S. 105 (1943), overruling *Jones v. Opelika*, 316 U.S. 584 (1942).

the spoken and printed word are not to be gauged by standards governing retailers or wholesalers of books. . . . It is plain that a religious organization needs funds to remain a going concern. But an itinerant evangelist, however misguided or intolerant he may be, does not become a mere book agent by selling the Bible or religious tracts to help defray his expenses or to sustain him. Freedom of speech, freedom of the press, freedom of religion are available to all, not merely to those who can pay their own way.[24]

Almost forty years later the Court in 1981 addressed a First Amendment challenge by the Hare Krishna sect to a Minnesota law governing conduct at a state fair. The rule required all persons seeking to sell literature or solicit funds at the fair to do so from a fixed booth. In *Heffron v. International Society for Krishna Consciousness*, the Court held that this rule was reasonable in light of the state's interest in maintaining order in a public place and that it was not an abridgement of the sect's freedom to exercise its religion. A few months later in 1981, similar considerations of evenhandedness guided the Court in *Widmar v. Vincent.* A state university must grant the same access to university buildings to an organized student group that wishes to hold religious meetings as it does to any organized group that wishes to meet for any reason, the Court said.[25]

RELIGION AND PATRIOTISM

Under what circumstances may government compel a person to set aside or subordinate his or her religious beliefs in order to fulfill some officially imposed duty? The Supreme Court usually has upheld statutes aimed clearly at maintaining or improving the public health and welfare even if those laws indirectly infringe on religious liberty.

In 1905 a state law requiring compulsory vaccination against smallpox was sustained against a challenge brought by Seventh-day Adventists opposed to it on religious grounds. The Court ruled in *Jacobson v. Massachusetts* that the legislature had acted reasonably to require vaccination in order to suppress a disease that threatened the entire population.[26]

The Supreme Court, however, has remained silent on the question whether the state can force a person to accept medical treatment, including blood transfusions, if such treatment would violate religious beliefs. Although a number of well-publicized cases have arisen in lower courts, the Supreme Court so far has chosen not to adjudicate the issue.

In several instances the Court has determined that the government's interest in imposing a duty upon individual citizens is not great enough to warrant the intrusion on their free exercise of religion. Two of the Court's early decisions on this issue illustrate the shifting weights accorded government interests and religious liberty in different situations.

In the 1925 case of *Pierce v. Society of Sisters,* the Court ruled that Oregon could not constitutionally compel all schoolchildren to attend public schools. Such compulsion violated the liberty of parents to direct the upbringing of their children, a liberty which includes the right to send children to parochial schools. But in 1934 the Court held that a college student's conscientious objection to war did not excuse him from attending mandatory classes in military science and tactics at the University of California.[27]

Flag Salute Cases - I

By far the most dramatic cases to pose the question of government compulsion versus religious liberty involved schoolchildren and the American flag. Could government demand that children be forced to salute the American flag against their religious beliefs? These cases arose as Europe and then the United States entered World War II.

Lillian and William Gobitas, aged twelve and ten, were expelled from a Minersville, Pennsylvania, school in 1936 for refusing to participate in daily flag salute ceremonies. The children were Jehovah's Witnesses who had been taught not to worship any graven image.

When school districts made the pledge of allegiance compulsory, Walter Gobitas's children, William and Lillian, Jehovah's Witnesses, were expelled for refusing to salute the flag. In *Minersville School District v. Gobitis* (1940)—the name was misspelled in the Court records—Harlan Fiske Stone wrote a lone dissent arguing that the pledge requirement was a violation of the children's freedom of religion. The Court reversed its ruling three years later.

Their parents appealed to the local school board to make an exception for their children to the flag salute requirement. When the school board refused, the parents placed the children in a private school and then sued to recover the additional school costs and to stop the school board from requiring the flag salute as a condition for attendance in the public schools.

A federal district court in Philadelphia and then the court of appeals upheld the parents' position. The school board appealed to the Supreme Court.

On three earlier occasions the Supreme Court in brief, unsigned opinions had dismissed challenges to flag salute requirements, saying that they posed no substantial federal question. But in each of those cases the result of the dismissal was to sustain the requirement.[28] A dismissal of the Gobitas case would have left the lower court decisions in place, striking down the requirement.

The Supreme Court granted review, and the case of *Minersville School District v. Gobitis* was argued in the spring of 1940. The Gobitas children were represented by attorneys for the American Civil Liberties Union; a "friend of the court" brief was filed by the American Bar Association in their behalf.

The Supreme Court voted 8–1, however, to reverse the lower courts and sustain the flag salute requirement.

Religious liberty must give way to political authority, wrote Justice Felix Frankfurter for the majority, at least so long as that authority was not used directly to promote or restrict religion.

"Certainly the affirmative pursuit of one's convictions about the ultimate mystery of the universe and man's relation to it is placed beyond the reach of the law," he wrote. On the other hand, he said, the "mere possession of religious convictions which contradict the relevant concerns of a political society does not relieve the citizen from the discharge of political responsibilities."[29]

Was the flag salute a relevant political concern? Frankfurter sidestepped the question, writing that national unity was the basis for national security and that the Court should defer to the local determination that a compulsory flag salute was an effective means of creating that unity:

The influences which help toward a common feeling for the common country are manifold. Some may seem harsh and others no doubt are foolish. Surely, however, the end is legitimate. And the effective means for its attainment are still so uncertain and so unauthenticated by science as to preclude us from putting the widely prevalent belief in flag-saluting beyond the pale of legislative power. It mocks reason and denies our whole history to find in the allowance of a requirement to salute our flag on fitting occasions the seeds of sanction for obeisance to a leader.

The wisdom of training children in patriotic impulses by those compulsions which necessarily pervade so much of the educational process is not for our independent judgment.[30]

Though the members of the Court might find "that the deepest patriotism is best engendered by giving unfettered scope to the most crotchety beliefs," it was not for the Court but for the school board to determine that granting the Gobitas children an exemption from the salute "might cast doubts in the minds of other children which would themselves weaken the effect of the exercise," Frankfurter wrote.[31]

Only Justice Stone dissented, choosing religious liberty over political authority. The compulsory salute, Stone said,

does more than suppress freedom of speech and more than prohibit the free exercise of religion, which concededly are forbidden by the First Amendment. . . . For by this law the state seeks to coerce these children to express a sentiment which, as they interpret it, they do not entertain, and which violates their deepest religious convictions.[32]

Moreover, Stone said the school board could have found ways to instill patriotism in its students without compelling an affirmation some students were unwilling to give:

The very essence of the liberty which they [the First and Fourteenth Amendments] guaranty is the freedom of the individual from compulsion as to what he shall think and what he shall say, at least where the compulsion is to bear false witness to his religion. If these guaranties are to have any meaning they must, I think, be deemed to withhold from the state any authority to compel belief or the expression of it where that expression violates religious convictions, whatever may be the legislative view of the desirability of such compulsion.[33]

The majority's reluctance to review legislative judgment was in this case "no more than the surrender of the constitutional protection of the liberty of small minorities to the popular will," Stone said.[34]

The press and the legal profession responded unfavorably to the decision. One commentator noted that more than 170 leading newspapers condemned the decision, while only a few supported it.[35] Law review articles almost universally opposed it.

Two years after the 1940 *Gobitis* decision, Justices Douglas,

RELIGION AND WAR

Since it instituted compulsory conscription in 1917, Congress has exempted from military service those persons who object to war for religious reasons.

In 1917 the exemption was narrow, extending only to adherents of a "well-recognized religious sect or organization . . . whose existing creed or principles [forbid] its members to participate in war in any form."

Congress expanded the exemption in 1940 to any persons who "by reason of their religious training and belief are conscientiously opposed to participation in war in any form." In 1948 Congress defined "religious training and belief" to mean "an individual's belief in a relation to a Supreme Being involving duties superior to those arising from any human relation but [not including] essentially political, sociological, or philosophical views or a merely personal moral code."

In 1965 this definition was challenged as discriminating against people who hold strong religious convictions but do not believe in a Supreme Being in the orthodox sense. The Supreme Court sidestepped the issue by interpreting Congress's definition very broadly.

The "test of belief 'in a relation to a Supreme Being' is whether a given belief that is sincere and meaningful occupies a place in the life of its possessor parallel to that filled by the orthodox belief in God of one who clearly qualifies for exemption," the Court said in *United States v. Seeger.*[1]

In 1970 the Court construed the exemption to include persons who objected to all war on moral and ethical grounds. To come within the meaning of the law, wrote Justice Hugo L. Black for the Court in *Welsh v. United States,* opposition to the war must "stem from the registrant's moral, ethical, or religious beliefs about what is right and wrong and . . . these beliefs [must] be held with the strength of traditional religious convictions."[2]

A year later, however, the Court refused to hold that conscription unconstitutionally infringed on the religious liberty of those opposed to a particular war as unjust. The Court acknowledged that the ruling impinged on those religions that counseled their members to fight only in those wars that were just. But the Court said that Congress had acted reasonably and neutrally when it decided that the danger of infringing religious liberty did not outweigh the government interest in maintaining a fairly administered draft service.

Fairness, the justices ruled, would be threatened by the difficulty of separating sincere conscientious objectors from fraudulent claimants.[3]

The Court in another case held that a federal law giving veterans' benefits only to persons who had performed active duty did not unconstitutionally discriminate against conscientious objectors who had performed alternative service.[4]

1. *United States v. Seeger,* 380 U.S. 163 at 165–166 (1965).
2. *Welsh v. United States,* 398 U.S. 333 at 340 (1970).
3. *Gillette v. United States,* 401 U.S. 437 (1971).
4. *Johnson v. Robison,* 415 U.S. 361 (1974).

Hugo L. Black, and Frank Murphy announced in a dissent from the majority's holding in an unrelated case that they had changed their minds about compulsory flag salutes.

In *Jones v. Opelika* (1942) the majority upheld a statute imposing peddler fees on Jehovah's Witnesses selling religious publications door to door. Dissenting from this decision as an unconstitutional suppression of the free exercise of religion, Black, Douglas, and Murphy described the majority position as a logical extension of the principles in the *Gobitis* ruling. They wrote:

Since we joined in the opinion in the *Gobitis* case, we think this is an appropriate occasion to state that we now believe that it was . . . wrongly decided. Certainly our democratic form of government functioning under the historic Bill of Rights has a high responsibility to accommodate itself to the religious views of minorities however unpopular and unorthodox those views may be. The First Amendment does not put the right freely to exercise religion in a subordinate position. We fear, however, that the opinion in these and in the *Gobitis* case do exactly that.[36]

Flag Salute Cases - II

Harlan Fiske Stone, the sole dissenter in *Gobitis*, became chief justice in 1941. The reversal of their position on *Gobitis* by Justices Douglas, Black, and Murphy in 1942 and the appointment in 1943 of Justice Rutledge, a libertarian with well-established views favoring freedom of religion, indicated that *Gobitis* might be overruled if the flag salute issue were reconsidered. That opportunity arose in 1943.

The case in which the Court overturned *Gobitis* was *West Virginia State Board of Education v. Barnette*. After the *Gobitis* decision, the West Virginia Board of Education required all schools to make flag salutes part of their daily routine in which all teachers and pupils must participate. Not only would children be expelled if they refused to salute the flag, they would be declared "unlawfully absent" from school and subject to delinquent proceedings. Parents of such children were subject to fine and imprisonment. Several families of Jehovah's Witnesses affected by this decree sued for an injunction to stop its enforcement. The federal district court agreed to issue the injunction, and the state school board appealed that decision directly to the Supreme Court.

By a 6–3 vote the Supreme Court upheld the lower federal court and reversed *Gobitis*. Writing the opinion, which was announced on Flag Day 1943, Justice Jackson rejected the *Gobitis* view that the courts should defer to the legislative judgment in this matter. "The very purpose of a Bill of Rights was to withdraw certain subjects from the vicissitudes of political controversy, to place them beyond the reach of majorities and officials and to establish them as legal principles to be applied by the courts," he said.[37]

Jackson then turned to the heart of the issue. "National unity as an end which officials may foster by persuasion and example is not in question," he wrote. "The problem is whether under our Constitution compulsion as here employed is a permissible means for its achievement." Jackson's answer was negative.

"Compulsory unification of opinion achieves only the unanimity of the graveyard."[38]

For Jackson the issues raised by the compulsory flag salute reached beyond questions of religious liberty to broader concerns for the individual's personal liberty. In one of the most elegant and eloquent passages in Supreme Court history, he wrote:

The case is made difficult not because the principles of its decision are obscure but because the flag involved is our own. Nevertheless, we apply the limitations of the Constitution with no fear that freedom to be intellectually and spiritually diverse or even contrary will disintegrate the social organization. To believe that patriotism will not flourish if patriotic ceremonies are voluntary and spontaneous instead of a compulsory routine is to make an unflattering estimate of the appeal of our institutions to free minds. We can have intellectual individualism and the rich cultural diversities that we owe to exceptional minds only at the price of occasional eccentricity and abnormal attitudes. When they are so harmless to others or to the State as those we deal with here, the price is not too great. But freedom to differ is not limited to things that do not matter much. That would be a mere shadow of freedom. The test of its substance is the right to differ as to things that touch the heart of the existing order.

If there is any fixed star in our constitutional constellation, it is that no official, high or petty, can prescribe what shall be orthodox in politics, nationalism, religion or other matters of opinion or force citizens to confess by word or act their faith therein. If there are any circumstances which permit an exception, they do not now occur to us.[39]

In dissent, Justices Owen J. Roberts and Stanley F. Reed simply stated that they agreed with the majority opinion in *Gobitis*.

But Justice Frankfurter's dissent rivaled Jackson's majority opinion in eloquence. Insisting that the majority had failed to exercise proper judicial restraint, Frankfurter maintained that it was within the constitutional authority of the state school board to demand that public school children salute the American flag. Reading the majority a lecture on their duties as interpreters of the Constitution, Frankfurter began with an unusual personal reference to his own heritage:

One who belongs to the most vilified and persecuted minority in history is not likely to be insensible to the freedoms guaranteed by our Constitution. Were my purely personal attitude relevant I should wholeheartedly associate myself with the general libertarian views in the Court's opinion, representing as they do the thought and action of a lifetime. But as judges we are neither Jew nor Gentile, neither Catholic nor agnostic. . . . As a member of this Court I am not justified in writing my private notions of policy into the Constitution, no matter how deeply I may cherish them or how mischievous I may deem their disregard. The duty of a judge who must decide which of two claims before the Court shall prevail, that of a State to enact and enforce laws within its general competence or that of an individual to refuse obedience because of the demands of his conscience, is not that of an ordinary person. It can never be emphasized too much that one's own opinion about the wisdom or evil of a law should be excluded altogether when one is doing one's duty on the bench. The only opinion of our own even looking in that direction that is material is our opinion whether legislators could in reason have enacted such a law. In the light of all the circumstances, including the history of this question in this Court, it would require more daring than I possess to deny that reasonable legislators could have taken the action which is before us for review. . . . I cannot bring my mind to believe that the "liberty" secured by the Due Process Clause gives this Court the authority to deny to the State of West Virginia the attainment of that which we all recognize as a legitimate legislative end, namely, the promotion of good citizenship, by employment of the means here chosen.[40]

RELIGION, WORK, AND SCHOOL

In 1961 the Court set out the modern rule for determining when a state may properly compel obedience to a secular law that conflicts with religious beliefs.

The rule was stated as the Court upheld the validity of Sunday closing laws, challenged as restricting the free exercise of religion. That claim was raised by an Orthodox Jew who observed the Jewish Sabbath, closing his clothing and furniture store on Saturday. To make up the lost revenue, he opened the store on Sunday. When Pennsylvania enacted a Sunday closing law in 1959, he challenged its constitutionality.

The Supreme Court found that the law did not violate the First Amendment. Sunday closing of commercial enterprises was an effective means for achieving the valid state purpose of providing citizens with a uniform day of rest. Although it operated indirectly to make observance of certain religious practices more expensive, the Sunday closing law did not make any religious practice illegal, the majority observed in *Braunfeld v. Brown* (1961).

The Court then announced the rule for judging whether a state law unconstitutionally restricts the exercise of religious liberty:

If the purpose or effect of a law is to impede the observance of one or all religions or is to discriminate invidiously between religions, that law is constitutionally invalid even though the burden may be characterized as being only indirect. But if the State regulates conduct by enacting a general law within its power, the purpose and effect of which is to advance the State's secular goals, the statute is valid despite its indirect burden on religious observance unless the State may accomplish its purpose by means which do not impose such a burden.[41]

Unemployment Compensation

Two years later the Court significantly modified *Braunfeld* by declaring that only a compelling state interest could justify limitations on religious liberty.

Sherbert v. Verner (1963) arose after Adell Sherbert was fired from her South Carolina textile mill job because, as a Seventh-Day Adventist, she refused to work on Saturdays. Because she refused available work, the state denied her unemployment compensation benefits.

Overturning the state ruling by a 7–2 vote, the Court, speaking through Justice William J. Brennan Jr., explained that the state's action forced Sherbert either to abandon her religious principles in order to work, or to maintain her religious precepts and forfeit unemployment compensation benefits. "Governmental imposition of such a choice puts the same kind of burden upon the free exercise of religion as would a fine imposed against appellant for her Saturday worship," Brennan wrote.[42]

Brennan contended that the state could limit the exercise of an individual's religion only for a compelling state interest.

"Only the gravest abuses, endangering paramount interests, give occasion for permissible limitation," he said. Prevention of fraudulent claims was the only reason the state advanced for denying benefits to Sherbert, Brennan noted. To justify that denial, he wrote, the state must show that it cannot prevent such fraud by means less restrictive of religious liberty.[43]

In dissent, Justices John Marshall Harlan and Byron R. White held that the Court should have abided by its *Braunfeld* rule. Unemployment compensation was intended to help people when there was no work available, not to aid those who, for whatever reason, refused available work. Maintenance of such a distinction was a valid goal of the state, which affected religion only indirectly, they said.

Twice in the mid-1980s the Court reaffirmed *Sherbert*, holding that a state could not deny unemployment benefits to a man in Indiana who quit his job because his religion forbade his participation in weapons production, or to a woman in Florida—like Sherbert—fired because she would not work on her Sabbath. On the other hand, the Court has also set limits to state action protecting the right of workers to have their Sabbath off from work. In 1985 the Court in *Thornton v. Caldor Inc.* ruled unconstitutional a state law giving all employees the right to refuse with impunity to work on their Sabbath. By giving those workers that right, the state gave religious concerns priority over all others in setting work schedules and thereby advanced religion, the Court held.[44]

Compulsory School Attendance

The *Sherbert* ruling was reinforced earlier by the Court's 1972 decision in *Wisconsin v. Yoder.* Old Order Amish parents refused to send their children to school beyond grade eight; this violated Wisconsin's law compelling all children to attend school until they reached age sixteen. The parents asserted that high school education engendered values contrary to Amish beliefs, which hold that salvation may be obtained only by living in religious, agrarian communities separate from the world and worldly influences.

Expert witnesses testified that compulsory high school education might result not only in psychological harm to Amish children confused by trying to fit into two different worlds, but also in destruction of the Amish community. Despite this testimony, the Wisconsin trial and appeals courts upheld compulsory attendance as a reasonable and constitutional means of promoting a valid state interest.

The state supreme court reversed, ruling that the state had not shown that its interest in compelling attendance was sufficient to justify the infringement on the free exercise of religion. The Supreme Court affirmed that holding.

Chief Justice Burger wrote the Court's opinion. He acknowledged that the provision of public schools was one of the primary functions of the state. But, he added,

a state's interest in universal education, however highly we rank it, is not totally free from a balancing process when it impinges on fundamental rights and interests, such as those specifically protected by the Free Exercise Clause of the First Amendment, and the traditional interest of parents with respect to the religious upbringing of their children so long as they . . . "prepare [them] for additional obligations."[45]

The Court accepted the evidence showing that the traditional Amish community life was based on convictions that would be weakened by forcing teenage children into public schools. The Court also noted that the Amish provided their children with alternative modes of vocational education that accommodated all the interests the state advanced in support of its compulsory attendance law.

Ruling in a case involving the sacramental use of the drug peyote, the Court in 1990 abandoned the "compelling interest" test from *Sherbert v. Verner.* But the effect of the ruling in *Employment Division v. Smith* was short-lived. Three years later Congress passed the Religious Freedom Restoration Act, which ensured a return to the rule that government may infringe on a person's exercise of religion only in furtherance of a compelling interest. *(See "Religion and Crime," pp. 476–478.)*

RELIGION AND OATH-TAKING

Article VI of the Constitution states that "no religious Test shall ever be required as a Qualification to any Office or public Trust under the United States."

The Supreme Court in 1961 ruled that under the First Amendment, states are prohibited from requiring religious test oaths.

Ray Torcaso, appointed a notary public in Maryland, was denied his commission when he refused to declare his belief in God, a part of the oath notaries public were required by Maryland law to take. Torcaso sued, challenging the oath as abridging his religious liberty.

A unanimous Supreme Court struck down the oath requirement in *Torcaso v. Watkins* (1961). Justice Black wrote:

We repeat and again affirm that neither a State nor the Federal Government can constitutionally force a person "to profess a belief or disbelief in any religion." Neither can constitutionally pass laws or impose requirements which aid all religions as against non-believers, and neither can aid those religions based on a belief in the existence of God as against those religions founded on different beliefs.[46]

The Supreme Court in *Torcaso* stated unequivocally that a state may not require a person to swear to a belief he or she does not hold. But may government require a person to swear a nonreligious oath contrary to religious beliefs? In a series of cases concerning pacifist applicants for U.S. citizenship, the Supreme Court first said yes but then changed its mind.

The naturalization oath requires applicants for citizenship to swear "to support and defend the Constitution and the law of the United States of America against all enemies, foreign and domestic."

The naturalization service interpreted the oath to require that prospective citizens must be willing to bear arms in defense of the country. It therefore denied citizenship to two women pacifists and to a fifty-four-year-old Yale Divinity School professor who said he would fight only in wars he believed to be morally justified.

Although the three were qualified in every other way to be citizens and were extremely unlikely ever to be called into active service, the Court upheld the naturalization service's position as reasonable in 1929 in *United States v. Schwimmer* and again in 1931.[47]

Following World War II, the Court reconsidered and reversed these holdings. Again the majority did not reach the constitutional issue but dealt only with the statutory interpretation of the oath.

Girouard v. United States (1946) concerned a Canadian Seventh-Day Adventist who agreed to serve as a noncombatant in the armed forces but refused to bear arms because killing conflicted with his religious beliefs. The majority noted that the oath did not expressly require naturalized citizens to swear to bear arms and ruled that this interpretation need not be read into the oath. Congress, the majority said, could not have intended to deny citizenship in a country noted for its protection of religious beliefs to persons whose religious beliefs prevented them from bearing arms.[48]

In 1945, the year before it overruled its early decisions in the pacifist naturalization cases, the Supreme Court upheld the Illinois bar's decision to deny admission to an attorney because its required oath conflicted with his beliefs. That decision has never been overruled, but its effect has been weakened by subsequent decisions.[49]

Among the more recent of these was the Court's 1978 ruling in *McDaniel v. Paty* in which the Court struck down as unconstitutional a Tennessee law that forbade clergy to hold state offices. Writing the Court's opinion, Chief Justice Burger relied on *Sherbert* as precedent, saying that the state law unconstitutionally restricted the right of free exercise of religion by making it conditional on a willingness to give up the right to seek public office.[50]

Justices Potter Stewart, Thurgood Marshall, and Brennan used *Torcaso* as precedent, and Marshall and Brennan held that the law also violated the establishment clause.[51] Justice White held that the law denied clergy equal protection of the laws.

Establishment of Religion

The establishment clause of the First Amendment prohibits Congress from making any law "respecting an establishment of religion." This has been interpreted to mean not only that Congress cannot designate a national church but also that it cannot act to give any direct support to religion.

There is considerable disagreement over how absolutely the two men most responsible for the establishment clause, Thomas Jefferson and James Madison, actually viewed it.[52] The Supreme Court, however, has never adopted an absolutist position in its interpretation of the clause.

Indeed, not for a century was the Court called on to rule on this part of the Bill of Rights. Its first decision, which came in 1899, sustained a federal construction grant to a Roman Catholic hospital. The Court held that the hospital's purpose was secular and that it did not discriminate among its patients on the basis of religion. The aid therefore only indirectly benefited the church.[53]

Most of the Court's establishment clause rulings have come since the Court declared the clause applicable to the states in 1947. A few of these cases have concerned taxation; some have concerned public displays of religious symbols, but most have concerned religion and education.

The Court has sustained the practice of exempting churches from taxes on the grounds that to tax them would be to entangle government excessively with religion. For much the same reason, the Court has also declined to review legal questions involving controversies within churches.

Three topics in the area of religion and education have drawn the Court's attention: religious readings and prayer in school, state aid to parochial schools, and equal treatment of student religious groups and publications.

The Court has barred religious exercises in tax-supported public schools as unconstitutional government advancement of religion. Prayer recitations, Bible readings, and religious instruction, when denominational, favor one religion over others; when nondenominational, they favor all religion over nonreligious beliefs, the Court has said.

The Court, however, has adopted what it describes as a "benevolent neutrality" toward government financial aid to parochial schools. If the aid is secular in its purpose and effect and does not entangle the government excessively in its administration, it is permissible, even if it indirectly benefits the church schools.

The Court also has held that access to school facilities, and in some cases school support, should be the same for all student groups. The First Amendment protection for free speech requires that religious groups not be treated differently because of the content of their meetings or messages.

TAX EXEMPTIONS

Historically, the federal government, every state, and the District of Columbia have exempted churches from paying property and income taxes. In 1970 the Supreme Court sustained these exemptions by an 8–1 vote. The case, *Walz v. Tax Commission*, arose when a property owner in New York challenged the state's property tax exemption for religious institutions as an establishment of religion. He contended that the exemption meant that nonexempt property owners made an involuntary contribution to churches.

Writing for the majority, Chief Justice Burger observed that churches were only one of several institutions—including hospitals, libraries, and historical and patriotic organizations—exempted from paying property taxes. Such exemptions reflected the state's decision that these groups provided beneficial and stabilizing influences in the community and that their activities might be hampered or destroyed by the need to pay property taxes. "We cannot read New York's statute as attempting to es-

---

INTERNAL CHURCH DISPUTES

The Supreme Court has been reluctant to involve itself in the internal disputes that occasionally arise within churches. Where judicial intervention is unavoidable, the Court has insisted that courts decline to resolve doctrinal questions.

This rule was first developed in *Watson v. Jones* (1872), a dispute over church property between a national church organization and local churches that had withdrawn from the national hierarchy.

The case was decided on common law grounds, but it had First Amendment overtones:

All who unite themselves to [the central church] do so with an implied consent to [its] government, and are bound to submit to it. But it would be a vain consent, and would lead to the total subversion of such religious bodies, if anyone aggrieved by one of their decisions could appeal to the secular courts and have [it] reversed.[1]

In 1952 the Court said that the First Amendment gave religious organizations "power to decide for themselves, free from state interference, matters of church government as well as those of faith and doctrine."[2]

In 1969 the Court held:

First Amendment values are plainly jeopardized when church property litigation is made to turn on the resolution by civil courts of controversies over religious doctrine and practice. If civil courts undertake to resolve such controversies . . . the hazards are ever present of inhibiting the free development of religious doctrine and of implicating secular interests in matters of purely ecclesiastical concern. . . . The Amendment therefore commands civil courts to decide church property disputes without resolving underlying controversies over religious doctrines.[3]

The judicial role is therefore limited to examining the church rules and determining that they have been applied appropriately. Justice Louis D. Brandeis wrote, "In the absence of fraud, collusion, or arbitrariness, the decisions of the proper church tribunals on matters purely ecclesiastical, although affecting civil rights, are accepted in litigation before the secular courts as conclusive."[4]

1. *Watson v. Jones*, 13 Wall. 679 at 728–29 (1872).
2. *Kedroff v. St. Nicholas Cathedral*, 344 U.S. 94 at 116 (1952); see also *Kreshik v. St. Nicholas Cathedral*, 363 U.S. 190 (1960).
3. *Presbyterian Church in the United States v. Mary Elizabeth Blue Hull Memorial Presbyterian Church*, 393 U.S. 440 at 449 (1969).
4. *Gonzalez v. Archbishop*, 280 U.S. 1 at 16 (1929).

---

tablish religion," Burger wrote; "it is simply sparing the exercise of religion from the burden of property taxation levied on private profit institutions."[54]

Thus the exemption met the existing test for determining whether government policy constituted improper establishment of religion. Both the purpose and effect of the exemption were primarily secular, having only an indirect benefit to religion.

But to this test the Court in *Walz* added a new one: whether the exemption resulted in excessive government involvement with religion. To answer this question, Burger said the Court must consider whether taxing the property would result in more or less entanglement than continuing the exemption.

Observing that taxation would require government valuation of church property, and possibly tax liens and foreclosures, Burger concluded that the "hazards of churches supporting government are hardly less in their potential than the hazards of government supporting churches." Tax exemption, on the other hand, created "only a minimal and remote involvement between church and state. . . . It restricts the fiscal relationship between church and state, and tends to complement and reinforce the desired separation insulating each from the other."[55]

As churches have moved into quasi-business areas in recent years, the tax question has returned to the Court in several new ways. In 1981 the Court ruled unanimously that church-run elementary and secondary schools were exempt from paying federal or state unemployment taxes. Four years later, however, the Court made clear that this exemption did not extend so far as to protect commercial enterprises of churches from minimum wage, overtime, and recordkeeping requirements of federal labor law.[56]

RELIGION AND PUBLIC SCHOOLS

"We are a religious people whose institutions presuppose a Supreme Being," wrote Justice Douglas in 1952.[57]

The nation's governmental institutions reflect this belief daily. Each session of the House and Senate opens with a prayer. The Supreme Court begins its sessions with an invocation asking that "God save the United States and this honorable Court." Our currency proclaims, "In God We Trust," and we acknowledge that we are "one nation, under God," each time we recite the pledge of allegiance.

These official and public affirmations of religious belief have not escaped legal challenge, but the Supreme Court has dismissed most of them summarily. In 1964 the Court refused to review a lower court decision that held that despite inclusion of the phrase "under God" in the pledge of allegiance, the First Amendment did not bar the New York Education Commission from recommending that the pledge be recited in schools. In 1971 the Court declined to stop astronauts from praying on television for God's blessing for a successful trip to the moon. In the same ruling, the lower court had rejected a challenge to the phrase "So help me God" contained in the oath witnesses are required to take in many courts. And in 1979 the Court refused to review a challenge to the words "In God We Trust" on currency.[58]

In 1983 the Court for the first time gave full consideration to a challenge to a state legislature's practice of opening sessions with a prayer. The Court upheld the practice, finding that it dated back to the First Congress of the United States, the one that also adopted the First Amendment, and had "become part of the fabric of our society."[59]

Although the Court has not proscribed government-sponsored public expression of religious belief on the part of adults, it has flatly prohibited states from requiring or permitting religious exercises by children in public elementary and secondary schools.

Released Time

The first two Supreme Court rulings concerning religious exercises in public schools involved "released time" programs. Employed by school districts across the country, these programs released students from regular classwork, usually once a week, to receive religious instruction. In some cases the students received the instruction in their regular classrooms; sometimes they met in another schoolroom; at other times they met in churches or synagogues. Students participated in the programs voluntarily. Students who did not participate had a study period during the time religious instruction was given.

The first of the released time cases was *Illinois ex rel. McCollum v. Board of Education* (1948). The Champaign, Illinois, school board operated a released time program in which religion teachers from the private sector came into the public schools once a week to give one half-hour of religious instruction to voluntary participants. The program was challenged as a violation of the First Amendment's establishment clause by the atheist mother of a fifth grader, the only pupil in his class who did not participate in the program.

By an 8–1 vote, the Supreme Court declared the program unconstitutional. "Pupils compelled by law to go to school for secular education are released in part from their legal duty upon the condition that they attend religious classes," wrote Justice Black for the majority. "This is beyond all question a utilization of the tax-established and tax-supported public school system to aid religious groups to spread their faith."[60]

Four justices concurred separately. They said the program not only violated the establishment clause by tending to advance certain religions over others, but it also threatened to impede the free exercise of religion. Justice Frankfurter explained:

Religious education so conducted on school time and property is patently woven into the working scheme of the school. The Champaign arrangement thus presents powerful elements of inherent pressure by the school system in the interest of religious sects. . . . That a child is offered an alternative may reduce the constraint; it does not eliminate the operation of influence by the school in matters sacred to conscience and outside the school's domain. The law of imitation operates, and nonconformity is not an outstanding characteristic of children. The result is an obvious pressure upon children to attend. Again, while the Champaign school population represents only a fraction of the more than two hundred and fifty sects of the nation, not even all the practicing sects in Champaign are willing or able to provide religious instruction. . . . As a result, the public school system of Champaign actively furthers inculcation in the religious tenets of some faiths, and in the process sharpens the consciousness of religious differences at least among some of the children committed to its care.[61]

Four years later the Court upheld, 6–3, New York City's released time program in which religious instruction was given during the school day but not in the public schools. In *Zorach v.*

Clausen (1952), the Court held that this program did not violate the establishment clause. "The First Amendment . . . does not say that in every and all respects there shall be a separation of Church and State," wrote Justice Douglas, noting that governments provided churches with general services such as police and fire protection and that public officials frequently said prayers before undertaking their official chores.[62]

The New York program did not significantly aid religion; it simply required that the public schools "accommodate" a program of outside religious instruction. Government, wrote Douglas,

may not coerce anyone to attend church, to observe a religious holiday, or to take religious instruction. But it can close its doors or suspend its operations as to those who want to repair to their religious sanctuary for worship or instruction. No more than that is undertaken here.[63]

Justices Black, Frankfurter, and Jackson held that the program was coercive and a direct aid to religion.

School Prayer

In 1962, a decade after *Zorach*, the Supreme Court set off an intense new round of controversy over church and state matters. *Engel v. Vitale* banned school prayer and Bible reading as regular devotional exercises in public schools. Such exercises, often coupled with recitation of the pledge of allegiance, had been common occurrences in classrooms across the country.

As early as 1930 the Supreme Court declined to review fully a state court's refusal to order the state school superintendent to require Bible reading in public schools. The question of Bible readings in public schools came to the Court again in 1952, and again the Court dismissed the suit, this time because the parents of the child involved no longer had standing to sue.[64]

Another ten years passed before the Court directly addressed the constitutionality of devotional practices in public schools. The case arose after New York's State Board of Regents recommended to school districts that they adopt a specified nondenominational prayer to be repeated voluntarily by students at the beginning of each school day. The brief prayer read: "Almighty God, we acknowledge our dependence upon Thee, and we beg Thy blessings upon us, our parents, our teachers, and our country."

The prayer was not universally adopted throughout the state. New York City, for example, chose instead to have its students recite the verse of the hymn "America" that asks God's protection for the country.

The school board of New Hyde Park, New York, adopted the recommended prayer. Parents of ten pupils in the school district, with the support of the New York Civil Liberties Union, brought suit, claiming that the prayer was contrary to their religious beliefs and practices and that its adoption and use violated the establishment clause. The state courts upheld the prayer on the condition that no student be compelled to participate.

The Supreme Court, 6–1, reversed the state courts, holding that this use of the prayer was "wholly inconsistent with the Es-

---

EVOLUTION OR CREATION?

One of the most celebrated trials in American history took place in 1925. John Scopes was convicted and fined $100 for teaching the Darwinian theory of evolution in violation of a Tennessee law that made it illegal to teach anything other than a literal biblical theory of human creation.

Although the state supreme court reversed Scopes's conviction, the Tennessee statute was left standing and was never challenged before the U.S. Supreme Court.[1]

Decades later the Supreme Court ruled twice on this issue. In *Epperson v. Arkansas* (1968) a public school biology teacher challenged a state law that forbade teachers in state-supported schools from teaching or using textbooks that teach "the theory or doctrine that mankind ascended or descended from a lower order of animals."

The Supreme Court unanimously held this law in violation of the First Amendment. "Arkansas law selects from the body of knowledge a particular segment which it proscribes for the sole reason that it is deemed to conflict with a particular religious doctrine; that is, with a particular interpretation of the Book of Genesis by a particular religious group," held the Court.[2]

In 1987 the Court, 7–2, held that Louisiana violated the First Amendment when it required that any public school teacher who taught evolution must also give equal time to teaching "creation-science." Writing for the majority in *Edwards v. Aguillard*, Justice William J. Brennan Jr. explained that it was clear that the purpose of the law was "to advance the religious viewpoint that a supernatural being created humankind."[3]

Dissenting were Chief Justice William H. Rehnquist and Justice Antonin Scalia, who criticized the Court for presuming the law unconstitutional because "it was supported strongly by organized religions or by adherents of particular faiths. . . . Political activism by the religiously motivated is part of our heritage," Scalia wrote. "Today's religious activism may give us [this law] . . . but yesterday's resulted in the abolition of slavery, and tomorrow's may bring relief for famine victims."[4]

1. *Scopes v. State*, 154 Tenn. 105, 289 S.W. 363 (1927).
2. *Epperson v. Arkansas*, 393 U.S. 97 at 103 (1968).
3. *Edwards v. Aguillard*, 482 U.S. 578 at 592 (1987).
4. Id. at 615.

---

tablishment Clause." In an opinion written by Justice Black, the majority explained its view:

[T]he constitutional prohibition against laws respecting an establishment of religion must at least mean that in this country it is no part of the business of government to compose official prayers for any group of the American people to recite as a part of a religious program carried on by government.[65]

The fact that the prayer was nondenominational and that students who did not wish to participate could remain silent or leave the room did not free the prayer "from the limitations of the Establishment Clause." Black wrote:

The Establishment Clause, unlike the Free Exercise Clause, does not depend upon any showing of direct governmental compulsion and is violated by the enactment of laws which establish an official religion whether those laws operate directly to coerce nonobserving individuals or not. This is not to say, of course, that laws officially prescribing a particular form of religious worship do not involve coercion of such individuals. When the power, prestige and financial support of government is placed behind a particular religious belief, the indirect coercive pressure upon religious minorities to conform to the prevailing officially approved religion is plain.[66]

In response to the argument that the prayer, if an establishment of religion at all, was a relatively insignificant and harmless encroachment, Black quoted Madison, the chief author of the First Amendment:

[I]t is proper to take alarm at the first experiment on our liberties. . . . Who does not see that the same authority which can establish Christianity, in exclusion of all other Religions, may establish with the same ease any particular sect of Christians, in exclusion of all other Sects?[67]

Asserting that "the Court has misapplied a great constitutional principle," Justice Stewart dissented. "I cannot see how an 'official religion' is established by letting those who want to say a prayer say it," he said.[68] Stewart compared the regents' prayer to other state-sanctioned religious exercises, such as the reference to God in the pledge to the flag, in the president's oath of office, and in the formal opening of each day's session of the Court itself:

I do not believe that this Court, or the Congress, or the President has by the actions and practices I have mentioned established an "official religion" in violation of the Constitution. And I do not believe the State of New York has done so in this case. What each has done has been to recognize and to follow the deeply entrenched and highly cherished spiritual traditions of our Nation—traditions which come down to us from those who almost two hundred years ago avowed their "firm Reliance on the Protection of divine Providence" when they proclaimed the freedom and independence of this brave new world.[69]

Bible Readings

A year later, in 1963, the Court affirmed its school prayer decision, declaring unconstitutional the practice of daily Bible readings in public school classrooms.

Two cases, *School District of Abington Township v. Schempp* and *Murray v. Curlett*, were considered together. The *Schempp* case concerned a Pennsylvania statute that required the reading of at least ten verses from the Bible each day, followed by recitation of the Lord's Prayer and the pledge to the flag. Pupils were excused from participating at the request of their parents. The Schempps asserted that certain literal Bible readings were contrary to their Unitarian religious beliefs and brought suit to stop the readings. In the *Murray* case, the challenged reading from the Bible was required not by state law but by a 1905 city rule. Madalyn Murray and her student son, William, were atheists. They contended that the daily religious exercises placed "a premium on belief as against non-belief and subject[ed] their freedom of conscience to the rule of the majority." They asked that the readings be stopped.

By 8–1 the Court held that the Bible readings in both cases were unconstitutional. The readings were clearly religious exercises prescribed as part of the school curriculum for students compelled by law to attend school. They were held in state buildings and supervised by teachers paid by the state. By these actions the state abandoned the neutrality toward religion demanded by the establishment clause. Justice Tom C. Clark wrote for the majority:

The place of religion in our society is an exalted one, achieved through a long tradition of reliance on the home, the church and the inviolable citadel of the individual heart and mind. We have come to recognize through bitter experience that it is not within the power of government to invade that citadel, whether its purpose or effect be to aid or oppose, to advance or retard. In the relationship between man and religion, the State is firmly committed to a position of neutrality.[70]

It was no defense that the Bible reading exercises might be "relatively minor" encroachments on the First Amendment. "The breach of neutrality that is today a trickling stream may all too soon become a raging torrent," Clark wrote.[71] Nor did the ruling set up a "religion of secularism" in the schools. Schools could permit the study of the Bible for its literary and historical merits; they were only prohibited from using the Bible as part of a devotional exercise.

Finally, Clark said that the ruling did not deny the majority its right to the free exercise of religion. "While the Free Exercise Clause clearly prohibits the use of state action to deny the rights of free exercise to *anyone*, it has never meant that a majority could use the machinery of the State to practice its beliefs."[72]

Opposition from the public to the two school prayer decisions, *Schempp* and *Murray,* ran high, encouraging both chambers of Congress to consider constitutional amendments that would overrule the decisions. Neither the House nor the Senate was able to produce the two-thirds votes needed to send a proposed amendment to the states for ratification.

For well over twenty years, the Court stayed away from school prayer cases. Then in 1985 in *Wallace v. Jaffree* it took a long, hard look at the new version of school prayer, a "moment-of-silence" law from Alabama. Twenty-three states had passed such laws. They varied in their particulars, but in general they permitted teachers to set aside a moment in each public school classroom each day for students to engage in quiet meditative activity.

When Alabama's law was challenged, a federal judge—in blithe disregard of a half-century of Supreme Court decisions—declared that the First Amendment did not preclude Alabama from establishing a state religion. Although an appeals court reversed that ruling, the state—backed by the Reagan administration—asked the Supreme Court to reinstate the law. The Court refused, 6–3, agreeing with the appeals court that the law violated the establishment clause.

Some moment-of-silence laws might pass muster, said Justices Lewis F. Powell Jr. and Sandra Day O'Connor, but not one that was so clearly just a subterfuge for returning prescribed prayer to the public schools. Writing for the majority, Justice John Paul Stevens declared that it was "established principle that the government must pursue a course of complete neutrality toward religion." Chief Justice Burger dissented, joined by Justices White and William H. Rehnquist, who said it was time for the Court to reassess its precedents on this issue.[73]

Two years later, in 1987, the Court took up the question of New Jersey's moment-of-silence law, which might have fallen into the category of those laws that passed constitutional examination.

But the Court did not address the school prayer issue head-on; it ruled that the individuals bringing the case, who were no longer members of the state legislature, lacked the authority to appeal this decision since new members of the legislature had decided to drop the matter.[74]

In 1992 a sharply divided Court confronted the issue and affirmed the prohibition on prayer in school. By 5–4, the Court in *Lee v. Weisman* sided with a Providence, Rhode Island, student who objected to an invocation and benediction by a rabbi at her junior high school graduation. The Court ruled unconstitutional the faculty-organized prayer.[75]

In his opinion for the majority, Justice Anthony M. Kennedy noted that the establishment clause was inspired by this lesson: "in the hands of the government what might begin as a tolerant expression of religious views may end in a policy to indoctrinate and coerce. A state-created orthodoxy puts at grave risk that freedom of belief and conscience which are the sole assurance that religious faith is real, not imposed."[76]

Kennedy stressed the vulnerability of children and said prayer exercises in elementary and secondary schools carry a particular risk of indirect coercion. He was joined by Justices Harry A. Blackmun, John Paul Stevens, Sandra Day O'Connor, and David H. Souter.

The majority distinguished the case from the 1983 *Marsh v. Chambers* case, in which the Court condoned a prayer at the opening of a state legislature's daily session: "The atmosphere at the opening of a session of a state legislature where adults are free to enter and leave with little comment and for any number of reasons cannot compare with the constraining potential of the one school event most important for the student to attend. The influence and force of a formal exercise in a school graduation are far greater than the prayer exercise we condoned in *Marsh*."[77]

Justices Antonin Scalia, William H. Rehnquist, Byron R. White, and Clarence Thomas dissented.

Scalia, writing for the group, emphasized the historical and unifying role of prayer in American celebrations: "The history and tradition of our Nation are replete with public ceremonies featuring prayers of thanksgiving and petition. . . . Most recently, President Bush, continuing the tradition established by President Washington, asked those attending his inauguration to bow their heads, and made a prayer his first official act as president."[78]

STATE AID TO CHURCH-RELATED SCHOOLS

The first suit challenging state aid to church-related schools reached the Supreme Court in the 1930 case of *Cochran v. Louisiana Board of Education.*[79]

Louisiana gave all schoolchildren in the state, including those attending parochial schools, secular textbooks paid for with public funds. Cochran, a taxpayer, challenged the statute. He contended that this use of public funds violated the Fourteenth Amendment's prohibition against state action depriving persons of their property without due process of law. (In 1930 the Court had not yet specifically stated that the Fourteenth Amendment incorporated the religious guarantees of the First Amendment.)

Rejecting Cochran's assertion, the Supreme Court adopted the "child benefit" theory. The provision of free textbooks was designed to further the education of all children in the state and not to benefit church-related schools, the Court maintained.

In *Everson v. Board of Education* (1947) the Court specifically applied the establishment clause to the states for the first time. This case was also the first one in which the Court was required to consider whether the clause barred public aid to church-operated schools.

Everson concerned a New Jersey statute that permitted local boards of education to reimburse parents for the costs of sending their children to school on public transportation. Arch Everson, a local taxpayer, challenged as an impermissible establishment of religion the reimbursement of parents of parochial school students.

The Court in *Everson* elaborated on its ruling in *Cochran*, decided seventeen years earlier. While the establishment clause forbade states from aiding religion, it did not prohibit the states from granting aid to all children in the state without regard to their religious beliefs.

Writing for the five-justice majority, Justice Black offered what would become an often quoted description of the meaning of the establishment clause:

The "establishment of religion" clause of the First Amendment means at least this: Neither a state nor the Federal Government can set up a church. Neither can pass laws which aid one religion, aid all religions or prefer one religion over another. Neither can force nor influence a person to go to or to remain away from church against his will or force him to profess a belief or disbelief in any religion. No person can be punished for entertaining or professing any religious beliefs or disbeliefs, for church attendance or non-attendance. No tax in any amount, large or small, can be levied to support any religious activities or institutions, whatever they may be called, or whatever form they may adopt to teach or practice religion. Neither a state nor the Federal Government can, openly or secretly, participate in the affairs of any religious organizations or groups and vice versa. In the words of Jefferson, the clause against establishment of religion by law was intended to erect "a wall of separation between Church and State."[80]

Having said that, however, the majority proceeded to uphold the New Jersey statute on the grounds that it did not aid religion

SCHOOL PRAYER AND CONGRESSIONAL BACKLASH

"The Supreme Court has made God unconstitutional," declared Sen. Sam Ervin, D-N.C. (1954–1974), after the Court's school prayer decision in *Engel v. Vitale*.[1]

Members of Congress, governors, even a former president all spoke out in opposition to the decision. And although the ruling was greeted favorably by the Jewish community and many Christian leaders, several members of the clergy expressed dismay. "I am shocked and frightened that the Supreme Court has declared unconstitutional a simple and voluntary declaration of belief in God by public school children," said Francis Cardinal Spellman. "The decision strikes at the very heart of the Godly tradition in which America's children have for so long been raised."[2]

Reaction to the Court's Bible reading decision in 1963 was equally adverse and outspoken. "Why should the majority be so severely penalized by the protests of a handful?" asked evangelist Billy Graham.[3]

With such proclamations began decades of debate in state legislatures and the halls of Congress over the issue of prayer and Bible reading in school. Despite the opposition of most major religious organizations to any constitutional amendment to overturn the rulings, mail advocating such an amendment began to pour into congressional offices in the days and months after the Supreme Court rulings.

Rep. Frank J. Becker, R-N.Y. (1953–1965), proposed a constitutional amendment in 1962. It provided that nothing in the Constitution should be interpreted to bar "the offering, reading from, or listening to prayer or biblical scriptures, if participation therein is on a voluntary basis, in any government or public school institution or place." The House Judiciary Committee took no action on the proposal, primarily because of the opposition of its chairman, Emanuel Celler, D-N.Y. (1923–1973).

Senate minority leader Everett McKinley Dirksen, R-Ill. (1951–1969), proposed in 1966 an amendment stating that the Constitution should not be interpreted to bar any public school authority from providing for or permitting the voluntary participation of students in prayer. His amendment specifically stated that it did not authorize any government official to prescribe the form or content of a prayer. When the Senate voted on this amendment, it fell nine votes short of approval.

In the early 1970s, at the urging of a grass-roots organization called the Prayer Campaign Committee, Rep. Chalmers P. Wylie, R-Ohio (1967–1993), supported another proposed amendment to the Constitution. He began to circulate among House members a petition to discharge this amendment, similar to the Dirksen amendment, from a still-opposed House Judiciary Committee. By September 1971 a majority of the House had signed Wylie's petition, and the amendment came to the House floor for debate. On November 8, 1971, the amendment failed by twenty-eight votes to win the approval of the necessary two-thirds majority.

A decade later the support of President Ronald Reagan for a constitutional amendment on school prayer revived efforts to win congressional approval. But in 1984 the Senate fell eleven votes short of approving the administration's amendment.[4]

In October 1994 Congress passed legislation that included a provision withholding federal funds from any public school that willfully violated a court order to allow constitutionally protected voluntary prayer.[5]

After the Republicans won majorities in both the House and Senate in November 1994, numerous proposals were offered for a constitutional amendment permitting organized school prayer. None had been adopted by the summer of 1996.

1. Quoted in Leo Pfeffer, *Church, State and Freedom*, rev. ed. (Boston: Beacon Press, 1967), 466.

2. Ibid., 467.

3. Quoted in Congressional Quarterly, "Restore Prayers in Schools: The Move that Failed," in *Education for a Nation* (Washington, D.C.: Congressional Quarterly, 1972), 38. The decision was *School District of Abington Township v. Schempp, Murray v. Curlett*, 374 U.S. 203 (1963).

4. *Congress and the Nation*, Vol. VI (Washington, D.C.: Congressional Quarterly, 1985), 703; *CQ Almanac 1985* (Washington, D.C.: Congressional Quarterly, 1986), 235.

5. *CQ Almanac 1994* (Washington, D.C.: Congressional Quarterly, 1995), 389–391.

but was instead public welfare legislation benefiting children rather than schools:

It is undoubtedly true that children are helped to get to church schools. There is even a possibility that some of the children might not be sent to the church schools if the parents were compelled to pay their children's bus fares out of their own pockets when transportation to a public school would have been paid for by the State. . . . Similarly, parents might be reluctant to permit their children to attend [church] schools which the state had cut off from such general government services as ordinary police and fire protection, connections for sewage disposal, public highways and sidewalks. Of course, cutting off church schools from these services, so separate and so indisputably marked off from the religious function, would make it far more difficult for the schools to operate. But such is obviously not the purpose of the First Amendment. That Amendment requires the state to be a neutral in its relations with groups of religious believers and nonbelievers; it does not require the state to be their adversary. State power is no more to be used so as to handicap religions, than it is to favor them.[81]

In his dissent, joined by Justices Jackson, Frankfurter, and Burton, Justice Rutledge agreed with the majority that the establishment clause "forbids state support, financial or other, of religion in any guise, form or degree. It outlaws all use of public funds for religious purposes." But to cast this particular case in terms of public welfare, as the majority does, is to ignore "the religious factor and its essential connection with the transportation, thereby leaving out the only vital element in the case," said Rutledge.[82]

Publicly supported transportation of parochial schoolchildren benefits not only their secular education but also their religious education, Rutledge asserted.

Two great drives are constantly in motion to abridge, in the name of education, the complete division of religion and civil authority which our forefathers made. One is to introduce religious education and observances into the public schools. The other, to obtain public funds for the aid and support of various private religious schools. . . . In my opinion, both avenues were closed by the Constitution. Neither should be opened by this Court.[83]

Textbooks

It was evident from *Everson* that despite Justice Black's extremely broad interpretation of the establishment clause, the line of separation between church and state was, as a later justice would put it, "a blurred, indistinct and variable barrier depending on all the circumstances of a particular relationship."[84]

The Court now needed to devise some criteria for assessing whether state aid to church schools breached that barrier.

In the twenty years between *Everson* and the next state aid case, *Board of Education of Central School District No. 1 v. Allen* (1968), the Supreme Court decided *Vitale, Schempp,* and *Murray,* ruling that the establishment clause did not permit public schools to use prayers and Bible reading as part of their daily exercises and that such exercises violated the clause because they were sectarian in purpose and their primary effect was to advance religion.

The Court first applied these guidelines to a question of state aid to church-related schools in the 1968 *Allen* case. The circumstances were similar to those of the *Cochran* case. New York required local school boards to lend textbooks purchased with public funds to seventh through twelfth grade students, including those attending parochial schools. The New York requirement was challenged as a violation of the establishment clause. The New York Court of Appeals upheld the requirement and, by a 6–3 vote, the Supreme Court agreed.

Writing for the majority, Justice White explained that the purpose of the requirement was secular, to further the educational opportunities of students at both public and private schools. Because the subject matter of the books was secular, the loan program neither advanced nor inhibited religion, White said.

To the claim that books were essential for teaching and that the primary goal of parochial schools was to teach religion, White observed that the Court "has long recognized that religious schools pursue two goals, religious instruction and secular education." Without more evidence, White said the majority could not state that "all teaching in a sectarian school is religious or that the processes of secular and religious training are so intertwined that secular textbooks furnished to students by the public are in fact instrumental in the teaching of religion."[85]

The majority also held that the loan program conformed to the *Everson* "child-benefit" precedent. "[N]o funds or books are furnished to parochial schools, and the financial benefit is to parents and children, not to schools," White wrote.[86]

In separate dissents, Justices William O. Douglas and Abe Fortas contended that although local public school boards would approve the books for use, in actual practice they would not choose the books to be used in the church schools; sectarian authorities would make that choice.

Justice Black also dissented, distinguishing between nonideological aid such as transportation or school lunch, which was permissible, and books, which were related to substantive religious views and beliefs and thus in his view impermissible.

"Parochiaid"

The *Allen* case was decided at a time when rising educational costs compelled more and more parochial school officials to seek direct financial aid from the states. Faced with their own fiscal problems, many states with large numbers of parochial school students were willing to comply on the premise that it would be less expensive to give the church schools aid than to absorb their students into the public system if they were forced to close.

Several states—notably New York, Pennsylvania, and Ohio—passed statutes authorizing direct aid such as teacher salary subsidies, tuition reimbursements, and tuition tax credits. The favorable decision in the *Allen* case and support for such programs from President Richard Nixon and many members of Congress encouraged church and state officials to hope that these so-called "parochiaid" programs might pass constitutional scrutiny. They were to be disappointed.

The first challenges to these direct aid laws reached the Court in 1971. *Lemon v. Kurtzman* and its companion cases concerned a Rhode Island statute that authorized a salary supplement to certain nonpublic school teachers and a Pennsylvania law that established a program to reimburse nonpublic schools for teachers' salaries, textbooks, and instructional materials. In practice the Rhode Island law benefited only Roman Catholic schools, while the Pennsylvania law affected more than 20 percent of the students in the state. Both laws stipulated that recipient teachers must teach only secular subjects. The Pennsylvania law stipulated that the textbooks and instructional materials also be secular in nature.

The Court struck down both state laws by unanimous votes. In doing so it added a new requirement to the test for permissible state aid. Writing the Court's opinion, Chief Justice Burger said such aid not only must have a secular legislative purpose and a primary effect that neither advanced nor inhibited religion, but it also must not foster "an excessive government entanglement with religion."[87] The latter requirement was drawn from a 1970 ruling upholding property tax exemptions for church property. (*See details of Walz v. Tax Commission, pp. 486–487.*)

To determine whether state entanglement with religion is excessive, Burger said, the Court "must examine the character and purposes of the institutions that are benefited, the nature of the aid that the State provides, and the resulting relationship between the government and the religious authority."[88]

Applying this new, three-part test to the Rhode Island statute, the majority found that teacher salary supplements did result in excessive state entanglement with religion. Without

THE *LEMON* DEMON

The Court's modern test for determining whether government policy or action violates the establishment clause was first set out in the 1971 ruling *Lemon v. Kurtzman* and hence is known as the *"Lemon"* test.[1]

In brief, the test permits government aid to religious entities only if the assistance has a secular purpose, neither advances nor inhibits religion, and does not foster excessive "entanglement" with the religious entity.

Many of the justices who came to the Court subsequent to *Lemon* believed it too strict a test. Because a majority could not agree on an alternative test, the Court used *Lemon* inconsistently during the 1980s and 1990s. In a 1993 opinion Justice Antonin Scalia mocked the Court's reluctance to rid itself of *Lemon*.

"Like some ghoul in a late-night horror movie that repeatedly sits up in its grave and shuffles abroad, after being repeatedly killed and buried, *Lemon* stalks our Establishment Clause jurisprudence once again, frightening the little children and school attorneys." He noted that five sitting justices (Scalia, Kennedy, O'Connor, Rehnquist, and White) "have, in their own opinions, personally driven pencils through the creature's heart."[2]

Scalia continued:

The secret of the *Lemon* test's survival, I think is that it is so easy to kill. It is there to scare us (and our audience) when we wish it to do so, but we can command it to return to the tomb at will. See, *e.g., Lynch v. Donnelly* (1984) (noting instances in which Court has not applied *Lemon* test).

When we wish to strike down a practice it forbids, we invoke it, see, *e.g., Aguilar v. Felton* (1985) (striking down state remedial education program administered in part in parochial schools); when we wish to uphold a practice it forbids, we ignore it entirely, *see Marsh v. Chambers* (1983) (upholding state legislative chaplains).

Sometimes, we take a middle course, calling its three prongs 'no more than helpful signposts,' *Hunt v. McNair* (1973). Such a docile and useful monster is worth keeping around, at least in a somnolent state; one never knows when one might need him.[3]

1. *Lemon v. Kurtzman*, 403 U.S. 602 (1971).
2. *Lamb's Chapel v. Center Moriches School District*, 508 U.S. 384 (1993).
3. Id.

continual monitoring, the state could not know with certainty whether a parochial school teacher was presenting subject matter to pupils in the required neutral manner, Burger said. Simple assurances were not sufficient, he said:

We need not and do not assume that teachers in parochial schools will be guilty of bad faith or any conscious design to evade the limitations imposed by the statute and the First Amendment. We simply recognize that a dedicated religious person, teaching in a school affiliated with his or her faith and operated to inculcate its tenets, will inevitably experience great difficulty in remaining religiously neutral.[89]

The only way to ensure that teachers remained neutral, Burger said, is through "comprehensive, discriminating and continuing state surveillance." Such contact between state and church amounted to excessive entanglement.[90]

By the same reasoning, the salary reimbursement portion of the Pennsylvania statute was invalid, Burger said. Furthermore, the portion of the Pennsylvania law reimbursing church schools for textbooks and instructional materials constituted direct aid to the school rather than to the pupils and their parents.

School Maintenance

Using the same three-part test, the Court in 1973 struck down New York statutes that authorized maintenance and repair grants to certain private and parochial schools, reimbursed low-income parents of nonpublic school students for a portion of the school tuition, and allowed tax credits to parents of nonpublic school students who did not qualify for the tuition reimbursements.

Writing for the majority in *Committee for Public Education and Religious Liberty v. Nyquist*, Justice Powell said that nothing in the statute stipulated that maintenance grants should be used only for secular purposes. Because the state grant could easily be used to "maintain the school chapel, or [cover] the cost of renovating classrooms in which religion is taught, or the cost of heating and lighting those same facilities," the majority could not deny that the primary effect of the grant was to subsidize directly "the religious activities of sectarian elementary and secondary schools" in violation of the establishment clause.[91]

Tuition Grants, Tax Credits

The tuition reimbursement law also unconstitutionally advanced religion, the majority held. Even though it appeared to aid parents, its obvious and primary effect was to aid church schools. Powell wrote:

[I]t is precisely the function of New York's law to provide assistance to private schools, the great majority of which are sectarian. By reimbursing parents for a portion of their tuition bill, the State seeks to relieve their financial burdens sufficiently to assure that they continue to have the option to send their children to religion-oriented schools. And while the other purposes for that aid—to perpetuate a pluralistic educational environment and to protect the fiscal integrity of overburdened public schools—are certainly unexceptionable, the effect of the aid is unmistakably to provide desired financial support for nonpublic, sectarian institutions.[92]

It made no difference to the majority that parents might spend the reimbursement money on something other than tuition:

[I]f the grants are offered as an incentive to parents to send their children to sectarian schools by making unrestricted cash payments to them, the Establishment Clause is violated whether or not the actual dollars given eventually find their way into the sectarian institutions. Whether the grant is labeled a reimbursement, a reward or a subsidy, its substantive impact is still the same.[93]

The majority concluded that the tax credit provisions served to advance religion for the same reasons tuition grants did. Under either the tuition reimbursement or the tax credit, the parent "receives the same form of encouragement and reward for sending his children to nonpublic schools," Powell wrote.[94]

Dissenting from the majority on tuition reimbursement and

tax credits, Chief Justice Burger and Justice Rehnquist contended that those two programs aided parents and not schools. Justice White would have upheld both programs as well as the grants for maintenance and repairs. He said that the primary effect of the New York statutes was not to advance religion but to "preserve the secular functions" of parochial schools.

Ten years after *Nyquist* the Court, 5–4, upheld a Minnesota state income tax deduction available to parents of children in public and private schools. In *Mueller v. Allen* (1983) the Court found permissible a deduction for parental costs of tuition, textbooks, and transportation for elementary and secondary school children up to $700 per older child and $500 per younger child. Critical to the ruling was the availability of this deduction both to public and private school patrons; it was not disputed that the major share of the benefit ran to the latter, since public schools charge no tuition.[95]

Testing Services

On the same day as the *Nyquist* decision, June 25, 1973, the Court also held invalid a New York law that provided per-pupil payments to nonpublic schools to cover the costs of testing and maintaining state-mandated pupil records. Most of the funds were spent on testing—state-mandated standardized tests and those prepared by teachers to measure the progress of students in regular course work.

The Court found that the statute was invalid as it related to this latter sort of testing. "Despite the obviously integral role of testing in the total teaching process," the statute made no attempt to ensure that teacher-prepared tests were "free of religious instruction." Thus the grants used for testing had the primary effect of advancing religion, the Court said. And because the Court could not determine which part of the grants was spent on potentially religious activities and which on permissible secular activities, it invalidated the entire statute.[96]

Several years later the Court found a permissible testing reimbursement arrangement that covered the costs of administering, grading, and reporting the results of standardized tests prepared by the state—as well as the costs of reporting pupil attendance and other basic data required by the state.[97]

Other State Services

In two other cases, *Meek v. Pittinger* (1975) and *Wolman v. Walter* (1977), the Court again used its three-level test to measure the constitutionality of a variety of state services. Under *Lemon's* three-part test, government aid must have a secular purpose; it can neither advance nor inhibit religion; and it must not foster excessive involvement with religion.

The Court in these rulings allowed states to provide church-affiliated schools with loaned textbooks, standardized testing and scoring services, and speech and hearing diagnostic services. Therapeutic, guidance, and remedial education services could be provided by public school board employees to parochial school students at sites away from the schools, although similar services provided at the schools were impermissible.

The Court in *Wolman* ruled unconstitutional an Ohio law that permitted the state to pay the costs of transportation for parochial school field trips. The majority held that because the schools determined the timing and destination of field trips, they and not parents were the true beneficiaries of the statute, and thus could not be reimbursed. "The field trips are an integral part of the educational experience," the majority said, "and where the teacher works within and for a sectarian institution, an unacceptable risk of fostering of religion is an inevitable byproduct."[98]

The Court also held impermissible as a violation of the establishment clause the loan of instructional materials and equipment either to sectarian schools themselves or to their pupils.

The Court ruled out direct loans to schools in *Meek*. Even though the materials were secular in nature, the loan "has the unconstitutional primary effect of advancing religion because of the predominantly religious character of the schools benefiting from the Act."[99] In the later *Wolman* case, the majority said it saw no significant difference between lending materials to schools and lending them to pupils; "the state aid inevitably flows in part in support of the religious role of the schools," it said.[100]

The perennial nature of the parochiaid issue—and the Court's firm stance—were illustrated afresh in 1985. On July 1 the Court held that Grand Rapids, Michigan, school officials had "established" religion by providing remedial and enrichment classes to students at forty-one nonpublic schools, forty of which were religiously affiliated. Writing for the majority, Justice Brennan said these classes—conducted during the school day by public school teachers, or after school by parochial school teachers who were paid for this work from public funds—were impermissible. The "symbolic union of church and state inherent in the provision of secular state-provided instruction in the religious school buildings threatens to convey a message of state support for religion," Brennan wrote in *Grand Rapids School District v. Ball*. The vote was 7–2 on the school-day classes, with Justices Rehnquist and White dissenting; it was 5–4 on the after-school classes, with Chief Justice Burger and Justice O'Connor finding them permissible.[101]

That same day the Court, 5–4, also held unconstitutional New York's system for providing remedial and counseling services to disadvantaged children in nonpublic schools.[102]

That ruling in *Aguilar v. Felton* set off events that produced a subsequent Court case, *Board of Education of Kiryas Joel Village School District v. Grumet* (1994). It involved the disabled youngsters of a New York community inhabited exclusively by members of a small, rigidly orthodox Jewish sect, the Satmar Hasidim. In this community, Kiryas Joel ("community of Joel"), religious rituals were scrupulously observed, and almost all the children were taught in religious schools.

RELIGIOUS SYMBOLS ON DISPLAY

In the closing years of the twentieth century, the Supreme Court repeatedly wrestled with the question of whether holiday displays of religious symbols violated the establishment clause of the First Amendment: "Congress shall make no law respecting an establishment of religion."

The first of three significant cases was *Lynch v. Donnelly* (1984). The establishment clause was invoked as a basis for challenging the decision of city officials in Pawtucket, Rhode Island, to include a crèche, or nativity scene, in their city's annual holiday display. Also included were other traditional Christmas symbols.

The Court, 5–4, upheld as permissible the inclusion of the crèche. Writing for the majority, Chief Justice Warren E. Burger declared that "the concept of a 'wall' of separation is a useful figure of speech . . . but . . . not a wholly accurate description of the practical aspects of the relationship that in fact exists between church and state."[1]

"No significant segment of our society and no institution within it can exist in a vacuum or in total or absolute isolation from all the other parts, much less from government," Burger continued. "Nor does the Constitution require complete separation of church and state; it affirmatively mandates accommodation, not merely tolerance, of all religions, and forbids hostility toward any."[2]

Justices William J. Brennan Jr., Harry A. Blackmun, Thurgood Marshall, and John Paul Stevens dissented. In their view the "primary effect of including a nativity scene in the city's display is . . . to place the government's imprimatur of approval on the particular religious beliefs exemplified by the crèche," which violated the First Amendment.[3]

Five years later the Court made clear the importance of context in determining whether the use of religious symbols by government was permissible. In a case involving a crèche and menorah displayed in separate locations, the Court held that the crèche display was unconstitutional, but the menorah display was permissible.[4]

The crèche display was unconstitutional, explained Justice Blackmun for the majority, because "unlike in *Lynch*, nothing in the context of the display detracts from the crèche's religious message" because it stood alone on the Grand Staircase of the Allegheny County Courthouse. By permitting its prominent display in this particular place, "the county sends an unmistakable message that it supports and promotes . . . the crèche's message." The Court divided 5–4 on that point; the dissenters were Chief Justice William H. Rehnquist and Justices Anthony M. Kennedy, Byron R. White, and Antonin Scalia.[5]

The menorah display was permissible, Blackmun continued, because it was part of an overall display of symbols of the winter holidays, including a Christmas tree, standing outside the City-County Building.

Unlike the crèche, he wrote, "the menorah's message is not exclusively religious."[6] The Court divided 6–3 on this point: Blackmun and Justice Sandra Day O'Connor were joined in the majority by the dissenters on the crèche issue; dissenting were Justices Stevens, Brennan, and Marshall.

The third case, which also implicated free speech rights, arose after Ohio officials denied Ku Klux Klan members a permit to put up a large wooden cross in front of the state capitol, where other private groups were permitted to erect a Christmas tree and a menorah.

By a 7–2 vote, the Court held that the state officials were wrong to exclude this one privately sponsored religious message from a public forum open to other privately sponsored messages. Justice Scalia, who wrote the opinion, said a reasonable observer would not think the state had endorsed the cross's message. He distinguished the case from *Allegheny County*, saying the "Grand Staircase" of the courthouse was not open to all on an equal basis, "so the County was *favoring* sectarian religious expression."[7]

Most of Scalia's opinion was joined by Chief Justice Rehnquist and Justices O'Connor, Kennedy, David H. Souter, Clarence Thomas, and Stephen G. Breyer. Justices Stevens and Ruth Bader Ginsburg dissented.

1. *Lynch v. Donnelly*, 465 U.S. 668 at 673 (1984).
2. Ibid.
3. Id. at 701.
4. *Allegheny County v. American Civil Liberties Union, Chabad v. American Civil Liberties Union, Pittsburgh v. American Civil Liberties Union*, 492 U.S. 573 (1989).
5. Id.
6. Id.
7. *Capitol Square Review and Advisory Board v. Pinette*, ____ U.S. ____ (1995).

Before the 1985 *Aguilar* ruling, the community's disabled youngsters received special services in an annex adjacent to one of the religious schools. The annex was operated by the region's public school district. After the Court's decision in *Aguilar*, the school district told the Hasidim that the youngsters had to attend a public school outside the community. Some of the students apparently felt traumatized by attending school in what the Hasidim leaders called a "foreign setting." The New York legislature responded in 1989 with a measure to make the village into its own school district so that it could set up a public school for its special-needs students.

The Supreme Court struck down the law as an unconstitutional establishment of religion. In the Court's main opinion, Justice David H. Souter said New York improperly had created a "fusion of governmental and religious functions." Justices Harry A. Blackmun, John Paul Stevens, and Ruth Bader Ginsburg joined that part of the opinion. Justice Sandra Day O'Connor signed a narrower part of Souter's opinion that said there was no assurance New York would provide the same benefit "equally to other religious (and nonreligious) groups." Providing a sixth vote for the judgment striking down the law, Justice Anthony M. Kennedy in a separate opinion called it "religious gerrymandering."[103] Justice Antonin Scalia, joined by Chief Justice William H. Rehnquist and Justice Clarence Thomas, dissented. Scalia depicted the challenged law as a neutral statute aimed at accommodating the villagers' cultural rather than religious views. He added that, in any event, a law acknowledging a group's religious beliefs promoted rather than violated religious freedom.

FEDERAL AID TO CHURCH-RELATED SCHOOLS

Federal taxpayers, the Court ruled in 1923, do not suffer direct injury from federal decisions on spending and therefore cannot challenge such decisions in Court.[104]

But in the 1968 case of *Flast v. Cohen*, the Court modified this rule to permit taxpayer suits under two circumstances: if they challenge a spending or tax program, rather than a regulatory policy, and if the taxpayer can show that the alleged misspending violated a constitutional restriction on congressional spending and taxing powers.

Mrs. Flast challenged as an unconstitutional establishment of religion a program of federal aid to both public and parochial schoolchildren. Congress in 1965 had based this education aid program on the "child benefit" theory, first espoused by the Court in *Cochran v. Louisiana Board of Education* (1930). Title I of the Elementary and Secondary Education Act of 1965, the major federal aid program, gave grants to educationally disadvantaged children regardless of whether they attended public or private schools.

The Supreme Court in 1968 ruled that Mrs. Flast could bring her suit challenging this program. The establishment clause "operates as a specific constitutional limitation upon the exercise by Congress of the taxing and spending power," barring Congress to act to establish religion.[105]

Flast's challenge never returned to the Supreme Court for a decision on the merits of her argument. Another case did, but the justices sidestepped the establishment clause issue.

Wheeler v. Barrera (1974) was brought by parents of nonpublic school students in Missouri who complained that their children were not receiving the same Title I benefits as eligible children attending public schools. The Court held that to continue receiving Title I funds, the state must comply with the federal requirement to provide parochial school students with remedial services comparable to those given public school students. But, the Court said, these services did not have to be identical.[106]

And because such a program had not yet been instituted, the Court declined to rule whether the provision of publicly employed teachers to teach parochial school students in their own schools would violate the establishment clause. When that question came up eleven years later, in *Aguilar v. Felton*, the answer was clear: such an arrangement did violate the establishment clause.

The Court in *Aguilar* said New York City could not use federal funds to send teachers into private and parochial schools to provide remedial and counseling services during the regular school day. This advanced religion in symbolic and practical fashion, held the Court, by providing services the private schools would otherwise lack. Moreover, by monitoring the program, the city became entangled in church-school affairs. Justices Burger, White, Rehnquist, and O'Connor dissented.[107]

In 1993 the Court ruled that the government could pay for a sign-language interpreter to accompany a deaf ninth-grade student in a Roman Catholic school. Arizona officials had refused the Tucson student's request for reimbursement under the state's administration of a federal law guaranteeing educational opportunities for the disabled. The state argued that funding the interpreter in a parochial school would violate the constitutional guarantee of separation of church and state. Writing for the 5–4 Court, Chief Justice William H. Rehnquist said such state funding would be constitutional as "part of a general government program that distributes benefits neutrally to any child qualifying as 'handicapped'" under the federal disabilities law.[108]

AID TO CHURCH COLLEGES

Unlike its lengthy deliberations over government aid to elementary and secondary schools, the Supreme Court had little difficulty in upholding direct government aid to church-affiliated colleges and universities. In three cases decided in the 1970s, the Court approved state and federal programs aiding sectarian institutions of higher education.

In *Tilton v. Richardson* (1971) the Court upheld federal construction grants to church-affiliated colleges under the Higher Education Facilities Act of 1963. This federal statute permitted church-related schools to receive grants with the understanding that no federally financed building would be used for sectarian purposes.

Writing the opinion for the majority of five, Chief Justice Burger said that because the grants were available to both secular and sectarian schools, the law met the test that government aid be secular in purpose. The majority did not find the involvement between the federal government and church-related schools likely to be excessive. The buildings themselves were religiously neutral in character, and since religious indoctrination was not the primary purpose of the colleges, the necessity for government surveillance to maintain the separation between religious and secular education was minimal.

Nor did the federal law advance religion. There was no evidence, said Burger, that "religion seeps into the use of any of these facilities."[109]

The majority, however, did declare unconstitutional a section of the law that permitted the schools to use the buildings for sectarian purposes after twenty years.

Underlying the majority's decision was its presumption that there is a significant difference between the religious aspects of church-related colleges and church-related primary and secondary schools, and between impressionable youngsters and more skeptical young adults. As Burger explained it:

[C]ollege students are less impressionable and less susceptible to religious indoctrination. . . . The skepticism of the college student is not an inconsiderable barrier to any attempt or tendency to subvert the

James Zobrest, right, signing with his parents. In *Zobrest v. Catalina Foothills School District* (1993) the Court ruled that Zobrest, a deaf student at a Roman Catholic high school, could be furnished with a state-funded sign-language interpreter.

congressional objectives and limitations. Furthermore, by their very nature, college and postgraduate courses tend to limit the opportunities for sectarian influence by virtue of their own internal disciplines. Many church-related colleges and universities are characterized by a high degree of academic freedom and seek to evoke free and critical responses from their students.[110]

Justice Douglas, speaking for three of the dissenters, objected to the federal law on the grounds that no federal tax revenues should be used to support religious activities of any sort. Justice Brennan also dissented.

Using the *Tilton* decision as a precedent, the Court subsequently upheld a South Carolina statute that allowed the state to issue revenue bonds to finance construction of secular facilities at secular and sectarian colleges and universities, and a Maryland program of general annual grants to private colleges, including church-related schools.[111]

EQUAL ACCESS

Although the Court generally forbids prayer in public schools, it has permitted public institutions to offer their facilities to religious organizations, as long as the benefits are provided neutrally to religious and nonreligious groups alike.

In four cases between 1981 and 1995, the Court rejected the arguments of school officials that the use of public school facilities to support religious programs would breach the establishment clause of the First Amendment.

In 1981 the Court said the University of Missouri should allow a student religious group to meet in school buildings on the same terms as other extracurricular clubs. The Court extended that decision to the public high schools in 1990 when it ruled that a federal "equal access" statute did not breach the Constitu-

tion's required separation of church and state. The justices said an Omaha high school student who wanted to start a Bible study group should have been given permission to do so on the same basis as a student who wished to start a scuba diving club.[112]

The next test of religious access, in 1993, went beyond student use of public school facilities. The Center Moriches Union Free School District on Long Island, New York, had allowed community groups to use its facilities after hours for social, civic, and recreational purposes. But the district had a formal policy against opening classrooms to groups for religious activities. It rejected a request from an evangelical Christian church that wanted to show a film series addressing various child-rearing questions.

This denial of access was unconstitutional, the Court ruled 9–0.

Writing for the majority, Justice Byron R. White said "it discriminates on the basis of viewpoint to permit school property to be used for the presentation of all views about family issues and child-rearing except those dealing with the subject matter from a religious standpoint."[113]

Two years later in 1995 the Supreme Court examined a University of Virginia policy that denied the use of student-activity funds to cover the costs of printing a Christian magazine on campus. These funds were used to support a broad range of extracurricular activities related to the university's educational purpose, such as the publication of student news, information, and opinion.

The Court, 5–4, struck down the policy as a violation of free speech. The justices said a program that distributes funds to religious and nonreligious publications would not violate the establishment clause. Justice Anthony M. Kennedy wrote the majority opinion in *Rosenberger v. University of Virginia*. "There is no difference in logic or principle, and no difference of constitutional significance, between a school using its funds to operate a facility to which students have access, and a school paying a third-party contractor [such as a printer] to operate the facility on its behalf. The latter occurs here," Kennedy explained.[114] "It is axiomatic that the government may not regulate speech based on its substantive content or the message it conveys," he continued.[115]

Kennedy was joined by Chief Justice William H. Rehnquist and Justices Sandra Day O'Connor, Antonin Scalia, and Clarence Thomas. Kennedy wrote:

Vital First Amendment speech principles are at stake here. The first danger to liberty lies in granting the State the power to examine publications to determine whether or not they are based on some ultimate idea and if so for the State to classify them. The second, and corollary, danger is to speech from the chilling of individual thought and expression. That danger is especially real in the University setting, where the State acts against a background and tradition of thought and experiment that is at the center of our intellectual and philosophic tradition.[116]

Justices David H. Souter, John Paul Stevens, Ruth Bader Ginsburg, and Stephen G. Breyer dissented. Justice Souter expressed their concern that "the Court today, for the first time, approves the direct funding of core religious activities by an arm of the State. . . . [T]here is no warrant for distinguishing among public funding sources for purposes of applying the First Amendment's prohibition on religious establishment. . . ." Souter concluded with a reference to the 1971 ruling that has defined the modern Court's approach to cases brought under the establishment clause: "[M]y apprehension is whetted by Chief Justice Burger's warning in *Lemon v. Kurtzman:* 'in constitutional adjudication some steps, which when taken were thought to approach "the verge," have become the platform for yet further steps. A certain momentum develops in constitutional theory and it can be a "downhill thrust" easily set in motion but difficult to retard or stop'."[117]

This vision of the Court on the verge of a slippery slope was not shared by the majority. Justice O'Connor's concurring opinion gives perhaps the best summary of the contemporary Court's approach to freedom of religion cases:

The Court's decision today . . . neither trumpets the supremacy of the neutrality principle nor signals the demise of the funding prohibition in Establishment Clause jurisprudence. As I observed last term, "experience proves that the Establishment Clause, like the Free Speech Clause, cannot easily be reduced to a single test." When bedrock principles collide, they test the limits of categorical obstinacy and expose the flaws and dangers of a Grand Unified Theory that may turn out to be neither grand nor unified. The Court today does only what courts must do in many Establishment Clause cases—focus on specific features of a particular government action to ensure that it does not violate the Constitution.[118]

NOTES

INTRODUCTION (PP. 409–414)

1. Zechariah Chafee Jr., *Free Speech in the United States* (Cambridge: Harvard University Press, 1941; reprint ed. New York: Atheneum, 1969), 33.

2. Thomas I. Emerson, *The System of Freedom of Expression* (New York: Random House, Vintage Books, 1970), 7.

3. Thomas M. Cooley, *A Treatise on Constitutional Limitations*, 8th ed., 2 vols. (Boston: Little, Brown, 1927), II: 901.

4. *Whitney v. California*, 274 U.S. 357 at 375–376 (1927).

5. *Barron v. Baltimore*, 7 Pet. 243 (1833).

6. Alpheus T. Mason and William M. Beaney, *The Supreme Court in a Free Society* (New York: Norton, 1968), 289.

7. *Gilbert v. Minnesota*, 254 U.S. 325 at 343 (1920).

8. *Prudential Insurance Co. v. Cheek*, 259 U.S. 530 at 538 (1922).

9. *Meyer v. Nebraska*, 262 U.S. 390 at 399–400 (1923).

10. *Gitlow v. New York*, 268 U.S. 652 at 666 (1925).

11. *Pierce v. Society of Sisters*, 268 U.S. 510 (1925).

12. *Cantwell v. Connecticut*, 310 U.S. 296 at 303 (1940); *Everson v. Board of Education*, 330 U.S. 1 (1947).

13. *Near v. Minnesota*, 283 U.S. 697 (1931); *DeJonge v. Oregon*, 299 U.S. 353 at 364 (1937).

14. William Blackstone, *Commentaries on the Laws of England*, quoted in Chafee, *Free Speech*, 9.

15. Cooley, *Constitutional Limitations*, II: 885–886.

16. *Cantwell v. Connecticut*, 310 U.S. 296 at 303–304 (1940).

17. *West Virginia State Board of Education v. Barnette*, 319 U.S. 624 at 642 (1943).

18. *Abrams v. United States*, 250 U.S. 616 at 630 (1919).

19. *Smith v. California*, 361 U.S. 147 at 157 (1959).

20. *Konigsberg v. State Bar of California*, 366 U.S. 36 at 61 (1961).

21. *Palko v. Connecticut*, 302 U.S. 319 at 327, 326 (1937).

22. *United States v. Carolene Products*, 304 U.S. 144 at 152, fn. 4 (1938).

23. *Schneider v. Irvington*, 308 U.S. 147 at 161 (1939).

24. *Murdock v. Pennsylvania*, 319 U.S. 105 at 115 (1943) overturning *Jones v. Opelika*, 316 U.S. 584 (1942).

25. *Thomas v. Collins*, 323 U.S. 516 at 529–530 (1945).

26. *Landmark Communications Inc. v. Virginia*, 435 U.S. 829 at 843–844 (1978).

27. *Kovacs v. Cooper*, 336 U.S. 77 at 90 (1949).

28. *Dennis v. United States*, 341 U.S. 494 at 539–540 (1951).

29. *Schenck v. United States*, 249 U.S. 47 at 52 (1919).

30. See, for example, *Abrams v. United States*, 250 U.S. 616 (1919); *Pierce v. United States*, 252 U.S. 239 (1920); *Gitlow v. New York*, 268 U.S. 652 (1925).

31. *Herndon v. Lowry*, 301 U.S. 242 at 261 (1937).

32. *Thornhill v. Alabama*, 310 U.S. 88 (1940).

33. *Cantwell v. Connecticut*, 310 U.S. 296 at 311 (1940).

34. *Terminiello v. Chicago* 337 U.S. 1 (1949); *Feiner v. New York*, 340 U.S. 315 (1951).

35. *Dennis v. United States*, 341 U.S. 494 at 510 (1951).

36. *Yates v. United States*, 354 U.S. 298 (1957).

37. *American Communications Association v. Douds*, 399 U.S. 382 at 399 (1950).

38. See, for example, *Konigsberg v. State Bar of California*, 366 U.S. 36 (1961).

39. *NAACP v. Alabama ex rel. Patterson*, 357 U.S. 449 (1958); *Edwards v. South Carolina*, 372 U.S. 229 (1963); *Cox v. Louisiana*, 379 U.S. 536 (1965); *Brown v. Louisiana*, 383 U.S. 131 (1966); *Adderly v. Florida*, 385 U.S. 39 (1966); *United States v. Robel*, 389 U.S. 258 (1967).

40. *Brandenburg v. Ohio*, 395 U.S. at 444 (1969).

41. *Shelton v. Tucker*, 364 U.S. 479 at 488 (1960).

42. *U.S. v. Eichman*, 496 U.S. 310 (1990).

FREEDOM OF SPEECH (PP. 415–446)

1. C. Herman Pritchett, *The American Constitution*, 3d ed. (New York: McGraw-Hill, 1977), 314.

2. Ibid., 317.

3. *Schenck v. United States*, 249 U.S. 47 at 51 (1919).

4. Id. at 52.

5. Id.

6. Id.

7. *Frohwerk v. United States*, 249 U.S. 204 at 208–209 (1919).

8. *Debs v. United States*, 249 U.S. 211 at 215 (1919).

9. Ibid.

10. *Abrams v. United States*, 250 U.S. 616 at 623 (1919).

11. Id. at 627, 628.

12. *Schaefer v. United States*, 251 U.S. 466 at 481 (1920).

13. Id. at 478.

14. Id. at 479.

15. Id. at 486.

16. Id. at 493–495.

17. *Pierce v. United States*, 252 U.S. 239 at 249 (1920).

18. Id. at 269.

19. Id. at 273; the three minor decisions in this series were *Sugarman v. United States*, 249 U.S. 182 (1919); *Stilson v. United States*, 250 U.S. 583 (1919); *O'Connell v. United States*, 253 U.S. 142 (1920).

20. *Hartzel v. United States*, 322 U.S. 680 (1944).

21. *Gitlow v. New York*, 268 U.S. 652 at 665 (1925).

22. Id. at 667.

23. Id. at 669.

24. Id. at 673.

25. *Whitney v. California*, 274 U.S. 357 at 371–372 (1927).

26. Id. at 373.

27. Id. at 376, 378.

28. *Fiske v. Kansas*, 274 U.S. 380 (1927).

29. *DeJonge v. Oregon*, 299 U.S. 353 at 365 (1937).

30. *Herndon v. Lowry*, 301 U.S. 242 at 258 (1937).

31. Id. at 263–64.

32. Id. at 276.

33. *Brandenburg v. Ohio*, 395 U.S. 444 at 447–448 (1969).

34. *Davis v. Massachusetts*, 167 U.S. 43 at 47 (1897).

35. *Hague v. C.I.O.*, 307 U.S. 496 at 515–516 (1939).

36. *Cox v. New Hampshire*, 312 U.S. 569 (1941).

37. *Cantwell v. Connecticut*, 310 U.S. 296 at 308 (1940).

38. Id. at 310, 311.

39. *Terminiello v. Chicago*, 337 U.S. 1 at 4–5 (1949).

40. Id. at 37.

41. *Feiner v. New York*, 340 U.S. 315 at 320–321 (1951).

42. *Near v. Minnesota*, 283 U.S. 697 (1931).

43. *Cantwell v. Connecticut*, 310 U.S. 296 (1940).

44. *Thomas v. Collins*, 323 U.S. 516 at 534–535 (1945).

45. Id. at 540.

46. *Kunz v. New York*, 340 U.S. 290 at 293 (1951).

47. Id. at 298.

48. *Stromberg v. California*, 283 U.S. 359 at 369 (1931).

49. *West Virginia State Board of Education v. Barnette*, 319 U.S. 624 at 632–633 (1943).

50. *Garner v. Louisiana*, 368 U.S. 157 (1961).

51. See, for example, *Peterson v. City of Greenville*, 373 U.S. 244 (1963); *Shuttlesworth v. City of Birmingham*, 373 U.S. 262 (1963); *Lombard v. Louisiana*, 373 U.S. 267 (1963); *Gober v. City of Birmingham*, 373 U.S. 374 (1963); *Avent v. North Carolina*, 373 U.S. 375 (1963).

52. *NAACP v. Claiborne Hardware Co.*, 458 U.S. 886 (1982).

53. *United States v. O'Brien*, 391 U.S. 367 at 376 (1968).

54. *Barnes v. Glen Theatre*, 501 U.S. 560 (1991).

55. *Tinker v. Des Moines School District*, 393 U.S. 503 at 508–509 (1969).

56. *Schacht v. United States*, 398 U.S. 58 at 63 (1970).

57. *Street v. New York*, 394 U.S. 576 (1969).

58. *Smith v. Goguen*, 415 U.S. 566 at 574 (1974).

59. *Spence v. Washington*, 418 U.S. 405 at 410–411 (1974).

60. *Texas v. Johnson*, 491 U.S. 397 (1989).

61. *United States v. Eichman*, 496 U.S. 310 (1990).

62. *City of Ladue v. Gilleo*, 114 S. Ct. 2038 (1994).

63. *United States v. Cruikshank*, 92 U.S. 542 at 552 (1876).

64. *DeJonge v. Oregon*, 299 U.S. 353 at 365 (1937).

65. *Hague v. C.I.O.*, 307 U.S. 496 (1939).

66. *Cox v. New Hampshire*, 312 U.S. 569 at 576 (1941).

67. *Forsyth County, Georgia v. Nationalist Movement*, 505 U.S. 123 (1992).

68. *Hurley v. Irish-American Gay, Lesbian and Bisexual Group of Boston*, 115 S. Ct. 2338 (1995).

69. *Edwards v. South Carolina*, 372 U.S. 229 (1963). See also *Fields v. South Carolina*, 375 U.S. 44 (1963); *Cameron v. Johnson*, 390 U.S. 611 (1968).

70. *Edwards v. South Carolina*, 372 U.S. 229 at 235, 237 (1963).

71. Id. at 237; *Terminiello v. Chicago*, 337 U.S. 1 (1949).

72. *Cox v. Louisiana*, 379 U.S. 536 (1965).

73. Id. at 559.

74. *Brown v. Louisiana*, 383 U.S. 131 at 142 (1966).

75. Id. at 166.

76. *Adderly v. Florida*, 385 U.S. 39 at 41, 47–48 (1966).

77. Id. at 49–51.

78. *Gregory v. City of Chicago*, 394 U.S. 111 at 112 (1969).

79. *Frisby v. Schultz*, 487 U.S. 474 (1988).

80. *United States v. Grace*, 461 U.S. 171 (1983).

81. *Clark v. Community for Creative Non-Violence*, 468 U.S. 288 (1984).

82. *Madsen v. Women's Health Center Inc.*, 114 S. Ct. 2516 (1994).

83. *American Steel Foundries v. Tri-City Central Trades Council*, 257 U.S. 184 at 204 (1921).

84. *Senn v. Tile Layers Union*, 301 U.S. 468 at 478 (1937).

85. *Thornhill v. Alabama*, 310 U.S. 88 at 102 (1940).

86. Id. at 104; see also *Carlson v. California*, 310 U.S. 106 (1940).

87. *AFL v. Swing*, 312 U.S. 321 (1941).

88. *Milk Wagon Drivers Union v. Meadowmoor Dairies Inc.*, 312 U.S. 287 at 293, 294 (1941).

89. *Bakery and Pastry Drivers v. Wohl*, 315 U.S. 769 at 775 (1942).

90. *Carpenters and Joiners Union v. Ritter's Cafe*, 315 U.S. 722 at 727 (1942).

91. *Bakery and Pastry Drivers v. Wohl*, 315 U.S. 769 at 776–777 (1942).

92. *Giboney v. Empire Storage & Ice Co.*, 336 U.S. 490 at 502 (1949).

93. *Hughes v. Superior Court of California*, 339 U.S. 460 at 465–466 (1950).

94. *Building Service Employees Union v. Gazzam*, 339 U.S. 532 (1950); *International Brotherhood of Teamsters v. Hanke*, 339 U.S. 470 (1950).

95. *Local Plumbers Union #10 v. Graham*, 345 U.S. 192 (1953).

96. *International Brotherhood of Teamsters, Local 695 v. Vogt*, 354 U.S. 284 at 294–295, 293 (1957).

97. Id. at 296.

98. *Amalgamated Food Employees Union Local 590 v. Logan Valley Plaza*, 391 U.S. 308 (1968), qualified by *Lloyd Corp. Ltd. v. Tanner*, 407 U.S. 551 (1972) and *Hudgens v. National Labor Relations Board*, 424 U.S. 507 (1976).

99. Zechariah Chafee Jr., *Free Speech in the United States* (Cambridge: Harvard University Press, 1941; reprint ed., New York: Atheneum, 1969), 405–406.

100. *Cantwell v. Connecticut*, 310 U.S. 296 at 306–307 (1940); see also *Schneider v. Irvington*, 308 U.S. 147 (1939); *Largent v. Texas*, 318 U.S. 418 (1943).

101. *Hynes v. Oradell*, 425 U.S. 610 (1976); *Village of Schaumburg v. Citizens for a Better Environment*, 444 U.S. 620 (1980).

102. *Secretary of State of Maryland v. Joseph H. Munson Co.*, 467 U.S. 947 (1984); *Riley v. National Federation of the Blind of North Carolina*, 487 U.S. 781 (1988).

103. *Thomas v. Collins*, 323 U.S. 516 at 534, 540 (1945). See also *Staub v. City of Baxley*, 355 U.S. 313 (1958).

104. *Martin v. City of Struthers*, 319 U.S. 141 at 145, 146, 154–155 (1943).

105. *International Society for Krishna Consciousness v. Lee; Lee v. International Society for Krishna Consciousness*, 505 U.S. 672 (1992).

106. Alex Kozinski and Stuart Banner, "Who's Afraid of Commercial Speech," 76 Va. L. Rev. 627 (May 1990).

107. *Schneider v. Irvington*, 308 U.S. 147 (1939).

108. *Valentine v. Chrestensen*, 316 U.S. 52 at 54 (1942).

109. *Breard v. City of Alexandria*, 341 U.S. 622 at 642 (1951).

110. *New York Times Co. v. Sullivan*, 376 U.S. 254 at 266 (1964).

111. *Bigelow v. Virginia*, 421 U.S. 809 (1975).

112. *Virginia State Board of Pharmacy v. Virginia Citizens Consumer Council Inc.*, 425 U.S. 748 at 765 (1976).

113. *Carey v. Population Services International*, 431 U.S. 678 (1977); *Bates v. Arizona State Bar*, 433 U.S. 350 (1977); *Linmark Associates Inc. v. Township of Willingboro*, 431 U.S. 85 (1977); *Bolger v. Youngs Drug Products Corp.*, 463 U.S. 60 (1983).

114. *Bates v. Arizona State Bar*, 433 U.S. 350 (1977); *Ohralik v. Ohio State Bar Association*, 436 U.S. 447 (1978). See also *Friedman v. Rogers*, 440 U.S. 1 (1979); *Zauderer v. Office of Disciplinary Counsel of the Supreme Court of Ohio*, 471 U.S. 626 (1985).

115. *In re R.M.J.*, 455 U.S. 191 (1982); *Shapero v. Kentucky Bar Assn.*, 486 U.S. 466 (1988).

116. *Florida Bar v. Went For It Inc.*, 115 S. Ct. 2371 (1995).

117. *Ibanez v. Florida Department of Business and Professional Regulation, Board of Accountancy*, 114 S. Ct. 2084 (1994); *Edenfield v. Fane* 507 U.S. 761 (1993).

118. *Central Hudson Gas & Electric Co. v. Public Service Commission of New York*, 447 U.S. 557 (1980).

119. Id. at 566.

120. *Consolidated Edison of New York v. Public Service Commission of New York*, 447 U.S. 530 (1980); *Pacific Gas & Electric Co. v. Public Utilities Commission*, 475 U.S. 1 (1986).

121. *Posadas de Puerto Rico Associates v. Tourism Council of Puerto Rico*, 478 U.S. 328 (1986).

122. *Liquormart v. Rhode Island*, —— U.S. —— (1996).

FREEDOM OF THE PRESS (PP. 447–474)

1. Quoted in Willard Grosvenor Bleyer, *Main Currents in the History of American Journalism* (Boston: Houghton Mifflin, 1927), 103.

2. Dissenting opinion in *Saxbe v. Washington Post*, 417 U.S. 843 at 863 (1974).

3. Thomas I. Emerson, *The System of Freedom of Expression* (New York: Random House, Vintage Books, 1970), 506.

4. *Near v. Minnesota*, 283 U.S. 697 at 713 (1931).

5. Id. at 716.

6. Id. at 720.

7. Id. at 721.

8. Id. at 722.

9. Id. at 735, 736.

10. Id. at 738.

11. *Simon & Schuster Inc. v. Members of New York State Crime Victims Board*, 502 U.S. 105 (1991).

12. *Grosjean v. American Press Co.*, 297 U.S. 233 at 244–245 (1936).

13. Id. at 250. See also *Minneapolis Star & Tribune Co. v. Minnesota Commissioner of Revenue*, 460 U.S. 575 (1983) and *Arkansas Writers' Project v. Ragland*, 481 U.S. 221 (1987).

14. *Lovell v. Griffin*, 303 U.S. 444 at 452 (1938).

15. Id. at 451.

16. *Schneider v. Irvington*, 308 U.S. 147 (1939); see also *Jamison v. Texas*, 318 U.S. 413 (1943). The other three cases are *Kim Young v. California, Snyder v. Milwaukee, Nichols v. Massachusetts*, 308 U.S. 147 (1939).

17. *Schneider v. Irvington*, 308 U.S. 147 at 160–161 (1939).

18. Id. at 163.

19. *Talley v. California*, 362 U.S. 60 at 64 (1960).

20. *McIntyre v. Ohio Elections Commission*, 115 S. Ct. 1511 (1995).

21. *Organization for a Better Austin v. Keefe*, 402 U.S. 415 at 418, 419, 420 (1971).

22. *Mills v. Alabama*, 384 U.S. 214 at 219 (1966).

23. *New York Times Co. v. United States*, 403 U.S. 713 at 714 (1971).

24. Id. at 715, 717.

25. Id. at 720.

26. Id. at 725–726.

27. Id. at 730.

28. Id. at 730–731, 732.

29. Id. at 742.

30. Id. at 749.

31. Id. at 751.

32. Id. at 757.

33. Id. at 759.

34. Id. at 761.

35. See Holmes's dissent in *Abrams v. United States*, 250 U.S. 616 at 630 (1919); Black's and Douglas's opinion in *Beauharnais v. Illinois*, 343 U.S. 250 at 272 (1952); majority opinion in *The New York Times Co. v. Sullivan*, 376 U.S. 254 (1964).

36. *Coleman v. MacLennan*, 98 P 281 at 281–282 (1908).

37. *Dun & Bradstreet Inc. v. Greenmoss Builders Inc.*, 422 U.S. 749 (1985).

38. *The New York Times Co. v. Sullivan*, 376 U.S. 254 at 257– 258 (1964).

39. Id. at 268, 269.

40. Id. at 270–271.

41. Id. at 271–272.

42. Id. at 279.

43. Id. at 279–280.

44. Id. at 288.

45. Id. at 293.

46. Id. at 300.

47. *Garrison v. Louisiana*, 379 U.S. 64 (1964); *Ashton v. Kentucky*, 384 U.S. 195 (1966); *St. Amant v. Thompson*, 390 U.S. 727 at 731 (1968); *Greenbelt Cooperative Publishing Assn. v. Bresler* 398 U.S. 6 (1970); *Time Inc. v. Pape*, 401 U.S. 279 (1971).

48. *Herbert v. Lando*, 441 U.S. 153 (1979).

49. *Rosenblatt v. Baer*, 383 U.S. 75 at 85–86 (1966).

50. Id. at 93.

51. *Monitor Patriot Co. v. Roy*, 401 U.S. 265 (1971); see also *Ocala Star-Banner Co. v. Damron*, 401 U.S. 295 (1971).

52. *Curtis Publishing Co. v. Butts, Associated Press v. Walker*, 388 U.S. 130 (1967).

53. Id. at 155.

54. Ibid.

55. Id. at 159.

56. *Wolston v. Reader's Digest Association Inc.*, 443 U.S. 157 (1979); *Hutchinson v. Proxmire*, 443 U.S. 111 (1979).

57. *Bose Corp. v. Consumers Union of the United States*, 466 U.S. 485 (1984); *Anderson v. Liberty Lobby*, 477 U.S. 242 (1986); *Hustler Magazine v. Falwell*, 485 U.S. 46 (1988).

58. *Milkovich v. Lorain Journal Co.*, 497 U.S. 1 (1990).

59. *Rosenbloom v. Metromedia Inc.*, 403 U.S. 29 at 43 (1971).

60. *Gertz v. Robert Welch Inc.*, 418 U.S. 323 at 345 (1974)

61. Id. at 347.

62. Id. at 352.

63. *Time Inc. v. Firestone*, 424 U.S. 448 at 453 (1976).

64. *Wolston v. Reader's Digest Assn. Inc.*, 443 U.S. 157 (1979); *Hutchinson v. Proxmire*, 443 U.S. 111 (1979); *Philadelphia Newspapers Inc. v. Hepps*, 475 U.S. 767 (1986).

65. *Masson v. New Yorker*, 501 U.S. 496 at 502 (1991).

66. *Cohen v. Cowles Media Co.*, 501 U.S. 663 (1991).

67. Id. at 672.

68. *Sheppard v. Maxwell*, 384 U.S. 333 at 350 (1966).

69. *Toledo Newspaper Co. v. United States*, 247 U.S. 402 (1918).

70. *Nye v. United States*, 313 U.S. 33 (1941).

71. *Patterson v. Colorado*, 205 U.S. 454 at 463 (1907).

72. *Bridges v. California, Times-Mirror Co. v. Superior Court of California,* 314 U.S. 252 at 269 (1941).

73. Id. at 270–271.

74. Id. at 273.

75. Id. at 278.

76. Id. at 284.

77. *Pennekamp v. Florida,* 328 U.S. 331 at 347 (1946).

78. *Craig v. Harney,* 331 U.S. 367 at 378 (1947).

79. *Wood v. Georgia,* 370 U.S. 375 at 389 (1962).

80. *Stroble v. California,* 343 U.S. 181 (1951).

81. *Marshall v. United States,* 360 U.S. 310 (1959).

82. *Irvin v. Dowd,* 366 U.S. 717 at 722–723 (1961).

83. *Beck v. Washington,* 369 U.S. 541 (1962).

84. *Rideau v. Louisiana,* 373 U.S. 723 (1963).

85. *Estes v. Texas,* 381 U.S. 532 at 536 (1965).

86. *Sheppard v. Maxwell,* 384 U.S. 333 at 355, 358 (1966).

87. Id. at 361–362.

88. *Nebraska Press Association v. Stuart,* 427 U.S. 539 at 559 (1976).

89. Id. at 568. See also *Cox Broadcasting Corp. v. Cohn,* 420 U.S. 469 (1975).

90. *Nebraska Press Association v. Stuart,* 427 U.S. 539 at 570 (1976).

91. Id. at 572.

92. *Seattle Times Co. v. Rhinehart,* 467 U.S. 1 (1984).

93. *Gentile v. State Bar of Nevada,* 501 U.S. 1030 (1991).

94. *Gannett Co. Inc. v. DePasquale,* 443 U.S. 368 (1979).

95. *Richmond Newspapers Inc. v. Commonwealth of Virginia,* 448 U.S. 555 (1980). See also *Globe Newspaper Co. v. Superior Court,* 457 U.S. 596 (1982); *Press-Enterprise Co. v. Superior Court of California, Riverside County,* 464 U.S. 501 (1984); *Press-Enterprise Co. v. Superior Court of California,* 464 U.S. 501 (1986).

96. *Chandler v. Florida,* 449 U.S. 560 (1981).

97. *Saxbe v. Washington Post Co.,* 417 U.S. 843 (1974); *Pell v. Procunier,* 417 U.S. 817 (1974).

98. *Pell v. Procunier,* 417 U.S. 817 at 834 (1974).

99. Id. at 835.

100. *Saxbe v. Washington Post Co.,* 417 U.S. 843 at 861 (1974).

101. *Houchins v. KQED Inc.,* 438 U.S. 1 at 15–16 (1978).

102. Id. at 32.

103. *Branzburg v. Hayes; In re Pappas; United States v. Caldwell,* 408 U.S. 665 at 689–690 (1972).

104. Id. at 681–682.

105. Id. at 690–691.

106. Id. at 691, 692.

107. Id. at 725.

108. Id. at 732–733.

109. Id. at 743.

110. *Zurcher v. The Stanford Daily,* 436 U.S. 547 at 565 (1978).

111. Id. at 566.

112. Id. at 571–573.

113. *Red Lion Broadcasting Co. v. Federal Communications Commission,* 395 U.S. 367 at 376 (1969).

114. *National Broadcasting Company v. United States,* 31 U.S. 190 at 226 (1943); see also *Federal Communications Commission v. SNCN Listeners Guild,* 450 U.S. 582 (1981).

115. *Red Lion Broadcasting Co. v. Federal Communications Commission,* 395 U.S. 367 at 388 (1969).

116. Id. at 389.

117. *Columbia Broadcasting System Inc. v. Democratic National Committee,* 412 U.S. 94 at 130 (1973).

118. Id. at 184, 187.

119. *Federal Communications Commission v. League of Women Voters of California,* 468 U.S. 364 (1984).

120. *Telecommunications Research and Action Center v. Federal Communications Commission,* 801 F 2d 501, review denied, June 8, 1987.

121. *Federal Communications Commission v. Pacifica Foundation,* 438 U.S. 726 at 744 (1978).

122. Id. at 748, 749.

123. *Federal Communications Commission v. National Citizens Committee for Broadcasting,* 436 U.S. 775 (1978).

124. *Turner Broadcasting System v. Federal Communications Commission,* 114 S. Ct. 2445 (1994).

125. *Denver Area Educational Telecommunications Consortium v. Federal Communications Commission,* —— U.S. —— (1996).

FREEDOM OF RELIGION (PP. 475–498)

1. Sources on the history of religious freedom in the United States include Loren P. Beth, *The American Theory of Church and State* (Gainesville: University of Florida Press, 1958); and Leo Pfeffer, *Church, State and Freedom,* rev. ed. (Boston: Beacon Press, 1967).

2. Joseph Story, *Commentaries on the Constitution of the United States,* Sec. 1879; cited in Charles Evans Hughes, *The Supreme Court of the United States: Its Foundations, Methods and Achievements, An Interpretation* (New York: Columbia University Press, 1928), 161.

3. *Walz v. Tax Commission,* 397 U.S. 664 at 669–670 (1970).

4. Marvin E. Frankel, *Faith and Freedom: Religious Liberty in America* (New York: Hill and Wang, 1994), 118.

5. *Lovell v. Griffin,* 303 U.S. 444 (1938); *Kunz v. New York,* 340 U.S. 290 (1951).

6. *Reynolds v. United States,* 98 U.S. 145 at 165 (1879).

7. *Davis v. Beason,* 133 U.S. 333 at 342–343 (1890).

8. Id. at 345; see also *Cleveland v. United States,* 329 U.S. 14 (1946).

9. *Cantwell v. Connecticut,* 310 U.S. 296 at 306–307 (1940).

10. *Martin v. City of Struthers,* 319 U.S. 141 (1943).

11. *United States v. Ballard,* 322 U.S. 78 at 86, 87 (1944).

12. *Prince v. Massachusetts,* 321 U.S. 158 at 166 (1944).

13. *Sherbert v. Verner,* 374 U.S. 398 (1963); *Employment Division v. Smith,* 494 U.S. 872 (1990).

14. *CQ Almanac 1993* (Washington, D.C.: Congressional Quarterly, 1994), 315.

15. *Church of the Lukumi Babalu Aye v. Hialeah,* 508 U.S. 520 (1993).

16. *Cantwell v. Connecticut,* 310 U.S. 296 at 308, at 311. (1940).

17. Id. at 307; see also *Schneider v. Irvington,* 308 U.S. 147 (1939); *Martin v. City of Struthers,* 319 U.S. 141 (1943).

18. *Cox v. New Hampshire,* 312 U.S. 569 (1941).

19. *Kunz v. New York,* 340 U.S. 290 at 293 (1951).

20. *Niemotko v. Maryland,* 340 U.S. 268 (1951).

21. *Fowler v. Rhode Island,* 345 U.S. 67 at 70 (1953).

22. *Jones v. Opelika,* 316 U.S. 584 at 597 (1942).

23. *Murdock v. Pennsylvania,* 319 U.S. 105 at 113, 109 (1943).

24. Id. at 111; see also *Follett v. City of McCormick,* 321 U.S. 573 (1944).

25. *Heffron v. International Society for Krishna Consciousness,* 452 U.S. 640 (1981); *Widmar v. Vincent,* 454 U.S. 263 (1981).

26. *Jacobson v. Massachusetts,* 197 U.S. 11 (1905).

27. *Pierce v. Society of Sisters,* 268 U.S. 510 (1925); *Hamilton v. California Board of Regents,* 293 U.S. 245 (1934).

28. *Leoles v. Landers,* 302 U.S. 656 (1937); *Hering v. State Board of Education,* 303 U.S. 624 (1938); *Gabrielli v. Knickerbocker, Johnson v. Town of Deerfield,* 306 U.S. 621 (1939).

29. *Minersville School District v. Gobitis,* 310 U.S. 586 at 593, 594–595 (1940).

30. Id. at 598.

31. Id. at 598, 600.

32. Id. at 601.

33. Id. at 604.

34. Id. at 606.

35. Irving Dilliard, "The Flag-Salute Cases," in *Quarrels That Have Shaped the Constitution,* ed. John A. Garraty (New York: Harper and Row, 1964), 234.

36. *Jones v. Opelika,* 316 U.S. 584 at 623–624 (1942).

37. *West Virginia State Board of Education v. Barnette,* 319 U.S. 624 at 638 (1943).

38. Id. at 640, 641.

39. Id. at 641–642.

40. Id. at 646–647.

41. *Braunfeld v. Brown*, 366 U.S. 599 at 607 (1961); see also *Gallagher v. Crown Kosher Super Market*, 366 U.S. 617 (1961).

42. *Sherbert v. Verner*, 374 U.S. 398 at 404 (1963).

43. Id. at 406 quoting *Thomas v. Collins*, 323 U.S. 516 at 530 (1945).

44. *Thomas v. Review Board of the Indiana Employment Security Division*, 450 U.S. 707 (1981); *Hobbie v. Unemployment Appeals Commission of Florida*, 480 U.S. 136 (1987); see also *Estate of Thornton v. Caldor Inc.*, 472 U.S. 703 (1985).

45. *Wisconsin v. Yoder*, 406 U.S. 205 at 214 (1972).

46. *Torcaso v. Watkins*, 367 U.S. 488 at 495 (1961).

47. *United States v. Schwimmer*, 279 U.S. 644 (1929); *United States v. Macintosh*, 283 U.S. 605 (1931); *United States v. Bland*, 283 U.S. 636 (1931).

48. *Girouard v. United States*, 328 U.S. 61 (1946), overturning *United States v. Schwimmer*, 279 U.S. 644 (1929).

49. *In re Summers*, 325 U.S. 561 (1945).

50. *McDaniel v. Paty*, 435 U.S. 618 (1978); *Sherbert v. Verner*, 374 U.S. 398 (1963).

51. *Torcaso v. Watkins*, 367 U.S. 488 (1961).

52. C. Herman Pritchett, *The American Constitution*, 3d ed. (New York: McGraw-Hill, 1977), 402; Robert L. Cord, *Separation of Church and State* (New York: Lambeth Press, 1982), 226.

53. *Bradfield v. Roberts*, 175 U.S. 291 (1899); see also *Quick Bear v. Leupp*, 210 U.S. 50 (1908).

54. *Walz v. Tax Commission*, 397 U.S. 664 at 673 (1970).

55. Id. at 675, 676.

56. *St. Martin Evangelical Lutheran Church and Northwestern Lutheran Academy v. State of South Dakota*, 452 U.S. 640 (1981); *Tony and Susan Alamo Foundation v. Secretary of Labor*, 471 U.S. 290 (1985). See also *Corporation of the Presiding Bishop of the Church of Jesus Christ of the Latter Day Saints v. Amos*, 483 U.S. 327 (1987).

57. *Zorach v. Clausen*, 343 U.S. 306 at 313 (1952).

58. *Lewis v. Allen*, 379 U.S. 923 (1964); *O'Hair v. Paine*, 401 U.S. 955 (1971); *O'Hair v. Blumenthal* 442 U.S. 930 (1979).

59. *Marsh v. Chambers*, 463 U.S. 783 (1983).

60. *Illinois ex rel. McCollum v. Board of Education*, 333 U.S. 203 at 210 (1948).

61. Id. at 227–228.

62. *Zorach v. Clausen*, 343 U.S. 306 at 312 (1952).

63. Id. at 315, 314.

64. *Clithero v. Schowalter*, 284 U.S. 573 (1930); *Doremus v. Board of Education*, 342 U.S. 429 (1952).

65. *Engel v. Vitale*, 370 U.S. 421 at 425 (1962).

66. Id. at 430–431.

67. Id. at 436, quoting James Madison, "Memorial and Remonstrance Against Religious Assessments."

68. Id. at 445.

69. Id. at 450.

70. *School District of Abington Township v. Schempp, Murray v. Curlett*, 374 U.S. 203 at 226 (1963).

71. Id. at 225.

72. Id. at 226.

73. *Wallace v. Jaffree*, 472 U.S. 38 (1985).

74. *Karcher v. May*, 484 U.S. 72 (1987).

75. *Lee v. Weisman*, 112 S. Ct. 2649 (1992).

76. Id. at 2658.

77. Id. at 2660.

78. Id. at 2679.

79. *Cochran v. Louisiana Board of Education*, 281 U.S. 370 (1930).

80. *Everson v. Board of Education*, 330 U.S. 1 at 15–16 (1947).

81. Id. at 17–18.

82. Id. at 33, 50.

83. Id. at 63.

84. *Lemon v. Kurtzman*, 403 U.S. 602 at 614 (1971).

85. *Board of Education of Central School District No. 1 v. Allen*, 392 U.S. 236 at 245, 248 (1968).

86. Id. at 243–244.

87. *Lemon v. Kurtzman*, 403 U.S. 602 at 613 (1971), quoting *Walz v. Tax Commission*, 397 U.S. 664 at 674 (1970).

88. Id. at 615.

89. Id. at 618.

90. Id. at 619.

91. *Committee for Public Education and Religious Liberty v. Nyquist*, 413 U.S. 756 at 774 (1973); *Sloan v. Lemon* 413 U.S. 825 (1973).

92. Id. at 783.

93. Id. at 786.

94. Id. at 791.

95. *Mueller v. Allen*, 463 U.S. 388 (1983); see also *Witters v. Washington Department of Services for the Blind*, 474 U.S. 481 (1986).

96. *Levitt v. Committee for Public Education and Religious Liberty*, 413 U.S. 472 at 480 (1973).

97. *Committee for Public Education and Religious Liberty v. Regan*, 444 U.S. 646 (1980).

98. *Wolman v. Walter*, 433 U.S. 229 at 254 (1977).

99. *Meek v. Pittinger*, 421 U.S. 349 at 363 (1975).

100. *Wolman v. Walter*, 433 U.S. 229 at 250 (1977).

101. *Grand Rapids School District v. Ball*, 473 U.S. 373 (1985).

102. *Aguilar v. Felton*, 473 U.S. 402 (1985).

103. *Board of Education of Kiryas Joel Village School District v. Grumet*, 114 S. Ct. 2481 at 2490–91, 2504 (1994).

104. *Frothingham v. Mellon*, 262 U.S. 447 (1923).

105. *Flast v. Cohen*, 392 U.S. 83 at 104 (1968).

106. *Wheeler v. Barrera*, 417 U.S. 402 (1974).

107. *Aguilar v. Felton*, 473 U.S. 402 (1985).

108. *Zobrest v. Catalina Foothills School District*, 509 U.S. 1 (1993).

109. *Tilton v. Richardson*, 403 U.S. 672 at 681 (1971).

110. Id. at 686.

111. *Hunt v. McNair*, 413 U.S. 734 (1973); *Roemer v. Maryland Board of Public Works*, 426 U.S. 736 (1976).

112. *Widmar v. Vincent*, 454 U.S. 263 (1981); *Board of Education of the Westside Community Schools (Dist. 66) v. Mergens*, 496 U.S. 226, (1990).

113. *Lamb's Chapel v. Center Moriches Union Free School District*, 508 U.S. 384 (1993).

114. *Rosenberger v. University of Virginia*, 115 S. Ct. 2510 (1995).

115. Id.

116. Id.

117. Id.

118. Id.

CHAPTER 10

The Rights of Political Participation

THE POLITICAL HISTORY of the United States is the story of the effort to translate the ideals of equality and freedom into political reality. The elusiveness of these goals is reflected in a long line of Supreme Court decisions that deal with the right to vote, the right to have that vote counted equally with all others, and the freedom to associate with persons of similar political views.

Although the right to vote is the cornerstone of the democratic political system, the Constitution until 1868 made almost no mention of that right. For well over a century, the Supreme Court maintained that state citizenship, not federal citizenship, was the source of the right to vote.

Five times the Constitution has been amended to extend and protect this basic political right:

• In 1868 the Fourteenth Amendment appeared to guarantee the right to vote to all citizens—including women and blacks—by forbidding any state to abridge the privileges and immunities of U.S. citizens.

• In 1870 the Fifteenth Amendment explicitly enfranchised former slaves.

• In 1920 the Nineteenth Amendment granted women the right to vote.

• In 1964 the Twenty-fourth Amendment prohibited use of a poll tax as a reason to deny anyone the right to vote in federal elections.

• In 1971 the Twenty-sixth Amendment lowered the voting age to eighteen.

In the nation's earliest years, the right to vote was the exclusive prerogative of white adult males who were free and owned property. Property qualifications were the first restriction abandoned, although vestiges of that requirement remained for more than a century in the form of poll taxes.

The Civil War—and the amendments that marked its close—seemed to promise a new age of broadened political participation. The privileges and immunities clause of the Fourteenth Amendment appeared to many to guarantee all citizens—female as well as male, black as well as white—the right to vote: "No state shall make or enforce any law which shall abridge the privileges or immunities of citizens of the United States."

But within a decade of its adoption in 1868, the Supreme Court made clear that the Fourteenth Amendment had no such practical effect. The Constitution of the United States, declared the Court, still granted no one the right to vote. That was a state prerogative. (The ruling, in a case brought on behalf of a woman seeking to vote, sparked a drive that lasted forty-five years until 1920, when a constitutional amendment granted women the right to vote.)

The Fifteenth Amendment, ratified in 1870, spoke plainly:

Section 1. The right of citizens of the United States to vote shall not be denied or abridged by the United States or by any State on account of race, color, or previous condition of servitude.

Section 2. The Congress shall have power to enforce this article by appropriate legislation.

Yet Court decisions perpetuated the view that voter qualifications and election regulations were exclusively state responsibilities. State officials, insulated from federal action by these decisions, successfully employed literacy tests, grandfather clauses, poll taxes, and white primaries to circumvent the amendment's intent for most of another century.

As early as 1915, the Supreme Court began to edge toward a new view of the amendments and the protection they provided for the right to vote. But it was Congress, spurred by the civil rights movement of the 1960s, that led in the eventual fulfillment of the promise of the Fifteenth Amendment. The Voting Rights Act of 1965 at last secured to the nation's black citizens the right to vote. To do so, the act asserted federal authority over electoral matters traditionally left in the hands of state officials.

Once Congress acted, the Supreme Court steadily backed its power to ensure the right to vote. The Court heard out the challenges of the states to the new law—and then rejected them resoundingly. A series of rulings in the 1960s were a mirror image of those postwar decisions of the 1870s and 1880s restricting federal power to protect the citizen's right to vote. The Court gave the broadest possible reading to the Fifteenth Amendment, the power of Congress to enforce it, and to the 1965 act, making it the most effective civil rights law ever enacted.

At the same time that the Court's modern voting rights decisions were underwriting the expansion of the right to vote, its plunge into the political morass of redistricting cases revolutionized the balance of political power both within Congress and in every state legislature in the nation.

Electoral districts within state boundaries had been a fact of life since early in the nineteenth century when Congress first directed all states with more than one member in the U.S. House of Representatives to elect those House members from separate, compact, and contiguous districts. Later in the century Congress required that these districts also be as nearly equal in population as was practicable.

But in 1929 Congress omitted those requirements from its revision of the law. A few years later the Supreme Court found the omission purposeful. Lifting these requirements for congressional districts came just as the nation's population was shifting from primarily rural areas to become an urban majority. For forty years this shift was not reflected in the nation's legislatures.

Farm and rural interests continued to dominate in Congress and in state legislatures. Efforts by urban residents to have district lines redrawn to reflect their new strength—and to win equal weight for their votes—failed.

In large part these attempts were blocked by the insistence of federal courts, led by the Supreme Court, that such challenges were political matters outside judicial power, best dealt with by the malapportioned legislatures that were the heart of the problem. As late as 1946, the Court explicitly reaffirmed this view, describing redistricting challenges as a "political thicket" it would not enter.

But within sixteen years the Court reversed itself. In 1962 it took the first step, ruling that redistricting cases might, after all, present questions susceptible to judicial resolution. This ruling opened the doors of the federal courts to a multitude of suits challenging state and congressional districting and apportionment structures.

As it dealt with these subsequent cases, the Court translated the Fourteenth Amendment's guarantee of equal protection into the rule of "one person, one vote" as the proper measure for redistricting plans. Within a decade it appeared that the standard was in some ways a dual one, applied to require that a state's congressional districts be almost precisely equal in population, while allowing a state's legislative electoral districts to vary further from the ideal of precise equality.

In subsequent rulings, the Court also extended the application of this "one person, one vote" rule to a variety of local electoral districts.

The freedom of political association receives no mention in the Constitution at all. Yet in its modern rulings, the Supreme Court has made clear in decisions concerning communists and civil rights activists, radicals and Republicans, that it considers the freedom to associate with persons of like political views—without penalty from the government—an essential corollary of the First Amendment freedoms of speech, peaceable assembly, and the right to petition the government for redress of grievances.

Like other First Amendment rights—but unlike the right to vote—the freedom of political association may legitimately be restricted by government to further other major interests. Thus political association cases present the Court with the task of reconciling individual freedom and the government's need to preserve public peace and national security.

Nowhere is this more obvious than in the decisions of the 1950s and 1960s concerning the efforts of Congress, the executive branch, and state legislatures to curtail the spread of domestic communism and to protect government against infiltration by disloyal persons.

Such reconciliation takes place through a process of weighing and balancing, which inevitably reflects the social and political context in which the justices live and work. During periods of severe external threat to the United States, the Court has upheld substantial restrictions upon the exercise of this right.

In its early 1950s rulings on these laws and programs, the Court found their restrictive impact on individual freedom justified. As the threat eased, however, the Court found challenges to these laws more and more persuasive. In response, it tightened the standards of proof to ensure that persons were not penalized simply for "guilt by association" or abstract advocacy of revolution, but only for actions that clearly threatened the nation's security. Eventually, this line of rulings vitiated the internal security laws.

The right of political association—finally recognized even in internal security cases—found its clearest definition in cases involving homegrown forms of activism and more traditional political activities. In the 1960s the Court forbade states to interfere with the right of civil rights activists to associate and work for the advancement of blacks and other minorities. Such associations could not be penalized by the state, held the Court. Later rulings recognized the right of national political parties to this freedom—interpreted to shield those parties from the interference of state courts—and the right of persons holding different views from those of an elected officeholder to keep their jobs nonetheless.

The Right to Vote: An Expanding Privilege

The gradually broadening suffrage is one of the most significant characteristics of the continuing American experiment in popular government.

In 1792 only propertied white males were granted the privilege of voting. By 1972 that right was possessed by all Americans eighteen or older—blacks and whites, women and men.

The Constitution barely mentions the right to vote. It provides for the direct election of members of the House of Representatives, permits states to set qualifications for voters, and gives the states the authority to set the times, places, and manner of elections for senators and representatives.

Article I, Section 4, however, does reserve to Congress the power to override, by law, such state-made election rules.

Early in the history of the republic, popular pressure forced states to drop the restrictive property qualification for voting. The Constitution subsequently has been amended five times to extend the vote to formerly disenfranchised groups.

The Fifteenth Amendment, added in 1870, prohibited denial of the right to vote for reasons of race, color, or previous condition of servitude.

Women, who had sought to win the right to vote through judicial interpretation of the "privileges and immunities" clause of the Fourteenth Amendment, were rebuffed in that effort by the Supreme Court.

Uniting into an organized women's suffrage movement, they worked and fought for half a century for the right to vote. Finally, in 1920, the addition of the Nineteenth Amendment forbade restriction of the suffrage on account of sex.

In 1961 the Twenty-third Amendment granted residents of the nation's capital, the District of Columbia, the right to vote in presidential elections. In 1964 the Twenty-fourth Amendment ended all efforts to restrict the right to vote because of lack of wealth or property, outlawing use of a poll tax as a means of abridging the right to vote in federal elections.

Then the age for political participation was formally lowered by the Twenty-sixth Amendment, ratified in 1971, granting all citizens eighteen and older the right to vote in federal elections.

With this amendment—and new civil rights legislation finally implementing the Fifteenth Amendment—virtually every adult citizen possessed the right to vote in the nation's elections by 1972.

The Right and the Power: A Narrow View

No other constitutional promise has gone so long unfulfilled as that of the Fifteenth Amendment. Despite the clear language forbidding abridgment of the right to vote because of race or color, state officials succeeded for almost a full century in denying black citizens the right to vote or to play any significant role in state or national politics. The Supreme Court, by its acqui-escence, played a critical role in creating this anomalous situation.

The right to vote was viewed by many as doubly guaranteed by the Civil War amendments—the Fourteenth Amendment safeguarding the privileges and immunities of citizens against state infringement and the Fifteenth Amendment forbidding abridgment of the right to vote because of race, color, or previous condition of servitude.

In addition, voting rights for blacks had been made a condition for readmission to the Union for the rebellious states of the Confederacy. And yet, after the presidential election of 1876, the issue of black voting rights was again left to state control. As the southern states returned to white rule under "restored" governments, they passed laws that effectively defeated the purposes of the amendments.

The Supreme Court created the environment for such systematic state obstruction with a set of rulings in which it adopted the narrowest possible view of federal power and responsibility for protecting the individual's right to vote. The Court held that the right to vote was chiefly governed by state laws; that its source was the state, not the U.S. Constitution; and that Congress had only limited power to interfere in state regulation of electoral matters.

NO PRIVILEGE OR IMMUNITY

The first of these restrictive rulings came in 1875 when the Court declared that the U.S. Constitution did not give anyone the right to vote.

Minor v. Happersett was brought by Francis Minor, a St. Louis attorney, on behalf of his wife, president of the Missouri Woman Suffrage Association. The Minors argued that the right to vote was a privilege of U.S. citizenship, protected by the first section of the Fourteenth Amendment. Therefore, the Minors concluded, states could not deny women the right to vote. Missouri law, however, limited suffrage to males. Happersett, an election registrar, refused to register Mrs. Minor, and the couple filed suit.

Just two years earlier, in the *Slaughterhouse Cases,* the Court had described the privileges and immunities of U.S. citizenship: "They may all . . . be comprehended under the following general heads: protection by the government, with the right to acquire and possess property of every kind, and to pursue and obtain happiness and safety, subject nevertheless to such restraints as the government may prescribe for the general good of the whole."[1] The right to vote was not mentioned.

In line with that decision, the Court rejected the Minors' argument. Chief Justice Morrison R. Waite wrote for the Court that the right to vote was not a privilege or immunity of federal citizenship. The suffrage, Waite stated, had never been coextensive with citizenship:

The United States has no voters in the States of its creation. . . .

[T]he Constitution of the United States does not confer the right of suffrage upon anyone.

It was still up to the states, Waite said, to define voter qualifications—even for federal elections:

The [Fourteenth] Amendment did not add to the privileges and immunities of a citizen. It simply furnished an additional guaranty for the protection of such as he already had.

It is clear, therefore, we think, that the Constitution has not added the right of suffrage to the privileges and immunities of citizenship as they existed at the time it was adopted.[2]

NO FEDERAL VOTING RIGHT

The following year the Court adopted a similar narrow view of the Fifteenth Amendment. In *United States v. Reese* and *United States v. Cruikshank,* the Court overturned federal convictions of persons charged with violating the Enforcement Act of 1870, the law enforcing the Fifteenth Amendment's guarantee against denial of voting rights because of race.

In the *Reese* case, state election officials were convicted for violating the law by refusing to receive or count a black man's vote. The Court overturned the convictions, finding the section of the law under which they were charged technically defective.

The Court, again through Chief Justice Waite, stated that "[t]he Fifteenth Amendment does not confer the right of suffrage upon anyone."[3] The right with which that amendment invests the citizens of the United States, he said, was the right to be free from discrimination (on account of race, color, or previous condition of servitude) in their exercise of the right to vote.

United States v. Cruikshank, decided that same day in 1876, dealt with one of the ninety-six indictments resulting from a massacre of sixty blacks in Colfax, Louisiana, in 1873. Disputes over local elections allegedly led William J. Cruikshank and others to shoot down a posse of blacks who had seized the Colfax Courthouse.

Cruikshank and his confederates were indicted under the 1870 Enforcement Act for conspiring to intimidate blacks to prevent their exercise of constitutional rights, including the right to vote. The Supreme Court declared the indictment defective because "it is nowhere alleged in these counts that the wrong contemplated against the rights of these citizens was on account of their race or color."[4]

Chief Justice Waite delivered the opinion of the Court. He declared again that the amendment added nothing to the rights a citizen possessed:

It simply furnishes an additional guaranty as against any encroachment by the States upon the fundamental rights which belong to every citizen as a member of society. . . . The power of the National Government is limited to the enforcement of this guaranty. . . .

The right to vote in the States comes from the States; but the right of exemption from the prohibited discrimination comes from the United States. The first has not been granted or secured by the Constitution of the United States; but the last has been.

Inasmuch, therefore, as it does not appear in these counts that the intent of the defendants was to prevent these parties from exercising

Despite adoption of the Fifteenth Amendment, making it illegal to bar citizens from voting because of their color, blacks were turned away from polls by a combination of Ku Klux Klan harassment, intimidation, and various legal gimmicks. The Supreme Court's ruling in *United States v. Reese* (1876) weakened the government's power to impose stiff penalties for interfering with the rights of blacks to vote.

their right to vote on account of their race . . . it does not appear that it was their intent to interfere with any right granted or secured by the Constitution or laws of the United States. We may suspect that race was the cause of the hostility; but it is not so averred.[5]

EXCEPTIONS TO THE VIEW

Despite this limiting interpretation of the new constitutional language concerning the right to vote, the Court upheld federal power to regulate elections under the provisions of Article I.

In 1880 in *Ex parte Siebold,* which did not involve charges of racial discrimination, the Court upheld federal power to ensure that elections of federal officials be fairly conducted. Albert Siebold, a state election official, was convicted of violating federal law by stuffing a ballot box in an election of state and federal officers.

The Court upheld his conviction, citing Article I, Section 4, to justify federal regulation of the actions of state election officials. Article I, Section 4, gave Congress broad concurrent powers to regulate elections along with and independent of state power in that area.[6]

Over the next three decades the Court reaffirmed this position in similar cases.[7]

The Court's narrow view of the Fifteenth Amendment broadened briefly in 1884. *Ex parte Yarbrough* was the only early case in which the Court backed the use of federal power to punish private individuals who obstructed the right to vote in a federal election. In *Yarbrough* the Court held that once an individual acquired the right to vote for federal officers—by meeting state-set voter qualifications—that right was accorded federal protection.

Jasper Yarbrough, a member of the Ku Klux Klan, and some fellow Klansmen attacked a black named Berry Saunders and beat him up to prevent his voting in a congressional election. Yarbrough was convicted and sentenced to prison for violating the 1870 Enforcement Act by conspiring to prevent a citizen from voting.

He challenged his conviction, arguing that the 1870 law was unconstitutional, because Congress lacked the authority to act to protect the right to vote in federal elections. The Court, however, upheld his conviction, the federal law, and congressional power to protect the right to vote.

Justice Samuel Miller, writing for the majority, made clear that the right to vote for members of Congress was derived from the federal Constitution—not state laws—and was subject to federal protection:

That a government whose essential character is republican . . . has no power to secure this election from the influence of violence, of corruption, and of fraud, is a proposition so startling as to arrest attention. . . .

If this government is anything more than a mere aggregation of delegated agents of other States and governments, each of which is superior to the General Government, it must have the power to protect the elections on which its existence depends from violence and corruption.

If it has not this power, it is left helpless before the two great natural and historical enemies of all republics, open violence and insidious corruption. . . .

The States in prescribing the qualifications for the most numerous branch of their own Legislatures, do not do this with reference to the election for members of Congress. . . . They define who are to vote for the popular branch of their own legislature, and the Constitution of the United States says the same persons shall vote for members of Congress in that State. It adopts the qualification thus furnished as the qualification of its own electors for members of Congress.

It is not true, therefore, that electors for members of Congress owe their right to vote to the state law in any sense which makes the exercise of the right to depend exclusively on the law of the State.[8]

The Fifteenth Amendment, said the Court, did operate in some circumstances as the source of a right to vote. And Congress did have the authority "to protect the citizen in the exercise of rights conferred by the Constitution of the United States essential to the healthy organization of the government itself."[9]

And so, the opinion concluded:

If the Government of the United States has within its constitutional domain no authority to provide against these evils [violence and corruption of elections], if the very sources of power may be poisoned by corruption or controlled by violence and outrage, without legal restraint, then, indeed, is the country in danger and its best powers, its highest purposes, the hopes which it inspires . . . are at the mercy of the combinations of those who respect no right but brute force, on the one hand, and unprincipled corruptionists on the other.[10]

But despite Justice Miller's strong words, the Court persisted for decades in its narrow view of the right to vote. In the absence of state action, the acts of private individuals to deny the rights of others to vote remained outside the reach of federal power.

In 1903 the Court stated that the provisions of the 1870 Enforcement Act, which might be interpreted "to punish purely individual action [to interfere with voting rights,] cannot be sustained as an appropriate exercise of the power conferred by the Fifteenth Amendment upon Congress."[11]

The Pattern of Exclusion

Encouraged by the Court's limiting view of the federal right to vote and of federal power to enforce that right, many southern states during the period from 1890 to 1910 excluded blacks from participation in the political process by rewriting their constitutions or adding new requirements for voters.[12] The Court by and large left major elements of the program of disenfranchisement untouched for decades.

The strategy of exclusion employed many methods, among them literacy tests, grandfather clauses, all-white primaries, poll taxes, and the racial gerrymander.

Grandfather clauses were held unconstitutional in 1915, and white primaries were finally ruled invalid in 1944. But not until Congress acted did the Court strike down the use of poll taxes and literacy tests.

ANCESTRY AND LITERACY

For seventy years, from 1898 until 1969, the Supreme Court upheld the validity of literacy tests for voters.

In *Williams v. Mississippi* (1898), a black man was indicted for murder by an all-white grand jury. The jurors were selected from the list of registered voters who had, among other qualifications, passed such a literacy test. Henry Williams challenged the use of the test as unconstitutional.

Williams's attorneys argued that his conviction was invalid because the laws under which the grand jury was selected allowed discrimination in voter registration, thereby violating the equal protection guarantee of the Fourteenth Amendment.

Justice Joseph McKenna, writing for the Court, refused to find the Mississippi statutes in violation of the equal protection clause. The "evil" was not the laws themselves, he wrote, for they did not on their face discriminate against blacks; the only evil resulted from the effect of their discriminatory administration.[13]

Grandfather Clauses

Seventeen years later, however, in *Guinn v. United States* (1915), the Supreme Court held impermissible Oklahoma's combined use of a literacy test and a "grandfather" clause.

"NAH, YOU AIN'T GOT ENOUGH EDJICCASHUN TO VOTE"

From 1898 to 1969, the Supreme Court upheld the validity of literacy tests for voters. Election officials in some states administered these tests in a racially discriminatory fashion. This cartoon observes that many blacks were deemed unqualified to vote by election officials less educated than they.

The state required all voters to pass a literacy test *or* to show that their ancestors were entitled to vote in 1866. This requirement was challenged as a violation of the Fifteenth Amendment, because in operation it exempted most white males from the literacy test requirement and permitted voter registrars to test primarily blacks, whose ancestors in most cases had not been eligible to vote in 1866.

The state defended its system by arguing that the clause did not deny blacks the right to vote outright; it simply required them all to take the literacy tests. The Fifteenth Amendment, the state continued, did not confer the right to vote on all blacks; it merely prevented states from denying them the right to vote on purely racial grounds.

With this decision the Court began moving toward its modern view of the amendment. Unanimously, the Court struck down Oklahoma's system as an unconstitutional evasion of the Fifteenth Amendment. Chief Justice Edward D. White wrote the Court's opinion.

In that opinion, however, the Court continued to affirm state power to require voters to demonstrate some measure of litera-

cy. The establishment of a literacy test requirement was "but the exercise by the state of a lawful power . . . not subject to our supervision."[14]

Guinn had limited impact on black voting rights in the South because it dealt only with the grandfather clause. The case, however, was the first in which the Court in a voting rights case looked beyond nondiscriminatory form to discover discriminatory substance.

In a second Oklahoma case decided the same day in 1915, the Court upheld the federal indictments—under the Reconstruction Civil Rights Acts—of county election officials who refused to count certain persons' votes. The Court, in *United States v. Mosely,* declared that "the right to have one's vote counted is as open to protection by Congress as the right to put a ballot in a box."[15]

Oklahoma subsequently adopted a requirement that all voters register within a twelve-day period, exempting from the requirement those who had voted in the 1914 elections, prior to *Guinn.* In 1939 the Court held this, too, was an unconstitutional attempt to disenfranchise blacks in violation of the Fifteenth Amendment.

Justice Felix Frankfurter, writing for the majority, said that the Fifteenth Amendment "nullifies sophisticated as well as simple-minded modes of discrimination. It hits onerous procedural requirements which effectively handicap exercise of the franchise by the colored race although the abstract right to vote may remain unrestricted as to race."[16]

Tests of Understanding

In addition to strict literacy tests, some states also required voters to "understand and explain" an article of the Constitution. The vagueness of one such provision was nullified by a federal court as an arbitrary grant of power to election officials who could and did administer the literacy test in a racially discriminatory fashion and thus violated the Fifteenth Amendment. The fact that the provision itself made no mention of race did not save it from being unconstitutional. The Supreme Court affirmed this ruling in 1949.[17]

But the Court continued to uphold the power of states to require that their voters demonstrate some measure of literacy. In 1959 the Supreme Court upheld North Carolina's requirement that all voters be able to read and write a section of the state constitution in English. Such a test was not, on its face, a violation of the Fourteenth, Fifteenth, or Seventeenth Amendments, the Court held in *Lassiter v. Northampton County Board of Elections.*

Justice William O. Douglas's opinion for the majority stressed that the state had an interest in securing an independent and intelligent electorate. How the state achieved that objective, Douglas said, was a policy question outside the Court's purview:

Literacy and intelligence are obviously not synonymous. Illiterate people may be intelligent voters. Yet in our society . . . a state might conclude that only those who are literate should exercise the franchise. . . . We do not sit in judgment on the wisdom of that policy. We cannot say, however, that it is not an allowable one measured by constitutional standards.

Of course a literacy test, fair on its face, may be employed to perpetuate that discrimination which the Fifteenth Amendment was designed to uproot. No such influence is charged here. . . . The present requirement, applicable to members of all races . . . seems to us one fair way of determining whether a person is literate. . . . Certainly we cannot condemn it on its face as a device unrelated to the desire of North Carolina to raise the standards for people of all races who cast the ballot."[18]

But six years later the Court held Louisiana's test requiring voters to display a reasonable knowledge and understanding of any section of the state or federal constitution to be a violation of the Fifteenth Amendment.

The Court's unanimous opinion, written by Justice Hugo L. Black, viewed the requirement in light of the history of voter discrimination in the state:

The applicant facing a registrar in Louisiana thus has been compelled to leave his voting fate to that official's uncontrolled power to determine whether the applicant's understanding of the Federal or State Constitution is satisfactory. As the evidence showed, colored people, even some with the most advanced education and scholarship, were declared by voting registrars with less education to have an unsatisfactory understanding of the Constitution of Louisiana or of the United States. This is not a test but a trap, sufficient to stop even the most brilliant man on his way to the voting booth. The cherished right of people in a country like ours to vote cannot be obliterated by the use of laws like this, which leave the voting fate of a citizen to the passing whim or impulse of an individual registrar.[19]

SUSPENSION OF LITERACY TESTS

In 1965 Congress, as part of the Voting Rights Act, suspended all literacy tests and similar devices in all areas where less than half the population of voting age had been registered or had voted in the 1964 presidential election.

The act was immediately challenged as infringing upon state power to oversee elections. In *South Carolina v. Katzenbach,* decided in 1966, the Supreme Court upheld Congress's power to pass the law and backed all its major provisions, including that suspending literacy tests.[20]

Chief Justice Earl Warren, who delivered the opinion of the Court, wrote that the provision of the act suspending literacy tests

was clearly a legitimate response to the problem. . . . Underlying the response was the feeling that States and political subdivisions which had been allowing white illiterates to vote for years could not sincerely complain about "dilution" of their electorates through the registration of Negro illiterates. Congress knew that continuance of the tests and devices in use at the present time, no matter how fairly administered in the future, would freeze the effect of past discrimination in favor of unqualified white registrants. Congress permissibly rejected the alternative of requiring a complete reregistration of all voters, believing that this would be too harsh on many whites who had enjoyed the franchise for their entire adult lives.[21]

The opinion was followed three months later by two decisions that prevented states from disqualifying potential voters simply because they were unable to read or write English.[22]

Then in 1969 the Court rejected, 7–1, the effort of a North Carolina county to have the literacy test reinstated. The Court declared in *Gaston County v. United States* that counties and states, by operating separate and unequal schools for blacks and whites, had denied blacks the opportunity to acquire the skills necessary to pass a literacy test. Reinstatement of a literacy test would simply perpetuate the effects of the dual, unequal educational system that had so long operated to disenfranchise blacks, the Court held.[23]

Justice John Marshall Harlan wrote for the majority:

Affording today's Negro youth equal educational opportunity will doubtless prepare them to meet, on equal terms, whatever standards of literacy are required when they reach voting age. It does nothing for their parents, however. From this record, we cannot escape the sad truth that throughout the years, Gaston County systematically deprived its black citizens of the educational opportunities it granted to its white citizens. "Impartial" administration of the literacy test today would serve only to perpetuate those inequities in a different form.[24]

The Voting Rights Act of 1965 was amended in 1970 to suspend literacy tests nationwide and to bring more areas under coverage of its provisions. The Supreme Court upheld the nationwide ban on literacy tests in *Oregon v. Mitchell* (1970).[25] Justice Black explained that such a ban, in light of the long history of discriminatory literacy tests, was well within the power of Congress to enforce the Fifteenth Amendment. In 1975 the law was amended to abolish all literacy tests permanently. *(See box, Requirements: Age, Residence, Property, p. 510.)*

WHITE PRIMARIES

Southern politics was completely dominated by the Democratic Party during the first half of the twentieth century. In many areas the Democratic primary was the only significant part of the election process. Winning the primary was tantamount to election. Being excluded from voting in the primary was equivalent to being excluded from voting altogether.

Not until 1941 was it clear, as the result of a Supreme Court ruling, that Congress had the power to regulate primary elections as well as general elections. In fact, in a 1921 decision involving campaign spending—*Newberry v. United States*—the Court seemed to say that Congress lacked this power.[26]

This Court-created doubt encouraged the eleven states that had comprised the Confederacy to begin systematic exclusion of blacks from participation in primaries. The Democratic Party was often organized on a statewide or county basis as a private club or association that could freely exclude blacks.

Texas's use of the white primary to shut blacks out of participation in the political process came before the Supreme Court five times.

Nixon v. Herndon: 1927

In 1923 the Texas legislature passed a law forbidding blacks to vote in the state Democratic primary. Dr. L. A. Nixon, a black resident of El Paso, challenged the law, arguing that it clearly violated the Fourteenth and Fifteenth Amendments.

In *Nixon v. Herndon,* decided in 1927, the Supreme Court

REQUIREMENTS: AGE, RESIDENCE, PROPERTY

States historically have imposed various nonracial qualifications upon voters. Supreme Court rulings, however, have limited the power to impose voter requirements related to age, to property ownership, and to residence for any extended period of time.

The Court has affirmed the power of states to exclude convicted felons from the exercise of the franchise. In 1968, in the case of *Green v. New York City Board of Elections*, the Court upheld a New York law that barred convicted, unpardoned felons from voting.[1] In 1974 the Court reaffirmed that position, ruling that denial of the right to vote to convicted felons did not violate the Fourteenth Amendment.[2]

In a 1959 decision the Court declared that states had broad powers to set age and residence rules for voters:

The states have long been held to have broad powers to determine the conditions under which the right of suffrage may be exercised. . . . Residence requirements, and age . . . are obvious examples indicating factors which a State may take into consideration in determining the qualification of voters.[3]

Then eleven years later the Court upheld the power of Congress to lower age and residence requirements for participation in federal, but not state or local, elections.[4]

Following that ruling, the Court in 1972 limited the ability of states to impose a residency requirement for an extended period. The Court invalidated a Tennessee law requiring people to be residents of the state for one year before qualifying to vote. The Court said residency requirements burden fundamental rights to vote and to travel and that the state had shown no compelling interest to justify its one-year demand.[5] This decision in *Dunn v. Blumstein* sidestepped but did not overrule a 1904 decision upholding a similar Maryland requirement that voters file a declaration of intent to register one year before their enrollment on the voter lists.[6]

The Court later upheld Arizona's rule cutting off voter registration fifty days before a primary. The Court indicated that the state had shown the fifty-day period necessary to permit preparation of accurate lists of voters.[7]

In an earlier ruling the Court had held that a state could not prevent military personnel stationed within its borders from establishing residence for purposes of voting.[8] And, the Court ruled in 1970, a state could not deny the right to vote to persons living in a federal enclave in the state, if those persons were otherwise treated as state residents.[9]

By the mid-1970s property requirements for voting in general elections had disappeared from the American electoral process.

In a set of modern rulings the Court made clear that the equal protection guarantee of the Fourteenth Amendment was infringed by state efforts to restrict the right to vote.

In 1969 the Court struck down Louisiana's law that limited to property tax payers the right to vote in elections to approve issuance of utility revenue bonds.[10]

The same day the Court held that the equal protection guarantee gave all residents—not merely those who owned or leased property or who had children in the public schools—the right to vote in school district elections.[11] In 1970 the Court applied the same principle to strike down state efforts to exclude those who did not own property from voting in elections held to approve the issue of general obligation bonds.[12]

The Court later struck down laws that limited the right to vote in city bond elections only to persons who owned taxable property.[13]

1. *Green v. New York City Board of Elections*, 389 U.S. 1048 (1968).
2. *Richardson v. Ramirez*, 418 U.S. 24 (1974).
3. *Lassiter v. Northampton County Board of Elections*, 360 U.S. 45 at 51 (1959).
4. *Oregon v. Mitchell, Texas v. Mitchell, United States v. Idaho, United States v. Arizona*, 400 U.S. 112 (1970).
5. *Dunn v. Blumstein*, 405 U.S. 330 (1972).
6. *Pope v. Williams*, 193 U.S. 621 (1904).
7. *Marston v. Lewis*, 410 U.S. 679 (1973); *Burns v. Fortson*, 410 U.S. 686 (1973).
8. *Carrington v. Rash*, 380 U.S. 89 (1965).
9. *Evans v. Cornman*, 398 U.S. 419 (1970).
10. *Cipriano v. City of Houma*, 395 U.S. 701 (1969).
11. *Kramer v. Union Free School District No. 15*, 395 U.S. 818 (1969).
12. *Phoenix v. Kolodzieski*, 399 U.S. 204 (1970).
13. *Hill v. Stone*, 421 U.S. 289 (1975); *Quinn v. Millsap*, 491 U.S. 95 (1989).

---

agreed with Nixon's Fourteenth Amendment claim. "A more direct and obvious infringement" of the equal protection guarantee would be hard to imagine, wrote Justice Oliver Wendell Holmes Jr. for a unanimous Court.[27]

Nixon v. Condon: 1932

After *Herndon* the Texas legislature authorized state political parties' executive committees to establish their own qualifications for voting in the primary. Dr. Nixon again sued successfully, challenging the law as racially discriminatory.

Attorneys for the state argued that the Fourteenth Amendment's equal protection clause did not apply because the party, not state officials, set up the allegedly discriminatory standards.

With Justice Benjamin N. Cardozo writing for the majority of five, the Court held that the executive committee of the Democratic Party acted as a delegate of the state in setting voter qualifications, that its action was equivalent to state action and thus within the scope of the equal protection guarantee it violated.[28]

Grovey v. Townsend: 1935

Undeterred, the Texas Democratic Party, without state direction or authorization, voted to limit party membership to whites.

This was permissible, all the justices agreed in *Grovey v. Townsend*. The Supreme Court unanimously held that the political party was not acting as a creature of the state and that its action was thus unreachable under either the Fourteenth or Fifteenth Amendments. The Court in this case viewed the political party as a private club, a voluntary association of private individuals, whose actions—even in controlling access to the vote—were not restricted by the Constitution.[29]

United States v. Classic: 1941

Only six years later, however, the Court began to cut away the foundation on which *Grovey v. Townsend* was based. In *United States v. Classic* (1941), the Court discarded the *Newberry* restriction on federal power to regulate primary elections.

Classic was not a racial discrimination case at all. Classic, an overzealous opponent of Louisiana governor Huey Long, was convicted of falsifying election returns. His conviction was based on the federal law that made it a crime "to injure, oppress, threaten or intimidate any citizen in the free exercise or enjoyment of any right or privilege secured to him by the Constitution."

He challenged his conviction, arguing that the right to vote in a primary election was not a right secured by the Constitution.

The prosecution in *Classic* was initiated by the newly formed civil rights section of the Justice Department set up by Attorney General Frank Murphy and later directed by Attorney General Robert Jackson, both of whom became members of the Supreme Court. The case was argued before the Court by Herbert Wechsler, a former law clerk to Justice Harlan Fiske Stone and by Jackson.

The Court upheld Classic's conviction and declared that the primary was an integral part of the election process. The authority of Congress under Article I, Section 4, to regulate elections included the authority to regulate primary elections, wrote Justice Stone, "when, as in this case, they are a step in the exercise by the people of their choice of representatives in Congress."[30]

Smith v. Allwright: 1944

Three years later, in 1944, the Court overturned *Grovey* and held the all-white primary unconstitutional. *Smith v. Allwright* arose out of the refusal of S. S. Allwright, a county election official, to permit Lonnie E. Smith, a black man, to vote in the 1940 Texas Democratic primary. Smith sued Allwright for damages. Lower federal courts denied Smith the right to bring suit; *Grovey v. Townsend*, they said, placed this sort of discrimination beyond federal control.

Smith was represented before the Supreme Court by two attorneys for the National Association for the Advancement of Colored People (NAACP), William H. Hastie and Thurgood Marshall. Both later became distinguished judges, and Marshall went on to become the first black member of the Court.

The Court heard arguments twice in the case. On April 3, 1944, the Court held the white primary unconstitutional as a violation of the Fifteenth Amendment.

The seven justices appointed by President Franklin Delano Roosevelt since the *Grovey* decision, along with Stone, who had voted with the majority in *Grovey*, found state action evident in the number of state laws regulating primary elections.

Writing for the majority, Justice Stanley Reed linked *Classic* and *Smith v. Allwright:* "The fusing by the *Classic* case of the primary and general elections into a single instrumentality for choice of officers has a definite bearing on the permissibility under the Constitution of excluding Negroes from primaries."[31] *Classic* bears upon *Grovey v. Townsend*, Reed explained, because the state had delegated so much responsibility for the primary to the political party that the party became an agent of the state in its actions conducting the primary. Thus, held the Court, Allwright's action was state action abridging Smith's right to vote just because of his race, a clear violation of the Fifteenth Amendment.

Only Justice Owen J. Roberts sounded a dissenting voice as the Court overturned *Grovey v. Townsend*, a decision not yet a decade old. Author of the Court's opinion in *Grovey*, Roberts warned that by overruling such a recent decision, the Court "tends to bring adjudications of this tribunal into the same class as a restricted railroad ticket, good for this day and train only."[32]

Terry v. Adams: 1953

In 1953 the relentless effort of Texas Democrats—and politicians in other southern states—to maintain the white primary came to an end at last.

Since 1889 the Jaybird Party, an all-white Democratic organization in one Texas county, had declared itself a private club and had submitted political candidates' names in an unofficial county primary for whites only. The successful candidate in the Jaybird primary invariably entered and won the following Democratic primary and general election.

The Court struck down this stratagem, finding the use of racially exclusive private clubs as a political caucus a violation of the Fifteenth Amendment. Justice Black wrote for the eight-justice majority in *Terry v. Adams:*

[T]he Jaybird primary has become an integral part, indeed the only effective part, of the elective process that determines who shall rule and govern in the county. The effect of the whole procedure, Jaybird primary plus Democratic primary plus general election, is to do precisely that which the Fifteenth Amendment forbids—strip Negroes of every vestige of influence in selecting the officials who control the local county matters that intimately touch the daily lives of citizens.[33]

POLL TAXES

In the early days of the republic, poll taxes—an annual assessment on each citizen—replaced landholding, property, and other more burdensome requirements for voters, but most poll taxes were eliminated by the time of the Civil War.

This sort of tax was revived in the early 1890s, as one of the devices used to restrict the suffrage to white voters in the South. The ostensible reason for reintroduction of the poll tax was to "cleanse" the state of such election abuses as repeat voting (one person in one election voting more than once).

A Legitimate Tax

In 1937 in *Breedlove v. Suttles*, the Supreme Court upheld the constitutionality of the poll tax against the challenge that it violated the equal protection guarantee of the Fourteenth Amendment. The tax assessed upon voters by Georgia was a legitimate means of raising revenue; it was not a denial of equal protection, held the Court, because on its face it applied to black and white voters alike.

The Court, for whom Justice Pierce Butler wrote the opinion, rejected the notion that the Georgia tax was an impermissible levy on a federally guaranteed right.[34]

After the Populist era many states had voluntarily dropped use of the poll tax. Proposals to abolish it were introduced in every Congress from 1939 to 1962. By 1960 only four states still required its payment by voters. In August 1962 the House approved a constitutional amendment—already accepted by the Senate—that outlawed poll taxes in federal elections.

Constitutional Amendment

The poll tax ban was ratified as the Twenty-fourth Amendment January 23, 1964. The first Supreme Court decision interpreting the amendment came in 1965. The Court in *Harman v. Forssenius* struck down Virginia's effort to anticipate the poll tax ban by giving voters in federal elections the option of paying the levy or filing a certificate of residence before each election.

The Court held that the reregistration/residence requirement for persons who chose to exercise their right to vote without paying a poll tax subverted the effect of the Twenty-fourth Amendment.[35]

In 1966 the Court held the poll tax an unconstitutional requirement for voting in state and local elections as well. "Wealth, like race, creed, or color is not germane to one's ability to participate intelligently in the electoral process," wrote Justice Douglas for the Court in *Harper v. Virginia State Board of Elections*. Thus the Court struck down Virginia's $1.50 poll tax as a violation of the equal protection clause, overruling *Breedlove v. Suttles*.[36]

Douglas explained the Court's reasoning.

We conclude that a State violates the Equal Protection Clause of the Fourteenth Amendment whenever it makes the affluence of the voter or payment of any fee an electoral standard. Voter qualifications have no relation to wealth nor to paying or not paying this or any other tax. . . .

To introduce wealth or payment of a fee as a measure of a voter's qualifications is to introduce a capricious or irrelevant factor. . . . In this context—that is, as a condition of obtaining a ballot—the requirement of fee paying causes an "invidious" discrimination . . . that runs afoul of the Equal Protection Clause.[37]

Justices Black and Harlan wrote dissents. Black argued that the majority was merely incorporating its notion of good government policy into the Constitution. Harlan, with whom Justice Potter Stewart concurred, described the majority opinion as "wholly inadequate" to explain why a poll tax was "irrational or invidious."[38]

THE RACIAL GERRYMANDER

Even as the white primary, literacy tests, and poll taxes were disappearing from the electoral framework of the South, the

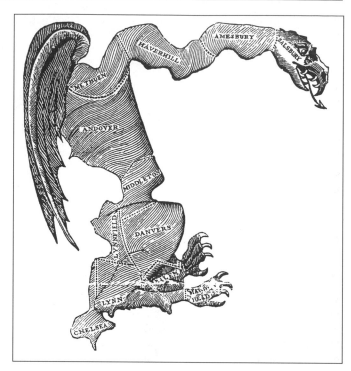

In 1812 Elkanah Tinsdale lampooned the political maneuverings of Gov. Elbridge Gerry of Massachusetts, who deftly engineered the construction of constituency boundaries to aid in the election of a member of his own party. Because the district resembled a mythological salamander in the cartoonist's illustration, the term *gerrymander* has come to mean the drawing of political district lines for partisan advantage. Racial gerrymandering was declared unconstitutional by the Supreme Court in *Gomillion v. Lightfoot* (1960).

Supreme Court struck down still another device used to disenfranchise black voters.

Northern and southern states both made some use of the racial gerrymander—the practice of drawing election district boundary lines to dilute or eliminate any concentration of black voting strength in a single district.

In 1960 the case of *Gomillion v. Lightfoot* brought this practice before the Supreme Court, which found it a clear violation of the Fifteenth Amendment. The Court's ruling was notable for two other reasons: it predated by two years the Court's abandonment of its traditional hands-off policy toward redistricting and reapportionment questions, and the majority opinion was written by Justice Frankfurter, who had been the Court's most articulate spokesman for this hands-off policy. *(See details of the case, p. 520.)*

Alabama had redefined the boundaries of the city of Tuskegee to exclude virtually all black voters. The excluded blacks sought a court order halting enforcement of the law, which had changed the shape of the city limits from a square to a twenty-eight-sided figure. The new boundary removed from within the city all but four or five qualified black voters yet not a single white voter.

Professor C. G. Gomillion of Tuskegee Institute and the other affected black citizens argued that the gerrymander denied them due process and equal protection under the Fourteenth

Amendment and infringed their right to vote in violation of the Fifteenth Amendment.

The Supreme Court unanimously declared the gerrymander unconstitutional. The right of the states to control the boundaries of their political subdivisions is subject to constitutional limitation, it held.

Justice Frankfurter wrote the Court's opinion. Frankfurter had been the author of the Court's opinion in the 1946 case of *Colegrove v. Green,* which declared that the Court ought not to enter the "political thicket" of redistricting questions because they were political questions beyond the competence of the Courts to resolve.[39]

Frankfurter distinguished between *Gomillion* and *Colegrove: Colegrove* involved involuntary nonracial disparities in districts created by population shifts, not state action; *Gomillion* involved intentional racial discrimination by the state.

When a legislature thus singles out a readily isolated segment of a racial minority for special discriminatory treatment, it violates the Fifteenth Amendment. In no case involving unequal weight in voting distribution that has come before the Court did the decision sanction a differentiation on racial lines whereby approval was given to unequivocal withdrawal of the vote solely from colored citizens. Apart from all else, these considerations lift this controversy out of the so-called "political" arena and into the conventional sphere of constitutional litigation. . . .

While in form this is merely an act redefining metes and bounds, if the allegations are established, the inescapable human effect of this essay in geometry and geography is to despoil colored citizens, and only colored citizens, of their theretofore enjoyed voting rights.[40]

Justice Charles E. Whittaker's concurring opinion pointed out that this application of the Fifteenth Amendment extended the meaning of that amendment, guaranteeing not only the right to vote but also the right to vote in a particular district. The equal protection clause of the Fourteenth Amendment would have been a preferable basis for the ruling, Whittaker wrote:

[I]nasmuch as no one has the right to vote in a political division, or in a local election concerning only an area in which he does not reside, it would seem to follow that one's right to vote in Division A is not abridged by a redistricting that places his residence in Division B if he there enjoys the same voting privileges as all others in that Division.

But it does seem clear to me that accomplishment of a State's purpose . . . of "fencing Negro citizens out of" Division A and into Division B is an unlawful segregation of races of citizens in violation of the Equal Protection Clause of the Fourteenth Amendment.[41]

In 1962 Manhattan voters brought suit charging that a New York congressional districting law was irrational, discriminatory, and unequal and segregated voters by race and national origin, concentrating white voters in the Seventeenth—"Silk Stocking"—District, and nonwhite and Puerto Rican voters in the Eighteenth, Nineteenth, and Twentieth Congressional Districts.

The Supreme Court in *Wright v. Rockefeller* (1964) found no constitutional violation. Since Manhattan was a mosaic of ethnic and racial groups, it said, almost any combination of arbitrarily drawn congressional district lines would result in some pattern of racial imbalance subject to challenge as unconstitutional.[42] *(See details of a later ruling, Wells v. Rockefeller, p. 526.)*

The Right and the Power: A Broad View

Although the Court had struck down the use of grandfather clauses and white primaries before 1950, it was Congress that at last asserted federal power to ensure the right of black citizens to vote.

A constitutional amendment ratified in 1964 outlawed the use of poll taxes in federal elections; the Voting Rights Act of 1965 suspended use of literacy tests and set up federal machinery to protect the opportunity of blacks to register and vote.

Congress began reasserting its authority to enforce the Fifteenth Amendment in 1957. The amendment authorizes Congress to pass appropriate legislation to enforce it. But in the years immediately after adoption of the amendment, efforts to pass enforcing legislation were proscribed by the Court's restrictive view of this power.

The Civil Rights Act of 1957 set up the Civil Rights Commission, which was charged, among other tasks, with studying the problem of voter discrimination. The act also authorized the attorney general to bring lawsuits to halt public and private interference with the right of blacks to vote, and it expanded federal jurisdiction over such suits. The Court upheld the investigatory procedures of the commission and the authorization of federal voting rights suits.[43]

Responding to reports that progress in securing voting rights for blacks was still slow even under the provisions of the 1957 act, Congress in 1960 passed a measure that permitted the U.S. attorney general to sue a state for deprivation of voting rights if the individuals named initially as defendants—usually voting registrars—should leave office. This provision remedied a situation that had arisen in a suit brought by the United States against Alabama voting officials who had subsequently relinquished their positions.[44]

In addition, Title VI of the 1960 law authorized the appointment of special federal "voting referees" to oversee voter registration in selected counties where a federal court found a pattern of voter discrimination.

The Civil Rights Act of 1964, in its first title, mandated state adoption of standard procedures and requirements for all persons seeking to register to vote. The law also required local officials to justify rejecting a potential voter who had completed the sixth grade or had equivalent evidence of intellectual competence. Other provisions of the 1964 law expedited the movement of voting rights cases to the Supreme Court.[45]

In two cases brought under the 1964 act, the Supreme Court sanctioned the federal government's efforts to break the pattern of case-by-case litigation of voting rights violations. The Court upheld federal power to challenge a state's entire constitutional legal framework for voter registration and conduct of elections.[46]

But progress was still slow. In Dallas County, Alabama, three new federal laws and four years of litigation produced the registration of only 383 black voters out of a potential pool of 15,000 blacks of voting age.

On March 8, 1965, the Rev. Martin Luther King Jr. led a "Walk for Freedom" to dramatize the need for more blacks to register to vote in the South. The violence of the reaction of local white law enforcement officers and white bystanders to King's peaceful demonstration drew nationwide attention to the problem.

A week later President Lyndon B. Johnson addressed a joint session of Congress to ask passage of a new voting rights measure to close the legal loopholes that had so long allowed local officials to stall black voter registration. Johnson explained that "no law that we now have on the books . . . can ensure the right to vote when local officials are determined to deny it."[47] Later that month NAACP official Roy Wilkins, appearing on behalf of the Leadership Conference on Civil Rights, testified before a Senate committee on the need for such legislation. He urged Congress to "transform this retail litigation method of registration into a wholesale administration procedure registering all who seek to exercise their democratic birthright."[48]

THE VOTING RIGHTS ACT

Within five months Congress had approved the sweeping Voting Rights Act of 1965. The law suspended literacy tests and provided for the appointment of federal supervisors of voter registration in all states and counties where literacy tests (or similar qualifying devices) were in effect as of November 1, 1964, and where fewer than 50 percent of the voting age residents were registered to vote or did vote in the 1964 presidential election.

The law established criminal penalties for persons found guilty of interfering with the voting rights of others. State or county governments brought under the coverage of the law were required to obtain federal approval of any new voting laws, standards, practices, or procedures. A covered state or county could "escape" from the law's provisions if it could convince a three-judge federal court in the District of Columbia that no racial discrimination in registration or voting had occurred in the previous five years.

The act placed federal registration machinery in six southern states (Alabama, Georgia, Mississippi, South Carolina, Louisiana, and Virginia), Alaska, twenty-eight counties in North Carolina, three counties in Arizona, and one in Idaho.

It was the most effective civil rights legislation ever enacted. Within four years almost one million blacks had registered to vote under its provisions.[49]

Rejecting the States' Challenge

Not surprisingly, this unprecedented assertion of federal power over electoral and voting matters was immediately challenged as exceeding congressional authority and encroaching on

One year after the Voting Rights Act of 1965 was passed, the Court upheld its constitutionality in *South Carolina v. Katzenbach.* The act, which abolished literacy tests for voters and called for federal approval of state election laws, was challenged on the grounds that it violated states' rights to specify qualifications for voters. In ruling against discrimination, the Court paved the way for egalitarian polling procedures. Here, staffers for the League of Women Voters work at a voter registration table.

states' rights. But times and the Court had changed since the post–Civil War era, and in 1966 the Supreme Court firmly backed the power of Congress to pass such a law.

In *South Carolina v. Katzenbach,* the state asked the Court to halt implementation of the law, charging that Congress had overstepped itself in suspending state voting standards, authorizing the use of federal election examiners, and adopting a "triggering" formula that resulted in its affecting some states but not others.

At the Court's invitation, Alabama, Georgia, Louisiana, Mississippi, and Virginia filed briefs in support of South Carolina's challenge. Twenty other states filed briefs in support of the law.

South Carolina charged that by suspending voter qualification "tests and devices" in some states, Congress violated the principle that all states were equal. It also alleged that the law denied the affected states due process of law by presuming that if the minority population was high and voter participation was low, racially discriminatory voting practices existed. Due process was also denied, argued South Carolina, by the law's failure to allow judicial review of the findings putting the law into effect in a state. Furthermore, the state maintained, the act was an unconstitutional bill of attainder, punishing certain states, and a violation of the separation of powers because it used legislative means to declare certain states guilty of discrimination.

Taking a far broader view both of the right to vote and congressional power to enforce and protect that right than had the Court of the 1870s and 1880s, the Supreme Court in 1966 rejected all challenges to the act.

"Congress," wrote Chief Justice Warren for eight members of the Court, "has full remedial powers to effectuate the constitutional prohibition against racial discrimination in voting."[50] He continued:

The Voting Rights Act was designed by Congress to banish the blight of racial discrimination in voting, which has infected the electoral process in parts of our country for nearly a century. . . . Congress assumed the power to prescribe these remedies from Section 2 of the Fifteenth Amendment, which authorizes the National Legislature to effectuate by "appropriate" measures the constitutional prohibition against racial discrimination in voting. We hold that the sections of the Act which are properly before us are an appropriate means for carrying out Congress' constitutional responsibilities and are consonant with all other provisions of the Constitution. We therefore deny South Carolina's request that enforcement of these sections of the act be enjoined.[51]

Warren then responded to the challenges to each particular provision. With respect to the triggering formula, Warren said that it was "rational in both practice and theory." The suspension of tests and devices "was a legitimate response to the problem for which there is ample precedent in Fifteenth Amendment cases." The federal approval requirement for new voting rules in the states covered by the act, Warren observed, "may have been an uncommon exercise of congressional power, as South Carolina contends, but the Court has recognized that exceptional conditions can justify legislative measures not otherwise appropriate." The appointment of federal election examiners was "clearly an appropriate response to the problem, closely related to remedies authorized in prior cases."[52]

Justice Black concurred in part and dissented in part. He agreed that Congress had the power under the Fifteenth Amendment to suspend literacy tests and to authorize federal

ELECTING JUDGES

The Voting Rights Act as passed by Congress in 1965 clearly applied to the election of judges as well as to lawmaking representatives. In 1982 Congress amended the act, using the term "representatives" in the amendment. This introduced an ambiguity that led to a pair of Supreme Court rulings on semantics and the scope of the act's protections: *Chisom v. Roemer* (1991) and *Houston Lawyers' Association v. Attorney General of Texas* (1991).[1] The amendment raised questions over whether judges were still covered by the act.

The cases began when voters in Louisiana and Texas challenged those states' system of electing judges through at-large districts. The districts, they said, diluted the power of black and Hispanic votes. State officials countered that judicial elections are not protected by federal voting rights law because judges are not "representatives" under the Voting Rights Act. Lower courts agreed.

The Supreme Court reversed in 1991 by a vote of 6–3 in *Chisom*. The act clearly applied to judicial elections before the 1982 amendments, it said, and those amendments were chiefly aimed at removing a requirement of proof of intentional discrimination for redress under the act. Therefore, no reason existed to believe that Congress intended to eliminate judges from the coverage of the act.

The justices noted that the main purpose of Congress's 1982 action was to overturn the Supreme Court's 1980 ruling in *Mobile v. Bolden*, which required challengers to a voting process to show it was intentionally discriminatory. In instituting a test that looked to the actual discriminatory "effects" of an election scheme, Congress happened to use the term "representatives."

Justice John Paul Stevens, who wrote for the majority, said, "It is difficult to believe that Congress, in an express effort to broaden the protection afforded by the Voting Rights Act, withdrew, without comment, an important category of elections from that protection."[2]

1. *Chisom v. Roemer*, 501 U.S. 380 (1991); *Houston Lawyers' Association v. Attorney General of Texas*, 501 U.S. 419 (1991).
2. *Chisom v. Roemer*, 501 U.S. 380 at 404 (1991).

Scope and Application

Although the basic constitutionality of the Voting Rights Act was now settled, a steady stream of voting rights cases came to the Court well into the mid-1990s, testing the scope and application of the law. The Court steadfastly backed the act through the 1970s and 1980s, but in the 1990s it began to cut back on its scope, concerned that the law was fostering "reverse discrimination."

In the 1969 case of *Gaston County v. United States*, the Court refused to allow a North Carolina county to reinstate a literacy test. Writing the Court's opinion, Justice Harlan linked the county's earlier maintenance of segregated schools and the literacy level of its blacks and declared that to reinstitute the literacy qualification for voters would simply perpetuate the inequality of the denial of equal educational opportunity.[55] (*See details of the case, p. 509.*)

In a number of other cases the Court upheld the preclearance requirement for a wide variety of laws and practices affecting the right to vote.[56] In 1978 the Court even extended the requirement to apply to a county school board's rule that any employee running for state office must take leave from his post without pay during the period of active candidacy. The Court held that the rule was a voting standard, practice, or procedure subject to the requirement and that the county school board was a political subdivision subject to the provisions of the Voting Rights Act. Four justices dissented on the first point, three on the second.[57]

Earlier, the Court held that annexation of contiguous areas by communities covered by the act was prohibited without prior federal approval.[58] In 1975, however, the Court held in *Richmond v. United States* that a federally approved annexation plan did not violate the Voting Rights Act—even if it reduced the percentage of black voters in the city's population—so long as there were legitimate objective reasons for the annexation.[59]

In two cases decided in 1977—*Briscoe v. Bell* and *Morris v. Gressette*—the Court also sustained the act's limits on judicial review of the formula that put the law into effect in certain areas, and on judicial review of the attorney general's decision to approve changes in voting laws or practices.[60]

Recent Interpretation

In 1980 the Court for the first time narrowed the reach of the Voting Rights Act, ruling 6–3 in *City of Mobile v. Bolden* that it did not reach a voting system that was found discriminatory in effect, unless there was evidence that the system was also discriminatory in its intent.

Justice Stewart wrote the opinion. "The Fifteenth Amendment does not entail the right to have Negro candidates elected," he declared. The amendment guaranteed only that blacks be able to "register and vote without hindrance." The fact that no black had ever been elected city commissioner under Mobile's challenged system of at-large elections was not enough to prove the system in violation of the Voting Rights Act or the Constitution.[61]

examiners to register qualified voters. But Black objected to the provisions that suspended any changes in state voting laws until the state obtained approval of the change from the attorney general or the federal district court in the District of Columbia. This provision, Black argued, "so distorts our constitutional structure of government as to render any distinction drawn in the Constitution between state and federal power almost meaningless."[53]

Also in 1966, in *Katzenbach v. Morgan*, the Court upheld the portion of the Voting Rights Act that permitted persons educated in accredited "American-flag" schools to vote even if they were unable to demonstrate literacy in English. The provision was aimed at enfranchising persons educated in schools in Puerto Rico, a commonwealth of the United States, who were unable to read or write English.[54]

Long lines of black voters in Cobb County, Georgia, casting ballots for the 1946 Democratic primary elections showed that when the government removed obstacles to voting, blacks turned up at the polls in large numbers. Nearly twenty years later, the Voting Rights Act of 1965 eliminated the remaining obstacles to voting. Within four years of the act's passage, almost one million blacks had registered to vote.

The dissenters were Justices Marshall, White, and William J. Brennan Jr. Marshall protested the Court's acquiescence in the "vote dilution" that occurred in this situation for black residents of Mobile. He was not arguing for proportional representation of blacks, he said, but simply that it was not permissible for "the right to vote [to be] . . . granted in form, but denied in substance."[62]

The Mobile decision set off an immediate reaction on Capitol Hill. In 1982 Congress extended the Voting Rights Act, writing into the law specific language to overturn *Mobile* by declaring that a voting practice or law that had the effect of discriminating against blacks or other minorities violated the law, whatever its intent.[63]

In 1986 the Court applied that new test in *Thornburg v. Gingles,* ruling that six of North Carolina's multimember state legislative districts impermissibly diluted the strength of black votes in the state. The fact that very few blacks had been elected from those districts was enough to prove that the system was in violation of the law, the Court held.[64]

Permissible Redistricting by Race

Despite its willingness to affirm the sweeping provisions of the Voting Rights Act of 1965 as originally enacted and as amended, the Court has refused to interpret it as forbidding all use of racial criteria in redistricting or as requiring that blacks be given proportional representation on elected bodies.

In its 1976 decision in *Beer v. United States,* the Court upheld a city's reapportionment of the districts from which city council members were chosen. The change resulted in an increase in the number of black council members but not in a proportional representation of black voters among the council members. The Court held that the Voting Rights Act was satisfied so long as such changes did not reduce the voting strength of racial minorities.[65]

In *United Jewish Organizations of Williamsburgh v. Carey* (1977), the Court held that states could use some racial criteria in drawing electoral districts for members of the state legislature.

The decision broadened lawful redistricting and undercut *Gomillion v. Lightfoot* (1960). The Court in that earlier decision had held as unconstitutional *any* redistricting that was clearly intended to deny or dilute the right of blacks to vote.[66]

In *Carey* the Court upheld New York's 1974 redistricting law that purposely redrew certain districts with nonwhite majorities of at least 65 percent. The county affected was one of three in the state brought under the coverage of the Voting Rights Act by the 1970 amendments to that law.

The Hasidic Jewish community of the Williamsburgh section of Brooklyn objected to the redrawn lines because the new boundaries divided its voting strength between two districts. The Jewish community argued that such use of racial criteria in the redistricting plan deprived them of equal protection guaranteed by the Fourteenth Amendment and diluted their voting strength in violation of the Fifteenth Amendment.

The Constitution does not prevent all use of racial criteria in districting and apportionment, wrote Justice Byron R. White for the seven-member majority. Nor, he continued, does it "prevent a State subject to the Voting Rights Act from deliberately creating or preserving black majorities in particular districts in order to ensure that its reapportionment plan complies with [the act]."[67]

"There is no doubt," White continued, that the state in drawing new district lines, "deliberately used race in a purposeful manner. But its plan represented no racial slur or stigma with respect to whites or any other race, and we discern no discrimination violative of the Fourteenth Amendment nor any abridgment of the right to vote on account of race within the meaning of the Fifteenth Amendment."[68]

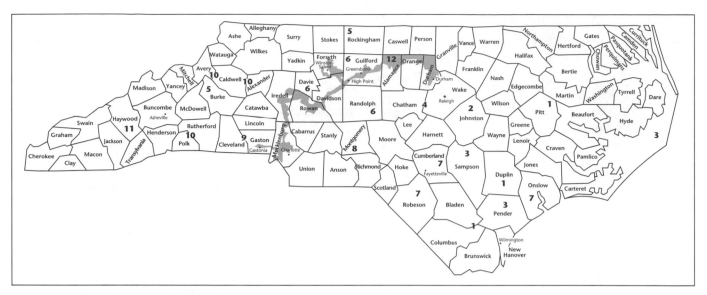

The irregular shape of North Carolina's Twelfth Congressional District was challenged in *Shaw v. Reno* (1993).

Majority-Minority Districts

The 1990 census and subsequent redistricting produced a record number of "majority-minority" voting districts and significantly boosted black and Hispanic representation in Congress.[69]

But the Supreme Court demonstrated in 1993 that some of these new districts that snaked through states collecting a majority of minority voters would come under tough legal scrutiny. By 5–4, the Court ruled that white voters could challenge as a violation of the equal protection clause any oddly shaped majority-minority district that appeared to be defensible only on grounds of race.[70] (Valid redistricting grounds include shared community interests and geographical compactness.)

The Court's ruling in *Shaw v. Reno* reinstated a challenge by white voters in North Carolina to the state's new Twelfth Congressional District. The serpentine 160-mile-long district was purposely drawn to create a majority of black voters, and it elected a black representative to Congress in 1992. But a group of white voters contended that the redistricting plan established "a racially discriminatory voting process" and deprived them of the right to vote in "a color-blind" election.

A lower court ruled against the whites, but the Supreme Court reinstated their complaint in June 1993. Justice Sandra Day O'Connor said for the majority, "[A] racial gerrymander may exacerbate the very patterns of racial bloc voting that majority-minority districting is sometimes said to counteract."[71] To justify such a plan, O'Connor said, the government must show that it is narrowly tailored to serve a compelling governmental interest. The case was remanded for further hearings before a three-judge federal district court that earlier had voted 2–1 to uphold the plan.

In 1995 the Court made it even more difficult to draw such districts by ruling that even when a district is not irregularly shaped a state's use of race must be "narrowly tailored to achieve a compelling interest," for example, to redress some proved discrimination.[72] By 5–4, the justices struck down a majority-black Georgia district in *Miller v. Johnson* because race was the predominant factor in redistricting.

Writing for the majority, Justice Anthony M. Kennedy said voters must be treated as individuals, not as members of a racial class: "When the state assigns voters on the basis of race, it engages in the offensive and demeaning assumption that voters of a particular race, because of their race, think alike, share the same political interests, and will prefer the same candidates at the polls."[73]

Looking at whether race was a predominant factor in drawing boundaries, as dictated by the *Miller* ruling, the justices in 1996 struck down one majority-Hispanic and two majority-black districts in Texas and invalidated a majority-black district in North Carolina.[74] In the two separate cases, one revisiting the serpentine North Carolina district scrutinized in 1993, the Court said state lawmakers had neglected traditional districting criteria, such as compactness, to create racially gerrymandered districts. The narrow five-justice majority, which had prevailed a year earlier in the Georgia case, rejected arguments that the oddly shaped districts reflected a state interest in preserving incumbents' constituencies or were necessary to eradicate the effects of past discrimination and required under federal voting rights law. Overall, the decisions, *Bush v. Vera* and *Shaw v. Hunt*, followed principles already articulated in the 1993 and 1995 cases, but they called into serious question whether any majority-minority district would pass constitutional muster. (*See "House Districts: Strict Equality," pp. 525–526.*)

The Right to an Equal Vote

In the early 1960s, as Congress was moving with judicial backing to fulfill at last the promise of the Fifteenth Amendment, the Supreme Court sparked a second revolution in the nation's electoral system. At issue in this revolution was not every American's right to vote but the right, based on the equal protection guarantee of the Fourteenth Amendment, to an equal vote.

In 1962 the Court abandoned its long-standing policy of noninterference in the malapportionment of population among a state's electoral districts. By the end of the decade, the Court's rulings had required that almost all the nation's legislative and congressional district lines be redrawn.

The equal protection guarantee meant that one person's vote should be counted equally with another's. Thus the standard by which these redistricting efforts were measured was that of "one person, one vote."

Congress, Districts, and People

Article I, Section 4, of the Constitution gives Congress the power to override state-set rules governing the election of senators and representatives. The section reads:

The Times, Places and Manner of holding Elections for Senators and Representatives shall be prescribed in each State by the Legislature thereof; but the Congress may at any time by Law make or alter such Regulations, except as to the Places of chusing Senators.

Congress exercised this power in 1842 to require that members of the House be elected from separate districts within each state. In 1872 Congress added the requirement that these congressional districts be of approximately equal population. Subsequent reapportionment statutes, including those enacted in 1901 and 1911, contained the specification that congressional districts be "contiguous and compact territory and containing as nearly as practicable an equal number of inhabitants."[1]

But the next such law, passed in 1929, omitted these requirements, and the Supreme Court in 1932 held the omission intentional and the standards thus no longer in effect. In *Wood v. Broom* the Court upheld a Mississippi redistricting law that failed to provide compact, contiguous, and population-equal districts.[2]

This decision came at a critical time in the nation's demographic history. The 1920 census showed that, for the first time, more Americans lived in cities than in rural settings. The implication was clear: the voice of the farmer in the legislature and in Congress would grow fainter, while that of the city dweller would increase in strength.

But for forty years, while the Supreme Court maintained a hands-off policy, rural interests delayed the political impact of this shift in population. The Court steadfastly held that challenges to malapportionment were political questions, outside its purview. In 1946 the Court refused to intervene in Illinois, reaffirming its intention to stay out of the "political thicket" of redistricting and reapportionment.

Within two decades, however, the Court reversed that stance of restraint. With the decision announced in *Baker v. Carr,* the Court abandoned its view that malapportionment was a strictly political question. In subsequent rulings the Court moved into the thicket, requiring the redrawing of state legislative and congressional district lines to ensure each voter's ballot equal weight in the state electoral process.

"THE POLITICAL THICKET"

The case of *Colegrove v. Green* was brought to the Supreme Court in 1946 by Kenneth W. Colegrove, a Northwestern University professor of political science. He challenged Illinois congressional districts as so unequal in population that they in fact denied voters in the more populous districts the equal protection of the law guaranteed by the Fourteenth Amendment. The numerical disparity between these districts, he pointed out, was as large as 800,000 persons.

The Supreme Court, 4–3, threw out his case without addressing the equal protection issue. Justice Robert H. Jackson did not take part in the decision; the seat of the chief justice was vacant—Chief Justice Harlan Fiske Stone died two months before the decision was announced.[3]

Justice Felix Frankfurter wrote the Court's opinion, joined by Justices Stanley F. Reed and Harold H. Burton. Frankfurter noted that the case could be resolved on the same basis as *Wood v. Broom.* Because Congress had omitted the equal population standard from the reapportionment law now in effect, there was no such requirement for states to follow in drawing district lines.

But practical considerations as well as judicial precedent dictated the Court's decision not to intervene. The issue in the case, Frankfurter noted, was "of a peculiarly political nature and therefore not meet for judicial determination." He continued:

Nothing is clearer than that this controversy concerns matters that bring courts into immediate and active relations with party contests. From the determination of such issues this Court has traditionally held aloof. It is hostile to a democratic system to involve the judiciary in the politics of the people. . . .

. . . due regard for the Constitution as a viable system precludes judicial correction [of the evils protested here]. Authority for dealing with such problems resides elsewhere. . . . The short of it is that the Constitution [Article I, Section 4] has conferred upon Congress exclusive authority to secure fair representation by the States in the popular House and left to that House determination whether States have fulfilled their responsibility. If Congress failed in exercising its powers, whereby standards of fairness are offended, the remedy ultimately lies with the people. Whether Congress faithfully discharges its duty or not, the subject has been committed to the exclusive control of Congress. . . .

To sustain this action would cut very deep into the very being of Congress. Courts ought not to enter this political thicket. The remedy for unfairness in districting is to secure State legislatures that will apportion properly, or to invoke the ample powers of Congress.[4]

The critical fourth vote was cast by Justice Wiley B. Rutledge, who wrote a separate opinion. He did not endorse the position set out by Frankfurter that issues of districting were not proper matters for judicial determination, but in this case he thought the Court properly dismissed the matter in order to avoid collision with the political departments of the government.[5]

Justices Hugo L. Black, William O. Douglas, and Frank Murphy dissented, finding Colegrove's complaint well within the power of the federal courts to redress constitutional grievances caused by state action.

Black wrote: "What is involved here is the right to vote guaranteed by the Federal Constitution. It has always been the rule that where a federally protected right has been invaded the federal courts will provide the remedy to rectify the wrong done."[6]

Population disparities such as those in this case clearly violated the Fourteenth Amendment, the dissenters concluded, and the Court should grant relief.

Colegrove stood for sixteen years as a firmly planted obstacle to judicial inquiry into the apportionment of state legislatures, as well as into the distribution of population among congressional districts.

RACE AND REDISTRICTING

But in 1960—with Justice Frankfurter speaking for the Court—the Supreme Court made an exception to its refusal to intervene in such matters. Civil rights and redistricting converged in the case of Gomillion v. Lightfoot, and the Supreme Court was persuaded by a claim of racial discrimination to strike down an Alabama law redrawing Tuskegee's voting boundary lines to eliminate nearly every black voter from the city's limits.[7] (See details of this case, p. 512.)

Justice Frankfurter drew a clear line between redistricting challenges based on the Fourteenth Amendment, like Colegrove, and those based on the Fifteenth Amendment, like Gomillion.

The decisive facts in this case . . . are wholly different from the considerations found controlling in Colegrove.

That case involved a complaint of discriminatory apportionment of congressional districts. The appellants in Colegrove complained only of a dilution of the strength of their votes as a result of legislative inaction over a course of many years. The petitioners here complain that affirmative legislative action deprives them of their vote and the consequent advantages that the ballot affords. . . .

When a state exercises power wholly within the domain of state interest, it is insulated from federal judicial review. But such insulation is not carried over when state power is used as an instrument of circumventing a federally protected right.[8]

BAKER V. CARR

By 1962 only three members of the Colegrove Court remained on the bench: Frankfurter, Black, and Douglas—the latter two, dissenters from the 1946 ruling.

By that year as well the once slight advantage in representation of rural voters in state legislatures had become extremely pronounced. Legislative districts in rural areas held nearly twice as many seats as they would have been entitled to by apportionment on a population basis alone. A similar degree of population imbalance existed with respect to congressional districts.

In the 1962 Tennessee redistricting case of Baker v. Carr, the Supreme Court took its first step into the political thicket of legislative reapportionment.[9]

The Tennessee legislature had failed to reapportion itself for sixty years, despite the fact that the state constitution required decennial reapportionment after each census. By 1960 population shifts from rural to urban regions of the state had created dramatic disparities in the pattern of representation for state house and senate seats. Justice Tom C. Clark in his concurring opinion in Baker v. Carr pointed out that two-thirds of the members of the state legislature were elected by slightly more than one-third of the state's population.[10]

Appeals to the legislature to reapportion itself were futile. A suit brought in state court was rejected on the grounds that state courts—like federal courts—should stay out of such legislative matters. The city dwellers who brought the state suit then appealed to the federal courts, charging that the "unconstitutional and obsolete" apportionment system denied them the equal protection of the laws promised by the Fourteenth Amendment.

In Baker v. Carr the Court ruled 6–2 that constitutional challenges to legislative malapportionment could properly be considered by federal courts. Such claims were "justiciable," held the Court, abandoning the view that they were political questions outside the competence of the courts.

The Court stopped there. It did not go on to address the merits of the challenge to malapportionment.

The Opinion

Justice William J. Brennan Jr. wrote the Court's opinion in Baker v. Carr. With surprising ease, the majority resolved the question of federal jurisdiction over the case. The complaint clearly arose under one of the provisions of the U.S. Constitution, Brennan wrote, so it fell within the federal judicial power as defined in Article III. "An unbroken line of our precedents sustains the federal courts' jurisdiction of the subject matter of federal constitutional claims of this nature."[11]

Then, turning to the question of the voters' standing to bring the case, Brennan explained that they did have standing because they had been deprived of an interest they sought to defend.

These appellants seek relief in order to protect or vindicate an interest of their own. . . . Their constitutional claim is, in substance, that the 1901 statute [setting up the existing districting and apportionment structure] constitutes arbitrary and capricious state action, offensive to the Fourteenth Amendment in its irrational disregard of the standard of apportionment prescribed by the State's Constitution or of any standard, effecting a gross disproportion of representation to voting population.[12]

To avoid addressing the issue of legislative malapportionment, the Supreme Court in *Colegrove v. Green* (1946) invoked the "political question" doctrine. Indeed, it is one of the oldest of the Court's rationales for *not* deciding a case.

In his classic discussion of judicial power in *Marbury v. Madison,* Chief Justice John Marshall declared:

The province of the court is, solely, to decide on the rights of individuals, not to inquire how the executive, or executive officers, perform duties in which they have a discretion. Questions in their nature political, or which are, by the Constitution and laws, submitted to the executive, can never be made in this court.[1]

In the ensuing years the Court used this doctrine as a convenient device for avoiding collisions with Congress, the president, or the states on matters ranging from foreign relations to malapportioned congressional districts.

The attributes of the political question doctrine are quite variable. One modern justice has observed that they "in various settings, diverge, combine, appear, and disappear in seeming disorderliness."[2]

The Constitution provides that the United States shall guarantee to every state a republican form of government. When the question of enforcing that guarantee came for the first time to the Supreme Court in 1849, however, the Court made clear that this was a "political question" beyond its reach.

The case of *Luther v. Borden* involved two competing groups, each asserting that it was the lawful government of Rhode Island. Writing for the Court, Chief Justice Roger B. Taney stated firmly that it was up to Congress to decide which government was the legitimate one. He explained:

when the senators and representatives of a State are admitted into the councils of the Union, the authority of the government under which they are appointed, as well as its republican character, is recognized by the proper constitutional authority.

And its decision is binding on every other department of the government and could not be questioned in a judicial tribunal.[3]

The Court has consistently applied the political question doctrine to avoid addressing Fourteenth Amendment "guaranty clause" challenges to state action.[4]

In another early nineteenth century ruling, the Court placed questions of foreign policy and foreign affairs firmly in the "political question" category.

In 1829 the Court refused to settle an international border question, stating that it was not the role of the courts to assert national interests against foreign powers.[5] Throughout its history, the Court has reaffirmed the view that in foreign affairs the nation should speak with a single voice.[6]

In similar fashion, the Court has generally invoked the political question doctrine to refuse to intervene in questions of legislative process or procedure, leaving their resolution to Congress or the states.

The exception to that general practice has come in cases raising questions of basic constitutional standards—such as the power of Congress to legislate on certain matters, or the propriety of one chamber's action excluding a member who meets constitutional qualifications[7]—or in matters where Congress and the president are deadlocked over an issue.[8]

For most of the nation's history, the Court also viewed challenges to state decisions allocating population among electoral districts as a political question. It was in this vein that Justice Felix Frankfurter wrote in *Colegrove* that for Courts to involve themselves in malapportionment controversies was "hostile to a democratic system."[9]

But sixteen years later the Court in *Baker v. Carr* found the *Colegrove* ruling based on too broad a definition of "political questions." For the new majority, Justice William J. Brennan Jr. explained:

[I]t is the relationship between the judiciary and the coordinate branches of the Federal Government, and not the federal judiciary's relationship to the States, which gives rise to the "political questions.". . . The nonjusticiability of a political question is primarily a function of the separation of powers.[10]

The basic question of fairness involved in *Baker v. Carr,* wrote Brennan, was constitutional, not political, and was therefore well within the jurisdiction of the Court. Simply "the presence of a matter affecting state government does not [in and of itself] render the case nonjusticiable."[11]

More recently the Court widened what it considered justiciable when it extended federal court jurisdiction to cover the issue of political gerrymanders.

In *Davis v. Bandemer* Justice Byron R. White applied the political questions standard set out in *Baker v. Carr.* Referring to political gerrymanders, he said:

Disposition of this question does not involve us in a matter more properly decided by a coequal branch of our Government. There is no risk of foreign or domestic disturbance, and . . . we are not persuaded that there are no judicially discernible and manageable standards by which political gerrymander cases are to be decided.[12]

1. *Marbury v. Madison,* 1 Cr. 137 at 170 (1803).
2. *Baker v. Carr,* 369 U.S. 186 at 210 (1962).
3. *Luther v. Borden,* 7 How. 1 at 42 (1849).
4. *Pacific States Telephone and Telegraph Co. v. Oregon,* 223 U.S. 118 (1912).
5. *Foster v. Neilson,* 2 Pet. 253 at 307 (1829).
6. *Oetjen v. Central Leather Co.,* 246 U.S. 297 at 302 (1918); *United States v. Curtiss-Wright Export Corporation,* 299 U.S. 304 (1936).
7. *Hawke v. Smith,* 253 U.S. 221 (1920); *Coleman v. Miller,* 307 U.S. 433 (1939); *Powell v. McCormack,* 395 U.S. 486 (1969).
8. *Pocket Veto Case,* 279 U.S. 655 (1929).
9. *Colegrove v. Green,* 328 U.S. 549 at 554 (1946).
10. *Baker v. Carr,* 369 U.S. 186 at 210 (1962).
11. Id. at 232.
12. *Davis v. Bandemer,* 478 U.S. 109 at 123 (1986).

This holding did not require the Court to decide the merits of the voters' allegations, Brennan wrote. But he did consider the critical question of the justiciability of the issue—its suitability to judicial solution.

Did this suit present a "political question" outside the proper scope of the Supreme Court's consideration? Brennan's answer was no.

He explained:

[T]he mere fact that the suit seeks protection of a political right does not mean it presents a political question. . . . It is argued that apportionment cases, whatever the actual wording of the complaint, can involve no federal constitutional right except one resting on the guaranty of a republican form of government, and that complaints based on that clause have been held to present political questions which are nonjusticiable.

We hold that the claim pleaded here neither rests upon nor implicates the Guaranty Clause and that its justiciability is therefore not foreclosed by our decisions of cases involving that clause. The District Court misinterpreted *Colegrove v. Green* and other decisions of this Court on which it relied.[13]

The guaranty clause to which Brennan referred is in Article IV, Section 4, of the Constitution: "The United States shall guarantee to every State in this Union a Republican Form of Government."

One of the first major expositions of the "political question" doctrine in the 1849 case of *Luther v. Borden* involved this guarantee. The Court held its enforcement to be a political question, left to the political branches—Congress and the president—and outside judicial competence.[14] *Baker v. Carr* rendered the guaranty clause virtually useless.

Justice Charles E. Whittaker did not participate in the decision, and one week later, suffering from physical exhaustion, he retired from the Court.

Concurring Opinions

Justices Douglas, Clark, and Potter Stewart wrote concurring opinions.

Douglas emphasized the Court's frequent role as protector of voting rights.

Clark would have gone further and considered the merits of the particular complaint and granted relief: "[No] one, not even the State nor the dissenters, has come up with any rational basis for Tennessee's apportionment statute."[15] Nevertheless, Clark recommended that federal courts intrude in reapportionment matters only as a last resort.

Stewart reiterated that the Court had decided only that such Fourteenth Amendment challenges to malapportionment were justiciable matters and that the persons bringing this case had standing to sue.

Dissenting Opinions

Justices Frankfurter and John Marshall Harlan dissented. In what was his last major opinion, Frankfurter criticized the majority for "[s]uch a massive repudiation of the experience of our whole past in asserting destructively novel judicial power." The Court had, he argued, allowed a "hypothetical claim resting on abstract assumptions" to become "the basis for affording illusory relief for a particular evil even though it foreshadows deeper and more pervasive difficulties in consequence."[16]

Frankfurter went on to say that to give judges the task of "accommodating the incommensurable factors of policy" involved in reapportionment plans was "to attribute . . . omnicompetence to judges." By this decision, he wrote, the Supreme Court gave the nation's courts the power "to devise what should constitute the proper composition of the legislatures of the fifty States." The Court had overlooked the fact, he added, "that there is not under our Constitution a judicial remedy for every political mischief, for every undesirable exercise of legislative power."[17]

Justice Harlan found the Tennessee plan rational. "Nothing in the Equal Protection Clause or elsewhere in the Federal Constitution," he wrote, "expressly or impliedly supports the view that state legislatures must be so structured as to reflect with approximate equality the voice of every voter. . . . In short, there is nothing in the Federal Constitution to prevent a State, acting not irrationally, from choosing any electoral legislative structure it thinks best suited to the interests, temper, and customs of its people."[18]

Harlan concluded with a strong criticism of the majority's action, saying that "what the Court is doing reflects more an adventure in judicial experimentation than a solid piece of constitutional adjudication."[19]

"ONE PERSON, ONE VOTE"

The decision in *Baker v. Carr* opened the doors of federal courtrooms across the country to litigants challenging state and congressional apportionment systems. But it provided no standards to guide federal judges in measuring the validity of challenged systems.

With its subsequent rulings in 1963 and 1964, the Supreme Court formulated a standard, known far and wide as the "one man, one vote" or "one person, one vote" rule.

Two new justices participated in these decisions. After *Baker v. Carr,* Justices Whittaker and Frankfurter retired. President John F. Kennedy appointed Byron R. White to succeed Whittaker and Arthur J. Goldberg to succeed Frankfurter.

The Rule Announced

The "one person, one vote" rule was first set out by the Court almost exactly one year after *Baker v. Carr.* But the case in which the announcement came did not involve legislative districts.

In *Gray v. Sanders* the Court found that Georgia's county-unit primary system for electing state officials—a system that weighted votes to give advantage to rural districts in statewide primary elections—denied voters the equal protection of the laws.

Justice Douglas's opinion for eight members of the Court rejected the state's effort to defend this weighted vote system by analogy to the electoral college system. The electoral college sys-

Cartoon showing the impact of the Supreme Court's decision in *Gray v. Sanders* on the rural vote in Georgia.

tem was included in the Constitution because of specific historical concerns, Douglas wrote, but that inclusion "implied nothing about the use of an analogous system by a State in a statewide election."[20]

All votes in a statewide election must have equal weight, held the Court:

How then can one person be given twice or 10 times the voting power of another person in a statewide election merely because he lives in a rural area or because he lives in the smallest rural county? Once the geographical unit for which a representative is to be chosen is designated, all who participate in the election are to have an equal vote—whatever their race, whatever their sex, whatever their occupation, whatever their income, and wherever their home may be in that geographical unit. This is required by the Equal Protection Clause of the Fourteenth Amendment. The concept of "we the people" under the Constitution visualizes no preferred class of voters but equality among those who meet the basic qualification. The idea that every voter is equal to every other voter in his State, when he casts his ballot in favor of one of several competing candidates, underlies many of our decisions. . . . The conception of political equality from the Declaration of Independence to Lincoln's Gettysburg Address, to the Fifteenth, Seventeenth, and Nineteenth Amendments can mean only one thing—one person, one vote.[21]

Justice Harlan again dissented:

The Court's holding surely . . . flies in the face of history . . . "one person, one vote" has never been the universally accepted political philosophy in England, the American Colonies, or in the United States. . . . I do not understand how, on the basis of these mere numbers, unillumi-

nated as they are by any of the complex and subtle political factors involved, a court of law can say, except by judicial fiat, that these disparities are in themselves constitutionally invidious.[22]

Congressional Districts

The Court's rulings in *Baker* and *Gray* concerned the equal weighting and counting of votes cast in state elections. In 1964, deciding the case of *Wesberry v. Sanders,* the Court applied the "one person, one vote" principle to congressional districts and set equality, not rationality, as the standard for congressional redistricting.

Voters in Georgia's Fifth Congressional District—which included Atlanta—complained that the population of their congressional district was more than twice the ideal state average of 394,312 persons per district. By its failure to redistrict, the state denied them equal protection of the laws, they charged. They also challenged Georgia's apportionment scheme as a violation of Article I, Section 2, of the Constitution that declares that members of the House of Representatives are to be elected "by the people."

A federal district court dismissed the case in 1962, but the Supreme Court, 6–3, reversed the lower court decision in 1964.

In the majority opinion Justice Black considered the historical context of the requirement in Article I, Section 2, of the Constitution, that representatives be chosen "by the People of the several States." This means, he wrote,

that as nearly as is practicable, one man's vote in a congressional election is to be worth as much as another's. . . .

To say that a vote is worth more in one district than in another would not only run counter to our fundamental ideas of democratic government, it would cast aside the principle of a House of Representatives elected "by the People."

While it may not be possible to draw congressional districts with mathematical precision, that is no excuse for ignoring our Constitution's plain objective of making equal representation for equal numbers the fundamental goal of the House of Representatives.[23]

Black's view was sharply attacked by Justice Harlan, who dissented:

The upshot of all this is that the language of Art. I, [Sections] 2 and 4, the surrounding text, and the relevant history are all in strong and consistent direct contradiction of the Court's holding. The constitutional scheme vests in the States plenary power to regulate the conduct of elections for Representatives, and, in order to protect the Federal Government, provides for congressional supervision of the States' exercise of their power. Within this scheme, the appellants do not have the right which they assert, in the absence of provision for equal districts by the Georgia Legislature or the Congress. The constitutional right which the Court creates is manufactured out of whole cloth.[24]

Justice Black did not invoke the equal protection clause in the case. Speculation as to why Black based this ruling on historical grounds rather than on the Fourteenth Amendment suggests that his choice was a compromise among members of the Court.[25]

Four months later, however, eight members agreed on the requirements of the Fourteenth Amendment for state reapportionment.

"ONE PERSON, ONE VOTE" AT CITY HALL

With several rulings the Supreme Court has extended the "one person, one vote" rule to some local districts as well as state and national districts.

In 1967 the Court ruled that county school board members (each representing a local board) from districts of disparate population were not subject to this rule because the county board performed administrative, not legislative, functions.[1]

But in *Avery v. Midland County* the Court ruled in 1968 that when a state delegates lawmaking power to local government and provides for election by district of the officials exercising that power, those districts must be of substantially equal population.[2]

Two years later the Court ruled that the "one person, one vote" rule must be applied to *any* election—state or local—of persons performing governmental functions:

If one person's vote is given less weight through unequal apportionment, his right to equal voting participation is impaired just as much when he votes for a school board member as when he votes for a state legislator. . . . [T]he crucial consideration is the right of each qualified voter to participate on an equal footing in the election process.[3]

In 1973, however, the Court held that the constitutional guarantee of equal protection did not demand that the "one person, one vote" rule be applied to special-purpose electoral districts such as those devised to regulate water supplies in the West. In such districts, the Court held, states may restrict the franchise to landowners and weigh the votes of each person according to the property he owns.[4]

1. *Sailors v. Board of Education,* 387 U.S. 105 (1967); see also *Dusch v. Davis,* 387 U.S. 112 (1967).

2. *Avery v. Midland County,* 390 U.S. 474 (1968).

3. *Hadley v. Junior College District of Metropolitan Kansas City, Mo.,* 397 U.S. 50 at 55 (1970); see also *New York Board of Estimate v. Morris,* 489 U.S. 688 (1989).

4. *Salyer Land Co. v. Tulare Water District; Associated Enterprises Inc. v. Toltec Watershed Improvement District,* 410 U.S. 719, 743 (1973).

State Legislative Districts

By a vote of 8–1, the Supreme Court ruled in *Reynolds v. Sims* (1964) that the Fourteenth Amendment required equally populated electoral districts for both houses of bicameral state legislatures.

The case, which concerned Alabama, was accompanied to the Supreme Court by a number of others concerning other state legislatures. Therefore, the Court's decision immediately affected reapportionment not only in Alabama but also in New York, Maryland, Virginia, Delaware, and Colorado. Ultimately, every state legislature felt the impact of *Reynolds v. Sims*.

Writing for the Court what he would often describe as the most significant opinion of his judicial career, Chief Justice Earl Warren stated that the "controlling criterion" for any reapportionment plan must be equal population.[26]

The Court rejected the suggestion that a state might, by analogy to the federal system, constitute one house of its legislature on the basis of population and the other on an area basis. Chief Justice Warren explained: "The system of representation in the two Houses of Congress is one conceived out of compromise and concession indispensable to the establishment of our federal republic . . . based on the consideration that in establishing our type of federalism a group of formerly independent states bound themselves together under one national government." Political subdivisions of states, like cities and countries, he continued, were never considered "sovereign entities" but are rather "subordinate governmental instrumentalities."[27]

The equal protection clause required substantially equal representation of all citizens. The Court did not provide any precise formula for defining "substantially equal" and left it to lower courts to work out a useful standard.

Justice Harlan, the lone dissenter, said that the Court's rule had no constitutional basis and that the drafters of the Fourteenth Amendment had not meant to give the federal government authority to intervene in the internal organization of state legislatures.

Majority Opinion. Chief Justice Warren set forth the reasoning behind the "one person, one vote" rule with clarity and firmness:

The right to vote freely for the candidate of one's choice is of the essence of a democratic society, and any restrictions on that right strike at the heart of representative government. And the right of suffrage can be denied by a debasement of suffrage or dilution of the weight of a citizen's vote just as effectively as by wholly prohibiting the free exercise of the franchise. . . .

Legislators represent people, not trees or acres. Legislators are elected by voters, not farms or cities or economic interests. As long as ours is a representative form of government, and our legislatures are those instruments of government elected directly by and directly representative of the people, the right to elect legislators in a free and unimpaired fashion is a bedrock of our political system. . . .

. . . The fact that an individual lives here or there is not a legitimate reason for overweighting or diluting the efficacy of his vote. The complexions of societies and civilizations change, often with amazing rapidity. A nation once primarily rural in character becomes predominantly urban. Representation schemes once fair and equitable become archaic and outdated. But the basic principle of representative government remains, and must remain, unchanged—the weight of a citizen's vote cannot be made to depend on where he lives. Population is, of necessity, the starting point for consideration and the controlling criterion for judgment in legislative apportionment controversies. A citizen, a qualified voter, is no more nor no less so because he lives in the city or on the farm. This is the clear and strong command of our Constitution's Equal Protection Clause. This is an essential part of the concept of a government of laws and not men. . . .

The Equal Protection Clause demands no less than substantially equal state legislative representation for all citizens, of all places as well as of all races.

We hold that as a basic constitutional standard, the Equal Protection Clause requires that the seats in both houses of a bicameral state legislature must be apportioned on a population basis. Simply stated, an individual's right to vote for state legislators is unconstitutionally impaired when its weight is in substantial fashion diluted when compared with votes of citizens living in other parts of the State.[28]

The Court recognized the impossibility of attaining mathematical precision in election district populations:

[T]he Equal Protection Clause requires that a State make an honest and good faith effort to construct districts, in both houses of its legislature, as nearly of equal population as is practicable. We realize that it is a practical impossibility to arrange legislative districts so that each one has an identical number of residents, or citizens, or voters. Mathematical exactness or precision is hardly a workable constitutional requirement.[29]

Warren wrote that in applying the equal population principle the Court, for the present, considered it

expedient not to attempt to spell out any precise constitutional tests. What is marginally permissible in one State may be unsatisfactory in another, depending on the particular circumstances of the case. Developing a body of doctrine on a case-by-case basis appears to us to provide the most satisfactory means of arriving at detailed constitutional requirements in the area of state legislative apportionment.[30]

Dissenting Opinion. Justice Harlan again dissented, arguing that judicial intervention in reapportionment questions was "profoundly ill advised and constitutionally impermissible." This series of decisions, Harlan said, would weaken the vitality of the political system and "cut deeply into the fabric of our federalism." The Court's ruling gave "support to a current mistaken view of the Constitution and the constitutional function of this Court. This view, in a nutshell, is that every major social ill in this country can find its cure in some constitutional 'principle,' and that this Court should 'take the lead' in promoting reform when other branches of government fail to act. The Constitution is not a panacea for every blot upon the public welfare, nor should this Court, ordained as a judicial body, be thought of as a haven for reform movements."[31]

House Districts: Strict Equality

Five years elapsed between the Court's admonition in *Wesberry v. Sanders* (1964), urging states to make a good-faith effort to construct congressional districts as nearly of equal population as is practicable, and the Court's next application of constitutional standards to redistricting.

In 1967 the Court hinted at the strict stance it would adopt two years later. With two unsigned opinions, the Court sent back to Indiana and Missouri for revision redistricting plans for congressional districts that allowed variations of as much as 20 percent from the average district population.[32]

Two years later Missouri's revised plan returned to the Court for full review. With its decision in *Kirkpatrick v. Preisler,* the Court, 6–3, rejected the plan. It was unacceptable, held the majority, because it allowed a variation of as much as 3.1 percent from perfectly equal population districts.[33]

The Court thus made clear its strict application of "one person, one vote" to congressional redistricting. Minor deviations from the strict principle of equal population were permissible only when the state provided substantial evidence that the variation was unavoidable.

Writing for the majority, Justice Brennan declared that there was no "fixed numerical or percentage population variance

---

POLITICAL GERRYMANDERS

The Supreme Court opened the door on a whole new category of political cases on June 30, 1986, when the Court ruled that political gerrymanders are subject to constitutional review by federal courts—even if the disputed districts meet the "one person, one vote" test.

"The issue is one of representation," wrote Justice Byron R. White in *Davis v. Bandemer,* "and we decline to hold that such claims are never justiciable."[1]

Davis v. Bandemer came to the Court as a challenge by Indiana Democrats to a 1981 reapportionment of seats for the state legislature. The Democrats argued that the Republican-drawn map so heavily favored the Republican Party that it effectively denied Democrats in the state appropriate representation.

In the 1982 election, based on the revised map, the Republicans won a disproportionate share of the seats in the state legislature.

The Republicans responded by arguing that this was a "political question" outside the jurisdiction of federal courts. The Court, 6–3, rejected that threshold argument, holding that such challenges were justiciable.

Dissenting on that point were Chief Justice Warren E. Burger and Justices Sandra Day O'Connor and William H. Rehnquist, who held that "the partisan gerrymandering claims of major political parties raise a nonjusticiable political question that the judiciary should leave to the legislative branch as the Framers of the Constitution unquestionably intended."[2]

They warned, in O'Connor's words, that "the losing party . . . in every reapportionment will now be invited to fight the battle anew in federal court."[3]

But the Court then went on to rule 7–2 on the specific question—rejecting the Democratic challenge to the alleged gerrymander.

"Relying on a single election to prove unconstitutional discrimination," White wrote, was "unsatisfactory." "Unconstitutional discrimination occurs," he continued, "only when the electoral system is arranged in a manner that will consistently degrade a voter's or a group of voters' influence on the political process as a whole."[4]

To prove unconstitutional discrimination through a political gerrymander, both discriminatory intent and effect must be shown, said White.

The question to be asked in evaluating such a challenge is "whether a particular group has been unconstitutionally denied its chance to effectively influence the political process. . . . Such a finding of unconstitutionality must be supported by evidence of continued frustration of the will of a majority of the voters or effective denial to a minority of voters of a fair chance to influence the political process."[5]

1. *Davis v. Bandemer,* 478 U.S. 109 at 124 (1986).
2. Id. at 144.
3. Id. at 147.
4. Id. at 135, 132.
5. Id. at 133.

small enough to be considered *de minimis*" and he emphasized the need "to satisfy without question the 'as nearly as practicable' standard."[34]

Brennan continued:

The whole thrust of the "as nearly as practicable" approach is inconsistent with adoption of fixed numerical standards which excuse population variances without regard to the circumstances of each particular case. . . .

The extent to which equality may practically be achieved may differ from State to State and from district to district. . . . Unless population variances among congressional districts are shown to have resulted despite such effort, the State must justify each variance, no matter how small. . . .

. . . to consider a certain range of variances *de minimis* would encourage legislators to strive for that range rather than for equality "as nearly as practicable." . . . to accept population variances, large or small, in order to create districts with specific interest orientations is antithetical to the basic premise of the constitutional command to provide equal representation for equal numbers of people.[35]

Justice Abe Fortas concurred with the majority but felt that the Court had set a standard of "near-perfection" difficult to achieve:

Whatever might be the merits of insistence on absolute equality if it could be obtained, the majority's pursuit of precision is a search for a will-o'-the wisp. The fact is that any solution to the apportionment and districting problem is at best an approximation because it is based upon figures which are always to some degree obsolete. No purpose is served by an insistence on precision which is unattainable because of the inherent imprecisions in the population data on which districting must be based.[36]

Justices Harlan, Stewart, and White dissented. White called the majority's ruling "an unduly rigid and unwarranted application of the Equal Protection Clause which will unnecessarily involve the courts in the abrasive task of drawing district lines."[37] Harlan wrote that the decision transformed "a political slogan into a constitutional absolute. Strait indeed is the path of the righteous legislator. Slide rule in hand, he must avoid all thought of county lines, local traditions, politics, history, and economics, so as to achieve the magic formula: one man, one vote."[38]

In another congressional redistricting case decided the same day, the Court in *Wells v. Rockefeller* rejected New York's redistricting plan as out of line with equal protection standards.

The New York plan resulted in districts of nearly equal size within regions of the state but not of equal population throughout the state. That was unacceptable, held the Court, because the state could not and did not claim that its legislators had made a good-faith effort to achieve precise mathematical equality among its congressional districts.

Brennan wrote again for the Court:

To accept a scheme such as New York's would permit groups of districts with defined interest orientations to be overrepresented at the expense of districts with different interest orientations. Equality of population among districts in a substate is not a justification for inequality among all the districts in the State.[39]

The effect of this line of rulings from *Baker* in 1962 through *Kirkpatrick* in 1969 was felt in every state. By the end of the 1960s, thirty-nine of the forty-five states that elect more than one member of the House had redrawn their district lines. But because the new districts were based on 1960 census figures, population shifts during the decade left the new districts far from equal in population.

The redistricting following the 1970 census, however, resulted in substantial progress toward population equality among each state's congressional districts. Three hundred eighty-five of the 435 members of the House of Representatives elected in 1972 were chosen from districts that varied less than 1 percent from their state's average congressional district population.[40]

In 1973 the Court unanimously reaffirmed the strict standard for congressional districts set out in *Kirkpatrick*. The Court invalidated Texas's 1971 redistricting plan that allowed a difference of almost 5 percent between the most populous and the least populous congressional district.[41]

Justice White, writing the opinion in *White v. Weiser*, said that these differences were avoidable. Chief Justice Warren E. Burger and Justices William H. Rehnquist and Lewis F. Powell Jr. concurred, but they added that had they been members of the Court in 1969, they would have dissented from the rule of strict equality set out in *Kirkpatrick v. Preisler*.

Ten years later, on June 22, 1983, the Court again emphasized the strict standard of "one person, one vote," but this time the Court was not at all unanimous. Divided 5–4 in *Karcher v. Daggett*, the Court struck down New Jersey's congressional redistricting plan that was based on the 1980 census. Although the variation between the most populous district and the least populous district was less than 1 percent, the Court held that the difference must be justified as necessary to achieve some important state goal. New Jersey had not provided that justification, held the Court. Justice Brennan wrote the opinion; Justices White, Powell, Rehnquist, and Burger dissented.[42]

In 1992 the Court rejected a challenge by the state of Montana to the allocation of U.S. House members under a 1941 federal law.[43] State officials argued that the statute violated the principle of "one person, one vote." After the 1990 census and subsequent reapportionment, Montana lost one of its two seats in the House. If it had kept both seats, each district would have been closer to the ideal size of a congressional district than was the reapportioned single district.

In a unanimous decision, the Court said precise equal representation is impossible to achieve because the Constitution guarantees each state at least one representative and prevents House districts from crossing state lines. Furthermore, the Court said Congress has broad discretion in apportioning representatives.

State Districts: More Leeway

In *Baker v. Carr* (1962), the Supreme Court said for the first time that federal courts could address the problem of unequal distribution of voters among legislative districts. This decision, which rejected the Court's view in *Colegrove v. Green* (1946) that it should stay out of the "political thicket" of redistricting, began the first phase of changes in state legislatures across the nation.

Reynolds v. Sims began the second phase in the process. This 1964 decision applied the "one person, one vote" apportionment rule set forth in *Gray v. Sanders* (1963) to both houses of a state legislature.

The third and longest phase was characterized by the Supreme Court's effort to resolve the tension between the goal of equal population, demanded by the Fourteenth Amendment, and state definitions of democratic representation that often took factors other than population into account.

In this effort, which extended for decades following *Reynolds v. Sims,* the Court indicated a preference for single-member, not multimember, districts for electing state legislators. It continues to insist that reapportionment is primarily a legislative responsibility. And since 1973, it has been willing to tolerate more deviation from absolute population equality for state legislative districts than for congressional districts.

MULTIMEMBER DISTRICTS

In 1965, in *Fortson v. Dorsey,* the Supreme Court rejected a constitutional challenge to Georgia's use of single-member and multimember districts for electing members of the state senate. This system was challenged as intended to minimize the voting strength of certain minority groups.

Although the Court held that those allegations had not been proved, Justice Brennan in the opinion made clear that the Court was not giving blanket approval to multimember districts:

It might well be that, designedly or otherwise, a multi-member constituency apportionment scheme, under the circumstances of a particular scheme, would operate to minimize or cancel out the voting strength of racial or political elements of the voting population. When this is demonstrated it will be time enough to consider whether the system still passes constitutional muster.[44]

The following year the Court refused to disturb a similar electoral system for Hawaii's senate, emphasizing that the task of setting up such systems should be left to legislators, not judges.[45]

Again in 1971, in a case from Indiana, the Court refused to hold multimember districts unconstitutional. It required proof that the challenged districts operated to dilute the votes of certain groups or certain persons.[46]

Two years later the Court did find unconstitutional two multimember districts for electing members of the Texas house; it held them impermissible in light of the history of political discrimination against blacks and Mexican-Americans residing in those areas.[47]

POPULATION EQUALITY

Beginning in 1967, with *Swann v. Adams,* the Court defined the outer limits of population variance for state legislative districts. In that case the Court held unconstitutional Florida's plan that permitted deviations of as much as 30 percent and 40 percent from population equality.

Minor variations from equality would be tolerated if there were special justifications for it, held the Court, but it would be left to the state to prove the justification sufficient. Justice White wrote the opinion:

Reynolds v. Sims . . . recognized that mathematical exactness is not required in state apportionment plans. *De minimis* variations are unavoidable, but variations of 30 percent among senate districts and 40 percent among house districts can hardly be deemed *de minimis* and none of our cases suggests that differences of this magnitude will be approved without a satisfactory explanation grounded on acceptable state policy.[48]

White said that the Court in *Reynolds* had limited the permissible deviations to "minor variations" brought about by "legitimate considerations incident to the effectuation of a rational state policy . . . such . . . as the integrity of political subdivisions, the maintenance of compactness and contiguity in legislative districts or the recognition of natural or historical boundary lines."[49]

Justice Harlan, joined by Justice Stewart, dissented, saying that Florida's plan was a rational state policy. Harlan complained that in striking down the plan because it found the relatively minor variations in population among some districts unjustified, the Court "seems to me to stand on its head the usual rule governing this Court's approach to legislative enactments, state as well as federal, which is . . . that they come to us with a wrong presumption of regularity and constitutionality."[50]

After the Court's insistence in the 1969 decision in *Kirkpatrick v. Preisler* that congressional districts be precisely equal in population, states doubted the flexibility left to them in drawing state legislative districts not absolutely equal in the number of inhabitants.

But in 1973 the Court in *Mahan v. Howell* reiterated the more relaxed application to state legislative districts of the "one person, one vote" standard. The Court declared that "in the implementation of the basic constitutional principle—equality of population among the districts—more flexibility was constitutionally permissible with respect to state legislative reapportionment than in congressional redistricting."[51]

Virginia's legislative reapportionment statute, enacted after the 1970 census, allowed as much as a 16.4 percent deviation from equal population in the districts from which members of the state house were elected. When this was challenged in federal court as too wide a disparity, the lower court agreed, citing *Kirkpatrick v. Preisler* and *Wells v. Rockefeller,* both of which concerned districts from which members of the U.S. House of Representatives were elected.

By a 5–3 vote the Supreme Court reversed the lower court, with Justice Rehnquist speaking for the majority. Justice Powell did not participate in the decision; Justices Brennan, Douglas, and Thurgood Marshall dissented.

The Court upheld the state districting plan, finding the population variance not excessive.

Justice Rehnquist cited *Reynolds v. Sims* in support of the majority's view that some deviation from equal population was permissible for state legislative districts so long as it was justified by rational state policy. He explained the reason behind the Court's application of different standards to state and congressional redistricting plans:

[A]lmost invariably, there is a significantly larger number of seats in state legislative bodies to be distributed within a State than congressional seats and . . . therefore it may be feasible for a State to use political subdivision lines to a greater extent in establishing state legislative districts while still affording adequate statewide representation. . . .

By contrast, the court in *Wesberry v. Sanders* . . . recognized no excuse for the failure to meet the objective of equal representation for equal numbers of people in congressional districting other than the practical impossibility of drawing equal districts with mathematical precision. Thus, whereas population alone has been the sole criterion of constitutionality in congressional redistricting under Art. I . . . broader latitude has been afforded the State under the Equal Protection Clause in state legislative redistricting because of the considerations enumerated in *Reynolds v. Sims*. . . . The dichotomy between the two lines of cases has consistently been maintained. . . .

Application of the "absolute equality" test of *Kirkpatrick* and *Wells* to state legislative redistricting may impair the normal functioning of state and local governments. . . .

We hold that the legislature's plan for apportionment of the House of Delegates may reasonably be said to advance the rational state policy of respecting the boundaries of political subdivisions. The remaining inquiry is whether the population disparities among the districts which have resulted from the pursuit of this plan exceed constitutional limits. We conclude that they do not.[52]

Rehnquist noted, however, that the 16 percent deviation from equality "may well approach tolerable limits."

In dissent, Justice Brennan, joined by Justices Douglas and Marshall, argued for a stricter application of the "one person, one vote" principle, saying:

The principal question presented for our decision is whether on the facts of this case an asserted state interest in preserving the integrity of county lines can justify the resulting substantial deviations from population equality. . . .

. . . The Constitution does not permit a State to relegate considerations of equality to secondary status and reserve as the primary goal of apportionment the service of some other state interest.[53]

Several months later in 1973, the Court, in the case of *Gaffney v. Cummings,* upheld Connecticut's reapportionment of its legislature, despite a maximum deviation of 7.8 percent from mathematical equality in the population of the districts.[54]

Justice White wrote for the majority that state legislative reapportionment plans need not place an "unrealistic emphasis on raw population figures" when to do so might "submerge . . . other considerations and itself furnish a ready tool for ignoring factors that in day-to-day operation are important to an acceptable representation and apportionment arrangement."[55]

White also warned that strict adherence to arithmetic could frustrate achievement of the goal of fair and effective represen-

tation "by making the standards of reapportionment so difficult to satisfy that the reapportionment task is recurringly removed from legislative hands and performed by federal courts."[56]

He continued:

We doubt that the Fourteenth Amendment requires repeated displacement of otherwise appropriate state decision making in the name of essentially minor deviations from perfect census population equality that no one, with confidence, can say will deprive any person of fair and effective representation in his state legislature.

That the Court was not deterred by the hazards of the political thicket when it undertook to adjudicate the reapportionment cases does not mean that it should become bogged down in a vast, intractable apportionment slough, particularly when there is little if anything to be accomplished by doing so.[57]

The same day it announced its decision upholding Connecticut's reapportionment in *Gaffney,* the Court in *White v. Regester* upheld a similar plan for the Texas legislature, despite a 9.9 percent variation in the populations of the largest and smallest districts. In the same case, however, the Court required revision of the plan to eliminate two multimember districts in areas with histories of discrimination against racial and ethnic minority-group voters.[58]

Ten years later the Court again affirmed its willingness to give states more leeway in drawing their legislative districts than in drawing their congressional district lines. The same day that it struck down, 5–4, New Jersey's congressional redistricting plan with less than 1 percent variation between districts, it upheld, 5–4, Wyoming's law that gave each county one representative in the state's lower house—even though the population variance among the counties was enormous. The Court said that this arrangement was permissible in light of the state interest in giving each county its own representative.[59]

County governments prevailed in two key voting rights cases in the early 1990s primarily because the Court majority did not view the challenged practices as covered by the Voting Rights Act. In the first, *Presley v. Etowah County Commission* (1992), the Court said changes in the responsibilities of elected county commissioners are not subject to federal approval under the act, even when the changes adversely affect the political power of black county commissioners.[60] In this Alabama case the Court ruled 5–4 that only modifications that directly affect voting itself are covered by the act.

The second case, *Holder v. Hall* (1994), also was decided by a 5–4 vote. The Court said the size of a governing body—in this case a single county commissioner with executive and legislative authority in Georgia—is not subject to challenge under the Voting Rights Act.[61]

The decision barred a challenge to the unusual governmental structure used in rural Bleckley County, Georgia. Blacks, who made up about 20 percent of the county population, claimed the single-member commission violated the Voting Rights Act by "diluting" their opportunity to elect blacks to office.

In an opinion joined by Justices Rehnquist and O'Connor, Anthony M. Kennedy said "no objective and workable standard" existed to decide how many members a county commission should have.

Thomas wrote a massive, fifty-nine-page concurring opinion that attacked the use of the Voting Rights Act in any legislative redistricting case. He said invoking the law to encourage "racially designated districts" had been a "disastrous adventure in judicial policymaking."[62] Scalia joined Thomas's opinion.

COURT-ORDERED REDISTRICTING

Since 1975 the Court has distinguished between the standards it applied to state redistricting plans drawn by legislators and to those drawn by judges. Stricter standards applied to the latter. In the North Dakota case of *Chapman v. Meier,* the Court disapproved a court-ordered plan for the state legislature that allowed up to 20 percent population variance among districts.[63]

Court-ordered redistricting plans should not include multimember districts or allow more than a minimal variation from the goal of equal population, held the Court, unless unique state features or significant state policy justified those characteristics.

Justice Harry A. Blackmun spoke for the unanimous Court, stating that "absent particularly pressing features calling for multimember districts, a United States district court should refrain from imposing them upon a State."[64]

A 20 percent population variance, he continued, was not permissible "simply because there is no particular racial or political group whose voting power is minimized or cancelled." Moreover, Blackmun stated, neither sparse population nor the geographic division of the state by the Missouri River, "warrant[ed] departure from population equality."[65]

Reaffirming this position in the 1977 case of *Connor v. Finch,* the Court, by a 7–1 vote, overturned a court-ordered reapportionment plan for the Mississippi state legislature because it allowed population variations of up to 16.5 percent in senate districts and of up to 19.3 percent among house districts. The population variance was defended as necessary to preserve the integrity of county lines within legislative districts.[66]

The Court found this insufficient in light of the stricter standards set out in *Chapman v. Meier* for court-ordered plans.

In 1993 the justices ruled unanimously that federal courts generally should defer to state courts if both are hearing legal challenges to a state redistricting plan. The justices also ruled 9–0 that states may create "majority-minority" districts even when such districts are not required to remedy previous Voting Rights Act violations.[67]

MAJORITY-MINORITY DISTRICTS: NEW SCRUTINY

On the last day of the October 1992 term, the Court issued a redistricting decision that would reshape the outlook for voting districts nationwide. White voters, the Court ruled, could challenge racially drawn districts as a violation of the Fourteenth Amendment's equal protection clause if the districts were "highly irregular" in shape and "lacked sufficient justification."[68] *Shaw v. Reno,* decided on a 5–4 vote, reflected the conservative

Court's belief that majority-minority districts can perpetuate the very patterns of racial bloc voting they are intended to counteract.

At issue in 1993 was a district that wound around in a snake-like fashion for 160 miles in central North Carolina, picking up black neighborhoods in four metropolitan areas. The district, about 57 percent black, had been drawn at the urging of the U.S. Justice Department, which under the Voting Rights Act's "preclearance" procedure was pushing states to maximize the number of black and Hispanic seats created.

A group of white voters alleged that North Carolina had set up "a racially discriminatory voting process" and deprived them of the right to vote in "a color-blind" election. A lower court dismissed the complaint. At the time the case came to the justices, the stakes were high: the creation of numerous majority-minority districts had nearly doubled the number of blacks and Hispanics in Congress in the early 1990s. Critics of such districts, however, contended the bizarre shapes reflected a racial quota system, violating white voters' rights.

Justice O'Connor, who wrote the Court's opinion, acknowledged that racial considerations are legitimately among the myriad of factors that go into redistricting. But she said that in "some exceptional cases," a plan could be "so highly irregular that, on its face, it rationally cannot be understood as anything other than an effort to segregate voters on the basis of race."[69]

O'Connor went on to say that "reapportionment is one area in which appearances do matter."

A reapportionment plan that includes in one district individuals who belong to the same race, but who are otherwise widely separated by geographical and political boundaries, and who may have little in common with one another but the color of their skin, bears an uncomfortable resemblance to political apartheid. It reinforces the perception that members of the same racial group—regardless of their education, economic status, or the community in which they live—think alike, share the same political interests, and will prefer the same candidates at the polls. We have rejected such perceptions elsewhere as impermissible racial stereotypes.[70]

O'Connor warned of the "lasting harm to our society" that can be caused by racial classifications.

They reinforce the belief, held by too many for too much of our history, that individuals should be judged by the color of their skin. Racial classifications with respect to voting carry particular dangers. Racial gerrymandering, even for remedial purposes, may balkanize us into competing racial factions; it threatens to carry us further from the goal of a political system in which race no longer matters—a goal that the Fourteenth and Fifteenth Amendments embody, and to which the Nation continues to aspire. It is for these reasons that race-based districting by our state legislatures demands close judicial scrutiny.[71]

Joining O'Connor were Chief Justice Rehnquist and Justices Scalia, Kennedy, and Thomas. Justices White, Blackmun, Stevens, and Souter dissented.

The decision in *Shaw v. Reno* returned the case to a lower court for further hearings to determine whether the reapportionment plan was narrowly tailored to serve a compelling government interest.

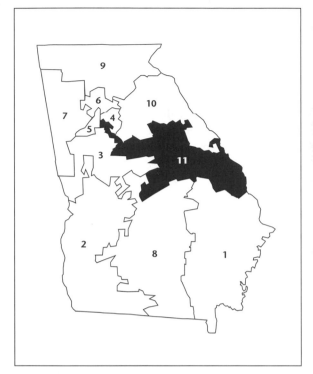

Georgia's Eleventh Congressional District *(above left)* was challenged in *Miller v. Johnson* (1995). Although the district is not generally irregular in shape, note the thin fingerlike extensions in the northwestern, northeastern, and western sections of the district. These were designed to incorporate high concentrations of black voters in Savannah, Augusta, and Atlanta. Pictured *(above right)* are Democratic representatives who protested the Court's decision *(from left to right):* Charles B. Rangel of New York; Cynthia A. McKinney, whose Georgia district was invalidated by the *Miller* decision; and Bobby L. Rush and Luis V. Gutierrez of Illinois.

In a dissenting opinion, White said the majority never identified the harm that the state's white voters had suffered: "Whites constitute roughly 76 percent of the total population and 79 percent of the voting age population in North Carolina. Yet, under the state's plan, they still constitute a voting majority in ten (or 83 percent) of the 12 congressional districts. Though they might be dissatisfied at the prospect of casting a vote for a losing candidate—a lot shared by many, including a disproportionate number of minority voters—surely they cannot complain of discriminatory treatment."[72]

Blackmun and Stevens both joined White's opinion and wrote biting opinions of their own. Blackmun said it was "ironic" that the Court's ruling came after North Carolina had elected its first black members of Congress since Reconstruction. Stevens called it "perverse" to permit redistricting plans drawn to provide adequate representation for other groups—mentioning rural voters, union members, Hasidic Jews, Polish Americans, and Republicans—but not for blacks.

Souter wrote a separate dissent, contending the majority had no reason for adopting the strict scrutiny test. Instead, he said, the Court should have stuck with previous decisions that required proof of a discriminatory intent and effect to invalidate a district plan because of racial considerations.

The following year the Court returned to the issue of racially drawn districts but ruled narrowly and avoided any reconsider-

ation or enhancement of *Shaw.* By 7–2, the Court in *Johnson v. DeGrandy* said the Voting Rights Act does not require legislative districting plans to maximize the number of districts in which minority groups are in the majority. Instead, the Court said state legislatures usually can satisfy the Voting Rights Act if minority voters form "effective voting majorities in a number of districts roughly proportional to the minority voters' respective shares in the voting-age population." The decision left in place a redistricting plan for the Florida legislature.[73]

In *Miller v. Johnson* (1995) the Court revisited *Shaw v. Reno* and expanded its scrutiny for districts drafted on racial lines.[74] The Court said any district in which race was a predominant factor in boundaries deserves strict scrutiny. That meant a larger group of districts would be challenged, not only those that were oddly shaped, as in *Shaw.* The Court said districts in which race is a predominant factor require government to show that its action is narrowly tailored to achieve a compelling interest.

By 5–4, the Court said Georgia's creation of a third majority-black congressional district, under pressure from the Justice Department, violated the equal protection rights of white voters in the district. (The boundaries of the central Georgian district were not bizarre or particularly distinctive.) The Justice Department twice had rejected state plans that included only two such majority-minority districts.

When a state follows a Justice Department determination

that race-based districting is necessary to comply with the Voting Rights Act, the majority said, federal judges still have an independent obligation to ensure that the state's action is narrowly tailored to achieve a compelling interest.

Justice Kennedy, who wrote for the majority, said government should not treat citizens as members of a racial class:

When the State assigns voters on the basis of race, it engages in the offensive and demeaning assumption that voters of a particular race, because of their race, think alike, share the same political interests, and will prefer the same candidates at the polls. Race-based assignments embody stereotypes that treat individuals as the product of their race, evaluating their thoughts and efforts—their very worth as citizens—according to a criterion barred to the government by history and the Constitution.[75]

Kennedy was joined in *Miller v. Johnson* by the rest of the majority in *Shaw v. Reno*: Chief Justice Rehnquist and Justices O'Connor, Scalia, and Thomas. Dissenting were Stevens, Souter, Ginsburg, and Breyer.

By the same 5–4 line-up the following year the Court invalidated one majority-Hispanic and two majority-black districts in Texas and struck down a majority-black district in North Carolina.[76] Relying on the principles laid down in earlier rulings and referring to traditional districting practices that until the 1990s had not been invoked in regard to race, Justice O'Connor wrote in the Texas case, "Those practices and our precedents, which acknowledge voters as more than mere racial statistics, play an important role in defining the political identity of the American voter. Our Fourteenth Amendment jurisprudence evinces a commitment to eliminate unnecessary and excessive governmental use and reinforcement of racial stereotypes."[77]

In dissent, Justice Stevens countered, "While any racial classification may risk some stereotyping, the risk of true 'discrimination' in this case is extremely tenuous in light of the remedial purpose the classification is intended to achieve and the long history of resistance to giving minorities a full voice in the political process. . . ."[78]

Freedom of Political Association

The freedom to espouse any political belief and to associate with others sharing that belief is, in the words of the modern Supreme Court, "the core of those activities protected by the First Amendment."[1]

Judicial recognition of this freedom is new, exclusively a development of the midtwentieth century. A corollary of the First Amendment freedoms of speech and belief, the right of political association was first expounded upon by the Court after World War I, when the Court attempted to reconcile the government's need to protect itself against internal subversion with the First Amendment protection for free speech.

This freedom is not absolute. The Court has condoned its curtailment, especially during times of national peril, when the line between freedom of political association and treasonable conspiracy blurs.

In its longest series of rulings on this freedom—those involving the antisubversive programs of the cold war era—the Court labored to strike the proper balance. Traced decision by decision, the constitutional freedom is ill defined. But by the end of that effort in the 1960s, the Court was firm on one point: guilt by association is impermissible. A person must not be found guilty simply because he or she belongs to a particular group. A government-imposed penalty is proper only after it is shown that the association involves active, knowing participation in efforts to bring about violent revolution.

The nation's first internal security laws were enacted within the same decade as the Bill of Rights. The Alien and Sedition Acts of 1798 set severe penalties for persons found guilty of criticizing the government or government officials. Convictions under these laws—some obtained before Supreme Court justices sitting as circuit judges—aroused public indignation, but the laws expired before they were ever challenged before the Supreme Court itself.

During the Civil War, military officials imposed many restrictions upon individual rights and expression. But, again, the constitutionality of those actions was never questioned before the Court.

The Supreme Court first found itself face to face with the question of permissible government restrictions upon political belief and expression in 1919. During World War I, Congress passed the Espionage Act of 1917 and the Sedition Act of 1918 to penalize persons who spoke or published statements with the intent of interfering with the nation's military success. In addition, persons who brought the flag, the Constitution, the government, or the military uniform into disrepute, or who promoted the cause of the enemy, could be charged under the act. Hundreds of persons were convicted.

In a series of cases decided after the end of the war, the Court upheld these laws but began to formulate tests to gauge when such restriction of speech and expression was permissible and when it was not.[2]

Concern about the threat of communism intensified after World War II, sparking the passage of federal laws intended to protect the nation against communist subversion. These laws restricted the exercise—by persons holding certain views—of the freedom of political belief, expression, and association. In cases arising under these laws, the modern Court attempted to reconcile the demands of political freedom with the requirements of internal security.

The famous if often-disregarded "clear and present danger" test for determining when official restriction or punishment may be imposed upon the exercise of the right to speak was set out by the Court in 1919 in *Schenck v. United States*. Schenck was convicted under the Espionage Act for mailing circulars to men eligible for the military draft. The circulars urged them to resist the draft, which he described as unconstitutional despotism.

Although the Court upheld his conviction, finding that his actions constituted a clear and present threat that illegal action would result, it did set out the new standard.

Writing for the unanimous Court, Justice Oliver Wendell Holmes Jr. declared:

The most stringent protection of free speech would not protect a man in falsely shouting fire in a theatre and causing a panic. It does not even protect a man from an injunction against uttering words that may have all the effect of force. . . . The question in every case is whether the words used are used in such circumstances and are of such a nature as to create a clear and present danger that they will bring about the substantive evils that Congress has a right to prevent.[3]

Later in 1919—and again in 1920—Holmes dissented with Justice Louis D. Brandeis when the Court upheld three more convictions under the World War I espionage and sedition acts. In these cases, to the dismay of Holmes and Brandeis, the Court relaxed its standard for government curtailment of free expression of political ideas.

In *Schaefer v. United States* (1920) the majority espoused the view that the "bad tendency" of an individual's speech or action, rather than the actual threat of danger, was sufficient to justify punishment. The new test, stated the majority, did not require that an utterance's "effect or the persons affected . . . be shown. . . . The tendency of the articles and their efficacy were enough for offense."[4]

In dissent Justice Brandeis opposed this "bad tendency" test both because it eliminated consideration of the speaker's intent and because it ignored the relevance of the likelihood that danger would result. The clear and present danger test, he said,

is a rule of reason. Correctly applied, it will preserve the right of free speech both from suppression by tyrannous majorities and from abuse by irresponsible, fanatical minorities.[5]

The 1920s were a period of intolerance in the United States. Many states, following the example of Congress, passed laws penalizing persons for expressing or acting upon views of political

In this 1918 cartoon Uncle Sam rounds up enemies of the United States. During World War I, Congress passed an amendment to the Espionage Act of 1917, imposing severe penalties on speech that interfered with the prosecution of the war. The Court ruled in *Schenck v. United States* (1919) that Schenck's words raised a "clear and present danger" and were not protected by the First Amendment.

truth that were perceived as subversive. In 1925 and again in 1927 the Court upheld convictions of persons holding such views. In both instances, Holmes and Brandeis disagreed with the majority's view that the clear and present danger test had no application at all to laws that punished advocacy of the forcible overthrow of government.

In *Gitlow v. New York* the Court in 1925 upheld the conviction of Benjamin Gitlow, a leader of the left wing of the Socialist Party. Gitlow violated provisions of the New York criminal anarchy statute by publishing thousands of copies of a manifesto setting out his beliefs.

In this case the Court for the first time assumed that the First Amendment freedoms of speech and the press—protected from abridgment by Congress—were also among the fundamental personal liberties protected by the Fourteenth Amendment against impairment by the states. But the Court made clear that the First Amendment "does not confer an absolute right to speak or publish, without responsibility, whatever one may choose."[6]

Challenges to state laws alleged to restrict the freedom of speech or the press must overcome a strong presumption in favor of the constitutionality of state legislation, the Court said. If the state thought the statute necessary, and the Court agreed, then the only other question was whether the language used or the action punished was prohibited by the state law.

In 1927 the Court upheld the conviction of Anita Whitney—who happened to be the niece of former Supreme Court justice Stephen J. Field—for violating the California Syndicalism Act of 1919 by her part in organizing the California Communist Labor Party. Whitney had participated in the convention setting up the state party and was an alternate member of its state executive committee. With the decision in *Whitney v. California,* the majority of the Court appeared to allow persons to be punished simply for associating with groups that espoused potentially illegal acts.

Justices Holmes and Brandeis agreed in upholding the conviction, because the clear and present danger test had not been used as part of Whitney's defense at trial. But in a concurring opinion that often read like a dissent, Brandeis challenged laws that exalted order over liberty:

Those who won our independence by revolution were not cowards. They did not fear political change. They did not exalt order at the cost of liberty. To courageous, self-reliant men, with confidence in the power of free and fearless reasoning applied through the processes of popular government, no danger flowing from speech can be deemed clear and present, unless the incidence of the evil apprehended is so imminent that it may befall before there is opportunity for full discussion. If there be time to expose through discussion the falsehood and fallacies, to avert the evil by the processes of education, the remedy to be applied is more speech, not enforced silence. Only an emergency can justify repression. Such must be the rule if authority is to be reconciled with freedom.[7]

During the 1930s the Supreme Court, now under the leadership of Chief Justice Charles Evans Hughes, extended *Gitlow's* protection of First Amendment freedoms against state action, while it repudiated the guilt-by-association rule it seemed to adopt in *Whitney.*

In 1931 the Court reversed the conviction of Yetta Stromberg, a supervisor in a youth camp operated by the Young Communist League in California, for violating the state law prohibiting display of a red flag as an "emblem of opposition to organized government." Such a flag was raised by Stromberg each morning at the camp for a flag-salute ceremony. In holding the state law invalid under the due process guarantee of the Fourteenth Amendment, the Court ignored Stromberg's Communist Party affiliation.[8]

Six years later, in 1937, the Court overturned the conviction of Dirk DeJonge for violating Oregon's criminal syndicalism law when he presided over a public meeting called by the Communist Party to protest police brutality in a longshoremen's strike. That same year the Court reversed the conviction of a communist organizer in Georgia for attempting to recruit members and distributing literature about the party.[9]

In each case the Court focused upon the actions of the individual, emphasizing personal guilt rather than guilt by association. In the Court's opinion in DeJonge's case, Chief Justice Hughes wrote that the state could not punish a person making a lawful speech simply because the speech was sponsored by an allegedly "subversive" organization.

Hughes's opinion made no reference to the clear and present

danger test. He assumed that incitement to violence would not be protected by the First Amendment. The unanimous Court opinion affirmed the political value of the rights of free speech and association:

The greater the importance of safeguarding the community from incitements to the overthrow of our institutions by force and violence, the more imperative is the need to preserve inviolate the constitutional rights of free speech, free press and free assembly in order to maintain the opportunity for free political discussion, to the end that government may be responsive to the will of the people and that changes, if desired, may be obtained by peaceful means. Therein lies the security of the Republic, the very foundation of constitutional government. . . . The question, if the rights of free speech and peaceable assembly are to be preserved, is not as to the auspices under which the meeting is held but as to its purpose; not as to the relations of the speakers, but whether their utterances transcend the bounds of the freedom of speech.[10]

Communism and Cold War

World communism posed a double-edged threat to the survival of the American system. Militarily, the spread of communist-dominated regimes across the globe posed the most serious external challenge the West had ever faced. And ideologically, the appeal of communist theory to some in the United States resulted in enactment of laws intended to curtail the advocacy of those ideas and penalize those who espoused them. Some observers of this reaction wondered if legislators at home would in fact strangle the very freedoms that military and diplomatic personnel abroad were working to preserve.

Justice William O. Douglas expressed this concern in 1951:

In days of great tension when feelings run high, it is a temptation to take shortcuts by borrowing from the totalitarian techniques of our opponents. But when we do, we set in motion a subversive influence of our own design that destroys us from within.[11]

The three major federal laws enacted to discourage the growth of communist-affiliated organizations in the United States were the Smith Act of 1940, the McCarran Act of 1950, and the Communist Control Act of 1954.

The Smith Act made it a crime to advocate the violent overthrow of the government or to organize or to belong to any group advocating such revolutionary action. The McCarran Act required all communist-action groups or communist-front groups to register with the Justice Department and disclose their membership lists. The act further penalized members of such groups by prohibiting them from holding government or defense-related jobs or using U.S. passports.

The Communist Control Act of 1954 declared that the Communist Party was an instrument of treasonable conspiracy against the U.S. government and thus deprived of all the rights and privileges of political parties and legal entities in the United States.

Debate over the constitutionality of these laws—and the loyalty-security programs and oath requirements that accompanied them—resounded frequently in the nation's courtrooms,

---

ALIENS AND COMMUNIST PARTY MEMBERSHIP

Congress, by virtue of its control over immigration and naturalization, has virtually unlimited power to regulate the activities of aliens in the United States and to deport those it finds undesirable. But in several decisions the modern Supreme Court has curtailed this power when it was used to penalize aliens for membership in the Communist Party.

Party membership alone—without evidence of the member's advocacy of forcible or violent overthrow of the government—was insufficient reason to revoke an individual's naturalization, the Court ruled in 1943. By a 6–3 vote in *Schneiderman v. United States,* the Court reversed the government's decision to revoke naturalization papers granted to William Schneiderman in 1927 when he was a member of the Communist Party.[1]

The Alien Registration Act of 1940 provided for deportation of aliens who were members of the party. In 1952 the Court upheld the application of this provision even to aliens whose membership had terminated before the 1940 law took effect.[2] Congress included similar provisions in the Internal Security Act of 1950 and the Immigration and Nationality Act of 1952.

In 1954 the Court upheld deportation of a resident alien because of his Communist Party membership, even though it was not clear that he was aware of the party's advocacy of the violent overthrow of the government. Congress, said the Court, had virtually unrestricted power to deport aliens.[3]

But in 1957 and 1963 the Court applied stricter standards to similar deportation decisions. In *Rowoldt v. Perfetto* and *Gastelum-Quinones v. Kennedy,* the Court required the government to prove not only that the alien was a member of the party but also that he understood the political implications of that membership before it might permissibly order him to leave the country.[4]

Writing for the Court in *Gastelum-Quinones,* Justice Arthur J. Goldberg explained:

[T]here is a great practical and legal difference between those who firmly attach themselves to the Communist Party being aware of all of the aims and purposes attributed to it, and those who temporarily join the Party, knowing nothing of its international relationships and believing it to be a group solely trying to remedy unsatisfactory social or economic conditions, carry out trade-union objectives, eliminate racial discrimination, combat unemployment, or alleviate distress and poverty.[5]

1. *Schneiderman v. United States,* 320 U.S. 118 (1943).
2. *Harisiades v. Shaughnessy,* 342 U.S. 580 (1952).
3. *Galvan v. Press,* 347 U.S. 522 (1954).
4. *Rowoldt v. Perfetto,* 355 U.S. 115 (1957); *Gastelum-Quinones v. Kennedy,* 374 U.S. 469 (1963).
5. *Gastelum-Quinones v. Kennedy,* 374 U.S. 469 at 473 (1963).

---

including that of the Supreme Court. Views of communism differed. Was it a valid political movement, espousal of which and association with which was protected by the First Amendment? Or was it a treasonable conspiracy, which the Constitution itself viewed as punishable?[12]

In the first decade of the cold war, 1947 to 1957, the Supreme

Court—reflecting the mood of the nation—generally upheld the provisions and application of the anticommunism laws. In so doing, the majority avoided ruling directly on the challenge that they impermissibly abridged the First Amendment guarantee of freedom of political association.

Then, beginning in 1957, as the cold war thawed, the Court began to restrict their application, finding them often used in too sweeping a fashion. The Constitution specifies that no one shall be found guilty of treason without evidence of overt treasonous acts. The Supreme Court began to insist that these internal security laws be used only to penalize persons who knowingly and actively sought to promote communist revolution in the United States, not simply to punish persons who had at some time found other social and economic or philosophical tenets of the movement attractive.

In the decade from 1957 through 1967, a libertarian majority coalesced on the Court under Chief Justice Earl Warren. Its decisions forced the government to cease prosecuting persons under the Smith Act, to abandon its effort to force registration of the Communist Party and other communist-affiliated groups, and to cease denying passports and defense industry jobs to members of such groups.

Although the Court had earlier condoned the use of loyalty oaths by state and local governments attempting to ensure the loyalty of their employees, it now struck many of them down as improper restrictions upon the freedom to believe and to speak freely and to associate with others of like belief.

Article VI of the Constitution requires state and federal officeholders to swear to uphold the Constitution of the United States. Congress and state legislatures during the cold war era in particular imposed other oaths deemed appropriate as a condition of public office.

THE SMITH ACT

The Alien Registration Act of 1940 required all aliens living in the United States to register with the government; any found to have past ties to "subversive organizations" could be deported. *(See box, Aliens and Communist Party Membership, p. 534.)* The act was known as the Smith Act after its sponsor, Rep. Howard Smith, D-Va. (1931–1967). Title I of the act affected citizens as well as aliens. Intended to thwart communist activity in the United States, the measure was the nation's first peacetime sedition law since the infamous Sedition Act of 1798. Yet it attracted little attention at the time of its passage in 1940. Thomas I. Emerson observed that "enactment of the bill reflected not so much a deliberate national determination that the measure was necessary to protect internal security as an unwillingness of members of Congress to vote against legislation directed at the Communist Party."[13]

The Smith Act made it a crime "to knowingly or willfully advocate, abet, advise, or teach the duty, necessity, desirability, or propriety of overthrowing or destroying any government in the United States by force or violence." It forbade the publication or display of printed matter teaching or advocating forcible over-

throw of the government. And in language directly curtailing the freedom of association, the law made it a crime to organize any group teaching, advocating, or encouraging the overthrow or destruction of government by force. It also was a crime to become a "knowing" member of any organization or group dedicated to the violent overthrow of any government in the United States.

In 1948 the government indicted eleven leaders of the Communist Party in the United States, charging them with violating the Smith Act by conspiring to form groups teaching the overthrow of the government. The eleven were convicted after a long and sensational trial.

In upholding the convictions, Judge Learned Hand spoke for the federal court of appeals and used a "sliding scale" rule for applying the clear and present danger test in sedition cases: "In each case [courts] must ask whether the gravity of the 'evil,' discounted by its improbability, justifies such invasion of free speech as is necessary to avoid the danger."[14]

The Act Upheld: Dennis

In 1951 the Supreme Court by a vote of 6–2 upheld the convictions—and the constitutionality of the Smith Act. Justice Tom C. Clark did not take part in the Court's decision in *Dennis v. United States.* The eight voting members of the Court disagreed widely over the proper way to measure the validity of sedition laws against the restraints they placed on First Amendment freedoms of expression and association.

The Majority Justices Chief Justice Fred M. Vinson, speaking for Justices Stanley F. Reed, Harold H. Burton, and Sherman Minton, gave lip service to the clear and present danger test from *Schenck* but seemed in fact to apply the "sliding scale" rule. The Smith Act, wrote Vinson, did not allow persons to be punished simply for peaceful study and discussion of revolutionary concepts: "Congress did not intend to eradicate the free discussion of political theories, to destroy the traditional rights of Americans to discuss and evaluate ideas without fear of governmental sanction."[15] But, he wrote:

Overthrow of the Government by force and violence is certainly a substantial enough interest for the Government to limit speech. Indeed, this is the ultimate value of any society, for if a society cannot protect its very structure from armed internal attack, it must follow that no subordinate value can be protected. If, then, this interest may be protected, the literal problem which is presented is what has been meant by the use of the phrase "clear and present danger" of the utterances bringing about the evil within the power of Congress to punish.

Obviously, the words cannot mean that before the Government may act, it must wait until the putsch is about to be executed, the plans have been laid and the signal is awaited. If Government is aware that a group aiming at its overthrow is attempting to indoctrinate its members and to commit them to a course whereby they will strike when the leaders feel the circumstances permit, action by the Government is required. . . . Certainly an attempt to overthrow the Government by force, even though doomed from the outset because of inadequate numbers or power of the revolutionists is a sufficient evil for Congress to prevent. . . .

The damage which such attempts create both physically and politi-

Eleven leaders of the American Communist Party were arrested and jailed in 1951 after Congress passed the Smith Act, which made it illegal to belong to a subversive organization. In *Dennis v. United States* (1951) Chief Justice Fred M. Vinson upheld the act by reason that the threat of communism justified a restriction on the rights of free expression.

cally to a nation makes it impossible to measure the validity in terms of the probability of success. . . .

The formation . . . of such a highly organized conspiracy, with rigidly disciplined members subject to call when the leaders . . . felt that the time had come for action, coupled with the inflammable nature of world conditions . . . convince us that their convictions were justified. . . . And this analysis disposes of the contention that a conspiracy to advocate, as distinguished from the advocacy itself, cannot be constitutionally restrained, because it comprises only the preparation. It is the existence of the conspiracy which creates the danger. . . . If the ingredients of the reaction are present we cannot bind the Government to wait until the catalyst is added. . . .

. . . Petitioners intended to overthrow the Government of the United States as speedily as the circumstances would permit. Their conspiracy to organize the Communist Party and to teach and advocate the overthrow of the Government of the United States by force and violence created a "clear and present danger" of an attempt to overthrow the Government by force and violence. They were properly and constitutionally convicted for violation of the Smith Act.[16]

Concurring, Justice Felix Frankfurter observed:

Suppressing advocates of overthrow inevitably will also silence critics who do not advocate overthrow but fear that their criticism may be so construed. No matter how clear we may be that the defendants now before us are preparing to overthrow our Government at the propitious moment, it is self-delusion to think that we can punish them for their advocacy without adding to the risks run by loyal citizens who honestly believe in some of the reforms these defendants advance. It is a sobering fact that in sustaining the convictions before us we can hardly escape restriction on the interchange of ideas.[17]

First Amendment guarantees must be balanced against the nation's need to protect itself, Frankfurter stated:

The appellants maintain that they have a right to advocate a political theory, so long, at least, as their advocacy does not create an immediate

danger of obvious magnitude to the very existence of our present scheme of society. On the other hand, the Government asserts the right to safeguard the security of the Nation by such a measure as the Smith Act. Our judgment is thus solicited on a conflict of interests of the utmost concern to the well-being of the country.[18]

The responsibility for reconciling this conflict of values lay primarily with Congress, not the Court, wrote Frankfurter. The Court should set aside the laws reflecting the judgment of Congress in such matters only if it found no reasonable basis for the judgment, or if it found the law too indefinite to meet the demands of due process or breaching the separation of powers. The Court was responsible for ensuring fair procedures in the enforcement of the law and for requiring substantial proof to justify conviction, but "[b]eyond these powers we must not go; we must scrupulously observe the narrow limits of judicial authority even though self-restraint is alone set over us."[19]

Justice Robert H. Jackson, in his concurring opinion, declared that the clear and present danger test was inadequate when applied to laws intended to curtail the spread of the communist conspiracy:

The authors of the clear and present danger test never applied it to a case like this, nor would I. If applied as it is proposed here, it means that the Communist plotting is protected during its period of incubation; its preliminary stages of organization and preparation are immune from the law; the Government can move only after imminent action is manifest, when it would, of course, be too late.[20]

The law of conspiracy was "an awkward and inept remedy" when applied to the threat of subversion presented by the Communist Party, which Jackson described as "a state within a state, an authoritarian dictatorship within a republic." But despite the awkwardness of the instrument, Jackson wrote, he

POLITICS AND THE RIGHT TO A PASSPORT

Cold war legislation forbade any member of the Communist Party to apply for a U.S. passport, but that was not the first time this privilege had been denied to people who seemed ideologically out of line with prevailing U.S. thought. The Passport Act of 1926, the basis for modern passport administration, authorized the State Department to deny travel documents to applicants with criminal records and to noncitizens.

From 1917 until 1931 passports generally were refused to members of the American Communist Party. During the cold war, the State Department resumed the practice. The 1950 McCarran Act forbade members of any registered communist political action or front organization to apply for or use a passport.

Although the registration provisions were successfully resisted, the State Department nevertheless denied passports to a number of individuals thought to be communists, acting under its own rules and the discretion granted it by the Immigration and Nationality Act of 1952.

FREEDOM TO TRAVEL

In *Kent v. Dulles* (1958) the Supreme Court held that Congress had not authorized the secretary of state to deny passports to persons because of their beliefs or associations. Furthermore, held the Court, the right to travel is an aspect of a citizen's protected personal liberty of which he cannot be deprived without due process.

The Court, 5–4, reversed the State Department's denial of a passport to artist Rockwell Kent, who refused to submit an affidavit disclaiming any affiliation with communist groups.

Justice William O. Douglas wrote:

[W]e are dealing here with citizens who have neither been accused of crimes or found guilty. They are being denied their freedom of movement solely because of their refusal to be subjected to inquiry into their beliefs and associations. They do not seek to escape the law nor to violate it. They may or may not be Communists. But assuming they are, the only law which Congress has passed expressly curtailing the movement of Communists across our borders has not yet become effective. It would therefore be strange to infer that pending the effectiveness of that law, the Secretary has been silently granted by Congress the larger, the more pervasive power to curtail in his discretion the free movement of citizens in order to satisfy himself about their beliefs or associations.[1]

The dissenting justices—Harold H. Burton, John Marshall Harlan, Charles E. Whittaker, and Tom C. Clark—found the denial proper.

In the wake of *Kent,* the Eisenhower administration asked Congress to authorize the State Department to deny passports to persons with communist affiliations. Congress did not do so.[2]

The Court's decision in 1961 in *Communist Party v. Subversive Activities Control Board* upheld the order to the party to register under the McCarran Act and made operative the provisions of the act that denied passports to Communist Party members. *(See details of this case, pp. 542–543.)*

The State Department revoked the passports of several leading communists including Herbert Aptheker, one of the party's leading intellectuals. In its 1964 decision in *Aptheker v. Secretary of State*, the Court, 6–3, declared the passport denial provisions of the McCarran Act unconstitutional as infringements of the freedom to travel.

Writing for the majority, Justice Arthur J. Goldberg explained that the law violated the guarantee of due process by failing to distinguish between knowing and unknowing party membership and by arbitrarily excluding any consideration of the purpose of the proposed travel.[3] Justices Harlan, Clark, and Byron R. White dissented.

The following year the Court in *Zemel v. Rusk* upheld the power of the State Department to impose geographic area limitations on the use of U.S. passports.[4] But subsequent decisions made clear that such limitations, forbidding Americans to travel to certain countries, although valid are unenforceable.[5]

FREEDOM TO TRAVEL DENIED

In 1981 the Court in *Haig v. Agee* upheld the power of the secretary of state to revoke a citizen's passport. Philip Agee was not a communist but a former Central Intelligence Agency official who had become disillusioned with the agency. He had worked as an undercover CIA agent and undertook, upon leaving the agency, to expose CIA agents abroad in order to drive them out of the countries where they were working.

The secretary of state revoked Agee's passport, stating that his activities caused serious damage to national security. Agee challenged the revocation as a violation of his First Amendment right to criticize the government, but the Court decided against him, 7–2.[6]

1. *Kent v. Dulles*, 357 U.S. 117 at 130 (1958).
2. *Congress and the Nation*, Vol. I (Washington, D.C.: Congressional Quarterly, 1965), 1650.
3. *Aptheker v. Secretary of State*, 378 U.S. 500 (1964).
4. *Zemel v. Rusk*, 381 U.S. 1 (1965).
5. *United States v. Laub*, 385 U.S. 475 (1967); *Travis v. United States*, 385 U.S. 491 (1967).
6. *Haig v. Agee*, 453 U.S. 280 (1981).

found no constitutional reason for denying the government its use: "There is no constitutional right to gang up on the Government."[21]

The Dissenters. Justices Hugo L. Black and William Douglas dissented. Black argued that the conspiracy section of the Smith Act should be held void as a prior restraint on the exercise of First Amendment freedoms of speech and the press.

Black noted that the eleven communist leaders had not been charged with an actual attempt to overthrow the government but only with agreeing "to assemble and to talk and publish certain ideas at a later date. The indictment is that they conspired to organize the Communist Party and to use speech or newspapers ... to teach and advocate the forcible overthrow of the Government. No matter how it is worded, this is a virulent form of prior censorship of speech and press, which I believe the First Amendment forbids."[22]

Douglas also reminded his colleagues that the defendants were not on trial for conspiring to overthrow the government but only for organizing groups advocating its overthrow. He warned of the "vice of treating speech as the equivalent of overt acts of a treasonable or seditious character," noting that the Constitution allowed punishment for treason only upon evidence of overt treasonable acts:

[N]ever until today has anyone seriously thought that the ancient law of conspiracy could constitutionally be used to turn speech into seditious conduct. Yet that is precisely what is suggested. . . . We deal here with speech alone, not with speech plus acts of sabotage or unlawful conduct. Not a single seditious act is charged in the indictment. . . .

Free speech has occupied an exalted position because of the high service it has given our society. Its protection is essential to the very existence of a democracy. . . . We have founded our political system on it. It has been the safeguard of every religious, political, philosophical, economic, and racial group amongst us. We have counted on it to keep us from embracing what is cheap and false; we have trusted the common sense of our people to choose the doctrine true to our genius and to reject the rest. . . . We have above all else feared the political censor. . . .

There comes a time when even speech loses its constitutional immunity. Speech innocuous one year may at another time fan such destructive flames that it must be halted in the interests of the safety of the Republic. That is the meaning of the clear and present danger test. When conditions are so critical that there will be no time to avoid the evil that the speech threatens, it is time to call a halt. Otherwise, free speech which is the strength of the Nation will be the cause of its destruction.

Yet free speech is the rule, not the exception. The restraint to be constitutional must be based on more than fear, on more than passionate opposition . . . on more than a revolted dislike for its contents. . . .

Free speech—the glory of our system of government—should not be sacrificed on anything less than plain and objective proof of danger that the evil advocated is imminent. On this record no one can say that petitioners and their converts are in such a strategic position as to have even the slightest chance of achieving their aims.[23]

In the wake of the *Dennis* decision, new conspiracy prosecutions under the Smith Act were brought involving 121 defendants—all second-rank officials in the U.S. Communist Party. Other prosecutions were brought against individuals for their party membership. Convictions were secured in every case brought to trial between 1951 and 1956. The courts of appeal affirmed the convictions and the Supreme Court denied petitions for review.

Strict Standards of Proof: Yates

Late in 1955, however, the Court agreed to review the convictions of fourteen persons charged with Smith Act violations. The decision of the Court in these cases, generally known by the name of one, *Yates v. United States,* was announced in June 1957. By imposing strict standards of proof upon the government in such prosecutions, the Court effectively curtailed further use of the Smith Act to prosecute members of the U.S. Communist Party.

The decision marked a major shift in the Court's attitude toward the Smith Act, although it left untouched its earlier declaration in *Dennis* that the act was constitutional.

This cartoon, published June 28, 1957, illustrated popular opinion that a Supreme Court's decision regarding alleged subversives was based on legal technicalities.

The defendants who brought before the Court the cases of *Yates v. United States, Schneiderman v. United States,* and *Richmond v. United States* were charged with organizing and participating in a conspiracy, namely the Communist Party of the United States, to advocate the overthrow of the government by force.

By a 6–1 vote the Supreme Court in *Yates* found that the government had waited too long to indict these persons for their involvement in the organization of the party in the United States, that the trial judge had erred in his instructions to the jury concerning what they must find to convict the defendants on the advocacy charges, and that the evidence in several cases was insufficient to prove the charges. The Court reversed all the convictions, acquitting those of the defendants against whom the evidence was insufficient and ordering new trials for the others.

Not participating in the ruling were Justice William J. Brennan Jr. and Justice Charles E. Whittaker.[24]

The majority took a narrow view of the scope of the Smith Act provision making it unlawful to organize a group advocating violent overthrow of the government. The majority, explained Justice John Marshall Harlan in the Court's opinion, defined "organize" with respect to the formation of the U.S. Communist Party as an activity that took place in 1945 with the party's founding in this country, rejecting the government's definition of "organize" as an ongoing process. Because the defendants were not indicted on this charge until 1951, the three-year statute of limitations on such charges rendered that part of the indictment invalid, held the Court.

Harlan wrote:

Stated most simply, the problem is to choose between two possible answers to the question: when was the Communist Party "organized"? Petitioners contend that the only natural answer to the question is the formation date—in this case, 1945. The Government would have us answer the question by saying that the Party today is still not completely "organized"; that "organizing" is a continuing process that does not end until the entity is dissolved. . . .

We conclude . . . that since the Communist Party came into being in 1945, and the indictment was not returned until 1951, the three-year statute of limitations had run on the "organizing" charge, and required the withdrawal of that part of the indictment from the jury's consideration.[25]

Furthermore, held the Court, the trial judge had misinterpreted the Court's meaning in the *Dennis* decision when he instructed the jury. He failed to distinguish properly between advocacy of an abstract doctrine, a protected activity, and advocacy intended to promote unlawful action, a punishable activity under the Smith Act. In restating Vinson's ruling in *Dennis*, Justice Harlan discarded the clear and present danger test altogether. In *Dennis*, he wrote, the punishable advocacy did not create any danger of immediate revolution but "was aimed at building up a seditious group and maintaining it in readiness for action at a propitious time."[26]

Harlan continued:

In failing to distinguish between advocacy of forcible overthrow as an abstract doctrine and advocacy of action to that end, the District Court appears to have been led astray by the holding in *Dennis* that advocacy of violent action to be taken at some future time was enough. . . . The District Court apparently thought that *Dennis* obliterated the traditional dividing line between advocacy of abstract doctrine and advocacy of action. . . .

The essence of the *Dennis* holding was that indoctrination of a group in preparation for future violent action, as well as exhortation to immediate action, by advocacy found to be directed to "action for the accomplishment" of forcible overthrow, to violence as "a rule or principle of action," and employing "language of incitement," . . . is not constitutionally protected when the group is of sufficient size and cohesiveness, is sufficiently oriented towards action, and other circumstances are such as reasonable to justify apprehension that action will occur.

This is quite a different thing from the view of the District Court here that mere doctrinal justification of forcible overthrow, if engaged in with the intent to accomplish overthrow, is punishable *per se* under the Smith Act. That sort of advocacy, even though uttered with the hope that it may ultimately lead to violent revolution, is too remote from concrete action to be regarded as the kind of indoctrination preparatory to action which was condemned in *Dennis*. . . .

The essential distinction is that those to whom the advocacy is addressed must be urged to do something, now or in the future, rather than merely to believe in something. . . .

We recognize that distinctions between advocacy and teaching of abstract doctrines, with evil intent, and that which is directed to stirring people to action, are often subtle and difficult to grasp, for in a broad sense, as Mr. Justice Holmes said . . . , "Every idea is an incitement." But the very subtlety of these distinctions required the most clear and explicit instructions with reference to them.[27]

The Court, wrote Harlan, also found the evidence of advocacy geared to action deficient in a number of the cases: "however much one may abhor even the abstract preaching of forcible overthrow or believe that forcible overthrow is the ultimate purpose to which the Communist Party is dedicated, it is upon the evidence in the record that the petitioners must be judged in this case."[28]

Justices Black and Douglas concurred in part and dissented in part. Both felt that all the prosecutions of these defendants should be dropped because the Smith Act provisions upon which the charges were based "abridge freedom of speech, press and assembly in violation of the First Amendment."[29]

"I believe that the First Amendment forbids Congress to punish people for talking about public affairs, whether or not such discussion incites to action, legal or illegal," Black wrote.[30]

In a separate dissenting opinion Justice Clark said that all of the convictions should be upheld, in line with *Dennis*. Clark noted that although the communists in *Yates* were lower in the hierarchy than those defendants in *Dennis*, they served "in the same army and were engaged in the same mission."[31]

The *Yates* requirement that the government show a connection between advocacy and action, between participation in the Communist Party and forcible overthrow of the government, ended most Smith Act prosecutions. The government decided to drop charges against those of the *Yates* defendants who, in light of the Court's ruling, could have been retried.

Membership Prosecutions

Despite the Court's narrow view of the Smith Act's "organizing" and "advocating" provisions, prosecutions remained possible under the clause that forbade "knowing" membership in any group advocating forcible overthrow of the government. When coupled with the registration provisions of the 1950 McCarran Act, this provision seemed to constitute compulsory self-incrimination in violation of the Fifth Amendment guarantee against such coercion. *(See "The McCarran Act," pp. 541–544.)*

In 1961 the Supreme Court for the first time reviewed convictions of persons under the membership clause of the Smith Act. In those rulings, the Court upheld the constitutionality of the provision but measured the government's proof in such cases against the strict *Yates* standard of evidence.

In the case of *Scales v. United States,* the Court affirmed the conviction of Junius Scales, director of a communist training school, and upheld the constitutionality of the membership clause. The vote was 5–4. Chief Justice Warren and Justices Black, Douglas, and Brennan dissented.

Justice Harlan, the spokesman for the majority as he had been in *Yates*, distinguished between active, "knowing" membership and passive, merely nominal membership in a subversive organization.

One of the few provisions of the original Constitution affecting individual rights is this terse sentence in Article I, Section 9: "No Bill of Attainder or ex post facto Law shall be passed."

Only three acts of Congress have been held to be bills of attainder, and one of those is the only instance in which the Court has found that Congress passed an ex post facto law. A bill of attainder, stated the Court in 1867, is "a legislative act which inflicts punishment without a judicial trial."[1] An ex post facto law makes an action a crime after it has already been committed or otherwise penalizes some past action.

EX PARTE GARLAND

In that year, with its ruling in *Ex parte Garland*, the Court struck down a law enacted in 1865 that barred attorneys from practicing before federal courts unless they swore an oath that they had remained loyal to the Union throughout the Civil War. Persons who swore falsely could be charged with and convicted of perjury.

A. H. Garland of Arkansas had been admitted to practice law before the federal courts during the 1860 Supreme Court term. When Arkansas seceded from the Union, Garland went with his state, becoming first a representative and later a senator in the Confederate Congress.

He received a full pardon in 1865 from President Andrew Johnson for his service to the Confederacy. In *Ex parte Garland* he argued that he should be allowed to resume his federal practice without taking the required oath.[2]

The Supreme Court agreed with him, 5–4, finding the test oath requirement invalid as a bill of attainder.

Justice Stephen J. Field explained that lawyers who had served the Confederacy could not take the oath without perjuring themselves. Therefore,

the act, as against them, operates as a legislative decree of perpetual exclusion. And exclusion from any of the professions or any of the ordinary avocations of life for past conduct can be regarded in no other light than as punishment for such conduct.[3]

In addition, the Court held the test oath invalid as an ex post facto law, prohibiting attorneys from practicing before a federal court if they did not take the oath—and thus punishing them for past acts not defined as illegal at the time they were committed.

UNITED STATES V. LOVETT

Almost eighty years passed before the Court again applied the bill of attainder clause to hold a law invalid. The 1946 case of *United States v. Lovett* arose after Rep. Martin Dies, D-Texas (1931–1945, 1953–1959), chairman of the House Committee on Un-American Activities, listed thirty-nine federal employees as "irresponsible, unrepresentative, crackpot, radical bureaucrats" who were affiliated with "communist front organizations."

Dies urged that Congress refuse to appropriate the funds necessary to pay these employees' salaries.

After a special subcommittee of the House Appropriations Committee heard testimony in secret session, it pronounced three of the thirty-nine federal employees—individuals named Lovett, Watson, and Dodd—guilty of subversive activities and unfit to hold their government jobs.

Congress then added specific language to an appropriations bill forbidding the use of any of the funds it contained to pay the salaries of the three. President Franklin D. Roosevelt signed the bill but made clear that he viewed that particular provision as an unconstitutional bill of attainder. In 1946 a majority of the Court agreed with Roosevelt.

Justice Hugo L. Black wrote that "legislative acts, no matter what their form, that apply either to named individuals or to easily ascertainable members of a group in such a way as to inflict punishment on them without a judicial trial are bills of attainder prohibited by the Constitution."[4]

UNITED STATES V. BROWN

The most recent of the Court's rulings striking down an act of Congress as a bill of attainder is the 1965 case of *United States v. Brown*, which concerned a provision of the Labor-Management Reporting and Disclosure Act of 1959.

The provision made it a crime for anyone to serve as an officer or employee of a labor union if he or she were a member of the Communist Party or had been a member at any time in the previous five years.[5]

Designed to prevent politically motivated strikes, the provision replaced a section of the Taft-Hartley Act of 1947 that had required unions seeking access to the National Labor Relations Board to file affidavits swearing that none of the union's officers was a member of or affiliated with the Communist Party.

In 1950 the Court had upheld that requirement.[6] *(See "Labor Affidavit Upheld," pp. 546–547.)*

The Court, however, found the successor provision unconstitutional as a bill of attainder. "The statute," wrote Chief Justice Earl Warren, "designates in no uncertain terms the persons who possess the feared characteristics and therefore cannot hold union office without incurring criminal liability—members of the Communist Party."[7]

Brown differed from *Douds*, Warren said, because the Taft-Hartley provision could be escaped by persons who resigned from the Communist Party. The newer provision applied to persons who had been members of the party before its enactment.[8]

1. *Cummings v. Missouri*, 4 Wall. 277 (1867).
2. *Ex parte Garland*, 4 Wall. 333 (1867).
3. Id. at 377.
4. *United States v. Lovett*, 328 U.S. 303 at 315 (1946).
5. *United States v. Brown*, 381 U.S. 437 (1965).
6. *American Communications Association v. Douds*, 339 U.S. 382 (1950).
7. *United States v. Brown*, 381 U.S. 437 at 450 (1965).
8. Id. at 457–458.

The membership clause, properly applied, did not violate the First Amendment guarantees of free political expression and association, he explained. In *Dennis* the Court had established two points in that regard:

the advocacy with which we are here concerned is not constitutionally protected speech, and . . . that a combination to promote such advocacy, albeit under the aegis of what purports to be a political party, is not such association as is protected by the First Amendment.

We can discern no reason why membership, when it constitutes a purposeful form of complicity in a group engaging in this same forbidden advocacy, should receive any greater degree of protection from the guarantees of that amendment.[32]

Harlan continued:

The clause does not make criminal all association with an organization which has been shown to engage in illegal advocacy. There must be clear proof that a defendant "specifically intend[s] to accomplish [the aims of the organization] by resort to violence." . . . Thus the member for whom the organization is a vehicle for the advancement of legitimate aims and policies does not fall within the ban of the statute: he lacks the requisite specific intent "to bring about the overthrow of the government as speedily as circumstances would permit." Such a person may be foolish, deluded, or perhaps merely optimistic, but he is not by this statute made a criminal.[33]

Justices Douglas and Brennan and Chief Justice Warren based their dissent primarily on the view that the 1950 Internal Security Act specifically immunized persons from prosecution under the Smith Act membership clause.

In a separate opinion Justice Douglas charged that the Court was legalizing guilt by association, an action with which he strongly disagreed. In his separate opinion Justice Black reiterated his view that the First Amendment "absolutely forbids Congress to outlaw membership in a political party or similar association merely because one of the philosophical tenets of that group is that the existing government should be overthrown by force at some distant time in the future when circumstances may permit."[34]

In a companion case, *Noto v. United States*, the Court reversed the membership clause conviction of John Francis Noto, holding the evidence insufficient under the *Yates* rule to justify the conviction. Justice Harlan wrote for the unanimous Court:

[T]he mere abstract teaching of Communist theory, including the teaching of the moral propriety or even moral necessity for a resort to force and violence, is not the same as preparing a group for violent action and steeling it to such action. There must be some substantial direct or circumstantial evidence of a call to violence now or in the future which is both sufficiently strong and sufficiently pervasive to lend color to the otherwise ambiguous theoretical material regarding Communist Party teaching, and to justify the inference that such a call to violence may fairly be imputed to the Party as a whole, and not merely to some narrow segment of it.[35]

THE MCCARRAN ACT

Deeming the Smith Act insufficient protection against the domestic communist movement, Congress in 1950 approved the Internal Security Act over the veto of President Harry S. Tru-

---

THE COURT AND STATE SEDITION LAWS

Loyalty oath requirements and loyalty dismissal programs were not the only state response to concern about communist subversion. Many states during the 1940s and 1950s passed their own sedition laws to punish persons for plotting to overthrow the U.S. government.

In 1956, however, the Supreme Court held that Congress had preempted such state laws, occupying the field of federal sedition prosecutions with passage of the Smith Act of 1940, the McCarran Act of 1950, and the Communist Control Act of 1954. This decision in *Pennsylvania v. Nelson* limited state sedition statutes to punishing sedition against state or local government—not the federal government.

Steve Nelson, an avowed communist, had been convicted for violating Pennsylvania's sedition law by his words and actions concerning the federal government. He was sentenced to serve twenty years in prison and to pay a $10,000 fine and prosecution costs of $13,000. The state supreme court held that the state law had been superseded by the Smith Act—a ruling the Supreme Court upheld and extended.

Chief Justice Earl Warren surveyed the relevant provisions of the Smith, McCarran, and Communist Control Acts and declared:

[T]he conclusion is inescapable that Congress has intended to occupy the field of sedition. Taken as a whole they evince a congressional plan which makes it reasonable to determine that no room has been left for the States to supplement it.

Therefore, a state sedition statute is superseded regardless of whether it purports to supplement the federal law.[1]

"Since 1939," he noted, "in order to avoid a hampering of uniform enforcement of its program by sporadic local prosecutions, the Federal Government has urged local authorities not to intervene in such matters, but to turn over to the federal authorities immediately and unevaluated all information concerning subversive activities."[2]

Justices Stanley F. Reed, Harold H. Burton, and Sherman Minton dissented.

Following the decision, all pending proceedings under state sedition laws were dismissed or abandoned. Congress considered a measure reversing the Court's decision but did not complete action on such a bill.

In 1965 the Court further curtailed state subversion laws, holding Louisiana's Subversive Activities Criminal Control Act unconstitutionally vague.[3] And in 1969 the Court in *Brandenburg v. Ohio* struck down Ohio's Criminal Syndicalism Act, declaring illegal the use of advocacy of violence, crime, sabotage, and terrorism to accomplish industrial or political reform. This ruling overturned the Court's 1927 decision in *Whitney v. California*, upholding an almost identical California law.[4] *(See details of this case, p. 533.)*

1. *Pennsylvania v. Nelson*, 350 U.S. 497 at 504 (1956).
2. Id. at 505–506.
3. *Dombrowski v. Pfister*, 380 U.S. 479 (1965).
4. *Brandenburg v. Ohio*, 395 U.S. 444 (1969), overturning *Whitney v. California*, 274 U.S. 357 (1927).

The House Un-American Activities Committee, which reported the bill that became the McCarran Act, holds a press conference December 3, 1948, after a closed session. Standing are two committee investigators. Seated are several reporters and, left to right, Richard Nixon, R-Calif., John Rankin, D-Miss., and John McDowell, R-Pa.

man, who felt its vague language endangered First Amendment freedoms of speech, press, and assembly.

The act was known as the McCarran Act after its sponsor, Sen. Pat McCarran, D-Nev. (1933–1954). Its purpose was to expose party leaders and members of communist-front groups by requiring that all communist-front and communist-action organizations register with the attorney general. Public exposure, it was thought, would curtail the activities of such groups.

The Subversive Activities Control Act of 1950 was Title I of the McCarran Act. It established a five-member Subversive Activities Control Board (SACB), appointed by the president, to determine, subject to judicial review, whether a particular organization was a communist-action or communist-front group and whether certain individuals were among the members.

Once the SACB decided that an organization was such a communist group, the organization was required to register with the Justice Department and provide to the government lists of its officers and members. Members of registered groups were barred from federal jobs, jobs in defense-related industries, and from applying for or using U.S. passports.[36]

The penalties for failure to register were heavy fines and long prison terms. Compliance with the law, however, made the subject a likely candidate for investigation by a legislative committee or prosecution under the Smith Act. The act did state, however, that holding offices in, or being a member of, a communist organization should not in itself be a crime and that registration should not be used as evidence against a person being prosecuted for violating any criminal law.

In November 1950 the attorney general filed a petition with the SACB to compel the Communist Party of the United States to register as a communist-action organization. That action began an unsuccessful fifteen-year battle to force registration of the party. The judicial record involved three decisions by the court of appeals and two reviews by the Supreme Court. The case record included 15,000 pages of testimony and 507 documentary exhibits. The SACB twice ordered the party to register. The party appealed both orders to the courts.[37]

Registration Upheld

In 1961 the Supreme Court upheld the second registration order in an apparent victory for the government. The case of *Communist Party v. Subversive Activities Control Board* was decided by a 5–4 vote. The majority rejected the party's arguments that the registration provisions were unconstitutional as a bill of attainder and as violations of the First Amendment's guarantees of freedom.[38]

Joined by Justices Clark, Harlan, Whittaker, and Potter Stewart, Justice Frankfurter wrote one of the longest opinions in the Court's history. The evidence, he said, confirmed the SACB ruling that the party was a communist-action group within the scope of the McCarran Act registration provisions. The provisions of that law, Frankfurter declared, did not constitute a bill of attainder (a legislative act pronouncing a particular individual guilty of a crime without trial or conviction and imposing a sentence upon him). The McCarran Act

attaches not to specified organizations but to described activities in which an organization may or may not engage. The singling out of an individual for legislatively prescribed punishment constitutes an attainder whether the individual is called by name or described in terms of conduct which, because it is past conduct, operates only as a designation of particular persons. . . . The Subversive Activities Control Act is not of that kind. It requires the registration only of organizations which, after the date of the Act, are found to be under the direction, domination, or control of certain foreign powers and to operate primarily to advance certain objectives.[39]

Nor, held the majority, did the law violate First Amendment guarantees. In requiring registration Congress balanced private rights of free speech and association against the public interest in disclosure.

Where the mask of anonymity which an organization's members wear serves the double purpose of protecting them from popular prejudice and of enabling them to cover over a foreign-directed conspiracy, infiltrate into other groups, and enlist the support of persons who would not, if the truth were revealed, lend their support . . . it would be a distortion of the First Amendment to hold that it prohibits Congress from removing the mask.[40]

Frankfurter emphasized the foreign-dominated character of the Communist Party in the United States:

There is no attempt here to impose stifling obligations upon the proponents of a particular political creed as such, or even to check the importation of particular political ideas from abroad for propagation here. The Act compels the registration of organized groups which have been made the instruments of a long-continued, systematic, disciplined activity directed by a foreign power and purposing to overthrow existing government in this country.[41]

The majority found it premature to consider the challenge that the registration provisions violated the Fifth Amendment privilege against compelled self-incrimination: "No person . . . shall be compelled in any criminal case to be a witness against himself." This privilege, it pointed out, must be claimed by an individual, and it was not now evident that the party officers would make such a claim. In similar fashion, the majority refused to rule on the constitutionality of any other sanctions that might be imposed upon members of the party, once it was registered.

Chief Justice Warren and Justices Brennan, Black, and Douglas dissented in separate opinions, citing a wide variety of reasons for their disagreement with the majority.

Warren would have remanded the case to the SACB for reconsideration of credibility of the testimony of two key government witnesses.

Justice Black protested that the Subversive Activities Control Act of 1950 effectively outlawed the Communist Party, a direct violation of the First Amendment:

The first banning of an association because it advocates hated ideas—whether that association be called a political party or not—marks a fateful moment in the history of a free country. That moment seems to have arrived for this country. . . . This whole Act, with its pains and penalties, embarks this country, for the first time, on the dangerous adventure of outlawing groups that preach doctrines nearly all Americans detest. When the practice of outlawing parties and various public groups begins, no one can say where it will end. In most countries such a practice once begun ends with a one-party government.[42]

Justices Douglas and Brennan found the registration provisions in violation of the Fifth Amendment. Justice Douglas wrote:

Signing as an officer or director of the Communist Party—an ingredient of an offense that results in punishment—must be done under the mandate of law. That is compulsory incrimination of those individuals and, in my view, a plain violation of the Fifth Amendment.[43]

Enforcing Provisions Nullified

But as subsequent rulings made clear, the Court had upheld only the power of Congress under the McCarran Act to require registration of communist-front and communist-action groups; it would not give similar sanction to the implementing provisions of the act.

In 1964 the Court held invalid the passport restrictions imposed by the act on members of registered organizations. *(See box, Politics and the Right to a Passport, p. 537.)* In 1965, in the case of *Albertson v. Subversive Activities Control Board,* the Court held that the registration requirements, when applied to individuals, violated the Fifth Amendment privilege against compelled self-incrimination.

And in 1967 the Court declared unconstitutional the provision that barred members of registered organizations from jobs in defense-related facilities.

Congress responded, first by rewriting the registration provisions, and eventually by allowing the SACB to die.[44]

Registration and Incrimination

The most severe of these Court-inflicted blows to the McCarran Act was its 1965 ruling in *Albertson v. Subversive Activities Control Board,* a sequel to the 1961 decision upholding the SACB registration order to the Communist Party.

Party officers refused to comply with a final notice from the Justice Department that set November 19, 1961, as the deadline for registration of the party. The government subsequently obtained criminal indictments against the party for its failure to register, and an SACB order directed party officers to register personally.

The officers refused and appealed to the federal courts, citing their Fifth Amendment privilege against self-incrimination as justification for their refusal.

With the Court's decision in *Albertson v. Subversive Activities Control Board,* the officers of the Communist Party won a clear-cut victory. The Court held unanimously that the information sought in the registration forms included material that was self-incriminating. Thus compulsion to register did violate the officers' Fifth Amendment privilege. Brennan wrote the Court's opinion.

The Court rejected the government's argument that the information sought through the registration forms was no more incriminating than that on a tax return. While questions on tax returns were "neutral on their face and directed at the public at large," wrote Brennan, the registration questions were aimed at "a highly selective group inherently suspect of criminal activities." In this case, he explained, the Fifth Amendment privilege was asserted "not . . . in an essentially non-criminal and regulatory area of inquiry, but against an inquiry in an area permeated with criminal statutes where response to any of the form's questions in context might involve the petitioners in the admission of a crucial element of a crime."[45]

This ruling effectively ended the long effort by the government to force registration of the party.[46]

Association and Jobs

Two years later, in *United States v. Robel,* the Court declared that the McCarran Act also abridged the right of political association insofar as it denied all members of communist-action or communist-front organizations the right to hold jobs in defense-related industries. The ban, held the Court 6–2, was too broad, taking in all types of members, not simply active and knowing advocates of violent revolution.

Robel, a member of the Communist Party, worked as a machinist in a Seattle shipyard determined by the secretary of defense to be a defense facility. Robel stayed on the job after the final registration deadline for the party and so was charged with violation of the act.

Chief Justice Warren's opinion for the majority viewed this portion of the law as establishing guilt purely by association:

When Congress' exercise of one of its enumerated powers clashes with those individual liberties protected by the Bill of Rights, it is our "delicate and difficult" task to determine whether the resulting restriction on freedom can be tolerated. . . . The Government emphasizes that the purpose of . . . [the contested ban] is to reduce the threat of sabotage and espionage in the nation's defense plants. The Government's interest in such a prophylactic measure is not insubstantial. But it cannot be doubted that the means chosen to implement that governmental purpose in this instance cut deeply into the right of association. [It] . . . put appellee to the choice of surrendering his organizational affiliation, regardless of whether his membership threatened the security of a defense facility or giving up his job. . . . The statute quite literally establishes guilt by association alone, without any need to establish that an individual's association poses the threat feared by the Government in proscribing it. The inhibiting effect on the exercise of First Amendment rights is clear.

Warren added, however, that "nothing we hold today should be read to deny Congress the power under narrowly drawn legislation to keep from sensitive positions in defense facilities those who would use their positions to disrupt the Nation's production facilities."[47]

Justices Byron R. White and Harlan dissented. White wrote that in Robel's case

the interest in anticipating and preventing espionage or sabotage would outweigh the deterrent impact of job disqualification. . . . In the case before us the Court simply disagrees with the Congress and the Defense Department, ruling that Robel does not present a sufficient danger to the national security to require him to choose between membership in the Communist Party and his employment in a defense facility. . . . I much prefer the judgment of Congress and the Executive Branch that the interest of respondent in remaining a member of the Communist Party . . . is less substantial than the public interest in excluding him from employment in critical defense industries.[48]

In the fall of 1967, Congress revised the definition of communist-front organization in the McCarran Act. Another amendment to the act eliminated the registration requirement and authorized the SACB to place on a public register the names of individuals and organizations it found to be communist.

In 1968 Attorney General Ramsey Clark asked the board to conduct hearings on seven individuals thought to be members of the Communist Party. The SACB issued orders against three of them, declaring they were members of a communist-action organization. The Board's order was set aside by the District of Columbia Court of Appeals in 1969, holding that membership in the Communist Party was protected by the First Amendment.[49]

FEDERAL LOYALTY PROGRAMS

To ensure that only "loyal" persons held federal jobs, Presidents Harry Truman and Dwight Eisenhower instituted federal loyalty programs that provoked considerable controversy.

Critics of the programs argued that through them the government penalized persons for a state of mind rather than for overt acts of disloyalty, and it dismissed persons from jobs purely on the grounds of guilt by association. Defenders of the programs pointed out that there was no constitutional right to hold a government job and that the government had a right to protect itself from internal subversion. Moreover, dismissal from a government job did not imply guilt but only that some question existed as to one's fitness for government employment.

The Truman Program

In 1947 President Truman by executive order established a loyalty program for all civilian employees of the executive branch. Executive Order 9835 established a Loyalty Review Board within the Civil Service Commission to coordinate agency loyalty policies and to serve as the final board of appeal in loyalty dismissal cases. Loyalty investigations were required for all persons employed by the government and for all applicants for government jobs. Dismissal of individuals from government posts or denial of a job was permitted when "on all the evidence, reasonable grounds exist for belief that the person involved is disloyal to the Government of the United States." (In 1951 this standard was modified to allow dismissal when "there is a reasonable doubt as to the loyalty of the person involved.")

In the 1940s Congress authorized summary dismissal of employees of the Departments of State, Defense, Army, Navy, and Air Force and the Atomic Energy Commission when dismissal was considered necessary or advisable in the interest of national security. In 1950 Congress extended this authority to the Departments of the Treasury, Commerce, and Justice.

The Eisenhower Program

In 1953 President Eisenhower extended this summary dismissal power to all executive branch agencies and replaced the Truman loyalty program with a more stringent loyalty-security program established by Executive Order 10450.

Under the Eisenhower program a suspected employee bore the burden of proving his employment "clearly consistent" with national security. The order also sanctioned dismissal for reasons other than disloyalty: for example, personal behavior, sexual misconduct, excessive use of drugs or alcohol, and physical or mental disorders.[50]

Loyalty Programs Sustained

The Supreme Court never squarely addressed the substantial constitutional questions raised by the federal loyalty and security programs, although it did rule in a number of cases during the 1950s concerning individual dismissals.

Three constitutional provisions were implicated in government loyalty programs: the First Amendment guarantees of freedom of expression and political association; the Fifth Amendment guarantee that government would not deprive one of liberty or property without due process of law; and the Article I ban on the passage of bills of attainder. Only the due process question received any extended consideration by the Court in these cases.

The first rulings came in 1951. In *Joint Anti-Fascist Refugee Committee v. McGrath* the Court upheld the authority of the attorney general, under the Truman loyalty program, to maintain and furnish to the Loyalty Review Board a list of allegedly subversive organizations. The Court held, however, that the attorney general had exceeded that authority and acted arbitrarily in placing the names of three particular organizations—including the Anti-Fascist Refugee Committee—on that list.

The vote was 5–3. Justice Clark, attorney general when the case was filed, did not participate in the decision. Justice Burton—joined only by Justice Douglas—wrote the opinion announcing the judgment of the Court. That opinion carefully avoided the First Amendment issues of political association raised by use of this list.

In concurring opinions, Justices Black, Douglas, Frankfurter, and Jackson questioned the constitutionality of the list in light of the guarantee of due process and the prohibition on a bill of attainder. Justice Frankfurter wrote that although the designation as "communist" actually imposed no legal sanction on the listed organizations,

in the conditions of our time such designation drastically restricts the organizations, if it does not proscribe them. . . . Yet, designation has been made without notice, without disclosure of any reasons justifying it, without opportunity to meet the undisclosed evidence or suspicion on which designation may have been based, and without opportunity to establish affirmatively that the aims and acts of the organization are innocent.

Frankfurter concluded that such action

to maim or decapitate, on the mere say-so of the Attorney General, an organization to all outward-seeming engaged in lawful objectives is so devoid of fundamental fairness as to offend the Due Process Clause of the Fifth Amendment.[51]

Justices Reed and Minton and Chief Justice Vinson dissented, finding the due process guarantee inapplicable and rejecting any First Amendment challenge to use of the list. Justice Reed explained:

So long as petitioners are permitted to voice their political ideas . . . it is hard to understand how any advocate of freedom of expression can assert that their right has been unconstitutionally abridged. As nothing in the orders or regulations concerning this list limits the teachings or support of these organizations, we do not believe that any right of theirs under the First Amendment is abridged by publication of the list.[52]

The same day the Court upheld the decision of the loyalty board to dismiss Dorothy Bailey, a training officer in the United States Employment Service. Justice Clark again did not participate in the decision. The vote was 4–4. There was no opinion from the Supreme Court, as is the practice in cases in which the justices are evenly divided.[53]

The even division within the Court left standing an appeals court ruling finding Bailey's removal valid. Because there was no constitutional right to federal employment, her dismissal did not violate due process, and, the majority of the lower court continued, the First Amendment did not bar removal of persons from office for political reasons.

In 1955 the Court ruled that the Loyalty Review Board had exceeded its authority in discharging a public health officer as a security risk, after the officer had twice been cleared of any suspicion of disloyalty by agency loyalty boards.[54] In 1956 the Court held unjustified the summary dismissal of an inspector with the Food and Drug Administration on loyalty grounds. The Court ruled that dismissal from a nonsensitive position could not be justified as necessary in the interest of national security.[55]

In 1959 the Court weakened the federal government's effort to carry out its loyalty program by casting doubt on the propriety of the procedures used in revoking security clearances and dismissing employees on the basis of information from anonymous sources. With its ruling in *Greene v. McElroy,* the Court forced the president to revise those procedures.[56]

William L. Greene lost his job as vice president of an engineering firm engaged in defense contract work after his security clearance was revoked. The review board revoking the clearance relied on confidential reports, never available to Greene, even though he appeared at the hearings of the board to respond to the charges against him.

When he lost his clearance, Greene was unable to find another job in the field of aeronautical engineering. He challenged the revocation of his clearance as depriving him of his livelihood and thus of liberty and property without due process of law guaranteed by the Fifth Amendment.

The Court, 8–1, agreed that the denial of access to the evidence against Greene had been improper, depriving him of the opportunity to respond and rebut the charges. Neither Congress nor the president had authorized the Defense Department thus to classify the employees of a contractor as security risks without giving them the opportunity to confront and examine the evidence against them, held the Court.

Chief Justice Warren, writing for five members of the majority, carefully narrowed the reach of the ruling:

[P]etitioner's work opportunities have been severely limited on the basis of a fact determination rendered after a hearing which failed to comport with our traditional ideas of fair procedure. The type of hearing was the product of administrative decision not explicitly authorized by either Congress or the President. Whether those procedures under the circumstances comport with the Constitution we do not decide. Nor do we decide whether the President has inherent authority to create such a program, whether congressional action is necessary, or what the limits on executive or legislative authority may be. We decide only that in the absence of explicit authorization from the President or Congress the respondents were not empowered to deprive petitioner of his job in a proceeding in which he was not afforded the safeguards of confrontation and cross-examination.[57]

Justices Frankfurter, Harlan, and Whittaker concurred with the Court's judgment.

Justice Clark dissented, arguing that no one has "a constitutional right to have access to the Government's military secrets. . . . What for anyone else would be considered a privilege at best has for Greene been enshrouded in constitutional protection. This sleight of hand is too much for me." Clark warned that the majority was casting a cloud over the entire federal loyalty-security program, which could result in "a rout of our internal security."[58]

Early in 1960 President Eisenhower issued an executive order restricting the use of informants whose identities must be protected. The order also granted to persons accused of being security risks the right to confront and crossexamine their accusers.[59]

In 1961, however, the Court upheld the national security dismissal of a short-order cook in a cafeteria on the premises of the Naval Gun Factory in Washington, D.C. The Court, 5–4, held this action well within the authority granted by Congress to the executive to control security on military bases.[60]

LOYALTY OATHS AND LABOR

Along with the institution of the federal loyalty-security program came the proliferation of requirements that persons holding certain posts take loyalty oaths or sign affidavits to demonstrate their loyalty to the U.S. government.

In a long line of rulings, the Supreme Court first upheld and then circumscribed both the use and the usefulness of such requirements.

Labor Affidavit Upheld

Concern over communist infiltration of the labor movement and "political strikes" spurred passage of the Labor Management Relations Act of 1947, sponsored by Sen. Robert Taft, R-Ohio (1939–1953), and Rep. Fred Hartley Jr., R-N.Y. (1929–1949). A provision in the Taft-Hartley Act required officers of all labor organizations wishing to benefit from the protections and guarantees of federal labor law to sign affidavits that they were not members of, or affiliated with, the Communist Party, and that they did not believe in or hold membership in any organization teaching or believing in the forcible, illegal, or unconstitutional overthrow of the federal government. Unions whose officers did

not sign such affidavits were denied all protection of and services from the National Labor Relations Board.

In *American Communications Association v. Douds* (1950) the Supreme Court, 5–1, upheld the affidavit requirement as within the power of Congress. Chief Justice Vinson wrote the opinion. Justices Clark, Minton, and Douglas did not take part.

"There can be no doubt that Congress may, under its constitutional power to regulate commerce among the several States, attempt to prevent political strikes and other kinds of direct action designed to burden and interrupt the free flow of commerce," Vinson said.[61] The affidavit requirement, he explained, was a reasonable means of attaining that end.

Vinson continued:

Congress could rationally find that the Communist Party is not like other political parties in its utilization of positions of union leadership as means by which to bring about strikes and other obstructions of commerce for purposes of political advantage.[62]

The affidavit requirement, "by exerting pressures on unions to deny office to communists and others identified therein,"

undoubtedly lessens the threat to interstate commerce, but it has the further necessary effect of discouraging the exercise of political rights protected by the First Amendment. Men who hold union offices often have little choice but to renounce Communism or give up their offices.[63]

Vinson rejected the challenge that the affidavit requirement was an unconstitutional curtailment of individual freedom. The requirement, Vinson wrote,

does not interfere with speech because Congress fears the consequences of speech; it regulates harmful conduct which Congress has determined is carried on by persons who may be identified by their political affiliations and beliefs. The [National Labor Relations] Board does not contend that political strikes, the substantive evil at which . . . [the requirement] is aimed, are the present or impending products of advocacy of the doctrines of Communism or the expression of belief in overthrow of the Government by force. . . . Speech may be fought with speech. Falsehoods and fallacies must be exposed, not suppressed, unless there is not sufficient time to avert the evil consequences of noxious doctrine by argument and education. That is the command of the First Amendment. But force may and must be met with force. . . . [The affidavit requirement] is designed to protect the public not against what Communists and others identified therein advocate or believe, but against what Congress has concluded they have done and are likely to do again.[64]

Justice Frankfurter concurred in upholding the membership portion of the affidavit but dissented from the majority opinion upholding the portion involving belief alone.

Justice Jackson also concurred in part and dissented in part, making a similar distinction between the membership and the belief portions of the affidavit:

[A]ll parts of this oath which require disclosure of overt acts of affiliation or membership in the Communist Party are within the competence of Congress to enact . . . any parts of it that call for a disclosure of belief unconnected with any overt act are beyond its power.[65]

Earlier in his opinion, Jackson had phrased his view in less abstract terms:

I think that under our system, it is time enough for the law to lay hold of the citizen when he acts illegally, or in some rare circumstances when his thoughts are given illegal utterance. I think we must let his mind alone.[66]

In a vigorous dissenting opinion, Justice Black criticized his colleagues for allowing the government to restrict the right to think:

Freedom to think is inevitably abridged when beliefs are penalized by imposition of civil disabilities. . . . Like anyone else, individual Communists who commit overt acts in violation of valid laws can and should be punished. But the postulate of the First Amendment is that our free institutions can be maintained without proscribing or penalizing political belief, speech, press, assembly, or party affiliation. This is a far bolder philosophy than despotic rulers can afford to follow. It is the heart of the system on which our freedom depends.[67]

Labor Office Ban Voided

In 1959 Congress replaced the affidavit requirement—which proved ineffective since some communists were willing to take the oath and risk prosecution for perjury—with a flat prohibition against members of the Communist Party holding any union office. The new section of the federal labor law, part of the Labor-Management Reporting and Disclosure Act of 1959, also disqualified anyone who had been a member of the party during the last five years.[68]

In 1965 the Supreme Court held this ban unconstitutional as a violation of the provision forbidding Congress to pass bills of attainder.

Archie Brown, a member of the Communist Party, challenged the operation of the law that forbade him to serve on the executive board of a local of the International Longshoremen's and Warehousemen's Union. He based his challenge on First and Fifth Amendment grounds, but the Court found it unnecessary to consider those. *(See box, Politics and Loyalty at the Bar, p. 548.)*

By a 5–4 vote in *United States v. Brown,* the Supreme Court ruled in his favor. Chief Justice Earl Warren wrote:

Congress undoubtedly possesses power under the Commerce Clause to enact legislation designed to keep from positions affecting interstate commerce persons who may use such positions to bring about political strikes. In . . . [this prohibition] however, Congress has exceeded the authority granted it by the Constitution. The statute does not set forth a generally applicable rule decreeing that any person who commits certain acts or possesses certain characteristics (acts and characteristics which, in Congress' view, make them likely to initiate political strikes) shall not hold union office, and leave to courts and juries the job of deciding what persons have committed the specified acts or possess the specified characteristics. Instead, it designates in no uncertain terms the persons who possess the feared characteristics and therefore cannot hold union office without incurring criminal liability—members of the Communist Party. . . .

We do not hold today that Congress cannot weed dangerous persons out of the labor movement. . . . Rather, we make again the point . . . that Congress must accomplish such results by rules of general applicability. It cannot specify the people upon whom the sanction it prescribes is to be levied. Under our Constitution, Congress possesses full legislative authority, but the task of adjudication must be left to other tribunals.[69]

In dissent, Justice White, joined by Justices Clark, Harlan, and Stewart, criticized the majority's distinction between the legislative function of making rules and the judicial function in applying those rules to particular individuals or groups. White wrote that the Court took "too narrow [a] view of the legislative process."[70]

In the 1960s the Court ruled on two other cases related to the Taft-Hartley Act requirement that labor organization officers sign affidavits that they were not Communist Party members. The decisions reversed convictions of union members who had sworn falsely that they were not communists. The Court decided both cases without dealing with the First Amendment claim of freedom of political association or the Fifth Amendment privilege protecting individuals against compelled self-incrimination.[71]

TEACHERS AND OATHS

The most frequent state reaction to the threat of communist subversion was passage of a law requiring public employees—particularly teachers—to take a loyalty oath affirming that they had not been and were not members of the Communist Party.

During the 1950s the Court upheld the constitutionality of such oaths, but by 1967 it had reversed itself, finding that most oaths came too close to guilt by association, demanding little evidence of actual subversive activity. In the 1970s the Court upheld several laws requiring state employees to take affirmative oaths promising to uphold the Constitution and to oppose the violent overthrow of the government.

Gerende and Garner

The Court's first loyalty oath rulings came in 1951. In *Gerende v. Board of Supervisors of Elections,* the Court upheld Maryland's law requiring every candidate for public office to file an affidavit disavowing involvement in any attempt to overthrow the government by force or violence.[72]

Two months later, on the same day that it upheld in *Dennis* the constitutionality of the Smith Act, the Court in *Garner v. Board of Public Works of the City of Los Angeles* upheld a Los Angeles ordinance requiring city employees to affirm their loyalty through oath and affidavit.

Public employees had to state whether they ever had been members of the Communist Party and to swear that they had not advocated the overthrow of state or federal government in the previous five years, that they had not and would not be affiliated with any group advocating such overthrow during the period they held a city job.

Seventeen employees refused to comply and were dismissed. They sued for reinstatement, challenging the oath and affidavit requirement as unconstitutional as a bill of attainder, an ex post facto law, and a violation of their freedom of speech, assembly, and right to petition the government for redress of grievances.[73]

The Court upheld the affidavit requirement 7–2, but the oath only 5–4. Justice Clark, writing for the majority, explained that they did not view the Los Angeles ordinance as a bill of attainder

Concerned about communist infiltration of the legal profession, several states in the 1950s began inquiring into the political affiliation and associations of individuals seeking admission to the practice of law.

This line of inquiry—and resulting state decisions to deny certain persons admission—produced a series of Supreme Court rulings that covered almost twenty years.

The first case was that of George Anastaplo. When Illinois bar examiners questioned him about his political beliefs, he refused on principle to respond, asserting that the questions invaded areas protected by the First and Fourteenth Amendments from state infringement. He was denied admission to the bar. In 1955 the Supreme Court upheld the denial by refusing to review his appeal.[1]

Two years later, however, the Court ruled in two cases that questionable political affiliations alone, or the simple refusal to answer questions about one's political associations, did not give a state a basis for concluding that an applicant lacked the proper moral character for admission to the practice of law.

In *Schware v. New Mexico Board of Bar Examiners,* the board had concluded that Rudolph Schware lacked the requisite "good moral character" because he had used aliases during the 1930s to obtain jobs in businesses that discriminated against Jews, because he had been arrested several times, and because he had been a member of the Communist Party from 1932 to 1940.

The Supreme Court unanimously reversed the board's decision. Justice Hugo L. Black wrote the opinion, refuting the board's inference that because Schware had belonged to the Communist Party he was of bad moral character.[2]

Raphael Konigsberg was denied admission to the California bar because he, like Anastaplo, refused to answer questions about his political affiliations. The Court overturned the state's action the same day it reversed the lower court decision in *Schware.*

Konigsberg's record of public and military service testified sufficiently to his loyalty, the Supreme Court held, reversing the state board's ruling as contrary to the evidence.[3]

ADMISSION NOT GUARANTEED

Supreme Court reversal of the state's initial refusal to admit both Anastaplo and Konigsberg to the practice of law did not guarantee their admission.

On the basis of *Schware* and *Konigsberg,* Anastaplo asked Illinois to reconsider his application for admission to the bar. After lengthy proceedings, the state again rejected it.

In 1961 the Supreme Court, 5–4, upheld the state's action. The majority said that the state had a legitimate interest in examining the qualifications of persons seeking to practice law in the state—and that questions about his political background were a proper element in that examination.

The Court held that by continuing to refuse to answer those questions, Anastaplo obstructed the state's inquiry; therefore, denial of admission was a legitimate response.[4]

A second ruling in Konigsberg's case was announced the same day.

Also 5–4, the Court upheld California bar officials' refusal to admit Konigsberg—not because of concern about his character but simply because he too persisted in his refusal to answer questions germane to its inquiry, thereby obstructing the state's examining process.[5]

EVIDENCE OF CHARACTER

Ten years later, in two decisions announced the same day in 1971, the Supreme Court marked the boundary line for such questioning.

By 5–4, the Court made it harder for a state to exclude an applicant from admission to the bar. Without any other evidence of the applicant's disloyalty or unfitness, a state may not refuse the applicant solely on the basis of his refusal to state whether he had ever belonged to an organization advocating the violent overthrow of the government.

Justice Black wrote the opinion; Justices John Marshall Harlan, Byron R. White, and Harry A. Blackmun and Chief Justice Warren Burger dissented.[6]

But the same day, with Justice Potter Stewart joining those dissenters, the Court, 5–4, held that states could require applicants for admission to the bar to be of good moral character and loyal to the Constitution.

It made no difference that the "loyalty" requirement included taking an oath in support of the state and federal constitutions and responding to two questions concerning membership in any organization advocating overthrow of the government by force or violence, with the specific intent of furthering that goal.[7]

In this case, the majority was careful to point out that there was no indication that any applicant had been denied admission to the bar because of his or her answers to these questions or the refusal to answer them.

"It is well settled," wrote Justice Stewart, "that Bar Examiners may ask about Communist affiliation as a preliminary to further inquiry into the nature of the association and may exclude an applicant for refusal to answer."[8]

---

1. *In re Anastaplo,* 348 U.S. 946 (1955).
2. *Schware v. New Mexico Board of Bar Examiners,* 353 U.S. 232 (1957).
3. *Konigsberg v. State Bar of California,* 353 U.S. 252 (1957).
4. *In re Anastaplo,* 366 U.S. 82 (1961).
5. *Konigsberg v. State Bar of California,* 366 U.S. 36 (1961).
6. *In re Stolar, Baird v. State Bar of Arizona,* 401 U.S. 23 (1971).
7. *Law Students Civil Rights Research Council v. Wadmond,* 401 U.S. 154 (1971).
8. Id. at 165–166.

because it did not punish anyone, but simply set standards of qualification and eligibility for city jobs. It was not an ex post facto law, he continued, because it involved activity that for the seven previous years had been proscribed for city employees. The majority did not address the First Amendment issues directly.

Justices Frankfurter and Burton concurred in the decision to uphold the affidavit requirement, but they dissented from the majority's ruling upholding the oath. Frankfurter wrote:

The Constitution does not guarantee public employment. City, State and Nation are not confined to making provisions appropriate for securing competent professional discharge of the functions pertaining to diverse governmental jobs. They may also assure themselves of fidelity to the very presuppositions of our scheme of government on the part of those who seek to serve it.[74]

Frankfurter explained that he would have overturned the oath requirement because it was "not limited to affiliation with organizations known at the time to have advocated overthrow of government. . . . How can anyone be sure that an organization with which he affiliates will not at some time in the future be found . . . to advocate overthrow of government by 'unlawful means'?"[75]

Burton found the retroactive nature of the oath invalid under the Court's decisions concerning bills of attainder and ex post facto laws.

Justices Black and Douglas found all aspects of the ordinance objectionable, holding both the oath and the affidavit requirements invalid as bills of attainder.

Loyalty Dismissals

Loyalty oath requirements for state or city employees were often linked with programs for the removal of public employees whose loyalty was suspect.

In 1952 the Supreme Court upheld a New York law setting up

POLITICS AND PUBLIC EMPLOYEES

Despite the First Amendment's guarantee of freedom for political association, the Supreme Court has consistently upheld the power of Congress and state legislatures to limit the political activity of public employees. The Court first made this point in 1947: the limited burden such laws place upon the right of political association is justified by the government's interest in having its employees chosen on the basis of merit, not political loyalty.

The end of the spoils system for filling federal posts brought with it laws limiting the political activities of government workers.

In 1876 Congress prohibited government employees from requesting, giving, or receiving money for political purposes from any federal official. The Civil Service Act of 1883 forbade federal officials to use their positions to influence the political action of their subordinates.

The Hatch Act of 1939 prohibited federal employees from taking active part in political campaigns or the management of political party activities. Office of Personnel Management (formerly the Civil Service Commission) regulations subsequently have denied government workers the right to participate in the following political activities: running for office, distributing campaign literature, taking an active role in political campaigns, circulating nominating petitions, attending political conventions as anything other than a spectator, and publishing or signing a letter soliciting votes for a candidate.

In 1947 the Supreme Court in *United Public Workers v. Mitchell* upheld, 4–3, these restrictions on the political activities of government employees. Justices Frank Murphy and Robert H. Jackson did not take part in the decision. Justices Wiley Rutledge, Hugo L. Black, and William O. Douglas dissented.

Justice Stanley F. Reed, speaking for the Court, declared that there was no constitutional objection to the finding of Congress that an efficient public service was best obtained by prohibiting active participation by public employees in political campaigns. The conclusion was a reasonable one, well within the power of Congress. Reed continued:

For regulation of employees it is not necessary that the act regulated be anything more than an act reasonably deemed by Congress to interfere with the efficiency of the public service. . . .

We have said that Congress may regulate the political conduct of Government employees "within reasonable limits," even though the regulation trenches to some extent upon unfettered political action. The determination of the extent to which political activities of governmental employees shall be regulated lies primarily in Congress. Courts will interfere only when such regulation passes beyond the generally existing conception of governmental power.[1]

Reed warned, however, that the concept of government power might change. Some future Court might find these restrictions impermissible.

But twenty-six years later in *Civil Service Commission v. Letter Carriers* (1973), the Court again rebuffed First Amendment challenges to federal and state prohibitions on partisan political activity by public employees. By 6–3, the Court reaffirmed the validity of the Hatch Act.

Justice Byron R. White wrote for the majority:

[I]t is in the best interest of the country, indeed essential, that federal service should depend upon meritorious performance rather than political service, and that the political influence of federal employees on others and on the electoral process should be limited.[2]

Justices Douglas, William J. Brennan Jr., and Thurgood Marshall dissented.

In a companion case, *Broadrick v. Oklahoma State Personnel Board*, the Court 5–4 sustained a state law prohibiting employees from partisan political activity.[3] Justice Potter Stewart, who voted with the majority in the Hatch Act case, joined the dissenters in this case.

1. *United Public Workers v. Mitchell*, 330 U.S. 75 at 101, 102 (1947).
2. *Civil Service Commission v. Letter Carriers*, 413 U.S. 548 at 557 (1973).
3. *Broadrick v. Oklahoma State Personnel Board*, 413 U.S. 601 (1973).

a state list of subversive organizations—those advocating the violent overthrow of the government—and providing that membership in any listed organization would constitute prima facie evidence justifying dismissal from a public post.

The law was intended to ensure the doctrinal orthodoxy of teachers and other officials in the New York public school system. Before dismissal, persons who were members of such an organization were entitled to a full hearing and judicial review of the decision to dismiss them. With its decision in *Adler v. Board of Education, City of New York,* the Court, 6–3, sustained the law.[76]

For the majority, Justice Minton wrote:

That the school authorities have the right and the duty to screen the officials, teachers and employees as to their fitness to maintain the integrity of the schools as a part of ordered society, cannot be doubted. One's associates, past and present, as well as one's conduct, may properly be considered in determining fitness and loyalty. From time immemorial, one's reputation has been determined in part by the company he keeps.[77]

Disqualification from a job under the law, wrote Minton, did not deny one the right of free speech and assembly. "His freedom of choice between membership in the organization and employment in the school system might be limited, but not his freedom of speech or assembly."[78]

Justices Frankfurter, Black, and Douglas dissented. Frankfurter argued that the Court should have dismissed the case without ruling on the law. Douglas and Black found the law a violation of the First Amendment. It "proceeds on a principle repugnant to our society—guilt by association," wrote Douglas.[79] He elaborated:

Youthful indiscretions, mistaken causes, misguided enthusiasms—all long forgotten—become the ghosts of a harrowing present. Any organization committed to a liberal cause, any group organized to revolt against a hysterical trend, any committee launched to sponsor an unpopular program becomes suspect. These are the organizations into which Communists often infiltrate. Their presence infects the whole, even though the project was not conceived in sin. A teacher caught in that mesh is almost certain to stand condemned. Fearing condemnation, she will tend to shrink from any association that stirs controversy. In that manner freedom of expression will be stifled. . . .

What happens under this law is typical of what happens in a police state. Teachers are under constant surveillance; their pasts are combed for signs of disloyalty; their utterances are watched for cues to dangerous thoughts. A pall is cast over the classrooms. There can be no real academic freedom in that environment. Where suspicion fills the air and holds scholars in line for fear of their jobs, there can be no exercise of the free intellect. . . .

Of course the school systems . . . need not become cells for Communist activities; and the classrooms need not become forums for propagandizing the Marxist creed. But the guilt of the teacher should turn on overt acts. So long as she is a law-abiding citizen, so long as her performance within the public school system meets professional standards, her private life, her political philosophy, her social creed should not be the cause of reprisals against her.[80]

Initial Limitation

But late in the same year as *Adler,* the Court unanimously struck down an Oklahoma loyalty program that penalized knowing *and* unknowing members of certain proscribed organizations. (The Smith Act of 1940 made it a crime to become a knowing member of any organization or group dedicated to the violent overthrow of any government in the United States.)

The law challenged in *Wieman v. Updegraff* required all state officers and employees to take a loyalty oath and excluded from public jobs those persons who had been members of certain organizations, regardless of their knowledge of the organization's purposes. With this ruling the Court began to impose limits upon state loyalty oaths. Membership in an organization could not be used as a basis for a state-imposed penalty, the Court said, unless the member consciously endorsed the organization's aims and doctrines.

Justice Clark, writing for the unanimous Court, made clear that in *Garner* and *Adler* only "knowing" membership resulted in disqualification for or dismissal from a public job. But under Oklahoma law, "membership alone disqualifies."[81] This was a critical difference.

Under the challenged law

the fact of association alone determines disloyalty and disqualification; it matters not whether association existed innocently or knowingly. To thus inhibit individual freedom of movement is to stifle the flow of democratic expression and controversy at one of its chief sources. . . . Indiscriminate classification of innocent with knowing activity must fall as an assertion of arbitrary power. The oath offends due process.[82]

Justice Jackson, who had not heard the case argued, did not participate in the decision.

Penalizing the Privilege

Four years later the Court held it unconstitutional for a state or city automatically to dismiss employees if they invoked their constitutional privilege against self-incrimination to avoid answering questions about their political associations.

At issue in *Slochower v. Board of Higher Education of New York City* was the city's summary dismissal of a Brooklyn College professor because, in testimony before the Senate internal security subcommittee, he had refused to answer questions about his political associations before 1941, invoking the Fifth Amendment.

Slochower was suspended without notice, hearing, or an opportunity to explain or discuss the reasons for the termination of his tenure. This action came under a provision of the city charter that automatically terminated the tenure of any public official who invoked the Fifth Amendment to avoid answering questions related to official conduct. Slochower sued, challenging his dismissal as improper and the city charter provision as unconstitutional because it penalized the exercise of a federally guaranteed constitutional right.

The Court ruled in his favor but on different grounds. Summary dismissal, the Court held 5–4, violated Slochower's right to due process of law. The city board of education, wrote Justice Clark for the majority, had erred in treating his assertion of his Fifth Amendment privilege as a "conclusive presumption of guilt."

Such interpretation of the assertion of a constitutional right was impermissible, Clark continued: "The privilege against self-incrimination would be reduced to a hollow mockery if its exercise could be taken as equivalent to a confession of guilt."[83] Because no valid inference of guilt could be made, the Court sustained Slochower's claim of privilege before the Senate subcommittee and ruled that there was no basis for his dismissal.

Justice Reed, speaking also for Justices Burton and Minton, dissented. He argued that "the city does have reasonable ground to require its employees either to give evidence regarding facts of official conduct within their knowledge or to give up the positions they hold."[84] Justice Harlan, in a separate dissenting opinion, wrote that the majority had "misconceived" the nature of the city charter provision in question and had "unduly circumscribed the power of the State to ensure the qualifications of its teachers."[85]

The State's Right to Inquire

In two 1958 decisions, however, the Court again upheld the right of states to question employees about their associations when examining their overall qualifications for state employment.

In *Lerner v. Casey* a subway conductor refused to tell his superiors whether he was a member of the Communist Party. He was dismissed as a person of doubtful loyalty and reliability.[86] In *Beilan v. Board of Public Education, School District of Philadelphia*, a school teacher, who refused to tell his superintendent whether he had earlier held a position in the Communist Party, was dismissed as incompetent.[87]

The five-man majority in both cases—Harlan, Burton, Frankfurter, Clark, and Whittaker—stressed that the subway conductor and the school teacher were dismissed because they refused to answer questions put by their employers—action that constituted evidence of incompetency and unreliability.

In a concurring opinion, Justice Frankfurter said the two employees were "terminated because of their refusals to answer questions relevant . . . to an inquiry by their supervisors into their dependability. When these two employees were discharged, they were not labeled 'disloyal.' They were discharged because governmental authorities, like other employers, sought to satisfy themselves of the dependability of employees in relation to their duties."[88]

In dissent, Chief Justice Warren and Justices Brennan, Black, and Douglas argued that the two employees had been branded disloyal by the inquiry into their political associations and activities. In his dissenting opinion, Brennan wrote that "more is at stake here than the loss of positions of public employment for unreliability or incompetence. Rather, it is the simultaneous public labeling of the employees as disloyal that gives rise to our concern."[89]

THE SHIFT OF THE SIXTIES

With a series of decisions beginning in 1958—initially involving civil rights, not communist, groups—the Supreme Court gave formal recognition to a First Amendment freedom of po-litical association. *(See box, The Right and Freedom of Association, pp. 420–421.)*

In line with this development came a clear shift in the Court's willingness to back government inquiry into the affiliations of its employees. The Court also was less willing to uphold government-imposed penalties for persons whose affiliations seemed suspect. The *Aptheker* and *Robel* rulings of 1964 and 1967 reflected the change. *(See details on these two cases, pp. 537, 544.)*

And the Court, in a set of rulings in the mid-1960s, effectively reversed most of its key decisions upholding state government loyalty oath and loyalty program requirements, finding that they were too broad to comport with the freedom guaranteed by the First Amendment. The first of these freedom-of-association rulings was the 1958 decision in *National Association for the Advancement of Colored People v. Alabama.*[90]

Two years later the Court struck down a state law that required public school teachers to file affidavits listing all their organizational memberships. In its opinion in *Shelton v. Tucker,* the Court found this requirement to go "far beyond what might be justified in the exercise of the State's legitimate inquiry into the fitness and competency of its teachers."[91]

The following year the Court first applied this new view to loyalty oaths, striking down a Florida law that required state employees to swear that they had never lent "aid, support, advice, counsel or influence to the Communist Party." Employees who did not sign the oath were fired.

In its opinion in *Cramp v. Board of Public Instruction, Orange County, Fla.,* the Court held this oath far too vague, "completely lacking in . . . terms susceptible of objective measurement."[92] A law describing prohibited acts "'in terms so vague that men of common intelligence must necessarily guess at its meaning and differ as to its application violates the first essential of due process of law,'" wrote Justice Stewart for the unanimous Court.[93]

In 1964 Washington State's loyalty oath for teachers was struck down on the basis of similar reasoning.[94] And in 1966 and 1967, this shift culminated in decisions effectively nullifying *Gerende, Garner,* and *Adler.*

Elfbrandt and Garner

The first of these rulings came in the case of *Elfbrandt v. Russell.* Barbara Elfbrandt, a Quaker teacher in Arizona, challenged the constitutionality of the state laws that required state employees to take a loyalty oath. The oath itself simply affirmed support for the constitutions and laws of the state and the United States, but the state legislature had by law provided that the oath would be considered violated by knowing membership in the Communist Party. The law made clear that any employee who took the oath and at the time or later became a willing, knowing member of the Communist Party could be prosecuted for perjury.

By 5–4 the Supreme Court held this combination of oath and interpretative statute too broad to meet constitutional standards. Justice Douglas explained that the major flaw was the failure of the state to acknowledge that many people might join organizations such as the Communist Party without actually sharing the organization's unlawful purposes. The challenged law, he continued, was predicated on the doctrine of guilt by association:

Those who join an organization but do not share its unlawful purposes and who do not participate in its unlawful activities surely pose no threat, either as citizens or as public employees. . . . This Act threatens the cherished freedom of association protected by the First Amendment, made applicable to the States through the Fourteenth Amendment. . . . A law which applies to membership without the "specific intent" to further the illegal aims of the organization infringes unnecessarily on protected freedoms. It rests on the doctrine of "guilt by association" which has no place here.[95]

With this ruling, the Court effectively, if implicitly, overturned *Garner*, which had upheld that sort of oath. The four dissenting justices, White, Clark, Harlan, and Stewart, said that the oath should be upheld in light of the Court's earlier decisions acknowledging the right of states to condition public employment upon the requirement that employees abstain from knowing membership in subversive organizations.

Keyishian and Adler

The following year the Court struck down the New York law it had upheld in *Adler*. The vote in *Keyishian v. Board of Regents of the University of the State of New York* was again 5–4. Justice Brennan wrote the majority opinion.

The law authorized the board of regents to prepare a list of subversive organizations and to deny jobs to teachers belonging to those organizations. The law made membership in the Communist Party prima facie evidence for disqualification from employment. Four university faculty members subject to dismissal under the law challenged its constitutionality.

The Court found the law too vague and too sweeping, penalizing "[m]ere knowing membership without a specific intent to further the unlawful aims" of the Communist Party.[96] The question of vagueness, noted Brennan, had not been placed before the Court in *Adler*. The majority described New York's complex of criminal anarchy and loyalty laws as "a highly efficient *in terrorem* mechanism" that operated to curtail First Amendment freedom:

It would be a bold teacher who would not stay as far as possible from utterances or acts which might jeopardize his living by enmeshing him in this intricate machinery. . . .
Our Nation is deeply committed to safeguarding academic freedom, which is of transcendent value to all of us and not merely to the teachers concerned. That freedom is therefore a special concern of the First Amendment, which does not tolerate laws that cast a pall of orthodoxy over the classroom.[97]

Four justices—Clark, Harlan, Stewart, and White—dissented. Justice Clark declared: "[T]he majority has by its broadside swept away one of our most precious rights, namely, the right of self preservation."[98]

A few months later the Court, 6–3, struck down the Maryland loyalty oath law it had upheld in *Gerende*. Justice Douglas explained that the oath was so vague that it violated the due process guarantee of the Fourteenth Amendment. Its capricious application could "deter the flowering of academic freedom as much as successive suits for perjury," he wrote.[99] Justices Harlan, Stewart, and White dissented.

Political Association: A Contemporary View

As the threat of domestic subversion faded, and questions of domestic politics came again to the foreground of national attention, the Supreme Court through the 1990s continued to define various aspects of this freedom of political association.

LOYALTY OATHS

The Court continued to support state requirements that employees take loyalty oaths that are worded affirmatively. The employees declare their support for the existing system of constitutional government rather than disavow any affiliation with groups intending to overthrow that system.

In 1971 the Court upheld a state requirement that teachers take such an oath, making clear in its opinion that persons could be properly dismissed for refusing to take such an oath only after they were given a hearing.[100] The following year the Court, 4–3, upheld a state requirement that all employees swear to "oppose the overthrow of the government by force, violence or by any illegal or unconstitutional method."[101]

Also in 1971 and 1972 the Court upheld state requirements that applicants for admission to the state bar take affirmative oaths of loyalty to the state and federal constitutions. But the Court at the same time limited strictly the power of state officials to penalize those who would not take such oaths.[102] (*See box, Politics and Loyalty at the Bar, p. 548.*)

In 1974 the Court held unanimously that a state infringed this freedom when it required political parties seeking a place on the ballot to swear that they did not advocate the violent overthrow of local, state, or federal government.

In *Communist Party of Indiana v. Whitcomb*, Justice Brennan reaffirmed the Court's view that "'the constitutional guarantees of free speech and free press do not permit a State to forbid or proscribe advocacy of the use of force or of law violation except where such advocacy is directed to inciting or producing imminent lawless action and is likely to incite or produce such action.'"[103]

POLITICAL PARTIES

Political parties—and in one case a radical student organization—have won Court rulings making clear their right of association, and the point at which state officials could limit its exercise. The 1972 case of *Healy v. James* concerned a local chapter of the radical organization Students for a Democratic Society. The Court held that, without evidence that the chapter would have adverse effects on campus life, university officials could not constitutionally refuse to recognize it.[104]

Several decisions in the next two years set out the Court's view of the permissible restrictions a state might place on voters or candidates wishing to change political parties. In 1973 the Court upheld a state requirement that voters who wish to vote in a party's primary enroll in that party at least thirty days before the last general election.[105]

Later in the year the Court held that the First Amendment limited the scope of such a state requirement. The Court struck down as abridging the right of political association a state rule forbidding persons to vote in the primary of one party if they had voted in that of another party within the preceding twenty-three months.[106] Early in 1974, however, the Court upheld a state requirement that independent candidates disaffiliate themselves from a party one year before the primary election of the year in which they wish to run as independents.[107]

In 1975 the Court held that national political parties, as well as individuals, have a constitutional right of political association. In *Cousins v. Wigoda* the Court held that Illinois law infringed the party's First Amendment right by penalizing one set of party delegates recognized and seated, instead of an alternative delegation, by the Democratic National Convention. The case arose out of the 1972 convention—to which two opposing sets of Democratic delegates went from Illinois, one committed to the presidential candidacy of Sen. George S. McGovern, D-S.D. (1963–1981), and the other set chosen and led by Mayor Richard J. Daley of Chicago.[108]

The right of association of political parties was further defined in 1981 when the Court, 6–3, upheld Wisconsin's right to hold an open primary in which voters participate without declaring their allegiance to a particular party. But, held the Court, the state could not compel the national party to recognize the primary results if to do so would violate the party's rules and infringe on its right of association.[109]

A year later the Court struck down Ohio's law requiring candidates for office to disclose the names and addresses of campaign contributors. By a 6–3 vote, the Court held that such disclosure, particularly of contributors to minor parties, might subject the persons whose names were disclosed to harassment, violating their freedom of association.[110]

And in 1986 the Court told the states they could not require political parties to hold "closed primaries" in which only party members could vote. A political party may make that decision, wrote Justice Thurgood Marshall, but the state may not do it for a party.[111]

PATRONAGE HIRING AND FIRING

Twice the Court has upheld laws restricting the partisan political activity of federal and state workers. Curtailment of their First Amendment rights may be justified, the Court has ruled, by the interest in having government jobs filled on the basis of merit, not political loyalty. *(See box, Politics and Public Employees, p. 549.)*

In the last quarter century, the Court dealt with the other side of the patronage hiring issue—patronage firing. And in those decisions the Court held that the freedom of political association was violated by that practice.

The case of *Elrod v. Burns*, like *Cousins*, arose in Illinois. At the time, all employees of the Cook County sheriff's office who were not covered by civil service regulations and who were not of the same party as the newly elected sheriff were fired by the incoming sheriff. He then would replace them with persons of political affiliation similar to his.

This practice, held the Court 5–3, violated the First Amendment.

In his opinion for the Court, Justice Brennan first quoted the Court's earlier declaration in *Buckley v. Valeo* (1976) that the "First Amendment protects political association as well as political expression." He then continued: "There can no longer be doubt that freedom to associate with others for the common advancement of political beliefs and ideas is a form of 'orderly group activity' protected by the First and Fourteenth Amendments."[112]

Brennan cited as precedent the decision in *Keyishian* nine years earlier, noting that in that case the Court "squarely held that political association alone could not, consistently with the First Amendment, constitute adequate ground for denying public employment."[113] *(See details of Keyishian v. Board of Regents of the University of the State of New York, p. 552.)*

Then, moving to weigh the state's justification for patronage firing against its curtailment of individual freedom, Brennan cited the cases in which the Court had upheld the Hatch Act limitations on partisan political activity by government employees—*United Public Workers v. Mitchell* and *Civil Service Commission v. Letter Carriers*.[114]

Those limitations were upheld, he explained, as a justifiable way of eliminating patronage, the very practice that Illinois now argued to preserve.

By forbidding the firing of persons simply because of their political affiliation, Brennan continued, the Court was not outlawing political parties.

Parties are free to exist and their concomitant activities are free to continue. We require only that the rights of every citizen to believe as he will and to act and associate according to his beliefs be free to continue as well.

In summary, patronage dismissals severely restrict political belief and association. Though there is a vital need for government efficiency and effectiveness, such dismissals are on balance not the least restrictive means for fostering that end. . . . [P]atronage dismissals cannot be justified by their contribution to the proper functioning of our democratic process through their assistance to partisan politics since political parties are nurtured by other, less intrusive and equally effective methods. More fundamentally, however, any contribution of patronage dismissals to the democratic process does not suffice to override their severe encroachment on First Amendment freedoms.[115]

Justices Lewis F. Powell Jr. and William H. Rehnquist dissented, as did Chief Justice Warren E. Burger. They held that the patronage system contributed to the democratization of politics and to sustaining grass-roots interest in government—considerations that outweighed the limited intrusion of patronage firing on First Amendment freedoms. Powell wrote: "Before patronage practices developed fully, an 'aristocratic' class dominated political affairs, a tendency that persisted in areas where patronage did not become prevalent. Patronage practices broadened the base of political participation by providing incentives to take part in the process, thereby increasing the volume of political discourse in society."[116]

Four years later in *Branti v. Finkel,* the Court expanded the First Amendment's protections for non–civil service workers.[117] Then in 1990 the Court went beyond the context of dismissals and held that it was unconstitutional for states, cities, or counties to hire, promote, or transfer most public employees based on party affiliation.[118]

The Court, 5–4, ruled that patronage violates the right of free association when government workers who are not in policy or confidential positions are denied advancement because of their party membership.

Justice Brennan, writing for the majority in *Rutan v. Republican Party of Illinois,* opened his opinion with this quip: "To the victor belong only those spoils that may be constitutionally obtained."[119] Brennan was joined by Justices Byron R. White, Thurgood Marshall, Harry A. Blackmun, and John Paul Stevens.

Justice Antonin Scalia's strongly worded dissent was joined by Chief Justice Rehnquist, Justice Anthony M. Kennedy, and in part by Justice Sandra Day O'Connor.

Wrote Scalia: "There is little doubt that our decisions in *Elrod* and *Branti,* by contributing to the decline of party strength, have also contributed to the growth of interest-group politics in the last decade. Our decision today will greatly accelerate the trend."[120]

Casting the discussion as a conflict between patronage and the merit principle, Scalia explained: "As the merit principle has been extended and its effects increasingly felt; as the Boss Tweeds, the Tammany Halls, the Pendergast machines, the Byrd machines and the Daley machines have faded into history; we find that political leaders at all levels increasingly complain of the helplessness of elected government . . . before the demands of small and cohesive interest-groups."[121]

The Court extended the protections of *Rutan v. Republican Party of Illinois* to independent contractors in 1996, ruling 7–2 that government may not retaliate against a contractor for political disloyalty.[122]

On the same day in a separate case, the Court 7–2 also gave some protection to contractors fired for speaking out on public issues. Declaring for the first time that government contractors have free speech rights similar to those of regular payroll employees, the majority said lower courts reviewing a contractor's complaint of illegal termination should weigh the government's legitimate interests against the contractor's free speech rights.[123]

NOTES

THE RIGHT TO VOTE: AN EXPANDING PRIVILEGE (PP. 505–518)

1. *Slaughterhouse Cases (Butchers' Benevolent Association of New Orleans v. The Crescent City Livestock Landing and Slaughterhouse Company; Esteben v. Louisiana),* 16 Wall. U.S. 36 at 75 (1873).

2. *Minor v. Happersett,* 21 Wall. 163 (1875).

3. *United States v. Reese,* 92 U.S. 214 at 564 (1876).

4. *United States v. Cruikshank,* 92 U.S. 542 at 555 (1876).

5. Id. at 554–556.

6. *Ex parte Siebold,* 100 U.S. 371 (1880).

7. *Ex parte Clarke,* 100 U.S. 399 (1880); *United States v. Gale,* 109 U.S. 65 (1883); *In re Coy,* 127 U.S. 731 (1888); *United States v. Mosely,* 238 U.S. 383 (1915).

8. *Ex parte Yarbrough,* 110 U.S. 651 at 657–658, 663–664 (1884).

9. Id. at 666.

10. Id. at 667.

11. *James v. Bowman,* 190 U.S. 127 at 139 (1903).

12. C. Vann Woodward, *The Strange Career of Jim Crow,* 2d rev. ed. (New York: Oxford University Press, 1966), 82–93.

13. *Williams v. Mississippi,* 170 U.S. 213 at 225 (1898).

14. *Guinn v. United States,* 238 U.S. 347 at 366 (1915).

15. *United States v. Mosley,* 238 U.S. 383 at 386 (1915).

16. *Lane v. Wilson,* 307 U.S. 268 at 275 (1939).

17. *Davis v. Schnell,* 336 U.S. 933 (1949).

18. *Lassiter v. Northampton County Board of Elections,* 360 U.S. 45 at 51–54 (1959).

19. *Louisiana v. United States,* 380 U.S. 145 at 152–153 (1965).

20. *South Carolina v. Katzenbach,* 383 U.S. 301 (1966).

21. Id. at 328, 334.

22. *Katzenbach v. Morgan,* 384 U.S. 641 (1966); *Cardona v. Power,* 384 U.S. 672 (1966).

23. *Gaston County v. United States,* 395 U.S. 285 (1969).

24. Id. at 296–297.

25. *Oregon v. Mitchell,* 400 U.S. 112 (1970).

26. *Newberry v. United States,* 256 U.S. 232 (1921).

27. *Nixon v. Herndon,* 273 U.S. 536 at 541 (1927).

28. *Nixon v. Condon,* 286 U.S. 73 (1932).

29. *Grovey v. Townsend,* 295 U.S. 45 (1935).

30. *United States v. Classic,* 313 U.S. 299 at 317 (1941).

31. *Smith v. Allwright,* 321 U.S. 649 at 660 (1944).

32. Id. at 669.

33. *Terry v. Adams,* 345 U.S. 461 at 469–470 (1953).

34. *Breedlove v. Suttles,* 302 U.S. 277 (1937).

35. *Harman v. Forssenius,* 380 U.S. 528 (1965).

36. *Harper v. Virginia State Board of Elections,* 383 U.S. 663 at 668 (1966).

37. Id. at 666, 668.

38. Id. at 683, 686.

39. *Colegrove v. Green,* 328 U.S. 549 (1946).

40. *Gomillion v. Lightfoot,* 364 U.S. 339 at 346–347 (1960).

41. Id. at 349.

42. *Wright v. Rockefeller,* 376 U.S. 52 (1964).

43. *United States v. Raines,* 362 U.S. 17 (1960); *Hannah v. Larch,* 363 U.S. 420 (1960).

44. *Congress and the Nation,* Vol. I (Washington, D.C.: Congressional Quarterly, 1965), 1628; *United States v. Alabama,* 362 U.S. 602 (1960).

45. *Congress and the Nation,* Vol. I, 1638.

46. *United States v. Louisiana,* 380 U.S. 145 (1965); *United States v. Mississippi,* 380 U.S. 128 (1965).

47. Lyndon B. Johnson, *Public Papers of the Presidents of the United States, Lyndon B. Johnson, 1965,* Book 1 (Washington, D.C.: U.S. Government Printing Office, 1966), March 15, 1965, 282.

48. U.S. Congress, Senate Judiciary Committee, *Voting Rights,* pt. 2, statement of Roy Wilkins, 89th Cong., 1st sess., 1965, 1005.

49. *Congress and the Nation,* Vol. II (Washington, D.C.: Congressional Quarterly, 1969), 354, 356–365.

50. *South Carolina v. Katzenbach,* 383 U.S. 301 at 326 (1966).

51. Id. at 308.

52. Id. at 330, 334, 336.

53. Id. at 358.

54. *Katzenbach v. Morgan,* 384 U.S. 641 (1966).

55. *Gaston County v. United States,* 395 U.S. 285 (1969).

56. *Allen v. Virginia Board of Elections,* 393 U.S. 544 (1969); *Hadnott v. Amos,* 394 U.S. 358 (1969); *McDaniel v. Sanchez,* 452 U.S. 130 (1981); *Hathorn v. Lovorn,* 457 U.S. 255 (1982); *City of Port Arthur, Texas v. United States,* 459 U.S. 159 (1982); *NAACP v. Hampton County Election Commission,* 470 U.S. 166 (1985); *Morse v. Republican Party of Virginia,* 000 U.S. 000 (1996).

57. *Dougherty County Board of Education v. White,* 435 U.S. 921 (1978).

58. *Perkins v. Mathews,* 400 U.S. 379 (1971); see also *City of Pleasant Grove v. United States,* 479 U.S. 462 (1987).

59. *Richmond v. United States,* 422 U.S. 358 (1975).

60. *Briscoe v. Bell,* 432 U.S. 404 (1977); *Morris v. Gressette,* 432 U.S. 491 (1977).

61. *City of Mobile v. Bolden,* 446 U.S. 55 at 65 (1980).

62. Id. at 141.

63. *Congress and the Nation,* Vol. VI (Washington, D.C.: Congressional Quarterly, 1985), 680.

64. *Thornburg v. Gingles,* 478 U.S. 30 (1986).

65. *Beer v. United States,* 425 U.S. 130 (1976).

66. *United Jewish Organizations of Williamsburgh v. Carey,* 430 U.S. 144 (1977); *Gomillion v. Lightfoot,* 364 U.S. 339 (1960).

67. *United Jewish Organizations of Williamsburgh v. Carey,* 430 U.S. 144 at 161 (1977).

68. Id. at 165.

69. *CQ Almanac 1993* (Washington, D.C.: Congressional Quarterly, 1994), 325.

70. *Shaw v. Reno,* 509 U.S. 630 (1993).

71. Id.

72. *Miller v. Johnson,* 115 S. Ct. 2475 (1995).

73. Id.

74. *Bush v. Vera,* 000 U.S. 000 (1996); *Shaw v. Hunt,* 000 U.S. 000 (1996).

THE RIGHT TO AN EQUAL VOTE (PP. 519–531)

1. For general background see *Congressional Quarterly's Guide to U.S. Elections,* 3d ed. (Washington, D.C.: Congressional Quarterly, 1994), 925–939.

2. *Wood v. Broom,* 287 U.S. 1 (1932).

3. *Colegrove v. Green,* 328 U.S. 549 (1946).

4. Id. at 552, 553–554, 556.

5. Id. at 564.

6. Id. at 574.

7. *Gomillion v. Lightfoot,* 364 U.S. 339 (1960).

8. Id. at 346, 347.

9. *Baker v. Carr,* 369 U.S. 186 (1962).

10. Id. at 253.

11. Id. at 201.

12. Id. at 207.

13. Id. at 209.

14. *Luther v. Borden,* 7 How. 1 (1849).

15. *Baker v. Carr,* 369 U.S. 186 at 258 (1962).

16. Id. at 267.

17. Id. at 268–270.

18. Id. at 332, 334.

19. Id. at 339.

20. *Gray v. Sanders,* 372 U.S. 368 at 378 (1963).

21. Id. at 379–381.

22. Id. at 384, 388.

23. *Wesberry v. Sanders,* 376 U.S. 1 at 7–8 (1964).

24. Id. at 42.

25. Richard O. Claude, *The Supreme Court and the Electoral Process* (Baltimore: John Hopkins University Press, 1970), 213n.–214n.

26. *Reynolds v. Sims,* 377 U.S. 533 at 567 (1964).

27. Id. at 573–574.

28. Id. at 555, 562, 567–568.

29. Id. at 577.

30. Id. at 578.

31. Id. at 624–625.

32. *Duddleston v. Grills,* 385 U.S. 155 (1967); *Kirkpatrick v. Preisler,* 385 U.S. 450 (1967).

33. *Kirkpatrick v. Preisler,* 394 U.S. 526 (1969).

34. Id. at 530.

35. Id. at 530–531, 533.

36. Id. at 538–539.

37. Id. at 553.

38. Id. at 549–550.

39. *Wells v. Rockefeller,* 394 U.S. 542 at 546 (1969).

40. *Guide to U.S. Elections,* 538.

41. *White v. Weiser,* 412 U.S. 783 (1973).

42. *Karcher v. Daggett,* 462 U.S. 725 (1983).

43. *United States Department of Commerce v. Montana,* 503 U.S. 442 (1992).

44. *Fortson v. Dorsey,* 379 U.S. 433 at 439 (1965).

45. *Burns v. Richardson,* 384 U.S. 73 (1966).

46. *Whitcomb v. Chavis,* 403 U.S. 124 (1971).

47. *White v. Regester,* 412 U.S. 755 (1973).

48. *Swann v. Adams,* 385 U.S. 440 at 444 (1967).

49. Ibid.

50. Id. at 447.

51. *Mahan v. Howell,* 410 U.S. 315 at 321 (1973).

52. Id. at 321–323, 328.

53. Id. at 339–340.

54. *Gaffney v. Cummings,* 412 U.S. 736 (1973).

55. Id. at 749.

56. Ibid.

57. Id. at 749–750.

58. *White v. Regester,* 412 U.S. 755 (1973).

59. *Brown v. Thomson,* 462 U.S. 835 (1983).

60. *Presley v. Etowah County Commission,* 502 U.S. 491 (1992).

61. *Holder v. Hall,* 114 S. Ct. 2581 (1994).

62. Id.

63. *Chapman v. Meier,* 420 U.S. 1 (1975).

64. Id. at 19.

65. Id. at 24–25.

66. *Connor v. Finch,* 431 U.S. 407 (1977).

67. *Growe v. Emison,* 507 U.S. 25 (1993); *Voinovich v. Quilter,* 507 U.S. 146 (1993).

68. *Shaw v. Reno,* 509 U.S. 630 (1993).

69. Id.

70. Id.

71. Id.

72. Id.

73. *Johnson v. DeGrandy,* 114 S. Ct. 2647 (1994).

74. *Miller v. Johnson,* 115 S. Ct. 2475 (1994).

75. Id.

76. *Bush v. Vera,* ____ U.S. ____ (1996); *Shaw v. Hunt,* ____ U.S. ____ (1996).

77. *Bush v. Vera.*

78. Id.

FREEDOM OF POLITICAL ASSOCIATION (PP. 532–554)

1. *Elrod v. Burns,* 427 U.S. 347 at 356 (1976).

2. *Schenck v. United States,* 249 U.S. 47 (1919); *Frohwerk v. United States,* 249 U.S. 204 (1919); *Debs v. United States,* 249 U.S. 211 (1919).

3. *Schenck v. United States*, 249 U.S. 47 at 52 (1919).

4. *Schaefer v. United States*, 251 U.S. 466 at 482 (1920).

5. Id. at 479.

6. *Gitlow v. New York*, 268 U.S. 652 at 666 (1925).

7. *Whitney v. California*, 274 U.S. 357 at 377 (1927).

8. *Stromberg v. California*, 283 U.S. 359 (1931).

9. *DeJonge v. Oregon*, 299 U.S. 353 (1937); *Herndon v. Lowry*, 301 U.S. 242 (1937).

10. *DeJonge v. Oregon*, 299 U.S. 353 at 365 (1937).

11. *Joint Anti-Fascist Refugee Committee v. McGrath*, 341 U.S. 123 at 174 (1951).

12. *Congress and the Nation*, Vol. I (Washington, D.C.: Congressional Quarterly, 1965), 1645–1670.

13. Thomas I. Emerson, *The System of Freedom of Expression* (New York: Random House, 1970), 110.

14. *Dennis v. United States*, 341 U.S. 494 at 510 (1951).

15. Id. at 502.

16. Id. at 509, 510–511, 516–517.

17. Id. at 549.

18. Id. at 518–520.

19. Id. at 525–526.

20. Id. at 570.

21. Id. at 577.

22. Id. at 579.

23. Id. at 584–585, 590.

24. *Yates v. United States*, 354 U.S. 298 (1957); see also the Court's review of Yates's conviction for contempt: *Yates v. United States*, 355 U.S. 66 (1957); 356 U.S. 363 (1958).

25. *Yates v. United States*, 354 U.S. 298 at 306–307, 312 (1957).

26. Id. at 321.

27. Id. at 320–322, 324–325, 326–327.

28. Id. at 329–330.

29. Id. at 339.

30. Id. at 340.

31. Id. at 345.

32. *Scales v. United States*, 367 U.S. 203 at 228–229 (1961).

33. Id. at 229–230.

34. Id. at 260.

35. *Noto v. United States*, 367 U.S. 290 at 297–298 (1961).

36. *Congress and the Nation*, Vol. I, 1650–1651.

37. Ibid., 1653.

38. *Communist Party v. Subversive Activities Control Board*, 367 U.S. 1 (1961).

39. Id. at 86.

40. Id. at 102–103.

41. Id. at 105.

42. Id. at 137, 145.

43. Id. at 181.

44. *Congress and the Nation*, Vol. II (Washington, D.C.: Congressional Quarterly, 1969), 413–415. See also Vol. III, published in 1973, 489; and Vol. IV, published in 1977, 570.

45. *Albertson v. Subversive Activities Control Board*, 382 U.S. 70 at 79 (1965).

46. *Congress and the Nation*, Vol. II, 418.

47. *United States v. Robel*, 389 U.S. 258 at 265, 266–267 (1967).

48. Id. at 285.

49. *Boorda v. Subversive Activities Control Board*, 421 F. 2d 1142 (D.C. Cir. 1969).

50. For general background on loyalty programs, see *Congress and the Nation*, Vol. I, 1663–1668.

51. *Joint Anti-Fascist Refugee Committee v. McGrath*, 341 U.S. 123 at 161 (1951).

52. Id. at 200.

53. *Bailey v. Richardson*, 341 U.S. 918 (1951).

54. *Peters v. Hobby*, 349 U.S. 331 (1955).

55. *Cole v. Young*, 351 U.S. 536 (1956); see also *Service v. Dulles*, 354 U.S. 363 (1957).

56. *Greene v. McElroy*, 360 U.S. 474 (1959).

57. Id. at 508.

58. Id. at 511, 524.

59. *Congress and the Nation*, Vol. I, 1667–1668.

60. *Cafeteria and Restaurant Workers Union v. McElroy*, 367 U.S. 886 (1961).

61. *American Communications Association v. Douds*, 339 U.S. 382 at 390 (1950).

62. Id. at 391.

63. Id. at 393.

64. Id. at 396.

65. Id. at 445.

66. Id. at 444.

67. Id. at 446, 452–453.

68. *Congress and the Nation*, Vol. I, 568, 611.

69. *United States v. Brown*, 381 U.S. 437 at 449–450, 461 (1965).

70. Id. at 474.

71. *Killian v. United States*, 368 U.S. 231 (1961); *Raymond Dennis et al. v. United States*, 384 U.S. 855 (1966).

72. *Gerende v. Board of Supervisors of Elections*, 341 U.S. 56 (1951).

73. *Garner v. Board of Public Works of the City of Los Angeles*, 341 U.S. 716 (1951).

74. Id. at 724–725.

75. Id. at 726, 728.

76. *Adler v. Board of Education, City of New York*, 342 U.S. 485 (1952).

77. Id. at 493.

78. Ibid.

79. Id. at 508.

80. Id. at 509, 510, 511.

81. *Wieman v. Updegraff*, 344 U.S. 183 at 190 (1952).

82. Id. at 191.

83. *Slochower v. Board of Higher Education of New York City*, 350 U.S. 551 at 557 (1956).

84. Id. at 561.

85. Id. at 565.

86. *Lerner v. Casey*, 357 U.S. 468 (1958).

87. *Beilan v. Board of Public Education, School District of Philadelphia*, 357 U.S. 399 (1958).

88. Id. at 410.

89. Id. at 418; see also *Speiser v. Randall*, 357 U.S. 513 (1958).

90. *National Association for the Advancement of Colored People v. Alabama*, 357 U.S. 449 (1958).

91. *Shelton v. Tucker*, 364 U.S. 479 at 490 (1960).

92. *Cramp v. Board of Public Instruction, Orange County, Fla.*, 368 U.S. 278 at 286 (1961).

93. Id. at 287.

94. *Baggett v. Bullitt*, 377 U.S. 360 at 367 (1964).

95. *Elfbrandt v. Russell*, 384 U.S. 11 at 17–19 (1966).

96. *Keyishian v. Board of Regents of the University of the State of New York*, 385 U.S. 589 at 606 (1967).

97. Id. at 601, 603.

98. Id. at 628.

99. *Whitehill v. Elkins*, 389 U.S. 54 at 62 (1967).

100. *Connell v. Higginbotham*, 403 U.S. 207 (1971).

101. *Cole v. Richardson*, 405 U.S. 676 (1972).

102. *In re Stolar, Baird v. State Bar of Arizona*, 401 U.S. 23, 1 (1971); *Law Students Civil Rights Research Council v. Wadmond*, 401 U.S. 154 (1971).

103. *Communist Party of Indiana v. Whitcomb*, 414 U.S. 441 at 448 (1974).

104. *Healy v. James*, 408 U.S. 169 (1972).

105. *Rosario v. Rockefeller*, 410 U.S. 752 (1973).

106. *Kusper v. Pontikes*, 414 U.S. 51 (1973).

107. *Storer v. Brown, Frommhagen v. Brown*, 415 U.S. 724 (1974).

108. *Cousins v. Wigoda*, 419 U.S. 477 (1975).

109. *Democratic Party of the United States v. La Follette*, 450 U.S. 107 (1981).

110. *Brown v. Socialist Workers '74 Campaign Committee*, 459 U.S. 81 (1982).

111. *Tashjian v. Republican Party of Connecticut*, 479 U.S. 208 (1986); see also *Eu v. San Francisco County Democratic Central Committee* 103 L.Ed. 2d 271 (1989).

112. *Elrod v. Burns*, 427 U.S. 347 at 357 (1976). See also *Buckley v. Valeo*, 424 U.S. 1 at 11 (1976). The reference to "orderly group activity" is from *National Association for the Advancement of Colored People v. Button*, 371 U.S. 415 at 430 (1963).

113. *Elrod v. Burns*, 427 U.S. 347 at 358 (1976).

114. *United Public Workers v. Mitchell*, 330 U.S. 75 (1947); *Civil Service Commission v. Letter Carriers*, 413 U.S. 548 (1973).

115. *Elrod v. Burns*, 427 U.S. 347 at 372–373 (1976).

116. Id. at 379.

117. *Branti v. Finkel*, 445 U.S. 507 (1980).

118. *Rutan et al. v. Republican Party of Illinois et al.*, 497 U.S. 62 (1990).

119. Id.

120. Id.

121. Id.

122. *O'Hare Truck Service v. Northlake*, _____ U.S. _____ (1996).

123. *Board of County Commissioners, Wabaunsee County v. Umbehr*, _____ U.S. _____ (1996).

CHAPTER 11

Due Process and Criminal Rights

D UE PROCESS of law embodies a promise that government will deal fairly with the individual. In the twentieth century the Supreme Court read into that guarantee a wide range of rights, including those granted in other provisions of the Bill of Rights—guarantees until then applicable only against federal, not state, infringement.

Due process is primarily a guarantee of *how* the government must act, not of *what* it must do. It is difficult to overestimate the importance of procedure, noted Justice William O. Douglas, pointing out that most of the provisions of the Bill of Rights were procedural. "It is procedure," he wrote, "that spells much of the difference between rule by law and rule by whim or caprice. Steadfast adherence to strict procedural safeguards is our main assurance that there will be equal justice under law."[1]

Procedural rights are of great significance for persons charged with crimes. The Bill of Rights assures an individual accused of a crime fair treatment. Every criminal case is a legal contest between the individual and government. A crime is an offense against society. Government is society's agency to prosecute the offender, but it is an uneven match. The power of the individual defendant is no match for the power of government unless the individual has guarantees he or she will be treated fairly.

Procedural rights are not based on sentimental concern for criminals. The guarantees were not devised to coddle them or to provide technical loopholes through which dangerous persons can escape the consequences of their acts. "Due process of law is not, primarily, the right of the accused," David Fellman has written. "It is basically the community's assurance that prosecutors, judges and juries will behave properly, within rules distilled from long centuries of concrete experience."[2]

Although the procedural safeguards of the Bill of Rights are known primarily for their importance to persons suspected or accused of crime, they operate as well to shield all individuals against arbitrary, despotic, or unduly intrusive government action. They assure an individual charged with a crime notice of the charge against him, a speedy and public trial by an impartial jury, the opportunity to confront witnesses accusing him and to compel witnesses in his favor to appear, and the aid of an attorney in preparing and presenting his defense.

Furthermore, these guarantees promise the individual that he will not be subjected to unreasonable search or arrest by government officials, compelled to incriminate himself, deprived of life, liberty, or property without due process of law, tried for a serious offense without being formally charged in an indictment, tried twice for the same action by the same sovereign, subject to excessive bail or excessive fines, or sentenced to suffer cruel and unusual punishment.

Originally, these guarantees applied directly only to persons tried in federal courts, even though most persons charged with crimes in the United States are tried in state and local courts. But since 1868 the Fourteenth Amendment has guaranteed the individual due process and equal protection from state, as well as federal, authorities. Beginning in the 1930s, the Court has read those guarantees as extending most of the specific procedural protections of the Bill of Rights to persons tried in state courts.

The judicial expansion of due process reached its climax in the 1960s, but the revolutionary decisions of that time had roots. In the 1920s and 1930s the Court, under the leadership of successive chief justices, William Howard Taft and Charles Evans Hughes, began to apply the fundamental requirements of fair procedure to state trials, even while individual justices wrangled over whether the Fourteenth Amendment guarantee of due process so "incorporated" the Bill of Rights as to extend all its specific guarantees to defendants in state cases.

At first, the Court rejected any wholesale incorporation theory, preferring a more selective approach. The majority began developing a list of fundamental rights that states must honor: the right to legal counsel, the ban on cruel and unusual punishment, and the guarantee against unreasonable search and seizure.

The selective incorporation debate came to a dramatic end in the 1960s. In a series of rulings, the Court resoundingly rejected any idea that only a watered-down Bill of Rights applied to the states. The Court extended to state defendants the protection of the controversial exclusionary rule, the right to appointed counsel, the privilege against compelled self-incrimination, the right to confront prosecution witnesses, the right to a speedy trial, the right to a jury trial, and the protection against double jeopardy.

EARLY VIEW

Early in its history, during the tenure of Chief Justice John Marshall, the Supreme Court held that the Bill of Rights limited only the federal government, not the states. In 1833 the Supreme Court set out this conclusion in *Barron v. Baltimore*, decided without dissent.[3]

With Marshall writing, the Court rejected the argument of a Baltimore wharf-owner that the Fifth Amendment guarantee of just compensation to persons whose private property was taken for public use applied against all governments, not just the federal government. This was not the intent of the Bill of Rights, according to Marshall.

> The Constitution was ordained and established by the people of the United States for themselves, for their own government, and not for the government of the individual States. . . . The powers they conferred on this government were to be exercised by itself; and the limitations on power, if expressed in general terms, are naturally, and, we think, necessarily applicable to the government created by the instrument.
>
> . . . the provision in the fifth amendment to the Constitution, declaring that private property shall not be taken for public use without just compensation, is intended solely as a limitation on the exercise of power by the government of the United States, and is not applicable to the legislation of the States.[4]

Congress and Due Process

Although the justices refused to extend the Fifth Amendment's guarantee of due process against *state* action, the Court in 1856 applied that guarantee to legislative action by Congress, making clear that all branches of the *federal* government were bound by it.

In *Murray's Lessee v. Hoboken Land and Improvement Company* the Court upheld an act of Congress authorizing the Treasury Department to issue warrants against the property of federal revenue collectors who were indebted to the federal government.[5] The law had been challenged as allowing the taking of property without due process. In the majority opinion by Justice Benjamin R. Curtis, the Court began its effort to define due process as any process that did not conflict with specific constitutional provisions or established judicial practices.

> That the warrant now in question is legal process, is not denied. It was issued in conformity with an act of Congress. But is it "due process of law?" The Constitution contains no description of those processes which it was intended to allow or forbid. It does not even declare what principles are to be applied to ascertain whether it be due process. It is manifest that it was not left to the legislative power to enact any process which might be devised. The article is a restraint on the legislative as well as on the executive and judicial powers of the government, and cannot be so construed as to leave Congress free to make any process "due process of law," by its mere will. To what principles, then, are we to resort to ascertain whether this process enacted by Congress, is due process? To this the answer must be twofold. We must examine the Constitution itself, to see whether this process be in conflict with any of its provisions. If not found to be so, we must look to those settled usages and modes of proceeding existing in the common and statute law of England, before the emigration of our ancestors and which are shown not to have been unsuited to their civil and political condition by having been acted on by them after the settlement of this country.[6]

Substantive Due Process

In 1868, twelve years after that ruling, the Fourteenth Amendment became part of the Constitution. It forbid the states to deprive any person of life, liberty, or property without due process of law.

Oddly, the due process guarantee was initially used with a great deal more effect to protect property than to protect life or liberty. This was the result of the development of the doctrine of substantive due process—the view that the substance, as well as the procedures, of a law must comply with due process. (*See box, The Protection of Substantive Due Process, pp. 688–689, in Chapter 12.*)

In the midtwentieth century, Justice Robert H. Jackson compared the two types of due process:

> Procedural due process is more elemental and less flexible than substantive due process. It yields less to the times, varies less with conditions, and defers much less to legislative judgment. Insofar as it is technical law, it must be a specialized responsibility within the competence of the judiciary on which they do not bend before political branches of the Government, as they should on matters of policy which comprise substantive law.[7]

DUE PROCESS AND THE STATES

For sixty-five years after the Fourteenth Amendment was ratified, its due process clause provided little protection to persons tried in state and local courts.

In 1884 the Court held that due process did not require states to use indictments to charge persons with capital crimes, despite the Fifth Amendment provision requiring indictments in similar federal cases. In 1900 the Court held that the due process guarantee did not require states to use twelve-man juries. In 1908 the Court held that the Fifth Amendment privilege against compelled self-incrimination did not protect state defendants.

Hurtado v. California

In the indictment case, *Hurtado v. California,* the Court upheld the murder conviction and death sentence of Joseph Hurtado, charged without an indictment.[8] He challenged his conviction, arguing that under Justice Curtis's definition of due process in *Hoboken,* he had been denied due process.

The Court's ruling, relaxing the earlier standard for the demands of due process upon state criminal procedures, blurred the *Hoboken* definition. Writing for the seven-justice majority, Justice Stanley Matthews redefined due process as "any legal proceeding enforced by public authority, whether sanctioned by age and custom, or newly devised in the discretion of the legislative power, in furtherance of the general public good, which regards, and preserves these principles of liberty and justice."[9]

However, "not every Act, legislative in form, . . . is law," Matthews explained:

> Law is something more than mere will exerted as an act of power. It must be not a special rule for a particular person or a particular case, . . . thus excluding, as not due process of law, Acts of attainder, Bills of pains and penalties, Acts of confiscation, Acts reversing judgments, and Acts directly transferring one man's estate to another, legislative judgments and decrees, and other similar, special, partial and arbitrary exertions of power under the forms of legislation. Arbitrary power, enforcing its edicts to the injury of the persons and property of its subjects, is not law, whether manifested as the decree of a personal monarch or of an impersonal multitude.[10]

Adopting reasoning diametrically opposed to that of Justice Curtis in *Hoboken,* the majority ruled that because the Fifth Amendment expressly included *both* the indictment requirement *and* the due process guarantee, the indictment requirement was obviously not included as an element of due process.

In lone dissent Justice John Marshall Harlan set out the "incorporation" approach. In his view the Fourteenth Amendment guarantee of due process incorporated many of the specific guarantees of the Bill of Rights, effectively nullifying *Barron v. Baltimore* by applying those guarantees against state action. Harlan argued that the Court's reasoning in *Hurtado* could open the door for states to deny defendants many other rights:

If the presence in the Fifth Amendment of a specific provision for grand juries in capital cases, alongside the provision for due process of law in proceedings involving life, liberty or property, is held to prove that "due process of law" did not, in the judgment of the framers of the Constitution, necessarily require a grand jury in capital cases, inexorable logic would require it to be, likewise, held that the right not to be put twice in jeopardy of life and limb for the same offense, nor compelled in a criminal case to testify against one's self—rights and immunities also specifically recognized in the Fifth Amendment— were not protected by that due process of law required by the settled usages and proceedings existing under the common and statute law of England at the settlement of this country. More than that, other Amendments of the Constitution proposed at the same time, expressly recognize the right of persons to just compensation for private property taken for public use; their right, when accused of crime, to be informed of the nature and cause of the accusation against them, and to a speedy and public trial, by an impartial jury of the State and district wherein the crime was committed; to be confronted by the witnesses against them; and to have compulsory process for obtaining witnesses in their favor. Will it be claimed that these rights were not secured by the "law of the land" or by "due process of law," as declared and established at the foundation of our government?[11]

Selective Incorporation

Eventually the Court would adopt an approach of "selective incorporation" of the guarantees of the Bill of Rights into the due process clause of the Fourteenth Amendment. Justice Samuel F. Miller wrote:

If . . . it were possible to define what it is for a State to deprive a person of life, liberty or property without due process of law, in terms which would cover every exercise of power thus forbidden to the State, and exclude those which are not, no more useful construction could be furnished by this or any other court to any part of the fundamental law.

But, apart from the imminent risk of failure to give any definition which would be at once perspicuous, comprehensive and satisfactory, there is wisdom, we think, in the ascertaining of the intent and application of such an important phrase in the Federal Constitution, by the gradual process of judicial inclusion and exclusion, as the cases presented for decision shall require, with the reasoning on which such decisions may be founded. This court is, after . . . nearly a century, still engaged in defining . . . other powers conferred on the Federal Government, or limitations imposed upon the States.[12]

Maxwell v. Dow

In 1900 the Court ruled in *Maxwell v. Dow* that the Fourteenth Amendment did not require state juries to be composed of twelve persons.

Justice Harlan again dissented, protesting the contrast between the Court's vigorous use of substantive due process and its reluctance to enforce procedural due process:

If then the "due process of law" required by the Fourteenth Amendment does not allow a State to take private property without just compensation, but does allow the life or liberty of the citizen to be taken in a mode that is repugnant to the settled usages and the modes of proceeding authorized at the time the Constitution was adopted and which was expressly forbidden in the National Bill of Rights, it would seem that the protection of private property is of more consequence than the protection of the life and liberty of the citizen.[13]

Twining v. New Jersey

Eight years later the Court in *Twining v. New Jersey* permitted a judge to call attention to defendants' failure to testify in their own defense. Despite the trial judge's implication that the silence was an admission of guilt, the Court ruled that due process was not denied the defendants. The defendants had claimed that the judge's comments violated their Fifth Amendment right to remain silent rather than incriminate themselves. They argued that this right was a fundamental "privilege or immunity" of federal citizenship protected against state action by the Fourteenth Amendment.

The Court rejected the claim and upheld the decision of the state court, sustaining conviction. Justice William H. Moody's opinion also denied that the Fourteenth Amendment guarantee of due process extended the protection of the first eight amendments against state action:

The essential elements of due process of law, already established . . . are singularly few, though of wide application and deep significance. . . . Due process requires that the court which assumes to determine the rights of parties shall have jurisdiction . . . and that there shall be notice and opportunity for hearing given the parties.[14]

But Justice Moody left open the possibility that additional due process requirements could be imposed upon the states.

It is possible that some of the personal rights safeguarded by the first eight Amendments against national action may also be safeguarded against state action, because a denial of them would be a denial of due process of law. . . . If this is so, it is not because those rights are enumerated in the first eight Amendments, but because they are of such a nature that they are included in the conception of due process of law.[15]

"Fundamental" Rights

In the 1920s and 1930s the Court began to rule that some rights were so fundamental to fair treatment that the due process guarantee required states to observe them.

In *Palko v. Connecticut,* decided in 1937, the Court explained that some rights were "implicit in the concept of ordered liberty" and thus protected by due process against state infringement. In *Palko*, however, the Court again rejected the "incorporation" theory, first expressed in Harlan's dissent from *Hurtado* (1884).

Frank Palko had been tried twice by Connecticut for the same murder. He challenged his conviction, arguing that the second trial violated the Fifth Amendment guarantee against double jeopardy. The Court refused to reverse his conviction, declaring that the protection against double jeopardy was not one of those rights which due process required the states to observe.

For the Court, divided 8–1, Justice Benjamin N. Cardozo gave a "status report" on due process and state action:

The right to trial by jury and the immunity from prosecution except as the result of an indictment may have value and importance. Even so, they are not of the very essence of a scheme of ordered liberty. To abolish them is not to violate a "principle of justice so rooted in the traditions and conscience of our people as to be ranked as fundamental." . . . What is true of jury trials and indictments is true also, as the cases show, of the immunity from compulsory self-incrimination. . . . This too might be lost, and justice still be done. . . . The exclusion of these immunities and privileges from the privileges and immunities protected against the action of the states has not been arbitrary or casual. It has been dictated by a study and appreciation of the meaning, the essential implications, of liberty itself.

We reach a different plane of social and moral values when we pass to the privileges and immunities that have been taken over from the earlier articles of the federal bill of rights and brought within the Fourteenth Amendment by a process of absorption. . . .[T]he process of absorption has had its source in the belief that neither liberty nor justice would exist if they were sacrificed. . . . This is true . . . of freedom of thought and speech. . . . Fundamental too in the concept of due process, and so in that of liberty, is the thought that condemnation shall be rendered only after trial. . . . The hearing, moreover, must be a real one, not a sham or a pretense, *Moore v. Dempsey.* . . . For that reason, ignorant defendants in a capital case were held to have been condemned unlawfully when in truth, though not in form, they were refused the aid of counsel, *Powell v. Alabama.*[16]

A decade later, with its decision in *Adamson v. California,* the Court reaffirmed its holding in *Twining* that the self-incrimination guarantee did not operate against state action—and its general view that the Fourteenth Amendment did not incorporate the Bill of Rights.[17]

Arguing for the "incorporation" theory and dissenting from *Adamson* were four members of the Court—Justices Hugo L. Black, Frank Murphy, William O. Douglas, and Wiley B. Rutledge. They argued that the Fourteenth Amendment was originally intended "to extend to all the people of the nation the complete protection of the Bill of Rights."[18]

Black and Douglas would continue to serve on the Court through the 1960s—and find their views at last espoused by a majority of the Court as it extended virtually all those protections to all persons.

A Fair Trial

Anyone accused of a crime is constitutionally guaranteed a hearing on the charges against him, an opportunity to force the government to prove the charges, and a chance to present a rebuttal to that evidence.

In the 1920s the Supreme Court began to use the due process clause of the Fourteenth Amendment to require that states ensure that trials be held free of mob domination and be conducted before an impartial judge and a fairly chosen jury.

As early as 1915 the Court acknowledged that a trial could be so dominated by outside pressures that its outcome would deny the defendant due process. But the Court refused to intervene in the case of *Frank v. Mangum,* finding that the state in that instance provided the defendant sufficient opportunity through appellate review to win correction of this denial of his rights.[1]

Eight years later, however, the Court approved federal intervention to order the release of five black men convicted of murder in Arkansas and sentenced to die after a trial so dominated by racial tensions that it became a travesty of justice. Justice Oliver Wendell Holmes Jr. explained in *Moore v. Dempsey* that such intervention was necessary when "the case is that the whole proceeding is a mask—that counsel, jury, and judge were swept to the fatal end by an irresistible wave of public passion, and that the state courts failed to correct that wrong." At that point, he went on, "neither perfection in the machinery for correction nor the possibility that the trial court and counsel saw no other way of avoiding an immediate outbreak of the mob can prevent this court from securing to the petitioners their constitutional rights."[2]

Four years after *Moore* the Court in 1927 applied the due process clause to require that state and local trials be held before impartial judges without any personal stake in their outcome. In *Tumey v. Ohio* the Court held unconstitutional a system that permitted the presiding judge to take a portion of every fine he assessed against persons found guilty of violating the state's prohibition law.[3]

Writing for the Court, Chief Justice William Howard Taft declared:

All matters of judicial qualification may not involve constitutional validity. Thus matters of kinship, personal bias, state policy, remoteness of interest would seem to generally be matters merely of legislative discretion. . . . But it certainly violates the 14th Amendment and deprives a defendant in a criminal case of due process of law to subject his liberty or property to the judgment of a court, the judge of which has a direct, personal, substantial pecuniary interest in reaching a conclusion against him in his case.[4]

The Court has emphasized that the judge's interest must be both personal and substantial to affect his or her impartiality. For example, in an Ohio town where the mayor-judge received a fixed salary for his duties, payment of half the fines to the town treasury did not violate due process of law, the Court ruled in 1928, limiting the effect of *Tumey.*[5]

In 1972, however, the Court ruled that persons charged with traffic offenses in another Ohio town were denied due process when the judge at their trial was the town mayor. The critical difference in this case was the fact that the fines collected from traffic violators provided a substantial portion of village revenues.

Justice William J. Brennan Jr. reasoned that although the mayor received no personal benefit or income from convictions, the "possible temptation" to convict "may . . . exist when the mayor's executive responsibilities for village finances may make him partisan to maintain the high level of contributions from the mayor's court."[6]

Although due process requires that a judge be impartial, it does not require that a judge be an attorney.

In *North v. Russell* (1976) the Court considered a due process challenge to Kentucky's two-tiered state court system under which small towns were permitted to employ nonlawyer judges for police courts. Such a court and a nonlawyer judge convicted Lonnie North for drunken driving. North challenged his conviction, claiming that it violated his right to due process. The Supreme Court rejected this argument and upheld the use of nonlawyer judges in cases involving minor offenses.

Chief Justice Warren E. Burger, speaking for five of the six members of the majority, wrote:

Our concern in prior cases with judicial functions being performed by nonjudicial officers has also been directed at the need for independent, neutral and detached judgment, not at legal training. . . .

We conclude that the Kentucky two-tier trial court system with lay judicial officers in the first tier in smaller cities and an appeal of right with a de novo trial before a traditionally law-trained judge in the second does not violate either the due process or equal protection guarantees of the Constitution of the United States.[7]

Justices Potter Stewart and Thurgood Marshall dissented. They found the use of nonlawyer judges a violation of the guarantees of due process and of the assistance of legal counsel.

The Right to a Jury Trial

The system of trial by jury is a distinctive feature of the Anglo-American system of justice, dating back as far as the fourteenth century.

The men who wrote the Constitution included in Article III the flat requirement that "the Trial of all Crimes, except in Cases of Impeachment, shall be by Jury."

Not content with this single provision, those who drafted the Bill of Rights included additional guarantees of that right in the grand jury requirement of the Fifth Amendment, in the "speedy and public trial by an impartial jury" requirement of the Sixth Amendment, and in the Seventh Amendment requirement of jury trials in common-law suits involving more than $20.

This right has been the subject of many Supreme Court rulings concerning the size, selection, and unanimity of juries, as well as a defendant's decision to waive the right to a jury trial, usually as a result of plea bargaining.

In federal cases, the Court has been unwavering in insisting that a jury in a criminal case must consist of twelve people and must reach a unanimous verdict. (In federal civil cases, however, juries may be as small as six members.)[8]

The Court in *Patton v. United States* explained that a jury trial "includes all the essential elements as they were recognized in this country and England when the Constitution was adopted."

Those elements were: 1) That the jury should consist of twelve men, neither more nor less; 2) that the trial should be in the presence and under the superintendence of a judge having power to instruct them as to the law and advise them in respect of the facts; and 3) that the verdict should be unanimous.[9]

STATE TRIALS

Not until 1968, a full century after ratification of the Fourteenth Amendment and its due process clause, did the Court apply the right to trial by jury to the states.

In *Walker v. Sauvinet,* decided in 1876, the Court held that the Seventh Amendment right to trial by jury in civil cases was not a privilege or immunity of federal citizenship protected against state action.[10] Then in *Maxwell v. Dow* (1900) the Court ruled that neither the privileges and immunities clause of the Fourteenth Amendment nor the due process clause required that state juries consist of twelve persons. "Trial by jury has never been affirmed to be a necessary requisite of due process of law," declared the Court.[11]

With a line of decisions beginning in the 1930s, however, the Court made clear that *if* a state provided a trial by jury to a defendant, it was required to use fair procedures in selecting a jury that would represent a cross section of the community and would be relatively unbiased.

In 1968, the centennial of the adoption of the Fourteenth Amendment, the Court finally held that the right to trial by jury for persons charged with serious crimes applied to the states. In *Duncan v. Louisiana* the Court applied the Sixth Amendment right to a jury trial to the states as a necessary ingredient of due process.[12] The Sixth Amendment's guarantee is as follows:

In all criminal prosecutions, the accused shall enjoy the right to a speedy and public trial, by an impartial jury of the State and district wherein the crime shall have been committed, which district shall have been previously ascertained by law, and to be informed of the nature and cause of the accusation; to be confronted with the witnesses against him; to have compulsory process for obtaining witnesses in his favor, and to have the Assistance of Counsel for his defence.

Gary Duncan, charged with battery in Louisiana courts, had been denied a jury trial; he was convicted and sentenced to a fine and two years in prison. Duncan appealed to the Supreme Court, arguing that this denial of a jury trial violated his right to due process.

The Court agreed. Justice Byron R. White wrote:

Because we believe that trial by jury is fundamental to the American scheme of justice, we hold that the Fourteenth Amendment guarantees a right of jury trial in all criminal cases which—were they to be tried in a federal court—would come within the Sixth Amendment's guarantee.[13]

By applying the right to jury trial to the states the Court created two new questions. Were states now required to use only twelve-person juries? Must all state jury verdicts be unanimous?

Small Juries

The answer to the first question came quickly—and it was no. In *Williams v. Florida,* decided in 1970, the Court held it proper for states to use juries composed of as few as six persons in noncapital cases.[14]

Johnny Williams was tried for robbery by a six-man jury, which Florida law allowed in all noncapital cases. Writing for the Court, Justice White acknowledged:

We do not pretend to be able to divine precisely what the word "jury" imported to the Framers, the First Congress, or the States in 1789. It may well be that the usual expectation was that the jury would consist of 12, and that hence, the most likely conclusion to be drawn is simply that little thought was actually given to the specific question we face today. But there is absolutely no indication in "the intent of the Framers" of an explicit decision to equate the constitutional and common law characteristics of the jury. Nothing in this history suggests, then, that we do violence to the letter of the Constitution by turning to other than purely historical considerations to determine which features of the jury system, as it existed at common law, were preserved in the Constitution. The relevant inquiry, as we see it, must be the function which the particular feature performs and its relation to the purposes of the jury trial. Measured by this standard, the 12-man requirement cannot be regarded as an indispensable component of the Sixth Amendment. . . .

. . . [T]he essential feature of a jury obviously lies in the interposition between the accused and his accuser of the common-sense judgment of a group of laymen, and in the community participation and shared responsibility which results from the group's determination of guilt or innocence. The performance of this role is not a function of the particular number of the body which makes up the jury. To be sure the number should probably be large enough to promote group deliberation, free from outside attempts at intimidation, and to provide a fair possibility for obtaining a representative cross section of the community. But we find little reason to think that these goals are in any meaningful sense less likely to be achieved when the jury numbers six, than when it numbers 12—particularly if the requirement of unanimity is retained. And, certainly the reliability of the jury as a factfinder hardly seems likely to be a function of its size.[15]

In 1978 the Supreme Court made plain that juries must consist of at least six persons, rejecting Georgia's use of a five-person jury.[16]

The same day the Court in *Williams* resolved the question of jury size, it answered another question: What crimes were serious enough to require states to provide a jury trial? In *Baldwin v. New York* the Court held that states must provide trial by jury for all persons charged with offenses that could be punished by more than six months in prison.[17]

DUE PROCESS FOR DELINQUENTS

Juveniles, the Court has ruled, possess some, but not all, of the due process rights assured to adults by the Fifth Amendment's due process clause and the Sixth Amendment. Juvenile court proceedings are considered civil, not criminal, hearings. They are designed to shelter young offenders from the exposure of a public trial, giving them the opportunity to begin anew without the handicap of publicity or a criminal record.

Until 1967 only general elements of due process and fair treatment were applied to these proceedings. But in 1967 the Court in *In re Gault* held that juveniles charged with violating the law did have the right to confront and crossexamine persons presenting the evidence against them. Furthermore, the Court declared that juveniles had the same rights as adults to notice, aid of counsel, and protection against self-incrimination.[1]

Juveniles must be found delinquent by proof "beyond a reasonable doubt" rather than by any lesser standard, the Court held in *In re Winship* (1970). The justices found that Samuel Winship, a twelve-year-old found guilty "by a preponderance of the evidence" of stealing money from a woman's pocketbook, had been denied his due process rights. The stricter standard of proof of guilt, "beyond a reasonable doubt" was an essential element of due process and fair treatment applicable to juvenile as well as adult proceedings, said the Court.[2]

The following year, however, in *McKeiver v. Pennsylvania* and *In re Burrus*, the Court refused to extend the right to trial by jury to juvenile court proceedings.[3]

Justice Harry A. Blackmun explained:

If the jury trial were to be injected into the juvenile court system as a matter of right, it would bring with it into that system the traditional delay, the formality and the clamor of the adversary system and, possibly, the public trial. . . .

If the formalities of the criminal adjudicative process are to be superimposed upon the juvenile court system, there is little need for its separate existence. Perhaps that ultimate disillusionment will come one day, but for the moment we are disinclined to give impetus to it.[4]

Four years later the Court extended the Fifth Amendment protection against double jeopardy to minors, ruling that a defendant found in juvenile court to have violated the law could not subsequently be tried for the same act as an adult.[5]

1. *In re Gault*, 387 U.S. 1 (1967).
2. *In re Winship*, 397 U.S. 358 (1970).
3. *McKeiver v. Pennsylvania, In re Burrus*, 403 U.S. 528 (1971).
4. Id. at 550–551.
5. *Breed v. Jones*, 421 U.S. 519 at 529 (1975).

Unanimous Juries

In 1972 the Court held that state juries need not reach their verdicts unanimously. This ruling came in *Johnson v. Louisiana* and *Apodaca v. Oregon*.[18]

In the Louisiana case the Court upheld a state jury's 9–3 verdict convicting a man of robbery. Writing for the majority, Justice White declared that "want of jury unanimity is not to be equated with the existence of a reasonable doubt" concerning a defendant's guilt.

The Court rejected the defendant's argument "that in order to give substance to the reasonable doubt standard which the State, by virtue of the Due Process Clause of the Fourteenth Amendment, must satisfy in criminal cases . . . that clause must be construed to require a unanimous jury verdict in all criminal cases."[19]

White wrote:

[T]his Court has never held jury unanimity to be a requisite of due process of law. . . . Appellant offers no evidence that majority jurors simply ignore the reasonable doubts of their colleagues or otherwise act irresponsibly in casting their votes in favor of conviction, and before we alter our own longstanding perceptions about jury behavior and overturn a considered legislative judgment that unanimity is not essential to reasoned jury verdicts, we must have some basis for doing so other than unsupported assumptions. . . .

Of course, the State's proof could perhaps be regarded as more certain if it had convinced all 12 jurors instead of only nine. . . . But the fact remains that nine jurors—a substantial majority of the jury—were convinced by the evidence. In our view disagreement of three jurors does not alone establish reasonable doubt. . . . That rational men disagree is not in itself equivalent to a failure of proof by the State, nor does it indicate infidelity to the reasonable-doubt standard.[20]

In the Oregon case Robert Apodaca and two other men had been convicted of burglary, larceny, and assault with a deadly weapon. The men had been convicted by twelve member juries voting 11–1 and 10–2 for a verdict of guilty. Oregon law required that juries reach their verdicts by no less a majority than 10–2. The Supreme Court affirmed these convictions, using reasoning similar to that in the Louisiana case.

In 1979 the Court in *Burch v. Louisiana* faced a question posed by the "intersection" of its decisions allowing states to use juries of fewer than twelve persons and those allowing state juries to reach their verdicts by less than unanimous votes. The Court held that a jury as small as six persons must reach its verdict unanimously. The Court held that a defendant charged with a nonpetty crime was denied his Sixth Amendment right to trial by jury if the state allowed him to be convicted by a less than unanimous vote of a six-man jury.[21]

AN IMPARTIAL JURY

The fairness of an individual's trial is further safeguarded by the selection of an impartial jury. The defendant is protected against prejudice based on race, sex, employment, or class by the "cross section" principle espoused in *Williams* (1970). That principle forbids systematic exclusion from juries of identifiable segments of the community.

Long before 1968, when *Duncan v. Louisiana* required states to provide jury trials, the Court was demanding that state juries, if provided, be fairly selected. "It is part of the established tradition in the use of juries as instruments of public justice," declared the Court in 1940, "that the jury be a body truly representative of the community. For racial discrimination to result in the exclusion from jury service of otherwise qualified groups

DUE PROCESS: THE RIGHT TO NOTICE

Formal notice of charges—or of legal proceedings affecting one's rights—is one of the essential elements of due process of law.

All parties who are to become involved in legal proceedings must be informed in advance of trial of the specific charges against them to give them time to prepare their defense or, in the case of modern class action cases, to withdraw from the affected class.

In civil and criminal proceedings alike, notice must be given promptly and with sufficient specificity to permit preparation of an adequate defense. In addition, the Court has extended the due process requirement of notice to protect consumers from a unilateral seizure of property by creditors and to shield individuals from some administrative actions.

The concept of notice is included in both the Fifth and Sixth Amendments. The Fifth Amendment provides that no one "shall be held to answer for a capital, or otherwise infamous crime, unless on a presentment or indictment of a Grand Jury, except in cases arising in the land or naval forces, or in the militia." The Court in its 1884 ruling in *Hurtado v. California* held that this requirement of an indictment applied only to persons charged with federal crimes. That decision has never been reversed.[1]

The Sixth Amendment states that in *all* criminal prosecutions the defendant has the right "to be informed of the nature and cause of the accusation." This more general rule has been accepted as basic to a fair trial.

Both the Sixth Amendment and due process require that laws describing certain actions as criminal be sufficiently specific to place persons on notice as to what acts are proscribed. As the Court wrote in 1926, "a statute which either forbids or requires the doing of an act in terms so vague that men of common intelligence must necessarily guess at its meaning and differ as to its application, violates the first essential of due process of law."[2]

Therefore, the Court has held "void for vagueness" laws that do not define with reasonable specificity the nature of forbidden conduct, and it has set aside indictments that are insufficiently precise in stating the charges against an individual.

In testing laws challenged as unconstitutionally vague, the Court balances the right to notice against the imprecise language and political considerations inherent in the process of writing laws. Justice Tom C. Clark in 1952 set out the Court's view of these factors:

A criminal statute must be sufficiently definite to give notice of the required conduct to one who would avoid its penalties, and to guide the judge in its application and the lawyer in defending one charged with its violation. But few words possess the precision of mathematical symbols, most statutes must deal with untold and unforeseen variations in factual situations, and the practical necessities of discharging the business of government inevitably limit the specificity with which legislators can spell out prohibitions. Consequently, no more than a reasonable degree of certainty can be demanded. Nor is it unfair to require that one who deliberately goes perilously close to an area of proscribed conduct shall take the risk that he may cross the line.[3]

In later rulings, the Supreme Court extended the concept of notice, holding that it is required in a variety of situations outside of those occurring in the enforcement of the criminal law.

In 1969 and 1972 the Court held that due process required that consumers be notified before their wages were garnished or property repossessed for nonpayment of debts.[4]

The Court in 1970 applied the notice requirement to termination of welfare benefits.[5] Two years later it held that a teacher fired after ten years of service was entitled to notice and a hearing.[6] And in 1975 the Court held that students were entitled to notice of charges before they were suspended from public schools for misbehavior.[7]

1. *Hurtado v. California*, 110 U.S. 516 (1884).
2. *Connally v. General Construction Co.*, 269 U.S. 385 at 391 (1926).
3. *Boyce Motor Lines Inc. v. United States*, 342 U.S. 337 at 340 (1952).
4. *Sniadach v. Family Finance Corp. et al.*, 395 U.S. 337 (1969); *Fuentes v. Shevin*, 407 U.S. 67 (1972).
5. *Goldberg v. Kelly*, 397 U.S. 254 (1970).
6. *Perry v. Sinderman*, 408 U.S. 593 (1972).
7. *Goss v. Lopez*, 419 U.S. 565 (1975).

---

not only violates our Constitution and the laws enacted under it but is at war with our basic concepts of a democratic society and a representative government."[22]

Three decades later the Court reiterated this point, holding that state laws were unconstitutional if they resulted in the exclusion of women from juries. In these rulings the Court reaffirmed the fair cross-section requirement as fundamental to the right to a jury trial.[23]

Congress incorporated this principle into the Federal Jury Selection and Service Act of 1968, which—a century after adoption of the Fourteenth Amendment—forbade discrimination in the selection of jury panels based on race, color, religion, sex, national origin, or economic status.[24]

Racial Bias

Racial discrimination in jury selection has been the subject of Supreme Court rulings for more than one hundred years. Both the due process and the equal protection guarantees of the Fourteenth Amendment furnish a basis for federal courts to review state jury selection practices alleged to be discriminatory. Most often the equal protection clause has served as the more effective of the two provisions in this area.

In 1880 the Court struck down Virginia and West Virginia laws that excluded blacks from jury service.[25] But the Court made clear in another decision the same year that it would not require state officials to ensure that blacks actually did serve on juries.[26] In other words, the mere absence of black jurors from

WITNESSES FOR THE DEFENSE

The right to present a defense includes the power to use subpoenas and similar legal means to compel witnesses to appear in one's behalf at trial.

In 1967 the Supreme Court ruled that this right applied in state as well as federal trials. In *Washington v. Texas* Chief Justice Earl Warren wrote for the unanimous Court:

The right to offer the testimony of witnesses, and to compel their attendance if necessary, is in plain terms the right to present a defense, the right to present the defendant's version of the facts as well as the prosecution's to the jury so it may decide where the truth lies. Just as an accused has a right to confront the prosecution's witnesses for the purpose of challenging their testimony, he has the right to present his own witnesses to establish a defense. This right is a fundamental element of due process of law. (388 U.S. 14 at 19, 1967)

any particular panel would not serve as a constitutional basis for challenging the jury's decision.

For the next half-century this superficial approach prevailed, and blacks continued to be excluded from local juries. Then in the "Second Scottsboro Case" (named for the town in which the trial was held)—*Norris v. Alabama* (1935)—the Court looked behind the language of the state law to its effect, finding it unconstitutional.[27]

One of the "Scottsboro boys," Clarence Norris, a black convicted of raping a white woman, challenged his conviction as a violation of equal protection. Norris pointed out that blacks were systematically eliminated from the pools of potential state jurors—including those who indicted and tried him. The Supreme Court reversed his conviction.

Chief Justice Charles Evans Hughes said the Court's responsibility was to decide whether the equal protection guarantee was denied "not merely . . . in express terms but also whether it was denied in substance and effect."[28] He noted that no black had served on a jury in that county within the memory of any person living. Hughes found that sufficient basis for reversing Norris's conviction.

Twelve years later, in *Patton v. Mississippi,* the Court found similar justification for reversing the murder conviction of a black man indicted and convicted by all-white juries.

The Supreme Court held the long exclusion of blacks from juries a denial of equal protection. Justice Hugo L. Black delivered the opinion of a unanimous Court:

When a jury selection plan, whatever it is, operates in such way as always to result in the complete and long-continued exclusion of any representative at all from a large group of negroes, or any other racial group, indictments and verdicts returned against them by juries thus selected cannot stand. . . . [O]ur holding does not mean that a guilty defendant must go free. For indictments can be returned and convictions can be obtained by juries selected as the Constitution commands.[29]

In subsequent cases, the Court upheld good-faith efforts by state officials to secure competent juries representative of the community. In 1953 the Court approved the use of taxpayers' rolls as the basis from which names were selected for jury service.[30]

The Court then began to rule against token selection of blacks for jury duty, or systems of jury selection that made it easy to exclude blacks. In *Avery v. Georgia* the Court struck down a system using different colored pieces of paper for black persons eligible for jury duty than for white persons. Juries were selected by a judge drawing pieces of paper from a box. In *Whitus v. Georgia* the justices invalidated the selection of jurors from racially separated tax records.[31]

In 1954 in *Hernandez v. Texas* the Court held that the Fourteenth Amendment forbade the systematic or arbitrary exclusion of any substantial racial group from jury service. A unanimous Court ruled that in a county where 14 percent of the population was of Mexican or Latin American descent, it violated equal protection to exclude all such persons from juries.[32]

In the mid-1980s the Court reaffirmed the importance of eliminating racial bias from the juryroom. In the 1986 case of *Vasquez v. Hillery,* the Court ruled that anyone indicted by a grand jury selected in racially discriminatory fashion had the right to a new trial, regardless of the length of time since the discriminatory indictment. Such discrimination is a "grave constitutional trespass," wrote Justice Marshall. It "undermines the structural integrity of the criminal tribunal itself."[33]

Later the same year the Court, 7–2, held it unconstitutional for prosecutors to use peremptory challenges to exclude blacks from juries in criminal cases. Overruling a 1965 decision in *Swain v. Alabama,* the Court held in *Batson v. Kentucky* that this practice could be successfully challenged even without evidence of a pattern or practice of such exclusions.[34]

The underlying premise of *Batson*—that racial bias in jury selection corrupts the integrity of the judicial system—was subsequently extended to apply in other trial contexts.

• In *Edmonson v. Leesville Concrete Co.* (1991) the Court said jurors in civil cases cannot be excluded because of their race.

• In another case that year, it ruled that a defendant may object to race-based exclusions even if he or she is not the same race as the excluded jurors.[35]

• The following year the Court, 7–2, completed the prohibition on race bias in jury selection, ruling that defense attorneys, as well as prosecutors, cannot eliminate prospective jurors because of race. The majority said any racially motivated approach to choosing a jury violates the constitutional guarantee of equal protection of the laws.[36]

Women on Juries

Although the Court as early as 1946 disapproved of the exclusion of women from federal jury panels, it took thirty more years before that disapproval extended to state juries. As recently as 1961, in the case of *Hoyt v. Florida,* the Court upheld a Florida statute that made jury service by women voluntary. Women interested in being included on jury lists had to record with the county their willingness to serve.[37]

THE DISRUPTIVE DEFENDANT

Inherent in the defendant's right to confront and cross-examine witnesses is the right to attend the trial.[1]

In 1970, however, the Supreme Court held that this right was not absolute and that a defendant who persistently disrupted trial proceedings by noisy and disorderly conduct was not denied his constitutional rights when the judge had him removed from the courtroom.

In *Illinois v. Allen* the defendant had repeatedly interrupted the trial proceedings with noisy outbursts and insulting language. The judge finally ordered him removed from the courtroom until he agreed to behave.

At the conclusion of the trial, which resulted in his conviction, the defendant filed a petition for habeas corpus relief, claiming that he had been denied his right to a fair trial because of his enforced absence from the courtroom during the presentation of most of the state's case against him.

A unanimous Supreme Court rejected that argument. Justice Hugo L. Black wrote:

It is essential to the proper administration of criminal justice that dignity, order, and decorum be the hallmarks of all court proceedings in our country. The flagrant disregard in the courtroom of elementary standards of proper conduct should not and cannot be tolerated. We believe trial judges confronted with disruptive, contumacious, stubbornly defiant defendants must be given sufficient discretion to meet the circumstances of each case. No one formula for maintaining the appropriate courtroom atmosphere will be best in all situations. We think there are at least three constitutionally permissible ways for a trial judge to handle an obstreperous defendant like Allen: 1) bind and gag him, thereby keeping him present; 2) cite him for contempt; 3) take him out of the courtroom until he promises to conduct himself properly.[2]

1. *Lewis v. United States,* 146 U.S. 370 (1892).
2. *Illinois v. Allen,* 397 U.S. 337 at 343–344 (1970); see also *Mayberry v. Pennsylvania,* 400 U.S. 455 (1971).

Gwendolyn Hoyt, accused of murdering her husband with a baseball bat, challenged the constitutionality of the voluntary jury service statute. Failure to include women on the jury, she claimed, denied women defendants the equal protection of the law.

The Court rejected this argument, saying that Florida law did not exclude all women from jury service but simply permitted them to avail themselves of a broad exemption from that duty. At the time, the Court noted, seventeen states made jury service by women voluntary.

For the unanimous Court Justice John Marshall Harlan wrote that "woman is still regarded as the center of home and family life." In light of that, he continued, "[w]e cannot say that it is constitutionally impermissible for a State . . . to conclude that a woman should be relieved from the civic duty of jury service unless she herself determines that such service is consistent with her own special responsibilities."[38]

Fourteen years later the Court reversed itself and overturned

Hoyt. In *Taylor v. Louisiana* the Court in 1975 found no rational, let alone compelling, reason for exempting women from jury duty. The Court found the law unconstitutional, in conflict with the Sixth Amendment right of a defendant to be tried by an impartial jury drawn from a fair cross section of the community.[39]

In 1979 the Court reaffirmed this position, striking down a Missouri law that exempted women from jury duty upon their request. Leaving room for states to exempt from jury duty persons responsible for the care of children and other dependents, the Court held that the broader, sex-based exemption denied defendants their right to a jury that fairly represented their community.[40]

The 1986 *Batson* prohibition of race discrimination in jury selection was extended to sex discrimination in 1994 in *J. E. B. v. Alabama.* By 6–3, the justices said the use of gender-based peremptory challenges to eliminate women jurors "serves to ratify and perpetuate invidious, archaic, and overbroad stereotypes about the relative abilities of men and women."[41]

Blue Ribbon Juries

The Supreme Court has upheld the use of specially qualified panels of jurors for difficult cases. In *Fay v. New York,* decided in 1947, the Court considered a New York law that forbade selection of jury panels on the basis of race, creed, color, or occupation but provided for the use of such "blue ribbon" juries. Two union officials convicted of conspiracy and extortion by a blue ribbon jury claimed that these panels excluded laborers, craftsmen, and service employees, discriminating against certain economic classes and thus violating the due process and equal protection guarantees.

The Court, 5–4, upheld the system and the convictions. Justice Robert H. Jackson explained:

We fail to perceive on its face any constitutional offense in the statutory standards prescribed for the special panel. The Act does not exclude, or authorize the clerk to exclude, any person or class because of race, creed, color or occupation. It imposes no qualification of an economic nature beyond that imposed by the concededly valid general panel statute. Each of the grounds of elimination is reasonably and closely related to the juror's suitability for the kind of service the special panel requires or to his fitness to judge the kind of cases for which it is most frequently utilized. Not all of the grounds of elimination would appear relevant to the issues of the present case. But we know of no right of defendants to have a specially constituted panel which would include all persons who might be fitted to hear their particular and unique case.[42]

In dissent Justices Frank Murphy, Hugo L. Black, Wiley B. Rutledge, and William O. Douglas protested that use of blue ribbon juries conflicted with the fair cross-section requirement. Murphy wrote:

There is no constitutional right to a jury drawn from a group of uneducated and unintelligent persons. Nor is there any right to a jury chosen solely from those at the lower end of the economic and social scale. But there is a constitutional right to a jury drawn from a group which represents a cross-section of the community. And a cross-section of the community includes persons with varying degrees of training and

---

THE RIGHT TO A PUBLIC TRIAL

The Sixth Amendment guarantees persons charged with crimes a public trial; the First Amendment guarantees the press and public the right to attend criminal trials.

In 1979 the Supreme Court held that the Sixth Amendment guarantee is solely for the benefit of the defendant, not for the public in general or the press. *(See "Access and Confidentiality," pp. 468–470; see also "Restrictions and Restraints," pp. 447–448.)*

In *Gannett Co. v. DePasquale* the Court held that a trial judge could close to the press and the public a pretrial hearing on evidence in a murder case, if closure was needed to protect the defendant's right to a fair trial.[1]

"To safeguard the due process rights of the accused, a trial judge has an affirmative constitutional duty to minimize the effects of prejudicial pretrial publicity," wrote Justice Potter Stewart, noting that one of the most effective means of minimizing publicity is to close pretrial proceedings to both the public and the press.[2]

"The Sixth Amendment," Stewart continued, "surrounds a criminal trial with guarantees . . . that have as their overriding purpose the protection of the accused from prosecutorial and judicial abuses. Among the guarantees that the Amendment provides to a person charged with the commission of a criminal offense, and to him alone, is the 'right to a speedy and public trial, by an impartial jury.' The Constitution nowhere mentions any right of access to a criminal trial on the part of the public; its guarantee, like the others enumerated, is personal to the accused."[3]

Gannett has not been overruled, but a series of subsequent decisions have established a growing presumption of openness. That series began the year after *Gannett*, when the Supreme Court found in the First Amendment the very guarantee of access that it had found absent in the Sixth.

In *Richmond Newspapers v. Virginia*, the Court agreed with a First Amendment challenge brought by the press and overturned the decision of a trial judge to close a murder trial to the press and public.[4]

"We hold that the right to attend criminal trials is implicit in the guarantees of the First Amendment," wrote Chief Justice Warren E. Burger. "[W]ithout the freedom to attend such trials, which people have exercised for centuries, important aspects of freedom of speech and 'of the press could be eviscerated.'"[5]

Burger acknowledged that in some situations the only way to preserve the right to a fair trial is to limit the access of press and public to the courtroom. But, said Burger, if such limitations were necessary they should be outlined clearly and backed by written findings on the part of the judge that closure was essential to preserve an overriding state interest.

In the 1984 case of *Waller v. Georgia*, the Court held that a defendant's right to a public trial means that a judge may close pretrial hearings to the public over a defendant's objection only if there is some overriding interest that will be prejudiced by an open hearing.[6]

Two years later, in still another case on these points, Burger declared that the defendant's right to a fair trial need not be in conflict with the public's right to access. In the case, *Press-Enterprise Co. v. Superior Court*, the justices ruled that a newspaper could have access to the transcript of a preliminary hearing in a criminal case. Chief Justice Burger wrote to emphasize that one important way to assure the defendant's right to a fair trial is to keep the process open to neutral observers.[7]

1. *Gannett Co. v. DePasquale*, 443 U.S. 368 (1979).
2. Id. at 378.
3. Id. at 379.
4. *Richmond Newspapers v. Virginia*, 448 U.S. 555 (1980).
5. Id. at 580.
6. *Waller v. Georgia*, 467 U.S. 39 (1984).
7. *Press-Enterprise Co. v. Superior Court*, 478 U.S. 1 (1986).

---

intelligence and with varying economic and social positions. Under our Constitution, the jury is not to be made the representative of the most intelligent, the most wealthy or the most successful, nor of the least intelligent, the least wealthy or the least successful. It is a democratic institution, representative of all qualified classes of people.[43]

The Right to a Speedy Trial

As early as 1905 the Supreme Court made clear that the right to a speedy trial is a relative matter, "consistent with delays and depend[ent] upon circumstances."[44]

The Court has adopted a balancing approach in cases alleging that a defendant has been denied this right. The justices weigh the particular facts to determine the reasons for the delay and the effect of the delay on the defendant.

In *United States v. Provoo* the Court in 1955 upheld dismissal of an indictment of a defendant who—although ready for trial since 1951 and protesting governmental requests for delay—had

not been tried. The Court explained that the lapse of time, the death or disappearance of witnesses, and the protracted confinement of the defendant had seriously jeopardized his opportunity to defend himself.[45]

Dismissal of the charges, the unanimous Court held firmly in 1973, is the only appropriate remedy for denial of this right. In *Strunk v. United States* the Court found reduction of sentence insufficient remedy for delay of trial.[46]

The right to a speedy trial does not apply to delays before a person is accused of a crime but only to the interval between arrest and trial.

In 1971 Justice White explained:

[T]he Sixth Amendment speedy trial provision has no application until the putative defendant becomes an "accused". . . .

. . . On its face, the protection of the amendment is activated only when a criminal prosecution has begun and extends only to those persons who have been "accused" in the course of that prosecution. These provisions would seem to afford no protection to those not yet accused, nor would they seem to require the Government to discover, investigate, and accuse any person within any particular period of time.[47]

In 1977 the Court reaffirmed this point. Its decision in *United States v. Lovasco* rejected the argument that a defendant was denied due process by a good-faith investigative delay between the commission of an offense and the time of his indictment.[48] Justice Marshall wrote:

[P]rosecutors do not deviate from "fundamental conceptions of justice" when they defer seeking indictments until they have probable cause to believe an accused is guilty; indeed it is unprofessional conduct for a prosecutor to recommend an indictment on less than probable cause. . . . From the perspective of potential defendants, requiring prosecutions to commence when probable cause is established is undesirable because it would increase the likelihood of unwarranted charges being filed, and would add to the time during which defendants stand accused but untried. . . .

Penalizing prosecutors who defer action . . . would subordinate the goal of "orderly expedition" to that of "mere speed." This the Due Process Clause does not require. We therefore hold that to prosecute a defendant following investigative delay does not deprive him of due process, even if his defense might have been somewhat prejudiced by the lapse of time.[49]

In *Klopfer v. North Carolina* the Court in 1976 held that the due process clause required protection of the right to speedy trial against abridgment by the states.[50] The Court unanimously struck down a North Carolina law that allowed indefinite postponement of a criminal prosecution without dismissal of the indictment. The defendant would remain at liberty, but the prosecutor could restore the case to the docket any time a judge agreed such action to be appropriate.

Speaking for the Court, Chief Justice Earl Warren explained that this procedure "clearly denies the petitioner the right to a speedy trial which we hold is guaranteed to him by the Sixth Amendment. . . . We hold here that the right to a speedy trial is as fundamental as any of the rights secured by the Sixth Amendment."[51]

Federal and state officials operated until the 1970s on the assumption that an accused's failure to demand a speedy trial meant that he acquiesced in delay of proceedings. In 1972 in *Barker v. Wingo*, the Court rejected the view "that a defendant who fails to demand a speedy trial forever waives his right."[52]

Justice Lewis F. Powell Jr. reaffirmed the Court's "balancing approach" to speedy trial claims:

The approach we accept is a balancing test, in which the conduct of both the prosecution and the defendant are weighed.

A balancing test necessarily compels courts to approach speedy-trial cases on an ad-hoc basis. We can do little more than identify some of the factors which courts should assess in determining whether a particular defendant has been deprived of his right. Though some might express them in different ways, we identify four such factors: Length of delay, the reason for the delay, the defendant's assertion of his right, and prejudice to the defendant. . . .

We regard none of the four factors identified above as either a necessary or sufficient condition to the finding of a deprivation of the right of speedy trial. Rather they are related factors and must be considered together with such other circumstances as may be relevant. In sum, these factors have no talismanic qualities; courts must still engage in a difficult and sensitive balancing process. But, because we are dealing with a fundamental right of the accused, this process must be carried out with full recognition that the accused's interest in a speedy trial is specifically affirmed in the Constitution.[53]

Barker v. Wingo prompted Congress—against the advice of the Justice Department and federal judges—to pass the Speedy Trial Act of 1974 to reduce delays in federal trials. The act established a deadline of one hundred days between arrest or indictment and trial. Failure to meet the deadline would result in dismissal of the charges.[54]

In *United States v. MacDonald* (1982) the Court further defined the right to a speedy trial, ruling that this guarantee applied to the period between arrest and indictment, not to a period after military charges have been dropped and before a civilian indictment has been obtained. The right was not intended to prevent prejudice to the defense as a result of the passage of time but to limit the impairment of liberty of an accused before trial and to shorten the disruption of life caused by pending criminal charges.[55]

In 1990 the Court said an eight-year delay between indictment and arrest violated the Sixth Amendment right to a speedy trial. The defendant in this case was indicted on federal drug charges in 1980 but left the country, apparently unaware of his indictment, before he could be arrested. After several years he returned to the United States, married, earned a college degree, found steady employment, and lived under his own name. He

---

JAIL BEFORE TRIAL

Twice during the 1980s the Supreme Court approved of preventive detention, the practice of holding certain defendants in jail before their trial. The first case involved the pretrial detention of dangerous juveniles; the second, the pretrial detention of organized crime figures.

In *Schall v. Martin, Abrams v. Martin* (467 U.S. 253, 1984), the Court voted 6–3 to uphold New York's law permitting pretrial detention of juveniles when there is a serious risk that the juvenile may commit a serious crime before trial. Detention fell well within the bounds of due process, wrote Justice William H. Rehnquist for the Court. In such a case, he continued, detention protects both the juvenile and society. Justices William J. Brennan Jr., Thurgood Marshall, and John Paul Stevens dissented.

Three years later the Court reaffirmed and broadened its approval for pretrial detention, upholding the relevant provisions of a 1984 federal law. The case of *United States v. Salerno* (481 U.S. 739, 1987) arose from the pretrial detention of Anthony Salerno and Vincent Cafaro, indicted in New York on racketeering charges. The Court ruled—again 6–3—that neither due process nor the ban on excessive bail was violated when a judge decided that freeing the suspect on bail pending trial would pose a danger to the community.

was arrested after a routine credit check. By 5–4, the Court ruled he could not be tried after such a long delay. The justices said U.S. officials were negligent in tracking the defendant.[56]

The Right to Confront Witnesses

The Sixth Amendment guarantees federal defendants the right to confront and crossexamine their accusers. In *Mattox v. United States*, decided in 1895, the Supreme Court defined the purpose of this confrontation rule:

The primary object . . . was to prevent depositions or ex parte affidavits . . . being used against the prisoner in lieu of a personal examination and cross-examination of the witness in which the accused has an opportunity, not only of testing the recollection and sifting the conscience of the witness, but of compelling him to stand face to face with the jury in order that they may look at him, and judge by his demeanor upon the stand and manner in which he gives his testimony whether he is worthy of belief.[57]

Subsequently, the Court struck down an act of Congress for violating this right. The act allowed the court record of a person convicted of stealing government property to be used against the person charged with receiving that property. The act said that the record from the first case could be used as evidence that the property was stolen. In the opinion the Court further explained the purpose of this confrontation clause:

[A] fact which can be primarily established only by witnesses cannot be proved against an accused . . . except by witnesses who confront him at the trial, upon whom he can look while being tried, whom he is entitled to cross-examine, and whose testimony he may impeach. . . . The presumption of the innocence of an accused attends him throughout the trial, and has relation to every fact that must be established to prove his guilt beyond a reasonable doubt.[58]

This presumption was denied the defendant in this case because "he was put upon the defensive almost from the outset of the trial by reason alone of what appeared to have been *said* in another criminal prosecution with which he was not connected and at which he was not entitled to be represented."[59]

Many of the Court's pronouncements on the confrontation clause have focused on efforts by prosecutors to use at trial hearsay evidence—prior, out-of-court statements of persons unavailable to testify and be crossexamined. In general, the Court allows use of such evidence only when there is sufficient reason to consider it credible.

In *Pointer v. Texas*, decided in 1965, the Court held this right of confrontation to be "a fundamental right essential to a fair trial in a criminal prosecution" and therefore applicable to defendants in state trials through the due process clause.[60] *Pointer* involved a trial in which a state prosecutor attempted to use the transcript of a witness's testimony taken at a preliminary hearing, where he was not subject to crossexamination. The prosecutor had made no effort to secure the personal appearance of the witness at the trial. The Court threw out that evidence.

Although in recent years the Court seems to have relaxed some of its earlier restrictions on the use of hearsay evidence or

TELEVISING TRIALS

Although he steadfastly opposed the introduction of cameras into the Supreme Court chamber, Chief Justice Warren E. Burger nonetheless wrote the Court's opinion in 1981 permitting states to televise trials.[1]

For almost half a century, cameras had been unwelcome in the nation's courtrooms, in reaction to some sensational news coverage during trials of the 1920s and 1930s. The American Bar Association (ABA) had in fact declared, as one of the canons of judicial ethics, that all photographic and broadcast coverage of trials should be prohibited.

But during the 1970s attitudes began to change. In 1978 the ABA began considering relaxation of this ban, and the Conference of State Chief Justices voted to allow each state to develop guidelines for the use of cameras in the courtroom.

Florida began to experiment with televised trials in 1977. One of the trials covered by television was that of Noel Chandler and Robert Granger, former Miami Beach police officers charged with burglary. They challenged their convictions, arguing that the television coverage had denied them a fair trial.

Chandler and Granger cited the Court's 1964 ruling in *Estes v. Texas*.[2] This decision, they said, had declared that all photographic or broadcast coverage of a criminal trial was a denial of due process. *(See details of the case, p. 467, in Chapter 9.)*

No, indeed, responded Chief Justice Burger for the Court in *Chandler v. Florida*. *Estes* "does not stand as an absolute ban on state experimentation with an evolving technology, which, in terms of modes of mass communication, was in its relative infancy in 1964, and is, even now, in a state of continuing change."[3]

He continued: "Any criminal case that generates a great deal of publicity presents some risks that the publicity may compromise the right of the defendant to a fair trial. The risk of juror prejudice in some cases does not justify an absolute ban on news coverage of trials by the printed media [or of] . . . all broadcast coverage."[4]

"Dangers lurk in this, as in most experiments, but unless we were to conclude that television coverage under all conditions is prohibited by the Constitution, the states must be free to experiment," Burger concluded.[5]

By 1996 most states allowed trials to be televised, typically at the judge's discretion, but the federal courts continued to oppose cameras in the courtroom in criminal cases.

In a small step toward greater public access, the Judicial Conference of the United States, which oversees the lower federal courts, voted in March 1996 to give appellate judges the option of allowing television coverage of appellate arguments. This action did not apply to the U.S. Supreme Court.

1. *Chandler v. Florida*, 449 U.S. 560 (1981).
2. *Estes v. Texas*, 381 U.S. 532 (1964).
3. *Chandler v. Florida*, 449 U.S. 560 at 574 (1981).
4. Ibid.
5. Id. at 582.

In 1990 the Supreme Court ruled
that child victims in abuse cases
may testify on closed-circuit
television. Antonin Scalia wrote
a dissent arguing that this practice violates the Sixth Amendment rights of a defendant to
confront his or her accuser.

out-of-court statements, it has reaffirmed the high priority it
places upon this right in ensuring a fair trial.[61]

In 1973 the Court, 8–1, held that a defendant on trial for murder had been denied a fair trial and due process by the state
judge's strict application of the hearsay rule. That application
wrongly prevented the introduction of testimony by three men
to whom a fourth had confessed the crime with which the defendant was charged.[62]

And in 1974, with Chief Justice Burger writing the opinion,
the Court held that a defendant was denied his right of confrontation when the trial judge forbade crossexamination of a
key witness, a juvenile, about his delinquency record and proba-
tionary status, matters that could have impeached the credibility
of his testimony.[63]

To protect the victims in child abuse cases from additional
trauma caused by testifying at the trial of the alleged attacker, a
number of states in the 1980s passed laws that permitted the victims to testify shielded from the view of the defendant.

In 1988, in *Coy v. Iowa,* the Supreme Court held unconstitutional Iowa's law that permitted the child victims to testify behind a screen because the law denied the defendant his right to
meet face-to-face with his accusers in front of a judge and a
jury.

This guarantee of confrontation, wrote Justice Antonin
Scalia, "serves ends related both to appearances and to
reality. . . . The perception that confrontation is essential to fairness has persisted over the centuries because there is much truth
to it. . . . That face-to-face presence may, unfortunately, upset

the truthful rape victim or abused child; but by the same token
it may confound and undo the false accuser, or reveal the child
coached by a malevolent adult. . . . Constitutional protections
have costs."[64]

But two years later Scalia was in the minority when the
Court ruled 5–4 that states may shield victims of child abuse by
allowing them to testify on closed-circuit television rather than
face the person accused of abusing them. Writing for the majority in *Maryland v. Craig,* Justice Sandra Day O'Connor said the
state interest in protecting child witnesses from the trauma of
testifying may justify permitting them to answer questions
without a confrontation with the defendant.[65]

In another 1990 decision the Court, again 5–4, ruled that
hearsay statements from a child who is unable to testify in an
abuse case can be admitted at trial if the child's story is tested for
trustworthiness, including how well the child knew the accused
and whether the child would make up the story.[66]

In another sensitive area, the Court ruled that while the confrontation clause does guarantee an alleged rapist the right to
face his accuser, it does not assure him the opportunity to
counter the charge by introducing evidence of their prior romantic relationship. The defendant in this 1991 case from Michigan was barred from introducing such evidence because he
failed to notify prosecutors within 10 days after arraignment
that he wished to introduce such testimony. The Court said the
state's "notice" requirement and ten-day rule served legitimate
interests of protecting rape victims against surprise, harassment, and unnecessary invasions of privacy.[67]

Search and Seizure

"The security of one's privacy against arbitrary intrusion by the police," wrote Justice Felix Frankfurter in 1946, "is basic to a free society."

"The knock at the door, whether by day or by night," he continued, "as a prelude to a search, without authority of law but solely on the authority of the police, did not need the commentary of recent history to be condemned as inconsistent with the conception of human rights enshrined in the history and the basic constitutional documents of English-speaking peoples."[1]

The Fourth Amendment's guarantee of the "right of the people to be secure in their persons, houses, papers and effects, against unreasonable searches and seizures" was intended to protect the individual against this sort of arbitrary invasion of privacy by police or other authorities. Fresh in the minds of the men who drafted that language was the British use of general warrants and "writs of assistance" to justify the searches of colonists' homes by government agents seeking smugglers and others who violated trade and navigation laws.

The guarantee of personal security against unreasonable search and seizure is buttressed by the second portion of the amendment, the warrant clause. It underscores the "reasonableness" requirement for searches and seizures by stating that "no Warrants shall issue, but upon probable cause, supported by Oath or affirmation, and particularly describing the place to be searched and the person or things to be seized."

The Supreme Court has held that a valid warrant—one issued by a neutral and detached magistrate upon his or her finding of probable cause—is an essential element of compliance with the Fourth Amendment prohibition against unreasonable search and seizure.

This is perhaps the single most stable element in Fourth Amendment doctrine. As the Court itself has acknowledged, "translation of the abstract prohibition against 'unreasonable searches and seizures' into workable guidelines for the decision of particular cases is a difficult task that for many years has divided the Court.

"Nevertheless, one governing principle, justified by history and by current experience, has consistently been followed: except in certain carefully defined classes of cases, a search of private property without proper consent is 'unreasonable' unless it has been authorized by a valid search warrant."[2]

The warrant must be sufficiently specific to remove the element of discretion from those persons who are to execute it. The Court has recognized two primary exceptions to the warrant requirement for searches: warrants are not required for a search related to a lawful arrest or a search of a moving vehicle that has been halted by police.

Although the Court generally has resisted arguments for new exceptions to the warrant requirement, it has held that neither aerial surveillance nor police searches of privately owned open fields need be authorized by warrant. And it has steadily lengthened the list of situations in which police are permitted to search cars without first obtaining warrants.[3]

The Court has adopted a controversial method of enforcing the Fourth Amendment guarantee. That method is the "exclusionary rule," the Court's insistence that evidence obtained in violation of the Fourth Amendment rights of a defendant may not be used as evidence against the defendant at trial. This rule has been in effect in federal courts since 1914. *(See box, The Exclusionary Rule, pp. 578–579.)*

Not until 1949 did the Supreme Court consider applying the Fourth Amendment guarantee and the exclusionary rule to state defendants. In *Wolf v. Colorado* the Court seemed to say that the rights protected by the Fourth Amendment were so basic to "the concept of ordered liberty" that they were protected against state action through the due process clause of the Fourteenth Amendment. Nevertheless, the Court in *Wolf* expressly declined to apply the exclusionary rule against state officials.[4]

In 1961, however, the Court reversed *Wolf* and in *Mapp v. Ohio* extended to state defendants the full protection of the guarantee.[5] Two years later in *Ker v. California* the Court stated that the Fourth Amendment guarantee as applied to state action was in all respects the same as that applied to federal action.[6]

The Neutral Magistrate

The Court has interpreted the Constitution to require that search and arrest warrants be issued by a neutral and detached magistrate.

Justice Robert H. Jackson in 1948 explained why:

The point of the Fourth Amendment, which often is not grasped by zealous officers, is not that it denies law enforcement the support of the usual inferences which reasonable men draw from evidence. Its protection consists in requiring that those inferences be drawn by a neutral and detached magistrate instead of being judged by the officer engaged in the often competitive enterprise of ferreting out crime. Any assumption that evidence sufficient to support a magistrate's disinterested determination to issue a search warrant will justify the officers in making a search without a warrant would reduce the Amendment to a nullity and leave the people's homes secure only in the discretion of police officers. . . . When the right of privacy must reasonably yield to the right of search is, as a rule, to be decided by a judicial officer, not by a policeman or Government enforcement agent.[7]

The Court emphasized the importance of this requirement again in 1971. In *Coolidge v. New Hampshire* the Court forbade the use of evidence obtained in a police search based on a warrant issued by the state official who was the chief investigator and prosecutor in the case. "Since he was not the neutral and detached magistrate required by the Constitution," stated the Court, "the search stands on no firmer ground than if there had been no warrant at all."[8]

PRIVATE SEARCH

The Fourth Amendment protects individuals only against searches and seizures by government agents, not by private individuals.

The Supreme Court set out this rule in 1921 in *Burdeau v. Mc-Dowell*. After J. C. McDowell was dismissed from his corporate job, his former employers blew open the lock on his private office safe, broke the lock on his desk drawer, and delivered the contents of the desk and safe to the Justice Department, which was investigating McDowell's role in a mail fraud scheme.

McDowell challenged the seizure of the evidence as a violation of his right to be secure in his "papers and effects" against unreasonable search and seizure. The Supreme Court rebuffed his challenge, holding that the Fourth Amendment reached only government action; acts committed by private individuals, as in McDowell's case, were outside the protection of that guarantee. McDowell could, the Court noted, institute a private suit against those individuals who took his papers and turned them over to the government. (*Burdeau v. McDowell*, 256 U.S. 465, 1921)

The following year, however, the Court ruled that municipal court clerks may issue search warrants in cases involving the breach of municipal laws. There was no Fourth Amendment "commandment . . . that all warrant authority must reside exclusively in a lawyer or judge." Justice Lewis F. Powell Jr. wrote the Court's opinion:

The substance of the Constitution's warrant requirements does not turn on the labeling of the issuing party. The warrant traditionally has represented an independent assurance that a search and arrest will not proceed without probable cause to believe that a crime has been committed and that the person or place named in the warrant is involved in the crime. Thus an issuing magistrate must meet two tests. He must be neutral and detached, and he must be capable of determining whether probable cause exists for the requested arrest or search. . . . If . . . detachment and capacity do conjoin, the magistrate has satisfied the Fourth Amendment's purpose.[9]

Probable Cause

A magistrate must find "probable cause" to issue a warrant. Probable cause has been variously defined. Although the term "means less than evidence which would justify condemnation,"[10] probable cause does require "belief that the law was being violated on the premises to be searched; and . . . the facts . . . are such that a reasonably discreet and prudent man would be led to believe that there was a commission of the offense charged."[11]

A warrant is not valid, the Court has held, if it is based only upon a sworn allegation without adequate support in fact. In the 1933 case of *Nathanson v. United States*, the Court set out this rule:

Under the Fourth Amendment, an officer may not properly issue a warrant to search a private dwelling unless he can find probable cause therefore from facts or circumstances presented to him under oath or affirmation. Mere affirmance of belief or suspicion is not enough.[12]

The Court has held valid, however, warrants based on hearsay, and it has not required direct personal observation of the facts or circumstances justifying the warrant by the individual who seeks it.[13] But the magistrate must be satisfied that the informant, whose identity need not be disclosed, is credible or his information reliable.[14]

In 1978 the Court granted the right to a trial court hearing to a defendant who claimed that police obtained evidence against him by using lies to convince a magistrate of probable cause. Justice Harry A. Blackmun, writing for the Court in *Franks v. Delaware*, made clear the majority's view that "a warrant . . . would be reduced to a nullity if a police officer was able to use deliberately falsified allegations to demonstrate probable cause."[15]

Only if an individual cannot or does not consent to a search are police required to obtain a warrant. Voluntary consent of the individual who owns or occupies the place to be searched validates the search.

But, the Court held in 1973, the individual who is asked to consent to a search need not be informed that he or she may refuse. In *Schneckloth v. Bustamonte* the Court discussed the elements of voluntary consent. Justice Potter Stewart wrote for the majority:

We hold only that when the subject of a search is not in custody and the State attempts to justify the search on the basis of his consent, the Fourth and Fourteenth Amendments require that it demonstrate that the consent was in fact voluntarily given, and not the result of duress or coercion, express or implied. Voluntariness is a question of fact to be determined from all the circumstances, and while the subject's knowledge of a right to refuse is a factor to be taken into account, the prosecution is not required to demonstrate such knowledge as a prerequisite to establishing a voluntary consent.[16]

Justices William J. Brennan Jr., William O. Douglas, and Thurgood Marshall dissented, saying that they failed to see "how our citizens can meaningfully be said to have waived something as precious as a constitutional guarantee without ever being aware of its existence."[17]

The following year, in *United States v. Matlock*, the Court held that when one occupant of a house consents to search of the premises, the search is proper, and evidence uncovered in it may be used against another occupant.[18]

In 1990, in another case involving multiple occupants of a residence, the Court ruled that an overnight house guest has a legitimate expectation of privacy and is entitled to Fourth Amendment protection against police intrusion at the house. By 7–2, the justices said the guest has sufficient interest in the home to challenge the legality of his warrantless arrest there.[19]

Property, Papers, and Effects

The Supreme Court's first major ruling on the scope of the Fourth Amendment's protection for individual privacy and security came in 1886. The case was *Boyd v. United States*.[20]

In *Boyd* the Court established that the Fourth Amendment

"STOP AND FRISK" SEARCHES HELD REASONABLE

The Supreme Court has held that the police practice of stopping suspicious persons and "frisking" them for weapons is a reasonable "search" within the boundaries of the Fourth Amendment. The Court has found such searches permissible even without a search warrant or enough information to constitute probable cause for arrest.

In *Terry v. Ohio* (1968) Chief Justice Earl Warren announced "that there must be a narrowly drawn authority to permit a reasonable search for weapons for the protection of the police officer, where he has reason to believe that he is dealing with an armed and dangerous individual, regardless of whether he has probable cause to arrest the individual for a crime. The officer need not be absolutely certain that the individual is armed; the issue is whether a reasonably prudent man in the circumstances would be warranted in the belief that his safety or that of others was in danger."[1]

The limited nature of this authority was emphasized by the Court in a companion case, *Sibron v. New York*. In *Sibron* the Court held impermissible a police officer's search of a suspect, finding it in violation of the *Terry* standard. Chief Justice Warren explained the difference in the two cases:

The search for weapons approved in *Terry* consisted solely of a limited patting of the outer clothing of the suspect for concealed objects which might be used as instruments of assault. Only when he discovered such objects did the officer in *Terry* place his hands in the pockets of the man he searched. In this case, with no attempt at an initial limited exploration for arms, [the] patrolman . . . thrust his hand into Sibron's pocket and took from him envelopes of heroin. . . . The search was not reasonably limited in scope to the accomplishment of the only goal which might conceivably have justified its inception—the protection of the officer by disarming a potentially dangerous man. Such a search violates the guarantee of the Fourth Amendment, which protects the sanctity of the person against unreasonable intrusions on the part of all government agents.[2]

Four years later the Court in *Adams v. Williams* upheld as proper the conduct of an officer who stopped a motorist, based upon an informant's tip, reached into the car, and took a handgun from the person's waistband. The gun was not visible from outside the car; the policeman would not have known of its existence without the informant's tip.[3]

The Court stated that "[s]o long as the officer is entitled to make a forcible stop and has reason to believe that the suspect is armed and dangerous, he may conduct a weapons search limited in scope to this protective purpose."[4]

In 1983 the Court ruled that police officers could conduct the same sort of protective search of the interior of a car they have stopped—just as they could pat down or frisk a suspect on the street.[5]

In 1985 the Court eased its rules about the length of time police could detain a suspect under *Terry*.

In *United States v. Sharpe* the Court held that it was not unreasonable or unconstitutional for police to detain for twenty minutes the driver of a car stopped on the highway and suspected of transporting drugs, while other law enforcement agents located a truck that had been traveling with the car and confirmed their suspicions that it carried narcotics.[6]

Several years later the Court broadened the type of search that could occur during a limited "stop-and-frisk" situation. It said in 1993 that police may seize drugs or other contraband from a suspect if they can feel the material.

Explaining the "plain feel" exception, Justice Byron R. White wrote that police could seize material only if they felt it through the suspect's outer clothing and if its identity as contraband was "immediately apparent."[7]

1. *Terry v. Ohio*, 392 U.S. 1 at 27 (1968).
2. *Sibron v. New York*, 392 U.S. 40 at 65–66 (1968).
3. *Adams v. Williams*, 407 U.S. 143 (1972).
4. Id. at 146.
5. *Michigan v. Long*, 463 U.S. 1032 (1983).
6. *United States v. Sharpe*, 470 U.S. 675 (1985).
7. *Minnesota v. Dickerson*,_____ U.S._____ at (1993).

---

protected individuals against subpoenas, as well as searches, for private business papers, and it forbade such subpoenas as unreasonable if they forced the person to whom they were directed to produce self-incriminating evidence.

E. A. Boyd and Sons had contracted with the federal government to furnish plate glass for a post office and courthouse building in Philadelphia. They agreed to discount the price of the glass in return for permission to import it duty-free. Subsequently, the government charged that the Boyds had taken advantage of the agreement by importing more glass than the contract permitted.

The government sought forfeiture of the contract. At trial the judge ordered the Boyds to produce the invoice showing the amount of imported glass they had received. Under protest, the Boyds complied with the order. They were convicted.

The Supreme Court reversed their conviction and ordered a new trial, declaring that the subpoena had violated the Boyds' Fourth Amendment and Fifth Amendment rights. For the majority, Justice Joseph P. Bradley explained that compulsory production of a man's private papers was an unreasonable search and seizure under the Fourth Amendment. He also explained how the Boyds' Fifth Amendment rights were infringed:

The principles laid down in this opinion affect the very essence of constitutional liberty and security . . . they apply to all invasions, on the part of the Government and its employees, of the sanctity of a man's home and the privacies of life. It is not the breaking of his doors and the rummaging of his drawers that constitutes the essence of the offence: but it is the invasion of his indefeasible right of personal security, personal liberty and private property, where that right has never been forfeited by his conviction of some public offense. . . . Breaking into a house and opening boxes and drawers are circumstances of aggravation; but any forcible and compulsory extortion of a man's own testimony or of his private papers to be used as evidence to convict him of crime or to forfeit his goods is within the condemnation of that judgment. In this regard the Fourth and Fifth Amendments run almost into each other. . . .

We have already noticed the intimate relation between the two Amendments. They throw great light on each other. For the "unreasonable searches and seizures" condemned in the Fourth Amendment are almost always made for the purpose of compelling a man to give evidence against himself, which in criminal cases is condemned in the Fifth Amendment; and compelling a man "in a criminal case to be a witness against himself," which is condemned in the Fifth Amendment, throws light on the question as to what is an "unreasonable search and seizure" within the meaning of the Fourth Amendment. And we have been unable to perceive that the seizure of a man's private books and papers to be used in evidence against him is substantially different from compelling him to be a witness against himself.[21]

THE EXCLUSIONARY RULE

To avoid the cumbersome and expensive remedy of retrial for persons convicted on the basis of evidence seized in violation of their Fourth Amendment rights, the Court in 1914 adopted the exclusionary rule.

Set out first by the Court in *Weeks v. United States,* the rule allows a defendant who feels that evidence obtained in violation of his rights will be used against him to require the trial court to exclude it from use.[22]

Fremont Weeks was arrested without a warrant. Federal agents searched his home, also without a warrant, and took from it documents and letters used as evidence against him at trial. After his conviction, he challenged the conviction as obtained in violation of his rights.

The Supreme Court agreed. In the Court's unanimous opinion Justice William R. Day explained that exclusion of such evidence was necessary to discourage unlawful practices by law enforcement agents:

The tendency of those who execute the criminal laws of the country to obtain conviction by means of unlawful seizures and enforced confessions . . . should find no sanction in the judgments of the courts, which are charged . . . with the support of the Constitution. . . .

. . . If letters and private documents can thus be seized and held and used in evidence against a citizen accused of an offense, the protection of the 4th Amendment, declaring his right to be secure against such searches and seizures, is of no value, and, so far as those thus placed are concerned, might as well be stricken from the Constitution.[23]

The Court concluded both that the seizure of the letters by a federal agent and the refusal of the judge to honor Weeks's request for their return before they were used as evidence were violations of his constitutional rights. *(See box, The Exclusionary Rule, pp. 578–579.)*

"MERE EVIDENCE" RULE

The Court's next major Fourth Amendment decision— *Gouled v. United States*—set out the rule that "mere evidence" could not properly be seized by government officials, even with a search warrant. In *Gouled* the Court also held that a search of a place to which access had been gained by stealth rather than force still fell within the searches prohibited by the Fourth Amendment.[24]

An acquaintance of Felix Gouled called upon him at his office on the pretext of paying a friendly visit. The visit, as it turned out, was at the direction of federal agents. Gouled was suspected of attempting to defraud the government in regard to some defense contracts. While Gouled was out of the room, the acquaintance removed some documents from the premises. Those documents were later introduced as evidence against Gouled, who was convicted of conspiracy to defraud the government. He challenged the use of the documents as evidence, arguing that it violated his Fourth and Fifth Amendment rights.

The Supreme Court upheld his challenge, applying *Weeks* to exclude both the letters taken by the visitor and additional evidence obtained as a result of the first seizure. The Court's ruling was based on the surreptitious and warrantless nature of the search, and on the nature of the letters seized. The letters were mere evidence and thus were outside the zone of reasonable seizures.

The Court of the late nineteenth and early twentieth centuries was very sensitive to property interests. Both in *Boyd* and *Gouled* the Court indicated that the government had a right to seize from an individual only that property to which the individual himself had no right—or a right inferior to the government's. With this reasoning, the only proper targets of search warrants were the fruits and instruments of crime and contraband.

Justice John H. Clarke set out this mere evidence rule:

Although search warrants have . . . been used in many cases ever since the adoption of the Constitution, and although their use has been extended from time to time to meet new cases within the old rules, nevertheless it is clear that, at common law and as the result of the *Boyd* and *Weeks Cases* . . . they may not be used as a means of gaining access to a man's house or office and papers solely for the purpose of making search to secure evidence to be used against him in a criminal or penal proceeding, but that they may be resorted to only when a primary right to such search and seizure may be found in the interest which the public or the complainant may have in the property to be seized, or in the right to the possession of it, or when a valid exercise of the police power renders possession of the property by the accused unlawful, and provides that it may be taken.[25]

Although this rule severely limits the use of search warrants, in practice its impact was less dramatic. Congress never authorized the use of search warrants for mere evidence, and the Federal Rules of Criminal Procedure limited the objects of federal warrants to instrumentalities and fruits of crime. Lower courts, however, construed those categories broadly, including many things only remotely connected with a crime.

By the time the Court discarded the mere evidence rule in 1967, confusion abounded over what was evidence and what was an instrument of crime. So many exceptions to the rule had been created, remarked Justice Brennan, that it was questionable what effect the rule still had.

SEARCHES AT THE BORDER AND BEYOND

Since the earliest days of the nation's history, Congress has authorized warrantless searches of persons entering the country at its borders. Until the last quarter century it was assumed that such searches were not subject to the limits of the Fourth Amendment guarantee.

But in a series of rulings in the mid-1970s, the Supreme Court held that the Fourth Amendment did apply to those searches that were part of the U.S. Border Patrol's effort to control illegal immigration.

In 1973 the Court in *Almeida-Sanchez v. United States* held that roving patrols violated the Fourth Amendment guarantee when they searched vehicles as far as one hundred miles from the border without a search warrant or probable cause to suspect that the car contained illegal aliens.[1]

Two years later the unanimous Court extended *Almeida-Sanchez* to hold that roving patrols could not even stop a car for questioning of its occupants unless there was more cause than the fact that the occupants appeared to be Mexican.[2] The same day, the Court held that border patrol officers at fixed checkpoints away from the border itself must have probable cause or a warrant before they searched cars at the checkpoint without the driver's consent.[3]

But in 1976 the Court held that border patrol officers need not have probable cause or a warrant before they stopped cars for brief questioning at fixed checkpoints. Justice Lewis F. Powell Jr. made clear the Court's distinction between searches and stops for questioning:

While the need to make routine checkpoint stops is great, the consequent intrusion on Fourth Amendment interests is quite limited. . . .

Neither the vehicle nor its occupants is searched, and visual inspection of the vehicle is limited to what can be seen without a search. This objective intrusion—the stop itself, the questioning, and the visual inspection—also existed in roving-patrol stops. But we view checkpoint stops in a different light because the subjective intrusion—the generating of concern or even fright on the part of lawful travelers—is appreciably less in the case of a checkpoint stop. . . .

. . . [T]he reasonableness of the procedures followed in making these checkpoint stops makes the resulting intrusion on the interests of the motorists minimal. On the other hand, the purpose of the stops is legitimate and in the public interest. . . . Accordingly, we hold that the stops and questioning at issue may be made in the absence of any individualized suspicion at reasonably located checkpoints.[4]

In 1990 the Supreme Court addressed the question of whether the Fourth Amendment limited searches outside the borders of the United States. In an opinion by Chief Justice William H. Rehnquist, the Court ruled, 5–4, that U.S. law-enforcement agents operating without warrants may search a foreigner's property in a foreign country without violating the constitutional prohibition against unreasonable searches and seizures. The Court's ruling in *United States v. Verdugo-Urquidez* overturned a federal appeals court decision that had excluded from trial evidence seized in a warrantless search in Mexico of a man who was arrested there and brought back to the United States on drug charges.

The Fourth Amendment's protection of the rights of "the people" was limited "to a class of persons who are part of a national community or who have otherwise developed sufficient connection with this country to be considered part of that community," wrote Rehnquist. The foreigner in this case did not fall within that group.[5] Justices Brennan, Marshall, Blackmun, and Stevens dissented.

1. *Almeida-Sanchez v. United States*, 413 U.S. 266 (1973).
2. *United States v. Brignoni-Ponce*, 422 U.S. 873 (1975).
3. *United States v. Ortiz*, 422 U.S. 891 (1975).
4. *United States v. Martinez-Fuerte, Sifuentes v. United States*, 428 U.S. 543 at 557–558, 561–562 (1976).
5. *United States v. Verdugo-Urquidez*, 494 U.S. 258 at 265 (1990).

Rule Abandoned

The Court abandoned the "mere evidence" rule in 1967, announcing this shift in *Warden v. Hayden*.[26] Bennie Joe Hayden, a robbery suspect, was arrested in his home. In a warrantless search of the house at the time of the arrest, police found clothing that matched that described by witnesses as worn by the robber and weapons allegedly used in the holdup.

Hayden was convicted of armed robbery on the basis of this evidence. He appealed, claiming that the clothing was seized in violation of *Gouled*. The Court, 8–1, rejected his challenge. Justice Brennan declared:

Nothing in the language of the Fourth Amendment supports the distinction between "mere evidence" and instrumentalities, fruits of crime, or contraband. On its face, the provision assures the "right of the people to be secure in their persons, houses, papers and effects . . . ," without regard to the use to which any of these things are applied. This "right of the people" is certainly unrelated to the "mere evidence" limitation. Privacy is disturbed no more by a search directed to a purely evidentiary object than it is by a search directed to an instrumentality, fruit, or contraband. A magistrate can intervene in both situations, and the requirements of probable cause and specificity can be preserved intact. Moreover, nothing in the nature of property seized as evidence renders it more private than property seized, for example, as an instrumentality; quite the opposite may be true. Indeed, the distinction is wholly irrational, since, depending on the circumstances, the same "papers and effects" may be "mere evidence" in one case and "instrumentality" in another.[27]

Brennan declared discredited the twin premises upon which the Court in *Gouled* based the mere evidence rule—"that property interests control the right of the government to search and seize" and "that government may not seize evidence simply for the purpose of proving crime."[28]

Privacy, not property, was the primary interest protected by the Fourth Amendment, reasoned the majority, and "[t]he requirements of the Fourth Amendment can secure the same pro-

In *Weeks v. United States*, decided in 1914, the Supreme Court announced the controversial "exclusionary rule," which prohibits the use in federal courts of evidence seized by federal agents in violation of the Fourth Amendment ban against unreasonable search and seizure.[1] Subsequently, the Court applied the rule to forbid use of evidence taken in violation of other constitutional rights, in particular the Fifth Amendment privilege against self-incrimination and the Sixth Amendment right to counsel. Not until 1961, with its ruling in *Mapp v. Ohio*, did the Court extend the exclusionary rule to state trials.[2]

Application of the rule has been the subject of continuing legal controversy. By denying prosecutors the use of certain evidence, the rule can cause the collapse of the government's case and allow a guilty person to go free. As Justice Benjamin Cardozo wrote before he came to the Supreme Court bench, "The criminal is to go free because the constable has blundered."[3]

Some, including Chief Justices Warren E. Burger and William H. Rehnquist, believed that this result is too high a price for society to pay for inadvertent violations of constitutional guarantees. Burger suggested that the rule should be abandoned and replaced with some less costly remedy—such as a law authorizing persons whose rights are so violated by law enforcement officers to sue the particular offending individuals for monetary damages.

In *Silverthorne Lumber Co. v. United States* (1920) the Court made clear that the exclusionary rule announced in *Weeks* forbade *all* use of illegally obtained evidence in federal courts. The Court ordered the government to return to the owner physical evidence illegally seized by federal officials, and it ordered the exclusion of evidence photocopied from the originals.[4]

Justice Oliver Wendell Holmes Jr., speaking for the majority, ruled the photocopied evidence inadmissible, saying, "The essence of a provision forbidding the acquisition of evidence in a certain way is that not merely evidence so acquired shall not be used before the court, but that it shall not be used at all."[5]

In 1954, however, the Court held that narcotics illegally seized by federal officials, while not admissible as evidence at trial, could be used to impeach a defendant's credibility after he had testified that he had never used them.[6] In other decisions, the Court made clear that only the person whose rights were violated by the search and seizure could invoke the exclusionary rule.[7]

WOLF V. COLORADO

In 1949 the Court held in *Wolf v. Colorado* that the Fourth Amendment guarantee protected individuals against state as well as federal action. The Court declined, however, to apply the exclusionary rule to enforce this guarantee against state officials.[8]

Julius Wolf challenged the use of such evidence, arguing that it had been illegally seized and should be excluded. The Supreme Court, however, sustained his conviction. In the case a deputy sheriff had seized Dr. Wolf's appointment book without a warrant, interrogated patients whose names he found in the book, and thereby obtained evidence to charge Wolf with performing illegal abortions.

Justice Felix Frankfurter wrote for the majority. "The immediate question," he said,

is whether the basic right to protect against arbitrary intrusion by the police demands the exclusion of logically relevant evidence obtained by an unreasonable search and seizure because, in a federal prosecution for a federal crime, it would be excluded. . . . When we find that in fact most of the English-speaking world does not regard as vital to such protection the exclusion of evidence thus obtained, we must hesitate to treat this remedy as an essential ingredient of the right. . . .

Granting that in practice the exclusion of evidence may be an effective way of deterring unreasonable searches, it is not for this Court to condemn as falling below the minimal standards assured by the Due Process Clause a State's reliance upon other methods which, if consistently enforced, would be equally effective. . . .

We hold, therefore, that in a prosecution in a State Court for a State crime the Fourteenth Amendment does not forbid the admission of evidence obtained by an unreasonable search and seizure.[9]

Shocking conduct by police, however, did cause the Court to reverse state convictions obtained by an unreasonable search and seizure, even before it applied the exclusionary rule to states. One such case was *Rochin v. California*, decided in 1952.

In *Rochin* state police officers had "seized" evidence from a suspect by pumping his stomach to recover two capsules of drugs he had swallowed at the time of his arrest. The Court held the resulting conviction invalid. Frankfurter wrote the opinion for the unanimous Court, decrying such methods as "conduct that shocks the conscience, . . . methods too close to the rack and the screw to permit of constitutional differentiation."[10]

But the Court's earlier refusal in *Wolf* to exclude *all* illegally obtained evidence was subsequently reaffirmed in cases involving eavesdropping, illegal entry, and the taking of a blood sample from an unconscious injured suspect.[11]

THE "SILVER PLATTER" DOCTRINE

The Supreme Court in *Weeks v. United States* announced two rules of evidence for federal courts.

One was the exclusionary rule: federal prosecutors could not use evidence obtained by federal agents in violation of the Fourth Amendment protection against unreasonable search and seizure.

The second rule became known as the "silver platter" doctrine: federal prosecutors *could* use evidence obtained by *state* agents through unreasonable search and seizure, if that evidence was obtained without federal participation and was turned over to the federal officials—in other words, handed to them on a silver platter.

The incongruity of these two rules was explained by the Court's view in 1914 that the Fourth Amendment did not apply to state action. But after the Court reversed that view in *Wolf v. Colorado* in 1949, the silver platter doctrine survived for eleven more years. Finally, in *Elkins v. United States* (1960) the Court repudiated the practice. Writing for the Court, Justice Potter Stewart declared:

[S]urely no distinction can logically be drawn between evidence obtained in violation of the Fourth Amendment and that obtained in violation of the Fourteenth [through which the ban against unreasonable search and seizure was applicable to the states]. The Constitution is flouted equally in either case. To the victim it matters not whether his constitutional right has been invaded by a federal agent or by a state officer.[12]

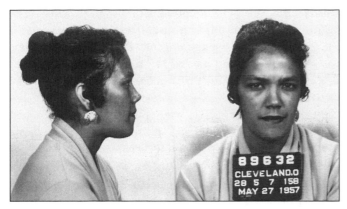

In 1957 Dollree Mapp was arrested for possession of obscene materials. The police seized vital evidence against her during an unconstitutional search. In *Mapp v. Ohio* (1961) the Supreme Court reversed her conviction holding that evidence obtained through an illegal search could not be admitted in court.

MAPP V. OHIO

The Supreme Court extended the exclusionary rule to the states in *Mapp v. Ohio*, decided in 1961. In *Mapp* the Court finally declared that "the exclusionary rule is an essential part of both the Fourth and Fourteenth Amendments."[13]

Cleveland police, suspecting that a criminal was hiding in a certain house, broke in the door, manhandled the woman resident, a Miss Mapp, and searched the entire premises without a warrant. A trunk containing obscene materials was found in the house. Mapp was tried and convicted for possession of obscene materials.

The Supreme Court overturned Mapp's conviction because the evidence used against her had been unconstitutionally seized. The majority opinion by Justice Tom C. Clark reversed *Wolf* insofar as it dealt with the exclusionary rule:

Nothing can destroy a government more quickly than its failure to observe its own laws, or worse, its disregard of the charter of its own existence. . . .

The ignoble shortcut to conviction left open to the State [by allowing use of illegally obtained evidence] tends to destroy the entire system of constitutional restraints on which the liberties of the people rest. Having once recognized that the right to privacy embodied in the Fourth Amendment is enforceable against the States, and that the right to be secure against rude invasions of privacy by state officers is, therefore, constitutional in origin, we can no longer permit that right to remain an empty promise.[14]

In 1965 the Court held that the *Mapp* decision would not be retroactively applied to overturn state criminal convictions that had occurred before the new standard was promulgated. In *Linkletter v. Walker* the Court stated that *Mapp* applied only to cases on direct review at the time of the 1961 ruling and to later cases.[15]

The Court in the 1970s limited the use of the exclusionary rule to overturn convictions, reflecting the lack of enthusiasm of some members of the Court for the rule. Chief Justice Burger said in *Bivens v. Six Unknown Named Agents*, decided in 1971, that he preferred an alternative remedy—perhaps a damage suit against the offending officials.[16]

The Court subsequently refused to forbid prosecutors to use illegally obtained evidence when questioning witnesses before grand juries. It also declined to direct federal judges to release persons challenging their state convictions as obtained with illegally seized evidence. So long as the state has provided an opportunity for a full, fair hearing of the defendant's challenge to that evidence, held the Court, there was no constitutional obligation for federal courts to use the writ of habeas corpus to enforce the exclusionary rule.[17]

In the 1980s the Court approved several exceptions to the exclusionary rule. A "good faith" exception, approved by the Court in 1984, permitted the use of illegally obtained evidence at trial if the police who seized it had a search warrant and thought they were acting legally—only to find that because of some "technical" flaw, their search was in fact illegal. In such a case where the police were acting in good faith, wrote Justice Byron R. White in *United States v. Leon*, the exclusion of valid evidence has no deterrent effect and exacts too high a price from society.[18]

The same year the Court also approved an "inevitable discovery" exception to the exclusionary rule—permitting evidence taken in violation of a defendant's rights to be used at trial if the prosecutor can show that the evidence ultimately would have been discovered by lawful means.[19]

In 1995 the Court extended the good faith exception to mistakes made by judicial personnel. The case of *Arizona v. Evans* involved a courthouse computer mistake, which led a police officer to believe that a warrant that actually had been quashed still was valid. After the officer arrested the individual involved, he discovered a bag of marijuana in the man's car. The Supreme Court ruled 7–2 that errors made by clerical employees resulting in an unconstitutional arrest do not invoke the exclusionary rule and that the drug evidence need not be suppressed.[20]

1. *Weeks v. United States*, 232 U.S. 383 (1914).
2. *Mapp v. Ohio*, 367 U.S. 643 (1961).
3. *People v. Defore*, 242 N.Y. 13 at 21, 150 N.B. 585 (1926).
4. *Silverthorne Lumber Co. v. United States*, 251 U.S. 385 (1921).
5. Id. at 392.
6. *Walder v. United States*, 347 U.S. 62 (1954); see also *Stefanelli v. Minard*, 342 U.S. 117 (1951).
7. *Goldstein v. United States*, 316 U.S. 114 (1942).
8. *Wolf v. Colorado*, 338 U.S. 25 (1949).
9. Id. at 28–29, 31, 33.
10. *Rochin v. California*, 342 U.S. 165 (1952).
11. *Irvine v. California*, 347 U.S. 128 (1954); *Breithaupt v. Abrams*, 352 U.S. 432 (1957).
12. *Elkins v. United States*, 364 U.S. 206 at 215 (1960).
13. *Mapp v. Ohio*, 367 U.S. 643 at 657 (1961).
14. Id. at 659, 660.
15. *Linkletter v. Walker*, 381 U.S. 618 (1965).
16. *Bivens v. Six Unknown Named Agents*, 403 U.S. 388 (1971); see also *Monroe v. Pape*, 365 U.S. 176 (1961).
17. *United States v. Calandra*, 414 U.S. 338 (1974); *Stone v. Powell, Wolff v. Rice*, 428 U.S. 465 (1976); see also *United States v. Janis*, 428 U.S. 433 (1976).
18. *United States v. Leon*, 468 U.S. 897 (1984); *Massachusetts v. Sheppard*, 468 U.S. 981 (1984); see also *Maryland v. Garrison*, 480 U.S. 79 (1987); *Illinois v. Krull*, 480 U.S. 340 (1987).
19. *Nix v. Williams*, 467 U.S. 431 (1984).
20. *Arizona v. Evans*, 115 S. Ct. 1185 (1995).

tection of privacy whether the search is for 'mere evidence' or for fruits, instrumentalities or contraband" [29]

In conclusion, Brennan wrote:

The "mere evidence" limitation has spawned exceptions so numerous and confusion so great, in fact, that it is questionable whether it affords meaningful protection. But if its rejection does enlarge the area of permissible searches, the intrusions are nevertheless made after fulfilling the probable cause and particularity requirements of the Fourth Amendment and after the intervention of "a neutral and detached magistrate." . . . The Fourth Amendment allows intrusions upon privacy under these circumstances, and there is no viable reason to distinguish intrusions to secure "mere evidence" from intrusions to secure fruits, instrumentalities, or contraband. [30]

Justice Abe Fortas, joined by Chief Justice Earl Warren, agreed that Hayden's clothing was properly used as evidence against him, but Fortas criticized the majority's repudiation of the mere evidence rule as needless and dangerous.

In dissent, Justice Douglas argued that there were two zones of privacy—one that was completely protected from official intrusion and one that could be invaded by a reasonable, usually warranted, search by government agents. Douglas would place personal effects like Hayden's clothes in the first category. He explained:

The right of privacy protected by the Fourth Amendment relates in part of course to the precincts of the home or the office. But it does not make them sanctuaries where the law can never reach. . . . A policeman in "hot pursuit" or an officer with a search warrant can enter any house, any room, any building, any office. The privacy of those places is of course protected against invasion except in limited situations. The full privacy protected by the Fourth Amendment is, however, reached when we come to books, phamphlets [sic], papers, letters, documents, and other personal effects. Unless they are contraband or instruments of the crime, they may not be reached by any warrant nor may they be lawfully seized by the police who are in "hot pursuit." By reason of the Fourth Amendment the police may not rummage around among these personal effects, no matter how formally perfect their authority may appear to be. They may not seize them. If they do, those articles may not be used as evidence. Any invasion whatsoever of those personal effects is "unreasonable" within the meaning of the Fourth Amendment. [31]

To Douglas, "the constitutional philosophy" was clear:

The personal effects and possessions of the individual (all contraband and the like excepted) are sacrosanct from prying eyes, from the long arm of the law, from any rummaging by police. Privacy involves the choice of the individual to disclose or to reveal what he believes, what he thinks, what he possesses. The article may be a nondescript work of art, a manuscript of a book, a personal account book, a diary, invoices, personal clothing, jewelry, or what not. [32]

Douglas concluded:

That there is a zone that no police can enter—whether in "hot pursuit" or armed with a meticulously proper warrant—has been emphasized by Boyd and by Gouled. They have been consistently and continuously approved. I would adhere to them and leave with the individual the choice of opening his private effects (apart from contraband and the like) to the police or keeping their contents and their integrity inviolate. The existence of that choice is the very essence of the right of privacy. Without it the Fourth Amendment and the Fifth are ready instruments for the police state that the Framers sought to avoid. [33]

Private Papers, Less Protection

The Court's abandonment of the mere evidence rule curtailed Fourth Amendment protection for private papers.

Two 1976 decisions made this point. In *United States v. Miller* the Court ruled that bank records of a depositor's transactions were not private papers protected by the amendment. [34] And in *Andresen v. Maryland* the Court undercut *Boyd* to allow use of an attorney's business records as evidence against him. [35] Because police had a warrant for the search in which they seized those papers, there was no valid Fourth Amendment challenge to their use, the Court held. And the justices rejected the attorney's argument that, as in *Boyd,* the use of these papers against him violated his Fifth Amendment privilege against compelled self-incrimination.

Two years later in *Zurcher v. The Stanford Daily* the Court rejected the argument of a campus newspaper that a search of its offices by police with a warrant violated the First and the Fourth Amendments. The *Stanford Daily* offices were searched by police looking for photographs or notes revealing the identity of individual demonstrators responsible for injuries to police during a protest. Such documents were clearly mere evidence, and there was no allegation that the newspaper or any of its employees had engaged in any wrongdoing.

The newspaper contended that police should have subpoenaed the information, rather than searching its offices. The Court ruled that the Fourth Amendment did not restrict permissible searches to those places occupied by persons suspected of crimes. "Under existing law," wrote Justice Byron R. White for the five-justice majority, "valid warrants may be issued to search *any* property, whether or not occupied by a third party, at which there is probable cause to believe that the fruits, instrumentalities, or evidence of a crime will be found." [36]

Justice John Paul Stevens, one of the dissenters from the *Zurcher* decision, took this opportunity to express his concern about the Court's departure in *Warden v. Hayden* from the mere evidence rule:

Countless law abiding citizens . . . may have documents in their possession that relate to an ongoing criminal investigation. The consequences of subjecting this large category of persons to unannounced police searches are extremely serious. [37]

Signaling his disagreement with the abandonment of the rule forbidding seizure of mere evidence, Stevens continued:

Possession of contraband or the proceeds or tools of crime gives rise to two inferences: that the custodian is involved in the criminal activity, and that, if given notice of an intended search, he will conceal or destroy what is being sought. The probability of criminal culpability justifies the invasion of his privacy; the need to accomplish the law enforcement purpose of the search justifies acting without advance notice and by force, if necessary. . . .

Mere possession of documentary evidence, however, is much less likely to demonstrate that the custodian is guilty of any wrongdoing. . . .

The only conceivable justification for an unannounced search of an innocent citizen is the fear that, if notice were given, he would conceal or destroy the object of the search. Probable cause to believe that the custodian is a criminal, or that he holds a criminal's weapons, spoils, or the like, justifies that fear. . . . But if nothing said under oath in the warrant application demonstrates the need for an unannounced search by force, the probable cause requirement is not satisfied. In the absence of some other showing of reasonableness, the ensuing search violates the Fourth Amendment.[38]

Arrests and Searches

The Supreme Court has never applied the warrant requirement of the Fourth Amendment as strictly to arrests—the seizure of one's person—as to searches. The Court has applied the common law rule to arrests, approving warrantless arrests by law enforcement officers for crimes committed in their presence and for other crimes where there are reasonable grounds for their action.[39]

In 1925 the Court stated that "[t]he usual rule is that a police officer may arrest without warrant one believed by the officer upon reasonable cause to have been guilty of a felony."[40]

Half a century later the Court noted that it had never invalidated an arrest supported by probable cause just because the arresting officer did not have an arrest warrant. To impose a warrant requirement on all arrests, the Court said, would "constitute an intolerable handicap for legitimate law enforcement."[41]

Probable cause, however, is essential to justify a warrantless arrest.[42] The Court has declared unconstitutional the warrantless detention of suspects apprehended in a police dragnet, declaring that such "investigatory arrests" must be authorized by warrants if the evidence they uncover is to be used in court.[43]

In *United States v. Watson* the Court in 1976 upheld the warrantless arrest of a suspect in a public place, based upon probable cause.[44] Justice White elaborated on the Court's view of the warrant requirement for arrests:

Law enforcement officers may find it wise to seek arrest warrants where practicable to do so, and their judgments about probable cause may be more readily accepted where backed by a warrant issued by a magistrate. . . . But we decline to transform this judicial preference into a constitutional rule when the judgment of the Nation and Congress has for so long been to authorize warrantless public arrests on probable cause rather than to encumber criminal prosecutions with endless litigation with respect to the existence of exigent circumstances, whether it was practicable to get a warrant, whether the suspect was about to flee, and the like.[45]

Joined by Justice Brennan, Justice Marshall dissented, saying:

A warrant requirement for arrests would . . . minimize the possibility that such an intrusion into the individual's sacred sphere of personal privacy would occur on less than probable cause. Primarily for this reason, a warrant is required for searches. Surely there is no reason to place greater trust in the partisan assessment of a police officer that there is probable cause for an arrest than in his determination that probable cause exists for a search.[46]

Later in the same term the Court in *United States v. Santana* upheld the warrantless arrest by police of a suspect in her own home.[47] Police officers followed her inside after they saw her standing on her front porch.

Justice William H. Rehnquist explained that under the Court's interpretation of the Fourth Amendment, the suspect's front porch was a "public" place:

She was not in an area where she had any expectation of privacy. . . . She was not merely visible to the public but as exposed to public view, speech, hearing and touch as if she had been standing completely outside her house. . . .

We thus conclude that a suspect may not defeat an arrest which has been set in motion in a public place, and is therefore proper under *Watson,* by the expedient of escaping to a private place.[48]

Justices Marshall and Brennan again dissented.

Four years later the Court rejected this type of warrantless arrest, ruling 6–3 in *Payton v. New York,* that police may not enter a home to arrest its occupant without a warrant for the arrest or the consent of the occupant. Chief Justice Burger and Justices White and Rehnquist dissented.[49]

Even when police have a warrant, the Court ruled in 1995, they must knock and announce their identity before entering a home. Ruling unanimously, the Court said in *Wilson v. Arkansas* that the guarantee against unreasonable searches and seizures includes the common law principle that the sheriff announce himself before invading a residence. The Court cautioned that some legitimate exceptions for an unannounced entry may arise, such as when lives are in danger or evidence could be destroyed.[50]

SEARCHES INCIDENT TO ARREST

When police arrest a suspect, the Court has held it reasonable—even without a search warrant—for them to search both the person arrested and, to some limited extent, the suspect's immediate surroundings. The justices have viewed such searches as necessary to protect the lives of the arresting officers, to prevent the fugitive's escape, and to prohibit the destruction of evidence.

In 1925 the Court in *Agnello v. United States* acknowledged this exception to the warrant requirement:

The right without a search warrant contemporaneously to search persons lawfully arrested while committing crime, and to search the place where the arrest is made in order to find and seize things connected with the crime as its fruits, or as the means by which it was committed, as well as weapons and other things to effect an escape from custody is not to be doubted.[51]

Twenty-two years later in 1947, in *Harris v. United States,* the Court read this exception broadly.[52] Harris was arrested in his apartment by FBI agents and charged with mail fraud and forgery. Without a search warrant, the agents searched his entire apartment for five hours. They found no evidence of mail fraud or forgery, but they did discover several stolen Selective Service draft cards. Harris was subsequently convicted for illegal possession of those cards.

He challenged the validity of the search and the seizure of the cards, but the Court upheld the search as valid, incident to his arrest. Harris was in control of the entire four-room apartment, it reasoned, and thus the search could extend beyond the room in which he was arrested.

Chief Justice Fred M. Vinson declared that "[s]earch and

The Fourth Amendment requires building, health, and fire inspectors to obtain warrants for administrative searches of private premises, the Court has ruled. But the justices have also held that warrants for such searches do not need to meet the same strict "probable cause" standards mandated for warrants in criminal investigations.

Further, the Court has held that warrants are not required when welfare workers enter the homes of clients for interviews, nor when inspectors visit regulated business establishments such as gun and liquor stores and junkyards.

In 1959 the Court in *Frank v. Maryland* upheld the warrantless inspection of a private dwelling by a city health official seeking the source of a rat infestation. In *Frank* the Court stated that the protection of the Fourth Amendment did not apply:

No evidence for criminal prosecution is sought. . . . Appellant is simply directed to do what he could have been ordered to do without any inspection, and what he cannot properly resist, namely, act in a manner consistent with the maintenance of minimum community standards of health.[1]

Only eight years later the Court overturned *Frank.* In *Camara v. Municipal Court* it declared that administrative searches were indeed "significant intrusions upon the interests protected by the Fourth Amendment."[2]

Roland Camara refused to permit a housing inspector of the San Francisco Health Department to make an inspection of his apartment without a search warrant. The Court upheld Camara's position, stating:

We may agree that a routine inspection of the physical condition of private property is a less hostile intrusion than the typical policeman's search for the fruits and instrumentalities of crime. For this reason alone, *Frank* differed from the great bulk of Fourth Amendment cases. . . . But we cannot agree that the Fourth Amendment interests at stake in these inspection cases are merely "peripheral." It is surely anomalous to say that the individual and his private property are fully protected by the Fourth Amendment only when the individual is suspected of criminal behavior.[3]

In a second ruling announced the same day, the Court declared that government agents must obtain a warrant for administrative entries into the nonpublic portions of commercial establishments. In *See v. City of Seattle* the Court established broad guidelines for such searches.[4]

The Court in the 1978 case of *Marshall v. Barlow's Inc.* denied government inspectors from the Occupational Safety and Health Administration the right to make warrantless random safety inspections of nonpublic working areas on business premises over the owner's objection. If consent was not given to the search, a warrant must be obtained, the Court held.

Relying on *Camara,* the Court held that the "Warrant Clause of the Fourth Amendment protects commercial buildings as well as private homes. . . . That an employee is free to report, and the Government is free to use, any evidence of non-compliance with OSHA that the employee observes furnishes no justification for federal agents to enter a place of business from which the public is restricted and to conduct their own warrantless search."[5]

The Court has made exceptions to the warrant requirement for administrative searches of premises occupied by gun dealers and liquor establishments, both of which are regulated by federal law. The premises of such business establishments may be inspected during regular business hours by government agents without a warrant.

In *Colonnade Catering Corp. v. United States* the Court held that in certain industries subject to particular government oversight there can be no expectation of privacy for the proprietor or the premises.

A federal agent of the alcohol and tobacco tax division of the Internal Revenue Service made a warrantless inspection of a locked storeroom and forcibly seized illegal liquor. Justice William O. Douglas declared that "Congress has broad power to design such powers of inspection under the liquor laws as it deems necessary to meet the evils at hand."[6]

In *United States v. Biswell* the Court upheld the warrantless search of a pawnbroker's storeroom by a federal agent who discovered two illegal weapons there. Relying on *Colonnade Catering,* the Court declared that in this case "regulatory inspections further urgent federal interest, and the possibilities of abuse and the threat to privacy are not of impressive dimensions." Therefore, "the inspection may proceed without a warrant where specifically authorized by statute."[7]

In *New York v. Burger* the Court in 1987 brought auto junkyards, which are regulated by the state, within this exception to the warrant requirement.[8]

Twice—in 1978 and again in 1984—the Court has insisted that fire officials inspecting the premises on which a suspicious fire occurred must have a warrant, unless the inspection occurs during or immediately after the fire. In *Michigan v. Tyler* the Court held:

[A]n entry to fight a fire requires no warrant, and . . . once in the building, officials may remain there for a reasonable time to investigate the cause of the fire. Thereafter, additional entries to investigate . . . must be made pursuant to the warrant procedures governing administrative searches.[9]

The Court underscored this point in *Michigan v. Clifford,* declaring that the warrantless entry and search of a burned residence five hours after the fire was extinguished, without notice to the absent residents, was a violation of the Fourth Amendment.[10]

In contrast, the Court has held since the 1970 case of *Wyman v. James* that home visits by a welfare worker to a prospective client raised no valid Fourth Amendment issues. The visit, agreed the Court, might be both "rehabilitative and investigative," but it nevertheless was not "a search in the traditional criminal law context" to which the warrant requirement applied.[11]

1. *Frank v. Maryland,* 359 U.S. 360 at 366 (1959).
2. *Camara v. Municipal Court,* 387 U.S. 523 at 530 (1967).
3. Ibid.
4. *See v. City of Seattle,* 387 U.S. 541 (1967).
5. *Marshall v. Barlow's Inc.,* 436 U.S. 307 at 311, 315 (1978).
6. *Colonnade Catering Corp. v. United States,* 397 U.S. 72 at 76 (1970).
7. *United States v. Biswell,* 406 U.S. 311 at 317 (1972).
8. *New York v. Burger,* 482 U.S. 691 (1987).
9. *Michigan v. Tyler,* 436 U.S. 499 at 511 (1978).
10. *Michigan v. Clifford,* 464 U.S. 287 (1984).
11. *Wyman v. James,* 400 U.S. 309 at 317–318 (1971).

seizure incident to lawful arrest is a practice of ancient origin and has long been an integral part of the law-enforcement procedures of the United States."[53]

Justices Frankfurter, Jackson, Wiley B. Rutledge, and Frank Murphy dissented. Murphy wrote:

The Court today has resurrected and approved, in effect, the use of the odious general warrant or writ of assistance, presumably outlawed forever from our society by the Fourth Amendment. A warrant of arrest, without more, is now sufficient to justify an unlimited search of a man's home from cellar to garret for evidence of any crime, provided only that he is arrested in his home. Probable cause for the search need not be shown; an oath or affirmation is unnecessary; no description of the place to be searched or the things to be seized need be given; and the magistrate's judgment that these requirements have been satisfied is now dispensed with. In short, all the restrictions put upon the issuance and execution of search warrants by the Fourth Amendment are now dead letters as to those who are arrested in their homes.[54]

The following year, however, the Court seemed to narrow the definition of a search which was permissible, without a warrant, pursuant to a valid arrest. *Trupiano v. United States* involved the arrest of several persons on a farm in New Jersey for operating an illegal still—and the seizure, without a warrant, of the still, which the arresting agents had observed in operation during the arrest.[55]

The Supreme Court held the warrantless arrest valid but not the seizure of the still. For the majority, Justice Murphy wrote that no reason was offered why the federal agents could not have obtained a search warrant before moving in to make the arrest "except [their] indifference to the legal process for search and seizure which the Constitution contemplated."[56] Murphy continued:

A search or seizure without a warrant as an incident to a lawful arrest has always been considered to be a strictly limited right. It grows out of the inherent necessities of the situation at the time of the arrest. But there must be something more in the way of necessity than merely a lawful arrest. . . . Otherwise the exception swallows the general principle, making a search warrant completely unnecessary wherever there is a lawful arrest, and so there must be some other factor in the situation that would make it unreasonable or impracticable to require the arresting officer to equip himself with a search warrant.[57]

Later in 1948 the Court reiterated this last point in its ruling in *McDonald v. United States*:

Where . . . officers are not responding to an emergency, there must be compelling reasons to justify the absence of a search warrant. A search without a warrant demands exceptional circumstances. . . . We cannot . . . excuse the absence of a search warrant without a showing by those who seek exemption from the constitutional mandate that the exigencies of the situation made that course imperative.[58]

Although the "exigent circumstances" requirement of *McDonald* for warrantless searches generally has survived, the *Trupiano* ruling that a warrant be required whenever obtaining one was practicable was short-lived.

In 1950 the Court in *United States v. Rabinowitz* declared that "[t]o the extent that *Trupiano* . . . requires a search warrant solely upon the basis of the practicability of procuring it rather than upon the reasonableness of the search after a lawful arrest, that case is overruled."[59]

In *Rabinowitz* the Court separated the question of the reasonableness of a search from the warrant requirement. Justice Sherman Minton explained:

What is a reasonable search is not to be determined by any fixed formula. The Constitution does not define what are "unreasonable" searches and, regrettably, in our discipline we have no ready litmus-paper test. The recurring questions of the reasonableness of searches must find resolution in the facts and circumstances of each case. . . .

The relevant test is not whether it is reasonable to procure a search warrant, but whether the search was reasonable. That criterion in turn depends on the facts and circumstances—the total atmosphere of the case.[60]

The attempted separation of the reasonableness standard from the warrant requirement and the use of the "total atmosphere" test resulted in considerable confusion over what warrantless searches were permissible incident to a valid arrest.[61]

In 1969 the Court overruled *Rabinowitz* and *Harris* and returned to the view that the warrant and reasonableness requirements were indeed linked. This shift was announced in *Chimel v. California*.[62] The Court overturned a burglary conviction because it was based on evidence seized without a warrant incident to arrest but the search was too extensive to be justified by the arrest alone.

Searches incident to arrest were only reasonable insofar as they involved the person arrested and the area immediately under his control—from which he could obtain a weapon or within which he could destroy evidence, declared the Court.

Justice Stewart wrote for the majority:

No consideration relevant to the Fourth Amendment suggests any point of rational limitation, once the search is allowed to go beyond the area from which the person arrested might obtain weapons or evidentiary items. The only reasoned distinction is one between a search of the person arrested and the area within his reach on the one hand, and more extensive searches on the other. . . .

The search here went far beyond the petitioner's person and the area from within which he might have obtained either a weapon or something that could have been used as evidence against him. There was no constitutional justification, in the absence of a search warrant, for extending the search beyond that area. The scope of the search was, therefore, "unreasonable" under the Fourth and Fourteenth Amendments, and the petitioner's conviction cannot stand.[63]

Justice White, joined by Justice Hugo L. Black, dissented:

[W]here as here the existence of probable cause is independently established and would justify a warrant for a broader search for evidence, I would follow past cases and permit such a search to be carried out without a warrant, since the fact of arrest supplies an exigent circumstance justifying police action before the evidence can be removed, and also alerts the suspect to the fact of the search so that he can immediately seek judicial determination of probable cause in an adversary proceeding and appropriate redress.[64]

The following year in *Vale v. Louisiana* the Court held that a street arrest of a narcotics suspect did not constitute an "exigent circumstance" to justify a warrantless search of his house.[65]

Then in *Coolidge v. New Hampshire*, decided in 1971, the Court ruled that the arrest of a suspect inside his house did not justify a search of his automobile parked in the driveway.[66]

But the Court has never retreated from its view that a suspect under lawful arrest may properly be subjected to full search of his person without a warrant, that such a search is reasonable under the Fourth Amendment, and that evidence found in such a search is admissible.

The Court reaffirmed these points in 1973 in *United States v. Robinson* and *Gustafson v. Florida*. These cases involved motorists stopped for violations of auto or traffic laws and found to possess illegal drugs. The subsequent narcotics convictions of both motorists were upheld.[67]

AUTOMOBILE SEARCHES

Warrants are not always required for searches incident to arrest, and since 1925 the Court has allowed some warrantless searches of moving vehicles, especially automobiles.

The landmark case in this area is *Carroll v. United States*, decided in 1925.[68] George Carroll was convicted of transporting liquor for sale in violation of the federal prohibition law and the Eighteenth Amendment. The contraband liquor used as evidence against him had been taken from his car by federal agents acting without a search warrant.

The Supreme Court sustained Carroll's conviction against his contention that this seizure violated his Fourth Amendment rights. Writing for the Court, Chief Justice William Howard Taft explained:

[T]he guaranty of freedom from unreasonable searches and seizures by the Fourth Amendment has been construed, practically since the beginning of the government, as recognizing a necessary difference between a search of a store, dwelling house, or other structure in respect of which a proper official warrant readily may be obtained and a search of a ship, motor boat, wagon, or automobile for contraband goods, where it is not practicable to secure a warrant, because the vehicle can be quickly moved out of the locality or jurisdiction in which the warrant must be sought.[69]

Subsequent rulings involving police searches of automobiles, without warrants, for contraband, have made clear the breadth of this exception to the warrant requirements. In 1931 the Court upheld the search of a parked car as reasonable because police could not know when the suspect might move it.[70] The Court in 1948 appeared to limit this exception to situations in which Congress had authorized warrantless searches of moving vehicles suspected of involvement in violating federal laws.[71] But the following year the justices in *Brinegar v. United States* upheld, as reasonable, warrantless searches of automobiles whenever police had probable cause to believe the cars were involved in illegal activity.[72]

This remains the rule, as the Court has repeatedly emphasized in cases in which it has refused to declare evidence to be admissible when it was discovered in a search for which there was no probable cause.[73]

After the Court in *Mapp v. Ohio* applied the exclusionary

"SEIZURE" OF TRAITS

The Supreme Court has consistently held that certain physical characteristics are not protected by the Fourth Amendment from government "seizure" for use as evidence.

Writing for the Court in 1910, Justice Oliver Wendell Holmes Jr. held that such revelations were not compelled self-incrimination. The Fifth Amendment, wrote Holmes, did not demand "an exclusion of his [the suspect's] body as evidence."[1] This principle has been invoked to rebut Fourth Amendment challenges to the use of evidence such as voice samples and handwriting examples obtained from suspects.[2]

The Court also has held that minor intrusions on a suspect's body do not violate the Fourth Amendment. But it has outlawed more drastic intrusions as offending both the Fourth Amendment and the sense of justice. Thus the Court has upheld the extraction of blood samples from suspects, but it has rejected the use of a stomach pump to obtain evidence of narcotics possession.[3]

That distinction between minor and major intrusions blurred in 1989 when the Court upheld mandatory drug testing for certain groups—not of suspects—but of federal employees in particular positions with responsibility for public safety or law enforcement. The Court acknowledged that such tests, which required the employee to provide a urine specimen, were searches within the meaning of the Fourth Amendment but held that it was reasonable for the government to conduct them, even without a warrant.[4]

1. *Holt v. United States*, 218 U.S. 245 at 253 (1910).
2. *United States v. Dionisio*, 410 U.S. 1 (1973); *United States v. Mara*, 410 U.S. 19 (1973); *United States v. Wade*, 388 U.S. 218 (1967); *Gilbert v. California*, 388 U.S. 263 (1967); see also *United States v. Euge*, 444 U.S. 707 (1980).
3. *Rochin v. California*, 342 U.S. 165 (1952); *Breithaupt v. Abrams*, 352 U.S. 432 (1957); *Schmerber v. California*, 384 U.S. 757 (1966); *Cupp v. Murphy*, 412 U.S. 291 (1973); *South Dakota v. Neville*, 459 U.S. 553 (1983); *Winston v. Lee*, 470 U.S. 753 (1985); but see *United States v. Montoya de Hernandez*, 473 U.S. 531 (1985).
4. *Skinner v. Railway Labor Executives' Association*, 489 U.S. 602 (1989); *National Treasury Employees Union v. Von Raab*, 489 U.S. 656 (1989).

---

rule to state proceedings—and in *Ker v. California* adopted a uniform standard for state and federal action under the Fourth Amendment—the Court applied the same rules for warrantless auto searches to state police and federal agents.

The Court gives police leeway in such searches. It has upheld the search of a car without a warrant as long as a week after the arrest of its owner, when the government had a proprietary interest in the car because it was subject to forfeiture under state law.[74] It has allowed police to make such searches of autos after they have been towed to the police garage from the site of an arrest.[75]

The justices have refused to exclude evidence obtained in the routine warrantless search of an impounded vehicle as inadmissible,[76] or to require that a warrant be obtained before police take paint samples from the exterior of a car parked in a public parking lot.[77]

In 1978 the Court in *Rakas v. Illinois* held that passengers did

Since 1925 the Court has made numerous decisions dealing with searches of automobiles, their oc cupants, and even closed packages found in a car. In general, the Court has decided that people and their paraphernalia are entitled to less privacy in cars than in their homes or places of business.

not have the right to challenge the warrantless search of the vehicle in which they were riding or the use of evidence seized in that search against them. That decision tied the Fourth Amendment rights of persons in cars more closely to ownership concepts than in earlier cases.

For the five-man majority, Justice Rehnquist emphasized that Fourth Amendment rights could be asserted only by the person whose privacy was invaded: "A person who is aggrieved by an illegal search and seizure only through the introduction of damaging evidence secured by a search of a third person's premises or property has not had any of his Fourth Amendment rights infringed."[78]

The warrantless search in this case was proper because it was based on probable cause: the car fit the description of a getaway car used in a nearby robbery. And because the passengers did not claim that they owned either the car or the items seized, they could not challenge the search, the seizure, or the use of discovered evidence against them as a violation of the Fourth Amendment guarantee.

The four dissenting justices, for whom Justice White wrote, criticized the majority for implying that the Fourth Amendment protected property interests rather than privacy interests. The Court in this ruling, wrote White, was declaring "open season" for auto searches.[79]

Four months later, however, the Court appeared to allay White's fears with its 8–1 decision in *Delaware v. Prouse.* With White writing the majority opinion, the Court held impermissible the state police practice of randomly stopping motorists—without any probable cause—to check licenses and registrations. The Court decided that such "seizures" of the person and any subsequent searches violated the Fourth Amendment and

that evidence of a drug law violation discovered in a car after such a random stop could not be admitted as evidence in state court.[80]

The difficulty of administering this exception was well illustrated with a pair of rulings in 1981 and 1982. On July 1, 1981, the Court in *Robbins v. California* ruled that police needed a search warrant to open a closed piece of luggage or other closed container found in a lawfully searched car. The vote was 6–3, with Justices Rehnquist, Stevens, and Harry A. Blackmun dissenting.[81]

On June 1, 1982, the Court reversed itself. Stevens wrote in *United States v. Ross* that police officers who have probable cause to suspect that drugs or other contraband are in a car they have stopped may search the entire vehicle as thoroughly as if they had a warrant, including all containers and packages in the car that might contain the object of the search. Justices White, Brennan, and Marshall dissented.[82]

Nine years later the Court, 6–3, allowed police even more leeway. The justices ruled in *California v. Acevedo* that police do not need a warrant to search a car and all closed containers inside if they have probable cause to believe that one of the containers holds contraband, even if they lack probable cause for the entire vehicle.[83]

During this same period, police accelerated their use of random searches at sobriety checkpoints. The use of such checkpoints was endorsed by the Court in a 1990 ruling.[84] In an opinion by Chief Justice Rehnquist, the Court said that states have a strong interest in deterring drunk driving, the checkpoints advance that interest, and the intrusion on motorists stopped is "slight."

Justices Brennan, Marshall, and Stevens dissented. Brennan

cited the Fourth Amendment protection not only to be free from police intrusion but the "right to be let alone." He said, "In the face of the 'momentary evil' of drunken driving, the Court today abdicates its role of protector of that fundamental right."[85]

The following year the Court, 6–3, said police may approach passengers on buses and ask to search their luggage for illegal drugs, even if police have no basis for suspicion that the passengers are engaged in wrongdoing. The Court said the rationale for permitting these searches was the same as the rationale in prior decisions allowing random searches in other public places.[86]

In a 1996 case with racial overtones, two black men from the District of Columbia said narcotics police officers had used a minor traffic violation as a pretext, or excuse, to actually investigate whether the men were engaged in illegal drug dealing. The men, who were caught with bags of crack cocaine, said that if such stops were allowed when the police lacked probable cause to investigate for drug dealing, police would tail certain motorists looking for minor traffic infractions. But the Court ruled unanimously that even if police have an ulterior motive, a traffic stop is permissible as long as there is probable cause to believe that the motorist had violated a traffic law, no matter how slight.[87]

That same term in another crack cocaine case, the Court ruled 8–1 that a black defendant who alleges selective prosecution based on racial discrimination is entitled to discovery, that is, the acquisition of facts and documents in a case, only if he makes a threshold showing that the government declined to prosecute similarly situated white suspects.[88]

Electronic Eavesdropping

Not until 1967 did the Supreme Court bring electronic eavesdropping and surveillance techniques within the scope of the Fourth Amendment guarantee of security against unreasonable search and seizure.

From 1928 until 1967, the Court held firmly that the Fourth Amendment applied only when there was physical entry and seizure of tangible items; it did not apply to overheard conversations. This rule was set out in *Olmstead v. United States.* Through the use of wiretaps, police had gathered evidence against a bootlegging operation. The defendants challenged this method of obtaining evidence, arguing that it violated their Fourth Amendment rights. The Court, with Chief Justice Taft writing its opinion, rejected that claim:

The well-known historical purpose of the 4th Amendment, directed against general warrants and writs of assistance, was to prevent the use of governmental force to search a man's house, his person, his papers, and his effects, and to prevent their seizure against his will. . . .

The Amendment itself shows that the search is to be of material things—the person, the house, his papers or his effects. The description of the warrant necessary to make the proceeding lawful is that it must specify the place to be searched and the person or things to be seized. . . .

The Amendment does not forbid what was done here. There was no searching. There was no seizure. The evidence was secured by the use of the sense of hearing and that only. There was no entry of the houses or offices of the defendants. . . .

The language of the Amendment can not be extended and expanded to include telephone wires reaching to the whole world from the defendant's house or office. . . .

Congress may, of course, protect the secrecy of telephone messages by making them, when intercepted, inadmissible in evidence in Federal criminal trials. . . . But the courts may not adopt such a policy by attributing an enlarged and unusual meaning to the 4th Amendment.[89]

In dissent Justice Oliver Wendell Holmes Jr. wrote, "[A]part from the Constitution, the government ought not to use evidence obtained, and only obtainable, by a criminal act. . . . I think it a less evil that some criminals should escape than that the government should play an ignoble part."[90]

Justice Louis D. Brandeis also dissented, arguing that wiretapping was clearly a search within the meaning of the Fourth Amendment, which he described as intended to protect "the sanctities of a man's home and the privacies of life." He added that the Fourth Amendment guarantee must, to retain its validity, be read with an awareness of new threats to the security it was intended to protect:

Subtler and more far-reaching means of invading privacy have become available to the government. Discovery and invention have made it possible for the government, by means far more effective than stretching upon the rack, to obtain disclosure in court of what is whispered in the closet.

Furthermore, Brandeis argued, wiretapping was itself a crime under federal law, and government agents should not be allowed to commit crimes to catch criminals:

Decency, security, and liberty alike demand that government officials shall be subjected to the same rules of conduct that are commands to the citizen. In a government of laws, existence of the government will be imperiled if it fails to observe the law scrupulously. Our government is the potent, the omnipresent, teacher. For good or ill, it teaches the whole people by its example. Crime is contagious. If the government becomes a law-breaker, it breeds contempt for law; it invites every man to become a law unto himself; it invites anarchy. To declare that in the administration of the criminal law the end justifies the means—to declare that the government may commit crimes in order to secure the conviction of a private criminal—would bring terrible retribution. Against that pernicious doctrine this court should resolutely set its face.[91]

In 1934 Congress included in the Federal Communications Act the statement that "no person not being authorized by the sender shall intercept any communication and divulge or publish the existence, contents, substance, purport, effect or meaning of such intercepted communication to any person."

Three years later, in *Nardone v. United States,* the Court read this provision as forbidding federal agents, as well as all other persons, to intercept and disclose telephone messages by the use of wiretaps. In that and a similar case in 1939, the Court excluded from use in federal courts any evidence obtained, directly or indirectly, from wiretaps.[92]

Two wartime rulings announced in 1942, however, allowed some use of evidence obtained by electronic surveillance. In *Goldstein v. United States* the Court held that wiretap evidence could be used against persons other than those whose conversations had been overheard. And in *Goldman v. United States* the Court held that the use of a "bug"—an electronic listening device, not a wiretap on telephone lines—was not in violation of the Communications Act provision, which applied only to actual interference with communication wires and telephone lines.[93]

In 1961 the Court began to take a tougher view of electronic surveillance as an impermissible intrusion into personal privacy. In *Silverman v. United States* the Court held that the Fourth Amendment was violated by the use of a "spike-mike" driven into a building wall to allow police to overhear conversations within the building. The fact that the device, although tiny, actually penetrated the building wall was sufficient to constitute physical intrusion in violation of the search-and-seizure provision.[94]

Six years later the Court finally abandoned *Olmstead* and brought electronic surveillance of all types within the proscription of the Fourth Amendment.

Katz v. United States involved evidence obtained by government agents who placed a listening device on the outside of a public telephone booth. The information from the telephone conversations led to the prosecution of individuals involved in illegal bookmaking activities.[95]

Justice Stewart explained: "The fact that the electronic device employed . . . did not happen to penetrate the wall of the booth can have no constitutional significance."[96] He continued:

[T]he Fourth Amendment protects people, not places. What a person knowingly exposes to the public, even in his own home or office, is not a subject of Fourth Amendment protection. . . . But what he seeks to preserve as private, even in an area accessible to the public, may be constitutionally protected. . . .

. . . [W]hat he [Katz] sought to exclude when he entered the booth

STUDENTS AND BUREAUCRATS

In the mid-1980s the Court for the first time explicitly applied the Fourth Amendment's guarantee against unreasonable searches and seizures to public school students and government workers.

In each case, however, the application seemed a hollow victory—at least to the particular students and workers involved in the cases of *New Jersey v. T. L. O.* and *O'Connor v. Ortega.* The Court, having applied the constitutional guarantee, found that the searches challenged in these cases did not require warrants.

The Fourth Amendment's protection for students seemed even less meaningful after the Court in 1995 ruled in *Vernonia School District 47J v. Acton* that public schools can require students to take drug tests as a condition of playing sports. The majority said that urinalysis testing did not impinge the students' constitutional rights to privacy and to be free from unreasonable searches.

In *New Jersey v. T. L. O.,* the Court held that school officials did not need a search warrant or probable cause to conduct a reasonable search of a student. Instead, wrote Justice Byron R. White for the Court, school officials may search a student so long as "there are reasonable grounds for suspecting that the search will turn up evidence that the student has violated or is violating either the law or the rules of the school."[1]

Two years later, the Court in *O'Connor v. Ortega* declared that "individuals do not lose Fourth Amendment rights merely because they work for the government instead of a private employer." But Justice Sandra Day O'Connor went on to say that supervisors do not need warrants for searching desk drawers and office files for routine work-related purposes or to investigate work-related misconduct.[2]

In the 1995 case from Vernonia, Oregon, the Court by a 6–3 vote said students' rights under the Fourth Amendment are outweighed by a school's interest in deterring drug abuse. Justice Antonin Scalia, who wrote for the majority, emphasized that young students lack adult rights. "Deterring drug use by our nation's schoolchildren is at least as important as enhancing efficient enforcement of the nation's laws against the importation of drugs," Scalia wrote.[3]

1. *New Jersey v. T. L. O.,* 469 U.S. 325 at 342 (1985).
2. *O'Connor v. Ortega,* 480 U.S. 709 (1987).
3. *Vernonia School District 47J v. Acton,* 115 S. Ct. 2386 (1995).

was not the intruding eye—it was the uninvited ear. He did not shed his right to do so simply because he made his calls from a place where he might be seen.[97]

Two years later, in 1969, the Court made clear its intention of penalizing government agents for engaging in improper electronic surveillance. In *Alderman v. United States, Butenko v. United States,* and *Ivanov v. United States,* the Court held that the government must turn over all material obtained by illegal surveillance to the defendant whose Fourth Amendment rights had been violated by its collection and against whom such evidence might be used. The defendant could then examine the information to ascertain what parts of it the government might plan to use against him and to challenge its use. The government, dismayed by this ruling, chose to drop a number of prosecutions rather than disclose the method and the content of some particular instances of surveillance.[98]

Following *Katz,* Congress in the 1968 Crime Control and Safe Streets Act provided statutory authorization for federal use of judicially approved electronic surveillance. The law set out procedures to be followed by federal agents in obtaining approval for such surveillance, first from Justice Department officials and then from a federal judge who would issue a warrant for this type of search and seizure.

The law provided that applications for warrants must be approved either by the attorney general or by a specially designated assistant attorney general.[99]

Twice in the 1970s the Court signaled its determination to apply the warrant requirement to wiretaps at least as strictly as it applied it to other types of searches. In 1972 the Court unanimously rejected the contention of the Nixon administration that the 1968 law did not require judicial approval of warrants for wiretaps or surveillance in national security cases.[100] Two years later the Court effectively nullified hundreds of criminal prosecutions based on evidence obtained by electronic surveillance. The reason was that Attorney General John N. Mitchell had not himself signed the applications for the warrants authorizing the surveillance and had allowed an aide other than the designated assistant attorney general to approve the applications.[101]

In 1979, however, the Court held that because Congress must have recognized that most electronic bugs can be installed only by agents who secretly enter the premises, warrants authorizing such surveillance need not explicitly authorize covert entry.[102]

The Fifth Amendment privilege against self-incrimination is stated clearly: no one "shall be compelled in any criminal case to be a witness against himself."

A person may not be forced to confess, required to testify, or provide evidence that could convict him. When charged with a crime, an individual defendant is free to plead not guilty. And no inference of guilt may be drawn either from his decision not to testify at his own trial or to remain silent when interrogated by police.[1]

The privilege is not an absolute right to silence. The right must be claimed; it is waived unless invoked. And when it is claimed, a judge decides whether its assertion is justified.[2] The accused waives that right when he agrees to testify in his own defense, and thus becomes subject to crossexamination.

A witness called to testify before a grand jury, a congressional committee, or an administrative hearing risks a contempt citation if he refuses to appear. Once on the stand, however, he may refuse to answer particular questions on the grounds that the answers will tend to incriminate him.[3] But he may not assert the privilege just because he fears other adverse consequences of his testimony, such as public ridicule or general disrepute.[4]

And once incriminating facts have been revealed voluntarily, a witness cannot then assert his Fifth Amendment privilege to avoid disclosure of further details.[5]

The privilege is a personal one and may not be invoked to protect anyone else. It is to be asserted only by "natural" persons, not by corporations, labor unions, or other organizations.[6] Individuals in possession of public records or those of an organization cannot claim the Fifth Amendment privilege to protect those records, even if they contain information incriminating to the witness. Only purely personal and private documents and papers in the possession of the owner are protected by the privilege.[7]

The Court has affirmed repeatedly that innocent persons as well as guilty ones may invoke this privilege. In doing so, the Court rejects the assumption that anyone who "takes the Fifth" must be guilty. The Court has declared it unconstitutional for a state to punish employees who refuse to testify about employment-related activities, after being ordered to waive their privilege against self-incrimination. It has reversed convictions of public employees based on testimony obtained through such coercion and held that states may not fire persons just because they invoke this privilege.[8] (See "Penalizing the Privilege," pp. 550–551.)

Congress, in the course of regulating certain forms of business and political activity found highly susceptible to illegal diversion or influence, has passed a number of federal laws requiring detailed records, reports, registration, and/or tax payments related to membership in some groups, to drug and firearms transactions, and to gambling.

Until the 1960s the Court generally upheld such registration and tax provisions,[9] but beginning with its decision in the Communist Party registration case of *Albertson v. Subversive Activities Control Board* in 1965, the Court held that compliance with such requirements violated the Fifth Amendment.[10] (See details of the case, pp. 543–544.)

In the late 1960s and early 1970s the Court struck down many of these registration provisions on Fifth Amendment grounds. Congress subsequently rewrote some of the offending laws and omitted the self-incriminatory provisions.[11]

Privilege and Immunity

Immunity statutes, in use throughout American history, represent the government's effort to reconcile its need for information with the Fifth Amendment privilege against compelled self-incrimination.

These laws protect individuals who furnish information to the government from prosecutions based on their own coerced testimony. Most immunity laws contain an exception for perjury: if immunized witnesses provide false information, they are subject to prosecution for perjury using their own words.

Justice Lewis F. Powell Jr. noted once that immunity laws "seek a rational accommodation between the imperatives of the privilege and the legitimate demands of government to compel citizens to testify."[12]

The modern Court has condoned as constitutional a narrower form of immunity than that approved during the nineteenth century. Early statutes allowed immunization of witnesses from prosecution for any crime revealed in their testimony, a so-called "immunity bath." Later statutes, however, allowed some indirect use of immunized testimony to obtain other evidence of wrongdoing by the witness.

In 1892, in one of its earliest rulings concerning the Fifth Amendment privilege, the Supreme Court held this more limited immunity insufficient protection for the witness. In *Counselman v. Hitchcock* the Court unanimously ordered the release from custody of Charles Counselman, a railroad official, held in contempt of court. Asserting his constitutional privilege against compelled self-incrimination, he had declined to answer certain questions from a grand jury. Counselman challenged his detention as a violation of his Fifth Amendment rights and sought release through a writ of habeas corpus. The Supreme Court agreed with his challenge.

In its opinion, written by Justice Samuel Blatchford, the Court held that grand jury witnesses, as well as persons already charged with crimes, could assert this privilege.

In addition, the Court found this limited immunity, which left the witness still subject to indirect use of his testimony against him, insufficient because it "does not supply a complete protection from all the perils against which the constitutional prohibition was designed to guard, and is not a full substitute for that prohibition."[13]

"In view of the constitutional provision," concluded Justice Blatchford, "a statutory enactment, to be valid, must afford absolute immunity against future prosecution for the offense to which the question relates."[14]

This decision was interpreted as a requirement that immunity must protect a witness from all prosecution for the criminal "transactions" revealed in immunized testimony, not just against the "use" of the testimony itself as evidence.

Concerned that the Fifth Amendment privilege could be used to block inquiry into alleged violations of the Interstate Commerce Act, Congress in 1892 provided that witnesses appearing in Interstate Commerce Commission investigations could be granted this type of "transactional" immunity.

In 1896 the Court, 5–4, upheld the new law in *Brown v. Walker.* In so doing, the Court made clear that the privilege was to be claimed only to protect the witness alone, not any third party, and only to protect the witness from prosecution, not simply from "personal odium and disgrace."

The Court upheld the contempt sentence of Brown, a railway company auditor. He had refused to answer certain questions from a grand jury, claiming his Fifth Amendment privilege. The Court held that this assertion was not appropriate, since the privilege was being claimed to shield others from prosecution.

Justice Henry B. Brown viewed the privilege as meaning only that the witness was secure from criminal prosecution. This interpretation, he said, established an appropriate equilibrium between the private right and the public welfare.

The clause of the Constitution in question is obviously susceptible of two interpretations. If it be construed literally, as authorizing the witness to refuse to disclose any fact that might tend to incriminate, disgrace, or expose him to unfavorable comments, then, as he must necessarily to a large extent determine upon his own conscience and responsibility whether his answer to the proposed question will have that tendency . . . the practical result would be, that no one could be compelled to testify to a material fact in a criminal case. . . . If, upon the other hand, the object of the provision be to secure the witness against a criminal prosecution, which might be aided directly or indirectly by his disclosure, then, if no such prosecution be possible,—in other words, if his testimony operate as a complete pardon for the offense to which it relates,—a statute absolutely securing to him such immunity from prosecution would satisfy the demands of the clause in question. . . .

It can only be said in general that the clause should be construed, as it was doubtless designed, to effect a practical and beneficent purpose—not necessarily to protect witnesses against every possible detriment which might happen to them from their testimony, nor to unduly impede, hinder, or obstruct the administration of criminal justice. . . .

The design of the constitutional privilege is not to aid the witness in vindicating his character but to protect him against being compelled to furnish evidence to convict him of a criminal charge. . . . While the constitutional provision in question is justly regarded as one of the most valuable prerogatives of the citizen, its object is fully accom-

plished by the statutory immunity, and we are therefore of opinion that the witness was compellable to answer.[15]

The issue of what constituted true immunity was again raised during the 1950s when the Eisenhower administration proposed, and Congress approved, the Immunity Act of 1954. Its purpose was to prevent witnesses, called to testify in government subversion inquiries, from refusing to answer questions on grounds of self-incrimination. The act granted immunity from prosecution for criminal activity revealed during compelled testimony.

But Communist Party members in congressional testimony challenged the law. They alleged that the 1954 act did not provide true immunity in light of the many disabilities—including loss of employment and public criticism—imposed on party members.

In 1956 the Court upheld the 1954 act in *Ullmann v. United States.* Justice Felix Frankfurter, citing *Brown v. Walker,* described the 1893 immunity statute upheld in *Brown* as now "part of our constitutional fabric."[16]

Frankfurter continued:

We are not dealing here with one of the vague, undefinable, admonitory provisions of the Constitution whose scope is inevitably addressed to changing circumstances. . . . [T]he history of the privilege establishes not only that it is not to be interpreted literally, but also that its sole concern is . . . with the danger to a witness forced to give testimony leading to the infliction of "penalties affixed to the criminal acts." . . . Immunity displaces the danger. Once the reason for the privilege ceases, the privilege ceases.[17]

Justices William O. Douglas and Hugo L. Black dissented, urging the Court to overrule *Brown v. Walker* and adopt the literal view "that the right of silence created by the Fifth Amendment is beyond the reach of Congress."[18] Douglas said:

[T]he Fifth Amendment was written in part to prevent any Congress, any court, and any prosecutor from prying open the lips of an accused to make incriminating statements against his will. The Fifth Amendment protects the conscience and the dignity of the individual, as well as his safety and security, against the compulsion of the government. . . .

The critical point is that the Constitution places the right of silence beyond the reach of government. The Fifth Amendment stands between the citizen and his government. When public opinion casts a person into the outer darkness, as happens today when a person is exposed as a Communist, the government brings infamy on the head of the witness when it compels disclosure. That is precisely what the Fifth Amendment prohibits.[19]

In the Organized Crime Control Act of 1970, Congress approved a more limited grant of "use" immunity to witnesses in organized crime cases. Rather than providing immunity from prosecution for any offense in which the witness was implicated through his testimony, the law simply forbade the use of any of his compelled testimony or derivative evidence against him. Under the 1970 Act, however, a witness could be prosecuted for crimes mentioned in his testimony if the evidence used in the prosecution was developed independently of his testimony.[20]

In *Kastigar v. United States* the Court found this narrower "use" immunity constitutional.

The privilege has never been construed to mean that one who invokes it cannot subsequently be prosecuted. Its sole concern is to afford protection against being forced to give testimony leading to the infliction of "penalties affixed to . . . criminal acts." Immunity from the use of compelled testimony, as well as evidence derived directly and indirectly therefrom, affords this protection.[21]

The Court found this use immunity sufficient, because the law required the state—in prosecuting an immunized witness—to show that its evidence had not been derived from his immunized testimony.

Justice Powell wrote:

A person accorded this immunity . . . , and subsequently prosecuted, is not dependent for the preservation of his rights upon the integrity and good faith of the prosecuting authorities. . . . This burden of proof which we reaffirm as appropriate . . . imposes on the prosecution the affirmative duty to prove that the evidence it proposes to use is derived from a legitimate source wholly independent of the compelled testimony.[22]

Justices Douglas and Thurgood Marshall dissented, and Douglas wrote:

When we allow the prosecution to offer only "use" immunity we allow it to grant far less than it has taken away. For while the precise testimony that is compelled may not be used, leads from that testimony may be pursued and used to convict the witness. My view is that the Framers put it beyond the power of Congress to compel anyone to confess his crimes. . . . Government acts in an ignoble way when it stoops to the end which we authorize today.[23]

Expanding Protection

Twice—in 1908 and 1947—the Supreme Court rejected arguments that the due process guarantee of the Fourteenth Amendment extended the privilege against self-incrimination to state defendants. In both cases the Court permitted state officials to draw unfavorable inferences from a defendant's failure to testify in his own behalf.

In *Twining v. New Jersey,* decided in 1908, the Court stated that the privilege was not inherent in due process, but "separate from and independent of" it.[24] In 1947 the Court reaffirmed this stance with its decision in *Adamson v. California,* refusing to find the privilege essential to a system of "ordered liberty."[25]

Furthermore, the Court in several cases held that the Fifth Amendment did not protect an individual from a state's use of testimony compelled by federal authority or from federal use of testimony compelled by state authority.[26] But in 1964 in *Malloy v. Hogan* the Court reconsidered *Twining* and *Adamson* and declared that the Fifth Amendment guarantee against self-incrimination did extend to state proceedings.

William Malloy, convicted of illegal gambling activities, refused to testify before a state investigation of gambling operations in Hartford County, Connecticut. Malloy claimed that to testify would compel him to incriminate himself. He was held in contempt and sentenced to prison.

Malloy appealed, but the Connecticut Supreme Court held that the Fifth Amendment's privilege against self-incrimination was not available to a witness in a state proceeding.

The Supreme Court, 5–4, reversed the state court and upheld Malloy's claim, holding that the Fourteenth Amendment guaranteed him the protection of the Fifth Amendment's privilege against self-incrimination.

Justice William J. Brennan Jr. wrote the majority opinion, declaring:

The Fourteenth Amendment secures against state invasion the same privilege that the Fifth Amendment guarantees against federal infringement—the right of a person to remain silent unless he chooses to speak in the unfettered exercise of his own will, and to suffer no penalty . . . for such silence. . . .

It would be incongruous to have different standards determine the validity of a claim of privilege based on the same feared prosecution, depending on whether the claim was asserted in a state or federal court. Therefore, the same standards must determine whether an accused's silence in either a federal or state proceeding is justified. . . . It must be considered irrelevant that the petitioner was a witness in a statutory inquiry and not a defendant in a criminal prosecution, for it has long been settled that the privilege protects witnesses in similar federal inquiries.[27]

Justices Byron R. White, Potter Stewart, John Marshall Harlan, and Tom C. Clark dissented from what they viewed as the step-by-step incorporation of the first eight amendments under the due process clause of the Fourteenth Amendment. Harlan stated:

The consequence of such an approach . . . is inevitable disregard of all relevant differences which may exist between state and federal criminal law and its enforcement. . . .

The Court's approach in the present case is in fact nothing more or less than "incorporation" in snatches. If, however, the Due Process Clause is something more than a reference to the Bill of Rights and protects only those rights which derive from fundamental principles . . . it is just as contrary to precedent and just as illogical to incorporate the provisions of the Bill of Rights one at a time as it is to incorporate them all at once.[28]

On the same day the Court announced its decision in *Malloy v. Hogan*—June 15, 1964—it decided *Murphy v. The Waterfront Commission of New York Harbor.* In that case the Court said the Fifth Amendment protects a state witness against incrimination under federal as well as state law and a federal witness against incrimination under state as well as federal law. Immunity granted under federal law protects against state prosecution and vice versa.

William Murphy, a labor union official subpoenaed to testify about a work stoppage at New Jersey piers, refused to answer questions on the grounds that his answers would tend to incriminate him. Granted immunity under New York and New Jersey laws, Murphy still refused to testify because the immunity failed to protect him from federal prosecution. The court held Murphy in contempt.

The Supreme Court vacated the contempt judgment. Justice Arthur J. Goldberg's opinion for a unanimous Court set out the constitutional rule:

JUSTICE AND THE PLEA BARGAIN . . . A GUILTY PLEA, A LESSER PENALTY

In a plea bargain, a defendant exchanges a plea of guilty for a prosecutor's promise of less severe punishment than could be expected after trial. This bargain has been described as "a mainstay of the criminal justice system in state and federal courts where 80 percent or more of the serious cases and 90 percent or more of the less serious offenses are resolved through pleas of guilty."[1]

There is no constitutional or statutory basis for plea bargaining. Its origin and survival are based on sheer pragmatism.

As the Supreme Court explained in 1977:

Properly administered, they [plea bargains] can benefit all concerned. The defendant avoids extended pretrial incarceration and the anxieties and uncertainties of a trial; he gains a speedy disposition of his case, the chance to acknowledge his guilt, and a prompt start in realizing whatever potential there may be for rehabilitation. Judges and prosecutors conserve vital and scarce resources. The public is protected from the risks posed by those charged with criminal offenses who are at large on bail while awaiting completion of criminal proceedings.[2]

RECOGNIZING THE PRACTICE

In 1970 the Court for the first time formally recognized the practice of plea bargaining. In *Brady v. United States* the Court upheld its use, finding that it provided a "mutuality of advantage" for the state and for the defendant.[3]

Robert Brady was charged with kidnapping under provisions of a federal law that provided for imposition of the death sentence for that crime upon the recommendation of a jury after trial. He pleaded guilty, foregoing trial and ensuring that he would not receive the death penalty.

Two years earlier the Court in *United States v. Jackson* had struck down that portion of the federal kidnapping law under which Brady had been charged, arguing that by allowing a death sentence *only* after trial, the law had the "inevitable effect" of penalizing both the exercise of the Fifth Amendment right *not* to plead guilty and the Sixth Amendment right to trial by jury.[4] Brady cited this ruling in challenging his conviction, claiming that his guilty plea was invalid be-

cause it was "coerced" by unconstitutional provisions and by his desire to avoid the death penalty.

With Justice Byron R. White as its spokesman, the Court unanimously sustained the plea bargaining process and Brady's conviction:

For a defendant who sees slight possibility of acquittal, the advantages of pleading guilty and limiting the probable penalty are obvious—his exposure is reduced, the correctional processes can begin immediately, and the practical burdens of a trial are eliminated. For the State there are also advantages—the more promptly imposed punishment after an admission of guilt may more effectively attain the objective of punishment; and with the avoidance of trial scarce judicial and prosecutorial resources are conserved. . . .

[W]e cannot hold that it is unconstitutional for the State to extend a benefit to a defendant who in turn extends a substantial benefit to the State and who demonstrates by his plea that he is ready and willing to admit his crime.[5]

KEEPING THE BARGAIN

In later rulings the Court has emphasized that guilty pleas are admissible only if knowingly and voluntarily made—although it has condoned some forms of pressure in plea negotiations—and it has usually required prosecutors to keep their bargains.

In *Santobello v. New York* the Court in 1971 held that the state's failure to keep its commitment to recommend a reduced sentence in exchange for a guilty plea required that the defendant be given the opportunity for a trial.

Chief Justice Warren E. Burger wrote:

[H]is phase of the process of criminal justice and the adjudicative element in accepting a plea of guilty, must be attended by safeguards to insure the defendant what is reasonably due in the circumstances. Those circumstances will vary, but a constant factor is that when a plea rests in any significant degree on a promise or agreement of the prosecutor, so that it can be said to be part of the inducement or consideration, such promise must be fulfilled.[6]

Two years later the Court in *Tollett v. Henderson* refused to allow a defendant who had pleaded guilty to murder to challenge his convic-

---

[A] state witness may not be compelled to give testimony which may be incriminating under federal law unless the compelled testimony and its fruits cannot be used in any manner by federal officials in connection with a criminal prosecution against him. We conclude, moreover, that in order to implement this constitutional rule and accommodate the interests of the State and Federal Governments in investigating and prosecuting crime, the Federal Government must be prohibited from making any such use of compelled testimony and its fruits.[29]

The following year the Court reinforced the *Malloy* ruling with *Griffin v. California*. Effectively reversing *Twining* and *Adamson* in their specific holdings concerning judicial or prosecutorial comment on the silence of defendants, the Court held that the Fifth Amendment "forbids either comment by the prosecution on the accused's silence or instructions by the Court

that such silence is evidence of guilt."[30] Writing for the Court in *Griffin*, Justice Douglas explained:

[C]omment on the refusal to testify is a remnant of the "inquisitorial system of criminal justice," . . . which the Fifth Amendment outlaws. It is a penalty imposed by courts for exercising a constitutional privilege. It cuts down on the privilege by making its assertion costly.[31]

Coerced Confessions

Confessions, the Court stated long ago, are "among the most effectual proofs in the law," but they are admissible as evidence only when given voluntarily.[32] This requirement has long been the rule in federal courts, where the Fifth Amendment clearly applies.[33]

Since 1936 the same rule has governed the use of confessions

tion by arguing that the grand jury that indicted him was unfairly selected.

Justice William H. Rehnquist explained that a guilty plea represented a break in the chain of events that preceded it:

When a criminal defendant has solemnly admitted in open court that he is in fact guilty of the offense with which he is charged, he may not thereafter raise independent claims relating to the deprivation of constitutional rights that occurred prior to the entry of the plea.[7]

In a similar vein, the Court in 1984 refused in *Mabry v. Johnson* to rule that once a plea bargain was made, a defendant had a constitutional right to have it enforced.

If a prosecutor decides to withdraw the bargain before a plea of guilty is entered, that withdrawal cannot serve as the basis for challenging a later guilty plea entered in keeping with another, less favorable, plea bargain.

In 1987 the Court held in *Ricketts v. Adamson* that when a defendant breaches a plea bargain and refuses to testify against others a second time, as he had promised, the state does not breach the double jeopardy guarantee when it prosecutes him for murder—even though he has already pleaded guilty to a lesser offense and begun serving time.[8]

PERMITTING THE PRESSURE

To be valid, a guilty plea must be voluntarily made and entered with full knowledge of its implications. The Court set aside a second-degree murder conviction of a man who pleaded guilty without realizing that he was admitting that he *intended* to kill his victim, holding that a defendant's failure to receive adequate notice of the offense to which he pleaded guilty resulted in an involuntary plea.[9]

The Court held in 1978, however, that due process does not deprive the prosecutor of valid bargaining tools. By a 5–4 vote, the justices backed a prosecutor's threat of an additional justified indictment if the defendant did not accept a plea bargain.

The Court announced this decision in *Bordenkircher v. Hayes*. Hayes had two prior felony convictions and had been charged with a third felony.

In plea negotiations the prosecutor offered to recommend a reduced sentence in return for a guilty plea—and threatened that if the bargain was not accepted he would reindict Hayes under a "habitual criminal" law that would have made him subject to a mandatory life sentence if convicted.

Hayes rejected the bargain, was reindicted, convicted, and received a life sentence. He challenged the prosecutor's actions as "vindictive"; the Court rejected that challenge.

Justice Potter Stewart explained that

in the "give-and-take" of plea bargaining, there is no . . . element of punishment or retaliation so long as the accused is free to accept or reject the prosecutor's offer. . . .

There is no doubt that the breadth of discretion that our country's legal system vests in prosecuting attorneys carries with it the potential for both individual and institutional abuse. And broad though that discretion may be, there are undoubtedly constitutional limits upon its exercise. We hold only that the course of conduct engaged in by the prosecutor in this case, which no more than openly presented the defendant with the unpleasant alternatives of foregoing trial or facing charges on which he was plainly subject to prosecution, did not violate the Due Process Clause of the Fourteenth Amendment.[10]

1. Alpheus T. Mason and William M. Beaney, *American Constitutional Law*, 6th ed. (Englewood Cliffs, N.J.: Prentice-Hall, 1978), 669.
2. *Blackledge v. Allison*, 431 U.S. 63 at 71 (1977).
3. *Brady v. United States*, 397 U.S. 742 at 752 (1970); see also *Boykin v. Alabama*, 395 U.S. 238 (1969).
4. *United States v. Jackson*, 390 U.S. 570 (1968).
5. *Brady v. United States*, 397 U.S. 742 at 752–753 (1970); see also *North Carolina v. Alford*, 400 U.S. 25 (1970).
6. *Santobello v. New York*, 404 U.S. 257 at 262 (1971).
7. *Tollett v. Henderson*, 411 U.S. 258 at 267 (1973).
8. *Mabry v. Johnson*, 467 U.S. 504 (1984); *Ricketts v. Adamson*, 483 U.S. 1 (1987).
9. *Henderson v. Morgan*, 426 U.S. 637 (1976).
10. *Bordenkircher v. Hayes*, 434 U.S. 357 at 363, 365 (1978); see also *Corbitt v. New Jersey*, 439 U.S. 212 (1978).

in state courts. The inevitable question is how to determine when a confession is voluntary.

The Court ruled on the use of confessions for the first time in 1884. An involuntary confession, it said, is one that "appears to have been made, either in consequence of inducements of a temporal nature . . . or because of a threat or promise . . . which, operating upon the fears or hopes of the accused . . . deprive him of that freedom of will or self-control essential to make his confession voluntary within the meaning of the law."[34]

A dozen years later the Court restated the standard for determining when a confession was admissible: "The true test of admissibility is that the confession is made freely, voluntarily, and without compulsion or inducement of any sort."[35]

This test, as the Court acknowledged in 1897, had to be applied every time the use of a confession was challenged. The

judge should consider "the circumstances surrounding, and the facts established to exist, in reference to the confession, in order to determine whether it was shown to have been voluntarily made." In all federal trials, the resolution of this issue was controlled by the Fifth Amendment command that no person be compelled to incriminate himself.[36]

Delay in charging a suspect with a crime is a significant factor in determining if a confession is admissible. Several federal laws made clear that when persons are arrested, they should be taken promptly before a magistrate and charged. In 1943 the Supreme Court gave compelling force to this requirement by holding that confessions obtained after "unnecessary delay" in a suspect's arraignment could not be used as evidence in federal court.

In *McNabb v. United States* the Court overturned the convic-

USE OF COERCED CONFESSIONS

In the 1967 case of *Chapman v. California,* the Court declared that it was a denial of due process ever to use a forced confession against a defendant, regardless of what other evidence might exist.

Use of a coerced confession could never be "harmless error," the Court said, and it must always result in reversal of any resulting conviction. (386 U.S. 18, 1967)

For twenty-four years that was the law of the land, but in 1991, the Court, 5–4, reversed *Chapman* and held that use of a coerced confession does not automatically require reversal of a conviction.

Writing for the Court in a key portion of *Arizona v. Fulminante,* Chief Justice William H. Rehnquist said that if other evidence was sufficient to convict, a compelled confession might be harmless error and its use would not dictate a new trial. Rehnquist was joined in that opinion by Justices Sandra Day O'Connor, Antonin Scalia, Anthony Kennedy, and David Souter.

The dissenting justices, Byron R. White, Thurgood Marshall, Harry A. Blackmun, and John Paul Stevens, criticized the majority. In White's words: "Today, a majority of the court, without any justification . . . dislodges one of the fundamental tenets of our criminal justice system. . . . Permitting a coerced confession to be part of the evidence on which a jury is free to base its verdict of guilty is inconsistent with the thesis that ours is not an inquisitorial system" of justice. (499 U.S. 279, 1991)

---

tions of several men for murdering a federal revenue agent. The most important elements in the prosecution's case were incriminating statements made by the defendants after three days of questioning by federal officers in the absence of any defense counsel and before they were formally charged with any crime.

The Court based its decision on the statutory requirements of prompt arraignment, and on the Court's general power to supervise the functioning of the federal judicial system, rather than on the Fifth Amendment.

Justice Frankfurter explained that the Court's supervisory role obligated it to establish and maintain "civilized standards of procedure and evidence" for federal courts.[37] The purpose of the ban on unnecessary delay between arrest and arraignment, he continued, was plain:

A democratic society, in which respect for the dignity of all men is central, naturally guards against the misuse of the law enforcement process. Zeal in tracking down crime is not in itself an assurance of soberness of judgment. Disinterestedness in law enforcement does not alone prevent disregard of cherished liberties. Experience has therefore counseled that safeguards must be provided against the dangers of the overzealous as well as the despotic. The awful instruments of the criminal law cannot be entrusted to a single functionary. The complicated process of criminal justice is therefore divided into different parts, responsibility for which is separately vested in the various participants upon whom the criminal law relies for its vindication. Legislation . . . requiring that the police must with reasonable promptness show legal cause for detaining arrested persons, constitutes an important safe-

guard—not only in assuring protection for the innocent but also in securing conviction of the guilty by methods that commend themselves to a progressive and self-confident society. For this procedural requirement checks resort to those reprehensible practices known as the "third degree" which, though universally rejected as indefensible, still find their way into use. It aims to avoid all the evil implications of secret interrogation of persons accused of crime. It reflects not a sentimental but a sturdy view of law enforcement. It outlaws easy but self-defeating ways in which brutality is substituted for brains as an instrument of crime detection.[38]

The Federal Rules of Criminal Procedure subsequently incorporated this rule, and in 1957 the Court in *Mallory v. United States* reaffirmed its importance. In *Mallory* the Court nullified a death sentence imposed upon a rapist who "confessed" to the crime during a delay of more than eighteen hours between his arrest and his arraignment. The Court warned that such "unwarranted detention" could lead "to tempting utilization of intensive interrogation, easily gliding into the evils of 'the third degree'"—precisely what the rule was intended to avoid.[39]

Mallory generated fierce criticism and prompted Congress to revise the statutory rule to allow some use of evidence obtained during such delays. In 1968 Congress included in the Crime Control and Safe Streets Act a provision stating that delay in arraignment was not an absolute bar to federal use of a confession obtained during the period of delay.

Decades before it applied the Fifth Amendment to state action, the Supreme Court unanimously forbade states to use coerced confessions to convict persons of crimes.

The concept of basic fairness implicit in the Fourteenth Amendment guarantee of due process served as the basis for the Court's declaration of this prohibition in its 1936 ruling in *Brown v. Mississippi.* With that decision the Court for the first time overturned a state conviction because it was obtained by using a confession extracted by torture.

Mississippi defended its use of this confession by citing *Twining v. New Jersey,* a 1908 ruling that state defendants did not enjoy the protection of the Fifth Amendment privilege against compelled self-incrimination.

The Court rejected that defense, stating flatly that "the question of the right of the state to withdraw the privilege against self-incrimination is not here involved."[40] Chief Justice Charles Evans Hughes saw a distinction between "compulsion" forbidden by the Fifth Amendment and "compulsion" forbidden by the Fourteenth Amendment's due process clause.

The compulsion to which the . . . [Fifth Amendment] refer[s] is that of the processes of justice by which the accused may be called as a witness and required to testify. Compulsion by torture to extort a confession is a different matter. . . .

Because a state may dispense with a jury trial, it does not follow that it may substitute trial by ordeal. The rack and torture chamber may not be substituted for the witness stand. . . . It would be difficult to conceive of methods more revolting to the sense of justice than those taken to procure the confessions of these petitioners, and the use of the confessions thus obtained as the basis for conviction and sentence was a clear denial of due process.[41]

Over the next three decades the Court judged each case in which state use of a confession was challenged by looking at the "totality of the circumstances" surrounding the arrest and interrogation. In these cases Chief Justice Hughes's neat distinction between physical coercion and other forms of compulsion soon blurred.

In 1940 the Court affirmed *Brown* in *Chambers v. Florida*. In *Chambers* four black men had been convicted of murder on the basis of confessions obtained after days of being held incommunicado and interrogated by law enforcement officials. The unanimous Court overturned their convictions, acknowledging that psychological coercion, as well as physical torture, could produce involuntary confessions whose use violated due process.

Justice Black wrote the Court's opinion, declaring:

The determination to preserve an accused's right to procedural due process sprang in large part from knowledge of the historical truth that the rights and liberties of people accused of crime could not be safely entrusted to secret inquisitorial processes. . . .

For five days petitioners were subjected to interrogations culminating in . . . [an] all night examination. Over a period of five days they steadily refused to confess and disclaimed any guilt. The very circumstances surrounding their confinement and their questioning without any formal charges having been brought, were such as to fill petitioners with terror and frightful misgivings. Some were practically strangers in the community. . . . The haunting fear of mob violence was around them in an atmosphere charged with excitement and public indignation. . . . To permit human lives to be forfeited upon confessions thus obtained would make of the constitutional requirement of due process of law a meaningless symbol. . . .

Due process of law, preserved for all by our Constitution, commands that no such practice as that disclosed by this record shall send any accused to his death.[42]

The Court in subsequent decisions acknowledged that some situations were so inherently coercive that evidence produced from them was inadmissible, but not until the mid-1960s did it develop any hard-and-fast rules concerning the admissibility of the products of prolonged interrogation of suspects in police custody.[43]

Voluntariness, not veracity, was the key to whether a confession was admissible. As Justice Frankfurter explained in the Court's 1961 decision in *Rogers v. Richmond*:

Our decisions . . . have made clear that convictions following the admission into evidence of confessions which are involuntary . . . cannot stand. This is so not because such confessions are unlikely to be true but because the methods used to extract them offend an underlying principle in the enforcement of our criminal law: that ours is an accusatorial and not an inquisitorial system—a system in which the State must establish guilt by evidence independently and freely secured and may not by coercion prove its own charge against an accused out of his own mouth.[44]

Confessions and Counsel

The Fifth Amendment privilege against compelled self-incrimination was inextricably linked with the Sixth Amendment right to counsel by the Court's mid-1960s rulings in *Escobedo v. Illinois* and *Miranda v. Arizona*.

The Court as late as 1958 had ruled that confessions could be voluntary and admissible even when obtained from a suspect who was denied the opportunity to consult with legal counsel during his interrogation by police.[45]

But in 1964 the Court reversed that view. In *Massiah v. United States* the Court declared that an indicted person could not properly be questioned or otherwise persuaded to make incriminating remarks in the absence of his lawyer.[46] Coupled with the Court's ruling later that term in *Malloy v. Hogan*, extending the Fifth Amendment privilege to state defendants, *Massiah* laid the groundwork for *Escobedo*.

ESCOBEDO V. ILLINOIS

A week after *Malloy* the Court announced its decision in the case of Danny Escobedo, convicted of murder in Illinois on the basis of his own words. In *Escobedo v. Illinois* the Court discarded the voluntarism standard for determining the admissibility of confessions, moving away from the "totality of the circumstances" approach to concentrate on the procedures followed by police in obtaining a confession.[47]

Escobedo repeatedly asked for and was denied the opportunity to see his attorney during his interrogation by police. Incriminating statements he made during this time were used as evidence against him. He challenged his conviction as a denial of his right to counsel. The Court agreed, saying a defendant has a right to remain silent rather than be forced to incriminate himself. The Court said that if police do not warn a suspect of his "absolute constitutional right to remain silent," he has been denied "the assistance of counsel" in violation of the Sixth Amendment.

Justice Goldberg wrote the majority opinion. Dissenting were Justices Harlan, White, Clark, and Stewart.

The year before, the Court had declared in *Gideon v. Wainwright* that the Sixth Amendment required that every person accused of a serious crime be provided the aid of an attorney.[48] Justice Goldberg reasoned in *Escobedo* that the right guaranteed in *Gideon* would be a hollow one if it did not apply until after police obtained a confession. Goldberg wrote:

We have . . . learned . . . that no system of criminal justice can, or should, survive if it comes to depend for its continued effectiveness on the citizens' abdication through unawareness of their constitutional rights. No system worth preserving should have to fear that if an accused is permitted to consult with a lawyer, he will become aware of, and exercise, these rights. If the exercise of constitutional rights will thwart the effectiveness of a system of law enforcement, then there is something very wrong with that system.

We hold, therefore, that where, as here, the investigation is no longer a general inquiry into an unsolved crime but has begun to focus on a particular suspect, the suspect has been taken into police custody, the police carry out a process of interrogations that lends itself to eliciting incriminating statements, the suspect has requested and been denied an opportunity to consult with his lawyer, and the police have not effectively warned him of his absolute constitutional right to remain silent, the accused has been denied "the Assistance of Counsel" in violation of the Sixth Amendment . . . and that no statement elicited by police during the interrogation may be used against him at a criminal trial.[49]

Danny Escobedo's 1960 arrest and conviction for the murder of his brother-in-law led to a Supreme Court decision that expanded constitutional protections for criminal defendants during police interrogations. This photograph of Escobedo was taken as he awaited processing on charges of burglarizing a hot dog stand not long after the Supreme Court issued its landmark ruling in *Escobedo v. Illinois* in 1964.

Justice White's dissenting opinion, joined by Justices Clark and Stewart, criticized the majority's holding that any incriminating statement made by an arrested suspect who was denied the opportunity to see his lawyer was inadmissible:

By abandoning the voluntary-involuntary test . . . the Court seems driven by the notion that it is uncivilized law enforcement to use an accused's own admissions against him at his trial. It attempts to find a home for this new and nebulous rule of due process by attaching it to the right of counsel guaranteed in the federal system by the Sixth Amendment and binding upon the States by virtue of the due process guarantee of the Fourteenth Amendment. . . . The right to counsel now not only entitles the accused to counsel's advice and aid in preparing for trial but stands as an impenetrable barrier to any interrogation once the accused has become a suspect.[50]

MIRANDA V. ARIZONA

Two years after *Escobedo* the Supreme Court in *Miranda v. Arizona* set out "concrete constitutional guidelines" for the custodial interrogation practices of state and local police.[51]

Ernesto Miranda was convicted of kidnapping and rape in Arizona. The prosecution used as evidence against him statements Miranda had made to police during his interrogation. He was not advised of his rights to remain silent and to consult an attorney. Miranda challenged his conviction as obtained in violation of the Fifth Amendment privilege.

By the same 5–4 vote as in *Escobedo*, the Court upheld his challenge. It ruled that prosecutors were constitutionally forbidden to use incriminating statements obtained from suspects during interrogation unless strict procedural safeguards had been followed to guarantee that the suspect was aware of his constitutional rights to remain silent and to have the aid of an attorney. "The presence of counsel," stated Chief Justice Earl Warren for the majority, was "the adequate protective device" to "insure that statements made in the government-established atmosphere are not the product of compulsion."[52]

No Warning, No Use

Warren, summarizing the Court's holding, said:

the prosecution may not use statements, whether exculpatory or inculpatory, stemming from custodial interrogation of the defendant unless it demonstrates the use of procedural safeguards effective to secure the privilege against self-incrimination. By custodial interrogation, we mean questioning initiated by law enforcement officers after a person has been taken into custody or otherwise deprived of his freedom of action in any significant way. As for the procedural safeguards to be employed, unless other fully effective means are devised to inform accused persons of their right of silence and to assure a continuous opportunity to exercise it, the following measures are required. Prior to any questioning, the person must be warned that he has a right to remain silent, that any statement he does make may be used as evidence against him, and that he has a right to the presence of an attorney, either retained or appointed. The defendant may waive effectuation of these rights, provided the waiver is made voluntarily, knowingly and intelligently. If, however, he indicates in any manner and at any stage of the process, that he wishes to consult with an attorney before speaking there can be no questioning. Likewise, if the individual is alone and indicates in any manner that he does not wish to be interrogated, the police may not question him. The mere fact that he may have answered some questions or have volunteered some statements on his own does not deprive him of the right to refrain from answering any further inquiries until he has consulted with an attorney and thereafter consents to be questioned.[53]

The Fifth Amendment, explained Warren, required that whenever a suspect indicated, before or during interrogation, that he wished to remain silent, all interrogation must cease. "At this point he has shown that he intends to exercise his Fifth Amendment privilege," wrote the chief justice. Therefore "any statement taken after the person invokes his privilege cannot be other than the product of compulsion, subtle or otherwise."[54]

As in *Escobedo* Justices Clark, Harlan, White, and Stewart dissented, arguing that they felt the Court should continue to use the "totality of the circumstances" approach to determining the admissibility of confessions. Justice Harlan criticized the ruling as "poor constitutional law." He continued:

I think it must be frankly recognized at the outset that police questioning allowable under due process precedents may inherently entail some pressure on the suspect and may seek advantage in his ignorance or weaknesses. . . . Until today, the role of the Constitution has been only to sift out undue pressure, not to assure spontaneous confessions. The Court's new rules aim to offset these minor pressures and disadvantages intrinsic to any kind of police interrogation. The rules do not serve due process interests in preventing blatant coercion since . . . they

```
PD 47
Rev.8/73   METROPOLITAN POLICE DEPARTMENT

           WARNING AS TO YOUR RIGHTS

You are under arrest. Before we ask you any questions, you must
understand what your rights are.

You have the right to remain silent. You are not required to say
anything to us at any time or to answer any questions. Anything
you say can be used against you in court.

You have the right to talk to a lawyer for advice before we ques-
tion you and to have him with you during questioning.

If you cannot afford a lawyer and want one, a lawyer will be pro-
vided for you.

If you want to answer questions now without a lawyer present
you will still have the right to stop answering at any time. You
also have the right to stop answering at any time until you talk
to a lawyer.
```

```
                        WAIVER

1.  Have you read or had read to you the warning as to your
    rights? _____

2.  Do you understand these rights? _____

3.  Do you wish to answer any questions? _____

4.  Are you willing to answer questions without having an
    attorney present? _____

5.  Signature of defendant on line below.

    _____

6.  Time _____      Date _____

7.  Signature of Officer _____

8.  Signature of Witness _____
```

As a result of the ruling in *Miranda v. Arizona* (1966) a police officer must advise a person placed under arrest of his or her right to remain silent and to be represented by an attorney.

do nothing to contain the policeman who is prepared to lie from the start.[55]

White said the majority misread the Fifth Amendment prohibition against compelled self-incrimination:

Confessions and incriminating admissions, as such, are not forbidden evidence; only those which are compelled are banned. I doubt that the Court observes these distinctions today. . . .

The obvious underpinning of the Court's decision is a deep-seated distrust of all confessions. . . .

The rule announced today . . . is a deliberate calculus to prevent interrogations, to reduce the incidence of confessions and pleas of guilty and to increase the number of trials. Criminal trials, no matter how efficient the police are, are not sure bets for the prosecution, nor should they be if the evidence is not forthcoming. . . . There is, in my view, every reason to believe that a good many criminal defendants, who otherwise would have been convicted on what this Court has previously thought to be the most satisfactory kind of evidence, will now, under this new version of the Fifth Amendment, either not be tried at all or will be acquitted if the State's evidence, minus the confession, is put to the test of litigation.[56]

A week after *Miranda* the Court held that it would not apply the decision retroactively to invalidate convictions obtained in trials begun before its announcement on June 13, 1966. A similar rule applied in cases to which *Escobedo* might apply, held the Court.[57]

Campaign Backlash

Mallory v. United States, Escobedo v. Illinois, and *Miranda v. Arizona,* together with rulings extending the specific protections of the Bill of Rights to state defendants, brought criticism of the Warren Court to a crescendo in the late 1960s.

One of the major themes of the 1968 presidential campaign was "law and order"—a phrase that Richard Nixon, the successful candidate, used as a basis for his criticism of the Court's rulings.

Many members of Congress were persuaded that the Court was, in fact, encouraging crime by impeding law enforcement officers in their duties. In the Crime Control and Safe Streets Act of 1968, Congress included provisions intended to blunt or overrule the effect of *Mallory* and *Miranda.* By stating that confessions could be used in federal courts whenever the judge

found them voluntary, Congress attempted to abandon the procedural guidelines set out in *Miranda* and return to the old voluntary-involuntary test for prosecutorial use of incriminating statements. The 1968 law, however, affected only federal trials, not state trials. The states remained bound by the *Miranda* requirements.

Despite opposition to *Miranda,* the Supreme Court stood by that decision. Early in 1969 the Court held that *Miranda* required that police, before questioning an individual in his own home, warn him of his constitutional rights as soon as he was effectively in custody.[58]

President-elect Nixon promised during his 1968 campaign to appoint justices to the Supreme Court who would be less receptive to the arguments of criminal defendants and more responsive to the reasoning of law enforcement officers. Even before the election, Chief Justice Warren had announced his plans to retire.

In the spring of 1969 Nixon named—and the Senate confirmed—Warren E. Burger, a conservative appeals court judge, as Warren's successor. In 1970 Burger was joined on the bench by another Nixon appointee, Harry A. Blackmun. And in 1971 Nixon filled two more seats on the Court with Justices Powell and William H. Rehnquist.

No Warning, Some Use

Although the Court with its new chief justice and new members did not overturn *Miranda,* it did, over the next twenty-five years, decline to extend *Miranda,* and it did allow a number of indirect uses of statements and other evidence obtained from persons not warned of their rights.

The first of these rulings came in 1971 in *Harris v. New York.* By a 5–4 vote, the Court held that although statements made by a defendant before he was advised of his rights could not be used as evidence against him, they could be used to impeach his credibility if he took the stand in his own defense and contradicted what he had said before trial.

Chief Justice Burger observed:

Some comments in the *Miranda* opinion can indeed be read as indicating a bar to use of an uncounseled statement for any purpose, but discussion of that issue was not at all necessary to the Court's holding, and cannot be regarded as controlling. *Miranda* barred the prosecution from making its case with statements of an accused while in custody prior to having or effectively waiving counsel. It does not follow from *Miranda* that evidence inadmissible against an accused in the prosecution's case in chief is barred for all purposes, provided of course that the trustworthiness of the evidence satisfies legal standards. . . .

The shield provided by *Miranda* cannot be perverted into a license to use perjury by way of a defense, free from the risk of confrontation with prior inconsistent utterances.[59]

Justices Black, Brennan, Douglas, and Marshall dissented, warning that this ruling "goes far toward undoing much of the progress made in conforming police methods to the Constitution."[60]

Three years later the Court in *Michigan v. Tucker* upheld the prosecution's use of a statement made by a suspect not fully warned of his rights as a "lead" for locating a prosecution witness. Writing the opinion, Justice Rehnquist emphasized that the procedures *Miranda* required were safeguards for constitutional rights but were not themselves constitutionally guaranteed.[61]

And in 1976 the Court in *United States v. Mandujano* refused to require that *Miranda* warnings be given to grand jury witnesses before they testify—even though they may be potential defendants.[62]

In 1984 the Court for the first time approved an exception to the strict requirement of *Miranda* that police advise a suspect in custody of his rights to remain silent and to have the aid of an attorney before the suspect can be questioned. That exception was called the "public safety" exception, and it was recognized in *New York v. Quarles.*

In that case police were arresting a suspect in a grocery store and did not see the gun they expected him to be carrying. Instead of first warning him of his rights under *Miranda,* police asked, "Where's the gun?" and only then advised him of his rights. The Court by votes of 5–4 and 6–3 held that the police acted appropriately to protect the public safety, and that the suspect's answer to the question of the gun's whereabouts, and any evidence that answer produced, could be used against him.[63] Rehnquist wrote the Court's opinion.

Justice Sandra Day O'Connor, then a junior member of the Court, wrote a dissenting opinion that attracted considerable attention. Demonstrating the degree to which *Miranda* had become an established part of American law, O'Connor refused to agree with the majority that this public safety exception should be permitted. "Were the Court writing from a clean slate, I could agree," she wrote. "But *Miranda* is now the law . . . and the Court

has not provided sufficient justification for blurring its now clear strictures."[64]

The following year the Court ruled that an initial unwarned admission of guilt—given voluntarily in a noncoercive environment—does not so taint any subsequent confession as to bar its use in a trial.[65]

And in 1990 the Court ruled 8–1 that videotaped sobriety tests can be used as evidence against a suspect even if he has not been warned of his rights before the test is administered. The Court said police may videotape people answering routine "booking" questions, including name, address, and date of birth, without first telling them they have a right to remain silent. The majority said their replies were physical evidence, comparable to blood or a handwriting sample, not evidence that is "testimonial."[66]

The Court has been asked on numerous occasions to define what action by a suspect constitutes assertion of his rights to counsel and to silence and what limits such action places on police. In 1975 the Court ruled that, although a suspect's assertion of his right to silence must terminate police interrogation of him about one crime, it does not foreclose subsequent police efforts, after an interval and a second warning of his rights, to question him about another crime.[67]

Fifteen years later, in 1990, the Court said again that once a suspect has invoked his right to counsel, police may not resume questioning about the crime of which he is suspected until his lawyer is present, even if the suspect has consulted with counsel in the meantime. The Court affirmed and extended the rule, established in *Edwards v. Arizona* (1981), requiring the police to stop interrogation after the accused asks for a lawyer.[68]

But only three years later the Court held 5–4 that police need not stop questioning unless a suspect makes "an unambiguous or unequivocal request for counsel."[69] If the suspect makes an ambiguous statement, one that is not clearly a request for counsel, the police are not required to ask the suspect for clarification, the majority said.

The Court had held earlier that a juvenile suspect's request to see his probation officer is not an assertion of his Fifth Amendment privilege against self-incrimination, requiring police to cease questioning him, and that a probationer does not need *Miranda* warnings before being asked about crimes by his probation officer.[70]

Mental illness, the Court has held, 7–2, does not necessarily disable someone from voluntarily and intelligently waiving his constitutional rights to silence and the aid of an attorney.[71]

The Aid of Legal Counsel

"In all criminal prosecutions," the Sixth Amendment stipulates, "the accused shall enjoy the right . . . to have the assistance of counsel for his defense."

Despite this unambiguous language, only persons charged with federal crimes punishable by death have been guaranteed this right throughout American history.[1] The right of all other defendants, federal and state, to the aid of an attorney traditionally depended upon their ability to hire and pay their own lawyer.

But beginning in the 1930s the Supreme Court vastly enlarged the class of persons who have the right to legal counsel—appointed and paid by the state if necessary—in preparing and presenting a defense. In 1932 the Court declared this right so fundamental that the Fourteenth Amendment's due process clause required states to provide the effective aid of counsel to all defendants charged with capital crimes.[2] Six years later the Court held that the Sixth Amendment required that all federal defendants be provided an attorney.[3]

This expansion of the Sixth Amendment right to counsel continued during the 1960s and 1970s, when the Court ruled that the amendment guaranteed the aid of an attorney to all state defendants charged with crimes that could be considered serious. In the 1980s the Court further expanded the right to include a guarantee that indigents who are defending themselves with a claim of insanity are entitled to the aid of a court-appointed and publicly paid psychiatrist.[4]

A Fundamental Right

The Court's first modern ruling on the right to counsel came in the "First Scottsboro Case"—*Powell v. Alabama*—in 1932.

Nine young illiterate black men, aged thirteen to twenty-one, were charged with the rape of two white girls on a freight train passing through Tennessee and Alabama. Their trial was held in Scottsboro, Alabama, where community hostility to the defendants was intense.

The trial judge appointed all the members of the local bar to serve as defense counsel. But when the trial began, no attorney appeared to represent the defendants. The judge, on the morning of the trial, appointed a local lawyer who undertook the task with reluctance. The defendants were convicted.

They challenged their convictions, arguing that they were effectively denied aid of counsel because they did not have the opportunity to consult with their lawyer and prepare a defense. The Supreme Court agreed, 7–2.

Writing for the Court, Justice George Sutherland explained:

It is hardly necessary to say that the right to counsel being conceded, a defendant should be afforded a fair opportunity to secure counsel of his own choice. Not only was that not done here, but such designation of counsel as was attempted was either so indefinite or so close upon the trial as to amount to a denial of effective and substantial aid.[5]

The plight of the nine "Scottsboro boys," arrested in rural Alabama in 1931 for allegedly raping two white females, spawned numerous legal actions including *Powell v. Alabama* (1932), which expanded the rights of indigents to legal representation. Samuel Leibowitz, a prominent attorney and later a judge, handled the defendants' cases after their original conviction. He is shown here conferring with his clients.

The action of the judge in appointing all members of the local bar as defense counsel was "little more than an expansive gesture" that resulted in no aid to the defendants in the critical pretrial period, the Court said.[6]

In *Twining v. New Jersey* two dozen years earlier, the Court acknowledged that some of the rights guaranteed in the Bill of Rights might be so fundamental that a denial of them by a state would be a denial of due process. Citing *Twining,* the Court declared that "the right to the aid of counsel is of this fundamental character."[7] *(See details of Twining v. New Jersey, p. 561.)*

In *Powell v. Alabama* the Court leaned heavily upon the circumstances of the case and the characteristics of the defendants in finding the denial of effective aid of counsel a denial of due process. Sutherland wrote:

In the light of the facts . . . the ignorance and illiteracy of the defendants, their youth, the circumstances of public hostility, the imprisonment and the close surveillance of the defendants by the military forces, the fact that their friends and families were all in other states and communication with them necessarily difficult, and above all that they stood in deadly peril of their lives—we think the failure of the trial court to give them reasonable time and opportunity to secure counsel was a clear denial of due process.

But . . . assuming their inability, even if opportunity had been given, to employ counsel, as the trial court evidently did assume, we are of opinion that, under the circumstances just stated, the necessity of counsel was so vital and imperative that the failure of the trial court to make an effective appointment of counsel was likewise a denial of due process within the meaning of the Fourteenth Amendment. Whether this would be so in other criminal prosecutions, or under other circumstances, we need not determine. All that it is necessary now to decide, as we do decide, is that in a capital case, where the defendant is unable to employ counsel, and is incapable adequately of making his own defense because of ignorance, feeblemindedness, illiteracy or the like, it is the duty of the court, whether requested or not, to assign counsel for him as a necessary requisite of due process of law; and that duty is not discharged by an assignment at such a time or under such circumstances as to preclude the giving of effective aid in the preparation and trial of the case.[8]

Since 1790 federal law implementing the Sixth Amendment guarantee has required that persons charged with capital crimes in federal courts be provided an attorney.[9] In 1938 the Court held that the Sixth Amendment required this assurance for *all* federal defendants. This was the ruling in *Johnson v. Zerbst.*[10]

John Johnson, a marine, was charged with passing counterfeit money. He was tried and convicted in civil court without the aid of an attorney to act in his defense. He challenged his conviction as obtained in violation of his constitutional rights.

The Supreme Court found his argument persuasive and upheld his claim. Justice Hugo L. Black spoke for a majority of the Court:

The Sixth Amendment . . . embodies a realistic recognition of the obvious truth that the average defendant does not have the professional legal skill to protect himself when brought before a tribunal with power to take his life or liberty, wherein the prosecution is presented by experienced and learned counsel. That which is simple, orderly and necessary to the lawyer—to the untrained laymen . . . may appear intricate, complex, and mysterious. . . .

. . . The Sixth Amendment withholds from federal courts, in all criminal proceedings, the power and authority to deprive an accused of his life or liberty unless he has or waives the assistance of counsel. . . .

. . . While an accused may waive the right to counsel, whether there is a proper waiver should be clearly determined by the trial court. . . .

Since the Sixth Amendment constitutionally entitles one charged with crime to the assistance of counsel, compliance with this constitutional mandate is an essential jurisdictional prerequisite to a federal court's authority to deprive an accused of his life or liberty [unless the right has been properly waived]. . . . If the accused, however, is not represented by counsel and has not competently and intelligently waived his constitutional right, the Sixth Amendment stands as a jurisdictional bar to a valid conviction and sentence depriving him of his life or his liberty.[11]

The Appointment of Counsel

Johnson v. Zerbst, with its emphatic declaration of the right of federal defendants to have an attorney, provided no aid to state defendants. And for thirty years after *Powell v. Alabama,*

"GUIDING HAND"

A classic description of the "guiding hand" of an attorney at trial came in the landmark 1932 decision in *Powell v. Alabama,* the "First Scottsboro Case." Writing for the Court, Justice George Sutherland discussed the basic requirements of due process and the importance, to the defendant, of the aid of counsel:

It has never been doubted by this court, or any other so far as we know, that notice and hearing are preliminary steps essential to the passing of an enforceable judgment, and that they, together with a legally competent tribunal having jurisdiction of the case, constitute basic elements of the constitutional requirement of due process. . . .

What, then, does a hearing include? Historically and in practice, in our own country at least, it has always included the right to the aid of counsel when desired and provided by the party asserting the right. The right to be heard would be, in many cases, of little avail if it did not comprehend the right to be heard by counsel. Even the intelligent and educated layman has small and sometimes no skill in the science of law. If charged with crime, he is incapable, generally, of determining for himself whether the indictment is good or bad. He is unfamiliar with the rules of evidence. Left without the aid of counsel he may be put on trial without a proper charge, and convicted upon incompetent evidence, or evidence irrelevant to the issue or otherwise inadmissible. He lacks both the skill and knowledge adequately to prepare his defense, even though he have a perfect one. He requires the guiding hand of counsel at every step in the proceedings against him. Without it, though he be not guilty, he faces the danger of conviction because he does not know how to establish his innocence. If that be true of men of intelligence, how much more true is it of the ignorant and illiterate, or those of feeble intellect. If in any case, civil or criminal, a state or federal court were arbitrarily to refuse to hear a party by counsel, employed by and appearing for him, it reasonably may not be doubted that such a refusal would be a denial of a hearing, and, therefore, of due process in the constitutional sense. (*Powell v. Alabama,* 287 U.S. 45 at 68–69, 1932)

the Court refused to rule that the Sixth Amendment, in addition to the general due process guarantee of the Fourteenth Amendment, extended the right to legal counsel to state defendants.

The primary effect of this judicial posture was to withhold the aid of counsel from indigent state defendants charged with noncapital crimes. The Court first declared, in the 1942 case of *Betts v. Brady,* that "appointment of counsel is not a fundamental right" for such state defendants.[12] The due process guarantee of the Fourteenth Amendment, held the Court, did not require states to appoint counsel in every criminal case where it was requested by the defendant. A state legislature might choose to write such a requirement into state law, the Court added. The vote was 6–3. Justice Owen J. Roberts declared for the majority:

The Sixth Amendment of the national Constitution applies only to trials in federal courts. The due process clause of the Fourteenth Amendment does not incorporate, as such, the specific guarantees found in the Sixth Amendment although a denial by a state of rights or privileges specifically embodied in that and others of the first eight amendments may, in certain circumstances, or in connection with other ele-

Clarence Earl Gideon *(right)*, a penniless convict who had not been able to afford a defense attorney, sent a handwritten petition *(left)* from prison to the Supreme Court to hear his case. The Supreme Court granted his petition, heard his case, and ruled unanimously in 1963 that every state must provide counsel to an indigent charged with a felony.

ments, operate, in a given case, to deprive a litigant of due process of law in violation of the Fourteenth. Due process of law is secured against invasion by the federal Government by the Fifth Amendment and is safeguarded against state action in identical words by the Fourteenth. The phrase formulates a concept less rigid and more fluid than those envisaged in other specific and particular provisions of the Bill of Rights. Its application is less a matter of rule. Asserted denial is to be tested by an appraisal of the totality of facts in a given case. That which may, in one setting, constitute a denial of fundamental fairness, shocking to the universal sense of justice, may, in other circumstances, and in the light of other considerations, fall short of such denial.[13]

Justice Roberts acknowledged that *Johnson v. Zerbst* raised the question "whether the constraint laid by the [Sixth] amendment upon the national courts expresses a rule so fundamental and essential to a fair trial, and so, to due process of law, that it is made obligatory upon the States by the Fourteenth Amendment."[14]

The Court's answer was no. Justice Roberts wrote that Smith Betts—unlike Powell of the Scottsboro case—was a man forty-three years old, "of ordinary intelligence and ability." He was not so handicapped by lack of counsel that he was denied the fundamental fairness promised by the due process clause. And so, concluded the Court, while "the Fourteenth Amendment prohibits the conviction and incarceration of one whose trial is

offensive to the common and fundamental ideas of fairness and right, and while want of counsel in a particular case may result in a conviction lacking in such fundamental fairness, we cannot say that the amendment embodies an inexorable command that no trial for any offense, or in any court, can be fairly conducted and justice accorded a defendant who is not represented by counsel."[15]

Justice Black, joined by Justices Frank Murphy and William O. Douglas in dissent, urged that the same rule apply in state as in federal courts:

A practice cannot be reconciled with "common and fundamental ideas of fairness and right," which subjects innocent men to increased dangers of conviction merely because of their poverty. . . .

Denial to the poor of the request for counsel in proceedings based on charges of serious crime has long been regarded as shocking to the "universal sense of justice" throughout this country.[16]

Under *Betts,* then, the Court considered the special circumstances of each case to determine if denial of counsel denied the defendant fair treatment. The Court upheld some of the state convictions challenged due to lack of counsel, but in most cases it found circumstances that warranted reversal. Among those were the conduct of the trial judge or the youth, ignorance, or lack of legal sophistication of the defendants.[17]

THE RIGHT TO REFUSE COUNSEL

In a case that seemed to turn inside-out the series of rulings expanding the right of defendants to have the assistance of an attorney, the Supreme Court in 1975 held that defendants also have the right to *refuse* legal assistance.

In *Faretta v. California* the Court ruled that individuals have the right to conduct their own defense and to reject counsel who have been appointed to represent them.

Justice Potter Stewart acknowledged that recognition of this right seemed "to cut against the grain of this court's decisions holding that the Constitution requires that no accused can be convicted and imprisoned unless he has been accorded the right to the assistance of counsel." However, Stewart continued, "it is one thing to hold that every defendant, rich or poor, has the right to the assistance of counsel, and quite another to say that a state may compel a defendant to accept a lawyer he does not want." *(Faretta v. California, 422 U.S. 806 at 832–833, 1975)*

In 1963 the Supreme Court unanimously discarded this case-by-case approach, overruling *Betts v. Brady* to hold that the right to the assistance of counsel was so fundamental that the Fourteenth Amendment due process clause extended the Sixth Amendment guarantee to state defendants. States were henceforth required to provide counsel for all defendants charged with felonies and unable to pay a lawyer. This was the decision in *Gideon v. Wainwright*.[18]

Clarence Earl Gideon, an indigent, was tried and convicted in a Florida state court of a felony—breaking and entering a poolroom to commit a misdemeanor. He requested and was denied a court-appointed attorney. The judge based his refusal on the fact that Gideon's crime—unlike that in the *Powell* case—was not a capital one. Gideon conducted his own defense.

Convicted and sentenced to spend five years in prison, Gideon prepared his own petitions asking a federal court to declare his conviction invalid because it was obtained in violation of his constitutional right to counsel, and to order his release. The Supreme Court finally agreed to hear Gideon's case, and appointed a well-known Washington attorney, Abe Fortas, to argue on his behalf. The Court also requested that both sides in the case argue the additional question: should *Betts v. Brady* be reconsidered?

The Court's opinion in *Gideon,* reconsidering and reversing *Betts v. Brady,* was written by Justice Black, who had dissented from *Betts.* Looking back to *Powell v. Alabama,* in which the Court had described the right to counsel as fundamental to a fair trial, Black wrote:

The fact is that the Court in *Betts v. Brady* made an abrupt break with its own well-considered precedents. In returning to these old precedents, sounder we believe than the new, we but restore constitutional principles established to achieve a fair system of justice. Not only these precedents but also reason and reflection require us to recognize that in our adversary system of criminal justice, any person haled into

court, who is too poor to hire a lawyer, cannot be assured a fair trial unless counsel is provided for him. This seems to us to be an obvious truth. . . . Lawyers to prosecute are everywhere deemed essential to protect the public's interest in an orderly society. . . .

That government hires lawyers to prosecute and defendants who have the money hire lawyers to defend are the strongest indications of the widespread belief that lawyers in criminal courts are necessities, not luxuries.[19]

"ADEQUATE PROTECTIVE DEVICE"

In 1964 the Supreme Court further tightened the requirement that states observe the right to counsel. With its controversial ruling in *Escobedo v. Illinois,* the Court linked that right to the Fifth Amendment privilege against self-incrimination. In *Escobedo* a divided Court held that a suspect in custody had an absolute right to the aid of an attorney during police interrogation.[20] *(See details of this case, pp. 595–596.)*

Two years later, with its decision in *Miranda v. Arizona,* the Court declared the presence of counsel "the adequate protective device necessary to make the process of police interrogation conform to the dictates of the [Fifth Amendment] privilege."[21] "Accordingly," wrote Chief Justice Earl Warren, "we hold that an individual held for interrogation must be clearly informed that he has the right to consult with a lawyer and to have the lawyer with him during interrogation."[22]

In 1972 the Court held that the right to counsel applied not only to state defendants charged with felonies but in all trials of persons for offenses serious enough to warrant a jail sentence. Speaking for the unanimous Court in *Argersinger v. Hamlin,* Justice Douglas looked back both to *Powell* and *Gideon:*

Both *Powell* and *Gideon* involved felonies. But their rationale has relevance to any criminal trial, where an accused is deprived of liberty. *Powell* and *Gideon* suggest that there are certain fundamental rights applicable to all such criminal prosecutions. . . .

The requirement of counsel may well be necessary for a fair trial even in a petty offense prosecution. We are by no means convinced that legal and constitutional questions involved in a case that actually leads to imprisonment even for a brief period are any less complex than when a person can be sent off for six months or more. . . .

Under the rule we announce today, every judge will know when the trial of a misdemeanor starts that no imprisonment may be imposed, even though local law permits it, unless the accused is represented by counsel.[23]

Seven years later, in 1979, the Court limited *Argersinger,* holding that the right to counsel did not apply in trials of lesser offenses where no sentence of imprisonment *was* imposed, even though such a sentence *could* have been imposed.

The Court was divided 5–4. For the majority, Justice William H. Rehnquist reaffirmed the key holding in *Argersinger,* that no one could receive a prison sentence if he had not been afforded the aid of an attorney at trial. But Rehnquist said that *Argersinger* did not require reversal of a man's conviction for shoplifting, a crime for which he was fined fifty dollars, even though he had not been provided an attorney, and even though a year in jail was a possible sentence for his crime.[24]

THE QUESTION OF QUESTIONING

Critical to the meaning of *Miranda v. Arizona,* the case that forbade police to continue questioning a suspect after he invoked his right to remain silent or to have his lawyer present, was the meaning of the term "interrogation."[1]

Fourteen years after *Miranda,* the Court adopted a broad definition of this word. Interrogation, the Court declared unanimously in *Rhode Island v. Innis,* means more than just the direct questioning of a suspect by police. It includes other "techniques of persuasion," such as staged lineups, intended to evoke statements from a suspect. Indeed, said the Court, interrogation occurs any time police use words or actions "that they *should have known* were reasonably likely to elicit an incriminating response" from a suspect.

This broad definition of interrogation did not encompass events that transpired in *Rhode Island,* the Court held 6–3. Thomas Innis, arrested for murder, led police to the murder weapon after he overheard policemen conversing among themselves about the possibility of children finding and being harmed by the weapon they were seeking. Because this evocative conversation occurred in a police car without Innis's attorney present, he challenged his eventually incriminating statements as obtained in violation of *Miranda.*

The Supreme Court rejected this argument, holding that the conversation he overheard did not qualify as interrogation.[2]

In 1981 the Court reaffirmed its broad view of interrogation, ruling that a defendant should be warned, prior to an interview with a state-appointed psychiatrist, that he had the right to refuse to answer the psychiatrist's questions and to have his attorney present during the interview.[3]

The whole area of police conversation with a suspect raises difficult points of distinction. In 1981 the Court in *Edwards v. Arizona* was unanimous in insisting that once a defendant has said he wants his attorney present, all interrogation must cease and may not resume until the attorney is present—or the defendant starts a new conversation with police.[4]

Two years later the Court emphasized the latter point, ruling 5–4 that a suspect who invokes his right to counsel but later, before counsel arrives, asks police "Well, what is going to happen to me now?" is not denied his rights when police remind him of his request for counsel—but then continue to talk with him.[5]

Police use of a well-placed informer can also constitute interrogation, the Court has held. In *United States v. Henry* in 1980, the Court held that a suspect was denied the right to counsel when the government obtained and used incriminating statements by planting an informer in his cell prior to trial.[6]

The Court reaffirmed this ruling in *Maine v. Moulton* in 1985, but a year later it drew the line between solicited and unsolicited incriminating statements, permitting police to use *unsolicited* remarks made by a suspect to a police informer in his cell.[7] *(See other rulings on invocation of privilege, p. 597.)*

1. *Miranda v. Arizona,* 384 U.S. 436 (1966), reaffirmed in *Michigan v. Jackson, Michigan v. Bladel,* 475 U.S. 625 (1986).
2. *Rhode Island v. Innis,* 446 U.S. 291 (1980).
3. *Estelle v. Smith,* 451 U.S. 454 (1981); *Satterwhite v. Texas,* 486 U.S. 249 (1988).
4. *Edwards v. Arizona,* 451 U.S. 477 (1981), applied retroactively to cases pending on appeal; *Shea v. Louisiana,* 470 U.S. 51 (1985). See also *Arizona v. Roberson,* 486 U.S. 675 (1988), *Patterson v. Illinois,* 487 U.S. 285 (1988).
5. *Oregon v. Bradshaw,* 462 U.S. 1039 (1983).
6. *United States v. Henry,* 447 U.S. 264 (1980).
7. *Maine v. Moulton,* 474 U.S. 159 (1985); *Kuhlmann v. Wilson,* 477 U.S. 436 (1986).

"CRITICAL STAGE"

In *Powell v. Alabama* the Court in 1932 indicated the importance of timing in the provision of legal assistance to a defendant.[25] The Court described the period between arrest and trial as a critical one in the preparation of a defense.

Many subsequent rulings on the right to counsel have worked to define the "critical stage" at which the right applies, the time counsel must be made available if requested by the suspect or defendant.

In *Hamilton v. Alabama,* decided in 1961, the Court held that arraignment was such a critical stage, at least in some states.[26] Later, *Escobedo* and *Miranda* emphatically held that the right applied once a suspect was in custody and subject to interrogation.[27]

In 1967 the Court in *United States v. Wade*—and its state counterpart, *Gilbert v. California*—held that police lineups also were such a critical stage.[28] The Court declared inadmissible any in-court identification of defendants based on pretrial lineups conducted in the absence of the defendant's attorney.

Justice William J. Brennan Jr., writing for a unanimous Court in *Wade,* observed:

[T]he principle of *Powell v. Alabama* and succeeding cases requires that we scrutinize any pretrial confrontation of the accused to determine whether the presence of his counsel is necessary to preserve the defendant's basic right to a fair trial as affected by his right meaningfully to cross-examine the witnesses against him and to have effective assistance of counsel at the trial itself.[29]

In *Gilbert* the Court applied the same rule to state proceedings.

Wade was undercut by Congress. In the Crime Control and Safe Streets Act of 1968, Congress included a provision allowing use of such lineup identification evidence at trial in federal courts, even if obtained in the absence of counsel.

And in 1972 the Court further limited the effect of *Wade* and *Gilbert.* The defendants in those cases had already been indicted when they were placed in the lineup. In *Kirby v. Illinois* the Court ruled that the right to counsel did not apply to persons in such lineups who had not yet been indicted.

The right did not take effect, the Court held, until "formal prosecutorial proceedings" were under way.[30] Justice Potter Stewart explained:

The initiation of judicial criminal proceedings is far from a mere formalism. It is the starting point of our whole system of adversary crimi-

nal justice. For it is only then that the Government has committed itself to prosecute and only then that the adverse positions of Government and defendant have solidified. It is then that a defendant finds
himself faced with the prosecutorial forces of organized society, and
immersed in the intricacies of substantive and procedural criminal law.
It is this point, therefore, that marks the commencement of the "criminal prosecutions" to which alone the explicit guarantees of the Sixth
Amendment are applicable.[31]

The principle of *Wade* and *Gilbert* was further eroded in 1973
when the Court held that it was not necessary for a defendant's
attorney to be present at a postindictment photographic identification session with potential witnesses.[32]

At the other end of the criminal justice process—appeal of
conviction—the Court in 1974 called a halt to the gradual extension of the right to appointed counsel. In *Ross v. Moffit* the
Court held that the state's constitutional obligation to provide
appointed counsel for indigents appealing their convictions did
not extend past the point where their right to appeal had been
effectively exhausted.[33]

"EFFECTIVE" AID

As the Court made clear in *Powell v. Alabama,* the effective
aid of counsel means more than the mere physical presence of
an attorney at trial.

In *Powell* the Court held that the judge's gesture of appointing the entire local bar as defense counsel—and the failure of
any particular individuals to assume that role before trial—deprived the defendants of the *effective* aid of counsel.

Other factors can deprive defendants of the sort of legal representation to which the Sixth Amendment—or due process
generally—entitles them. Conflict of interest is one. In the 1942
case of *Glasser v. United States,* the Court found that a judge had
denied defendants the effective aid of counsel by requiring a single attorney to represent them both.[34] In that opinion, the majority declared:

Upon the trial judge rests the duty of seeing that the trial is conducted
with solicitude for the essential rights of the accused. . . . Of equal importance with the duty of the court to see that an accused has the assistance of counsel is its duty to refrain from embarrassing counsel in the
defense of an accused by insisting, or indeed, even suggesting, that
counsel undertake to concurrently represent interests which might diverge from those of his first client, when the possibility of that divergence is brought home to the court.[35]

In 1978 the Court elaborated on that point, stating in *Holloway v. Arkansas:*

Joint representation of conflicting interests is suspect because of what
it tends to prevent the attorney from doing. . . . Generally speaking, a
conflict may . . . prevent an attorney from challenging the admission of
evidence prejudicial to one client but perhaps favorable to another, or
from arguing at the sentencing hearing the relative involvement and

culpability of his clients in order to minimize the culpability of one by
emphasizing that of another. . . . The mere physical presence of an attorney does not fulfill the Sixth Amendment guarantee when the advocate's conflicting obligations has [sic] effectively sealed his lips on crucial matters.[36]

Competence of counsel, however, is more difficult to challenge. The Court in the 1970s rejected the argument of several
persons that their convictions, based on guilty pleas, were the
result of advice from incompetent counsel. The Court declared
that defendants must assume a certain degree of risk that their
attorneys would make some "ordinary error" in assessing the
facts of their case and the law that applied, and that such error
was not a basis for reversing a conviction.[37]

A RULE OF REASON

In 1984, however, the Supreme Court for the first time set out
a standard for use in reviewing a defendant's claim that he had
been denied the effective aid of an attorney. Justice Sandra Day
O'Connor, who had been a trial judge in Arizona prior to her
appointment to the Court, wrote the opinion in *Strickland v.
Washington.*

"The benchmark for judging any claim of ineffectiveness,"
wrote O'Connor, "must be whether counsel's conduct so undermined the proper functioning of the adversarial process that the
trial cannot be relied on as having produced a just result." She
explained that to win reversal of a conviction or invalidation of
a sentence, a defendant must show that his attorney made errors
so serious at trial that they resulted in his being denied a fair trial. The proper standard, O'Connor continued, is "reasonably
effective assistance." The lawyer, she said, deserves the benefit of
the doubt. "Judicial scrutiny of counsel's performance must be
highly deferential. . . . Because of the difficulties inherent in
making the evaluation, a court must indulge a strong presumption that counsel's conduct falls within the wide range of reasonable professional assistance."[38]

The Court applied that standard to another case decided the
same day, May 14, 1984. In *United States v. Cronic,* it unanimously held that an appeals court was wrong to infer that a defendant was denied the right to counsel because the appointed
counsel lacked criminal law experience and was given only a
brief time to prepare for trial. Such a conclusion, wrote Justice
John Paul Stevens, must be supported by evidence of serious errors by the lawyer so prejudicial that the defendant was denied a
fair trial.[39]

In 1985 the Court for the first time found a case in which this
standard worked to prove the defendant's claim. In *Evitts v.
Lucey* the Court held that an attorney's failure to file a statement
of appeal by the legal deadline constituted evidence that he was
not providing his client the effective aid of counsel.[40]

Double Jeopardy

To restrain the government from repeated prosecutions of an individual for one particular offense, the prohibition against double jeopardy was included in the Fifth Amendment: "nor shall any person be subject for the same offense to be twice put in jeopardy of life or limb." The Supreme Court has held that this guarantee protects an individual both against multiple prosecutions for the same offense and against multiple punishments for the same crime.

Until 1969 the double jeopardy clause applied only to federal prosecutions. In that year the Supreme Court in *Benton v. Maryland* held that the due process guarantee of the Fourteenth Amendment extended this protection to persons tried by states as well.[1]

A defendant is placed in jeopardy at the time his jury is sworn in,[2] although if a mistrial is declared under certain circumstances[3] or if the jury fails to agree on a verdict,[4] the double jeopardy clause does not forbid his retrial.

If he is convicted, he may waive his immunity against double jeopardy and seek a new trial, or he may appeal the verdict to a higher court. If the conviction is set aside for a reason other than insufficient evidence, he may be tried again for the same offense.[5]

If he is acquitted, the double jeopardy clause absolutely bars any further prosecution of him for that crime, even if the acquittal was the result of error.[6]

One Trial Per Sovereign

The double jeopardy guarantee, however, protects only against repeated prosecutions by a single sovereign government. Thus, it is not violated when a person is tried on both state and federal charges arising from a single offense. Many acts are offenses under both federal and state laws.

The Court established this rule in the 1922 case of *United States v. Lanza.* Vito Lanza was convicted for violating Washington State's prohibition law. Then he was indicted on the same grounds for violating the federal prohibition law. The federal district judge dismissed his indictment as a violation of the double jeopardy guarantee. The government appealed the dismissal, and the Supreme Court reversed it, 6–3.

Chief Justice William Howard Taft wrote:

We have here two sovereignties, deriving power from different sources, capable of dealing with the same subject-matter within the same territory. Each may, without interference by the other, enact laws to secure prohibition. . . . Each government, in determining what shall be an offense against its peace and dignity, is exercising its own sovereignty, not that of the other.

It follows that an act denounced as a crime by both national and state sovereignties is an offense against the peace and dignity of both, and may be punished by each. The 5th Amendment, like all the other guaranties in the first eight amendments, applies only to proceedings by the Federal government . . . and the double jeopardy therein forbidden is a second prosecution under authority of the Federal government after a first trial for the same offense under the same authority. Here the same act was an offense against the state of Washington, because a violation of its law, and also an offense against the United States under the National Prohibition Act. The defendants thus committed two different offenses by the same act, and a conviction by a court of Washington of the offense against that state is not a conviction of the different offense against the United States, and so is not double jeopardy.[7]

The *Lanza* rule survives. The Court repeatedly has reaffirmed that multiple prosecutions by different sovereigns—including two states—for the same offense did not violate the double jeopardy clause.[8] However, because a state and a city are not separate sovereigns, the double jeopardy guarantee does protect an individual against prosecution by both for one offense.[9]

The separate sovereignties doctrine was applied by the Court in the 1978 case of *United States v. Wheeler.* There the Court ruled that the double jeopardy clause did not protect an American Indian defendant convicted in tribal court from being tried by federal authorities for the same offense.[10]

In 1985 the Court allowed a defendant to be tried in two different states for two parts of the same crime—the murder of his wife. One state—where the murder was committed—charged him for the murder; the second—where he dumped the body—charged him for that crime. The Supreme Court, with Justice Sandra Day O'Connor writing the opinion in *Heath v. Alabama,* found nothing to violate the double jeopardy guarantee.[11]

The double jeopardy clause also protects an individual who successfully appeals his conviction on a lesser charge from being retried on the original charge.

In the 1957 case of *Green v. United States,* the Court ruled that Everett Green—tried for first-degree murder but convicted of murder in the second degree, a verdict that he successfully appealed—could not be tried again for first-degree murder after he won a new trial on appeal. The Court said that Green had been once in jeopardy for first-degree murder and that appeal of his conviction for a different crime did not constitute a waiver of his protection against double jeopardy. The Court explained:

The underlying idea, one that is deeply ingrained in at least the Anglo-American system of jurisprudence, is that the State with all its resources and power should not be allowed to make repeated attempts to convict an individual for an alleged offense, thereby subjecting him to embarrassment, expense and ordeal and compelling him to live in a continuing state of anxiety and insecurity, as well as enhancing the possibility that even though innocent he may be found guilty.[12]

State Action

In 1937—in the often-cited decision in *Palko v. Connecticut*—the Court rejected the idea that the Fourteenth Amendment due process clause applied the double jeopardy guarantee to state action.

Frank Palko was convicted of second-degree murder and sentenced to life imprisonment. The state sought and won a new trial claiming that legal errors had occurred at trial. At a second trial Palko was found guilty of first-degree murder and sentenced to die. He challenged his second conviction as a violation of the double jeopardy guarantee and of due process.

The Court rejected this argument, excluding the double jeopardy guarantee from the list of guarantees that had been "absorbed" into due process. That protection, Justice Benjamin N. Cardozo wrote for the majority, was not "of the very essence of a scheme of ordered liberty."[13] He then elaborated:

Is that kind of double jeopardy to which the statute has subjected him a hardship so acute and shocking that our polity will not endure it? Does it violate those "fundamental principles of liberty and justice which lie at the base of all our civil and political institutions?"... The answer surely must be "no."... The state is not attempting to wear the accused out by a multitude of cases with accumulated trials. It asks no more than this, that the case against him shall go on until there shall be a trial free from the corrosion of substantial legal error.... This is not cruelty at all, nor even vexation in any immoderate degree. If the trial had been infected with error adverse to the accused, there might have been review at his instance, and as often as necessary to purge the vicious taint. A reciprocal privilege, subject at all times to the discretion of the presiding judge..., has now been granted to the state. There is here no seismic innovation. The edifice of justice stands, its symmetry, to many, greater than before.[14]

Thirty-two years later, in 1969, the Court overruled *Palko* by a vote of 6–2. In its last announced decision under Chief Justice Earl Warren, the Court in *Benton v. Maryland* declared that the double jeopardy clause did apply to the states through the due process guarantee of the Fourteenth Amendment. Justice Thurgood Marshall delivered the majority opinion:

Our recent cases have thoroughly rejected the *Palko* notion that basic constitutional rights can be denied by the States so long as the totality of the circumstances does not disclose a denial of "fundamental fairness." Once it is decided that a particular Bill of Rights guarantee is "fundamental to the American scheme of justice,"... the same constitutional standards apply against both the State and Federal Governments. *Palko's* roots had thus been cut away years ago. We today only recognize the inevitable.[15]

Justices John Marshall Harlan and Potter Stewart dissented from this "march toward 'incorporating' much, if not all, of the Federal Bill of Rights into the Due Process Clause."[16]

Resentencing Restrictions

A dozen years later a case similar to *Palko* came to the Court. *Bullington v. Missouri* arose after Robert Bullington was convicted of murder, for which he could have been sentenced to death. Instead, the jury sentenced him to life in prison without eligibility for parole for fifty years.

Bullington won a new trial, and the state declared that it would again seek a death sentence for him. Bullington objected, arguing that the double jeopardy clause precluded his being once again placed in jeopardy of a death sentence—after a jury had already decided that he should not be executed.

The Supreme Court, 5–4, agreed with him. The state should not have a second chance to try to convince a jury to sentence Bullington to die, wrote Justice Harry A. Blackmun. Once a jury had decided that he should not die for his crime, Bullington's right to be secure against double jeopardy forbade the state, even at a new trial, to seek the death penalty. Dissenting were Chief Justice Warren E. Burger and Justices Byron R. White, Lewis F. Powell Jr., and William H. Rehnquist.[17]

The same day the Court announced its decision in *Benton*—June 23, 1969—it held in *North Carolina v. Pearce* that the double jeopardy guarantee limited the authority of a judge to impose a harsher sentence than the original upon a defendant whose first conviction had been set aside for a new trial.[18]

Unless there were objective reasons related to the conduct of the defendant after the imposition of the first sentence, and unless those reasons were set out in the record of the case, a judge could not impose a harsher sentence after retrial, the Court held. Furthermore, time already served on the first sentence must be credited against the new sentence.

Clifton Pearce was convicted of assault with intent to rape and sentenced to twelve to fifteen years in prison. After serving several years, he won reversal of his conviction and a new trial. Convicted in the second trial, Pearce was sentenced to eight years in prison. When this new sentence was added to the time he had already served, it amounted to a longer sentence than the original one.

Justice Stewart wrote the Court's opinion, holding the new sentence a violation of the double jeopardy guarantee unless the time already served was credited against it:

The Court has held today, in *Benton v. Maryland* . . . that the Fifth Amendment guarantee against double jeopardy is enforceable against the States through the Fourteenth Amendment. That guarantee has been said to consist of three separate constitutional protections. It protects against a second prosecution for the same offense after acquittal. It protects against a second prosecution for the same offense after conviction. And it protects against multiple punishments for the same offense. This last protection is what is necessarily implicated in any consideration of the question whether, in the imposition of sentence for the same offense after retrial, the Constitution requires that credit must be given for punishment already endured. . . .

We hold that the constitutional guarantee against multiple punishments for the same offense absolutely requires that punishment already exacted must be fully "credited" in imposing sentence upon a new conviction for the same offense. If upon a new trial, the defendant is acquitted, there is no way the years he spent in prison can be returned to him. But if he is reconvicted, those years can and must be returned—by subtracting them from whatever new sentence is imposed.[19]

In 1973, however, the Court refused to apply these limitations to resentencing by a *jury* after retrial.[20]

Appealing Dismissals

In the mid-1970s the Supreme Court began to expand the government's right to appeal a judge's decision to dismiss charges against a defendant after the trial was under way. Such appeals had been thought impermissible under the general rule that the prosecution may not appeal a verdict of acquittal.

In 1975 the Court in *United States v. Wilson* held that the double jeopardy guarantee did not foreclose a government appeal of a trial judge's decision to dismiss charges against a defendant who had already been found guilty.[21]

The Court reasoned that the double jeopardy clause did not foreclose an appeal of such a postverdict dismissal of charges inasmuch as the success of the appeal would only result in reinstatement of the verdict, not in a new trial.

In another case decided that same day, the Court seemed to make the possibility of further proceedings against the defendant a crucial element in determining the permissibility of such appeals. In *United States v. Jenkins* the Court held that the double jeopardy clause did forbid the government to appeal a ruling dismissing an indictment when a successful appeal might result in further proceedings.[22]

Three years later, however, the Court overruled *Jenkins* with its decision in *United States v. Scott*.[23] By a 5–4 vote the Court held that the government could appeal a trial judge's decision to grant a defendant's motion to dismiss charges in midtrial. The Court held that the double jeopardy guarantee did not forbid an appeal of that ruling—or retrial of the defendant—because a defendant, in seeking dismissal of the charges based on grounds unrelated to his guilt or innocence, had made a voluntary choice to risk retrial for the same offense.

The double jeopardy clause, held the majority, protected an individual against government oppression through multiple prosecutions but not against the consequences of his own voluntary choice.

One Offense, Two Trials?

For a brief few years in the early 1990s, the Court broadened the double jeopardy provision to bar multiple prosecutions whenever the two offenses charged involved the same conduct.

In 1990 the Court ruled, 5–4, that the test for double jeopardy was whether a second prosecution was based on conduct that had already been prosecuted. Writing for the Court in *Grady v. Corbin*, Justice William J. Brennan Jr. said a defendant should be protected from repeated government attempts to convict him for a single action. In this case, a driver was ticketed and fined for the misdemeanors of driving while intoxicated and failing to keep right of the road median. Later, prosecutors who were unaware of the earlier court action sought to try the driver for the death of a motorist he allegedly hit in the oncoming lane.[24]

Joining Brennan in the majority were Justices White, Thurgood Marshall, Harry A. Blackmun, and John Paul Stevens. Chief Justice William H. Rehnquist and Justices Sandra Day O'Connor and Anthony M. Kennedy dissented, as did Antonin Scalia. Scalia wrote that the double jeopardy clause protects an individual against a second prosecution for the same offense, not the same conduct.

Three years later Scalia and the three other *Grady* dissenters, joined by a new justice, Clarence Thomas, reversed the 1990 ruling. They held that multiple prosecutions are permitted if the two offenses contain different elements. Dissenting were Justices White, Blackmun, Stevens, and David H. Souter, who had succeeded Brennan in the interim.[25]

Taxes

In 1994 the Court for the first time used the double jeopardy clause to strike down a tax. By 5–4 it ruled that Montana's tax on illegal drugs was punitive and violated the constitutional prohibition against multiple punishments. The state set a tax of $100 per ounce on marijuana and similarly high levies on other illegal drugs.

Montana tried to collect the tax from persons who had been prosecuted for criminal dealings in drugs. In this case Montana was attempting to collect $181,000 from a family prosecuted for growing marijuana on a ranch in central Montana.

Writing for the majority, Justice Stevens said the tax had "an unmistakable punitive character" because it was so high, was imposed only after a criminal proceeding, and was based on the value of property that the government presumably had already confiscated and destroyed.[26] Rehnquist, O'Connor, Scalia, and Thomas dissented, each for different reasons.

Two years later, the Court upheld the seizure of property in a civil forfeiture proceeding for defendants who already had been prosecuted in a criminal trial. The Court distinguished the new case from the Montana dispute, saying the Montana tax was the functional equivalent of a successive criminal prosecution. In the new ruling, *United States v. Ursery*, the Court said forfeiture—an action technically taken against a piece of property—does not constitute "punishment" for double jeopardy purposes.[27]

Cruel and Unusual Punishment

The Eighth Amendment prohibits "cruel and unusual" punishment but does not specify what is cruel and unusual. The Supreme Court has interpreted this prohibition flexibly, measuring punishments against "evolving standards of decency." Although it has refused, for example, to outlaw the death penalty as invariably cruel and unusual, it has applied the constitutional standard to prohibit states from imposing prison sentences upon those found "guilty" only of drug addiction, not drug-related crimes. The Court has said that it views the amendment as prohibiting punishments it found barbaric or disproportionate to the crime.

Since early in the twentieth century, the Supreme Court has weighed the severity of a challenged sentence against the seriousness of the crime. In 1910 the Court overturned a law that allowed a person convicted of falsifying a public record to be assessed a heavy fine and fifteen years at hard labor.[1]

Nearly a half century later the Court reversed a military court's decision to strip of U.S. citizenship a man who had been convicted of desertion. The majority, for whom Chief Justice Earl Warren spoke, found such "denationalization" a cruel and unusual punishment "forbidden by the principle of civilized treatment guaranteed by the Eighth Amendment."[2] Warren then set out an often quoted description of this provision:

The exact scope of the constitutional phrase "cruel and unusual" has not been detailed by this Court. . . . The basic concept underlying the Eighth Amendment is nothing less than the dignity of man. While the State has the power to punish, the Amendment stands to assure that this power be exercised within the limits of civilized standards. Fines, imprisonment and even execution may be imposed depending upon the enormity of the crime, but any technique outside the bounds of these traditional penalties is constitutionally suspect. . . . The Court [has] recognized . . . that the words of the Amendment are not precise, and that their scope is not static. The Amendment must draw its meaning from the evolving standards of decency that mark the progress of a maturing society.[3]

The Eighth Amendment and the States

One of the Court's earliest Eighth Amendment decisions came in 1892 when the Court refused to apply the ban on cruel and unusual punishment to state action.[4] Despite that refusal, cases challenging state action as violating that guarantee continued to come to the Court from time to time. In the midtwentieth century, the Court quietly began applying the ban to states, but not until 1962 did it strike down a state-imposed punishment as a violation of the Eighth Amendment.

One of the most bizarre of the Court's early Eighth Amendment cases was that of *Louisiana ex rel. Francis v. Resweber*, decided in 1947. It was in this case that the Court assumed for the first time that the Eighth Amendment ban on cruel and unusual punishment could be enforced against the states.

Willie Francis was sentenced by a Louisiana court to be elec-

trocuted. On the appointed day Francis was put in the electric chair, the switch was thrown—and nothing happened. A failure in the operating mechanism prevented the electricity from reaching Francis.

Francis appealed to the Supreme Court, asking them to forbid the state a second execution attempt because it would constitute cruel and unusual punishment. The Court denied Francis's appeal, by a vote of 5–4.[5]

Justice Stanley F. Reed, who wrote for the majority, clearly saw the Eighth Amendment ban as applicable to state action, but he did not find that action in Francis's case to be cruel and unusual.

[T]he fact that petitioner has already been subjected to a current of electricity does not make his subsequent execution any more cruel in the constitutional sense than any other execution. The cruelty against which the Constitution protects a convicted man is cruelty inherent in the method of punishment, not the necessary suffering involved in any method employed to extinguish life humanely. The fact that an unforeseeable accident prevented the prompt consummation of the sentence cannot, it seems to us, add an element of cruelty to a subsequent execution. There is no purpose to inflict unnecessary pain nor any unnecessary pain involved in the proposed execution. . . . We cannot agree that the hardship imposed upon the petitioner rises to that level of hardship denounced as denial of due process because of cruelty.[6]

Justice Harold H. Burton, joined by Justices William O. Douglas, Frank Murphy, and Wiley B. Rutledge, dissented.

It was fifteen years later that the Court for the first time used the Eighth Amendment to invalidate a state law. In *Robinson v. California* the Court held it impermissibly cruel and unusual punishment for a state to impose prison sentences upon persons found to be drug addicts.

Justice Potter Stewart wrote the majority opinion for six members of the Court:

This statute . . . is not one which punishes a person for the use of narcotics, for their purchase, sale or possession, or for antisocial or disorderly behavior resulting from their administration. It is not a law which even purports to provide or require medical treatment. Rather, we deal with a statute which makes the "status" of narcotic addiction a criminal offense. . . .

It is unlikely that any State . . . would attempt to make it a criminal offense for a person to be mentally ill, or a leper, or to be afflicted with a venereal disease . . . in the light of contemporary human knowledge, a law which made a criminal offense of such a disease would doubtless be universally thought to be an infliction of cruel and unusual punishment in violation of the Eighth and Fourteenth Amendments. . . .

. . . We hold that a state law which imprisons a person thus afflicted as a criminal . . . inflicts a cruel and unusual punishment in violation of the Fourteenth Amendment.[7]

Justices Byron R. White and Tom C. Clark dissented.

In 1968 the Court refused to apply *Robinson* to forbid states to punish public drunkenness. The Court upheld a Texas law under which Leroy Powell was convicted of being intoxicated in a public place. He attacked the law as cruel and unusual punishment, because it punished him for being a chronic alcoholic.

By a 5–4 vote in *Powell v. Texas,* the Court rejected that challenge. Justice Thurgood Marshall delivered the majority opinion, distinguishing the law in *Powell* from that in *Robinson.*

[A]ppellant was convicted, not for being a chronic alcoholic, but for being in public while drunk on a particular occasion. The State of Texas thus has not sought to punish a mere status, as California did in *Robinson;* nor has it attempted to regulate appellant's behavior in the privacy of his home. Rather, it has imposed upon appellant a criminal sanction for public behavior which may create substantial health and safety hazards, both for appellant and for members of the general public, and which offends the moral and esthetic sensibilities of a large segment of the community.[8]

Justice Abe Fortas, in a dissent joined by Justices Douglas, Stewart, and William J. Brennan Jr., said the appellant was powerless to avoid drinking and, once intoxicated, could not prevent himself from appearing in public places.

Capital Punishment

Time and time again in the last half of the twentieth century, convicted criminals sentenced to death have challenged state (and sometimes federal) capital punishment laws as violating the Eighth Amendment ban on cruel and unusual punishment.

While the Court often seemed to be zigzagging its way through a succession of death penalty cases, it ultimately upheld the ultimate punishment. Decision by decision, it became clear that a continuing majority of the members of the modern Court accepted the death penalty as consistent with contemporary standards of punishment and decency.

The first in this modern line of rulings on capital punishment was *Witherspoon v. Illinois,* decided in 1968. In *Witherspoon* the Court held that states could not exclude from juries in capital cases all persons opposed to the death penalty. Such exclusion of a sizable group, held the Court, resulted in a jury that was not fairly representative of the community. By permitting opponents of the death penalty to serve on juries in capital cases, the Court made it more difficult for prosecutors to obtain death sentences. *(See details on jury selection, "The Right to a Jury Trial," pp. 563–569.)*

Justice Stewart spoke for the majority:

[I]n a nation less than half of whose people believe in the death penalty, a jury composed exclusively of such people [those favoring capital punishment] cannot speak for the community. Culled of all who harbor doubts about the wisdom of capital punishment—of all who would be reluctant to pronounce the extreme penalty—such a jury can speak only for a distinct and dwindling minority. . . . In its quest for a jury capable of imposing the death penalty, the State produced a jury uncommonly willing to condemn a man to die.[9]

Witherspoon would remain law for the next seventeen years, but in 1985 the Court discarded it and adopted a rule that made it easier for prosecutors to exclude death penalty opponents from juries. *(See details of this case, p. 614.)*

In 1971 the Court upheld, against a due process challenge, state laws that left it completely to the discretion of the jury whether to impose a sentence of death. This was the Court's ruling in *McGautha v. California,* reached by a 6–3 vote.

Justice John Marshall Harlan wrote for the majority:

In light of history, experience, and the present limitations of human knowledge, we find it quite impossible to say that committing to the untrammeled discretion of the jury the power to pronounce life or death in capital cases is offensive to anything in the Constitution.[10]

In dissent, Justices Brennan, Marshall, and Douglas argued that states should be required to set guidelines for this irrevocable decision by a jury.

The decision in *McGautha,* however, was even shorter-lived than *Witherspoon.* Only a year later the Court effectively reversed it.

By a 5–4 vote in *Furman v. Georgia, Jackson v. Georgia,* and *Branch v. Texas,* the Court invalidated the death penalty statutes of Georgia and Texas and, by extension, those in every state.[11] The Court that had rejected a Fourteenth Amendment due process challenge in *McGautha* upheld an Eighth Amendment challenge in *Furman.*

Death penalty laws, held the majority, left too much discretion to juries in imposing this ultimate penalty. The result was a "wanton and freakish" pattern of its use that violated the Eighth Amendment ban on cruel and unusual punishments.

The majority was composed of the five justices who had served under Chief Justice Warren: Douglas, Brennan, Stewart, White, and Marshall. Each wrote a separate opinion. Dissenting were the four members named to the Court by President Richard Nixon—Chief Justice Warren E. Burger and Justices Harry A. Blackmun, Lewis F. Powell Jr., and William H. Rehnquist.

Under the death penalty laws existing in Georgia and Texas, Justice Douglas wrote,

no standards govern the selection of the penalty. People live or die, dependent on the whim of one man or of 12. . . .

. . . these discretionary statutes are unconstitutional in their operation. They are pregnant with discrimination and discrimination is an ingredient not compatible with the idea of equal protection of the laws that is implicit in the ban on "cruel and unusual" punishments.[12]

Justice Brennan found the death penalty "uniquely degrading to human dignity" no matter how the decision was reached.[13] He continued:

Death is an unusually severe and degrading punishment; there is a strong probability that it is inflicted arbitrarily; its rejection by contemporary society is virtually total; and there is no reason to believe that it serves any penal purpose more effectively than the less severe punishment of imprisonment. The function of these principles is to enable a court to determine whether a punishment comports with human dignity. Death, quite simply, does not.[14]

Justice Stewart found critical how this penalty was applied under existing law:

These death sentences are cruel and unusual in the same way that being struck by lightning is cruel and unusual. For, of all the people con-

CRUEL PUNISHMENT

The Supreme Court in the 1980s and 1990s addressed a number of cases in which punishments other than the death penalty were challenged as in violation of the Eighth Amendment.

In 1980 the Court, 5–4, rejected the argument that it was unconstitutionally cruel and unusual punishment for a state to impose a mandatory life sentence upon a "three-time loser"—even though the three crimes of which this defendant had been convicted were all considered relatively petty, nonviolent crimes. Justice William H. Rehnquist wrote the opinion in *Rummel v. Estelle;* Justices William J. Brennan Jr., Thurgood Marshall, Lewis F. Powell Jr., and John Paul Stevens dissented.[1]

That same year, however, the Court ruled that individuals who felt that federal officials had violated their Eighth Amendment right had the right to sue those officials for damages.[2]

Just three years later the Court reversed *Rummel* by a 5–4 vote in *Solem v. Helm.* This time Justice Harry A. Blackmun joined the *Rummel* dissenters. It did constitute cruel and unusual punishment, wrote Justice Powell for the majority, when South Dakota imposed a life sentence without possibility of parole on a man convicted on seven separate occasions of nonviolent felonies. This decision was the first time this provision had been used to judge the relative severity of a prison sentence.[3] In a second ruling a few years later, the Court, 5–4, held that a state does not violate the Eighth Amendment ban when it imposes a sentence of life in prison without parole on a first-time drug offender.[4]

In response to a number of inmate cases challenging prison conditions as cruel and unusual, the Court instituted a high standard for such challenges. To make their case, prisoners must show a culpable state of mind, "deliberate indifference" and "wanton" conduct on the part of prison officials who acted "maliciously and sadistically for the very purpose of causing harm."[5]

Applying that standard, the Court ruled that the use of excessive physical force against a prison inmate may constitute cruel and unusual punishment even if the prisoner does not suffer "significant injury." In a 1993 case, the justices, 7–2, sided with a Louisiana inmate who had been beaten by guards while handcuffed and shackled.[6]

Further refining its standard for such claims, the Court held unanimously in 1994 that prison officials may be held liable for injuries to an inmate only if they know the prisoner faces a substantial risk of harm and fail to take reasonable measures to prevent it. The ruling reinstated a lawsuit brought by a male transsexual who was raped after being placed in the general population of a high-security penitentiary.[7]

1. *Rummel v. Estelle,* 445 U.S. 263 (1980).
2. *Carlson v. Green,* 446 U.S. 14 (1980).
3. *Solem v. Helm,* 463 U.S. 277 (1983).
4. *Harmelin v. Michigan,* 501 U.S. 957 (1991).
5. *Wilson v. Seiter,* 501 U.S. 294 (1991).
6. *Hudson v. McMillian,* 503 U.S. 1 (1992); see also *Helling v. McKinney,* 509 U.S. 25 (1993).
7. *Farmer v. Brennan,* 114 S. Ct. 1970 (1994).

victed of rapes and murders in 1967 and 1968, many just as reprehensible as these, the petitioners are among a capriciously selected random handful upon whom the sentence of death has in fact been imposed. . . . [T]he Eighth and Fourteenth Amendments cannot tolerate the infliction of a sentence of death under legal systems that permit this unique penalty to be so wantonly and so freakishly imposed.[15]

Justice White took a similar view:

The imposition and execution of the death penalty are obviously cruel in the dictionary sense. But the penalty has not been considered cruel and unusual punishment in the constitutional sense because it was thought justified by the social ends it was deemed to serve. At the moment that it ceases realistically to further these purposes, however, the emerging question is whether its imposition . . . would violate the Eighth Amendment. It is my view that it would, for its imposition would then be the pointless and needless extinction of life with only marginal contributions to any discernible social or public purposes. . . .

It is . . . my judgment that this point has been reached with respect to capital punishment as it is presently administered under the statutes involved in these cases.[16]

Justice Marshall found the death penalty both "excessive" and "morally unacceptable." He wrote that "the average citizen would, in my opinion, find it shocking to his conscience and sense of justice. For this reason alone capital punishment cannot stand."[17]

Justice Burger, writing for the dissenting justices, based their

position in large part on their view of the respective roles of judges and legislators:

If legislatures come to doubt the efficacy of capital punishment, they can abolish it, either completely or on a selective basis. If new evidence persuades them that they have acted unwisely, they can reverse their field and reinstate the penalty to the extent it is thought warranted. An Eighth Amendment ruling by judges cannot be made with such flexibility or discriminating precision.[18]

Furman effectively struck down all existing death penalty laws. In enacting new laws, states were given two options by the Court. They could remove almost all jury discretion from the decision by making death the mandatory punishment for certain crimes. Or the states could provide a two-stage procedure in capital cases—a trial at which the issue of guilt or innocence was determined and then, for those persons found guilty, a second proceeding at which evidence might be presented before the decision was reached on whether to impose a sentence of death.

Thirty-five states passed new death penalty statutes. Ten chose the mandatory route; the other twenty-five, the two-stage procedure. By 1976 both types of new laws were back before the Supreme Court, and the Court again was asked to declare whether death in and of itself was a cruel and unusual—hence unconstitutional—punishment for any crime in the United States.

The Eighth Amendment states that "[e]xcessive bail shall not be required." Throughout U.S. history, federal law has provided that persons arrested for noncapital offenses shall be granted the right to post bail and win release to participate in preparing their defense.

Bail is money or property pledged by an accused person to guarantee his or her appearance at trial. Failure to appear at trial—"jumping bail"—carries criminal penalties, plus forfeiture of the pledged bond.

The Supreme Court has held that a presumption in favor of granting bail exists in the Bill of Rights. Justice Horace Gray wrote in 1895:

The statutes of the United States have been framed upon the theory that a person accused of crime shall not, until he has been finally adjudged guilty in the court of last resort, be absolutely compelled to undergo imprisonment or punishment, but may be admitted to bail, not only after arrest and before trial, but after conviction and pending a writ of error.[1]

The Eighth Amendment's bail provisions limit federal courts, not state courts. In 1894 the Court ruled in *McKane v. Durston* that the Eighth Amendment provision on bail did not apply to the states.[2]

The Federal Rules of Criminal Procedure provide that the amount of bail shall be determined by the nature and circumstances of the offense, the weight of the evidence, the defendant's ability to pay, and his or her general character.[3] Under the 1966 Bail Reform Act, almost all persons charged with noncapital federal offenses are able to obtain release on personal recognizance or unsecured bond.[4]

The leading Supreme Court decision on the question of excessive bail is *Stack v. Boyle,* decided in 1951. Twelve communist leaders in California were indicted for conspiracy under the Alien Registration Act of 1940. Bail was fixed at $50,000 for each defendant. The defendants moved to reduce the amount of bail on the grounds that it was excessive in violation of the Eighth Amendment.

The Supreme Court agreed. Chief Justice Fred M. Vinson delivered the opinion of the unanimous Court. He wrote:

This traditional right to freedom before conviction permits the unhampered preparation of a defense, and serves to prevent the infliction of punishment prior to conviction. . . . Unless this right to bail before trial is preserved, the presumption of innocence, secured only after centuries of struggle, would lose its meaning.

The right to release before trial is conditioned upon the accused's giving adequate assurance that he will stand trial and submit to sentence if found guilty. . . . Bail set at a figure higher than an amount reasonably calculated to fulfill this purpose is "excessive" under the Eighth Amendment. . . .

If bail in an amount greater than that usually fixed for serious charges of crimes is required in the case of any of the petitioners, that is a matter to which evidence should be directed in a hearing. . . .

In the absence of such a showing, we are of the opinion that the fixing of bail before trial in these cases cannot be squared with the statutory and constitutional standards for admission to bail.[5]

The following spring, however, the Court held that the Eighth Amendment did not guarantee an absolute right to bail. Certain alien communists had been detained prior to a final determination on their deportation. Their application for bail was denied by the attorney general acting under provisions of the Internal Security Act of 1950.

The Court divided 5–4 in rejecting their argument that bail should be granted. Justice Stanley F. Reed, writing for the majority in *Carlson v. Landon*, stated that the Eighth Amendment did not guarantee everyone detained by federal authority the right to be released on bail:

The bail clause was lifted . . . from the English Bill of Rights Act. In England that clause has never been thought to accord a right to bail in all cases, but merely to provide that bail shall not be excessive in those cases where it is proper to grant bail. When this clause was carried over into our Bill of Rights, nothing was said that indicated any different concept. The Eighth Amendment has not prevented Congress from defining the classes of cases in which bail shall be allowed in this country. Thus, in criminal cases, bail is not compulsory where the punishment may be death. . . . We think, clearly, here that the Eighth Amendment does not require that bail be allowed.[6]

Justices Hugo L. Black, Felix Frankfurter, William O. Douglas, and Harold H. Burton dissented. Black wrote, "The plain purpose of our bail Amendment was to make it impossible for any agency of Government, even the Congress, to authorize keeping people imprisoned a moment longer than was necessary."[7]

Twice in the 1980s the Supreme Court approved the denial of bail to certain suspects. In 1984 it upheld the denial to dangerous juveniles, and in 1987 to organized crime figures.[8] In *United States v. Salerno*, Chief Justice William H. Rehnquist discussed the Eighth Amendment guarantee, pointing out that it "says nothing about whether bail shall be available at all."[9]

The primary function of bail, he acknowledged, "is to safeguard the courts' role in adjudicating the guilt or innocence of the defendants [by preventing flight]." But the Eighth Amendment does not deny the government the opportunity to regulate pretrial release for other reasons. "We believe," Rehnquist concluded, "that when Congress has mandated detention on the basis of a compelling interest other than prevention of flight, as it has here, the Eighth Amendment does not require release on bail."[10]

1. *Hudson v. Parker,* 156 U.S. 277 at 285 (1895).
2. *McKane v. Durston,* 153 U.S. 684 (1894).
3. Federal Rules of Criminal Procedure, Rule 46(c).
4. *Congress and the Nation,* Vol. II (Washington, D.C.: Congressional Quarterly, 1969), 315–316.
5. *Stack v. Boyle,* 342 U.S. 1 at 4–5, 6, 7 (1951).
6. *Carlson v. Landon,* 342 U.S. 524 at 545–546 (1952).
7. Id. at 557–558.
8. *Schall v. Martin, Abrams v. Martin,* 467 U.S. 253 (1984); *United States v. Salerno,* 481 U.S. 739 (1987).
9. *United States v. Salerno,* 481 U.S. 739 at 752 (1987).
10. Id. at 753, 755.

FORFEITING THE GOODS

As part of the 1980s war against drug trafficking, Congress and many states gave law enforcement agencies new power to seize money, goods, and property from criminal defendants or suspects.

While these laws permitted confiscation of billions of dollars of property, they also provoked charges from defense lawyers and civil libertarians that the government was seizing the property not only of criminals but also of people who had unknowingly received the proceeds of criminal activities. Critics also charged that the value of the property seized sometimes far outweighed the seriousness of the offense.

Several disputes percolated up to the Supreme Court, and in June 1993 the justices ruled that the Eighth Amendment limits the government's power to seize assets. The Court held unanimously that the prohibition against excessive fines restricts the government's power in civil forfeiture proceedings.

The case of *Austin v. United States* involved a South Dakota man whose mobile home and auto body shop, valued at about $38,000, were seized in a civil forfeiture after he had pleaded guilty to selling two grams of cocaine to an undercover agent.

Rejecting the government's arguments to the contrary, the Court held that the Eighth Amendment did apply to civil proceedings and that its excessive fines clause did apply to forfeiture. "The purpose of the Eighth Amendment . . . was to limit the government's power to punish," wrote Harry A. Blackmun for the five-justice majority. He said that it should be left to lower courts to set the standard that should be used to determine when a forfeiture is "excessive."[1]

In a separate case, the Court said that the government cannot seize property brought with drug money by someone who did not know the source of the funds.[2]

The following December, the Court ruled that a property owner is ordinarily entitled to notice and a hearing before the government can seize real estate through civil forfeiture.[3]

In 1996 the Court moved in another direction, rejecting, in two separate cases, challenges to government's aggressive use of civil forfeiture. The first case was brought by a Michigan woman, Tina Bennis, who lost the family car after her husband, John, was caught in it committing a sex act with a prostitute. The automobile, which was jointly owned by the Bennises, was seized under a state public nuisance statute. Mrs. Bennis, as an innocent owner, protested the seizure, contending she did not know her husband would use their car to break the law. By a 5–4 vote, the Court said that a co-owner's lack of knowledge of the wrongdoing is not sufficient defense. The majority emphasized that Michigan wanted to deter activity that contributed to neighborhood deterioration and unsafe streets, and that the Bennis car had indeed facilitated such activity.[4]

In a separate case, the Court ruled that the seizure of property in a civil forfeiture proceeding is not "punishment" within the scope of the constitutional guarantee against double jeopardy. The justices overturned two lower court decisions that said government could not both punish a defendant for a criminal offense and seize his property for that same offense in a separate civil proceeding. The justices distinguished the case from the 1993 ruling in *Austin v. United States* by noting that the earlier case challenged seizure of assets under the Excessive Fines Clause of the Eighth Amendment. The different constitutional grounds required a different legal analysis from that triggered by a challenge based on the Fifth Amendment's double jeopardy provision.[5]

1. *Austin v. United States*, 509 U.S. 602 (1993). See also *Alexander v. United States*, 509 U.S. ____ (1993).
2. *United States v. A Parcel of Land, Buildings, Appurtenances and Improvements, known as 92 Buena Vista Ave.*, ____ U.S. ____ (1993).
3. *United States v. James Daniel Good Real Property*, 510 U.S. 43 (1993).
4. *Bennis v. Michigan*, 516 U.S. ____ (1996).
5. *United States v. Ursery*, ____ U.S. ____ (1996). See also *Libretti v. United States*, 516 U.S. ____ (1996).

The Court refused to outlaw capital punishment in 1976. In *Gregg v. Georgia* and two companion cases, *Proffitt v. Florida* and *Jurek v. Texas*, the Court refused to declare the death penalty unconstitutional in all circumstances.

Justice Stewart set out the majority position:

[W]e are concerned here only with the imposition of capital punishment for the crime of murder, and when a life has been taken deliberately by the offender, we cannot say that the punishment is invariably disproportionate to the crime. It is an extreme sanction, suitable to the most extreme of crimes.[19]

So the Court would not overrule the judgment of state legislatures and declare capital punishment *per se* unconstitutional. Justice Stewart continued:

Considerations of federalism, as well as respect for the ability of a legislature to evaluate, in terms of its particular State, the moral consensus concerning the death penalty and its social utility as a sanction, require us to conclude, in the absence of more convincing evidence, that the infliction of death as a punishment for murder is not without justification and thus is not unconstitutionally severe. . . .

. . . We hold that the death penalty is not a form of punishment that may never be imposed, regardless of the circumstances of the offense, regardless of the character of the offender, and regardless of the procedure followed in reaching the decision to impose it.[20]

Justices Brennan and Marshall dissented. Brennan argued that death was now an uncivilized and unconstitutional punishment. The Court "inescapably has the duty, as the ultimate arbiter of the meaning of our Constitution, to say whether . . . 'moral concepts' require us to hold that the law has progressed to the point where we should declare that the punishment of death, like punishments on the rack, the screw and the wheel, is no longer morally tolerable in our civilized society."[21]

Justice Marshall found death an excessive, shocking, and unjust punishment in all cases, and would declare it invariably cruel and unusual punishment, forbidden by the Eighth Amendment.

Of equal or greater practical significance, the Court in *Gregg, Jurek,* and *Proffitt* approved as constitutional the new two-stage procedure adopted by Georgia, Florida, Texas, and twenty-two other states for imposing the death sentence. This procedure, wrote Justice Stewart, met the objections that had caused the Court in *Furman* to invalidate the existing state laws:

The basic concern of *Furman* centered on those defendants who were being condemned to death capriciously and arbitrarily. Under the procedures before the Court in that case, sentencing authorities were not directed to give attention to the nature or circumstances of the crime committed or to the character or record of the defendant. Left unguided, juries imposed the death sentence in a way that could only be called freakish. The new . . . sentencing procedures, by contrast, focus the jury's attention on the particularized nature of the crime and the particularized characteristics of the individual defendant. While the jury is permitted to consider any aggravating or mitigating circumstances, it must find and identify at least one statutory aggravating factor before it may impose a penalty of death. In this way the jury's discretion is channeled. No longer can a jury wantonly and freakishly impose the death sentence; it is always circumscribed by the legislative guidelines.[22]

The same day—July 2, 1976—the Court struck down state laws that made death the mandatory penalty for first-degree murder. This ruling came in *Woodson v. North Carolina* and *Roberts v. Louisiana.*[23]

The Court divided 5–4; Justices Brennan and Marshall became part of the majority with Justices Stewart, Powell, and John Paul Stevens. Chief Justice Burger and Justices Blackmun, White, and Rehnquist dissented.

The Court held that mandatory death penalty statutes "simply papered over the problem of unguided and unchecked jury discretion" and were constitutionally unsatisfactory because they failed to allow room for consideration of the individual defendant and the particular crime.[24]

The majority refused to approve "[a] process that accords no significance to relevant facets of the character and record of the individual offender or the circumstances of the particular offense." Such a process "excludes from consideration in fixing the ultimate punishment of death the possibility of compassionate or mitigating factors stemming from the diverse frailties of humankind."[25]

In capital cases, the majority opinion concluded, "the fundamental respect for humanity underlying the Eighth Amendment . . . requires consideration of the character and record of the individual offender and the circumstances of the particular offense as a constitutionally indispensable part of the process of inflicting the penalty of death."[26]

Subsequently, the Court used similar reasoning in striking down a state law that made death the mandatory sentence for anyone convicted of the first-degree murder of a police officer, or for a prison inmate serving a life sentence without possibility of parole and yet convicted of murdering a fellow inmate.[27]

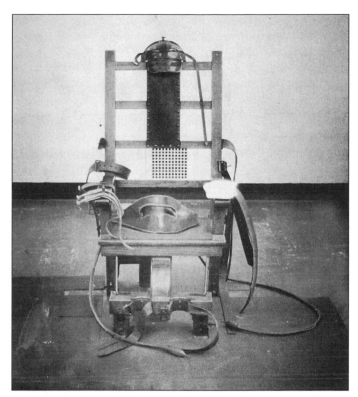

This electric chair once was used to carry out death sentences in Washington, D.C.

The Continuing Review

Although *Gregg* and *Woodson* left little doubt about the Court's belief in the constitutionality of the death penalty, a steady stream of capital punishment cases continued to come to the Court over the next several decades. Some argued that laws approved in *Gregg* had been misapplied in a particular case, others brought broad new challenges to the death penalty itself.

As the Court resolved these cases, it defined more closely the scope of crimes for which death might be an appropriate punishment—and the procedures by which that sentence might be imposed.

One set of cases involved the question of what crimes merited the penalty of death. In 1977 in *Coker v. Georgia* the Court held that death was an excessive penalty for the crime of rape, striking down state laws that made rape a capital crime.[28]

Can a death sentence be imposed upon someone who participated in a crime that included murder but who was not the killer? That question was addressed several times by the Court. In *Enmund v. Florida* in 1982, the Court, 5–4, overturned a death sentence imposed upon the driver of a getaway car who neither killed anyone nor witnessed the killings. It was disproportionate, and therefore cruel and unusual, for him to be sentenced to death, wrote Justice White for the majority. Chief Justice Burger and Justices Rehnquist, Powell, and Sandra Day O'Connor dissented.[29]

Five years later, however, the Court narrowed *Enmund* in another 5–4 decision, *Tison v. Arizona.* O'Connor wrote the opinion. Justice White joined the majority in this case. The Court ruled that accomplices could indeed be executed if their participation in the crime was major and if they displayed reckless indifference to the value of human life.[30]

RELEVANT FACTORS

In 1978 the Court invalidated Ohio's death penalty law for murder because it limited too strictly the sort of mitigating factors that could be considered in the decision whether to impose the death penalty. Chief Justice Burger wrote for the Court in *Lockett v. Ohio, Bell v. Ohio.* Only Justice Rehnquist dissented.[31]

The Eighth Amendment requires that the sentencing judge or jury consider *all* relevant aspects of an individual offender's character, record, and crime—particularly any mitigating factors—before rendering a sentence.[32]

The Court in 1987 held unconstitutional the use of "victim impact statements" describing to the jury the effect of a murder on a victim's family. This, the Court held 5–4, created a risk that a jury might impose a sentence of death in arbitrary and capricious fashion.[33]

Only four years later, however, the Court reversed that decision and ruled that evidence of a victim's character and the impact of a crime on a victim's family may be used against a murder defendant in the sentencing phase of a capital case. The vote was 6–3. Writing for the majority, Chief Justice Rehnquist said, "We are now of the view that a state may properly conclude that for the jury to assess meaningfully the defendant's moral culpability and blameworthiness, it should have before it at the sentencing phase evidence of the specific harm caused by the defendant."[34]

JURY QUESTIONS

The power and the composition of juries in capital cases also drew the Court's attention. In 1984 the Court, 6–3, held that a judge was free to disregard a jury's recommendation of a life sentence and to impose a sentence of death instead. Nothing in the Constitution gave juries sole power to impose a death sentence, the Court held in *Spaziano v. Florida.*[35]

And the following year the Court overturned its 1968 ruling in *Witherspoon,* which made it difficult for prosecutors to exclude jurors with scruples about the death penalty. The new rules adopted by the Court made exclusion of death penalty opponents easier, and hence made it more likely that juries would impose a sentence of death.

With Rehnquist as its spokesman, the Court, 7–2, declared that a juror could be excluded when his views would "prevent or substantially impair the performance of his duties as a juror in accordance with his instructions and oath." This rule, adopted in *Wainwright v. Witt* (1985), was much more permissive than *Witherspoon,* which permitted exclusion only if it was unmistakable that a juror's opposition to the death penalty was so strong as to prevent the juror from making an impartial decision on the defendant's guilt.[36]

The following year the Court reaffirmed the more relaxed

INNOCENTS ON DEATH ROW

Does the Constitution permit the execution of an innocent person? This question came to the Court in the 1993 case of Texas prisoner Leonel Herrera, sentenced to death for killing a police officer.

Ten years after his conviction, Herrera filed a federal habeas corpus petition—his second—claiming that newly discovered evidence showed someone else committed the crime. On that basis, he argued that his execution would violate the Eighth Amendment's ban on cruel and unusual punishment and the Fourteenth Amendment's due process clause.

By 6–3, the justices said a death row inmate ordinarily is not entitled to federal habeas corpus relief based solely on a claim of innocence, rather than a claim of constitutional error in his state court trial or other proceedings.

The Court said federal courts should not consider Herrera's "actual innocence" claim. "[F]ederal habeas courts sit to ensure that individuals are not imprisoned in violation of the Constitution—not to correct errors of fact," Chief Justice William H. Rehnquist wrote. In the majority's view, the refusal of Texas courts to consider Herrera's new evidence so long after his conviction did not violate "principles of fundamental fairness."

Instead of seeking help through this remedy in the courts, Rehnquist suggested that Herrera seek executive clemency, which Rehnquist called the "historic remedy for preventing miscarriages of justice." (*Herrera v. Collins,* 506 U.S. 390, 1993)

---

stance taken in *Wainwright.* Exclusion of opponents of the death penalty from juries, it said, did not offend the constitutional requirement that the jury be drawn from a cross section of the community and that it be impartial.

But in 1987 the Court ruled that if a potential juror was wrongly disqualified for expressing doubts about capital punishment, the defendant was entitled to a new trial. And in the case of *Morgan v. Illinois* in 1992, the Court, 6–3, said a criminal defendant has a constitutional right to ask potential jurors if they automatically would impose the death penalty if they found the defendant guilty of murder. A potential juror answering in the affirmative rightfully can be excluded by the defendant.[37]

EQUITY ISSUES

Questions of proportionality and equity in the treatment of capital defendants were addressed in several cases. In 1984 the Court rebuffed the argument that the Constitution required state courts to review a death sentence to ensure that it was proportional to the punishment imposed on others convicted of similar crimes. Such review was permitted but not required by the Constitution, the Court held, 7–2, in *Pulley v. Harris.*[38]

Three years later the Court held, 5–4, that statistics showing race-related disparities in the imposition of the death penalty

Warren McCleskey based the appeal of his death sentence on a study showing that someone convicted of killing a white person was four times more likely to receive the death penalty than someone convicted of killing a black person. His appeal was rejected in *McCleskey v. Kemp* (1987), and he was executed in 1991.

were not enough to sustain constitutional challenges to state death penalty laws.

For the majority Justice Powell wrote that "apparent disparities in sentencing are an inevitable part of our criminal justice system."

The disparities shown in this case, *McCleskey v. Kemp*, were not so great as to warrant striking down the entire system. Justices Brennan, Marshall, Blackmun, and Stevens dissented.[39]

QUESTIONS OF RESPONSIBILITY

Another category of capital punishment cases has focused on the question of responsibility: are there groups of persons who by reason of youth, disability, or illness cannot constitutionally be executed for their crimes?

The Court has held that the Constitution forbids the execution of prisoners who are insane and cannot understand the reason for their execution. But just three years after that ruling, it permitted execution of a person who was mentally retarded but had been found competent to stand trial.[40]

In 1988 the Court ruled that a state could not execute a defendant who was younger than sixteen at the time of the crime. Indicators of contemporary standards of decency, wrote Justice Stevens in *Thompson v. Oklahoma*, "confirm our judgment that such a young person is not capable of acting with the degree of culpability that can justify the ultimate penalty." Of the eighteen states that in 1988 set a minimum age for the death penalty, all of them required that age to be at least sixteen, he noted.[41] The following year, however, the Court drew the line at sixteen years of age, refusing to bar a state from executing a convicted criminal who was only sixteen or seventeen at the time he or she committed a capital crime.[42]

And in 1991 the Court held that no one should be sentenced

to death who has not been informed that his crime is a capital one and that a sentence of death is a possibility for him. The Court ruled that an Idaho murder defendant's right to due process was violated when a judge sentenced him to death without his knowing the death penalty was under consideration. Separately, the justices held that if prosecutors are using a defendant's dangerousness as an argument for imposing the death sentence, the jury must be told it has the option of sentencing the defendant to life in prison without parole as well as death.[43]

NOTES

INTRODUCTION (PP. 559–562)

1. *Joint Anti-Fascist Refugee Committee v. McGrath*, 341 U.S. 123 at 179 (1951).
2. David Fellman, *The Defendant's Rights* (New York: Rinehart, 1958), 3–4.
3. *Barron v. Baltimore*, 7 Pet. 243 (1833).
4. Id. at 247, 250–251.
5. *Murray's Lessee v. Hoboken Land and Improvement Co.*, 18 How. 272 (1856).
6. Id. at 276–277.
7. *Shaughnessy v. United States ex rel. Mezei*, 345 U.S. 206 at 224 (1953).
8. *Hurtado v. California*, 110 U.S. 516 (1884); see also *Pennoyer v. Neff*, 95 U.S. 714 (1878).
9. *Hurtado v. California*, 110 U.S. 516 at 537 (1884).
10. Id. at 535–536.
11. Id. at 547–548.
12. *Davidson v. New Orleans*, 95 U.S. 97 at 104 (1878).
13. *Maxwell v. Dow*, 1976 U.S. 581 at 614 (1900).
14. *Twining v. New Jersey*, 211 U.S. 78 at 110–111 (1908).
15. Id. at 99.
16. *Palko v. Connecticut*, 302 U.S. 319 at 325 (1937).
17. *Adamson v. California*, 332 U.S. 46 at 53 (1947).
18. Id. at 89.

A FAIR TRIAL (PP. 563–572)

1. *Frank v. Mangum*, 237 U.S. 309 (1915).
2. *Moore v. Dempsey*, 261 U.S. 86 at 91 (1923).
3. *Tumey v. Ohio*, 273 U.S. 510 (1927).
4. Id. at 523.
5. *Dugan v. Ohio*, 277 U.S. 261 (1928).
6. *Ward v. Village of Monroeville*, 409 U.S. 57 at 60 (1972).
7. *North v. Russell*, 427 U.S. 328 at 337, 339 (1976); see also *Fisher v. Pace*, 336 U.S. 155 (1949); *Sacher v. United States*, 343 U.S. 1 (1952).
8. *Colgrove v. Battin*, 413 U.S. 149 (1973).
9. *Patton v. United States*, 281 U.S. 276 at 288 (1930); see also *Singer v. United States*, 380 U.S. 24 (1965).
10. *Walker v. Sauvinet*, 92 U.S. 90 (1876).
11. *Maxwell v. Dow*, 176 U.S. 581 at 603 (1900).
12. *Duncan v. Louisiana*, 391 U.S. 145 (1968); but see *Blanton v. City of North Las Vegas*, 489 U.S. 538 (1989).
13. Id. at 149.
14. *Williams v. Florida*, 399 U.S. 78 (1970).
15. Id. at 98–101.
16. *Ballew v. Georgia*, 435 U.S. 223 (1978).
17. *Baldwin v. New York*, 399 U.S. 66 (1970).
18. *Johnson v. Louisiana*, 406 U.S. 356 (1972); *Apodaca v. Oregon*, 406 U.S. 404 (1972).
19. *Johnson v. Louisiana*, 406 U.S. 356 at 359 (1972).
20. Id. at 359, 362.
21. *Burch v. Louisiana*, 441 U.S. 130 (1979); *Brown v. Louisiana*, 447 U.S. 323 (1980).
22. *Smith v. Texas*, 311 U.S. 128 at 130 (1940).
23. *Taylor v. Louisiana*, 419 U.S. 522 (1975); *Duren v. Missouri*, 439 U.S. 357 (1979).
24. *Congress and the Nation*, Vol. II (Washington, D.C.: Congressional Quarterly, 1969), 385.
25. *Ex parte Virginia*, 100 U.S. 339 (1880); *Strauder v. West Virginia*, 100 U.S. 303 (1880); see also *Rose v. Mitchell*, 443 U.S. 545 (1979).
26. *Virginia v. Rives*, 100 U.S. 313 (1880).
27. *Norris v. Alabama*, 294 U.S. 587 (1935).
28. Id. at 590.
29. *Patton v. Mississippi*, 332 U.S. 463 at 469 (1947).
30. *Brown v. Allen*, 344 U.S. 443 (1953).
31. *Cassell v. Texas*, 339 U.S. 282 (1950); *Whitus v. Georgia*, 385 U.S. 545 (1967); *Avery v. Georgia*, 345 U.S. 559 (1952).
32. *Hernandez v. Texas*, 347 U.S. 475 (1954).
33. *Vasquez v. Hillery*, 474 U.S. 254 (1986).
34. *Batson v. Kentucky*, 476 U.S. 79 (1986); see also *Griffith v. Kentucky, Brown v. United States*, 479 U.S. 314 (1987).
35. *Edmonson v. Leesville Concrete Co.*, 500 U.S. 614 (1991), *Powers v. Ohio*, 499 U.S. 400 (1991).
36. *Georgia v. McCollum*, 505 U.S. 42 (1992).
37. *Ballard v. United States*, 329 U.S. 187 (1946); *Hoyt v. Florida*, 368 U.S. 57 (1961).
38. Id. at 62.
39. *Taylor v. Louisiana*, 419 U.S. 522 (1975).
40. *Duren v. Missouri*, 439 U.S. 357 (1979).
41. *J. E. B. v. Alabama*, 114 S. Ct. 1419 (1994).
42. *Fay v. New York*, 332 U.S. 261 at 270–272 (1947); see also *Moore v. New York*, 333 U.S. 565 (1948).
43. Id. at 299–300.
44. *Beavers v. Haubert*, 198 U.S. 77 at 87 (1905).
45. *United States v. Provoo*, 350 U.S. 857 (1955); see also *Pollard v. United States*, 352 U.S. 354 (1957); *United States v. Ewell*, 383 U.S. 116 (1966).
46. *Strunk v. United States*, 412 U.S. 434 (1973).
47. *United States v. Marion*, 404 U.S. 307 at 313 (1971).
48. *United States v. Lovasco*, 431 U.S. 783 (1977).
49. Id. at 790–791, 795–796.
50. *Klopfer v. North Carolina*, 386 U.S. 213 (1967).
51. Id. at 222–223.
52. *Barker v. Wingo*, 407 U.S. 514 (1972).
53. Id. at 530, 533.
54. *Congress and the Nation*, Vol. IV (Washington, D.C.: Congressional Quarterly, 1977), 576; see also *United States v. Taylor*, 485 U.S. 902 (1988).
55. *United States v. MacDonald*, 435 U.S. 850 (1982); see also *United States v. Loud Hawk*, 474 U.S. 302 (1986).
56. *Doggett v. United States*, 505 U.S. 647 (1990).
57. *Mattox v. United States*, 156 U.S. 237 at 242–243 (1895).
58. *Kirby v. United States*, 174 U.S. 47 at 55 (1899).
59. Id. at 56.
60. *Pointer v. Texas*, 380 U.S. 400 (1965); see also *Douglas v. Alabama*, 380 U.S. 415 (1965).
61. *California v. Green*, 399 U.S. 149 (1970); *Dutton v. Evans*, 400 U.S. 74 (1970). See also *Harrington v. California*, 395 U.S. 250 (1969); *Nelson v. O'Neil*, 402 U.S. 622 (1971); *Schneble v. Florida*, 405 U.S. 427 (1972); *United States v. Inadi*, 475 U.S. 387 (1986); *Delaware v. Van Arsdall*, 475 U.S. 673 (1986); *Richardson v. Marsh*, 481 U.S. 200 (1987), *Cruz v. New York*, 482 U.S. 186 (1987).
62. *Chambers v. Mississippi*, 410 U.S. 284 (1973).
63. *Davis v. Alaska*, 415 U.S. 308 (1974).
64. *Coy v. Iowa*, 487 U.S. 1012 (1988).
65. *Maryland v. Craig*, 110 S.Ct. 3157 (1990).
66. *Idaho v. Wright*, 497 U.S. 805 (1990); see also White v. Illinois, 502 U.S. 346 (1992).
67. *Michigan v. Lucas*, 500 U.S. 145 (1991).

SEARCH AND SEIZURE (PP. 573–588)

1. *Wolf v. Colorado*, 338 U.S. 25 at 27–28 (1949).
2. *Camara v. Municipal Court*, 387 U.S. 523 at 528–529 (1967).
3. *GM Leasing Corporation v. United States*, 429 U.S. 338 (1977); *Michigan v. Tyler*, 436 U.S. 499 (1978); *Mincey v. Arizona*, 437 U.S. 385 (1978); but see also *Oliver v. United States, Maine v. Thornton*, 466 U.S. 170 (1984); *California v. Ciraolo*, 476 U.S. 207 (1986); *Dow Chemical v. United States*, 476 U.S. 227 (1986); *California v. Acevedo*, 500 U.S. 565 (1991).
4. *Wolf v. Colorado*, 338 U.S. 25 (1949).
5. *Mapp v. Ohio*, 367 U.S. 643 (1961).
6. *Ker v. California*, 374 U.S. 23 (1963).
7. *Johnson v. United States*, 333 U.S. 10 at 13–14 (1948).
8. *Coolidge v. New Hampshire*, 403 U.S. 443 at 453 (1971); see also *Lo-Ji Sales v. New York*, 442 U.S. 319 (1979).
9. *Shadwick v. City of Tampa, Fla.*, 407 U.S. 345 at 350 (1972).
10. *Locke v. United States*, 7 Cr. 339 at 348 (1813); see *Arizona v. Hicks*, 480 U.S. 321 (1987).
11. *Dumbra v. United States*, 268 U.S. 435 at 441 (1925); see also *Byars v. United States*, 273 U.S. 28 (1927); *Draper v. United States*, 358 U.S. 307 (1959).
12. *Nathanson v. United States*, 290 U.S. 41 at 47 (1933); see also *Giordanello v. United States*, 357 U.S. 480 (1958); *Aguilar v. Texas*, 378 U.S. 108 (1964); *Spinelli v. United States*, 393 U.S. 410 (1969); *United States v. Ventresca*, 380 U.S. 102 at 108–109 (1965).
13. *Jones v. United States*, 362 U.S. 257 (1960).
14. *Rugendorf v. United States*, 367 U.S. 528 (1964); *McCray v. Illinois*, 386 U.S. 300 (1967); see also *Whitely v. Warden*, 401 U.S. 560 (1971); *United States v. Harris*, 403 U.S. 573 (1971); *Adams v. Williams*, 407 U.S. 143 (1972); *Alabama v. White*, 496 U.S. 325 (1990).
15. *Franks v. Delaware*, 438 U.S. 154 at 168 (1978).
16. *Schneckloth v. Bustamonte*, 412 U.S. 218 at 248–249 (1973).
17. Id. at 277.
18. *United States v. Matlock*, 415 U.S. 164 (1974).
19. *Minnesota v. Olson*, 495 U.S. 91 (1990); see also *United States v. Padilla*, 508 U.S. 77 (1993).
20. *Boyd v. United States*, 116 U.S. 616 (1886).
21. Id. at 630, 633.
22. *Weeks v. United States*, 232 U.S. 383 (1914).
23. Id. at 392–393.

24. *Gouled v. United States*, 255 U.S. 298 (1921).

25. Id. at 309.

26. *Warden v. Hayden*, 387 U.S. 294 (1967).

27. Id. at 301–302.

28. Id. at 304, 306.

29. Id. at 306–307.

30. Id. at 309–310.

31. Id. at 320.

32. Id. at 323.

33. Id. at 325.

34. *United States v. Miller*, 425 U.S. 435 (1976).

35. *Andresen v. Maryland*, 427 U.S. 463 (1976).

36. *Zurcher v. The Stanford Daily*, 436 U.S. 547 at 554 (1978).

37. Id. at 579.

38. Id. at 581–583.

39. *Ex parte Burford*, 3 Cr. 448 (1805); *Kurtz v. Moffitt*, 115 U.S. 487 (1885).

40. *Carroll v. United States*, 267 U.S. 132 at 156 (1925).

41. *Gerstein v. Pugh*, 420 U.S. 103 at 113 (1975).

42. *Ker v. California*, 374 U.S. 23 (1963).

43. *Davis v. Mississippi*, 394 U.S. 721 at 727 (1969); *Dunaway v. New York*, 442 U.S. 200 (1979).

44. *United States v. Watson*, 423 U.S. 411 (1976).

45. Id. at 423–424.

46. Id. at 447.

47. *United States v. Santana*, 427 U.S. 38 (1976). For use of the term "hot pursuit," see *Johnson v. United States*, 333 U.S. 10 at 16, note 7 (1948).

48. *United States v. Santana*, 427 U.S. 38 at 42–43 (1976).

49. *Payton v. New York, Riddick v. New York*, 445 U.S. 573 (1980); see also *Welsh v. Wisconsin*, 466 U.S. 740 (1984).

50. *Wilson v. Arkansas*, 115 S. Ct. 1914 (1995).

51. *Agnello v. United States*, 269 U.S. 20 at 30 (1925); *Marron v. United States* 275 U.S. 192 (1927).

52. *Harris v. United States*, 331 U.S. 145 (1947)

53. Id. at 150–151.

54. Id. at 183.

55. *Trupiano v. United States*, 334 U.S. 699 at 706 (1948).

56. Id. at 708.

57. Id.

58. *McDonald v. United States*, 335 U.S. 451 at 454, 456 (1948).

59. *United States v. Rabinowitz*, 339 U.S. 56 at 66 (1950).

60. Id. at 63, 66.

61. *Kremen v. United States*, 353 U.S. 346 (1957); *Abel v. United States*, 362 U.S. 217 at 238 (1960); *Chapman v. United States*, 365 U.S. 610 (1961); *Ker v. California*, 374 U.S. 23 (1963).

62. *Chimel v. California*, 395 U.S. 752 (1969).

63. Id. at 766, 768.

64. Id. at 780.

65. *Vale v. Louisiana*, 399 U.S. 30 (1970).

66. *Coolidge v. New Hampshire*, 403 U.S. 443 (1971); see also *United States v. Edwards*, 415 U.S. 800 (1974).

67. *United States v. Robinson*, 414 U.S. 218 (1973); *Gustafson v. Florida*, 414 U.S. 260 (1973).

68. *Carroll v. United States*, 267 U.S. 132 (1925).

69. Id. at 153.

70. *Husty v. United States*, 282 U.S. 694 (1931); see also *Scher v. United States*, 305 U.S. 251 (1938).

71. *United States v. Di Re*, 332 U.S. 581 (1948).

72. *Brinegar v. United States*, 338 U.S. 160 (1949); see also *California v. Carney*, 471 U.S. 386 (1985).

73. *Henry v. United States*, 361 U.S. 98 (1959); *Rios v. United States*, 364 U.S. 253 (1960).

74. *Cooper v. California*, 386 U.S. 58 (1967).

75. *Chambers v. Maroney*, 399 U.S. 42 (1970); *Preston v. United States*, 376 U.S. 364 (1964).

76. *Cady v. Dombrowski*, 413 U.S. 433 (1973); *South Dakota v. Opperman*, 428 U.S. 364 (1976).

77. *Cardwell v. Lewis*, 417 U.S. 583 (1974).

78. *Rakas v. Illinois*, 439 U.S. 128 (1978).

79. Id. at 409.

80. *Delaware v. Prouse*, 440 U.S. 648 (1979).

81. *Robbins v. California*, 453 U.S. 420 (1981).

82. *United States v. Ross*, 456 U.S. 798 (1982).

83. *California v. Acevedo*, 500 U.S. 565 (1991).

84. *Michigan v. Sitz*, 496 U.S. 444 (1990).

85. Id.

86. *Florida v. Bostick*, 501 U.S. 429 (1991).

87. *Whren v. United States*, ____ U.S. ____ (1996).

88. *United States v. Armstrong*, ____ U.S. ____ (1996).

89. *Olmstead v. United States*, 277 U.S. 438 at 463 466 (1928).

90. Id. at 469–470.

91. Id. at 473, 485.

92. *Nardone v. United States*, 302 U.S. 379 (1937); *Weiss v. United States*, 308 U.S. 321 (1939); *Nardone v. United States*, 308 U.S. 338 (1939); see also *Rathbun v. United States*, 355 U.S. 107 (1957); *Benanti v. United States*, 355 U.S. 96 (1957).

93. *Goldstein v. United States*, 316 U.S. 114 (1942); *Goldman v. United States*, 316 U.S. 129 (1942); see also *On Lee v. United States*, 343 U.S. 747 (1952).

94. *Silverman v. United States*, 365 U.S. 505 (1961); see also *Wong Sun v. United States*, 371 U.S. 471 (1963); *Berger v. New York*, 388 U.S. 41 (1967); *Osborn v. United States*, 385 U.S. 323 (1966).

95. *Katz v. United States*, 389 U.S. 247 (1967).

96. Id. at 353.

97. Id. at 351.

98. *Alderman v. United States, Butenko v. United States, Ivanov v. United States*, 394 U.S. 165 (1969).

99. *Congress and the Nation*, Vol. II (Washington, D.C.: Congressional Quarterly, 1969), 326–327.

100. *United States v. U.S. District Court, Eastern Michigan*, 407 U.S. 297 (1972).

101. *United States v. Giordano*, 416 U.S. 505 (1974).

102. *Dalia v. United States*, 441 U.S. 238 (1979).

SELF-INCRIMINATION (PP. 589–598)

1. *Bruno v. United States*, 308 U.S. 287 (1939); *Griffin v. California*, 380 U.S. 609 (1965); *United States v. Hale*, 422 U.S. 171 (1975); *Doyle v. Ohio, Wood v. Ohio*, 427 U.S. 610 (1976).

2. *Hoffman v. United States*, 341 U.S. 479 (1951); *Mason v. United States*, 244 U.S. 362 (1917); *Rogers v. United States*, 340 U.S. 367 (1951); *United States v. Monia*, 317 U.S. 424 (1943).

3. *Emspak v. United States*, 349 U.S. 190 (1955).

4. *Heike v. United States*, 227 U.S. 131 (1913); *Brown v. Walker*, 161 U.S. 591 (1896).

5. *Rogers v. United States*, 340 U.S. 367 at 372–374 (1951); see also *Blau v. United States*, 340 U.S. 159 (1950).

6. *Hale v. Henkel*, 201 U.S. 43 (1906); *United States v. White*, 322 U.S. 694 (1944); *Bellis v. United States*, 417 U.S. 85 (1974).

7. *Wilson v. United States*, 221 U.S. 361 (1911); *Shapiro v. United States*, 335 U.S. 1 (1948); see also *Mancusi v. DeForte*, 392 U.S. 364 (1968); *Couch v. United States*, 409 U.S. 322 (1973); *United States v. Kasmir, Fisher v. United States*, 425 U.S. 391 (1976).

8. *Garrity v. New Jersey*, 385 U.S. 493 (1967); *Spevack v. Klein*, 385 U.S. 511 (1967); *Slochower v. Board of Higher Education of New York City*, 350 U.S. 551 (1956); *Garner v. Broderick*, 392 U.S. 273 (1968); *Lefkowitz v. Cunningham*, 431 U.S. 801 (1977).

9. *United States v. Doremus*, 249 U.S. 86 (1919); *United States v. Sanchez*, 340 U.S. 42 (1950); *Sonzinsky v. United States*, 300 U.S. 506 (1937); *United States v. Kahriger*, 345 U.S. 22 (1953).

10. *Albertson v. Subversive Activities Control Board*, 382 U.S. 70 (1965).

11. *Grosso v. United States*, 390 U.S. 62 (1968); *Marchetti v. United States*, 390 U.S. 39 (1968); *Haynes v. United States*, 390 U.S. 85 (1968); *Leary v. Unit-

ed States, 395 U.S. 6 (1969); see also *Minor v. United States, Buie v. United States*, 396 U.S. 87 (1969); *United States v. Freed*, 41 U.S. 601 (1971).

12. *Kastigar v. United States*, 406 U.S. 441 at 446 (1972).

13. *Counselman v. Hitchcock*, 142 U.S. 547 at 585–586 (1892).

14. Id.

15. *Brown v. Walker*, 161 U.S. 591 at 595, 596, 605–606, 610 (1896).

16. *Ullmann v. United States*, 350 U.S. 422 at 438 (1956).

17. Id. at 438–439.

18. Id. at 440.

19. Id. at 449, 454.

20. *Congress and the Nation*, Vol. III (Washington, D.C.: Congressional Quarterly, 1973), 273.

21. *Kastigar v. United States*, 406 U.S. 441 at 453 (1972).

22. Id. at 460.

23. Id. at 466–467.

24. *Twining v. New Jersey*, 211 U.S. 78 at 106 (1908).

25. *Adamson v. California*, 332 U.S. 46 at 54 (1947).

26. *United States v. Murdock*, 284 U.S. 141 (1931); *Feldman v. United States*, 322 U.S. 487 (1944); *Knapp v. Schweitzer*, 357 U.S. 371 (1958).

27. *Malloy v. Hogan*, 378 U.S. 1 at 8, 11 (1964).

28. Id at 16, 27.

29. *Murphy v. The Waterfront Commission of New York Harbor*, 378 U.S. 52 at 79 (1964).

30. *Griffin v. California*, 380 U.S. 609 at 615 (1965).

31. Id. at 614; see also *Lakeside v. Oregon*, 435 U.S. 333 (1978).

32. *Hopt v. Utah*, 110 U.S. 574 at 585 (1884).

33. *Bram v. United States*, 168 U.S. 532 (1897).

34. *Hopt v. Utah*, 110 U.S. 574 at 584–585 (1884).

35. *Wilson v. United States*, 162 U.S. 613 at 623 (1896).

36. *Bram v. United States*, 168 U.S. 532 at 561, 542 (1897).

37. *McNabb v. United States*, 318 U.S. 332 at 340 (1943).

38. Id. at 343–344.

39. *Mallory v. United States*, 354 U.S. 449 at 453 (1957).

40. *Brown v. Mississippi*, 297 U.S. 278 at 285 (1935).

41. Id. at 285–286.

42. *Chambers v. Florida*, 309 U.S. 227 at 237, 239–240, 241 (1940).

43. *Lisenba v. California*, 314 U.S. 219 (1941); *Ashcraft v. Tennessee*, 322 U.S. 143 (1944); *Fikes v. Alabama*, 352 U.S. 191 (1957); *Spano v. New York*, 360 U.S. 315 (1959); *Lynumn v. Illinois*, 372 U.S. 528 (1963); *Townsend v. Sain*, 372 U.S. 293 (1963); *Haynes v. Washington*, 373 U.S. 503 (1963).

44. *Rogers v. Richmond*, 365 U.S. 534 at 540–541 (1961); see also *Stein v. New York*, 346 U.S. 156 (1953); *Jackson v. Denno*, 378 U.S. 368 (1964).

45. *Crooker v. California*, 357 U.S. 433 (1958); *Cicencia v. LaGay*, 357 U.S. 504 (1958), overruled by *Miranda v. Arizona*, 384 U.S. 436 (1966).

46. *Massiah v. United States*, 377 U.S. 201 (1964).

47. *Escobedo v. Illinois*, 378 U.S. 478 (1964).

48. *Gideon v. Wainwright*, 372 U.S. 335 (1963).

49. *Escobedo v. Illinois*, 378 U.S. 478 at 490–491 (1964).

50. Id. at 496.

51. *Miranda v. Arizona*, 384 U.S. 436 at 441–442 (1966). *Miranda* was one of four cases reviewed by the Court and resolved together. The others were *Vignera v. New York, Westover v. United States, California v. Stewart*.

52. Id. at 466.

53. Id. at 444–445.

54. Id. at 474.

55. Id. at 515–516.

56. Id. at 536, 537, 541–542.

57. *Johnson v. New Jersey*, 384 U.S. 719 (1966).

58. *Orozco v. Texas*, 394 U.S. 324 (1969).

59. *Harris v. New York*, 401 U.S. 222 at 224, 226 (1971).

60. Id. at 232.

61. *Michigan v. Tucker*, 417 U.S. 433 (1974); see also *Oregon v. Hass*, 420 U.S. 714 (1975).

62. *United States v. Mandujano*, 425 U.S. 564 (1976).

63. *New York v. Quarles*, 467 U.S. 649 (1984).

64. Id. at 660.

65. *Minnesota v. Murphy*, 465 U.S. 420 (1984); see also *Oregon v. Elstad*, 470 U.S. 298 (1985).

66. *Pennsylvania v. Muniz*, 496 U.S. 582 (1990).

67. *Michigan v. Mosley*, 423 U.S. 96 (1975).

68. *Minnick v. Mississippi*, 498 U.S. 146 (1990); *Edwards v. Arizona*, 451 U.S. 477 (1981).

69. *Davis v. United States*, 114 S. Ct. 2350 (1994).

70. *Fare v. Michael C.*, 442 U.S. 707 (1979).

71. *Colorado v. Connelly*, 479 U.S. 157 (1986).

THE AID OF LEGAL COUNSEL (PP. 599–604)

1. 1 Stat. 73, 92 (1789); 1 Stat. 112, 118 (1790), now 18 United States Code 563.

2. *Powell v. Alabama*, 287 U.S. 45 (1932).

3. *Johnson v. Zerbst*, 304 U.S. 458 (1938).

4. *Gideon v. Wainwright*, 372 U.S. 335 (1963); *Argersinger v. Hamlin*, 407 U.S. 25 (1972); *Ake v. Oklahoma*, 470 U.S. 68 (1985).

5. *Powell v. Alabama*, 287 U.S. 45 at 53 (1932).

6. Id. 56–57.

7. Id. at 68.

8. Id. at 71.

9. 1 Stat. 73, 92 (1789); 1 Stat. 112, 118 (1790); now 18 United States Code 563.

10. *Johnson v. Zerbst*, 304 U.S. 458 (1938).

11. Id. at 462–463, 465, 467–468.

12. *Betts v. Brady*, 316 U.S. 455 (1942).

13. Id. at 461–462.

14. Id. at 465.

15. Id. at 473.

16. Id. at 476.

17. *Canizio v. New York*, 327 U.S. 82 (1946); *Bute v. Illinois*, 333 U.S. 640 (1948); *Tomkins v. Missouri*, 323 U.S. 485 (1945); *Townsend v. Burk*, 334 U.S. 736 (1948); *White v. Ragen*, 324 U.S. 760 (1945); *DeMeerleer v. Michigan*, 329 U.S. 663 (1947); *Marino v. Ragen*, 332 U.S. 561 (1947); *Rice v. Olsen*, 324 U.S. 786 (1945).

18. *Gideon v. Wainwright*, 372 U.S. 335 (1963).

19. Id. at 343–344.

20. *Escobedo v. Illinois*, 378 U.S. 478 (1964).

21. *Miranda v. Arizona*, 384 U.S. 436 at 466 (1966).

22. Id. at 471.; see also *Duckworth v. Eagan*, 492 U.S. 195 (1989).

23. *Argersinger v. Hamlin*, 407 U.S. 25 at 32–33, 40 (1972).

24. *Scott v. Illinois*, 440 U.S. 367 (1979).

25. *Powell v. Alabama*, 287 U.S. 45 (1932).

26. *Hamilton v. Alabama*, 368 U.S. 52 (1961).

27. *Escobedo v. Illinois*, 378 U.S. 478 (1964); *Miranda v. Arizona*, 384 U.S. 436 (1966).

28. *United States v. Wade*, 388 U.S. 218 (1967); *Gilbert v. California*, 388 U.S. 263 (1967).

29. *United States v. Wade*, 388 U.S. 218 at 227 (1967).

30. *Kirby v. Illinois*, 406 U.S. 682 (1972); but see also *Coleman v. Alabama*, 399 U.S. 1 (1970).

31. *Kirby v. Illinois*, 406 U.S. 682 at 689–690 (1972).

32. *United States v. Ash*, 413 U.S. 300 (1973).

33. *Ross v. Moffit*, 417 U.S. 600 (1974).

34. *Glasser v. United States*, 315 U.S. 60 (1942).

35. Id. at 71, 76.

36. *Holloway v. Arkansas*, 435 U.S. 475 at 489–490 (1978).

37. *Mann v. Richardson*, 397 U.S. 759 (1970); *Tollett v. Henderson*, 411 U.S. 258 (1973).

38. *Strickland v. Washington*, 466 U.S. 668, at 689 (1984).

39. *United States v. Cronic*, 466 U.S. 648 (1984).

40. *Evitts v. Lucey*, 469 U.S. 387 (1985).

DOUBLE JEOPARDY (PP. 605–607)

1. *Benton v. Maryland*, 395 U.S. 784 (1969).

2. *Downum v. United States*, 372 U.S. 734 (1963); *Crist v. Bretz*, 437 U.S. 28 (1978).

3. *Wade v. Hunter*, 336 U.S. 684 (1949); *United States v. Dinitz*, 424 U.S. 600 (1976); *Lee v. United States*, 432 U.S. 23 (1977); *Oregon v. Kennedy*, 456 U.S. 667 (1982).

4. *United States v. Perez*, 9 Wheat. 579 (1824); *Richardson v. United States*, 468 U.S. 317 (1984).

5. *United States v. Ball*, 163 U.S. 662 (1896); *Hudson v. Louisiana*, 450 U.S. 40 (1981); *Smalis v. Pennsylvania*, 476 U.S. 140 (1986); but see *Tibbs v. Florida*, 457 U.S. 31 (1982).

6. *United States v. Sanges*, 144 U.S. 310 (1892); *United States v. Ball*, 163 U.S. 662 (1896); *Fong Foo v. United States*, 369 U.S. 141 (1962); *Sanabria v. United States*, 437 U.S. 54 (1978).

7. *United States v. Lanza*, 260 U.S. 377 at 382 (1922).

8. *Abbate v. United States*, 359 U.S. 187 (1959); *Bartkus v. Illinois*, 359 U.S. 121 (1959); see also *Petite v. United States*, 361 U.S. 529 (1960); *Heath v. Alabama*, 474 U.S. 82 (1985).

9. *Waller v. Florida*, 397 U.S. 387 (1970).

10. *United States v. Wheeler*, 435 U.S. 313 (1978).

11. *Heath v. Alabama*, 474 U.S. 82 (1985); see also *Grady v. Corbin*, 495 U.S. 508 (1990); *United States v. Dixon*, 509 U.S. 688 (1993).

12. *Green v. United States*, 355 U.S. 184 at 187–188 (1957); see also *Price v. Georgia*, 398 U.S. 323 (1970).

13. *Palko v. Connecticut*, 302 U.S. 319 at 325 (1937).

14. Id. at 328.

15. *Benton v. Maryland*, 395 U.S. 784 at 795 (1969).

16. Id. at 808.

17. *Bullington v. Missouri*, 451 U.S. 430 (1981); see also *Arizona v. Rumsey*, 467 U.S. 203 (1984); *Poland v. Arizona*, 476 U.S. 147 (1986).

18. *North Carolina v. Pearce*, 395 U.S. 711 (1969); but see *Texas v. McCullough*, 475 U.S. 134 (1986); *Alabama v. Smith*, 490 U.S. 794 (1989).

19. *North Carolina v. Pearce*, 395 U.S. 711 at 717.

20. *Chaffin v. Stynchcombe*, 412 U.S. 17 (1973).

21. *United States v. Wilson*, 420 U.S. 332 (1975).

22. *United States v. Jenkins*, 420 U.S. 358 (1975).

23. *United States v. Scott*, 437 U.S. 82 (1978).

24. *Grady v. Corbin*, 495 U.S. 508 (1990).

25. *United States v. Dixon*, 509 U.S. 688 (1993).

26. *Montana Department of Revenue v. Kurth Ranch*, 114 S. Ct. 1937 (1994).

27. *United States v. Ursery*, ____ U.S. ____ (1996).

CRUEL AND UNUSUAL PUNISHMENT (PP. 608–615)

1. *Weems v. United States*, 217 U.S. 349 (1910).

2. *Trop v. Dulles*, 356 U.S. 86 at 99 (1958).

3. Id. at 99–101.

4. *O'Neil v. Vermont*, 144 U.S. 323 (1892).

5. *Louisiana ex rel. Francis v. Resweber*, 329 U.S. 459 (1947).

6. Id. at 464.

7. *Robinson v. California*, 370 U.S. 660 at 666, 667 (1962).

8. *Powell v. Texas*, 392 U.S. 514 at 532 (1968).

9. *Witherspoon v. Illinois*, 391 U.S. 510 at 520–521 (1968); reversed by *Wainwright v. Witt*, 469 U.S. 412 (1985).

10. *McGautha v. California*, 402 U.S. 183 at 207 (1971).

11. *Furman v. Georgia, Jackson v. Georgia, Branch v. Texas*, 408 U.S. 238 (1972).

12. Id. at 253, 256–257.

13. Id. at 291.

14. Id. at 305.

15. Id. at 309–310.

16. Id. at 312–313.

17. Id. at 369.

18. Id. at 404.

19. *Gregg v. Georgia*, 428 U.S. 153 at 187 (1976); *Proffitt v. Florida*, 428 U.S. 242 (1976); *Jurek v. Texas*, 428 U.S. 262 (1976).

20. *Gregg v. Georgia*, 428 U.S. 153 at 186–187 (1976).

21. Id. at 229.

22. Id at 206–207.

23. *Woodson v. North Carolina*, 428 U.S. 280 (1976); *Roberts v. Louisiana*, 428 U.S. 325 (1976).

24. *Woodson v. North Carolina*, 428 U.S. 280 at 302 (1976).

25. Id. at 304.

26. Id.

27. *Roberts v. Louisiana*, 431 U.S. 633 (1977); *Sumner v. Shuman*, 483 U.S. 66 (1987).

28. *Coker v. Georgia*, 433 U.S. 583 (1977).

29. *Enmund v. Florida*, 458 U.S. 782 (1982).

30. *Eddings v. Oklahoma*, 455 U.S. 104 (1982); *Skipper v. South Carolina*, 476 U.S. 1 (1986); *Hitchcock v. Dugger*, 481 U.S. 393 (1987).

31. *Lockett v. Ohio*, 438 U.S. 586 (1978); *Bell v. Ohio*, 438 U.S. 637 (1978); *Mills v. Maryland*, 486 U.S. 367 (1988).

32. *Tison v. Arizona*, 481 U.S. 137 (1987).

33. *Booth v. Maryland*, 482 U.S. 496 (1987); see also *South Carolina v. Gathers*, 490 U.S. 805 (1989).

34. *Payne v. Tennessee*, 501 U.S. 808 (1991).

35. *Spaziano v. Florida*, 468 U.S. 447 (1984).

36. *Wainwright v. Witt*, 469 U.S. 412 (1985).

37. *Lockhart v. McCree*, 476 U.S. 162 (1986); *Gray v. Mississippi*, 481 U.S. 648 (1987), *Morgan v. Illinois*, 504 U.S. 719 (1992).

38. *Pulley v. Harris*, 465 U.S. 37 (1984).

39. *McCleskey v. Kemp*, 481 U.S. 279 (1987).

40. *Ford v. Wainwright* 477 U.S. 399 (1986); *Penry v. Lynaugh*, 492 U.S. 302 (1989).

41. *Thompson v. Oklahoma*, 487 U.S. 815 (1988).

42. *Stanford v. Kentucky*, 492 U.S. 361 (1989).

43. *Lankford v. Idaho*, 500 U.S. 110 (1991); *Simmons v. South Carolina*, 114 S. Ct. 2187 (1994).

CHAPTER 12

Equal Rights and Personal Liberties

THE FOURTEENTH AMENDMENT to the Constitution forbids a state to "deny any person within its jurisdiction the equal protection of the laws." Upholding that guarantee of equal protection, the Supreme Court in 1954 struck down state laws segregating public schools, touching off a civil rights revolution that has widened to include discrimination against women, the aged, the handicapped, and aliens.

The guarantee of equal protection prohibits arbitrary discrimination, such as laws that restrict a person's right to vote, to travel from state to state, or to marry whomever he or she pleases. The equal protection clause is both the weapon securing and the armor safeguarding the civil rights of many distinct groups of people.

In the closing years of the twentieth century, the equal protection clause has become so well established as a shield against discrimination that it may be forgotten that this interpretation of the clause is a modern development. The Fourteenth Amendment, ratified in 1868, was intended primarily to prevent discrimination against the blacks whose citizenship it confirmed. But the Supreme Court soon interpreted it into uselessness.

Segregation of the races was an unassailable fact of life in the late nineteenth century and for most of the twentieth century. The equal protection clause was invoked primarily, although not often successfully, against allegedly unfair and unequal taxation and regulation of economic and commercial affairs. Not until the late 1930s did the clause begin to protect those persons and groups intended to be its primary beneficiaries.

Whether applied to civil rights or property rights, the equal protection clause has never been interpreted by the Court to require a law to treat all groups it affects just the same. Laws by their very nature distinguish between categories of people, classes of property, and kinds of actions. For the most part, such distinctions are desirable, even necessary, in an organized society. But some may be capricious or malicious and thereby deny equal protection to the classified group. Thus the question a court must answer whenever a law is challenged as a violation of equal protection is whether the classification is permissible.

TRADITIONAL STANDARD

The first standard developed by the Supreme Court for measuring a particular classification against the equal protection guarantee grew largely out of its review of state tax and economic regulation. Here the Court deferred more often than not to the judgment of the states.

Not surprisingly, its standard for review of such alleged violations was minimal. The Court was satisfied that a classification was valid if a state could show that it had a reasonable basis. This traditional standard for testing the validity of classifications—still pertinent to appropriate cases today—was summarized by the Court in 1911:

The equal protection clause of the Fourteenth Amendment does not take from the State the power to classify in the adoption of police laws, but admits of the exercise of a wide scope of discretion in that regard, and avoids what is done only when it is without any reasonable basis and is therefore purely arbitrary. . . .

A classification having some reasonable basis does not offend against the clause merely because it is not made with mathematical nicety or because in practice it results in some inequality. . . .

When the classification in such a law is called in question, if any state of facts reasonably can be conceived that would sustain it, the existence of that state of facts at the time the law was enacted must be assumed. . . .

One who assails the classification in such a law must carry the burden of showing that it does not rest upon any reasonable basis, but is essentially arbitrary.[1]

Invoking only this permissive standard, the Court upheld few challenges to laws on equal protection grounds. The Court noted in 1927 the clause had become no more than "the usual last resort of constitutional arguments."[2]

MODERN STANDARD

The Court's shift in focus from property rights to individual rights in the late 1930s led it to develop a more probing standard for examining charges of denial of equal protection. Under this so-called active standard, classifications that are "inherently suspect" or that affect what the Court considers to be fundamental rights or interests require a greater degree of justification for their existence than simple rationality. A state must prove not only that it has a compelling governmental interest for making the challenged classification, but also that the classification is narrowly tailored to achieve that interest.

The development of this modern standard came in distinct stages. In 1944 the Court declared race to be a suspect category requiring this heightened judicial scrutiny. But the Court then did not expressly apply this standard in its most important decision on racial discrimination, the 1954 ruling striking down state-imposed school segregation as a violation of equal protection. Classifications by alienage came in for heightened review as early as 1948, but not until 1971 did the Court explicitly describe alienage as a suspect category.

As early as 1942 the Court indicated that the equal protection

622 PART III THE COURT AND THE INDIVIDUAL

FEDERAL EQUAL PROTECTION

Nowhere does the Constitution explicitly require the federal government to ensure equal protection of its laws against arbitrary discrimination. The Supreme Court, however, has found this requirement implicit in the Fifth Amendment's guarantee of due process of law. The Court explained this finding in the 1954 case of *Bolling v. Sharpe* in which it struck down the federal government's requirement that black and white pupils in the District of Columbia attend separate schools:

The Fifth Amendment . . . does not contain an equal protection clause as does the Fourteenth Amendment which applies only to the states. But the concepts of equal protection and due process, both stemming from our American ideal of fairness, are not mutually exclusive. The "equal protection of the law" is a more explicit safeguard of prohibited unfairness than "due process of law," and, therefore, we do not imply that the two are always interchangeable phrases. But, as this Court has recognized, discrimination may be so unjustifiable as to be violative of due process. (347 U.S. 483 at 499, 1954)

The Court reaffirmed this finding in several later cases: *Weinberger v. Wiesenfeld*, 420 U.S. 636 at 638, note 2 (1975); *Buckley v. Valeo*, 424 U.S. 1 at 93 (1976); *Hampton v. Mow Sun Wong*, 426 U.S. 88 at 100 (1976); *Davis v. Passman*, 442 U.S. 228 (1979).

clause protected all individuals from state deprivation of certain fundamental rights. But twenty years passed before the Court began to elaborate on this premise.

Much of the development of this modern equal protection standard began after Congress passed the 1964 Civil Rights Act, which prohibited discrimination on the grounds of race, color, national origin, or religion in most privately owned public accommodations. It also prohibited job discrimination on these grounds and on the basis of sex.

Passage of the 1965 Voting Rights Act authorized federal action to enforce the rights of blacks to vote. In 1968 Congress barred discrimination in the sale and rental of housing.

As a result of these federal laws, minorities and other groups traditionally victimized by discrimination brought more and more lawsuits charging a denial of equal protection. In reviewing these cases, the Court has moved further and further from the traditional "reasonable basis" standard.

Race and alienage are the only two categories to which the Supreme Court has accorded suspect status.

RACIAL CLASSIFICATIONS

The Court first declared race a suspect category in 1944. The case was *Korematsu v. United States,* and it involved a U.S. citizen of Japanese descent who defied a World War II military order requiring all persons of Japanese descent living on the West Coast to report to relocation centers. The Court ruled against Toyosaburo Korematsu and held that the wartime emergency necessitated the unusual detention. But in so deciding, it an-

nounced that it would give classifications by race increased attention:

It should be noted . . . that all legal restrictions which curtail the civil rights of a single racial group are immediately suspect. That is not to say that all such restrictions are unconstitutional. It is to say that courts must subject them to the most rigid scrutiny. Pressing public necessity may sometimes justify the existence of such restrictions; racial antagonism never can.[3]

Ten years later, its 1954 school desegregation decisions made abundantly clear the meaning of "rigid scrutiny."

But it was not until 1967 that the Court expressly acknowledged that all racial classifications were "inherently suspect." This rather anticlimactic declaration came in a case in which the Court struck down a Virginia statute that made it a crime for residents to enter into interracial marriages. *(See details of Brown v. Board of Education, p. 631; Loving v. Virginia, p. 690.)*

DISCRIMINATION AGAINST ALIENS

As early as 1886 the Court held that the Fourteenth Amendment protected aliens as well as citizens. But during the next sixty years, the Court, applying the traditional standard of review, found that most statutes challenged as discriminating against aliens were in fact based on some reasonable—and therefore permissible—objective.

In 1948 the Court began to require more than simple rationality to justify such laws. But not until 1971 did the Court explicitly acknowledge that such classifications were inherently suspect, requiring a compelling interest as justification.

"Aliens as a class are a prime example of a 'discrete and insular' minority . . . for whom . . . heightened judicial solicitude is appropriate," said the Court.[4]

However, because the Constitution gives Congress exclusive authority over naturalization and, by extension, immigration, the Court has been reluctant to judge federal alienage classification laws as strictly as similar state laws. *(See "Aliens and the Law," pp. 669–673.)*

SEX DISCRIMINATION

All the modern cases challenging discrimination on the basis of sex have occurred since 1969. In the earliest of those cases, the Court applied the traditional standard of review and more often than not found that the state had a rational basis to justify treating women differently from men.

But in a line of cases involving the defense of administrative efficiency, the Court held that classifications by sex were impermissible. The statutes struck down in these cases presumed that all men behaved in one way and all women in another, failing to allow for any variation from the unproved assumption. The Court found such presumptions arbitrary, too broad, and unjustified by mere administrative convenience.

In a case decided in 1976, a slim majority of the Court adopted a test that fell between the "reasonable basis" standard and the "compelling governmental interest" test. This standard requires the state to show that its sex-based classification was necessary to achieve some "important governmental objective."[5] Ever since then, the Court has used such "intermediate" scrutiny for classifications based on gender. Regulations that discriminate against women are usually held invalid if they serve no important interest of government. The Court stressed in 1996 that governments defending gender-based action must demonstrate an "exceedingly persuasive justification."

The Court has upheld both the 1964 Civil Rights Act ban on job discrimination on the grounds of sex and the 1963 Equal Pay Act requiring that men and women be paid the same for the same work.

But the Court has steadily refused to describe differential treatment of pregnant women as sex discrimination. Such a classification is based not on gender but on physical condition, a majority of the Court has held, ruling that classification by physical condition did not violate either the equal protection clause or the 1964 Civil Rights Act. (See "Romantic" Paternalism, pp. 677–678.)

The Court has refused to apply the compelling interest standard to test laws that discriminate against illegitimate children and the poor. Nonetheless, it has treated most cases involving classification by legitimacy with more than minimal scrutiny, striking down several laws distinguishing illegitimate children from their legitimate siblings on the grounds that such classifications were arbitrary and archaic. The Court has found discrimination against the poor unconstitutional when it deprives the indigent of a fundamental right or interest. But the Court has not applied the equal protection clause to protect the poverty-stricken from deprivation of rights not considered "fundamental."

FUNDAMENTAL INTERESTS

The Court first articulated its "fundamental interest" standard in the 1942 case of *Skinner v. Oklahoma*. The decision not only advanced the concept of equal protection but contributed to the contemporary interpretation of an implicit constitutional right of privacy. *Skinner* marked the first time the Court declared a fundamental right to marriage and procreation. The justices were unanimous as they struck down an Oklahoma statute that authorized sterilization of criminals who had committed two felonies "involving moral turpitude":

We are dealing here with legislation which involves one of the basic civil rights of man. Marriage and procreation are fundamental to the very existence and survival of the race. The power to sterilize, if exercised, may have subtle, far-reaching and devastating effects. In evil or reckless hands it can cause races or types which are inimical to the dominant group to wither and disappear. There is no redemption for the individual whom the law touches. . . . He is forever deprived of a basic liberty. We mention these matters . . . merely in emphasis of our view that strict scrutiny of the classification which a State makes in a sterilization law is essential, lest unwittingly or otherwise invidious discriminations are made against groups or types of individuals in violation of the constitutional guaranty of just and equal laws.[6]

The expansive ruling in *Skinner,* merging due process values and equal protection, would lead two decades later to signifi-

cant decisions in the areas of personal liberty and electoral equality.

Substantive Due Process and the Right to Privacy

The Court had applied a theory of "substantive due process" in the early 1900s to protect economic and property rights, in effect "a liberty to contract." But the era of economic rights ended in the 1930s, and when the Court revived "substantive due process" in the 1960s, personal liberties, rather than economic ones, were at stake.

"Substantive due process" extends judicial scrutiny beyond the procedures, or methods, of government to the substance, or fundamental value, at the heart of the law. In its first modern invocation of substantive due process in 1965, the Supreme Court struck down a ban on the use of contraceptives. That law, it said, infringed on "the zone of privacy" protected by fundamental constitutional guarantees.

Justice Douglas wrote in *Griswold v. Connecticut:*

Would we allow the police to search the sacred precincts of marital bedrooms for telltale signs of the use of contraceptives? The very idea is repulsive to the notions of privacy surrounding the marriage relationship. We deal with a right of privacy older than the Bill of Rights— older than our political parties, older than our school system. Marriage is a coming together for better or for worse, hopefully enduring, and intimate to the degree of being sacred. The association promotes a way of life, not causes; a harmony in living, not political faiths; a bilateral loyalty, not commercial or social projects. Yet it is an association for as noble a purpose as any involved in our prior decisions.[7]

Eight years later that generous view of the right of privacy exploded into public consciousness. The Court made abortion legal nationwide in *Roe v. Wade,* the most controversial ruling of the modern era. Justice Blackmun wrote that the right of privacy implicit in the Fourteenth Amendment guarantee of liberty is "broad enough to encompass a woman's decision whether or not to terminate her pregnancy."[8]

Despite intense political pressure to repudiate that ruling and that position, the belief in the right of privacy endured through the ensuing decades. In 1992, almost twenty years after *Roe v. Wade,* the Court reaffirmed:

Our law affords constitutional protection to personal decisions relating to marriage, procreation, contraception, family relationships, child rearing, and education. . . . These matters, involving the most intimate and personal choices a person may make in a lifetime, choices central to personal dignity and autonomy, are central to the liberty protected by the Fourteenth Amendment. At the heart of liberty is the right to define one's own concept of existence, of meaning, of the universe, and of the mystery of human life. Beliefs about these matters could not define the attributes of personhood were they formed under compulsion of the state.[9]

Electoral Equality

The fundamental interest doctrine, set forth in *Skinner v. Oklahoma* (1942), next emerged in the area of equal protection in 1964, when the Court held that state electoral districts must each contain substantially the same number of voters. In *Reynolds v. Sims* the Court wrote:

Undoubtedly, the right of suffrage is a fundamental matter in a free and democratic society. Especially since the right to exercise the franchise in a free and unimpaired manner is preservative of other basic civil and political rights, any alleged infringement of the right of citizens to vote must be carefully and meticulously scrutinized.[10]

In 1969 the Court elaborated:

[I]f a challenged state statute grants the right to vote to some bona fide residents of requisite age and citizenship and denies the franchise to others, the Court must determine whether the exclusions are necessary to promote a compelling state interest.

. . . [T]he deference usually given to the judgment of legislators does not extend to decisions concerning which resident citizens may participate in the election of legislators and other public officials. . . . [W]hen we are reviewing statutes which deny some residents the right to vote, the general presumption of constitutionality afforded state statutes and the traditional approval given state classifications if the Court can conceive of a "rational basis" for the distinctions made are not applicable.[11]

Applying this stricter standard, the Court has struck down a number of statutes because they restricted the right to vote. States have no compelling reason to deny the right to vote to persons simply because they have not resided in the state for a certain period of time, or because they are too poor to pay a poll tax. Filing fees that prevent poor candidates from seeking office also are unconstitutional, as are statutes that keep off the ballot all candidates except those belonging to the two major political parties. *(See voting participation cases, p. 675.)*

The Right to Travel

Durational residency requirements also violate another fundamental interest guarded by the equal protection clause—the right to travel unrestricted from state to state. The Court has debated for several decades the source of this right, sometimes finding it in the interstate commerce clause of Article I of the Constitution, at other times in the privileges and immunities clause of the Fourteenth Amendment. In 1966 the Court abandoned the debate:

The constitutional right to travel from one State to another . . . occupies a position fundamental to the concept of our Federal Union. It is a right that has been firmly established and repeatedly recognized. . . . Although there have been recurring differences in emphasis within the Court as to the source of the constitutional right of interstate travel, there is no need here to canvass those differences further. All have agreed that the right exists.[12]

Using this reasoning, the Court in 1969 declared requirements that persons live in a state for a certain period of time before becoming eligible for welfare benefits to be a violation of equal protection and thus unconstitutional. The Court said such requirements unconstitutionally restricted the poor in the exercise of their right to travel interstate.

Access to Justice for the Poor

The Supreme Court has designated one other such matter a fundamental right. That right—access to justice—has been foreclosed at times to poor people who could not afford the fees required either to file suit or hire an attorney, or pay for a transcript to prepare an appeal.

In many of these instances, the Court has held that requiring a fee impermissibly violated the indigent's guarantee of due process as well as equal protection of the laws. *(See "Access to Justice," pp. 673–675.)*

Doctrine Criticized

The fundamental interest doctrine has been criticized from the bench, first by Justice John Marshall Harlan and then by Justice William H. Rehnquist, who replaced him on the Court. Both contended that the Court exceeds its power when it singles out certain rights and interests for special protection. Harlan wrote in 1969:

[W]hen a statute affects only matters not mentioned in the Federal Constitution and is not arbitrary or irrational, I must reiterate that I know of nothing which entitles this Court to pick out particular human activities, characterize them as "fundamental," and give them added protection under an unusually stringent equal protection test.[13]

In 1972 Rehnquist added that "[t]his body of doctrine created by the Court can only be described as a judicial superstructure, awkwardly engrafted upon the Constitution itself."[14]

Since 1969 the Court has refused to classify any other right or interest as fundamental. Although it hinted in 1969 that it might place "food, shelter and other necessities of life" in the fundamental right category, the Court in 1972 held that the assurance of adequate housing was not a fundamental interest.[15] And in 1973 a majority of the Court held that the right to an education was neither explicitly nor implicitly guaranteed by the Constitution. The majority added that it was "not the province of this Court to create substantive constitutional rights in the name of guaranteeing equal protection of the laws."[16]

The Fourteenth Amendment, said the Supreme Court in 1880,

> was designed to assure to the colored race the enjoyment of all the civil rights that under the law are enjoyed by white persons, and to give to that race the protection of the general government, in that enjoyment, whenever it should be denied by the States. It not only gave citizenship and the privileges of citizenship to persons of color, but it denied to any State the power to withhold from them the equal protection of the laws, and authorized Congress to enforce its provisions.[1]

Another seventy-five years would pass before black people would receive any substantial benefit from the Fourteenth Amendment's protections. Even as the Court spoke in 1880, southern states had begun to separate white from black in what would result in almost complete social, legal, and political segregation of the two races.

The Court itself played a role in creating the climate that allowed segregation to flourish. In its first actions regarding blacks after the Civil War, the Court admitted a black attorney to the Supreme Court bar and ruled that a black woman could sue for damages a railroad company that had forcibly removed her from a train after she refused to sit in the "colored" car.[2]

But in the 1873 *Slaughterhouse Cases,* the Court divided 5–4 in ruling that citizens held two distinct types of citizenship, one federal and one state. The Fourteenth Amendment, the majority held, protected a person only from state infringement on such privileges and immunities of national citizenship as the right to petition the federal government and the right to vote in federal elections. The privileges and immunities conferred by citizenship in a state were outside federal protection. This decision, intact today, divested the privileges and immunities clause of any substantive protection it might have afforded citizens of either race.[3]

In the *Slaughterhouse* opinion, the majority characterized the amendment's equal protection clause as primarily of use to protect blacks from unjust discrimination. In deciding the 1880 case of *Strauder v. West Virginia,* the Court utilized the clause to strike down a state law that barred blacks from jury service.

Three years later, however, the Court significantly narrowed the protection of the clause for blacks. In the 1883 *Civil Rights Cases,* the Court nullified an 1875 federal law that gave all persons, regardless of color, "the full and equal enjoyment" of public transportation, inns, theaters, and "other places of public amusement."[4]

The Court held that the Fourteenth Amendment prohibited only state-imposed discrimination and not that imposed by individuals acting privately. Congress therefore had overstepped its authority when it sought to stop private business persons from discriminating against blacks. Furthermore, the Court said, the amendment only empowered Congress to remedy acts of state discrimination; Congress could not enact a general law in anticipation of discriminatory state actions.

By 1883 the fervor of Reconstruction had worn thin. As one historian wrote, "Other than Negroes and their faithful friends, the people were tired of giving special protection to the former slaves. It was felt to be time for the return to power of the dominant factions in the several communities."[5]

Against this background, the decision in the *Civil Rights Cases* had particular significance. Political scientist Alan F. Westin attributed two primary effects to it:

> [F]irst, it destroyed the delicate balance of federal guarantee, Negro protest and private enlightenment which was producing a steadily widening area of peacefully integrated public facilities in the North and South during the 1870s and early 1880s. Second, it had an immediate and profound effect on national and state politics as they related to the Negro. By denying Congress power to protect the Negro's rights to equal treatment, the Supreme Court wiped the issue of civil rights from the Republican party's agenda of national responsibility. At the same time, those Southern political leaders who saw anti-Negro politics as the most promising avenue to power could now rally the "poor whites" to the banner of segregation.[6]

Thirteen years later, in 1896, the Supreme Court sanctioned the "separate but equal" doctrine developed to justify state-imposed racial segregation. In its decision in *Plessy v. Ferguson,* a majority of the Court held that so long as the facilities provided blacks were equal to those provided whites, state laws requiring segregation did not violate the equal protection or due process clauses of the Fourteenth Amendment. Nor did the Court view separation of the races as pinning on blacks a badge of slavery in violation of the Thirteenth Amendment.[7]

In the wake of this decision, state-ordered segregation invaded almost every aspect of daily life in the former Confederate states. Blacks throughout the South were required to use separate streetcars, waiting rooms, toilets, and water fountains. They attended different schools and were segregated in parks and theaters, mental hospitals, and prisons. At the same time, blacks were almost completely disenfranchised in those states by devices such as the poll tax, property and literacy tests, and the white primary. *(See "The Right to Vote," pp. 505–518, in Chapter 10.)*

Although there was comparatively little official segregation in northern and western states, whites there generally regarded blacks as inferiors, and there was little intermingling of the two races.

When the United States entered its brief but intense period of imperialism at the end of the nineteenth century, bringing some eight million nonwhites under its domination, northern attitudes grew steadily more sympathetic to the racist views of southern whites.

As the U.S. Commission on Civil Rights wrote in understatement: at the end of the nineteenth century, the "very concept of civil rights seemed to have passed out of existence, and the prospects for the future were not encouraging."[8]

Segregation Under Attack

During the first third of the twentieth century, segregation by law appeared firmly entrenched, but the events that would lead to its demise were taking shape. The National Association for the Advancement of Colored People (NAACP), which would lead the court fight to end racial discrimination, was founded in 1909, and the National Urban League in 1911. World War I contributed markedly to the rising aspirations of blacks.

Many of the 360,000 blacks who fought to make the world safe for democracy began to wonder when they might begin to enjoy democracy's benefits. The Great War also spurred a black migration to the North where blacks found defense industry work.

Racial tension escalated. In the first year after the war's end, more than seventy blacks were lynched. The Ku Klux Klan enjoyed revived popularity in the North and South. In 1919 bloody race riots broke out in twenty-five cities across the nation. Historian John Hope Franklin described this time as "the greatest period of interracial strife the nation had ever witnessed."[9]

In three school segregation cases the Supreme Court refused to review the separate but equal doctrine, although in 1914 it did strike down a state law because it did not provide blacks with exactly the same train accommodations it provided whites.

In 1917 the Court struck down a municipal ordinance that prohibited blacks from living on the same streets as whites. This decision did not end residential segregation, however, because private restrictive covenants quickly replaced the illegal ordinances. These covenants, attached to the deed or title to property, forbade the white owner to sell to blacks. The Supreme Court upheld the covenants in 1926, reiterating its view that the Fourteenth Amendment did not reach private discrimination.

Blacks as a group were among the most severely burdened by the Great Depression of the 1930s. Although many blacks had left the Republican Party to vote for Woodrow Wilson in 1912, only to be disillusioned when he did little to advance their civil rights, many thousands more swung their support to Franklin Delano Roosevelt in the 1936 and 1940 elections. The Democratic administration did try to improve the economic condition of both races, but segregation continued unabated. Blacks nonetheless had won recognition as a political power, and by the 1940s militant individuals and organized groups demanding an end to segregation were beginning to make themselves heard.

These demands steadily gained adherents as the ironies of World War II became increasingly apparent. The inconsistency of sending black and white soldiers to fight against Germany's vile racial policies while continuing to practice racial segregation at home became too obvious to ignore.

The cold war further intensified this paradox. Communist countries pointed to American racial policies in an effort to undermine the appeal of the democratic system. No reasonable person could deny the irony, as C. Vann Woodward observed, of the United States competing with the Soviet Union for the friendship of the people of the Orient and Africa while continuing to treat Orientals and blacks in the United States as second-class citizens.

SUPREME COURT SHIFTS FOCUS

Against this backdrop the Supreme Court began to take a closer look at the laws that discriminated on the basis of race.

From the end of the Civil War until 1937, the Supreme Court's primary concern was the protection of business from what it considered excessive regulation by the federal government. When these laissez-faire views jeopardized Roosevelt's New Deal programs, the president threatened in 1937 to "pack" the Court with additional justices who would construe the Constitution to support his economic policies.

The Court responded by relaxing its vigilant attitude toward economic regulation and shifting its focus to individual rights and liberties. A harbinger of this shift came in a 1938 footnote to an otherwise routine decision. In that note Justice Harlan Fiske Stone implied that the Court might soon be required to decide whether

statutes directed at particular religious . . . or national . . . or racial minorities . . . [or] whether prejudice against discrete and insular minorities may be a special condition which tends seriously to curtail the operation of those political processes ordinarily to be relied upon to protect minorities, and which may call for a correspondingly more searching judicial inquiry.[10]

That same year the Court ruled that the separate but equal rule required a state to provide law schools for blacks if it provided them for whites, even though there might be only a single black law student. The Court also upheld the right of blacks to picket an employer to persuade the employer to hire more black workers.

In 1944, six years after Stone's footnote comment, the Court announced that it would give closer scrutiny to laws that treated one race differently from another, upholding such distinctions only if they were justified by a pressing governmental need. In that same year the Court held it unconstitutional for states to exclude black voters from primary elections, and in the first modern decision on job discrimination, the Court ruled in favor of black railroad workers.

In 1948 the Court took another look at restrictive covenants, ruling that although the Fourteenth Amendment did not prohibit them, it did prohibit states from enforcing them. With this decision, the Court began to expand its definition of state action covered by the Fourteenth Amendment to include private discrimination promoted in any way by official state action, even if the state action itself was not discriminatory.

But the decisions that portended the most for the future of black civil rights dealt with the question of whether separate facilities could be equal.

On June 5, 1950, the Court held that Texas violated the equal protection clause because its black state law school was not the equivalent of the white school either in tangible aspects (such as the number of books in the library) or in intangible aspects (such as the prestige of its faculty and alumni). In a second case

Dred Scott, a slave seeking his freedom, brought about the first major individual rights ruling from the U.S. Supreme Court. Scott lost his case, but the Court's decision inflamed public opinion and contributed to the outbreak of the Civil War, which finally settled the question of slavery in the United States.

Dred Scott v. Sandford was brought with the financial support of Scott's owners to test whether a slave who lived for a time on free soil would become free as a result. Scott had lived in Illinois and Wisconsin, where slavery was not permitted. He later returned to the slave state of Missouri, contending that he was free.

The Missouri supreme court held that under state law, Scott remained a slave. The case moved into the federal courts. The first federal court dismissed the case, finding that Scott, as a slave, was not a citizen of Missouri and so could not invoke the jurisdiction of the federal courts over suits between citizens of different states. By this time Scott had been sold outside of Missouri.

Scott appealed his case to the U.S. Supreme Court, which heard it argued twice in 1856. The nine justices voted 7–2 against him.

The majority would have resolved the case simply by declaring that Scott's status was a matter for Missouri, not federal officials, to decide. But the two dissenters, both fiercely antislavery, announced that their dissents would address broader issues: whether a slave could ever become a citizen, whether a stay on free soil made a slave free, and whether Congress had the power to ban slavery in the territories.

In response, each of the seven majority justices wrote his own opinion, setting out his views on these matters. The result was confusion. On March 6, 1857, the Court announced its decision. The opinion, by Chief Justice Roger B. Taney, is generally considered the official majority view.

Dred Scott could not be a citizen, declared Taney, nor could any slave or his descendant. Thus, the chief justice continued, blacks could "claim none of the rights and privileges which . . . [the Constitution] provides for and secures to citizens of the United States."[1]

When the Constitution used the word "citizens," it did not include slaves, Taney explained, reasoning from the fact that slaves "had for more than a century before [ratification of the Constitution] been regarded as being of an inferior order, and altogether unfit to associate with the white race, either in social or political relations; and so far inferior, that they had no rights which the white man was bound to respect."[2]

This last statement, taken out of its context as Taney's observation upon the historical view of slaves, was quoted time and again in the incendiary debates of the years before the war. Northern abolitionists were particularly incensed by it, viewing it as a statement of Taney's own belief in the inferiority of blacks.

Furthermore, wrote Taney, slaves were not included in the statement in the Declaration of Independence that "all men are created equal."[3]

Indeed, slaves were viewed as property, and the Constitution reflects this view. "The only two provisions which point to them and include them, treat them as property, and make it the duty of the government to protect it; no other power, in relation to this race, is to be found in the Constitution."[4]

Taney could have stopped there. He had given ample reason for

Dred Scott

dismissing Scott's case on the grounds that he was not a citizen. But Taney continued.

Congress lacked the power to declare certain territory "free" of slavery, he wrote, and so the "free territory" in which Scott had lived could not actually be so designated.

For Congress to do so, Taney reasoned, deprived slave-owning citizens of their property when they came into that territory—and thus denied slave owners due process of law, in violation of the Fifth Amendment.[5] Congress was officially declared powerless to stop the spread of slavery through the expanding nation.

The Civil War rendered moot the question of congressional power over slavery. And in 1868 ratification of the Fourteenth Amendment reversed the Court's declaration that blacks were not and could not be citizens under the Constitution.

The first section of the amendment declares that all persons born or naturalized in the United States and subject to its jurisdiction are citizens of the United States and the state in which they live. That same section prohibits states from making any law abridging the privileges and immunities of citizens, depriving any person of life, liberty, or property without due process of law, or denying to anyone equal protection of the law.

This set of guarantees, indirectly the legacy of Dred Scott, a slave who sought to be free, provides the basis for the modern revolution in civil rights.

1. *Dred Scott v. Sandford,* 19 How. 393 at 404 (1857).
2. Id. at 407.
3. Id. at 410
4. Id. at 425.
5. Id. at 450.

decided the same day, the Court ruled that Oklahoma violated the equal protection guarantee when it separated a black from his white colleagues in classes, the library, and the cafeteria.

Four years later in the public school desegregation cases, familiarly known as *Brown v. Board of Education,* the unanimous Court declared that separation of the races in public schools was "inherently unequal."[11] After sixty years the *Plessy* doctrine—and a way of life for an entire section of the nation—had been officially renounced.

The *Brown* decisions, wrote G. Theodore Mitau,

acknowledged judicially what many people had known or felt for a long time: Segregation was morally indefensible, socially irrational and politically undemocratic. It perpetuated a racial myth which imprisoned American values at home and weakened America's leadership abroad. Equally important to many, it defiled this country's claim to stand as a world model of freedom and human dignity in defense of which whites and Negroes fought side by side in all of this nation's major wars.[12]

In 1955 the Court issued guidelines directing school officials to desegregate schools with "all deliberate speed." Although many states complied with the Court order, many others embarked on programs of "massive resistance" in defiance of the Supreme Court order.

The governor of Arkansas in 1958 called out the state's national guard to prevent black students from entering a formerly all-white high school in Little Rock. In an extraordinary session, the Supreme Court demanded unanimously that the state cease its resistance and that the students be admitted to the school.

For ten years after *Brown,* the Court left it to lower courts to implement school desegregation. The pace was slow: by 1964 less than 2 percent of black pupils in the former Confederate states were in desegregated schools.[13]

CIVIL RIGHTS REVOLUTION

During this same decade, however, the Court frequently cited *Brown* as precedent for rulings striking down other forms of segregation throughout the South, in parks and beaches, traffic courts and theaters, railroad cars and bus terminals.

These decisions spurred a revolution in civil rights. Blacks were no longer willing to let whites deny them their rights. Beginning in 1957 with a Montgomery, Alabama, bus boycott led by Dr. Martin Luther King Jr., blacks organized to protest racial segregation and discrimination in jobs, housing, and public accommodations. The student sit-ins and "freedom rides" of the early 1960s sensitized the rest of the nation to the black dilemma; the violence with which whites frequently countered black demonstrations drew the nation's sympathy.

The year that marked the 100th anniversary of the Emancipation Proclamation was particularly turbulent. In May 1963 police loosed dogs and turned high-pressure fire hoses on demonstrators in Birmingham, Alabama. Sympathy protests soon spread in several other cities. In August 200,000 blacks and whites marched peacefully in Washington, D.C., to present blacks' demands for equal treatment to Congress, the president,

On August 28, 1963, after leading 200,000 blacks and whites in a peaceful march in Washington, D.C., Martin Luther King Jr. delivered a now-famous speech from the steps of the Lincoln Memorial. "I have a dream," he said, "that one day this nation will rise up and live out the true meaning of its creed: 'We hold these truths to be self-evident: that all men are created equal.'"

and a closely watching country. One month later a bomb thrown into a black church in Birmingham killed four little girls. On November 22, an assassin shot and killed President John F. Kennedy, an unequivocal advocate of civil rights.

Hope, frustration, and outrage impelled Congress in 1964 to approve the most comprehensive civil rights act since Reconstruction. It barred discrimination in most public accommodations, prohibited job discrimination on the basis of race, and established a procedure for withholding federal funds from any program, including schools, that continued to discriminate against blacks.

That year also marked the end of the Court's silence on continuing questions of school desegregation. There has been "too much deliberation and not enough speed" in desegregating public schools, the Court declared in 1964, holding that a county could not close its schools to avoid desegregating them. Later in the year the Court upheld that section of the 1964 Civil Rights Act barring racial discrimination in most private accommodations. In 1966 the Court upheld Congress's 1965 Voting Rights Act.

In 1968 the Court reinterpreted an 1866 civil rights law as barring private individuals from refusing to sell their homes to persons of a different race. The Court also declared that state and school officials must do more than simply end segregation, that they had a duty to take affirmative action to ensure effective school desegregation. The Court also gave lower courts new guidelines for determining if desegregation efforts were sincere.

THE COURT'S REMEDIES

Chief Justice Earl Warren's replacement in 1969 by Chief Justice Warren E. Burger coincided with a new phase in the civil rights movement and the Court's role in it. It was clear that racial discrimination was illegal; the Court's task was now to define the scope of remedies available to its victims.

The Burger Court approved a wide variety of measures to remedy school segregation, including busing, gerrymandered attendance zones, limited use of mathematical ratios, and compensatory education programs. The Court also extended the obligation to desegregate to nonsouthern school districts where existing segregation had not been required by law but rather imposed as a matter of school-board policy.

At the same time, however, the Court insisted that these remedies be tailored to fit the extent of the proven discrimination. Thus a multidistrict busing plan was found too sweeping a remedy when deliberate discrimination had been found in only one of the affected districts. In another instance, a districtwide plan was held to be too broad because the proven discrimination had not been shown to infect the entire school district. The Court also held that once a school district was desegregated, school officials were not required to remedy its resegregation so long as it did not result from official state action.

After the Court reinterpreted the 1866 Civil Rights Act to bar housing discrimination by private individuals, it also read the act to prohibit private schools from refusing to admit black pupils and to invalidate neighborhood recreational association policies excluding black homeowners and renters from membership. In a major case in which federal and city housing officials admitted they had been guilty of intentional racial segregation, the Court backed a lower court's remedy that covered a metropolitan area. But in a second case, where a community was charged with exercising its zoning power to exclude blacks by omitting low-income housing, the Court held there was no constitutional violation because there was no evidence that the charges were true and that the zoning decision was motivated by racial considerations.

When charges of racial discrimination in employment have been brought under Title VII of the Civil Rights Act of 1964, the Court has placed the burden of proving nondiscrimination on the employer. Few employers have met this test. But when charges of job discrimination have been brought under the Fourteenth Amendment, the Court shifted the burden to the employees, requiring them to prove that the employer intended to discriminate; the discriminatory effect of an employment policy is not sufficient proof of intent. Few employees have met this test. Where job discrimination has been proved, however, the Court has sanctioned far-reaching remedies, including awards of back pay and retroactive seniority.

The success of the black civil rights movement encouraged other victims of discrimination, particularly women, to assert their right to equal treatment. It has also prompted some members of the majority to complain that they have suffered from "reverse discrimination," that is, that affirmative action programs to remedy past discrimination against minorities have in turn discriminated against whites.

The Court has held that the 1964 Civil Rights Act provides remedies to whites as well as blacks who have been discriminated against in employment because of their race and that it bars universities receiving federal funds from setting aside a specific number of seats in each class for minority applicants. But the Court has endorsed as within the bounds of the Constitution and the law the use of affirmative action, a program that deliberately takes into account the personal characteristics of an individual (such as race, color, or sex) to remedy society's past discrimination against racial minorities or women.

Equal Opportunity for Education

When the Supreme Court in 1896 ruled that separate public facilities for blacks and whites did not violate the equal protection clause of the Fourteenth Amendment, it pointed to the nation's schools as "the most common instance" of segregation. "Establishment of separate schools for white and colored children has been held to be a valid exercise of the legislative power," the Court said in *Plessy v. Ferguson*, "even by courts of States where the political rights of the colored race have been longest and most earnestly enforced." [14]

BOSTON, 1849

The Court was referring to Massachusetts, and it used *Roberts v. City of Boston* to support its decision in *Plessy*. In this 1849 ruling a Massachusetts court first sanctioned separate schools for the two races. The city of Boston had maintained separate schools for blacks and whites since 1820. Sarah Roberts, a five-year-old black child, was forced, as a result of this segregation, to walk past five white primary schools on her way to the black school. When repeated attempts to place her in one of the closer white schools failed, Sarah's father hired Charles Sumner, the future senator and abolitionist, and went to court.

Appearing before Chief Justice Lemuel Shaw of Massachusetts, Sumner made one of his most eloquent pleas, contending that the segregated schools violated state law which held all persons, "without distinction of age or sex, birth or color, origin or condition," to be equal before the law. Noting the general soundness of Sumner's contention, the state supreme court nonetheless rejected Roberts's challenge.

Shaw wrote that

when this great principle [of equality before the law] comes to be applied to the actual and various conditions of persons in society, it will not warrant the assertion, that men and women are legally clothed with the same civil and political powers, and that children and adults are legally to have the same functions and be subject to the same treatment; but only that the rights of all, as they are settled and regulated by law, are equally entitled to the paternal consideration and protection of the law, for their maintenance and security. What those rights are, to which individuals, in the infinite variety of circumstances by which they are surrounded in society, are entitled, must depend on laws adapted to their respective relations and conditions. [15]

To Sumner's contention that segregation "brand[s] a whole race with the stigma of inferiority and degradation," Shaw responded:

Under the rule of law established in *Plessy v. Ferguson* (1896), states could require racial separation if facilities for blacks and whites were of equal quality. In public education black schools were not always equal to those reserved for whites.

It is urged, that this maintenance of separate schools tends to deepen and perpetuate the odious distinction of caste, founded in a deep-rooted prejudice in public opinion. This prejudice, if it exists, is not created by law, and probably cannot be changed by laws.[16]

Massachusetts prohibited dual school systems six years after *Roberts.* In citing this case to support *Plessy,* the Court overlooked the fact that the state case was decided almost twenty years before ratification of the Fourteenth Amendment made blacks citizens and required the states to give all citizens equal protection of the laws.

PLESSY AND SCHOOLS

While the *Plessy* decision did not deal directly with school segregation, the Supreme Court in that opinion clearly condoned the practice. The Court confirmed this position in three subsequent cases challenging the "separate" half of the "separate but equal" doctrine as states applied it to schools. In all three instances the Court bowed to the right of the state to run its own schools, refusing to consider the constitutional question of whether state-required segregation denied black children equal protection of the laws.

The first of these cases was *Cumming v. Richmond (Ga.) County Board of Education,* decided in 1899, three years after *Plessy.* The school board had discontinued operating the black high school in order to use the building as an additional facility for black primary school pupils. The board continued to operate a high school for white girls and one for white boys. Blacks in the county sought an injunction to prevent taxes from being used to operate the white schools until a black high school was reestablished.

Refusing to grant the injunction, the Court said it would not address the issue of equal protection because it was not raised in the case. The Court then said:

[W]hile all admit that the benefits and burdens of public taxation must be shared by citizens without discrimination against any class on account of their race, the education of the people in schools maintained by state taxation is a matter belonging to the respective States, and any interference on the part of the federal authority with the management of such schools cannot be justified except in the case of a clear and unmistakable disregard of rights secured by the supreme law of the land.[17]

Ironically, this opinion was written by Justice John Marshall Harlan, who had so vigorously dissented from *Plessy.* *(See details of Plessy v. Ferguson, pp. 648–649.)*

In 1908 Berea College, a private Christian school incorporated in Kentucky, challenged in the Supreme Court a state law requiring that any institution that taught both blacks and whites conduct separate classes for the two races.

The school said the state had illegally impaired the school's charter by denying it the right to teach students of both races together. The Court rejected the challenge, holding that since the college could still teach members of both races, the law had not significantly injured the school's charter.[18]

Twenty years later a girl of Chinese descent challenged her assignment to an all-black school in Mississippi as a denial of equal protection. In *Gong Lum v. Rice* (1927) the Court upheld her assignment to the black school, saying that the question raised "has been many times decided to be within the constitutional power of the state legislature to settle without intervention of the federal courts under the Federal Constitution."[19]

SEPARATE AND UNEQUAL

In none of these early cases did the Court consider whether the segregated facilities were in fact equal. Nor was school segregation challenged on that specific basis. During the 1930s the NAACP determined that the separate-but-equal doctrine was most vulnerable on this point. Studies of dual school systems, particularly in the South, showed disproportionate amounts of money spent on white and black school facilities, materials, salaries, and transportation.

The NAACP decided first to attack the lack of equality in institutions of higher education. Inequality of facilities and instruction was even more apparent at the university level than at the primary and secondary school levels. Many states provided no school at all to blacks seeking certain advanced degrees. And NAACP officials reasoned that integration of a college or university by a few black students represented less of a threat to the segregated southern lifestyle than did wholesale integration of entire school districts.[20]

In 1938 the Supreme Court decided the first of these cases, *Missouri ex rel. Gaines v. Canada.* Because there were no black law schools in Missouri, Lloyd Gaines, a qualified black undergraduate, applied to the all-white University of Missouri Law School, which refused him admission solely because of his race. The school said it would pay Gaines's tuition at any law school in an adjacent state that would accept him. At the time, law schools in Kansas, Nebraska, Iowa, and Illinois accepted black out-of-state students. This solution was unacceptable to Gaines, who sued to compel the University of Missouri to admit him.

The Supreme Court ruled, 6–2, that Gaines had been denied equal protection and that he was entitled to be admitted to the state's all-white law school. Dismissing the state's contention that it intended to establish a black law school when it became practical, Chief Justice Charles Evans Hughes wrote:

The question here is not of a duty of the State to supply legal training, or of the quality of the training which it does supply, but of its duty when it provides such training to furnish it to the residents of the State upon the basis of an equality of right. By the operation of the laws of Missouri, a privilege has been created for white law students which is denied to Negroes by reason of their race.[21]

The majority also rejected as inadequate the state's promise to pay tuition at an out-of-state school:

We find it impossible to conclude that what otherwise would be an unconstitutional discrimination, with respect to the legal right to the enjoyment of opportunities within the State, can be justified by requiring resort to opportunities elsewhere. That resort may mitigate the inconvenience of the discrimination but cannot serve to validate it.[22]

Ten years later the Court reaffirmed this ruling in *Sipuel v. Board of Regents of the University of Oklahoma* (1948). A law school applicant had been refused admission to the University of Oklahoma because she was black. In a *per curiam* opinion, the Court said the state must provide Ada Lois Sipuel with legal training "in conformity with the equal protection clause."[23]

The next case, *Sweatt v. Painter* (1950), focused on the inequality of two state institutions at which legal training was provided. Refused admission to the all-white University of Texas law school, Heman Marion Sweatt sued in state court. The Court agreed that Sweatt had been denied equal protection but gave the state time to create a black law school. Sweatt refused to apply to the new school on the ground that its instruction would be inferior to the education he would receive at the University of Texas. After state courts held the new school "equal" to the long-established university law school, Sweatt appealed to the Supreme Court.

Unanimously, the Court ordered that Sweatt be admitted to the University of Texas. The Court "cannot find substantial equality in the educational opportunities offered white and Negro law students by the state," wrote Chief Justice Fred M. Vinson. He elaborated:

In terms of number of the faculty, variety of courses and opportunity for specialization, size of the student body, scope of the library, availability of law review and similar activities, the University of Texas Law School is superior. What is more important, the University of Texas Law School possesses to a far greater degree those qualities which are incapable of objective measurement but which make for greatness in a law school. Such qualities, to name but a few, include reputation of the faculty, experience of the administration, position and influence of the alumni, standing in the community, traditions and prestige. It is difficult to believe that one who had a free choice between these law schools would consider the question close.[24]

For the first time the Court had ordered a state to admit a black to an all-white school because the education provided by a black school was inferior. But Vinson said the Court saw no necessity to go on—as Sweatt's attorney, Thurgood Marshall, had asked it to do—to re-examine the separate but equal doctrine "in the light of contemporary knowledge respecting the purposes of the Fourteenth Amendment and the effects of racial segregation."[25]

A second case decided the same day, June 5, 1950, cast even more doubt upon the premise that separate could be equal. A black student named G. W. McLaurin was admitted to the all-white University of Oklahoma as a candidate for a doctorate in education and assigned to a special seat in the classroom and to special tables in the library and cafeteria. The Supreme Court held that such state-imposed requirements produced inequities that could not be tolerated. The restrictions, the Court wrote, "impair and inhibit [McLaurin's] ability to study, to engage in discussion and exchange views with other students, and, in general, to learn his profession."[26] It was only McLaurin's segregation from the rest of the students that made his treatment unequal, the Court recognized. He heard the same lectures, had access to the same books, and ate the same food.

BROWN V. BOARD OF EDUCATION

Even as the Court announced its decisions in *Sweatt* and *McLaurin,* the five cases in which the Court would make the implicit explicit were taking shape. In each of the five cases, parents of black schoolchildren asked lower courts to order school boards to stop enforcing laws requiring or permitting segregated schools.

FAMOUS FOOTNOTE: *PLESSY* REFUTED

One of the more controversial footnotes in Supreme Court history is footnote 11 in *Brown v. Board of Education* (1954). That footnote cited seven sociological and psychological studies of the effects of racial segregation, support for the unanimous Court's contention that segregation on the basis of race generated a feeling of inferiority among blacks that might never be erased. The text of the footnote follows:

11. K. B. Clark, *Effect of Prejudice and Discrimination on Personality Development* (Midcentury White House Conference on Children and Youth, 1950); Witner and Kotinsky, *Personality in the Making* (152), c. VI; Deutscher and Chein, *The Psychological Effects of Enforced Segregation; A Survey of Social Science Opinion*, 26 *J. Psychol.* 259 (1948); Chein, *What are the Psychological Effects of Segregation Under Conditions of Equal Facilities?*, 3 *Int. J. Opinion and Attitude Res.* 229 (1949); Brameld, Educational Costs, in *Discrimination and National Welfare* (McIver, ed., 1949), 44–48; Frazier, *The Negro in the United States* (1949), 674–681. And see generally Myrdal, *An American Dilemma* (1944).[1]

In his book *Simple Justice*, Richard Kluger quotes Chief Justice Earl Warren as saying of the footnote: "We included it because I thought the point it made was the antithesis of what was said in *Plessy*. They had said there that if there was any harm intended, it was solely in the mind of the Negro. I thought these things—these cited sources—were sufficient to note as being in contradistinction to that statement in *Plessy*."[2]

In *Brown v. Board of Education*, Warren restated that point with poignant clarity:

We then come to the question presented: Does segregation of children in public schools solely on the basis of race, even though the physical facilities and other "tangible" factors may be equal, deprive the children of the minority group of equal educational opportunities? We believe that it does. . . . To separate them from others of similar age and qualifications solely because of their race generates a feeling of inferiority as to their status in the community that may affect their hearts and minds in a way unlikely ever to be undone.[3]

Kluger's research indicates that at least two of the justices questioned inclusion of the footnote in the school desegregation opinion, but their objections were minor compared to those that came from critics of the decision. Democratic senator James O. Eastland of Mississippi, (1941, 1943–1979), in a May 27, 1954, speech in the Senate, said:

The Supreme Court could not find the authority for its decisions in the wording of the 14th Amendment, in the history of the amendment or in the decision of any court. Instead, the Court was forced to resort to the unprecedented authority of a group of recent partisan books on sociology and psychology. If this is the judicial calibre of the Court, what can the Nation expect from it in the future? What is to prevent the Court from citing as an authority in some future decision the works of Karl Marx?[4]

Even some who favored desegregation were displeased with the footnote. "It is one thing to use the current scientific findings, however ephemeral they may be, in order to ascertain whether the legislature has acted reasonably, in adopting some scheme of social or economic regulation. . . . It is quite another thing to have our fundamental rights rise, fall or change along with the latest fashions of psychological literature," wrote Professor Edmond Cahn.[5]

Another respected law professor, Alexander Bickel, concluded:

It was a mistake to do it this way. If you're going to invoke sociology and psychology, do it right. . . . No matter how it had been done, no doubt, the enemies of the opinion were certain to seize upon it and proclaim the ruling unjudicial and illegal. The opinion therefore should have said straightforwardly that *Plessy* was based on a self-invented philosophy, no less psychologically oriented than the Court was being now in citing these sources that justify the holding that segregation inflicted damage. It was clear, though, that Warren wanted to present as small a target as possible, and that was wise. He did not want to go out to the country wearing a Hussar's uniform.[6]

More recently, Thurgood Marshall biographer Mark V. Tushnet reexamined the footnote and its importance:

Warren later denied that the material was crucial to the Court's decision, and in some sense it clearly was not. The footnote references were asides. And yet, [the] strategy of introducing the evidence [at trial] paid off. Something had to bridge the gap between the intangibles of [a college's] reputation and the [opportunities for] networking in the university cases and the intangibles in lower schools. Warren's statement about damage to hearts and minds shows that psychological intuitions, if not necessarily the trial court testimony, provided the bridge.[7]

1. *Brown v. Board of Education*, 347 U.S. 483 at 495 (1954).
2. Richard Kluger, *Simple Justice: The History of* Brown v. Board of Education *and Black America's Struggle for Equality* (New York: Knopf, 1976), 706.
3. *Brown v. Board of Education*, 347 U.S. 483 at 493 (1954).
4. U.S. Senate, *Congressional Record*, May 27, 1954, 100: 7252.
5. Edmond Cahn, "Jurisprudence" 30, *New York University Law Review* 150, 159 (1955).
6. Kluger, *Simple Justice*, 707.
7. Mark V. Tushnet, *Making Civil Rights Law: Thurgood Marshall and the Supreme Court, 1946–1961* (New York: Oxford University Press, 1994), 214.

The Cases

The challenge that gave the landmark school desegregation decision its name, *Brown v. Board of Education of Topeka*, was brought in 1951 by Oliver Brown in behalf of his daughter Linda.[27] Under Kansas law permitting cities with populations over 15,000 to operate dual school systems, Topeka had opted to segregate its primary schools. As a result Linda Brown was forced to walk twenty blocks to an all-black grade school rather than attend an all-white school in her neighborhood. Several other black families joined the challenge.

In 1951 a federal district court found Topeka's segregation detrimental to black children but found no constitutional violation because the black and white primary schools were substantially equal with respect to buildings, curricula, transportation, and teachers.

The case of *Briggs v. Elliott* was actually the first to reach the Supreme Court. Federal proceedings began in 1950 when parents of black elementary and secondary school-aged children in Clarendon County, South Carolina, asked a federal district court to enjoin enforcement of state constitutional and statutory provisions requiring segregation in public schools. The court denied the request, but it found the black schools inferior to the white and ordered the school board to equalize them immediately. The court refused, however, to order the school board to admit black children to the white school while the equalization took place.

The children's parents then appealed to the Supreme Court, which in 1952 returned the case to the lower court to consider a report on the progress of the equalization program. The lower court found that the school board had either achieved substantial equality in all areas or soon would, and it again upheld the separate but equal doctrine. The case then returned to the Supreme Court.

Davis v. County School Board of Prince Edward County, Va. was almost identical to *Briggs v. Elliott.* Parents of black high school students sued to stop enforcement of the state's constitutional provisions requiring separate schools. While the district court found the black high school to be inferior and ordered its equalization, it upheld the validity of the segregation provisions. It also refused to admit the black students to white high schools while the black schools were being brought up to par with the white schools.

The fourth case, *Gebhart v. Belton,* involved the schools of New Castle County, Delaware. As in the other cases, parents of black children sued to stop enforcement of the constitutional provisions mandating a dual school system, but unlike the other cases, the state court granted the request. Finding the black schools inferior on a number of points, the court ordered white schools to admit black children. The state supreme court affirmed the decree, which the school board then appealed to the U.S. Supreme Court.

The fifth case, although argued with the other four, was decided separately.[28] *Bolling v. Sharpe* concerned public schools in the District of Columbia. Because the Fourteenth Amendment's guarantee of equal protection of the laws applies only to states, parents of black pupils based their challenge to school segregation in the District on the Fifth Amendment's guarantee of due process. A district court dismissed the suit, and the Supreme Court granted review of the dismissal. *(See box, Federal Equal Protection, p. 622.)*

Together, the five cases brought to the Court grade school pupils and high school students, mandatory segregation laws and more permissive laws, the equal protection clause of the Fourteenth Amendment and the due process clause of the Fifth Amendment.

Geographically, the five cases came from two southern states, one border state, a plains state, and the nation's capital. As one commentator noted, the "wide geographical range gave the anticipated decision a national flavor and would blunt any claim that the South was being made a whipping boy."[29]

In all five cases the lower courts found that education offered black students was substantially equal, or soon would be, to that given in the white schools. Thus the question presented to the

This photograph of Linda Brown, plaintiff in *Brown v. Board of Education,* was taken in 1952 when she was nine years old.

Court was whether public school segregation per se was unconstitutional.

The Arguments

The school cases were argued in December 1952. In June 1953 the Court requested reargument, asking the attorneys to address themselves to three main questions.

• What historical evidence was there that the Framers of the Fourteenth Amendment intended it to apply to segregation in public schools?

• If the answer to the first question was inconclusive, was it within the power of the Court to abolish segregation?

• If school segregation was found unconstitutional, what approach should the Court take to end it?

The cases were reargued in December 1953. Two months earlier former California governor Earl Warren had become chief justice, replacing Vinson, who had died in September. Because Congress had already adjourned when he was named, Warren presided over the Court by virtue of a recess appointment until his unanimous confirmation on March 1, 1954.

Although there were several lawyers on both sides, the two leading adversaries were Marshall, director of the NAACP Legal Defense and Educational Fund, which had been instrumental in guiding the challenge to school segregation through the courts,

Pictured on the steps of the U.S. Supreme Court are the NAACP Legal Defense Fund lawyers who argued the school segregation cases resulting in the May 17, 1954, *Brown v. Board of Education* decision. *Left to right:* Howard Jenkins, James M. Nabrit, Spottswood W. Robinson III, Frank Reeves, Jack Greenberg, Special Counsel Thurgood Marshall, Louis Redding, U. Simpson Tate, and George E. C. Hayes. Missing from the photograph is Robert L. Carter, who argued the Topeka, Kansas, case.

and John W. Davis, U.S. representative, D-W.Va. (1911–1913), solicitor general (1913–1918), and ambassador to Great Britain (1918–1921). In addition to being the 1924 Democratic presidential nominee, he had argued more cases before the Supreme Court than any other lawyer of his era.

Marshall, then forty-five, would become in 1967 the first black to sit *on* the Supreme Court. Davis, at age eighty, was making his final appearance before the Court, arguing in behalf of South Carolina in *Briggs* for the continuation of school segregation.

It is one of the ironies of these cases that in 1915 Davis as solicitor general had successfully persuaded the Court to strike down Oklahoma's "grandfather clause" that prohibited blacks from voting. In that case the fledgling NAACP supported Davis's position in its first friend-of-the-court brief.[30] *(See details of Guinn v. United States, pp. 507–508, in Chapter 10.)*

Davis was first to present an answer to the Court's three questions. He contended that the Fourteenth Amendment was never intended to bar segregation in the nation's public schools. In addition to an intensive examination of the legislative history surrounding enactment of the amendment, Davis also recited the names of the states both North and South that instituted or continued to conduct segregated schools after the amendment was ratified; several of these same states had voted to ratify.

To the question whether the Court had the authority on its

own to overturn the separate but equal doctrine, Davis reminded the Court that the doctrine had been upheld not only by the lower courts but by the Supreme Court, and had therefore become part of the law of the land. "[S]omewhere, sometime to every principle comes a moment of repose when it has been so often announced, so confidently relied upon, so long continued, that it passes the limits of judicial discretion and disturbance," he said.[31]

Making clear what he thought of earlier expert testimony concerning the detrimental effects of segregation on black children, Davis rhetorically asked what impact a desegregation order might have on a predominantly black school district such as Clarendon County:

If it is done on the mathematical basis, with 30 children as a maximum . . . you would have 27 Negro children and three whites in one school room. Would that make the children any happier? Would they learn any more quickly? Would their lives be more serene?

Children of that age are not the most considerate animals in the world, as we all know. Would the terrible psychological disaster being wrought, according to some . . . to the colored child be removed if he had three white children sitting somewhere in the same school room?

Would white children be prevented from getting a distorted idea of racial relations if they sat with 27 Negro children? I have posed that question because it is the very one that cannot be denied.[32]

Davis also said he did not believe the courts had the power to tell the states how to desegregate their schools. "Your Honors do not sit, and cannot sit as a glorified Board of Education for the State of South Carolina or any other state. Neither can the District Court," he declared. Davis then concluded:

Let me say this for the State of South Carolina. . . . It believes that its legislation is not offensive to the Constitution of the United States.

It is confident of its good faith and intention to produce equality for all of its children of whatever race or color. It is convinced that the happiness, the progress and the welfare of these children is best promoted in segregated schools, and it thinks it a thousand pities that by this controversy there should be urged the return to an experiment which gives no more promise of success today than when it was written into their Constitution during what I call the tragic era.

I am reminded—and I hope it won't be treated as a reflection on anybody—of Aesop's fable of the dog and the meat: The dog, with a fine piece of meat in his mouth, crossed a bridge and saw the shadow in the stream and plunged for it and lost both substance and shadow.

Here is equal education, not promised, not prophesied, but present. Shall it be thrown away on some fancied question of racial prestige?[33]

Marshall's response to Davis the following day illustrated the difference between the two men's styles and philosophies:

I got the feeling on hearing the discussion yesterday that when you put a white child in a school with a whole lot of colored children, the child would fall apart or something. Everybody knows that is not true.

Those same kids in Virginia and South Carolina—and I have seen them do it—they play in the streets together, they play on their farms together, they go down the road together, they separate to go to school, they come out of school and play ball together. They have to be separated in school.

There is some magic to it. You can have them voting together, you can have them not restricted because of law in the houses they live in. You can have them going to the same state university and the same college, but if they go to elementary and high school, the world will fall apart. . . . They can't take race out of this case. From the day this case was filed until this moment, nobody has in any form or fashion . . . done anything to distinguish this [segregation] statute from the Black Codes, which they must admit, because nobody can dispute . . . the Fourteenth Amendment was intended to deprive the states of power to enforce Black Codes or anything else like it.

. . . [T]he only way that this Court can decide this case in opposition to our position, is that there must be some reason which gives the state the right to make a classification that they can make in regard to nothing else in regard to Negroes, and we submit the only way to arrive at this decision is to find that for some reason Negroes are inferior to all other human beings. . . .

It can't be because of slavery in the past, because there are very few groups in this country that haven't had slavery some place back in the history of their groups. It can't be color because there are Negroes as white as the drifted snow, with blue eyes, and they are just as segregated as the colored man.

The only thing [it] can be is an inherent determination that the people who were formerly in slavery, regardless of anything else, shall be kept as near that stage as possible, and now is the time, we submit, that this Court should make it clear that that is not what our Constitution stands for.[34]

The Decision

All nine justices—including Robert H. Jackson, who had left a hospital bed—were present May 17, 1954, when Chief Justice Warren read the unanimous decision in *Brown v. Board of Education.* The opinion, described by many as the most socially and ideologically significant decision in the Court's history, was just thirteen paragraphs long.

Warren quickly disposed of the Court's first question—

whether the Framers of the Fourteenth Amendment intended it to bar school segregation. The evidence was inconclusive.

The chief justice then turned to the "separate but equal" doctrine. Children attending the segregated public schools in these cases (unlike *Sweatt*) were—or soon would be—receiving substantially equal treatment so far as "tangible" factors were concerned. Therefore, said Warren, the Court must look at the "effect of segregation itself on public education."[35] That assessment could not be made by turning the clock back to 1868 when the amendment was adopted or to 1896 when the *Plessy* decision was written.

"We must consider public education in the light of its full development and its present place in American life throughout the Nation," wrote Warren. "Only in this way can it be determined if segregation in public schools deprives these plaintiffs of the equal protection of the laws."[36]

The Court found that education was "perhaps the most important function" of state and local government, as evidenced by their compulsory attendance laws and considerable expenditures. Education, wrote Warren, was the foundation of good citizenship and the basis for professional training and adjustment to society.

"In these days, it is doubtful that any child may reasonably be expected to succeed in life if he is denied the opportunity of an education," said Warren, adding that where the state had undertaken to make education available it must be available to all on equal terms.[37]

Warren then posed this question: "Does segregation of children in public schools solely on the basis of race, even though the physical facilities and other 'tangible' factors may be equal, deprive the children of the minority group of equal educational opportunities?"

The Court's answer: "We believe that it does."[38]

Observing that intangible factors were considered in finding the treatment accorded Sweatt and McLaurin unequal, Warren said:

Such considerations apply with added force to children in grade and high schools. To separate them from others of similar age and qualifications solely because of their race generates a feeling of inferiority as to their status in the community that may affect their hearts and minds in a way unlikely ever to be undone.[39]

This belief "was amply supported by modern authority," Warren asserted. In a footnote he cited seven sociological studies on the detrimental effects of enforced racial segregation. *(See box, Famous Footnote, p. 632.)*

Warren then stated:

We conclude that in the field of public education the doctrine of "separate but equal" has no place. Separate educational facilities are inherently unequal. Therefore, we hold that the plaintiffs and others similarly situated for whom the actions have been brought are, by reason of the segregation complained of, deprived of the equal protection of the laws guaranteed by the Fourteenth Amendment.[40]

In the District of Columbia case, considered separately from the other four because it involved a question of due process under the Fifth Amendment, Warren wrote:

The Fourteenth Amendment prohibits state action denying anyone the equal protection of the law. It clearly applies to de jure segregation—that which is imposed by law. It was de jure segregation that the Court declared unconstitutional in *Brown v. Board of Education* (1954). De jure segregation existed throughout most southern and border states.

School segregation also existed in the North and West, particularly in major cities. But most of the northern and western communities had never required segregation by law or had repealed their segregation laws decades before the *Brown* decision. Their so-called de facto segregation resulted from economic status, residential patterns, and other factors outside the usual scope of the equal protection clause.

DENVER, 1973

Almost twenty years after *Brown,* the Court decided the first school segregation case from a state that had not imposed separation by law.

In *Keyes v. School District #1, Denver* (1973), the Court, 7–1, ruled that under certain circumstances segregation in such school systems was unconstitutional.

The case concerned two sets of schools in the Denver school system that were governed by one school board. The first were schools segregated by deliberate actions of the school board, and core city schools that were segregated but not—a lower court had held—as a result of school board action.

The Supreme Court directed the lower court to determine whether the school board's deliberate action in regard to the first set of schools so affected the other schools that it made the entire district a dual (that is, segregated) system. If not, the lower court was to consider proof that the core city schools were not intentionally segregated. If this proof produced by the school board was not persuasive, the court should order desegregation.

With this decision the Court expanded the definition of de jure segregation to include that fostered by intentional school board policies, even in the absence of state law.

Without a showing of intent to segregate, however, no constitutional wrong existed. "We emphasize that the differentiating factor between *de jure* segregation and so-called *de facto* segregation . . . is *purpose or intent to* segregate," Justice William J. Brennan Jr. wrote.[1]

The majority indicated that the deliberate segregation of some of a system's schools could make the entire system a segregated one:

[C]ommon sense dictates the conclusion that racially inspired school board actions have an impact beyond the particular schools that are the subjects of those actions. . . . Plainly a finding of intentional segregation as to a portion of a school system is not devoid of probative value in assessing the school authorities' intent with respect to other parts of the same school system.[2]

Justice Lewis F. Powell Jr. agreed with the decision but not with retention of the de jure, de facto distinction. He contended that the Court should adopt instead the rule that

where segregated public schools exist within a school district to a substantial degree, there is a prima facie case that the duly constituted public authorities . . . are sufficiently responsible [for the segregation] to warrant imposing upon them a nationally applicable burden to demonstrate they nevertheless are operating a genuinely integrated school system.[3]

DISCRIMINATORY INTENT

Disregarding Powell's suggestion, the Court in 1976 and 1977 continued to maintain the distinction between de jure and de facto segregation.

In 1976, in *Austin Independent School District v. United States,* the Supreme Court told lower federal court judges to reconsider the school case of Austin, Texas, in light of *Washington v. Davis,* decided earlier in 1976. In that case the Court ruled that discriminatory intent, as well as discriminatory effect, must be shown for a denial of equal protection to be proved.[4]

DAYTON, 1979

In its 1977 decision in *Dayton (Ohio) Board of Education v. Brinkman,* the Court held that a lower court had erred in holding that the simple existence of racial imbalance in a city's schools constituted proof of deliberate segregation.[5]

But when the Dayton case, along with a case from Columbus returned to the Court two years later, the Court abandoned its effort to distinguish between de jure and de facto segregation. The Court upheld massive court-ordered busing for both school systems, backing the finding of lower courts that both systems were unconstitutionally segregated.[6]

The majority stated that because the Dayton and Columbus systems had been largely segregated by race in 1954—at the time of *Brown*—the school boards in those cities had an affirmative constitutional responsibility to end that segregation. Because they had not, the busing orders were justified, declared the majority: the board's actions after 1954 "having foreseeable and anticipated disparate [racial] impact" were relevant evidence "to prove . . . forbidden purpose."[7]

1. *Keyes v. School District #1, Denver,* 413 U.S. 189 at 208 (1973); see also *Columbus (Ohio) Board of Education v. Penick,* 443 U.S. 449 (1979).

2. Id. at 203, 207 passim.

3. Id. at 224.

4. *Austin Independent School District v. United States,* 429 U.S. 990 (1976); *Washington v. Davis,* 426 U.S. 229 (1976).

5. *Dayton (Ohio) Board of Education v. Brinkman,* 433 U.S. 406 (1977).

6. *Dayton Board of Education v. Brinkman, Columbus Board of Education v. Penick,* 443 U.S. 526 (1979).

7. Id.

Liberty under law extends to the full range of conduct which the individual is free to pursue, and it cannot be restricted except for a proper governmental objective. Segregation in public education is not reasonably related to any proper governmental objective, and thus it imposes on Negro children of the District of Columbia a burden that constitutes an arbitrary deprivation of their liberty in violation of the Due Process Clause.

In view of our decision that the Constitution prohibits the states from maintaining racially segregated public schools, it would be unthinkable that the same Constitution would impose a lesser duty on the Federal Government.[41]

In the four state cases and in the District of Columbia suit, the Court postponed its decision on a remedy for the school segregation until after the parties presented their views on that question.

"ALL DELIBERATE SPEED"

Among the issues the Court asked the parties to address in argument on appropriate remedies were:

• Should the Supreme Court formulate a detailed decree in each of the five cases, and if so, what specific issues should be addressed?

• Should the Court appoint a special master to take evidence and then make specific recommendations to the Court on the contents of the decrees?

• Should the Court remand the cases to the lower courts to fashion the decrees, and if so, what directions and procedural guidelines should the Supreme Court give the lower courts?

• Should black pupils be admitted to schools of their choice "forthwith" or might desegregation be brought about gradually?

In addition to hearing from the parties involved in the five cases, the Court invited the Eisenhower administration and every state that required or permitted segregated public schools to submit their answers to these questions. The administration, Florida, North Carolina, Arkansas, Oklahoma, Maryland, and Texas accepted the invitation and participated in the oral argument in April 1955. Several other states declined the invitation.

On May 31, 1955, Chief Justice Warren announced the Court's final decision in an opinion commonly known as *Brown II*, to distinguish it from the 1954 decision. Warren first noted that the District of Columbia and the school districts in Kansas and Delaware had made substantial progress toward desegregation in the year since the first *Brown* decision was handed down. Virginia and South Carolina, he said, were awaiting the Court's final decision before acting. Warren then moved to the heart of the matter:

Full implementation of these constitutional principles may require solution of varied local school problems. School authorities have the primary responsibility for elucidating, assessing, and solving these problems; courts will have to consider whether the action of school authorities constitutes good faith implementation of the governing constitutional principles. Because of their proximity to local conditions and the possible need for further hearings, the courts which originally heard these cases can best perform this judicial appraisal. Accordingly, we believe it appropriate to remand the cases to those courts.

In fashioning and effectuating the decrees, the courts will be guided by equitable principles. . . . At stake is the personal interest of the plaintiffs in admission to public schools as soon as practicable on a nondiscriminatory basis. To effectuate this interest may call for elimination of a variety of obstacles in making the transition to school systems operated in accordance with the constitutional principles set forth in our May 17, 1954, decision. Courts of equity may properly take into account the public interest in the elimination of such obstacles in a systematic and effective manner. But it should go without saying that the vitality of these constitutional principles cannot be allowed to yield simply because of disagreement with them.

While giving weight to these public and private considerations, the courts will require that the defendants make a prompt and reasonable start toward full compliance with our May 17, 1954, ruling. Once such a start has been made, the courts may find that additional time is necessary to carry out the ruling in an effective manner. The burden rests upon the defendants to establish that such time is necessary in the public interest and is consistent with good faith compliance at the earliest practicable date. To that end, the courts may consider problems related to administration, arising from the physical condition of the school plant, the school transportation system, personnel, revision of school districts and attendance areas into compact units to achieve a system of determining admission to the public schools on a nonracial basis, and revision of local laws and regulations which may be necessary in solving the foregoing problems. They will also consider the adequacy of any plans the defendants may propose to meet these problems and to effectuate a transition to a racially nondiscriminatory school system. During this period of transition, the courts will retain jurisdiction of these cases.[42]

Desegregation of public schools, Warren concluded, was to proceed "with all deliberate speed."[43]

Reaction and Resistance

Reaction to the two *Brown* decisions was immediate.

At one extreme were those committed to segregation as a way of life. They castigated the Court, called the decisions a usurpation of state prerogatives, and urged defiance. The height of the rhetoric opposing the *Brown* decisions may have been the March 1956 "Declaration of Constitutional Principles," a tract signed by 101 of 128 members of Congress from eleven southern and border states. The signers called the *Brown* decisions "a clear abuse of judicial power," and they commended those states that intended to "resist enforced integration by any means."[44]

At the other end of the spectrum were those who hailed the demise of the "separate but equal" doctrine as long overdue but felt that the Court seriously erred in *Brown II* by not ordering immediate desegregation. Many found themselves somewhere in the middle, unhappy with the command to desegregate but unwilling to defy it.

Massive resistance—a phrase coined by Democratic senator Harry F. Byrd of Virginia (1933–1965)—did not begin in earnest until late 1955 and early 1956.

Relieved that the Court had not ordered immediate desegregation, many southern leaders opposed to desegregation apparently presumed that lower courts would ignore or otherwise delay implementation of the *Brown* decisions. By January 1956, however, nineteen lower courts had used the *Brown* precedents to invalidate school segregation and, as historian C. Vann

Woodward characterized it, "[s]omething very much like panic seized many parts of the South . . . a panic bred of insecurity and fear."[45] White citizens councils, created to preserve segregation, spread throughout the South. The NAACP was barred from operating in some states. And many state and local officials sought ways to delay desegregation in the schools.

Official resistance took three main paths. Several states enacted "interposition" statutes declaring the *Brown* decisions of no effect. Mississippi and Louisiana also passed laws requiring school segregation in order to promote public health and morals and preserve the public peace.

Several states also adopted superficially neutral laws that resulted in separation of pupils by race. Among these types of statutes were laws that assigned pupils to specific schools and classes on the basis of their scholastic aptitude and achievement. Since black children had rarely received adequate educations, they were thus easily isolated.

Another tactic was to allow pupils to attend any public school (of the correct grade level) they chose. Few blacks had the courage to attend hostile white schools, and even fewer whites chose to attend black schools. Some states barred public funds to any school district that integrated; others permitted public schools to close rather than to accept black children.

In some instances compulsory attendance laws were repealed, and in still other cases states and localities allocated public funds to private segregated schools. Many states employed more than one of these methods to perpetuate segregation in their public schools.

Brown as Precedent

Adverse reaction to the desegregation decision did not deter the Court from applying it to other areas of life. In 1955 the Court ordered the University of Alabama to admit two blacks to its undergraduate program.[46] In March 1956 the Court in a per curiam opinion declared in *Florida ex rel. Hawkins v. Board of Control* that it would not permit institutes of higher education to delay desegregation.[47] Beginning with the 1954 case of *Muir v. Louisville Park Theatrical Assn.*, the Court, in brief orders that cited *Brown* as authority, struck down the separate but equal doctrine as it applied to state-imposed segregation of public places, such as parks, and vehicles of interstate transportation.[48] *(See "Travel and Public Accommodations," pp. 647–653.)*

RESISTANCE REBUKED

In 1958 the Court first addressed the problem of massive resistance. The occasion was the case of *Cooper v. Aaron,* in which Arkansas officials openly defied the Court's order to abandon segregation.

Less than a week after the Supreme Court struck down the separate but equal doctrine, the Little Rock school board announced its intention to develop a desegregation plan for the city schools. One year later—a week before the Court announced its decision in *Brown II*—the school board approved a plan that called for gradual desegregation beginning with Cen-

In 1957, facing massive resistance in the South to school desegregation, President Eisenhower ordered federal troops to protect black students as they integrated Central High School in Little Rock, Arkansas.

tral High School in the fall of 1957. Meanwhile, the state adopted a constitutional amendment commanding the legislature to oppose the *Brown* decisions. In response, the state legislature enacted a law permitting children in racially mixed schools to ignore compulsory attendance laws.

On September 2, 1957, Governor Orval Faubus sent units of the Arkansas National Guard to Central High to prevent nine black students scheduled to attend the school from entering. Obeying a federal district court order, the school board proceeded with its integration plan, and on September 4 the nine students tried to enter the school, only to find their way blocked by guardsmen standing shoulder to shoulder, along with a mob of hostile onlookers. This situation prevailed until September 20, when Faubus decided to obey a court order and withdraw the troops.

On September 23 the black students entered the high school but were quickly removed by police when a mob outside grew unruly. Two days later President Dwight D. Eisenhower sent federal troops to protect the blacks as they entered and left the school. Federal troops remained there until November 27, when they were replaced by federalized national guardsmen who remained for the duration of the school year.

In the face of both official and public hostility to its desegregation plan, the school board in February 1958 asked the district court for permission to withdraw the black students from Central High and to postpone any further desegregation for two and a half years. Finding the situation at Central intolerable, the court agreed to the request. An appeals court reversed the decision, and the school board appealed to the Supreme Court.

A Special Term

The Court convened a special summer term August 28, 1958, to render its opinion before the school year began. Arguments were heard September 11. The next day the Court issued an unsigned per curiam opinion affirming the appeals court's denial of the postponement. On September 29 the Court issued its formal opinion, which sharply rebuked Faubus and the Arkansas legislature for their obstructive actions.[49]

The Court indicated its sympathy for the Little Rock school board, which it said had acted in good faith, but the Court added that the "constitutional rights of [black] respondents are not to be sacrificed or yielded to the violence and disorder which have followed upon the actions of the Governor and Legislature."[50] The Court then reminded those officials that the Fourteenth Amendment prohibited state officials from denying anyone equal protection of the laws and said that it would not tolerate any state action perpetuating segregation in schools:

State support of segregated schools through any arrangement, management, funds or property cannot be squared with the [Fourteenth] Amendment's command that no State shall deny to any person within its jurisdiction the equal protection of the laws. . . . The basic decision in *Brown* was unanimously reached by this Court only after the case had been briefed and twice argued and the issues had been given the most serious consideration.

Since the first *Brown* opinion three new Justices have come to the Court. They are at one with the Justices still on the Court who participated in that basic decision as to its correctness, and that decision is now unanimously reaffirmed. The principles announced in that decision and the obedience of the States to them, according to the command of the Constitution, are indispensable for the protection of the freedoms guaranteed by our fundamental charter for all of us. Our constitutional ideal of equal justice under law is thus made a living truth.[51]

To emphasize the gravity with which they viewed the defiance of the Arkansas officials, each of the nine justices personally signed the opinion.

Governor Faubus and the Arkansas legislature chose to ignore this warning. With approval of the legislature, Faubus closed all four Little Rock high schools, which remained closed for the entire 1958–1959 school year. In June 1959 a federal district court declared the statute authorizing the closing a violation of due process and equal protection, and the Supreme Court affirmed that opinion.[52] Little Rock high schools opened to black and white students in the fall of 1959.

Other Decisions

Despite its protestation in the Arkansas case that it would not tolerate schemes to evade segregation, the Court in November 1958 affirmed without opinion an appeals court decision upholding Alabama's pupil placement law as constitutional on its face. (The lower court had made clear, however, that the law might be found unconstitutional if its application resulted in racial discrimination.)[53]

In two 1959 cases the Supreme Court refused to review lower court rulings requiring that all state remedies for segregation be exhausted before a case could move into federal court.[54]

Over the next three years the Court affirmed lower court decisions striking down Louisiana laws clearly designed to continue school segregation.[55]

Then in June 1963 the Court began to express its impatience with dilatory school boards. In the first signed opinion on school desegregation since *Cooper v. Aaron,* the Court struck down a transfer scheme that worked to preserve segregated schools. Its decision in *Goss v. Board of Education of Knoxville* reversed the lower courts' approval of transfer plans in two Tennessee cities that allowed students assigned to schools where they were in the minority to transfer to schools where their race was in the majority. The unanimous Court declared that because it was "readily apparent" that the plan would continue segregation, it was unconstitutional.[56]

In a second case in 1963, *McNeese v. Board of Education,* the Court ruled that where federal rights were at stake, all state remedies need not be exhausted before relief was sought in federal court.[57]

TOO MUCH DELIBERATION

The following year, a full ten years after *Brown I,* the Court announced that there had been too much deliberation and not enough speed in the effort to desegregate the nation's public schools.

The case of *Griffin v. County School Board of Prince Edward County* (1964) originated in the same Virginia county involved in *Brown.* Despite that decision in 1954, the county's schools remained segregated. In 1959 the county closed its schools rather than obey a lower court order to desegregate. The county then replaced the public schools for whites with private schools, partially financed by public funds.

The county offered to set up similar schools for blacks. The blacks refused the offer and pursued the legal battle for integrated public schools. Consequently, black children in Prince Edward County could not attend public school there from 1959 until 1963. Finally, federal, state, and local officials cooperated to open some desegregated public schools in the county.

In 1961 a federal district court ordered a halt in the flow of public funds to the all-white private schools. In 1962 it ordered the county to reopen the public schools, ruling that it could not constitutionally close the schools to avoid segregating them while all the other public schools in the state remained open. The county appealed the ruling to the Supreme Court.

"Whatever nonracial grounds might support a State's allowing a county to abandon public schools, the object must be a constitutional one, and grounds of race and opposition to desegregation do not qualify as constitutional," the Court said in 1964 affirming the lower court order.[58]

Dismissing the county's contention that the state courts

should have been given an opportunity to determine whether the schools should be opened before the federal district court acted, the Court declared:

[W]e hold that the issues here imperatively call for decision now. The case has been delayed since 1951 by resistance at the state and county level, by legislation, and by lawsuits. The original plaintiffs have doubtless all passed high school age. There has been entirely too much deliberation and not enough speed in enforcing the constitutional rights which we held in Brown . . . had been denied Prince Edward County Negro children.[59]

The Court spoke even more sharply in a November 1965 ruling. "Delays in desegregating public school systems are no longer tolerable," the justices declared in a per curiam opinion in *Bradley v. School Board of City of Richmond*.[60] Three weeks later, in *Rogers v. Paul*, the Court in another per curiam opinion ordered an Arkansas school district to permit a black student "immediate transfer" to an all-white high school, adding that "those similarly situated" might transfer as well.[61] In December 1967 the Court affirmed without opinion lower court rulings requiring Alabama to desegregate its schools. It was the first time that a state was ordered to take such action; previously, desegregation orders had been directed only to local school systems.[62]

"Affirmative Duty"

In May 1968 the Supreme Court put its foot down. The unanimous Court ordered still-segregated school systems to devise desegregation plans that promised to be effective. In *Green v. County School Board of New Kent County, Va.*, the Court held that the county's freedom of choice plan did not accomplish the goals set out in *Brown I* and *Brown II*.

Freedom of choice plans allowed students to choose which school within the district they wanted to attend. Details varied from district to district, but in most instances custom and residential patterns served to keep the schools under such plans racially segregated.

Rural New Kent County, with a population divided almost evenly between whites and blacks, was originally segregated by Virginia law. In 1965 the school board adopted a freedom of choice plan, but, as the Supreme Court noted, in three years of operation no white pupil chose to attend the black school and only 15 percent of the black children were enrolled in the formerly all-white school.

In an opinion written by Justice William J. Brennan Jr., the Court said the school board's adoption of a freedom of choice plan did not fulfill its obligation to desegregate the county schools:

In the context of the state-imposed segregated pattern of long standing, the fact that in 1965 the Board opened the doors of the former "white" school to Negro children and of the "Negro" school to white children merely begins, not ends, our inquiry whether the Board has taken steps adequate to abolish its dual, segregated system. Brown II was a call for the dismantling of well-entrenched dual systems tempered by an awareness that complex and multifaceted problems would arise which would require time and flexibility for a successful resolution. School boards such as the respondent then operating state-compelled dual systems were nevertheless clearly charged with the affirma-

tive duty to take whatever steps might be necessary to convert to a unitary system in which racial discrimination would be eliminated root and branch.[63]

Observing that it had taken eleven years after *Brown I* for the district to begin desegregating, Brennan continued:

This deliberate perpetuation of the unconstitutional dual system can only have compounded the harm of such a system. . . . Moreover, a plan that at this late date fails to provide meaningful assurance of prompt and effective disestablishment of a dual system is also intolerable. . . . The burden on a school board today is to come forward with a plan that promises realistically to work, and promises realistically to work now.[64]

Effective Remedy

The Court refused to say that any one type of desegregation plan promised to be more effective than another, leaving it up to each individual school district to fashion a remedy best suited to its situation and needs. But it did give the district courts some guidance in assessing the effectiveness of desegregation plans. Brennan wrote:

It is incumbent upon the district court to weigh that claim [of plan effectiveness] in light of the facts at hand and . . . any alternatives which may be shown as feasible and more promising in their effectiveness. Where the court finds the board to be acting in good faith and the proposed plan to have real prospects for dismantling the state-imposed dual system "at the earliest practicable date," then the plan may be said to provide effective relief. Of course, the availability to the board of other, more promising courses of action may indicate a lack of good faith; and at the least it places a heavy burden upon the board to explain its preference for an apparently less effective method.[65]

Although it did not rule out freedom of choice plans entirely, the Court said experience indicated they were usually ineffective. Certainly, the Court said, New Kent County's plan was ineffective. There "the plan has operated simply to burden children and their parents with a responsibility which *Brown II* places squarely on the School Board." The Court ordered the board to formulate a new plan that promised to convert the county schools "to a system, without a 'white' school and a 'Negro' school, but just schools."[66]

In two other cases decided the same day, the Court applied *Green* to find a freedom of choice plan in an Arkansas school district and a free transfer plan in Jackson, Tennessee, unlikely to achieve desegregation.[67]

Green was the last major school desegregation case in which Chief Justice Warren participated; he retired in June 1969. In the first case heard by Chief Justice Burger, the Court reversed an appeals court order that allowed indefinite postponement of desegregation in thirty-three Mississippi school districts so long as they took "significant steps" in the forthcoming school year to dismantle their dual school systems.

The Court's brief decision in *Alexander v. Holmes Board of Education* (1969) took on added significance because the administration of President Richard Nixon had argued for allowing delay. In an unsigned opinion, the Court said that the standard of "all deliberate speed" was "no longer constitutionally permissible," and it ordered the school districts to begin immediate operation of unitary school systems. The Court defined these as "systems within which no person is to be effectively excluded from any school because of race or color."[68]

THE SCOPE OF THE REMEDY

Chief Justice Burger's appointment to the Court coincided with a shift in the focus of school desegregation cases. With *Green* it became clear that schools could no longer avoid the duty to desegregate; the question now was what methods could be used to accomplish that end? A major issue was whether schools were required to reflect the racial balance that existed in the community. Would neighborhood schools, whatever their racial balance, satisfy the desegregation requirement so long as they were open to students of all races? Or must pupils be transported beyond their normal geographic school zones to achieve some sort of racial balance?

The Swann Decision

School officials, the Court held in 1971, could choose from a broad range of desegregation tools those that would most effectively eliminate segregation in their district. In a unanimous decision the Court ruled in *Swann v. Charlotte-Mecklenburg County Board of Education* that busing, racial balance quotas, and gerrymandered school districts were all appropriate interim methods of eliminating the vestiges of school segregation.

The case arose from controversy over the desegregation of the Charlotte-Mecklenburg County, North Carolina, school system. That system in the 1969–1970 school year had 84,000 students, 71 percent white and 29 percent black. In that year almost 29,000 of those students were bused to school in an effort to desegregate the school system.

Of the 24,000 black students, 21,000 lived within the city of Charlotte. Because of the smaller number and dispersed residences of black pupils in the rural part of the county, there were no all-black schools in that part of the system. But in the city, most schools remained racially identifiable, and two of every three of the city's black students attended one of twenty-five schools that were 98 percent to 100 percent black. Three of every four of the area's white students attended schools that were primarily white.

In February 1970 a federal district judge ordered 13,000 additional students bused. More than 9,000 of these pupils were elementary school children. Under the order, no school remained all black, and the effort was made to reach a 71:29 white-black ratio in each school, reflecting the overall white-black ratio in the system.

The Fourth Circuit Court of Appeals first delayed, then reversed the elementary school part of the plan as imposing an unreasonable burden upon the school board. The NAACP Legal Defense Fund, representing the black parents concerned, appealed to the Supreme Court, arguing that the order should have been left intact. The school board also appealed, arguing that more of the order should have been modified.

Chief Justice Burger wrote the Court's opinion. He pointed

TWO RACES, TWO DISTRICTS?

One way some towns and cities avoided desegregation was to divide a school district so that most black children would attend the schools of one district and most white children the other. The Supreme Court did not view this ploy sympathetically. In two cases decided in 1972, it struck down such efforts.

Wright v. Emporia City Council concerned a Virginia city whose schools were part of the surrounding county school system. When the county was ordered to desegregate its schools, the city petitioned to operate its own school system. Although both city and county school systems would have had a majority of black students, the county schools would have been more heavily black if the city school district were created than if the city's students were part of a countywide plan.

By a 5–4 vote the Court ruled the city's proposal impermissible because it would hinder desegregation. "Certainly desegregation is not achieved by splitting a single school system operating 'white schools' and 'Negro schools' into two new systems, each operating unitary schools within its borders, where one of the two new systems is, in fact, 'white' and the other is, in fact, 'Negro,'" the majority stated.[1]

The four dissenters denied that creation of the second school system would interfere with the desegregation process. A second system should not be rejected if its only effect was a slightly greater racial imbalance in both school systems, they said.

In the second case, the Court was unanimous in its opinion that the creation of a new school district was impermissible. *United States v. Scotland Neck City Board of Education* involved the North Carolina legislature's creation of a school district for the city of Scotland Neck, which had been part of a county school system that was in the process of implementing a desegregation plan. The Court said there was no question that the statute was motivated by a desire to create a predominantly white school system in the city and so it must be struck down.[2]

1. *Wright v. Emporia City Council,* 407 U.S. 451 at 463 (1972).
2. *United States v. Scotland Neck Board of Education,* 407 U.S. 484 (1972).

---

out that federal courts became involved in the desegregation process only when local school authorities failed to fulfill their obligation to eliminate the dual school system. If school authorities did so default—as the lower federal court found that the Charlotte school board had in *Swann*—then the federal judge had wide discretion to select the means of desegregating the school system. Burger then discussed the four main issues *Swann* presented: racial balance, one-race schools, attendance zones, and busing.

Racial Balance. The Court held that the federal district court had properly used mathematical ratios of whites and blacks as "a starting point in the process of shaping a remedy."

However, Burger wrote, a court could not require "as a matter of substantive constitutional right" any specific degree of racial mixing. "The constitutional command to desegregate schools does not mean that every school in every community must always reflect the racial composition of the school system as a whole."[69]

One-Race Schools. The Court acknowledged that residential patterns often result in schools that were attended only by children of one race. The presence of such schools did not necessarily indicate a system that was still segregated, but, wrote Burger, school authorities or the district court

should make every effort to achieve the greatest possible degree of actual desegregation and will thus necessarily be concerned with the elimination of one-race schools. No per se rule can adequately embrace all the difficulties of reconciling the competing interests involved; but in a system with a history of segregation, the need for remedial criteria of sufficient specificity to assure a school authority's

compliance with its constitutional duty warrants a presumption against schools that are substantially disproportionate in their racial composition. . . . [T]he burden upon the school authorities will be to satisfy the court that their racial composition is not the result of present or past discriminatory action on their part.[70]

The Court endorsed plans that allowed a child attending a school where his or her race was a majority to transfer to a school where the child's race was a minority. But to be successful, the justices added, such plans must ensure the transferring pupil available space in the school and free transportation.

Attendance Zones. To overcome the effects of segregated residential patterns, the Court endorsed drastic gerrymandering of school districts and pairing, clustering, and grouping of schools that were not necessarily contiguous. "As an interim corrective

---

DISCRIMINATION AND PRIVATE SCHOOLS . . . TEXTBOOKS TO TAXES

Private schools proliferated in most areas under pressure to desegregate public schools. Many of the private schools were created specifically as havens for whites fleeing desegregation.

As early as 1925 the Supreme Court acknowledged the right of parents to send their children to private schools. In *Pierce v. Society of Sisters* the Court ruled that an Oregon statute requiring all children to attend public schools "unreasonably interferes with the liberty of parents and guardians to direct the upbringing and education of children under their control."[1]

This holding, coupled with the Court's view that the Fourteenth Amendment did not prohibit acts of private discrimination, appeared to immunize private schools with racially discriminatory admissions policies from desegregation efforts.

But two Supreme Court rulings in the 1970s curtailed the forms of support that state and local governments could provide to racially discriminatory private schools. In a third case the Court significantly narrowed the freedom of such schools to discriminate. And in 1983 the Court held that racial discrimination by a private university was grounds for denial, or withdrawal, of that university's tax-exempt status.

TEXTBOOKS

In *Norwood v. Harrison* (1973) a unanimous Court held that it was not permissible for Mississippi to lend textbooks to private schools that discriminated on the basis of race. Lending textbooks was direct state aid in violation of the Fourteenth Amendment. (In other cases the Court has held that the First Amendment's clause prohibiting government establishment of religion bars states from lending textbooks to parochial schools but not from lending them to children who attend those schools.) *(See "State Aid to Church-Related Schools," pp. 490–496, in Chapter 9.)*

Noting that it had affirmed lower court rulings barring state tuition grants to students attending racially discriminatory private schools, Chief Justice Warren E. Burger wrote:

Free textbooks, like tuition grants directed to private school students, are a form of financial assistance inuring to the benefit of the private schools themselves. An inescapable educational cost for students in both public

and private schools is the expense of providing all necessary learning materials. When, as here, that necessary expense is borne by the State, the economic consequence is to give aid to the enterprise; if the school engages in discriminatory practices the State by tangible aid in the form of textbooks thereby supports such discrimination. Racial discrimination in state-operated schools is barred by the Constitution and "[i]t is also axiomatic that a State may not induce, encourage or promote private persons to accomplish what it is constitutionally forbidden to accomplish."[2]

The Court rejected Mississippi's contention that to deny such private schools state aid would deny them equal protection of the laws. "It is one thing to say that a State may not prohibit the maintenance of private schools and quite another to say that such schools must, as a matter of equal protection, receive state aid," declared the Court.[3]

ATHLETIC FACILITIES

In 1974 the Court affirmed a lower court order forbidding Montgomery, Alabama, to permit racially discriminatory private schools to have exclusive use of its park and recreational facilities. Such permission "created, in effect, 'enclaves of segregation,'" which deprived black children and their families of equal access to the parks.[4]

Furthermore, the city's action ran counter to the intent of a court order directing it to desegregate its public schools. Justice Harry A. Blackmun explained that the city, by permitting these schools to have exclusive use of public recreational facilities, enhanced the attractiveness of segregated private schools—formed in reaction to the desegregation order—by enabling them to offer athletic programs to their students at public expense.

Because the city provided the schools with stadiums and other recreational facilities, the schools were able to spend money they would have spent on athletic programs or other educational projects. At the same time, the schools realized revenue from the concessions operated at the stadiums and other facilities.

"We are persuaded," concluded Blackmun in *Gilmore v. City of Montgomery*, ". . . that this assistance significantly tended to undermine the federal court order mandating the establishment and maintenance of a unitary school system in Montgomery."[5]

measure, this cannot be said to be beyond the broad remedial powers of a court," the chief justice wrote.[71]

Busing. Bus transportation of students had been an "integral part of the public education system for years," Burger wrote, and was a permissible remedial technique to help achieve desegregation. The Court conceded that objections to busing might be valid "when the time or distance of travel is so great as to either risk the health of the children or significantly impinge on the educational process." The limits to busing would vary with many factors, "but probably with none more than the age" of the children, the Court said.[72]

The Court acknowledged that some of these remedies might be "administratively awkward, inconvenient and even bizarre in some situations and may impose burdens on some; but all awkwardness and inconvenience cannot be avoided in the interim period when the remedial adjustments are being made to eliminate the dual school systems."[73]

The Court was careful to say that its decision did not deal with de facto segregation, discrimination resulting from factors other than state law. Nor did it reach the question of what action might be taken against schools that were segregated as a result of "other types of state action, without any discriminatory action by the school authorities."[74]

In reference to the potential problem of resegregation, which might occur after achievement of a unitary school system, the Court concluded:

However, the Court was unable to decide whether it was unconstitutional for the state to allow the segregated private schools to use the facilities in common with other schoolchildren and private nonschool organizations.

ADMISSIONS POLICIES

Racially discriminatory admissions policies of private schools were directly challenged in the 1976 cases of *Runyon v. McCrary* and *Fairfax-Brewster School v. Gonzales.* Two private schools in northern Virginia, Bobbe's Private School and Fairfax-Brewster School, refused to admit Michael McCrary and Colin Gonzales solely because they were black. Their parents filed suit on behalf of the boys, charging that discriminatory admissions policies violated the 1866 Civil Rights Act that gives "all persons within the jurisdiction of the United States the same right . . . to make and enforce contracts . . . as is enjoyed by white citizens." A federal district court and court of appeals agreed with the parents, and the Supreme Court affirmed the lower courts by a 7–2 vote.[6]

The majority, with Justice Potter Stewart as its spokesman, rejected the argument that the 1866 law did not reach private contracts. That claim was inconsistent with the Court's earlier rulings, said Stewart, in particular the 1968 decision in *Jones v. Alfred H. Mayer Co.* In that decision the Court held that a companion provision of the 1866 act forbade private racial discrimination in the sale or rental of property.[7] *(See details of this case, pp. 655–656.)*

The Court also rejected the arguments that application of the 1866 law to admissions policies violated the constitutional right of parents to have their children associate only with certain persons and to send their children to schools that promote racial segregation. "[P]arents have a First Amendment right to send their children to educational institutions that promote the belief that racial segregation is desirable, and . . . the children have an equal right to attend such institutions," Stewart wrote. "But it does not follow that the *practice* of excluding racial minorities from such institutions is also protected" by the right of association.[8]

Dissenting for himself and Justice William H. Rehnquist, Justice Byron R. White took issue with the extension of the contract provision of the 1866 law to private action. No person, black or white, has a right to enter into a contract with an unwilling party, White said.[9]

In 1989 the Court unanimously reaffirmed its decision in *Runyon.* This time Rehnquist, now chief justice, and White agreed with the majority. Kennedy's opinion stressed adherence to precedent, *stare decisis.* He said that the antique Civil Rights Act of 1866 did indeed continue to prohibit racial discrimination in the making and enforcing of private contracts.[10]

TAX-EXEMPT STATUS

Citing the national interest in ending race discrimination, the Court had ruled in 1983 that the federal government could deny tax-exempt status to private schools, including universities, that discriminated against blacks. By an 8–1 vote in *Bob Jones University v. United States,* the justices upheld the decision of the Internal Revenue Service in 1970 to stop granting tax-exempt status to discriminatory private schools.

The school in this case argued that its policy of discriminating against black students was based upon sincerely held religious beliefs. Writing for the Court, Chief Justice Burger countered that the national interest in eradicating racial discrimination in education "substantially outweighs whatever burden denial of tax benefits places" on the exercise of the freedom of religion.[11] Only Justice Rehnquist dissented.

1. *Pierce v. Society of Sisters,* 268 U.S. 510 at 534–535 (1925).

2. *Norwood v. Harrison,* 413 U.S. 455 at 463–465 (1973); for state tuition grants cases, see *Brown v. South Carolina Board of Education,* 296 F. Supp. 199 (S.C. 1968), affirmed per curiam 393 U.S. 222 (1968); *Poindexter v. Louisiana Finance Commission,* 275 F. Supp. 833 (E D La. 1967), affirmed per curiam 389 U.S. 571 (1968).

3. *Norwood v. Harrison,* 413 U.S. 455 at 462 (1973).

4. *Gilmore v. City of Montgomery,* 417 U.S. 556 at 566 (1974).

5. Id. at 569.

6. *Runyon v. McCrary, Fairfax-Brewster School v. Gonzales,* 427 U.S. 160 (1976).

7. *Jones v. Alfred H. Mayer Co.,* 392 U.S. 409 (1969).

8. *Runyon v. McCrary,* 427 U.S. 160 at 176 (1976).

9. Id. at 195.

10. *Patterson v. McLean Credit Union,* 491 U.S. 164 (1989).

Neither school authorities nor district courts are constitutionally required to make year-by-year adjustments of the racial composition of student bodies once the affirmative duty to desegregate has been accomplished and racial discrimination through official action is eliminated from the system. This does not mean that federal courts are without power to deal with future problems; but in the absence of a showing that either the school authorities or some other agency of the state has deliberately attempted to fix or alter demographic patterns to affect the racial composition of the schools, further intervention by a district court should not be necessary.[75]

Related Rulings

The Court handed down three other related school desegregation decisions the same day—April 20, 1971. In *North Carolina State Board of Education v. Swann* the Court struck down a state law that forbade school systems to bus or assign students to schools on the basis of race. The Court said the law was invalid because it prevented implementation of desegregation plans.

[I]f a state-imposed limitation on a school authority's discretion operates to inhibit or obstruct the operation of a unitary school system or impede the disestablishing of a dual school system, it must fall; state policy must give way when it operates to hinder vindication of federal constitutional guarantees. . . . [T]he statute exploits an apparently neutral form to control school assignment plans by directing that they be "color-blind"; that requirement, against the background of segregation, would render illusory the promise of *Brown*. . . . Just as the race of students must be considered in determining whether a constitutional violation has occurred, so also must race be considered in formulating a remedy. To forbid, at this stage, all assignments made on the basis of race would deprive school authorities of the one tool absolutely essential to fulfillment of their constitutional obligation to eliminate existing dual school systems.[76]

In *Davis v. Board of School Commissioners of Mobile County, Ala.*, the Court ordered an appeals court to reexamine its desegregation order for Mobile, Alabama, in light of the guidelines set down in *Swann*. The Court said the appeals court had not considered all the available techniques for desegregation. The plan included no busing for black children attending predominantly black high schools, and its insistence on geographically unified school zones tended to preserve single-race schools.[77]

In the third case, *McDaniel v. Barresi*, the Court upheld a Georgia county desegregation plan that assigned black pupils living in heavily black areas to schools in other attendance zones. The state supreme court had declared the plan invalid on the grounds that busing only black pupils denied equal protection of the laws. But the Supreme Court said the school board had acted properly in considering race as a factor in a desegregation plan.[78]

"TAILORING" THE REMEDY

In the early 1970s opposition to court-ordered desegregation focused on the school bus. The nearly universal antipathy to busing did not cause the Supreme Court to retract its opinion that busing was an appropriate remedy for segregation, but in 1974 the Court began to insist that the scope of the remedy not exceed the extent of the violation causing the segregation.

Busing Across Boundaries: Richmond and Detroit

The first time the Court considered whether federal courts could require busing between school districts as part of a desegregation plan, it did not reach a conclusion.

The Supreme Court ruled in *Swann v. Charlotte-Mecklenburg County Board of Education* (1971) that busing is an appropriate method of eliminating the vestiges of school segregation. In this photograph, motorcycle police escort buses from South Boston High School in Boston, Massachusetts.

The case of *Richmond School Board v. Virginia State Board of Education* (1973) came to the Court after a federal district judge ordered school officials to consolidate the predominantly black Richmond school district with the two neighboring, mostly white county systems in order to desegregate the city schools.[79] The court of appeals overturned the order as too drastic.

The Supreme Court divided 4–4, automatically upholding the court of appeals. Justice Lewis F. Powell Jr. did not participate in the case; he had formerly served on both the Richmond and Virginia school boards. There was no Court opinion, and because of the even vote, the case carried no weight as precedent.

Little more than a year later, the Court, 5–4, struck down a district court plan to desegregate Detroit, Michigan, schools by busing students among fifty-four school districts in three counties. The majority held that a multidistrict remedy was not appropriate unless all of the districts were responsible for the segregation.

Milliken v. Bradley (1974) originated when a federal district judge concluded that both the Detroit school board and state officials had taken actions that fostered school segregation in the city. Because the city school system was predominantly black, the judge declared that a plan limited to its boundaries would fail to provide meaningful desegregation of the schools. He therefore ordered the multidistrict remedy. "[S]chool district lines are simply matters of political convenience and may not be used to deny constitutional rights," the judge ruled.[80] A court of appeals affirmed the order.

The Supreme Court majority overturned the order. Chief Justice Burger explained that both lower courts erred when they assumed that desegregation could not be achieved unless the Detroit schools reflected the racial balance of the surrounding metropolitan area. Although "boundary lines may be bridged where there has been a constitutional violation calling for interdistrict relief," wrote Burger, ". . . the notion that school district lines may be casually ignored or treated as a mere administrative convenience is contrary to the history of public education in our country."[81]

In any school desegregation case, said Burger, the scope of the remedy should not exceed the extent of the violation. He continued:

Before the boundaries of separate and autonomous school districts may be set aside by consolidating the separate units for remedial purposes or by imposing a cross-district remedy, it must first be shown that there has been a constitutional violation within one district that produces a significant segregative effect in another district. Specifically, it must be shown that racially discriminatory acts of the state or local school districts, or of a single school district, have been a substantial cause of interdistrict segregation. Thus an interdistrict remedy might be in order where the racially discriminatory acts of one or more school districts caused racial segregation in an adjacent district or where district lines have been deliberately drawn on the basis of race. In such circumstances, an interdistrict remedy would be appropriate to eliminate the interdistrict segregation directly caused by the constitutional violation. Conversely, without an interdistrict violation and in-

terdistrict effect, there is no constitutional wrong calling for an interdistrict remedy.[82]

Since none of the other fifty-three school districts had been shown to practice segregation or to have been affected by Detroit's segregation, the proposed remedy was "wholly impermissible," the majority concluded.

Nor did the fact that state officials contributed to the segregation empower the federal court to order the multidistrict remedy. "Disparate treatment of white and Negro students occurred within the Detroit school system, and not elsewhere, and on this record the remedy must be limited to that system," Burger wrote.[83]

Without an interdistrict remedy, wrote Justice Marshall in a dissenting opinion, "Negro children in Detroit will receive the same separate and inherently unequal education in the future as they have been unconstitutionally afforded in the past."[84] Marshall insisted that the segregative actions of state officials justified the multidistrict remedy:

The essential foundation of interdistrict relief in this case was not to correct conditions within outlying districts. . . . Instead, interdistrict relief was seen as a necessary part of any meaningful effort by the State of Michigan to remedy the state-caused segregation within the city of Detroit.[85]

Remedying the System: Detroit and Dayton

The Supreme Court remanded *Milliken* to the district court to fashion a new remedy that affected only the Detroit city schools. In an opinion affirmed by the appeals court, the district court ordered the school board as part of the new remedy to institute comprehensive remedial education, testing, training, counseling, and guidance programs in the city schools. It also directed the state to pay half the costs of implementing these programs. These two parts of the remedy were appealed to the Supreme Court, which upheld them in 1977 by a 9–0 vote.

The Court found the comprehensive remedial programs appropriate to remedy the educational conditions caused by the segregation. "Pupil assignment alone does not automatically remedy the impact of previous unlawful educational isolation; the consequences linger and can be dealt with only by independent measures," the Court said.[86]

The justices also held that the order to the state to pay half the costs was not equivalent, as the state claimed, to an award for damages. In a nonschool-related case, the Court in 1974 had ruled that the Eleventh Amendment protected states against such payments of damages.[87] But the school payments were permissible, held the Court, because they amounted to prospective relief "designed to wipe out continuing conditions of inequality" caused by the state.[88]

In the 1974 *Milliken* decision the Court held that where segregation affected only one school district, a multidistrict remedy was excessive. In 1977 the Court held that where segregation did not affect an entire school district, a systemwide desegregation plan was excessive.

A federal district court found in *Dayton (Ohio) Board of Ed-*

ucation v. Brinkman that the city school board had discriminated against minority students in three specific instances. After a court of appeals rejected more limited remedies, the district court proposed a desegregation plan that involved the entire school district. The appeals court affirmed this plan, but the Supreme Court struck it down, 8–0.

In an opinion written by Justice William H. Rehnquist, the Court questioned the validity of the district court's finding of discrimination in two of the instances and observed that the discrimination in the third affected only high school students. Under these circumstances, the Court said, the appeals court overstepped its proper role when it ordered the district court to develop a systemwide plan without disputing the district court's findings of fact or legal opinion. Rehnquist wrote:

The duty of both the District Court and of the Court of Appeals in a case such as this, where mandatory segregation by law of the races in the schools has long since ceased, is to first determine whether there was any action in the conduct of the business of the school board which was intended to, and did in fact, discriminate against minority pupils, teachers or staff. . . . If such violations are found, the District Court in the first instance, subject to review by the Court of Appeals, must determine how much incremental segregative effect these violations had on the racial distribution of the Dayton school population as presently constituted, when that distribution is compared to what it would have been in the absence of such constitutional violations. The remedy must be designed to redress that difference, and only if there has been a systemwide impact may there be a systemwide remedy.[89]

In 1979 the Court held that the board's discrimination had a systemwide impact and thus necessitated a systemwide remedy. (*See box, De Facto Segregation, p. 636.*)

Balance, Not Rebalance: Pasadena

The Court in *Swann* said that once a school system was desegregated, school authorities would not be required to make annual adjustments in order to maintain a specific racial balance in each school. In the 1976 case of *Pasadena City Board of Education v. Spangler,* the Court elaborated on that point.

The Pasadena, California, school board adopted a desegregation plan stipulating that as of the 1970–1971 school year, no school in the district could have a majority of students of a minority race. In 1974 the school board asked the district court to lift or modify the "no-majority" requirement. Observing that the board had complied with that requirement only in the initial year of the plan's implementation, the district court refused the request. It held that the requirement was applicable every year, even though residential patterns and other factors outside the school board's control resulted in a changing racial composition of the schools.

The Supreme Court, 6–2, reversed the district court, holding that its literal interpretation required the board to maintain a specific racial balance, something that the Court in *Swann* said it would disapprove. The majority wrote:

No one disputes that the initial implementation of the plan accomplished [its] objective. That being the case, the District Court was not entitled to require the [school district] to rearrange its attendance zones each year so as to ensure that the racial mix desired by the court was maintained in perpetuity. For having once implemented a racially neutral attendance pattern in order to remedy the perceived constitutional violations on the part of the defendants [the school board], the District Court has fully performed its function of providing the appropriate remedy for previous racially discriminatory attendance patterns.[90]

Joined in dissent by Justice Brennan, Justice Marshall noted that the desegregation plan fulfilled the no-majority requirement only for one year and that without its continued maintenance immediate resegregation of the school system was likely. Because a lasting unitary school system had apparently not been achieved, Marshall said the majority's application of *Swann* was improper. *Swann*, wrote Marshall,

recognizes on the one hand that a fully desegregated school system may not be compelled to adjust its attendance zones to conform to changing demographic patterns. But on the other hand, it also appears to recognize that until such a unitary system is established, a district court may act with broad discretion—discretion which includes the adjustment of attendance zones—so that the goal of a wholly unitary system might be sooner achieved.[91]

Judicial Withdrawal: Kansas City

For the next twenty years the Court continued down the path of *Milliken* and *Pasadena*, easing judges out of the business of desegregating schools. In a 1991 Oklahoma City case, the Court emphasized that desegregation decrees were meant to be temporary.[92] In that decision the justices, 5–3, said formerly segregated school districts may free themselves of court orders directing school busing if they can prove that elements of past discrimination have been removed to all "practicable" extent.

Federal judges' role in local school desegregation was likely to be further diminished as a result of the Court's 1995 ruling in *Missouri v. Jenkins*.[93]

Five years earlier, when the Kansas City, Missouri, case was first before the Court, the justices endorsed broad judicial authority to move school systems toward desegregation. By 5–4, the Court allowed a judge to order a local government to levy taxes in excess of state statutory limits to correct school segregation.[94]

But in 1995, when the Court again reviewed the situation in Kansas City, the conservative majority prevailed. Writing for the Court, Chief Justice William H. Rehnquist said the federal judge overseeing the Kansas City schools had exceeded his authority by ordering salary increases and the creation of magnet schools to attract white students from neighboring districts. Rehnquist was joined by Justices Sandra Day O'Connor, Antonin Scalia, Anthony M. Kennedy, and Clarence Thomas. Justices David H. Souter, John Paul Stevens, Ruth Bader Ginsburg, and Stephen G. Breyer dissented.

The decision required lower courts to reconsider parts of a showcase plan aimed at increasing the attractiveness of a predominantly black school district. The state of Missouri, which had challenged the judge's remedial plan, specifically attacked two orders requiring salary increases for most of the school district's employees and converting all high schools and middle schools and half of the district's elementary schools into magnet schools.

The Court held that the orders went beyond federal courts' power to remedy the "vestiges" of previous legal segregation. Rehnquist said the effort to attract white students from adjoining suburban districts amounted to an impermissible "interdistrict remedy." He criticized the judge's use of below-normal achievement scores to justify his continued supervision over the school system. "Insistence upon academic goals unrelated to the effects of legal segregation unwarrantably postpones the day when the [Kansas City district] will be able to operate on its own," the chief justice wrote.[95]

Justice Souter, writing for the four dissenters, asserted that the majority had not followed proper procedure in reviewing the judge's remedy. On the merits, he contended that the lower courts had properly concluded that past segregation had contributed to white flight and that the desegregation decree could include steps to draw them back to the Kansas City system.

Travel and Public Accommodations

During the first few years after the Civil War, blacks in many localities were treated substantially the same as whites. In the 1870s there was little state-imposed segregation of the races in transportation or public accommodations; in fact, three states—Massachusetts, New York, and Kansas—specifically prohibited separation of the races in public places. Whether to accept the patronage of blacks was left largely to individual choice, and the majority of operators of public transport systems, hotels, restaurants, theaters, and other amusements admitted blacks—if not always to first class accommodations, then at least to second class.[96]

Nonetheless, many proprietors, especially in the rural South, refused to serve blacks. Enactment of the 1866 Civil Rights Act granting blacks the same rights as whites to bring lawsuits encouraged blacks to challenge such exclusion. Although many of these suits were successful, some courts upheld the right of individual proprietors to deny service to whomever they chose.

In an attempt to reverse such rulings, the Republican Congress enacted the Civil Rights Act of 1875, declaring that "all persons within the jurisdiction of the United States shall be entitled to the full and equal enjoyment of the accommodations . . . of inns, public conveyances on land or water, theaters, and other places of public amusement; subject only to the conditions and limitations established by law, and applicable alike to citizens of every race or color." Persons violating the act were subject to fine or imprisonment.

THE *CIVIL RIGHTS CASES*

This law became the basis for several dozen suits protesting denial of equal treatment to blacks. Federal courts in some states upheld the constitutionality of the act, while others found it invalid.

Five of these cases—known collectively as the *Civil Rights Cases*—reached the Supreme Court. They involved theaters in New York and California that would not seat blacks, a hotel in Missouri and a restaurant in Kansas that would not serve blacks, and a train in Tennessee that prohibited a black woman from riding in the "ladies" car *(United States v. Singleton, United States v. Ryan, United States v. Nichols, United States v. Stanley,* and *Robinson & Wife v. Memphis and Charleston Railroad Company).*

Deciding these cases by an 8–1 vote, the Court in 1883 declared that Congress had exceeded its authority to enforce the Thirteenth and Fourteenth Amendments in passing the 1875 act, and so it was invalid.

The Fourteenth Amendment applied only to discriminatory *state* actions, the Court reminded Congress. "Individual invasion of individual rights is not the subject-matter of the amendment," the Court asserted.[97]

Furthermore, said the majority, private discrimination against blacks did not violate the Thirteenth Amendment abolishing slavery:

[S]uch an act of refusal has nothing to do with slavery or involuntary servitude. . . . It would be running the slavery argument into the ground to make it apply to every act of discrimination which a person may see fit to make as to the guests he will entertain, or as to the people he will take into his coach or cab or car, or admit to his concert or theater.[98]

Although public opinion generally supported the Court's decision in these *Civil Rights Cases,* four states in 1884 barred discrimination in public places. By 1897, eleven more states, all in the North and West, had enacted similar laws. Those that were challenged were sustained as a proper exercise of state police power.[99]

SEGREGATION AND COMMERCE

The decision in the *Civil Rights Cases* left open the possibility that Congress, through its commerce power, might bar private discrimination against blacks on public carriers.

The Constitution gave Congress authority to regulate interstate commerce. By the close of the Civil War, the Court had interpreted that authority to deny the states power to regulate anything other than local commerce with no significant impact on other states.

In 1878 a unanimous Supreme Court had declared unconstitutional a Louisiana law *forbidding* segregation on public carriers.

So far as the state law required desegregation on carriers that traveled interstate, it was a burden on interstate commerce, the Court said in *Hall v. DeCuir*. Prohibition of segregation in interstate transportation was a matter on which there should be national uniformity, and thus only Congress could adopt that policy. "If each state was at liberty to regulate the conduct of carriers while within its jurisdiction, the confusion likely to follow could not but be productive of great inconvenience and unnecessary hardship," the Court concluded.[100]

Hoping that the Court would apply this same reasoning to strike down state segregation laws, opponents of segregation in 1890 challenged a Mississippi law *requiring* segregation on public transportation. Their hopes went unfulfilled.

Distinguishing the 1890 case of *Louisville, New Orleans & Texas Railway v. Mississippi* from *DeCuir,* the Court ruled that the Mississippi law applied only to intrastate traffic and was therefore within a state's power to regulate local commerce.[101]

PLESSY V. FERGUSON

Six years later the Supreme Court gave its blessing to segregation in the case of *Plessy v. Ferguson.* The case was a deliberate test of the constitutionality of a Louisiana statute requiring separate but equal railroad accommodations for the races. Louisiana was one of six states that by 1896 had enacted such "Jim Crow" laws segregating blacks from whites on trains.

The suit was brought by Homer Plessy, a citizen of the United States and a Louisiana resident who was one-eighth black and appeared white. Plessy bought a first class ticket to travel from New Orleans to Covington, Louisiana, and took a seat in the coach reserved for whites. When he refused to move to the black coach, he was arrested. The state courts upheld the constitutionality of the state law. Plessy then appealed to the Supreme Court, which in 1896 affirmed the holdings of the state courts.

A Reasonable Rule

Writing for the majority, Justice Henry B. Brown said the state law did not infringe on congressional authority over commerce. "In the present case," said Brown, "no question of interference with interstate commerce can possibly arise, since the East Louisiana Railway appears to have been purely a local line, with both its termini within the State."[102]

Nor did the state statute violate the Thirteenth Amendment:

A statute which implies merely a legal distinction between the white and colored races—a distinction which is founded in the color of the two races, and which must always exist so long as white men are distinguished from the other race by color—has no tendency to destroy the legal equality of the two races, or reestablish a state of involuntary servitude.[103]

Plessy's challenge to the law as a violation of the Fourteenth Amendment also failed, the majority said, because that amendment guaranteed only political equality and did not encompass what the Court considered social distinctions:

The object of the [Fourteenth] Amendment was undoubtedly to enforce the absolute equality of the two races before the law, but in the nature of things it could not have been intended to abolish distinctions based upon color, or to enforce social, as distinguished from political equality, or a commingling of the two races upon terms unsatisfactory to either. Laws permitting, and even requiring, their separation in places where they are liable to be brought into contact do not necessarily imply the inferiority of either race to the other, and have been generally recognized as within the competency of the state legislatures in the exercise of their police powers.[104]

The question then, Brown continued, was whether the law was an unreasonable use of the state's police power. Noting that the Court thought it reasonable for a state to consider the traditions and customs of its people and to want to protect their comfort and peace, Brown wrote:

[W]e cannot say that a law which authorizes or even requires the separation of the two races in public conveyances is unreasonable, or more obnoxious to the Fourteenth Amendment than the act of Congress requiring separate schools for colored children in the District of Columbia, the constitutionality of which does not seem to have been questioned, or the corresponding acts of state legislatures.

We consider the underlying fallacy of [Plessy's] argument to consist in the assumption that the enforced separation of the two races stamps the colored race with a badge of inferiority. If this be so, it is not by reason of anything found in the act, but solely because the colored race chooses to put this construction upon it. . . . Legislation is powerless to eradicate racial instincts or to abolish distinctions based upon physical differences, and the attempt to do so can only result in accentuating the difficulties of the present situation. If the civil and political rights of both races be equal one cannot be inferior to the other civilly, or politically. If one race be inferior to the other socially, the Constitution of the United States cannot put them upon the same plane.[105]

A Colorblind Constitution

In lone dissent, as in the *Civil Rights Cases,* Justice Harlan predicted that the decision would prove "quite as pernicious" as had the 1857 Dred Scott decision. The Kentucky-born Harlan, himself a former slaveholder, acknowledged that whites were the dominant race in prestige, education, wealth, and power. "But in view of the Constitution," he declared, "in the eye of the law, there is in this country no superior, dominant, ruling class of citizens. There is no caste here. Our Constitution is colorblind and neither knows nor tolerates classes among citizens."[106] (See box, The Dred Scott Case, p. 627.)

Charging that the majority had glossed over the fact that the Louisiana law segregated blacks because whites considered them inferior, Harlan wrote:

The arbitrary separation of citizens, on the basis of race, while they are on a public highway, is a badge of servitude wholly inconsistent with the civil freedom and the equality before the law established by the Constitution. It cannot be justified upon any legal grounds. . . . We boast of the freedom enjoyed by our people above all other peoples. But it is difficult to reconcile that boast with a state of the law, which, practically, puts the brand of servitude and degradation upon a large class of our fellow-citizens, our equals before the law. The thin disguise of "equal" accommodations for passengers in railroad coaches will not mislead any one, nor atone for the wrong this day done.[107]

EQUAL TREATMENT

For sixty years the Court's stance in regard to segregation on public carriers was similar to the stance it maintained on school segregation. The Court upheld the right of the states to separate the races while requiring that their treatment be equal.

This insistence on equal treatment in transportation was first apparent in the 1914 case of *McCabe v. Atchison, Topeka & Santa Fe Railroad.* Oklahoma law required companies operating trains within the state to provide separate coaches for whites and blacks. McCabe sued the railroad because it provided sleeping cars for whites but none for blacks.

The railroad argued that there was not sufficient demand by blacks for sleeping car accommodations. The Court rejected this defense. In an opinion written by Justice Hughes, the Court said the railway's contention

makes the constitutional right depend upon the number of persons who may be discriminated against, whereas the essence of the constitutional right is that it is a personal one. Whether or not particular facilities shall be provided may doubtless be conditioned upon there being a reasonable demand therefore, but, if facilities are provided, substantial equality of treatment of persons traveling under like conditions cannot be refused. It is the individual who is entitled to the equal protection of the laws, and if he is denied by a common carrier, acting in the matter under the authority of a state law, a facility or convenience in the course of his journey which under substantially the same circumstances is furnished to another traveler, he may properly complain that his constitutional privilege has been invaded.[108]

In 1941 the Court extended this principle to the case of an interstate traveler. A black member of the U.S. House of Representatives, Arthur W. Mitchell, D-Ill. (1935–1943), held a first class ticket for a trip from Chicago to Hot Springs, Arkansas. When the train reached the Arkansas border, Mitchell was required by state law to move to a car reserved for blacks where there were no first class accommodations.

Mitchell challenged the state law as a violation of the Interstate Commerce Act of 1887, which prohibited public carriers from subjecting "any person . . . to any undue or unreasonable prejudice or disadvantage in any respect whatsoever." The Interstate Commerce Commission (ICC) dismissed the complaint, but Mitchell appealed to the Supreme Court, which held he was entitled to first class accommodations just as any white would be. The Court, however, did not question Arkansas's right to require the segregated coaches.[109]

Five years later the Court took a significant step toward overturning segregation in public interstate transportation. The case

DISCRIMINATORY WILLS

In two sets of cases, the Supreme Court has held that the Fourteenth Amendment forbids a state agency, but not a private one, from acting as trustee for wills that discriminate against blacks.

The 1957 case of *Pennsylvania v. Board of Directors of City Trusts of Philadelphia,* concerned a will that left money in trust for the establishment and maintenance of a school for poor white orphan boys. The trust was administered by a state agency. The case arose when the agency refused admittance to two black orphan boys.

In a per curiam opinion, the Court said the agency's refusal to admit the two boys amounted to state discrimination in violation of the Fourteenth Amendment. Administration of the school was then turned over to private trustees who continued to follow the discriminatory terms of the will. This policy was again challenged, but the Court in 1958 refused to review it.[1]

A decade later in 1966 the Court decided a case concerning a park in Macon, Georgia, which, under the terms of the will bequeathing the land, could serve only whites. In this case the Court held that even though the city, refusing to operate the park on a segregated basis, had turned over its management to private trustees, the park retained a public character that made it subject to the prohibitions of the Fourteenth Amendment.[2]

As a result, the park reverted to the original heirs and was closed. A group of blacks sued, claiming the closing violated their right to equal protection of the laws. But the Court in 1970 found no constitutional violation. Closing the park to the public did not treat one race differently from the other but deprived both blacks and whites equally of the facility, the majority said.[3]

1. *Pennsylvania v. Board of Directors of City Trusts of Philadelphia,* 353 U.S. 230 (1957); 357 U.S. 570 (1958).
2. *Evans v. Newton,* 382 U.S. 296 (1966).
3. *Evans v. Abney,* 396 U.S. 435 (1970); see also *Palmer v. Thompson,* 403 U.S. 217 (1971).

of *Morgan v. Virginia* (1946) concerned a black woman traveling on a bus from Virginia to Maryland. Upon entering Virginia, she defied that state's law when she refused to move to the back of the bus to make her seat available to whites.

Noting that ten states specifically required segregation in interstate bus travel and that eighteen specifically prohibited it, the Court said that a "burden [on interstate commerce] might arise from a state statute which requires interstate passengers to order their movements on the vehicle in accordance with local rather than national requirements."[110] The Court held that "seating arrangements for the different races in interstate motor travel require a single, uniform rule to promote and protect national travel."[111] The state law violated the commerce clause.

In 1948 the Court upheld a Michigan law prohibiting segregation in public transportation. The law did not interfere with Congress's power to regulate interstate and foreign commerce, it said. In 1950 the Court struck down segregated but unequal dining facilities on trains. In 1953 the Court applied two seldom-used laws to prohibit restaurants in the District of Columbia from discriminating against blacks.[112]

PLESSY OVERTURNED

Then, in 1954, the Supreme Court renounced the separate but equal doctrine as it applied to public schools.[113] Beginning with *Muir v. Louisville Park Theatrical Assn.* (1954), the Court summarily declared that state-imposed segregation in public accommodations and transportation was unconstitutional as well. Relying on *Brown,* the Court ordered an end to state-imposed segregation on public beaches, municipal golf courses, vehicles of interstate transportation, in public parks, municipal auditoriums and athletic contests, seating in traffic court, and in prisons and jails.[114]

Most of these decisions were issued without opinion. In 1963, however, the Court issued a full opinion in one case to emphasize its expectation that the states would proceed expeditiously to eliminate state-imposed segregation in public areas. The question in *Watson v. Memphis* (1963) was whether the Tennessee city should be granted more time to desegregate its public parks and other municipal facilities. Warning that it would not countenance indefinite delays, the Court said:

The rights here asserted are, like all such rights, present rights; they are not merely hopes to some future enjoyment of some formalistic constitutional promise. The basic guarantees of our Constitution are warrants for the here and now and, unless there is an overwhelmingly compelling reason, they are to be promptly fulfilled.[115]

In contrast to its continued insistence on school desegregation, a sharply divided Court held in 1971 that a city under a court order to desegregate its public facilities could close its public swimming pools rather than operate them on an integrated basis.

For the five-man majority in *Palmer v. Thompson,* Justice Hugo L. Black maintained that the Fourteenth Amendment did not impose an affirmative obligation on a local government to maintain public swimming pools. And, said Black, so long as the city government denied the same facility to both races, it was not denying either equal protection.

For the dissenters, Justice Byron R. White said that "a state may not have an official stance against desegregating public facilities in response to a desegregation order.... The fact is that closing the pools is an expression of public policy that Negroes are unfit to associate with whites."[116]

SEMIPUBLIC BUSINESS

In a pair of cases, the Court in 1960 and 1961 prohibited racial discrimination by privately owned businesses operated on public property. *Boynton v. Virginia* (1960) concerned a privately owned restaurant in an interstate bus terminal. The restaurant refused to serve a black interstate traveler. The question presented to the Court was whether the refusal violated the Interstate Commerce Act. The Court decided it did:

[I]f the bus carrier has volunteered to make terminal and restaurant facilities and service available to its interstate passengers as a regular part of their transportation, and the terminal and restaurant have acquiesced and cooperated in this undertaking, the terminal and restaurant must perform these services without discriminations prohibited by the Act. In performance of these services under such conditions, the terminal and the restaurant stand in the place of the bus company.[117]

The second case involved an intrastate situation and a constitutional question rather than a question of statutory law. The case of *Burton v. Wilmington Parking Authority* (1961) concerned the Eagle restaurant, which leased space in a city-owned parking building. The parking authority rented out the space in order to procure additional revenue to redeem its bonds. When the restaurant refused to serve a black, the question was whether the restaurant was so closely associated with the municipal parking authority as to make its discriminatory action state action in violation of the equal protection clause.

"Only by sifting facts and weighing circumstances can the nonobvious involvement of the State in private conduct be attributed its true significance," the Court said in answering the question.[118] It then pointed out that the land on which the parking garage and restaurant sat was publicly owned and that the restaurant was there for the purpose of maintaining the public garage as a self-sustaining entity. Thus, the Court concluded:

The State has so far insinuated itself into a position of interdependence with [the] Eagle [restaurant] that it must be recognized as a joint participant in the challenged activity, which, on that account, cannot be considered to have been so "purely private" as to fall without the scope of the Fourteenth Amendment.[119]

THE SIT-IN CASES

Boynton and *Burton* served as precedent for a series of cases decided in 1962 and commonly known as the *Sit-In Cases.* Four of these concerned young blacks who had been convicted of criminal trespass after they had protested racially discriminatory policies of privately owned stores and restaurants by seeking service at "whites only" lunch counters and tables. The fifth case involved two ministers convicted of aiding and abetting persons to commit criminal trespass by encouraging them to sit in.

The Supreme Court earlier had decided such cases involving civil rights activists on First Amendment grounds. The *Sit-In Cases* were the only major cases decided on equal protection grounds. In each, a majority of the Court found sufficient state involvement with the private act of discrimination to warrant coverage by the Fourteenth Amendment's equal protection clause.

In the first case, *Peterson v. City of Greenville,* an eight-justice majority overturned the convictions of ten youthful protesters who attempted to desegregate a department store lunch counter in Greenville, South Carolina. A city ordinance required racial segregation of public eating places. By having the protesters arrested, the store's managers did what the ordinance required, and therefore, held the Court, the subsequent convictions amounted to state enforcement of the city ordinance denying equal protection. It was no defense that the store managers would have brought criminal trespass charges in the absence of the ordinance, the majority said.

As the civil rights movement gained strength, demonstrators demanding service at whites-only lunch counters were not only arrested and convicted but also ill-treated by private citizens, as in this 1963 incident in Jackson, Mississippi.

When a state agency passes a law compelling persons to discriminate against other persons because of race, and the State's criminal processes are employed in a way which enforces the discrimination mandated by that law, such a palpable violation of the Fourteenth Amendment cannot be saved by attempting to separate the mental urges of the discriminators.[120]

The *Peterson* case then became the rule for overturning similar criminal trespass convictions in *Gober v. City of Birmingham* and *Avent v. North Carolina*.[121] In both cases, city ordinances required separation of the races in eating places. Then, having overturned the trespass convictions in *Gober,* the Court overturned the aiding and abetting convictions of the two ministers who had urged participation in that sit-in. "It is generally recognized that there can be no conviction for aiding and abetting someone to do an innocent act," the majority wrote in *Shuttlesworth v. Birmingham.*[122]

In the final case, *Lombard v. Louisiana,* there was no law requiring segregated eating places in New Orleans. Nonetheless, the Court found that public statements of the city mayor and police chief effectively "required" that public eating facilities be segregated. If it is constitutionally impermissible for a state to enact a law segregating the races, "the State cannot achieve the same result by an official command which has at least as much coercive effect as an ordinance," the justices said.[123]

INDIVIDUAL DISCRIMINATION

Despite the Court's rulings in the *Sit-In Cases,* most private owners of hotels, stores, restaurants, theaters, and other public accommodations remained "without the scope of the Four-

teenth Amendment" until passage in 1964 of the most comprehensive civil rights act since 1875. The act barred discrimination in employment, provided new guarantees to ensure blacks the right to vote, and authorized the federal government to seek court orders for the desegregation of public schools.

Title II of the act was aimed at discrimination in public accommodations. It prohibited discrimination on grounds of race, color, religion, or national origin in public accommodations if the discrimination was supported by state law or other official action, if lodgings or other service were provided to interstate travelers, or if a substantial portion of the goods sold or entertainment provided moved in interstate commerce.

There was no question that the Fourteenth Amendment barred state officials from requiring or supporting segregation in public places. But the power of Congress to use the commerce clause as authority for barring private discrimination was uncertain. A case challenging that exercise of the commerce power reached the Supreme Court just six months after the Civil Rights Act of 1964 was enacted.

Heart of Atlanta Motel

The case of *Heart of Atlanta Motel v. United States* (1964) involved a motel in downtown Atlanta that refused to serve blacks in defiance of the new federal law. The motel owner charged that Congress had exceeded its authority under the commerce clause when it enacted Title II, and that the property owner's Fifth Amendment rights were denied when Congress deprived him of the freedom to choose his customers.

A unanimous Supreme Court upheld Title II. Writing for the

PRIVATE CLUBS

The freedom to associate with persons of one's own choosing is protected by the First Amendment, at least up to a point. Consequently, private clubs with racially discriminatory admissions policies are generally considered beyond the reach of the Fourteenth Amendment.

In 1972 the Supreme Court held, 6–3, that the issuance of a liquor license by the state to a private club that discriminated against blacks was not discriminatory state action in violation of the Fourteenth Amendment. In *Moose Lodge 107 v. Irvis* the majority said the Court had never forbidden a state to provide services to a private individual or group that practiced discrimination.[1] Such a ruling would mean that the state could not provide vital essentials such as fire and police protection, electricity, and water to private individuals who discriminate.

The degree of state involvement necessary to constitute state action varies from case to case, the majority continued. In this situation the liquor regulations, with one exception, in no way promoted discrimination and therefore did not involve the state in the private discriminatory policy, it concluded. The exception was the liquor board's requirement that all club bylaws be obeyed. The majority found that in cases where the bylaws restricted membership by race, the state regulation amounted to enforcement of a discriminatory practice and the requirement should not be applied to the private club.

In a second case, the Court rejected the claim of a community recreation association that it was a private club exempt from the 1964 Civil Rights Act. The association limited membership in its swimming pool to white residents of the community and their white guests. In *Tillman v. Wheaton-Haven Recreation Association* (1973) the Court ruled that the association was not entitled to the exemption because it had no selection criteria for membership other than race and residence in the community.[2]

1. *Moose Lodge 107 v. Irvis,* 407 U.S. 163 (1972).
2. *Tillman v. Wheaton-Haven Recreation Association,* 410 U.S. 431 (1973).

Court, Justice Tom C. Clark first outlined the interstate aspect of the motel's business, noting that it was accessible to interstate travelers, that it sought out-of-state patrons by advertising in nationally circulated publications, and that 75 percent of its guests were interstate travelers. Clark then cited the testimony at the congressional hearings on the act that showed that blacks were frequently discouraged from traveling because of the difficulty encountered in obtaining accommodations. Congress had reasonably concluded that discrimination was an impediment to interstate travel, the Court said.

Clark next turned to the commerce power of Congress, finding that Congress had the authority not only to regulate interstate commerce but also to regulate intrastate matters that affected interstate commerce:

[T]he power of Congress to promote interstate commerce includes the power to regulate the local incidents thereof, including local activities in both the States of origin and destination, which might have a substantial and harmful effect upon that commerce. One need only examine the evidence . . . to see that Congress may—as it has—prohibit racial discrimination by motels serving travelers, however "local" their operations may appear.[124]

The Court also said that it made no difference that Congress had used its power under the commerce clause to achieve a moral goal. That fact, wrote Clark,

does not detract from the overwhelming evidence of the disruptive effect that racial discrimination has had on commercial intercourse. It was this burden which empowered Congress to enact appropriate legislation, and, given this basis for the exercise of its power, Congress was not restricted by the fact that the particular obstruction to interstate commerce with which it was dealing was also deemed a moral and social wrong.[125]

The Court also rejected the claim that Title II violated the motel owner's Fifth Amendment rights. Congress acted reasonably to prohibit racial discrimination, the Court said, noting that thirty-two states had civil rights laws that were similar to the 1964 federal law. Furthermore, "in a long line of cases this Court has rejected the claim that the prohibition of racial discrimination in public accommodations interferes with personal liberty."[126]

The Court's decision upholding the constitutionality of the use of the commerce power to bar private discrimination seemed to conflict with its decision in the 1883 *Civil Rights Cases* that Congress lacked the power to enforce the Thirteenth and Fourteenth Amendments by barring private acts of discrimination in public accommodations. The Court said in its 1964 ruling that it found the 1883 decision "without precedential value" since Congress in 1875 had not limited prohibition of discrimination to those businesses that impinged on interstate commerce. Wrote Clark of that case:

Since the commerce power was not relied on by the Government and was without support in the [trial] record it is understandable that the Court narrowed its inquiry and excluded the Commerce Clause as a possible source of power. In any event, it is clear that such a limitation renders the opinion devoid of authority for the proposition that the Commerce Clause gives no power to Congress to regulate discriminatory practices now found substantially to affect interstate commerce.[127]

Ollie's Barbecue

In the companion case of *Katzenbach v. McClung* (1964), the Court upheld the section of Title II barring discrimination by private proprietors who served to their clientele goods that moved in interstate commerce. Ollie's Barbecue, a Birmingham, Alabama, restaurant that discriminated against blacks, did not seek to serve customers from out of state, but 46 percent of the food it served was supplied through interstate commerce.

The restaurant claimed that the amount of food it purchased in interstate commerce was insignificant compared to the total amount of food in interstate commerce. The Court rejected this argument. The restaurant's purchase might be insignificant, the Court said, but added to all other purchases of food through interstate commerce by persons who discriminate against blacks, the impact on interstate commerce was far from insignificant.[128]

Commerce and Recreation

Five years later in *Daniel v. Paul* (1969), the Court, 7–1, upheld Title II as applied to a small recreational area near Little Rock, Arkansas. The area admitted only whites, but claimed it did not fall under Title II because it did not seek interstate travelers and sold little food purchased through interstate commerce.

The Court disagreed, pointing out that the food sold was composed of ingredients produced in other states. Moreover, the facility advertised in Little Rock and at a military base, and it was unreasonable to think that the ads would not attract some interstate travelers.[129]

Justice Black, the sole dissenter, objected to connecting the recreational area to interstate commerce, saying he would have supported a decision based on the Fourteenth Amendment.

The Right to Fair Housing

Even as the Supreme Court in the *Civil Rights Cases* of 1883 held that Congress lacked authority to protect blacks against persons who refused them public accommodations, it acknowledged in those cases the power of Congress to erase "the necessary incidents of slavery" and "to secure to all citizens of every race and color, without regard to previous servitude, those fundamental rights which are the essence of civil freedom." Among these, the Court said, was the right "to inherit, purchase, lease, sell and convey property."[130]

With this statement the Court by indirection upheld the Civil Rights Act of 1866, enacted by Congress to enforce the Thirteenth Amendment, which abolished slavery. The act gave blacks the same rights as whites to buy, lease, hold, and sell property. *(See box, Civil Rights Act of 1866, p. 654.)*

STATE DISCRIMINATION

As states and cities adopted more laws segregating whites from blacks, even these fundamental rights fell victim to "Jim Crow" laws. In 1917 the Supreme Court struck down one such housing law.

Buchanan v. Warley (1917) began in Louisville, Kentucky, where a city ordinance forbade members of one race to buy, reside on, or sell property on streets where a majority of the residents were of the other race. Charles Buchanan, a white property owner, entered into a contract for the sale of his property to a black man named William Warley. When Warley found the Louisville law prevented him from living on the property, he exercised a contract proviso allowing him to break his agreement to purchase. Buchanan then sued for performance of the contract and charged that the Louisville ordinance violated the Fourteenth Amendment. Defenders of the ordinance claimed that it was a valid exercise of the city's police power to prevent racial conflict, maintain racial purity, and prevent deterioration in property values.

The Supreme Court acknowledged a broad police power but also recalled the Court's 1883 opinion that acquisition, use, and disposal of property were fundamental rights available to all citizens without regard to race or color. The Court then unanimously struck down the city ordinance. Justice William R. Day wrote for the Court.

That there exists a serious and difficult problem arising from a feeling of race hostility which the law is powerless to control, and to which it must give a measure of consideration, may be freely admitted. But its solution cannot be promoted by depriving citizens of their constitutional rights and privileges. . . . The right which the ordinance annulled was the civil right of a white man to dispose of his property if he saw fit to do so to a person of color, and of a colored person to make such disposition to a white person. . . . We think this attempt to prevent the alienation of the property in question . . . was not a legitimate exercise of the police power of the state, and is in direct violation of the fundamental law enacted in the Fourteenth Amendment of the Constitution preventing state interference with property rights except by due process of law.[131]

Citing *Buchanan,* the Court subsequently upheld several lower court decisions invalidating similar laws.[132]

RESTRICTIVE COVENANTS

Officially imposed housing segregation was quickly replaced in many localities by private restrictive covenants. Under such covenants, the white residents of a particular block or neighborhood agreed to refuse to sell or lease their homes to blacks.

A challenge to the constitutional validity of such private covenants came before the Supreme Court in 1926. Adhering to its earlier rulings that Congress had no authority to protect individuals from private discrimination, the Court dismissed *Corrigan v. Buckley* (1926), effectively upholding as valid private restrictive covenants. The arguments that the covenant violated the Fifth, Thirteenth, and Fourteenth Amendments, the Court said, were

entirely lacking in substance or color of merit. The Fifth Amendment "is a limitation only upon the powers of the General Government," . . . and is not directed against the action of individuals. The Thirteenth Amendment denouncing slavery . . . does not in other matters protect the individual rights of persons of the Negro race. . . . And the prohibitions of the Fourteenth Amendment "have reference to state action exclusively, and not to any action of private individuals."[133]

No State Enforcement

Twenty-two years later the Court effectively nullified restrictive covenants by forbidding states to enforce them. *Shelley v. Kraemer* (1948) arose when a black couple bought property to which a restrictive covenant applied. A white couple who owned restricted property in the same neighborhood sued to stop the Shelleys from taking possession of the property. The trial court denied that request, holding that the covenant was not effective because it had not been signed by all the property owners in the affected area. The supreme court of Missouri reversed the decision, ruling the covenant effective and not a violation of the Shelleys' rights under the Fourteenth Amendment. The Shelleys appealed to the Supreme Court, where their case was combined with a similar one, *McGhee v. Sipes.*[134]

CIVIL RIGHTS ACT OF 1866

Congress enacted the Civil Rights Act of 1866 to enforce the newly ratified Thirteenth Amendment prohibiting slavery. Following is the text of the portion of the act that, the Supreme Court ruled in 1968, barred individuals from discriminating against racial minorities in the sale or rental of housing:

Section 1. Be it enacted by the Senate and House of Representatives of the United States of America in Congress assembled, That all persons in the United States and not subject to any foreign power, . . . are hereby declared to be citizens of the United States; and such citizens, of every race and color, without regard to any previous condition of servitude . . . shall have the same right, in every State and Territory in the United States, to make and enforce contracts, to sue, be parties, and give evidence, to inherit, purchase, lease, sell, hold, and convey real and personal property, and to full and equal benefit of all laws and proceedings for the security of person and property, as is enjoyed by white citizens, and shall be subject to like punishment, pains, and penalties, and to none other, any law, statute, ordinance, regulation, or custom, to the contrary notwithstanding.

Section 2. That any person who, under color of any law, statute, ordinance, regulation, or custom, shall subject, or cause to be subjected, any inhabitant of any State or Territory to the deprivation of any right secured or protected by this act, or to different punishment, pains, or penalties on account of such person having at any time been held in a condition of slavery or involuntary servitude, . . . or by reason of his color or race, than is prescribed for the punishment of white persons, shall be deemed guilty of a misdemeanor, and, on conviction, shall be punished by fine not exceeding one thousand dollars, or imprisonment not exceeding one year, or both, in the discretion of the court.

Writing for a unanimous Court (although three members did not participate), Chief Justice Vinson repeated the Court's earlier opinion that the Fourteenth Amendment does not reach "private conduct, however discriminatory or wrongful." Therefore, Vinson wrote, private restrictive covenants "effectuated by voluntary adherence to their terms" are not in violation of the amendment.[135]

Official actions by state courts and judicial officers, however, have never been considered to be outside the scope of the Fourteenth Amendment, the chief justice continued. In the two cases before the Court, Vinson said,

the States have made available to [private] individuals the full coercive power of government to deny to petitioners, on the grounds of race or color, the enjoyment of property rights in premises which petitioners are willing and financially able to acquire and which the grantors are willing to sell. The difference between judicial enforcement and nonenforcement of the restrictive covenants is the difference to petitioners between being denied rights of property available to other members of the community and being accorded full enjoyment of these rights on an equal footing. . . .

We hold that in granting judicial enforcement of the restrictive agreements in these cases, the States have denied petitioners the equal protection of the laws and that, therefore, the action of the state courts cannot stand.[136]

Two companion cases, *Hurd v. Hodge* and *Urciola v. Hodge* (1948), challenged restrictive covenants in the District of Columbia. Because the Fourteenth Amendment applied only to states, the District covenants could not be challenged on that

In 1948 the Supreme Court held that the state of Missouri had engaged in unconstitutional discrimination when it enforced a restrictive covenant that prevented J. D. and Ethel Lee Shelley and their six children from retaining ownership of their newly purchased St. Louis home.

basis. Instead, the covenants were alleged to violate the due process clause of the Fifth Amendment. But the Court found it unnecessary to address the constitutional issue, holding that the district courts were barred from enforcing the covenants by the Civil Rights Act of 1866.[137]

No Penalty

The Court expanded *Shelley v. Kraemer* five years later in *Barrows v. Jackson* (1953) when it ruled that state courts could not require a person who had violated a restrictive covenant to pay damages to other covenantors who claimed her action had reduced the value of their property.

Court enforcement of such a damage claim constitutes state action that violates the Fourteenth Amendment if it denies any class the equal protection of the laws, the Court said. "If a state court awards damages for breach of a restrictive covenant," the Court reasoned, "a prospective seller of restricted land will either refuse to sell to non-Caucasians or else will require non-Caucasians to pay a higher price to meet the damage which the seller may incur."[138] In either event, the Court concluded, non-Caucasians would be denied equal protection.

HOUSING REFERENDA

In the 1967 case of *Reitman v. Mulkey,* the Court applied *Shelley v. Kraemer* to nullify a 1964 California constitutional amendment barring the state from interfering with the right of any person to sell or refuse to sell his property to anyone for any reason. The amendment effectively had nullified several state fair housing laws.

When the Mulkeys sued Neil Reitman on the grounds that he had declined to rent them an apartment solely because they were black, Reitman moved for dismissal of the complaint, citing the newly enacted constitutional amendment. The California supreme court, however, held that by the amendment the state had acted "to make private discriminations legally possible" and thus had violated the equal protection clause.

By a 5–4 vote the Supreme Court affirmed that ruling. For the majority, Justice White wrote that adoption of the amendment meant:

The right to discriminate, including the right to discriminate on racial grounds, was now embodied in the State's basic charter, immune from legislative, executive or judicial regulation at any level of the state government. Those practicing racial discriminations need no longer rely solely on their personal choice. They could now invoke express constitutional authority, free from censure or interference of any kind from official sources.[139]

Justice Harlan, writing for the dissenters, said the amendment was neutral on its face and did not violate the equal protection clause. By maintaining that the amendment actually encourages private discrimination, Harlan said, the majority "is forging a slippery and unfortunate criterion by which to measure the constitutionality of a statute simply permissive in purpose and effect, and inoffensive on its face."[140]

Two years later the Court struck down a newly added provision of the Akron, Ohio, city charter that required a majority of voters to approve any ordinance dealing with racial, religious, or ancestral discrimination in housing.

Noting that the charter did not require similar referenda for other housing matters, such as rent control, public housing, and building codes, the majority in *Hunter v. Erickson* (1969) held that the charter singled out a special class of people for special treatment in violation of the equal protection clause. "[T]he State may no more disadvantage any particular group by making it more difficult to enact legislation in its behalf than it may dilute any person's vote or give any group a smaller representation than another of comparable size," the majority wrote.[141]

Justice Black dissented, protesting "against use of the Equal Protection Clause to bar States from repealing laws that the Court wants the States to retain."[142]

In the 1971 case of *James v. Valtierra,* however, the Court upheld a California constitutional amendment providing that no local government agency could construct low-income housing projects without first receiving the approval of a majority of those voting in a local referendum. Distinguishing this case from *Hunter,* the majority said the city charter at issue in *Hunter* created a classification based solely upon race, while the constitutional amendment involved in the *James* case "requires referendum approval for any low-rent public housing project, not only for projects . . . occupied by a racial minority."[143]

In dissent, Justice Marshall contended that the California amendment created a classification based on poverty that violated the equal protection clause just as much as classifications based on race. "It is far too late in the day to contend that the Fourteenth Amendment prohibits only racial discrimination," Marshall wrote, "and, to me, singling out the poor to bear a burden not placed on any other class of citizens tramples the values that the Fourteenth Amendment was designed to protect."[144] *(See "Poverty and Equal Protection," pp. 673–676.)*

INDIVIDUAL DISCRIMINATION

Despite the Court's rulings on state enforcement of restrictive covenants and housing referenda, blacks and other minorities still had little protection from housing discrimination by individual home and apartment owners.

Old Law, New Life

Then, in 1968, just weeks after Congress enacted the first federal fair housing law, the Supreme Court, 7–2, held that the 1866 Civil Rights Act barred individual as well as state-backed discrimination in the sale and rental of housing. The case was brought by Joseph Lee Jones, who contended that the Alfred H. Mayer Company violated the 1866 act by refusing to sell him a home in the Paddock Woods section of St. Louis County, Missouri, because he was black.

A federal district court dismissed the case; the court of appeals affirmed the dismissal on the grounds that the 1866 act (in

THE RIGHT TO CHALLENGE

Ordinarily, the Supreme Court does not allow a person to come before it to defend someone else's rights. However, the Court has sometimes bent this rule in housing discrimination cases.

Barrows v. Jackson (1953) concerned a woman who violated a restrictive covenant by selling her property to blacks. Other covenantors in the neighborhood sued her for damages, claiming that her action reduced their property values.

The restrictive covenant did not affect the constitutional rights of the white seller who had breached its terms, but in defense of her action, she argued that the covenant infringed on the rights of racial minorities by forbidding them to buy homes in the neighborhood.

The Court allowed her to make this defense in behalf of minority group members. The reasons for ordinarily prohibiting such a third-party defense were "outweighed [in this case] by the need to protect the fundamental rights which would be denied by permitting the damages action to be maintained," the Court said.[1]

In 1972 the Court again took a broad view of the right to bring housing discrimination cases. Two white tenants in an apartment building claimed that their landlord's discriminatory policy against nonwhites harmed them by denying them social, business, and professional advantages gained from association with minorities. The tenants filed a complaint with the U.S. Department of Housing and Urban Development (HUD) under Section 810 of the 1968 Civil Rights Act.

When the complaint came to trial, a federal judge held that the tenants were not within the class of persons entitled to sue under the 1968 act. The Supreme Court reversed.

"We can give vitality to [section] 810....," wrote Justice William O. Douglas, "only by a generous construction which gives standing to sue to all in the same housing unit who are injured by racial discrimination in the management of those facilities within the coverage of the stature."[2]

But the Court has not been consistently generous in construing standing to challenge alleged housing discrimination. In the 1975 case of *Warth v. Seldin*, a five-justice majority deflected an effort to attack a town's zoning ordinance that effectively excluded low-income and moderate-income persons from living in the town. The majority held that none of the groups or individuals seeking to bring the suit had the legal standing because none could show that a decision in their favor would have a direct ameliorative effect on the injury they claimed to suffer as a result of the zoning ordinance.[3]

1. *Barrows v. Jackson*, 346 U.S. 249 at 257 (1953).
2. *Trafficante v. Metropolitan Life Insurance Company*, 409 U.S. 205 at 212 (1972); see also *Gladstone Realtors v. Village of Bellwood*, 441 U.S. 91 (1979).
3. *Warth v. Seldin*, 422 U.S. 490 (1975).

---

modern form Section 1982 of Title 42 of the U.S. Code) applied only to state discrimination and not to the segregative actions of private individuals.

The Supreme Court reversed the court of appeals. Writing in *Jones v. Alfred H. Mayer Co.* (1968), Justice Potter Stewart said that the legislative history of the 1866 act persuaded the Court that Congress intended to ban private and state-backed discrimination:

In light of the concerns that led Congress to adopt it and the contents of the debates that preceded its passage, it is clear that the Act was designed to do just what its terms suggest: to prohibit all racial discrimination, whether or not under color of law, with respect to the rights enumerated therein—including the right to purchase or lease property.[145]

The question was then: Did Congress have the power to enact the 1866 act? For the answer, Stewart looked to the Thirteenth Amendment rather than to the equal protection clause of the Fourteenth Amendment. The Thirteenth Amendment was adopted to remove the "badges of slavery" from the nation's blacks, Stewart observed, and it gave Congress the power to enforce that removal.

If Congress has power under the Thirteenth Amendment to eradicate conditions that prevent Negroes from buying and renting property because of their race or color, then no federal statute calculated to achieve that objective can be thought to exceed the constitutional power of Congress simply because it reaches beyond state action to regulate the conduct of private individuals. . . . Surely Congress has the power under the Thirteenth Amendment rationally to determine what are the badges and the incidents of slavery, and the authority to translate that determination into effective legislation. Nor can we say that the determination Congress has made is an irrational one. . . . [W]hen racial discrimination herds men into ghettoes and makes their ability to buy property turn on the color of their skin, then it too is a relic of slavery. . . .

At the very least, the freedom that Congress is empowered to secure under the Thirteenth Amendment includes the freedom to buy whatever a white man can buy, the right to live wherever a white man can live. If Congress cannot say that being a free man means at least this much, then the Thirteenth Amendment made a promise the Nation cannot keep.[146]

Justice Harlan, in a dissent joined by Justice White, said that the 1866 act was meant only to protect people from state-imposed discrimination.

Community Clubs, Pools

In 1969 the Court held that the 1866 act also prohibited a community recreational club from refusing membership to a black man who received membership as part of his lease of a home in the neighborhood.[147]

And in 1973 the Court ruled that a community recreation area violated the 1866 Civil Rights Act when it limited membership in its swimming pools to white residents of the community and their white guests.

In *Tillman v. Wheaton-Haven Recreation Association* a unanimous Court wrote:

THE ZONING POWER AND FAIR HOUSING

Since 1926, when it first upheld a comprehensive local zoning law, the Supreme Court has seldom interfered with state power over land use, even when those laws were challenged as violating the equal protection clause of the Fourteenth Amendment.

Such a challenge was raised in 1974 against a New York village's zoning ordinance that prohibited more than two unrelated persons from sharing a single-family home. The ordinance placed no limit on the number of family members that could share a house. Rejecting an equal protection challenge to the ordinance, the Court wrote that the law was a reasonable means of attaining a permissible objective—the preservation of the family character of the village.[1]

DISCRIMINATORY INTENT

In 1977 the Court again turned back an equal protection challenge to a local zoning decision. The case of *Village of Arlington Heights v. Metropolitan Housing Development Corporation* arose when a housing developer requested the predominantly white Chicago suburb of Arlington Heights to rezone certain land so that he could build housing for low- and moderate-income persons of both races there. When zoning officials refused the request, the developer went to court, charging the denial was motivated by a desire to keep black families from moving into the suburb.

By 5–3, the Supreme Court upheld the village's refusal to rezone, finding no evidence that it was racially motivated. Instead the evidence showed that the zoning decision was the result of the legitimate desire to protect property values.[2]

Without discriminatory intent, wrote Justice Lewis F. Powell Jr., the fact that the refusal to rezone had a racially discriminatory effect was "without independent constitutional significance." The Court referred to its 1976 job discrimination ruling in *Washington v. Davis*.[3] There, said Powell, the Court made clear "that official action will not be held unconstitutional solely because it results in a racially disproportionate impact. . . . Proof of racially discriminatory intent or purpose is required to show a violation of the Equal Protection Clause."[4] *(See box, The Question of Intent, p. 659.)*

Powell said that the factors that might be examined to determine whether a decision had been motivated by racial discrimination included its potential impact, the historical background, the sequence of events leading up to the decision, departures from normal procedures, and the legislative or administrative history.

For example, Powell said, the Arlington Heights decision to refuse to rezone would appear in a different light if the village had not consistently applied its zoning policy, if unusual procedures had been followed in handling this particular request, or if the zoning for the particular parcel had been recently changed from multi-family to single-family use.

Justice Byron R. White, author of the Court's opinion in *Washington v. Davis*, dissented, saying that the majority should not have applied that ruling to this case.

DISCRIMINATORY EFFECT

The Court sent the case back to the court of appeals to consider whether the zoning decision violated the Fair Housing Act of 1968. In July 1977 that court held that the village's refusal to rezone would violate the act if it had a discriminatory effect even though there was no intent to discriminate. "Conduct that has the necessary and foreseeable consequences of perpetuating segregation can be as deleterious as purposefully discriminating conduct in frustrating" the national goal of integrated housing, the appeals court wrote.[5]

1. *Village of Belle Terre v. Boraas*, 416 U.S. 1 (1974).
2. *Village of Arlington Heights v. Metropolitan Housing Development Corporation*, 429 U.S. 252 (1977).
3. *Washington v. Davis*, 426 U.S. 229 (1976).
4. *Village of Arlington Heights v. Metropolitan Housing Development Corporation*, 429 U.S. 252 at 264–265 (1977).
5. *Metropolitan Housing Development Corporation v. Village of Arlington Heights*, 558 F. 2d 1283 at 1289 (1977).

When an organization links membership benefits to residence in a narrow geographical area, that decision infuses those benefits into the bundle of rights for which an individual pays when buying or leasing within the area. The mandate of [the 1866 Civil Rights Act] then operates to guarantee a nonwhite resident, who purchases, leases or holds this property, the same rights as are enjoyed by a white resident.[148]

REMEDIES FOR DISCRIMINATION

Although the Court has struck down several varieties of housing discrimination, it has had little occasion to consider remedies for that discrimination.

In the one case the Court has heard on the remedy issue, however, it unanimously upheld the power of a federal judge to order a metropolitan areawide remedy for segregated public housing in Chicago.

The question in *Hills v. Gautreaux* (1976) was whether the remedy for racial discrimination in public housing caused by state and federal officials must be confined to the city in which the discrimination occurred or could include the surrounding metropolitan area.[149] In holding that the remedy need not be restricted to the city alone, the Court made an important distinction between the facts in this case and those in the 1974 case of *Milliken v. Bradley*, which overturned a metropolitan areawide plan of school desegregation.[150] *(See details of Milliken v. Bradley, p. 645.)*

In *Hills* the Chicago Housing Authority (CHA) was found guilty of discrimination in placing most of the city's public housing in black ghettoes, and the Department of Housing and Urban Development (HUD) was found guilty of sanctioning and aiding this discriminatory public housing program. A court of appeals ordered a metropolitan areawide plan to eliminate the segregated public housing system, but HUD asked the Supreme Court to reverse it, citing *Milliken v. Bradley*.

Distinguishing between the two cases, Justice Stewart said the Court struck down the school desegregation plan because "there was no finding of unconstitutional action on the part of the suburban school officials and no demonstration that the violations committed in the operation of the Detroit school system had any significant segregative effects in the suburbs."[151]

The situation in the Chicago housing case was different, Stewart said. HUD did not contest the finding that it had violated the Constitution and the 1964 Civil Rights Act, nor did it dispute the appropriateness of its being ordered to help develop public housing:

The critical distinction between HUD and the suburban school districts in *Milliken* is that HUD has been found to have violated the Constitution. . . . Nothing in the *Milliken* decision suggests a *per se* rule that federal courts lack authority to order parties found to have violated the Constitution to undertake remedial efforts beyond the municipal boundaries of the city where the violation occurred.[152]

The Court's opinion continued:

[I]t is entirely appropriate and consistent with *Milliken* to order CHA and HUD to attempt to create housing alternatives for the respondents [the black plaintiffs] in the Chicago suburbs. Here the wrong committed by HUD confined the respondents to segregated public housing. The relevant geographic area for purposes of the respondents' housing option is the Chicago housing market, not the Chicago city limits. . . . To foreclose such relief solely because HUD's constitutional violation took place within the city limits of Chicago would transform *Milliken's* principled limitation on the exercise of federal judicial authority into an arbitrary . . . shield for those found to have engaged in unconstitutional conduct.[153]

A metropolitan remedy need not impermissibly interfere with local governments that had not been involved in the unconstitutional segregation, Stewart continued:

The remedial decree would neither force suburban governments to submit public housing proposals to HUD nor displace the rights and powers accorded local government entities under federal or state housing statutes or existing land-use laws. The order would have the same effect on the suburban governments as a discretionary decision by HUD to use its statutory powers to provide the respondents with alternatives to the racially segregated Chicago public housing system created by CHA and HUD.[154]

In 1977 the Court seemed to limit the potential impact of *Gautreaux*. In *Village of Arlington Heights v. Metropolitan Housing Development Corporation* the Court said that, without a showing of discriminatory motive, the village's refusal to rezone property to permit building of a housing development for low- and moderate-income persons of both races did not violate the Fourteenth Amendment.[155] The Court's decision left open the possibility that the zoning decision might have violated the 1968 Fair Housing Act. (*See box, The Zoning Power and Fair Housing, p. 657.*)

Equal Employment Opportunity

Civil war and emancipation did little to free blacks from job discrimination. Most of the southern states enacted Black Codes restricting the kinds of jobs blacks could hold, thereby limiting competition with white workers and forcing blacks to continue as farm and plantation workers.

South Carolina enacted one of the harshest of these codes. It prohibited a black from working as an artisan or mechanic unless he obtained a license that cost ten dollars and from becoming a shopkeeper unless he had a license costing one hundred dollars. Licenses were issued by judges who decided whether the black applicants were skilled and morally fit for the work.

The only jobs that blacks could obtain without a license were as farm workers or servants, and in both cases they were required to sign labor contracts with their employers. In South Carolina, as in many other southern states, failure to fulfill the labor contract was a crime, and a black worker could avoid a jail term only by agreeing to work off the original contract, his or her fine for defaulting, and court costs. The Supreme Court struck down such peonage laws as unconstitutional in the early 1900s.[156]

Despite industrialization, blacks remained relegated to low-paying, unskilled jobs that promised little, if any, advancement. Even if blacks qualified for a better job, they were often passed over in favor of white employees. Until the enactment of state fair employment laws in the mid-1940s, few blacks who had been refused jobs because of their race had any legal recourse. The employer-employee relationship was considered private, outside the protection of the Fourteenth Amendment. Private employers and labor unions could discriminate against blacks with impunity and many of them did.[157]

EARLY RULINGS

Because there were so few legal protections available, only a handful of employment discrimination cases reached the Court before 1964, the year that Congress prohibited such job bias. In almost all of these early cases, however, the Supreme Court interpreted available law to protect blacks.

The first of these cases came in 1938. Blacks organized a picket line outside a District of Columbia grocery to force the proprietor to hire blacks. A federal court ordered the picketing stopped; the blacks charged that the order violated the Norris-LaGuardia Act, which prohibited federal courts from issuing injunctions in legal labor disputes. The issue was whether picketing to force someone to hire blacks was a legal labor objective within the meaning of the law. By 7–2, the Court held that it was:

Race discrimination by an employer may be reasonably deemed more unfair and less excusable than discrimination against workers on the ground of union affiliation. There is no justification . . . for limiting [the act's] definition of labor disputes and cases arising therefrom by excluding those which arise with respect to discrimination in terms and condition of employment based upon differences of race or color.[158]

The Court modified this position in 1950 when it held that picketing to demand that a store owner increase the number of blacks he employed constituted discrimination against already-hired white clerks.[159]

The first case involving union discrimination came in 1944 when the Court was asked to decide whether a union acting under federal law as the exclusive bargaining agent for a class of workers was obligated by that law to represent all workers without regard to race.

Steele v. Louisville and Nashville Railroad Co. involved the Brotherhood of Locomotive Firemen, the exclusive bargaining representative for train firemen of twenty-one railroad companies. The union, which excluded blacks from membership, agreed with the railroad companies to amend the work contract to end all employment of blacks as firemen. As a result, Steele, a black fireman, was reassigned to more difficult, less remunerative work, and his job was given to a white man with less seniority and no more qualifications.

In an opinion that carefully avoided any constitutional issues, the Court ruled that the Railway Labor Act of 1930 compelled the exclusive bargaining agent for an entire class of employees to represent all those employees fairly "without hostile discrimination" against any of them.[160]

The Court reached a similar conclusion in the 1952 case of *Brotherhood of Railroad Trainmen v. Howard*. A white brakemen's union threatened to strike unless the railroad company fired all its black "train porters," who performed the same functions as brakemen, and replaced them with white union members. Unlike the blacks in the *Steele* case, however, the black train porters had long been represented by their own union. Nonetheless, a majority of the Supreme Court saw no significant difference in the two cases. The black "train porters are threatened with loss of their jobs because they are not white and for no other reason," wrote Justice Black. "The Federal [Railway Labor] Act . . . prohibits bargaining agents it authorizes from using their position and power to destroy colored workers' jobs in order to bestow them on white workers."[161]

STATE ANTIDISCRIMINATION LAWS

Black workers won another measure of job protection in 1945 when the Court upheld the validity of state fair-employment laws. The New York Civil Rights Act contained a provision—one of the first of its kind ever enacted—prohibiting a union from denying membership on the basis of race, creed, or color. The Railway Mail Association, which represented postal clerks in New York and other states and which limited its membership to whites and Indians, appealed the state's judgment that this law applied to its policy of excluding blacks. The association claimed the state law violated the organization's right to due process and equal protection and encroached on Congress's power to regulate the mails. The Supreme Court denied all three claims:

We see no constitutional basis for the contention that a state cannot protect workers from exclusion solely on the basis of race, color or creed by an organization functioning under the protection of the state, which holds itself out to represent the general business needs of employees.[162]

The question whether a state fair-employment practices act placed an impermissible burden on interstate commerce came to the Court in *Colorado Anti-Discrimination Commission v. Continental Airlines* (1963).[163]

THE QUESTION OF INTENT

Distinguishing between cases based on the Constitution's guarantee of equal protection and those based on civil rights laws, the Supreme Court has made clear that it is sometimes more difficult to prove actions unconstitutional than to prove them illegal.

The seminal case was *Washington v. Davis,* decided in 1976. In order to prove an employer guilty of unconstitutional discrimination, his action must be shown to be discriminatory in effect and intent, the Court held. The case arose when two blacks challenged as unconstitutionally discriminatory the District of Columbia police department's requirement that recruits pass a verbal ability test. The two men argued that the number of black police officers did not reflect the city's large black population, that more blacks than whites failed the test, and that the test was not significantly related to job performance.

Their challenge was based, not on the Civil Rights Act of 1964, but on the due process clause of the Fifth Amendment, which implicitly includes the equal protection guarantee. *(See box, Federal Equal Protection, p. 622.)*

A federal district court rejected the challenge because there was no evidence of intent to discriminate. The appeals court reversed, citing *Griggs v. Duke Power* (1971). *(See details of this case, p. 660.)*

The Supreme Court, however, reversed again, agreeing with the district court, 7–2, that there was no constitutional violation without proof of discriminatory intent.

Justice Byron R. White wrote that the Court had "not held that a law, neutral on its face and serving ends otherwise within the power of the government to pursue, is invalid under the Equal Protection Clause simply because it may affect a greater proportion of one race than another."[1]

The Court subsequently applied this principle—that a law or other official action must reflect some racially discriminatory intent to violate the equal protection guarantee—in other areas of discrimination, including schools and housing.[2] *(See Austin Independent School District v. United States, p. 636; Village of Arlington Heights v. Metropolitan Housing Development Corporation, p. 657.)*

In 1980 the Court extended this intent requirement to challenged voting practices in *Mobile v. Bolden*. The Court ruled, 6–3, that before it would strike down an at-large system for electing city officials as a violation of the equal protection guarantee or of the law barring racial discrimination in voting, the system must be found intentionally discriminatory as well as discriminatory in effect. Congress quickly overrode this ruling with its 1982 amendments to the Voting Rights Act, which made plain that there was no need for this finding of intent to justify holding a voting practice impermissible under that law.[3]

Two years later the Court again applied the intent requirement in the job area, ruling 5–4 that workers challenging a seniority system as discriminatory under the 1964 act must prove both a discriminatory intent and effect.[4]

1. *Washington v. Davis,* 426 U.S. 229 at 242 (1976).

2. *Austin Independent School District v. United States,* 429 U.S. 990 (1976); *Village of Arlington Heights v. Metropolitan Housing Development Corporation,* 429 U.S. 252 (1977).

3. *City of Mobile, Ala. v. Bolden,* 446 U.S. 55 (1980); *Congress and the Nation,* vol. 6 (Washington, D.C.: Congressional Quarterly, 1985), 680.

4. *American Tobacco Co. v. Patterson,* 456 U.S. 63 (1982); see also *U.S. Postal Service Board of Governors v. Aikens,* 460 U.S. 711 (1983).

A black man named Marion Green applied for a job as a pilot with the interstate airline, which had its headquarters in Denver. He was rejected solely because of his race. The Colorado Anti-Discrimination Commission found the company had discriminated in violation of state law and ordered it to give Green the first opening in its next training course. A state court overruled the order because the law unduly burdened interstate commerce.

The Supreme Court reversed the trial court and upheld the commission's order. The state antidiscrimination law did not conflict with or frustrate any federal law that might also regulate employment discrimination by airlines, said the Court. Nor did it deny the airlines any rights granted by Congress. Unlike several cases in which the Court has found that state-required racial separation of passengers in public transportation unduly burdened interstate commerce, the Court found hiring within a state, even for an interstate job, a "much more localized matter." Furthermore, the potential for diverse and conflicting hiring regulations among the states, which might hamper interstate commerce, was "virtually nonexistent." *(See details of Plessy v. Ferguson and McCabe v. Atchison, Topeka and Santa Fe Railroad, pp. 648–650.)*

THE 1964 CIVIL RIGHTS ACT

The following year Congress enacted the first federal law prohibiting job discrimination. Title VII of the Civil Rights Act of 1964 prohibited employers of and unions representing more than twenty-five workers, union hiring halls, and employment agencies from discriminating on the grounds of race, color, religion, sex, or national origin in the hiring, classification, training, or promotion of anyone. The act also created the Equal Employment Opportunities Commission (EEOC) to hear complaints and seek compliance with the law.

In 1972 Congress extended coverage to employers and unions with fifteen or more employees or members, state and local governments, and educational institutions. The only major group left uncovered were federal government employees. The 1972 act also authorized the EEOC to go into federal courts to enforce the law. Federal courts were authorized to order employers to remedy proven discrimination by reinstating or hiring the employees concerned, with or without back pay, and by any other remedial measures the courts found appropriate.

Job Qualifications

The Supreme Court first fully discussed the scope of Title VII in its 1971 decision in *Griggs v. Duke Power Co.* Black employees charged that the North Carolina power company had unfairly discriminated when it required them to have a high school diploma or pass a generalized intelligence test as a condition for employment or promotion. The black workers claimed that neither requirement was related to successful job performance, that the requirements disqualified a substantially higher number of blacks than whites, and that the jobs in question had been filled

---

BLACK *AND* WHITE

Title VII of the 1964 Civil Rights Act prohibits racial discrimination against whites as well as blacks in the workplace, the Court ruled in 1976.

In *McDonald v. Santa Fe Trail Transportation Co.* a freight company fired two white men who had stolen sixty cans of antifreeze, but the company did not dismiss a black man who had also participated in the theft.

The Court held this differential treatment a clear violation of Title VII. The law in its language and its legislative history makes plain that whites are to be protected as well as members of racial minorities, said Justice Thurgood Marshall. "While Santa Fe may decide that participation in a theft of cargo may render an employee unqualified for employment, this criterion must be 'applied alike to members of all races,' and Title VII is violated if . . . it was not." (427 U.S. 273 at 283, 1976)

The Court held, 7–2, that the two white men were also protected from such treatment by a provision of the 1866 Civil Rights Act, embodied in existing law as Section 1981 of Title 42 of the United States Code. The section declares that "all persons within the jurisdiction of the United States shall have the same right . . . to make and enforce contracts . . . as is enjoyed by white citizens." *(See box, Civil Rights Act of 1866, p. 654.)*

---

by whites under the company's former long-standing policy of giving whites first preference.

By 8–0 the Court ruled that under those circumstances the job qualification requirements were discriminatory. Chief Justice Burger set out the Court's interpretation of Title VII:

[T]he Act does not command that any person be hired simply because he was formerly the subject of discrimination, or because he is a member of a minority group. Discriminatory preference for any group, minority or majority, is precisely and only what Congress has proscribed. What is required by Congress is the removal of artificial, arbitrary, and unnecessary barriers to employment when the barriers operate invidiously to discriminate on the basis of racial or other impermissible classification.[164]

Any test that operates to exclude blacks, even one that is neutral on its face, must be shown to have a significant relation to job performance, Burger continued. Neither the requirement for a high school diploma nor the intelligence test had this relation. The Court agreed that there was no evidence that the company had intended to discriminate against its black employees, but, wrote Burger, "Congress directed the thrust of the Act to the consequences of employment practices, not simply the motivation."[165]

The Supreme Court in 1975 reaffirmed its view that tests that excluded more blacks than whites and were not proven to be job-related were discriminatory.[166]

More than a decade later the Court backed away from *Griggs.* In *Wards Cove Packing Co. v. Atonio* (1989) the Court, 5–4, held that workers charging an employer with discrimination had to do more to prove the charge than simply show that there was a high proportion of nonwhite workers in low-status jobs and a high proportion of white workers in high-status jobs. To hold otherwise, wrote Justice White for the Court, would be to encourage employers to adopt racial quotas to make certain that no portion of the workforce deviated in racial composition from the other parts of the workforce. Congress and the Court had rejected that idea, he said. The dissenting justices criticized the majority for "tipping the scales in favor of employers."[167] Two years later Congress reversed some of the effects of the *Wards Cove* decision by easing the burden of proof for aggrieved workers in its Civil Rights Act of 1991.[168]

Proving Bias

A unanimous Court held in 1973 that the 1964 Civil Rights Act did not require a company to rehire a black employee who had engaged in deliberate unlawful protests against it. But neither was the company permitted to use the protests as a pretext for refusing to rehire the employee just because of his race. The former employee should have an opportunity to prove that the employer was using the illegal protest as an excuse to carry out a discriminatory hiring policy, the Court said in *McDonnell Douglas Corp. v. Green* (1973). If he could not show this, the refusal to rehire him could stand.[169]

Twenty years later the Court held that a worker is not automatically entitled to a judgment when a judge or jury rejects his employer's explanations for an adverse employment action. Instead, the Court held, the worker must prove a discriminatory motive for the action taken against him or her.[170]

In a 1978 case of *Furnco Construction Corp. v. Waters,* the Supreme Court held that an appeals court erred in ordering a construction company to adopt nondiscriminatory hiring practices before the company had been found guilty of job discrimination. The Court also said that an employer may point to the fact that he has hired a substantial number of black workers as part of his proof that he is not guilty of discrimination. But, wrote the Court, "a racially balanced work force cannot immunize an employer from liability for specific acts of discrimination."[171]

Remedies

The Supreme Court has upheld the broad authority of lower federal courts under Title VII of the Civil Rights Act of 1964 to award back wages and retirement benefits to persons who have suffered illegal job discrimination.

Back Pay. The first such case was *Albemarle Paper Co. v. Moody* (1975). A federal district court found that the North Carolina paper mill had discriminated against blacks prior to enactment of Title VII and that the effects of that discrimination were apparent for several years afterward. But because the company no longer discriminated, the lower court decided against a back pay award. A court of appeals reversed the decision, and the paper mill appealed.

By 7–1 the Court ruled that back pay was a proper remedy for past job discrimination. Justice Stewart wrote:

If employers faced only the prospect of an injunctive order, they would have little incentive to shun practices of dubious legality. It is the reasonably certain prospect of a backpay award that "provide[s] the spur or catalyst which causes employers and unions to self-examine and to self-evaluate their employment practices and to endeavor to eliminate, so far as possible, the last vestiges of an unfortunate and ignominious page in this country's history.". . . It is also the purpose of Title VII to make persons whole for the injuries suffered on account of unlawful employment discrimination.[172]

Back pay should be awarded in most cases where job discrimination in violation of Title VII has been proved, the majority held, even in cases such as this one, where the employer had acted in good faith to end discrimination. If back pay were awarded only for acts of bad faith, the majority said, "the remedy would become a punishment for moral turpitude, rather than a compensation for workers' injuries. . . . [A] worker's injury is no less real simply because his employer did not inflict it in "bad faith."[173]

In *Fitzpatrick v. Bitzer* (1976) the Court upheld the award of retroactive retirement benefits to male employees of the state of Connecticut who had been required to work longer than women employees before they could retire.[174]

One of the first Supreme Court opinions by Justice Sandra Day O'Connor concerned back pay awards. In *Ford Motor Co. v. Equal Employment Opportunity Commission* she explained the Court's view that an employer charged with job bias can terminate the period for which he may be held liable for back pay by unconditionally offering the person charging bias the job he had previously refused to offer. "The victims of job discrimination want jobs, not lawsuits," she wrote, expressing the hope that this ruling would encourage employers to make such offers.[175]

Seniority Rights. The Court also has upheld the authority of federal courts to award retroactive seniority rights to persons denied employment or promotion by biased policies.

In *Franks v. Bowman Transportation Co. Inc.* (1976) the Court, 5–3, approved seniority awards by lower courts dating back to rejection of the job application. Retroactive seniority was an appropriate remedy, and such awards should be made in most cases where a seniority system exists and discrimination is proved, the Court said.

Such awards fulfill the "make-whole" purposes of Title VII, held the Court. Without them, Justice Brennan wrote, the victim of job discrimination "will never obtain his rightful place in the hierarchy of seniority according to which these various employment benefits are distributed. He will perpetually remain subordinate to persons who, but for the illegal discrimination, would have been in respect to entitlement to these benefits his inferiors."[176]

The Court did not distinguish between benefit seniority, which determines matters such as length of vacation and pension benefits, and competitive seniority, which determines issues such as the order in which employees are laid off and re-hired, promoted, and transferred.

In dissent Justice Powell opposed the award of retroactive competitive seniority because it did not affect the employer but rather "the rights and expectations of perfectly innocent employees. The economic benefits awarded discrimination victims would be derived not at the expense of the employer but at the expense of other workers."[177]

Retroactive Seniority Limited. Little more than a year later the Court qualified its holding in *Franks.* Its decision in *Teamsters v. United States, T.I.M.E.-D.C. v. United States* (1977) barred the award of retroactive seniority benefits dating before July 2, 1965, the effective date of the 1964 Civil Rights Act.

In Title VII Congress specifically included language that immunized existing bona fide seniority systems from attack as discriminatory. By 7–2 the Court held that this immunity precluded any award of retroactive seniority benefits that would have been accumulated prior to July 2, 1965, absent racial discrimination.

This case concerned a nationwide trucking firm and the truckers' union.[178] Lower courts found that the firm systematically denied intercity-line driver jobs to blacks and Spanish-surnamed employees and applicants. Seniority became an issue in determining the remedy for this discrimination.

Under the company's collective bargaining agreement with the Teamsters, competitive seniority for a line driver was counted from the time he took the post, not from the time he joined the company. Thus a black employee transferring to the line driver job would be required to give up any competitive seniority he had accumulated.

Citing *Franks,* the unanimous Court held that persons discriminated against after the effective date of the 1964 act were entitled to retroactive seniority as far back as that date. But with Justices Brennan and Marshall dissenting, the Court refused to order seniority awards stretching back further than July 2, 1965, for victims of discrimination.

Were it not for the specific immunity granted by the act to bona fide seniority systems, wrote Stewart for the majority, the seniority system challenged in this case would probably have been found invalid. But both the language of the immunization provision and the legislative history demonstrated that an

otherwise neutral, legitimate seniority system does not become unlawful under Title VII simply because it may perpetuate pre-Act discrimination. Congress did not intend to make it illegal for employees with vested seniority rights to continue to exercise those rights, even at the expense of pre-Act discriminatees.[179]

Marshall and Brennan based their dissent on their view that a seniority system that perpetuated the effect of pre-1965 discrimination was not a bona fide system protected by Title VII.

In 1983 the Court, by a splintered majority, held that without proof of intent to discriminate, private persons suing their employer, a recipient of federal funds, for discrimination in violation of Title VI of the 1964 Civil Rights Act, may not win back pay or retroactive seniority, but only an injunction against the continuation of such conduct.[180]

Affirmative Action

Affirmative action cases began to dominate the Court's civil rights agenda in the latter decades of the twentieth century, reflecting the fact that this question of appropriate remedy had become one of the most contentious issues in American society.

On the one hand, the public's focus on this matter, a question not of right but of remedy, reflected the progress the nation had made into the second generation of the civil rights movement. On the other hand, the resentment that the use of affirmative action engendered in some areas threatened to undercut the gains of earlier decades.

From 1974—when the issue first came to the Supreme Court—until 1995, the Court considered thirteen affirmative action cases.

Over these years the Court and the country wrestled with the questions of fairness and equal protection presented by a remedy designed to compensate for past discrimination. Was it proper to deny members of the majority fair treatment to make up for past unequal treatment of minorities? How did such a remedy fit within the equal protection guarantee?

Not until 1987 did the Court take a firm stance. Until that point its record on the issue was mixed to the point of confusion. Between 1974 and 1987, the Court struck down as many affirmative action plans as it upheld. Never with the agreement of more than six justices, the Court had approved some use of affirmative action in school admissions, job training, contract set-asides, admission to union membership, and promotions. It had forbidden the use of affirmative action in layoffs to preserve the jobs of blacks at the expense of more senior white employees.

In 1987 the Court came down firmly on the side of affirmative action, ruling that so long as it was carefully used, affirmative action was an appropriate remedy violating neither the Constitution nor any federal civil rights law.

Over the next eight years the Court steadily tightened the standard of care by which use of this controversial remedy was judged. In 1989 the Court struck down Richmond, Virginia's, decision to set aside a certain percentage of public contract dollars to be awarded to minority businesses. This set-aside had been adopted by the city without any clear evidence of discrimination against black construction contractors. Therefore, there was no showing of any public interest compelling enough to justify allocating public money on the basis of race, the Court ruled.

Racial classifications carry the danger of "stigmatic harm," declared Justice O'Connor in the Richmond case. Race-based classifications must be used only when demanded by evidence of past discrimination.

Six years later in 1995, the Court brought affirmative action fully under the equal protection requirement of strict scrutiny. That standard limits the use of affirmative action to situations in which it is demonstrated that affirmative action serves a compelling governmental interest and is narrowly tailored to achieve that goal. "[A]ll governmental action based on race . . . should be subjected to detailed judicial inquiry to ensure that the personal right to equal protection of the laws has not been infringed," wrote Justice O'Connor for the Court.[181]

BEGINNING WITH *BAKKE*

The first time the issue of affirmative action came to the Court, in the 1974 case of *DeFunis v. Odegaard,* a five-justice majority sidestepped the issue. The Court avoided ruling on the reverse discrimination issue by finding the case moot, no longer presenting a live controversy.

The white plaintiff, who charged that he was denied admission to a state law school so that the school might accept a less-qualified minority student, had been admitted under court order. He was scheduled to graduate from law school in the spring of 1974, only months after the Court heard arguments in his case.

The majority held that the case was moot because their decision on the equal protection issue would have no effect on the plaintiff. The dissenting justices would have preferred to resolve the substantive question.[182]

When the Court in 1978 finally dealt with a live case of reverse discrimination—*University of California Regents v. Bakke*—it found itself just as divided as the country was over the issue.

On one point, the Court, 5–4, told state universities that they may not set aside a fixed quota of seats in each class for minority group members, denying white applicants the opportunity to compete for those places.

On a second point, a different five-justice majority held that admissions officers do not violate the equal protection guarantee when they consider race as one of many factors that determine which applicant is accepted and which rejected.

Background

Allan Bakke, a thirty-eight-year-old white engineer, was twice denied admission to the medical school at the University of California at Davis. To ensure minority representation in the student body, the university had set aside sixteen seats for minority applicants in each medical school class of one hundred students.

Challenging the set-aside as a violation of his constitutional right to equal protection of the laws, Bakke contended that he would have been admitted had it not been for this rigid preference system. In each year his application was rejected, the school had accepted some minority applicants with qualifications inferior to Bakke's.

Justice Powell's Votes

Justice Powell was the key to the Bakke decision. He was the only justice who was in both majorities in *University of California Regents v. Bakke.*

On the first point—the decision to strike down the Davis quota system—Powell voted with Chief Justice Burger and Justices Rehnquist, Potter Stewart, and John Paul Stevens, who saw *Bakke* as a controversy between litigants that could be settled by

Twice rejected for admission to the medical school of the University of California at Davis, Allan Bakke filed suit challenging school policy that admitted minority students with grades and test scores inferior to his. Bakke's suit led to the Supreme Court's first major statement on the constitutionality of affirmative action programs. Bakke was awarded his medical degree from the university in 1982.

applying the 1964 Civil Rights Act without involving constitutional issues. Title VI of the act, they pointed out, barred any discrimination on the grounds of race, color, or national origin in any program receiving federal financial assistance. When that ban was placed alongside the facts of the case, it was clear to them that the university had violated the statute. Stevens explained:

The University, through its special admissions policy, excluded Bakke from participation in its program of medical education because of his race. The University also acknowledges that it was, and still is, receiving federal financial assistance. . . . The meaning of the Title VI ban on exclusion is crystal clear: Race cannot be the basis of excluding anyone from participation in a federally funded program.[183]

Powell's reasoning on this point differed from the view of the four dissenters. Where they found no constitutional involvement, he found the scope of the Title VI ban and the equal protection clause of the Fourteenth Amendment identical—what violated one therefore violated the other. And so he based his vote against the university's preference system on both the law and the Constitution.

The Davis special admissions program used an explicit racial classification, Powell noted. Such classifications were not always unconstitutional, he continued, "[b]ut when a state's distribution of benefits or imposition of burdens hinges on . . . the color of a person's skin or ancestry, that individual is entitled to a demonstration that the challenged classification is necessary to promote a substantial state interest." Powell could find no substantial interest that justified establishment of the university's specific quota system. Not even the desire to remedy past discrimination was a sufficient justification, he said; such a desire was based on "an amorphous concept of injury that may be ageless in its reach into the past."[184]

But Powell did not believe that all racial classifications were unconstitutional. He voted with Justices Brennan, Marshall, White, and Harry A. Blackmun to approve the use of some race-conscious affirmative action programs.

Powell's vote endorsing this position was cautious; he would limit the use of these programs to situations in which past discrimination had been proved. The other four contended that the university's wish to remedy past societal discrimination was sufficient justification. For the four, Brennan wrote:

> Government may take race into account when it acts not to demean or insult any racial group, but to remedy disadvantages cast on minorities by past racial prejudice, at least when appropriate findings have been made by judicial, legislative, or administrative bodies with competence to act in this area.[185]

The four endorsed the broad remedial use of race-conscious programs, even in situations where no specific constitutional violation had been found.

VOLUNTARY AFFIRMATIVE ACTION

The Court's next affirmative action case, *United Steelworkers of America v. Weber,* decided in 1979, did not raise the constitutional issue of equal protection. It posed only the question whether the Civil Rights Act of 1964 barred an employer from voluntarily establishing an affirmative action training program that preferred blacks over whites.

By a 5–2 vote the Court held that Title VII did not bar such a program. Stewart, who had voted against racial quotas in the *Bakke* case, joined the four justices who had endorsed use of race-conscious programs in that case to form the majority in *Weber.* Burger and Rehnquist dissented; Powell and Stevens did not participate in the case.

Background

In 1974 Kaiser Aluminum and the United Steelworkers of America agreed upon an affirmative action plan that reserved 50 percent of all in-plant craft training slots for minorities. The agreement was a voluntary effort to increase the number of minority participants holding skilled jobs in the aluminum industry.

Brian Weber, a white, applied for a training program at the Kaiser plant where he worked in Gramercy, Louisiana. He was rejected. Weber, who had more seniority than the most junior black accepted for the program, charged that he had been a victim of "reverse discrimination." He won at both the federal district court and the court of appeals levels. The union, the company, and the Justice Department then asked the Supreme Court to review the appeals court decision.[186]

Permissible Plan

Reversing the lower courts, the majority said that in passing Title VII Congress could not have intended to prohibit private employers from voluntarily instituting affirmative action plans to open opportunities for blacks in job areas traditionally closed to them:

> It would be ironic indeed if a law triggered by a Nation's concern over centuries of racial injustice and intended to improve the lot of those who had "been excluded from the American dream for so long" . . . constituted the first legislative prohibition of all voluntary, private, race-conscious efforts to abolish traditional patterns of racial segregation and hierarchy.[187]

The majority carefully distinguished between the language of Title VII prohibiting racial discrimination in employment and Title VI, the section of the act reviewed in *Bakke* and held to mean that programs receiving federal aid could not discriminate on the basis of race.

In Title VI, Brennan said for the majority, "Congress was legislating to assure federal funds would not be used in an improper manner. Title VII, by contrast, was enacted pursuant to the Commerce power to regulate purely private decisionmaking and was not intended to incorporate and particularize the commands of the Fifth and Fourteenth Amendments" that guarantee equal protection of the laws against federal and state infringement.[188]

In separate dissents Chief Justice Burger and Justice Rehnquist objected to the majority's interpretation of Title VII and its legislative history. The Court's judgment, Burger wrote,

> is contrary to the explicit language of the statute and arrived at by means wholly incompatible with long-established principles of separation of powers. Under the guise of statutory "construction," the Court effectively rewrites Title VII to achieve what it regards as a desirable result. It "amends" the statute to do precisely what both its sponsors and its opponents agreed the statute was not intended to do.[189]

Rehnquist charged that the majority had contorted the language of Title VII. Its opinion, he said, is "reminiscent not of jurists such as Hale, Holmes and Hughes, but of escape artists such as Houdini."

The Court, he continued, "eludes clear statutory language, 'uncontradicted' legislative history, and uniform precedent in concluding that employers are, after all, permitted to consider race in making employment decisions."[190]

FEDERAL AFFIRMATIVE ACTION

The following year, 1980, the Court faced a constitutional challenge to affirmative action that was not voluntary but mandated by federal law. In the Public Works Employment Act of 1977, Congress set aside a certain percentage of federal funds for contracts with minority-owned businesses. The Court, 6–3, held the set-aside permissible.

This program, explained Chief Justice Burger, "was designed to ensure that, to the extent federal funds were granted under . . . [this law], grantees who elect to participate would not employ procurement practices that Congress had decided might result in perpetuation of the effects of prior discrimination which had impaired or foreclosed access by minority businesses to public contracting opportunities."[191]

"In the continuing effort to achieve the goal of equality of economic opportunity," wrote Burger, "Congress has necessary latitude to try new techniques such as the limited use of racial and ethnic criteria to accomplish remedial objectives; this is especially so in programs where voluntary cooperation with remedial measures is induced by placing conditions on federal expenditures."[192]

The justices in the majority were Burger, Brennan, Powell, Marshall, White, and Blackmun. Rehnquist, Stewart, and Stevens dissented.

THE LAYOFF CASES

Affirmative action was anathema to Ronald Reagan's administration, which saw it as impermissible reverse discrimination, penalizing innocent whites—usually white men—for past discrimination by others against blacks and women.

The first two affirmative action cases heard by the Court during the Reagan years brought results the administration found quite congenial. Twice, the Court ruled that affirmative action was not appropriately used in layoff situations to protect the jobs of more recently hired blacks at the cost of the jobs of more senior white employees.

Background

In December 1983 the Court heard arguments in the first affirmative action case of the Reagan years, *Firefighters Local Union No. 1784 v. Stotts, Memphis Fire Department v. Stotts.*

After the Memphis fire department, operating under a consent decree settling charges of racial discrimination against the department, hired a number of black firefighters, budget cutbacks required some firemen to be laid off. The black fire captain, Carl Stotts, who had won the consent decree, persuaded a federal judge to order that whites with more seniority be laid off in order to preserve the jobs of more recently hired blacks.

With the backing of the Reagan administration, the city and the firefighters' union came to the Court seeking reversal of this order. They argued that layoffs should proceed along the general rule of "last hired, first fired."

The administration's friend-of-the-court argument contended that the firefighters' seniority system was immunized by the 1964 Civil Rights Act against such judicial tampering—unless the system was shown to have been designed to discriminate against minority employees, a finding not made in the Memphis case.

Stotts Ruling

In June 1984 the Court agreed with the challenge, holding that the federal judge had overstepped his powers when he overrode the usual seniority rule to preserve the jobs of the junior firefighters who were black. The administration hailed the decision as a victory, reading into it a broad disavowal of affirmative action.

In fact, Justice White tied the Court's opinion closely to the particular facts of this case, namely, the court order directing the city to ignore its usual rules for layoffs in order to preserve gains achieved under a consent decree.[193]

But White and the four other justices in the majority—Burger, Powell, Rehnquist, and O'Connor—did declare that Congress, in the 1964 Civil Rights Act, had intended to provide remedies of this affirmative sort only to persons who had themselves been the victims of illegal discrimination. Because there was no finding in this case that any of the newly hired black firefighters had suffered such personal rejection, the judge's order was unwarranted, they said. Justice Stevens joined the majority but not White's opinion. Justices Brennan, Blackmun, and Marshall dissented.

Wygant Decision

Two years later the Court underscored its doubts about any use of affirmative action in layoff situations, ruling 5–4 that it was unconstitutional for a school board to lay off white teachers to preserve the jobs of blacks with less seniority. That, the Court held in *Wygant v. Jackson Board of Education,* denied the whites equal protection.[194]

The voluntary adoption of an agreement protecting blacks' jobs in time of layoffs was not based on any showing by the board of actual past discrimination, nor was it narrowly tailored enough to be permitted, the majority held. It was one thing to use affirmative action in hiring, when "the burden to be borne by innocent individuals is diffused . . . generally," wrote Powell, but quite another to use it to deprive people of their existing jobs.[195]

It was notable, in light of the Reagan administration's position, that the Court went out of its way to point out that although the school board's use of affirmative action in this case was not permissible, some affirmative action was appropriate.

"We have recognized . . . that in order to remedy the effects of prior discrimination, it may be necessary to take race into account," wrote Justice Powell. "As part of this nation's dedication to eradicating racial discrimination, innocent persons may be called upon to bear some burden of the remedy."[196]

Justice O'Connor also wrote to emphasize the Court's agreement on "core principles" concerning affirmative action. "The Court is in agreement," she wrote, that "remedying past or present racial discrimination by a state actor is a sufficiently weighty state interest to warrant the remedial use of a carefully constructed affirmative action program."[197]

O'Connor's opinion rejected the administration's position, which *Stotts* had seemed to endorse, that affirmative action was constitutional only when used to benefit specific identified victims of bias.

Her opinion, her first substantive writing on the issue, moved her into the decisive "swing" position between the four justices who usually favored affirmative action—Brennan, Marshall, Blackmun, and Stevens—and the four who generally disapproved it—Burger, Rehnquist, White, and Powell.

AFFIRMATIVE ACTION UPHELD

Wygant marked a turning point. Within the next ten months the Court removed all doubt that affirmative action, properly used in the proper circumstance, was a constitutionally permissible remedy for past discrimination.

Six weeks after *Wygant,* on July 2, 1986, the Court ruled in two more affirmative action cases. In both the Court rebuffed the administration's argument against affirmative action. Only Chief Justice Burger and Justice Rehnquist accepted the administration's view.

Justice Brennan, the Court's most staunchly liberal member, spoke for the majority in both cases, holding that neither court-ordered minority quotas for union admission nor race-based job promotions violated the 1964 Civil Rights Act.

In *Local #28 of the Sheet Metal Workers' International v. Equal Employment Opportunity Commission* the Court, 5–4, upheld an order requiring the union, which had persistently refused to admit blacks, to increase its nonwhite membership to 29.23 percent by August 1987.[198] In *Local #93, International Association of Firefighters v. City of Cleveland and Cleveland Vanguards* the Court, 6–3, held that the Civil Rights Act did not prevent the city from resolving a bias complaint by agreeing to promote one black firefighter for every white promoted.[199]

O'Connor, who had dissented in the sheet metal workers' case, criticized racial quotas as impermissible in the Cleveland case. She joined the majority, leaving Burger, Rehnquist, and White in dissent.

Paradise: Promotion Quota

For the third time in less than a year, the Supreme Court in February 1987 upheld a challenged affirmative action plan. Against a challenge that a one-black-for-one-white promotion quota denied white troopers the equal protection of the law, the Court, 5–4, upheld the plan imposed on Alabama's state troopers by a federal judge.[200]

Brennan spoke for the Court in *United States v. Paradise:* "Strong measures were required in light of the . . . long and shameful record of delay and resistance." The Alabama Department of Public Safety had hired no blacks before it was sued for discrimination in 1972. Eleven years later a federal judge found racial discrimination still pervasive and conspicuous in the department and therefore imposed the promotion quota. This quota "was amply justified and narrowly tailored to serve the legitimate and laudable purposes" of eradicating this history of discrimination, wrote Brennan.[201]

Powell, but not O'Connor, joined the majority in this case. Dissenting with O'Connor were Rehnquist, now chief justice, White, and Antonin Scalia, then the Court's newest member.

Johnson: A Boost for Women

In *Johnson v. Transportation Agency, Santa Clara County, Calif.,* the Court laid to rest any remaining doubts about its endorsement of the careful use of affirmative action. This 1987 case was the first one before the Court concerning the use of affirmative action to benefit women.

The vote was 6–3. O'Connor and Powell joined the usual foursome of affirmative action advocates—Brennan, Marshall, Blackmun, and Stevens. Their decision upheld a voluntary affirmative action plan adopted by the Santa Clara County Transportation Department to move women into higher ranking positions than they had held before. The plan resulted in the promotion of Diane Joyce to road dispatcher. Competing with Joyce for the job was Paul Johnson, who scored two points higher on a qualifying interview but, because of the affirmative action plan, lost out on the promotion.

It was appropriate, under the circumstances, to take Joyce's sex into account as a plus, wrote Justice Brennan for the majority. "The decision to do so was made pursuant to an affirmative action plan that represents a moderate, flexible, case-by-case approach to effecting a gradual improvement in the representation of minorities and women in the agency's work force. . . . Such a plan is fully consistent with Title VII [of the Civil Rights Act of 1964], for it embodies the contribution that voluntary employer action can make in eliminating the vestiges of discrimination in the workplace."[202]

Brennan looked back to the 1979 *Weber* ruling in writing this opinion, extending its approval of voluntary affirmative action to include public as well as private employers. As in *Weber,* the plan in *Johnson* was permissible because it did not require white men to be fired and replaced by blacks or women nor impose an absolute bar to advancement by white males, and it was only a temporary remedy.

Dissenting were Rehnquist, White, and Scalia.

A TIGHTENING STANDARD

After the Court's 1980 ruling in *Fullilove,* dozens of state and local governments set aside a certain portion of their public works dollars for minority-owned businesses. Those programs boosted the economic prospects of racial minorities and women but sometimes at the expense of more established contractors, a number of whom went to court to protest.

Richmond: Rigid Set-Aside

In 1989 the Court struck down Richmond, Virginia's, rigid set-aside plan. The program required the prime contractor on every city construction project to subcontract at least 30 percent of the dollar amount of the contract to minority-owned businesses. The case of *City of Richmond v. J. A. Croson Co.* was a challenge to that plan by a company that had lost a contract for installing plumbing fixtures at the city jail because it could not find a qualified minority subcontractor.

The states do not share Congress's broad power to enforce the Fourteenth Amendment, which operates as a direct restriction on the power of the states to use racial classifications, said the Court. Therefore, *Fullilove* does not govern city and state minority set-aside plans, it declared.

Richmond's plan violated the Fourteenth Amendment promise that "no state shall . . . deny to any person within its jurisdiction the equal protection of the laws," wrote Justice O'Connor, joined by Chief Justice Rehnquist and Justices White, Stevens, and Anthony M. Kennedy. Justice Scalia concurred; Justices Marshall, Brennan, and Blackmun dissented.

The plan's primary defect, O'Connor explained, was its lack of justification by specific evidence of racial discrimination within the city's construction industry. Echoing her opinion in *Wygant*, she wrote, "a generalized assertion that there has been past discrimination in an entire industry provides no guidance for a legislative body to determine the precise scope of the injury it seeks to remedy."[203]

"While there is no doubt that the sorry history of both private and public discrimination in this country has contributed to a lack of opportunities for black entrepreneurs, this observation, standing alone, cannot justify a rigid racial quota in the awarding of public contracts in Richmond, Virginia. . . . An amorphous claim that there has been past discrimination in a particular industry cannot justify the use of an unyielding racial quota. . . . The 30 percent quota cannot in any realistic sense be tied to any injury suffered by anyone."[204]

States and cities "may take remedial action when they possess evidence that their own spending practices are exacerbating a pattern of prior discrimination," said O'Connor, but "they must identify that discrimination, public or private, with some specificity before they use race-conscious relief."[205]

"To accept Richmond's claim that past societal discrimination alone can serve as the basis for rigid racial preferences would be to open the door to competing claims for 'remedial relief' for every disadvantaged group. The dream of a Nation of equal citizens in a society where race is irrelevant to personal opportunity and achievement would be lost in a mosaic of shifting preferences based on inherently immeasurable claims of past wrongs," she added.[206]

"Proper findings in this regard are necessary to define both the scope of the injury and the extent of the remedy necessary to cure its effects. Such findings also serve to assure all citizens that the deviation from the norm of equal treatment for all racial and ethnic groups is a temporary matter, a measure taken in the service of the goal of equality itself. Absent such findings, there is a danger that a racial classification is merely the product of unthinking stereotypes or a form of racial politics."[207]

Later in 1989 the Court seemed to encourage the testing of affirmative action plans when it ruled that such settlements could be challenged, after their adoption, by white workers who felt themselves adversely affected by the terms. Until the Court's ruling in *Martin v. Wilks,* a suit between black firefighters and the city of Birmingham, such "third-party" challenges generally were not permitted.[208]

Writing for the Court, divided 5–4, Chief Justice Rehnquist declared that the Court felt it must permit such challenges in order to honor the principle that a person could not be deprived of his legal rights in a proceeding to which he was not a party.

Two editorial cartoonists respond to the Supreme Court's recent rulings on affirmative action. In *Adarand Constructors Inc. v. Peña* (1995), the Court decided that federal affirmative action policies are subject to strict scrutiny.

Federal Preferences

Continuing to defer far more readily to congressional decisions than to municipal decisions to adopt affirmative action measures, the Court in 1990 ruled that Congress may order preferential treatment of racial minorities to increase their ownership of broadcast licenses.

By a 5–4 vote, the justices said "benign race-conscious measures," including those that do not compensate victims of past discrimination, are constitutional as long as they further important government objectives—a standard easier to meet than the heightened scrutiny required in Croson for a state set-aside program. Central to the Court's opinion in *Metro Broadcasting Inc. v. Federal Communications Commission* was the fact that Congress had mandated the preferential treatment. Justice William J. Brennan Jr. wrote the opinion. Chief Justice Rehnquist and Justices O'Connor, Scalia, and Kennedy dissented.[209]

Strict Scrutiny

Just five years later, in 1995, the Court overruled *Metro Broadcasting* and brought all governmental action based on race under the most searching judicial inquiry.

By 5–4, with O'Connor writing for the majority, the Court

held that affirmative action policies, including federal minority contracting provisions, are subject to strict scrutiny by the courts. That means that such policies will survive judicial scrutiny only if they serve a compelling governmental interest and are narrowly tailored to achieve that goal.[210]

With that decision in *Adarand Constructors Inc. v. Peña,* the justices returned to lower courts the case begun by a white contractor in Colorado. His guardrail construction company had challenged a U.S. Department of Transportation program that gave contractors a financial incentive to award subcontracts to minority-owned businesses. Adarand Constructors sued after it lost a bid on a federal highway project to an Hispanic-owned company.

Not surprisingly, the lower federal courts hearing the case rejected the challenge and upheld the program, applying the intermediate standard of review used by the Court in *Metro Broadcasting.* The Supreme Court overruled them.

The Decision

In her opinion Justice O'Connor said the Court was generally skeptical of racial classifications and had imposed identical standards under the equal protection clause on federal, state, or local governments. *Metro Broadcasting,* she said, had departed from those precedents.

"[W]henever the government treats any person unequally because of his or her race, that person has suffered an injury that falls squarely within the language and spirit of the Constitution's guarantee of equal protection," she wrote.[211]

O'Connor stopped short of saying that strict scrutiny would prevent the government from ever using racial classifications. ". . . [W]e wish to dispel the notion that strict scrutiny is 'strict in theory, but fatal in fact,'" she said, quoting a passage by Justice Marshall in *Fullilove.* "The unhappy persistence of both the practice and lingering effects of racial discrimination against minority groups in this country is an unfortunate reality, and government is not disqualified from acting in response to it."[212]

Chief Justice Rehnquist and Justices Antonin Scalia, Anthony M. Kennedy, and Clarence Thomas joined most of O'Connor's opinion. (Thomas, who succeeded Thurgood Marshall, one of the five justices in the *Metro Broadcasting* majority, effectively made the difference in shifting the Court toward strict judicial scrutiny for federal affirmative action programs.)

Dissenting in *Adarand* were Justices John Paul Stevens, David H. Souter, Ruth Bader Ginsburg, and Stephen G. Breyer. Stevens, the most senior of the group, criticized the majority's "inability to differentiate between 'invidious' and 'benign' discrimination." The ruling, Stevens said, "would disregard the difference between a 'No Trespassing' sign and a welcome mat. It would treat a Dixiecrat Senator's decision to vote against Thurgood Marshall's confirmation in order to keep African Americans off the Supreme Court as on a par with President Johnson's evaluation of his nominee's race as a positive factor."[213]

Equal Protection, the Alien and the Poor

More than a half century ago, in 1944, the Court declared that discrimination or any classifications based on race should be subject to strict judicial scrutiny. It was not until a decade later that the Court actually applied that standard to strike down segregation in public schools.

The Supreme Court uses one of three tests for measuring the validity of laws challenged as violations of the due process and equal protection guarantees. The strictest test is applied when the law involves a suspect classification (race or alienage) or a fundamental right. Under this "strict scrutiny" test, a law is upheld only if it is found necessary to achieve a compelling or overriding government purpose.

The Court's intermediate test, usually called "intermediate scrutiny," allows a law to be upheld so long as it is substantially related to an important government purpose. This test, usually applied in cases involving gender or legitimacy, is easier to meet than the "strict scrutiny" test.

The easiest standard applied by the Court in these cases is the "rational basis" test. Laws tested against that standard are upheld if they are rationally related to a legitimate purpose.

For aliens, like blacks and other racial minorities, the Court's protection expanded gradually. In time, laws discriminating against aliens, persons born in another country who have not become U.S. citizens, would receive the greatest scrutiny under the Fourteenth Amendment's guarantee of equality. Other cases would test whether strict scrutiny applied to discrimination based on sex, relative wealth, or education. By the mid-1990s, the Court still reserved the greatest protection, and strictest judicial scrutiny, for race and alienage alone. *(See "Compromise Standard," pp. 681–682.)*

Aliens and the Law

Congress has exclusive authority to determine who may enter the country, but once an alien is admitted to the United States, he or she is entitled to the equal protection of its laws. In 1886 the Court declared that the Fourteenth Amendment protected persons, not just citizens. The Supreme Court in *Yick Wo v. Hopkins* wrote that the Civil War amendment applied "to all *persons* within the territorial jurisdiction, without regard to any differences of race, of color, or of nationality; and the equal protection of the laws is a pledge of the protection of equal laws."[1]

It was eighty-five years before the Supreme Court in 1971 declared alienage, like race, a "suspect" category justifiable only by a compelling government interest. Still, even before then, beginning with *Yick Wo,* the Court—with one period of exception—required states to show more than a merely rational basis for a legal distinction between aliens and citizens. As a result, aliens initially fared better under the Court's application of the Fourteenth Amendment's equal protection clause than did the blacks

In *Yick Wo v. Hopkins* (1886), involving a Chinese laundry owner whose license to operate in San Francisco had not been renewed by city officials, the Supreme Court ruled that the Fourteenth Amendment protects all persons, not just citizens of the United States.

who were expected by the authors of the clause to be its prime beneficiaries.

Yick Wo involved a San Francisco ordinance, which, to minimize fire hazards, required operators of wooden laundries to obtain a license from the city. Although his laundry had been declared safe by city fire and health officials, Yick Wo was denied a renewal of his license. When he discovered that most Chinese owners of wooden laundries had been denied permits, while most white laundry owners were granted them, he sued, charging that he had been denied equal protection of the laws.

Sustaining the charge, a unanimous Supreme Court wrote:

Though the law itself be fair on its face and impartial in appearance, yet, if it is applied and administered by public authority with an evil eye and an unequal hand, so as practically to make unjust and illegal discriminations between persons in similar circumstances, material to their rights, the denial of equal justice is still within the prohibition of the Constitution.[2]

Because the city offered no explanation for its discrimination, "the conclusion cannot be resisted, that no reason for it exists except hostility to the race and nationality to which the petitioners belong, and which in the eye of the law is not justified," the Court wrote.[3]

Yick Wo's case involved his right to earn a living, a right the Court said was "essential to the enjoyment of life." The Court amplified this holding in the 1915 case of *Truax v. Raich.* Arizona law required that 80 percent of the workers in establishments with more than five employees be U.S. citizens. When a restaurant owner fired Mike Raich, an Austrian native, in order to comply with the statute, Raich charged that he had been denied equal protection. Agreeing, the Supreme Court declared the state law unconstitutional. Justice Charles Evans Hughes wrote the opinion:

It requires no argument to show that the right to work for a living in the common occupations of the community is of the very essence of the personal freedom and opportunity that it was the purpose of the [Fourteenth] Amendment to secure. . . . If this could be refused solely upon the ground of race or nationality, the prohibition of the denial to any person of the equal protection of the laws would be a barren form of words."[4]

Within twelve years *Raich* itself would prove rather barren. In 1915 the country was already growing suspicious of and antagonistic toward immigrants from certain countries. The prejudice, which would peak in the 1920s, is described by historians Alfred H. Kelly and Winfred A. Harbison:

The average middle class "old American" of the twenties believed firmly that both the Communist and anarchist menaces and the contemporary alarming increase in urban crime were due to the presence of undesirable aliens in the country. Much contemporary xenophobic sentiment also was laden with religious and racial prejudice. Conservative Protestants feared and resented the recent heavy influx of Catholic immigrants from Italy and Poland, while the swarthy new-comers from southern and eastern Europe as well as those from Japan and Asia were looked upon as "unassimilable" and a threat to American racial purity."[5]

In response, Congress passed laws requiring deportation for aliens convicted of crimes and subversive activity. Congress also established immigration quotas based on national origin; the quotas heavily favored the immigrants of northwest Europe. In 1924 Congress passed a second law that effectively barred most immigration from Asia.

ALIENS AND STATE GOVERNMENT

The Supreme Court was not immune to public prejudice against aliens. Beginning in 1914, it condoned state laws excluding aliens from certain activities and jobs cloaked with a special public interest.

In 1877 the Court had ruled in *McCready v. Virginia* that Virginia could prohibit residents of other states from planting oysters in its tidal streams. The right to use such streams was a property right, and the privilege and immunity clause did not invest "the citizens of one state . . . with any interest in the common property of the citizens of another state."[6]

The Court extended this special public interest rule to aliens in 1914 when it upheld a Pennsylvania statute forbidding aliens to shoot wild game and, to that end, to possess shotguns and rifles. Wild game, like a tidal stream, was a natural resource that a state may preserve for its own citizens "if it pleases," the Court said in *Patsone v. Pennsylvania.* To that purpose, the state may make classifications, and if the class "discriminated against is or reasonably might be considered to define those from whom the evil mainly is to be feared," the classification is permissible,

wrote Justice Oliver Wendell Holmes Jr.[7] No evidence was presented to support a contention that aliens shot more game than any other class, but the majority would not say the state was wrong in identifying aliens "as the peculiar source of the evil that it desired to prevent."[8]

In 1915 the Court used the special public interest test to uphold the right of a state to confine hiring on state public works projects to U.S. citizens.[9]

In the early 1920s several western states seeking to discourage Japanese immigration passed laws barring aliens ineligible for citizenship from owning or leasing agricultural lands. The Court in 1922 interpreted the federal laws restricting citizenship as allowing only whites and blacks of African descent to become citizens.[10] As a result, the alien land laws applied primarily to Japanese aliens.

In 1923 the Court upheld these laws. Because the federal government recognized two classes of aliens—those who were eligible for citizenship and those who were not—the states were not required to justify similar state laws. "The rule established by Congress on this subject, in and of itself, furnishes a reasonable basis for classification in a state law," the Court said in *Terrace v. Thompson.*[11]

In 1927 the Court appeared to abandon its 1915 decision that states may not deny aliens opportunities to hold "the common occupations of the community" solely because they were aliens. At the same time the Court adopted a more relaxed standard of review for state classifications based on alienage.

Clarke v. Deckebach (1927) concerned a Cincinnati ordinance that barred aliens from operating pool and billiards halls. The city justified this classification by arguing that pool halls were evil places frequented by lawbreakers and were the scenes of many crimes. Because aliens were less familiar with the laws and customs of the country, their operation of these pool halls constituted a menace to the public, the city claimed.

Upholding the ordinance, the unanimous Court said that while the Fourteenth Amendment prohibits "plainly irrational discrimination against aliens . . . it does not follow that alien race and allegiance may not bear in some instances such a relation to a legitimate object of legislation as to be made the basis of a permissible classification."[12]

Enunciating its new standard of scrutiny, the Court wrote:

It is enough for present purposes that the ordinance, in the light of facts admitted or generally assumed, does not preclude the possibility of a rational basis for the legislative judgment and that we have no such knowledge of local conditions as would enable us to say that it is clearly wrong.

It was competent for the city to make such a choice, not shown to be irrational, by excluding from the conduct of a dubious business an entire class rather than its objectionable members selected by more empirical means.[13]

The Fourteenth Amendment no longer protected aliens seeking to work at ordinary jobs. The Court now allowed a city or state to deny rights to all aliens on the presumption that some aliens would act in an unacceptable manner. It was left to the alien class to prove the presumption irrational. Fortunately for aliens, this standard was relatively short-lived.

A CLOSER SCRUTINY

The Court first indicated a changed attitude toward questions of alienage and national origin in two World War II cases that concerned U.S. citizens of Asian descent. Both involved Japanese-Americans who had failed to comply with military orders first restricting the movements of Japanese-Americans living on the West Coast and then confining them to detention camps for eventual relocation away from the coast. In both cases the Court held that such extreme discrimination against these citizens was justified by the necessities of war and the need to protect the country from the possibility that some disloyal Japanese-Americans might collaborate with the Japanese enemy. But in both cases the Court said distinctions based on race and ancestry merited close scrutiny and could be justified only by such "pressing public necessity" as the war.[14]

In 1948 the Court effectively reversed its position on alien land laws. *Oyama v. California* involved a Japanese alien, Kajiro Oyama, who had purchased some agricultural property as a gift to his minor son, Fred Oyama, a U.S. citizen by birth. Kajiro Oyama was then appointed his son's guardian, which allowed him to work the land for the benefit of his son. The state charged Oyama with attempting to evade the alien land law, and Oyama in turn charged that both he and his son were denied equal protection of the laws by that law.

The Supreme Court ruled, 6–3, that the state law did deprive the citizen son of equal protection:

There remains the question of whether discrimination between citizens on the basis of their racial descent, as revealed in this case, is justifiable. Here we start with the proposition that only the most exceptional circumstances can excuse discrimination on that basis in the face of the equal protection clause and a federal statute giving all citizens the right to own land. . . . The only justification urged upon us by the State is that the discrimination is necessary to prevent evasion of the Alien Land Law. . . . In the light most favorable to the State, this case presents a conflict between the State's right to formulate a policy of landholding within its bounds and the right of American citizens to own land anywhere in the United States. When these two rights clash, the rights of a citizen may not be subordinated merely because of his father's country of origin.[15]

The majority did not decide whether the alien father had been denied equal protection of the laws. But the decision stripped the law of much of its effectiveness.

Six months later the Court, 7–2, rejected its reasoning in *Deckebach* and returned to its earlier position that the right to earn a living was a liberty that could not be denied an alien solely on the basis of race or national origin.

Takahashi v. Fish and Game Commission (1948) involved a 1943 California law that prohibited alien Japanese from fishing in the state's coastal waters. In 1945 the state amended the law to extend the ban to all aliens ineligible for citizenship. In effect, this meant Japanese aliens because a 1946 federal law made Filipinos and persons of races indigenous to India eligible for citi-

zenship. Torao Takahashi, a fisherman denied a license, charged that he had been denied equal protection by the 1945 state law.

Sustaining the charge, the Court reversed its previous position that a state could make the same alienage classifications as the federal government. "It does not follow," wrote Justice Hugo L. Black for the majority, "that because the United States regulates immigration and naturalization in part on the basis of race and color classifications, a state can adopt one or more of the same classifications."[16]

The Constitution gave Congress complete authority over admission and naturalization of aliens. "State laws which impose discriminatory burdens upon the entrance or residence of aliens lawfully within the United States conflict with this constitutionally derived federal power to regulate immigration," Black wrote.[17]

Furthermore, the majority rejected California's claim that the fish in its offshore waters were a natural resource that the state could reserve for its own citizens under the special public interest rule:

To whatever extent the fish in the three-mile belt off California may be "capable of ownership" by California, we think that the "ownership" is inadequate to justify California in excluding any or all aliens who are lawful residents of the State from making a living by fishing in the ocean off its shores while permitting all others to do so.[18]

THE MODERN STANDARD

Questions of discrimination against aliens did not come before the Court again until the 1970s. In its first important aliens case of this period, *Graham v. Richardson* (1971), a unanimous Court asserted that

classifications based on alienage, like those based on nationality or race, are inherently suspect and subject to close judicial scrutiny. Aliens as a class are a prime example of a "discrete and insular" minority . . . for whom such heightened judicial solicitude is appropriate.[19]

Graham concerned an Arizona statute that restricted certain welfare benefits to citizens and aliens who had resided in the United States for at least fifteen years. A second case, consolidated with *Graham,* tested a Pennsylvania statute that denied certain welfare benefits to all aliens. By its declaration that classification by alienage was inherently suspect, the Court required states to show a compelling governmental interest to justify making that distinction.

The claim that the special public interest rule allowed a state to "preserve limited welfare benefits for its own citizens is inadequate" to justify the classification, the Court said.[20]

Aliens as well as residents pay state and federal taxes. "There can be no 'special public interest' in tax revenues to which aliens have contributed on an equal basis with the residents of the State," the Court said.[21]

Over the next few years, the Court applied close judicial scrutiny and found no compelling interest in several state laws denying aliens certain benefits or the opportunity to work in certain professions. The Court struck down a Connecticut law that barred aliens from being licensed as lawyers, a Puerto Rico law that barred them from becoming engineers, a New York law that excluded aliens from the state's competitive civil service, and a Texas law barring resident aliens from the job of notary public. It also struck down a New York law that excluded resident aliens who did not intend to become citizens from eligibility for state financial aid for higher education.[22]

In *Sugarman v. Dougall,* the case concerning its competitive civil service, New York contended it should be allowed to exclude aliens from governmental policy-making positions because aliens might not be "free of competing obligations to another power."[23] The Court observed that not all members of the competitive civil service held policy-formulating positions. At the same time, the state allowed aliens to serve in other branches of the state civil service in both policy-making and nonpolicy-making jobs. Applying strict scrutiny, the Court held that the statute must fall because it "is neither narrowly confined nor precise in its application."[24]

But in *dicta* at the end of that unanimous opinion, the Court said states might require a person to be a citizen in order to exercise certain rights, such as voting, or to hold certain positions essential to the maintenance of representative government. Among these positions were "state elective or important non-elective executive, legislative, and judicial positions, for officers who participate directly in the formulation, execution, or review of broad public policy perform functions that go to the heart of representative government."[25]

The Court further stated that its scrutiny would "not be so demanding where we deal with matters resting firmly within the State's constitutional prerogatives."[26]

In 1978 this statement provided the basis for a decision in which the Supreme Court, 6–3, upheld a New York statute requiring all its state police to be U.S. citizens. Writing for the majority, Chief Justice Warren E. Burger found police among the category of those who participated in making or carrying out governmental policy. Therefore, the state could require them to be citizens. Burger explained: "The essence of our holdings to date is that although we extend to aliens the right to education and public welfare, along with the ability to earn a livelihood and engage in licensed professions, the right to govern is reserved to citizens."[27]

And because the right to govern fell within the state's constitutional prerogatives, the state needed only to prove that it had a rational basis for excluding aliens from police positions. Because police generally execute public policy and exercise a wide variety of discretionary powers that have a significant impact on citizens, the majority felt it was rational for the state to restrict such jobs to citizens. "Clearly the exercise of police authority calls for a very high degree of judgment and discretion, the abuse or misuse of which can have serious impact on individuals," Burger said. "In short, it would be as anomalous to conclude that citizens may be subjected to the broad discretionary powers of noncitizen police officers as it would be to say that judicial officers and jurors with power to judge citizens may be aliens."[28]

In 1979 the Court, 5–4, sustained a New York law prohibiting aliens who refuse to apply for U.S. citizenship the opportunity to work as public school teachers. Because teachers played a critical role in developing the attitudes of their students toward government, society, and the political process, they fell into the category of occupations "so bound up with the operation of the State as a governmental entity" as to permit the restriction of those jobs to citizens, the majority wrote.[29]

Subsequently, the Court, 5–4, upheld a California requirement that all peace officers (that is, persons with law enforcement responsibilities) be U.S. citizens. These officers, explained Justice Byron R. White in *Cabell v. Chavez-Salido,* exercise and symbolize the power of the political community and it is reasonable to require that they be citizens.[30]

But the Court did not see the education of public school age children the same way. By refusing to educate illegal alien children in the public schools, Texas sought to curtail the costs those residents imposed on the state budget. This policy was challenged, and in 1982 the Supreme Court, 5–4, ruled it unconstitutional in *Plyler v. Doe, Texas v. Certain Named and Unnamed Undocumented Alien Children.*

Illegal aliens present in the United States are accorded the full protection of the equal protection clause, wrote Justice William J. Brennan Jr. for the majority. Regardless of their illegal status, they are clearly persons and may not be denied the right to a free public education. There is no national policy nor state interest sufficient to justify denying them this right, held the Court.[31]

Brennan wrote:

It is difficult to understand precisely what the State hopes to achieve by promoting the creation and perpetuation of a subclass of illiterates within our boundaries, surely adding to the problems and costs of unemployment, welfare, and crime. It is thus clear that whatever savings might be achieved by denying these children an education, they are wholly insubstantial in light of the costs involved to these children, the State, and the Nation. . . . If the State is to deny a discrete group of innocent children the free public education that it offers to other children residing within its borders, that denial must be justified by a showing that it furthers some substantial state interest.[32]

ALIENS AND THE FEDERAL GOVERNMENT

The Court has traditionally allowed the federal government to treat citizens and aliens differently. Because the Constitution gives Congress absolute authority over immigrants' admission to the United States and their naturalization, the Supreme Court requires Congress only to present some rational basis for making a distinction between citizen and alien or between some aliens and other aliens.

In 1976 a unanimous Court in *Mathews v. Diaz* upheld a Medicare regulation that made aliens who were not permanent residents of the country for at least five years ineligible for supplementary medical benefits. The Court wrote:

[T]he fact that Congress has provided some welfare benefits for citizens does not require it to provide like benefits for all aliens. Neither the overnight visitor, the unfriendly agent of a hostile foreign power, the resident diplomat, nor the illegal entrant, can advance even a colorable constitutional claim to a share in the bounty that a conscientious sovereign makes available to its own citizens and some of its guests. The decision to share that bounty with our guests may take into account the character of the relationship between the alien and this country: Congress may decide that as the alien's tie grows stronger, so does the strength of his claim to an equal share of the munificence. . . .

. . . In short, it is unquestionably reasonable for Congress to make an alien's eligibility depend on both the character and the duration of his residence. Since neither requirement is wholly irrational, this case essentially involves nothing more than a claim that it would have been more reasonable for Congress to select somewhat different requirements of the same kind.[33]

And because the benefit issue raised was a question of degree rather than kind, the Court said it was "especially reluctant to question the exercise of congressional judgment."[34]

In a second case decided the same day, the Court, 5–4, ruled that the Civil Service Commission violated the Fifth Amendment due process guarantee by excluding all aliens from the federal competitive civil service and therefore denying them the opportunity for employment in a major sector of the economy. The denial affected an aspect of liberty protected by the Fifth Amendment, the majority said in *Hampton v. Mow Sun Wong.*

Since these resident . . . [aliens] were admitted as a result of decisions made by the Congress and the President . . . due process requires that the decision to impose that deprivation of an important liberty be made either at a comparable level of government or, if it is permitted to be made by the Civil Service Commission, that it be justified by reasons which are properly the concern of that agency.[35]

The only reason offered that properly concerned the agency was administrative efficiency, the majority continued. And while it was reasonable for the agency to make a single rule applicable to all aliens, such an arbitrary rule did not outweigh "the public interest in avoiding the wholesale deprivation of employment opportunities caused" by the rule, which therefore must fall.[36]

Three months later, on September 2, 1976, President Gerald R. Ford issued an executive order authorizing the Civil Service Commission to continue to exclude noncitizens from the federal competitive civil service.

Poverty and Equal Protection

Discrimination against poor people because of their poverty has not been declared inherently unconstitutional by the Supreme Court, even though individual justices have endorsed that belief. The Court, however, has found wealth-based classifications in violation of the equal protection guarantee when they deprive poor people of fundamental rights and interests with no compelling state interest to justify the discrimination.

On this basis the Court has invalidated classifications by wealth that impede access to justice, the right to travel freely between states, and the right to vote and run for public office.

Efforts to persuade the Court to classify all distinctions based on wealth as inherently suspect and to raise vital interests, such as education, to the status of fundamental rights have been un-successful. Where the Court has found that a classification by wealth does not involve a fundamental interest, it has applied the traditional equal protection test in which the state must only show a rational basis to justify the distinction between rich and poor.

ACCESS TO JUSTICE

In 1956 the Court said for the first time that a wealth-based classification violated the equal protection guarantee. In the case of *Griffin v. Illinois,* Judson Griffin and James Crenshaw were convicted of armed robbery. Because they were indigent, the two asked for a free transcript of their trial for use in preparing an appeal. After their request was refused, the two charged that the refusal denied them due process and equal protection. The Supreme Court agreed, 5–4.

Justice Hugo L. Black wrote the opinion, joined by only three other justices. Justice Felix Frankfurter concurred in the judgment with a separate opinion.

Black wrote:

Both equal protection and due process emphasize the central aim of our entire judicial system—all people charged with crime must, so far as the law is concerned, "stand on an equality before the bar of justice in every American court." . . . [*Chambers v. Florida,* 309 U.S. 227 at 241 (1940)] Surely no one would contend that either a State or the Federal Government could constitutionally provide that defendants unable to pay court costs in advance should be denied the right to plead not guilty or to defend themselves in court. Such a law would make the constitutional promise of a fair trial a worthless thing. Notice, the right to be heard, and the right to counsel would under such circumstances be meaningless promises to the poor. In criminal trials a State can no more discriminate on account of poverty than on account of religion, race, or color. Plainly the ability to pay costs in advance bears no rational relationship to a defendant's guilt or innocence and could not be used as an excuse to deprive a defendant of a fair trial.[37]

A state is not required by the Constitution to provide an appeals procedure. But if it chooses to do so it may not limit access to it on the basis of wealth, Black continued. "There can be no equal justice where the kind of a trial a man gets depends on the amount of money he has."[38]

The four dissenters held that so long as Illinois followed its established procedure for appellate review, due process had not been denied. And so long as the state opened its appeals procedure to all defendants convicted of the same crime, it did not violate equal protection even though

some may not be able to avail themselves of the full appeal because of their poverty. . . . The Constitution requires the equal protection of the law, but it does not require the States to provide equal financial means for all defendants to avail themselves of such laws.[39]

An Equal Right to Appeal

By 1971, however, the entire Court agreed that poverty alone should not bar an indigent from appealing his or her conviction. In *Mayer v. Chicago* a unanimous Court expanded *Griffin* to hold that a state's refusal to provide a free transcript to a man so that he might appeal his misdemeanor conviction was a violation of equal protection. "The size of the defendant's pocketbook bears no more relationship to his guilt or innocence in a nonfelony than in a felony case," the Court declared.[40]

But in 1976 the Court limited the circumstances under which the federal government must provide transcripts at public expense. In *United States v. MacCollum* the Court declared that indigent convicts did not have an unlimited constitutional right to a free transcript of their trial. Congress did not violate the equal protection guarantee implicit in the Fifth Amendment when it made provision of such a transcript conditional upon a finding that the challenge to the conviction was not frivolous and that the transcript was necessary to resolve the issues presented.

These conditions, the five-justice majority conceded,

place an indigent in somewhat less advantageous position than a person of means. But neither the Equal Protection Clause of the Fourteenth Amendment nor . . . the Fifth Amendment . . . guarantees "absolute equality or precisely equal advantages." . . . [*San Antonio School District v. Rodriguez*, 411 U.S. 1 at 24 (1973)] In the context of a criminal proceeding, they require only an "adequate opportunity to present [one's] claims fairly." [*Ross v. Moffitt*, 417 U.S. 600 at 616 (1974)][41]

The Right to Legal Counsel

In 1963 the Supreme Court held in *Gideon v. Wainwright* that a state violated due process when it refused to provide court-appointed attorneys to indigents charged with felonies. On the same day the Court also held that a state violated equal protection if it provided attorneys to indigents appealing convictions only when the appellate court decided legal counsel would be advantageous to the success of the appeal.

For the majority in *Douglas v. California*, Justice William O. Douglas wrote:

There is lacking that equality demanded by the Fourteenth Amendment where the rich man, who appeals as of right, enjoys the benefit of counsel's examination into the record, research of the law, and marshaling of arguments on his behalf, while the indigent, already burdened by a preliminary determination that his case is without merit, is forced to shift for himself.[42]

Justice John Marshall Harlan, who dissented in *Griffin,* also dissented in *Douglas.* He argued that the Court should have relied on the due process clause rather than the equal protection guarantee to invalidate the state law:

The States, of course, are prohibited by the Equal Protection Clause from discriminating between "rich" and "poor" as such in the formulation and application of their laws. But it is a far different thing to suggest that this provision prevents the State from adopting a law of general applicability that may affect the poor more harshly than it does the rich, or, on the other hand, from making some effort to redress economic imbalances while not eliminating them entirely.[43]

In subsequent cases the Court held that neither due process nor equal protection required a state to provide a convicted defendant with counsel so that he could seek discretionary review of his case in the state's higher courts or in the Supreme Court—rather than in an appeal to which he had a right. Nor did a state deny equal protection when it required a convicted indigent who subsequently became capable of repayment to reimburse the state for the costs of his court-appointed attorney.[44]

Court Costs

Justice Harlan eventually persuaded a majority of the Court that due process was the proper constitutional basis for striking down state laws discriminating against the poor.

People who could not afford the sixty dollars in court costs associated with divorce proceedings were barred by Connecticut from filing for separation. Ruling against the state in *Boddie v. Connecticut,* Justice Harlan for the majority pointed out that the only way to obtain a divorce was in court. By denying access to court to persons too poor to pay the fees, the state—in the absence of a "sufficient countervailing" justification—denied them due process. Harlan acknowledged that the state had an interest in curbing frivolous suits and in using court fees to offset court costs. But these reasons were not sufficient, he said, "to override the interest of these [indigents] in having access to the only avenue open for dissolving their . . . marriages."[45]

Justices Douglas and William J. Brennan Jr. concurred in the result but argued that the case presented a classic denial of equal protection. "Affluence does not pass muster under the Equal Protection Clause for determining who must remain married and who shall be allowed to separate," wrote Douglas.[46]

Bankruptcy

By a 5–4 vote the Court sustained a federal law that required indigents to pay a fee to declare bankruptcy. "There is no constitutional right to obtain a discharge of one's debts in bankruptcy," the majority wrote in *United States v. Kras* (1973).[47]

Because the right to file for bankruptcy was not a fundamental one, the majority ruled that the federal government need only meet the rationality test. And since it was reasonable that the bankruptcy system be self-sufficient, the government met the test.

In dissent, Justice Potter Stewart said he could not agree with a decision that made "some of the poor too poor even to go bankrupt."[48]

Fines and Terms

In two unanimous decisions the Court has held that states may not substitute imprisonment for a fine that an indigent is unable to pay. In *Williams v. Illinois* (1970) the Court said that states could not hold poor people in prison beyond the length of the maximum sentence merely to work off a fine they were unable to pay. Forty-seven of the fifty states allowed such further imprisonment.

For the Court, Chief Justice Warren E. Burger said:

On its face the statute extends to all defendants an apparently equal opportunity for limiting confinement to the statutory maximum simply by satisfying a money judgment. In fact, this is an illusory choice for Williams or any indigent who . . . is without funds. . . . By making the maximum confinement contingent upon one's ability to pay, the State has visited different consequences on two categories of people.[49]

In 1971 the Court ruled that a "$30 or 30 days" sentence was also an unconstitutional denial of equal protection. That provision of the Fourteenth Amendment, held the Court, barred any state or municipality from limiting punishment for an offense to a fine for those who could pay, but expanding punishment for the same offense to imprisonment for those who could not.[50]

RIGHT TO TRAVEL, POLITICAL RIGHTS

Although the Supreme Court has not settled on which clause of the Constitution protects an individual's right to travel from state to state, since 1966 it has been established that this is a fundamental protected right.[51]

In 1969 the Court struck down two state laws and a District of Columbia statute setting residence requirements for welfare recipients. In *Shapiro v. Thompson* the Court ruled, 6–3, that the residency requirements infringed on the right of poor people to move from state to state and thereby denied them due process and equal protection of the laws. "[A]ny classification which serves to penalize the exercise of that right [to travel], unless shown to be necessary to promote a *compelling* governmental interest is unconstitutional," the majority said.[52] The majority recognized the state's valid interest in maintaining the fiscal integrity of its welfare plan but found this interest not a compelling justification for making "invidious distinctions between classes of its citizens."[53]

The Court reiterated its *Shapiro* holding in 1974 when it ruled that Arizona violated the equal protection clause by requiring indigent persons to live in a county for a year before becoming eligible for free nonemergency medical care.[54]

The Court has ruled consistently that states may not place financial impediments in the way of a person's right to vote or otherwise participate in the political process. Rights associated with political participation are of fundamental interest to citizens, and classifications that prevent a group of people from participating may be justified only by a compelling governmental interest. (*See "Fundamental Interests," pp. 623–624.*)

The poll tax was the major financial barrier to voting for many people for years. Originally conceived of as an additional source of revenue, the poll tax became in the early 1900s a discriminatory tool to bar blacks from voting.

In *Breedlove v. Suttles* (1937) the Court turned aside a charge that the poll tax denied equal protection of the laws, upholding it as a valid source of revenue.[55] In the 1966 case of *Harper v. Virginia State Board of Elections*, the Court overruled its 1937 decision on the ground that the poll tax denied equal protection to the poor by depriving them of the freedom to exercise their right to vote. "Wealth, like race, creed, or color, is not germane to one's ability to participate intelligently in the electoral process," the majority declared.[56] (*See "Poll Taxes," pp. 511–512, in Chapter 10.*)

Twice the Court has held that states may not use filing fee requirements to keep poor candidates off the ballot for public office. Such restrictions violate the guarantee of equal protection not only to candidates but also to voters by limiting the choice of candidates, the Court reasoned. *Bullock v. Carter* (1972) concerned a Texas statute that based the size of primary election filing fees on the costs of conducting those elections. The fees ran as high as $8,900 for some races.

FAMILY MATTERS

Because some matters of family and marital relations are of fundamental interest, classifications that restrict these relationships can be justified only by a compelling reason. However, in 1970 the Supreme Court ruled that a state statute that appeared to discriminate against large families was constitutional because it had a rational basis.

Dandridge v. Williams concerned a Maryland law that limited the maximum amount of welfare a family could receive. This meant that large families received less per child in benefits than families with fewer children. Large poor families consequently charged that the state had impermissibly denied them equal protection.

The Court held that the statute did not deliberately discriminate against large families but was simply a reasonable means for a state to use to allocate scarce welfare funds. *Dandridge v. Williams*, 397 U.S. 471, 1970)

Although keeping spurious candidates off the ballot was a legitimate state objective, the method selected to achieve that objective was arbitrary, the Court held, since some serious candidates were unable to pay the high filing fees while some frivolous candidates could afford them.

The test applied to the challenged law was not as demanding as the compelling interest test generally used for classifications affecting fundamental interests, but it was more rigorous than the traditional equal protection test that simply required the state to show that the challenged classification had a rational basis.[57]

Bullock was expanded in 1974 when the Court held that California could not deny an indigent candidate a ballot spot simply because he was too poor to pay the filing fee, no matter how reasonable that fee was. In *Lubin v. Panish* the Court said the state must provide alternative means for indigents to qualify for a ballot position.[58]

EDUCATION AND WEALTH

In 1973 the Court refused to make classifications by wealth inherently suspect or to give education the status of a "fundamental interest." This meant that the Court did not closely scrutinize a state's decision to continue financing public schools from local property taxes—even though that resulted in wide disparities in the amount spent per pupil in different districts. Nor did the state have to prove that its financing system served a compelling state interest.

In *San Antonio School District v. Rodriguez* the Court, 5–4, upheld this system of financing public education, challenged as a denial of equal protection of the laws.

In the early 1970s, school districts in every state but Hawaii operated primarily with money raised from taxing the real property within the district. Variations in districts—the amount of taxable property, the value of the property, and the tax rate—

resulted in widely differing amounts that school districts in the same state could spend for the education of their children. In Texas, where the case arose, the wealthiest district spent $594 for each schoolchild while the poorest spent only $356.

A bombshell shook the foundations of public school financing on August 30, 1971, when the California Supreme Court declared the traditional fee structure unconstitutional because it resulted in less being spent to educate a child in one school district than in another.[59]

Similar rulings followed from other state and federal courts. In Texas the parents of Mexican-American pupils in San Antonio brought a similar suit, and in December 1971 a federal court found the Texas system unconstitutional. The state appealed to the Supreme Court.

Critical to the holding of the five-justice majority, for whom Justice Lewis F. Powell Jr. wrote, were its findings that the Texas system did not disadvantage an identifiable group of poor persons and that the Constitution makes no mention of a right to education.

In previous cases classifications by wealth were found unconstitutionally discriminatory, wrote Powell, because the groups or individuals affected "were completely unable to pay for some desired benefit, and as a consequence, they sustained an absolute deprivation of a meaningful opportunity to enjoy that benefit."

But in *Rodriguez,* Powell continued, there was no showing that the financing system disadvantaged any definable indigent group or that the poorest people were concentrated in the poorest school districts. He explained:

The argument here is not that the children in districts having relatively low assessable property values are receiving no public education; rather, it is that they are receiving a poorer quality education than that available to children in districts having more assessable wealth. Apart from the unsettled and disputed question whether the quality of education may be determined by the amount of money expended for it, a sufficient answer . . . is that at least where wealth is involved, the Equal Protection Clause does not require absolute equality or precisely equal advantages.[60]

"It is not the province of this Court to create substantive constitutional rights in the name of guaranteeing equal protection of the laws," Powell said. "[T]he undisputed importance of education will not alone cause this Court to depart from the usual standard for reviewing a State's societal and economic legislation."[61]

The question remaining was whether it was reasonable for the state to use the property tax to finance public schools. The majority concluded that it was rational:

[T]o the extent that the Texas system of school finance results in unequal expenditures between children who happen to reside in different districts, we cannot say that such disparities are the product of a system that is so irrational as to be invidiously discriminatory. . . . The Texas plan is not the result of hurried, ill-conceived legislation. It certainly is not the product of purposeful discrimination against any group or class. On the contrary, it is rooted in decades of experience in Texas and elsewhere, and in major part is the product of responsible studies by qualified people. . . . One must also remember that the system here challenged is not peculiar to Texas. . . . In its essential charac-

In 1973 the Supreme Court upheld the Texas public school financing system challenged by Demetrio Rodriguez and other Mexican-American parents as being discriminatory on the basis of economic status.

teristics, the Texas plan for financing public education reflects what many educators for a half century have thought was an enlightened approach to a problem for which there is no perfect solution. We are unwilling to assume for ourselves a level of wisdom superior to that of legislators, scholars, and educational authorities in 50 States, especially where the alternatives proposed are only recently conceived and nowhere yet tested. The constitutional standard under the Equal Protection Clause is whether the challenged state action rationally furthers a legitimate state purpose or interest. . . . We hold that the Texas plan abundantly satisfies this standard.[62]

The four dissenters wanted to overturn the Texas system. Justices Douglas and Thurgood Marshall contended that classification by wealth demanded strict scrutiny and that education was a fundamental interest. Children in property-poor districts were unconstitutionally discriminated against, wrote Marshall, and the Court should not judge the instrument of their discrimination against the "lenient standard of rationality which we have traditionally applied . . . in the context of economic and commercial matters."[63]

Marshall rejected "the majority's labored efforts to demonstrate that fundamental interests . . . encompass only established rights which we are somehow bound to recognize from the text of the Constitution itself."[64]

The right to an education was fundamental, he said, because it was so intimately related to such rights as the right of expressing and receiving information and ideas as guaranteed by the First Amendment. Justices Douglas, Brennan, and Byron R. White said that the school financing system was not rational.

Sex Discrimination

It took the Supreme Court almost a century to extend the guarantee of equal protection to blacks, but it took even longer for it to extend the same guarantee to women.

Not until the 1970s did the Court begin to apply the equal protection guarantee to gender-based discrimination. And more than twenty-five years later this form of discrimination was still measured against a lower standard than was racial discrimination. The Court had taken important steps toward placing men and women on an equal footing before the law, but it continued to uphold some laws—most notably those excluding women from the military draft—based on traditional beliefs about the respective roles of men and women.

"Romantic" Paternalism

The Supreme Court's attitude toward women and their role in the political and economic life of the nation reflects prevailing societal attitudes. Early on, the Court adopted a protectionist philosophy, described as "romantic paternalism," to justify discrimination against women. Relying on the view of woman as wife, mother, and homemaker, the Court in 1873 upheld a state's refusal to let a woman practice law. In *Bradwell v. Illinois* a Chicago woman appealed to the Supreme Court to overturn the state's refusal to license her to practice law.

In the Court's opinion, Justice Samuel F. Miller did not discuss the gender issue but simply held that the Fourteenth Amendment did not affect state authority to regulate admission of members to its bar. In a concurring opinion, Justice Joseph P. Bradley gave judicial cognizance to the then-common belief that women were unfit by nature to hold certain occupations:

[T]he civil law, as well as nature herself, has always recognized a wide difference in the respective spheres and destinies of man and woman. Man is, or should be, woman's protector and defender. The natural and proper timidity and delicacy which belongs to the female sex evidently unfits it for many of the occupations of civil life. The constitution of the family organization, which is founded in divine ordinance, as well as in the nature of things, indicates the domestic sphere as that which properly belongs to the domain and functions of womanhood.[1]

The Fourteenth Amendment did not compel the states to admit women to the bar or to allow women to vote or serve on juries. In *Minor v. Happersett* (1875) the Court held that, although women were citizens, the right to vote was not a privilege or immunity of national citizenship before adoption of the Fourteenth Amendment, nor did the amendment add suffrage to the privileges and immunities of national citizenship. Therefore, the national government could not require states to permit women to vote.[2] In this respect, women fared worse than blacks, whose right to vote was specifically protected by the Fifteenth Amendment. Not until ratification in 1920 of the Nineteenth Amendment were women assured of the right to vote. *(See "No Privilege or Immunity," pp. 505–506, in Chapter 10.)*

The Court in 1880 ruled that the Fourteenth Amendment did not prohibit the states from excluding women from jury duty. This position, reaffirmed as recently as 1961, was overturned by the Court's 1975 decision in *Taylor v. Louisiana*.[3] *(See box, Women on Jury Duty, p. 681.)*

"Romantic paternalism" again came into play when the Court upheld laws intended to protect women's morals. In 1904 it affirmed the validity of a Denver ordinance prohibiting the sale of liquor to women and barring women from working in bars or stores where liquor was sold.[4] Four decades later in the 1948 case of *Goesaert v. Cleary,* the Court sustained a Michigan law that forbade a woman to serve as a bartender unless she was the wife or daughter of the bar's owner. The majority thought it was reasonable for Michigan to believe "that the oversight assured through ownership of a bar by a barmaid's husband or father minimizes hardships that may confront a barmaid without such protecting oversight."[5]

But three justices disagreed, contending that the statute made an unjustifiable and therefore unconstitutional distinction between male and female bar owners. "A male bar owner, although he himself is always absent from his bar, may employ his wife and daughter as barmaids," they wrote, while a "female [bar] owner may neither work as a barmaid herself nor employ her daughter in that position."[6] The real purpose of the statute, implied the dissenters, was not to protect women's morals but men's jobs.

Paternalism was also evident in the Court's response to other cases involving working women. In the early 1900s the Court upheld state laws setting maximum hours and minimum wages for women while holding similar regulations for men a violation of the right to contract their labor. The typical justification of this distinction was provided by the Court's 1908 decision in *Muller v. Oregon,* backing a state law that set maximum hours for women laundry workers. The unanimous Court wrote:

The two sexes differ in structure of body, in the functions to be performed by each, in the amount of physical strength, in the capacity for long-continued labor, particularly when done standing, the influence of vigorous health upon the future well-being of the race, the self-reliance which enables one to assert full rights, and in the capacity to maintain the struggle for subsistence. This difference justifies a difference in legislation and upholds that which is designed to compensate for some of the burdens which rest upon [women].[7]

The civil rights movement of the 1950s and 1960s aroused a new national sensitivity to all forms of discrimination, including that based on sex. Even a cursory examination showed that the traditional protectionist view of women as wives and mothers had contributed substantially to the discrimination they suffered in a modern era where more and more women worked to support themselves and their families.

Because women had been expected to remain at home, they were generally less well educated than men. As a result, women seeking jobs outside the home usually qualified only for low-paying, low-skill jobs where opportunities for advancement were limited. Frequently women were paid less than men who performed the same job, often on the theory that women's earnings were less vital to the support of their families than were men's. Certain legal rights and benefits accrued to women only through their presumed dependency on their husbands and not to them as individuals. As a lower court wrote in 1971: "The pedestal upon which women have been placed has, . . . upon closer inspection, been revealed as a cage."[8]

Congress began to act to remedy some of the more obvious inequities in 1963 when it adopted the Equal Pay Act. Title VII of the 1964 Civil Rights Act prohibited employment discrimination on the basis of sex. In 1972 Congress barred gender-based discrimination in all education programs that received federal support. It also passed the proposed Equal Rights Amendment to the Constitution, which would guarantee women and men equal rights under the law if ratified by three-fourths of the states. In 1973 it approved a bill prohibiting lenders from denying credit on the basis of sex or marital status.

Challenges to laws and practices that discriminated against women, and occasionally against men, began to reach the Court in the 1970s. While the Court consistently held that classifications based on sex could be challenged as violating the equal protection guarantee, the justices were unable for several years to agree on the standard to use in deciding whether such classifications were justified and constitutional. An "intermediate scrutiny" test, used first in a 1976 case and adopted by majorities in the 1980s, eventually became the rule. Some individual justices, however, continued to press for measuring sex discrimination against the same tough standard of strict scrutiny that is applied to charges of racial bias.

The Search for a Standard

Rationality was the standard applied in the first case, *Reed v. Reed*, decided in 1971. The case arose after a minor child in Idaho died intestate (without a will). His adoptive parents, Sally and Cecil Reed, were separated; both filed competing petitions to serve as administrator of the child's estate. The Court awarded the appointment to the father because the Idaho statute designating those eligible to administer intestate estates gave preference to males. Sally Reed challenged the statute as a violation of the equal protection clause of the Fourteenth Amendment.

For the first time the Supreme Court held a state law invalid because it discriminated against women. In an opinion written by Chief Justice Warren E. Burger, a unanimous Supreme Court struck down the Idaho statute. Quoting from a 1920 decision, Burger said that to be constitutionally permissible, a gender-based classification "must be reasonable, not arbitrary, and must rest upon some ground of difference having a fair and substantial relation to the object of the legislation so that all persons similarly circumstanced shall be treated alike."[9]

Applying that standard, the Court could find no rational basis for giving men preference over women. The statute's purpose was to reduce the work of probate courts by eliminating one source of controversy in probate cases, the Court said. But "[t]o give a mandatory preference to members of either sex over members of the other, merely to accomplish the elimination of hearings on the merits, is to make the very kind of arbitrary legislative choice forbidden by the Equal Protection Clause," the Court concluded.[10]

Using the rationality standard, the Court in several cases upheld gender-based classifications, sustaining:

• A Florida property tax exemption for widows but not for widowers. The majority found the exemption "reasonably designed to further the state policy of cushioning the financial impact of spousal loss upon the sex for whom that loss imposes a disproportionately heavy burden." *(Kahn v. Shevin,* 1974)[11]

• A federal law that allows certain female naval officers to serve longer than male officers before mandatory discharge upon failure to win promotion. Observing that female officers could not compete with male officers to win promotion through combat or sea duty, the majority thought it reasonable for Congress to give them a longer period in which to earn advancement. *(Schlesinger v. Ballard,* 1975)[12]

• A Social Security regulation that denies survivors' benefits to widows married less than three months before their husband's death. The majority said such denials were a rational means of preventing sham marriages solely for the purpose of obtaining Social Security benefits. *(Weinberger v. Salfi,* 1975)[13]

• A Social Security regulation providing benefits to married women under age sixty-two with a minor dependent whose husbands were retired or disabled but not to divorced women in the same circumstances. *(Mathews v. deCastro,* 1976)[14]

In 1975 the Court used the rationality standard to strike down a Utah law that required divorced fathers to support their sons to age twenty-one but their daughters only to age eighteen. The Court in *Stanton v. Stanton* rejected arguments that boys needed the longer period of parental support to obtain education and training and that girls needed a shorter period of support because they tended to mature and marry earlier than males.

Present realities make education for girls as important as for boys, the majority said. "And if any weight remains in this day in the claim of earlier maturity of the female, with a concomitant inference of absence of need for support beyond 18, we fail to perceive its unquestioned truth or its significance," the Court added.[15]

STRICTER STANDARD ADVOCATED

As early as 1973, four members of the Court argued for adoption of a stricter standard for gender-based laws. *Frontiero v. Richardson* involved a female air force officer who sought increased benefits for her husband as a dependent. Her request was denied because the law stipulated that while wives of members of the uniformed services were assumed to be dependents eligible for additional benefits, husbands were not and must prove actual dependence in order to be eligible.

Because a federal law was involved, the officer could not challenge it under the Fourteenth Amendment's guarantee of equal protection of the laws against state action. Instead she challenged the law as a violation of the due process clause of the Fifth Amendment, which applies to federal action. Although the Fifth Amendment does not specifically guarantee equal protection, the Court has long held that some discriminations are so unjustifiable as to be violations of the amendment's promise of due process. *(See box, Federal Equal Protection, p. 622.)*

The Supreme Court struck the law down 8–1. In a plurality opinion announcing the decision, Justice William J. Brennan Jr. contended that gender-based classifications, like distinctions based on race and alienage, were inherently suspect. Brennan observed that a person's sex was a noncontrollable and immutable characteristic, and added:

what differentiates sex from such nonsuspect statuses as intelligence or physical disability, and aligns it with the recognized suspect criteria, is that the sex characteristic frequently bears no relation to ability to perform or contribute to society. As a result, statutory distinctions between the sexes often have the effect of invidiously relegating the entire class of females to inferior legal status without regard to the actual capabilities of its individual members.[16]

Such inherently suspect classifications may be justified only by a compelling governmental interest, argued Brennan. But the government's only purpose for the gender-based distinction in this case appeared to be administrative convenience, he said. Even under the less exacting standard of rationality, gender-based classifications made solely to suit administrative convenience were constitutionally impermissible.

Only three other justices agreed with Brennan's reasoning, and so his view that gender-based classifications were inherently suspect remained simply an opinion without the force of law.

Justice Lewis F. Powell Jr., joined by Chief Justice Burger and Justice Harry A. Blackmun, said he agreed that the classification under consideration violated the due process clause. He objected, however, to placing sex-based classifications among those considered inherently suspect and justifiable only by a compelling government interest. He maintained that application of the rationality standard to this case would have resulted in the same outcome.

Justice Potter Stewart concurred in the result without subscribing to either opinion.

ARBITRARY PRESUMPTIONS

In *Frontiero* the law fell because the legislators had made the unproven assumption that wives depended on their husbands for support while men did not so depend on their wives. Because this assumption did not take into account those situations where wives were financially independent of their husbands and where husbands were in fact dependent on their wives, the Court held that the law was too broad and therefore a violation of the equal protection guarantee.

In three subsequent cases, the Court found similar presumptions invalid.

In 1975 the Court struck down that portion of the Social Security Act that provided survivors' benefits to widows with small children but not to widowers with small children. Finding this distinction the same as the invalid classification in *Frontiero,* the Court ruled that it violated the due process clause by providing working women fewer benefits for their Social Security contributions than working men received.

The distinction challenged here was based on an "archaic and overbroad" generalization, said the Court in *Weinberger v. Wiesenfeld.* The idea that men more frequently than women are the primary supporters of their families is "not without empirical support," Justice Brennan wrote. "But such a gender-based generalization cannot suffice to justify the denigration of the efforts of women who do work and whose earnings contribute significantly to their families' support."[17]

Pointing out that the intended purpose of the benefit was to allow a mother to stay home to care for her young children, Brennan said the distinction between surviving mothers and surviving fathers was "entirely irrational.... It is no less important for a child to be cared for by its sole surviving parent when that parent is male rather than female."[18]

Two years later a five-justice majority invalidated a Social Security Act provision that provided survivors' benefits to widows regardless of their financial dependence on their husbands, but to widowers only if they proved they had received more than half their income from their wives. In *Califano v. Goldfarb* four members of the majority found that this impermissibly discriminated against female wage earners by diminishing the protection, relative to male wage earners, that they provided for their families.

Justice Brennan wrote:

The only conceivable justification for writing the presumption of wives' dependency into the statute is the assumption, not verified by the Government ... but based simply on "archaic and overbroad" generalizations ... that it would save the Government time, money and effort simply to pay benefits to all widows, rather than to require proof of dependency of both sexes. We held in *Frontiero,* and again in *Wiesenfeld,* and therefore hold again here, that such assumptions do not suffice to justify a gender-based discrimination in the distribution of employment-related benefits.[19]

The fifth member of the majority, Justice John Paul Stevens found that the provision impermissibly discriminated against the dependent widowers.

For the minority, Justice William H. Rehnquist argued that the classification was a rational one substantially related to the intended goal, which Rehnquist defined as a wish to aid "the characteristically [economically] depressed condition of aged widows."[20]

Again in 1980 the Court struck down such a law, this time a state law making widows automatically eligible for death benefits after the work-related death of their husband, but requiring widowers—in order to be eligible for such benefits—to prove that they were physically or mentally unable to earn a living or that they were dependent upon their wives' earnings.[21]

Beginning with cases in the late 1960s and early 1970s, the Supreme Court has allowed illegitimate and legitimate children the same rights under the equal protection clause of the Fourteenth Amendment.

The Court requires more than a rational basis to justify different treatment of legitimate and illegitimate children. But it has not made illegitimacy a suspect classification justifiable only by a compelling government interest. In most instances the Court has rejected a statute as unconstitutional when it irrationally punishes the child for something the parents did.

For example, in 1972 it struck down a state law that denied illegitimate children any share in workers' compensation survivors' benefits paid automatically to legitimate children. "The status of illegitimacy has expressed through the ages society's condemnation of irresponsible liaisons beyond the bonds of marriage," the Court said.

But visiting this condemnation on the head of an infant is illogical and unjust. Moreover, imposing disabilities on the illegitimate child is contrary to the basic concept of our system that legal burdens should bear some relationship to individual responsibility or wrongdoing. Obviously, no child is responsible for his birth and penalizing the illegitimate child is an ineffectual—as well as an unjust—way of deterring the parent.[1]

Using similar reasoning, the Court rejected state laws forbidding illegitimate children to recover damages in the wrongful death of their mother and, conversely, a mother from recovering damages for the wrongful death of her illegitimate child.[2] It also voided a state law giving legitimate, but not illegitimate, children an enforceable right to support from their natural fathers.[3]

THE RIGHT TO INHERIT

The Court has been ambivalent about laws restricting the rights of illegitimate children to inherit from their fathers when their fathers die without a written will—in legal terms, intestate.

In 1971 the Court, 5–4, upheld a state law that prevented an acknowledged illegitimate child from inheriting property from her father, who died with no will. To strike down the law, said the majority, would be an unwarranted interference with an exercise of state power. The father could have written a will designating his illegitimate child as an heir or could have legitimated her, the majority pointed out.[4]

But six years later the Court appeared to repudiate this decision when it struck down an Illinois statute that allowed illegitimate children to inherit intestate only from their mothers while legitimate children could inherit from both parents in the absence of a will.[5] In 1978 the Court wavered again on this point, upholding, 5–4, a New York law that forbade illegitimate children to inherit from their intestate fathers unless the father had acknowledged his paternity in a Court proceeding during his lifetime.[6]

The Court has evidenced similar indecision in its rulings on federal laws that distinguish between legitimate and illegitimate children. Although it struck down a provision that denied disability insurance benefits to some illegitimate children,[7] it upheld a provision requiring certain illegitimate children to prove actual dependence on their deceased parent in order to be eligible for surviving children's benefits. Such proof was not required for legitimate children.[8]

RIGHTS OF UNWED FATHERS

The fathers of illegitimate children also were brought under the scope of the equal protection clause in the 1970s. Many state laws had presumed that fathers had no fundamental interest in their illegitimate offspring.

In *Stanley v. Illinois* an unwed father of children whose mother had died challenged a state statute that made his children wards of the state without giving him an opportunity to prove his fitness as a parent. The law provided a fitness hearing in such circumstances for legitimate parents and unwed mothers. The Court ruled in the 1972 case that due process entitled him to a hearing and that denial of the hearing would violate equal protection. Administrative convenience was insufficient reason to justify denying unwed fathers such hearings.[9]

The Court also has held that states need not grant unwed fathers a veto over the adoption of their children—unless they had been legitimated—nor need they notify unwed fathers of a child's adoption unless the father had established some legal relationship to his child.[10] In 1979, however, the Court struck down a state law that gave the natural mother, but not the natural father, the right to veto an adoption.[11]

Questions concerning the relationship of a father to his illegitimate child recur. The Court has held that once a state grants children the right to support from their fathers, equal protection denies the state the power to make the exercise of that right any more difficult for illegitimate children than for legitimate children.[12] And the justices struck down a Tennessee law that required all paternity and support actions on behalf of illegitimate children to be filed by the time the child is two years old. No similar time limit was imposed on such actions on behalf of legitimate children.[13]

In 1989 the Court narrowly divided over the rights of a man claiming to be the father of a child, whose mother already was married to another man. The child's father, known as Michael H., sought visitation rights with the child. A state court had rejected the man's claim of paternity, and the high court agreed, 5–4.

A plurality of justices rejected Michael H.'s arguments that his right to due process had been violated. Writing for Chief Justice Rehnquist and Justices O'Connor and Kennedy, Justice Scalia said the Constitution protects traditional societal interests and emphasized the value of "relationships that develop within the unitary family."[14] (Justice Stevens joined in the judgment.)

The dissenting justices argued that the child's biological father should have an opportunity to rebut the presumption that the mother's husband was the father and to prove his paternity in court, thereby opening the door to visitation rights.

1. *Weber v. Aetna Casualty and Surety Co.*, 406 U.S. 164 at 175 (1972).
2. *Levy v. Louisiana*, 391 U.S. 68 (1968); *Glona v. American Guarantee and Liability Insurance Co.*, 391 U.S. 73 (1968); see also *Parham v. Hughes*, 441 U.S. 347 (1979).
3. *Gomez v. Perez*, 409 U.S. 535 (1973).
4. *Labine v. Vincent*, 401 U.S. 532 (1971).
5. *Trimble v. Gordon*, 430 U.S. 762 (1977).
6. *Lalli v. Lalli*, 439 U.S. 259 (1978).
7. *Jimenez v. Weinberger*, 417 U.S. 628 (1974).
8. *Mathews v. Lucas*, 427 U.S. 495 (1976).
9. *Stanley v. Illinois*, 405 U.S. 645 (1972).
10. *Quilloin v. Walcott*, 434 U.S. 246 (1978); *Lehr v. Robertson*, 463 U.S. 248 (1983).
11. *Caban v. Mohammed*, 441 U.S. 380 (1979).
12. *Mills v. Habluetzel*, 456 U.S. 91 (1982).
13. *Pickett v. Brown*, 462 U.S. 1 (1983).
14. *Michael H. v. Gerald D.*, 491 U.S. 110 at 123 (1989).

COMPROMISE STANDARD

Although he had been unable to convince a majority of the Court that gender-based discrimination was so invidious as to require a compelling government interest to justify it, Justice Brennan in 1976 won majority support for a standard that was midway between the standards of rationality and a compelling governmental interest.

Craig v. Boren (1976) involved a challenge to an Oklahoma law that permitted the sale of 3.2 beer to women at age eighteen but not to men until age twenty-one. Four justices agreed with Brennan that to "withstand constitutional challenge . . . classifications by gender must serve important governmental objectives and must be substantially related to achievement of those objectives."[22] It was not enough that the classification was rational, Brennan said; the distinction must serve some "important governmental objective."

Applying this standard, the majority found that Oklahoma's desire to promote traffic safety was an important goal but that the gender-based distinction prohibiting the sale, but not the possession, of a low-alcohol beverage to males under age twenty-one was not substantially related to the attainment of that objective. The classification was therefore invalid.

Five years later the Court upheld a sex-based distinction in criminal law, finding it justified as an appropriate means of accomplishing an important state end. California's statutory rape law permitted a man to be prosecuted for having sexual relations with a woman younger than eighteen to whom he is not married. The woman was exempted from criminal liability. Challenged as discriminating against the man, the state law was upheld by the Court, 5–4, as an appropriate means of preventing illegitimate teenage pregnancies.[23]

Also in 1981 the Court gave at least lip service to this standard when it decided, 6–3, that Congress was well within its authority when it decided to exclude women from the military draft. Writing for the majority in *Rostker v. Goldberg*, Justice Rehnquist declared this distinction justified because women were barred from combat and thus were not "similarly situated" with men for the purposes of maintaining a ready military force.[24]

Brennan's position gained strength when Justice Sandra Day O'Connor joined the Court in 1981. The following year, in one of her first opinions for the Court, O'Connor described the test for determining the validity of a classification based on sex as "straightforward." She then went on to invoke the "important governmental objectives" test.

The case involved a Mississippi state statute that barred men from enrolling in a state-supported nursing school.[25] "Our decisions . . . establish that the party seeking to uphold a statute that classifies individuals on the basis of their gender must carry the burden of showing an 'exceedingly persuasive justification' for the classification. The burden is met only by showing at least that the classification serves 'important governmental objectives and that the discriminatory means employed' are 'substantially related to the achievement of those objectives.'"[26] The Court

WOMEN ON JURY DUTY

For nearly one hundred years, the Supreme Court held that because a woman's place was in the home, she did not have to perform jury duty unless she expressed a wish to do so. Further, the exclusion of women from state court jury panels did not violate the Fourteenth Amendment, the Court ruled in *Strauder v. West Virginia* (1880).[1]

In *Hoyt v. Florida* (1961) Gwendolyn Hoyt sought to overturn her murder conviction, arguing that Florida's jury selection procedures were unconstitutional because only women who had registered for jury duty could be called, which excluded most women from service. The Court majority found the statute valid. "[W]oman is still regarded as the center of home and family life," wrote Justice John Marshall Harlan. "We cannot say that it is constitutionally impermissible for a State . . . to conclude that a woman should be relieved from the civic duty of jury service unless she herself determines that such service is consistent with her own special responsibilities."[2]

Fourteen years later the Court reversed itself. In *Taylor v. Louisiana* (1975) it ruled unconstitutional the automatic exemption of women. Billy Taylor, convicted of a crime by an all-male jury, challenged the Louisiana law that exempted women from jury service unless they volunteered. He said the law denied him his right to a fair trial. The Court agreed, reasoning that a jury comprised of a fair cross section of the community was fundamental to the right to jury trial guaranteed by the Sixth Amendment.

That guarantee was denied "if the jury pool is made up of only special segments of the populace or if large, distinctive groups are excluded from the pool," the majority said. Because 53 percent of the community was female—a large, distinctive group—the question then became whether women served "such a distinctive role" that their exclusion from jury service was justifiable.

The majority answered that it was "no longer tenable to hold that women as a class may be excluded or given automatic exemptions based solely on sex if the consequence is that criminal jury venires are almost totally male. . . . If it was ever the case that women were unqualified to sit on juries or were so situated that none of them could be required to perform jury service, that time has long since passed."[3]

In 1994 the Court ruled that lawyers may not exclude people from serving on juries solely because of their sex. The decision in *J.E.B. v. Alabama* extended the reasoning of a line of cases beginning in 1986 that barred lawyers from excluding potential jurors on account of race. Referring to the guarantee of the equal protection clause, the Court said, "Discrimination in jury selection, whether based on race or on gender, causes harm to the litigants, the community, and the individual jurors who are wrongfully excluded from participation in the judicial process."[4]

1. *Strauder v. West Virginia*, 100 U.S. 303 (1880).
2. *Hoyt v. Florida*, 368 U.S. 57 at 62 (1961).
3. *Taylor v. Louisiana*, 419 U.S. 522 at 537 (1975).
4. *J. E. B. v. Alabama*, 114 S. Ct. 1419 (1994).

struck down the admissions policy and said excluding males from nursing training "tends to perpetuate the stereotyped view of nursing as an exclusively women's job."[27]

That same year, 1982, saw the deadline pass for ratification by the states of the Equal Rights Amendment, cleared by Congress and submitted to the states a decade earlier. The proposed amendment failed when three-fourths of the states failed to ratify it. The amendment said, "Equality of rights under the law shall not be denied or abridged by the United States or by any State on account of sex."

The standard of "intermediate" scrutiny as articulated in *Mississippi University for Women v. Hogan* would prevail through 1996.

The Court in 1996 declined to raise the judicial standard to strict scrutiny for classifications based on sex. However, in striking down the Virginia Military Institute's traditional policy excluding women students, the Court broadly interpreted the standards for protecting victims of sex discrimination. The Court stressed that government must demonstrate an "exceedingly persuasive justification" for gender-based action.[28] The opinion in *United States v. Virginia* was written by Justice Ruth Bader Ginsburg, a well-known advocate for women's rights before her appointment to the Court in 1993.

Since its founding in 1839, Virginia's publicly funded, military-style academy had admitted only men. It had become one of the state's most prestigious colleges, boasting the largest per-student endowment of any undergraduate institution in the nation.

VMI attracted the interest of some women who wished to apply for admission, and in 1990, the U.S. Justice Department sued Virginia alleging that VMI's exclusively male admission policy violated the Fourteenth Amendment's guarantee of equal protection. VMI countered that its distinctive approach, marked by a mentally and physically grueling regimen and an absence of student privacy, would be compromised by the admission of women. Midway through the litigation, in response to an initial federal appeals court ruling, Virginia developed a parallel program for women, the Virginia Women's Institute for Leadership (VWIL), at the nearby Mary Baldwin College, a private liberal arts school for women. Although the women's program lacked VMI's distinctive "adversative" training, its well-credentialed faculty, and high admissions standards, the U.S. Court of Appeals for the Fourth Circuit said the dual programs met the test of whether students at the respective institutions could obtain "substantially comparable benefits."

In reversing that decision and ordering VMI to choose between admitting women and retaining its state support or going private and continuing as a male-only institution, the Supreme Court said that while the state's educational options may be serving "the state's sons, it makes no provision whatever for her daughters. That is not *equal* protection."[29]

The vote against VMI was 7–1. Ginsburg was joined by Justices John Paul Stevens, Sandra Day O'Connor, Anthony M. Kennedy, David H. Souter, and Stephen G. Breyer. Chief Justice

William H. Rehnquist wrote a statement concurring in the judgment but disagreeing with the "exceedingly persuasive justification" legal standard used by the majority. Justice Antonin Scalia dissented, and Justice Clarence Thomas, whose son Jamal was attending VMI at the time, took no part in the case.

In explaining the standard used for judging sex discrimination, the Ginsburg majority adopted language from precedent but cast the constitutional protection broadly:

[T]he reviewing court must determine whether the proffered justification is exceedingly persuasive. The burden of justification is demanding and it rests entirely on the State. The State must show at least that the challenged classification serves important governmental objectives and that the discriminatory means employed are substantially related to the achievement of those objectives. The justification must be genuine, not hypothesized or invented *post hoc* in response to litigation. And it must not rely on overbroad generalizations about the different talents, capacities, or preferences of males and females.[30]

Rejecting VMI's defense that women were not suited to the arduous program, Ginsburg noted that similar concerns were voiced when women first sought admission to law schools and the bar. She wrote, "There is no reason to believe that the admission of women capable of all the activities required of VMI cadets would destroy the Institute rather than enhance its capacity to serve the 'more perfect Union.'"[31]

Rehnquist referred to the state's asserted justification of educational diversity: "The difficulty with its position is that the diversity benefitted only one sex; there was single-sex public education available for men at VMI, but no corresponding single-sex public education available for women."[32] He added, however, that the majority's broad rendering of the constitutional protection for sex discrimination left the "intermediate" scrutiny traditionally used for sex discrimination muddled.

Scalia's dissent targeted both the majority's legal analysis and its rejection of the values underlying the venerable military institute: "In an odd sort of way, it is precisely VMI's attachment to such old-fashioned concepts as manly 'honor' that has made it, and the system it represents, the target of those who today succeed in abolishing public single-sex education."[33] He said Virginia was appropriately providing different programs to meet the different developmental needs of men and women students.

Discrimination in Employment

Because women traditionally have had the primary responsibility for raising children, employers have used potential pregnancy as an argument against hiring, training, and promoting women. Employers' policies on pregnancy have been a major target of women's rights advocates who see this issue as the heart of sex discrimination.

The Supreme Court has found it difficult to deal with cases involving pregnancy-related discrimination. For a time the Court declared that pregnancy classifications did not discriminate between men and women but rather between pregnant persons and nonpregnant persons. After Justice John Paul

Stevens took issue with that view, lecturing his brethren in 1976 that "it is the capacity to become pregnant which primarily differentiates the female from the male," it was rarely invoked again.[34]

HIRING STANDARDS

Title VII of the 1964 Civil Rights Act forbids discrimination on the basis of sex as well as race in employment. It took seven years for the first Title VII sex discrimination case to come to the Supreme Court, *Phillips v. Martin Marietta Corp.* (1971).

Martin Marietta refused to hire women with preschool children, although it hired men regardless of the age of their children. The Court said that Title VII did not permit such a distinction unless it was "a bona fide occupational qualification reasonably necessary to the normal operation of that particular business or enterprise."[35]

Six years later, in *Dothard v. Rawlinson,* the Court struck down as discrimination on the basis of sex a state law that set minimum height and weight requirements for certain jobs, in this case that of a prison guard.

Dianne Rawlinson was rejected for a job as a prison guard in Alabama because she did not meet the requirement that guards be at least five feet, two inches tall and weigh at least 120 pounds. She challenged the law on the grounds that it would disqualify more than 40 percent of the women in the country but less than 1 percent of the men.

The Court ruled this prima facie evidence of sex discrimination because the apparently neutral physical requirements "select applicants for hire in a significantly discriminatory pattern."

The state was then required to show that the height and weight requirements had a "manifest relationship" to the job in question. This the state failed to do, the Court said.[36]

The Court did uphold, however, a provision of the Alabama statute that prohibited women from filling positions that brought them into close proximity with inmates. In this case, the majority said an employee's "very womanhood" would make her vulnerable to sexual and other attacks by inmates and thus "undermine her capacity to provide the security that is the essence of a correctional counselor's responsibility."[37]

Justices Brennan and Marshall dissented. The majority decision "perpetuates one of the most insidious of the old myths about women—that women, wittingly or not, are seductive sexual objects," wrote Marshall. The majority, he said, makes women "pay the price in lost job opportunities for the threat of depraved conduct by prison inmates.... The proper response to inevitable attacks on both female and male guards is ... to take swift and sure punitive actions against the inmate offenders."[38]

MATERNITY LEAVE

The Court's first major modern constitutional decisions on sex discrimination in the workplace came in 1974 and required employers to be more flexible in administering maternity leave. The Court, 7–2, held that it violated the due process guarantee to require all pregnant women to leave their jobs at the same point in pregnancy.

Cleveland Board of Education v. LaFleur and *Cohen v. Chesterfield County School Board,* decided together, involved school board policies that forced teachers to stop teaching midway through pregnancy.

"[F]reedom of personal choice in matters of marriage and family life is one of the liberties protected by the due process clause," the majority wrote. Due process requires that maternity leave regulations "not needlessly, arbitrarily, or capriciously impinge upon this vital area of a teacher's constitutional liberty."[39]

The Court rejected the school boards' arguments that mandatory leave policies ensured continuity of instruction by giving the school time to find qualified substitute teachers. Such an absolute requirement violated the test of rationality, the Court said, because in many instances it would interrupt continuity by requiring a teacher to leave her classroom in the middle of a term.

"As long as the teachers are required to give substantial advance notice of their condition, the choice of firm dates later in pregnancy would serve the boards' objectives just as well, while imposing a far lesser burden on the women's exercise of constitutionally protected freedom," the majority wrote.[40]

The Court also held that the regulations were too broad because they presumed that all women reaching the fifth or sixth month of pregnancy were physically incapable of continuing in their jobs. Such a presumption, which denies a pregnant woman the opportunity to prove she is fit to continue working, is contrary to the due process guarantees of the Fifth and Fourteenth Amendments.

"If legislative bodies are to be permitted to draw a general line anywhere short of the delivery room, I can find no judicial standard of measurement which says the lines drawn here are invalid," said Justice Rehnquist, dissenting for himself and Chief Justice Burger.[41]

PREGNANCY AND DISABILITY

When the Court turned to look at an employer's obligation to provide disability payments to women unable to work because of pregnancy and childbirth, it was distinctly less sympathetic to the needs of working women. After the Court twice ruled against women workers in this context, Congress stepped in to correct the trend: it amended Title VII to prohibit discrimination against pregnant women in all areas of employment.

Six months after the maternity leave decision, the Court in *Geduldig v. Aiello* upheld a state disability insurance program excluding coverage of disabilities related to normal pregnancy and childbirth. The six-justice majority said the exclusion was based on physical condition, not sex:

The California insurance program does not exclude anyone from benefit eligibility because of gender but merely removes one physical condition—pregnancy—from the list of compensable disabilities. While it is true that only women can become pregnant, it does not follow that every legislative classification concerning pregnancy is a sex-based classification. . . . Normal pregnancy is an objectively identifiable physical condition with unique characteristics. Absent a showing that distinctions involving pregnancy are mere pretexts designed to effect an invidious discrimination against the members of one sex or the other, lawmakers are constitutionally free to include or exclude pregnancy from the coverage of legislation such as this on any reasonable basis, just as with respect to any other physical condition.[42]

The question then became simply whether the exclusion was reasonable. Stewart observed that disability coverage for pregnancy would increase costs that would have to be offset by increased contributions by employees, changes in other coverage, or lower benefit levels. He continued:

The state has a legitimate interest in maintaining the self-supporting nature of its insurance program. Similarly, it has an interest in distributing the available resources in such a way as to keep benefit payments at an adequate level for disabilities that are covered, rather than to cover all disabilities inadequately. Finally, California has a legitimate concern in maintaining the contribution rate at a level that will not unduly burden participating employees, particularly low-income employees who may be most in need of the disability insurance.

These policies provide an objective and wholly non-invidious basis for the State's decision not to create a more comprehensive insurance program than it has. There is no evidence in the record that the selection of the risks insured by the program worked to discriminate against any definable group or class in terms of the aggregate risk protection derived by that group or class from the program. There is no risk from which men are protected and women are not. Likewise, there is no risk from which women are protected and men are not.

The appellee simply contends . . . she has suffered discrimination because she encountered a risk that was outside the program's protection. . . . [W]e hold that this contention is not a valid one under the Equal Protection Clause of the Fourteenth Amendment.[43]

In dissent Justice Brennan argued as he had in previous sex discrimination cases that the Court should regard gender-based classifications as inherently suspect, justifiable only to achieve a compelling government interest that could not otherwise be met. He also asserted that the Court misapplied the more lenient standard it did use:

[T]he economic effects caused by pregnancy-related disabilities are functionally indistinguishable from the effects caused by any other disability: wages are lost due to a physical inability to work, and medical expenses are incurred for the delivery of the child and for post-partum care. In my view, by singling out for less favorable treatment a gender-linked disability peculiar to women, the State has created a double standard for disability compensation: a limitation is imposed upon the disabilities for which women workers may recover, while men receive full compensation for all disabilities suffered, including those that affect only or primarily their sex. . . . Such dissimilar treatment of men and women, on the basis of physical characteristics inextricably linked to one sex, inevitably constitutes sex discrimination.[44]

Two years later the Court upheld a similar exclusion from a disability plan maintained by a private employer, General Electric. "[E]xclusion of pregnancy from a disability benefits plan providing general coverage is not a gender-based discrimination at all," wrote Rehnquist for the six-justice majority in *General Electric Co. v. Gilbert* (1976).[45] The plan covered some risks, but not others; there was no risk from which men were protected, but not women, or vice versa. Rehnquist wrote:

[I]t is impossible to find any gender-based discriminatory effect in this scheme simply because women disabled as a result of pregnancy do not receive benefits; that is to say, gender-based discrimination does not result simply because an employer's disability benefits plan is less than all-inclusive. . . . To hold otherwise would endanger the common-sense notion that an employer who has no disability benefits program at all does not violate Title VII [of the 1964 Act].[46]

"Surely it offends common sense to suggest . . . that a classification revolving around pregnancy is not, at the minimum, strongly 'sex related,'" wrote Justice Brennan in dissent. "Pregnancy exclusions . . . both financially burden women workers and act to break down the continuity of the employment relationship, thereby exacerbating women's comparatively transient role in the labor force."[47]

SICK PAY AND SENIORITY

Almost exactly one year after *General Electric* the Court ruled that employers can refuse sick pay to women employees absent from work due to pregnancy and childbirth, but they cannot divest those women of their accumulated seniority for taking maternity leave. All the justices concurred in the ruling in *Nashville Gas Co. v. Satty* (1977).

For the Court, Justice Rehnquist wrote that the divestiture of seniority clearly violated the 1964 Civil Rights Act's Title VII, which prohibited employment discrimination on the basis of sex.

Although the policy appeared neutral—divesting of seniority all persons who took leaves of absence from work for any reason other than illness, a category from which childbirth-related absences were excluded—its effect was clearly discriminatory, depriving far more women than men of job opportunities and adversely affecting their status as employees.

The denial of sick pay was permissible, wrote Rehnquist, under the *General Electric* reasoning, which permitted disabilities arising from pregnancy to be treated differently from similar disabilities caused by other medical conditions. Attempting to distinguish the seniority policy from the sick pay and disability benefits policies, Rehnquist emphasized that the gas company

has not merely refused to extend to women a benefit [sick pay, disability insurance] that men cannot and do not receive, but has imposed on women a substantial burden that men need not suffer. The distinction between benefits and burdens is more than one of semantics. We held in *Gilbert* that . . . [Title VII] did not require that greater economic benefits be paid to one sex or the other "because of their differing roles in the scheme of human existence." . . . But that holding does not allow us to read . . . [Title VII] to permit an employer to burden female employees in such a way as to deprive them of employment opportunities because of their different role.[48]

Finding Rehnquist's distinction between General Electric's seniority policy and its sick pay and disability benefits policy somewhat confusing, Justice Stevens said he saw the difference between the two policies as one of short-term versus long-term effect. Denial of sick pay did not affect the woman worker beyond the period of her leave; loss of seniority resulted in permanent disadvantage.

In a concurring opinion, Justices Brennan, Powell, and Thurgood Marshall suggested that the combination of the seniority and sick pay policies violated Title VII by resulting in less net compensation for women than for men employees.

Frustrated by the Court's complicated position, women's rights activists turned to Congress for relief. Congress responded in 1978 by amending Title VII to prohibit discrimination against pregnant women in any area of employment, including hiring, promotion, seniority rights, and job security.

The Pregnancy Discrimination Act of 1978 also required employers who offered health insurance and temporary disability plans to provide coverage to women for pregnancy, childbirth, and related medical conditions.[49]

That meant, the Court held later, that employers must provide health insurance pregnancy coverage for the wives of male employees that was as comprehensive as that provided for the female employees.

On the other hand, the Court held in 1987, the new law did not preclude states from requiring more benefits for workers disabled by pregnancy than for other temporarily disabled workers.[50]

Four years later, in the Court's first "fetal protection" case, the justices ruled unanimously that companies may not exclude women from jobs that might harm a developing fetus. The justices, however, divided over whether an employer could restrict working conditions for pregnant women, but not for other workers, and still satisfy the standards of Title VII.

Five members of the Court, led by Justice Blackmun, said Congress had intended to forbid any discrimination based on a worker's ability to have children. He wrote that "Congress has left this choice to the woman as hers to make," and he was joined by Justices Marshall, Stevens, O'Connor, and Souter.[51]

Justices White, Rehnquist, Kennedy, and Scalia said that situations could arise in which a company, because of personal injury liability and workplace costs, could exclude women based on hazards to the unborn.

Pension Rights, Sexual Harassment

Women, as a group, live longer than men as a group. Traditionally, that disparity has been reflected in differing treatment of men and women by life insurance plans. But the Supreme Court has made clear that the 1964 Civil Rights Act bars the use of this collective difference to discriminate, in premiums or annuities, against women by charging them more than the generally shorter lived men.

In 1978 the Court, 5–3, ruled that a municipal employer could not require female employees to make higher contributions to a pension fund than male employees earning the same salary.

In *Los Angeles v. Manhart* the city contended that the differential contributions were not based on sex but on longevity. Justice Stevens for the majority acknowledged that women usually lived longer than men and that without the differential, men

would, in effect, subsidize the pension benefits eventually paid to women. However, such subsidies, Stevens said, are the essence of group insurance:

Treating different classes of risk as though they were the same for purposes of group insurance is a common practice which has never been considered inherently unfair. To insure the flabby and the fit as though they were equivalent risks may be more common than treating men and women alike; but nothing more than habit makes one "subsidy" seem less fair than the other.[52]

It is the individual that the 1964 Civil Rights Act protects from discrimination: "Even a true generalization about the class is an insufficient reason for disqualifying an individual to whom the generalization does not apply."[53] Even though most women live longer than most men, many women workers who paid the larger contribution would not, in fact, live longer than some of their male colleagues, Stevens pointed out.

In dissent, Chief Justice Burger said if employers

are to operate economically workable group pension programs, it is only rational to permit them to rely on statistically sound and proven disparities in longevity between men and women. Indeed, it seems to me irrational to assume Congress intended to outlaw use of the fact that, for whatever reasons or combination of reasons, women as a class outlive men. . . .

An effect upon pension plans so revolutionary and discriminatory—this time favorable to women at the expense of men—should not be read into the statute without either a clear statement of that intent in the statute, or some reliable indication in the legislative history that this was Congress' purpose.[54]

The majority may have been influenced by Burger's warning of the decision's revolutionary effect on pension plans. By a 7–1 vote, the Court reversed the lower court order awarding retroactive relief to the women contributors. In this instance the majority felt that retroactive relief was inappropriate because it "could be devastating for a pension fund."[55] Payment of the award from the pension fund would diminish the fund's assets; that might then prove inadequate to meet obligations, which in turn might decrease benefits to all employees or increase the contribution rates for current employees, the Court said.

In lone dissent on this point, Justice Marshall said the majority had been shown no proof of the predicted "devastating" effect. Repayment to women of their earlier excessive contributions was the only way to make them whole for the discrimination they had suffered, he said.

In an earlier case involving remedies for proven sex discrimination, the Court held that the Eleventh Amendment, which prohibits private suits in federal courts against unwilling states, did not protect a state from an order to pay retroactive benefits to employees who were discriminated against by the state.

In *Fitzpatrick v. Bitzer* (1976) the Court upheld a federal court order to Connecticut to pay retroactive benefits to men who had been forced by state law to work longer than women employees before they could retire.[56]

The Court said Congress had the power to enforce the guarantees of the Fourteenth Amendment by authorizing orders requiring expenditures of states' funds. States, by ratifying that amendment, surrendered some of their sovereign immunity to federal orders, it said.

The proper allocation of retirement rights and costs is still a matter that closely divides the Court. In 1983 the Court divided twice, 5–4, in resolving a challenge to an employer's retirement plan under which women workers upon retirement received smaller monthly payments than did men who had contributed the same amounts during their working years.

In *Arizona Governing Committee for Tax Deferred Annuity and Deferred Compensation Plans v. Norris* the Court held—with reasoning similar to that set out by Stevens in *Manhart*—that the greater longevity of women than men was not a permissible basis for paying them different monthly benefits.[57]

Voting together on that point were Justices Marshall, Brennan, Stevens, Sandra Day O'Connor, and Byron R. White.

But on a second point, of considerable practical importance to women who had already retired under this plan, the Court held that this decision would apply only to retirement benefits derived from contributions made after this ruling. O'Connor joined the dissenters from the other point—Burger, Blackmun, Powell, and Rehnquist—to form this majority.

In June 1986, the week Rehnquist was promoted to chief justice, the Court unanimously applied Title VII to ban sexual harassment in the workplace as a form of sexual discrimination, and the usually conservative Rehnquist wrote the majority's opinion. Such harassment is illegal not only when it results in the loss of a job or promotion but also when it creates an offensive or hostile working environment, Rehnquist wrote.

The language of Title VII is not limited to "economic" or "tangible" discrimination. The phrase "terms, conditions, or privileges of employment" evinces a congressional intent "to strike at the entire spectrum of disparate treatment of men and women" in employment.[58]

An employee claiming sexual harassment must prove the existence of a hostile or abusive work environment, said the unanimous Court in 1993, but there is no need for a showing that he or she suffered serious psychological injury as a result. The prohibition on sex discrimination contained in Title VII of the Civil Rights Act of 1964 "comes into play before the harassing conduct leads to a nervous breakdown," explained Justice O'Connor in *Harris v. Forklift Systems Inc.* She added, "So long as the environment would reasonably be perceived, and is perceived, as hostile or abusive, there is no need for it also to be psychologically injurious."[59]

Liberty and Privacy

The belief that an individual has a constitutionally protected right to privacy has evolved from the Court's interpretation of the Fourteenth Amendment guarantee that no state shall "deprive any person of life, liberty, or property, without due process of law." The Court has found embedded in the guarantee of liberty a right to privacy with which government may not casually interfere.

The roots of this privacy doctrine run back a full century, but it was not until the mid-1960s that the Court plainly recognized an individual's right to privacy in decisions concerning marriage, procreation, and abortion. In perhaps its best-known modern ruling, the Court held, 7–2, that pregnant women have a constitutional right to end a pregnancy through abortion. That ruling, in the 1973 case of *Roe v. Wade,* set off a public firestorm that has roared steadily through the ensuing decades. The furor is fueled by the strong emotions that surround the intensely personal nature of abortion, the related issues of life and death, the continuing struggle of women for sexual equality, and the unique political and social character of America.

"The war over abortion seems fiercer and more violent in America than anywhere else," notes Professor Ronald Dworkin. He attributes this reaction to a combination of America's contradictory public and private attitudes toward religion and the nature of the women's movement. While the country demands strict separation of church and state, Dworkin observes, religious faith is nonetheless a powerful force in American life. Meanwhile, the women's movement has sought to free women from traditional notions of sexuality and duty.[1]

The Court's decision in *Roe v. Wade* has remained at the political forefront year after year. Ronald Reagan campaigned on an antiabortion platform for president in 1980, and throughout his two terms he appointed to the judiciary candidates who opposed *Roe v. Wade.* His Supreme Court appointees were chosen carefully with an eye to reversing *Roe v. Wade,* but in 1992 the Court acknowledged the strength of precedent and affirmed the essential holding of *Roe.*

Some of the controversy over *Roe v. Wade* flows from the difficult area of legal reasoning known as "substantive due process." Substantive due process extends the concept of due process beyond its literal meaning of ensuring fair procedures to an examination of the substance, the fundamental values, affected by a particular law or official action. *(See "Substantive Due Process," p. 560, in Chapter 11.)*

At various times in the twentieth century, the Court has wrestled with the question of what rights are so fundamental that laws impinging on those rights violate the due process guarantee because of the "substance" they affect. The result has been rulings in which the Court invoked the Fourteenth Amendment guarantee of "liberty" to protect fundamental values, such as privacy, unmentioned in the Constitution or its history. *(See box, The Protection of Substantive Due Process, pp. 688–689.)*

In *Roe v. Wade* Justice Harry A. Blackmun declared that the due process guarantee for personal liberty included an implicit right of privacy that protected a woman's decision whether or not to end her pregnancy:

The Constitution does not explicitly mention any right to privacy. . . . [But] the Court has recognized that a right of personal privacy, or a guarantee of certain areas or zones of privacy, does exist under the Constitution. In varying contexts, the Court or individual Justices have, indeed, found at least the roots of that right in the First Amendment; in the Fourth and Fifth Amendments; in the penumbras of the Bill of Rights; in the Ninth Amendment; or in the concept of liberty guaranteed by the first section of the 14th Amendment. These decisions make it clear that only personal rights that can be deemed "fundamental" or "implicit in the concept of ordered liberty" are included in this guarantee of personal privacy. They also make it clear that the right has some extension to activities relating to marriage, procreation, contraception, family relationship, and child rearing and education.[2]

When the Court reaffirmed constitutional protection for abortion in 1992, it relied again on the due process clause of the Fourteenth Amendment. The plurality opinion in that case also acknowledged the social implications of the abortion right. Men and women, said the justices, could disagree about "the profound moral and spiritual implications of terminating a pregnancy, even in its earliest stage. Some of us as individuals find abortion offensive to our most basic principles of morality, but that cannot control our decision. Our obligation is to define the liberty of all, not to mandate our own moral code."[3]

In 1990 the Court applied the concept of substantive due process to personal decisions outside the context of reproductive rights. In its first "right to die" case, the Court recognized "the principle that a competent person has a constitutionally protected liberty interest in refusing unwanted medical treatment."[4] That same year the Court recognized that prisoners possess "a significant liberty interest" in avoiding unwanted antipsychotic drugs or other medication.[5]

ORIGINS OF PERSONAL PRIVACY

Judicial recognition of a protected category of personal rights dates back to 1923, during the era when the Court interpreted the liberty guarantee as "the liberty to contract." In *Meyer v. Nebraska* the Court extended the liberty guarantee to cover rights that were personal as well as economic. That case involved a Nebraska law that forbade any school from teaching a modern foreign language other than English to children in the first eight grades. The Court held that the statute violated the Fourteenth Amendment's due process guarantee by depriving the teacher who had been convicted and the affected parents and children of a measure of personal liberty, the right to choose this area of instruction:

The concept of "substantive due process" has produced a number of important rulings by the Supreme Court involving fundamental personal rights and liberties. But this idea—that the Constitution not only demands that government follow fair procedures but also protects certain substantive values—has bitterly divided the Court and the nation.

The Court rejected the concept of substantive due process in the *Slaughterhouse Cases* in 1873. But around the turn of the century it without fanfare began to develop a theory of substantive due process to protect a liberty to contract, to protect economic and property rights.

This development transformed a guarantee of procedural fairness for individuals into a legal foundation from which the Court monitored state economic regulation. One of the best-known decisions of this era, during which the justices scrutinized *what* states choose to regulate rather than *how* they regulated, is the 1905 case of *Lochner v. New York,* which struck down a maximum-hours law for bakers.

The economic-rights trend fell into disfavor in the 1930s, and when substantive due process was revived in the 1960s, it was to protect personal liberties—most controversially, the right to abort a pregnancy. As in the *Lochner* era, the value judgments in the wake of *Roe v. Wade* have engendered considerable legal controversy and social tumult.

A DEVELOPING CONCEPT

The first hint of the doctrine of substantive due process came in a dissenting opinion in the *Slaughterhouse Cases* in 1873. The Court rejected this Fourteenth Amendment challenge. New Orleans butchers challenged a state-granted slaughterhouse monopoly as denying them due process, the opportunity to practice their trade. In dissent, Justice Joseph P. Bradley agreed that "a law which prohibits a large class of citizens from adopting . . . or from following a lawful employment . . . does deprive them of liberty as well as property, without due process of law."[1]

Four years later in *Munn v. Illinois,* the Court edged closer to Bradley's view. Although the justices upheld a state law that regulated grain elevator rates, they did so only after considering the substance of the business regulated. The Court found that grain storage was one of a class of businesses "affected with a public interest" and therefore subject to state regulation.[2]

In this decision, the first in a line of rulings stretching over half a century, the Court looked to the character of the activity regulated to determine whether it was properly within the state's domain. In *Mugler v. Kansas* (1887), concerning a state prohibition law, Justice John Marshall Harlan explained the Court's view:

The courts are not bound by mere forms, nor are they to be misled by mere pretenses. They are at liberty—indeed, are under a solemn duty—to look at the substance of things, whenever they enter upon the inquiry whether the legislature has transcended the limits of its authority. If, therefore, a statute purporting to have been enacted to protect the public health, the public morals, or the public safety, has no real or substantial relation to those objects, or is a palpable invasion of rights secured by the fundamental law, it is the duty of the courts to so adjudge, and thereby give effect to the Constitution.[3]

In *Chicago, Milwaukee and St. Paul R. R. Co. v. Minnesota* (1890) the Court first used substantive due process to strike down a state law regulating economic matters. It ruled that the courts should have the final word on the reasonableness of railroad rates.[4] And in 1898 the Court declared that courts should review public utility rates for reasonableness and to see that they allowed a fair return to the utility.[5]

FREEDOM OF CONTRACT

Although many laws in which states exercised their police power were challenged as a denial of due process, the Supreme Court generally found those laws valid.[6]

In the areas of rate-setting, price regulation, and wage-and-hour laws, however, the Court was far less disposed to defer to the judgment of state legislators.[7]

Two key doctrines emerged: business in which there is a public interest could be regulated by the state, and government should not interfere with the freedom of contract. With those doctrines, the Supreme Court plunged into a new role as judge of the substance of state economic regulation.

Under the public interest rubric, the Court upheld state regulation of such varied matters as insurance and stockyards.[8] But beginning in the 1920s, the Court found fewer and fewer areas of economic life to be properly included in this category.[9]

To protect the freedom of contract, the Court struck down a number of the first wage-and-hour laws passed by the states. In 1898, in *Holden v. Hardy,* the Court upheld a law setting the eight-hour day as the maximum that miners might work.[10]

But seven years later, in *Lochner v. New York,* the Court struck down a law setting the ten-hour day and the sixty-hour week as the maximum for bakers.[11]

The Court saw a critical difference between the working conditions of mines and bakeries. Miners worked in palpably unhealthy conditions, to which their exposure should be limited; bakers were subject to less risk of injury or illness in their working environment. Subsequently, the Court dropped its opposition to maximum-hour laws.[12]

But it was not so tolerant when it considered the first minimum-wage statutes. In its 1923 decision in *Adkins v. Children's Hospital,* the Court struck down the District of Columbia's minimum-wage law for women. Justice George Sutherland, for the five-man majority, described the law as "simply and exclusively a price-fixing law" in violation of the freedom of contract.[13]

DEMISE OF SUBSTANTIVE DUE PROCESS

The Great Depression and the New Deal created pressures that inexorably forced the Supreme Court to drop its use of substantive due process to monitor economic regulation.

Beginning in 1934 with *Nebbia v. New York*, the Court abdicated its role as "super-legislature," leaving decisions on the wisdom and appropriateness of economic legislation to legislators. In *Nebbia* the Court upheld a state law regulating milk prices, even though the milk industry was not one "affected with a public interest."[14] The Court thus ceased to distinguish between some lines of business and others for the purpose of finding some subject to state regulation and others exempt.

Nevertheless, the Court continued to use the "freedom of contract" doctrine to nullify a state minimum-wage law for women. In *Morehead v. New York ex rel. Tipaldo* a five-man majority in 1936 declared:

The right to make contracts about one's affairs is a part of the liberty protected by the due process clause. Within this liberty are provisions of contracts between employer and employee fixing the wages to be paid.[15]

But the tide of public opinion had already turned against this sort of judicial second-guessing. In 1936 both major parties repudiated the *Morehead* decision.

Then in *West Coast Hotel v. Parrish* the Court upheld a Washington state minimum-wage law for women, overruling *Adkins* and *Morehead*.[16]

FROM PROPERTY TO PRIVACY

Yet even as the Court sounded the epitaph for the use of substantive due process to justify its supervision of economic regulation, it was developing a line of rulings under the equal protection guarantee that led it again to consider the substance of state legislation.

In 1942 the Court in *Skinner v. Oklahoma* struck down a state law that allowed habitual criminals to be sterilized. This law was a denial of equal protection, held the Court, because of its substance—because it allowed the state to deprive an individual of "one of the basic civil rights of man."[17]

Matters of personal choice in family life have been the primary beneficiary of the "new substantive due process" approach foreshadowed in *Skinner*.

One landmark in this area was the 1965 declaration in *Griswold v. Connecticut* that privacy was a value protected by the Constitution.[18] In that case the Court struck down a state law forbidding all use of birth control devices.

Although Justice Douglas, writing the majority opinion, was careful not to rest the conclusion upon the due process clause, Justice Hugo L. Black—in dissent—found the ruling a direct descendant of *Lochner v. New York*. This too was substantive due process,

he warned, and it was "no less dangerous when used to enforce this Court's views about personal rights than those about economic rights."[19]

Eight years later Justice William H. Rehnquist sounded the same complaint, dissenting from the Court's 1973 decision in *Roe v. Wade*, which struck down state laws banning abortion. "As in *Lochner* and similar cases applying substantive due process standards," Rehnquist wrote, the standard adopted in *Roe v. Wade* "will inevitably require this Court to examine the legislative policies and pass on the wisdom of these policies."[20]

In 1992 the Court narrowly affirmed the essential holding of *Roe*, voting 5–4 in the case of *Planned Parenthood of Southeastern Pennsylvania v. Casey, Governor of Pennsylvania*. The three justices whose votes effectively preserved the right to abortion wrote in their plurality opinion: "Neither the Bill of Rights nor the specific practices of the States at the time of the adoption of the Fourteenth Amendment marks the outer limits of the substantive sphere which the Fourteenth Amendment protects. . . . It is settled now, as it was when the Court heard arguments in *Roe v. Wade*, that the Constitution places limits on a State's right to interfere with a person's most basic decisions about family and parenthood."[21]

1. *Slaughterhouse Cases*, 16 Wall. 36 at 122 (1873).

2. *Munn v. Illinois*, 94 U.S. 113 (1877).

3. *Mugler v. Kansas*, 123 U.S. 623 at 661 (1887).

4. *Chicago, Milwaukee and St. Paul R. R. Co. v. Minnesota*, 134 U.S. 418 (1890); see also *Smyth v. Ames*, 169 U.S. 466 (1898).

5. *Smyth v. Ames*, 169 U.S. 466 (1898).

6. *Powell v. Pennsylvania*, 127 U.S. 678 (1888); *Jacobson v. Massachusetts*, 197 U.S. 11 (1905); *Austin v. Tennessee*, 179 U.S. 343 (1900); *Packer Corp. v. Utah*, 285 U.S. 105 (1932); *Euclid v. Ambler Realty Co.*, 272 U.S. 365 (1926).

7. *Allgeyer v. Louisiana*, 165 U.S. 578 at 589 (1897).

8. *German Alliance Insurance Co. v. Lewis*, 233 U.S. 389 (1914); *Cotting v. Godard*, 183 U.S. 79 (1901).

9. *Tyson & Brother v. Banton*, 273 U.S. 418 (1927); *Ribnik v. McBride*, 277 U.S. 350 (1928); *Wolff Packing Co. v. Court of Industrial Relations*, 262 U.S. 522 (1923); *Burns Baking Co. v. Bryan*, 264 U.S. 504 (1924).

10. *Holden v. Hardy*, 169 U.S. 366 (1898).

11. *Lochner v. New York*, 198 U.S. 45 (1905).

12. *Muller v. Oregon*, 208 U.S. 412 (1908); *Bunting v. Oregon*, 243 U.S. 426 (1917). For examples of substantive due process and labor matters, see *Adair v. United States*, 208 U.S. 161 (1908); *Coppage v. Kansas*, 236 U.S. 1 (1915); *Lincoln Federal Labor Union v. Northwestern Iron & Metal Co.*, 335 U.S. 525 (1949).

13. *Adkins v. Children's Hospital*, 261 U.S. 525 at 554 (1923).

14. *Nebbia v. New York*, 291 U.S. 502 (1934); see also *Petersen Baking Co. v. Burns*, 290 U.S. 570 (1934).

15. *Morehead v. New York ex rel. Tipaldo*, 298 U.S. 587 at 610 (1936).

16. *West Coast Hotel v. Parrish*, 300 U.S. 379 (1937); see also *United States v. Darby Lumber Co.*, 312 U.S. 100 (1941); *Olsen v. Nebraska*, 313 U.S. 236 (1941); *Federal Power Commission v. Hope Natural Gas*, 320 U.S. 551 (1944); *Day-Brite Lighting Inc. v. Missouri*, 342 U.S. 421 at 423 (1952); *Williamson v. Lee Optical of Oklahoma*, 348 U.S. 483 (1955).

17. *Skinner v. Oklahoma*, 316 U.S. 535 (1942).

18. *Griswold v. Connecticut*, 381 U.S. 479 (1965); see also *Eisenstadt v. Baird*, 405 U.S. 438 (1972); *Roe v. Wade*, 410 U.S. 113 (1973); *Doe v. Bolton*, 410 U.S. 179 (1973).

19. *Griswold v. Connecticut*, 381 U.S. 479 at 522 (1965).

20. *Roe v. Wade*, 410 U.S. 113 at 174 (1973).

21. *Planned Parenthood of Southeastern Pennsylvania v. Casey*, 505 U.S. 833 (1992).

Without doubt, it [liberty] denotes not merely freedom from bodily restraint but also the right of the individual to contract, to engage in any of the common occupations of life, to acquire useful knowledge, to marry, establish a home and bring up children, to worship God according to the dictates of his own conscience, and generally to enjoy those privileges long recognized at common law as essential to the orderly pursuit of happiness by free men.[6]

Two years later the Court struck down an Oregon law that required all children to attend public schools. The challenge was brought by the Society of the Sisters of the Holy Names of Jesus and Mary, which ran orphanages and parochial schools. The Court in *Pierce v. Society of Sisters* declared that the statute "unreasonably interferes with the liberty of parents . . . to direct the upbringing and education of [their] children."[7]

The Court said parents may educate children as they choose: "The child is not the mere creature of the State; those who nurture him and direct his destiny have the right, coupled with the high duty, to recognize and prepare him for additional obligations."[8]

MARRIAGE AND PROCREATION

In 1942 the Court recognized another fundamental right of liberty that had no clear constitutional roots—the freedom to marry and procreate.

Oklahoma law provided that persons convicted three times of crimes of "moral turpitude" were to be sterilized. The Supreme Court in *Skinner v. Oklahoma* invalidated the law because it did not treat all persons convicted of similar crimes in a similar way:

We are dealing here with legislation which involves one of the basic civil rights of man. Marriage and procreation are fundamental to the very existence and survival of the race. The power to sterilize, if exercised, may have subtle, far-reaching and devastating effects. In evil or reckless hands it can cause races or types which are inimical to the dominant group to wither and disappear. . . . [T]he individual whom the law touches . . . is forever deprived of a basic liberty.[9]

As a result of this decision, laws that affected such fundamental rights as marriage and procreation were now subject to close scrutiny and could be justified only by a pressing governmental objective. Such protection for the right of personal privacy was reinforced by the Court's evolving fundamental interest standard for equal protection cases.

Twenty-five years after *Skinner,* the Court in 1967 affirmed the Constitution's protection for choice in marriage. In the case of *Loving v. Virginia,* the Court struck down a Virginia law that punished persons for marrying someone of a different race. This law, the unanimous Court held, violated the equal protection clause and denied those it affected due process:

The freedom to marry has long been recognized as one of the vital personal rights essential to the orderly pursuit of happiness by free men. . . . To deny this fundamental freedom on so unsupportable a basis as the racial classification embodied in these statutes . . . is surely to deprive all the State's citizens of liberty without due process of law. The Fourteenth Amendment requires that the freedom of choice to marry not be restricted by invidious racial discriminations. Under our Con-

stitution, the freedom to marry or not marry a person of another race resides with the individual and cannot be infringed by the State.[10]

CONTRACEPTIVES

In 1965 two years before *Loving,* the Court held that the Constitution forbade a state to prohibit married couples from using contraceptives. The case was *Griswold v. Connecticut.* Estelle Griswold, the executive director of the Planned Parenthood League of Connecticut, gave medical advice to married persons who wished to prevent conception, and she challenged the Connecticut law.

The progeny of this case would greatly expand the scope of constitutional liberties. The individual votes in the seven-justice majority rested on a variety of reasons.

Justice William O. Douglas, for the Court, found the basis for his vote in a right of personal privacy, an independent right implicit in the First, Third, Fourth, Fifth, and Ninth Amendments. "[S]pecific guarantees in the Bill of Rights have penumbras, formed by emanations from those guarantees that help give

Estelle Griswold opened a birth control clinic in New Haven in violation of an 1879 Connecticut law prohibiting the use of contraceptives. She challenged the constitutionality of the statute, and in *Griswold v. Connecticut* (1965) the Supreme Court struck down the law and established a constitutionally protected right to privacy.

Norma McCorvey was the real "Jane Roe" behind the Supreme Court's controversial 1973 abortion decision, *Roe v. Wade*. She is pictured here in 1989, more than fifteen years after she challenged the Texas antiabortion statute.

them life and substance," he wrote. "Various guarantees create zones of privacy."[11]

Marriage was within a protected zone of privacy, Douglas continued, and the state impermissibly invaded that zone by prohibiting married couples from using contraceptives. "Would we allow the police to search the sacred precincts of marital bedrooms for telltale signs of the use of contraceptives? The very idea is repulsive to the notions of privacy surrounding the marriage relationship," he concluded.[12]

In a convincing opinion by Justice Arthur J. Goldberg for himself, Chief Justice Earl Warren, and Justice Brennan, the right to personal privacy was declared to be one of those rights "retained by the people" under the Ninth Amendment, which states that the "enumeration in the Constitution of certain rights shall not be construed to deny or disparage others retained by the people."[13]

Justice John Marshall Harlan saw marriage as one of the basic values that the Court had found "implicit in the concept of ordered liberty" protected by the Fourteenth Amendment.[14] Justice Byron R. White held that because marriage was a fundamental interest, the Connecticut law deprived married couples of "liberty" without due process of law.[15]

The dissenting justices, Potter Stewart and Hugo L. Black, found no right of personal privacy expressed or implied in the Constitution.

In 1972 the Court struck down a state law that permitted the distribution of contraceptives to single persons to prevent the spread of disease but not to prevent conception, finding it a violation of the equal protection guarantee.[16]

ABORTION: *ROE V. WADE*

The most controversial decision of the 1970s vastly enlarged a woman's right of privacy, striking down all state laws banning abortion. The Court's 1973 ruling in *Roe v. Wade* extended the

right of personal privacy to embrace the right of a woman to have an abortion. Once again the Court reached a conclusion based on a constitutional right of privacy without agreeing on the precise location within the Constitution for that right.

"The Constitution does not explicitly mention any right of privacy," wrote Justice Blackmun. "[H]owever, . . . the Court has recognized that a right of personal privacy, or a guarantee of certain areas or zones of privacy does exist under the Constitution."[17]

Whatever its source, Blackmun declared, "[t]his right of privacy . . . is broad enough to encompass a woman's decision whether or not to terminate her pregnancy."[18] But, Blackmun cautioned, the woman's right to have an abortion is a qualified one:

[A] state may properly assert important interests in safeguarding health, in maintaining medical standards, and in protecting potential life. At some point in pregnancy, these respective interests become sufficiently compelling to sustain regulation of the factors that govern the abortion decision.[19]

The state's interest changed as the pregnancy progressed, Blackmun explained. In the first trimester of pregnancy, the state had no interest sufficiently compelling to warrant interfering with this decision. In the second trimester, when an abortion was more likely than continuation of the pregnancy to affect the health of the mother adversely, the state had a compelling interest in protecting her and could therefore regulate the abortion procedure, by requiring, for example, that it be performed in a hospital.[20]

In the third trimester, when the fetus presumably could live on its own, the state's compelling interest lay in protecting that life. To that end the Court said a state could forbid abortions in the third trimester except when necessary to protect the life or health of the mother.[21]

In a 1976 case the Court said a mature woman has a right to

have an abortion, even in the face of strong family opposition. The Court held that states cannot require either the consent of the husband or, if the woman was an unmarried minor, the consent of her parents, as an essential condition for a first-trimester abortion.[22]

However, the Court has declined to require that public funds be used for abortions for poor women.[23] It has upheld state and federal funding bans.

Justices White and Rehnquist dissented from *Roe v. Wade*. Rehnquist was particularly critical of the vague grounding of the right of personal privacy in the Constitution.

ABORTION: STATE RESTRICTIONS

Sixteen years later White and Rehnquist were joined by three other justices, all new to the Court since 1973, whose votes created a majority willing to give states more authority to regulate abortions.

Rehnquist, now chief justice, wrote the Court's opinion in *Webster v. Reproductive Health Services* (1989), pointedly omitting any discussion—indeed, any mention—of the right of privacy. The Court, 5–4, upheld the state's right to prohibit the use of public facilities or public employees to perform abortions. It also upheld the state's right to require physicians to test for fetal viability before permitting an abortion on a woman believed to be as much as twenty weeks pregnant.

In an impassioned dissent, Justice Blackmun criticized the majority for refusing to debate whether the Constitution includes a general right to privacy. "A chill wind blows," he warned, as the majority "casts into darkness the hopes and visions of every woman in this country who had come to believe that the Constitution guaranteed her the right to exercise some control over her unique ability to bear children." They did so, he continued, "either oblivious or insensitive to the fact that millions of women and their families have ordered their lives around this right to reproductive choice, and that this right has become vital to the full participation of women in the economic and political walks of American life."[24]

In the term immediately after the *Webster* decision, the Court upheld state laws requiring teen-age girls to notify their parents of abortion decisions.[25] A more fundamental battle would come two years later in 1992.

ABORTION: RIGHT REAFFIRMED

Even as *Roe v. Wade* neared its twentieth anniversary, the abortion controversy continued to be a driving force in American politics and in the courts. In 1992 President George Bush asked the Supreme Court, as Ronald Reagan before him had, to overturn *Roe v. Wade*. The opportunity came in the case of *Planned Parenthood of Southeastern Pennsylvania v. Casey*. But the conservative-dominated bench defied all predictions and upheld the 1973 landmark. While abortion remains contentious socially and politically, as a constitutional matter, *Roe v. Wade* endures.

In the 1992 case the Court, 5–4, affirmed a right to abortion.

PROTECTING PRIVACY: ABORTION PROTESTS

Opponents of abortion have often tried to close health clinics where abortions are performed by engaging in demonstrations, taunting patients, and harassing medical workers as they enter the buildings. These highly effective and sometimes violent efforts have caused abortion rights groups to look for help to the courts. In the early 1990s the Supreme Court heard three complaints against clinic blockades. The Court decided two of these cases on statutory grounds and a third on free speech issues. None of these cases turned on the due process guarantee of privacy at issue in *Roe v. Wade*.

In 1993 the Court rejected an effort by a group of clinics to invoke a Reconstruction-era civil rights law against demonstrators. By a 6–3 vote in *Bray v. Alexandria Women's Health Clinic*, the justices said the law prohibiting conspiracies to deprive any person or class of equal protection of the laws cannot be used to prevent blockades by antiabortion demonstrators. The clinic blockades do not involve "invidious discrimination" against women by reason of their sex, wrote Justice Scalia for the majority. For that reason, the demonstrations did not fall under the 1871 law as interpreted by the Court in a decision a century later, *Griffin v. Breckenridge* (1971).[1]

In early 1994 the Court unanimously upheld civil damage suits against antiabortion protesters based on a federal antiracketeering law. The decision in *National Organization for Women Inc. v. Scheidler* reinstated a lawsuit by two abortion clinics against a coalition of antiabortion groups called the Pro-Life Action Network. The clinics contended the protesters were using force and violence to try to close them down, and they asked for damages under the Racketeer Influenced and Corrupt Organizations Act, commonly called RICO. Two lower federal courts had said RICO could not be used because the antiabortion groups had no economic motive for their actions.

But the high court rejected the argument. Chief Justice Rehnquist wrote that RICO may be used even if there is no evident economic motive. He said the abortion clinics could sue as long as they showed that the defendants constituted an "enterprise" that was engaged in "a pattern of racketeering."[2]

In the 1994 case of *Madsen v. Women's Health Center Inc.*, the Court held 6–3 that judges can set up "buffer zones" requiring protesters to keep a minimum distance away from clinics. However, Chief Justice Rehnquist, again writing for the Court, said judges must be careful that they do not restrict "more speech than necessary" to protect access to clinics or other government interests. Rehnquist listed "a woman's freedom to seek lawful medical counseling or counseling services in connection with her pregnancy" as one of the interests that would justify "an appropriately tailored injunction."[3]

On that basis the Court upheld a thirty-six-foot buffer zone around most of the clinic and a broad noise ban during hours when abortions were performed.

1. *Bray v. Alexandria Women's Health Clinic*, 506 U.S. 263 (1993).
2. *National Organization for Women Inc. v. Scheidler*, 114 S. Ct. 798 (1994).
3. *Madsen v. Women's Health Center Inc.*, 114 S. Ct. 2516 (1994).

States, the Court said, may not prohibit abortions performed early in pregnancy before the fetus has a reasonable chance of survival outside of the womb. There was no majority opinion in this case. The plurality opinion, written jointly by O'Connor, Kennedy, and Souter, constitutes the rule of *Casey.*

They adopted a new, more lenient standard for determining whether particular state restrictions infringe too far on the right to abortion. The decision in *Casey* upheld Pennsylvania abortion regulations that had earlier been found to conflict with the standard adopted in *Roe v. Wade* to protect the "fundamental" right to abortion.[26]

The decision to uphold *Roe v. Wade* was the result of unexpected votes by Justices O'Connor, Kennedy, and Souter. Until 1992 O'Connor's position on abortion had been unclear. She had described the legal framework of *Roe v. Wade* as "problematic" but had stopped short of saying it should be overruled. Souter, appointed to the Court in 1990, had never voted in an abortion rights case. Kennedy's vote was perhaps the most surprising. He had signed the plurality opinion in the 1989 case of *Webster v. Reproductive Health Services,* which would have overturned *Roe v. Wade* had a fifth justice joined it. But in *Casey* Kennedy sided with O'Connor and Souter to affirm *Roe.*

Using its new, more lenient standard, the Court upheld a list of requirements that Pennsylvania placed on a woman seeking an abortion, including a twenty-four-hour waiting period between being given certain information and having the abortion and parental or judicial approval for minors seeking abortions. The Court struck down a requirement that a woman seeking an abortion notify her husband.

Justices Blackmun and Stevens joined O'Connor, Souter, and Kennedy to declare that *Roe v. Wade* created a "rule of law and a component of liberty we cannot renounce."[27] Blackmun, the author of *Roe,* praised the three-justice opinion as an "act of personal courage and Constitutional principle."[28] But he dissented from all the portions upholding the state regulations. In that position he was joined by Justice Stevens on all but one point.

Dissenting from the affirmation of *Roe* and agreeing to the sections of the opinion upholding the Pennsylvania regulations were Chief Justice Rehnquist and Justices White, Scalia, and Thomas.

In the first paragraph of the plurality opinion that spoke for the Court, the justices noted that five times in the past decade presidents had asked the Court to overturn *Roe v. Wade.* The justices said, "Liberty finds no refuge in the jurisprudence of doubt."[29]

The three-justice opinion affirmed what it called the "essential holding" of *Roe v. Wade*: recognition of a woman's right to obtain an abortion without undue interference from the state before a fetus becomes viable; confirmation of the state's power to restrict abortions after viability, if the law contains exceptions for abortions necessary to save the mother's life or health; and affirmation of legitimate state interests in protecting the health of the woman and the life of the fetus.

"Some of us as individuals find abortion offensive to our most basic principles or morality," wrote O'Connor, Kennedy, and Souter, "but that cannot control our decision. Our obligation is to define the liberty of all, not to mandate our own moral code."[30] They upheld *Roe v. Wade* because of their regard for individual liberty and their adherence to precedent. To overturn *Roe* would have serious social repercussions, they acknowledged. For twenty years people have lived with the idea that abortion is available if contraception fails. By making it more possible for women to control their reproductive lives, *Roe* has helped women achieve economic and social equality, they noted.

Altering the legal test for determining whether a state is interfering with an abortion choice, the justices abandoned the *Roe* standard allowing interference only when the state had a "compelling interest." Under that strict standard, virtually all restrictions on abortion through the first two trimesters—six months—of a pregnancy were invalid.

The plurality in *Casey* said the standard should be whether the regulation puts an "undue burden" on a woman seeking an abortion. An undue burden exists if the law places substantial obstacles in the path of a woman before the fetus is viable. The Court said a state may put regulations in place to further the health or safety of a woman, but it may not impose unnecessary health regulations.

The plurality rejected *Roe*'s trimester framework but said a state may not prohibit any woman from deciding to end her pregnancy before viability. The Court effectively overruled two earlier decisions that struck down "informed consent" provisions—*City of Akron v. Akron Center for Reproductive Health Inc.* (1983) and *Thornburgh v. American College of Obstetricians and Gynecologists* (1986).[31] Informed consent refers to written consent from a woman who is about to have an abortion, indicating she understands the abortion procedure, its risks, and the alternatives.

Dissenting from the affirmation of *Roe* were Rehnquist, White, Scalia, and Thomas. Rehnquist wrote: "Because abortion involves the purposeful termination of potential life, the abortion decision must be recognized as *sui generis,* different in kind from the rights protected in earlier cases under the rubric of personal or family privacy and autonomy."[32]

In a separate dissent, Scalia said the abortion issue should be returned to state legislatures. "[B]y foreclosing all democratic outlet for the deep passions this issue arouses, by banishing the issue from the political forum that gives all participants, even the losers, the satisfaction of a fair hearing and an honest fight, by continuing the imposition of a rigid national rule instead of allowing for regional differences, the Court merely prolongs and intensifies the anguish."[33]

RIGHTS OF HOMOSEXUALS

The concern for both individual privacy and public morality, evident in the Court's abortion cases, resonated in its rulings on the rights of homosexuals. Two cases, one decided in 1986 and the second in 1996, produced the Court's first pronouncements on gay rights. The contexts of the two cases, their outcomes, and the majority's reasoning were strikingly different. The first case challenged a state law as violating the right of privacy embodied in the guarantee of due process; the second challenged an amendment to a state constitution as violating the guarantee of equal protection. Both inspired decisions reflecting the morality and evolving standards of a diverse country.

The 1986 case of *Bowers v. Hardwick* began when Michael Hardwick deliberately challenged a Georgia law that forbade sodomy, defined as "any sexual act involving the sex organs of one person and the mouth or anus of another." Hardwick was charged with violating the law by engaging in sexual activity with another man in his house.

A district court threw out Hardwick's challenge to the constitutionality of the law, but a federal appeals court reversed. It agreed with Hardwick that the Georgia statute violated his fundamental rights because his homosexual activity was private and beyond the reach of the state. The appeals court relied on the due process guarantee of privacy as articulated in reproductive rights cases such as *Griswold v. Connecticut* (1965) and *Roe v. Wade* (1973).

The Supreme Court reversed by a narrow vote. In the majority were Chief Justice Burger and Justices White, Powell, Rehnquist, and O'Connor. Dissenting were Brennan, Marshall, Blackmun, and Stevens.

Writing for the majority, Justice White framed the case as presenting "whether the federal Constitution confers a fundamental right upon homosexuals to engage in sodomy and hence invalidates the laws of the many states that still make such conduct illegal and have done so for a very long time."[34]

White emphasized that the country had a long history of proscribing consensual sodomy:

Sodomy was a criminal offense at common law and was forbidden by the laws of the original thirteen states when they ratified the Bill of Rights. In 1868, when the Fourteenth Amendment was ratified, all but 5 of the 37 states in the Union had criminal sodomy laws. In fact, until 1961, all states outlawed sodomy, and today, 24 states and the District of Columbia continue to provide criminal penalties for sodomy performed in private and between consenting adults. Against this background, to claim that a right to engage in such conduct is "deeply rooted in this Nation's history and tradition" or "implicit in the concept of ordered liberty" is, at best, facetious.[35]

His references were to the Court's earlier descriptions of fundamental liberties.

The majority upheld the Georgia law as rational, saying it was enough that Georgia lawmakers believed sodomy immoral and unacceptable.

Justice Blackmun, who had taken the lead in the justices' abortion rights cases, wrote for the dissenting justices, describing the central issue as "the right to be let alone." He said the fact that

individuals define themselves in a significant way through their intimate sexual relationships with others suggests, in a Nation as diverse as ours, that there may be many "right" ways of conducting those relationships, and that much of the richness of a relationship will come

from the freedom an individual has to *choose* the form and nature of these intensely personal bonds.[36]

For a decade this gay rights case stood as the Court's sole statement on the issue. For some of the justices, it was a sore subject. Justice Powell publicly regretted his vote, saying the *Bowers* ruling was inconsistent with the principles of privacy in *Roe v. Wade*.[37] And when the Court in 1996 decided its second gay rights case, it made no reference to *Bowers v. Hardwick*.

At issue in 1996 was an amendment to the Colorado constitution, adopted by the voters in a 1992 statewide referendum. The amendment barred all legislative, executive, or judicial action at any governmental level designed to protect the status of persons based on their "homosexual, lesbian or bisexual orientation, conduct, practices or relationships." The targets of the provision were controversial ordinances adopted in various Colorado municipalities, including Aspen and Boulder, that banned discrimination in housing, employment, and education based on sexual orientation. Supporters of the constitutional amendment, Amendment 2, asserted that the measure was necessary to counter the gay rights efforts that they deemed harmful to the country's traditions and morals.

After the law was challenged by Richard G. Evans, a gay man who worked for the City of Denver, and other homosexuals, the Colorado Supreme Court ruled that the law infringed the fundamental right of gays and lesbians to participate in the political process.

By a 6–3 vote in the case of *Romer v. Evans,* the Supreme Court agreed that Amendment 2 was invalid but on different grounds.[38] The Court said the amendment violated the federal equal protection guarantee. In the majority were Justices Stevens, O'Connor, Kennedy, Souter, Ginsburg, and Breyer. Dissenting were Chief Justice Rehnquist and Justices Scalia and Thomas.

Indicative of the generous civil rights approach of the majority, Kennedy, who wrote for the Court, opened with reference to Justice Harlan's admonishing dissent in *Plessy v. Ferguson* (1896) that the Constitution "neither knows nor tolerates classes among citizens."[39]

Kennedy said Amendment 2 deprived gay people of rights enjoyed by others:

Sweeping and comprehensive is the change in legal status effected by this law. . . . Homosexuals, by state decree, are put in a solitary class with respect to transactions and relations in both the private and governmental spheres. The amendment withdraws from homosexuals, but no others, specific legal protection from the injuries caused by discrimination, and it forbids reinstatement of these laws and policies.[40]

Supporters of Amendment 2 had wanted to stop cities from giving "special protection" to gays, but the Court said, "We find nothing special in the protections taken for granted by most people either because they already have them or do not need them; these are protections against exclusion from an almost limitless number of transactions and endeavors that constitute ordinary civil life in a free society."[41]

As in *Bowers v. Hardwick,* the Court used the test of rationality to measure the constitutionality of Amendment 2. But when the Court asked whether the amendment bore a rational relationship to some legitimate end, it found that it did not. In Kennedy's words:

Amendment 2 fails, indeed defies, even this conventional inquiry. First, the amendment has the peculiar property of imposing a broad and undifferentiated disability on a single named group, an exceptional and . . . invalid form of legislation. Second, its sheer breadth is so discontinuous with the reasons offered for it that the amendment seems inexplicable by anything but animus toward the class that it affects; it lacks a rational relationship to legitimate state interests.[42]

In an unusual display of unity among the justices in the majority, no one wrote a concurring opinion to dilute the force of Kennedy's statement, which ended on this note: "We must conclude that Amendment 2 classifies homosexuals not to further a proper legislative end but to make them unequal to everyone else. This Colorado cannot do. A state cannot so deem a class of persons a stranger to its laws."[43]

The breadth of the decision and absence of references to precedent, notably *Bowers v. Hardwick,* outraged the dissenting justices. Scalia, writing for himself, Rehnquist, and Thomas, said, "In holding that homosexuality cannot be singled out for disfavored treatment, the Court contradicts a decision, unchallenged here, pronounced only 10 years ago . . . and places the prestige of this institution behind the proposition that opposition to homosexuality is as reprehensible as racial or religious bias."[44]

Only two of the justices in the *Bowers* majority were still on the Court in 1996, Rehnquist and O'Connor. Rehnquist's position was consistently against gay rights. O'Connor, who viewed the Colorado case differently, did not write separately to explain how she reconciled the two rulings.

While Scalia's opinion carried a clear tone of great moral indignation, his legal reasoning stressed the importance of leaving it to legislatures and voters to deal with such a divisive topic as gay rights, rather than allowing the Court to dictate policy:

Since the Constitution of the United States says nothing about this subject, it is left to be resolved by normal democratic means, including the democratic adoption of provisions in state constitutions. This Court has no business imposing upon all Americans the resolution favored by the elite class from which the Members of this institution are selected, pronouncing that "animosity" toward homosexuality is evil.[45]

Referring to *Bowers v. Hardwick,* Scalia wrote that if it is constitutionally permissible for a state to make homosexual conduct criminal, it must be constitutionally permissible for a state to enact other laws disfavoring that conduct. He concluded, "Amendment 2 is designed to prevent piecemeal deterioration of the sexual morality favored by a majority of Coloradans, and is not only an appropriate means to that legitimate end, but a means that Americans have employed before. Striking it down is an act, not of judicial judgment, but of political will."[46]

THE RIGHT TO DIE

In 1990, the first year of its third century, the Court confronted the question of withdrawing artificial life supports from a co-

THE RIGHT TO REFUSE MEDICATION

Interpreting the Fourteenth Amendment guarantee of liberty, the Court in 1990 recognized that even prison inmates possess "a significant liberty interest in avoiding the unwanted administration of antipsychotic drugs." (*Washington v. Harper,* 494 U.S. 210, 1990.) In that case, however, the Court ruled, 6–3, that state prison officials may force a mentally ill inmate to take antipsychotic drugs if he is a danger to himself or others and the treatment is in his medical interest. The Court said mentally ill prisoners are not entitled to a judicial-style hearing before the drugs are given.

Two years later the Court held, 7–2, that a state cannot force a defendant to take an antipsychotic drug during his murder trial without an "overriding justification." If there is no such justification, such medication violates the defendant's liberty rights under the Fourteenth Amendment and the Sixth Amendment guarantee of a fair trial. (*Riggins v. Nevada,* 504 U.S. 127, 1992.)

The murder defendant in this case admitted fighting with his victim but said the individual was trying to kill him and that voices in his head said the retaliatory killing would be justified. Over the defendant's objections, the trial court allowed the defendant to be given high doses of an antipsychotic drug. The defendant argued that the medication deprived him of a "full and fair" trial because he could not show jurors his true mental state when he offered an insanity defense.

The Supreme Court agreed. The state, it said, must demonstrate that the treatment is medically appropriate and "essential" for the safety of the defendant or others.

matose patient. Like the difficult issues of life and death involved in the abortion cases, this case involved the Constitution's implied right of privacy.

While the Court unanimously found a "right to die" within the Fourteenth Amendment concept of protected personal liberty, it also set a strict standard for such cases. By a 5–4 vote, the justices held that a state can require clear and convincing evidence of a patient's previously expressed wish to die, before allowing family members to disconnect life-support systems.[47]

Thirty-two-year-old Nancy Beth Cruzan, the victim of an automobile accident, had suffered irreversible brain damage. For several years she lay helpless in a state hospital bed. Physicians said she was in a "persistent vegetative state," exhibiting motor reflexes but no cognitive function. When it became clear that Nancy Cruzan would not regain her mental faculties, her parents sought to stop her artificial feedings. Hospital officials refused, and the Cruzans went to court.

A Missouri trial court ruled for the parents, citing some of Nancy's pre-accident remarks to friends as indicating her desire not to be kept alive in this fashion. The Missouri supreme court reversed, saying Cruzan's statements were "unreliable for determining her intent."

The Supreme Court upheld Missouri's statute requiring that evidence of a person's wishes for the withdrawal of treatment be clear and convincing. Rehnquist wrote, "The choice between life and death is a deeply personal decision of obvious and overwhelming finality. We believe Missouri may legitimately seek to safeguard the personal element of this choice through the imposition of heightened evidentiary requirements."[48] He was joined in the majority by Justices White, Kennedy, O'Connor, and Scalia.

Rehnquist began with the premise that an individual has a constitutionally protected right to refuse lifesaving food and water: "It cannot be disputed that the Due Process Clause protects an interest in life as well as an interest in refusing life-sustaining medical treatment."[49] But the chief justice emphasized the need for a clear expression of the person's wishes, acknowledging that some persons' true desires will be frustrated if they are not in writing.

Justice Brennan, joined by Justices Marshall, Blackmun, and Stevens, dissented. Cruzan had a fundamental right to be free of the feeding tube and "to choose to die with dignity," Brennan wrote.

Dying is personal. And it is profound. For many, the thought of an ignoble end, steeped in decay, is abhorrent. . . . Although the right to be free of unwanted medical intervention, like other constitutionally protected interests, may not be absolute, no state interests could outweigh the rights of an individual in Nancy Cruzan's position. Whatever a state's possible interests in mandating life-support treatment under other circumstances, there is no good to be obtained here by Missouri's insistence that Nancy Cruzan remain on life-support systems if it is indeed her wish not to do so.[50]

O'Connor, who was in the majority, wrote separately to observe that the Court and the country was only beginning to address troubling questions of medical ethics. "[N]o national consensus has yet emerged on the best solution for this difficult and sensitive problem. Today, we decide only that one state's practice does not violate the Constitution; the more challenging task of crafting appropriate procedures for safeguarding incompetents' liberty interests is entrusted to the 'laboratory' of the states," she said.[51]

NOTES

INTRODUCTION (PP. 621–624)

1. *Lindsley v. Natural Carbonic Gas Co.*, 220 U.S. 61 at 78–79 (1911); see also *McGowan v. Maryland*, 366 U.S. 420 (1961); *Williamson v. Lee Optical of Oklahoma*, 348 U.S. 483 (1955); *Kotch v. Board of River Pilot Commissioners*, 330 U.S. 552 (1947); *Royster Guano Co. v. Virginia*, 253 U.S. 412 (1920).

2. *Buck v. Bell*, 274 U.S. 200 at 208 (1927).

3. *Korematsu v. United States*, 323 U.S. 214 at 216 (1944).

4. *Graham v. Richardson*, 403 U.S. 365 at 372 (1971).

5. *Craig v. Boren*, 429 U.S. 190 at 197 (1976).

6. *Skinner v. Oklahoma*, 316 U.S. 535 at 541 (1942).

7. *Griswold v. Connecticut*, 381 U.S. 479 (1965).

8. *Roe v. Wade*, 410 U.S. 113 (1973).

9. *Planned Parenthood of Southeastern Pennsylvania v. Casey*, 505 U.S. 833 (1992).

10. *Reynolds v. Sims*, 377 U.S. 533 at 561–562 (1964).

11. *Kramer v. Union Free School District*, 395 U.S. 621 at 627–628 (1969).

12. *United States v. Guest*, 383 U.S. 745 at 757, 759 (1966).

13. *Shapiro v. Thompson*, 394 U.S. 618 at 662 (1969).

14. *Weber v. Aetna Casualty & Surety Co.*, 406 U.S. 164 at 179 (1972).

15. *Shapiro v. Thompson*, 394 U.S. 618 at 627 (1969); *Lindsey v. Normet*, 405 U.S. 56 (1972).

16. *San Antonio Independent School District v. Rodriguez*, 411 U.S. 1 at 33 (1973).

RACIAL EQUALITY (PP. 625–668)

1. *Strauder v. West Virginia*, 100 U.S. 303 at 306–307 (1880).

2. John P. Frank, *Marble Palace: The Supreme Court in American Life* (New York: Knopf, 1961), 204. Other sources include John Hope Franklin, *From Slavery to Freedom: A History of Negro Americans*, 3d ed. (New York: Random House, Vintage Books, 1969); John A. Garraty, ed., *Quarrels That Have Shaped the Constitution* (New York: Harper and Row, 1964); United States Commission on Civil Rights, *Freedom to the Free: Century of Emancipation, 1863–1963* (Washington, D.C.: U.S. Government Printing Office, 1963); C. Vann Woodward, *The Strange Career of Jim Crow*, 2d rev. ed. (New York: Oxford University Press, 1966).

3. *Slaughterhouse Cases*, 16 Wall. 36 (1873).

4. *Civil Rights Cases*, 109 U.S. 3 (1883).

5. Carl B. Swisher, "Dred Scott One Hundred Years After," *Journal of Politics*, May 1957, 167–174, quoted in *Marble Palace*, 205.

6. Alan P. Westin, "The Case of the Prejudiced Doorkeeper," in *Quarrels That Have Shaped the Constitution*, 143.

7. *Plessy v. Ferguson*, 163 U.S. 537 (1896).

8. United States Commission on Civil Rights, *Freedom to the Free*, 71.

9. Franklin, *From Slavery to Freedom*, 480.

10. *United States v. Carolene Products Co.*, 304 U.S. 144 at 152–153, footnote 4 (1938).

11. *Brown v. Board of Education of Topeka*, 347 U.S. 483 (1954).

12. G. Theodore Mitau, *Decade of Decision: The Supreme Court and the Constitutional Revolution, 1954–1964* (New York: Scribner's, 1967), 62–63.

13. Franklin, *From Slavery to Freedom*, 644.

14. *Plessy v. Ferguson*, 163 U.S. 537 at 544 (1896).

15. *Roberts v. City of Boston*, 59 Mass. 198 at 206 (1849).

16. *Id*. at 209.

17. *Cumming v. Richmond County Board of Education*, 175 U.S. 528 at 545 (1899).

18. *Berea College v. Kentucky*, 211 U.S. 45 (1908).

19. *Gong Lum v. Rice*, 275 U.S. 78 at 86 (1927).

20. For general background, see Alfred H. Kelly and Winfred A. Harbison, *The American Constitution: Its Origins and Development*, 5th ed. (New York: Norton, 1976), 860; Richard Kluger, *Simple Justice* (New York: Knopf, 1976), 126–137.

21. *Missouri ex rel. Gaines v. Canada*, 305 U.S. 337 at 349 (1938).

22. *Id*. at 350.

23. *Sipuel v. Board of Regents of the University of Oklahoma*, 332 U.S. 631 at 633 (1948).

24. *Sweatt v. Painter*, 339 U.S. 629 at 633–634 (1950).

25. *Id*. at 636.

26. *McLaurin v. Oklahoma State Regents for Higher Education*, 339 U.S. 637 at 641 (1950).

27. *Brown v. Board of Education of Topeka, Briggs v. Elliott, Davis v. County School Board of Prince Edward County, Va., Gebhart v. Belton*, 347 U.S. 483 (1954).

28. *Bolling v. Sharpe*, 347 U.S. 497 (1954).

29. Loren Miller, *The Petitioners: The Story of the Supreme Court of the United States and the Negro* (New York: Random House, Pantheon Books, 1966), 345.

30. *Guinn v. United States*, 238 U.S. 347 (1915); see also Kluger, *Simple Justice*, 527.

31. Quoted in Leon Friedman, ed., *Argument: The Oral Argument Before the Supreme Court in Brown v. Board of Education of Topeka, 1952–55* (New York: Chelsea House, 1969), 215.

32. Ibid.

33. Ibid., 216.

34. Ibid., 239–240.

35. *Brown v. Board of Education of Topeka*, 347 U.S. 483 at 492 (1954).

36. Id. at 492–493.

37. Id. at 493.

38. Id.

39. Id. at 494.

40. Id. at 495.

41. *Bolling v. Sharpe*, 347 U.S. 497 at 499–500 (1954).

42. *Brown v. Board of Education of Topeka*, 349 U.S. 294 at 299–301 (1955).

43. Id. at 301.

44. U.S. Congress, Senate, "Declaration of Constitutional Principles," March 12, 1956, *Congressional Record*, 102:4460.

45. Woodward, *Strange Career of Jim Crow*, 154.

46. *Lucy v. Adams*, 350 U.S. 1 (1955).

47. *Florida ex rel. Hawkins v. Board of Control*, 350 U.S. 413 (1956).

48. *Muir v. Louisville Park Theatrical Assn.*, 347 U.S. 971 (1954); see also *Mayor and City Council of Baltimore v. Dawson*, 350 U.S. 877 (1955); *Holmes v. City of Atlanta*, 350 U.S. 879 (1955); *New Orleans City Park Improvement Assn. v. Detiege*, 358 U.S. 54 (1959); *Gayle v. Browder*, 352 U.S. 903 (1956); *Wright v. Georgia*, 373 U.S. 284 (1963).

49. *Cooper v. Aaron*, 358 U.S. 1 (1958).

50. Id. at 16.

51. Id. at 19–20.

52. *Faubus v. Aaron*, 361 U.S. 197 (1959).

53. *Shuttlesworth v. Birmingham Board of Education*, 162 F. Supp. 372, affirmed 358 U.S. 101 (1958).

54. *Holt v. Raleigh*, 265 F. 2d 95, cert. denied, 361 U.S. 818 (1959); *Covington v. Edwards*, 264 F. 2d 780, cert. denied, 361 U.S. 840 (1959).

55. *Bush v. Orleans Parish School Board*, 364 U.S. 500 (1960); *Orleans Parish School Board v. Bush*, 365 U.S. 569 (1961); *St. Helena Parish School Board v. Hall*, 368 U.S. 515 (1962).

56. *Goss v. Board of Education of Knoxville*, 373 U.S. 683 (1963).

57. *McNeese v. Board of Education for Community School District 187, Cahokia, Ill.*, 373 U.S. 668 (1963).

58. *Griffin v. County School Board of Prince Edward County*, 377 U.S. 218 at 231 (1964).

59. Id. at 229.

60. *Bradley v. School Board, City of Richmond*, 382 U.S. 103 (1965).

61. *Rogers v. Paul*, 382 U.S. 198 (1965).

62. *Wallace v. United States, Bibb County Board of Education v. United States*, 386 U.S. 976 (1967).

63. *Green v. County School Board of New Kent County, Va.*, 391 U.S. 430 at 437–438 (1968).

64. Id. at 438–439.

65. Id. at 439.

66. Id. at 441, 442.

67. *Raney v. Board of Education of Gould School District*, 391 U.S. 443 (1968); *Monroe v. Board of Commissioners, City of Jackson*, 391 U.S. 450 (1968).

68. *Alexander v. Holmes Board of Education*, 396 U.S. 19 (1969); see also *Carter v. West Feliciana Parish School Board*, 396 U.S. 290 (1970); *Northcross v. Board of Education, City of Memphis*, 397 U.S. 232 (1970).

69. *Swann v. Charlotte-Mecklenburg County Board of Education*, 402 U.S. 1 at 25, 24 (1971).

70. Id. at 26.

71. Id. at 27.

72. Id. at 30–31.

73. Id. at 28.

74. Id. at 23.

75. Id. at 31–32.

76. *North Carolina State Board of Education v. Swann*, 402 U.S. 43 at 45–46 (1971).

77. *Davis v. Board of School Commissioners of Mobile County, Ala.*, 402 U.S. 33 (1971).

78. *McDaniel v. Barresi*, 402 U.S. 39 (1971).

79. *Richmond School Board v. Virginia State Board of Education*, 412 U.S. 92 (1973).

80. Quoted by Chief Justice Warren E. Burger in *Milliken v. Bradley*, 418 U.S. 717 at 733 (1974).

81. Id. at 741.

82. Id. at 744–745.

83. Id. at 746.

84. Id. at 752.

85. Id. at 789.

86. *Milliken v. Bradley*, 433 U.S. 267 at 287–288 (1977).

87. *Edelman v. Jordan*, 415 U.S. 651 (1974).

88. *Milliken v. Bradley*, 433 U.S. 267 at 290 (1977).

89. *Dayton (Ohio) Board of Education v. Brinkman*, 433 U.S. 406 at 420 (1977); *Dayton Board of Education v. Brinkman* 443 U.S. 526 (1979).

90. *Pasadena City Board of Education v. Spangler*, 427 U.S. 424 at 437 (1976).

91. Id. at 443.

92. *Board of Education of Oklahoma City Public Schools v. Dowell*, 498 U.S. 237 (1991).

93. *Missouri v. Jenkins*, 115 S. Ct. 2038 (1995).

94. *Missouri v. Jenkins*, 495 U.S. 33 (1990).

95. *Missouri v. Jenkins*, 115 S. Ct. 2038 (1995).

96. For general historical background in this area, see Commission on Civil Rights, *Freedom to the Free*, 60–71; Woodward, "The Case of the Louisiana Traveler," *Quarrels That Have Shaped the Constitution*, 145; Woodward, *Strange Career of Jim Crow*.

97. *Civil Rights Cases*, 109 U.S. 3 at 11 (1883).

98. Id. at 24.

99. Milton Konvitz and Theodore Leskes, *A Century of Civil Rights, with a Study of State Law Against Discrimination* (New York: Columbia University Press, 1961), 157. The states that passed antidiscrimination laws were Connecticut, Iowa, New Jersey, and Ohio in 1884; Colorado, Illinois, Indiana, Michigan, Minnesota, Nebraska, and Rhode Island in 1885; Pennsylvania in 1887; Washington in 1890, Wisconsin in 1895, and California in 1897.

100. *Hall v. DeCuir*, 95 U.S. 485 at 489 (1878).

101. *Louisville, New Orleans and Texas Railway v. Mississippi*, 133 U.S. 587 (1890).

102. *Plessy v. Ferguson*, 163 U.S. 537 at 548 (1896).

103. Id. at 543.

104. Id. at 544.

105. Id. at 550–551.

106. Id. at 559.

107. Id. at 560–561.

108. *McCabe v. Atchison, Topeka and Santa Fe Railroad*, 235 U.S. 151 at 161–162 (1914).

109. *Mitchell v. United States*, 313 U.S. 80 (1941).

110. *Morgan v. Virginia*, 328 U.S. 373 at 380–381 (1946).

111. Id. at 386.

112. *Bob-Lo Excursion Co. v. Michigan*, 333 U.S. 28 (1948); *Henderson v. United States*, 339 U.S. 816 (1950); *District of Columbia v. Thompson Co.*, 346 U.S. 100 (1953).

113. *Brown v. Board of Education of Topeka*, 347 U.S. 483 (1954).

114. *Mayor and City Council of Baltimore v. Dawson*, 350 U.S. 877 (1955); *Holmes v. City of Atlanta*, 350 U.S. 879 (1955); *New Orleans City Park Improvement Assn. v. Detiege*, 358 U.S. 54 (1959); *Gayle v. Browder*, 352 U.S. 903 (1956); *Muir v. Louisville Park Theatrical Assn.*, 347 U.S. 971 (1954); *Wright v. Georgia*, 373 U.S. 284 (1963); *Schiro v. Bynum*, 375 U.S. 395 (1964); *State Athletic Commission v. Dorsey*, 359 U.S. 533 (1959); *Johnson v. Virginia*, 373 U.S. 61 (1963); *Lee v. Washington*, 390 U.S. 333 (1968).

115. *Watson v. City of Memphis*, 373 U.S. 526 at 533 (1963).

116. *Palmer v. Thompson*, 403 U.S. 217 (1971).

117. *Boynton v. Virginia*, 364 U.S. 454 at 460–461 (1960).

118. *Burton v. Wilmington Parking Authority*, 365 U.S. 715 at 722 (1961).

119. Id. at 725.

120. *Peterson v. City of Greenville*, 373 U.S. 244 at 248 (1963).

121. *Gober v. City of Birmingham*, 373 U.S. 374 (1963); *Avent v. North Carolina*, 373 U.S. 375 (1963).

122. *Shuttlesworth v. Birmingham*, 373 U.S. 262 at 265 (1963).

123. *Lombard v. Louisiana*, 373 U.S. 267 at 273 (1963).

124. *Heart of Atlanta Motel v. United States*, 379 U.S. 241 at 258 (1964).

125. Id. at 257.

126. Id. at 260.

127. Id. at 252.

128. *Katzenbach v. McClung*, 379 U.S. 294 (1964).

129. *Daniel v. Paul*, 395 U.S. 298 (1969).

130. *Civil Rights Cases*, 109 U.S. 3 at 22 (1883).

131. *Buchanan v. Warley*, 245 U.S. 60 at 80–82 (1917).

132. See, for example, *Harmon v. Tyler*, 273 U.S. 668 (1927); *City of Richmond v. Deans*, 281 U.S. 704 (1930).

133. *Corrigan v. Buckley*, 271 U.S. 323 at 330 (1926).

134. *Shelley v. Kraemer, McGhee v. Sipes*, 334 U.S. 1 (1948).

135. Id. at 13.

136. Id. at 19–20.

137. *Hurd v. Hodge, Urciola v. Hodge*, 334 U.S. 24 (1948).

138. *Barrows v. Jackson*, 346 U.S. 254 (1953).

139. *Reitman v. Mulkey*, 387 U.S. 369 at 377 (1967).

140. Id. at 393.

141. *Hunter v. Erickson*, 393 U.S. 385 at 393 (1969).

142. Id. at 396–397.

143. *James v. Valtierra*, 402 U.S. 137 at 141 (1971).

144. Id. at 145.

145. *Jones v. Alfred H. Mayer Co.*, 392 U.S. 409 at 436 (1968).

146. Id. at 438–443, passim.

147. *Sullivan v. Little Hunting Park Inc.*, 396 U.S. 229 (1969).

148. *Tillman v. Wheaton-Haven Recreation Association*, 410 U.S. 431 at 437 (1973).

149. *Hills v. Gautreaux*, 425 U.S. 284 (1976).

150. *Milliken v. Bradley*, 418 U.S. 717 (1974).

151. *Hills v. Gautreaux*, 425 U.S. 284 at 294 (1976).

152. Id. at 297.

153. Id. at 298–300.

154. Id. at 306.

155. *Village of Arlington Heights v. Metropolitan Housing Development Corporation*, 429 U.S. 252 (1977).

156. *Bailey v. Alabama*, 219 U.S. 219 (1911); *United States v. Reynolds*, 235 U.S. 133 (1914); see also *Taylor v. Georgia*, 315 U.S. 25 (1942); *Pollock v. Williams*, 322 U.S. 4 (1944).

157. For general historical accounts of job discrimination against blacks, see Miller, *The Petitioners*; Woodward, *Strange Career of Jim Crow*.

158. *New Negro Alliance v. Sanitary Grocery Co.*, 303 U.S. 552 at 561 (1938).

159. *Hughes v. Superior Court*, 339 U.S. 460 (1950).

160. *Steele v. Louisville and Nashville Railroad Company*, 323 U.S. 192 (1944); see also *Tunstall v. Brotherhood*, 323 U.S. 210 (1944); *Graham v. Brotherhood*, 338 U.S. 232 (1949); *Conley v. Gibson*, 355 U.S. 41 (1957).

161. *Brotherhood of Railroad Trainmen v. Howard*, 343 U.S. 768 at 774 (1951); see also *Syres v. Oil Workers International Union*, 350 U.S. 892 (1955).

162. *Railway Mail Association v. Corsi*, 326 U.S. 88 (1945).

163. *Colorado Anti-Discrimination Commission v. Continental Airlines*, 372 U.S. 714 (1963).

164. *Griggs v. Duke Power Co.*, 401 U.S. 424 at 430–431 (1971).

165. Id. at 432.

166. *Albemarle Paper Company v. Moody*, 422 U.S. 405 (1975).

167. *Wards Cove Packing Co. v. Atonio*, 490 U.S. 642 (1989); see also *Lorance v. AT&T Technologies Inc.*, 490 U.S. 900 (1989).

168. *CQ Almanac 1991* (Washington, D.C.: Congressional Quarterly, 1992), 251–261.

169. *McDonnell Douglas Corporation v. Green*, 411 U.S. 807 (1973).

170. *St. Mary's Honor Center v. Hicks*, 509 U.S. 502 (1993).

171. *Furnco Construction Corporation v. Waters*, 438 U.S. 567 at 579 (1978).

172. *Albemarle Paper Company v. Moody*, 422 U.S. 405 at 417–418 (1975).

173. Id. at 422.

174. *Fitzpatrick v. Bitzer*, 427 U.S. 445 (1976).

175. *Ford Motor Co. v. Equal Employment Opportunity Commission*, 458 U.S. 219 (1982).

176. *Franks v. Bowman Transportation Co. Inc.*, 424 U.S. 747 at 768 (1976).

177. Id. at 788–789.

178. *Teamsters v. United States, T.I.M.E.-D.C. v. United States*, 431 U.S. 324 (1977).

179. Id. at 354.

180. *Guardians Association v. Civil Service Commission of City of New York*, 463 U.S. 482 (1983).

181. *Adarand Constructors Inc. v. Peña*, 115 S. Ct. 2097 (1995).

182. *DeFunis v. Odegaard*, 416 U.S. 312 (1974).

183. *University of California Regents v. Bakke*, 438 U.S. 265 at 412, 418 (1978).

184. Id. at 320, 307.

185. Id. at 325.

186. *United Steelworkers of America v. Weber, Kaiser Aluminum & Chemical Corp. v. Weber, United States v. Weber*, 443 U.S. 193 (1979).

187. Id. at 204.

188. Id. at 206, footnote 6.

189. Id. at 216.

190. Id. at 222.

191. *Fullilove v. Klutznick*, 448 U.S. 448 at 473 (1980).

192. Id. at 490.

193. *Firefighters Local No. 1784 v. Stotts*, 467 U.S. 561 (1984).

194. *Wygant v. Jackson Board of Education*, 476 U.S. 267 (1986).

195. Id. at 282.

196. Id. at 280–281.

197. Id. at 286.

198. *Local #28 of the Sheet Metal Workers' International v. Equal Employment Opportunity Commission*, 478 U.S. 421 (1986).

199. *Local #93, International Association of Firefighters v. City of Cleveland and Cleveland Vanguards*, 478 U.S. 501 (1986).

200. *United States v. Paradise*, 480 U.S. 149 (1987).

201. Id.

202. *Johnson v. Transportation Agency of Santa Clara County, Calif.*, 480 U.S. 616 (1987).

203. *City of Richmond v. J. A. Croson Co.*, 488 U.S. 469 at 498 (1989).

204. Id. at 499.

205. Id. at 504.

206. Id. at 505–506.

207. Id. at 510.

208. *Martin v. Wilks*, 490 U.S. 755 (1989).

209. *Metro Broadcasting Inc. v. Federal Communications Commission*, 497 U.S. 547 (1990).

210. *Adarand Constructors Inc. v. Peña*, 115 S. Ct. 2097 (1995).

211. Id.

212. Id.

213. Id.

EQUAL PROTECTION, THE ALIEN AND THE POOR (PP. 669–676)

1. *Yick Wo v. Hopkins*, 118 U.S. 356 at 369 (1886).

2. Id. at 373–374.

3. Id. at 374.

4. *Truax v. Raich*, 239 U.S. 33 at 41 (1915).

5. Alfred H. Kelly and Winfred A. Harbison, *The American Constitution: Its Origins and Development*, 5th ed. (New York: Norton, 1976), 666.

6. *McCready v. Virginia*, 94 U.S. 391 at 395 (1877).

7. *Patsone v. Pennsylvania*, 232 U.S. 138 at 144 (1914).

8. Ibid.

9. *Heim v. McCall*, 239 U.S. 175 (1915); *Crane v. New York*, 239 U.S. 195 (1915).

10. *Ozawa v. United States*, 260 U.S. 178 (1922).

11. *Terrace v. Thompson*, 263 U.S. 197 at 220 (1923); see also *Porterfield v. Webb*, 263 U.S. 225 (1923); *Webb v. O'Brien*, 263 U.S. 313 (1923); *Frick v. Webb*, 263 U.S. 326 (1923); *Cockrill v. California* 268 U.S. 258 (1925).

12. *Clarke v. Deckebach*, 274 U.S. 392 at 396 (1927).

13. Id. at 397.

14. *Hirabayashi v. United States*, 320 U.S. 81 (1943); *Korematsu v. United States*, 323 U.S. 214 (1944).

15. *Oyama v. California*, 332 U.S. 633 at 646 (1948).

16. *Takahashi v. Fish and Game Commission*, 334 U.S. 410 at 418 (1948).

17. Id. at 419.

18. Id. at 421.

19. *Graham v. Richardson*, 403 U.S. 365 at 372 (1971).

20. Id. at 374.

21. Id. at 376.

22. *In re Griffiths*, 413 U.S. 717 (1973); *Examining Board of Engineers, Architects and Surveyors v. de Otero*, 426 U.S. 572 (1976); *Sugarman v. Dougall*, 413 U.S. 634 (1973); *Nyquist v. Mauclet*, 432 U.S. 1 (1977); *Bernal v. Fainter*, 467 U.S. 216 (1984).

23. *Sugarman v. Dougall*, 413 U.S. 634 at 641 (1973).

24. Id. at 643.

25. Id. at 647.

26. Id. at 648.

27. *Foley v. Connelie*, 435 U.S. 291 at 297 (1978).

28. Id. at 298–299.

29. *Ambach v. Norwick*, 441 U.S. 68 (1979).

30. *Cabell v. Chavez-Salido*, 454 U.S. 432 (1982).

31. *Plyler v. Doe, Texas v. Certain Named and Unnamed Undocumented Alien Children*, 457 U.S. 202 (1982).

32. Id. at 230.

33. *Mathews v. Diaz*, 426 U.S. 67 at 80–83, passim (1976).

34. Id. at 84.

35. *Hampton v. Mow Sun Wong*, 426 U.S. 88 at 1 (1976).

36. Id. at 115.

37. *Griffin v. Illinois*, 351 U.S. 12 at 12–13 (1956).

38. Id. at 19.

39. Id. at 28–29.

40. *Mayer v. Chicago*, 404 U.S. 189 at 196 (1971).

41. *United States v. MacCollum*, 426 U.S. 317 at 324 (1976).

42. *Douglas v. California*, 372 U.S. 353 at 357–358 (1963).

43. Id. at 361.

44. *Ross v. Moffitt*, 417 U.S. 600 (1974); *Fuller v. Oregon*, 417 U.S. 40 (1974).

45. *Boddie v. Connecticut*, 401 U.S. 371 at 381 (1971).

46. Id. at 386.

47. *United States v. Kras*, 409 U.S. 434 at 446 (1973).

48. Id. at 457.

49. *Williams v. Illinois*, 399 U.S. 235 (1970).

50. *Tate v. Short*, 401 U.S. 395 (1971).

51. *United States v. Guest*, 383 U.S. 745 (1966).

52. *Shapiro v. Thompson*, 394 U.S. 618 at 634 (1969).

53. Id. at 633.

54. *Memorial Hospital v. Maricopa County*, 415 U.S. 250 (1974).

55. *Breedlove v. Suttles*, 302 U.S. 277 (1937).

56. *Harper v. Virginia State Board of Elections*, 383 U.S. 663 at 668 (1966).

57. *Bullock v. Carter*, 405 U.S. 134 (1972).

58. *Lubin v. Panish*, 415 U.S. 709 (1974).

59. *Serrano v. Priest*, 96 Cal. Rptr. 601, 487 P. 2d 1241; 5 Cal. 3d 584 (1971).

60. *San Antonio Independent School District v. Rodriguez*, 411 U.S. 1 at 23–24 (1973); see also *Kadrmas v. Dickinson Public Schools*, 487 U.S. 450 (1988).

61. Id. at 33, 35.

62. Id. at 54–55.

63. Id. at 98.

64. Id. at 99.

SEX DISCRIMINATION (PP. 677–686)

1. *Bradwell v. Illinois*, 16 Wall. 130 at 141 (1873).

2. *Minor v. Happersett*, 21 Wall. 162 (1875).

3. *Strauder v. West Virginia*, 100 U.S. 303 (1880); *Hoyt v. Florida*, 368 U.S. 57 (1961), overruled by *Taylor v. Louisiana*, 419 U.S. 522 (1975).

4. *Cronin v. Adams*, 192 U.S. 108 (1904).

5. *Goesaert v. Cleary*, 335 U.S. 464 at 466 (1948).

6. Id. at 468.

7. *Muller v. Oregon*, 208 U.S. 412 at 422–423 (1908); see also *Riley v. Massachusetts*, 232 U.S. 671 (1914); *Miller v. Wilson*, 236 U.S. 373 (1915); *Bosley v. McLaughlin*, 236 U.S. 385 (1915); *West Coast Hotel v. Parrish*, 300 U.S. 379 (1937).

8. *Sail'er Inn Inc. v. Kirby*, 5 Cal. 3d 1.20, 485 P. 2d 529 (1971).

9. *Reed v. Reed*, 404 U.S. 71 at 76 (1971), quoting *Royster Guano Co. v. Virginia*, 253 U.S. 412 at 415 (1920).

10. *Reed v. Reed*, 404 U.S. 71 at 76 (1971).

11. *Kahn v. Shevin*, 416 U.S. 351 (1974).

12. *Schlesinger v. Ballard*, 419 U.S. 498 (1975).

13. *Weinberger v. Salfi*, 422 U.S. 749 (1975).

14. *Mathews v. deCastro*, 429 U.S. 181 (1976).

15. *Stanton v. Stanton*, 421 U.S. 7 at 15 (1975).

16. *Frontiero v. Richardson*, 411 U.S. 677 at 686–687 (1973).

17. *Weinberger v. Wiesenfeld*, 420 U.S. 636 at 645 (1975).

18. Id. at 651–652.

19. *Califano v. Goldfarb*, 430 U.S. 199 at 217 (1977).

20. Id. at 242.

21. *Wengler v. Druggists Mutual Insurance Co.*, 446 U.S. 142 (1980).

22. *Craig v. Boren*, 429 U.S. 190 at 197 (1976); see also *Orr v. Orr*, 440 U.S. 268 (1979).

23. *Michael M. v. Superior Court of Sonoma County*, 450 U.S. 464 (1981).

24. *Rostker v. Goldberg*, 453 U.S. 57 (1981).

25. *Mississippi University for Women v. Hogan*, 458 U.S. 718 (1982).

26. Id. at 724.

27. Id. at 729.

28. *United States v. Virginia*, _____ U.S. _____ (1996).

29. Id.

30. Id.

31. Id.

32. Id.

33. Id.

34. *General Electric Co. v. Gilbert*, 429 U.S. 125 at 162 (1976).

35. *Phillips v. Martin Marietta Corp.*, 400 U.S. 542 (1971).

36. *Dothard v. Rawlinson*, 433 U.S. 321 at 329 (1977).

37. Id. at 336.

38. Id. at 345–346.

39. *Cleveland Board of Education v. LaFleur, Cohen v. Chesterfield County School Board*, 414 U.S. 632 at 639–640 (1974).

40. Id. at 643.

41. Id. at 660.

42. *Geduldig v. Aiello*, 417 U.S. 484 at 496–497, footnote 20 (1974).

43. Id. at 496–497.

44. Id. at 500–501.

45. *General Electric Co. v. Gilbert*, 429 U.S. 125 at 136 (1976).

46. Id. at 138–139.

47. Id. at 149, 158.

48. *Nashville Gas Co. v. Satty,* 434 U.S. 136 at 142 (1977).

49. *Congress and the Nation,* Vol. V (Washington, D.C.: Congressional Quarterly, 1981), 796.

50. *Newport News Shipbuilding & Dry Dock Co. v. Equal Employment Opportunity Commission,* 462 U.S. 669 (1983); *California Federal Savings & Loan v. Guerra,* 479 U.S. 272 (1987).

51. *UAW v. Johnson Controls,* 499 U.S. 187 (1991).

52. *Los Angeles v. Manhart,* 435 U.S. 702 at 710 (1978).

53. Id. at 708.

54. Id. at 726.

55. Id. at 722.

56. *Fitzpatrick v. Bitzer,* 427 U.S. 445 (1976).

57. *Arizona Governing Committee for Tax Deferred Annuity and Deferred Compensation Plans v. Norris,* 463 U.S. 1073 (1983); see also *Florida v. Long,* 487 U.S. 223 (1988).

58. *Meritor Savings Bank v. Vinson,* 477 U.S. 57 (1986).

59. *Harris v. Forklift Systems Inc.,* 510 U.S. 17 (1993).

LIBERTY AND PRIVACY (PP. 687–696)

1. Ronald Dworkin, *Life's Dominion: An Argument about Abortion, Euthanasia, and Individual Freedom* (New York: Knopf, 1993), 6.

2. *Roe v. Wade,* 410 U.S. 113 (1973).

3. *Planned Parenthood of Southeastern Pennsylvania v. Casey,* 505 U.S. 833 (1992).

4. *Cruzan v. Missouri Department of Health,* 497 U.S. 261 at 000 (1990).

5. *Washington v. Harper,* 494 U.S. 210 (1990).

6. *Meyer v. Nebraska,* 262 U.S. 390 at 399 (1923).

7. *Pierce v. Society of Sisters,* 268 U.S. 510 at 534–535 (1925).

8. Ibid.

9. *Skinner v. Oklahoma,* 316 U.S. 535 at 541 (1942).

10. *Loving v. Virginia,* 388 U.S. 1 at 12 (1967).

11. *Griswold v. Connecticut,* 381 U.S. 479 at 484 (1965).

12. Id. at 485–486.

13. Id. at 499.

14. Id. at 500, quoting from *Palko v. Connecticut,* 302 U.S. 319 at 325 (1937).

15. Id. at 502.

16. *Eisenstadt v. Baird,* 405 U.S. 438 (1972).

17. *Roe v. Wade,* 410 U.S. 113 at 152 (1973).

18. Id. at 153.

19. Id. at 154.

20. Ibid. See also *Simopoulos v. Virginia,* 462 U.S. 506 (1983).

21. *Roe v. Wade,* 410 U.S. 113 (1973); see also *Thornburgh v. American College of Obstetricians and Gynecologists,* 476 U.S. 747 (1986).

22. *Planned Parenthood of Central Missouri v. Danforth,* 428 U.S. 52 (1976); *Bellotti v. Baird,* 443 U.S. 622 (1979); *H. L. v. Matheson,* 450 U.S. 398 (1981); *City of Akron v. Akron Center for Reproductive Health Inc.,* 462 U.S. 416 (1983); *Planned Parenthood Association of Kansas City, Mo. v. Ashcroft,* 462 U.S. 476 (1983).

23. *Harris v. McRae,* 448 U.S. 297 (1980); *Williams v. Zbaraz,* 448 U.S. 358 (1980).

24. *Webster v. Reproductive Health Services,* 492 U.S. 490 (1989).

25. *Hodgson v. Minnesota,* 497 U.S. 417 (1990), *Ohio v. Akron Center for Reproductive Health Inc.,* 497 U.S. 502 (1990).

26. *Planned Parenthood of Southeastern Pennsylvania v. Casey,* 505 U.S. 833 (1992).

27. Id.

28. Id.

29. Id.

30. Id.

31. *City of Akron v. Akron Center for Reproductive Health Inc.,* 462 U.S. 416 (1983); *Thornburgh v. American College of Obstetricians and Gynecologists,* 476 U.S. 747 (1986).

32. *Planned Parenthood of Southeastern Pennsylvania v. Casey,* 505 U.S. 833 (1992).

33. Id.

34. *Bowers v. Hardwick,* 478 U.S. 186 (1986).

35. Id. at 192–194.

36. Id. at 205.

37. John C. Jeffries Jr., *Justice Lewis F. Powell, Jr.: A Biography* (New York: Scribner's, 1994), 530.

38. *Romer v. Evans,* _____ U.S. _____ (1996).

39. *Plessy v. Ferguson,* 163 U.S. 537 (1896).

40. *Romer v. Evans,* _____ U.S. _____ (1996).

41. Id.

42. Id.

43. Id.

44. Id.

45. Id.

46. Id.

47. *Cruzan v. Missouri Department of Health,* 497 U.S. 261 (1990).

48. Id. at 281.

49. Id.

50. Id. at 310, 312.

51. Id. at 292.

Case Index

Subject Index

P

Pacifica Foundation, 474
Pacifists. *See also* Conscientious objectors
    employment in arms production, 484
    naturalization denial, 152
Packers and Stockyards Act of 1921, 100
Palko, Frank, 561, 605–606
Panama Canal, 150 (box), 196
Panama invasion, 194
Pappas, Paul, 471
Parades, 436, 479. *See also* Protest demonstra-
    tions
Paraguay, 211
Pardons
    acceptance, 232, 235
    conditional pardons, 234–236
    criminal contempt, 294
    effect, 232–234
    executive powers, 231–236
    innocents on death row, 614 (box)
    sentence commutation, 235–236
    subsequent offenses, 234
Parens patriae suits, 302
Parental rights
    abortion consent, notice, 64, 692, 693
    education
        compulsory attendance, 484–485
        foreign language, 40, 687–690
        mandatory public schooling, 410, 481,
            690
        religious school tuition aid, 493–494
        school library books, 453
    illegitimate children, 680
    unwed fathers, 680
Paris Accords of 1973, 206
Parker, John J., 40, 707 (box), 708, 858 (box)
Parochial schools. *See* Religious school aid
Parrish, Elsie, 342
Parsons, Richard C., 825 (box)
Parvin, Albert, 714, 821
Pasadena, Calif., 646
Passport Act of 1926, 537 (box)
Passports
    denial to communists, 534, 725 (box)
    travel freedom, 537 (box)
Patents
    congressional powers, 115 (box)
    federal court jurisdiction, 266 (box)
Paterson, William
    career, 7, 8, 9, 11, 243, 744
        biography, 864–865
        foreign birth, 852 (box)
        impeachment threat, 10
        political experience, 849, 851
        service in Congress, 179 (box)
        unconfirmed nomination, 707 (box)
    executive powers in foreign policy, 210, 211
Patronage jobs, 549 (box), 553–554
Pawtucket, R.I., 479, 495
Pearce, Clifton, 606
Pearl Harbor Review Commission, 822
Peck, James H., 290
Peckham, Rufus Wheeler
    antitrust law, 34, 101, 100
    career, 32, 35
        biography, 909–910
    criminal rights, 34
    federal police powers, 34
    state police powers, 34, 341
    substantive due process, 356
Peckham, Wheeler Hazard, 32, 707 (box), 708,
    742, 858 (box)
Peddlers' licenses, 347
Pennsylvania
    abortion, 357 (box), 692–693

alien discrimination, 670, 671
Bible reading in schools, 489
commerce regulation, 330–331
    oleomargarine, 337 (box)
    railroad freight, 346
    sugar trust, 98
federal-state relations, 317
flag salute, 46
fugitive slave laws, 395
justices' state of origin, 740
military base closings, 86 (box)
religious school aid, 492–493
sedition laws, 541 (box), 722, 725
Sunday closing laws, 484
Pennsylvanian (newspaper), 765
Pensions and retirement
    contract obligation, 328
    judicial administration, 7, 76
    railroad system, 42, 89, 97, 249
    retirement age, 380
    sex discrimination, 661, 685–686
    Supreme Court justices, 25, 43, 252, 714 (box),
        819–821, 842, 852
        mandatory age proposal, 820 (box)
Pentagon Papers, 55, 174, 240, 254, 401, 447,
    454–456, 789
Peonage, 352, 658
Peremptory juror challenges, 59, 283, 567, 568,
    681 (box)
Perjury, 83, 291
Perkins, Dexter, 822
Perlman, Philip B., 831 (box)
Perovich, Vuco, 235
Perpich, Rudy, 207 (box)
Persian Gulf War
    congressional authorization, 134, 194, 195
        (box), 207 (ill.)
    injunction to compel declaration of war, 208
    protest displays, 434–435
Personal liberty. *See also* Privacy rights and
    issues
    education of children, 39–40, 687–690
Personal property taxes, 119
Personnel Management, U.S. Office of, 218, 549
    (box)
Peters, Richard, 317
Peters, Richard Jr., 14, 20, 826
Peterson, William, 845
Petition rights
    civil rights demonstrations, 437
    summary, 435 (box)
Peyote, 478, 485, 735
Pfeffer, Leo, 480 (box)
Phelps, Timothy, 780
Philadelphia & Reading Railroad, 346
Philadelphia Naval Shipyard, 86 (box)
Philadelphia, Pa.
    garbage disposal, 334 (box)
    port pilots, 330–331
    Supreme Court quarters, 835
Philippines
    criminal rights, 150
    habeas corpus suspension, 84 (box)
    McKinley policies
    U.S. citizenship, 152
Phillips, Samuel F., 831 (box)
Physicians
    abortion counseling ban, 446 (box)
    advice, treatment restrictions, 302
    practice ban for felons, 351
Pickering, John, 244, 711
Picketing
    illegal conduct, 441
    prior restraints, 439
    protected actions, 438–439

    residences, 438
    shopping malls, 441 (box)
    state regulation, 442–443
    third-party pickets, 439–440
Pierce, Franklin
    executive privilege, 239
    foreign policy, 195
    slavery crisis, 227
    Supreme Court appointments, 20, 708, 742,
        750, 767, 847, 849
Pinckney, Charles, 821, 842
Pitney, Mahlon
    career, 35, 39, 742
        biography, 919–920
        confirmation vote, 858 (box)
        service in Congress, 179 (box)
    congressional primary elections, 178–179
    First Amendment rights, 422
    habeas corpus writs, 281
    wage and hour regulation, 37
Planned Parenthood, 446 (box), 690
Plea bargains, 592–593 (box)
Pledge of allegiance
    flag salute, 46, 358, 431–432, 433 (box),
        481–484
    "under God" phrase, 487
Plessy, Homer, 648
Pocket vetoes, 230–231
Poindexter, John M., 169 (box)
Points of Rebellion (Douglas), 713–714, 821
Police and law enforcement agencies
    choke holds, 299
    employment discrimination
        affirmative action, 666
        aliens, 364, 672
        effect-intent issue, 659 (box)
    First Amendment protections
        civil rights movement libel case, 457–461
        newsroom searches, 448, 472–473
        speech rights, 429
        speech rights of officers, 445 (box)
    lineups, 603, 733
    mandatory sentence for murder, 613
    protection of justices, 225–226
    search and seizure, 573–588
        border searches, 577 (box)
        deadly force, 586 (box)
        exclusionary rule, 578–579 (box)
        "stop and frisk" searches, 575 (box)
    suspect self-incrimination
        confessions, 592–598, 733
        interrogation definition, 603 (box)
        Miranda warnings, 53, 596–598
        right to counsel, 53, 602, 603
Police power. *See* Federal police powers; State
    police powers
Political action committees, 443 (box)
Political advertising, 444, 454
Political parties. *See also* Campaign finance;
    Primary elections
    association rights, 403, 504, 552–554
    ballot access, 514 (box), 552
    federal employee participation, 549 (box)
    patronage hiring and firing, 553–554
    state employees, 126
    subversive organizations, 48
    Supreme Court
        justices' activities, 821–822
        nominee qualifications, 741, 744, 846–847,
          850 (box)
        press coverage, 759–760
Political questions
    Congress membership, 173, 181
    executive immunity, 237–238
    foreign affairs, 74, 209, 210